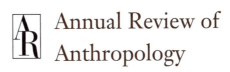

Annual Review of
Anthropology

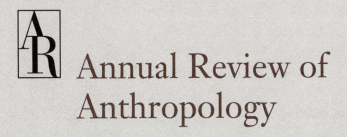

Annual Review of Anthropology

Volume 39, 2010

Donald Brenneis, *Co-Editor*
University of California, Santa Cruz

Peter T. Ellison, *Co-Editor*
Harvard University

www.annualreviews.org • science@annualreviews.org • 650-493-4400

Annual Reviews
4139 El Camino Way • P.O. Box 10139 • Palo Alto, California 94303-0139

Annual Reviews
Palo Alto, California, USA

International Standard Serial Number: 0084-6570
International Standard Book Number: 978-0-8243-1939-7
Library of Congress Catalog Card Number: 72-821360

TYPESET BY APTARA
PRINTED AND BOUND BY MALLOY INCORPORATED, ANN ARBOR, MICHIGAN

Preface: Searching for Serendipity

Both Co-Editors remember, even more recently than graduate school, the excitement of holding the newest copy of a journal in hand, turning eagerly to the table of contents and focusing in on our own particular fascinations while simultaneously considering the broader intellectual context represented by the other articles. At times nothing leaped out, but occasionally a quick glance at possibly relevant articles led to new ways of thinking about our own work—and about the field more broadly. We also both relish the capacity for quick and focused search, which especially online versions of the *ARA* and other significant publications afford. It has become a commonplace luxury to follow topical threads with speed and precision, finding generative routes through the welter of likely extraneous materials.

How might these different media, print and digital, shape distinctive browsing and reading practices and, further, influence the ways in which we both find and interpret scientific and scholarly writing? Printed journals provide considerable potential for reading outwards, suggesting possible connections and unexpected paths to pursue, whereas the searchability and connection characteristic of electronic publications provide different affordances, making access much easier than in print while often depending on much more tightly defined starting points. As readers, we browse as well as rely increasingly on machinic browsers; how do these practices and their outcomes differ and complement each other? Are we free-range readers, or do we pursue more linear paths?

Many years ago, Robert Merton (1948) emphasized the significant role of serendipity in science, noting that "[t]he unanticipated, anomalous, and strategic [often] exerts a pressure for initiating theory" (p. 506). It is not surprising that one of the cases he uses to illustrate the "recasting of theory" (p. 509) through such serendipity is Malinowski's consideration of Trobriand fishing magic; two hallmarks of anthropology have long been our attention to unexpected and apparently anomalous cases and our willingness to remold our thinking through paying serious attention to them. Although Merton was initially concerned with those unexpected findings that catalyze theoretical refiguring, it is also clear that serendipity figures signally in other domains, including our own ways of browsing and making connections in our reading. Discovering articles that speak, perhaps somewhat surprisingly, to each other in interesting ways is a key element of such readerly serendipity. As Co-Editors, we hope to help make possible such generative juxtapositions.

One strategy for pursuing this goal is through the use of themes in the *Annual Review of Anthropology*. These themes outline shared general topics for examination across the subfields; however, they are also intended to provide the opportunity for surprise— and for thinking beyond the individual articles themselves. This issue's two themes are

"Modalities of Capitalism" and "Anthropology of the Senses." The articles under each rubric address a range of specific topics from various perspectives; we strongly encourage readers to check out the whole array. Although the themes themselves may seem quite disparate, as Co-Editors we have recognized quite lively points of intersection between the two. "Reorganization of the Sensory World," for example, speaks directly to new media and the complex nexus of technology and capital with which they are entangled; the "Semiotics of Brand," conversely, reflects in lively ways on sensory experience. A further strategy for encouraging serendipitous reading can be seen in the list of Related Articles from other *Annual Review* series. As the reader will see, between the two of us we came up with a perhaps startling collection of possible connections.

Whether you are reading the *Annual Review* online or on paper, and however your search may be guided, we encourage exploratory reading. Browse on!

We want to take this opportunity to thank John Bowen for five years of great ideas and lively conversation on the Editorial Committee, and we also thank Jennifer Mann for her ongoing acute and amiable shepherding of the *Annual Review of Anthropology* as Production Editor and for the particular generosity and clarity with which she has helped guide us as still-novice Co-Editors.

Don Brenneis and Peter Ellison
Co-Editors

LITERATURE CITED

Merton RK. 1948. The bearing of empirical research upon the development of social theory. *Am. Soc. Rev.* 13(5):505–15

**Annual Review of
Anthropology**

Volume 39, 2010

Contents

Theme I: Modalities of Capitalism

Theme II: The Anthropology of the Senses

Soundscapes: Toward a Sounded Anthropology

Indexes

Errata

An online log of corrections to *Annual Review of Anthropology* articles may be found at http://anthro.annualreviews.org/errata.shtml

Related Articles

From the ***Annual Review of Political Science***, Volume 13 (2010)

From the ***Annual Review of Psychology***, Volume 61 (2010)

Geoffrey A. Harrison

A Life of Research in Biological Anthropology

Geoffrey A. Harrison

Institute of Human Sciences, University of Oxford, Oxford OX2 6QS, United Kingdom; email: EJandGAHarrison@talktalk.net

Annu. Rev. Anthropol. 2010. 39:1–16

The *Annual Review of Anthropology* is online at anthro.annualreviews.org

This article's doi: 10.1146/annurev.anthro.012809.105020

Key Words

variation, adaptation, well-being

Abstract

I much appreciated being invited to write a contribution for this journal, but initially presumed that what was required was a comprehensive review of some major issue in biological anthropology. Indeed I drafted a contribution on the history of the subject during the second part of the twentieth century. I was then firmly told that this was not what was wanted, rather something much more autobiographical. Well that is what you have got: an extremely personal account of my own research career over some 50 years in biological anthropology. I have summarized the results of what I consider the main projects I and my colleagues have undertaken and tried to document successes and failures. I cannot claim any earth-shattering discovery but hope that we have contributed in a substantial way to the further understanding of the nature of human variation, a main concern of biological anthropology in the second half of the twentieth century.

FROM BONES TO HORMONES

Like many other biological anthropologists I first became attracted to the field by learning of human evolution as evidenced in the fossil record. I well remember a fascinating lecture, on Australopithecus, given in Cambridge by Robert Broome. Before that, I had been intending a quite different career.

In the first half of the twentieth century biological anthropology (then termed physical anthropology) was largely concerned with the study of bones, not only in ancient fossils, but also in examining the variety of skeletal and especially skull shapes in relatively recent modern populations. This, of course, is easily understandable considering the focus on human origins. My first research as a Cambridge student was to compare the cranial features of a group of modern Palestinian Arabs with Iron Age remains from a site at Lachish. In about half of the metrical characters measured, the two groups were not significantly different, but in the other half, the groups were different. I remember pondering hard what might be the explanation, but of four quite different explanations, I couldn't decide which was the more likely. At that juncture I became rather disillusioned with craniometry.

Later, however, I did have two quite different experiences with fossil bones. The first concerned the remains found at Swanscombe in Kent in the valley of the River Thames and of great interglacial date. Originally discovered in 1935, these remains consisted of an occipital bone and one parietal bone and showed some remarkably modern features. Some 20 years later the other parietal was found and a great search was launched to find the frontal bone to see whether there was a supraorbital torus: a feature that distinguished modern from ancient forms. As a graduate student, I was one of many recruited for the search. The main revelation was the state of bones preserved in the Swanscombe gravels; they were like cream cheese and totally disintegrated even on gentle brushing. For preservation, they needed to be progressively implanted with plastic and that was both time-consuming and expensive. I do not think I was responsible for the destruction of the Swanscombe frontal, but none was ever found and other helpers may not have been so lucky.

My second experience was not of finding a fossil but of making one. My first formal employment was as a temporary departmental demonstrator in the Anatomy department at Oxford and where, in my first week in post, J.S. Weiner instructed me to "make another Piltdown jaw." He had concluded on a night drive from London that the inconsistencies in the Piltdown fossils were explicable only by being fraudulent. The following day, I was given my task, which turned out to be remarkably easy. Using a modern Orang jaw as a basis, I was able to re-create a good imitation of the Piltdown jaw in about a week. I had some difficulty with tooth wear, but so did the fraudster. I accompanied Weiner on many of the visits he made to Sussex to interview anyone who had been associated with the original finds and to examine possible leads and connections. It felt more like being in a detective agency than in a laboratory of physical anthropology.

That concluded my study of bones, but it did lead me to some collaborative work on the principles and methods of animal taxonomy with A.J. Cain in the Zoology department at Oxford. At this time, numerical taxonomy was in its infancy, and investigators were making attempts to bring some objectivity to the view "that a taxon was what a good taxonomist judged to be a good taxon." We devised a rather simple way to combine different characters measured on different scales into a single measure of relationship (Cain & Harrison 1958). As far as I am aware, the method was never widely used and was quickly replaced by more sophisticated mathematical treatments. But it did lead us to a much better understanding of the purposes and nature of classifications and of the meaning of the word "affinity" (Cain & Harrison 1960). We clearly identified the distinctions between a phenetic classification (i.e., "natural" one) and a phylogenetic one and indicated methods by which the former could be converted to the latter. More significantly, we recognized that the terms evolutionary affinity or relationship were being used in two quite different ways: first, in the genealogical sense of the time of divisions of evolutionary branches, which we called cladistic affinity, and second, as a measure of the number of shared characters derived from the common ancestry, i.e., patristic affinity. Much of the controversy over the status of Australopithecus was due to protagonists defining affinity in these two different ways. They are identical only if all evolution is divergence at a constant rate, which clearly is rarely if ever the case. We subsequently applied the arguments to hominid evolution (Harrison & Weiner 1963).

Following completion of this work, the direction of my research changed greatly. We increasingly recognized that many features of variation in human body size and shape were related to climate and, in particular, that humans like many other geographically wide-ranging homeothermic species obeyed the ecology rules of Bergmann and Allen with body surface area relatively decreasing with increasing latitude. Much of this relationship was genetically determined and produced by natural selection, but it also raised the question of whether actual exposure to varying climate during individual development played any part.

To examine the extent by which mammalian development was affected by temperature, J.S. Weiner suggested that I compare the growth and development of mice in a hot environment to those of a temperate one. Mice were chosen because of their short generation time and rapid development and most importantly because of the availability of inbred and F1 hybrid lines within which there was little if any genetic variance. The possible complication of genetic contributions to relationships could thus be ignored. The most striking finding was that heat-reared animals developed much longer tails, by 2 to 3 cm, than did the controls. The degree to which this occurred was dependent on strain, but the phenomenon was universal. So far as body weight was concerned, heat appeared to promote the growth of young animals, but by

the time they reached sexual maturity heat-reared animals tended to be lighter. Again there were significant differences between the strains; F1 hybrid animals tended to show smaller differences by age (Harrison et al. 1959, 1964).

I mention these results in some detail because they raise important questions about the nature of any direct effect of environment on human biology: (a) To what extent is the effect adaptive by facilitating survival and reproduction in the environment that produces it? (b) To what extent is the effect indicative of somatic fitness and the capacity of homeostatic mechanisms to be effective? And (c) what is the relationship between adaptability and fitness according to variation in environmental quality? The tail growth response is a clear example of adaptability because it is an important structure in mouse thermoregulation (Harrison 1958a,b). The rapid early growth in body weight in heat-reared mice would seem to reflect favorable environmental conditions, but the later slower growth is more ambiguous. It may be indicative of diminished homeostasis, but because small adult size appears to be advantageous in the heat, it could be a component of adaptability. The fact that the hybrids showing heterosis appear to be less affected than the inbred strains suggests that the former explanation is the main one, but it does not rule out some element of the latter (Harrison 1962). Then there is the issue of how much making an adaptive response at one stage in the life history causes a comparative reduction of fitness at a later stage.

These questions, of course, relate to all organisms including humans and are practically important when considering nutritional issues including intervention programs. Plenty of evidence indicates that people adapt to nutritional variation, and it is strikingly obvious that changes in nutritional status cause differences in overall fitness (Harrison 1988, Harrison & Waterlow 1990). However, when one observes slow child growth and small body size in a particular population, can one attribute everything to loss of fitness in a poor nutritional environment, or might there be some component of adaptability in these responses

(Harrison 1990a,b; 2000)? The essential question is not whether indicators of fitness are related to environmental quality but whether variation in them in any one environment differentiates levels of adaptation. A fast-growing heavy individual in nutritionally poor conditions may well have a poorer chance of survival than would a slowly growing light individual. If intervention produces an improved fitness at one age, one probably needs to ensure that the intervention is available at all ages including adulthood. Gerry Brush and I tried to examine environmental quality and fitness not by analyzing child growth in various populations in terms of mean values of weight and stature but by looking at their variance within a population (Brush et al. 1992, Brush & Harrison 2001). The mouse work had shown that whereas adaptive characters demonstrated a lower variance in demanding conditions, fitness characters tended to show an increased variance particularly within inbred genotypes. This outcome of course is because chance perturbations in environmental quality are likely to have a much more important effect on fitness when conditions are difficult than when they are easy. The proposition tended to be fulfilled by comparing growth in a number of different human populations, but the findings were not unequivocal. One possible factor that could not be controlled for was differences in levels of genetic heterogeneity in population structure, but a much more likely influence was comparative mortality. In the worst conditions, many individuals are likely to die before measurement, and such mortality could cause a profound reduction of variance in the survivors.

The mouse work prompted me to find the nearest equivalent situation in natural human populations. The environmental variation chosen had to be altitude (Harrison 1966). Altitude causes profound climatic changes, especially in the partial pressure of atmospheric oxygen, in short geographical distances. These short distances mean that genetically similar people can be found in very different environments, so any developmental differences found are likely to be due entirely to immediate environmental effects. Preparatory studies with rats in decompression chambers showed that varying pressures did have a marked developmental effect on them (Clegg & Harrison 1966). The particular human populations chosen for study were in the Simien regions of Ethiopia. Here one finds quite large numbers of people living at altitudes varying from 5000 ft to 12,000 feet in virtually zero geographical distance. Furthermore, local movement between zones ensured genetic homogeneity, which was confirmed by genetic marker investigations over the course of the study.

The results of the study (Harrison et al. 1969) showed marked differences in the physiology and morphology of the peoples. As was to be expected, the blood picture showed great contrast; red cell counts and hemoglobin levels were much greater in highland peoples. There were also notable differences in physique. Thorax development was particularly affected, which was related to the striking contrast in levels of forced vital capacity and forced expiratory volume, factors that measure lung function. Clearly this is an adaptable response to variation in levels of atmospheric oxygen. The outcome is most evident in those who have lived all their lives at one altitude, but it is also shown in adult migrants between highlands and lowlands, indicating that it is not dependent only on experience during growth.

Other differences in physique between altitude zones were probably not directly related to atmospheric oxygen levels. The agricultural practice was necessarily different between highlands and lowlands; the former were mainly pastoralists and the latter cultivators. This difference inevitably caused a big contrast in diets. Infectious disease patterns were also different: Malaria was endemic in the lowlands, and respiratory diseases were prevalent in the highlands. Many of the responses to these environmental components were not adaptive and reflected the optimality of the total environment for human existence; thus they were indicators of comparative fitness. Thus, the conclusions from the human study were very comparable to those of the mouse experiments.

In early physical anthropology studies, when concern was almost exclusively directed to identifying evolutionary relationships, the possible direct effects of environmental variation on development were seen as a nuisance that could conceal genetic affinities. They certainly could have been the cause for the differences I observed in the Palestinian skulls because environmental factors can affect skeletal development in many ways. One of the biggest breakthroughs in affinity studies and classifications was the discovery of genetic systems from blood groups to DNA where phenotypic development is totally free of environmental variation and populations can be characterized solely in terms of gene frequencies.

I trust that my own studies with mice and altitude contributed to the realization that although environmental effects were a nuisance in determining population relationships, they were extremely important in considering human evolution as well as human health and well-being. After all, the capacity to make adaptable responses is one of the major factors contributing to the success of the human species in colonizing so many different environments, and this ability, of course, is genetically determined; factors that influence health and well-being are clear determinants of reproductive fitness (Harrison 1979).

Nevertheless studies of genetic variation within and between populations are the only domains that are totally exclusive to anthropologists and are at the core of understanding human evolution. We now have very detailed descriptions of most world populations, and interestingly enough, the patterns of variation displayed by single gene markers are not all that different from those shown by craniometrical and similar multifactorial characters. Certainly, broad geographical classifications are more or less identical. However, the concept of distinct races is no longer generally regarded as scientifically meaningful because gene frequencies tend to change gradually over geographical distances as "clines"; thus while widely separated groups may be very different, they tend to be connected by groups

showing every degree of intermediacy. That said, whereas many characters follow similar distributions, some may show quite different patterns (Harrison 1963, 1989).

I contributed in only a minor way to the documentation of geographical variance in blood polymorphisms with collections during field trips to Namibia, Ethiopia, Brazil, and Papua New Guinea. In fact, my main contribution to a specific genetic analysis was with a multifactorial system: skin color.

In the late 1950s to early 1960s, I was teaching at the University of Liverpool, which provided a remarkable opportunity for analyzing skin color. Liverpool was a major U.K. port and had particularly large-volume trade with West Africa. This led, during first decades of the twentieth century, to many African seamen settling in the city and marrying white women. Their children were genuine F1 hybrids. Sufficient time had elapsed for some of these themselves to have married, producing children who were F2 hybrids or "back cross white" or "back cross black" hybrids: the perfect composition for the analysis of a quantitative trait. One would also have liked, of course, access to F3 and later hybrids, but the immigration after the war of many West Indians, whose hybrid status was unknown, prevented this level of study. With my colleague J.J.T. Owen we did, however, manage to measure the skin color of many of the first- and second-generation hybrids with a reflectance spectrometer. Such instruments allowed, for the first time, objective and accurate measurements of skin pigmentation. Studying hybrids of known ancestry allowed us both to determine the reflectance scale on which skin color genes were acting additively and, from there, to determine the number of effective factors responsible for the variation in skin color between West African blacks and Liverpool whites. Effective factors might represent pairs of major genes or groups of linked genes. Without deeper knowledge of ancestry, one cannot determine linkage levels. In our analysis, we concluded that two or three effective factors were involved, a number that seems to correspond with more recent DNA analysis (Harrison & Owen 1964). The identification of appropriate scales of measurement also allowed a much more meaningful comparison of skin color differences among all populations (Weiner et al. 1964, Harrison & Salzano 1966, Harrison et al. 1967).

An issue that has dominated biological anthropology throughout the past century has been the causes for genetic variation between populations: To what extent is this variation due to the chance effects of genetic drift, as first identified by Sewell Wright, or due to the deterministic effects of natural selection, as championed particularly by R.A. Fisher. Selectionist arguments need to demonstrate that genetic differences affect reproductive fitness and, as far as between-population differences are concerned, that different genes have different values in different environments.

The amount of genetic variation within populations is now known to be so great that it seems most of it cannot be affecting fitness and must be subject to drift. However, natural selection is very hard to detect in long-generation-time organisms such as humans. The most definitive evidence must come by identifying relationships between particular gene differences on the one hand and demographic measures such as viability and fertility on the other hand. Even where selection is very strong, such as in the hemoglobinopathies such as sickle cell, it took many years to obtain definitive evidence. The more common approach has been to search for associations between genetic variation and other biological characters that may influence Darwinian fitness, such as various pathologies and functional attributes.

My colleagues and I searched for such associations in various populations and situations. Some of the strongest evidence came from a multidisciplinary study in Papua New Guinea. On the island of Karkar and at Lufa in the Eastern Highlands District, teams from Papua New Guinea, Australia, and the United Kingdom collected information on a large number of human biological characteristics: demography, genetics, physiology, nutrition, and epidemiology (Harrison & Walsh 1974, Harrison 1976).

This study produced a wealth of data, but initial publications were concerned largely with results obtained in each discipline. We were therefore charged to examine interrelationships among the results of the different disciplines. One major undertaking involved examining the interrelationships among the genetic blood polymorphisms and other characteristics. We found many interrelationships of which two were particularly strong: an association between ABO blood groups and thyroid goiter (Boyce et al. 1976) and between haptoglobin polymorphisms and the probability of developing splenomegaly and heptomegaly. The latter occurred significantly not only in both sexes but also in each of three different age groups. In studies elsewhere, we recorded a number of other associations (Harrison et al. 1976a,b,c; Brush et al. 1983; Mascie-Taylor et al. 1985), but all need much further examination before a causal relationship is established. The fundamental difficulty with such approaches is that they can also arise from heterogeneity in the structure of the populations being examined, and no population can ever be regarded as strictly homogenous (Gibson et al. 1975).

Other results from the New Guinea synthesis included a demographic explanation for the distribution of polymorphisms on the island of Karkar with its circular distribution of villages (Harrison et al. 1974b) and an interesting relationship between amounts and distribution of body fat in women and the length of their breastfeeding and parity status (Harrison et al. 1975).

Overall, the study emphasized the importance of population structure and history in examining human biological variety. In early physical anthropology research, attention was focused largely on documenting the patterns of differences among populations, which were then exclusively explained in descent terms. But the differences and similarities among populations arise from what is happening within populations, and it has increasingly been recognized that studies in what causes genetic diversity in single groups or closely related groups such as neighboring villages are fundamental to understanding all human variety (Harrison & Boyce 1972, Harrison 1977).

The ultimate causes for the biological structure of populations are primarily demographic: migration and intermixture, population size, mating patterns and differential fertility, and mortality (Harrison 1970). These parameters must always be measured, but interpretation is still difficult because it takes time, i.e., numerous generations, for results of one demographic structure to equilibrate. They probably rarely do so because the demographic forces themselves are constantly changing. The situation is made even more difficult by the comparative long generation time of humans. There is, however, one compensation: the fact that many human societies have written records of more than a few hundred years at least. Many of these records, particularly church records, document such demographic features as individual births, marriages, and deaths, from which family structure and history can be reconstituted (Kuchemann & Harrison 1972).

It was quite by chance that I discovered, while having a beer with a local vicar, that there are a group of ecclesial parishes in the Otmoor region of Oxfordshire, which have excellent parish records extending back, in some cases, more than 400 years and are more or less complete. Otmoor is distinct because the land is relatively impoverished as compared with surrounding areas because it suffers from widespread flooding in winter. The villages, first established in Anglo-Saxon times, lie on outcrops of stony land, which rise above the surrounding glacial clays. They have never been owned by lords of the manor and have a distinct history and sense of common ethnicity (Harrison 1995).

All the parish records were diligently copied, mainly by C.F. Kuchemann, who also undertook the formidable task of putting together single life histories and then undertaking family reconstitution. With these data, we traced changing patterns of fertility and mortality and related them to prevailing socioeconomic conditions (Kuchemann et al. 1967). Our main interest, however, focused on movement and particularly marital movement because, for most of the recorded history of the villages, this was the main form of long-term movement and a major determinant of villages' genetic structure. Throughout the recorded time, the frequency of village exogamy constantly increased, but the mean distances over which exogamous unions occurred remained remarkably constant at ~5–6 miles for two centuries, i.e., representing marriages between neighboring villages. Around 1850, however, the mean distance rose to 20–30 miles, which coincided with the arrival of the railway to the region. Since then, though other forms of movement have, of course, increased considerably, the distribution of marital distance in the early period fit well with a model based on the likely experience and knowledge people had of their neighborhood when daily movement before mechanical transport would not have been much more than ~12 miles, and people who walked or rode horses inevitably met others on the way and on the way back (Boyce et al. 1967).

The main purpose of the analysis, however, was to determine the relationships between the villages and predict which levels of genetic heterogeneity they would show. For this purpose, we collaborated with our colleague in biomathematics at Oxford, R.W. Hiorns, who devised a matrix approach to demonstrate how long it would take for villages to share a 95% common ancestry were there no such original common ancestry at the beginning of their exchanges, and how the pattern of such relatedness would develop between the villages (Hiorns et al. 1969).

The analysis concluded overall that no genetic heterogeneity was to be expected in the region for genes that were not associated with the movement. This finding was mainly because of the amount of intermixture that had been occurring with populations outside Otmoor. This occurrence had increased considerably in recent decades; however, even before the development of mechanical transport, it was substantial. If one considered only the exchanges between the Otmoor villages themselves, a distinct local pattern of relationship was evident, based partly on distance but also on geographical settlement patterns. Until very recently, there was no direct route across the swampy moor, and movement was forced into a circular pattern. The local pattern would have taken much longer to produce ancestral homogeneity, but even under it alone, one would not have expected genetic variation between the villages.

The Otmoor predictions clearly needed to be tested empirically; as a second phase of the Otmoor research, volunteers were sought who would provide blood samples for genetic analysis. We received an excellent response from the volunteers, and some 680 samples were tested for 14 genetic symptoms. None of them produced any evidence of significant genetic heterogeneity among the three least related village groups (Hiorns et al. 1977). What did emerge was that among those who were Otmoor born, the blood group O gene was at a lower frequency than in those who were immigrants to the region.

In addition to blood collection, information on many other biological characteristics were also collected including various anthropomorphic measures, Wechsler I.Q.s, and Eysenk personality scores (Harrison et al. 1974a). These characteristics not only have some genetic determination but also may be profoundly affected by environmental factors. And unlike the blood markers, many showed considerable between-village heterogeneity. Thus, for example, the mean I.Q. of the 10 different parishes ranged from 100 to 112 in males and 98–113 in females. This kind of variation could be attributed largely to different proportions of immigrants in the different villages because immigrants tend to have higher IQs than do the locally born. Only for stature was there evidence of village heterogeneity among the locally born. However, I.Q. is strongly related to occupation and social class, and the proportion of immigrants of higher social class differs considerably from village to village. Also, locally born villagers have themselves been subject to outmigration, but following up these outmigrants was beyond our capacity.

Our interest on mobility focused not only on geographical mobility but also on social mobility, i.e., movement among the five different social classes recognized by the British Registrar General's Classification of Occupations (Harrison et al. 1970, 1971). In overall terms, the amount of movement between the classes was, and has been since the beginning of records, so high that no genetic heterogeneity between the classes could be expected unless the genetic heterogeneity affected the probability and direction of social mobility. The expectation was fully realized for blood groups and the like, but because I.Q. appears to be associated with social mobility and its direction, any genetic component to I.Q. variation is likely to have become stratified by class. The classes differ by I.Q. from 122 to 98 in men and 121 to 93 in women, and although social mobility, as judged by differences in occupations of fathers and sons, has been increasing in recent times, class has long been an important determinant of demographic structure.

Marriage can also be an important factor. There is strong evidence today not only for assortative marriage for I.Q. and for many other social characteristics (Harrison et al. 1976a, Harrison & Palmer 1981) but also for women who move up the social ladder in marriage to be of higher I.Q. than those who remain in their birth class (Harrison et al. 1971, Harrison et al. 1974c, Kuchemann et al. 1974).

In an overall examination of the blood markers with I.Q., a small but statistically significant association between the blood groups and I.Q. variation was found with people of blood group O tending to have a somewhat higher I.Q. If this finding represented some genetic connection between the two systems, it would be very interesting, but it may instead arise solely from population structure because, as already mentioned, blood group O is somewhat higher in frequency in immigrants than in the locally born population, and the immigrants have a higher I.Q. This is perhaps the most likely explanation, although it does not explain why immigrants have a higher frequency of blood group O. Most of them come from the nearby towns and also from all directions. A similar analysis of outmigrants would have been helpful.

These studies of variation clearly brought us into close contact with the present-day people of Otmoor. Many of them enjoyed the association, expressed interest in the results of the analysis, and welcomed further collaboration. Of course, some people had no wish to be involved, and one must be concerned that studies of at least some of the features were not representative of the entire population. However, varying degrees of cooperation did, of course, occur by village and by test, and where it was possible to make an analysis, there were no significant differences associated with the level of cooperation.

The fact that there was such wide interest and willingness to help (which, for example, could involve providing six timed urine samples), however, made possible a third phase of investigation. I had become much interested in the striking variation in human well-being. My interest was not only because of its profound practical importance but also because it could provide an important vehicle for human evolution through natural selection (Harrison 1982; Harrison 1990a,b). Well-being is determined by environmental factors, but well-being itself can clearly affect such factors. How rich a person becomes, for example, will affect the quality of his or her environment, and quality of environment is likely to affect how rich one becomes. Evidence from Otmoor itself suggests that, in the past, farm laborers had more children than did farm owners, but infant mortality was substantially higher in the laborer class (Harrison 1996).

With such thoughts in mind, we attempted to document the lifestyle of the present Otmoor population and see to what extent this was associated with well-being. By well-being, we meant variation in general health status, which may not be recognized as a medically morbid status. To document these data, we designed questions that examined many aspects of general lifestyle: e.g., occupation, including what the job actually entailed; social networks, including the fre-

quency with which they were used; leisure activities; and various habits such as alcohol consumption, smoking, and food habits.

We also measured well-being in three different ways: (a) a well-being questionnaire in which subjects were asked to record their general feelings about their lives, as well as recognized ailments; (b) a sleep questionnaire focusing on the components of sleep duration and sleep latency but also providing information on the perception of sleep quality (plenty of evidence emphasizes the importance of sleep in well-being); and (c) determination of the level of various stress hormones in urinary samples. We initially hoped to include corticosteroids in the assay, but various technical difficulties involved in urine collection prevented this, and the analysis was ultimately performed only on the catecholamines, adrenaline and noradrenaline (also known in the United States as epinephrine and norepinephrine).

The results of the study are summarized in Harrison (1995). Briefly, the sleep analysis revealed a rather slight relationship between sleep duration in the main sleep period and occupation: Students and the unemployed had the longest sleep, and heavy-goods vehicle drivers experienced the shortest. The latter, however, made up for their loss by substantial daytime napping. Sleep latency showed a rather strong relationship with how people generally felt about their state of well-being (Palmer et al. 1980a,b; Palmer & Harrison 1983a,b).

The hormone analysis, particularly of adrenaline output, was more interesting (Jenner et al. 1980; Harrison et al. 1980, 1981; Reynolds et al. 1981). In this analysis, there was a clear difference between work day and rest day in men. The work-day levels, but not the rest-day levels, associated with type of occupation and social class: Professional and managerial men had greater outputs than did manual workers. No similar relationship was detectable in women, many of whom were only part-time workers or housewives. However, on the rest day, adrenaline levels in women, although not associated with their own occupation, were correlated with their husbands' occupation. Of course, spouses usually spent their rest days together.

Adrenaline is frequently referred to as a stress hormone with the implication that high levels are to be avoided. It is well known as the flight-and-fight hormone, states that are clearly hazardous and best avoided, if possible. However, the hormone response to these conditions is surely adaptive and helps provide the additional energy that conditions demand. It is much better seen as an arousal hormone, and aroused states can be both good and bad. The people in Otmoor who show the lowest output are those who report being endlessly bored, hardly a desirable state.

The results of the Otmoor studies prompted further investigation of variation in stress hormone levels in other populations and other environmental situations. Investigations were initially limited to urinary catecholamines, but later we were able to examine the corticoids cortisol and cortisone even by HPLC in urine and later still by radioimmunoassay in saliva. Cortisol would, less ambiguously, appear to be an indicator of negative stress than would adrenaline.

We first wanted to establish the range of population variation in these hormones across different societies. For this purpose, we needed to have full 24-h urine collections because activity patterns and circadian rhythms differ from situation to situation. Such samples are difficult to obtain, particularly from nonhospitalized groups, but with the help of colleagues from all over the world, a few free-living populations were examined in this way (Jenner et al. 1987). These samples showed marked differences in mean adrenaline levels; people in technically modern societies excreted, on average, nearly twice as much as did people with traditional lifestyles. A particularly interesting situation was revealed in an analysis of 24-h urine samples collected by Ian Prior and his colleagues in New Zealand for their blood pressure studies (Jenner et al. 1987). They examined three groups of Tokelau islanders, one of which was composed of migrants from the islands to New Zealand; the other two were composed of individuals who still resided on two of the

islands. The migrants had significantly greater outputs than did the sedentes, but among the latter, the subjects from the traditional island demonstrated higher outputs than did those from the more modernized island. Social anthropologists provided the explanation because they found that the people from the more modern situation had completely accepted their new situation, whereas on the other island the process of modernization was causing severe social conflicts among different groups of people.

Findings such as this led me, in collaboration with L. Schmitt, of the University of Western Australia, to undertake work with the Aboriginal peoples of the Kimberley Region of northwest Australia. Here the health situation is dreadful despite the provision of excellent medical and educational programs. It is particularly evident in the small towns where drunkenness and violence are widely found. To defeat alcoholism, the Australian government has encouraged people to take up residence in small outstations located some distance from the towns and where the Aboriginal councils have, themselves, banned the sale of alcohol. Our immediate impression on visiting these outstations is one of piece and tranquility. Urine analysis, however, indicates that cortisol levels in the outstations are significantly greater than in the towns. This surprising finding probably comes from the fact that in the outstations there is little or no work or play for the adults ever. It is not hard to imagine the demoralizing effects of having nothing to do for the whole of an adult lifetime. And this is the fate of many of the outstation inhabitants (Schmitt et al. 1995, 1998).

Finally, I should mention a long-standing interest in determinants of human growth (Harrison & Schmitt 1989). This interest originated from early mouse work, but it also seems to me that growth patterns generally afford the best insights into the long-term interaction of adaption, fitness, and environmental quality. Short-term growth reflects the totality of immediate environmental experience, but long-term growth offers insight into the integrated effects of all these experiences: to the successes and failures in adaptation. Two of our studies seem particularly worthy of mention. Data collected in Khartoum by F. Zumrawi offered an excellent opportunity for identifying, by path analysis, the interaction between many factors, social and biological, affecting infant growth during the first years of life. The situation here is remarkable because there is practically no correlation between birth weight and weight at one year of life (Brush et al. 1993; Harrison et al. 1993b, 1994). Furthermore, measurements collected by M. Henneberg on child growth in affluent and poor South African children allowed us to compare the effects of genetic and environmental factors in determining physical fitness. The comparison showed that both muscular development and muscular strength in children of the same muscular development were poorer in the deprived children (Henneberg et al. 1998).

How can we put these various endeavors into a coherent lifetime contribution? At one level, they are really no more than a potpourri of unrelated projects that do not obviously represent a single specific objective. Many of them were indeed undertaken simply because they interested me. However, they are all concerned with understanding the nature of human variation, which is surely one of the main aims of biological anthropology. Variation in all forms is the raw material of adaptation, homeostasis, and evolution.

I do not think I had realized until writing this overview how much the initial mouse work, which also included aspects of immunology, had influenced my subsequent thinking. It set the agenda for all my research on adaptation and fitness. The power of this work lay, of course, in it being experimental, an approach that is typically impossible in human population biology. Here one must rely on fieldwork, and practically every problem in the subject requires it. Indeed, as others have said, the one thing that binds together all anthropologists, social as well as biological, is fieldwork.

As must be evident from this account of my research, I was fortunate in being able to undertake fieldwork in many places, both in the United Kingdom and worldwide. I was particularly helped by the fact that obtaining measurements and body fluid samples was possible without much knowledge of local languages: just "please" and "thank you." How different the situation is today: All ecological research demands real competence in languages.

Nevertheless, fieldwork was often far from easy, needed careful planning, and required a capacity to handle considerable physical if not social privation. I learned most of the things one should not do in my first overseas expedition to Namibia when everything that could go wrong did go wrong. The main mistake was in changing the objectives of the expedition while in the field. The initial plan was to document the genetic characteristics of the various populations in the Kalahari, including the black Bushmen. On arrival, however, we learned that there had been an outbreak of bubonic plague in the dense populations bordering the Okavango river. This outbreak more or less coincided with a publication claiming antigen overlap between the plague bacillus and ABH blood-group substances. We thought we had been offered a heaven-sent opportunity to test for natural selection, and we started collecting hundreds of blood samples from infected areas. Most of those samples spoiled because we were not properly equipped to refrigerate such large numbers; however, even if this had not been the case, the exercise was pointless. Some simple calculations indicated that one would need thousands not hundreds of samples to detect disturbances from Hardy-Weinberg equilibrium with likely levels of selection (Hiorns & Harrison 1970). Clearly, experience may require field modifications, but changing the basic purpose of one's mission while in the field is not recommended. Chronic discomfort and adversity are not good companions for clear thinking.

Fortunately, my other fieldwork studies were more successful. On the primary genetic issues, we obtained comprehensive insight into the nature and consequences of human movement, particularly at the local level.

Both in Otmoor and on Karkar Island, Papua New Guinea, patterns of village exogamy were the main factors used to determine genetic structure, and in Otmoor, various characteristics associated with the movement were identified.

I should note here that I.Q. measurements were included in the Otmoor survey, not because we had any specific interest in I.Q. itself but rather because it possessed general elements in which we were interested: it represented a mix of nature and nurture in its development and was relatively easy to measure, and most importantly, it was likely to affect movement patterns, both spatially and socially. I trust that the summary of results provided above illustrates how interesting the analysis was, but in passing, one cannot help but notice that the mean I.Q.s for the different villages have ranges not too dissimilar to those among major ethnic groups.

Our other main genetic interest, in addition to the skin color analysis, was to detect natural selection by looking for associations between gene markers and conditions that might affect reproductive fitness. Although a few such associations were discovered, the exercise could hardly be called successful. They certainly drew little attention perhaps because there can be causes other than selection for such associations. The only association considered worthy of debate was the observed correlation between I.Q. and ABO blood group in Oxfordshire villages. This observation was by no means the strongest association we reported, but it clearly caused some upset. It seems unfortunate to me that in the present socio-political atmosphere any identification of genes with I.Q. variance is unacceptable. Whatever one's belief or judgment about the magnitude of a heritable component to I.Q., few would deny that there is at least some genetic involvement. And if there is any contribution at all, it is likely that associations will be manifest because pleiotropy or close linkage is bound to occur.

A final contribution on the genetic side was to consider the relationship between geographical movement and selection on the assumption that selection has played a significant role in determining between-population differences. In this analysis, we (Hiorns & Harrison 1977) modeled the development of gene distributions when gene flow was reinforced by favorable selection or was opposed by it. Two significant findings emerged: First, although the final equilibrium of gene frequency is very different under the two models of selection, i.e., complete loss of a polymorphism versus a stable cline, the gene distributions in the passage states may be extremely similar; second, it became clear that local movements between closely neighboring populations would not spread new genes very far geographically, even over numerous generations and when supported by selection. A fundamental requirement for major geographical spread is at least some long-range movement, and this must have happened to maintain the integrity of the human species.

Although I trust that the genetic contributions we have made are useful, it is with our increased understanding of the relationships between adaptability, fitness, and environmental quality that I am most pleased. Components of adaptability are strikingly evident in human responses to climate and infection, and increasingly evidence indicates that they occur in nutritional ecology. In each component, there appears to be a rough hierarchy dependent on an inverse relationship between speed of response and economy of maintenance. Some responses occur almost immediately on exposure to the environment change but are costly to maintain. They are progressively replaced by physiological acclimatizations, which take weeks to develop fully but which are more economical. Then there are developmental responses, which can occur only during the growing period but need no additional maintenance. And maximum economy will occur through the inheritance of adaptive genes (Harrison 1993b). Our work with mice and in Ethiopia exemplifies these various elements of adaptation. Overall, I recognize, of course, that in humans it is the components of behavior and culture that are ultimately responsible for the success of the human species and its widespread geographical distribution. But the biological components should not be ignored.

And, interest in adaptability is not merely academic; it is an essential element in the determination of health and well-being, both of which are determinants not only of evolution but also of human happiness. One of the most seminal insights into the biology of the human condition was made by S. Boyden when he examined the impact of modern lifestyles and genetic constitutions, which were evolved to cope with hunter-gatherer lifestyles. It has given me great pleasure to follow some of these ideas by examining theoretically the impact of modern urbanization on human health (Harrison 1978; 1982; 1990a,b; 1996).

But perhaps most important for the future is further investigation of the interrelationship between biological adaptation and social processes. Such work has been pioneered by Brooke Thomas, but I am pleased to note that a number of Oxford-trained students are now in this field. They include A. Almedon, G. Brush, G. Garrard, D. Jenner, C. Kuchemann, B. Long, H. Macbeth, C. Palmer, C. Panter-Brick, M. Parker, T. Pollard, M. Ryan, P. Sells, D. Sief, L. Singh, and K. Summers. I am also proud of the many undergraduate students I have taught, particularly in our Human Sciences program at Oxford, who have gone on to practical work to improve the lot of human beings: surely the ultimate goal of biological anthropology.

DISCLOSURE STATEMENT

The author is not aware of any affiliations, memberships, funding, or financial holdings that might be perceived as affecting the objectivity of this review.

ACKNOWLEDGMENTS

I greatly value all the subjects, officials, and colleagues that have made my research possible and thank them most sincerely for their invaluable contributions. I particularly wish to acknowledge the assistance of my two long-standing colleagues in biological anthropology at Oxford, Dr. A.J. Boyce and Professor V. Reynolds. They were critically involved in many of the research projects here described. I also thank my daughter, Clare, and wife, Elizabeth, for putting this piece together and Dr. John Clarke for his most helpful comments on it.

LITERATURE CITED

Boyce AJ, Harrison GA, Platt CM, Hornabrook RW. 1976. Association between PTC taster status and goitre in a Papua New Guinean population. *Hum. Biol.* 48:769–73

Boyce AJ, Kuchemann CF, Harrison GA. 1967. Neighbourhood knowledge and the distribution of marriage distance. *Ann. Hum. Genet.* 30:335–38

Brush G, Boyce AJ, Harrison GA. 1983. Associations between anthropometric variables and reproductive performance in a Papua New Guinea highland population. *Ann. Hum. Biol.* 10:223–34

Brush G, Harrison GA. 2001. Components of length growth variation in infants from the same population but different environments. *Am. J. Hum. Biol.* 13:197–203

Brush G, Harrison GA, Baber FM, Zumrawi FY. 1992. Comparative variability and interval correlation in linear growth of Hong Kong and Sudanese infants. *Am. J. Hum. Biol.* 291–99

Brush G, Harrison GA, Zumrawi FY. 1993. A path analysis of some determinants of infant growth in Khartoum. *Ann. Hum. Biol.* 20:381–87

Cain AJ, Harrison GA. 1958. An analysis of the taxonomist's judgement of affinity. *Proc. Zoolog. Soc.* 131:85–98

Cain AJ, Harrison GA. 1960. Phyletic weighting. *Proc. Zool. Soc.* 135:1–31

Clegg EJ, Harrison GA. 1966. Changes in body weight as a parameter of fitness in mice exposed to diminished atmospheric pressure. *Proc. Int. Congr. Biometeorol.*, *3rd*, pp. 184—89. Oxford/New York: Pergamon

Gibson JB, Harrison GA, Hiorns RW. 1975. Population stratification as an explanation of IQ and ABO association—reply to G Thompson and WF Bodmer. *Nature* 254:363–64

Harrison GA. 1958a. The adaptability of mice to high environmental temperatures. *J. Exp. Biol.* 35:892–901

Harrison GA. 1958b. High temperature responses of inbred and hybrid mice. *Proc. Int. Congr. Genet., 10th, Montreal,* Vol. II

Harrison GA. 1962. Heterosis and adaptability in the heat tolerance of mice. *Genetics* 47:427–34

Harrison GA. 1963. Temperature adaptation as evidenced by the growth of mice. *Fed. Proc.* 22:691–98

Harrison GA. 1966. Human adaptability with reference to the IBP proposals for high altitude research. In *The Biology of Human Adaptability*, ed. PT Baker, JS Weiner, pp. 509–19. Oxford: Clarendon

Harrison GA. 1970. Human variation and its social causes and consequences. *Proc. R. Anthropol. Inst. G. B. Irel.,* pp. 501–3

Harrison GA. 1976. Genetic and anthropological studies in the human adaptability section of the International Biological Program. *Phil. Trans. R. Soc.* B274:437–45

Harrison GA. 1977. Structure and function in the biology of human populations. In *Population Structure and Human Variation*, ed. GA Harrison, pp. 1–8. Cambridge, UK: Cambridge Univ. Press

Harrison GA. 1978. Biological aspects of life's quality in modern environments. *Urban Ecol.* 3:292–98

Harrison GA. 1979. Human evolution and the environment. In *The Biological Environment*, ed. J Lenihan, WW Fletcher, pp. 32–48. Glasgow: Blackie

Harrison GA. 1982. Lifestyles, well-being and stress. *Hum. Biol.* 54(2):193–202

Harrison GA. 1988. Seasonality and human population biology. In *Coping with Uncertainty in Food Supply*, ed. I deGarine, GA Harrison, pp. 26–31. Oxford: Oxford Univ. Press

Harrison GA. 1989. Human geographical variation. In *Evolutionary Studies: A Centenary Celebration of the Life of Julian Huxley*, ed. M Keynes, GA Harrison, pp. 158–67. London: Macmillan

Harrison GA. 1990a. The biology of human well-being. In *Is Our Future Limited by Our Past? Proc. Australas. Soc. Hum. Biol., No. 3.*, ed. L Freedman, pp. 3–10. Nedlands, Aust.: Univ. West. Aust.

Harrison GA. 1990b. Lifestyle, health, well-being and natural selection. In *Primate Life History and Evolution*, ed. J DeRousseau, pp. 221–28. New York: Wiley-Liss

Harrison GA, ed. 1993a. *Human Adaptation*. Oxford: Oxford Univ. Press

Harrison GA. 1993b. Physiological adaptation. See Harrison 1993a, pp. 55—72

Harrison GA. 1995. *The Human Biology of the English Village*. Oxford: Oxford Univ. Press

Harrison GA. 1996. The biology of everyday living: Pearl lecture. *Am. J. Hum. Biol.* 8:291–300

Harrison GA. 2000. Gene/environmental interrelationships in adaptation and fitness. *Jpn. J. Health Hum. Ecol.* 66:13–20

Harrison GA, Boyce AJ, eds. 1972. *The Structure of Human Populations*. Oxford: Oxford Univ. Press

Harrison GA, Boyce AJ, Hornabrook RW, Craig WJ. 1976a. Associations between polymorphic variety and anthropometric and biochemical variation in two New Guinea populations. *Ann. Hum. Biol.* 3(6):557—68

Harrison GA, Boyce AJ, Hornabrook RW, Craig WJ. 1976b. Associations between polymorphic variety and disease susceptibility in two New Guinea populations. *Ann. Hum. Biol.* 3(3):253–67

Harrison GA, Boyce AJ, Hornabrook RW, Serjeantson S, Craig WJ. 1976c. Evidence for an association between ABO blood group and goitre. *Hum. Genet.* 32:335–37

Harrison GA, Boyce AJ, Platt CM, Serjeantson S. 1975. Body composition changes during lactation in a New Guinea population. *Ann. Hum. Biol.* 2(4):395–98

Harrison GA, Brush G, Zumrawi FY. 1993. Motherhood and infant health in Khartoum. *Bull. WHO* 71:529–33

Harrison GA, Brush G, Zumrawi FY. 1994. Comparative length and weight growth in Khartoum infants. *Ann. Human Biol.* 21:399–405

Harrison GA, Gibson JB, Hiorns RW, Wigley M, Hancock C, et al. 1974a. Psychometric, personality and anthropometric variation in a group of Oxfordshire villages. *Ann. Hum. Biol.* 1:365—81

Harrison GA, Hiorns RW, Boyce AJ. 1974b. Movement, relatedness and the genetic structure of the population of Karkar Island. *Phil. Trans. R. Soc.* B 268:241–49

Harrison GA, Hiorns RW, Kuchemann CF. 1970. Social class relatedness in a group of Oxfordshire parishes. *J. Biosoc. Sci.* 2:71–80

Harrison GA, Hiorns RW, Kuchemann CF. 1971. Social class and marriage patterns in some Oxford populations. *J. Biosoc. Sci.* 3:1–12

Harrison GA, Hiorns RW, Weiner JS. 1964. The growth of mice in a fluctuating temperature environment. *Proc. R. Soc. B* 160:137–48

Harrison GA, Kuchemann CF, Hiorns RW, Carrivick PJ. 1974c. Social mobility, assortative marriage and their interrelationships with marital distance and age in Oxford City. *Ann. Hum. Biol.* 1:211–23

Harrison GA, Kuchemann CF, Moore MSA, Boyce AJ, Baju T, et al. 1969. Studies on the effects of altitudinal variation in Ethiopia. *Phil. Trans. R. Soc. B* 256:147–82

Harrison GA, Morton RJ, Weiner JS. 1959. The growth in weight and tail length of inbred and hybrid mice reared at two different temperatures. *Phil. Trans. R. Soc. B* 242:479–516

Harrison GA, Owen JJT. 1964. Studies on the inheritance of human skin color. *Ann. Hum. Genet.* 28:27–37

Harrison GA, Owen JJT, DaRocha FJ, Salzano FM. 1967. Skin color in Southern Brazilian populations. *Hum. Biol.* 39:21–31

Harrison GA, Palmer CD. 1981. Husband-wife similarities among Oxfordshire villagers. *MAN* 16:130–34

Harrison GA, Palmer CD, Jenner D, Reynolds V. 1980. Similarities between husbands and wives in rates of catecholamine excretion. *Ann. Hum. Biol.* 7(4):379–80

Harrison GA, Palmer CD, Jenner DA, Reynolds V. 1981. Associations between rates of urinary catecholamine excretions and aspects of lifestyle among adult women in some Oxfordshire villages. *Hum. Biol.* 53:617–33

Harrison GA, Salzano FM. 1966. The skin color of the Caingang and Guarani Indians of Brazil. *Hum. Biol.* 38:104–11

Harrison GA, Schmitt LH. 1989. Variability in stature growth. *Ann. Hum. Biol.* 16(1):45–51

Harrison GA, Walsh RJ. 1974. Human adaptability in a tropical ecosystem. *Phil. Trans. R. Soc.* 268:221–400

Harrison GA, Waterlow JC, eds. 1990. *Diet and Disease in Traditional and Developing Societies*. Cambridge, UK: Cambridge Univ. Press

Harrison GA, Weiner JS. 1963. Some considerations in the formulation of theories of human phylogeny. In *Classification and Human Evolution*, ed. SL Washburn, pp. 75–84. Viking Fund Publ. 37. Chicago: Aldine

Henneberg M, Harrison GA, Brush G. 1998. The small child: anthropometric and physical performance characteristics of short-for-age children growing in food and poor socio-economic conditions. *Eur. J. Clin. Nutr.* 52:286–91

Hiorns RW, Harrison GA. 1970. Sampling for the detection of natural selection by age group genetic differences. *Hum. Biol.* 42:53–64

Hiorns RW, Harrison GA. 1977. The combined effects of selection and migration in human evolution. *MAN* 12:438–45

Hiorns RW, Harrison GA, Boyce AJ, Kuchemann CF. 1969. A mathematical analysis of the effects of movement on the relatedness between populations. *Ann. Hum. Genet.* 32:237–50

Hiorns RW, Harrison GA, Gibson JB. 1977. Genetic variation in some Oxfordshire villages. *Ann. Hum. Biol.* 4:197–210

Jenner DA, Harrison GA, Prior IAM. 1987. Catecholamine excretion in Tokelauans living in three different environments. *Hum. Biol.* 59(1):165–72

Jenner DA, Reynolds V, Harrison GA. 1980. Catecholamine excretion rates and occupation. *Ergonomics* 23(3):237–46

Kuchemann CF, Boyce AJ, Harrison GA. 1967. The demographic and genetic structure of a group of Oxfordshire Villages. *Hum. Biol.* 39:251–75

Kucheman CF, Harrison GA. 1972. Historical demography in relation to human biology. *Dyn* 2:1–22

Kuchemann CF, Harrison GA, Hiorns RW, Carrivick PJ. 1974. Social class and marital distance in Oxford City. *Ann. Hum. Biol.* 1(1):13–27

Mascie-Taylor CGN, Gibson JB, Hiorns RW, Harrison GA. 1985. Associations between some polymorphic markers and variation in IQ and its components in Otmoor villagers. *Behav. Genet.* 15(4):371–83

Palmer CD, Harrison GA. 1983a. Intercorrelation between sleep and activity patterns in Otmoor villagers. *Hum. Biol.* 55(4):749–62

Palmer CD, Harrison GA. 1983b. Sleep latency and lifestyle in Oxfordshire villages. *Ann. Hum. Biol.* 10(5):417–28

Palmer CD, Harrison GA, Hiorns RW. 1980a. Association between smoking and drinking and sleep duration. *Ann. Hum. Biol.* 7(2):103–08

Palmer CD, Harrison GA, Hiorns RW. 1980b. Sleep patterns and lifestyle in Oxfordshire villages. *J. Biosoc. Sci.* 12:437–67

Reynolds V, Jenner DA, Palmer CD, Harrison GA. 1981. Catecholamine excretion rates in relation to lifestyles in the male population of Otmoor, Oxfordshire. *Ann. Hum. Biol.* 8(3):197–209

Schmitt LH, Harrison GA, Spargo RM. 1998. Variation in epinephrine and cortisol excretion rates associated with behavior in an Australian Aboriginal community. *Am. J. Phys. Anthropol.* 106:249–53

Schmitt LH, Harrison GA, Spargo RM, Pollard T, Ungpakorn G. 1995. Patterns of cortisol and adrenaline variation in Australian Aboriginal communities of the Kimberley region. *J. Biosoc. Sci.* 27:107–16

Weiner JS, Harrison GA, Singer R, Harris R, Jopp W. 1964. Skin color in South West Africa. *Hum. Biol.* 36:294–307

Enactments of Expertise

E. Summerson Carr

School of Social Service Administration, University of Chicago, Chicago, Illinois 60637;
email: esc@uchicago.edu

Annu. Rev. Anthropol. 2010. 39:17–32

First published online as a Review in Advance on
May 3, 2010

The *Annual Review of Anthropology* is online at
anthro.annualreviews.org

This article's doi:
10.1146/annurev.anthro.012809.104948

0084-6570/10/1021-0017$20.00

Key Words

apprenticeship, institution, language, naturalization, value

Abstract

Every society recognizes expertise, and anthropologists have long documented the culturally and historically specific practices that constitute
it. The anthropology of expertise focuses on what people do rather
than what people possess, even in the many circumstances where the
former is naturalized as the latter. Across its many domains, expertise
is both inherently interactional, involving the participation of objects,
producers, and consumers of knowledge, and inescapably ideological,
implicated in the evolving hierarchies of value that legitimate particular
ways of knowing as "expert." This review focuses on the semiotics of expertise, highlighting four constitutive processes: socialization practices
through which people establish intimacy with classes of cultural objects
and learn to communicate that familiarity; evaluation, or the establishment of asymmetries among people and between people and objects;
institutionalization, wherein ways of knowing are organized and authorized; and naturalization, or the essentialization of expert enactments
as bodies of knowledge.

INTRODUCTION

The ethnographic record demonstrates that every society recognizes forms of expertise. The very practice of ethnography entails mapping and representing social distributions of knowledge, including the sites where modes of expertise are practiced and deployed. After all, the key informant is a kind of cultural expert on whom the anthropologist—as another kind of cultural expert—has long relied. From the canoe technologists of Melanesia (see Malinowski 1922, Mead 1928, Mishkin 1937, Scoditti 1982) to the medical specialists of the contemporary United States (see Dumit 2004, Saunders 2008), experts have taught anthropologists about (a) socialization practices such as training and apprenticeship; (b) cultural processes of evaluation, validation, and authentication; (c) the institutionalization of ways of seeing and speaking into authorized and authorizing domains; and (d) the naturalization of specified activities as specialized knowledge.

In an age defined by mass dissemination and proliferation, many contemporary anthropologists have turned to the study of how different kinds of expertise encounter each other (e.g., Choy 2005; Epstein 1996; Good 2004, 2007; Gusterson 1996; Haviland 2003; Hess 2007; Hogle 2002a,b; Irwin & Jordan 1987; Rapp 2000) and work to anticipate, or at least keep pace with, the world's revolutions (e.g., Fortun 2001, Holmes & Marcus 2005, Kelty 2008, Knorr Cetina 1999, Lakoff 2008, Nader 1996, Ong 2005, Redfield 2006, Strathern 2006, Timura 2004). Indeed, with the emergence of what Urban (2001) calls a "metaculture of newness," in which social totality is achieved through the aggregation of "mass-mediated individual performative epiphanies" (Lee 2001, p. xv), contemporary social experience is simply unimaginable without expertise to categorize and rank these responses. As it turns out, the enactment of expertise not only determines the value of cultural objects, whether mental states, real estate, wine, disease, or gold; it also confers value on those who interact with these objects, including the experts so enacted.

This review begins with the simple premise that expertise is something people do rather than something people have or hold (compare Collins & Evans 2002, 2007). From the medico-religious (Lambek 1993, Simpson 1997) to the biogenetic (Brodwin 2002, Rapp 1988, Simpson 2004), expertise is inherently interactional because it involves the participation of objects, producers, and consumers of knowledge. Expertise is also always ideological because it is implicated in semistable hierarchies of value that authorize particular ways of seeing and speaking as expert. Expertise is arguably the exemplar of what Silverstein calls "second order indexicality" (1992, 2003)—that is, historically constituted and contingent metadiscursive practices (e.g., rationalizations, evaluations, diagnoses) that mediate between would-be experts and some set of cultural goods. These practices are routinized and organized as institutional boundaries are forged between different ways of knowing the very same thing, spawning the social configurations we call profession, craft, and discipline (Abbott 1988, 1995; Brenneis 1994; Gal & Irvine 1995).

Foucault has influenced many contemporary anthropological accounts of expertise (e.g., Fassin & D'Halluin 2005, 2007; Gusterson 1996; Ilcan & Phillips 2003; Lakoff 2005; Ong 2005; Schwegler 2008). These studies consistently assert that expertise manifests in power relations that are both repressive and productive, and it reproduces these relations when expressed by disciplined social actors (i.e., experts and laypeople). For instance, in her study of public health officials in Brazil, Wayland draws on Foucault to suggest that "[t]hose who control valued knowledge are viewed as experts, and expertise often conveys authority" (Wayland 2003, p. 484; compare Scott 2009). And in his study of East German journalists, Boyer draws on Foucault's theorization of discipline as a positive economy—in which bodies are made docile to exploit the resource of time—as a "useful way of thinking about the decorporealized body of the professional intellectual" (2005a, p. 250; see also

Boyer 2005b). Foucauldian studies have repeatedly demonstrated how expert opinion, as a poignant intersection of knowledge and power, both formulates and compels individual bodies and populations. Yet, to the extent that anthropologists follow Foucault (1984) in jettisoning an archaeological method, which reconstructs intradiscursive relations in favor of a genealogy devoted to plotting "the hazardous play of dominations" (p. 83) across vast spans of time and space, we risk overlooking the dynamics of expertise-in-practice that we are especially well positioned to document and analyze. Indeed, to attend archaeologically to the "anticipatory power of meaning" (p. 83) is also to appreciate the way that expertise emerges in real-time interaction as actors and institutions struggle to author and authorize powerful texts that will be read as such by others (see Redfield 2006).

After all, to be an expert is not only to be authorized by an institutionalized domain of knowledge or to make determinations about what is true, valid, or valuable within that domain; expertise is also the ability to "finesse reality and animate evidence through mastery of verbal performance" (Matoesian 1999, p. 518). Accordingly, this review approaches expertise as intensively citational institutional action, rather than as a powerful cache of individual knowledge that is simply expressed in social interaction. To this end, I highlight how expert actors use linguistic and metalinguistic resources—such as jargons and acronyms—and poetically structure real-time interaction. I also address the role of gesture, uniforms, and other visual media in the enactment of expertise (Goodwin 1994, 1996; Matoesian 2008).

Given the ubiquity of expertise, and the richness and range of anthropological treatments of it, I have organized this review around four conceptual themes, each of which contributes to an understanding of expertise as accomplished, or enacted, through linguistic practices. The first section addresses socialization processes, such as training and apprenticeship, by which people learn to act as experts. Apprenticeship invariably involves a period of intensive interaction with objects of knowledge, as well as with other people who have putatively mastered those objects. However, the reader will see that people become experts not simply by forming familiar—if asymmetrical—relationships with people and things, but rather by learning to communicate that familiarity from an authoritative angle. An emphasis on semiotic mediation is carried through the discussion of evaluation and authentication, to which the second section of the review is devoted. Considering the relative agency of people, both expert and lay, and the objects of knowledge they engage, I highlight the collaborative labor involved in sustaining expertise in situated practice. A third section on institutionalization and authorization focuses on how certain ways of knowing come to be institutionally authorized as expert, and the fourth section touches on the naturalization of expertise by posing the following question: Why are the highly collaborative and institutionally organized dynamics of expert enactment so often understood as a property that elite individuals have or hold within them? Rather than concluding that "actual social relations are obscured or misrecognized by the actors" (Irwin & Jordan 1987, p. 319; see also Bourdieu & Johnson 1993), I underscore the basic premise of the review. That is, expertise requires the mastery of verbal performance, including—perhaps most importantly—the ability to use language to index and therefore instantiate already existing inner states of knowledge. In conclusion, I offer methodological principles for studying expertise as enactment.

APPRENTICESHIP, TRAINING, AND SOCIALIZATION

If expertise is enactment, it is also fundamentally a process of becoming rather than a crystallized state of being or knowing. So although certain forms of expertise may be culturally cast as natural or spiritual endowment, it is clear that one can learn to be an expert. Indeed, the development of expertise generally begins with a period of training, which takes an array of forms cross-culturally as well as across historically specific domains of expertise. Consider Lave's study of Liberian tailors. It documents the five-year period during which apprentices work in master tailors' shops, learning the process of garment production in reverse. Each step, Lave shows, involves "the unstated opportunity to consider how the previous step contributes to the present one...[an] ordering that minimizes experiences of failure" (1997, p. 21; see also Lave 1988).

This is one of several case studies reviewed by Lave & Wenger (1991), in their efforts to "rescue the idea of apprenticeship" from the notion that it is an outmoded form of training and theorize it as part of a ubiquitous cultural process of "situated learning" (p. 29; see also Hanks 1991). Frink (2009) has recently responded by rescuing a so-called subsistence technology—namely, herring processing in Native Alaska—and outlining how mastery is acquired through a lifetime of training in a gender- and age-stratified apprenticeship system. My own current work documents that apprenticeship is alive and well in the rapidly proliferating therapeutic field of Motivational Interviewing. In this case, learning to expertly incite behavioral change in others commonly involves observing experienced practitioners conduct video-taped, simulated sessions with client-actors, practicing the technique through a variety of role-playing exercises, and carefully evaluating one's audio-taped sessions with clients alongside an experienced trainer, who elaborately codes the recorded work (E.S. Carr, forthcoming).

The social organization of training has arguably been of enduring interest to anthropologists, at least since Malinowski (1964 [1922]; see also Scoditti 1982) described the range of skills that one must master to initiate a ritually and technically sound canoe—from the selecting, felling, and transporting of trees to the recitation of rites during the piecing together of ribs, poles, and planks. Contemporary technologies continue to galvanize the cultivation and dissemination of expertise. Saunders (2008) illustrates how diagnostics are cultivated at computerized tomography (CT) viewboxes around which clinicians huddle, ritually transforming seemingly mysterious images into powerful evidence that testifies to, among other things, the viewers' developing expertise. Indeed, becoming an expert invariably involves building an intimate relationship with a valuable class of cultural objects (Knorr Cetina 1999, Lee & Roth 2003, Urban 2001). Yet because a single kind of object, such as a CT scan, can play a number of roles across institutional contexts (see Dumit 2004)—generating opportunities for would-be experts to distinguish themselves from laypersons and novices along the way—apprenticeship involves learning how to define and frame, as well as to interpret and engage objects in an expert way.

Because being socialized as an expert involves establishing a deliberate stance in relation to a set of culturally valued or valuable objects, novices must master a register—that is, a recognizable, if specialized, linguistic repertoire that can include technical terms or acronyms, specific prosodic practices, and non-verbal signs such as facial expressions or gestures (Agha 1998, 2001, 2007; Silverstein 2003, 2004, 2006). For instance, to "constitute themselves as hair experts," students in an African American cosmetology school learn "to distinguish between specialized and lay hair terminology" (Jacobs-Huey 2003, p. 277); they also distinguish their knowledge from that of lay-clients by "renam[ing] commonly known black hair care procedures" (p. 278). Indeed, jargons are often not attempts to guard or obfuscate expert knowledge, as many have suggested, but are rather a way to signify it. Consider that in the course of American medical training, "[n]ovices simulate expertise by projecting a sense of authority or control over information and motor skills and especially by the way they use particular words, asking questions while trying to achieve a poised demeanor and speech delivery to mask any anxiety or uncertainty about what is happening" (Cicourel 2001, p. 68; compare Bosk 2003). Given such examples, we can define an expert register as a way of speaking that is recognized as a special kind of knowledge and manifests in interaction as such.

Indeed, socialization into a domain of expertise involves learning how to control interactional texts as much as determining the content of denotational ones. That is, apprentices learn not only what to say in representing the objects of their expertise, but how to say it as well. This point is keenly illustrated in Mertz's examination of "learning to think like a lawyer," which involves pragmatically mobilizing legal texts, such as case law, rather than simply learning its "content" (1993, 1996, 2007). Mertz further argues that the pedagogical routines of American law school classrooms—in which professors successively engage students in intensive dyadic exchanges—are structured attempts to undermine the semantic-interpretive orientation with which students enter the classroom. Not unlike law students and beauty school students, Motivational Interviewing novices commonly engage in elaborate role-play exercises to anticipate future interactions with clients and practice expert communication, as do magicians' apprentices (Jones & Shweder 2003).

Of course, the degree to which socialization as an expert involves mastering verbal routines, whether ritual incantation or diagnostic explication, or mobilizing lexical resources such as jargons, depends on local ideologies of language, as well as the specific form of expertise at stake. In the medical domain, Cicourel (1981, 1995) finds that attending physicians do not directly observe medical students interviewing patients and interpreting their symptoms; instead, attendings determine the degree to which novices have acquired expert knowledge by evaluating the oral presentation of their work. By contrast, in studying Mexicano woodcarvers in Cordova, Briggs (1986) quickly learned of a form of expertise transmitted not through verbal exchange between masters and apprentices, but instead through observation, internalization, and imitation of patterned behaviors.

Even when people engage in training routines that ritually transform them into experts, and often also officially render them as such by bestowing various credentials (e.g., diplomas, badges, passwords, titles, offices, keys, uniforms), they must consistently act as experts if they are to maintain their status. As Lambek's (1993) study of ritual experts in Mayotte makes clear, there is no precise threshold between being a novice and expert, nor does expertise entail an irreversible progression. Because expertise is always subject to public evaluation, "the appellation is [not] in most cases absolute; rather it is relative and situational, a matter of social context" (p. 86; see also Hogle 2002a). And because "attributing minimal or natural expertise to someone assumes training and experience associated with a title and a prior credentialing process" (Cicourel 2001, p. 27), a crucial question arises: How is one's training actively invoked across the communicative events in which expertise is at stake? Indeed, whether referencing the sites of one's training, carrying credentialing initials before or behind one's family name, or hanging certificates bearing institutional affiliations on one's walls, would-be experts must continuously work to authenticate themselves as experts as well as to authenticate the objects of their expertise.

AUTHENTICATION AND EVALUATION

As Urban (2001) notes, experts are people who make it their business to become intimate with classes of culturally valuable things that are relatively inaccessible or illegible to laypeople, such as art (Myers 1994), weapons (Cohn 1987, Gusterson 1996, Masco 2006), wine (Silverstein 2004, 2006), mental states (Carr 2010, Lakoff 2005, Smith 2005, Young 1997), cosmological conditions (Hanks 1996, Lambek 1993), brains and bodies (Bosk 2003, Dumit 2004, Rapp 1999, Smardon 2008), endangered or proper language (Gal 1995, Hill 2002, Silverstein 1996), hair (Jacobs-Huey 2003), odds (Modell 1989), and gold (Putnam 1973). As reviewed above, establishing this intimacy, as well as a way to relay it publicly, is part of learning to be an expert across diverse terrains of practice. To the extent that practitioners are successful in establishing their expertise, both in the actual process of training and their continual real-time evocation of it, they can create hierarchies and distinctions by determining the qualities, authenticity, or value of the objects within their purview. This holds true whether experts base their assessments on the intrinsic qualities or on future circulations of the things they evaluate, with the latter increasingly serving as the basis of the former in conditions of late capitalism.

In line with what Bateson (2000) provocatively identified as the fundamental "error in the thinking and attitudes of Occidental culture" (p. 498)—that is, the privileging of mind over matter—it is all too easy to presume that expertise is a matter of people interpreting, establishing the value of, and thereby managing, if not totally mastering, the objects of their expert interest. However, as some anthropologists have elegantly shown, the culturally ascribed qualities of the things that engage experts profoundly shape the manifestation of expertise (e.g., Lambek 1993). For instance, in line with the Latourian impulse to assign agency to objects (see especially, Johnson 1988; Latour 1988, 2005; compare Abbott 1995, p. 323), Dumit (2004) asserts the existence of "expert objects"—such as brain scans—that actively confer opportunities for the enactment of expertise. He further suggests that "objects. . .that require help in interpreting even though they may appear to be legible to a layperson" (p. 112; see also Dumit 2000) may be particularly powerful. Other anthropologists of science have averred that objects thought to be obscure or inaccessible to laypeople—such as nano-materials (Kelty 2008) or beamtimes (Traweek 1988)—generate high degrees of expert agency. Their ethnographic accounts therefore represent such things, along with the people who interact with them, as expert actors.

Likewise, we should consider how things that everyone is thought to have—such as language or mental states—are expertly translated by those who claim to have special knowledge of them (see, for example, Carr 2010, Gal 1995). Indeed, some objects of expertise are widely, if not universally, accessible but still offer elite opportunities for authorized people to enact expertise. In such cases, distinctions about the relative legibility of these objects are commonly drawn. For example, in cultures in which gender is thought to be a natural property of individual bodies (compare Strathern 1988, Rosaldo 1982), to enact gender expertly is to decipher and deploy it in an especially reflexive way (Hall 1995, McCloskey 1999; compare McCloskey 1992). Similarly, in the case of mainstream American addiction treatment, therapists' efforts to help and heal their clients, and establish themselves as experts, commonly hinge on their claim that they intimately know the inner states that their clients, as addicts, deny (Carr 2006, 2010; compare Lakoff 2005, p. 85). Other kinds of clinical expertise cast clients as experts of their own bodily experience, while retaining the authority to read that experience as evidence.

If anthropological accounts of the relative agency of expert persons and expert objects differ, so do theories about the role of laypeople in the enactment of expertise. After all, expertise is not only a relationship between a special kind of person and a special kind of thing. It is also a relationship between at least two types of people: experts and laities. Knorr Cetina (1999) calibrates these two orders of expertise by suggesting that the expert's discernment of objects necessarily involves the creation of distinctions among people; she considers the role of expert colleagues as well, writing, "Experts are those who have learned to engage with objects in reliable trust relationships and who, therefore, are trusted by colleagues who cannot engage in those relationships directly" (p. 135). However, realizing one's self as an expert can hinge on casting other people as less aware, knowing, or knowledgeable. Indeed, expertise emerges in the hoary intersection of claims about types of people, and the relative knowledge they contain and control, and claims about differentially knowable types of things. As Mitchell (2002) argues, the rise of modern Egyptian techno-political expertise would have been impossible without the figuring of the Egyptian peasant as nonintellectual Other.

The enactment of expertise can also involve the performance of uncertainty. Consider Bergmann's (1992) fascinating case of the clinicians who, in performing intake interviews in a mental hospital, frame their own knowledge of the patient and her troubles as uncertain and in need of confirmation. This strategy, Bergmann argues, works to elicit a firsthand account from the patient, which is of course both the function of the intake process and the initiation of the diagnostic processes that constitute the "uncertain" clinicians' expertise (see Peräkylä 1995).

This example illustrates that successful enactments of expertise hinge on the would-be expert's ability to establish an interpretive frame through which to view that object. As Silverstein (2004, 2006; see also Goodwin 1994, Urban 2001) points out, it may seem that evaluative principles are read directly off things, but people emerge as more or less expert not in unmediated relationships to culturally valued objects (such as wine), but instead through the discursive processes of representing them (such as wine talk). Thus, it is not simply in the realm of the culinary that "you are what you say about what you eat" (Silverstein 2004, p. 644; compare Bourdieu 1984). Ayurvedic experts in India differentiate themselves from quacks not through direct interaction with patients or their illnesses, but through metadiagnostic activities that painstakingly differentiate authentic and inauthentic ways of knowing (Langford 1999). Similarly, Mayan shamanic expertise is enacted during exorcism events—and exorcism is thereby achieved—through the citing and reworking of other shamans' prayers (Hanks 1996). Another explicitly citational realm of social practice—that is, social scientific expertise—follows suit. Bauman & Briggs (2003) demonstrate the metadiscursive nature of late-seventeenth-century European regimes of intellectual authority, which were constituted by ways of speaking about ways of knowing. And, as Gal & Irvine (1995; see also Gal 2006) note, the achievement and maintenance of our academic disciplines rely on the same kind of metalinguistic practices that differentiate languages from dialects. (I suppose, then, the writing of an *Annual Review* article is a particularly poignant case in point, at least for this putative expert).

As Silverstein's discussions of Mr. A and Mr. B demonstrate so well (1998, 2003, 2004), would-be experts work to establish their expertise not so much by trying to out-denote each other, in verbal or written displays of what they know about an object of mutual interest. Instead, they must engage in less predictable, real-time performances, which often take the form of one-upmanship (Silverstein 2004). The enactment of expertise may involve talking to even more than it entails talking about. This point is demonstrated with particular acuity by linguistic anthropologists who carefully attend to the role of gesture in the enactment of expertise. Consider Matoesian's (2008) brilliant demonstration of how a doctor, acting as an expert witness, trumps a prosecuting attorney not by providing incontrovertible evidence that satisfies the referential demands of the prosecution's increasingly insistent questions. Instead, the doctor emerges as an expert through a careful calibration of verbal and bodily conduct—including lip protrusions, "thinking face displays," and more or less dramatic shakes of his head—which gears the questioning in a more favorable direction.

Matoesian's work—especially when read alongside Mertz's (1993, 1996, 2007) discussion of law students and Philips's (1991) ethnography of American judges—suggests that institutional contexts (such as courtrooms) and professional affiliations (such as doctor and lawyer) do not magically or automatically confer expert statuses onto their inhabitants. It is arguably only when we rigorously attend to real-time semiotic interaction—where struggles between law, science, magic, and medicine play out in improvisational and contingent if always already conventionally controlled ways—that we can also discern just what role institutions play in the organization, authorization, and enactment of expertise.

INSTITUTIONS AND AUTHORIZATION

As long as anthropologists have been interested in the institution of training and apprenticeship, we have also recognized how evaluative and authenticating practices are institutionally authorized. After all, anthropologists know that institutions not only host ritual ceremonies, such as ordinations and graduations; institutions also provide certificates, badges, feathers, tools, technologies, special clothing, and credentialing letters (e.g., PhD) that signify these expert rites of passage in future expert enactments. Indeed, well after novices have been officially rendered experts by the institutions that sponsored their training, the emblems of expertise provide access to other institutional sites and the equipment, artifacts, and objects contained therein (Cicourel 2001, p. 27).

Expertise also links institutions, paving the way for things to travel by assigning them meaning and value. For example, Myers (1994) examines how art criticism deals in aesthetic, ethnic, and monetary value, categorizing things as art or its reproductions and derivatives and shaping the markets in which these things flow. One need only to watch a single episode of "Antiques Roadshow" to see how appraisers subsume individual distinctions in an elaborate system of values (authenticity, biographical history, cultural origin, aesthetic beauty, market worth, etc.), thereby institutionalizing them. In doing so, appraisers also project themselves, the objects they evaluate, and the laypeople who possess them far beyond the sets of the Public Broadcasting System.

Some have argued that institutions, such as professions, schools, and disciplines, provide boundaries between ways of knowing the very same object (Abbott 1988, 1995; Douglas 1986; Hogle 2002b). In these accounts, the role of institutions is not just to cultivate and authorize certain knowledge practices, but also to organize them. Others have further demonstrated that institutions' ability to organize ways of knowing rests on their ability to manage ways of speaking by providing participants with semi-

otic resources (Carr 2009; Collins 2008; Gal & Irvine 1995; Goodwin 1994; Mehan 1996; Silverstein 2004, 2006). As Goodwin (1994) incisively notes, "Discursive practices are used by members of a profession to shape events in the domains subject to their professional scrutiny. The shaping process creates objects of knowledge that become the insignia of a profession's craft: The theories, artifacts, and bodies of expertise that distinguish it from other professions" (p. 606).

In line with Matoesian's analysis of expert testimony (2008), Goodwin further suggests that it is not the law that decides what counts as expertise. Nor do institutions—such as professions—automatically instantiate a prestructured power dynamic just because they can rest their claims on a collective, already always authorized Us versus a singular, lay You (see Desjarlais 1996). Institutions also help people to cultivate and strategically deploy what Goodwin calls "professional vision": the interpretive frameworks that allow, for instance, testifying police to expertly transform the brutal beating of Rodney King into discrete professional responses (e.g., kicks, clubbings, punches) or archaeologists to determine the color of the artifacts they retrieve in line with the categories provided by Munsell.

Thus, if we are indeed what we say about what we eat, "interested institutional forces are, however, hard at work to give directionality to this process, seeking to establish a solid foundation of 'true' worth of the object by naturalizing (essentializing) hierarchies of distinctions" (Silverstein 2006, p. 485). Indeed, institutions trade in "onomic" knowledge, terms that simultaneously index specialized areas of cultural knowledge and special types of people (p. 485). Those who participate in status-conferring institutions have greater access to and experience with -onomic knowledge, which suggests a fundamentally linguistic division of knowledge and labor (Putnam 1975; compare Barth 2002) as much as a prestructured organization of more-or-less knowing people in relation to more-or-less knowable things. It is in this sense that we can say that "professional vision is perspectival, lodged within specific social entities, and unevenly allocated" (Goodwin 1994, p. 626), which holds true across the many terrains of expertise that anthropologists study.

Consider what Mehan (1996), in his studies of special education meetings among parents, teachers, and school psychologists, calls "stratifying registers of representation" (p. 268). Given these parties' competing versions of a particular child, Mehan asks why it is that the technical discourse of the psychologist, which defines the child as "learning disabled," is never called on to clarify its terms. By way of an answer, Mehan suggests that "the psychologist's discourse obtains its privileged status because it is ambiguous, because it is shot full of technical terms, because it is difficult to understand" (p. 269), thereby removing it from the grounds of the potential challenges. Negating the tendency of American speakers to make their intentions, ideas, and interests maximally understood, Mehan concludes that the expert register is allowed to speak for itself in the context of the special education meeting.

Furthermore, once an individual's situated speech is "devoiced" as expert opinion (Mehan 1996), it can travel far from its interactional and institutional origin—a powerful phenomenon glossed by linguistic anthropologists in the twin terms of entextualization, or "the rendering of a given instance of discourse as text, detachable from its local context" (Urban 1996, p. 21), and contextualization, the accommodation of those texts to new institutional surrounds (Bauman & Briggs 1990; Carr 2010; Collins 1996; Gal 2005; Hanks 1996; Kuipers 1989; Mehan 1996; Philips 2010; Silverstein & Urban 1996; Urban 1992). Sometimes it is possible to track ethnographically how expert messages travel across institutional contexts or even to identify specific messengers. Yet perhaps what institutions do best is naturalize the expertise that has been produced in real-time interactions between putatively expert people and potentially valuable objects, allowing it to float across evermore empowering contexts (compare Foucault 1978, 1984). As Brenneis (1994) points out, even the bureaucracies that we perhaps know best as anthropologists work not so much to organize, but instead to naturalize knowledge.

NATURALIZATION

In his own masterful project, *Keywords*, Williams (1985) explains that the word "expert"—derived from the Latin *expertus* (to try)—first appeared in the English language as an adjective and was closely related to the word "experience." Ever suspicious of the transformation of verbs and adjectives into nouns, Williams historically anchors the rendering of "expertise" as a noun in the specialization and division of labor ushered in by the nineteenth-century industrialization of Western nations.

Although anthropologists have studied modes of expertise the world over, some have followed Williams in expressing a certain distrust of its contemporary manifestations, especially in highly industrialized and technocratic societies. Following Bourdieu (1984, Bourdieu & Johnson 1993), for instance, some have asserted that regimes of expertise obscure actual social relations, leading experts and laities alike to misrecognize the nature of things as well as their own interests in and evaluations of them (see, for instance, Irwin & Jordan 1987). Others have approached expertise as disciplined perception, showing how generations of experts differentially make sense of what they see given the ever-changing conditions of their labor. For instance, Masco (2004) argues that as the technical aspects of nuclear weapons research went underground and then virtual, weapons scientists suffered a "diminishing sensory experience" (p. 1) that blinded them to the political nature of their work.

Yet in documenting the production of a new sensibility, called "technoaesthetics," which arises precisely out of the diminishment of outmoded sensory and technical returns, Masco's work theoretically advances Cohn's (1987) chilling portrait of the hypermasculinist jargon of defense intellectuals. In her brilliant study, Cohn focuses on a "technostrategic" language that abstracts the realities of nuclear war by preventing certain questions to be asked or values to be expressed, thereby allowing defense intellectuals to escape the idea that they too could be the victims of their very own weapons. Suggesting the mystifying and even violent qualities of professional jargon, Cohn concludes, "the problem, then, is not only that the language is narrow but also that it is seen by its speakers as complete or whole unto itself—as representing a body of truths that exist independently of any other truth or knowledge" (p. 712; compare Latour & Woolgar 1986, Mehan 1996).

All modes of expertise arguably have coding systems, like jargons, that both produce categorical distinctions and erase the debate that inevitably went into producing them. Goodwin (1994) indicates as much in his study of those near and dear: professional archaeologists. Like Cohn, he suggests that a "coding scheme typically erases from subsequent documentation the cognitive and perceptual uncertainties" (p. 609) of expert actors and leads them to view the world (and its artifacts) in line with the perspective it establishes. And, much like Cohn implies in her comment about defense intellectuals' investment not only in their jargon, but also in the grounding idea that truth is independent of its representation, Goodwin's work suggests that the anthropology of expertise must always account for the language ideologies—that is, cultural constellations of ideas about the functions and effects of language—that organize and naturalize expertise. It is precisely the widely held ideas that language primarily functions to denote preexisting states and that those states are the inner property of speakers that so frequently naturalize expertise as something one has rather than something one does. My own ethnographic work on mainstream American addiction therapeutics suggests as much by documenting the semiotic processes that erase the real-time interactional routines by which people enact and establish expert knowledge of psychic interiors (Carr 2006, 2009, 2010).

Indeed, although telling people what they want to hear is precisely what experts do so well, as earlier sections of this review have proffered, expertise is nonetheless widely naturalized as the simple speaking of what one knows. This practice is precisely why American politicians, as professionals who commonly and quite tellingly fall outside of the cultural recognition of expertise, work so hard to master the performance of inner reference (see Fliegalman 1993). Indeed, to emerge as an expert within a linguistic community that privileges the ability of language to denote already existing states, one must master the performance of what is putatively remembered in uncluttered and context-relevant ways (Cicourel 2001). So thank goodness, dear reader, you are not witness to the messy stacks of the much loved, copiously underlined, and even soiled papers and dog-eared books that surround me as I conclude my very own expert enactment.

CONCLUSION: METHODS FOR THE STUDY OF EXPERTISE AS ENACTMENT

The premise that expertise is not something one has but something one does has been demonstrated by anthropologists of science and technology (Fortun 2001, Knorr Cetina 1999, Latour 1988, Latour & Woolgar 1986), medical anthropologists (Briggs & Mantini Briggs 2003, Rapp 2000, Young 1997), and anthropologists who study professionals (Benner et al. 1990; Bishara 2008; Brodwin 2008; Goodwin 1994, 1996; Mehan 1983, 1993, 1996; Smardon 2008), apprentices (Jacobs-Huey 2003; Mertz 1993, 1996, 2007; Lave 1997), intellectuals (Bauman & Briggs 2003, Boyer & Lomnitz 2005), and ritual specialists (Lambek 1993, Hanks 1996). Anthropologists and ethnographers dedicated to showing the expertise of seemingly mundane or subsistence activities (Becker 1953, Boster & Johnson 1989, Frink 2009, Kataoka 1998, Srinivasan Shipman & Boster 2008) have lent much support to this thesis as well. Lambek (1993) nicely summarizes the bottom line of the anthropology of expertise when he notes, "to be recognized publicly as [a ritual specialist in Mayotte] is to perform as one, to act the part, and to provide assistance in the appropriate manner when it is needed" (p. 87).

Across a wide array of sites, linguistic anthropologists have shown how expertise is enacted in the real-time course of communicative practice, which is never insulated nor isolated from institution and ideology. Indeed, a linguistic anthropological method assumes that culture and its many institutional forms and formulas manifest in semiotic interaction rather than simply controlling and containing it. It follows that linguistic anthropologists who study various forms of expertise are similarly driven to answer this question: What are the semiotic processes by which expertise is realized, and what cultural and linguistic resources are deployed in this inherently improvisational, interactional, and institutional work?

Studying expertise as semiotically accomplished allows us to reflect on our own expertise as anthropologists. Working in the long shadow of the colonial encounter, anthropologists should be especially aware of "the way in which professional coding schemes for constituting control and asymmetry in interaction" might be deployed "at the service of another profession, thereby amplifying its voice and the power it can exert on those who become the objects of its scrutiny" (Goodwin 1994, p. 626). Furthermore, attending to how native ideas about communicative competence, as they inform our interviews and interactions in the field, is crucial. When Cordovan carvers answered Briggs's questions about the skills involved in wood carving by handing him a piece of wood and a knife, they schooled him on and in a native mode of expert enactment (see Briggs 1986, 2007). They also provided Briggs the impetus to reflect on his native ideology of language, which was instantiated in his widely held belief that he could learn by asking before "learning how to ask." Indeed, the semiotic study of expertise and its constitutive processes of socialization, evaluation, institutionalization, and naturalization must not be confined to the examination of verbal signs at the expense of visual ones. It must also understand that the acquisition of a way of representing things, on the one hand, and knowing things, on the other, should not be conflated and that the former is the proper methodological loci for the study of expertise as enactment.

DISCLOSURE STATEMENT

The author is not aware of any affiliations, memberships, funding, or financial holdings that might be perceived as affecting the objectivity of this review.

ACKNOWLEDGMENTS

I offer special thanks to Susan Gal, Gregory Matoesian, and Michael Silverstein for their ongoing engagement with this piece. Paul Brodwin, Amahl Bishara, and Susan U. Philips contributed valuable input on initial formulations and outlines, and Joseph Masco, Daniel Listoe, and Yvonne Smith offered wise words in its latest stages. Flaws and omissions remain solely my own.

LITERATURE CITED

Abbott AD. 1988. *The System of Professions*. Chicago: Univ. Chicago Press

Abbott AD. 1995. Boundaries of social work and the social work of boundaries. *Soc. Serv. Rev.* 69:545–62

Agha A. 1998. Stereotypes and registers of honorific language. *Lang. Soc.* 27:151–93

Agha A. 2001. Register. See Duranti 2001, pp. 212–15

Agha A. 2007. *Language and Social Relations*. New York: Cambridge Univ. Press

Barth F. 2002. An anthropology of knowledge. *Curr. Anthropol.* 43:1–18

Bateson G. 2000. *Steps to an Ecology of Mind*. Chicago: Univ. Chicago Press

Bauman R, Briggs CL. 1990. Poetics and performances as critical perspectives on language and social life. *Annu. Rev. Anthropol.* 19:59–88

Bauman R, Briggs CL. 2003. *Voices of Modernity: Language Ideologies and the Politics of Inequality*. New York: Cambridge Univ. Press

Becker H. 1953. Becoming a marihuana user. *Am. J. Sociol.* 59:235–42

Benner P, Tanner C, Chesla C. 1990. The nature of clinical expertise in intensive care nursing units. *Anthropol. Work Rev.* 11:16–19

Bergmann JR. 1992. Veiled morality: notes on discretion in psychiatry. In *Talk at Work: Interaction in Institutional Settings*, ed. P Drew, J Heritage, pp. 137–62. Cambridge, UK: Cambridge Univ. Press

Bishara A. 2008. Watching U.S. television from the Palestinian street: the media, the state, and representational interventions. *Cult. Anthropol.* 23:488–530

Bosk CL. 2003. *Forgive and Remember: Managing Medical Failure*. Chicago: Univ. Chicago Press

Boster JS, Johnson JC. 1989. Form or function: a comparison of expert and novice judgments of similarity among fish. *Am. Anthropol.* 91:866–89

Bourdieu P. 1984. *Distinction: A Social Critique of the Judgment of Taste*. Cambridge, MA: Harvard Univ. Press

Bourdieu P, Johnson R. 1993. *The Field of Cultural Production: Essays on Art and Literature*. New York: Columbia Univ. Press

Boyer D. 2005a. The corporeality of expertise. *Ethnos* 70:243–66

Boyer D. 2005b. *Spirit and System: Media, Intellectuals, and the Dialectic in Modern German Culture*. Chicago: Univ. Chicago Press

Boyer D, Lomnitz C. 2005. Intellectuals and nationalism: anthropological engagements. *Annu. Rev. Anthropol.* 34:105–20

Brenneis D. 1994. Discourse and discipline at the National Research Council: a bureaucratic Bildungsroman. *Cult. Anthropol.* 9:23–36

Briggs CL. 1986. *Learning How to Ask: A Sociolinguistic Appraisal of the Role of the Interview in Social Science Research*. New York: Cambridge Univ. Press

Briggs CL. 2007. Anthropology, interviewing, and communicability in contemporary society. *Curr. Anthropol.* 48:551–80

Briggs CL, Mantini-Briggs C. 2003. *Stories in the Time of Cholera: Racial Profiling During a Medical Nightmare*. Berkeley: Univ. Calif. Press

Brodwin P. 2002. Genetics, identity, and the anthropology of essentialism. *Anthropol. Q.* 75:323–30

Brodwin P. 2008. The coproduction of moral discourse in US community psychiatry. *Med. Anthropol. Q.* 22:127–47

Carr ES. 2006. "Secrets keep you sick": metalinguistic labor in a drug treatment program for homeless women. *Lang. Soc.* 35:631–53

Carr ES. 2009. Anticipating and inhabiting institutional identities. *Am. Ethnol.* 36:317–36

Carr ES. 2010. *Scripting Addiction: The Politics of Therapeutic Talk and American Social Work*. Princeton, NJ: Princeton Univ. Press

Choy TK. 2005. Articulated knowledges: environmental forms after universality's demise. *Am. Anthropol.* 107:5–18

Cicourel AV. 1981. Language and the structure of belief in medical communication. *Stud. Ling.* 35:71–85

Cicourel AV. 1995. Medical speech events as resources for inferring differences in expert-novice diagnostic reasoning. In *Aspects of Oral Communication*, ed. U Quasthoff, pp. 364–87. New York: Walter de Gruyter

Cicourel AV. 2001. Expert. See Duranti 2001, pp. 67–70

Cohn C. 1987. Sex and death in the rational world of defense intellectuals. *Signs: J. Women Cult. Soc.* 12:687–718

Collins HM, Evans R. 2002. The third wave of science studies: studies of expertise and experience. *Soc. Stud. Sci.* 32:235–96

Collins HM, Evans R. 2007. *Rethinking Expertise*. Chicago: Univ. Chicago Press

Collins J. 1996. Socialization to text: structure and context in schooled literacy. See Silverstein & Urban 1996a, pp. 203–28

Collins J. 2008. "You don't know what they translate": language contact, institutional procedure, and literacy practice in neighborhood health clinics in urban Flanders. *J. Ling. Anthropol.* 16:249–68

Desjarlais R. 1996. The office of reason: on the politics of language and agency in a shelter for the "homeless mentally ill." *Am. Ethnol.* 23:880–900

Douglas M. 1986. *How Institutions Think*. Syracuse, NY: Syracuse Univ. Press

Dumit J. 2000. When explanations rest: "good-enough" brain science and the new socio-medical disorders. See Lock et al. 2000, pp. 209–32

Dumit J. 2004. *Picturing Personhood: Brain Scans and Biomedical Identity*. Princeton, NJ: Princeton Univ. Press

Duranti A, ed. 2001. *Key Terms in Language and Culture*. Malden, MA: Blackwell

Epstein S. 1996. *Impure Science: AIDS, Activism, and the Politics of Knowledge*. Berkeley: Univ. Calif. Press

Fassin D, d'Halluin E. 2005. The truth from the body: medical certificates as ultimate evidence for asylum seekers. *Am. Anthropol.* 107:597–608

Fassin D, d'Halluin E. 2007. Critical evidence: the politics of trauma in French asylum policies. *Ethos* 35:300–29

Fliegelman J. 1993. *Declaring Independence: Jefferson, Natural Language, and the Culture of Performance*. Stanford, CA: Stanford Univ. Press

Foucault M. 1978. *The History of Sexuality*. Vol. 1, *An Introduction*. New York: Random House

Foucault M. 1984. Nietzsche, genealogy, and history. In *The Foucault Reader*, ed. P Rabinow, pp. 76–100. New York: Pantheon

Fortun K. 2001. *Advocacy After Bhopal: Environmentalism, Disaster, New Global Orders*. Chicago: Univ. Chicago Press

Frink L. 2009. The identity division of labor in Native Alaska. *Am. Anthropol.* 111:21–29

Gal S. 1995. Lost in a Slavic sea: linguistic theories and expert knowledge in nineteenth century Hungary. *Pragmatics* 5:155–66

Gal S. 2005. Language ideologies compared: metaphors of public/private. *J. Ling. Anthropol.* 15:23–37

Gal S. 2006. Language, its stakes, and its effects. In *The Oxford Handbook of Contextual Political Analysis*, ed. R Goodin, C Tilly, pp. 376–91. New York: Oxford Univ. Press

Gal S, Irvine JT. 1995. The boundaries of languages and disciplines: how ideologies construct difference. *Soc. Res.* 62:967–1001

Good A. 2004. "Undoubtedly an expert"? Anthropologists in British asylum courts. *J. R. Anthropol. Inst.* 10:113–33

Good A. 2007. *Anthropology and Expertise in the Asylum Courts*. London: Routledge-Cavendish

Goodwin C. 1994. Professional vision. *Am. Anthropol.* 96:606–33

Goodwin C. 1996. Transparent vision. In *Interaction and Grammar*, ed. E Ochs, EA Schegloff, SA Thompson, pp. 370–404. New York: Cambridge Univ. Press

Gusterson C. 1996. *Nuclear Rites: A Weapons Laboratory at the End of the Cold War*. Berkeley, CA: Univ. Calif. Press

Hall K. 1995. Lip service on the fantasy lines. In *Gender Articulated: Language and the Socially Constructed Self*, ed. K Hall, M Bucholtz, pp. 183–216. New York: Routledge

Hanks WF. 1991. Forward. In *Situated Learning: Legitimate Peripheral Participation*, ed. J Lave, E Wenger, pp. 13–24. New York: Cambridge Univ. Press. 138 pp.

Hanks WF. 1996. Exorcism and the description of participant roles. See Silverstein & Urban 1996a, pp. 160–202

Haviland JB. 2003. Ideologies of language: some reflections on language and US law. *Am. Anthropol.* 105:764–74

Hess DJ. 2007. Crosscurrents: social movements and the anthropology of science and technology. *Am. Anthropol.* 109:463–72

Hill JH. 2002. "Expert rhetorics" in advocacy for endangered languages: Who is listening, and what do they hear? *J. Ling. Anthropol.* 12:119–33

Hogle LF. 2002a. Claims and disclaimers: Whose expertise counts? *Med. Anthropol.* 21:275–306

Hogle LF. 2002b. Introduction: jurisdictions of authority and expertise in science and medicine. *Med. Anthropol.* 21:231–46

Holmes DR, Marcus GE. 2005. Cultures of expertise and the management of globalization: toward the refunctioning of ethnography. See Ong & Collier 2005, pp. 235–53

Ilcan S, Phillips L. 2003. Making food count: expert knowledge and global technologies of government. *Can. Rev. Soc. Anthropol.* 40:441–62

Irwin S, Jordan B. 1987. Knowledge, practice, and power: court-ordered cesarean sections. *Med. Anthropol. Q.* 1:319–34

Jacobs-Huey L. 2003. Ladies are seen, not heard: language socialization in a southern, African American cosmetology school. *Anthropol. Ed. Q.* 34:277–99

Johnson J. 1988. Mixing humans and nonhumans together: the sociology of a door-closer. *Soc. Prob.* 35:298–310

Jones G, Shweder L. 2003. The performance of illusion and illusionary performatives: learning the language of theatrical magic. *J. Ling. Anthropol.* 13:51–57

Kataoka K. 1998. Gravity or levity: vertical space in Japanese rock climbing instructions. *J. Ling. Anthropol.* 8:222–48

Kelty C. 2008. Allotropes of fieldwork in nanotechnology. In *Emerging Conceptual, Ethical and Policy Issues in Bionanotechnology*, ed. F Jotterand, pp. 157–80. Dordrecht, The Neth.: Springer

Knorr Cetina K. 1999. *Epistemic Cultures: How the Sciences Make Knowledge.* Cambridge, MA: Harvard Univ. Press

Kuipers JC. 1989. "Medical discourse" in anthropological context: views of language and power. *Med. Anthropol. Q.* 3:99–123

Lakoff A. 2005. *Pharmaceutical Reason: Knowledge and Value in Global Psychiatry.* New York: Cambridge Univ. Press

Lakoff A. 2008. The generic biothreat, or, how we became unprepared. *Cult. Anthropol.* 23:399–428

Lambek M. 1993. *Knowledge and Practice in Mayotte.* Toronto: Univ. Toronto Press

Langford JM. 1999. Medical mimesis: healing signs of a cosmopolitan "quack." *Am. Ethnol.* 26:24–46

Latour B. 1988. *Science in Action.* Cambridge, MA: Harvard Univ. Press

Latour B. 2005. *Reassembling the Social: An Introduction to Actor-Network Theory.* Oxford: Oxford Univ. Press

Latour B, Woolgar S. 1986. *Laboratory Life: The Construction of Scientific Facts.* Princeton, NJ: Princeton Univ. Press

Lave J. 1988. *Cognition in Practice: Mind, Mathematics, and Culture in Everyday Life.* Cambridge, UK: Cambridge Univ. Press

Lave J. 1997. The culture of acquisition and the practice of understanding. In *Situated Cognition: Social, Semiotic, and Psychological Perspectives*, ed. D Kirshner, JA Whitson, pp. 17–36. Mahwah, NJ: Lawrence Erlbaum

Lave J, Wenger E. 1991. *Situated Learning: Legitimate Peripheral Participation.* New York: Cambridge Univ. Press

Lee B. 2001. Foreword. In *Metaculture: How Culture Moves Through the World*, ed. G Urban, pp. ix–xvi. Minneapolis: Univ. Minn. Press. 336 pp.

Lee Y-J, Roth W-M. 2004. They've gotta learn something unless they're just out to lunch: becoming an expert in a salmon hatchery. *Anthropol. Work Rev.* 25:15–21

Lock M, Young A, Combrosio A, eds. 2000. *Living and Working with the New Medical Technologies: Intersections of Inquiry.* Cambridge, UK: Cambridge Univ. Press

Malinowski B. 1964 [1922]. *Argonauts of the Western Pacific.* London: Routledge/Kegan Paul

Masco J. 2004. Nuclear technoaesthetics: sensory politics from trinity to the virtual bomb in Los Alamos. *Am. Ethnol.* 31:1–25

Masco J. 2006. *The Nuclear Borderlands: The Manhattan Project in Post-Cold War New Mexico.* Princeton, NJ: Princeton Univ. Press

Matoesian GM. 1999. The grammaticalization of participant roles in the constitution of expert identity. *Lang. Soc.* 28:491–521

Matoesian GM. 2008. Role conflict as an interactional resource in the multimodal emergence of expert identity. *Semiotica* 171:15–49

McCloskey DN. 1992. *If You're So Smart: The Narrative of Economic Expertise.* Chicago: Univ. Chicago Press

McCloskey DN. 1999. *Crossing: A Memoir.* Chicago: Univ. Chicago Press

Mead M. 1928. *An Inquiry into the Question of Cultural Stability in Polynesia.* New York: Columbia Univ. Press

Mehan H. 1983. The role of language and the language of role in institutional decision making. *Lang. Soc.* 12:187–211

Mehan H. 1993. Beneath the skin and between the ears: a case study in the politics of representation. In *Understanding Practice: Perspectives on Activity and Context*, ed. S Chaiklin, J Lave, pp. 241–68. Cambridge, UK: Cambridge Univ. Press

Mehan H. 1996. The construction of an LD student: a case study in the politics of representation. See Silverstein & Urban 1996a, pp. 253–76

Mertz E. 1993. Learning what to ask: metapragmatic factors and methodological reification. In *Reflexive Language: Reported Speech and Metapragmatics*, ed. JA Lucy, pp. 159–74. New York: Cambridge Univ. Press

Mertz E. 1996. Recontextualization as socialization: text and pragmatics in the law school classroom. See Silverstein & Urban 1996a, pp. 229–52

Mertz E. 2007. *The Language of Law School: Learning to "Think Like a Lawyer."* New York: Oxford Univ. Press

Mishkin B. 1937. The Maori of New Zealand. In *Cooperation and Competition among Primitive Peoples*, ed. M Mead, pp. 428–57. New York: McGraw Hill

Mitchell T. 2002. *Rule of Experts: Egypt, Techno-Politics, Modernity*. Berkeley: Univ. Calif. Press

Modell J. 1989. Last chance babies: interpretations of parenthood in an in vitro fertilization program. *Med. Anthropol. Q.* 3:124–38

Myers F. 1994. Beyond the intentional fallacy: art criticism and the ethnography of aboriginal acrylic painting. *Vis. Anthropol. Rev.* 10:10–43

Nader L, ed. 1996. *Naked Science: Anthropological Inquiry into Boundaries, Power, and Knowledge*. New York: Routledge

Ong A. 2005. Ecologies of expertise: assembling flows, managing citizenship. See Ong & Collier 2005, pp. 337–53

Ong A, Collier SJ, eds. 2005. *Global Assemblages: Technology, Politics, and Ethics as Anthropological Problems*. Oxford, UK: Blackwell

Peräkylä A. 1995. *AIDS Counseling: Institutional Interaction and Clinical Practice*. Oxford: Oxford Univ. Press

Philips SU. 1998. *Ideology in the Language of Judges: How Judges Practice Law, Politics, and Courtroom Control*. New York: Oxford Univ. Press

Philips SU. 2010. Semantic and interactional indirectness in Tongan lexical honorification. *J. Pragmatics* 42:317–36

Putnam H. 1973. Meaning and reference. *J. Philos.* 70:699–711

Putnam H. 1975. The meaning of meaning. In *Philosophical Papers*, Vol. 2: *Mind, Language and Reality*, 2:215–71. New York: Cambridge Univ. Press

Rapp R. 1988. Chromosomes and communication: the discourse of genetic counseling. *Med. Anthropol. Q.* 2:143–57

Rapp R. 1999. *Testing Women, Testing the Fetus: The Social Impact of Amniocentesis in America*. New York: Routledge

Rapp R. 2000. Extra chromosomes and blue tulips: medico-familial interpretations. See Lock et al. 2000, pp. 184–208

Redfield P. 2006. A less modest witness. *Am. Ethnol.* 33:3–26

Rosaldo M. 1982. The things we do with words: Illongot speech acts and speech act theory in philosophy. *Lang. Soc.* 11:203–37

Saunders BF. 2008. *CT Suite: The Work of Diagnosis in the Age of Noninvasive Cutting*. Durham, NC: Duke Univ. Press

Schwegler TA. 2008. Take it from the top (down)? Rethinking neoliberalism and political hierarchy in Mexico. *Am. Ethnol.* 35:682—700

Scoditti GMG. 1982. The significance of apprenticeship in Kitawa. *Man* 17:74–91

Scott S. 2009. The metrological mountain: "translating" tuberculosis in periurban Bolivia. PhD thesis, Univ. Chicago, 520 pp.

Silverstein M. 1992. The uses and utility of ideology: some reflections. *Pragmatics* 2:311–23

Silverstein M. 1996. Monoglot "standard" in America: standardization and metaphors of linguistic hegemony. In *The Matrix of Language: Contemporary Linguistic Anthropology*, ed. D Brenneis, RKS Macaulay, pp. 284–306. Boulder, CO: Westview

Silverstein M. 1998. The improvisational performance of culture in realtime discursive practice. In *Creativity in Performance*, ed. K Sawyer, pp. 265–312. Greenwich, CT: Ablex

Silverstein M. 2003. Indexical order and the dialectics of sociolinguistic life. *Lang. Comm.* 23:193–229

Silverstein M. 2004. Cultural concepts and the language-culture nexus. *Curr. Anthropol.* 45:621–52

Silverstein M. 2006. Old wine, new ethnographic lexicography. *Annu. Rev. Anthropol.* 35:481–96

Silverstein M, Urban G, eds. 1996a. *Natural Histories of Discourse.* Chicago: Univ. Chicago Press

Silverstein M, Urban G. 1996b. The natural history of discourse. See Silverstein & Urban 1996a, pp. 1–17

Simpson B. 1997. Possession, dispossession and the social distribution of knowledge among Sri Lankan ritual specialists. *J. R. Anthropol. Inst.* 3:43–59

Simpson B. 2004. Acting ethically, responding culturally: framing the new reproductive and genetic technologies in Sri Lanka. *Asia Pac. J. Anthropol.* 5:227–43

Smardon R. 2008. Broken brains and broken homes: the meaning of special education in an Appalachian community. *Anthropol. Educ. Q.* 39:161–80

Smith B. 2005. Ideologies of the speaking subject in the psychotherapeutic theory and practice of Carl Rogers. *J. Ling. Anthropol.* 15:258–72

Srinivasan Shipman AC, Boster JS. 2008. Recall, similarity judgment, and identification of trees: a comparison of experts and novices. *Ethos* 36:171–93

Strathern M. 1988. *The Gender of the Gift: Problems with Women and Problems with Society in Melanesia.* Berkeley: Univ. Calif. Press

Strathern M. 2006. A community of critics? Thoughts on new knowledge. *J. R. Anthropol. Inst.* 12:191–209

Timura CT. 2004. Negotiating expertise: the globalizing cultures of British and American conflict resolution experts. *PoLAR: Pol. Leg. Anthropol. Rev.* 27:160–71

Traweek S. 1988. *Beamtimes and Lifetimes: The World of High Energy Physicists.* Cambridge, MA: Harvard Univ. Press

Urban G. 1992. Two faces of culture. In *Working Papers and Proceedings of the Center for Psychosocial Studies No. 49.* Chicago: Cent. Psychol. Stud.

Urban G. 1996. Entextualization, replication, power. See Silverstein & Urban 1996a, pp. 21–44

Urban G. 2001. *Metaculture: How Culture Moves Through the World.* Minneapolis: Univ. Minn. Press

Wayland C. 2003. Contextualizing the politics of knowledge: physicians' attitudes toward medicinal plants. *Med. Anthropol. Q.* 17:483–500

Williams R. 1985. *Keywords: A Vocabulary of Culture and Society.* New York: Oxford Univ. Press

Young A. 1997. *The Harmony of Illusions: Inventing Post-Traumatic Stress Disorder.* Princeton, NJ: Princeton Univ. Press

The Semiotics of Brand

Paul Manning

Department of Anthropology, Trent University, Toronto, Ontario M6H 3Y3, Canada;
email: paulmanning@trentu.ca

Annu. Rev. Anthropol. 2010. 39:33–49

First published online as a Review in Advance on
June 14, 2010

The *Annual Review of Anthropology* is online at
anthro.annualreviews.org

This article's doi:
10.1146/annurev.anthro.012809.104939

Key Words

materiality, trademark, production, circulation, fetish

Abstract

Approaches to the semiotics of brand are troubled by the lack of any
accepted analytic definition of the phenomenon, as well as capacious,
almost metaphysical, extensions in which brand becomes identified with
semiosis as such, and thus everything is a brand. In addition, studies of
brand tend to focus on highly visible or successful brands, as often as
not as a proxy for a real object of analytic interest that lies elsewhere.
Brand discourse defines brand in opposition to the material properties of
the product, leading to a dematerialization of brand, which erases the
messy materialities, contingencies, and hybrids that continually arise
in the material semiosis of brand. Rather than attempt a definition of
brand, the recent literature on brand semiotics is explored along several
material and semiotic dimensions of the variousness of its relationship
to its universes of circulation and in different professional discourses
and historical and cultural contexts.

INTRODUCTION

Any discussion of the semiotics of brand confronts the basic problem that there is virtually no agreement on what brand is or means (Davis 2008). Brand stands at the intersection of the interested discourses of brand owners, producers, and consumers, as well as diverse groups of professionals, each of whom has a stake both in the specific definition of brand as well as in promoting the concept as a whole. In addition, brand is often deployed as an unexamined transparent proxy for the real object of analytical interest that lies elsewhere. For example, Ritzer's (1993) famous "McDonaldization thesis" uses a global brand, McDonalds, to capture not primarily the specificity of the "symbolic universe constructed by branding" but rather the extension of corporate "control mechanisms"—such as efficiency, calculability, predictability, and control typical of the capitalist labor process (what is sometimes called Taylorism)—to the consumer (Askegaard 2006, p. 95; also Heilbrunn 2006, pp. 109–10). Brand becomes virtually synonymous with global capitalism. Therefore, much analytic attention is given to specific highly salient western brands (Coca-Cola, Nike) that serve as what Miller (1998) calls "meta-symbols" of aspects of this global culture of circulation: "So Coca-Cola is not merely material culture, it is a symbol that stands for a debate about material culture" (p. 170). Furthermore, as a privileged semiotic object that is felt to epitomize the contemporary period of capitalism (Lury 2004, Arvidsson 2006), brand is frequently extended to a whole new range of experiences, services, and quasi-commodities that are not in themselves conventional economic objects (including experiences, selves, nations, political programs, and revolutions) (Moore 2003, p. 332; for specific examples, see Lury 2004, Arvidsson 2006, Hearn 2008, Jansen 2008, Manning 2009). Such claims for the ubiquity and importance of brand discourse can be treated as being themselves interested product claims of brand producers, "puffery" (on the semiotics of which generally, see Parmentier 1994, Hoffman 2006), in which the properties of the most successful iconic brands are treated as being characteristic of the phenomenon as a whole: "The stories that get told about brands in the professional and other literature are almost always success stories, not least because failed brands by definition are the ones that nobody knows, that do not, in fact, exist (anymore)" (Moore 2003, p. 334). Indeed, the most enthusiastic pronouncements about brand are often akin to a new-age wisdom literature, what Arvidsson calls the "metaphysical line of managerial literature" (Arvidsson 2006, p. 126), where "brands take on religious dimensions" (Askegaard 2006, p. 96) and key thinkers are often called gurus, and their pronouncements often called mantras (Askegaard 2006, Wang 2007). Thus, the semiotic language of brand has undergone a curious form of genericide (on which see below) in which a specific kind of semiosis (brand) becomes coextensive with semiosis as such: "Everything is a brand....A brand is any label that carries meaning and associations" (Kotler 2003, p. 8).

Recent ethnographic approaches to the semiotics of brand appear to fall into a few major (and not exclusive) tendencies, which can be roughly characterized as consumption-centered, production-centered, and product-centered. Of these, the consumption-centered approach is certainly most dominant, following the mid-1990s turn to privileging consumer agency and resistance (e.g., Miller 1995), "producing a discourse that had uncanny similarities with contemporary Thatcherite enthusiasm about the sovereign consumer" (Arvidsson 2006, p.18). Here, a virtual identification of the equally capaciously and vaguely defined concepts of consumption and brand under contemporary capitalism (Arvidsson 2006, Johanssen & Holm 2006) makes brand a privileged point of entry into such diverse subjects as the mediatization of everyday life worlds in consumption (Arvidsson 2006, pp. 35–40), subcultural styles (Elliot & Davies 2006, Wang 2007), the sundry antinomies of contemporary global capitalism itself (Lury 2004; Foster 2005, 2007, 2008; Arvidsson 2006; Wang 2007), or a "mere psychoanalytic shorthand for a 'discourse of desire'" (Wang 2007, p. xiiii).

An alternate approach is represented by more recent production-centered methodologies (Moore 2003; Mazzarella 2003; Meneley 2004, 2007; Manning & Uplisashvili 2007; Wang 2007), which, while not ignoring the consumer, show the production of brand and definitions of brand to be a privileged site for the production of professional self-definition within a "system of professions" (Abbott 1988). As Moore (2003) shows, "the procedures used to get at the 'brand personality' reveal much about the 'semiotic ideology' of branding in the corporate culture of the 'New Economy', as does the division of branding labor at the Firm, where brand strategists coordinated their efforts with anthropologists and graphic designers" (p. 336). The "division of branding labor" within a single firm reproduces asymmetric professional jurisdictions over brand within a system of professions so that brand becomes a composite semiotic object where designers take care of the qualitative dimensions of brand, anthropologists address the indexical associative dimensions of brand, and brand strategists manage the assembly of these iconic and indexical moments into a coherent typification, a "brand personality" (Moore 2003). In addition, the specific procedures and semiotic "technologies of the imagination" (Ito 2007) used to produce brand, a list including free association, personalization, and collages, reveal "the strongly associationist character of . . . assumptions about consumers' thought processes" (Moore 2003, p. 343). However, the roles of these different professionals involved in the production of brand is asymmetric: Brand managers' control over the unifying "brand personality" (which represents a financial asset as "brand equity") gives them a central position compared with designers and creatives, whose closer relation to the product makes them peripheral to and subordinate within the brand production process (Johanssen & Holm 2006; Wang 2007, pp. 24–25).

Last, many recent product-centered approaches seek to embed the phenomenon within the context of global product networks and commodity biographies, shifting the focus from persons (consumers, producers) to "worldly things," worldly because they are both physically present here and now and yet "bear traces of their simultaneous existence elsewhere, over and beyond one's immediate horizons" (Foster 2008, p. xvii), allowing the often incommensurable perspectives of diverse agents (brand producers and consumers) to be treated within a single framework. Such approaches (Miller 1998; Foster 2005, 2007, 2008; also Meneley 2004, 2007, 2008; Heath & Meneley 2007) promise to move beyond ontologies of producers and consumers (and even hybrids such as prosumers), treating exchange as a continuous series of qualitative "transformations" (Munn 1986) or processes of "qualification and requalification" (Callon et al. 2002).

THE DEMATERIALIZATION OF BRAND

Because brand is thus everywhere, and yet nowhere, the phenomenon comes to be represented as an essentially immaterial form of mediation, a kind of globalized interdiscursivity, an indexical icon of the virtual nature of the global capitalist economy itself, which is often compared with virtual worlds on the Internet (Lury 2004, Arvidsson 2006). This virtualized brand starkly contrasts the messy materiality of "messages on bottles" as they are often encountered on the individual token level, illustrating a tendency toward what Robert Moore has dubbed the "dematerialization of brand" (R. Moore, personal communication). This tendency erases the "semiotic vulnerabilities" of brand, Moore argues, that come into view when the semiotic ideology of brand is confronted with the contingent world of its materializations (Moore 2003, p. 336). Because of the metaphysical expansiveness of brand discourse and its tendency toward dematerialization, it becomes difficult to decide where brand lives as a semiotic phenomenon:

How should a semiotic analysis of branding take account of the seemingly quite different ontological statuses of brands as such, versus branded products (as types), versus individual instances (tokens) of branded products, these last being what actual people engage with in activities of consumption, use, enjoyment, display, and so on? How can the concrete sensuous reality (e.g., color) of such tokens in use act as a relay for the more abstract associations (Young! Fresh! Edgy!) that branding professionals try to "encode" in consumer experience. (Moore 2003, p. 332)

The tendency for brand to be conceived as an immaterial form of mediation essentially identical to semiosis as such is partially due to the way that brand is defined in opposition to the product. "The product and the brand" (Gardner & Levy 1955) form a privileged doublet, expressed in popular marketing mantras such as "a product is made in a factory: a brand is bought by a consumer" (Wang 2007, p. 23; Lury 2004, pp. 31, 72). As mantras such as this show, the definition of brand develops over time by a kind of mystical *via negativa*, defining itself not so much by saying what brand is as what it is not: the product. By degrees, brand moves from being a "symbolic extension" of a product (Arvidsson 2006, p. 95; Askegard 2006, p. 100), as brand guru David Ogilvy put it in 1955, the "intangible sum of a product's attributes, its name, packaging, and price, its history, reputation, and the way it is advertised" (cited in Wang 2007, pp. 23–24), to leaving behind the dull, passive, generic, inert utility and materiality of the product entirely, taking on an "enchanting, sometimes religious character," adding a "spiritual dimension to what used to be 'merely a product'" (Askegard 2006, p. 96). The opposition brand/product condenses a folk-ontological opposition between immaterial/material, form/function, distinctive/descriptive, decorative/functional, symbolic/technical, properties of subjects/properties of objects; the pervasive dematerialization of brand recapitulating in broad outlines the dematerialization of meaning itself in western secular and religious discourse (Irvine 1989, Pfaffenberger 1992,

Masuzawa 2000, Keane 2003, Manning & Meneley 2008).

In addition to the complementary schizmogenesis in which brand drifts away from the product, leading to a dematerialization of brand, brand undergoes several other parallel semiotic shifts. Earlier, primarily legal, discourses tend to treat brand as an arbitrary and distinctive trademark indexing a producer, whereas more recent marketing discourses tend to treat the essence of brand as a set of associations held in the minds of consumers (Hanby 1999, Moore 2003). This treatment is sometimes linked to an opposition between an earlier "positivistic," "mechanistic" view of brands as "lifeless manipulable artefacts," "inert physical objects," which serve primarily as differentiating marks for products and which are "owner-oriented, reductionistic and grounded in economics" (Hanby 1999, p. 9; Csaba & Bengsston 2006, p. 121), and more recent quasi-animistic discourses that treat brand as a "person" (Lury 2004, p. 75) in which the pervasive associations based on the role brands play in consumers' lives are transformed into actual anthropomorphic characteristics imputed to brands understood as holistic, organic, living, growing entities with which consumers can form actual social relationships directly (Hanby 1999, Csaba & Bengsston 2006). We also see historical changes in which trademarks and brands move from being a category of communication to objects of property (Lury 2004, Bently 2008a). The discourse of brand is much addicted to epochalism so that in the 1960s we move from the "product era" to the "image era," and in the 1980s the "brand image" gives way to a financially quantifiable "brand equity" (Arvidsson 2006, pp. 41–65; Wang 2007, pp. 23–25). All these shifts broadly recapitulate moves away from earlier Saussurean structuralist semiotic theories privileging the arbitrariness and distinctiveness of the sign to later poststructuralist accounts in which the omnivorous associationism of brand (for homologies between semiotic theories and trademark law, see Beebe 2004), not to mention rampant anthropomorphism, comes to approximate the fetish (Beebe 2004, p. 681;

2008, p. 52; Hearn 2008). However, the brand fetish is not easily assimilated to the Marxian "commodity fetish" to which it is frequently compared (Manning 2009, p. 926n6). Rather, I am taking the fetish here as a general semiotic figure "standing for an amorphous collection of 'hybrid' semiotic phenomena united only in their inability to be assimilated to the Saussurean 'purification' of the sign" (Manning & Meneley 2008, p. 292; on the semiotic polysemy of the fetish, see also Pietz 1985, Masuzawa 2000).

Whereas these different views of brand are often presented in epochal shifts globally affecting the imagination of brand, mechanistic views of brands as lifeless signs and organic views of brands as living persons are often mixed in contemporary marketing discourse (Hanby 1999, Csaba & Bengtsson 2006). As with other dichotomies such as nature/culture (Latour 1993 [1991]), if brand discourse seems preoccupied with ontological purification of brand from its connection, *inter alia*, to products, brand practice confronts us with a phenomenal proliferation of semiotic hybrids. Given these difficulties of analytic specification, I follow Moore (2003) by presenting the various semiotic moments of brand on the model of the communicative act itself, replacing speakers with producers, consumers with addressees, referents with products, and messages with the brand itself.

TRADEMARKS: INDEXES OF THE PRODUCER OR SOURCE

Because brand is often defined as a "conceptual extension of trademark" (Mazzarella 2003, p. 185; Beebe 2008, p. 47; Davis 2008, p. 81), the simplest way to begin would be to explore those functions of brand that approximate the functions of the trademark in legal discourse, where the "primary and proper function of a trademark" is "to identify the origin or ownership of the goods to which it is affixed" (Schechter 1927, pp. 183–84). As Schechter notes, this original definition collapses two different sorts of marks, proprietary marks optionally affixed

to goods by merchants and regulatory production marks affixed by statute to identify the work of a single craftsman (Schechter 1927, p. 184). However, the producer or source indexed is, in fact, usually a fictive person such as a corporation and therefore does not correspond precisely to either of these earlier figures of mercantile capitalism, although as imagined figures they both continue to haunt the modern imaginary of brand, as discussed below. In addition, the referent indexed is often not the source itself but the goodwill associated with that source, in essence, functioning as a guarantee of quality, even if the source is unknown (Coombe 1996, Dinwoodie 1997, Beebe 2004), so that trademark names and logos become "visible or materialized goodwill" (Foster 2008, pp. 79–80). In addition to indexing such personalistic sources, trademark-like protections have long been conferred on geographical places (Bently 2008b), including separately evolved sets of protections such as geographical indications and *terroir* (Meneley 2004, 2007; Parry 2008). Moreover, as trademarks move from a communicative understanding—as inalienable, nontransferrable, and rigid source indicators [where personal or geographic names become the archetypal trademark (Bently 2008b)] related to notions of fraud and confusion, to alienable, transferrable forms of property (Lury 2004; Bently 2008a, 2008b), which can operate entirely through licensing without any involvement or regulation of product quality (Lury 2004, Beebe 2008)—it becomes debatable whether trademarks indicate any specific source at all or whether they even act as guarantees of quality relative to, for example, the actual locus of production (Vann 2005): "The modern trademark does not function to identify the true origin of goods. It functions to obscure that origin, to cover it with a *myth* of origin" (Beebe 2008, p. 52).

If, following Moore, we broaden this semiotic aspect of brand to any "source-identifying indexical" (Moore 2003, p. 339), it remains that different kinds of indexical relation may be involved. As Coombe (1996) points out, type-mediated indexes such as logos act as "a signature of authenticity, indicating that the good that bears it is true to its origins—that is, that the good is a true or accurate copy" and token-mediated indexes which mark "a real contact, a making, a moment of imprinting by one for whom it acts as a kind of fingerprint" (p. 205). As Meneley (2004, 2007) and Manning & Uplisashvili (2007) make clear, these two different kinds of indexes become enregistered as distinctions among different kinds of production [which are also adumbrated, for example, in styles of trade dress (Meneley 2004, pp. 167–69; Meneley 2007, p. 682)]: the authenticity of the distinctive variability of artisanal craft production versus the guarantee of absolutely identical quality of industrial production, respectively (also Kapferer 2006). Although authenticity serves as a constitutive element of western brand discourse, Vann (2006) shows the various ways that production-centered Vietnamese market models treat branded goods in different ways depending on whether they are "model" goods (brand source-identifying goods), "mimic" goods (inferior goods that emulate the brand model in product qualities), or "fake" goods (useless nongoods that imitate the brand, but not the product qualities), thereby showing alternate vernacular models for reckoning source-identifying indexicality outside of the hegemonic framework of authenticity.

These two kinds of indexes not only differentiate kinds of production, but also index different, but equally imaginary, kinds of producer: the traditional craftsman using traditional forms of production within a circumscribed *terroir*, whose identity is indexed in the product, and the industrial modernist abstraction of a corporation where the indexes serve more to guarantee consistent product quality (goodwill), but at the same time erase the real producers (Meneley 2004). In addition, goods that are actually produced using mass production can be associated with traditional producers and production with varying effects (Manning & Uplisashvili 2007, Meneley 2007, Renne 2007). Thus, the source-indexing function of trademark does not connect physically distant producers and consumers but serves

to create, consolidate, and unify these as substitute "figures" (Manning & Uplisashvili 2007, p. 631), "surrogate identities" (Coombe 1996, p. 210), or "prosthetic personalities" (Mazzarella 2003, pp. 187–92). As prosthetic personas, brands also mediate a complex distribution context, allowing producers to extend a prosthetic persona into a retail context, "to reach over the shoulder of the retailer straight to the consumer" (H.G. Wells, cited in Lury 2004, p. 46). But because the unitary producer indexed by trademark is, of course, typically itself a prosthetic quasi-persona (a legal entity, "the undertaking" or corporation) whose "very existence is a legal formality," (Foster 2008, p. 80), and which may have no actual role in production, some scholars have suggested that rather than index the modern corporation as a unitary source, trademarks actually create it (Griffiths 2008, p. 248), even as these prosthetic producers effectively erase the actual producers from sight (Foster 2005, 2007, 2008; Beebe 2008; for vernacular production-centered market models that privilege locus of production or product quality over brand identity, see Vann 2005, 2006). Similarly, independently evolved geographical source-identifying indexicals such as *terroir*—cognate with trademarks because they act as guarantors of quality—must construct localities as sharply bounded, naturalized, essentialized "hermetically sealed" containers, each attribute of which [whether natural (soil, climate, varietal), cultural (traditional techniques of production), or "spiritual"] must be made to sit still in order to be included (Parry 2008).

BRAND WORLDS: BRANDS AS CONDENSED SPACE TIMES

Brands index the dimensions, contours, and horizons of their own circulatory space times (for space times, see Munn 1986, pp. 8–16). Brands can align themselves with respect to social imaginaries such as the nation by situating themselves within local or global trajectories of circulation (Iwabuchi 2002, 2004; Mazzarella 2003; Özkan & Foster 2005; Vann 2005; Wang

2007; Foster 2008), or they can gesture to diasporic, aspirational, or exotic elsewheres on the horizons of imaginative geographies of alterity (Mazzarella 2003; Meneley 2004, 2007; Manning & Uplisashvili 2007; Renne 2007). Brand as a semiotic feature of an individual circulatory object can act as what Munn calls "condensed spacetime, and may be analyzed to give a fuller account of the wider intersubjective spacetime in which it operates" (Munn 1986, p. 10). For example, with respect to the global traffic in purified bottled water, Wilk (2006) has recently shown how the branding strategies of bottled water marketers condense a social ontology shot through with antinomies—contradictory attitudes about nature and technology, the state and the market, the public and the private—and provides ample illustrations of the very obvious material differences between first- and third-world economies. Similarly, Meneley (2004, 2007) shows how the positive imaginings of the Mediterranean and the healthful Mediterranean diet makes Tuscan Extra Virgin Olive Oil an object of desire that partakes of the other imagined properties associated with Tuscany as the picturesque center of this regional imagining. But she also shows how this imagining, which places Tuscany at the center of the imaginary Mediterranean, is mirrored by negative Orientalist imaginings of place that lower the value of other Mediterranean olive oils produced in Palestine, Tunisia, Libya, or Turkey (Meneley 2004, p. 167). But the problems of the latter producers do not end there. In other work, Meneley shows how Palestinian fair trade olive oil serves as an index and an icon of the time-space distortion of the Israeli occupation: "[O]live oil is an icon of arrested circulation, as the movement of bottles of oil, bottled Palestinian labor time, is itself bottled up within the occupation time of the Israeli state" (Meneley 2008, p. 23).

Many recent studies show how strategies of localization locate brands within the imagined cultural specificities of cities, regions, and nations, even as they, at the same time, ambivalently position themselves as world-class aspirational brands with strategies of globalization (Mazzarella 2003, Özkan & Foster 2005, Vann 2005, Manning & Uplisashvili 2007, Wang 2007, Foster 2008). By contrast, Iwabuchi (2002, 2004) shows how some Japanese products (consumer technologies, comics and cartoons, and computer games) are marketed with a self-consciously cosmopolitan global strategy (*mukokuseki* "no nationality"), which specifically erases such distinctive cultural characteristics to produce "culturally odorless commodities" such as the Sony Walkman (Iwabuchi 2002, p. 28; 2004, p. 58). Thus, although Japaneseness does indeed become the object of a certain "techno-orientalism" by its association with technology (Iwabuchi 2004, p. 59), Iwabuchi (2002, pp. 32–33) argues that it is fallacious to treat this cosmopolitan *mukokuseki* strategy as being a mirror-image of the equally self-consciously global strategies of Americanization (in which the culturally specific characteristics of America are universalized as expressing global desires and aspirations; e.g., Foster 2008, pp. 40–47).

The semiotic material out of which trademarks and brands are fashioned, too, can index the dimensions of alterity of a culture of circulation. Coombe (1996) shows how early American trademarks draw on "symbolic fields of social alterity" drawn from embodied images of racial and ethnic others of the imagined space of the frontier against which American consumers define themselves, but they could also be drawn from the colonial field of alterity of empire in the British imperial context (McClintock 1995), nostalgic diasporic or folkloric images of traditional production (Renne 2007, Manning & Uplisashvili 2007), and even the entirely fanciful characters of folklore and mythology (Olivier 2007).

Such metaphoric consumption of alterity, the use of images and figures of elsewhere, is matched by metonymic alterity, the desire for actual objects from elsewhere, exemplified in the way that labels and containers of western goods, often detached from the use value, came to be self-valuable mediums of "contact" with the "Imaginary West" in the USSR (Yurchak 2006, Fehervary 2009, Manning

2009) or the way that socialist products index a particular apperception of temporal alterity in East German (N)*Ostalgie* (Berdahl 1999, Bach 2002). Invidious essentialized distinctions between elsewheres of orientalist and occidentalist imaginary geographies pervade the discourse of brand (Mazzarella 2003; Meneley 2004, 2007; Vann 2005, 2006; Pelkmans 2006; Manning & Uplisashvili 2007; Wang 2007; Manning 2009), sometimes becoming enregistered in distinct or hybrid brand strategies. Mazzarella argues that whereas some Indian brands involve a kind of "auto-orientalism," which he defines as "the use of globally recognized signifiers of Indian 'tradition' to facilitate the aspirational consumption, by Indians, of a culturally marked self" (Mazzarella 2003, p. 138), by contrast, western goods mark a kind of aspirational occidentalist consumption comparable to that observed by Lemon (1998) or Yurchak (2006): "Much of the mystique associated with these [western] goods depended on their capacity to serve as physical embodiments of a source of value that was understood to reside *elsewhere*" (Mazzarella 2003, p. 256, original emphasis). As Mazzarella notes for Indian brands, this invidious Orientalist distinction produces unique problems for brands that seek to locate themselves simultaneously as Indian (oriental) and world-class (occidental) (Mazzarella 2003, p. 98; compare Özkan & Foster 2005; Vann 2005, 2006; Manning & Uplisashvili 2007).

INDEXING THE PRODUCT: THE PRODUCT AND THE BRAND

Even if the brand is defined partly in opposition to both trademarks and products, brands usually include the names and logos of trademarks as their sign vehicles (Beebe 2004, p. 47); therefore, like trademarks, they must be affixed to the products, wherever else they may be found. Brands function as token-level indexicals (each instance of brand is existentially associated with one instance of a product). Insofar as these tokens are identical replicas of a type, they guarantee that each product will be of the same quality as every other (Lury 2004). The realization of brand thus depends on the materiality of the product (producing Latourian hybrids), but the brand and the product must also be kept separate (purification). The difficulties of separating the two modalities occur on the linguistic plane [the difference between distinctive (brand/trademark) versus descriptive (product) predicates] and on the plane of trade dress (between distinctive and functional aspects of product design and packaging), but they become especially pronounced when the product indexed is itself a new kind of object, a place, an experience, a service, or a sociality itself (for the problems presented by "ingredient branding" and "viral marketing," see Moore 2003, pp. 347–51).

Logos and Names: Linguistic Distinctiveness

The ability of linguistic trademarks to act as signifiers is partially evaluated on the basis of legal doctrines such as distinctiveness, dilution, and genericide (Moore 2003, pp. 344–46; Beebe 2004, 2008). All these categories define the distinctive semiotic properties of trademark or brand in opposition to the generic product. The traditional doctrine of inherent distinctiveness relates to a specifically linguistic aspect of brand, namely that "suggestive, arbitrary, or fanciful words" are more singular and distinctive than terms generically descriptive or referential or in common usage. Thus trademarks are protected to the extent that they lack a descriptive or referential relationship to properties or qualities of the product. Note that the legal category of puffery, which protects optimistic or exaggerated, but not referentially falsifiable, product claims, is defined by a referential ideology of commercial speech involving distinctions of referentiality homologous to those that separate brand distinctiveness from descriptive product claims. As a result, optimistic product claims are protected as noninformational puffs (indexical signs of seller bias), even though evidence shows that consumers are likely to regard them as informational (Parmentier 1994, Hoffman 2006). This particular formulation of the doctrine inherent distinctiveness is generally referred to as the Abercrombie spectrum of trademarks because its formulation derives from the decision in Abercrombie & Fitch v. Hunting World (1976; Dinwoodie 1997, pp. 485–888; Beebe 2004, pp. 670–74; Beebe 2008, pp. 54–56). However, earlier trademark taxonomies are also based on similar oppositions between "original, arbitrary and fanciful" words and generic, descriptive, or semidescriptive words (Schechter 1927, pp. 826–27), and similar distinctions found in early American and British trademark law (Coombe 1996, Bently 2008b) show these categories to be revelatory of remarkably durable linguistic ideologies. The early protection afforded by arbitrary or fanciful names explicitly favored exoticism so that "foreign words, words in dead languages" as well as the exotic images of alterity discussed above figure prominently as trademarks (Coombe 1996, p. 211), alongside the vaguely suggestive Esperanto-like neologisms common today.

The highly contentious category of dilution, instead, "occurs when, because two signifiers are similar, they lessen each other's differential distinctiveness" (Beebe 2008, p. 58). The definition of dilution crucially involves the properties of not only the distinctive signifiers used by two different undertakings, but also the products themselves. Schechter originally defined dilution as the "gradual whittling away or dispersion of the identity and hold upon the public mind of the mark or name by its use upon noncompeting goods" (Schechter 1927, p. 825). The distance between the qualities of the products designated by the mark is at issue here: The name Kodak applied to cameras and bicycles, Aunt Jemima to pancake flour and syrup; there is no competition between the products, but there is a loss of differential distinctiveness. Genericide relates to a loss of differential distinctiveness when a brand name has become "a term identifying not a single producer's products but the product class to which they belong (hence, generic)" (Moore 2003, p. 336). To avoid genericide, the brand must also be separated from the product on

the syntactic plane as well. Thus advertisers are reminded by lawyers never to use the brand name as a noun, but always as an attributive adjective modifying a noun that denotes the product class (not Legos but Lego blocks), often inserting the word "brand" (Lego brand blocks) (Moore 2003, p. 345).

Design and Trade Dress: Nonlinguistic Dimensions of Brand

The inherent distinctiveness of brand may be realized through a variety of markings, including linguistic and nonlinguistic signs, trademarks (words or pictorial symbols) versus trade dress (packaging and product design) (Dinwoodie 1997, p. 477), signs that can be graphically represented and those that cannot (Davis 2008, p. 68). As the indexical relationship between the mark and the product moves from separable to inseparable, contiguous to coextensive, the manner of realization of the different material exponents of brand increasingly will vary according to the variable form of the product, leading to what one might call the morphology of brand.

In the prototypical case recognized in older trademark laws, the trademark is arbitrarily related to the product referentially, but it is also separable, affixed to the product as a segmentable material sign, like a morphological affix, which is potentially distinct, even removable, from the product. However, some of those exponents of brand may be materially continuous with, or only formally abstractable from, the product itself, which is where we find some of the most recondite exercises in legal semiosis (Denicola 1983; Dinwoodie 1997, 1999). Trade dress represents one of the greatest challenges to primarily linguistic models of trademark distinctiveness, where the deployment of linguistic categories such as "suggestive" and "arbitrary" of the Abercrombie spectrum to product shapes produces only immense confusion (Dinwoodie 1997, pp. 485–520). In addition, here we see legal semiotic ideologies seeking to distinguish between form (brand) and function (product), aesthetic notions of styling, ornamentation, or decoration as opposed to technical function or utility (compare Pfaffenberger 1992). Often these legal semiotic ideologies emphasizing physical or conceptual separability of trademark and product are in conflict with modernist aesthetic ideologies among designers, who seek to blur those same boundaries between form and function (Denicola 1983; Dinwoodie 1997, pp. 561–62). The problem is that just as legal regimes of inherent distinctiveness tend to prefer linguistic signs of trademark that are fanciful and arbitrary, but not referential or descriptive, so too legal regimes tend to prefer nonlinguistic aspects of brand that are clearly nonfunctional, decorative, and physically or conceptually separable from the technical or utility dimension of the use value or product. Particular problems arise with attempts to register colors, odors, shapes, and other qualities that have no independent existence (Davis 2008, pp. 70–71) regardless of whether they are distinctive exponents of trademark or brand or product. The limiting case of convergence is represented by (failed) attempts to register distinctive shapes not of packages, but of food commodities [such as distinctively shaped cheese or "impressions upon a piece of gingerbread" (Bently 2008b, p. 27)] themselves, rejected because "[c]onsumers do not expect to eat trade marks or part of them" (Davis 2008, p. 79).

Here Jain (2003, 2007) presents an interesting case in her study of the use of Indian sacred Puranic images in packaging as part of different registers of commodity aesthetics. For western companies, such Puranic imagery rendered in secularizing western naturalistic representational mode was "adopted as an instant cipher of Indianness . . . to tap into the 'native' market," but also to establish a "thematic relationship between the product and the image used to promote it, creating an allegorical, if not playfully ironic, correspondence between gods and mortals" (Jain 2003, p. 50). On the other hand, indigenous deployment of such sacred images was more arbitrarily connected to the product, instead associating the product with a divinity "in an indexical register to seek the deity's blessings and impart auspiciousness" to both the product and the transactions in which it is involved (pp. 51–52). Puranic imagery in product packaging is thus appropriated through two distinct (secular/western and sacred/Indian) registers of signification existing side by side or even sometimes juxtaposed, "a representational mode which uses perspectival naturalism to narrative and allegorical ends, and an indexical mode whose frontal address acknowledges the viewer and institutes an iconic (that is, divine) presence" (p. 49). But using a sacred image in profane product packaging is sometimes avoided "because a package is meant to be thrown away—a disrespectful and inauspicious act" (p. 51).

As Fehervary (2009) argues, modernist product design both in the west and particularly under state socialism also has brandlike qualities; the modernist design of late socialist production serves as a kind of "brand of socialism" consolidating a whole range of products in relation to a single producer, the socialist state (pp. 452–53). Because socialism also produced "branded goods," Fehervary argues that the socialist state was unable to capitalize on the goodwill of some of its own named brands, even as other named state brands suffered by comparison with capitalist brands of which they were understood to be imitations (p. 442). Fehervary (2009) particularly notes that the modernist design of state socialist goods was often paired with an ideology of product presentation that emphasized a technocratic socialist transparency in contrast with the deceitful dualistic opposition between product and brand characteristic of capitalism (which is reflected in western legal ideologies that emphasize strict separability of brand and product in a manner antithetical to principles of modernist design) (pp. 438–40).

Floating Brands: Self-Referential Brands and Counterfeit Brands

In contemporary discourses of brand, brands are often represented as self-valuable objects separate from products, "floating signifiers" or "self-referential signs" (Beebe 2004, p. 626). However, this abstract postmodern commonplace of the referential separability of brand from product can be mobilized to illustrate other more concrete semiotic possibilities and contingencies for brand when brand is considered as a material object that can be physically separated from the product and take on a circulatory life of its own (Foster 2008, pp. 8–17). As Yurchak (2006) argues, under late socialism the material semiotic apparatus of western brand was treated by late socialist youth as being entirely separable from products so that brands encountered in the form of empty packages and labels did not index any specific product but provided contact with the imaginary place of origin, "The Imaginary West": "Most of these packages and bottles [displayed by Soviet youth] were empty—they could not be purchased in regular Soviet stores and often circulated as pure packaging free of original products. However, this empty status did not matter because their original meaning as consumable commodities (the actual liquor, beer, or cigarettes) was largely irrelevant. They were not commodities but shells of commodities whose role was to link the here and now to an 'elsewhere'" (Yurchak 2006, pp. 194–95; see also Lemon 1998, Fehervary 2009, Manning 2009).

However, after socialism, this very separability of the material apparatus of brand, labels and packaging, from products becomes a problem, creating intense fears regarding counterfeiting often blamed on nefarious invisible forces such as "the Mafia" (Pelkmans 2006, pp. 171–94; also Lemon 1998), as well as the obvious absence of the state under postsocialism as an ultimator guarantor of goodwill. As a result, "Georgian concepts of brand remain strongly rooted in a generally productivist model of the economy, particularly because there is no sense that a 'generalized goodwill' exists in the economy: because of brandlessness, falsification of brands, and unreliability of producers, all branded products are to some extent suspect" (Manning & Uplisashvili 2007, p. 631; compare Vann 2006 for a very different set of possibilities for the reception of counterfeit goods in equally productivist market models in postsocialist Vietnam).

Branding Experience: Services and Sociality

In the case of the branding of services and sociality, because the product is typically an autonomous activity (often a linguistic one, say, talk), the categories of quality associated with branding by definition must be realized in tandem with that activity. This notion raises questions similar to those raised by design and trade dress, blurs the lines between producer and consumer as coproducers or coperformers of the brand, and shows the extension of branding concepts not only to services, but also to everyday consumption in general.

With respect to branding services, Cameron (2000) has shown the consequences for an autonomous activity such as conversation when it becomes a marketed, branded service. She shows how real subsumption of an autonomous activity as a service within a specifically capitalist labor process produces not only changes related to labor discipline (scripting, efficiency, surveillance) typical of any labor process subsumed under capitalism, but also "styling," changes of verbal behavior and physical self-presentation that act to produce a uniform brand image of an activity presented to a customer. Under such circumstances, due to extensive top-down scripting and styling of speech and other behavior, the style agent is in a very real sense not the person who performs the branded service style: "Service styles are designed by one set of people (managers on site or at head office, or not uncommonly outside consultants) to be enacted in speech by a different set of people (frontline customer-service workers)" (Cameron 2000, p. 326).

With corporate branding, the concept of brand is extended to branding service work and also extended to include "[aspects of] the context of use and wider environment," including practices of "brandscaping" (Lury 2004, pp. 32–44; Arvidsson 2006, pp. 77–80), which can include "lights, design, music and the demeanour of personnel to encourage consumers to coperform a particular ambience" (Arvidsson 2006, p. 80). Here the concept of brand is extended to include service work, and even includes the customers themselves who coperform the brand. For example, multiple-player online games represent what Arvidsson calls "branding sociality" in which much of the commodified content is produced by consumers (prosumers) themselves (Arvidsson 2006, pp. 104–14; Herman et al. 2006). In the case of Starbucks, brandscaping includes branding store ambience and consumer sociality (Gaudio 2003; Arvidsson 2006, p. 80) and extends even to the scripting and styling of the service interaction with the customer, who is expected to confabulate in the coperformance of the Starbucks brand in the process of formulating orders, which generates its own peculiar interactional dilemmas for the baristas and often recalcitrant customers (Manning 2008).

LOVEMARKS: INDEXING CONSUMER DESIRE

Through brands, products are also attached to figures of consumption: idealized consumers. This attention to the figure of the consumer is often treated again as an epochal shift from a social ontology of productivism to one of consumerism: a semiotic transition from trademarks of production to what Foster (borrowing from brand guru Kevin Roberts) calls "lovemarks" of consumer loyalty (Foster 2005, 2008). Understood as brands, the legally protected semiotic apparatus of trademark (e.g., logos and names) serves as a sign vehicle not only for legally protected source-identifying indexicals and the goodwill associated with that source (traditional trademarks), but also for a cloud of regimented consumer associations that have monetized value as intangible assets and clamor for legal recognition through doctrines such as "dilution" (Moore 2003, p. 339; Bently 2008a, p. 34; Beebe 2008, pp. 45–47; Davis 2008, pp. 66–68). Thus, branded objects attract to themselves properties of the subjects ("person-alities") that produce them and also,

by association, the subjects that consume them. Foster describes this as the

> reattachment of the alienated product to another personality, that is, to the consumer. It is this reattachment that is achieved through branding. I hasten to add that branding involves more than the labor of special workers who design logos and devise advertising campaigns....Branding also involves the work of consumers, whose meaningful use of the purchased products invests these products with the consumer's identity....Put differently, the persons of consumers enhance the value of brands. (Foster 2005, p. 11)

As this quote shows, perspectives such as these seek to see the value of brands as being a product of the joint labor of both producers and consumers (Lury 2004; Foster 2005, 2007, 2008; Arvidsson 2006). These commentators are careful to point out, however, that this consumer labor is policed and ultimately appropriated by the brand proprietor, what Mazzarella calls "keeping-while-giving the brand" (Mazzarella 2003, pp. 192–95). As Arvidsson (2006) puts it pithily, "For consumers, brands are means of production....For Capital, brands are a means of appropriation" (pp. 93–94). Thus, regulating, regimenting, and appropriating this two-way flow of associations between brand and consumer becomes a crucial component of brand management (Moore 2003, p. 343; Lury 2004, pp. 80–92; Arvidsson 2006, pp. 66–94).

The western discourse of brands tends to imagine brand as an almost universal articulation of the infinite particularity of consumer desire, which interpellates consumers in terms of "cool," "aspirational" lifestyles (Arvidsson 2006, pp. 68–73). But there are certainly other models for how brands interpellate consumers: For example, Japanese "cute" character brands interpellate generalized consumer identity on the model of the idealized girl consumer (Allison 2000, 2004; see Iwabuchi 2004, pp. 70–72, on the opposition between American/global "coolness" and Japanese/Asian "cuteness"), but brands can also interpellate consumers as citizens within socialist, developmentalist, or neo-liberal models of consumption and govermentality, as well as locate the brands and their consumers as being coeval with those elsewhere (Kelly & Volkov 1998, Gronow 2003, Mazzarella 2003, Özkan & Foster 2005). Because the model of aspirational consumption associated with brand becomes a sign of participation in universal normative models of desire, not responding to it becomes a diagnostic of uncivilized backwardness (Foster 2008, pp. 39–47). Socialist branded production is linked to an attempt to civilize the socialist citizen as a cultured consumer coeval with the western consumer by generalizing presocialist aristocratic models of consumption by making available branded goods that are competitive with those produced in capitalist societies (Kelly & Volkov 1998, Gronow 2003, Manning & Uplisashvili 2007, Fehervary 2009, Manning 2009). With respect to India, Mazzarella shows how the new western consumerist dispensation of "aspiration" mediated by "aspirational brands" parallels the developmentalism of earlier models of the consumer citizen, showing how it "equates the generality of consumer desire with the particular norms and forms of the nascent middle-class imaginary" and mimics developmental discourse by producing an "alternative temporality with its own language of progress and evolution" (Mazzarella 2003, p. 101). As Wang (2007) argues, the universalization of culturally particular models of consumer desire can lead to problems, for example, for transnational agencies in China who "mistake Chinese consumers for their Western counterparts by overselling them lifestyle aspirations while underrating the importance of safety appeal" (p. 309). These different models that emphasize consumer desires and consumer fears, respectively, lead to different branding strategies: In western "house of brands" strategies, brands identify specific product lines addressed to specific aspirational lifestyle market segments, but the parent company itself is anonymous; by contrast, in Asian "branded house" strategies, brands identify a single well-known and trusted producer whose goodwill is distributed across completely unrelated and potentially unlimited product lines (Wang 2007).

FIGURES AND FETISHES: LIFESTYLE AND CHARACTER BRANDING

As brands as objects attract more properties of consumers as subjects, and vice versa, these associations become the attributes of brands as subjects. Brands move from being lifeless symbols of these complex associations (figures) to living "persons" who embody them as personal attributes (fetishes) (Hanby 1999, Lury 2004). As brands move from being prosthetic figures mediating relations between subjects (producers and consumers) to becoming autonomous subjects in their own right, it becomes possible for consumers to form affective relationships with these figures directly. But brands as persons can be imagined in rather different ways, and the kinds of personalistic relationships they mediate also vary. Lury (2004) distinguishes between indexical and iconic modes of personalization: The former are source-identifying indexicals that are often figural, that is, they sometimes present "the organization as if it were an individual" (e.g., Betty Crocker) (p. 80), whereas the latter are really little more than unordered lists or bundles of abstract personalistic signs of qualitative possibility (Peircean qualisigns) [e.g., the brand Orange is "refreshing, honest, straightforward, dynamic, friendly" (p. 84)]. The nonfigural iconic mode of personalization characteristic of lifestyle branding shows very little integration into a coherent character or narrative development. In this way, they are much like the graphic collages often used in marketing to model or discover these unordered complexes of "unspoken emotional and symbolic" associations (Foster 2007, p. 707; see also Moore 2003, p. 243, Wang 2007, p. 86). Such techniques of representation permit "the decomposition of individual consumers into 'data clouds' and their recomposition into representations of the context of consumption" (Arvidsson 2006, p. 65).

By contrast, figural fictional or fantastic characters such as Betty Crocker (Lury 2004, pp. 79–80) or especially the eponymous Brownies of the Eastman Kodak "Brownie Camera" (Olivier 2007) are perhaps more comparable to the kind of personalization shown in Japanese character branding. Japanese character branding involves specific forms of cute figuration to produce, for example, corporate mascots, but these figures are also developed as characters of narratives in *manga* and *anime*, producing an interdiscursive narrative framework that helps these figures to be continually redeployed across diverse product lines. However, here too there are key differences: Character branding personas often embody affectively engaging attributes of cuteness [*chara-moe* (Azuma 2009 [2001], pp. 39–47)] that afford kinds of affective bonds and relationships between consumer and product quite different from desires enabled by western-brand personas that embody abstract aspirational cool lifestyles, or even the animated Disney characters to which they might otherwise be compared (Allison 2000, 2004; Iwabuchi 2002, 2004; Ito 2007; Wang 2007). Furthermore, as Azuma (2009 [2001]) shows, what begins as character branding can develop into autonomous forms of consumption of derivative (fan) works whose value derives only from their consistency with the narrative or character and certainly not from

their connection to the original product or producer.

Brands serve as semiotic figures for the characters on the stage of the global economy; however, they are frequently taken to figure the logic of the global economy itself: Lury (2004) deploys the punning opposition between brands as logos ("the signs or slogans that mark brands") and brand as *logos* ["the kind of thought or rationality that organizes the economy" (Lury 2004, p. 5)]. Thus both Lury (2004, pp. 5–6) and Arvidsson (2006, p. 124) argue that brand not only functions as a semiotic object that figures specific relations between producers and consumers, but also serves as a focal metasemiotic object that figures the indigenous categories (the *logos*) of the culture of circulation itself. However, as Mazzarella persuasively argues, the consumer of brand in the first sense (the consumers who buy the branded goods) may be quite distinct from the consumer of brand in the second sense ("the corporate client who 'buys into' the categories of marketing discourse") (Mazzarella 2003, pp. 186–87). Determining who the customer of brand is raises the question of what is the purpose or object of the semiotics of brand: Brands and their definitions thus reveal very different things depending on whether they are approached at work as semiotic objects within the economy or as metasemiotic objects that can be interrogated to reveal the folk ontologies and semiotic ideologies latent in economic categories. *Caveat emptor.*

DISCLOSURE STATEMENT

The author is not aware of any affiliations, memberships, funding, or financial holdings that might be perceived as affecting the objectivity of this review.

LITERATURE CITED

Abbott A. 1988. *The System of Professions: An Essay on the Division of Expert Labor.* Chicago: Univ. Chicago Press

Abercrombie & Fitch v. Hunting World. 1976. *Legal decision.* **http://www.altlaw.org/v1/cases/549267**

Allison A. 2000. A challenge to Hollywood? Japanese character goods hit the US. *Jpn. Stud.* 20(1):67–88

Allison A. 2004. Cuteness as Japan's millennial product. See Tobin 2004, pp. 34–52

Arvidsson A. 2006. *Brands: Meaning and Value in Media Culture.* Oxford: Routledge

Askegaard S. 2006. Brands as a global ideoscape. See Schroeder & Salzer-Mörling 2006, pp. 91–102

Azuma H. 2009 [2001]. *Otaku: Japan's Database Animals*, transl. JE Abel, S Kion. Minneapolis: Univ. Minn. Press (from Japanese)

Bach J. 2002. "The taste remains": consumption, (n)ostalgia, and the production of East Germany. *Public Cult.* 14(3):545–56

Beebe B. 2004. The semiotic analysis of trademark law. *UCLA Law Rev.* 51(3):621–704

Beebe B. 2008. The semiotic account of trademark doctrine and trademark culture. See Dinwoodie & Jamis 2008, pp. 42–64

Bently L. 2008a. From communication to thing: historical aspects of the conceptualisation of trade marks as property. See Dinwoodie & Jamis 2008, pp. 3–41

Bently L. 2008b. The making of modern trade mark law: the construction of the legal concept of trade mark (1860–80). See Bently et al. 2008, pp. 3–41

Bently L, Davis J, Ginsburg JC, eds. 2008. *Trade Marks and Brands: An Interdisciplinary Critique*. Cambridge, UK: Cambridge Univ. Press

Berdahl D. 1999. "(N)Ostalgie" for the present: memory, longing, and East German things. *Ethnos* 64(3):192–211

Callon M, Méadel C, Rabeharisoa V. 2002. The economy of qualities. *Econ. Soc.* 31(2):194–217

Cameron D. 2000. Styling the worker: gender and the commodification of language in the globalized service economy. *J. Sociolinguist.* 4(3):323–47

Coombe R. 1996. Embodied trademarks: mimesis and alterity on American commercial frontiers. *Cult. Anthropol.* 11(2):202–24

Csaba FF, Bengtsson A. 2006. Rethinking identity in brand management. See Schroeder & Salzer-Mörling 2006, pp. 118–35

Davis J. 2008. Between a sign and a brand: mapping the boundaries of a registered trade mark in European Union trade mark law. See Bently et al. 2008, pp. 65–91

Denicola R. 1983. Applied art and industrial design: a suggested approach to copyright in useful articles. *Minn. Law Rev.* 67:707–48

Dinwoodie G. 1997. Reconceptualizing the inherent distinctiveness of product design trade dress. *N. C. Law Rev.* 75:471–606

Dinwoodie G. 1999. The death of ontology: a teleological approach to trademark law. *Iowa Law Rev.* 84:611–752

Dinwoodie G, Jamis M, eds. 2008. *Trademark Law and Theory: A Handbook of Contemporary Research*. Cheltenham, UK: Edward Elgar

Elliot R, Davies A. 2006. Symbolic brands and authenticity of identity performance. See Schroeder & Salzer-Mörling 2006, pp. 155–71

Fehervary K. 2009. Goods and states: the political logic of state-socialist material culture. *Comp. Stud. Soc. Hist.* 51(2):426–59

Foster RJ. 2005. Commodity futures: labour, love, and value. *Anthropol. Today* 21(4):8–12

Foster RJ. 2007. The work of the new economy: consumers, brands and value-creation. *Cult. Anthropol.* 22(4):707–31

Foster RJ. 2008. *Coca-Globalization: Following Soft Drinks from New York to New Guineau*. New York: Palgrave

Gardner BB, Levy SJ. 1955. The product and the brand. *Harv. Bus. Rev.* March–April:33–39

Gaudio R. 2003. Coffeetalk: Starbucks[TM] and the commercialization of casual conversation. *Lang. Soc.* 32(5):659–91

Griffiths A. 2008. A law-and-economics perspective on trade marks. See Bently et al. 2008, pp. 241–66

Gronow J. 2003. *Caviar with Champagne: Common Luxury and the Ideals of the Good Life in Stalin's Russia*. Oxford: Berg

Hanby T. 1999. Brands—dead or alive? *J. Mark. Res. Soc.* 41(1):7–18

Hearn A. 2008. "Meat, mask, burden": probing the contours of the branded "self". *J. Consum. Cult.* 8(2):197–217

Heath D, Meneley A. 2007. Techne, technoscience, and the circulation of comestible commodities: an introduction. *Am. Anthropol.* 109(4):593–602

Heilbrunn B. 2006. Brave new brands: cultural branding between utopia and a-topia. See Schroeder & Salzer-Mörling 2006, pp. 103–17

Herman A, Coombe R, Kaye L. 2006. Your *Second Life?* goodwill and the performativity of intellectual property in online digital gaming. *Cult. Stud.* 20(2–3):184–210

Hoffman DA. 2006. The best puffery article ever. *Iowa Law Rev.* 91:101–51

Irvine J. 1989. When talk isn't cheap: language and political economy. *Am. Ethnol.* 16(2):248–67

Ito M. 2007. Technologies of the childhood imagination: *Yu-Gi-Oh!* media mixes, and everyday cultural production. In *Structures of Participation in Digital Culture*, ed. J Karaganis, pp. 88–111. Durham, NC: Duke Univ. Press

Iwabuchi K. 2002. *Recentering Globalization: Popular Culture and Japanese Transnationalism*. Durham, NC: Duke Univ. Press

Iwabuchi K. 2004. How "Japanese" is Pokemon? See Tobin 2004, pp. 53–79

Jain K. 2003. New visual technologies in the bazaar: reterritorialisation of the sacred in popular print culture. In *Sarai Reader 03: Shaping Technologies*, ed. R Vasudevan, R Sundaram, J Bagchi, M Narula, S Sengupta, et al., pp. 44–57. Delhi: Sarai

Jain K. 2007. *Gods in the Bazaar: The Economies of Indian Calendar Arts*. Durham, NC: Duke Univ. Press

Jansen SC. 2008. Designer nations: neo-liberal nation branding—Brand Estonia. *Soc. Identities* 14(1):121–42

Johanssen U, Holm LS. 2006. Brand management and design management: a nice couple or false friends? See Schroeder & Salzer-Mörling 2006, pp. 136–52

Kapferer JN. 2006. The two business cultures of luxury brands. See Schroeder & Salzer-Mörling 2006, pp. 67–76

Keane W. 2003. Semiotics and the social analysis of material things. *Lang. Commun.* 23(3–4):409–25

Kelly C, Volkov V. 1998. Directed desires: *kult'urnost'* and consumption. In *Constructing Russian Culture in the Age of Revolution, 1881–1940*, ed. C Kelly, D Shepherd, pp. 291–313. New York: Oxford Univ. Press

Kotler P. 2003. Brands. In *Marketing Insights from A to Z*, pp. 8–14. New York: Wiley

Latour B. 1993 [1991]. *We Have Never Been Modern*, transl. C Porter. Cambridge, MA: Harv. Univ. Press (from French)

Lemon A. 1998. "Your eyes are green like dollars": counterfeit cash, national substance, and currency apartheid in 1990s Russia. *Cult. Anthropol.* 13(1):22–55

Lury C. 2004. *Brands: The Logos of the Global Economy*. London: Routledge

Manning P. 2008. Barista rants about stupid customers at Starbucks: what imaginary conversations can teach us about real ones. *Lang. Commun.* 28(2):101–26

Manning P. 2009. The epoch of Magna: capitalist brands and postsocialist revolutions in Georgia. *Slav. Rev.* 68(4):924–45

Manning P, Meneley A. 2008. Material objects in cosmological worlds: an introduction. *Ethnos* 73(3):285–302

Manning P, Uplisashvili A. 2007. "Our beer": ethnographic brands in postsocialist Georgia. *Am. Anthropol.* 109(4):626–41

Masuzawa T. 2000. Troubles with materiality: the ghost of fetishism in the nineteenth century. *Comp. Stud. Soc. Hist.* 42(2):242–67

Mazzarella W. 2003. *Shoveling Smoke: Advertising and Globalization in Contemporary India*. Durham, NC: Duke Univ. Press

McClintock A. 1995. *Imperial Leather: Race, Gender and Sexuality in the Colonial Contest*. London: Routledge

Meneley A. 2004. Extra-virgin olive oil and slow food. *Anthropologica* 46(2):165–76

Meneley A. 2007. Like an extra virgin. *Am. Anthropol.* 109(4):678–87

Meneley A. 2008. Time in a bottle: the uneasy circulation of Palestinian olive oil. *Middle East Rep.* 248:18–23

Miller D. 1995. Consumption as the vanguard of history: a polemic by way of an introduction. In *Acknowledging Consumption: A Review of New Studies*, ed. D Miller, pp. 1–57. London: Routledge

Miller D. 1998. Coca-Cola: a black sweet drink from Trinidad. In *Material Cultures: Why Some Things Matter*, ed. D Miller, pp. 169–88. Chicago: Univ. Chicago Press

Moore R. 2003. From genericide to viral marketing: on "brand". *Lang. Commun.* 23(3–4):331–57

Munn N. 1986. *The Fame of Gawa: A Symbolic Study of Value Transformations in a Massim (Papua, New Guinea) Society*. Durham, NC: Duke Univ. Press

Olivier M. 2007. George Eastman's modern stone-age family: snapshot photography and the Brownie. *Technol. Cult.* 48(1):1–19

Özkan D, Foster RJ. 2005. Consumer citizenship, nationalism, and neoliberal globalization in Turkey: the advertising launch of *Cola Turka*. *Advert. Soc. Rev.* 6:3

Parmentier R. 1994. *Signs in Society: Studies in Semiotic Anthropology*. Bloomington: Ind. Univ. Press

Parry B. 2008. Geographical indications: not all "champagne and roses." See Bently et al. 2008, pp. 361–80

Pelkmans M. 2006. *Defending the Border: Identity, Religion, and Modernity in the Republic of Georgia*. Ithaca, NY: Cornell Univ. Press

Pfaffenberger B. 1992. The social anthropology of technology. *Annu. Rev. Anthropol.* 21:491–516

Pietz W. 1985. The problem of the fetish, I. *Res: J. Anthropol. Aesthet.* 9:5–17

Renne E. 2007. Mass producing food traditions for West Africans abroad. *Am. Anthropol.* 109(4):616–25

Ritzer G. 1993. *The McDonaldization of Society: An Investigation into the Changing Character of Contemporary Social Life*. Thousand Oaks, CA: Pine Forge

Schechter F. 1927. The rational basis of trademark protection. *Harv. Law Rev.* 40:813–33

Schroeder JE, Salzer-Mörling M, eds. 2006. *Brand Culture*. Oxford: Routledge

Tobin J, ed. 2004. *Pikachu's Global Adventure: The Rise and Fall of Pokemon*. Durham, NC: Duke Univ. Press

Vann EF. 2005. Domesticating consumer goods in the global economy: examples from Vietnam and Russia. *Ethnos* 70(4):465–88

Vann EF. 2006. The limits of authenticity in Vietnamese consumer markets. *Am. Anthropol.* 108(2):286–96

Wang J. 2007. *Brand New China: Advertising, Media, and Commercial Culture*. Cambridge, MA: Harv. Univ. Press

Wilk R. 2006. Bottled water: the pure commodity in the age of branding. *J. Consumer Cult.* 6(3):303–25

Yurchak A. 2006. *Everything Was Forever, Until It Was No More: The Last Soviet Generation*. Princeton, NJ: Princeton Univ. Press

The Reorganization of the Sensory World

Thomas Porcello,[1] Louise Meintjes,[2]
Ana Maria Ochoa,[3] and David W. Samuels[4]

[1]Department of Anthropology, Vassar College, Poughkeepsie, New York 12604;
email: thporcello@vassar.edu

[2]Departments of Music and Cultural Anthropology, Duke University, Durham,
North Carolina 27708-0665; email: meintjes@duke.edu

[3]Department of Music, Columbia University, New York, NY 10027;
email: ao2110@columbia.edu

[4]Department of Music, New York University, New York, NY 10003;
email: dws2004@nyu.edu

Annu. Rev. Anthropol. 2010. 39:51–66

First published online as a Review in Advance on
June 14, 2010

The *Annual Review of Anthropology* is online at
anthro.annualreviews.org

This article's doi:
10.1146/annurev.anthro.012809.105042

0084-6570/10/1021-0051$20.00

Key Words

senses, mediation, discourse, multisensory, materiality

Abstract

Although anthropological and critical social theory have a long interest in sensory experience, work on the senses has intensified within the past 20 years. This article traces three sensory genealogies within anthropology: the work of Ong and McLuhan as critiqued and advanced by David Howes and the Concordia Project; phenomenological studies as advanced by Paul Stoller; and a focus on materialities as advanced by Nadia Seremetakis. Studies of individual senses, which we survey, led to calls for a more integrated approach to the senses, both within anthropology and from cinema and media studies. In various ways, the senses are constituted by their imbrication in mediated cultural practices, whether mediated by technology, discourse, or local epistemologies. We argue that integrating language and discourse into the study of the senses along with new media insights more fully articulates the significance of body-sensorial knowledge.

INTRODUCTION

Anthropological and critical social theory have a long but spotty history of interest in sensory experience. Franz Boas (1901), for example, noted that, "it has been observed by many travelers that the senses of primitive man are remarkably well trained" (p. 4). Boas turned away from the senses, however, to focus on the importance of distinct forms of cultural association through which new sensory experiences were given meaningful import in different cultural formations. Karl Marx wrote in "Private Property and Communism" (1988 [1844], p. 109) that "the forming of the five senses is a labor of the entire history of the world down to the present," but he never followed through on the implications of this insight. Similarly, in *The Raw and the Cooked*, Claude Lévi-Strauss (1969) wrote a "Fugue for the Five Senses" as part of his analysis of Ge mythology. Even though the general tenor of his work remained highly abstract, two things are crucial in his analysis: The senses are not understood in isolation; rather each sense "suggests other sensory coding systems" (p. 153). Furthermore, the senses act as key articulators between the binary pairs of his structural analysis. Along with Marx and Lévi-Strauss, Sigmund Freud is sometimes cited as an important precursor to an anthropology of the senses (see Howes 2003, pp. xiv–xx).

More recently, numerous anthropologists have made a concerted effort to address the senses as a central object of research (Classen 2005; Classen et al. 1994; Howes 1991, 2003, 2005; Jackson 1989, 1996; Seremetakis 1994; Stoller 1989, 1997; Taussig 1993, 2009). Their work grapples with the materiality and sociality of the senses as culturally constituted and constitutes the sensorium as a cultural entity. But a reorganization of modes of thinking about the senses does not come solely from this work. Scholarship on technology and mediation that has prompted a reconsideration of the senses in modernity and postmodernity; the anthropology of ritual that addresses its aesthetic, performative, and perceptual dimensions; attention to the ethnopoetic and performative aspects of expressive culture; the turn to the body as a site of knowledge; and the recasting of the nature-culture divide in recent anthropological work have all played a role in rethinking the place of the senses in anthropological scholarship.

We begin by tracing three genealogies that in tandem articulated an anthropology of the senses in the late 1980s, drawing on earlier considerations of the importance of the senses for understanding cultural experience. As the field then developed through explorations of individual senses, we discuss research on taste, smell, touch, hearing, and vision, with an eye toward the work of anthropologists as well as an interdisciplinary literature in which anthropology has been a participant. We discuss subsequent calls for an integrative approach to the senses; although this call has come from within anthropology, it has also followed from other disciplines' explorations of relationships among the body, technology, and mediation. We conclude with what we see as an avenue of further development for an anthropology of the senses. While in its initial stages, the anthropology of the senses repeatedly cast itself as a critical response to discourse-centered approaches to culture. We believe that creating an opening to allow language and discourse into an approach to the senses adds important insights to understanding the cultural constitution of the sensorium. Thus we echo the call for an integrative approach to the senses that considers the work of scholars of mediation and technology, but we argue that the turn away from incorporating language and discourse into the anthropology of the senses forecloses potentially productive connections between language and the senses. We propose that the most productive of these connections can derive from work on aesthetic practices that mobilize both language and expressive-sensorial practices.

THE SENSES IN ANTHROPOLOGY: THREE GENEALOGIES

Anthropological work focused on the senses is founded on the insistence that the senses are not merely a biological ground on which cultural meanings are constructed. Rather, the senses are always already fully cultural, and "sensory perception is a cultural as well as physical act" (Classen 1997, p. 401). Responding to the static and textual nature of previous anthropological interpretations of cultural experience, anthropologists working on the senses since the 1980s, sharing some ground with the field of performance studies, have considered various ways of framing, researching, and writing about experience, emphasizing the lived and emergent nature of the senses, the cultural embeddedness of sensory experience, and the historical and political relations between sensory orders and social orders.

One impetus for the emergence of an anthropology of the senses came out of a growing dissatisfaction with anthropologists' analyses of the role of ritual and ceremony in everyday life (e.g., Stoller 1989). Examining aesthetics and performance in the constitution of the social, scholars within the anthropology of religion responded to two growing difficulties with anthropological interpretations of ritual in the late 1970s (Basso 1985, Bauman 1977). The first was the perceived overemphasis of functionalism on equilibrium, represented most clearly by Victor Turner's focus on conflict as social disruption that is reparable through ritual performance (Crapanzano 1992). The second was the sense that structuralism's textuality neglected the sensory processes of lived, encultured experiences of myth and ritual (Feld 1990 [1982]). Despite these critiques, Turner and Lévi-Strauss remain important precursors for work in the anthropology of the body and senses, especially in ethnographies of religion and healing. In fact, their modes of analysis prefigure types of relations developed as a critical creative response to their work by subsequent anthropologists (Farquhar 2002; Lambek 2003; Lambek & Strathern 1998; Viveiros de Castro 1992, 2004).

Another thread linking anthropological work on the senses has been a critique of western ocularcentrism that has created fertile points of cross-disciplinary contact. Challenging the philosophical and theological histories that posited sight as the highest of the sensory faculties, as the privileged means of coming to know God, or as the sense most closely linked to epistemological certainty as well as rationality (Jay 1993, Synnott 1991), anthropologists worked to document and analyze other cultural organizations of sensory knowledge, experience, and configuration. Some of these studies challenged ocularcentrism by focusing on other senses, leading to books and articles focused solely on one sense; others sought to challenge presuppositions of the senses as rigidly separate phenomena or of the sensorium as necessarily constituted of only five senses and of these particular senses (Geurts 2002, Howes 2009). Of the three genealogies that lie behind much of this work, one comes out of communication, another originates in phenomenology, and a third concerns materiality. We focus on three scholars whose work particularly strongly embodies these genealogies. Because several other excellent works address the emergence of the anthropology of the senses (Herzfeld 2001, Howes 2003), what follows is not intended to be comprehensive, but illustrative of what we see as the lines of thinking that have had the most impact on anthropological research.

Communication

Howes (1991, 2003, 2005) links an anthropology of the senses to a critical engagement with the media insights of Ong and McLuhan. Although he notes precursors in Marx and Freud, Howes argues that it was not until Ong's and McLuhan's discussions of media's agency in shaping forms of social being that an understanding of the sensorium as historically and socially constituted in specific ways became possible. Howes also credits, to a lesser extent, Carpenter's work in cross-cultural aesthetics (1973), and Leavitt & Hart (1990) have emphasized the work of Goody (1977) as well.

For Howes (2003), the sensorium is "the most fundamental domain of cultural expression, the medium through which all the values and practices of society are enacted" (p. 1).

Relations between the senses "are also social relations" (p. 55). Howes argues (2005) that the "ratios" of the senses—the relationships between vision, hearing, taste, touch, and smell—are socially constituted (p. 10) and that cultural productions constitute social relations through sensuous experience (p. 3). He critiques the lack of nuance in McLuhan's idea of ratios as technologically determined and dominated by one particular sense at a time. His support of the senses as sources of cultural experience and anthropological knowledge is coupled with a distrust of the antisensual nature of the discipline's turn to discourse (2005) and "the detour represented by the rise of the textual model of cultural analysis in the 1970s" (2003, p. xiv).

The collaborative and synthetic work of Howes and his colleagues at Concordia University, Classen and Synott, has substantially raised the presence of the senses within anthropology, leading to conferences, papers, a special edition of *Anthropologie et Sociétés* (1990), as well as the establishment of the journal, *The Senses & Society*, a book series, *Sensory Formations*, and a series of readers about the senses. This work has drawn together European and North American cross-disciplinary research that is historical and ethnographic, and it has engaged cultural and media studies scholars in a dialogue with humanists and social scientists. Much of their work can be found at **http://alcor.concordia.ca/~senses/**.

Phenomenology

Stoller originally set out to conduct research about the ritual language of the Songhay of Niger in 1976/1977. Through years of field research and an eventual immersion into the worlds of sorcery and possession, he turned from linguistics to a focus on knowledge held in multisensory experience. He drew especially on Merleau-Ponty's critique of the Cartesian mind/body split, arguing that perceptual knowledge played a crucial role in the ways in which the senses mediate the worlds of the material, social, and spiritual. In integrating perceptual knowledge into his analysis, Stoller lent equivalent epistemic weight to local material, social, and spiritual truths (Stoller 1989, 1997).

Stoller calls for a new kind of scholarship that comprehensively sensorializes the fieldwork and ethnographic practices of cultural anthropologists. He advocates for anthropologists to consider the sensory worlds of others (not only their language), but also to attend to the full range of their own senses, not just to sight, which he considers to be the "privileged sense of the West" (Stoller 1989, p. 5). "Sensuous scholarship," however, is not only about attending to questions of voice and taking critical account of the senses: These are a means by which to get at the "phenomenology of the fieldwork encounter" (Stoller 1997, p. 43) and the politics of representation, and thereby to recognize "the increasingly political implications of our works" (p. 34).

Materiality

Another stream contributing to the anthropology of the senses, most notably in the work of Seremetakis, derives from a reformulation of Fernand Braudel's notion of the historical unconscious and Ernst Bloch's and Walter Benjamin's insights concerning the political significance of the relations between technology, perception, the everyday, and the sensorium (Seremetakis 1994, p. 24). She uses their work as the basis to explore the historical as a sensory dimension in which cultural artifacts considered useless and discarded by a utilitarian and functional modernity, and imposed through colonial and postcolonial annulment of other modes of historical memory and practice, come to constitute a vast social unconscious of sensory-emotive experience that potentially offers up counternarratives of once-valued lifeworlds (1994, pp. 1–17). For Seremetakis, the senses provide an alternate entry point into the history of memory, a site for recovering forgotten or erased experiences that reintegrate the sensorial with the material, contra the fragmentation of the senses proposed by a modernity characterized by the division of the senses and labor and subsumed under the consumerist politics of commodification. In this argument, the material artifact is a sensory form in itself and also functions as "meta-sense" (1994, p. 9). Other work on materiality cautions, however, that one must not locate all understandings of the relation between things, perception, knowledge, and being in an epistemology of the senses and proposes the "thing" as ontologically significant (Henare et al. 2007).

THE SENSES SEPARATED

Among anthropologists who have produced ethnographies of the senses, it is common to find that the reorganization of the sensory domain is entangled with the different materialities of specific sensory practices. Much of this literature is interdisciplinary, engaging anthropologists in dialogue with scholars across the humanities, arts, media studies, and social sciences and theorizing through psychoanalytic, feminist, philosophical, and artistic approaches. In spite of recent calls for a more expansive and integrated conception of the senses, most social and cultural studies of the senses have treated them in relative isolation from one another.

Taste has been foregrounded in various forms of anthropological argument (Mintz 1985, Seremetakis 1994, Stoller 1989). It is framed as a component of symbolic action (Reed-Danahay 1996); as important to the dissemination of ideology and linked through its materiality to politics (Hayes-Conroy & Hayes-Conroy 2008); as an embodiment of experiences and patterns of migration and displacement (Choo 2004, Highmore 2008) or nationalism (Caldwell 2002); as tied to space and community (Gvion & Trostler 2008), aesthetics (Jain & Lochlann 2003), and health (Ferzacca 2004, Guthman 2003); or as embedded in production and consumption (Korsmeyer 2005). Classen et al. (1994) assert taste's equivalence and parallel history to other senses.

The philosophical placement of smell as a lower and elusive sense may account for a lag in its investigation (Curtis 2006). Classen et al. (1994) argue that "smell is cultural," although it possesses a quality of "radical interiority" (Classen et al. 1994, pp. 3, 5). Corbin (1986) initiated a social, historical, and interpretive approach to odor, fragrance, and the sense of smell. Europe's past has been a primary site of study, with an emphasis on class analysis. Drobnick (2006) provides a succinct history of smell research.

In the west, touch seems to encompass the other senses and has either been debased by its intense corporeality or sublimated in association to feeling and spirituality (Harvey 2003). The corporeality of touch has led to its theorization at the intersection of physical and cultural anthropology (Montagu 1971). Although touch is considered as located primarily in the skin and the hand, the conflation of touch with sensation, feeling, and emotion (Heller-Roazen 2007) leads to a western understanding of touch as a ubiquitous sense. The anthropology of healing and medical diagnosis (Desjarlais 1992, Kuriyama 1999), of life and death (Desjarlais 2003), and of the body (Lock 1995, Lock & Farquhar 2007) has productively explored touch. Its relation to other senses has been frequently noted (Classen 2005, p. 3), and it has been crucial in arguments for the integration of and thinking beyond the five senses (Howes 2009, pp. 22–29).

The proliferation of scholarship on listening in the past two decades has been characterized as an "auditory turn" that explores "the increasing significance of the acoustic as simultaneously a site for analysis, a medium for aesthetic engagement, and a model for theorization" (Drobnick 2004, p. 10). Feld (1982, 1988, 1991, 1996) pioneered the ethnography of listening with his work on Kaluli acoustemology, expanding it into an ethnographically rich and detailed exploration of the significance of listening in different cultural settings (Feld & Brenneis 2004). Some research has explored how forms of audition mark the divide between the secular and the religious in modernity (Corbin 1998, Schmidt 2000, Taussig 1993). Consideration of the role of audition in various Islamic spiritual practices has been particularly productive owing to the importance of audition in such traditions (Corbin 1958, Corbin &

Pearson 1977, During 1989, Hirschkind 2006, Kapchan 2007, Shannon 2003). Finally, hearing has been treated historically (Erlmann 2004; Samuels et al. 2010, this volume; Sterne 2003; Szendy 2009).

Hearing is often articulated not as a separate sense but as one part of the multisensorial dimensionality of ritual performances (Howes 2005, Leavitt & Hart 1990, Stoller 1997). Ethnographies that explore local distinctions among the natural, human, and spiritual worlds note that the transformation between worlds often occurs through acts of listening to songs, sounds, and noises (Descola 1994, Lévi-Strauss 1969, Seeger 1987, Stoller 1997, Taussig 1993, Viveiros de Castro 1992). Work on politics of the production of recorded sound has addressed listening as a cultural practice, in the auditory practices of recording studio engineers (Meintjes 2003, Porcello 2005), through the sampling and creation of hiphop beats (Schloss 2004), and via explorations of timbre or noise through the electronic manipulation of sound (Fales 2005, Larkin 2008). Ethnomusicological studies of the politics of musical "identities" (Wong 2004) and musical genres (Novak 2008) address the culture of listening.

No sense has been more thoroughly interrogated by anthropologists than sight. Visual anthropology has a more explicitly elaborated metadiscourse than do anthropologies of the other senses. It is also constructed around, and aware of the plasticity (and textualizing practices) of, its specific presentational mediums: on the one hand, film, photography, video, and digital media (Buckley 2006, Edwards et al. 2006, Pinney & Peterson 2003); on the other hand, visual artistic mediums such as painting and sculpture (Myers 2001, 2005). Perhaps owing to the disciplinary conversations that led to and followed from the establishment of the Society for Visual Anthropology (El Guindi 2004, pp. 23–49), sight is also the sense that has been least separable from the theorization of its relationship to various mediums of representation. Furthermore, the material means of visual representation became quickly linked to theories of seeing and to technologies of looking and of image capture (MacDougall 2006, pp. 240–53; Mead & Bateson 1977), as well as to concerns in cultural anthropology with modes of textual representation, cultural poetics, and their role in practices of othering, along with a growing interrogation of the colonialist enterprise that underlay much of anthropology's early use of visual media (Edwards 1992, Pinney 1992, Taussig 2009) and an attendant ocularcentrism.

Since the turn of the twenty-first century, many visual anthropologists (Edwards et al. 2006, Grimshaw & Ravetz 2005, MacDougall 2006, Ruby 2000) have joined in calls from other anthropologists not directly involved in visual anthropology per se (Ingold 2000, Taussig 1993)—many working on sexuality (Kulick 1998, Valentine 2007)—for a more sensorially embodied and integrated ethnography. Pink's (2006) discussion of this move notes that one of the challenges to sensorial ethnography is that "sensory workshops or performance anthropology in which spoken, visual, olfactory and tactile experiences [could be] incorporated" do not "fall within the tradition of creating anthropological publications we disseminate in the form of film or writing" (p. 58). Her suggestion is to explore further "how writing and video might combine to represent sensory experience theoretically and ethnographically" (p. 58). Pink's solution undermines the critique of ocularcentrism implicit in many calls for a multisensory anthropology; it is the very visuality of text and image that stands in for and recovers perceptions not available to the eye.

INTEGRATING THE SENSES

Leavitt & Hart (1990) argue against particular forms of sensory determinism that they perceive in studies growing out of McLuhan and Ong, a determinism also found, they suggest, in Febvre (1942), who proposes that the Middle Ages were more acoustic, whereas modernity is more visual. Moreover, not only do McLuhan and Ong insist on finding examples of senses that are supposedly privileged across different cultures or historical periods, but they also tend to describe the senses a priori when proposing, for example, that vision is abstract and distant, whereas hearing is comparatively concrete and emotional, without considering either neurobiological findings or specific understandings and uses of the senses in different cultures.

Against such reductionism in the relations between senses and communication and technology, Leavitt & Hart (1990) propose reclaiming the creative ambiguity of the term aesthetics (from the Greek *aisthesis*, which means simultaneously sensation, senses, and beauty), through an "ethno-aesthetics that would involve both a study of the senses in their cultural context, and of sensorial prolongations and elaborations operating in the arts" (p. 83, translated by AMO). They argue that because all societies engage with the senses at both a technological and an artistic level, the aesthetic is a privileged site for understanding specific cultural tendencies in the understanding and uses of the senses. The aesthetic elaboration and prolongation of the senses thus provide access to myths, rituals, and ultimately a way of entering into contact with the world of the sacred. Leavitt & Hart (1990) present "the prodigious aesthetic elaboration of certain sensorial practices" (p. 85, translated by AMO) as a means of communication with the divine in different ritual practices in North India, contrasting different aesthetic (pictorial and sung) and ritual practices of men and women. Finally, ethnoaesthetic studies provide the means of integrating semantics, ritual, and a multisensorial approach to a study of the senses that explores the specific and complementary use of each sense.

The overt politics of many earlier ethnographies of the senses (Feld 1982 [1990]; Howes 1991), as well as some historicizing work (Classen 1993, Curtis 2006), gravitated toward a critique of ocularcentrism. This critique illuminated the dominance of the eye as an idea specific to Enlightenment philosophy, rather than as a fact of modernity, or as empirically grounded in the social world or in physiological experience. Successive work was less concerned with this critique, instead refining understandings of the everyday practice of the senses. Here

the sensorium is represented as a world of affect, spirituality, ways of knowing, and sensory interplay situated in a fractured political world.

The earlier sensory ethnographies act as a bridge from the layeredness of Turnerian and Lévi-Straussian interpretations of ritual, performance, and symbol to this growing literature that refines the idea of the multisensory (Feld 1996, Howes 2003; and see below). "Multisensory" here evokes different points of apprehension, interpretation, knowledge construction, and memory making in relation to the world but does not imply their integration under one symbolic dimension. As such, "synaesthesia" need not necessarily entail a conflation of the experience of the senses to a point beyond recognition of their differences. Rather, dynamic cross-relationships are mediated by discursive codes and a plurality of receptivity within a culture (Stroeken 2008).

Contemporary sense ethnographies also benefit from three anthropologists who pushed multisensoriality in new political directions. Taussig (1993) brought dimensions of power, technology, and postcolonial studies together with an argument for the primacy of the senses in formations of knowledge and experience. Csordas (1994a,b, 1997) conjoined practice theory and phenomenology in his exploration of heightened bodily experiences and charismatic healing. Jackson (1989, 1996) brought the emotions and phenomenal experience into contact with the senses. His later focus on encounter, networks of relationships, movement, and living with contradictions presents multisensoriality as not only an embodied concept, but also gestural, agentive (Herzfeld 2001), transient, partial, and full of contradictions (2004, 2007, 2009).

Within this new theoretical terrain, scholars have carved out space for gender (Geurts 2002, Sanders 2008); extraordinary experience (Straight 2007); sensory cosmopolitanisms (Farquhar & Zhang 2005); refigurations of the nature/culture divide (Viveiros de Castro 1992) and of the interactive human and spirit ontology (Parkin 2007); various forms of synaesthetic experience (Meneley 2008); the social production of heightened mind-body awareness (Chau 2008); healing, diagnosis, and well-being (Desjarlais 2003, Farquhar 2002, Kuriyama 1999, Stroeken 2008); and truth-making in ethnographic encounters (Straight 2007, West 2007). The multisensory becomes a primary means of understanding conflict and suffering, not as a social aberration as in Turner's model but as a component of lives lived in struggle in relation to a fractured globalized political economy (Frykman et al. 1998, Herzfeld 2001). Contradiction and movement become productive of personhood and sociality rather than being exclusive or in opposition to their constitution. Working in the legacy of Foucault, contemporary multisensorial anthropology seeks to sensorialize Foucauldian ideas about politics. In turn, body politics and sexuality, knowledge archives, surveillance and discipline, and biopower become implicated in sensory experience.

Other calls for a multisensorial scholarship have arisen outside of anthropology, most notably from the study of digital media technologies and its examination of technologically mediated individual and collective experiences. Much of this work argues that the sensorium becomes fully constituted only in its contact with forms of mediation and simultaneously critiques vestiges of media determinism that characterized much early theorization of media, stretching as far back as the work of Benjamin (2008) and Horkheimer & Adorno (1976). Since the 1990s, digital media studies has centrally considered the ways in which mediums and perceptions are linked. Scholars investigate this linkage in relation to interfaces of artists and audiences and the technologies that produce and constitute contemporary media-based arts. One finds a concern with examining "the sensual," often framed in terms of "sensation" and "sensuality" (Massumi 2002), which Jones (2006) and Munster (2006) explicitly treat as a residue of modernism's segmentation, bureaucratization, and sterilization of the body in the twentieth-century plastic arts (especially painting and sculpture). They wonder about the potentials that exist for tech-

nological mediation to reinsert the body into art. What might a techno-embodied art mean for a politics of the senses, for example (Munster 2006)? Media theorists also recognize the potential that new media technologies carry to destabilize presumptions of ocularcentrism, as modes of interaction with media increasingly rely on body, voice, hand, or other body-and-sense interfaces (Hansen 2006). Embodied knowledge—of technologies and of the self that technologies reveal and produce—prompts a scholarly inquiry into the fully integrated sensorium (Jones 2006, p. 8). Deleuze & Guattari's concept of the haptic (1987) has gained particular traction in this work (e.g., Marks 2002) as a way to enfold touch and kinesthetics into encounters with images. Especially in analyses of virtual reality, the visual is treated as inseparable from tactile, kinesthetic, and proprioceptive dimensions of mediated encounters and objects (Fisher 1997).

Cinema studies, psychoanalytically influenced literary theory, and art criticism are the immediate antecedents of much new media theory that engages with the senses and embodiment. Within this work, laudable attention is given to the materiality and specificity of media and how objects and their production and consumption are inseparable from them. Delving down to contrast ratios and pixel density, for example, Marks (2002) argues that video is more likely to evoke a "haptic visuality" than an "optic visuality" (pp. 2–3) because, in comparison to film's greater contrast ratio and 20-fold greater detail, video is less able to render the detail of human vision. Engaging at this level of materiality, Marks argues, one is pulled away from symbolic—and therefore contested—understandings of the object into a more immediate, and therefore less contested, experience of its particularities.

However, the technological determinism lurking in this analysis is where the correctives of anthropology are especially valuable. Murray & Sixsmith (1999), in their examination of the nature of embodied experience in virtual reality, are quick to remind readers that "people bring their everyday, real-world understandings and social experiences to new virtual encounters" (p. 320). The universalizing "we" that permeates much of new media theory presupposes that individuals bring no culture, no social positioning, and no skill differences to encounters with new media. A more fully developed cyberanthropology that considers, for example, how avatars allow for the adoption of new identity-surfaces even as people bring their deeper and more corporeally embodied social identities to them (Boellstorff 2008), and that foregrounds an ethnographic accountability to how social positioning intersects with the senses, sensations, and sensualities of new media makes a critical contribution to this burgeoning media studies literature.

INTEGRATING DISCOURSE INTO THE STUDY OF THE SENSES

Myerhoff (2009 [1978]), writing about the Huichol Indians' peyote hunt, argues,

> one of the recurring explanations of the power of drugs is their ability to loosen cognitive social categories. Conceptualizations are socially provided and given in language. One of the sources of wonder and ecstasy in the mystic experience is the direct perception of the world, without the intervention and precedence of language and interpretation. The mystic experience is nonverbal precisely because it takes one back behind the word, or more accurately, before the word, to the stunning immediacy of sense data. (p. 305)

Meyerhoff's opposition between language and the senses is reprinted in Howes's *The Sixth Sense Reader* (2009). In the introduction, Howes stresses that the idea of five specific, discrete senses is culturally and historically determined, not a biological fact. He argues for replacing the term "senses" with "sensorium," a term that "straddles the divide between mind and body, cognition and sensation" (p. 1) and speculates that it is reasonable to ask whether, "in lieu of language, animals—or certain species—have

developed extrasensory modalities for staying in touch with each other" (p. 12). After describing Aristotle's model of sentience by stating that "sensation takes the form of 'a kind of mean' between two extremes...: sight between white and black, hearing between shrill and dull, and so on...'," Howes inserts a footnote that, while acknowledging the Saussurean notion of *différence* behind this phraseology, reads, "I would be the last to suggest we import a linguistic model into studies of how the senses function" (p. 39). These passages are indicative of the uncomfortable space occupied by the study of language, speech, and discourse in much research about the senses.

Arguably, a recurring feature in the anthropology of the senses is its rejection of language, discourse, and semiotics as modes for encountering and understanding the sensuous cultural world [notable exceptions include Classen's (1993) chapter on words and metaphoric terminology; Stoller's (1997) recognition of the significance of listening to the words of Songhay griots; as well as Csordas (1994c, 1997), Engelke (2007), and Geurts (2002)]. Recall, for example, Howes's distrust of the "antisensual" nature of anthropology's turn to "discourse" (2005) and "the detour represented by the rise of the textual model of cultural analysis in the 1970s" (2003). Similarly, Seremetakis (1994) posits clear differences between the construction of meaning and truth through sensorial experience and that constructed through language. The relation between the body and things "points to the perceptual construction of truth as an involuntary disclosure of meaning through the senses" (p. 6) so that truth is "extralinguistic and revealed through expression, performance, material culture and conditions of embodiment" (p. 6). Seremetakis, however, affirms that the history of the senses can be uncovered through contact with people via "fairy tales, anecdotes, folklore, and myth" (p. 9). As such, her work demonstrates an ambiguity between the narration of the senses through performative and historicizing linguistic genres and a critique of language as the sole repository of truth and meaning.

On a broader level, the opposition between language and body in much work on the senses derives from a critique of western epistemologies that locates thinking as a logo-centric activity based on the semantic content of words, in which the idea of (rational) thought is based on a separation between culture and nature, between man as the observer, and nature or the universe as the observed. Latour (1993) refers to this process of separation of an object and a knowing subject from its surroundings as "epistemologies of purification." In Latour's epistemologies, the object is made amenable to knowledge constructions, while the knower as an articulator of power relations is enacted through such knowledge practices. The anthropology of the senses positions itself as speaking back to such purificatory practices by reinserting sensorial perception as a site of knowledge construction. It often does so, however, through a critique of text-centered approaches to culture and language as the privileged site for the (de)construction of knowledge. Although we agree with the general critique of such purificatory practices and the inclusion of the body proposed by the anthropology of the senses, we argue that centering a return to the senses on an opposition between text-centered approaches to culture and body-centered approaches to culture neglects broad areas of overlap and agreement between various approaches to the embodied sensuous nature of human experience and sociability. Much recent work on language and discourse has similarly rejected a mentalist framing of language, strongly emphasizing its sensuous and sociable properties.

The three genealogies we identified above for work on the senses have strong traction in linguistics and linguistic anthropology as well. The life of discourse is physical, material, and emotional as well as intellectual. Communication is a multisensory experience, including not only the ears and eyes, but all sensory apparati. Speech is not simply the manifestation of thoughts to be transferred from the head of one individual into the head of another (although it may indeed serve that communicative purpose), but is rather the acoustic signature of the whole person (Truax 2001), including embodied and sensory markers of emotional state (Lutz & Abu-Lughod 1990, Ochs & Schieffelin 1989), age (Eckert 1998), social class (Fox 2004), geographic region (Wolfram & Schilling-Estes 2005), and gender identification (Bucholz et al. 1999). Far from a secondary ratiocination of experience, language and discourse exist as key components of experience in the unfolding of everyday life. [Schutz's (1982) discussion of Kurt Goldstein's theory of aphasia and experience shows this to be the case.] The link between sensory experience and language is not limited to lexical categorization. Grammatical, morpho-syntactic, intonation contour, metrical, generic, gesture and bodily hexis, and other sensory organizational aspects of discourse are all orchestrated for the purposes of presenting multilayered messages to the senses.

Nor is language simply an encoding of rational thought transferred from mind to mouth. It is produced physically, by lungs, diaphragm, lips, teeth, tongue, and glottis, fully embodied in its manifestation of physical presence (Perkell 1997, Stone et al. 2003). Phonologists and phoneticians have developed sophisticated methods for describing the precise physical aspects of vocal production and proprioception that result in particular utterances (Bolinger 1986, Sundberg & Thalen 2001). But the description is not limited to a scientific or biological discourse. Here we return to Pink's (2006) call for performance ethnography because performance ethnographers are surely aware of the embodied and material aspects that bring discourse and language to sensory presence.

It seems to us that much of the anthropology of the senses confuses two notions of discourse. As expressed by Bauman & Briggs (1992) with respect to linguistic anthropology, "highly divergent conceptualizations of the nature and significance of 'discourse' have often widened the gap between research agendas" (p. 159). Bauman & Briggs are referring to a confusion between a discourse-centered approach to culture (Sherzer 1987, Urban 1991, Woodbury 1992) and a Foucauldian poststructuralist approach to discourse. The former, with its careful attention to language use, treats language as "formal and functional patterning and dimensions of social interaction, social structure and cultural processes" (Bauman & Briggs 1992, p. 160). The Foucauldian poststructuralist approach is concerned with the deconstruction of social power rather than with paying specific attention to the details of expressive culture events. The anthropological discourse-centered approaches to culture have yielded sophisticated analyses of aesthetic aspects of expressive culture that can be intertwined with sensorial modes of knowing and embodied expressive-sensorial practices (Basso 1985, Feld 1996, Fox 2004, Kapchan 2007, Meintjes 2004, Novak 2008, Porcello 1998, Samuels 2004). Furthermore, the deconstruction of discourses of the body (Foucault 1988–1990, Lock & Farquhar 2007), of the sensorial practices of colonialism (Seremetakis 1994, Taussig 1993), of the politics of media circulation (Meintjes 2003), and of the notion of personhood (Descola 1994, Desjarlais 1992, Geurts 2002, Straight 2007) have been foundational for enabling us to think about the senses. It is more productive to treat discourse as part and parcel of processes of embodiment and knowledge and sense-making, rather than to dichotomize bodily sensorial knowledge and linguistic expression.

In conclusion, as the multisensory nature of embodied experience is increasingly recognized, the supremacy of sight as the historical articulator of modernity is increasingly challenged by an anthropology of the senses. We wish to emphasize the existence of productive synergies among scholars working in the anthropology of the senses, those researching mediated sensorial experiences in the arts and cinema studies, and linguistic anthropologists who examine language as an embodied expressive practice. Some scholars call for an integrative approach to the anthropology of the senses that attends to aesthetics (Leavitt & Hart 1990, Herzfeld 2001, Howes 2009). However, close formal analysis of expressive forms has increasingly incorporated body-sensorial knowledge. We suggest a complementary detailed attention to expressive forms across cultures—including discourse, new media arts, and cinema—and multisensory ethnography. Transdisciplinary ethnographic studies of the senses are ideal sites in which to question the relationship among artifacts, technologies, personhood, and the body, enabling an understanding of the senses not only as a means of knowing the world, but also as an ontological object of anthropological study. Such an approach acknowledges the importance of the senses in the postcolonial rethinking of modernity.

DISCLOSURE STATEMENT

The authors are not aware of any affiliations, memberships, funding, or financial holdings that might be perceived as affecting the objectivity of this review.

ACKNOWLEDGMENTS

The authors thank Debborah Battaglia, Richard Bauman, Steven Feld, and Susan Lepselter for reading various iterations of this article, as well as Alessandra Ciucci, for research support, and Sowmya Krishnamoorthy, a conversational partner throughout much of this article's preparation.

LITERATURE CITED

Basso EB. 1985. *A Musical View of the Universe: Kalapalo Myth and Ritual Performances*. Philadelphia: Univ. Penn. Press
Bauman R. 1977. *Verbal Art as Performance*. Long Grove, IL: Waveland

Bauman R, Briggs CL. 1992. Genre, intertextuality, and social power. *J. Ling. Anthropol.* 2(2):131–72

Benjamin W. 2008 [1935–1936]. The work of art in the age of its technological reproducibility (second version). In *The Work of Art in the Age of its Technological Reproducibility and Other Writings on Media*, ed. MW Jennings, TY Levin, B Doherty, pp. 19–55. Cambridge, MA: Harvard Univ. Press

Boas F. 1901. The mind of primitive man. *J. Am. Folk.* 14(52):1–11

Boellstorff T. 2008. *Coming of Age in Second Life: An Anthropologist Explores the Virtually Human*. Princeton, NJ: Princeton Univ. Press

Bolinger D. 1986. *Intonation and its Parts: Melody in Spoken English*. Stanford, CA: Stanford Univ. Press

Bucholz M, Liang AC, Sutton L. 1999. *Reinventing Identities: The Gendered Self in Discourse*. New York: Oxford Univ. Press

Buckley L. 2006. Studio photography and the aesthetics of citizenship in The Gambia, West Africa. See Edwards et al. 2006, pp. 61–85

Caldwell ML. 2002. The taste of nationalism: food politcs in postsocialist Moscow. *Ethnos* 67(3):295–319

Carpenter ES. 1973. *Eskimo Realities*. New York: Holt, Rinehart and Winston

Chau AY. 2008. The sensorial production of the social. *Ethnos* 73(4):485–504

Choo S. 2004. Eating satay babi: sensory perception of transnational movement. *J. Intercult. Stud.* 25(3):203–13

Classen C. 1993. *Worlds of Sense: Exploring the Senses in History and Across Cultures*. London: Routledge

Classen C. 1997. Foundations for an anthropology of the senses. *Int. Soc. Sci. J.* 153:401–12

Classen C. 2005. *The Book of Touch*. Oxford/New York: Berg

Classen C, Howes D, Synnott A. 1994. *Aroma: The Cultural History of Smell*. New York: Routledge

Corbin A. 1986. *The Foul and the Fragrant: Odor and the French Social Imagination*, transl. M Kochan, R Porter, C Prendergast. Cambridge, MA: Harvard Univ. Press

Corbin A. 1998. *Village Bells: Sound and Meaning in the Nineteenth Century French Countryside*. New York: Columbia Univ. Press

Corbin H. 1958. *Imagination Créatrice dans le Soufisme d'Ibn 'Arabi*. Paris: Flammarion

Corbin H, Pearson N. 1977. *Spiritual Body and Celestial Earth: From Mazden Iran to Shi'ite Iran*. Princeton, NJ: Princeton Univ. Press

Crapanzano V. 1992. *Hermes' Dilemma and Hamlet's Desire: On the Epistemology of Interpretation*. Cambridge, MA: Harvard Univ. Press

Csordas TJ, ed. 1994a. *Embodiment and Experience: The Existential Ground of Culture and Self*. Cambridge, UK: Cambridge Univ. Press

Csordas TJ. 1994b. *The Sacred Self: A Cultural Phenomenology of Charismatic Healing*. Berkeley: Univ. Calif. Press

Csordas TJ. 1994c. Words from the Holy People: a case study in cultural phenomenology. See Csordas 1994a, pp. 269–90

Csordas TJ. 1997. *Language, Charisma, and Creativity: The Ritual Life of a Religious Movement*. Berkeley: Univ. Calif. Press

Curtis B. 2006. "I can tell by the way you smell": dietetics, smell, social theory. *Senses Soc.* 3(1):5–22

Deleuze G, Guattari F. 1987. *A Thousand Plateaus: Capitalism and Schizophrenia*, transl. B Massumi. Minneapolis: Univ. Minn. Press

Descola P. 1994. *In the Society of Nature: A Native Ecology in Amazonia*. Cambridge, UK/New York: Cambridge Univ. Press

Desjarlais RR. 1992. *Sensory Biographies: Lives and Deaths among Nepal's Yolmo Buddhists*. Berkeley: Univ. Calif. Press

Desjarlais RR. 2003. *Body and Emotion: The Aesthetics of Healing in the Nepali Himalayas*. Philadelphia: Univ. Penn. Press

Drobnick J. 2004. Listening awry. In *Aural Cultures*, ed. J Drobnick, pp. 9–18. Toronto: YYZ Books

Drobnick J, ed. 2006. *The Smell Culture Reader*. Oxford/New York: Berg

During J. 1989. *Musique et Mystique dans les Traditions de l'Iran*. Paris: Inst. Fr. Rech. Iran/Diffusion, Ed. Peters

Eckert P. 1998. Age as a sociolinguistic variable. In *The Handbook of Sociolinguistics*, ed. F Coulmas, pp. 151–67. London: Blackwell

Edwards E. 1992. *Anthropology and Photography 1860–1920*. New Haven/London: Yale Univ. Press

Edwards E, Gosden C, Phillips RB, eds. 2006. *Sensible Objects: Colonialism, Museums and Material Culture*. Oxford: Berg

El Guindi F. 2004. *Visual Anthropology: Essential Method and Theory*. New York: Alta Mira

Engelke M. 2007. *A Problem of Presence: Beyond Scripture in an African church*. Berkeley: Univ. Calif. Press

Erlmann V. 2004. But what of the ethnographic ear? Anthropology, sound and the senses. In *Hearing Cultures: Essays on Sound, Listening and Modernity*, ed. V Erlmann, pp. 1–20. Oxford/New York: Berg

Fales C. 2005. Short-circuiting perceptual systems: timbre in ambient and techno music. See Greene & Porcello 2005, pp. 156–80

Farquhar J. 2002. *Appetites: Food and Sex in Postsocialist China*. Durham, NC: Duke Univ. Press

Farquhar J, Zhang Q. 2005. Biopolitical Beijing: pleasure, sovereignty and self-cultivation in China's capital. *Cult. Anthropol.* 20(3):303–27

Febvre L. 1942. *Le Probleme de l'incroyance au XVIe siecle. La religión de Rabelais*. Paris: Albin Michel

Feld S. 1988. Aesthetics as iconicity of style, or 'lift-up-oversounding': getting into the Kaluli groove. *Yr. Trad. Mus.* 20:74–113

Feld S. 1990 [1982]. *Sound and Sentiment: Birds, Weeping, Poetics, and Song in Kaluli Expression*. Philadelphia: Univ. Penn. Press

Feld S. 1991. Sound as a symbolic system: the Kaluli drum. See Howes 1991, pp. 79–99

Feld S. 1996. Waterfalls of song: an acoustemology of place resounding in Bosavi, Papua New Guinea. In *Senses of Place*, ed. S Feld, KH Basso, pp. 91–136. Santa Fe, NM: Sch. Am. Res. Press

Feld S, Brenneis D. 2004. Doing anthropology in sound. *Am. Ethnol.* 31(4):461–74

Ferzacca S. 2004. Lived food and judgments of taste at a time of disease. *Med. Anthropol.* 23:41–67

Fisher J. 1997. Relational sense: toward a haptic aesthetics. *Parachute* 87:4–11

Foucault M. 1988–1990. *History of Sexuality*. New York: Vintage

Fox AA. 2004. *Real Country: Music and Language in Working-Class Culture*. Durham, NC: Duke Univ. Press

Frykman J, Seremetakis N, Ewert S, eds. 1998. *Identities in Pain*. Lund, Swed.: Nordic Acad. Press

Geurts KL. 2002. *Culture and the Senses: Embodiment, Identity, and Well-Being in an African Community*. Berkeley: Univ. Calif. Press

Goody J. 1977. *The Domestication of the Savage Mind*. Cambridge, UK: Cambridge Univ. Press

Greene PD, Porcello T, eds. 2005. *Wired for Sound: Engineering and Technologies in Sonic Cultures*. Middletown, CT: Wesleyan Univ. Press

Grimshaw A, Ravetz A, eds. 2005. *Visualizing Anthropology*. Bristol, UK: Intellect

Guthman J. 2003. Fast food/organic food: reflexive tastes and the making of 'yuppie chow.' *Soc. Cult. Geogr.* 4(1):45–58

Gvion L, Trostler N. 2008. From spaghetti and meatballs through Hawaiian pizza to sushi: the changing nature of ethnicity in American restaurants. *J. Pop. Cult.* 41(6):950–74

Hansen MBN. 2006. *Bodies in Code: Interfaces with Digital Media*. New York: Routledge

Harvey ED. 2003. *Sensible Flesh: On Touch in Early Modern Culture*. Philadelphia: Univ. Penn. Press

Hayes-Conroy A, Hayes-Conroy J. 2008. Taking back taste: feminism, food and visceral politics. *Gender Place Cult.* 15(5):461–73

Heller-Roazen D. 2007. *Inner Touch: Archaeology of a Sensation*. New York: Zone

Henare A, Holbraa M, Wastell S. 2007. *Thinking through Things, Theorising Artifacts Ethnographically*. London: Routledge

Herzfeld M. 2001. *Anthropology: Theoretical Practice in Culture and Society*. Oxford: Blackwell

Highmore B. 2008. Alimentary gents: food, cultural theory and multiculturalism. *J. Intercult. Stud.* 29(4):381–98

Hirschkind C. 2006. *The Ethical Soundscape: Cassette Sermons and Islamic Counterpublics*. New York: Columbia Univ. Press

Horkheimer M, Adorno TW. 1976. *The Culture Industry: Enlightenment as Mass Deception*. New York: Continuum Int.

Howes D, ed. 1990. Les <<cinq>> sens. *Anthropolog. Soc.* 14(2):Spec. issue

Howes D, ed. 1991. *Varieties of Sensory Experience: A Sourcebook in the Anthropology of the Senses*. Toronto/Buffalo: Univ. Tor. Press

Howes D. 2003. *Sensual Relations: Engaging the Senses in Culture and Social Theory*. Ann Arbor: Univ. Mich. Press

Howes D. 2005. *Empire of the Senses: The Sensual Culture Reader*. Oxford/New York: Berg

Howes D, ed. 2009. *The Sixth Sense Reader*. Oxford: Berg

Ingold T. 2000. *The Perception of the Environment: Essays in Livelihood, Dwelling, and Skill*. London: Routledge

Jackson M. 1989. *Paths Toward a Clearing: Radical Empiricism and Ethnographic Enquiry*. Bloomington: Ind. Univ. Press

Jackson M, ed. 1996. *Things as They Are: New Directions in Phenomenological Anthropology*. Bloomington: Ind. Univ. Press

Jackson M. 2004. *In Sierra Leone*. Durham, NC: Duke Univ. Press

Jackson M. 2007. *Excursions*. Durham, NC: Duke Univ. Press

Jackson M. 2009. *The Palm at the End of the Mind: Relatedness, Religiosity and the Real*. Durham, NC: Duke Univ. Press

Jain S, Lochlann S. 2003. "Come up to the Kool taste": African American upward mobility and the semiotics of smoking menthols. *Public Cult.* 15(2):295–322

Jay M. 1993. *Downcast Eyes: The Denigration of Vision in Twentieth Century French Thought*. Berkeley: Univ. Calif. Press

Jones C, ed. 2006. *Sensorium: Embodied Experience, Technology, and Contemporary Art*. Cambridge, MA: MIT Press

Kapchan DA. 2007. *Traveling Spirit Masters: Moroccan Gnawa Trance and Music in the Global Marketplace*. Middletown, CT: Wesleyan Univ. Press

Korsmeyer C, ed. 2005. *The Taste Culture Reader: Experiencing Food and Drink*. Oxford/New York: Berg

Kulick D. 1998. *Travesti: Sex, Gender, and Culture Among Brazilian Transgendered Prostitutes*. Chicago: Univ. Chicago Press

Kuriyama S. 1999. *Expressiveness of the Body and the Divergence of Greek and Chinese Medicine*. New York: Zone

Lambek M. 2003. *The Weight of the Past: Living with History in Mahajanga, Madagascar*. New York: Palgrave Macmillan

Lambek M, Strathern A, eds. 1998. *Bodies and Persons: Comparative Perspectives from Africa and Melanesia*. Cambridge, UK: Univ. Cambridge Press

Larkin B. 2008. *Signal and Noise: Media, Infrastructure and Urban Culture in Nigeria*. Durham, NC/London: Duke Univ. Press

Latour B. 1993. *We Have Never Been Modern*. New York/London: Harvester, Wheatsheaf

Leavitt J, Hart LM. 1990. Critique de la 'raison' sensorielle, l'élaboration esthétique des sens dans une société himalayenne. *Anthropol. Soc.* 14(2):77–98

Lévi-Strauss C. 1969. *The Raw and the Cooked*. New York: Harper and Row

Lock M. 1995. *Encounters with Aging: Mythologies of Menopause in Japan and North America*. Berkeley: Univ. Calif. Press

Lock M, Farquhar J. 2007. *Beyond the Body Proper: Reading the Anthropology of Material Life*. Durham, NC/London: Duke Univ. Press

Lutz CA, Abu-Lughod L, eds. 1990. *Language and the Politics of Emotion*. Cambridge, UK: Cambridge Univ. Press

Marks LU. 2002. *Touch: Sensuous Theory and Multisensory Media*. Minneapolis: Univ. Minn. Press

Marx K. 1988 [1844]. Private property and communism. In *The Economic and Philosophic Manuscripts of 1844 of Karl Marx*, transl. M Millgan, pp. 99–114. Amherst, NY: Prometheus

Massumi B. 2002. *Parables for the Virtual: Movement, Affect, Sensation*. Durham, NC: Duke Univ. Press

McDougall D. 2006. *The Corporeal Image: Film, Ethnography and the Senses*. Princeton, NJ: Princeton Univ. Press

Mead M, Bateson G. 1977. Margaret Mead and Gregory Bateson on the use of the camera in anthropology. *Stud. Anthropol. Vis. Cult.* 4(2):78–80

Meintjes L. 2003. *Making Music Zulu in a South African Studio*. Durham, NC/London: Duke Univ. Press

Meintjes L. 2004. Shoot the sergeant, shatter the mountain: the production of masculinity in Zulu ngoma song and dance in postapartheid South Africa. *Ethnomusicol. Forum* 13(3):173–201

Meneley A. 2008. Oleo-signs and quali-signs: the qualities of olive oil. *Ethnos* 73(3):303–26

Mintz SW. 1985. *Sweetness and Power. The Place of Sugar in Modern History*. London: Penguin

Montagu A. 1971. *Touching: The Human Significance of the Skin*. New York: Columbia Univ. Press

Munster A. 2006. *Materializing New Media: Embodiment in Information Aesthetics*. Hanover, NH: Dartmouth Coll. Press

Murray C, Sixsmith J. 1999. The corporeal body in virtual reality. *Ethos* 27(3):315–43

Myerhoff B. 2009 [1978]. Peyote and the mystic vision. See Howes 2009, pp. 297–310

Myers F, ed. 2001. *The Empire of Things*. Santa Fe, NM: Sch. Am. Res.

Myers F. 2005. 'Primitivism', anthropology, and the category of 'primitive art'. In *Handbook of Material Culture*, ed. C Tilly, W Keane, S Küchler, M Rowlands, P Spyer, pp. 267–84. London: Sage

Novak D. 2008. 2.5 × 6 meters of space: Japanese music coffeehouses and experimental practices of listening. *Pop. Music* 27(1):15–34

Ochs E, Schieffelin B. 1989. Language has a heart. *Text* 99(1):7–25

Parkin D. 2007. Wafting on the wind: smell and the cycle of spirit and matter. *J. R. Anthropol. Inst.* pp. S39–53

Perkell J. 1997. Articulatory processes. In *The Handbook of Phonetic Sciences*, ed. W Hardcastle, J Laver, pp. 333–70. Malden, MA: Blackwell

Pink S. 2006. *The Future of Visual Anthropology: Engaging the Senses*. New York: Routledge

Pinney C. 1992. The parallel histories of anthropology and photography. See Edwards 1992, pp. 74–95

Pinney C, Peterson N, eds. 2003. *Photography's Other Histories*. Durham, NC: Duke Univ. Press

Porcello T. 1998. Tails out: social phenomenology and the ethnographic representation of technology in music making. *Ethnomusicology* 42(3):485–510

Porcello T. 2005. Music mediated as live in Austin: sound, technology and recording practice. See Greene & Porcello 2005, pp. 103–17

Reed-Danahay D. 1996. Champagne and chocolate: "taste" and inversion in a French wedding ritual. *Am. Anthropol.* 98(4):750–61

Ruby J. 2000. *Picturing Culture*. Chicago: Univ. Chicago Press

Samuels D. 2004. *Putting a Song on Top of It: Expression and Identity on the San Carlos Apache Reservation*. Tucson: Univ. Ariz. Press

Samuels DW, Porcello T, Meintjes L, Ochoa AM. 2010. Soundscapes: toward a sounded anthropology. *Annu. Rev. Anthropol.* 39:329–45

Sanders T. 2008. *Beyond Bodies: Rainmaking and Sense Making in Tanzania*. Toronto: Univ. Tor. Press

Schloss JG. 2004. *Making Beats, The Art of Sample-Based Hip Hop*. Middletown, CT: Wesleyan Univ. Press

Schmidt LE. 2000. *Hearing Things: Religion, Illusion and the American Enlightenment*. Cambridge, MA: Harvard Univ. Press

Schutz A. 1982. Language, language disturbances, and the texture of consciousness. In *Collected Papers I: The Problem of Social Reality*, ed. M Natanson. pp. 260–86. Hingham, MA: Kluwer

Seeger A. 1987. *Why Suya Sing. A Musical Anthropology of an Amazonian People*. Cambridge, UK: Cambridge Univ. Press

Seremetakis NC. 1994. *Perception and Memory as Material Culture in Modernity*. Boulder, CO: Westview

Shannon J. 2003. Emotion, performance, and temporality in Arab music: reflections on Tarab. *Cult. Anthropol.* 18(1):72–98

Sherzer J. 1987. A discourse-centered approach to language and culture. *Am. Anthropol.* 89:295–309

Sterne J. 2003. *The Audible Past: Cultural Origins of Sound Reproduction*. Durham, NC: Duke Univ. Press

Stoller P. 1989. *Taste of Ethnographic Things: The Senses in Anthropology*. Philadelphia: Univ. Penn. Press

Stoller P. 1997. *Sensuous Scholarship*. Philadelphia: Univ. Penn. Press

Stone RE, Cleveland T, Sundberg J, Prokop J. 2003. Aerodynamic and acoustical measures of speech, operatic and Broadway styles in a professional female singer. *J. Voice* 17:283–98

Straight B. 2007. *Miracles and Extraordinary Experience in Northern Kenya*. Philadelphia: Univ. Penn. Press

Stroeken K. 2008. Sensory shifts and 'synaesthetics' in Sukuma healing. *Ethnos* 73(4):466–84

Sundberg J, Thalén M. 2001. Describing different styles of singing: a comparison of a female singer's voice source in "classical," "pop," "jazz" and "blues." *Logoped. Phoniatr. Vocol.* 26:82–93

Synnott A. 1991. Puzzling over the senses: from Plato to Marx. See Howes 1991, pp. 61–76

Szendy P. 2009. *The auditory return (the point of listening)*. Presented at Think. Listening Conf., Oct. 2–4, Univ. Tex., Austin

Taussig M. 1993. *Mimesis and Alterity: A Particular History of the Senses*. New York: Routledge

Taussig M. 2009. *What Color is the Sacred?* Chicago: Univ. Chicago Press

Truax B. 2001. *Acoustic Communication*. Westport: Ablex

Urban G. 1991. *A Discourse-Centered Approach to Culture: Native South American Myths and Rituals*. Austin: Univ. Tex. Press

Valentine D. 2007. *Imagining Transgender: An Ethnography of a Category*. Durham, NC: Duke Univ. Press

Viveiros de Castro E. 1992. *From the Enemy's Point of View: Humanity and Divinity in an Amazonian Society*. Chicago: Univ. Chicago Press

Viveiros de Castro E. 2004. Exchanging perspectives: the transformation of objects into subjects in Amerindian ontologies. *Common Knowl.* 10(3):463–84

West HG. 2007. *Ethnographic Sorcery*. Chicago: Univ. Chicago Press

Wolfram W, Schilling-Estes N. 2005 [1991]. *American English: Dialects and Variation*. Oxford, UK: Wiley-Blackwell

Wong DA. 2004. *Speak it Louder: Asian Americans Making Music*. New York: Routledge

Woodbury A. 1992. Prosodic elements and prosodic structures in natural discourse. In *Proceedings of the IRCS Workshop on Prosody in Natural Speech. Institute for Research in Cognitive Science Technical Report No. 92–37*, ed. M Liberman, C McLemore. pp. 241–53. Philadelphia: Inst. Res. Cogn. Sci., Univ. Penn.

Miocene Hominids and the Origins of the African Apes and Humans

David R. Begun

Department of Anthropology, University of Toronto, Toronto, Ontario M5S 2S2, Canada;
email: begun@chass.utoronto.ca

Annu. Rev. Anthropol. 2010. 39:67–84

First published online as a Review in Advance on
June 14, 2010

The *Annual Review of Anthropology* is online at
anthro.annualreviews.org

This article's doi:
10.1146/annurev.anthro.012809.105047

Key Words

fossil apes, hominines, paleobiogeography, hominid origins,
Dryopithecus, *Griphopithecus*

Abstract

In the past 20 years, new discoveries of fossil apes from the Miocene
have transformed our ideas about the timing, geography, and causes of
the evolution of the African apes and humans. Darwin predicted that
the common ancestor of African apes and humans would be found in
Africa. Yet the majority of fossil great apes are from Europe and Asia. I
briefly review the fossil record of great apes and then examine the main
competing hypotheses of our origins, African or European, inspired
by these recent discoveries, concluding that elements of both ideas are
likely to be correct. Given current interpretations of the paleobiology of
fossil apes and relationships among living hominids, I suggest that the
last common ancestor of chimpanzees and humans was morphologically
unique, but more chimpanzee-like than hominin-like: a knuckle-walker
with a chimpanzee-sized brain, canine sexual dimorphism, and many
probable behavioral similarities to living chimpanzees.

INTRODUCTION

The First 137 Years

The history of research on the origins of the great apes and humans is over 150 years old. In 1856 Edouard Lartet published an account of a new fossil ape from France that he called *Dryopithecus fontani* (Lartet 1856). By the end of the nineteenth century a handful of specimens had been recovered from Germany and France, and many authorities recognized evolutionary links between these fossils and living apes. Even Darwin, who predicted that the fossilized antecedents of African apes and humans would be found in Africa, speculated that *Dryopithecus* may in fact be that ancestor, despite being from Europe (Darwin 1871).

Darwin's African prediction nevertheless seemed to be validated by discoveries in Kenya in the 1920s, and much of the attention of researchers of great ape and human origins has been focused on Africa ever since. *Proconsul*, named by Arthur Hopwood in 1933, was widely accepted as a direct ancestor of Africa apes, and when *Kenyapithecus* was discovered and described by Louis Leakey in 1962, many believed that the earliest member of the human family had been found in Africa as well (Hopwood 1933, Leakey 1962). It was not until the 1970s that attention returned to Europe, with the discoveries of Louis de Bonis and colleagues in Greece and Miklós Kretzoi in Hungary. In both cases, the describers of these new taxa, *Ouranopithecus* and *Rudapithecus*, argued that these fossil great apes are closely related to African apes and humans, or even directly related to humans (Bonis et al. 1974, Kretzoi 1969).

Despite those new discoveries in Europe, most researchers continued to prefer Darwin's idea that the African ape and human clade originated in Africa, the European genera representing evolutionary dead ends that migrated to Europe at some point after the origin of the lineage (e.g., Szalay & Delson 1979). The discovery of more complete fossil specimens from Pakistan in the 1980s led most researchers to conclude that fossil apes referred to variously as *Kenyapithecus*, *Ramapithecus*, or *Rudapithecus* are in fact not closely related to humans, as Leakey and Kretzoi had proposed. One of these taxa, *Ramapithecus*, was reinterpreted as a close relative of orangutans, and in fact the genus name was synonymized with the previously named *Sivapithecus* (Greenfield 1974, 1980; Pilbeam 1982). *Kenyapithecus* was soon reinterpreted as a basal (stem) ape without a direct relationship to any individual member of the great ape and human group, and *Rudapithecus* came to be viewed as synonymous with *Dryopithecus*, and was most commonly seen as an evolutionary dead end (Andrews & Martin 1987; Harrison 2010). It was not until the discovery of several very well-preserved specimens from Europe that a serious reexamination of the fossil record of apes in Europe took place, the "Renaissance of Europe's ape" (Martin & Andrews 1993). In the 17 years since then, many new discoveries in both Europe and Africa have contributed to a lively debate on the topic of the origins and evolution of the African ape and human clade.

The Past 17 Years

Most authorities accept the hypothesis that fossil apes from Asia are members of the lineage that includes the living orangutan, which is usually referred to the subfamily Ponginae (Kelley 2002) (**Table 1**). A much more animated debate characterizes interpretations of the fossil record of apes in Europe and Africa. There are three main points of view in the current literature. Some researchers support the idea that no known fossil ape has any specific evolutionary relationship to living great apes and humans. As noted, most authorities accept the evolutionary link between *Sivapithecus* and *Pongo*, but the idea that all Eurasian apes are evolutionary dead ends has some supporters (Benefit & McCrossin 1995, Pilbeam 1997, Pilbeam & Young 2004). However, most researchers view the fossil apes of Europe as close relatives of living great apes. Moyà-Solà and colleagues have suggested that *Dryopithecus*, like *Sivapithecus*, is a member of the orangutan clade (Moyà-Solà & Köhler 1995). This suggestion is based on the sample of fossil apes from Spain, which are now

Table 1 A classification of taxa discussed in the text

Magnafamily Hominidea[a]
Superfamily Proconsuloidea
  Proconsul
  Afropithecus
  Heliopithecus
Superfamily Hominoidea
  Family Hominidae
    Subfamily Griphopithecinae
     Griphopithecus
     Equatorius
     Nacholapithecus
     Kenyapithecus
    Subfamily Homininae
     Tribe Dryopithecini
      Dryopithecus
      Hispanopithecus
      Rudapithecus
      Ouranopithecus
     Tribe Hominini
      Subtribe Hominina
       Homo
       Australopithecus
       Paranthropus
       Ardipithecus
       Sahelanthropus
       Orrorin
       Pan
      Subtribe Gorillina
       Gorilla
    Subfamily Pongidae
     Pongo
     Tribe *Sivapithecini*[b]
      Sivapithecus
      Ankarapithecus
      Gigantopithecus
     Tribe Lufengpithecini[b]
      Lufengpithecus
      Khoratpithecus
  Family Hylobatidae

[a]Follows Begun (2007).
[b]Follows the classification of Kelley (2002) except for *Khoratpithecus*, which was not known at the time, and *Ankarapithecus*, following Begun & Güleç (1998).

related to humans than to any great ape, and represents the ancestor of australopithecines and living humans (Bonis & Koufos 1994, Koufos 2007). They interpret *Dryopithecus* (today *Dryopithecus* is split into at least three genera, *Hispanopithecus*, *Rudapithecus*, and *Dryopithecus*) as closely related to African apes. Begun and Kordos have argued that all European fossil great apes are closely related to one another and are the sister group to the African apes and humans (Begun 2007, 2009; Begun & Kordos 1997). This interpretation is based mostly on the sample of fossil great apes from Hungary now attributed once again to *Rudapithecus*.

Most recently, new discoveries have refueled proponents of the African origins hypothesis. Suwa and colleagues describe new remains from Ethiopia that they interpret as early members of the African ape and human clade, possibly closely related to living gorillas (Suwa et al. 2007). Kunimatsu and colleagues describe a new genus of fossil ape from Kenya that they interpret as a close relative of *Ouranopithecus* (Kunimatsu et al. 2007). In both cases, these authors suggest that the African ape and human clade originated in Africa perhaps 12 to 13 Ma (Mega-annum, or millions of years ago), and that some branches of this group moved to Europe, only to become extinct without leaving descendents a few million years later. Here I survey the evidence for both of these hypotheses and in the end I suggest that although both have merit, the preponderance of evidence today favors a European origin of the African ape and human clade and an African origin of the last common ancestor (LCA) of the African apes and humans.

HOMINID ORIGINS

Taxonomy

Before discussing the evidence for hominid origins, and the origins of all other lineages or clades covered in this review, I need to clarify the terminology used here (**Table 1**). By hominid I mean great apes and humans and all their fossil relatives. In other words,

referred to the genus *Hispanopithecus*. Other researchers interpret the European fossil great apes to be more closely related to African apes and humans. De Bonis and Koufos offer the hypothesis that *Ouranopithecus* is more closely

anything more closely related to a living great ape or human than to a hylobatid (gibbons and siamangs). Hominids as defined here are genetically as similar to one another as are members of many other mammalian families (Begun 1999, Goodman et al. 1998). Furthermore, if we are to continue to use the traditional dichotomy of hominid (for humans and our ancestors) and pongid (for the great apes), we would run counter to the laws of biological classification, one of the principles of which is that members of a group (e.g., pongids) must be more closely related to each other than to members of any other group. Because, as traditionally defined, some pongids (African apes), are more closely related to non-pongids (humans) than to the other pongid (orangutans), the pongid-hominid dichotomy breaks the law. African apes must be classified with humans because they are more closely related to each other than either one is to orangutans. That being the case, we have two choices. We could continue to reify humans as hominids, in which case we would need a category for humans and African apes (somewhere between the family and the superfamily), a similar rank for orangutans and their fossil relatives, and another higher level taxonomic rank to unify great apes and humans to the exclusion of the hylobatids. It gets very complicated. The simple alternative is to recognize one family (consistent with the genetics) and two subfamilies (consistent with the genetics, morphology, and fossil evidence) (**Table 2**). To summarize, herein hominine refers to African apes and humans and their fossil relatives, pongine to orangutans and their fossil relatives, and hominin to humans and our fossil relatives. This is a widely recognized classification scheme (Begun 2007, Kelley 2002, Strait & Grine 2004, Wood & Richmond 2000), though there are prominent holdouts for the more traditional classification that excludes all but humans and our ancestors from membership in the Hominidae (White 2002). Nevertheless, here, hominid origin refers to the origin of the clade that includes all great apes and humans and all their fossil relatives, while excluding hylobatids.

Griphopithecus

In my view, the best candidate for the earliest hominid is *Griphopithecus*, a genus of thickly enameled, robust-jawed ape that first appeared approximately 16 to 16.5 Ma (Begun et al. 2003a, Heizmann & Begun 2001). *Griphopithecus* or *Griphopithecus*-like apes (griphopithecins) are known first from sites in Germany and Turkey (**Table 2**, **Figure 1**). One to 1.5 Ma later similar apes are found in Africa, again with robust jaws and thickly enameled teeth (Ishida et al. 2000, Ward et al. 1999). The teeth are more modern than those of older apes such as *Proconsul*, especially in the development of the cingulum, a ridge of enamel that rims the buccal or outer edge of lower molars and the lingual or inner edge of upper molars. The disappearance of cingula, which is beginning in *Griphopithecus* and related taxa such as *Equatorius*, may be related to the broadening and flattening of the enamel cusps and the substance that supports them from below, the dentine.

Although they are dentally more like living hominids than *Proconsul*, *Griphopithecus* and its relatives retain primitive postcrania. They are more monkey-like than ape-like, as is *Proconsul*, in having fore and hind limbs of roughly equal length, without any indications of the suspensory capabilities of all later fossil and living great apes (Begun 1992b, 2003; Ishida et al. 2004; Nakatsukasa et al. 1998, 2003; Rose 1988, 1997; Rose et al. 1996; Ward 1997a, 2007; Ward et al. 1999). The one big exception with regard to the monkey-like anatomy of these early apes is that they lacked a tail, or, more precisely, they had a coccyx, as in all living hominoids (hylobatids and hominids) (Nakatsukasa et al. 2003, Ward et al. 1991).

Proconsul and middle Miocene hominoids show signs in the hip, wrist, and hand of greater ranges of mobility and more powerful grasping capabilities than those seen in a typical monkey (Beard et al. 1986; Begun et al. 1994; Ward 1993; Ward 1997a, 2007). However, the best-known middle Miocene taxon, *Nacholapithecus*, while having limb proportions closer to those of

Table 2 Fossil apes discussed in the text

Ma	Genera	Important localities (bold = type localities)	Country
19–17	*Proconsul*[a]	Rusinga, Songhor, **Koru**	Kenya
17.5	*Afropithecus*	**Kalodirr**	Kenya
17	*Heliopithecus*	**Ad Dabtiyah**	Saudi Arabia
16.5–14	*Griphopithecus*	Engelswies, **Děvínská Nová Ves**, Çandır, Paşalar	Germany, Slovakia, Turkey
15	*Equatorius*	**Maboko**	Kenya
15	*Nacholapithecus*	**Nachola**	Kenya
13.5	*Kenyapithecus*	Paşalar, **Fort Ternan**	Turkey, Kenya
12.5–7	*Sivapithecus*	Potwar Plateau	India, Pakistan
9–8	*Lufengpithecus*	**Lufeng**	China
?13.5–7	*Khoratpithecus*[b]	**Khorat**, Ba Sa	Thailand
10	*Ankarapithecus*	**Sinap**	Turkey
6.5	aff. *Gigantopithecus*[c]	Potwar Plateau	India
12	*Dryopithecus*[d]	**St. Gaudens**, Pierola, Can Vila, Can Mata, St. Stefan	France, Spain, Austria
10	*Hispanopithecus*	Can Llobateres, Can Ponsic, **La Tarumba**	Spain
10	*Rudapithecus*	**Rudabánya**	Hungary
9.5	*Ouranopithecus*	**Ravin de la Pluie**, Xirochori, Nikiti	Greece
?7–8	*Udabnopithecus*	**Udabno**	Georgia
?7–8	aff. *Ouranopithecus*[e]	**Çorakyerler**	Turkey
?7–8	aff. *Ouranopithecus*[e]	**Chirpan**	Bulgaria
9.8	*Nakalipithecus*	**Nakali**	Kenya
10	*Chororapithecus*	**Chorora**	Ethiopia
7–6	*Sahelanthropus*	**Toros-Menalla**	Chad
6	*Orrorin*	**Lukeino**	Kenya
5.8	aff. *Ardipithecus*[f]	**Alayla**	Ethiopia

[a]This is a simplified taxonomy. There may well be more than one genus present in this sample.

[b]The older age for *Khoratpithecus* is less certain.

[c]This material is sometimes attributed to *Indopithecus*.

[d]*Dryopithecus* includes the synonymous genera *Pierolapithecus* and *Anoiapithecus*.

[e]These fossils are most similar to *Ouranopithecus* from Greece but probably represent one or more new taxa.

[f]This material is much older and more primitive than *Ardipithecus ramidus* from Aramis, and probably represents a different genus. It may be more closely related to *Orrorin* and/or *Sahelanthropus*.

a monkey than of an ape, has much more powerfully built arms compared to its legs, suggesting the beginning of a shift in importance in locomotion to the forelimbs. Despite this shift in morphology, *Nacholapithecus* shows no signs of having been suspensory (Ishida et al. 2004).

Griphopithecins are the first cosmopolitan hominoid taxon, probably as a result of their powerful jaws and teeth that allowed them to exploit a wide variety of resources. They may have evolved from *Afropithecus*, which had morphologically different but also powerfully built jaws, and was distributed as far north as Saudi Arabia (**Figure 1**) (Begun 2002, Leakey & Walker 1997, Leakey et al. 1988). While moving more or less as a large arboreal monkey, griphopithecins may have been quite adept in the trees, perhaps slow-moving, with postures that would have allowed them access to terminal branches, where much of the food is, despite their relatively large body masses. I see the entire region from Germany and Turkey in the north to Kenya in the south as a potential core area in which early hominids could have

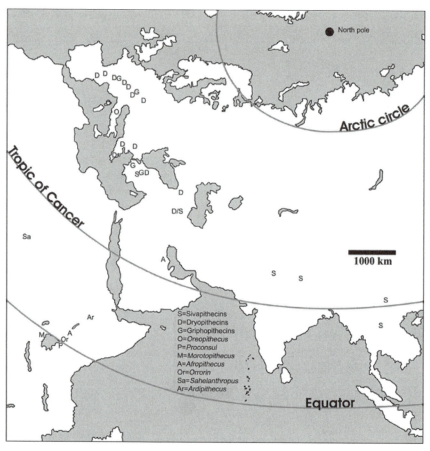

Figure 1

Hominoid localities discussed in this review article.

evolved. But there are major gaps in the record. For example, one species of *Kenyapithecus* is known from 16–16.5 Ma in Turkey and another from Kenya at about 13.5 Ma (Begun et al. 2003a, Kelley et al. 2008, Pickford 1986, Pickford & Morales 1994, Pickford et al. 2006). It was probably present elsewhere in the intervening interval of time but we have not yet found the fossils. This is likely the case for other members of this early radiation. From this core area these stem hominids (not specifically related to either living group of hominids, pongines, or hominines) eventually split, with one segment of the distribution of species dispersing to the north and east and another to the north and west. The causes of

this dispersal are unknown, but griphopithecins are the most primitive hominids we know. The later-occurring sivapithecins of Asia and dryopithecins of Europe are more modern, and strong cases can be made that they are related to living orangutans and African apes and humans, respectively.

ASIAN FOSSIL GREAT APES

As the focus here is on African ape and human origins, I only briefly cover the fossil record of the pongines. *Pongo*, the extant genus of orangutan, is thought by most researchers to be the end of a long and highly diverse radiation of great apes that originated at about

13–16 Ma (Kappelman et al. 1991, Kelley 2002). *Sivapithecus*, the best-known genus of fossil pongine, bears a remarkable resemblance to *Pongo* in its facial morphology, but is different in details of the structure of the jaws, teeth, and certain aspects of the postcranial skeleton (Kelley 2002; Madar et al. 2002; Pilbeam 1982; Rose 1986, 1989; Ward & Brown 1986; Ward 1997b; Ward & Pilbeam 1983). *Lufengpithecus* and *Khoratpithecus*, from south China and Thailand, respectively, more closely resemble *Pongo* in details of their tooth morphology, but less so in the face (only known for *Lufengpithecus*) (Chaimanee et al. 2003, 2004; Kelley 2002; Schwartz 1997). So it is not clear to which, if any, of these fossil apes *Pongo* is most directly related, but it is almost universally agreed that they are all pongines. *Ankarapithecus* from Turkey represents the most western of the siva-pithecins and is the only one that overlaps with the geographic ranges of the griphopithecins and dryopithecins (Begun & Güleç 1998, Begun et al. 2003b) (**Figure 1**). I would be remiss in discussing fossil pongines without referring to the most impressive of all of them, *Gigantopithecus* and its relatives. This lineage of huge apes lived from about 6.5 Ma to 300,000 years ago, eventually attaining a size equivalent to two to three big male gorillas. Curiously, despite their huge size and, one would think, large, durable limb bones and skulls, *Gigantopithecus* is known only from isolated teeth (numbering in the thousands) and a small number of partial mandibles. The traditional Chinese apothecary market, which includes medicines made from the ground remains of fossil mammals, may account in large part for this dearth of specimens, given that the first teeth of *Gigantopithecus* known to western biologists came from these shops.

There is much to resolve in the details of the evolution of Asian great apes, but very few researchers doubt that they are pongines. On the other hand, the case for the European side of the dispersal of griphopithecins as members of the African ape/human clade has met with much more debate (**Table 3**).

Table 3 Shared derived characters of the hominines found in one or more dryopithecins

Character state	Fossil taxon[a]
Biconvex premaxilla	R, D, O
Stepped subnasal fossa	R, D, O
Patent incisive canals	R, D, O
Broad, flat nasal aperture base	R, D, O, H
Moderate alveolar prognathism	R, D, O, H
Shallow canine fossa	R, D, O, H
Supraorbital torus	R, D, O, H
Inflated glabella	R, D, O, H
Ethmoidal frontal sinus	R, H
Elongated neurocranium	R
Inclined frontal squama	R, D
Klinorhynchy	R
Broad temporal fossa	R
Projecting entoglenoid process	R
Fused articular and tympanic temporal	R
Deep glenoid fossa	R

[a]R: Rudapithecus; D: Dryopithecus; H: Hispanopithecus; O: Ouranopithecus.

EUROPEAN GREAT APES

Dryopithecus

As noted in the introduction, *Dryopithecus* is one of the first described fossil apes, and the only one about which Darwin comments. But it was not until the mid 1970s when sufficiently well preserved fossils began to be found that the significance of *Dryopithecus* began to be more completely understood.

The older sample of *Dryopithecus* from Europe consists of three partial male mandibles and a humeral shaft from the type locality of St. Gaudens, France and a motley collection of isolated teeth and fragmentary jaws from sites in Spain, Germany, Austria, and the Republic of Georgia (Begun 2002) (**Table 2, Figure 1**). Other specimens that have at one time or another been attributed to *Dryopithecus* (Simons & Pilbeam 1965, Szalay & Delson 1979) from Europe, Asia, and Africa are now considered to represent different genera. With the discovery of more complete specimens from Greece, Spain, and Hungary, attention turned back to Europe among those researchers interested in great ape and human origins (Martin & Andrews 1993).

New, more informative *Dryopithecus* have been recovered over the past five years from a cluster of localities near the village of Els Hostalets de Pierola (Catalonia, northern Spain). The Hostalets de Pierola locality has produced a partial skeleton, and two sites at Can Mata yielded an upper and lower jaw, a proximal femur, and a fragmentary facial skeleton (Moyà-Solà & Köhler 1995; Moyà-Solà et al. 2004, 2009a,b). These specimens have attributed to three different genera (*Pierolapithecus, Anoiapithecus,* and *Dryopithecus*). I have argued elsewhere that they are most likely to be the same genus and very possibly the same species, *Dryopithecus fontani,* and that is how they are treated here (Begun 2009; Begun et al. 2006, 2008).

Dryopithecus from Spain closely resembles *Dryopithecus fontani* from France in details of its dental anatomy. In both cases the dentitions are more primitive than in later-occurring dryopithecins (**Table 1**) and are to some extent intermediate between these and more ancient genera such as *Kenyapithecus* (Begun 2009; Begun et al. 2006, 2008; Moyà-Solà et al. 2009a). The most obvious differences from later dryopithecins are the slightly more pronounced expression of molar cingula, the more robust male canines, and the relatively small size of the first molars (Begun 2009). *Anoiapithecus* is said to be primitive in the shortness of its face, but the specimen is too poorly preserved to make an accurate measurement, and dryopithecins in general have short faces below the nose, most closely resembling those of gorillas (Begun 1994, 2007, 2009). *Pierolapithecus* is said to be primitive in the orientation of its face relative to the tooth row, but in my view, the upward rotation of the face is due to distortion in the fossil, and with that corrected it would closely resemble the faces of other dryopithecins (Begun 2009).

The appearance of *Dryopithecus* at about 12 Ma parallels the first appearance of *Sivapithecus* at nearly the same time, suggesting that they diverged from a common ancestor possibly 13 to 16 Ma. *Dryopithecus* from St. Gaudens, Hostalets de Pierola, and Can Mata is known from postcranial remains, which are dramatically different from those of the griphopithecins and *Proconsul.* They show unambiguous indications of the importance of highly mobile limbs and suspensory positional behavior (Begun 1992b; Deane & Begun 2008; Moyà-Solà et al. 2004, 2009b; Pilbeam & Simons 1971; Rose 1997). This represents a significant departure from previous fossil apes, and provides clear evidence that *Dryopithecus* is an early great ape of modern aspect, with a broad thorax, stiff lower back, a well-developed capacity for powerful grasping and climbing and the ability to move about in the trees below the branches, though perhaps less efficiently than in later dryopithecins and living apes. I interpret this change to be extremely important in the evolution of the African and human clade. It allowed *Dryopithecus* to remain relatively large and yet retain the capacity to exploit terminal branch resources, by spreading its weight among the branches and by hanging below them to conserve energy, as do other larger highly arboreal animals (e.g., sloths). It also represents the evolutionary origins of human mobile and highly dexterous upper limbs.

In addition to being relatively primitive compared to later species, the teeth of *Dryopithecus* differ from those of the griphopithecins in having a thin layer of enamel and less rounded cusps. They more closely resemble the teeth of chimpanzees and have been interpreted as adaptations to a soft fruit diet, as in modern chimpanzees (Begun 1994, Deane 2007, Kay & Ungar 1997, Ungar 1996, Ungar & Kay 1995). The later occurring dryopithecins *Hispanopithecus, Rudapithecus,* and *Ouranopithecus* share even more postcranial derived characters with living great apes, and cranial characters with African apes.

Hispanopithecus

Hispanopithecus is now known from a partial skeleton that reveals numerous details of its anatomy unknown to previous researchers. The trunk and limbs of *Hispanopithecus* are even better preserved than in the Pierola *Dryopithecus* specimen, and show that the limb proportions were not only great ape-like (long arms, short legs), but even extreme in this regard, being most similar to the limb proportions of *Pongo* (Moyà-Solà & Köhler 1996). The lower back has more strongly developed adaptations for stiffness than in *Dryopithecus*, and the hands are huge, with phalanges (finger bones) that closely resemble those of living orangutans in terms of their length and structure (Almécija et al. 2007, Deane & Begun 2008, Moyà-Solà & Köhler 1996). This was an ape with a fully developed adaptation to suspensory positional behavior, with hooks for hands and highly flexible, mobile limbs for clambering among the branches. It is likely that *Hispanopithecus* was as arboreal as living *Pongo* and, given its size—roughly that of a modern female *Pongo*—it may rarely have ventured to the ground. The teeth of *Hispanopithecus* are very similar to those of *Dryopithecus* and *Rudapithecus* (see below), in being basically chimpanzee-like and indicative of a broad-based soft fruit diet (Ungar 1996).

The cranial morphology of *Hispanopithecus* reveals its evolutionary relationship to the African ape and human clade (**Table 3**). *Hispanopithecus* has an incipient supraorbital torus, which distinguishes African apes and humans from *Pongo*, and it has a large frontal sinus positioned low between the orbits, which, once again, is seen only in African apes and humans (Begun 2009). However, the cranium of *Hispanopithecus* is not as well preserved as in another late Miocene great ape, *Rudapithecus*. This sample consists of three cranial specimens including one skull (cranium and mandible) and two brain cases, and provides many more details of the anatomy of the face and the brain case (Kordos & Begun 2001a,b).

Rudapithecus

Rudapithecus provides the earliest evidence of a major reorganization of the skull, klinorhychy, which distinguishes African apes and humans from all other hominoids. A klinorhychous skull has the face tilted downwards relative to the long axis of the brain case. An airorhynchous skull has the face rotated upwards, as in *Pongo* and to a lesser extent *Hylobates* among extant apes (Begun 2007, 2009; Kordos & Begun 2001a; Shea 1985,1988). *Rudapithecus* is distinctly African ape-like in this regard. This fundamental reorganization of the skull is, in my view, a very important shared derived characteristic linking *Rudapithecus*, and by extension, other dryopithecins, with the African ape and human clade.

In addition, two of the *Rudapithecus* crania preserve portions of the anterior part of the palate, the premaxilla in most primates (Ashley-Montagu 1935; Krogman 1930a,b; Schultz 1926, 1936). The morphology of the premaxilla and its position and orientation with regard to the maxilla clearly distinguishes genera among extant apes (Begun 2007, Ward & Kimbel 1983, Ward & Pilbeam 1983). African apes have moderate (*Gorilla*) to elongated (*Pan* and *Australopithecus*) premaxilla that overlap the roof of the palate, forming a step into the nasal fossa. In two *Rudapithecus* specimens the position, length, and orientation of the premaxilla are most similar to the condition in *Gorilla*. From what is preserved in *Dryopithecus* from Can Mata and *Ouranopithecus*, the same can be said for these taxa (**Table 3**).

Another striking similarity between dryopithecins and African apes and humans is the configuration of the frontal sinus, one of the paranasal sinuses that are ubiquitous among mammals (Begun 1994, 2007, 2009; Begun & Kordos 1997; Cave 1949, 1961; Cave & Haines 1940; Rossie 2005). In African apes, humans, and dryopithecins there is a large and direct connection between the sinuses of the ethmoid region, between the orbits, and the frontal sinuses. Therefore, it appears that dryopithecins grew their frontal sinuses directly from the ethmoid, as in African apes and humans, representing another important shared derived character of this clade (Cave & Haines, 1940). **Table 3** lists a total of 16 shared derived characters that serve to link dryopithecins to extant African apes and humans.

It is noteworthy that they are spread across many different areas of the cranium, from the premaxilla to the neurocranium and basicranium, and are very unlikely to have evolved in parallel.

Ouranopithecus

Ouranopithecus is a larger great ape from slightly younger sites in Greece (**Table 1**). It shares a number of characters with australopithecines that have led de Bonis and colleagues to conclude that it is an early hominin (Bonis 1983; Bonis et al. 1990; Bonis & Koufos 1993, 1994, 1997; Koufos 2007) (**Table 1**). These include enlarged and thickly enameled molars with broad, flat cusps, small male canines with apical (tip) wear, a robust maxilla and especially zygomatic region of the face, and a comparatively flat condylar process of the mandible. In *Ouranopithecus* all of the similarities to fossil humans can be attributed to selection for a single functional complex, powerful mastication, which has produced parallel adaptations in many fossil and extant primates (*Cebus, Pongo, Australopithecus, Sivapithecus, Gigantopithecus*) (Begun & Kordos 1997). Other than the characters that appear to be directly related to powerful chewing, *Ouranopithecus* is very similar to other dryopithecins, and it is for this reason that I place them in the same tribe (Begun 1994, 1996, 2002, 2007, 2009) (**Table 1**).

Ouranopithecus has a premaxilla that closely resembles that of other dryopithecins and gorillas, and it has large, flat cusped, very thickly enameled molars resembling those of australopithecines. In *Ouranopithecus* males the lower canines are similar to those of other dryopithecins, though perhaps smaller relative to body size, but the male upper canines are undeniably reduced in size and in height. Whereas this attribute is one of the principal reasons that *Ouranopithecus* is attributed to the hominin clade by some, the pattern is different from that seen in any hominin, given that the obvious reduction in canine crown height is restricted to the upper dentition.

In the final analysis, *Ouranopithecus* probably evolved from a more typical dryopithecin such as *Rudapithecus*, following selection for more robust masticatory adaptations in an environment that was more open than for other dryopithecins (Begun 2009; Bonis et al. 1986; Bonis & Koufos 1994; Fortelius et al. 1996; Koufos 2003, 2007; Solounias et al. 1999).

Recently, two more European hominines have been added to the list, both most strongly resembling *Ouranopithecus* (**Table 2**). A very large hominine, dentally the size of Miocene *Gigantopithecus*, has been described from the site of Çorakyerler in Turkey. It is similar to *Ouranopithecus*, but differs in details of the morphology of the incisors, canines, and premolars and in the structure of the premaxilla and palate (Begun 2009, Begun et al. 2003b, Güleç et al. 2007). The paleoecology of the locality suggests that it was even more open, that is, less forested, than the *Ouranopithecus* localities from Greece (Güleç et al. 2007). The association of mammals from the site also suggests that it is younger than any *Ouranopithecus* locality, possibly by as many as two million years (Güleç et al. 2007). Another site in Bulgaria has yielded a hominoid upper premolar that looks very similar to *Ouranopithecus*, and a specimen of *Mesopithecus*, a primitive colobine monkey (Spassov 2009, Spassov & Geraads 2008). The significance of these new hominines is that they occur at a time and place where hominines were thought to have gone extinct, owing to the widely documented drying out of late Miocene Eurasia (Agustí 2007, Agustí et al. 2003, Begun 2009, Bernor 2007). That an ape from Turkey and another from Bulgaria managed to survive and adapt to these dramatic climatic fluctuations is a strong indication of the adaptability of the European hominines and anticipates the diversification of hominines in Africa. If confirmed, the co-occurrence of an Old World monkey and a fossil ape in Bulgaria would be a first in Eurasia.

There are no hominines known from Africa between 13.5 and 10 Ma, and there are many characteristics shared by dryopithecins and extant African apes. Nevertheless, two newly described samples have led some to call into question the hypothesis that the African apes and humans evolved and experienced their first radiation in Europe.

AFRICAN FOSSIL GREAT APES

Chororapithecus

A handful of isolated teeth discovered at the 10 Ma site of Chorora in Ethiopia have been attributed to the Homininae (Suwa et al. 2007). Suwa and colleagues speculate that *Chororapithecus* may represent an ancestor of gorillas given the presence of a ridge on one molar that appears to them to be the precursor of a slicing crest on the teeth of modern gorillas. However, the ridge in question is only partially developed, and is mainly visible on the enamo-dentine junction, the surface directly below the enamel (visualized using microCT scans). There is no way to be confident that this very subtle character is a homology with *Gorilla*, especially given the fact that the anatomy of the dentition of *Chororapithecus* overall is distinctly unlike gorillas both in terms of morphology and functional anatomy. Suwa and colleagues also indicate that the presence of a hominine or a gorilla ancestor as represented by *Chororapithecus* effectively falsifies the hypothesis that the African ape and human clade originated or even existed for any time in Eurasia (see also Harrison 2010). However, even if *Chororapithecus* is a hominine, which is far from certain, it is still 2 Ma younger than the earliest hominine, *Dryopithecus*, and nothing about the anatomy of *Chororapithecus* calls into question the hominine affinities of the dryopithecins (Begun 1992a, 2007, 2009; Hill & Ward 1988; Moyà-Solà et al. 2009b).

Nakalipithecus

Another possible hominine from Africa is *Nakalipithecus*, from Nakali in Kenya (Kunimatsu et al. 2007). The sample includes a partial mandible with worn teeth and several isolated teeth. The female upper canine bears a strong resemblance to the same tooth in *Ouranopithecus*, lending support to the hypothesis that *Nakalipithecus* is related to *Ouranopithecus* (Kunimatsu et al. 2007). These authors have argued that because *Nakalipithecus* is slightly older than *Ouranopithecus* (9.8 versus 9.5 Ma) it

might be ancestral to the latter, and that European great apes in general represent extinct side branches of the hominines. However, as with *Chororapithecus*, *Nakalipithecus* is about 2 million years younger than *Dryopithecus* (Begun 2009, Moyà-Solà et al. 2009b). Even if *Nakalipithecus* is ancestral to *Ouranopithecus* it has no direct bearing on the question of hominine origins.

THE PALEOBIOGEOGRAPHY OF HOMININE ORIGINS

In this review I have emphasized the evidence for a European origin of the Africa ape and human clade. In contrast to the simplistic interpretation that hominines could not have evolved in Europe (Bernor 2007, Harrison 2010), the fossil record shows that the circumstances of hominine origins are very complex. The fossil and molecular evidence of the other Old World catarrhine radiation, the cercopithecoids, shows a similar pattern of complexity, with genetic and fossil evidence of multiple dispersals starting in the late Miocene (Jablonski 2002, Stewart & Disotell 1998). The earliest hominines are European and there are no fossil hominines in Africa for at least two million years after they first appear in Spain and France. Although it has been argued that the absence of evidence is not evidence of absence, and that Africa is vast and relatively unexplored, the bottom line is that we have to base hypotheses on actual data and not on expectations of future discoveries. The absence of hominines in Africa does not explain the large number of hominine characters found in the European sample (**Table 3**).

Hominids first occur in Europe at about 16.5 Ma, as represented by *Griphopithecus* in Germany and Turkey (Begun 2002, Begun et al. 2003a, Heizmann & Begun 2001). Hominids were not alone in dispersing into Europe in the middle Miocene and eventually expanding their range to Africa. Numerous lineages of mammals including ungulates, carnivores, proboscideans, aardvarks, and small mammals disperse and expand their ranges between Europe and Africa at this time (Begun 2009; Begun et al. 2003a,b; Begun & Nargolwalla 2004, 2009; Nargolwalla et al. 2006). Europe from the Mediterranean to northern France, Germany, and Central Europe was subtropical in climate, and these conditions appear to have favored the evolution of the early great apes.

It is not clear where the ancestor of hominines originated, in Europe, Anatolia, or Africa, but by about 12.5–13 Ma hominines are present in Spain, France, and Austria. They thrived in Europe and expanded their range east over the next two to three million years. At first they are always found in contexts that indicate densely forested conditions, and often in proximity to the shores of the ancient inland sea, the Central Parathethys (Nargolwalla et al. 2006).

The best-known samples of late Miocene European hominines are about 10 to 9.5 Ma in age (Rudabánya, Can Llobateres, Ravin de la Pluie). By this time hominines had diversified substantially and in some ways mimic the diversity that existed among Pliocene hominins. *Ouranopithecus* was substantially larger, with much more robust jaws, thickly enameled teeth, and many other adaptations to a diet that must have emphasized the consumption of hard or tough food objects, like australopithecines. *Rudapithecus* and *Hispanopithecus* were highly suspensory, arboreal soft fruit frugivores, with cheek teeth closely resembling those of living chimpanzees. The brain of *Rudapithecus* is known to have been as large as that of modern chimpanzees, and it is possible that this fossil ape had cognitive capabilities similar to those of chimpanzees (Begun & Kordos 2004). *Ouranopithecus* inhabited areas that were more open compared with the habitats of *Rudapithecus* and *Hispanopithecus*, and newly discovered *Ouranopithecus*-like apes probably inhabited even more open habitats (Güleç et al. 2007, Spassov 2009, Spassov & Geraads 2008). These discoveries effectively falsify the hypothesis that apes could not have lived in Europe after the beginning of the climatic deterioration that characterizes the late Miocene, and that they could not have dispersed from Europe into Africa at

this time (Bernor 2007, Bernor & Rook 2003, Rook & Bernor 2004). In fact, there is much evidence to show that forested conditions persisted locally in various areas of Europe and the eastern Mediterranean that could very well have accommodated both the more forest-adapted and more open country–adapted dryopithecins (Begun 2009).

Nevertheless, by about 9 Ma fossil hominines from Europe have all but disappeared, with remnants remaining in Turkey and Bulgaria. A taxon that I have not mentioned before, *Oreopithecus*, survives until about 8 Ma, but in my view this genus is not a hominine but rather evolved from a distinct ancestor (Begun 2001, 2002, 2007). A dryopithecin with teeth closely resembling those of *Rudapithecus*, *Udabnopithecus*, survives in Georgia until about 9 Ma (Begun 2007, Burchak-Abramovitsch & Gabashvili 1950). Despite their adaptability, most late Miocene European hominines disappear from Europe following ecological changes that led to much more open and seasonal conditions (Agustí et al. 2003). As in the middle Miocene, faunal exchanges between Europe and Africa are ubiquitous in the late Miocene, and many modern African mammals disperse from Eurasia into Africa at this time (Begun 2001, 2005, 2009; Nargolwalla 2009). A hominine was very probably among those taxa that moved south into Africa sometime between about 9 and 10 Ma, but whether it more closely resembled *Ouranopithecus* and *Australopithecus* or *Rudapithecus* and chimpanzees is impossible to say at this time.

Darwin was almost certainly correct in his hypothesis that the LCA of the living African apes and humans evolved in Africa. There is no evidence that this clade had already split by 10 Ma before entering Africa. However, a very substantial body of evidence from the morphology of European fossil hominines as well as dispersal patterns of other mammals and the paleoecology of the circum-Mediterranean region in the late Miocene all strongly suggest that hominines first evolve in Europe, or at least that they radiate and acquire their most significant adaptations there. As it stands today, the preponderance of evidence indicates that the hominine clade originates and experiences its initial radiation in Europe, but that after dispersing back to Africa, the LCA of living African apes and humans splits to form the modern clades of hominines in Africa sometime after 10 Ma.

Finally, with regard to the nature of the LCA of humans and chimpanzees, it has recently been suggested that it was very much unlike either living taxa, being instead a palmigrade quadruped, like monkeys, with no anatomical specializations for suspension (White et al. 2009). This suggestion is based on the analysis of *Ardipithecus ramidus*, the oldest and most primitive Pliocene hominin (Lovejoy 2009; Lovejoy et al. 2009a,b,c,d; Suwa et al. 2009a,b; White et al. 2009). *Ardipithecus* is clearly a hominin, as indicated by its small canines, by its more centrally positioned foramen magnum, and probably by its pelvic morphology, although the bone is horribly distorted (Lovejoy et al. 2009b,d; Suwa et al. 2009a,b; White et al. 2009). However, it also had very powerfully built upper limbs, was about the same size and had similar levels of sexual dimorphism as in modern chimpanzees, and had a brain about the same size as a modern chimp's. The feet have highly divergent, mobile, powerful grasping big toes and the hand and foot phalanges are long and curved, as in all suspensory hominoids (Lovejoy et al. 2009b,d; Suwa et al. 2009a,b; White et al. 2009). *Ardipithecus* lived about three million years after the LCA of chimpanzees and humans. Speculations about the morphology of that ancestor should not be based exclusively on the evidence of this one partial skeleton, without considering the anatomy of Miocene apes, australopithecines,

and the living descendents as well. There are in fact numerous hallmarks of a suspensory ancestry in the skeleton of *Ardipithecus*. If it is correct that *Ardipithecus* and chimpanzees evolved from a palmigrade quadruped (Lovejoy 2009, White et al. 2009), then all of the characters related to suspensory positional behavior present in all living apes and all of the similarities between living apes and humans would have to have evolved in parallel, as would those of the numerous Miocene taxa that show the same adaptations. Although this is possible, it would represent a spectacular amount of homoplasy, unlike anything we see in any other lineage of vertebrates, and it would also call into question the very premise that it is possible to reconstruct evolutionary history and behavior using the fossil evidence.

From the perspective of the Miocene and its diversity of taxa, *Ardipithecus* actually fits in well as an intermediate genus between arboreal, suspensory, knuckle-walking chimpanzee-like common ancestors and our fully bipedal more direct ancestors. In my opinion, there is nothing to exclude the possibility that *Ardipithecus* is a surviving relict of an early branch of the hominins without a direct relationship to later taxa. Chimps are neither living fossils nor are they our ancestors. Nevertheless, the evidence from *Ardipithecus* does not falsify the most parsimonious hypothesis about the basically chimp-like nature of the common ancestor of chimpanzees and humans (Begun 2004, Richmond et al. 2001). As the search continues for additional sites with new hominines in both Europe and Africa (hopefully in the period between 10 and 8 Ma), further discoveries will surely shed light on many of the hypotheses presented herein.

DISCLOSURE STATEMENT

The author is not aware of any affiliations, memberships, funding, or financial holdings that might be perceived as affecting the objectivity of this review.

LITERATURE CITED

Agustí. 2007. The biotic environments of the late Miocene hominids. See Henke & Tattersall 2008, pp. 979–1009

Agustí J, Sanz de Siria A, Garcés M. 2003. Explaining the end of the hominoid experiment in Europe. *J. Hum. Evol.* 45:145–53

Almécija S, Alba DM, Moyà-Solà S, Köhler M. 2007. Orang-like manual adaptations in the fossil hominoid *Hispanopithecus laietanus*: first steps towards great ape suspensory behaviours. *Proc. R. Soc. Ser. B* 274:2375–84

Andrews P, Martin L. 1987. Cladistic relationships of extant and fossil hominoids. *J. Hum. Evol.* 16:101–18

Ashley-Montagu MF. 1935. The premaxilla in the primates. *Q. Rev. Biol.* 10:32–59; 181–208

Beard KC, Teaford MF, Walker A. 1986. New wrist bones of *Proconsul africanus* and *Proconsul nyanzae* from Rusinga Island, Kenya. *Folia Primatol.* 47:97–118

Begun DR. 1992a. Miocene fossil hominids and the chimp-human clade. *Science* 257:1929–33

Begun DR. 1992b. Phyletic diversity and locomotion in primitive European hominids. *Am. J. Phys. Anthropol.* 87:311–40

Begun DR. 1994. Relations among the great apes and humans: new interpretations based on the fossil great ape *Dryopithecus*. *Yearb. Phys. Anthropol.* 37:11–63

Begun DR. 1996. Events in European hominoid evolution. *Europal* 10:16–20

Begun DR. 1999. Hominid family values: morphological and molecular data on relations among the great apes and humans. In *The Mentalities of Gorillas and Orangutans: Comparative Perspectives*, ed. ST Parker, RW Mitchell, HL Miles, pp. 2–42. Cambridge, UK: Cambridge Univ. Press

Begun DR. 2001. African and Eurasian Miocene hominoids and the origins of the Hominidae. In *Hominoid Evolution and Environmental Change in the Neogene of Europe*. Vol. 2. *Phylogeny of the Neogene Hominoid Primates of Eurasia*, ed. L de Bonis, G Koufos, P Andrews, pp. 231–53. Cambridge, UK: Cambridge Univ. Press

Begun DR. 2002. European hominoids. In *The Primate Fossil Record*, ed. W Hartwig, pp. 339–68. Cambridge: Cambridge Univ. Press

Begun DR. 2003. Planet of the Apes. *Sci. Am.* 289:74–83

Begun DR. 2004. Knuckle-walking and the origin of human bipedalism. In *From Biped to Strider: The Emergence of Modern Human Walking*, ed. DJ Meldrum, CE Hilton, pp. 9–33. New York: Kluwer

Begun DR. 2005. *Sivapithecus* is east and *Dryopithecus* is west, and never the twain shall meet. *Anthropol. Sci.* 113:53–64

Begun DR. 2007. Fossil record of Miocene hominoids. See Henke & Tattersall 2007, pp. 921–77. Berlin: Springer

Begun DR. 2009. Dryopithecins, Darwin, de Bonis, and the European origin of the African apes and human clade. *Geodiversitas* 31:789–816

Begun DR, Geraads D, Güleç E. 2003a. The Çandır hominoid locality: Implications for the timing and pattern of hominoid dispersal events. *Cour. Forschung. Inst. Senckenberg.* 240:251–65

Begun DR, Güleç E. 1998. Restoration of the Type and Palate of *Ankarapithecus meteai*: Taxonomic, Phylogenetic, and Functional Implications. *Am. J. Phys. Anthropol.* 105:279–314

Begun DR, Güleç E, Geraads D. 2003b. Dispersal patterns of Eurasian hominoids: Implications from Turkey. *Deinsea* 10:23–39

Begun DR, Kordos L. 1997. Phyletic affinities and functional convergence in *Dryopithecus* and other Miocene and living hominids. See Begun et al. 1997, pp. 291–316

Begun DR, Kordos L. 2004. Cranial evidence of the evolution of intelligence in fossil apes. In *The Evolution of Thought: Evolutionary Origins of Great Ape Intelligence*, ed. AE Russon, DR Begun, pp. 260–79. Cambridge: Cambridge Univ. Press

Begun DR, Nargolwalla M, Kordos L. 2008. Revision of the Dryopithecinae: Phylogenetic and paleobiogeographic implications. *Am J. Phys. Anthropol.* S46:66

Begun DR, Nargolwalla MC. 2004. Late Miocene hominid biogeography: some recent perspectives. *Evol. Anthropol.* 13:234–38

Begun DR, Teaford MF, Walker A. 1994. Comparative and functional anatomy of *Proconsul* phalanges from the Kaswanga primate site, Rusinga Island, Kenya. *J. Hum. Evol.* 26:89–165

Begun DR, Ward CV, Deane AS, Kivell TL, Nargolwalla MC, Taylor ND. 2006. Stem hominine or hominid? The phylogeny and functional anatomy of *Pierolapithecus*. *Am. J. Phys. Anthropol.* S42:63

Begun DR, Ward CV, Rose MD, eds. 1997. *Function, Phylogeny and Fossils: Miocene Hominoid Evolution and Adaptations*. New York: Plenum

Benefit BR, McCrossin ML. 1995. Miocene Hominoids and hominid origins. *Annu. Rev. Anthropol.* 24:237–56

Bernor RL. 2007. New apes fill the gap. *Proc. Natl. Acad. Sci. USA* 104:19661–62

Bernor RL, Rook L. 2003. Palaeozoogeography of the Rudabanya fauna. *Palaeontolograph. Ital.* 89(2002):21–25

Bonis L de.1983. Phyletic relationships of Miocene hominoids and higher primate classification. See Corruccini & Ciochon 1983, pp. 625–49

Bonis L de, Bouvrain G, Geraads D, Koufos G. 1990. New hominid skull material form the late Miocene of Macedonia in Northern Greece. *Nature* 345:712–14

Bonis L de, Bouvrain G, Geraads D, Melentis J. 1974. Première découverte d'un primate hominoïde dans le Miocène supérieur de Macédoine (Grèce). *C. R. Acad. Sci. Paris Ser. D* 278:3063–66

Bonis L de, Bouvrain G, Koufos G, Malentis J. 1986. Succession and dating of the late Miocene primates of Macedonia. See Else & Lee 1986, pp. 107–14

Bonis L de, Koufos G. 1993. The face and mandible of *Ouranopithecus macedoniensis*: description of new specimens and comparisons. *J. Hum. Evol.* 24:469–91

Bonis L de, Koufos G. 1994. Our ancestors' ancestor: *Ouranopithecus* is a Greek link in human ancestry. *Evol. Anthropol.* 3:75–83

Bonis L de, Koufos G. 1997. The phylogenetic and functional implications of *Ouranopithecus macedoniensis*. See Begun et al. 1997, pp. 317–26

Burchak-Abramovitsch NO, Gabashvili EG. 1950. Discovery of a fossil anthropoid in Georgia (in Russian). *Priroda, Moscow* 9:70–72

Cave AJE. 1949. Notes on the nasal fossa of a young Chimpanzee. *Proc. Zool. Soc. London* 119:61–63

Cave AJE. 1961. The frontal sinus of the gorilla. *Proc. Zool. Soc. London* 136:359–73

Cave AJE, Haines RW. 1940. The paranasal sinues of the anthropoid apes. *J. Anat.* 74:493–523

Chaimanee Y, Jolly D, Benammi M, Tafforeau P, Duzer D, et al. 2003. A middle Miocene hominoid from Thailand and orangutan origins. *Nature* 422:61–65

Chaimanee Y, Suteethorn V, Pratueng J, Vidthayanon C, Marandat B, Jaeger J-J. 2004. A new orang-utan relative from the Late Miocene of Thailand. *Nature* 427:439–41

Corruccini RL, Ciochon RS, eds. 1983. *New Interpretations of Ape and Human Ancestry*. New York: Plenum

Darwin C. 1871. *The Descent of Man*. London: Murray

Deane AS. 2007. *Inferring dietary behavior from Miocene hominoids: a high resolution morphometric approach to incisal crown curvature*. PhD thesis. Univ. Toronto, Toronto. 338 pp.

Deane AS, Begun DR. 2008. Broken fingers: retesting locomotor hypotheses for fossil hominoids using fragmentary proximal phalanges and high-resolution polynomial curve fitting (HR-PCF). *J. Hum. Evol.* 55:691–701

Else JC, Lee PC, eds. 1986. *Primate Evolution*. New York: Cambridge Univ. Press

Fortelius M, Werdelin L, Andrews P, Bernor RL, Gentry A, et al. 1996. Provinciality, diversity, turnover, and paleoecology in land mammal faunas of the later Miocene of Western Eurasia. In *The Evolution of Western Eurasian Neogene Mammal Faunas*, ed. RL Bernor, V Fahlbusch, H-W Mittmann, pp. 415–48. New York: Columbia Univ. Press

Goodman M, Porter CA, Czelusniak J, Page SL, Schneider H, et al. 1998. Toward a phylogenetic classification of primates based on DNA evidence complemented by fossil evidence. *Mol. Phylogen. Evol.* 9:585–98

Greenfield LO. 1974. Taxonomic reassessment of two *Ramapithecus* specimens. *Folia Primatol.* 22:97–115

Greenfield LO. 1980. A late divergence hypothesis. *Am. J. Phys. Anthropol.* 52:351–65

Güleç E, Sevim A, Pehlevan C, Kaya F. 2007. A new great ape from the late Miocene of Turkey. *Anthropol. Sci.* 115:153–58

Harrison T. 2010. Apes among the tangled branches of human origins. *Science* 327:532–34

Hartwig W, ed. 2002. *The Primate Fossil Record*. Cambridge: Cambridge Univ. Press

Heizmann E, Begun DR. 2001. The oldest European hominoid. *J. Hum. Evol.* 41:465–81

Henke W, Tattersall I, eds. 2007. *Handbook of Palaeoanthropology*. Vol. 2: *Primate Evolution and Human Origins*. Berlin: Springer

Hill A, Ward S. 1988. Origin of the Hominidae: the record of African large hominoid evolution between 14 my and 4 my. *Yearb. Phys. Anthropol.* 31:48–83

Hopwood AT. 1933. Miocene primates from Kenya. *Zool. J. Linnean Soc. London* 38:437–64

Ishida H, Kunimatsu Y, Takano T, Nakano Y, Nakatsukasa M. 2004. *Nacholapithecus* skeleton from the middle Miocene of Kenya. *J. Hum. Evol.* 46:1–35

Ishida H, Nakatsukasa M, Kunimatsu Y. 2000. Erection of a new genus and species: *Nacholapithecus kerioi* for a middle Miocene hominoid from Nachola area, northern Kenya. *Anthropol. Sci.* 108:92

Jablonski NG. 2002. Fossil Old World monkeys: the late Neogene. See Hartwig 2002, pp. 255–99

Kappelman J, Kelley J, Pilbeam D, Sheikh KA, Ward S, et al. 1991. The earliest occurrence of *Sivapithecus* from the middle Miocene Chinji Formation of Pakistan. *J. Hum. Evol.* 21:61–73

Kay RF, Ungar PS. 1997. Dental evidence for diet in some Miocene catarrhines with comments on the effects of phylogeny on the interpretation of adaptation. See Begun et al. 1997, pp. 131–51

Kelley J. 2002. The hominoid radiation in Asia. See Hartwig 2002, pp. 369–84

Kelley J, Andrews P, Alpagut B. 2008. A new hominoid species from the middle Miocene site of Pasalar, Turkey. *J. Hum. Evol.* 54:455–79

Kordos L, Begun DR. 2001a. A new cranium of *Dryopithecus* from Rudabánya, Hungary. *J. Hum. Evol.* 41:689–700

Kordos L, Begun DR. 2001b. Primates from Rudabánya: allocation of specimens to individuals, sex and age categories. *J. Hum. Evol.* 40:17–39

Koufos GD. 2003. Late Miocene mammal events and biostratigraphy in the Eastern Mediterranean. *Deinsea* 10:343–71

Koufos GD. 2007. Potential hominoid ancestors for Hominidae. In *Handbook of Palaeoanthropology*. Vol. 3: *Phylogeny of Hominids*, ed. W Henke, I Tattersall, pp. 1347–77. Berlin: Springer

Kretzoi M. 1969. Geschichte der Primaten und der Hominisation. *Symp. Biol. Hung.* 9:3–11

Krogman WM. 1930a. Studies in the growth change in the skull and face of Anthropoids. II Ectocranial and endocranial suture closure in the anthropoids and apes. *Am. J. Anat.* 46:315–53

Krogman WM. 1930b. Studies in the growth change in the skull and face of Anthropoids. V. Growth changes in the skull and face of the ourang-utan. *Am. J. Anat.* 47:343–65

Kunimatsu Y, Nakatsukasa M, Sawada Y, Sakai T, Hyodo M, et al. 2007. A new Late Miocene great ape from Kenya and its implications for the origins of African great apes and humans. *Proc. Natl. Acad. Sci. USA* 104:19220–25

Lartet E. 1856. Note sur un grand singe fossile qui se rattache au groupe des singes supérieurs. *C. R. Acad. Sci.* 43:219–23

Leakey LSB. 1962. A new Lower Pliocene fossil primate from Kenya. *Ann. Mag. Nat. Hist.* 13:689–96

Leakey M, Walker A. 1997. *Afropithecus*: function and phylogeny. See Begun et al. 1997, pp. 225–39

Leakey REF, Leakey MG, Walker AC. 1988. Morphology of *Afropithecus turkanesis* from Kenya. *Am. J. Phys. Anthropol.* 76:289–307

Lovejoy CO. 2009. Reexamining human origins in light of *Ardipithecus ramidus*. *Science* 326:74e1–8

Lovejoy CO, Latimer B, Suwa G, Asfaw B, White TD. 2009a. Combining prehension and propulsion: the foot of *Ardipithecus ramidus*. *Science* 326:72e1–8

Lovejoy CO, Simpson SW, White TD, Asfaw B, Suwa G. 2009b. Careful climbing in the Miocene: The forelimbs of *Ardipithecus ramidus* and humans are primitive. *Science* 326:70e1–8

Lovejoy CO, Suwa G, Simpson SW, Matternes JH, White TD. 2009c. The great divides: *Ardipithecus ramidus* reveals the postcrania of our last common ancestors with African apes. *Science* 326:73–106

Lovejoy CO, Suwa G, Spurlock L, Asfaw B, White TD. 2009d. The pelvis and femur of *Ardipithecus ramidus*: the emergence of upright walking. *Science* 326:71e1–6

Madar SI, Rose MD, Kelley J, MacLatchy L, Pilbeam D. 2002. New *Sivapithecus* postcranial specimens from the Siwaliks of Pakistan. *J. Hum. Evol.* 42:705–52

Martin L, Andrews P. 1993. Renaissance of Europe's ape. *Nature* 365:494

Moyà-Solà M, Köhler M. 1995. New partial cranium of *Dryopithecus* Lartet, 1863 (Hominoidea, Primates) from the upper Miocene of Can Llobateres, Barcelona, Spain. *J. Hum Evol.* 29:101–39

Moyà-Solà S, Alba DM, Almecija S, Casanovas-Vilar I, Köhler M, et al. 2009a. A unique middle Miocene European hominoid and the origins of the great ape and human clade. *Proc. Natl. Acad. Sci. USA* 106:9601–6

Moyà-Solà S, Köhler M. 1996. A *Dryopithecus* skeleton and the origins of great ape locomotion. *Nature* 379:156–59

Moyà-Solà S, Köhler M, Alba DM, Casanovas-Vilar I, Galindo J. 2004. *Pierolapithecus catalaunicus*, a new middle Miocene great ape from Spain. *Science* 306:1339–44

Moyà-Solà S, Köhler M, Alba DM, Casanovas-Vilar I, Galindo J, et al. 2009b. First partial face and upper dentition of the middle Miocene hominoid *Dryopithecus fontani* from Abocador de Can Mata (Vallès-Penèdes Basin, Catalonia, NE Spain): taxonomic and phylogenetic implications. *Am. J. Phys. Anthropol.* 139:126–45

Nakatsukasa M, Yamanaka A, Kunimatsu Y, Shimizu D, Ishida H. 1998. A newly discovered *Kenyapithecus* skeleton and its implications for the evolution of positional behavior in Miocene East African hominoids. *J. Hum. Evol.* 34:659–64

Nakatsukasa M, Tsujikawa H, Shimizu D, Takano T, Kunimatsu Y, et al. 2003. Definitive evidence for tail loss in *Nacholapithecus*, an East African Miocene hominoid. *J. Hum. Evol.* 45:179–86

Nargolwalla MC. 2009. *Euasian middle and late Miocene hominoid paleobiogeography and the geographic origins of the Homininae.* PhD thesis. Univ. Toronto, Toronto. 259 pp.

Nargolwalla MC, Hutchison MP, Begun DR. 2006. Middle and late Miocene terrestrial vertebrate localities and paleoenvironments in the Pannonian Basin. *Beitr. Paläontolog.* 30:319–32

Pickford M. 1986. The geochronology of Miocene higher primate faunas of East Africa. See Else & Lee 1986, pp. 21–33

Pickford M, Morales J. 1994. Biostratigraphy and palaeobiogeography of East Africa and the Iberian peninsula. *Palaeogeog. Palaeoclimatol. Palaeoecol.* 112:297–322

Pickford M, Sawada Y, Tayama R, Matsuda Y-K, Itaya T, et al. 2006. Refinement of the age of the Middle Miocene Fort Teman Beds, Western Kenya, and its implications for Old World biochronology. *C. R. Geosci.* 338:545–55

Pilbeam D, Young N. 2004. Hominoid evolution: synthesizing disparate data. *C. R. Palevol.* 3:305–21

Pilbeam DR. 1982. New hominoid skull material from the Miocene of Pakistan. *Nature* 295:232–34

Pilbeam DR. 1997. Research on Miocene hominoids and hominid origins: the last three decades. See Begun et al. 1997, pp. 13–28

Pilbeam DR, Simons EL. 1971. Humerus of *Dryopithecus* from Saint Gaudens, France. *Nature* 229:406–7

Richmond BG, Begun DR, Strait DS. 2001. Origin of human bipedalism: the knuckle-walking hypothesis reconsidered. *Yearb. Phys. Anthropol.* 44:70–105

Rook L, Bernor RL. 2004. Recent advances on multidisciplinary research at Rudabánya, late Miocene (MN 9), Hungary: a compendium. Ancestry of the African ape/human clade? *Palaeontolograph. Ital.* 89:30–31

Rose MD. 1986. Further hominoid postcranial specimens from the Late Miocene Nagri Formation of Pakistan. *J. Hum. Evol.* 15:333–67

Rose MD. 1988. Another look at the anthropoid elbow. *J. Hum. Evol.* 17:193–224

Rose MD. 1989. New postcranial specimens of catarrhines from the Middle Miocene Chinji Formation, Pakistan: description and a discussion of proximal humeral functional morphology in anthropoids. *J. Hum. Evol.* 18:131–62

Rose MD. 1997. Functional and phylogenetic features of the forelimb in Miocene hominoids. See Begun et al. 1997, pp. 79–100

Rose MD, Nakano Y, Ishida H. 1996. *Kenyapithecus* postcranial specimens from Nachola, Kenya. *Afr. Study Monog.* 24:3–56

Rossie JB. 2005. Anatomy of the nasal cavity and paranasal sinuses in *Aegyptopithecus* and Early Miocene African catarrhines. *Am. J. Phys. Anthropol.* 126:250–67

Schultz AH. 1926. Fetal growth of man and other primates. *Q. Rev. Biol.* 1:465–521

Schultz AH. 1936. Characters common to higher primates and characters specific to man. *Q. Rev. Biol.* 11:425–55

Schwartz JH. 1997. *Lufengpithecus* and hominoid phylogeny. Problems in delineating and evaluating phylogenetically relevant characters. See Begun et al. 1997, pp. 363–88

Shea BT. 1985. On aspects of skull form in African apes and orangutans, with implications for hominoid evolution. *Am. J. Phys. Anthropol.* 68:329–42

Shea BT. 1988. Phylogeny and skull form in the hominoid primates. In *Orang-Utan Biology*, ed. J Schwartz, pp. 233–45. New York: Oxford Univ. Press

Simons EL, Pilbeam DR. 1965. Preliminary revision of the Dryopithecinae (Pongidae, Anthropoidea). *Folia Primatol.* 3:81–152

Solounias N, Plavcan JM, Quade J, Witmer L. 1999. The paleoecology of the Pikermian Biome and the Savanna myth. In *The Evolution of Neogene Terrestrial Ecosystems in Europe*, ed. J Agusti, L Rook, P Andrews, pp. 436–53. Cambridge: Cambridge Univ. Press

Spassov N. 2009. Bulgaria, national museum of natural history. *Soc. Vert. Paleontol. News Bull.* 197:12

Spassov N, Geraads D. 2008. The latest prehumans of Europe: discovery of a late Miocene hominoid in Bulgaria of about 7 Ma. *Bul. Acad. Sci.* 2:2–4

Stewart C-B, Disotell TR. 1998. Primate evolution—in and out of Africa. *Curr. Biol.* 8:582–88

Strait DS, Grine FE. 2004. Inferring hominoid and early hominid phylogeny using craniodental characters: the role of fossil taxa. *J. Hum. Evol.* 47:399–452

Suwa G, Asfaw B, Kono RT, Kubo D, Lovejoy CO, White TD. 2009a. The *Ardipithecus ramidus* skull and its implications for hominid origins. *Science* 326:68–87

Suwa G, Kono RT, Katoh S, Asfaw B, Beyene Y. 2007. A new species of great ape from the late Miocene epoch in Ethiopia. *Nature* 448:921–24

Suwa G, Kono RT, Simpson SW, Asfaw B, Lovejoy CO, White TD. 2009b. Paleobiological implications of the *Ardipithecus ramidus* dentition. *Science* 326:69–99

Szalay F, Delson E. 1979. *Evolutionary History of the Primates*. New York: Academic

Ungar PS. 1996. Dental microwear of European Miocene catarrhines: evidence for diets and tooth use. *J. Hum. Evol.* 31:335–66

Ungar PS, Kay RF. 1995. The dietary adaptations of European Miocene catarrhines. *Proc. Natl. Acad. Sci. USA* 92:5479–81

Ward CS, Brown B. 1986. The facial skeleton of *Sivapithecus indicus*. In *Comparative Primate Biology*, ed. DR Swindler, J Erwin, pp. 413–52. New York: Alan R. Liss

Ward CV. 1993. Torso morphology and locomotion in *Proconsul nyanzae*. *Am. J. Phys. Anthropol.* 92:291–328

Ward CV. 1997a. Functional anatomy and phyletic implications of the hominoid trunk and hindlimb. See Begun et al. 1997, pp. 101–30

Ward CV. 2007. Postcranial and locomotor adaptations of hominoids. See Henke & Tattersall 2007, pp. 1011–30

Ward CV, Walker AC, Teaford MF. 1991. *Proconsul* did not have a tail. *J. Hum. Evol.* 21:215–20

Ward S. 1997b. The taxonomy and phylogenetic relationships of *Sivapithecus* revisited. See Begun et al. 1997, pp. 269–90

Ward S, Brown B, Hill A, Kelley J, Downs W. 1999. *Equatorius*: a new hominoid genus from the middle Miocene of Kenya. *Science* 285:1382–86

Ward SC, Kimbel WH. 1983. Subnasal alveolar morphology and the systemic postion of *Sivapithecus*. *Am. J. Phys. Anthropol.* 61:157–71

Ward SC, Pilbeam DR. 1983. Maxillofacial morphology of Miocene Hominoids from Africa and Indo-Pakistan. See Corruccini & Ciochon 1983, pp. 211–38

White TD. 2002. Earliest hominids. See Hartwig 2002, pp. 407–17

White TD, Asfaw B, Beyene Y, Haile-Selassie Y, Lovejoy CO, et al. 2009. *Ardipithecus ramidus* and the paleobiology of early hominids. *Science* 326:64–86

Wood B, Richmond BG. 2000. Human evolution: taxonomy and paleobiology. *J. Anat.* 196:19–60

The Anthropology of Secularism

Fenella Cannell

Department of Anthropology, London School of Economics and Political Science, London WC2A 2AE, United Kingdom; email: f.cannell@lse.ac.uk

Annu. Rev. Anthropol. 2010. 39:85–100

First published online as a Review in Advance on June 14, 2010

The *Annual Review of Anthropology* is online at anthro.annualreviews.org

This article's doi: 10.1146/annurev.anthro.012809.105039

Key Words

religion, modernity, spirituality, Christianity, Islam, Hinduism

Abstract

Recent debates on this topic have been heavily shaped by two paradigms: Asad's deconstructivism and Taylor's Catholic/Hegelian revisionism. This article outlines the arguments of each but frames them within the longer history of arguments that make claims for the reality of secularization and alternate sources for claims that "the secular" is a historically constructed category, including arguments from radical theology and (differently) in the anthropology of India. It is argued that implicit claims for the hierarchical ordering of reality in modernity, in which the political is seen as more real than the religious, continue to create disjunctures in the range of debate that new ethnography has the opportunity to address.

INTRODUCTION

I begin by putting my cards on the table. I do not myself write from a faith position, but I am a sceptic about secularism as some of my fellow social scientists are sceptics about religion. I am not convinced that there is such a thing as an absolutely secular society nor that there can be such a thing as a perfectly secular state of mind. I agree with those who argue that the secular is a historically produced idea, a theory about how things are or could be, and not an inescapable or inevitable process or fact (compare Dumont 1985, Milbank 1990). Like other powerful ideas, however, it has many centrally important material effects, as when it is politically institutionalized and becomes programmatic. These material effects have been intensified where people hope or fear that secularism may be an inevitable condition, linked with the processes of modernity. That is to say, its effects—like the effects of some religious faiths—vary according to how far people believe in it and in which ways.

This review is not centrally concerned with my own opinions. But stating them in these simple terms may help because the literature considered here circles constantly around the problem of the relation of religion to modernity. Thus although much of this discussion is beyond our scope here, the reader should note that the meanings of "secular" and "secularism" are constantly shifting in the literature, depending on whether a given author believes that they are real. Two linked discussions are (a) the question of whether social science can proceed only through a thoroughly secular theory and (b) the question of whether it is true, as some think, that, although the reality of the secular is moot, it is necessary to act as though we believed in it to limit conflict between faith groups or to defend other treasured values in the public sphere, including, but not confined to, democratic politics and human rights.

I begin with a brief survey of secularization theory, which mounts the most committed defense of the reality of the secular. I then consider the recent and highly influential body of writing by Asad, Hirschkind, and Mahmood, which questions this and all the terms of the older debate in the context of the discussion of contemporary Islam, drawing on the ideas of Foucault and others. Next, I discuss the important body of work on Indian secularism, which examines the ethnographic meaning of the secular in a given context and thus relativizes it differently from deconstructivism. In the last section, I touch on some of the thinkers outside anthropology who have written key works on the problem of secularism, works that often set the terms of anthropological debate at one remove; I also consider writing now emerging on other parts of the world, which may allow us to begin to develop a genuine comparative anthropology of secularisms based on particular historical and local studies.

SECULARIZATION THEORY AND ITS LEGACIES

The terms of the current anthropological literature on secularism are set in relation to both classic and recent developments in secularization theory. This debate could in itself exceed the space allotted for this article (see, e.g., Casanova 1994, chapter one; Dobellaere 1998), so I give only a brief discussion here.

Classic secularization theory derives mainly from anglophone sociological work conducted in the 1960s by Luckmann (1970), Berger (1990), Talcott Parsons (1960), Luhmann (1982) and others. These authors produced various interpretations of the foundational sociology of Durkheim (1971) and Weber (1946, 1963, 1976), which had explored the links between Western modernity and the decline of traditional religions. Bryan Wilson (1966) and others then continued to synthesize these propositions, producing a widespread consensus among sociologists over four decades.

Neither Durkheim nor Weber offered a strongly teleological view of modernity. Weber's focal interest was in the unique features of Western historical development, which he maintained could never be literally repeated elsewhere, although comparable forms of rationalization might occur within different regional or religious traditions. Weber also clearly distinguished between the analysis of the origin of an idea or institution (e.g., Christianity) and the analysis of its historical spread or transposition (e.g., in colonial conversion). Commentators such as Parsons recognized these features of Weber's thought (Parsons 1963) and drew attention to his famous essay on the *Protestant Ethic* (Weber 1976) as a specific case study of historical Europe, not as a template for the universal study of modernities. Both Luhmann and Berger also focused on Western modernity, arguing that religious modalities transformed in complex ways, rather than simply being discarded. Nevertheless, interpretations of this work often drifted toward a convergence theory view that Western modernity would provide a template for modernization processes elsewhere; secularization was understood as both sign and consequence of an inevitable modernity. The definition of secularity often remained implicit.

Although the debate has now moved on considerably, some influential scholars still defend classic secularization positions. For instance, Bruce proposes that the key issue to be addressed is still what he suggests is the convincing empirical evidence of decreasing religious participation and increasing religious indifference in the Western world. The pluralism of modern society compared with a more socially homogeneous past is crucial; it is the perception of the possibility of choice that propels the splitting and decline of religion "[f]rom [c]athedrals to [c]ults" (Bruce 1996). Bruce believes that institutional fissure (rather than modern science per se) is causally linked to the rise of religious indifference. Religion can no longer be taken so seriously, and (redeploying Nietzsche's famous phrase), for Bruce, "God is dead" (2002) in modern Britain.

Whereas changes in institutional forms and congregational attendance in Britain are well documented, their connection to religious indifference in Britain or elsewhere is contested (e.g., Davie 1994). Bruce's later work makes less-clear-cut claims about the uniformity of secularization at the global level than does his earlier writing, but he continues to argue that Britain and indeed the United States confirm his views. In the U.S. case, he asserts that the persistently high levels of church affiliation and faith in God in America compared with levels in Europe are a transitional phenomenon linked to the history of U.S. immigration and the role of religion as a marker of ethnic identity. Rejecting the criticism that his views are teleological, Bruce nevertheless predicts that trends in American Protestantism indicate a repetition of the European experience: "Privatization, individualism and relativism are now affecting the US churches in the way they did the British churches in the middle of the twentieth century" (Bruce 2002, p. 227).

This kind of argument was criticized by an early and continuing dissenter on secularization among sociologists: Martin (2005). Martin's work has stressed that secularization can take quite different routes within different global contexts, has argued for the value of seeing modernity as capable of taking religious forms (for instance, in Latin America), and has been alert to continued Christian valences in apparently secular Western Europe. However, such views were shared by few other sociologists before the late 1980s.

Since the resurgence of so-called political religion in the 1980s, academic positions have changed considerably. Thus Casanova, writing in 1994, described a volte-face in sociological opinion and asked, "Who still believes in the *myth* of secularization?" (Casanova 1994, p. 11). I propose that somewhat uncritical oppositions between religion and secularism and between the past and modernity, in fact, continue to be constitutive of many public areas of debate and some important academic arenas.

Secularization arguments appear to be a default position at the borders of the academic, the journalistic, and the political (compare Benthall 2009). Convergence theory interpretations have often been combined with subtraction theory interpretations of modernity in which, as Milbank (1990) has argued, some scholars claimed or assumed that the contemporary world has acquired a privileged grasp of reality compared to the past, by discarding religious illusion. Modern science is cast as offering access to material reality, whereas religion is cast as an expression of (personal) childishness or (collective) immaturity. As Taylor (2007, p. 636) has noted, some individuals are drawn to the idea (based on a misinterpretation of Nietzsche) that facing man's aloneness in the universe is the most crucial guarantee of toughness of character and of mind. Thus we can understand the glee with which some commentators greeted the American Religious Identification Survey (ARIS) of 2001 (**http://www.americanreligionsurvey-aris.org**) and its follow-ups to 2009, which appear to show statistically that the number of Americans who believe in God, although still overwhelming, is gradually decreasing; refutations from the opposite camp were equally vocal. The trends recorded by ARIS are clearly important, although the survey actually measures a rise in the numbers of Americans who answer that they are of "no religion," which leaves open the question of what this statement means emically. But where liberal political positions are often aligned with "secular" outlooks and conservative positions with "religious" outlooks (compare Harding 1987, 1994, 2001), as in the United States, both sides have a high stake in interpretation.

A perception that the link between modernity and secularization is somehow obvious has also played into the enormous interest in the debates over the "new atheists" (Beattie 2007). Dawkins (2006) argues at length both that religion is responsible for most of the atrocities in world history and that religion is a form of fallacious explanation of the origins of the world, now superceded by scientific accounts such as neo-Darwinism. His critics have opined that Dawkins does not understand theology well; as Terry Eagleton puts it, "Christianity was never meant to be an *explanation* of anything in the first place. It is rather like saying that thanks to the electric toaster we can forget about Chekhov" (Eagleton 2009, p. 7, emphasis

in original). Nevertheless, the popular appeal of the idea that the relative truth claims of religion and science can be somehow settled in straight contest is clearly strong, and this mindset accounts for the unusual mainstream success of books such as cognitive anthropologist Boyer's *Religion Explained*, which seeks to show that religion is simply an unwanted "side effect" of diverse human mental processes, which evolved for other reasons (Boyer 2001, p. 330; for an important critique, see Bloch 2008).

Certain ideas about secularization, therefore, have entered popular culture and have themselves become a form of ethnographic datum. Insofar as many people believe secularization to be inevitable in modernity, it may even become in some places a partly self-fulfilling prophecy (Cannell 2006). In other cases, it is clear that people are rejecting the term religion itself, while attempting (sometimes in contradictory ways) to create forms of practice that many anthropologists would still classify as religion (e.g., Luhrmann 1989, Pike 2001). An unusual degree of overlap exists between terms social science uses in the analysis of contemporary forms of religious and secular experience and the terms that informants may use in daily life. Anthropologists are potentially well placed to record this ethnographically and so perhaps exit from some of the circular aspects of general-order analysis.

If for some secularization theorists the institutional changes in mainstream Western religion are causally linked to the rise of religious indifference, other trends of thinking, drawing on Luckmann (1970) and ultimately on Durkheim (1971 [1915]), have stressed instead the transmutation of collective religion into a modern, nontheistic religion of the individual. Perhaps the best-known current proponent of this view is Heelas (1996), who revisits this line of analysis via a distinctive emphasis on the importance of 1960s counter-culture; for Heelas, this is a key period in which people began to abandon the mainstream churches primarily because they disliked churches' claims to authority, and people redirected their energies toward multifarious individual quests, often preferring to define these as spiritual but not religious. Heelas has worked with Woodhead (Heelas et al. 2004) to analyze the decline in U.K. Christian congregations from this perspective (but compare Smith 2008 who summarizes the case against). Heelas's most recent book presents a significant revision to his earlier views; in replacing his earlier uses of the terms self-spiritualities and New Age with the phrase "spiritualities of life" (Heelas 2008, p. 26), he seeks to correct any implication that new religious formations are trivial and to illuminate their connections with Romantic philosophy.

The widespread popular avoidance of the term religion is clearly an important fact. Yet the potential hazard with this debate is that it becomes tautologous; some analysts claim to demonstrate from it that religion is clearly declining, whereas others claim that spiritual practices are ultimately (implicitly) religious. There is scope for reading the evidence either way, depending on the definition of religion considered allowable. The material presented is therefore interesting and valuable, but the debate is unlikely to provide an unequivocal definition of the relationship between secularity and modernity.

Classic secularization arguments have raised crucial questions about modernity, but they have not always been historically nuanced. There is a tendency toward broad-brush contrasts between a religious past and a secular present, which disregards many inconvenient facts. One problem is a relative indifference to the history of secularization itself, as an idea, and not just as an automatic mechanism. At the political level, it is clear that claims to be secular became closely bound up with the ideologies and policies of nation-states, especially in the nineteenth century. Such ideas may have been most characteristic of West European nations, but they were exported to many other parts of the world, both in European colonialism and in many noncolonized indigenous states, which saw secularism as one means to emulate and overtake European progress. To anticipate,

this history of transmission is one of Asad's central concerns, whereas much of the recent work by anthropologists of India understands secularism as an aspect of state ideology, colonial or local.

Casanova's central book, *Public Religions in the Modern World*, offered a considerable advance on most previous sociological writers except Martin, precisely because Casanova is interested in historical variation. Casanova suggests that secularization theory has confused three premises that should, in fact, be kept separate: (*a*) the historical process of differentiation in Western modernity through which religion has come to be objectified and separated out from other functions, particularly politics and economics; (*b*) the idea that religion necessarily exits the public sphere in modernity and becomes privatized; and (*c*) the claim (dating back to Enlightenment philosophy) that religion as sentiment and practice will "tend to dissipate with progressive modernization" (Casanova 1994, p. 7).

For Casanova, the third claim is patently false, and he argues that much previous discussion has proceeded against overwhelming evidence of continued religious activity in Europe and America only because the myth of secularization had been taken to be axiomatic. The second claim he views as only one possibility among a range of actual historical outcomes to be explored. The first claim, the idea of differentiation of functions in modernity, however, he accepts as a historical reality.

The central section of the book is given over to a close examination of five case studies: the cases of Spain, Poland, and Brazil, followed by discussions of evangelical Protestantism and of American Catholicism. The focus on Catholic contexts is important to Casanova partly because these contexts are often backgrounded in Protestant-inflected Whig history. Casanova argues that the claims of the nation-state to autonomy from religion conceal absolutist monarchs' actual reliance on the annexation of religious mana. He further claims that the decline of a public role for religion has been exaggerated everywhere and may be central where (as in Soviet Poland) the population has regarded the secular government as illegitimate. Finally, Casanova argues that both Catholicism and Pentecostal Protestantism are growing in new, deterritorialized forms.

On the question of religious values in modernity, Casanova proposes that decline is a possible, perhaps a majoritarian, but not a necessary consequence of differentiation. He suggests that where churches have accepted disestablishment most rapidly, they may in fact have suffered the least decline in popular support and participation as they found other arenas of public discourse in which to engage.

In a more recent article, Casanova (2006) revisits and updates his arguments in the light of intervening events and in response to Asad. He identifies three limitations of his earlier position: (*a*) His focus was restricted to Western Christendom and its inheritors, (*b*) he emphasized civil society as the key public space of religions in modernity, and (*c*) he focused on the nation-state rather than the transnational dimensions of modern religion. His response is ready acknowledgment of the importance of wider comparisons and rephrases some earlier conclusions. For example, he comments that "the European concept of secularization is not a particularly relevant category for the 'Christian' United States" (Casanova 2006, p. 9) because in the United States the advance of the secular (as differentiation) has, in fact, been accompanied both by continued high levels of religious adherence and by continued public roles for religion. He also underlines the diversity of European developments. He further acknowledges that other religious traditions may not construct the same tension between the categories of religious and secular (i.e., worldly) and therefore that the relationship between modern differentiation and religion may unfold quite differently in, for example, Chinese Confucianism and Daoism. We will see in the third section below that this issue has, in fact, already been taken up in a tradition of Indianist and other regional anthropologies, which is apparently not familiar to Casanova.

ASAD AND THE DECONSTRUCTION OF RELIGION AND THE "SECULAR"

Asad has defined much of the recent anthropological discussion of the secular. His *Formations of the Secular* (2003) and, by anticipation, his *Genealogies of Religion* (1993) explicitly challenge anthropologists to contribute more fully to a debate that had long been dominated by political science and political philosophy. Invoking the comparative tradition of Mauss, which permits the setting side by side of "lifeways" from different times and places (Asad 2007, p. 17), Asad offers a vigorous challenge to the seeming obviousness and inevitability of the secular in the modern. His anthropology of secularism (as a form of political constitution that follows the development of the concept of the secular) and secularization (as a particular historical instance of the adoption of secular logic) unravels some of its component concepts and reveals their development as historically contingent rather than as fatefully necessary.

Asad focuses closely on the entanglement of secularism with capitalist liberal democracies in nation-states, of whose politics and rhetorics he is an incisive critic. Indeed, he is less hopeful of benevolent outcomes from the liberal public sphere than is either Connolly (1999) or Taylor (1999, 2007), with each of whom he engages mainly on this particular question. While discarding any essentialist definitions of West versus non-West, Asad also retains a clear grip on the idea that secularism was a concept with particular geographical and historical locations and patterns of export, first from Europe and then from America, following lines of global capitalist inequality.

Asad asserts that liberal secularism is characterized by the claim to know what nature, including universal human nature, is (but see Das 2006) and by the myth of progress, which suggests that all societies should be traveling toward this same understanding. Secularism, he tells us, has become a hegemonic cluster of projects in the contemporary world. It permits and develops certain ways of being and living, while disdaining, tacitly prohibiting, or stunting others. The central sections of *Formations of the Secular: Christianity, Islam, Modernity* attempt to show this line of thinking in relation to concepts of subjectivity, agency, and rights. Asad pays particular attention to claims that democractic politics alleviates human suffering. On one hand, he argues that suffering has not been reduced, but merely deflected onto alternate (often non-Western) targets and managed through a different aesthetic. On the other, he draws our attention toward ways in which secular logics refuse to permit certain kinds of "passionate" agency, which involve attributing meaning to pain (the key example here is religious asceticism, but he also discusses childbirth), but instead outlaw these as irrational and therefore unjustified.

Asad thus rephrases the dilemma often discussed as the clash between universal rights and minority rights by asking under which conditions some people come to be considered as minorities at all. Liberal secularism's claims to tolerance, he argues, will always reach a limit when the fundamental premises of its worldview are challenged; at this point, "minorities" are prevented from speaking about alternate realities, either by persuasion or by force.

Yet although he often seems to sympathize with the practitioners of counter-hegemonic ways of life in the modern world, those whose passionate and embodied experiences work against the grain of liberal rationalism, Asad has also argued for the preservation in political life of a reconstructed secularism (Asad 2001, p. 147; compare Bangstad 2009, p. 192), and he distances himself from the views of theologians and others for whom religion is a greater reality than secularism is. He dislikes, for instance, any arguments that suggest there may be an underlying and transformed religious component to apparently secular ideas including nationalism because, as he says, "I am arguing that 'the secular' should not be thought of as the space in which *real* human life gradually emancipates itself from the controlling power of 'religion' and thus achieves the latter's relocation" (Asad 2003, p. 191). Rather, he maintains that the contrast between religious and secular, like that between disenchantment and enchantment (but see Lambek 2005), is a false binary produced posthoc by the ideological lens through which the Western present views the past and elsewhere as premodern.

As in his earlier work on religion, Asad's interest in Foucault is evidenced by his particular attention to the constraining and productive powers of practice as well as of ideology; he writes, 'we should look to what makes certain practices conceptually possible, desired, mandatory—including the everyday practices by which the subject's experience is disciplined" (Asad 2003, p. 36). His own books, of course, are not first-hand ethnographies of such practices, but two of his former students have each responded to the call for such ethnography with widely admired results. Both anthropologists study the Islamic pietist movement in Egypt. Mahmood's densely considered book (2005) and her key articles (2001a,b) conduct an ethnographic examination of the women's piety movement in Cairo against the grain (as she tells us) of Mahmood's own secular progressivist and feminist assumptions about what female agency should be (Mahmood 2005, p. xi). The mosque movement Mahmood studies strikingly includes precisely the constituency of women—middle class and increasingly educated, often professional—who might be expected to adopt secular values (2005, p. 66). The movement is also innovative in allowing women to teach women on Islamic matters. While always allowing for the macropolitical context in which many Egyptians are critical of the post-Sadat secular government, and especially of its Western leanings, Mahmood finds narrowly political explanations inadequate; the aim of this movement is to become more pious. Although the dominance of secular logic makes it inevitable that alternative self-fashionings must engage state politics if they are to succeed, these ethical practices of self-fashioning are not reducible to their political means (2005, p. 194). These aims are pursued through a program of prayer that begins with the deliberate awakening of conscience and the rousing of the will, but whose success can be gauged by the degree to which prayer becomes an embodied desire and need in itself. Understanding such practices, Mahmood argues, facilitates a critique of many of the binaries through which the anthropology of religion may often be expressed, including the opposition between ritual and sponteneity and that between autonomous agency and subordination. Hirschkind's absorbing study (2006) similarly explores embodied disciplines within current Islam but focuses on the (male) use of cassette sermons and the distinctive practices of audition cultivated by their users.

These authors have sought to counter stereotypical views of Islamic pietism in the public debate on Islam and secular politics (Hirschkind & Mahmood 2002, and see interventions by each author at **http://www.theimmanentframe.org**). Their theoretical approaches do have limitations as well as gains, however. Mahmood attends to the comparative implications of the Egyptian case with respect to the construction of women's agency and identity politics (2005, chapter 5 and epilogue) but sometimes claims that a cross-cultural comparative approach to prayer and religious self-construction would inevitably mislead (2001b, p. 844). Despite his invocation of Mauss, Asad's own Foucauldian antiessentialism tends to produce a resistance to the search for similarities and a preference for the highlighting of irreducible differences across contexts. Connectedly, his focus on the contrast between the discontinuities of Christianity as an object and the potentialities of Islamic tradition sometimes appears as an inconsistency in his work and even risks reproducing the dualistic contrast between them, which he seeks to unravel (compare Bangstad 2009, Caton 2006).

In another vein is Bowen's recent research on French Islam, published as a lucid account of the development of the specific French state view of secularism, or *laicité*, and its consequences for the crisis over veiling in public schools (2008) and an ethnography of understandings of being Muslim and of being French (2009) in the suburbs of Paris, the location of the 2005 clashes between police and French Muslims. Bowen's first study brings to life the point made by many commentators: that there is wide variation between secularisms even within Europe. French *laicité* is grounded not only in the French Revolution's production of a particular idea of citizenship, but also in the extended efforts by the state to disentangle itself from reliance on French Catholic institutions, particularly in the field of education. In France, Bowen tells us, citizenship and the dignity of the individual are guaranteed by a certain compulsory Republican homogeneity of self-presentation in public domains, including all domains of public employment such as hospitals and schools. By contrast, variation of opinion on matters that may implicitly challenge Republican assumptions must be reserved to the private sphere. These are not merely theoretical issues; Bowen tells us that abstract and elite discourse is woven into media and popular debate in France to an unusual extent, defining the ways in which (for instance) documentary portrayals of French Muslims are produced and consumed. The French *affaire du voile* and the law that banned the wearing of religious signs in French schools may have conspicuously avoided the issues of the economic and social disadvantage of France's immigrant workforce, the legacy of colonialism, etc., but it did so through a deeply felt French horror of public displays of religious affiliation. Bowen argues that (as well as transgressing French feminism) headscarves were experienced by non-Muslim French people as a deliberate communication of difference and claim of (moral) superiority in a public context in which all should relate as equal citizens. It is for these historically constructed yet viscerally felt reasons, he argues, that the French state finds it so difficult to accommodate the claim of large numbers of people in the Parisian suburbs and elsewhere to identify themselves as both French citizens and visibly observant Muslims. Yet the reasons for wearing the veil among French schoolgirls are complex, highly various, and often less concerned with communication to non-Muslim others than with the production of a certain kind of self-formation.

Among other contributions, Hefner & Zaman's (2006) *Schooling Islam: The Culture and Politics of Modern Muslim Education* offers valuable comparisons from inside and outside Europe, with a clear-sighted introduction by Hefner, and these issues are usefully related to the public sphere debates by Taylor and others (Taylor et al. 2008).

INDIAN SECULARISM

Before the recent explosion of debates on Islam, however, secularism was already being considered comparatively in the context of Indian politics. This literature is especially thought provoking for anthropologists. Indian politicians and intellectuals almost universally remarked that secularism was an idea that devolved from European history and philosophy and was imported into India under British colonialism. Its relevance to the Indian situation could therefore not be assumed. This indigenous debate has shaped the academic literature on the subject, giving it helpful analytic purchase.

We may consider the current literature to have started with Smith's (1963) *India as a Secular Nation*, which took as its topic the observation made by the then-Indian President Dr. S. Radhakrishnan: "It may appear somewhat strange that our government should be a secular one, while our culture is rooted in spiritual values" (quoted in Smith 1963, p. 146). Smith explores a wide range of possible explanatory factors. Beginning with what he takes to be the central feature of Western secularism—that is, the historical assertion by the state of its autonomy from the church and religion—he reviews the major Asian religions to consider whether some would be more likely to provoke or tolerate parallel moves in Asian states. Smith concludes that Hinduism, with no centralized clerical institutions likely to compete with those of the state and with a cyclical view of history that does not encourage religious intervention in political fields, was indeed an unlikely precursor for secularism. Smith reviews the three central explanations (and justifications) offered for secularism in

India itself. First, he quotes the argument of many supporters of the Congress Party. All Indians must be able to commit to a civic identity not based on any religious precept so that the nation is not threatened by perceived differences between Hindu and Muslim. Second, there is the argument that Indian secularism rests largely on Western models and is rooted in British policies of religious neutrality. This view, like the first, tends to accompany a belief that state and religion must be separate if freedom of religion and equal rights are to be protected. The third view differs: It argues that ancient values of tolerance inherent in Hindu culture are the best guarantee of religious freedoms because Hinduism acknowledges that aspects of the universal divinity are discernible in all forms of worship. In this definition, secularism comes to be defined as a form of pluralism with metaphysical foundations and not, in any sense, as the replacement of religious values by irreligious ones. Smith himself leans toward the view that the separation of state and religion is a firmer defense against potential interreligious violence. He points to aspects of the Hindu formula that would not be acceptable to Muslims, Christians, and others (perhaps even Buddhists). Smith tends to link Western secularism with democratic modernity and progress.

His discussion was nevertheless prescient. It was only after the eruption in 1992 of Hindu fundamentalist violence at the Ayodhya mosque that writers turned again to the topic of Indian secularism. How had Hindu tolerance degenerated into the actions of the Rashtriya Swayamsevak Sangh (RSS) and other radical groups? Madan (1997) argued that fundamentalist movements in religions including Hinduism and (earlier) Islam and Sikhism were a response to the hidden intolerance of Western-style secularist policies. Madan is among a number of scholars who argue that the European Enlightenment was not simply a humane and liberating movement; it also contained oppressive potentials, in particular, the tendency to portray religious thinking as false with respect to science and the accompanying stereotyping of religious people as backward. Madan is somewhat sceptical of romantic views of Hinduism as perfectly tolerant. Hinduism may extend tolerance to other faiths, but encounters with Western objectifications of religion can awaken its own defensive, nationalist, and territorialist potentials. Western models of a state freed from religion cannot, in Madan's view, succeed in India. This ideal was "a gift of Christianity," specific to and only feasible within a particular European, post-Protestant context (Madan 1997, p. 754).

The founder of Indian independence and Indian secularism, Mahatma Gandhi, was, of course, a deeply religious Hindu who argued that faith-based respect for all religions was the best foundation for tolerance and peace in India. Gandhi argued that the state should not support any religious organization and that it should govern on areas of common citizen interest, permitting the free expression of religious practices. His successor Jawarharlal Nehru amended this position according to his own agnostic and progressive views. Nehru argued that India could be ruled only by a government that afforded equal protection and respect to those of all faiths and none and that the Indian Constitution should strive to afford equal protection to all its citizens. This objective, however, has frequently been in tension with India's personal laws, dating back to administrative arrangements resorted to in the British period. These allow for the application of different systems of Hindu law (also applicable to Jains, Sikhs, and Buddhists) and Muslim and Christian laws to issues such as marriage, divorce, caste, and other issues deemed religious. Determining and maintaining the boundary between religious and civil jurisdictions continue to be difficult, and the tension between Gandhian and Nehruvian visions of Indian secularism plays out in complex ways. Thus the Hindutva (Hinduness) Bharatiya Janata Party (BJP) has advocated the universal application of the civil code in questions of law and alimony, partly as an opportunistic strike against Muslims defending shari'a-based personal law in these contexts.

Mahajan (2003) provides a lucid statement of a Nehruvian position. He argues that the debate on Indian secularism has been falsely premised on a Western model of separation between state and religion. Secularism's critics (Madan 1987; Mitra 1991; Nandy 1985, 1992) claim that politics without religion is without moral basis; its advocates (e.g., Chatterji 1984, d'Souza 1985, Kumar 1989, Singh & Chandra 1985) insist that such a separation is a condition of continued democracy and civil rights. Mahajan does not agree that the separation of the state from religion can only occur in the West; this mindset merely underwrites essentialized distinctions between East and West. Mahajan argues that the state can guarantee civil freedom by affording equal protection to citizens of all faiths and none. In Mahajan's view, the Western attempt to make religion uncontentious by making it private cannot work (in India or the West) because religions require public expression. Such freedoms can be balanced only against the protection of other citizens case by historical case (Mahajan 2003, p. 934).

The range of this debate is considerable. Chatterjee (1993) tries to find a middle ground to resolve arguments for discarding and retaining the idea of Indian secularism. Among defenders of secularism, Corbridge & Harriss (2000) is an important critique; Beteille (1994) claims that Indian secularism has suffered from the "bad advocacy" of academics.

Indian secularism has also been importantly contextualized by recent works examining Hindu nationalism and religious revival. Fuller (1983, 2003) offers a revealing account of the revival in status of the priests of the Minakshi temple in Tamil Nadu, reversing an earlier sharp decline between independence and the late 1970s. Fuller lucidly demonstrates how misleading it would be to see the secular Indian state as simply antireligious. State clashes with the temple were driven by a combination of Congress Party commitment to the promotion of Harijan ("untouchable") rights of temple access and local Dravidian sentiment against North Indian Brahmanism. Conversely, the priests did not oppose state regulation of the temple per se, but they did contest the Indian government's representation of itself as heir to the local Nyata royal dynasty. As it happened, state modernization of priestly status via the demand for more formal education in the Agamic ritual texts has opened a path for priests' self-assertion. The robust confidence of the temple priests today is upheld by the recognition that although the revival of temple endowments by contemporary Indian politicians may sometimes be self-interested, it is necessitated by the atmosphere of heightened Hindu religious devotion among voters; there is thus no sense of religion moving out of the public sphere in this setting (compare Van der Veer 2001, Veer & Lehmann 1999). Chatterjee (1993) suggested that the category of religion became central to the imagination since colonialism of a distinctive Indian national culture by its elite, whereas Hansen (1999, p. 52) argues that early-twentieth-century nationalist claiming of religion as a transcendent moral space paved the way for its opportunistic annexation by the BJP. Like Fuller, each scholar notes an important impact of imported and indigenized understandings of secularism on historical developments, but they conclude that what happened in India cannot be fully conceptualized in terms of the workings of Western states. We may recall here Das's comment that Asad's definitions sometimes suffer from "a restricted notion of context" (Das 2006, p. 101). Asad's close focus on the history of the secular in the West, logical for his own project, means that he does not engage at length with polytheistic (or nontheistic) formations of religion or with the unexpected forms of secularity, which might emerge in such contexts.

It continues to prove difficult to separate the anthropological recognition of the asymmetrical history of colonialism from the assumption that modernity has an asymmetrical and homogeneous effect on tradition (Fuller 1984, 2003), or secularism on religion. As Spencer (1995) notes in a thoughtful review of Tambiah's (1992) account of Sinhala nationalism, these problems are heightened where religious violence is to be explained. The apparent paradox of aggressive nationalism promoted by Buddhist monks must steer between "unacceptable primordialism" and "unacceptable constructivism" (Spencer 1995, p. 358).

"A SECULAR AGE"

As Asad notes, debates on secularism were dominated for many years by writers in political science and political philosophy (e.g., Habermas 1992) whose interests had been in forms of justice, the definition and potentials of the public sphere, etc. These writers have not been concerned primarily with a radical critique of the concept or origin of secularism as such. Connolly (1999) and Taylor (2007) are clear exceptions, but Asad engages each of them on their divergences from his position rather than on their commonalities. Asad considers Taylor insufficiently critical of liberal democracies, especially their claims to be "direct-access" societies. Asad also suggests that, for Taylor, something like secularism is likely to accompany modern democratic states all over the world and may guarantee pluralism (Taylor 1999), which from Asad's point of view is a naïve and potentially dangerous formulation (Asad 2006). An astute close reading of these differences between Taylor and Asad is given in a recent article by Bangstad (2009), although Bangstad perhaps oversimplifies in claiming that Taylor views modern life as benign (Taylor 2007, p. 675).

Like Asad, Taylor sets out to deconstruct the notion of the secular. Unlike Asad, he does so with the premise that there may be something like a universal human search for religious experience, often defined by Taylor as a search for fullness of life. In this view, religious experience cannot be understood as an aspect of the transformations of (state) power and the forms of knowing these transformations permit. Taylor's position clearly differs from Weber's careful avoidance of truth claims about, or specific definitions of, religion. However, to an anthropologist, and for all the range of his philosophical sources (especially Hegel), Taylor's project often reads as an extended meditation on the Weberian concept of "disenchantment" (Weber 1946, 1963; Kippenberg 2005) in its interest in accounting for the phenomenology of modern Western experience of religion and secularity.

We earlier noted a tendency of classic secularization theory to exaggerate contrasts between a "relatively stable" (Bruce 2002, p. 8) European past where religion was "a single, moral universe" and a fragmented, unstable present. The plea is that, in a broad-brush argument, differences between periods in the past are relatively unimportant. This misleads not only because preindustrial European history was scarcely marked by social stasis, but also because the possibility of radical scepticism within the allegedly homogeneous lifeworlds of the traditional past has been charted by several historians (e.g., Fulton 2002, p. 65). It is a mistake to imply that religious pluralism is found only in modern contexts because the comparison with the pluralism of the ancient world is well known; Taylor, for instance, discusses it at length, evolving the argument that classical pluralism and atheism did not appeal to a mass audience, whereas European movements after humanism were able to do so (Taylor 2007, pp. 80–84). In fact, the more detailed historical information we have, the more complex it becomes to answer the central question Taylor himself sets: Why is it difficult to believe in God in the Western present, and why was it difficult not to at periods of the European past (Taylor 2007, p. 25)? For Taylor, it requires 896 pages to begin to trace the unfolding historical processes through which the modern secular came to be thinkable and to feel normal. He attempts to trace these transformations in the North Atlantic world (the heir to Latin Christianity), viewed not as the subtraction of illusion from reality but as the creation of new forms of experience that had never previously existed but which nonetheless come to seem like the obvious medium in which we live.

Taylor maintains that secularity did not develop in a simple linear fashion, but rather through a series of doublings-back, reprises and ironies that allow, even in modern times, for the existence of multiple strands of experience or "cross-pressures" (Taylor 2007, pp. 595, 772). Nevertheless, he picks a central strand, which he (sometimes) calls the Reform Master Narrative (p. 774). Although the long history of Reform goes back to at least the eleventh century (pp. 786 n.7; 92), he also picks a crucial period, including what we usually call the Reformation and Counter-Reformation (pp. 77ff) but centrally motivated by the previous (fifteenth) century, when heightened anxieties about death helped create the subsequent "rage for order." For Taylor, as for Dumont (1985) and again here recalling Weber (1946), the origins of the secular therefore do not only lie with developments in state politics, nor indeed with the Enlightenment, but with earlier developments in which Christian theology ironically played a crucial part (Taylor 2007, pp. 19, 75).

The vast synthetic reach of Taylor's text is a feature of his argument. He wishes to demonstrate that Christian belief and contemporary atheistic humanism are philosophical cousins, not irreconcilable opposites, and thus (contra Dawkins et al.) to restore the possibility that Christian thinking contributes to modern debate on equal terms. Taylor thus expresses sympathy for the views of the radical orthodox theologians including Milbank (1990) and Pickstock (1998), Milbank having argued some time ago that "once there was no secular; the secular as a domain had to be instituted or *imagined*" (Milbank 1990, p. 9, emphasis in original). Milbank's perspective differs from Taylor's in locating the crucial turn in Western thinking much earlier: in deformations of the theology of Augustine. Dumont (1985) and others have also suggested an early medieval turning point for the crucial developments of Western secularism. Taylor (2007) recognizes these views in an epilogue that argues for the validity of "the many stories" (p. 773). One consequent difficulty with Taylor's text is determining where exactly he differs from many of the authors he discusses or why some issues and approaches, which might seem equally consequential (such as the development of capitalist institutions), are discussed relatively little.

MANY STORIES?

Like Asad, although for different theoretical reasons, Taylor is concerned primarily with the origin of "the secular" as a Western historical phenomenon; however, as Indianists have clearly shown, what happens to such categories once exported is unpredictable, especially where the context is no longer a monotheistic faith.

At this juncture, anthropologists must surely contribute to the expansion of the repertoire of ethnographic studies of actual, lived situations (in the West and outside it) in which local peoples enact their understandings of, interest in, or perhaps total indifference to the secular and the religious.[1] Ethnographies of particular forms of secularism are now gradually increasing. Navaro-Yashin (2002) offers a thought-provoking account of the ways in which ordinary people experience the Turkish state. Constructed on a rhetoric of nationalist secularism that casts Islam as "unprogressive," the Turkish state nevertheless revolves around the "uncanny" cult of Kemal Ataturk, a hybrid conceiveable only within this particular view of religion. Navaro-Yashin charts the ways in which "fantasies for the state" (p. 155) are produced and reproduced in daily life, even through the idioms of cynicism that attempt to puncture its pretensions. Tambar (2009, p. 519) considers recent developments in Turkey, reviewing the ways in which secularism has become a populist movement that defines itself against an elite Islamic leadership and proceeds through the mechanism of the crowd as much as the vote.

An explicit discussion of secularism has begun among anthropologists of the formerly atheist Communist states. Feuchtwang (2009) compares Chinese and Indian secularisms, whereas McBrien & Pelkmans (2008) examine the ways in which secularism has come to be understood as a religion in post-Soviet Krygystan. Others have examined the view that modernity in African settings is typically religious (e.g., Meyer 1999).

At a different point of conjuncture to these debates, Palmié (2007) and Rutherford (2009) are among those scholars asking in what American secular experience might consist (compare Engelke 2009 on aspects of English secularism). Rutherford's argument—that the category of belief, which has lately been avoided by many anthropologists for its Christocentric bias, is actually a constitutive aspect of secular American understandings of action—underscores the current degree of disjuncture between the secularism debates and the more established literature on religious modernity, even including work on Christian fundamentalisms (e.g., Harding 1987, 1994, 2001). Perhaps this failure of engagement is, in part, a consequence of Asad's focus on the constitutive differences between Islam and Christianity, but it also appears to be part of a more general divergence of orientation. Although the anthropology of secularism still turns toward interdisciplinary interlocutors who consider themselves to be writing on politics, works such as Keane's provocative and fascinating *Christian Moderns* (2007 and see Cannell 2008) most obviously engage fellow anthropologists, still tolerant of the discussion of transformations of religion, kinship, and exchange. But if this debate reminds us of anything, it is that these categorical distinctions, particularly that between the apparently urgent world of the political and the seemingly arcane or private domain of the religious, are themselves only a fiction of the historical processes we are examining.

---

[1]One would welcome new perspectives on secularism and Judaism, Orthodox Christianity, and other faiths and practices not prominent in the current literature.

DISCLOSURE STATEMENT

The author is not aware of any affiliations, memberships, funding, or financial holdings that might be perceived as affecting the objectivity of this review.

ACKNOWLEDGMENTS

The author offers particular thanks to Chris Fuller and to Simon Jarvis.

LITERATURE CITED

Asad T. 1993. *Genealogies of Religion: Discipline and Reasons of Power in Christianity and Islam*. Baltimore, MD: Johns Hopkins Univ. Press

Asad T. 2001. Reading a Modern Classic; W.C. Smith's *The Meaning and End of Religion*. In *Religion and Media*, ed. H De Vries, S Weber, pp. 131–50. Stanford, CA: Stanford Univ. Press

Asad T. 2003. *Formations of the Secular: Christianity, Islam, Modernity*. Stanford, CA: Stanford Univ. Press

Asad T. 2006. Trying to understand French Secularism. In *Political Theologies: Public Religions in a Post-Secular World*, ed. H de Vries, LE Sullivan, pp. 494–526, 763–72. New York: Fordham Univ. Press

Bangstad S. 2009. Contesting Secularism(s): secularism and Islam in the work of Talal Asad'. *Anthropol. Theory* 9(2):188–208

Beattie T. 2007. *The New Atheists: The Twilight of Reason and the War on Religion*. London: Orbis

Benthall J. 2009. Review of "Beyond belief." *Times Lit. Suppl.* Dec. 9, pp. 3–5

Berger P. 1990 [1967]. *The Sacred Canopy*. New York: Anchor

Beteille A. 1994. Secularism and intellectuals. *Econ. Pol. Wkly.* 29:559–66

Bloch M. 2008. Why religion is nothing special, but is central. *Phil. Trans. R. Soc B* 363:2055–61

Bowen J. 2008. *Why the French Don't Like Headscarves: Islam, the State and Public Space*. Princeton, NJ: Princeton Univ. Press

Bowen J. 2009. *Can Islam be French? Pluralism and Pragmatism in Secularist State*. Princeton, NJ: Princeton Univ. Press

Boyer PL. 2001. *Religion Explained: The Human Instincts that Fashion Gods, Spirits and Ancestors*. London: Heinemann

Bruce S. 1996. *Religion in the Modern World: Cathedrals to Cults*. Oxford: Oxford Univ. Press

Bruce S. 2002. *God is Dead: Secularization in the West*. Oxford: Oxford Univ. Press

Cannell F. 2006. Introduction. In *The Anthropology of Christianity*, pp. 1–50. Durham, NC: Duke Univ. Press

Cannell F. 2008. Review of Keane, "Christian Moderns: Freedom and Fetish in the Mission Encounter." *Indonesia* 85:147–60

Casanova J. 1994. *Public Religions in the Modern World*. Chicago: Chicago Univ. Press

Casanova J. 2006. Secularization revisited: a reply to Talal Asad. In *Powers of the Secular Modern*, ed. D Scott, C Hirschkind, pp. 12–30. Stanford, CA: Stanford Univ. Press

Caton S. 2006. What is an "authorizing discourse"? See Hirschkind & Scott 2006, pp. 31–57

Chatterjee P. 1993. *The Nation and its Fragments: Colonial and Postcolonial Fragments*. Princeton, NJ: Princeton Univ. Press

Chatterji PC. 1984. *Secular Values for Secular India*. Delhi: L. Chatterji

Connolly W. 1999. *Why I Am Not a Secularist*. Minneapolis: Univ. Minn. Press

Corbridge S, Harriss J. 2000. *Reinventing India: Liberalization, Hindu Nationalism and Popular Democracy*. Cambridge, UK: Polity

Das V. 2006. Secularism and the argument from nature. See Hirschkind & Scott 2006, pp. 93–112

Davie G. 1994. *Britain Since 1945: Believing Without Belonging*. Oxford: Blackwell

Dawkins R. 2006. *The God Delusion*. Boston: Houghton and Miffin

Dobellaere K. 1998. Secularization. In *Encyclopedia of Religion and Society*, ed. WH Swatos Jr. London: Sage. **http://hirr.hartsem.edu/ency/secularization.htm**

D'Souza PR. 1985. The church and politics. In *Secularism and Liberation: Perspectives and Strategies for India*. ed. RC Heredia, E Mathias. New Delhi: Ind. Soc. Inst.

Dumont L. 1985. A modified view of our origins: the Christian beginnings of modern individualism. In *The Category of the Person: Anthropology, Philosophy, History*, ed. M Carrithers, S Collins, S Lukes, pp. 93–122. Cambridge, UK: Cambridge Univ. Press

Durkheim E. 1971 [1915]. *The Elementary Forms of the Religious Life*. London: George Allen & Unwin

Eagleton T. 2009. *Reason, Faith and Revolution: Reflections on the God Debate*. New Haven/London: Yale Univ. Press

Engelke M. 2009. Strategic secularism: Bible advocacy in England. *Soc. Anal.* 53(1):39–51

Feuchtwang S. 2009. India and China as spiritual nations: a comparative anthropology of histories. In *Anthropology of Contemporary China*, ed. F Pieke. *Soc. Anthropol.* 19(1):100–8

Fuller C. 1984. *Servants of the Goddess: The Priests of a South Indian Temple*. Cambridge, UK: Cambridge Univ. Press

Fuller C. 2003. *The Renewal of the Priesthood: Modernity and Traditionalism in a South Indian Temple*. Princeton, NJ: Princeton Univ. Press

Fulton R. 2002. *From Judgment to Passion: Devotion to Christ and the Virgin Mary, 800–1200*. New York: Columbia Univ. Press

Habermas J. 1992. *The Structural Transformation of the Public Sphere*. London: Polity

Hansen T. 1999. *The Saffron Wave: Democracy and Hindu Nationalism in Modern India*. Princeton, NJ: Princeton Univ. Press

Harding S. 1987. Convicted by the Holy Spirit: the rhetoric of fundamental Baptist conversion. *Am. Ethnol.* 14(1):167–81

Harding S. 1994. Imagining the last days: the politics of apocalyptic language. In *Accounting for Fundamentalisms: The Dynamic Character of Movements*, ed. M Marty, RS Appleby, pp. 57–78. Chicago: Chicago Univ. Press

Harding S. 2001. *The Book of Jerry Falwell: Fundamentalist Language and Politics*. Princeton, NJ: Princeton Univ. Press

Heelas P. 1996. *The New Age Movement: The Celebration of the Self and the Sacralization of Modernity*. Oxford, UK: Blackwell

Heelas P. 2008. *Spiritualities of Life: New Age Romanticism and Consumptive Capitalism*. Malden/Oxford: Blackwell

Heelas P, Woodhead L, Seel B, Tusting K, Szerszynski B. 2004. *The Spiritual Revolution: Why Religion Is Giving Way to Spirituality*. London: Wiley Blackwell

Hefner R, Zaman MQ, eds. 2006. *Schooling Islam: The Culture and Politics of Modern Muslim Education*. Princeton, NJ: Princeton Univ. Press

Hirschkind C. 2006. *The Ethical Soundscape: Cassette Sermons and Islamic Counterpublics*. New York: Columbia Univ. Press

Hirschkind C, Mahmood S. 2002. Feminism, the Taliban, and politics of counter-insurgency. *Anthropol. Q.* 75(2):339–54

Hirschkind C, Scott D, eds. 2006. *Power of the Secular Modern: Talal Asad and his Interlocutors*. Stanford, CA: Stanford Univ. Press

Keane W. 2007. *Christian Moderns: Freedom and Fetish in the Mission Encounter*. Berkeley: Univ. Calif. Press

Kippenberg HG. 2005. Religious continuities and the path to disenchantment: the origin, sources and theoretical core of the religion section. In *Max Weber's "Economy and Society": A Critical Companion*, ed. C Camic, PS Gorski, DM Trubek, pp. 164–82. Stanford, CA: Stanford Univ. Press

Kumar R. 1989. *The Making of a Nation: Essays in Indian History and Politics*. Delhi: Manohar

Lambek M. 2005. Review of Talal Asad, *Formations of the Secular*. *Am. Anthropol.* 107(2):276–77

Luckmann T. 1970. *The Invisible Religion: The Problem of Religion in Modern Society*. New York: MacMillan

Luhmann N. 1982. *Religious Dogmatics and the Evolution of Societies*, transl. P Beyer. New York: Mellen

Luhrmann T. 1989. *Persuasions of the Witch's Craft: Ritual Magic in Contemporary England*. Oxford: Blackwell

Madan TN. 1987. Secularism in its place. *J. Asia Stud.* 46(4):747–58

Madan TN. 1997. *Modern Myths: Locked Minds: Secularism and Fundamentalism in India*. Delhi: Oxford Univ. Press

Mahajan G. 2003. Secularism. In *The Oxford India Companion to Sociology and Social Anthropology*, ed. V Das, pp. 908–36. Oxford/New York: Oxford Univ. Press

Mahmood S. 2001a. Feminist theory, embodiment and the docile agent: some reflections on the Egyptian Islamic Revival. *Cult. Anthropol.* 6(2):202–36

Mahmood S. 2001b. Rehearsed sponteneity and the conventionality of ritual: disciplines of salat. *Am. Ethnol.* 28(4):827–53

Mahmood S. 2005. *The Politics of Piety: The Islamic Revival and the Feminist Subject*. Princeton, NJ: Princeton Univ. Press

Martin D. 2005. *On Secularization: Towards a Revised Theory*. Aldershot, UK: Ashgate

McBrien J, Pelkmans M. 2008. Turning Marx on his head: missionaries, "extremists" and archaic secularists in Post-Soviet Krygyzstan. *Crit. Anthropol.* 28:87–103

Milbank J. 1990. *Theology and Social Theory: Beyond Secular Reason*. Oxford: Blackwell

Mitra SK. 1991. Desecularising the State: religion and politics in India after independence. *Comp. Stud. Soc. Hist.* 33(4):755–77

Meyer B. 1999. *Translating the Devil: Religion and Modernity among the Ewe in Ghana*. Edinburgh: Edinburgh Univ. Press

Nandy A. 1985. An antisecularist manifesto. *Seminar* 315:1–12

Nandy A. 1992. The politics of secularism and the recovery of religious tolerance. In *Mirrors of Violence: Communities, Riots and Survivors in South Asia*, ed. V Das, pp. 69–93. Delhi: Oxford Univ. Press

Navaro-Yashin Y. 2002. *Faces of the State: Secularism and Public Life in Turkey*. Princeton, NJ: Princeton Univ. Press

Palmié S. 2007. Genomics, divination, "racecraft". *Am. Ethnol.* 34:203–20

Parsons T. 1960. *Structure and Process in Modern Society*. New York: Free Press

Parsons T. 1971. Introduction. See Weber 1963, pp. iii–lxxiv

Pickstock C. 1998. *After Writing: On the Liturgical Consummation of Philosophy*. Oxford: Blackwell

Pike S. 2001. Desert goddesses and apocalyptic art: making sacred space at the Burning Man Festival. In *God in the Details: American Religion in Popular Culture*, ed. K McCarthy, EM Mazur, pp. 155–76. New York: Routledge

Rutherford D. 2009. *An absence of belief?* Posting on *Christian Moderns* in The Immanent Frame; secularism, religion and the public sphere. **http://blogs.ssrc.org/tif/2009/12/01/an-absence-of-belief/**

Singh K, Chandra B. 1985. *Many Faces of Communalism*. Delhi: Voice of India

Smith DE. 1963. *India as a Secular State*. Princeton, NJ: Princeton Univ. Press

Smith G. 1980. *A Short History of Secularism*. London: Tauris

Spencer J. 1995. The past in the present in Sri Lanka: a review article. *Comp. Stud. Soc. Hist. I* 37(2):358–67

Tambar K. 2009. Secular populism and the semiotics of the crowd in Turkey. *Public Cult.* 21(3):517–37

Tambiah S. 1992. *Buddhism Betrayed? Religious Politics and Violence in Sri Lanka*. Chicago: Chicago Univ. Press

Taylor C. 1999. Two theories of modernity. *Public Cult.* 11:153–74

Taylor C. 2007. *A Secular Age*. Cambridge, MA/London: Belknap Press of Harvard Univ. Press

Taylor C, Levey B, Modood T, eds. 2008. *Secularism, Religion and Multicultural Citizenship*. Cambridge, UK: Cambridge Univ. Press

Van Der Veer P. 2001. *Imperial Encounters: Religion and Modernity in India and Britain*. Princeton, NJ: Princeton Univ. Press

Van Der Veer P, Lehmann H, eds. 1999. *Nation and Religion*. Princeton, NJ: Princeton Univ. Press

Weber M. 1946 [1918]. Science as a vocation. In *From Max Weber: Essays in Sociology*, transl./ed. HH Gerth, C Wright Mills, pp. 129–56. New York: Oxford Univ. Press

Weber M. 1963. *The Sociology of Religion*, transl. E Fischer. London: Beacon

Weber M. 1976 [1905]. *The Protestant Ethic and the Spirit of Capitalism*. London: Allen Unwin

Wilson B. 1966. *Religion in Secular Society*. London: Watts

The Commodification of Language

Monica Heller

CREFO, OISE, University of Toronto, Toronto, Ontario M5S 1V6, Canada;
email: monica.heller@utoronto.ca

Annu. Rev. Anthropol. 2010. 39:101–14

The *Annual Review of Anthropology* is online at
anthro.annualreviews.org

This article's doi:
10.1146/annurev.anthro.012809.104951

Key Words

new economy, globalization, neoliberalism, market, multilingualism

Abstract

Although language can always be analyzed as a commodity, its salience
as a resource with exchange value has increased with the growing importance of language in the globalized new economy under the political
economic conditions of late capitalism. This review summarizes how
and in which ways those conditions have a commodifying effect on language and focuses on contemporary tensions between ideologies and
practices of language in the shift from modernity to late modernity. It
describes some of these tensions in key sites: tourism, marketing, language teaching, translation, communications (especially call centers),
and performance art.

WHAT IS MEANT BY COMMODIFICATION OF LANGUAGE? WHY WORRY ABOUT IT NOW?

Publications on the subject of the commodification of language have recently increased, including an edited volume devoted entirely to the subject (Tan & Rubdy 2008). This review article is, of course, also a product of this upsurge. One could argue that we could always have analyzed language in many ways using those terms. Why, then, has attention increased now?

Indeed, Bourdieu (1977, 1982) pointed to the many ways in which language forms part of the symbolic capital that can be mobilized in markets as interchangeable with forms of material capital. How one speaks and writes is one basis for deciding one's worth as a scholar, an employee, or a potential marriage partner. Gal (1989) and Irvine (1989) also argued that the study of language needs to be framed in terms of not only the making of meaning, of social categories (or identities), and of social relations, but also the political economic conditions that constrain the possibilities for making meaning and social relations. They further argue that these conditions underlie ideologies of language and therefore help explain why certain linguistic forms and practices play the role they do in the production and reproduction of the social order and of the moral order that legitimates it. Language, in this view, is not a reflection of the social order but is part of what makes it happen; in that sense, we cannot abstract away from the value attached to linguistic forms and practices or from their links to all kinds of social activities and to the circulation of resources of all kinds that social order mediates.

However, the recent interest in language as commodity points to a specific and emergent form of this exchange value and requires explanation on two levels. One level relates to the extent to which forms of exchange (standardized language for jobs, for example) that used to be treated discursively as matters of breeding, taste, intellectual competence, good schooling, or rational thought are now treated as directly exchangeable for material goods, and, especially, for money. The other concerns the extent to which the circulation of goods that used to depend (mainly or exclusively) on the deployment of other kinds of resources now depends on the deployment of linguistic resources (for example, in some areas getting a job used to depend on physical strength, but now many jobs require communicative skills instead).

Both of these levels are generally understood to be a feature of late capitalism. Put more generally, what we are witnessing is not a rupture with the ideology of language as a whole, bounded system, consistent with the territorial boundaries of the nation-state and the historical continuity of a putatively culturally (and, often, genetically) unified population, and repository of its distinct worldview, but rather an appropriation and extension of that ideology under new conditions that test the limits of its capacity to explain and orient social activity (Heller 2003, Pujolar 2007). We see this shift, for example, in the way struggles over social difference and social inequality on the terrain of language move away from political frames and toward economic ones, changing the nature of discourses that legitimize power and the nature of criteria used in social selection, and therefore also having an impact on the constraints on access to symbolic and material resources for actors occupying different social positions (Fairclough 2002, 2006; Urciuoli 2008). But because this shift emerges out of the expansion of existing political economies rather than from the creation of radically new ones, commodification remains in tension with formerly dominant liberal tropes of language, culture, citizenship, and nation (Bauman & Briggs 2003, Budach et al. 2003, Alsagoff 2008, Wee 2008, Silva & Heller 2009).

Finally, current shifts commodify languages in two, often competing ways: as a technical skill, manageable through taylorist techniques invented for industrialization (Cameron 2001, 2005), and as a sign of authenticity (Coupland 2003a), useful as added value for niche markets and for distinguishing among standardized products that have saturated markets (Bishop et al. 2005, Jaworski & Pritchard 2005, Comaroff & Comaroff 2009, McLaughlin et al. 2010). This leads to competition over who defines what counts as legitimate and commodifiable language, over what counts as such, and over who controls the production and distribution of linguistic resources (Heller & Boutet 2006).

The following section of this review discusses the nature of the changes in late capitalism (or high or late modernity) that led to these forms of commodification of language. Specifically, I review the argument that late capitalism consists of the expansion of markets and their progressive saturation, resulting in an increased importance for language in (*a*) managing the flow of resources over extended spatial relations and compressed space-time relations, (*b*) providing symbolic added value to industrially produced resources, (*c*) facilitating the construction of and access to niche markets, and (*d*) developing linguistically mediated knowledge and service industries.

The third section discusses the ways in which these processes are tied to struggles to preserve neocolonial relations on new grounds, that is, how relations of power established earlier in the political, social, and cultural terms characteristic of colonialism and the immediate postcolonial period are being recast in economic terms to relegitimize and preserve them. The national and imperial markets set up in previous centuries still operate, but they are reframed as collaborative rather than hierarchical and as aimed at economic development and competition rather than at servicing the nation or the imperial center. This act requires the erasure of the problem of who defines the value of linguistic commodities or, more broadly, of who regulates the market.

The fourth section focuses on the tensions between standardization and variability in the space between language-as-skill and language-as-identity, both of which are commodifiable in the globalized new economy. This tension represents a gap, or troubled space of contradiction, between established nationalist

discursive regimes and emergent destabilizations of those regimes. The literature certainly provides evidence of new ways of producing late capitalist subjectivities focused on performances (notably communicative ones) as skills that are marketable commodities rather than as expressions of true selves or of relatively good or poor accomplishments of socially located personae (whether within broad categories such as gender, class, or race or within kinship, institutional, political, religious, or other structures, such as femininity, or fatherhood, or adolescence, etc.). It also provides evidence of tensions around this shift, notably in the zone around attempts to use the taylorist techniques of industrial management to regulate and measure the value of linguistic skills at the same time that older regimes of authenticity are brought in to play in the same endeavor (think, for example, of the native speaker as the gold standard of language learning) or, alternatively, in the development of niche markets and their servicing. These tensions are visible in strategies used to manage them, from the concatenation of forms from formerly distinct spheres in a blurring of boundaries variously labeled hybridity, multiplicity, complexity, polynomia, metrolingualism, or transnationalism, just to give some examples; compartmentalization; irony and other distancing stance mechanisms; and transgression.

The fifth section examines how these processes play out in key language-centered economic spaces characteristic of the globalized new economy (tourism; marketing; language teaching; translation; communications, call centers in particular; and performance art). The case studies cited in this section provide much of the empirical material that serves as a basis for making or testing some of the claims made in the fourth section; these studies are also windows into the processes discussed in the second and third sections.

The final section uses this overview to raise questions about what it means for linguistic anthropology to confront these new forms and practices in terms of both its theoretical framework and its methodological tools. It focuses in particular on how it has become necessary to engage with the ways in which the processes of late capitalism call into question some foundational ideas about linguistic systems and cultural communities as relatively fixed and bounded, producing some alternative approaches centered on practices, speakers, resources, processes, and mobility.

LANGUAGE IN LATE CAPITALISM

The literature on late capitalism and high modernity points to specific features of the globalized new economy that, commentators have argued, lead to an increasingly central economic role for language, both as the means through which work is accomplished (the work process) and as a product of labor (the work product). The interlocked features in question include (a) capitalist expansion or globalization, requiring the management of communication (involving producers, consumers, and national or supranational regulating bodies) across linguistic difference; (b) computerization of the work process, requiring new kinds of language and literacy skills among workers; (c) the growth of the service sector, in largely communication-based form; and (d) responses to the saturation of markets in the form of the development of niche markets (which require localized approaches often including a focus on linguistic specificity) and of the use of symbolic, often linguistic, resources to add value to standardized products.

Theorists of the globalized new economy, such as Giddens (1990), Harvey (1989), Appadurai (1996), and Castells (2000), have argued that the contemporary era is not in rupture with industrial-era modernity, but rather represents its logical continuation. If the central trope of capitalism is growth, then expansion and intensification are unsurprising effects. One particular issue, however, is concerned with the regulation of expanded and intensified economic conditions, given that industrial-era modernity was predicated on markets regulated by the nation-state. The standardized

and vernacular languages (or dialects, patois, etc.) created by the discursive formation of the nation-state now therefore find themselves in greater conjunction as the "time-space compression," as Harvey terms it, of intensified and expanded exchange produces breaches in formerly less permeable boundaries, and as the networks described by Castells or the flows and scapes proposed by Appadurai allow for the penetration of those breaches or the evasion of those boundaries (Coupland 2003b). In addition, Castells argues, making these flows happen requires more communicative work than the industrial-era economy required, involving a greater proportion and number of workers. This development is linked, in part, to the outsourcing and off-shoring of the two central features of modern economies: the extraction of primary resources and their industrial transformation.

Gee et al. (1996) have argued that one of the ways in which global expansion was facilitated was through the application of computerized technologies; others (Horst & Miller 2006) have argued that communicative technologies, such as the cell phone, have also played an important role. In both cases, work itself, and the wide variety of activities involved in sustaining the relationships on which the circulation of resources depends, now requires degrees and forms of literacy new to our era.

Off-shoring has also opened up space in the First World for work aimed not just at managing the globalized production and circulation of industrialized goods, but also at producing resources aimed at an increasingly saturated market. Intensification takes the form of pressures toward adding value to goods; this added value can be symbolic as well as material. Sometimes a comb made by hand in Amazonia is worth more than a comb inlaid with gold, and sometimes consuming experiences is more valuable than consuming goods. Intensification is also manifested in the development of niche markets, in which it makes sense to sell targeted products at higher values. In both cases (symbolic added value and niche markets), as discussed below, older nation-state ideologies of language, identity, and culture are appropriated and mobilized in the commodification of authenticity, notably in tourism. T-shirts with linguistic forms indexing English are also popular items in many parts of the world, as are Chinese-language tattoos or multilingual yogurt labels. (The mocking they engender is symptomatic of the tension between old and new discursive regimes.)

One important result of the many ways in which communication in general, and language and multilingualism in particular, has become central to the globalized new economy is the emergence of language work, and therefore of the language worker (Boutet 2001, 2008, Heller & Boutet 2006, Duchêne 2009). Communication is more involved in moving people and goods around, that is, as part of the work process, but information in linguistic form (think call centers, translations, localization) and language as a form of commodified authenticity are also equally products of work.

In the next section, we look at some of the dilemmas the globalized new economy poses for the nation-state, with a focus on some strategies neo-liberal states have developed to mobilize linguistic capital in the preservation of neo-colonial relations.

NEW FORMS OF EMPIRE? OR THE OLD EMPIRE IN NEW CLOTHES?

Linguistic anthropological literature on postcolonialism often focuses on problems connected to the management of multilingualism by postcolonial elites or on the ways in which former colonial powers have used cultural aspects of language to legitimize continued influence. However, the issues raised above point to a new set of concerns, specifically some newer ways in which former colonial powers explicitly attempt to reconstitute their former empires as economic markets and to recast the former language of empire as a neutral and equitable means for gaining access to the global economy.

Among the earliest critiques of globalization are those about the use of English by British and American corporations to open up markets and create consumers, indeed, to eliminate competition and impose the tastes and habits of the English-speaking world on the rest of the planet in ways that, not coincidentally, leave control of products and their circulation squarely in the hands of British and American English-speaking citizens; this process is often referred to as "McDonaldization." Phillipson (1992) undertook a detailed critique of the work of the British Council in particular in facilitating such expansion, showing how agencies of the state initially invented as agents of postindependence neocolonialism could be mobilized to good effect in this new form of neo-colonialism (neo-neo-colonialism?) based on market share rather than on the *mission civilisatrice* or development work. Texts such as Pennycook (1994, 1998), Canagarajah (1999), Makoni & Meinhof (2003), Lin & Martin (2005), and Tupas (2008) have pursued this line of inquiry, asking difficult questions about what the possibilities may be for appropriation and resistance and what the consequences are for the formation of postcolonial subjectivities. This inquiry has led to heated debate, particularly in applied linguistics, where the issue of what it means to teach a language, or to be a speaker of that language, is framed increasingly in these political economic terms (Singh 1998, Block & Cameron 2002, Kubota 2002, Pomerantz 2002, Shin 2006, Liddicoat 2007, Martin-Jones et al. 2009, Park 2009; see Language Teaching, below).

Similar work has been done for the Spanish-speaking world (Mar-Molinero & Stewart 2006), notably on the Instituto Cervantes, Spain's corollary agency to the British Council (alongside, of course, the Alliance française, the Goethe Institut, the Japan Foundation, and, most recently, China's Confucius Institute). [See Delamotte (1999) on the economic role of the Alliance française in Brazil; on postnationalism, language, and the francophone world, see Dubois et al. (2006), Moïse (2006), Heller (2010).]

Del Valle (2005, 2006; del Valle & Villa 2006) has turned his attention to the mobilization not of such paragovernmental cultural agencies but of recently privatized corporations in such sectors as the media or transportation. These also, of course, played an important role in state unification and centralization, and now seek to establish new markets in areas of the former empire on the basis of shared language. Thus, the shared language imposed by colonialism becomes available for the maintenance of privileged market control and access under new conditions. Under these conditions, however, legitimacy can no longer be framed in terms of the greater value of the language of the empire, or its greater suitability for the activities of civilization or modernity, but rather in terms of democratic access to a shared market that can respond better to the specific needs and interests of Spanish-speaking producers and consumers than can its English-speaking global competitors. However, the English-language market is sometimes approached from the position of the added value (usually exotic in some way) of producers and products from the non-English-speaking world, drawing on old stereotypes about German efficiency, Italian design expertise, or French romance (Kelly-Holmes 2005; see Marketing and Advertising, below).

The work that needs to be done in the neo-neo-colonial project is thus focused less on the language teaching and translation that was the hallmark of earlier forms of empire (although those remain) than on relegitimizing those activities and constructing new subjectivities (Gal & Woolard 2001, Urciuoli 2008). Equally important and difficult is the work of managing the debates about what counts as legitimate English (or Spanish, or French, or Portuguese) and who defines it—debates opened up by reframing colonial relations on a supposedly more equitable basis and by extending the construction of consumers beyond the former colonial elite necessitated by the expansion of capital. Finally, as former colonial powers argue for multilingualism as a way to resist the domination of English, they open themselves up to similar claims from within their own putative zones of

influence and are obliged as much as anyone to cope with the management of multilingual networks of production and niche markets.

STANDARDIZATION, VARIABILITY, AND AUTHENTICITY

The previous sections have outlined some of the ways in which the globalized new economy provokes tensions between standardization and variability and triggers debates over which kinds of language, and which kinds of speakers, have legitimacy or authority, or value as commodities, under these new conditions. Although former languages of empire retain value as a means of controlling far-flung and complex networks, niche markets and symbolically added value introduce linguistic variability, both for managing workers and for selling products. Neo-liberal emphases on flattened hierarchies and flexibility open up the possibilities for staking claims for the value not only of a wide range of linguistic resources but also for the very possibility of being able to navigate them expertly (Gee et al. 1996; McEwan-Fujita 2005, 2008).

An increasingly strong literature on world Englishes (Bhatt 2001, Melchers & Shaw 2003, Rubdy & Saraceni 2006) and the foundation of a journal of that title attest to the by now well-organized claims to redistributing the locus of legitimacy of the language formerly known as English. These efforts can be read as attempts at staking a claim to legitimate participation in a global market on multiple terms. The long-standing debates between France and Quebec over who owns French (Deshaies & Ouellon 1998, Moïse 2006, Heller 2010) also opened the door to similar decentralization in the French-speaking world. It seems increasingly possible to appropriate Marcellesi's ideas about "polynomia" (allowing for multiple coexisting sources of authority regarding linguistic legitimacy; Marcellesi 1989). His idea was originally developed to resolve the contradiction between constructing a Corsican language that could resist the imposition of French on its own terms (that is, serve as an alternate basis for state-building) and yet still resonate in the ears of Corsican speakers who attach legitimacy to authenticity and authenticity to local ties (Jaffe 1999a). However, his idea now makes sense to speakers far beyond the borders of Corsica who are caught in a similar dilemma, albeit from a somewhat different source.

By the same token, countries formerly concentrated on building their own monolingual nation-states now explore a variety of ways of promoting multilingualism, whether for ease of navigation across national boundaries in supranational polities and markets such as the European Union or simply to compete on global markets (Extra & Gorter 2008, Francheschini 2009). Of course, this new affection for multilingualism mainly concerns access to English, but it also has room to develop commodifiable local or regional authenticities (Alcaras et al. 2001, Pujolar 2006, Le Menestrel 1999). It is also a terrain of struggle because its distribution is usually unequal (and inequitable). In the European Union, for example, the burden of bilingualism is usually borne by the managers of Eastern European branches of Western European companies in search of cheap materials and cheap labor (Nekvapil & Nekula 2006, Nekvapil & Sherman 2009), just as was the case in the internal colonial regimes of Western Europe (Hechter 1975, McDonald 1990) and the colonial regimes of Africa, Asia, and the Americas (Irvine 2001, Errington 2008).

Dilemmas also arise in the management of linguistic resources and practices in everyday life, especially in the world of language work. Attempts to import standardized, taylorist modes of management into the regulation of language-focused work processes and work products encounter both forms of linguistic variability that are simply hard to standardize and conflicting ideologies of the new service economy that emphasize employee flexibility (and hence variability) and niche marketing (hence meeting expectations of customers constituted as variable consumers). Language has been as subjected to taylorist regimes of regulation as have other forms of work, especially through language standardization. However,

as Boutet (2008) points out, taylorist regulation of language usually meant suppressing its use; industrial workers were not expected to talk and were even punished for doing so. Schoolchildren are taught not to interrupt and to leave their minority language at home (if even that). The globalized new economy tries, as discussed in greater detail in the next section, to apply taylorist regulation to language, not always comfortably; and it does so even as, in an echo of the generalized contradictions of late capitalism, it attempts to encourage workers to be flexible, to respond to the specific needs of niche markets, and to manage the movement of resources across linguistically diverse spaces. The commodification of language confronts monolingualism with multilingualism, standardization with variability, and prestige with authenticity in a market where linguistic resources have gained salience and value.

The next section examines empirical ethnographic work in some specific areas of the globalized new economy, work that illustrates the points raised in the previous sections and constitutes much of the empirical basis for it. It considers some reasons why recent work has been concentrated in these areas, reasons concerning economic importance (for example, tourism is often cited as one of the fastest-growing industries today); symbolic importance regarding current shifts (for example, call centers are highly charged symbols of the shift from industrial, white, masculine, working-class first-world culture to feminized and racialized, off-shore production); and discursive importance as sites of reimagining legitimizing discourses of identity.

SPECIFIC FIELDS

This section focuses on five areas of particular salience for illustrating the ways in which the commodification of language is tied to late capitalism, as well as some of the tensions and contradictions of commodifying language. Some, like tourism, translation, marketing, and language teaching, have been around for a long time and had particular forms and values as products of modernity. Today, they are increasingly involved in the symbolic dimensions of added value (notably in tourism and marketing), in the distribution of commodified linguistic resources (as in language teaching), or both (translation). Call centers are canonical sites of the globalized new economy, producing and distributing information. The attention they attract from the media and from comedians reveals the many ways in which they function as condensation symbols for the tensions of globalization. Finally, performance art serves more directly for the expression of these tensions, commodifying language while critiquing the alienation that it produces, claiming the local and the authentic on a global market for world music, and hybridizing linguistic forms beyond recognition within a globally recognized performance genre.

Tourism

Tourism is one of the canonical growth activities of the globalized new economy (Rojek and Urry 1997). As an industry, tourism has gone from the standardized product (e.g., the package tour) focusing on leisure, to niche markets focusing on heritage, experience (e.g., extreme sports), and the environment. It has become attractive to economically peripheral regions, which are also those from which linguistic minorities were produced by forms of state nationalism inherited from the nineteenth century, and who now seek to commodify politically produced identities (Macdonald 1997, Coupland et al. 2005, Rinaudo 2005). This process is not without its own contradictions because the commodification of forms of language and culture produced under industrial modernity must face new audiences, new publics, and new Others when mobilized as sources of profit. This can be felt as a tension between authenticity and alienation (Taylor 2001), whether in individual subjectivity (Bunten 2008) or more broadly within the frame of a problem of redefining collective projects of political empowerment into projects

of economic development (Phillips 2000, Roy & Gélinas 2004, Moïse et al. 2006, Malaborza & McLaughlin 2008, Heller & Pujolar 2009).

Marketing and Advertising

In much the same way as with call centers, language has become central to niche marketing and to the localization dimensions of globalization (Kelly-Holmes 2000, 2005). In particular, it addresses the linguistic and cultural specificities often found in heritage tourism (as a means of both adding value to products and reaching niche markets), as well as the forms of multilingualism symbolic of globalized cosmopolitanism (Sengès 2003, Bishop et al. 2005, Piller 2007). Finally, language emerges as a central element in the marketing of new forms of globalized circulation, notably the market for female labor and intimacy (as domestic servants, caregivers, or wives; Piller & Takahashi 2006).

Language Teaching

Through the various ways in which language has acquired centrality in the work process and work products of the new economy, language has become a commodity itself and, therefore, acts as a resource to be produced, controlled, distributed, valued, and constrained. Language teaching has become increasingly more about this kind of process, as it becomes involved in attempts to control what counts as legitimate language and who count as legitimate speakers of any given language, whether regarding varieties of what is usually considered one language (Urciuoli 2008) or in terms of access to various multilingual repertoires (Martin-Jones 2007). The tension between the ideology of language as a technical, universally available skill and the ideology of language as tied to identity and to individual talent is most evident in this field (Jaffe 2001, Block & Cameron 2002).

One manifestation of this tension is the growth of the language-teaching industry, in particular in the form of what Yarymowich (2005) terms "language edutourism." This notion is described as tourism for the purpose of appropriating authentic linguistic resources or of longer-term forms of language learning–related migration that stem from class-related strategies for the building of multilingual repertoires for access to global markets as well as to local ones affected by globalization. As Park (2009) and Shin (2009) have shown in their analyses of the Korean linguistic marketplace, understanding this phenomenon requires examination of the complex interrelations of regional class dynamics and the globalized linguistic market. A second important manifestation is debate over national and supranational language education policy, especially as it relates to bilingual education (Phillipson 2003, Martin-Jones 2007).

Translation

Translation as an activity also grew out of modern ideas about ethnonational boundaries and how to manage them (Jaffe 1999b). Some countries, such as Canada, long accustomed to such boundary maintenance, now seek to commodify their expertise in the service of the management of the more complex boundary crossing required in the new economy: for example, by promoting the development of language industries as an alliance of translators, language-teaching institutions, and developers of translation technologies (Gov. Canada 2003, Silva et al. 2007). As a field, translation is also experiencing the tension between attempts at introducing taylorist management practices (notably through technology, through speech recognition, and through machine translation) and constructing translation as a form of cultural practice (Cronin 2003, Simon 2006), processes increasingly of interest to ethnographers seeking to determine how translation operates as a site of struggle over who controls what counts as legitimate language and over who controls what counts as knowledge (Sturge 2007, LeBlanc 2008).

Call Centers

Call centers, those outsourced, off-shored, centralized service and information distributors, have been among the most heavily publicized forms of new economy activity, generating dozens of newspaper and television reports, as well as documentaries (Stitt 2002, Addelman 2005, Golati 2005, Belkhodja 2006) and even a feature film (Jeffcoat 2007), not to mention more new media satires than one might imagine (one can simply do a search on **http://www.youtube.com** to find such material). From a first-World center perspective, call centers condense many of the threats entailed in off-shoring, feminizing, and racializing labor as symbols of shifts from an emphasis on production of material goods to production of information and communications-mediated services. The disembodied voice has thus become a kind of condensation symbol for anxieties about the globalized new economy, notably regarding the loss of economic control on the part of the nation-state and of those who formerly were its ideal citizens (Larner 2002, Sonntag 2006). From a global south periphery perspective, they may represent opportunity and access to globalization and white-collar jobs or at least economic opportunities that do not require massive labor migration, but often at the high price of the racialization and feminization used in the service of exploitation (Roy 2003, Mirchandani 2004, Taylor & Bain 2005). In addition, as a field, call centers are traversed by tensions between standardization (the famous scripts that call center representatives are expected to follow, the personae that they are asked to perform; see Cameron 2001, Dubois et al. 2006, Cowie 2007), flexibility (in performing a variety of services for a variety of customers at a variety of times; Poster 2007, Rahman 2009) and variability (in the nature of customers and products; Duchêne 2009). These expectations raise issues for both consumers and front-line producers, who are left to manage the resulting tensions in interaction mediated by telephone and computer technology, whether through transgressive behavior (Chassey & Case 2003, Mulholland 2004) or by a variety of verbal and nonverbal means of compartmentalizing, distancing, or ironizing (or joking, as documented by material found on **http://www.youtube.com**).

Performance Art

Performance art, and notably art forms linked to popular culture and new media (Androutsopoulos 2007), is a final site for working out the tensions surrounding language in the globalized, postnational new economy. Sociolinguists and anthropologists have examined in particular the appearance of multilingualism and linguistic hybridity in the hip-hop cultural sphere, especially as concerns postcolonial and neocolonial sites as well as sites of new labor migration (Gross et al. 1996, Billiez 1998, Davies & Bentahila 2006, Sarkar & Winer 2006, Caubet 2007, LeBlanc et al. 2007). Performance art is understood as a space for reimagining old relations of power through transcending boundaries and breaking old taboos. Although much of this work attends mainly to the ideological dimensions of linguistic practice in this field, these performances must also be seen as commodified products with value on the world market. Their skillful juxtaposition of recognizable authentic (locally anchored) linguistic and musical resources within a standardized globally recognized performance frame (rap and hip-hop) facilitates their circulation while offering a critique of the nation-state from the perspective of the local.

CHALLENGES TO LINGUISTIC ANTHROPOLOGY

What does this material mean for linguistic anthropology? It certainly poses a challenge for traditional modes of linguistic anthropological inquiry focused on communities and cultures, with its emphasis on the detachment of language-as-skill from language-as-identity in the commodification process in a number of fields and those focused on the importance of flexible combinations of resources within discursive spaces, in individual trajectories, and in the tension between anchoring and mobility that emerges time and time again. This material also suggests that the attention linguistic anthropology has traditionally paid to the fine-grained workings of semiosis in specific sites needs to be tied to analyses of political economic conditions, and more particularly to the circulation of symbolic and material resources, to their active (albeit constrained) deployment, and to the complex interpenetrations of the construction of subjectivities, of categorizations (that is, of social difference), and of relations of power (that is, of social inequality). It provides a new purchase on the classic question of the relationship between social difference and social inequality, principally by opening up the means by which speakers claim ownership of linguistic resources or at least the right to control their production, their circulation, and the value attributed to them. Finally, it argues for a more central place for the study of linguistic practices in approaches to understanding the globalized new economy from a social theory point of view.

DISCLOSURE STATEMENT

The author is not aware of any affiliations, memberships, funding, or financial holdings that might be perceived as affecting the objectivity of this review.

LITERATURE CITED

Addelman B. 2005. *Bombay Calling: Life on the Other End of the Line*. Thornhill, Ont.: Mongrel Media. DVD
Alcaras JR, Blanchet P, Joubert J, eds. 2001. *Cultures régionales et développement économique*. Aix-en-Provence: Press. Univ. Aix-Marseille
Alsagoff L. 2008. The commodification of Malay: trading in futures. See Tan & Rubdy 2008, pp. 44–56

Androutsopoulos J. 2007. Bilingualism in the mass media and on the Internet. See Heller 2007, pp. 207–32

Appadurai A. 1996. *Modernity at Large: Cultural Dimensions of Globalization*. Minneapolis: Univ. Minn. Press

Bauman R, Briggs C. 2003. *Voices of Modernity: Language Ideologies and the Politics of Inequality*. Cambridge, UK: Cambridge Univ. Press

Belkhodja C. 2006. *Au bout du fil*. Canada: Off. Natl. Film. DVD

Bhatt R. 2001. World Englishes. *Annu. Rev. Anthropol.* 30:527–50

Billiez J. 1998. L'alternance des langues en chantant. *LIDIL* 18:125–40

Bishop H, Coupland N, Garrett P. 2005. Globalisation, advertising and language choice: shifting values for Welsh and Welshness in Y Drych, 1851–2001. *Multilingua* 24(4):343–78

Block D, Cameron D, eds. 2002. *Globalization and Language Teaching*. London: Routledge

Bourdieu P. 1977. The economics of linguistic exchanges. *Soc. Sci. Inf.* 16(6):645–68

Bourdieu P. 1982. *Ce que parler veut dire*. Paris: Fayard

Boutet J. 2001. Le travail devient-il intellectuel? *Travailler. Revue Int. Psychopathol. Psychodynamique Travail* 6:55–70

Boutet J. 2008. *La vie verbale au travail. Des manufactures aux centres d'appels*. Toulouse: Octares

Budach G, Roy S, Heller M. 2003. Community and commodity in French Ontario. *Lang. Soc.* 32(5):603–28

Bunten A. 2008. Sharing culture or selling out? Developing the commodified persona in the heritage industry. *Am. Ethnol.* 35(3):380–95

Cameron D. 2001. *Good to Talk?* London: Sage

Cameron D. 2005. Communication and commodification: global economic change in sociolinguistic perspective. In *Language, Communication and the Economy*, ed. G Erreygers, pp. 9–23. Amsterdam: John Benjamins

Canada, Government of. 2003. *Le prochain acte: un nouvel élan pour la dualité linguistique canadienne. Le plan d'action pour les langues officielles 2003*. Ottawa: Off. Privy Counc.

Canagarajah S. 1999. *Resisting Linguistic Imperialism in English Teaching*. Oxford: Oxford Univ. Press

Castells M. 2000. *The Information Age: Economy, Society and Culture*. Oxford: Blackwell. 3 vols.

Caubet D. 2007. Langues et musiques de France depuis les années 80. In *Les langues de France au XXIe siècle: vitalité sociolinguistique et dynamiques culturelles*, ed. CA Garabato, H Boyer, pp. 51–76. Paris: L'Harmattan

Chassey C, Case P. 2003. Talking shop: contact centres and dimensions of "social exclusion." *Telematics Inf.* 20:275–96

Comaroff J, Comaroff J. 2009. *Ethnicity, Inc.* Chicago: Univ. Chicago Press

Coupland N. 2003a. Sociolinguistic authenticities. *J. Sociolinguist.* 7(3):417–31

Coupland N, ed. 2003b. Sociolinguistics and globalisation. Special issue. *J. Sociolinguist.* 7(4):465–623

Coupland N, Garrett P, Bishop H. 2005. Wales underground: discursive frames and authenticities in Welsh mining heritage tourism events. See Jaworski & Pritchard 2005, pp. 199–221

Cowie C. 2007. The accents of outsourcing: the meanings of "neutral" in the Indian call centre industry. *World Engl.* 26(3):316–30

Cronin M. 2003. *Translation and Globalization*. London: Routledge

Davies E, Bentahila A. 2006. Code switching and the globalization of popular music: the case of North African rai and rap. *Multilingua* 25(4):367–92

Delamotte E. 1999. *Le commerce des langues*. Paris: Didier

del Valle J. 2005. La lengua, patria comun: politica lingüistica, politica esterior y el post-nacionalismo hispanico. In *Studies on Ibero-Romance Linguistics Dedicated to Ralph Penn*, ed. R Wright, P Ricketts, 7:391–416. Newark: Juan de la Cuesta Monogr./Estudios Ling.

del Valle J. 2006. US Latinos, la hispanofonia, and the language ideologies of high modernity. See Mar-Molinero & Stewart 2006, pp. 27–46

del Valle J, Villa L. 2006. Spanish in Brazil: language policy, business and cultural propaganda. *Lang. Policy* 5:369–92

Deshaies D, Ouellon C. 1998. *Les linguistes et les questions de langue au Québec: points de vue*. Québec: Cent. Int. Rech. Aménagement Ling.

Dubois L, LeBlanc M, Roy S, White C. 2006. La langue comme ressource productive et les rapports de pouvoir entre communautés linguistiques. *Lang. Soc.* 118:17–42

Duchêne A. 2009. Marketing, management and performance: multilingualism as a commodity in a tourism call center. *Lang. Policy* 8(1):27–50

Errington J. 2008. *Linguistics in a Colonial World: A Story of Language, Meaning and Power*. Oxford: Blackwell

Extra G, Gorter D, eds. 2008. *Multilingual Europe: Facts and Policies*. Berlin: Mouton de Gruyter

Fairclough N. 2002. Language in new capitalism. *Discourse Soc.* 13(2):163–66

Fairclough N. 2006. *Language and Globalization*. London: Routledge

Francheschini R. 2009. The genesis and development of research in multilingualism: perspectives for future research. In *The Exploration of Multilingualism: Development of Research on L3, Multilingulism and Multiple Language Acquisition*, ed. L Aronin, B Hufeisen, pp. 27–61. Amsterdam: John Benjamins

Gal S. 1989. Language and political economy. *Annu. Rev. Anthropol.* 18:345–67

Gal S, Woolard K, eds. 2001. *Languages and Publics: The Making of Authority*. Manchester, UK: St. Jerome

Gee J, Hull G, Lankshear C. 1996. *The New Work Order: Behind the Language of the New Capitalism*. Boulder, CO: Westview

Giddens A. 1990. *The Consequences of Modernity*. Berkeley/Los Angeles: Univ. Calif. Press

Golati S. 2005. *Nalini by Day, Nancy by Night: A Film*. New York: Women Make Movies. DVD

Gross J, McMurray D, Swedenburg T. 1996. Arab noise and Ramadan nights: rai, rap and Franco-Maghrebi identity. In *Displacement, Diaspora and the Geographies of Identity*, ed. S Levie, T Swedenburg, pp. 119–56. Durham, NC: Duke Univ. Press

Harvey D. 1989. *The Condition of Postmodernity*. Oxford: Blackwell

Hechter M. 1975. *Internal Colonialism: The Celtic Fringe in British National Development*. Berkeley: Univ. Calif. Press

Heller M. 2003. Globalization, the new economy and the commodification of language and identity. *J. Sociolinguist.* 7(4):473–92

Heller M, ed. 2007. *Bilingualism: A Social Approach*. London: Palgrave Macmillan

Heller M. 2010. La francophonie et ses contradictions. *Sociolinguist. Stud.* In press

Heller M, Boutet J. 2006. Vers de nouvelles formes de pouvoir langagier? Langue(s) et identité dans la nouvelle économie. *Lang. Soc.* 118:5–16

Heller M, Pujolar J. 2009. The political economy of texts: a case study in the structuration of tourism. *Sociolinguist. Stud.* 3(2):177–201

Horst H, Miller D. 2006. *The Cell Phone: An Anthropology of Communication*. Oxford: Berg

Irvine J. 1989. When talk isn't cheap: language and political economy. *Am. Ethnol.* 16(2):248–67

Irvine J. 2001. Linguistics in a colonial world: gender and family in nineteenth century representation of African languages. See Gal & Woolard 2001, pp. 13–29

Jaffe A. 1999a. *Ideologies in Action: Language Politics on Corsica*. Berlin: Mouton de Gruyter

Jaffe A. 1999b. Locating power: Corsican translators and their critics. In *Language Ideological Debates*, ed. J Blommaert, pp. 39–66. Berlin: Mouton de Gruyter

Jaffe A. 2001. Authority and authenticity: Corsican discourse on bilingual education. In *Voices of Authority: Education and Linguistic Difference*, ed. M Heller, M Martin-Jones, pp. 269–96. Greenwood, CT: Ablex

Jaworski A, Pritchard A, eds. 2005. *Discourse, Communication and Tourism*. Clevedon, UK/Buffalo/Toronto: Channel View

Jeffcoat J. 2007. *Outsourced*. Seattle, WA: Shadowcatcher Entertain. DVD

Kelly-Holmes H. 2000. Bier, parfum, kaas: language fetish in European advertising. *Cult. Stud.* 3(1):67–82

Kelly-Holmes H. 2005. *Advertising as Multilingual Communication*. London: Palgrave Macmillan

Kubota R. 2002. The impact of globalization on language teaching in Japan. See Block & Cameron 2002, pp. 13–26

Larner W. 2002. Calling capital: call centre strategies in New Brunswick and New Zealand. *Glob. Netw.* 2:133–52

LeBlanc M. 2008. *Pratiques langagières et bilinguisme dans la fonction publique fédérale: le cas d'un milieu de travail bilingue en Acadie du Nouveau-Brunswick*. PhD thesis, Univ. Moncton. 496 pp.

LeBlanc MN, Boudreault-Fournier A, Djerrahian G. 2007. Les jeunes et la marginalisation à Montréal: la culture hip-hop francophone et les enjeux de l'intégration. *Divers. Urbaine. Rev. Groupe Rech. Ethn. Soc.* 7(1):9–30

Le Menestrel S. 1999. *La voie des Cadiens*. Paris: Belin

Liddicoat A. 2007. Internationalising Japan: Nihonjinron and the intercultural in Japanese language-in-education policy. *J. Multicult. Discourses* 2(1):32–46

Lin A, Martin P, eds. 2005. *Decolonisation, Globalisation: Language-in-Education Policy and Practice*. Clevedon, UK: Multiling. Matters

Macdonald S. 1997. A people's story: heritage, identity and authenticity. See Rojek & Urry 1997, pp. 155–75

Makoni S, Meinhof U, eds. 2003. *Africa and Applied Linguistics*. Amsterdam: John Benjamins

Malaborza S, McLaughlin M. 2008. Les spectacles à grand déploiement et les représentations du passé et de l'avenir. *Cahiers Fr.-Can. OUEST* 18(2):191–204

Mar-Molinero C, Stewart M, eds. 2006. *Globalization and Language in the Spanish-Speaking World*. London: Palgrave Macmillan

Marcellesi JB. 1989. Corse et théorie sociolinguistique: reflets croisés. In *L'Île miroir*, ed. G Ravis-Giordani, pp. 165–74. Ajaccio, France: La Marge

Martin-Jones M. 2007. Bilingualism, education and the regulation of access to linguistic resources. See Heller 2007, pp. 161–82

Martin-Jones M, Hughes B, Williams A. 2009. Bilingual literacy in and for working lives on the land: case studies of young Welsh speakers in North Wales. *Int. J. Sociol. Lang.* 195:39–62

McDonald M. 1990. *We Are Not French*. London: Routledge

McEwan-Fujita E. 2005. Neoliberalism and minority-language planning in the Highlands and islands of Scotland. *Int. J. Sociol. Lang.* 171:155–71

McEwan-Fujita E. 2008. "9 to 5 Gaelic": speakers, context and ideology of an emerging minority language register. In *Sustaining Linguistic Diversity: Endangered and Minority Languages and Language Varieties*, ed. K King, N Schilling-Estes, L Fogle, JK Lou, B Soukup, pp. 81–93. Washington, DC: Georgetown Univ. Press

McLaughlin M, LeBlanc M, Heller M, Lamarre P, eds. 2009. Les mots du marché: l'inscription de la francophonie canadienne dans la nouvelle économie. Special issue. *Francoph. Am.* 27:11–155

Melchers G, Shaw P. 2003. *World Englishes: An Introduction*. London: Arnold

Mirchandani K. 2004. Practices of global capital: gaps, cracks and ironies in transnational call centres in India. *Glob. Netw.* 4(4):355–73

Moïse C. 2006. Protecting French: the view from France. In *Discourses of Endangerment: Ideology and Interest in the Defense of Languages*, ed. A Duchêne, M Heller, pp. 216–41. London: Continuum

Moïse C, McLaughlin M, Roy S, White C. 2006. Le tourisme patrimonial: la commercialisation de l'identité franco-canadienne et ses enjeux langagiers. *Lang. Soc.* 118:85–108

Mulholland K. 2004. Workplace resistance in an Irish call centre: slammin', scammin', smokin' and leavin'. *Work Employ. Soc.* 18(4):709–24

Nekvapil J, Nekula M. 2006. On language management in multilingual companies in the Czech Republic. *Curr. Issues Lang. Plann.* 7(2–3):307–27

Nekvapil J, Sherman T. 2009. Pre-interaction management in multinational companies in Central Europe. *Curr. Issues Lang. Plann.* 19(2):181–98

Park J. 2009. *Unspeakable Tongue: Ideologies of English in South Korea*. Berlin: Mouton de Gruyter

Pennycook A. 1994. *The Cultural Politics of English as an International Language*. London: Longman

Pennycook A. 1998. *English and the Discourses of Colonialism*. New York: Routledge

Phillips D. 2000. We'll keep a welcome? The effects of tourism on the Welsh language. In *"Let's Do Our Best for the Ancient Tongue": The Welsh Language in the 20th Century*, ed. GH Jenkins, MA Williams, pp. 527–50. Cardiff: Univ. Wales Press

Phillipson R. 1992. *Linguistic Imperialism*. Oxford: Oxford Univ. Press

Phillipson R. 2003. *English-Only Europe? Challenging Language Policy*. London/New York: Routledge

Piller I. 2007. English in Swiss tourism marketing. In *Wildern in luso-austro-deutschen Sprach- und Textgefilden: Festschrift zum 60. Geburtstag von Erwin Koller*, ed. C Flores, O Grossegesse, pp. 57–73. Braga, PT: CEHUM- Cent. Estudos Humanisticos

Piller I, Takahashi K. 2006. A passion for English: desire and the language market. In *Bilingual Minds: Emotional Experience, Expression and Representation*, ed. A Pavlenko, pp. 59–83. Clevedon, UK: Multiling. Matters

Pomerantz A. 2002. Language ideologies and the production of identities: Spanish as a resource for participation in a multilingual marketplace. *Multilingua* 21(2,3):275–302

Poster W. 2007. Who's on the line? Indian call centre agents pose as Americans for U.S.-outsourced firms. *Ind. Relat.* 46(2):271–304

Pujolar J. 2006. *Language, Culture and Tourism: Perspectives in Barcelona and Catalonia*. Barcelona: Turisme de Barcelona

Pujolar J. 2007. Bilingualism and the nation-state in the post-national era. See Heller 2007, pp. 71–95

Rahman T. 2009. Language ideology, identity and the commodification of language in the call centers of Pakistan. *Lang Soc.* 38(2):233–58

Rinaudo C. 2005. Carnaval de Nice et carnavals indépendants. Les mises en scène festives du spectacle de l'authentique. *Sociol. Soc.* 37(1):55–68

Rojek C, Urry J, eds. 1997. *Touring Cultures: Transformation of Travel and Theory*. Oxford: Routledge

Roy S. 2003. Bilingualism and standardization in a Canadian call center: challenges for a linguistic minority community. In *Language Socialization in Multilingual Societies*, ed. R Bayley, S Schecter, pp. 269–87. Clevedon, UK: Multiling. Matters

Roy S, Gélinas C. 2004. Le tourisme pour les Franco-Albertans: une porte d'entrée au monde. *Francoph.Am.* 17(1):131–40

Rubdy R, Saraceni M, eds. 2006. *English in the World: Global Rules, Global Roles*. London: Continuum

Sarkar M, Winer L. 2006. Multilingual code-switching in Quebec rap: poetry, pragmatics and performativity. *Int. J. Multiling.* 3(3):173–92

Sengès A. 2003. *Ethnik, la marketing de la différence*. Paris: Éditions Autrement

Shin H. 2006. Rethinking TESOL from a SOL's perspective: indigenous epistemology and decolonizing praxis in TESOL. *Crit. Inq. Lang. Stud.* 3(2–3):147–67

Shin H. 2009. *"Girogi Gajok": transnationalism and language learning*. PhD thesis. Univ. Tor. 227 pp.

Silva E da, Heller M. 2009. From protector to producer: the role of the state in the discursive shift from minority rights to economic development. *Lang. Policy* 8:95–116

Silva E da, McLaughlin M, Richards M. 2007. Bilingualism and the globalized new economy: the commodification of language and identity. See Heller 2007, pp. 183–206

Simon S. 2006. *Translating Montreal: Episodes in the Life of a Divided City*. Montreal, Kingston: McGill-Queen's Univ. Press

Singh R, ed. 1998. *The Native Speaker: Multilingual Perspectives*. New Dehli: Sage

Sonntag S. 2006. Appropriating identity or cultivating capital? Global English in offshoring service industries. *Anthropol. Work Rev.* 26(1):13–19

Stitt G. 2002. *Diverted to Delhi*. New York: Filmakers Libr. DVD

Sturge K. 2007. *Representing Others: Translation, Ethnography and the Museum*. Manchester, UK: St. Jerome

Tan P, Rubdy R, eds. 2008. *Language as Commodity: Global Structure, Local Marketplaces*. London: Continuum

Taylor JP. 2001. Authenticity and sincerity in tourism. *Ann. Tourism Res.* 28(1):7–26

Taylor P, Bain P. 2005. "India calling to the far away towns": the call centre labour process and globalization. *Work. Employ. Soc.* 19(2):261–82

Tupas TRF. 2008. Anatomies of linguistic commodification: the case of English in the Philippines vis-à-vis other languages in the multilingual marketplace. See Tan & Rubdy 2008, pp. 89–105

Urciuoli B. 2008. Skills and selves in the new workplace. *Am. Ethnol.* 35(2):211–28

Wee L. 2008. Linguistic instrumentalism in Singapore. See Tan & Rubdy 2008, pp. 31–43

Yarymowich M. 2005. "Language tourism" in Canada: a mixed discourse. In *La communication touristique. Approches discursives de l'identité et de l'alterité*, ed. F Baider, M Burger, D Goutsos, pp. 257–73. Paris: L'Harmattan

Sensory Impairment

Elizabeth Keating[1] and R. Neill Hadder[2]

[1]Department of Anthropology, University of Texas, Austin, Texas 78712;
email: ekeating@mail.utexas.edu

[2]Department of Anthropology, Texas State University, San Marcos, Texas 78666;
email: neill@txstate.edu

Annu. Rev. Anthropol. 2010. 39:115–29

The *Annual Review of Anthropology* is online at
anthro.annualreviews.org

This article's doi:
10.1146/annurev.anthro.012809.105026

Key Words

blindness, deafness, disability, embodiment, language

Abstract

Anthropological studies of sensory impairment address biological conditions and cultural disablement while contributing to theoretical discussions of cultural competence, communicative practices, the role of narrative, and features of identity, ideologies, and technology. As boundary cases, impairments can disclose essential aspects of the senses in human life. Sensory impairment studies navigate the complexities of comparing dominant sensory discourses with individual sense differences, cross-linguistic incomparabilities among sense categories, and how impairment categories tend to fuse together highly diverse conditions. The category of disability, which includes sensory impairment, comprises chronic deficit relative to priority competencies. With special emphasis on blindness/visual impairment and deafness/hearing impairment, we overview sensory impairment on three levels: the social partitioning of the sensorium, differential ramifications of sensory impairments cross-culturally, and the classification of the person based on cultural priorities. We identify ten common themes in ethnographically oriented studies.

INTRODUCTION

An anthropologically oriented investigation into sensory impairment articulates with a number of key cross-cultural issues. These include the notion of the individual, illness, the body and its relation to the environment, the relationship of present experience to the past, how views of the body change over human history, gender, difference, inequality, and deviance, as well as the potential role of globalization. The understanding of sensory impairment is complicated by the usual anthropological challenges of comparing categories cross-linguistically, a problem compounded with a term such as "impairment," which gathers many radically different physical and cultural conditions under one umbrella term in both the scholarly and the popular literatures. This conflation tends to obscure the fact that, for individuals within and across cultures, these embodied experiences can be quite different, with independent biological origins, supporting institutions, impacts on life, and political agendas. Nevertheless, looking at sensory impairment as a broad category across societies has the advantage of highlighting crucial differences and similarities in the human experience of the sensorium. Because most people experience diminished sensory capacities and some form of sensory impairment with aging, sensory impairment is relevant to almost all human beings. Cross-cultural investigations make clear the diversity of human experience and the role that culture plays in organizing meaning and mediating environmental information, including what normality is or how to experience and talk about the sacred, difficult, or puzzling character of altered sensory worlds.

Although the privileged role of language in understanding and interpreting the senses has been recently critiqued (Howes 2003, Serres 2009), it is difficult to study the senses without resorting to language forms and expression. Attention to the interactional ground of impairment can refine anthropological understanding of culturally organized intercorporealities and somatic modes of attention (Csordas 1993) because the body is a domain in which struggles over power and control are frequently waged (e.g., Zola 1982, Scheper-Hughes & Lock 1987, Frank 2000). Communicative practices such as narrative play an important role in formulating autobiographical memory and experience of people classed as dysfunctional (Desjarlais 1997, Mattingly 1998, Hadder 2007). The studies we discuss here participate in a widespread anthropological critique of the ideology that sensation provides unmediated experiential material, theorizing instead that experience comprises an accomplishment of discourse and social practice. This focus highlights sensory impairment as a mutual constitution of sensory, communicative, and social fields.

Our discussion overviews sensory impairment on three levels: the social partitioning of the sensorium, the differential ramifications of sensory impairments in cultural contexts, and the classification of the disabled person on the basis of the cultural priority of an impaired sense. We identify ten common themes in ethnographically oriented impairment studies. We focus additional attention on issues of blindness and deafness, drawing on our own ethnographic, and in the case of Hadder experiential, backgrounds (Keating & Mirus 2003a,b; Keating 2005; Hadder 2007). The terms blindness and deafness are labels that accrue around very significant degrees of impairment in these two senses, engaging with problems of communication, space, information, mobility, and identity (note that we often use blind or deaf as categories subsuming visual or hearing impairment for comparative purposes, although quantitative measures of impairment frequently pass over substantive qualitative differences in experience and analysis).

THEORIZING DISABILITY AND IMPAIRMENT

The terms impairment and disability are embedded within dominant sociological discourses and are used by scholarly, advocacy, and activist groups in multiple ways. The term person with a disability, some argue, objectifies disablement, whereas the term disabled person highlights the role of society and the built environment as disabling agents (Dijani 2001). Disability classifications, which typically center on a person's exclusion from paid labor, can render invisible some forms of labor that are traditional to women (Wendell 1996). The World Health Organization International Classification of Functioning, Disability, and Health (ICF), a 2001 revision of the earlier ICIDH (International Classification of Impairments, Disabilities, and Handicaps), recognizes that impairment, conceived as a functional deficit, can result in multiple disabilities, depending on the social environment. Kasnitz & Shuttleworth (2001) offer an alternative set of definitions grounded in a cultural-contextual approach to disability and impairment. From an anthropological perspective, disability can, at its broadest conception, comprise any ideologically or analytically figured location that identifies a particular human somatic condition as being at odds with a normativized relationship among biology, culture, and the individual. Like race and gender, both of which can be disabling, disabilities can, for certain purposes, be glossed as historically produced and ideologically motivated symbolizations on the basis of selected genetic expressions that are neither necessary nor sufficient causes for the resulting cultural category. Impairment presents a larger theoretical challenge because the body itself can be an effect of discourse and power (Hughes & Patterson 1997), and impairment-disability is not an entirely predictable relationship (Barnes et al. 1999, p. 2; Corker & French 1999, p. 2). Frequently, terminological switches employed by activist groups seek to guide medical and rehabilitation apparatuses toward client-centered rather than deficit-centered models. Within the disabled community itself, nondisabled persons are sometimes described pointedly as "temporarily able bodied" (Kirschbaum 1991).

Since the 1980s, the growing field of disability studies has productively integrated disability and impairment with mainstream social science and humanistic theoretical models. The social model (Oliver 1990, Thomas & Corker 2002) located disablement as a by-product of Fordist and Taylorist capitalism, and the minority model, pioneered by Harlan Hahn, conceptualized disability-related access as a civil rights matter and contributed, in the United States, to the Rehabilitation Act of 1973 and the Americans with Disabilities Act of 1990. Subsequent explorations include postmodern attention to the discursive construction of disability (Wilson & Wilson 2001), the Foucauldian framing of the disabled subject (Tremain 2005), integration with queer theory (Clare 2001, McRuer 2006), embodiment (Paterson & Hughes 1999, Snyder & Mitchell 2001, Iwakuma 2002), post-Freudian psychoanalytics (Marks 1999), and gender (Thomas 1999, Corker 2001, Hutchinson & Smith 2004). Disability studies literature often references elements of oppression, emancipation, and social construction (Shakespeare 1994, Marks 1999, Davis 2000), including the linkage of disability to explicit and implicit eugenics projects (Snyder & Mitchell 2005). Recent authors, as noted above, have argued that early social model theorists left impairment unproblematized, whereas others argue that constructionist considerations should not overshadow the physiological basis of impairment (Bickenbach et al. 1999).

Although social and minority models have been highly influential since the 1970s, the centrality they give to individualism and civil rights raises the issue of conceptual relativism in nonindustrial, non-Western ethnographic contexts. A group-oriented rather than individual-oriented view of the person in Polynesian and Micronesian societies, for example, presents a challenge to the concept of impairment that is widely used in the West; there, an impairment such as blindness is not a disability because the impaired person establishes new roles for active contributions to household and community life (Marshall 1996). Especially in developing societies, class likewise imposes specific experiences of health, equal rights, and expectations that frame understandings of impairment.

Sensory impairment has constituted a resource for interpretive positioning by blind (Steiner 1994) and deaf (Mills 1994) ethnographers, whereas experience narratives by sensory-impaired authors have provided rich sources of data about impairment, narrative, sense processing, and cultural values. Sacks (2003) contrasts several blindness memoirs to question neurological assumptions about the relationship between blindness and mental imagery. More fundamentally, reports of sensory experience in such memoirs reflect rhetorical factors in experience narrative generally and disability memoirs in particular (Couser 2001). Because the cultural resources for conceptualizing impairment circulate among people with normative bodies, formulation of a communicable experience of disability often represents a substantial achievement, one that must leverage the reflexive potentials of writing (Zola 1982, p. 2; Murphy 1987, pp. 3–4; Mehta 2001, p. 2). Literary memoirs of visual impairment (Clarke 1977, Hull 1992, Lusseyran 1999, Kuusisto 2006), in addition to articulating the social production of disability, explicitly use writing to work toward a phenomenology rooted in the author's individualistic embodiment. This literature can be considered a particularly forceful and theoretical form of autoethnography (Ellis & Bochner 2000, Sparkes 2002, Jones 2005) in which the body of a disabled ethnographer becomes the material for displaying not only beliefs about the disabled body but also many aspects of culture (Preston 1994, Michalko 1998, Kleege 1999, Wikan 2000, Titchkosky 2002, Hadder 2007). Memoirs of sensory impairment and disability contribute to anthropological understandings of related literatures surrounding the narration of individual experience (Linde 1993, Battaglia 1995, Bal et al. 1999), chronic conditions (Kleinman 1988, Good 1994, Frank 1995, Desjarlais 1997, Mattingly 1998, Mattingly & Garro 2000), emotion and affect (Reddy 2001, Stewart 2007, Wilce 2009), and dissociation (Spiegel 1994, Antze & Lambek 1996, Stern 1997).

THEMES IN STUDIES OF SENSORY IMPAIRMENT

The anthropological literature evidences longstanding but sporadic attention to disability, dating from Benedict's 1934 cross-cultural comparison of epilepsy, Edgerton's extensive work on intellectual disability, Goffman's *Stigma* (1963), and Ablon's studies of dwarfism. Several recent reviews of anthropological work have been published (Scheer & Groce 1988, Armstrong & Fitzgerald 1996, Schacht 2001, Klotz 2003, Shuttleworth & Kasnitz 2004, Reid-Cunningham 2009). Recent literature engages not only impairment but also the nature of ethnographic authority, deconstructing enculturated processes of remembering and experience, often using alternative or innovative work to convey the basic elements of reality employed by people with sensory impairments (Corker 2001). Cross-cultural investigations make clear the diversity of the role culture and language play in organizing experience (sense making) and in mediating sensory information (the life-world). In the following section, we discuss ten common themes of crosscultural ethnographic work relevant to sensory impairment.

Categories Are Not Limited to Sight, Smell, Touch, Taste, and Hearing, but Constructed Within Particular Cultural Contexts

The sensorium is variously conceptualized to include, for example, categories such as balance and sentiment, the Buddhist sense of the mental perception of things, and the Western popular notion of the sixth sense as intuition and can be expressed as a holistic perceptual system (Gibson 1966). Ideologies of the senses influence impairment to the extent that the cultural histories of sensation and sociality contribute to views of what is natural. The senses are instruments for perceiving information from the environment, including information about where we are in space or body position (proprioception) and anatomical processes such as signals of pain, pressure, and temperature. The Hausa of Nigeria linguistically mark only two senses, one referring to sight and one for experiencing (which encompasses intuition, emotion, smell, touch, taste, and hearing), and they grant great importance to taste

(Ritchie 1991). Howes (1991) has compared different cultural interpretations of the senses as shared "ratios of sense," a hierarchical sensorium members of a culture learn to inhabit (p. 8), which can vary significantly even between cultures sharing similar worldviews. Codability of sense impressions varies cross-culturally, and some sensory experiences may be ineffable (Majid & Levinson 2009). The senses are a kind of communicative resource for developing relationships with material things and are implicated in a culture's "perceptual construction of truth" (Serematakis 1994, p. 6).

Sense Priorities Differ Across Cultures

Western visual-centrism belongs to a particular heritage encoded in the Greek hierarchy of senses that elevates sight while associating smell and touch with lower aspects of life. In contrast, Feld (1982) describes the preeminence of sound in forest-dwelling groups in New Guinea, also noted for Inuit and Andaman Islanders. Roseman's work (1991) similarly describes the important role of music in expressing aspects of Temiar perception, including their experience of illness. Music (the ordering of sounds) is significantly linked to disability in classical Western tradition, where Straus (2006) argues that "language about music and music itself may be understood to both represent and construct disability" (p. 114) through marking the disabilities of influential musicians. To the Desana of Colombia, smell is a prioritized sense; they speak about the odor of a tune (Reichel-Dolmatoff 1981), whereas in Western societies, the sense of smell is suppressed or mostly ignored (Classen et al. 1994). In terms of linguistic representation, those forms associated with olfaction, taste, and touch tend to evidence an inventory of linguistic forms that is less rich than forms associated with vision and hearing (Slobin 1971). Metaphors commonly recruit sensory experience, such as the use of properties of vision in phrases such as "I see what you mean" or "eye of the storm." As a cultural category, impairment reflects biological

dysfunction at the root of social disablement, but variability in the cultural prioritization of various sensory, manual, and cognitive abilities determines which somatic differences impair activities enough to receive recognition.

Meanings of Disability and Cultural Lives of Impairments Change Over Time

Deafness is one example of shifting signs of difference over centuries. During the early nineteenth century, deaf people were thought to be able to achieve a moral life not open to hearing people because they were cut off from the evil influences of the world (Batson & Bergman 1985), although St. Augustine had earlier written of deafness that "this impairment prevents faith" (Lane 1984, p. 58). In 1884, Alexander Graham Bell advocated forbidding deaf people to marry or to use sign language, creating what Barnes (1991) has described for impaired people as a hostile world. In Medieval England, the restoration of sense impairment was often featured in miracles (Woolgar 2006, p. 8). The historical record provides many examples of changes in the significance of disabled traits (McDermott & Varenne 1995, Longmore & Umansky 2001, Burch 2005).

Sensory-Impaired Individuals Are Socialized to Employ Mainstream Sensory Discourses, but Shared Discursive Practices Mask Sensations Patterned in Radically Different Ways

A hearing person may have the same sensation of vibration as a deaf person experiencing music but may lack a schema for interpreting the vibrations as musical. Macpherson (2009) demonstrates that blind walkers associate inquiries about touch with hand-touch, but touch through the feet constitutes a more pertinent corporeal schema delivering specialized knowledge about the body and environment. Corker (2001) describes an experience of embodied uncertainty, instability, and transience owing to communicative differences for deaf people in a hearing-speaking world. Translating or interpreting for tactile signing deaf-blind must include the interpreter conveying essential background aspects of a scene, including details about manner and attitude of non-speaking participants considered by those blind and deaf to be key to understanding, and these nonlinguistic aspects are challenging to characterize (Edwards 2007). Such issues can become the methodological site for new understandings of embodiment and communication.

Disjuncture from the Normal Sensorium Does Not Automatically Produce Impairment; the Cultural Category of Disability Comprises Deficit Relative to Priority Competencies

Labeling and terminological practices reflect local interpretations of biocultural relationships and deficit relationships. Western medicine, for example, has a diagnostic label to mark individuals who lack a sense of smell (anosmiac), but the condition is related to particular contexts rather than marking the person as globally impaired. Synesthesia, where stimulus of one sense causes a perception by another unrelated sense—for example, musicians who taste the intervals between notes they hear (Beeli et al. 2005) or artists who smell color differences—is a distinctive individual difference in sensory stimulation not considered an impairment. Nabokov wrote about his "colored" hearing in his autobiography *Speak, Memory*. Imagining the outline of a letter as he spoke it produced a color sensation, such as the long "a" in English producing the tint of weathered wood and the French "a" a polished ebony (Ackerman 1990, p. 291). In Palau, someone who has a physical, mental, or sensory disability is understood as being different, but the term used for difference (*ngodech*) does not convey beliefs about etiology, potential, or stigmatization, but is instead a descriptor similar to blond or freckled (Rengiil & Jarrow 1994). In Zimbabwe, physical limitations are suggested by the use of a word meaning to become heavy, to fail, or to

experience difficulty (Mpofu & Harley 2002). As noted by Edgerton (1970), small-scale communities thought to have simpler technological surrounds are not necessarily more likely to discriminate less against those with impairments, emphasizing the need for cross-cultural research.

High Incidences of Sensory Impairment Can Lead to a Kind of Sensory Specialization that Lessens or Renders Invisible Distinction Based on Sensory Modes

In the town of Chilmark on Martha's Vineyard, owing to a recessive gene for deafness in the early colonial population, 1 in 25 members of the community was born deaf. Until the early twentieth century, when demographics changed, nearly everyone on the island possessed some fluency in the local sign language (Groce 1985). Likewise, Kisch (2004) describes the Al-Sayyid community in the Negev, where hearing loss is high, at 3% of the population, owing to recessive traits of deafness. Members of the community recognize the indigenous sign language as a second language of the village, routinely praising those with greater skills (Sandler et al. 2005). On the island of Pingelap in Micronesia, achromotopsia, a condition leading to a lack of cells specialized for perception of color and fine detail (called locally *maskun* or "don't see"), affects 10% of the population, who are blinded in bright sunlight and virtually cannot read or see fine detail (Sacks 1996). Onchocerciasis was common enough in the Mexican community studied by Gwaltney (1970) to make blindness part of negative expectations alongside other maladies under local pervasive conditions of extreme poverty. Its prevalence led to cultural accommodations that incorporated blind elders socially, including a tradition in which children routinely served as ad hoc sighted guides [Gwaltney's later study (1980) shows modernization to have greatly diminished the degree of cultural accommodation]. Ottenberg (1996) studies how the same form of blindness common in Mexico impacts the dynamics of structure and agency within a Sierra Leone chiefdom. These studies use blind or deaf informants to talk about culture, not primarily to offer generalizations about blindness or the blind as ethnographic objects.

Temporary Sensory Impairments or Alterations Have Different Meanings than Chronic Impairments of the Same Sense

Temporary impaired or altered sense conditions include drug- and alcohol-induced states, religious and ceremonial activities, curing practices, and scientific experiments. Spirit-possession practices have been described as "assaults on the sensory system" (Kennedy 1974, p. 1171), and Salish spirit dance initiations result in altered vision as initiates link the experience of pain to spiritual ways of knowing. Curing the Latin American illness *susto* (fright) involves hot and cold shocks to the body, and some Pentecostals and others utilize fire to mediate experiences of touch in fire-handling or fire-walking rituals. Also, some groups frequently use chemicals to restrict sensory impulses to the brain by inhibiting neural messages associated with hearing, smell, taste, and touch. In a well-known study at McGill in the 1950s, student volunteers who were isolated and deprived of perceptual experiences reported vivid hallucinations and body image disturbances (Bexton et al. 1954). The investigators concluded that a person undergoing sensory deprivation is in an altered life situation that affects self-systems, defenses, fantasies, motivations, and cognitive and interpersonal strategies. Benedict (1934) discusses variations in the cultural interpretation of the temporary trance state in epileptic seizures, which vary from shame responses to linkages with the power and authority of spirit mediums.

Biomedical and Biocultural Models of Cause and Cure Vary

In several ethnographies that note impairment, sorcery, witchcraft, acts of spirits, or moral transgression are reported as the root cause (see, e.g., Armstrong & Fitzgerald 1996), and in some cases, discovering exact cause is a critical part of treating the condition. Causes might include failure to follow tradition, to fulfill a responsibility, or to appease an ancestor. Treatment begins by families seeking guidance in determining what mistake was made and how atonement can be accomplished. After remedial action, the mistake may be forgiven, but the individual remains disabled as a reminder, although they are likely to be seen as a victim of circumstance and not as a guilty party (Rengiil & Jarrow 1994). Navajo tend to classify impairments by cause rather than by symptoms (e.g., animals, natural phenomena, evil spirits, or disharmony). Ceremonies to restore harmony, such as a curing ceremony for a blind person, are considered successful because the person has been made whole again, though still blind (Connors & Donnellan 1993). In Pingelap, color blindness in a fetus is related to carelessness during pregnancy or some kind of contagion, including contagion from Europeans (Sacks 1996, p. 47). Impairments can also be linked positively to the supernatural, as noted above. Ottenberg's study of Sierra Leone evidences a common ideology that sensory impairment does or should, perhaps for one's own peace of mind, be compensated by another, often supernormal ability (although music is also the means by which these blind individuals attain at least marginal social incorporation).

Disabilities, and Especially Sensory Impairments, Involve Social Complexities Disclosed Only by Systematic Observation

Stigma, as an ideological reduction of social complexities, refers to negative and limiting "social information" that accrues around the impairment once it becomes transacted as a sign (Goffman 1963). The stigma attached to an impairment will ultimately encompass far more aspects of self and personhood than will the sphere of impaired activities, a phenomenon the disability literature labels the spread effect.

For example, deaf or blind people will frequently be treated as if they lack mental competence as well. Virtually all forms of competence are assumed to require sight or hearing because in many cases alternate strategies for accomplishing those tasks have not been imagined, and the outward display of those strategies will not readily be recognized as displays of competence. Methodically tracing impairment's ramifications across social domains elucidates both sides of the able-disabled horizon of practice, in addition to offering important opportunities for studying sign systems.

Ordinary communicative practices, simply from their seeming transparency and their unreflexive character, are key tools in the disabling impacts of sensory impairment. Lack of reflexivity about spoken communication and lack of understanding regarding sign language communication, for example, significantly impair deaf-hearing interactions among children in public school settings (Keating & Mirus 2003b). Indexical use of conversational participants' bodies, such as pointing "over there" and "that way," along with similar assumptions that the hearer and speaker share visual access to their space, are very difficult for sighted people to bring to consciousness in verbal interaction and thereby thwart sighted–visually impaired interactions (Hadder 2007).

Impairment Requires that Analysts Reconsider the Attribution of Competence and Independence to an Individual Acting Alone

Technologies, social interactions, assistance animals, and even reliable routines coordinate, with varying degrees of dependability, to achieve competence despite impairment, just as tools, language, the built environment, and other aspects of culture routinely establish the preconditions for competent action more widely. The role of specialized assistive technologies in the lives of the sensory impaired can be profound in terms of both independence and social inclusion, although accessibility can be thwarted by often-inaccessible technological innovations. As multifunction digital sensors replace knobs and switches, for instance, these devices become more inaccessible to some impaired users. Speech and Braille output have allowed the visually impaired population to benefit from the information age, yet the computer hardware and software are generally expensive and difficult to retrofit onto mainstream technology. Universal or inclusive design can often provide accessibility in concert with increased usability for other users, presenting an area for further anthropological involvement (e.g., Gerber 2009). The deaf were early adopters of visual technologies such as Web cameras for communication (Keating & Mirus 2003a), and the Internet is now a key tool for interaction with hearing communities with and without online sign language interpreters. Assistive technologies change dependency relationships and, as a potential negative consequence, can free the able-bodied from the need to understand and engage with sensory impairment.

Technology can redefine impairment conditions and communities. Hard-of-hearing individuals share many experiences with deaf people, but the development of hearing aid technologies has resulted in a categorical distinction between deaf and hard-of-hearing. Woodward & Allen (1993) argue that hard-of-hearing and deaf people represent two different linguistic communities that cannot be subsumed under the category of hearing impaired. This method of labeling can have an adverse effect on hard-of-hearing students who do not feel aligned with Deaf culture or advocacy groups (Grushkin 2003). Cochlear implants to provide hearing to deaf or hard-of-hearing people have been a source of tremendous controversy in the Deaf community, raising concerns about the endangerment of sign language, the ethics of medical intervention, and ideological support for considering deaf people impaired rather than different. Thus impairment can be a site for disclosing some of the prosthetic dimensions of cultural competence.

In terms of the attribution of competence solely to individuals in isolation rather than within a larger participation framework, Goode's (1990) ethnographic study of a deaf-blind child describes a conflict between professionals and parents about the child's communication skills and behavioral competence. At home, parents interpreted the child's gestures or affective displays as indexical expressions, transforming the limited expressions into specific context-relevant content (see also Goodwin 2004; more broadly on context, see Hanks 1990). Devlieger (1998), in his study of the Nyole of Africa, notes that competency is recognized to be a property of social relations rather than of an individual in isolation.

In the final section, we focus more particularly on deafness and blindness and note ways that sensory impairments or people characterized by them are influenced by dominant social institutions and values, experiences of sensory conditions, socialization processes, and in some cases, a reflexive self-identification employed for purposes of political recognition or the construction of a valued counter-discourse.

CULTURE, PERSONHOOD, AND IDENTITY: THE CASE OF DEAFNESS AND BLINDNESS

Culturally iconic characteristics of blind and deaf populations are produced by various social and environmental contexts. For blind people, educational and rehabilitation institutions play a significant role in socializing them to embody and reproduce behaviors, limitations, and stereotypic attitudes about blindness (Scott 1969). In the case of the Deaf community, educational institutions have also been central in producing notions of Deafness and sign language development (Woll et al. 2001, Senghas & Monaghan 2002, Polich 2005). In Ireland, separate deaf boys' and girls' schools led to the development of unique forms of gendered sign languages (LeMaster 2003), whereas in Nicaragua the development of a deaf school

in 1980 provided an environment for the emergence of a new indigenous sign language and for a sense of Deaf personhood (Senghas 2003).

Many Deaf people do not think of themselves as impaired, and rigorously resist this characterization, yet they recognize that claiming equal access and individual rights can depend on disability framings (Lane et al. 1996). A cultural rather than pathological view of Deafness (Padden & Humphries 1988, Padden 1996) is promoted by the American Deaf community to recapture the terms of what it means to be deaf in a hearing society, to assert a visual communication mode, to emphasize bilingual and bicultural aspects of being Deaf (Parasnis 1996), as well as to counter discrimination. In this case, sensory impairment is at the core of particular cultural practices and relations within a population. Deaf culture stems not only from shared impairment, stigmatization, institutional affiliations, and shared technologies, but much more fundamentally from unique shared forms of communication that evolve within the community of practice (e.g., Padden & Humphries 1988, Ladd 2003), including Deaf poetry and theater. Investigating life-history narratives of deaf people in Norway, Breivik (2005) shows the diverse ways Deaf people define themselves through deafness as dependent on age of onset of deafness. One critical issue in Deafness is local language policies because most deaf children are born to nonsigning hearing parents, which can impact not only language and cognitive development (in the absence of visual language input), but also transmission of Deaf traditions. Deaf culture is mostly applicable to industrialized Western societies; however, within the past 30 years, the concept of Deaf culture and identity has had increasing influence worldwide (Erting et al. 1994, although see Nakamura 2006 for a discussion of generational differences). Studies on Deaf communities (Johnson 1991, Senghas & Monaghan 2002, Nakamura 2006, Nonaka 2009, Padden et al. 2010) focus on language creation over generations with recently emerged sign languages, language documentation, historical development, variation, language endangerment, and ethnographies of sign communities. The volume *Many Ways to Be Deaf* (Monaghan et al. 2003), for example, collects works by 24 scholars on a wide variety of Deaf communities. The linguistic description of sign languages has contributed theoretically to understanding language and communication in general (e.g., Meier et al. 2009); contact language issues (Lucas & Valli 1992); relationships between manual signs and gesture (Casey & Emmorey 2009), including the emergence of family home signs (see review in Morford 1996); and other topics. Stokoe's (1980) and Washabaugh's (1981) reviews of early sign language communication research and that of Senghas & Monaghan (2002), who particularly focus on issues of the role of language in Deaf identity and how to best approach research, are valuable summaries.

The question of whether it is accurate or useful to identify the blind as a culture group has been at issue among authors, blind and sighted. As a case in point, Deshen's (1992) study of blind Israelis documents the cultural process that creates the blind as a culture group, looking at a small sample in specific blindness-related voluntary organizations to produce a general model. Visually impaired guide dog users and other assistance animal users have been said to constitute a subculture on the grounds of shared experiences, dog-related practices, affiliations, and ways of talking about relevant experiences (Eames & Eames 2001). To assume that such a culture group exists anthropologically, however, can render invisible significant cultural aspects of this same population. Foss (2006) found the role of blind culture not to be a factor correlated with quality of life among those with sight loss late in life.

Because visually impaired individuals seldom have reason to prefer social interactions with blind over nonblind people, studies that use visual impairment as the criterion for informant selection tend automatically to yield an emphasis on data about the technologies, institutions, services, and practical strategies keyed to the individual's career of coping with this aspect of life. Opportunities or restrictions in a society may be the most common means of identifying the blind collectively, when they are mentioned in ethnographic texts. Scheer & Groce (1988) cite sub-Saharan African evidence that blind Kanuri engaged in robe making and lived with their families in a particular area of town, whereas blind Besongy often worked as musicians. Until recently, adolescent blind girls in Japan could become a spirit medium known as an Itako (Vaughan 2002), again exemplifying the ideology that impairment is compensated by supernatural sensitivity. Vaughan (2000), in a survey of rehabilitation programs and organizations of the blind and blind indigenous organizations in many countries, describes several special occupations open to, appropriated by, or sometimes virtually reserved for blind people today in various cultures, including massage in China and operating the lottery in Spain. These same examples problematize what is meant by social inclusion, however. Best estimates available after 1995 indicate a 70% unemployment rate among legally blind working-age Americans, although, according to the American Foundation for the Blind, no definitive statistical measures are as yet available. A significant percentage of deaf and blind are underemployed, unemployed, or, in the case of the blind, work in sheltered workshops. Blind men in the Sierra Leone chiefdom were considered ineligible as husbands (Ottenberg 1996), and, to an even greater extent, blind women in Uganda and in several other developing regions are likewise deemed ineligible for marriage because they are disabled with respect to traditional women's roles (Sentumbwe 1995). People with various impairments are often expected to abide by and reproduce limitations on personhood, including rights to adult status, ritual participation, reproduction, or choice of occupation. These aspects of personhood and its relationship to impairment are culturally diverse (Ingstad & Whyte 1995) and situationally variable.

CONCLUDING COMMENTS

The description of diverse sensory abilities and impairments can contribute to a more complete understanding of perception and embodied experience. However, using sensory-impaired groups as the basis for constituting an ethnographic study can potentially portray membership as based on sensory affinities or traditions, whereas the historic, economic, discursive, and institutional aspects of this identity are less well investigated. A persistent question for an anthropology of the senses concerns how impairment of a single sense leads to cultural impairment of the person across multiple intersecting domains. With more widespread incorporation of sensory impairment into ethnography, the potential exists for understanding a wide range of strategies for daily social practices, for clarifying the role of vision, hearing, and other senses in sense making, and for understanding the limits of vision-centric, sound-centric discourses for articulating experiences of partial vision or hearing or modes of spatial perception that blend mental imagery with nonvisual sensation.

DISCLOSURE STATEMENT

The authors are not aware of any affiliations, memberships, funding, or financial holdings that might be perceived as affecting the objectivity of this review.

LITERATURE CITED

Ackerman D. 1990. *A Natural History of the Senses*. New York: Vintage Books

Antze P, Lambek M, eds. 1996. *Tense Past: Cultural Essays in Trauma and Memory*. New York: Routledge

Armstrong J, Fitzgerald M. 1996. Culture and disability studies: an anthropological perspective. *Rehabil. Educ.* 10(4):247–304

Bal M, Crewe J, Spitzer L, eds. 1999. *Acts of Memory: Cultural Recall in the Present*. Hanover, NH: Univ. Press N. Engl.

Barnes C. 1991. *Disabled People in Britain and Discrimination: A Case for Anti-Discrimination Legislation*. London: Hurst

Barnes C, Mercer G, Shakespeare T. 1999. *Exploring Disability: A Sociological Introduction*. London: Polity

Batson T, Bergman E, eds. 1985. *Angels and Outcasts: An Anthology of Deaf Characters in Literature*. Washington, DC: Gallaudet Coll. Press

Battaglia D, ed. 1995. *Rhetorics of Self-Making*. Berkeley: Univ. Calif. Press

Beeli G, Esslen M, Jancke L. 2005. Synaesthesia: when colored sounds taste sweet. *Nature* 434:38

Benedict R. 1934. Anthropology and the abnormal. *J. Gen. Psychiatry* 10:59–80

Bexton WH, Heron W, Scott RH. 1954. Effects of decreased variation in the sensory environment. *Can. J. Psychol.* 8(2):70–76

Bickenbach JE, Chatterji S, Badley EM, Ustun TB. 1999. Models of disablement, universalism, and the ICIDH. *Social Sci. Med.* 48(9):1173–87

Breivik JK. 2005. *Deaf Identities in the Making: Local Lives, Transnational Connections*. Washington, DC: Gallaudet Univ. Press

Burch S. 2005. Disability history: suggested readings—an annotated bibliography. *Public Hist.* 27(2):63–74

Casey S, Emmorey K. 2009. Co-speech gesture in bimodal bilinguals. *Lang. Cogn. Process.* 24(2):290–312

Clare E. 2001. Stolen bodies, reclaimed bodies: disability and queerness. *Public Cult.* 13(3):359–65

Clark E. 1977. *Eyes, Etc.: A Memoir*. New York: Pantheon Books

Classen C, Howes D, Synott A. 1994. *Aroma: The Cultural History of Smell*. London/New York: Routledge

Connors JL, Donnellan AM. 1993. Citizenship and culture: the role of disabled people in Navajo society. *Disabil. Handicap Soc.* 8(3):265–80

Corker M. 2001. Sensing disability. *Hypatia* 16(4):34–52

Corker M, French S. 1999. *Disability Discourse*. Buckingham: Open Univ. Press

Couser GT. 2001. Conflicting paradigms: the rhetoric of disability memoirs. See Wilson & Lewiecki-Wilson 2001, pp. 78–91

Csordas TJ. 1993. Somatic modes of attention. *Cult. Anthropol.* 8:135–56

Davis L. 2000. *My Sense of Silence*. Chicago: Univ. Ill. Press

Deshen S. 1992. *Blind People: The Private and Public Lives of Sightless Israelis*. Albany: State Univ. N. Y. Press

Desjarlais R. 1997. *Shelter Blues: Sanity and Selfhood Among the Homeless*. Philadelphia: Univ. Penn. Press

Devlieger PJ. 1998. (In)competence in America in comparative perspective. In *Questions of Competence: Culture, Classification and Intellectual Disability*, ed. R Jenkins, pp. 54–75. Cambridge, UK: Cambridge Univ. Press

Dijani KF. 2001. What's in a name? Terms used to refer to people with disabilities. *Disabil. Stud. Q.* 21(3):196–209

Eames E, Eames T. 2001. Bridging differences within the disability community: the assistance dog movement. *Disabil. Stud. Q.* 21(3):55–66

Edgerton RB. 1970. Mental retardation in non-western societies: toward a cross-cultural perspective on incompetence. In *Social-Cultural Aspects of Mental Retardation*, ed. HC Haywood, pp. 523–59. New York: Meredith

Edwards T. 2007. *Language, affect, and politics in the deaf-blind community of Seattle, Washington*. MA thesis. Univ. Tex., Austin

Ellis C, Bochner A. 2000. Autoethnography, personal narrative, reflexivity: researcher as subject. In *Handbook of Qualitative Research*, ed. N Denzin, Y Lincoln, pp. 733–68. Thousand Oaks, CA: Sage

Erting CJ, Johnson RC, Snider BD, eds. 1994. *The Deaf Way: Perspectives from the International Conference on Deaf Culture*. Washington, DC: Gallaudet Univ. Press

Feld S. 1982. *Sound and Sentiment: Birds, Weeping, Poetics, and Song in Kaluli Expression*. Philadelphia: Univ. Penn. Press

Foss PD. 2006. *Exploring blind culture and life quality with seniors experiencing late-life sight loss*. PhD diss. Univ. Col., Boulder

Frank AW. 1995. *The Wounded Storyteller: Body, Illness, and Ethics*. Chicago: Chicago Univ. Press

Frank J. 2000. *Venus on Wheels: Two Decades on Disability, Biography, and Being Female in America*. Berkeley: Univ. Calif. Press

Gerber E. 2009. Describing tragedy: the information access needs of blind people in emergency-related circumstances. *Hum. Organ.* 68(1):73–81

Gibson JJ. 1966. *The Senses Considered as Perceptual Systems*. Boston: Houghton Mifflin

Goffman E. 1963. *Stigma: Notes on the Management of Spoiled Identity*. Penguin: Harmondsworth

Good B. 1994. *Medicine, Rationality, and Experience: An Anthropological Perspective*. Cambridge, UK: Cambridge Univ. Press

Goode DA. 1990. On understanding without words: communication between a deaf-blind child and her parents. *Hum. Stud.* 13:1–37

Goodwin C. 2004. A competent speaker who can't speak: the social life of aphasia. *J. Linguist. Anthropol.* 14(2):151–70

Groce NE. 1985. *Everyone Here Spoke Sign Language: Hereditary Deafness on Martha's Vineyard*. Cambridge, MA: Harvard Univ. Press

Grushkin D. 2003. A dual identity critical for students. *Odyssey* 4(2):48–49

Gwaltney J. 1980. Darkly through the glass of progress. *Pap. Anthropol. 21*, Anthropol. Dep., Univ. Okla.

Gwaltney JL. 1970. *The Thrice Shy: Cultural Accommodation to Blindness and Other Disasters in a Mexican Community*. New York: Columbia Univ. Press

Hadder RN. 2007. *Apparitions of difference: essays on the vocation of reflexive anthropology*. PhD diss. Univ. Tex., Austin, Dep. Anthropol.

Hanks W. 1990. *Referential Practice: Language and Lived Space among the Maya*. Chicago: Univ. Chicago Press

Howes D, ed. 1991. *The Varieties of Sensory Experience*. Toronto: Univ. Tor. Press

Howes D. 2003. *Sensual Relations: Engaging the Senses in Culture and Social Theory*. Ann Arbor: Univ. Mich. Press

Hughes B, Paterson K. 1997. The social model of disability and the disappearing body: towards a sociology of impairment. *Disabil. Soc.* 12:325–40

Hull JM. 1992. *Touching the Rock: An Experience of Blindness*. New York: Vintage

Hutchinson B, Smith B, eds. 2004. *Gendering Disability Studies*. New Brunswick, NJ: Rutgers

Ingstad B, Whyte SR, eds. 1995. *Disability and Culture*. Berkeley: Univ. Calif. Press

Iwakuma M. 2002. The body as embodiment: an investigation of the body by Merleau-Ponty. In *Disability/Postmodernity*, ed. M Corker, T Shakespeare, pp. 76–87. London: Continuum

Johnson RE. 1991. Sign language, culture and community in a traditional Yucatec Maya village. *Sign Lang. Stud.* 73:461–74

Jones SH. 2005. Autoethnography: making the personal political. In *The Sage Handbook of Qualitative Research*, ed. N Denzin, Y Lincoln, pp. 762–92. Thousand Oaks, CA: Sage

Kasnitz D, Shuttleworth RP. 2001. Anthropology and disability studies. In *Semiotics and Dis/ability: Interrogating Categories of Difference*, ed. L Rogers, B Swadener, pp. 19–41. Albany: SUNY Press

Keating E. 2005. Homo prostheticus: problematizing the notions of activity and computer-mediated interaction. *Discourse Stud.* 7(4–5):527–45

Keating E, Mirus G. 2003a. American Sign Language in virtual space: interactions between deaf users of computer-mediated video communication and the impact of technology on language practices. *Lang. Soc.* 32:693–714

Keating E, Mirus G. 2003b. Examining interactions across language modalities: deaf children and hearing peers at school. *Anthropol. Educ. Q.* 34(2):115–35

Kennedy J. 1974. Cultural psychiatry. In *Handbook of Social and Cultural Anthropology*, ed. JJ Honigmann, pp. 1119–98. Chicago: Rand McNally

Kirschbaum H. 1991. Disability and humiliation. *J. Prim. Prev.* 12:169–81

Kisch S. 2004. Negotiating (genetic) deafness in a Bedouin community. In *Genetics, Disability and Deafness*, ed. J van Cleve, pp. 148–73. Washington, DC: Gallaudet Univ. Press

Kleege G. 1999. *Sight Unseen*. New Haven: Yale Univ. Press

Kleinman A. 1988. *The Illness Narrative. Suffering, Healing and the Human Condition*. New York: Basic Books

Klotz J. 2003. *The culture concept: anthropology, disability studies and intellectual disability*. Paper presented at Disabil. Stud. Res. Inst. Symp., Disabil. Cutting Edge. Univ. Technol., Sydney, Aust.

Kuusisto S. 2006. *Eavesdropping: A Memoir of Blindness and Listening*. New York: Norton

Ladd P. 2003. *Understanding Deaf Culture. In Search of Deafhood*. Toronto: Multiling. Matters

Lane H. 1984. *When the Mind Hears*. New York: Random House

Lane H, Hoffmeister R, Bahan B. 1996. *A Journey into the Deaf-World*. San Diego, CA: Dawn Sign Press

LeMaster B. 2003. School language and shifts in Irish deaf identity. See Monaghan et al. 2003, pp. 153–72

Linde C. 1993. *Life Stories: The Creation of Coherence*. New York: Oxford Univ. Press

Longmore PK, Umansky L, eds. 2001. *The New Disability History: American Perspectives*. New York: N. Y. Univ. Press

Lucas C, Valli C. 1992. *Language Contact in the American Deaf Community*. New York: Academic

Lusseyran J. 1999. *Against the Pollution of the I: Selected Writings of Jacques Lusseyran*. New York: Parabola Books

Majid A, Levinson S. 2009. *An overview of the senses across languages and cultures*. Presented at Annu. Meet. Am. Anthropol. Assoc., 108th, Phila.

Macpherson H. 2009. Articulating blind touch: thinking through the feet. *Senses Soc.* 4(2):179–93

Marks D. 1999. *Disability: Controversial Debates and Psychosocial Perspectives*. London/New York: Routledge

Marshall M. 1996. Problematizing impairment: cultural competence in the Carolines. *Ethnology* 35(4):249–63

Mattingly C. 1998. *Healing Dramas and Clinical Plots: The Narrative Structure of Experience*. Cambridge, UK: Cambridge Univ. Press

Mattingly C, Garro LC, eds. 2000. *Narrative and the Cultural Construction of Illness and Healing*. Berkeley: Univ. Calif. Press

McDermott R, Varenne H. 1995. Culture 'as' disability. *Anthropol. Educ. Q.* 26(3):324–48

McRuer R. 2006. *Crip Theory: Cultural Signs of Queerness and Disability*. New York: N. Y. Univ. Press

Mehta V. 2001. *All For Love*. New York: Thunder's Mouth/Nation Books

Meier RP, Quinto D, Cormier K, eds. 2009. *Modality and Structure in Signed and Spoken Languages*. Cambridge, UK: Cambridge Univ. Press

Michalko R. 1998. *The Mystery of the Eye and the Shadow of Blindness*. Toronto: Univ. Tor. Press

Mills W. 1994. Silent bodies: the intricacies of sub-oral communication. *Anthropol. Work Rev.* 15:15–18

Monaghan LF, Nakamura K, Schmaling C, Turner GH, eds. 2003. *Many Ways to be Deaf: International Variation in Deaf Communities*. Washington, DC: Gallaudet Univ. Press

Morford J. 1996. Insights to language from the study of gesture: a review of research on the gestural communication of non-signing Deaf people. *Lang. Commun.* 16(2):165–78

Mpofu E, Harley D. 2002. Disability and rehabilitation in Zimbabwe: lessons and implications for rehabilitation practice in the US. *J. Rehabil.* 68(4):26–33

Murphy R. 1987. *The Body Silent*. New York: Holt

Nakamura K. 2006. *Deaf in Japan: Signing and the Politics of Identity*. Ithaca, NY: Cornell Univ. Press

Nonaka A. 2009. Estimating size, scope, and membership of the speech/sign communities of undocumented indigenous/village sign languages: the Ban Khor case study. *Lang. Commun.* 29:210–29

Oliver M. 1990. *The Politics of Disablement: A Sociological Approach*. New York: St. Martin's

Ottenberg S. 1996. *Seeing with Music: The Lives of 3 Blind African Musicians*. Seattle: Univ. Wash. Press

Padden C. 1996. From the cultural to the bicultural: the modern Deaf community. In *Cultural and Language Diversity: Reflections on the Deaf Experience*, ed. I Parasnis, pp. 79–98. New York: Cambridge Univ. Press

Padden C, Humpries T. 1988. *Deaf in America: Voices from a Culture*. Cambridge, MA: Harvard Univ. Press

Padden C, Meir I, Aronoff M, Sandler W. 2010. The grammar of space in two new sign languages. In *Sign Languages: A Cambridge Survey*, ed. D Brentari. New York: Cambridge Univ. Press. In press

Parasnis I, ed. 1996. *Cultural and Language Diversity and the Deaf Experience*. Cambridge, UK: Cambridge Univ. Press

Paterson K, Hughes B. 1999. Phenomenology: the carnal politics of everyday life. *Disabil. Soc.* 14(5):597–610

Polich L. 2005. *The Emergence of the Deaf Community in Nicaragua*. Washington, DC: Gallaudet Univ. Press

Preston P. 1994. *Mother Father Deaf: Living Between Sound and Silence*. Cambridge, MA: Harvard Univ. Press

Reddy WM. 2001. *The Navigation of Feeling: A Framework for the History of Emotions*. New York: Cambridge Univ. Press

Reichel-Dolmatoff G. 1981. Brain and mind in Desana shamanism. *J. Lat. Am. Lore* 7(1):73–98

Reid-Cunningham AR. 2009. Anthropological theories of disability. *J. Hum. Behav. Soc. Environ.* 19(1):99–111

Rengiil Y, Jarrow J. 1994. Culture and disability in Palau. *Int. Rehabil. Digest* 37(6):1–3

Ritchie I. 1991. Fusion of the faculties: a study of the language of the senses in Hausaland. See Howes 1991, pp. 192–202

Roseman M. 1991. *Healing Sounds from the Malaysian Rainforest: Temiar Music and Medicine*. Berkeley: Univ. Calif. Press

Sacks O. 1996. *The Island of the Colorblind*. New York: Knopf

Sacks O. 2003. The mind's eye. *New Yorker*, July 28:48–59

Sandler W, Meir I, Padden C, Aronoff M. 2005. The emergence of grammar: systematic structure in a new language. *Proc. Natl. Acad. Sci. USA* 102:2661–65

Schacht RM. 2001. Engaging anthropology in disability studies: American Indian issues. *Disabil. Stud. Q.* 21(3):17–36

Scheer J, Groce N. 1988. Impairment as a human constant: cross-cultural and historical perspectives on variation. *J. Soc. Issues* 44:23–37

Scheper-Hughes N, Lock MM. 1987. The mindful body: a prolegomenon to future work. *Med. Anthropol. Q.* 1(1):6–41

Scott RA. 1969. *The Making of Blind Men: A Study of Adult Socialization*. New York: Russell Sage Found.

Senghas RJ. 2003. New ways to be deaf in Nicaragua: changes in language, personhood, and community. See Monaghan et al. 2003, pp. 260–82

Senghas RJ, Monaghan L. 2002. Signs of their times: Deaf communities and the culture of language. *Annu. Rev. Anthropol.* 31:69–97

Sentumbwe N. 1995. Sighted lovers and blind husbands: experiences of blind women in Uganda. See Ingstad & Whyte 1995, pp. 159–73

Serematakis CN. 1994. *The Senses Still*. Chicago: Univ. Chicago Press

Serres M. 2009. *The Five Senses*. New York: Continuum Int.

Shakespeare T. 1994. Cultural representation of disabled people: dustbins for disavowal? *Disabil. Soc.* 9(3):283–99

Shuttleworth R, Kasnitz D. 2004. Stigma, community, ethnography: Joan Ablon's contribution to the anthropology of impairment-disability. *Med. Anthropol. Q.* 18(2):139–61

Slobin DI. 1971. *Psycholinguistics*. Glenview, IL: Scott Foresman

Snyder S, Mitchell D. 2005. *Cultural Locations of Disability*. Chicago: Univ. Chicago Press

Snyder SL, Mitchell DT. 2001. Re-engaging the body: disability studies and the resistance to embodiment. *Public Cult.* 13:367–89

Sparkes A. 2002. Autoethnography: self-indulgence or something more? In *Ethnographically Speaking: Autoethnography, Literature, and Aesthetics*, ed. A Bochner, C Ellis, pp. 209–32. Walnut Creek, CA: AltaMira

Spiegel D, ed. 1994. *Dissociation: Culture, Mind, and Body*. Washington, DC: Am. Psychiatr. Press

Steiner M. 1994. When an other meets an other: coming I-to-I. *Anthropol. Work Rev.* 15:10–11

Stern DB. 1997. *Unformulated Experience: From Dissociation to Imagination in Psychoanalysis*. Hillsdale, NJ: Academic

Stewart K. 2007. *Ordinary Affects*. Durham, NC: Duke Univ. Press

Stokoe WC. 1980. Sign language structure. *Annu. Rev. Anthropol.* 9:365–90

Straus JN. 2006. Normalizing the abnormal: disability in music and music theory. *J. Am. Musicol. Soc.* 59(1):113–84

Thomas C. 1999. *Female Forms: Experiencing and Understanding Disability*. Philadelphia: Open Univ. Press

Thomas C, Corker M. 2002. A journey around the social model. In *Disability/Postmodernity: Embodying Disability Theory*, ed. M Corker, T Shakespeare, pp. 18–31. London: Continuum

Titchkosky T. 2002. *Disability, Self, and Society*. Toronto: Univ. Tor. Press

Tremain S, ed. 2005. *Foucault and the Government of Disability*. Ann Arbor: Univ. Mich. Press

Vaughan CE. 2000. *Social and Cultural Perspectives on Blindness: Barriers to Community Integration*. Washington, DC: Natl. Libr. Serv. Blind Phys. Handicap.

Vaughan CE. 2002. The Itako—a spiritual occupation for blind Japanese girls. *Braille Monit.* May: **http://nfb.org/legacy/bm/bm02/bm0205/bm020511.htm**

Washabaugh W. 1981. Sign language in its social context. *Annu. Rev. Anthropol.* 10:237–52

Wendell S. 1996. *The Rejected Body: Feminist Philosophical Reflections on Disability*. New York: Routledge

Wikan U. 2000. With life in one's lap: the story of an eye/i (or two). See Mattingly & Garro 2000, pp. 212–36

Wilce J. 2009. *Language and Emotion*. Cambridge, UK: Cambridge Univ. Press

Wilson JC, Lewiecki-Wilson CL, eds. 2001. *Embodied Rhetorics: Disability in Language and Culture*. Carbondale: South. Ill. Univ. Press

Woll B, Sutton-Spence R, Elton F. 2001. Multilingualism: the global approach to sign languages. In *The Sociolinguistics of Sign Languages*, ed. C Lucas, pp. 8–32. Cambridge, UK: Cambridge Univ. Press

Woodward J, Allen T. 1993. Models of deafness compared: a sociolinguistic study of deaf and hard of hearing teachers. *Sign Lang. Stud.* 79:113–25

Woolgar C. 2006. *The Senses in Late Medieval England*. New Haven, CT: Yale Univ. Press

Zola IK. 1982. *Missing Pieces: A Chronicle of Living with a Disability*. Philadelphia: Temple Univ. Press

Peopling of the Pacific:
A Holistic Anthropological
Perspective

Patrick V. Kirch

Departments of Anthropology and Integrative Biology, University of California, Berkeley, California 94720; email: kirch@berkeley.edu

Annu. Rev. Anthropol. 2010. 39:131–48

First published online as a Review in Advance on June 14, 2010

The *Annual Review of Anthropology* is online at anthro.annualreviews.org

This article's doi: 10.1146/annurev.anthro.012809.104936

Key Words

Near Oceania, Remote Oceania, cultural phylogeny, historical anthropology, voyaging

Abstract

The human colonization of the Pacific is an enduring problem in historical anthropology. Recent advances in archaeology, historical linguistics, and bioanthropology have coalesced to form a set of models for population movements and interactions in Oceania, which have been tested on independent data sets. Earliest human movements into Near Oceania began about 40,000 years ago, resulting in great cultural, linguistic, and genetic diversity in this region. About 4000 years ago, the expansion of Austronesian speakers out of Southeast Asia led to the emergence of the Lapita cultural complex in Near Oceania. The Lapita expansion into Remote Oceania, commencing about 1200 BC, led ultimately to the settlement of the vast eastern Pacific, ending with the colonization of New Zealand about AD 1250. Polynesians probably reached the coast of South America, returning with the sweet potato and possibly the bottle gourd. Polynesian influences on New World cultures remain a topic of debate.

*In these Proes or Pahee's as the[y] call them...
these people sail in those seas from Island to Island
for several hundred Leagues, the Sun serving them
for a compass by day and the Moon and Stars by
night. When this comes to be prov'd we Shall be
no longer at a loss to know how the Islands lying in
those Seas came to be people'd, for... it cannot be
doubted but that the inhabitants of those western
Islands may have been at others as far to westward
of them and so we may trace them from Island to
Island quite to the East Indias.*

James Cook, 1769 (In Beaglehole 1955, p. 154)

In the late eighteenth century, James Cook and
other European voyagers of the Enlightenment
puzzled at how even the most remote of Pacific
islands had been discovered and peopled by indigenous populations, spawning varied theories
and a sizeable literature (Howard 1967). A century later, scholars such as Fornander (1878)
synthesized Polynesian oral traditions into
historical accounts of dubious veracity, tracing
Polynesians back to mythical homelands in
South Asia. The advent of modern anthropology in the early twentieth century led to a
re-engagement with the "problem of Polynesian origins" (Kirch 2000, pp. 20–27). However,
with the methods of archaeology and physical
anthropology still underdeveloped, comparative ethnology dominated. The results ranged
from Handy's (1930) *Kulturkriese* diffusionism
to Rivers's (1914) division of Oceanic peoples
into the "Kava" and the "Betel people." Buck's
(1938) sweeping synthesis, forged in a mid-
twentieth century cauldron of racial prejudice,
invoked flawed essentialist notions of human
biological types to trace "Caucasoid" Polynesian migrations around the fringe of "Negroid"
Melanesia (see Kirch 2000, pp. 24–27).

As stratigraphic archaeology commenced in
the Pacific following World War II, the ethnologists lost interest in historical questions,
and the search to trace the origins of Oceanic
peoples shifted increasingly to anthropology's
other subdisciplines. Archaeological fieldwork
began in earnest in Polynesia in the 1950s
and 1960s, and began to make major strides
in Melanesia and Micronesia in the 1970s and

1980s. At the same time, a small but energetic group of linguists tackled the historical
relationships among the 2000 or more languages spoken throughout the Pacific. This
launched a productive and continuing engagement between linguists and prehistorians, who
recognized the potential of testing each other's
models against independent data (Green 1999).
And, as the old physical anthropology was
transformed into a modern bioanthropology,
the unparalleled human biological diversity of
the Pacific proved fertile ground for testing
new methods of population genetics (Hill &
Serjeantson 1989, Friedlaender 2007).

The past 30 years, especially, have seen
an explosion of new archaeological, linguistic,
and bioanthropological data and interpretation
bearing on the long-standing questions of when
and how people entered the Pacific and managed to discover and colonize virtually every
one of its thousands of islands. The founders of
four-field anthropology, such as Sapir (1916),
envisioned the power that a holistic approach
could bring to historical questions, but they
lacked the tools to fully implement it. In the
Pacific, this potential has now been realized
through the interdisciplinary collaboration of
archaeology, historical linguistics, and bioanthropology. To be sure, not all of the questions
have been answered, but immense forward mo-
mentum has been gained, as this essay seeks to
demonstrate.

MULTIDISCIPLINARY ADVANCES IN KNOWLEDGE

Archaeology

By 1980, three major conclusions could be advanced based on accumulating evidence from
archaeological excavations, accompanied by an
increasingly robust radiocarbon chronology:
(*a*) Polynesia was the last part of the Pacific to
have been settled, and the immediate homeland of the Polynesians was in the Tonga-
Samoa region; (*b*) a distinctive ceramic series
named Lapita linked the earliest sites in Tonga
and Samoa with sites scattered throughout

island Melanesia, thus bridging the classic ethnographic divide between Melanesia and Polynesia; and (c) the large island of New Guinea had the greatest time depth, with demonstrated Pleistocene settlement (Golson 1972). However, significant debate ensued about whether Lapita represented a population intrusion into Melanesia from Southeast Asia, or whether it was an indigenous development in the New Guinea-Bismarck Archipelago region (Allen 1984). This debate has at times been caricatured as competing "fast train to Polynesia" versus "tangled bank" models (Terrell 1986, Diamond 1988, Oppenheimer 2004). In part, the debate revolves around the question of whether phylogenetic signals of human history (i.e., homologous changes) are detectable in linguistic and genetic patterns of variation in the Pacific, or whether intergroup contact and reticulation has been so pervasive as to have erased such phylogenetic history (Bellwood 1996, Terrell et al. 1997, Kirch & Green 2001, Greenhill & Gray 2005).

The multi-institutional Lapita Homeland Project (LHP), launched in 1984, sought to address this debate within the ambit of the Bismarck Archipelago. The project's several field teams acquired invaluable new data on Lapita sites (Gosden et al. 1989), but also demonstrated that human populations had moved into the large islands of New Britain and New Ireland in the Pleistocene, by about 36,000 BP (Wickler & Spriggs 1988, Allen & Gosden 1991, Smith & Sharp 1993). Building on the impetus of the LHP, archaeological excavations in both pre-Lapita and Lapita sites throughout island Melanesia have continued unabated over the past three decades (Kirch 1997, Galipaud & Lilley 1999, Clark et al. 2001, Summerhayes 2007, Sheppard et al. 2009). One outcome has been a resolution of the fast train/tangled bank debate in favor of the interpretation of Lapita as the outcome of a population intrusion (specifically, of Austronesian language speakers) into the New Guinea–Bismarck region. At the same time, Lapita is seen as something more complex than demic expansion alone, summed up in Green's Triple-I model of intrusion, innovation, and integration (Green 1991, Kirch 1997).

A fundamental conceptual revision to come out of the LHP and subsequent research is the abandonment of the nineteenth century, racist division of Oceania into Melanesia, Micronesia, and Polynesia (proposed by the French explorer Dumont D'Urville in 1832) and its replacement with the categories of *Near Oceania* and *Remote Oceania* (Green 1991). Near Oceania incorporates New Guinea, the Bismarck Archipelago, and the Solomon Islands as far as San Cristobal and Santa Anna, whereas Remote Oceania includes the rest of the Pacific proper. These new divisions are based on the archaeological demonstration that Near Oceania has a significantly greater time depth of human settlement, extending back into the Pleistocene, whereas human incursions into Remote Oceania did not begin until around 4000 BP (in western Micronesia) and were not completed until as recently as 1000 BP. The old tripartite categories still find use as geographical shorthand terms, and Polynesia has proven to be a meaningful culture-historical category, as all Polynesian populations and languages prove to be descendants of a common clade (Kirch & Green 2001). But Melanesia has no explanatory value other than as a geographic space; to speak of Melanesian peoples implies nothing about common origins or relationships in any genetic sense.

Historical Linguistics

The integrity of a widespread *Austronesian* language family (sometimes referred to in older literature as Malayo-Polynesian), including approximately 1200 modern languages spread from Madagascar to Easter Island, was well established by the mid-twentieth century (Blust 1996). Significant advances came from the 1970s onwards with delineation of the place of the *Oceanic* subgroup of Austronesian, and of the internal branching structure and relationships of the Oceanic languages, which include most of the languages spoken in island Melanesia (outside of New Guinea) and

Micronesia, and all of those in Polynesia (Pawley 1972; Ross 1988, 1989). The Oceanic subgroup and the historical relationships among its languages are now well understood, even to the point of detailed reconstructions of Proto Oceanic vocabulary and culture (Pawley & Ross 1993). Moreover, it is widely accepted that Proto Oceanic was the language of the earliest Lapita populations in Near Oceania (Pawley & Green 1984; Kirch 1997, pp. 88–96). Recently, work on the genetic relationships of Oceanic and other Austronesian languages has benefited not only from traditional comparative linguistic methods but also from the application of cladistic procedures derived from biology (Gray & Jordan 2000, Hurles et al. 2003, Greenhill & Gray 2005, Gray et al. 2009).

A large group of languages centered in New Guinea with a few isolates in the Bismarcks and Solomons (numbering perhaps 950 languages) proved more refractory to historical linguistic analysis due to their immense variation. Initially lumped as non-Austronesian, this negatively defined category has been replaced with the term Papuan, while recognizing that this is not a single language family (Foley 1986, Pawley 2007). Rather, Papuan incorporates at least 23 distinct families that appear to be unrelated to each other (at least such relationships are not detectable on present evidence), and another 10 isolates (Ross 2005). The largest single family grouping within Papuan is the Trans-New Guinea Phylum, which includes between 350 and 450 languages dispersed across the island of New Guinea (Pawley 2007).

The emerging picture of Pacific historical linguistics is thus one of extraordinary diversity confined within Near Oceania (the Papuan languages), along with the Oceanic subgroup of Austronesian that displays clear internal relationships due to relatively shallow time depth, but is dispersed from Near Oceania all the way to the geographic extremes of Remote Oceania. At the broadest level, there is remarkable congruence between the archaeological and linguistic evidence for deep-time, Pleistocene settlement of Near Oceania (giving rise to the protean Papuan languages), and late Holocene expansion of Lapita and post-Lapita populations into Remote Oceania (corresponding to the spread of Oceanic languages).

Bioanthropology

Physical anthropologists in the early decades of the twentieth century attempted to describe and classify Pacific peoples based on such categories as skin color, hair type, and through large series of metric indices. Beginning in the 1970s, some of these older data were reanalyzed using new multivariate statistical methods (Howells 1970, Pietrusewsky 1970, Houghton 1996) yielding new insights into the relationships among Pacific populations. These methods, however, had their limitations, and Howells, for example, was still led to write that the Melanesians "were so protean and varied as to resist satisfactory analysis" (1970, p. 192). The major breakthrough came with a modern bioanthropology that adopted the methods of population genetics and molecular biology, especially through sequencing of mitochondrial DNA (mtDNA) and nonrecombining Y-chromosome (NRY) DNA (Hill & Serjeantson 1989, Martinson et al. 1993, Boyce et al. 1995, Martinson 1996, Melton et al. 1998, Friedlaender 2007, Friedlaender et al. 2008). One of the first major discoveries was that Polynesians and island Southeast Asians shared a particular nine-base-pair deletion in mtDNA, sometimes called the Polynesian motif (Hertzberg et al. 1989, Lum et al. 1998, Lum & Cann 1998, Merriwether et al. 1999). This evidence appeared to strengthen the archaeolinguistic argument in favor of a fast-train dispersal out of Southeast Asia. Subsequent work on NRY variations, however, showed that the dominant Y haplotype in Polynesians is likely to be of Melanesian (Near Oceanic) origin (Kayser et al. 2000, Su et al. 2000, Hurles et al. 2002). This apparent contradiction in the mtDNA and NRY evidence can be resolved through a model of matrilocal residence in the early Oceanic-speaking (i.e., Lapita) populations, whereby Melanesian men were recruited into Lapita communities (Hage

& Marck 2003; Kayser et al. 2006, 2008; Jordan et al. 2009). These data also provide support for a slow-boat model of Polynesian origins, whereby "... Polynesian ancestors originated from East Asia but genetically mixed with Melanesians before colonizing the Pacific" (Kayser et al. 2008, p. 1362; Vilar et al. 2008). A period of sustained gene flow between ancestral Polynesian and Melanesian populations is also evidenced by the presence of an α-thalassemia deletion, which confers resistance to malaria, and must have been transferred to the ancestral Polynesian populations in Near Oceania before their dispersal to Remote Oceania, where malaria is generally absent (Hill et al. 1985, Martinson 1996).

In addition to testing models of Austronesian expansion into the Pacific, recent molecular studies have made significant contributions to understanding genetic diversity within Near Oceania. The various studies of mtDNA and NRY variation in northern Melanesia summarized above support an interpretation of great time depth in this region; microsatellite diversity gives estimated divergence ages of between 32,000 and 50,000 years for haplotypes that developed in Near Oceania (Friedlaender 2007, p. 92). Moreover, Papuan-speaking language groups (typically inland populations) are genetically the "most distinctive" in island Melanesia (Friedlaender 2007, p. 232). These findings correlate well with the archaeolinguistic model of Pleistocene settlement of Near Oceania by ancestors of Papuan-speaking groups.

Finally, the new molecular methods have also been applied to other organisms as proxies for human movement. The Pacific rat (*Rattus exulans*) was carried by voyagers from Near Oceania into Remote Oceania, either as a food item or as an inadvertent stowaway. mtDNA phylogenies of *R. exulans* show the presence of three major haplogroups, the distributions of which are consistent with the Triple-I model of Lapita origins in Near Oceania (Matisoo-Smith & Robins 2004). Recent genetic analysis of a human bacterial parasite, *Helicobacter pylori*, showed two distinct populations: (*a*) an hpSahul population with an estimated divergence age of 23,000–32,000 years, which is confined to Near Oceania; and (*b*) hpMaori, which is believed to have accompanied Austronesian expansion out of Taiwan at about 5,000 years ago (Moodley et al. 2009).

NEAR OCEANIA

Pleistocene Arrivals

The first arrival of people in Near Oceania must be understood within the context of Pleistocene biogeography and dynamic sea levels. For much of the later Pleistocene, lowered sea levels resulted in New Guinea being joined to Australia (and the latter to Tasmania), making up the supercontinent of Sahul. To the east, the Malay Peninsula was similarly joined to the Indonesian island arc as far east as Bali, along with Kalimantan, a vast area known as Sunda. Between Sunda and Sahul lies the island world of Wallacea in which water gaps were continuously present, making Wallacea a major barrier to plant and animal dispersal. The human colonization of Sahul, including Near Oceania, thus required some form of water-crossing ability, and it is increasingly evident that some kinds of simple watercraft—such as bamboo rafts, bark boats, or dugout canoes—must have been involved (Irwin 1993). This was true not only for crossing Wallacea, but for moving from New Guinea into the Bismarck Archipelago and the Solomons, where the islands were also always separated from each other by water gaps (**Figure 1**).

Upwards of 150 archaeological sites dating to the Pleistocene have been recorded in Sahul (Smith & Sharp 1993). Once humans had entered the continent, they spread rapidly over all of its varied ecosystems from the tropical north to the temperate south, displaying a remarkable adaptability. Within Near Oceania proper, the earliest archaeological evidence remains that at Huon on the northern coast of New Guinea, where split-cobble waisted blades have been bracketed between 60,000 and 40,000 years BP (Groube et al. 1986). The large islands of New Britain and New Ireland both have evidence

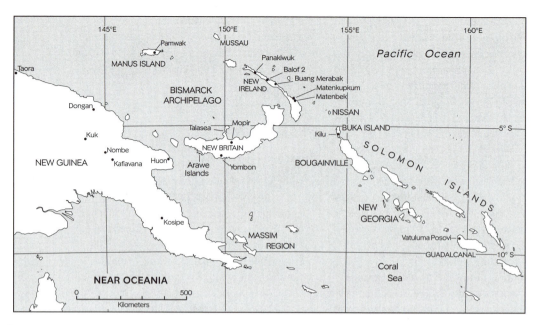

Figure 1

Map of Near Oceania, showing the location of key archaeological sites.

for occupation by around 35,000 BP (Allen & Gosden 1991, Pavlides & Gosden 1994, Allen 1996), Buka in the northern Solomons was settled by around 28,000 BP (Wickler & Spriggs 1988), and Manus sometime before 13,000 BP (Fredericksen et al. 1993).

Space limitations preclude a review here of cultural developments within Near Oceania during the late Pleistocene and early Holocene (but see Kirch 2000, pp. 70–84; Spriggs 1997). Suffice it to say that this period of thirty millennia provided the time depth necessary both for the emergence of a high degree of linguistic diversity (the Papuan languages), and for the evolution of human biological diversity including the various indigenous Near Oceanic mtDNA and NRY haplogroups referred to earlier (Friedlaender 2007).

Austronesian Incursion and Lapita Origins

It was into this landscape of cultural, linguistic, and biological diversity that a new population (or populations) with origins in island Southeast Asia moved beginning around 4000–3500 years BP, an eastwards advancing prong of the larger Austronesian expansion (Bellwood 2005, Donohue & Denham 2010). Aside from being marked by their obvious linguistic identity, these immediately pre-Oceanic speakers possessed at least two critical technological complexes: (*a*) ceramics and (*b*) the sailing outrigger canoe. Although there have been claims for pre-Lapita ceramics on New Guinea, there is no evidence thus far throughout the Bismarcks or Solomons for pottery making prior to Lapita. The Austronesian origins of the outrigger sailing canoe, or *waŋka* to use the Proto Austronesian word, are especially well attested on linguistic evidence (Pawley & Pawley 1994). Although these pre-Oceanic speaking voyagers also possessed a horticultural economy, this was not new to Near Oceania, where various tuber, fruit, and nut-bearing plants had already been domesticated. Nor was sophisticated shell working necessarily an Austronesian innovation, as there is evidence for shell tool manufacture in the Bismarcks at a quite early date.

The aceramic to ceramic transition in Near Oceania is still a phenomenon of active research and debate, in part exacerbated by violent eruptive events on New Britain that blanketed parts of that island with thick tephra (the W-K2 event) around 3600 BP, probably causing major population disruptions (Specht 2009). However, sites containing the distinctive dentate-stamped Lapita ceramics appear quite rapidly in the Bismarck Archipelago, possibly as early as 3500 BP in Mussau (Kirch 2001), but certainly by 3300–3000 BP at a number of localities (Specht & Gosden 1997, Summerhayes 2001). The immediate homeland of these pottery-making groups is likely to be the Sulawesi-Halmahera region, where similar pottery (but lacking the distinctive dentate stamped decoration) has been recovered (Kirch 1995). This is also consistent with linguistic evidence, since the closest external subgroup to the Oceanic languages are those of the South Halmahera-West New Guinea subgroup; both of these are branches of the Eastern Malayo-Polynesian languages (Kirch & Green 2001, figure 2.1).

As noted earlier, the emergence of Lapita in the Bismarcks has been debated in terms such as "fast train," "tangled bank," and "slow boat." While there is little doubt that a demic intrusion of pre-Oceanic speakers from island Southeast Asia was a key part of the process, a strictly fast train model can be rejected in favor a slow boat in which the intrusive populations not only interacted with pre-existing Papuan-speaking communities in the Bismarcks, but intermarried with them as well. The complex patterns of genetic and linguistic diversity found today in Near Oceania (Friedlaender 2007, Friedlaender et al. 2008) can only be explained as the outcome of such complex cultural, linguistic, and genetic exchanges. (The tangled bank model is also rejected, as it implies that no phylogenetic signals of the homologous relationships among these populations can be detected.) The best overall model for Lapita origins remains Green's (1991) Triple-I hypothesis, which posits that Lapita emerged out of a combination of intrusion, innovation, and integration processes.

REMOTE OCEANIA

The Lapita Expansion

Throughout the late Pleistocene and most of the Holocene, humans were confined to the geographically restricted region of Near Oceania, not venturing farther than the eastern end of the Solomons (San Cristobal and Santa Anna islands). Even the main Solomons may have been quite sparsely populated until the advent of Lapita, in part due to the rapid decline in terrestrial biodiversity as one moves from New Guinea and Bismarcks eastwards, limiting the potential resources for hunters and gatherers. Nonetheless, the Bismarcks to the Solomons comprise a chain of almost continuously intervisible island masses, which would have facilitated discovery of new islands and subsequent voyaging between them. Beyond Santa Anna, however, one encounters the first significant gap of 380 km of open ocean before landfall is reached in the Santa Cruz group. Beyond this, distances become even more formidable—some 800 km from northern Vanuatu to Fiji, for example. Making such long ocean crossings required seaworthy sailing craft, which the Lapita people had evidently perfected with a variant of the *waŋka outrigger canoe. Moreover, the colonization of Remote Oceania—which is far more biotically depauperate than is Near Oceania—also necessitated the ability to transport both crop plants and domestic animals to newfound islands. Although island colonizers may have relied heavily for the first few months on abundant wild birds and seafood, in the long run the success of new colonies depended on the establishment of horticultural production systems.

The timing of the Lapita expansion out of Near Oceania into the southwestern archipelagoes of Remote Oceania (**Figure 2**) has been narrowed down by extensive radiocarbon dating to the three centuries between 3200 and 2900 BP, a time span equivalent to roughly 15 human generations. The earliest Lapita settlement in the Reef-Santa Cruz group, the Nanggu site (SE-SZ-8), was occupied around

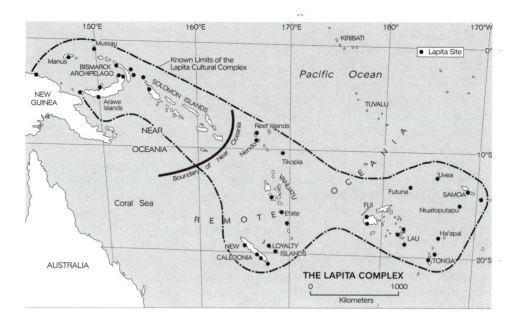

Figure 2

Map of the southwestern Pacific, showing the division between Near Oceania and Remote Oceania, and the extent of the Lapita Cultural Complex.

3200 BP (Green et al. 2008). From there colonization seems to have proceeded rapidly down through Vanuatu, across to the Loyalty Islands, and to La Grande Terre of New Caledonia. Sand (1997) puts the initial settlement of La Grande Terre at between 3000 and 2900 BP The wide ocean gap between Vanuatu and Fiji was crossed by between 3050 and 2950 BP (Anderson & Clark 1999, Clark & Anderson 2009), and Lapita colonization continued rapidly into the Lau and Tongan archipelagoes. Extensive dates from Lapita sites in the Ha'apai group of Tonga indicate initial settlements in place by 2850 BP (Burley et al. 1999). Samoa, along with Futuna and 'Uvea, were also settled at approximately this same time. Thus the Lapita expansion brought human settlement as far east as the Tonga-Samoa region, what is commonly known as Western Polynesia. At this point, further long-distance exploration to the east apparently halted, and would not be resumed until the later Polynesian diaspora in the first millennium AD.

Micronesia

Micronesia, one of D'Urville's three original divisions of Oceania, lies mostly north of the equator, stretching from Palau and the Marianas in the west, through the Caroline Islands, to the Marshall and Kiribati archipelagoes in the east, a distance of nearly 5000 km. Many of its islands are coral atolls, punctuated by such high volcanic islands as Chuuk, Pohnpei, and Kosrae. Biologically, Micronesian populations tend to share many traits with Polynesians based on either traditional morphometric analyses (Pietrusewsky 1970), or on more recent mtDNA analyses (Lum & Cann 1998, 2000).

The historical linguistic picture for Micronesia, which has been greatly clarified in recent years (Jackson 1986, Rehg 1995), is critical for understanding the settlement history of this vast region. Although all extant Micronesian languages are Austronesian, they do not all fall within the Oceanic subgroup, an exception within Remote Oceania. Specifically, the Chamorro (Marianas) and Palauan languages spoken in the westernmost archipelagoes belong to the Western Malayo-Polynesian subgroup of Austronesian, and are thus more closely related to many of the languages spoken in the Philippines and Indonesia. In contrast, all of the languages spoken in the Carolines, Marshalls, and Kiribati constitute a distinct subgroup of Oceanic languages, referred to as Nuclear Micronesian (Bender & Wang 1985), which is inferred to have derived from the initial breakup of Proto Oceanic. Finally, the language of Yap, which lies between Palau and the Carolines, has been shown to be an Oceanic language that has been modified through several phases of external contacts and borrowings (Ross 1996).

The historical linguistic evidence thus offers a three-part sequence for the peopling of Micronesia. An initial group (or groups) of Western Malayo-Polynesian speakers moved into Palau and the Marianas directly from island Southeast Asia. A second population (or closely related populations) would likely have originated in the Solomons-Vanuatu region, as a northern extension of the Lapita phenomenon at the time that the Proto Oceanic speech community was breaking up. This Proto Nuclear-Micronesian speech community may have been emplaced on more than a single island, possibly constituting a dialect chain spanning at least the high islands (and probably some atolls) of the central-eastern Micronesian region. Finally, Yap is likely to have been settled directly from the Bismarck Archipelago, but was then in later contact with islands both west and east.

Archaeological evidence increasingly supports the model offered by historical linguistics. The western island chains were the first to have been colonized, and early ceramics in the Marianas, such as those from the Achugao Point site radiocarbon dated to 1930–1630 BC (Butler 1994), display stylistic similarities with pottery from the Philippines and Sulawesi. In Palau, sediment cores with evidence for anthropogenic disturbance have been dated to as early as 2350 BC (Athens & Ward 2001), and pottery-bearing sites are known by 1250 BC (Liston 2009). In the Carolines, the earliest

documented settlements appear on the volcanic islands of Chuuk, Pohnpei, and Kosrae, all marked by calcareous sand-tempered ceramics associated with *Tridacna*-shell adzes and *Conus*-shell ornaments, all similar to late Lapita forms (Kirch 2000, pp. 173–175). Radiocarbon dates indicate settlement of these high islands in the last century or two of the first millennium BC. Similar-aged deposits have been excavated in the Marshall Islands (Weisler 2001), although these lack pottery. However, many atolls throughout central and western Micronesia may not have begun to form stable *motu* islets until well into the first millennium AD, following a late Holocene drop of about 1 m in sea level. Thus the atoll adaptations so characteristic of Micronesia are likely to be relatively recent developments. The archaeological picture for Yap is still enigmatic, as no primary settlement sites have as yet been identified or excavated.

The Polynesian Diaspora

Of the three regions defined by D'Urville in 1832, only Polynesia has stood the test of time as a meaningful unit of cultural history. As Kirch & Green (2001, pp. 53–91) argue, Polynesia constitutes a phylogenetic unit, a distinct clade. Biologically, Polynesian populations have long been noted for their relative homogeneity (Houghton 1996). Molecular analysis suggests that the founding population entering the Western Polynesian region passed through a constricted demographic bottleneck (Flint et al. 1989, Martinson et al. 1993, Harding & Clegg 1996). Linguistically, it is well established that all of the extant Polynesian languages form a single, well-defined subgroup of the Oceanic branch of Austronesian (Marck 1996). The Proto Polynesian interstage, which developed in the Tonga-Samoa region during the first millennium BC, is marked by roughly 1300 lexical innovations (Marck 2000). The initial breakup of Proto Polynesian (which probably constituted a dialect chain linking the islands from Tongatapu in the south up through Vava'u and Niuatoputapu to Samoa) led to two distinct branches: Tongic and Proto Nuclear Polynesian. The Eastern Polynesian languages derive from the Nuclear Polynesian subgroup, as do the Outlier Polynesian languages.

Whereas Western Polynesia is well established as the homeland region within which Ancestral Polynesian culture and Proto Polynesian language developed (Green 1981), debate has centered on the question of when Polynesians began to expand beyond the core homeland to settle Eastern Polynesia (Kirch 1986, Irwin 1992, Spriggs & Anderson 1993, Anderson 2001a). A long pause of at least 1000 years' duration lapsed between the initial Lapita settlement of Tonga-Samoa, and the subsequent expansion of Polynesian populations to the east. However, questions of just when long-distance voyages of colonization to the east commenced, how rapid was expansion into Eastern Polynesia, and how much time elapsed before Eastern Polynesia had been completely settled have been the focus of much recent research. Archaeological work in the 1950s and 1960s, in the Marquesas, Easter Island, and Hawai'i, led to interpretations of Eastern Polynesian colonization as early as AD 300, but the validity of many of the earlier radiocarbon dates has been called into question (Spriggs & Anderson 1993).

A considerably later chronology for initial Eastern Polynesian settlement has now emerged from the redating of key sites and assemblages, using improved methods such as accelerator mass spectrometry (AMS) ^{14}C. Among these are Ha'atuatua and Hane in the Marquesas (Anderson et al. 1994, Rolett & Conte 1995, Rolett 1998, Conte & Anderson 2003), the Bellows Dune and Halawa Dune sites in Hawai'i (Tuggle & Spriggs 2000, Kirch & McCoy 2007), the Maupiti and Vaito'otia sites in the Society Islands (Anderson & Sinoto 2002), along with several Archaic sites in New Zealand (Anderson & Wallace 1993, Anderson et al. 1996, Higham et al. 1999, Hogg et al. 2003). Newly discovered early sites in the Cooks, Mangareva, and Henderson-Pitcairn groups have added significantly to the corpus of chronological data (Kirch et al. 1995, Weisler 1995, Conte & Kirch 2004, Green & Weisler

2002), as have excavations in the Anakena beach site on Easter Island (Steadman et al. 1994, Hunt & Lipo 2006). The emerging picture is one of a fairly rapid Polynesian colonization of the chain of islands stretching from the Australs to Mangareva, Pitcairn-Henderson, and finally to Easter Island that occurred between roughly AD 800 and 1000. Hawai'i also seems to have been settled no earlier than AD 800 based on evidence from sediment cores and AMS dating of Pacific rat bones (Athens 1997, Athens et al. 2002). New Zealand was clearly the last of the major Polynesian islands to be discovered and settled, between about AD 1250 and 1300 (Hogg et al. 2003). However, the large and centrally situated Society Islands archipelago remains a gap in our knowledge of early sites, with the oldest evidence consisting of anaerobically preserved domesticated coconuts in a coastal swamp on Mo'orea Island (Lepofsky et al. 1992); clearly, more investigation in the Society Islands is warranted.

In contrast with earlier views that the settlement of Eastern Polynesia was accomplished by random drift (Sharp 1956), it is now certain that these widely dispersed islands were discovered as the result of purposive voyages of exploration enabled by a sophisticated canoe technology and navigational abilities (Finney 1996, 1997; Anderson 2001a,b). Here prehistorians have been aided by the knowledge gained from the experimental voyages of the *Hokule'a* and other replicated Polynesian double-hulled voyaging canoes (Finney 1994). Although there is some disagreement on this point, it is likely that the large ocean-going double-hulled sailing canoe (as opposed to the simpler sailing canoe with outrigger) was invented and perfected in the Western Polynesian homeland during the so-called "long pause" (Finney 2006). It was certainly the existence of this canoe type, with its vastly expanded range and cargo capacity that enabled the peopling of Eastern Polynesia. Moreover, it is increasingly evident that long-distance voyaging continued to link many of the Eastern Polynesian islands well after initial settlement, and the geochemical sourcing of basalt adzes in particular has demonstrated the existence of widespread interaction networks (Weisler 1998, Collerson & Weisler 2007).

The sequencing of mtDNA from extant populations and archaeological remains of the Pacific rat has also contributed to the emerging picture of Eastern Polynesian dispersals (Matisoo-Smith 1994, Matisoo-Smith et al. 1999, Matisoo-Smith & Robins 2004). These results indicate two separate introductions of *R. exulans* into the Hawaiian archipelago, lending independent support to archaeological and linguistic claims that Hawai'i had multiple voyages from central Eastern Polynesia. Hinkle (2004) analyzed molecular diversity in the Polynesian transported *ti* plant (*Cordyline fruticosa*), showing distinct Western and Eastern Polynesian clades; low levels of difference between the sterile Eastern Polynesian *ti* populations are consistent with a shallow time depth.

CONTACTS WITH THE AMERICAS

The theory that Eastern Polynesia, if not the Pacific islands more broadly, might have been peopled from the Americas has been proposed many times over the past two centuries (Howard 1967). It was most famously championed by Thor Heyerdahl (1952) who popularized the theory with his *Kon-Tiki* raft voyage. Most archaeologists never took Heyerdahl's ideas seriously, and none of the archaeological, linguistic, or biological evidence reviewed above lends any support to the intrusion of indigenous Native American populations into the Pacific in pre-Columbian times. However, the reverse proposition—that Polynesians sailed to the coasts of South and/or North America, making contact with populations there—seems increasingly likely, and has provoked recent debates.

The strongest evidence for Polynesian contact with South America is the sweet potato (*Ipomoea batatas*), a plant of undoubted American origins that was widely cultivated in Eastern Polynesia (especially in New Zealand, Hawai'i, and Easter Island) at the time of European contact. Yen's (1974) extensive

research on sweet potato distribution and variation led him to propose a "tripartite hypothesis" of the plant's distribution, in which sweet potato arrived in Eastern Polynesia in pre-European times, with the Polynesians themselves as the most likely transferors. The discovery and dating of carbonized sweet potato tubers (parenchyma) in the Tangatatau Rockshelter on Mangaia in the Southern Cooks (Hather & Kirch 1991) provided direct evidence that sweet potato had been transferred into central Polynesia by around AD 1000. Subsequently, many archaeobotanical samples of sweet potato have been radiocarbon dated to precontact contexts in New Zealand and Hawai'i. Given the evidence for rapid Polynesian expansion throughout southeastern Polynesia between about AD 800 and 1000, it is entirely plausible that at least one voyaging canoe reached South America to establish contact and return with sweet potato tubers, which then entered the Polynesian horticultural complex. Indeed, the adoption of sweet potato (as opposed to other American crops such as maize or beans) is culturally plausible, given that the plant is both morphologically and ecologically similar to the *Dioscorea* yams with which the Polynesians were already familiar. The Proto Eastern Polynesian name for sweet potato, *kuumara*, is almost certainly a borrowing from a South American dialect where the term for the crop is *kumar* or similar variants (Yen 1974, appendix; Green 2005).

A second possible botanical transfer into Polynesia is the bottle gourd (*Lagenaria siceraria*), a useful plant known to have been present in the Americas by at least 9900 BP. Archaeobotanical remains of bottle gourd (gourd fragments and seeds) have been recovered in precontact contexts in Hawai'i and elsewhere in Eastern Polynesia. A recent effort to test the hypothesis of a pre-Columbian American origin for the Polynesian bottle gourd using molecular evidence (Clarke et al. 2006) proved inconclusive, owing to the likelihood of postcontact hybridization with Asian cultivars. Nonetheless, *Lagenaria* remains a likely candidate for Polynesian transfer from South America.

If Polynesians made contact with coastal peoples in the Americas, the question arises whether this resulted in the flow of ideas, organisms, or even genes into the New World. One recent claim for such a Polynesia-to-America transfer concerns the jungle fowl (*Gallus gallus*), a species carried from Southeast Asia throughout the Pacific during the Austronesian expansion. Whether chickens were present in South America in pre-Columbian times has been debated, but Storey et al. (2007) report an AMS-dated chicken bone from the El Arenal site in south-central Chile, which, they argue, is evidence for Polynesian contact and introduction of *G. gallus*. The reported date, calibrated to AD 1321–1407, would fall toward the end of the period of extensive Eastern Polynesia voyaging, but certainly predates Spanish occupation (Pizarro reached Peru in 1532). This claim has provoked strong debate (Gongora et al. 2008, Storey et al. 2008), and more evidence from El Arenal or other sites will be required before a pre-Columbian transfer of chickens from Polynesia to South America can be firmly accepted.

A second case for Polynesian cultural influence in the New World has been made by Jones & Klar (2005), who argue that the sewn plank canoes of the Channel Islands region of California resulted from Polynesian contacts. They adduce both archaeological and linguistic evidence in support of their argument, which has again resulted in vigorous debate (Anderson 2006, Arnold 2007).

In short, some contact between Eastern Polynesians and indigenous American populations seems incontrovertible based on the evidence of the sweet potato. But much more research will be necessary to refine our understanding of such contact, and whether the Polynesians made any significant contributions to New World culture history.

CONCLUSION

The founders of an integrated, holistic approach to anthropology, including Sapir (1916), were confident that deep time problems of human history would be amenable to coordinated investigation by the discipline's several subfields. A century later, methodological advancements in archaeology, historical linguistics, and bioanthropology have made that vision a reality. The enduring problem of the peopling of the Pacific demonstrates the strength of building and testing models based on multiple lines of independent evidence. Moreover, claims that the genetic, linguistic, and cultural complexity of Oceania is so great (a "tangled bank") that no signals of homologous history may be detected has been shown to be false. While cultural contact, borrowings, and gene flow are indeed important parts of the history of Oceanic peoples, phylogenetic relationships can nonetheless be determined. In many ways, the Pacific serves as a model region for historical anthropology.

DISCLOSURE STATEMENT

The author is not aware of any affiliations, memberships, funding, or financial holdings that might be perceived as affecting the objectivity of this review.

LITERATURE CITED

Allen J. 1984. In search of the Lapita homeland. *J. Pac. Hist.* 19:186–201

Allen J. 1996. The pre-Austronesian settlement of island Melanesia: implications for Lapita archaeology. In *Prehistoric Settlement of the Pacific*, ed. WH Goodenough, pp. 11–27. *Trans. Am. Philos. Soc.* 86(5). Philadelphia

Allen J, Gosden C, ed. 1991. *Report of the Lapita Homeland Project. Occas. Pap. Prehist.*, No. 20. Canberra: Dep. Prehist., Aust. Natl. Univ.

Anderson A. 2001a. The chronology of prehistoric colonization in French Polynesia. In *Pacific 2000: Proc. Int. Conf. Easter Island Pac., 5th, Los Osos*, ed. CM Stevenson, G Lee, FJ Morin, pp. 247–52. Easter Island Found.

Anderson A. 2001b. Towards the sharp end: the form and performance of prehistoric Polynesian voyaging canoes. In *Pacific 2000: Proc. Int. Conf. Easter Island Pac., 5th, Los Osos*, ed. CM Stevenson, G Lee, FJ Morin, pp. 29–36. Easter Island Found.

Anderson A. 2006. Polynesian seafaring and American horizons: a response to Jones and Klar. *Am. Antiq.* 71:759–63

Anderson A, Allingham B, Smith I, ed. 1996. *Shag River Mouth: The Archaeology of an Early Southern Maori Village*. Res. Pap. Archaeol. Natl. Hist., No. 27, Aust. Natl. Univ., Canberra

Anderson A, Clark G. 1999. The age of Lapita settlement in Fiji. *Archaeol. Oceania* 34:31–39

Anderson A, Leach H, Smith I, Walter R. 1994. Reconsideration of the Marquesan sequence in East Polynesian prehistory, with particular reference to Hane (MUH1). *Archaeol. Oceania* 29:29–52

Anderson A, Sinoto Y. 2002. New radiocarbon ages of colonization sites in East Polynesia. *Asian Perspect.* 41:242–57

Anderson A, Wallace R. 1993. The chronology of Mount Camel Archaic site, Northland, New Zealand. *N.Z. J. Archaeol.* 15:5–16

Arnold JE. 2007. Credit where credit is due: the history of the Chumash oceangoing plank canoe. *Am. Antiq.* 72:196–209

Athens JS. 1997. Hawaiian native lowland vegetation in prehistory. In *Historical Ecology in the Pacific Islands: Prehistoric Environmental and Landscape Change*, ed. PV Kirch, TL Hunt, pp. 248–70. New Haven: Yale Univ. Press

Athens JS, Tuggle HD, Ward JV, Welch DJ. 2002. Avifaunal extinctions, vegetation change, and Polynesian impacts in prehistoric Hawai'i. *Archaeol. Oceania* 37:57–78

Athens JS, Ward JV. 2001. Paleoenvironmental evidence for early human settlement in Palau: The Ngerchau core. In *Pacific 2000: Proc. Int. Conf. Easter Island Pac., 5th, Los Osos*, ed. CM Stevenson, G Lee, FJ Morin, pp. 165–178. Easter Island Found.

Beaglehole JC, ed. 1955. *The Journals of Captain James Cook on His Voyages of Discovery, Vol. I, The Voyage of the Endeavor 1768–1771*. Hakluyt Soc. Extra Ser. No. XXXIV. Cambridge: Cambridge Univ. Press

Bellwood P. 1996. Phylogeny versus reticulation in prehistory. *Antiquity* 70:881–90

Bellwood P. 2005. *First Farmers: The Origins of Agricultural Societies*. Oxford: Blackwell

Bender BW, Wang JW. 1985. The status of Proto-Micronesian. In *Austronesian Linguistics at the 15th Pacific Science Congress*, ed. A Pawley, L Carrington, pp. 53–92. Pac. Linguist. C-88. Canberra: Aust. Natl. Univ.

Blust R. 1996. Austronesian culture history: The windows of language. In *Prehistoric Settlement of the Pacific*, ed. WH Goodenough, pp. 28–35. *Trans. Am. Philos. Soc.* 86(5). Philadelphia

Boyce AJ, Harding RM, Martinson JJ. 1995. Population genetics of the α-globin complex in Oceania. In *Human Populations: Diversity and Adaptation*, ed. AJ Boyce, V Reyonds, pp. 217–32. Oxford: Oxford Univ. Press

Buck PH. 1938. *Vikings of the Sunrise*. New York: Frederick Stokes

Burley DV, Nelson E, Shutler R Jr. 1999. A radiocarbon chronology for the Eastern Lapita frontier in Tonga. *Archaeol. Oceania* 34:59–72

Butler BM. 1994. Early prehistoric settlement in the Marianas Islands: new evidence from Saipan. *Man Cult. Oceania* 10:15–38

Clark G, Anderson A, eds. 2009. *The Early Prehistory of Fiji*. Terra Australis 31. Canberra: Pandanus

Clark GR, Anderson AJ, Vunidilo T, eds. 2001. *The Archaeology of Lapita Dispersal in Oceania*. Terra Australis 17. Canberra: Pandanus

Clarke AC, Burtensaw MK, McLenachan PA, Erickson DL, Penny D. 2006. Reconstructing the origins and dispersal of the Polynesian bottle gourd (*Lagenaria siceraria*). *Mol. Biol. Evol.* 23:893–900

Collerson KD, Weisler MI. 2007. Stone adze compositions and the extent of ancient Polynesian voyaging and trade. *Science* 317:1907–11

Conte E, Anderson AJ. 2003. Radiocarbon ages for two sites on Ua Huka, Marquesas. *Asian Perspect.* 42:155–60

Conte E, Kirch PV, eds. 2004. *Archaeological Investigations in the Mangareva Islands, French Polynesia*. Contrib. Archaeol. Res. Facil., No. 62, Univ. Calif. Berkeley

Davidson J, Irwin G, Leach F, Pawley A, Brown D, eds. 1996. *Oceanic Culture History: Essays in Honor of Roger Green*. Dunedin: N.Z. J. Archaeol.

Diamond J. 1988. Express train to Polynesia. *Nature* 336:307–8

Donohue M, Denham T. 2010. Farming and language in Island Southeast Asia. *Curr. Anthropol.* 51:223–56

Finney BR. 1994. *Voyage of Rediscovery: A Cultural Odyssey Through Polynesia*. Berkeley: Univ. Calif. Press

Finney BR. 1996. Putting voyaging back into Polynesian prehistory. See Davidson et al., pp. 365–76

Finney BR. 1997. Experimental voyaging, oral traditions and long-distance interaction in Polynesia. In *Prehistoric Long-Distance Interaction in Oceania: An Interdisciplinary Approach*, ed. MI Weisler, pp. 38–52. Auckland: N.Z. Archaeol. Assoc. Monogr. 21

Finney BR. 2006. Ocean sailing canoes. In *Vaka Moana: Voyagers of the Ancestors*, ed. KR Howe, pp. 100–153. Auckland: David Bateman

Flint J, Boyce AJ, Martinson JJ, Clegg JB. 1989. Population bottlenecks in Polynesia revealed by minisatellites. *Hum. Genet.* 83:257–63

Foley WA. 1986. *The Papuan Languages of New Guinea*. Cambridge: Cambridge Univ. Press

Fornander A. 1878. *An Account of the Polynesian Race*. London: Trubner

Fredericksen C, Spriggs M, Ambrose W. 1993. Pamwak rockshelter: a Pleistocene site on Manus Island, Papua New Guinea. See Smith et al., pp. 144–54

Friedlaender JS, ed. 2007. *Genes, Language, and Culture History in the Southwest Pacific*. Oxford: Oxford Univ. Press

Friedlaender JS, Friedlaender FR, Reef FA, Kidd KK, Kidd JR, et al. 2008. The genetic structure of Pacific islanders. *PLOS Genet.* 4:1–18

Galipaud J-C, Lilley I, eds. 1999. *The Pacific from 5000 to 2000 BP: Colonization and Transformations*. Paris: Éd. IRD

Golson J. 1972. The Pacific islands and their prehistoric inhabitants. In *Man in the Pacific Islands: Essays on Geographical Change in the Pacific Islands*, ed. RG Ward, pp. 5–33. Oxford: Oxford Univ. Press

Gongora J, Rawlence NJ, Mobegi VA, Jianlin H, Alcade JA, et al. 2008. Indo-European and Asian origins for Chilean and Pacific chickens revealed by mtDNA. *Proc. Natl. Acad. Sci. USA* 105:10308–13

Gosden C, Allen J, Ambrose W, Anson D, Golson J, et al. 1989. Lapita sites of the Bismarck Archipelago. *Antiquity* 63:561–86

Gray RD, Drummond AJ, Greenhill JS. 2009. Language phylogenies reveal expansion pulses and pauses in Pacific settlement. *Science* 323:479–83

Gray RD, Jordan FM. 2000. Language trees support the express-train sequence of Austronesian expansion. *Nature* 405:1052–55

Green RC. 1981. Location of the Polynesian homeland: a continuing problem. In *Studies in Pacific Languages & Cultures in Honor of Bruce Biggs*, ed. J Hollyman, A Pawley, pp. 133–58. Auckland: Linguist. Soc. N.Z.

Green RC. 1991. Near and Remote Oceania: disestablishing "Melanesia" in culture history. In *Man and a Half: Essays in Pacific Anthropology and Ethnobiology in Honor of Ralph Bulmer*, ed. A Pawley, pp. 491–502. Auckland: Polyn. Soc.

Green RC. 1999. Integrating historical linguistics with archaeology: insights from research in Remote Oceania. *Bull. Indo-Pac. Prehist. Assoc.* 18:3–16

Green RC. 2005. Sweet potato transfers in Polynesian prehistory. In *The Sweet Potato in Oceania: A Reappraisal*, ed. C Ballard, P Brown, RM Bourke, T Harwood, pp. 43–62. Oceania Monogr. 56. Sydney: Univ. Sydney

Green RC, Jones M, Sheppard P. 2008. The reconstructed and absolute dating of SE-SZ-8 Lapita site on Nendö, Santa Cruz, Solomon Islands. *Archaeol. Oceania* 43:49–61

Green RC, Weisler MI. 2002. The Mangarevan sequence and dating of the geographic expansion into Southeast Polynesia. *Asian Perspect.* 41:213–41

Greenhill SJ, Gray RD. 2005. Testing population dispersal hypotheses: Pacific settlement, phylogenetic trees and Austronesian languages. In *The Evolution of Cultural Diversity: A Phylogenetic Approach*, ed. R Mace, CJ Holden, S Shennan, pp. 31–52. London: Routledge

Groube LM, Chappell J, Muke J, Price D. 1986. A 40,000 year-old human occupation site at Huan Peninsula, Papua New Guinea. *Nature* 324:453–55

Hage P, Marck J. 2003. Matrilineality and the Melanesian origin of Polynesian Y chromosomes. *Curr. Anthropol.* 44:121–27

Handy ESC. 1930. The problem of Polynesian origins. *Bernice P. Bishop Mus. Occas. Pap.* 9:1–27

Harding RM, Clegg JB. 1996. Molecular population genetic studies of the island peoples of the South Pacific. *Am. J. Hum. Biol.* 8:587–97

Hather J, Kirch PV. 1991. Prehistoric sweet potato (*Ipomoea batatas*) from Mangaia Island, Central Polynesia. *Antiquity* 65:887–93

Hertzberg M, Mickleson KPN, Sergjeantson SW, Prior JF, Trent RJ. 1989. An Asian-specific 9-bp deletion of mitochondrial DNA is frequently found in Polynesians. *Am. J. Hum. Genet.* 44:504–10

Heyerdahl T. 1952. *American Indians in the Pacific: The Theory Behind the Kon-Tiki Expedition*. London: Allen & Unwin

Higham T, Anderson A, Jacomb C. 1999. Dating the first New Zealanders: the chronology of Wairau Bar. *Antiquity* 73:420–27

Hill AVS, Bowden DK, Trent RJ, Higgs DR, Oppenheimer SJ, et al. 1985. Melanesians and Polynesians share a unique α-thalassemia mutation. *Am. J. Hum. Genet.* 37:571–80

Hill AVS, Serjeantson SW, ed. 1989. *The Colonization of the Pacific: A Genetic Trail*. Oxford: Clarendon

Hinkle A. 2004. The distribution of a male sterile form of ti (*Cordyline fruticosa*) in Polynesia: a case of human selection? *J. Polyn. Soc.* 113:263–90

Hogg AG, Higham TG, Lowe DJ, Palmer JG, Reimer PJ, Newnham RM. 2003. A wiggle-match date for Polynesian settlement of New Zealand. *Antiquity* **77**:116–25

Houghton P. 1996. *People of the Great Ocean: Aspects of Human Biology of the Early Pacific*. Cambridge: Cambridge Univ. Press

Howard A. 1967. Polynesian origins and migrations. In *Polynesian Culture History*, ed. GA Highland, pp. 45–101. Bernice P. Bishop Mus. Spec. Publ. 56. Honolulu: Bishop Mus. Press

Howells WW. 1970. Anthropometric grouping analysis of Pacific peoples. *Archaeol. Phys. Anthropol. Oceania* 5:192–217

Hunt TL, Lipo CP. 2006. Late colonization of Easter Island. *Science* 311:1603–6

Hurles ME, Matisoo-Smith E, Gray RD, Penny D. 2003. Untangling Oceanic settlement: the edge of the knowable. *Trends Ecol. Evol.* 18:531–40

Hurles ME, Nicholson J, Bosch E, Renfrew C, Sykes BC, Jobling MA. 2002. Y chromosomal evidence for the origins of Oceanic-speaking peoples. *Genetics* 160:289–303

Jones TL, Klar KL. 2005. Diffusionism reconsidered: linguistic and archaeological evidence for prehistoric Polynesian contact with southern California. *Am. Antiq.* 70:457–84

Irwin G. 1992. *The Prehistoric Exploration and Colonization of the Pacific*. Cambridge: Cambridge Univ. Press

Irwin G. 1993. Voyaging. See Smith et al., pp. 73–87

Jackson FH. 1986. On determining the external relationships of the Micronesian languages. In *FOCAL II: Pap. Int. Conf. Austronesian Linguist., 4th*, ed. P Geraghty, L Carrington, SA Wurm, pp. 201–38. *Pac. Linguist.* C-94. Canberra: Aust. Natl. Univ.

Jordan FM, Gray RD, Greenhill SJ, Mace R. 2009. Matrilocal residence is ancestral in Austronesian societies. *Proc. R. Soc. B* 276:1957–64

Kayser M, Brauer S, Cordaux R, Casto A, Lao O, et al. 2006. Melanesian and Asian origins of Polynesians: mtDNA and Y chromosome gradients across the Pacific. *Mol. Biol. Evol.* 23:2234–44

Kayser M, Brauer S, Weiss G, Underhill PA, Roewer L, et al. 2000. Melanesian origin of Polynesian Y chromosome. *Curr. Biol.* 10:1237–46

Kayser M, Choi Y, van Oven M, Mona S, Brauer S, et al. 2008. The impact of the Austroniesan expansion: evidence from mtDNA and Y chromosome diversity in the Admiralty Islands of Melanesia. *Mol. Biol. Evol.* 25:1362–74

Kirch PV. 1986. Rethinking East Polynesian prehistory. *J. Polyn. Soc.* 95:9–40

Kirch PV. 1995. The Lapita culture of western Melanesia in the context of Austronesian origins and dispersals. In *Austronesian Studies Relating to Taiwan*, ed. P Li, pp. 255–294. Taipei: Acad. Sin.

Kirch PV. 1997. *The Lapita Peoples: Ancestors of the Oceanic World*. Oxford: Blackwell

Kirch PV. 2000. *On the Road of the Winds: An Archaeological History of the Pacific Islands before European Contact*. Berkeley: Univ. Calif. Press

Kirch PV, ed. 2001. *Lapita and its Transformations in Near Oceania: Archaeological Investigations in the Mussau Islands, Papua New Guinea, 1985–88. Vol. I, Introduction, Stratigraphy, Chronology*. Archaeol. Res. Facil. Contrib. No. 59. Berkeley: Univ. Calif.

Kirch PV, Green RC. 2001. *Hawaiki, Ancestral Polynesia: An Essay in Historical Anthropology*. Cambridge: Cambridge Univ. Press

Kirch PV, McCoy MD. 2007. Reconfiguring the Hawaiian cultural sequence: results of redating the Halawa dune site (MO-A1–3), Moloka'i Island. *J. Polyn. Soc.* 116:385–406

Kirch PV, Steadman DW, Butler VL, Hather J, Weisler MI. 1995. Prehistory and human ecology in Eastern Polynesia: excavations at Tangatatau rockshelter, Mangaia, Cook Islands. *Archaeol. Oceania* 30:47–65

Lepofsky D, Harries HC, Kellum M. 1992. Early coconuts on Mo'orea Island, French Polynesia. *J. Polyn. Soc.* 101:299–308

Liston J. 2009. Cultural chronology of earthworks in Palau, Western Micronesia. *Archaeol. Oceania* 44:56–73

Lum JK, Cann RL. 1998. mtDNA and language support a common origin of Micronesians and Polynesians in Island Southeast Asia. *Am. J. Phys. Anthropol.* 105:109–19

Lum JK, Cann RL. 2000. mtDNA lineage analyses: Origins and migrations of Micronesians and Polynesians. *Am. J. Phys. Anthropol.* 113:151–68

Lum JK, Cann RL, Martinson JJ, Jorde LB. 1998. Mitochondrial and nuclear genetic relationships among Pacific Island and Asian populations. *Am. J. Hum. Genet.* 63:613–24

Marck J. 1996. Eastern Polynesian subgrouping today. See Davidson et al., pp. 491–511

Marck J. 2000. *Topics in Polynesian Language and Culture History*. Canberra: Pac. Linguist., Aust. Natl. Univ.

Martinson JJ. 1996. Molecular perspectives on the colonization of the Pacific. In *Molecular Biology and Human Diversity*, ed. AJ Boyce, CGN Mascie-Taylor, pp. 171–95. Cambridge: Cambridge Univ. Press

Martinson JJ, Harding RM, Philippon G, Flye Sainte-Marie F, Roux J, et al. 1993. Demographic reductions and genetic bottlenecks in humans: minisatellite allele distributions in Oceania. *Hum. Genet.* 91:445–50

Matisoo-Smith E. 1994. The human colonization of Polynesia: a novel approach: genetic analyses of the Polynesian rat (*Rattus exulans*). *J. Polyn. Soc.* 103:75–87

Matisoo-Smith E, Allen JS, Roberts RM, Irwin GJ, Lambert DM. 1999. Rodents of the sunrise: mitochondrial DNA phylogenies of Polynesian *Rattus exulans* and the settlement of Polynesia. See Galipaud & Lilley, pp. 259–76

Matisoo-Smith E, Robins JH. 2004. Origins and dispersals of Pacific peoples: evidence from mtDNA phylogenies of the Pacific rat. *Proc. Natl. Acad. Sci. USA* 101:9167–72

Melton T, Clifford S, Martinson JJ, Batzer M, Stoneking M. 1998. Genetic evidence for the Proto-Austronesian homeland in Asia: mtDNA and nuclear DNA variation in Taiwanese Aboriginal tribes. *Am. J. Hum. Genet.* 63:1807–23

Merriwether DA, Friedlaender JS, Mediavilla J, Mgone C, Gentz F, Ferrell RE. 1999. Mitochondrial DNA variation is an indicator of Austronesian influence in Island Melanesia. *Am. J. Phys. Anthropol.* 110:243–70

Moodley Y, Linz B, Yamaoka Y, Windsor HM, Breurec S, et al. 2009. The peopling of the Pacific from a bacterial perspective. *Science* 323:527–30

Oppenheimer S. 2004. The 'Express Train from Taiwan to Polynesia': on the congruence of proxy lines of evidence. *World Archaeol.* 36:591–600

Pavlides C, Gosden C. 1994. 35000-year-old sites in the rainforests of West New Britain, Papua New Guinea. *Antiquity* 68:604–10

Pawley AK. 1972. On the internal relationships of Eastern Oceanic languages. *Pac. Anthropol. Rec.* 13:1–142

Pawley AK. 2007. Recent research on the historical relationships of the Papuan languages, or, What does linguistics day about the prehistory of Melanesia? See Friedlaender, pp. 36–58

Pawley AK, Green RC. 1984. The Proto-Oceanic language community. *J. Pac. Hist.* 19:123–46

Pawley AK, Pawley M. 1994. Early Austronesian terms for canoe parts and seafaring. In *Austronesian Terminologies: Continuity and Change*, ed. AK Pawley, MD Ross, pp. 329–61. Pac. Linguist. Ser. C-127. Canberra: Aust. Natl. Univ.

Pawley AK, Ross M. 1993. Austronesian historical linguistics and culture history. *Annu. Rev. Anthropol.* 22:425–59

Pietrusewsky M. 1970. An osteological view of indigenous populations in Oceania. In *Studies in Oceanic Culture History*, ed. RC Green, M Kelly, vol. 1, pp. 1–12. Pac. Anthropol. Records 11. Honolulu: Bishop Mus.

Rehg KL. 1995. The significance of linguistic interaction spheres in reconstructing Micronesian prehistory. *Oceanic Linguist.* 34:305–26

Rivers WHR. 1914. *The History of Melanesian Society*. Cambridge: Cambridge Univ. Press. 2 vols.

Rolett BV. 1998. *Hanamiai: Prehistoric Colonization and Cultural Change in the Marquesas Islands (East Polynesia)*. Yale Univ. Publ. Anthropol. No. 84. New Haven

Rolett BV, Conte E. 1995. Renewed investigation of the Ha'atuatua dune (Nukuhiva, Marquesas Islands): a key site in Polynesian prehistory. *J. Polyn. Soc.* 104:195–228

Ross MD. 1988. *Proto Oceanic and the Austronesian Languages of Western Melanesia*. Pac. Linguist. C-98. Canberra: Aust. Natl. Univ.

Ross MD. 1989. Early Oceanic linguistic prehistory. *J. Pac. Hist.* 24:135–49

Ross MD. 1996. Is Yapese oceanic? In *Reconstruction, Classification, Description: Festschrift in Honor of Isidore Dyen*, ed. B Nothofer, pp. 121–66. Hamburg: Abera Verlag Meyer

Ross MD. 2005. Pronouns as a preliminary diagnostic for grouping Papuan languages. In *Papuan Pasts: Cultural, Linguistic and Biological Histories of Papuan Speaking Peoples*, ed. AK Pawley, R Attenborough, J Golson, R Hide, pp. 15–66. Canberra: Aust. Natl. Univ.

Sand C. 1997. The chronology of Lapita ware in New Caledonia. *Antiquity* 71:539–47

Sapir E. 1916. *Time Perspective in Aboriginal American Culture: A Study in Method*. Dep. Mines, Geol. Surv. Mem. 90 Anthropol. Ser. No. 13. Ottawa: Gov. Print. Bur.

Sharp A. 1956. *Ancient Voyagers in the Pacific*. Wellington, N.Z.: Polyn. Soc.

Sheppard PJ, Thomas T, Summerhayes GR, eds. 2009. *Lapita: Ancestors and Descendants*. N.Z. Archaeol. Assoc. Monogr. 28. Auckland

Smith MA, Sharp ND. 1993. Pleistocene sites in Australia, New Guinea and Island Melanesia: geographic and temporal structure of the archaeological record. See Smith et al., pp. 37–59

Smith MA, Spriggs M, Fankhauser B, eds. 1993. *Sahul in Review: Pleistocene Archaeology in Australia, New Guinea and Island Melanesia*. Canberra: Dep. Prehist., Aust. Natl. Univ.

Specht J. 2009. The aceramic to ceramic boundary in the Bismarck Archipelago. See Sheppard et al., pp. 11–34

Specht J, Gosden C. 1997. Dating Lapita pottery in the Bismarck Archipelago, Papua New Guinea. *Asian Perspect.* 36:175–99

Spriggs M. 1997. *The Island Melanesians*. Oxford: Blackwell

Spriggs MJT, Anderson A. 1993. Late colonization of East Polynesia. *Antiquity* 67:200–217

Steadman DW, Vargas PC, Cristino CF. 1994. Stratigraphy, chronology, and cultural context of an early faunal assemblage from Easter Island. *Asian Perspect.* 33:79–96

Storey AA, Ramirez JM, Quiroz D, Burley DV, Addison DJ, et al. 2007. Radiocarbon and DNA evidence for a pre-Columbian introduction of Polynesian chickens to Chile. *Proc. Natl. Acad. Sci. USA* 104:10335–39

Storey AA, Quiroz D, Ramirez JM, Beavan-Athfield N, Addison DJ, et al. 2008. Pre-Columbian chickens, dates, isotopes, and mtDNA. *Proc. Natl. Acad. Sci. USA* 105:E99

Su B, Jin L, Underhill P, Martinson JJ, Saha N, et al. 2000. Polynesian origins: insights from the Y chromosome. *Proc. Natl. Acad. Sci. USA* 97:8225–28

Summerhayes GR. 2001. Defining the chronology of Lapita in the Bismarck Archipelago. See Clark et al., pp. 25–38

Summerhayes GR. 2007. Island Melanesian pasts: a view from archaeology. See Friedlaender, pp. 36–58

Terrell J. 1986. *Prehistory in the Pacific Islands*. Cambridge: Cambridge Univ. Press

Terrell J, Hunt TL, Gosden C. 1997. The dimensions of social life in the Pacific: human diversity and the myth of the primitive isolate. *Curr. Anthropol.* 38:155–96

Tuggle HD, Spriggs MJ. 2000. The age of the Bellows Dune Site O18, O'ahu, Hawai'i and the antiquity of Hawaiian colonization. *Asian Perspect.* 39:165–88

Vilar MG, Kaneko A, Hombhanje FW, Tsukahara T, Hwaihwanje I, Lum JK. 2008. Reconstructing the origin of the Lapita Cultural Complex: mtDNA analyses of East Sepik Province, PNG. *J. Hum. Genet.* 53:698–708

Weisler MI. 1995. Henderson Island prehistory: colonization and extinction on a remote Polynesian island. *Biol. J. Linnean Soc.* 56:377–404

Weisler MI. 1998. Hard evidence for prehistoric interaction in Polynesia. *Curr. Anthropol.* 39:521–32

Weisler MI. 2001. *On the Margins of Sustainability: Prehistoric Settlement of Utrok Atoll, Northern Marshall Islands.* BAR Int. Ser. 967. Oxford, UK: Archaeopress

Wickler S, Spriggs M. 1988. Pleistocene human occupation of the Solomon Islands, Melanesia. *Antiquity* 62:703–6

Yen DE. 1974. *The Sweet Potato and Oceania: An Essay in Ethnobotany.* Bernice P. Bishop Mus. Bull. 236. Honolulu: Bishop Mus. Press

Anthropological Perspectives on Structural Adjustment and Public Health

James Pfeiffer[1] and Rachel Chapman[2]

[1]Department of Global Health, Department of Health Services, School of Public Health, University of Washington, Seattle, Washington 98195-7660; email: jamespf@u.washington.edu

[2]Department of Anthropology, University of Washington, Seattle, Washington 98195-3100; email: rrc4@uw.edu

Annu. Rev. Anthropol. 2010. 39:149–65

First published online as a Review in Advance on June 14, 2010

The *Annual Review of Anthropology* is online at anthro.annualreviews.org

This article's doi: 10.1146/annurev.anthro.012809.105101

0084-6570/10/1021-0149$20.00

Key Words

globalization, global health, neoliberalism, critical medical anthropology, political economy, economic reform

Abstract

Thirty years since its first public use in 1980, the phrase structural adjustment remains obscure for many anthropologists and public health workers. However, structural adjustment programs (SAPs) are the practical tools used by international financial institutions (IFIs) such as the International Monetary Fund (IMF) and the World Bank to promote the market fundamentalism that constitutes the core of neoliberalism. A robust debate continues on the impact of SAPs on national economies and public health. But the stories that anthropologists tell from the field overwhelmingly speak to a new intensity of immiseration produced by adjustment programs that have undermined public sector services for the poor. This review provides a brief history of structural adjustment, and then presents anthropological analyses of adjustment and public health. The first section reviews studies of health services and the second section examines literature that assesses broader social determinants of health influenced by adjustment.

INTRODUCTION

SAP: structural
adjustment program

IFI: International
Financial Institution

OPEC: Organization
of Petroleum-
Exporting Countries

Thirty years since its first public use in 1980, the phrase structural adjustment remains obscure for many anthropologists and public health workers. Related terms such as globalization, economic reform, and neoliberalism are more widely circulated and often better understood in both development and academic circles (Harvey 2005). However, structural adjustment programs (or SAPs) are the practical tools used by international financial institutions (IFIs) such as the International Monetary Fund (IMF) and the World Bank at country level to promote the market fundamentalism that constitutes the core of neoliberalism. While other instruments such as global and regional trade pacts, military interventions, and embargos are essential to enforce the neoliberal project more broadly, SAPs refer to the country-specific agreements negotiated by the IFIs with local ministries of finance that have produced a cascade of profound political, economic, and social changes in the Third World. The primary tenets of neoliberalism—promotion of free markets, privatization, small government, and economic deregulation—have been operationalized at country level through concerted, formulaic, and strategically harmonized action by the IMF and World Bank through SAPs. The advent of structural adjustment came on the heels of colonialism and independence in much of the developing world, especially Africa, and signaled a definitive shift in the relationship of the West to its former colonies; a shift characterized by novel tools of extraction and new strategies of abandonment. A robust debate continues on the impact of SAPs on national economies and public health. But the stories that anthropologists tell from the field overwhelmingly speak to a new intensity of immiseration produced by adjustment programs that have ravaged public sector services for the poor.

A BRIEF HISTORY OF ADJUSTMENT

The IFIs were established as sister institutions at the end of World War II. Although most nations are IMF members, rich countries have far greater voting power formally calibrated to the size of their economies. The IMF's role is to maintain stability in the global monetary system, whereas the World Bank acts primarily as a lender for development projects. SAPs negotiated between the IFIs and national governments ostensibly seek to help governments restructure their economies to control inflation, repay international debt, and stimulate economic growth. The IFIs provide loans and debt relief to a target country if certain conditions are met; governments must reduce their public sector workforce and lower remaining salaries, cut public sector budgets, remove subsidies and price controls, devalue local currency, sell state-owned enterprises and services, reduce taxes on foreign investment, weaken state environmental and labor regulations, and deregulate movement of capital (Gershman & Irwin 2000).

A brief review of the history of adjustment and the cornerstone institutional literature helps map out anthropological engagements with SAPs. The emergence of the SAP idea as both a policy and a process is intimately bound up with the global economic downturn of the 1970s, the ensuing international debt crisis, the shift among economic elites from Keynesianism to monetarism, and the political realization of this shift with the election of the Reagan and Thatcher administrations in the early 1980s (see Harvey 2005; also see Gershman & Irwin 2000). OPEC's hike in oil prices in the early 1970s led to increased borrowing by oil-importing countries and a sharp increase in lending to poor countries by commercial banks flush with petrodollars. With global recession, prices for raw materials exported by poor countries declined, rich country markets shrank, and interest rates on loans increased. The debt crisis spiraled out of control and eventually threatened the stability of Western lenders and the global financial system.

As a result, the IFIs moved away from Keynesian principles of government intervention to free-market approaches espoused by monetarists, led by University of Chicago economist Milton Friedman, who claimed that economies free of regulation would grow more quickly and that benefits would trickle down to the poor (Harvey 2005). An influential World Bank (1981) policy paper, entitled *Accelerated Development in Sub-Saharan. Africa: an Agenda for Action* by Elliot Berg (and widely known as the *Berg Report*), laid blame for Africa's economic crisis squarely on African state intervention, protectionism, and price subsidies that distorted market forces and undercut economic growth (Arrighi 2002).

In 1980, the IFIs produced a new tool known as the Enhanced Structural Adjustment Facility (or ESAF); a credit package to be offered by IFIs if macroeconomic conditionalities were met by recipient governments. With the emergence of the ESAF, IFIs began negotiating with local Ministries of Finance to create SAPs, which were remarkably uniform across countries. By 1991, 75 of the poorest countries in the world had received adjustment loans, 30 in Africa and at least 18 in Latin America (Gershman & Irwin 2000). The term Washington Consensus was coined in 1989 to refer to the Washington, D.C.–based IMF, World Bank, and U.S. Treasury consortium, and came to signify the austerity economies that SAPs produced.

Structural adjustment coincided with another key moment in the public health world. In 1978, the concept of Primary Health Care (PHC) was embraced by 134 countries (including the United States) attending the landmark World Health Organization (WHO)/UNICEF Alma Ata conference in the former Soviet Union (now Kazakhstan) (Paluzzi 2004). The PHC concept promoted "Health for All" by 2000 through a package of basic health care services made available to all, especially the poor, through a public tiered health system. The package included vaccination, maternal-child health services, family planning, endemic and epidemic disease control, first aid, and referral systems for complex cases. It recognized the importance of multisectoral development to public health, and celebrated community participation as a core principle. But PHC immediately ran up against the new constraints imposed by SAPs. Debates erupted between those promoting a selective PHC that called for realistic priority setting in light of severe resource constraints and abandonment of the grand vision of comprehensive PHC (Rifkin & Walt 1986, Justice 2000).

In 1987, in a further blow to PHC, the World Bank's *Financing Health Services in Developing Countries* (World Bank 1987) provided the blueprint for the privatization of health services that included (*a*) user fees for government facilities; (*b*) introduction of private insurance; (*c*) encouragement of non-governmental organizations (NGOs and other private entities) to provide services; and (*d*) decentralization of government services. These prescriptions laid the groundwork for a generation of health and development policy in the adjustment era. That same year, UNICEF published its seminal but soft critique of SAPs entitled *Adjustment with a Human Face* (UNICEF 1987) that documented their negative effects and argued for greater protections for the poor. Also in 1987, the WHO and UNICEF crafted the Bamako Initiative at a conference in Mali, which provided guidelines to establish community-based health care financing in Africa, based on imposition of local user fees, to purchase drugs (UNICEF 1988).

In 1993, the World Bank's annual report, *Investing in Health*, introduced the disability adjusted life year (DALY) as a measure of health and promoted the principle of cost-effectiveness to guide health investment (World Bank 1993). The DALY provides a common unit, or metric, of health loss that accounts for the duration and severity of health conditions in order to measure the overall burden of disease to prioritize investment of scarce resources in poor countries (Murray & Lopez 1996). The report signaled that the Bank now superseded the WHO as the primary driver of global health policy.

As part of the push toward privatization, SAPs sought to redirect foreign aid to NGOs and away from governments. The World

PHC: primary health care

WHO: World Health Organization

DALY: disability adjusted life year

PRSPs: Poverty
Reduction Strategy
Papers

Bank, USAID and other major donors began channeling large proportions of their health funding to NGOs, producing an NGO explosion that is now the *sine qua non* of the neoliberal period in Africa (Turshen 1999, Green & Mathias 1997, Buse & Walt 1997).

Throughout the 1990s, as health indicators were deteriorating across Africa, economies remained anemic, and political opposition was brewing in Latin America (Kim et al. 2000). Under increasing criticism in 1996, the IFIs created the Heavily Indebted Poor Countries (HIPC) initiative that included 41 countries deemed to have unrepayable debt levels (Gershman & Irwin 2000). They could receive additional debt restructuring support if they agreed to IFI conditionalities. By 1999, however, even the HIPC was seen by many as too constraining and the ESAF was replaced by the euphemistic Poverty Reduction and Growth Facility (PRGF) implemented through Poverty Reduction Strategy Papers (PRSPs) (IMF/World Bank 2002, Craig & Porter 2003). The new approach sought to redirect debt relief toward poverty reduction programs. The creation of PRSPs would be a consultative process with local civil society to achieve a sense of national ownership. However, critics maintain that the essential aspects of structural adjustment remain intact in the PRSP approach (Wamala et al. 2007, Craig & Porter 2003, Hammonds & Ooms 2004).

In *Healthy Development: The World Bank Strategy for Health, Nutrition, and Population* (World Bank 2007), the Bank sought to reposition itself vis-à-vis the new architecture of global health aid. The adoption of the Millenium Development Goals (MDGs) as global benchmarks by the United Nations in 2000 established new health targets and challenged the effectiveness of adjustment (Freedman 2005). Major new funding for health and the AIDS crisis from other sources has reduced the World Bank's relative contribution to global heath. However, PRSPs continue to provide the basic aid and development framework in most poor countries.

THE IMPACT OF SAPs ON HEALTH

Critics of SAPs hypothesize a number of pathways through which adjustment policies can harm public health including cuts to basic public sector health care services; imposition of fees for health care services; cuts to other public sector services such as education, agriculture, water and public works; unemployment caused by lay-offs of public sector workers and income declines resulting from wage cuts for those remaining; privatization of state industries that often leads to layoffs; removal of state subsidies for essentials and liberalized markets for transport and food leading to price increases; currency devaluation that often leads to immediate and dramatic price increases for basic commodities, especially food; and increases in social inequality and economic vulnerability (Breman & Shelton 2007).

The World Bank and its supporters, on the other hand, argue that adjustment policies may cause hardship in the short run, but will eventually stabilize economies, promote new investment, and generate economic growth, which will lead to greater tax income for services (Sahn & Bernier 1995, Sahn et al. 1997, Haddad et al. 1995). Privatization and user fees for some services (such as health) will help them become more efficient and lead to better access. Greater economic growth will lead to higher incomes, less distorted pricing for basic needs, and more resources overall for health and development.

The task of epidemiologically disentangling and isolating the many influences on a nation's health is enormously challenging, so conclusive findings on the impact of SAPs on specific population-level health outcomes have been elusive and controversial (Breman & Shelton 2007, Cornia et al. 2009, Harris & Seid 2004). However, there is a more definitive literature outside of anthropology that documents how SAPs affect a wide range of proximate social determinants of health. Important volumes that address these determinants include Labonte et al. (2009), Harris & Seid (2004), and Kawachi

& Wamala (2007). [See Sahn et al. (1997) for a more favorable view.]

Social epidemiologists have provided useful perspectives on the relationships among structural adjustment programs, increases in social inequality, and population health outcomes (Coburn 2000, Kawachi & Wamala 2007). Public health and policy experts have provided valuable insights into the NGO phenomenon (Green & Mathias 1997, Buse & Walt 1997, Mburu 1989, Cliff 1993). [See also Gwatkin et al. (1999), and Anand & Hanson (1998) for discussions on the ethics of DALYs.]

Analysis of IFI policy can be found in De Beyer et al. (2000) who have provided a more sanguine assessment of SAPs and the role of the Bank. But this contrasts with a chorus of criticism in Fort et al. (2004), Chabot et al (1996), Navarro (2004), Hanlon (1996), Laurell (2000), Loewenson (1993), Hammonds & Ooms (2004), and Ooms & Schrecker (2005).

There is a rich literature that documents and examines the impact of structural adjustment on health services. Turshen's (1999) *Privatizing Health Services in Africa* is a critical touchstone treatise. Especially valuable contributions also include McCoy et al. (2005), McCoy et al. (2008), Jitta et al. (2003) for Uganda, Birn et al. (2000) for Nicaragua, Gloyd (1996) for Mozambique, Bassett et al. (1997) for Zimbabwe, and Handa & King (2003) on Jamaica. Literature assessing PRSPs has grown in recent years and is best summarized in Wamala et al. (2007) and Craig & Porter (2003). Health economists of course have weighed in on adjustment. Joseph Stiglitz (2002) offers a scathing criticism of the World Bank as its former chief economist (see also Sachs 2005, WHO 2001). [For a more positive economist's views of adjustment, see Sahn et al. (1997).]

ANTHROPOLOGICAL APPROACHES AND CONTRIBUTIONS

Specific use of the term structural adjustment is still sparse in the anthropology literature

on global health. Janes & Corbett (2009) have offered a recent valuable review of anthropology and global health more broadly. While there is some important overlap with this work, the review offered here focuses instead on anthropological research that identifies structural adjustment policies in national settings and either directly examines their effect on health services, tracks their broader impact on social and cultural life in ways that affect public health, or describes processes of policy development and resistance.

Several anthropological volumes outside the medical anthropology literature speak to the broader social processes of adjustment in ways that can inform our approach to health. These include Comaroff & Comaroff's (2001) *Millennial Capitalism and the Culture of Neoliberalism*, Ferguson's (2006) *Global Shadows: Africa in the Neoliberal World Order*, and Escobar's (1995) *Encountering Development*. Most of the anthropological work on SAPs and health has been produced by scholars writing in the critical medical anthropology (CMA) tradition that brings together, sometimes uncomfortably, political economic, poststructuralist, and critical theory approaches to health and society. CMA insists on locating sociocultural and health phenomena in the context of historical, political economic, and social forces that shape and constrain individual agency (Singer & Baer 1995), often drawing on Marxian political economy or Foucauldian notions of biopower and biopolitics. The structural violence analytic, popular among CMA adherents, offers an alternative lens to reinterpret disease and mortality among the poor as a form of violence that derives from structured inequality (Farmer 2001). CMA provides a corrective to mainstream international public health still rooted in narrow behaviorist and cognitive models of health disparities.

Several important collections on SAPs and health led by anthropologists have recently appeared. Most prominent of these is Kim et al.'s (2000b) *Dying for Growth* that unites the work of anthropologists, economists, and historians in a sweeping indictment of adjustment and neoliberalism. Castro & Singer's (2004)

Unhealthy Health Policy includes several chapters on SAPS; Baer et al.'s (2003) volume examines the intersection of world system's theory and medical anthropology. The Manderson & Whiteford (2000) collection contains case studies of global health policy and neoliberalism. Whiteford & Whiteford (2005) provides a collection of ethnographies about water privatization in poor countries. Nichter's (2008) recent volume offers a meditation on the power of representation in the shaping of recent health policy, including structural adjustment. The themes that have emerged in this and other anthropological literature on SAPs are elaborated below.

The Impact of SAPs on Health Care Services

Medical anthropologists have described community-level experiences and responses to the contraction of public sector health services and the emergence of private care. This work has focused primarily on imposition of fees for service, the Bamako Initiative, the discourse on cost-effectiveness, private sector and informal market services, the proliferation of NGOs to deliver services, and dynamics of community participation so important to the PHC concept. Woven within many of these accounts are stories and exploration of how patterns of health seeking have been transformed in local communities.

The experience and performance of public sector health workers themselves has emerged as an important theme. Harriet Birungi (1998) describes how biomedical injection technology migrated to the private and informal sectors in Uganda as the health system and quality of care weakened under adjustment. Streefland (2005) describes an emergent puvate zone in Uganda in which public sector health workers scratch out a living in the private and informal sectors to subsidize their low salaries. Kira Foster (2005) documents the effects of the neoliberal shift since 1997 on provision of care in postapartheid South Africa, highlighting strained relations between health staff and local communities

created by state budget cuts. Kyaddondo & Whyte depict the demoralization among Ugandan health workers as the health system was decentralized and privatized (2003). Lundy (1996) dissects the effects of health system budget cuts on health staff morale in Jamaica as salaries were reduced and work conditions deteriorated. Bassett et al. (1997) describe how Zimbabwe's SAP led to worsening conflict between nurses and patients as workloads increased, salaries declined, and work conditions eroded.

Maupin (2008) explains how adjustment constraints on Guatemala's maternal child health services led to promotion of ineffective traditional birth attendant (TBA) programs. Towghi (2004) depicts the difficulties in developing a TBA program in Pakistan under a SAP as formal services have disappeared for referrals of high-risk pregnancies. Chapman (2003) reveals how declines in service quality, such as longer waiting times and poor treatment, in Mozambique often delay women's use of antenatal care. Further notable country-specific anthropological accounts of adjustment and health service quality decline include Nigeria (Adulana & Olomajeye 1999), Malawi (Kalipeni 2004), Zaire (Schoepf et al. 1991), Peru (Kim et al. 2000), Haiti (Farmer 2001, Maternowska 2006), Brazil (Biehl 2007), and Mongolia (Janes 2004).

Ellen Foley (2009) provides one of the few book-length ethnographies that explicitly traces the impact of structural adjustment on health service delivery. She describes the bankrupting of a local health center in Senegal after adoption of the Bamako Initiative and exposes the new official discourse of state-citizen partnership and responsibilization as a gloss for passing on health costs to poor communities. Keshavjee (2004) describes a similar failure of a Bamako Initiative approach in post-Soviet Tajikistan as fees were introduced to recover costs. Ridde (2008) tracks the failings of the Bamako Initiative in Burkina Faso. [See additional reports on the negative consequences of user fees on the poor in Zambia (Van der Geest et al. 2000), Senegal (Desclaux 2004), and Zimbabwe (Bassett et al. 1997).]

Smith-Nonini (1998) describes the embrace of NGOs in El Salvador in the 1990s. The right-wing ARENA government at the time welcomed neoliberal reforms but was hesitant to cede control of health provision to NGOs. Janes (2004) questions the efficacy of the NGO model of service delivery in market-based health reform in Mongolia and challenges anthropologists to cast a critical eye toward the emergence of civil society in development discourse as a cover for privatization. Drawing on fieldwork in Mozambique, Pfeiffer (2003) claims that proliferation of NGOs in the Mozambique has fragmented the health sector and created an internal brain drain from the public sector to NGOs, which pay higher salaries. The contracting out of services by national governments to NGOs, most famously in Cambodia, is a newer dimension of the NGO phenomenon (Loevinsohn & Harding 2005). Maupin's (2009) study of contracting in Guatemala offers one of the few available case studies by an anthropologist. Maupin describes how contracting of services to NGOs in Guatemala may have undermined civil participation in health reform. The NGOs that were selected assumed primarily administrative roles and remained heavily dependent on the Ministry of Health, thereby losing their civil participation and service delivery roles.

Morgan (1993) argues for a political economic assessment of community participation in PHC in Costa Rica. Morgan's thorough (book-length) ethnography of participatory processes in Costa Rica reveals the contested nature of the concept itself among the World Bank, local governments, and NGOs. The language of decentralization, public/private partnership, civil society, community participation, and sustainability entered the development discussion, in part to justify passing on the costs of health care to communities. Similarly, Janes (2004) argues for an activist/advocacy approach to participation in health in the context of privatization in Mongolia to ensure that the poor are heard.

Medical anthropologists have provided important critiques of the cost-effectiveness argument by tying it to concerns for human rights, equity, and ethics. Paul Farmer's eloquent broadsides offer the strongest indictment against the cost-effectiveness logic that has delayed the provision of antiretroviral treatment (ART) to the poor, undermined tuberculosis (TB) programs, and otherwise prevented the improvement of basic services in poor countries (Farmer 2005, 2004, 2008; Castro & Farmer 2005). Janes & Chuluundorj (2004), Nichter (2008), and Allotey et al. (2003) criticize the use of DALYs for obscuring the social nature of suffering—the social and economic losses far exceed what is measured in the DALY.

The coincidence of the AIDS epidemic with the imposition of structural adjustment exposed global fault lines of inequality that were deepened by SAPs. As Comaroff (2007, p. 197) points out, "In retrospect, the timing of its [AIDS] onset was uncanny: the disease appeared like a *memento mori* in a world high on the hype of Reaganomics, deregulation, and the end of the Cold War." Analysts pointed out how SAPs and neoliberalism exacerbated the social conditions that propelled the epidemic, and undermined the public infrastructure needed to scale-up AIDS treatment in poor countries (Poku 2006, Piot 2001, Farmer 2001, Ooms et al. 2008, Lurie et al. 1995, Singer 1997). Parker et al.'s (2000) review of environmental influences on HIV prevention offers a good early snapshot of work assessing the impact of SAPs on the epidemic. Schoepf's (2001) review of anthropological research on HIV/AIDS highlights how the inequality and economic insecurity created by SAPs promotes HIV transmission. Ida Susser's (2009) recent volume connects the politics of global health governance to the growth of survival sex. See similar studies for Lesotho (Romero-Daza & Himmelgreen 1998), Haiti (Farmer et al. 1996), Zaire (Schoepf 2001), and South Africa (Hunter 2007). This important body of work belies the behaviorist and racist portrayals of a promiscuous Africa, common in international public health, that conjures a distinct African sexuality to explain the severity of the African AIDS crisis.

ART: antiretroviral treatment

TB: tuberculosis

PEPFAR: President's Emergency Program for AIDS Relief

GFATM: Global Fund to Fight AIDS, TB and Malaria

The surge in major funding over the past six years for scale-up of life-saving ART in poor countries from the President's Emergency Program for AIDS Relief (PEPFAR), the Global Fund to Fight AIDS, TB and Malaria (GFATM), and other major foundations has collided directly with structural adjustment on the ground. The struggles to scale-up ART through dilapidated and underresourced health systems, and the difficulties in patient follow-up and adherence have foregrounded the role of SAPs in impeding an effective response in spite of the new resources made available. Castro (2006) assesses social factors that influence ART adherence such as user fees, poverty, lack of income, and lack of food often exacerbated by SAPs. Castro & Farmer (2005) argue that AIDS stigma must be understood in terms of inequality and structural violence—often worsened by SAPs (see also Abadía-Barrero & Castro 2006). Desclaux (2004) describes challenges related to payment for ART in Senegal and Whyte et al. (2004) discuss dilemmas around charging for drugs in Uganda.

The scale-up of life-saving ART has stimulated a growing poststructuralist and Foucauldian literature on the pharmaceuticalization of public health, therapeutic citizenship, and biopolitics within the context of neoliberalism. Fassin (2007) provides a book-length analysis of the biopolitics of the AIDS crisis in South Africa with a special emphasis on AIDS denialism and the legacy of apartheid—in relation to the embrace of neoliberalism by the ANC (2007). Biehl is concerned with the pharmaceuticalization of AIDS and public health in Brazil created through a narrowly defined vertical scale-up of ART by an activist yet neoliberal Brazilian state. He seeks to track the creation of a new biomedical citizenship based on assessment of risk for HIV care (2007). Nguyen et al. (2007) have proposed a notion of therapeutic citizenship that points to the growing transnational influence of biomedical knowledge and practice in the government of human and non-human affairs. Petryna et al. (2006) have produced a volume of anthropological case studies that examine the global pharmaceutical nexus in the context of neoliberalism, of which the ARV drug industry plays a key role.

SAPs and Inequality Beyond Healthcare

The broader effects of economic reform on local societies that impact health—growing inequality and rapid class formation, land access and food, water rights, gender disparities, the commodification of social relations, unemployment, and the drops in income associated with economic austerity measures—have attracted the attention of anthropologists who explore the political and social ecology of adjustment.

Janes (2004) examines the social ecology of women's reproductive health in Mongolia as it reeled under free-market reform in the post-Soviet period characterized by high unemployment, famine, and the collapse of the public health system. Biehl (2005) describes the zones of social abandonment around Brazilian cities where the sick, mentally ill, and homeless are left to die. Maternowska (2006) offers a book-length examination of fertility choices and low levels of contraception use by poor women in neoliberal Haiti in terms of inequality, uncertainty, and vulnerability. Chapman's (2003, 2004) ethnography of pregnancy in central Mozambique uncovers how free-market economics have commodified important social relationships and ritual processes throughout the reproductive process, from virginity fees to bridewealth, to pregnancy protection rituals and traditional midwife support. Poor women without access to money react by hiding their pregnancies and avoiding biomedical antenatal services. Pfeiffer (2002a, 2004, 2005; Pfeiffer et al. 2007) argues that structural adjustment, inequality, and economic insecurity in Mozambique have fueled the growth of faith-healing Pentecostal and African Independent churches with important implications for public health and HIV/AIDS that are not yet well understood. Sanders describes the commodification of "occult" practices (2001) in Tanzania as insecurity and inequality increased under its SAP, and Whyte et al. (2004) similarly examines the experience of misfortune and uncertainty in Uganda exacerbated by neoliberalism. See also Okuonzi (2004) for Uganda and Schoepf et al. (2000) who describe the political ecology of adjustment and its impact on health in Congo, Rwanda, Ghana, and Senegal. Gill's (2000) ethnography of a peripheral migrant city in Bolivia reveals the urban spoilation produced by 15 years of neoliberal neglect in Bolivia's peri-urban neighborhoods.

Whiteford & Whiteford (2005) have produced a valuable collection of anthropological work that focuses on adjustment, access to water, and health in poor countries. Briggs & Mantini-Briggs (2003) examine the cholera epidemic of 1991 in Venezuela under structural adjustment and deconstruct the language, imagery, and rubric of representation elaborated by the government to deflect blame onto neighboring countries and the local poor, and to obfuscate the links between the epidemic and adjustment policies that had also provoked wide-spread riots two years earlier. [See also Loftus (2006) for discussion of the political ecology of water access in South Africa.]

Gladwin's (1991) edited volume, *Structural Adjustment and African Women Farmers*, presents a series of early case studies from around Africa that document the increased workloads for women, loss of land access to privatization schemes, and consequent declines in nutritional status associated with adjustment. Schoepf's chapter is a poignant case study of Zaire where land privatization intersected with local patriarchal ideologies to further undermine women farmers' rights to land and to intensify intrahousehold conflict. Johan Pottier (1999) reviews how structural adjustment programs have reconfigured rural small holder production by promoting failed cash-cropping, removing price subsidies, and ending state-run trading programs in ways that have undermined producers. Pfeiffer (2002b) similarly argues that in rural Mozambique, SAP policies that removed subsidized purchase of rural produce by the state, eliminated women's cooperatives, and privatized land, undermined women's ability to secure food. Commoditization of

social relationships made reliance on male cash income even more important for nutrition in the family. Janes (2004) describes how free-market changes in Mongolia led to widespread famine and food insecurity as the society was decollectivized and households turned toward self-provisioning. Vavrus (2005) discusses how access to secondary education declined in Tanzania as school fees were introduced and subsidized prices for food were removed. Nwajiuba et al. (2007) examine the SAP in Nigeria and its influence on migration and public health.

Wamala & Kawachi (2007) have provided a concise summary of globalization, neoliberalism, and women's health. Gender biases in the health costs of adjustment cover a broad range of sites, from the intensification of women's domestic and market work to the interruption of children's (especially girls') and women's education to increases in time inputs either to obtain basic services or self-provision them (Gladwin 1991, Connelly 1996). Pamela Sparr's (1994) seminal volume, *Mortgaging Women's Live: Feminist Critiques of Structural Adjustment*, uses diverse case studies to document the interrelated consequences of restructuring and privatization. Included is anthropologist Takiyiwaa Manuh's review of the problematic employment consequences and compensation measures of SAPs in Ghana, and Mervat Hatem's analysis of the impact of SAPS on women's health in Egypt. Feminist theorists have argued that the politics of international restructuring have had the greatest effect on the sphere of social reproduction, and thus, on women, while "amplifying" patriarchy (Bakker & Gill 2003, Sassen 2003). Austerity programs necessarily target poor, rural women, whose lack of access to good land and small chances of intensifying production would limit their ability to benefit from the new market conditions created by adjustment (Cliff 1991). Without ways to boost their own incomes, women suffer the hardships caused by inflation and rising prices as subsidies and price controls are dismantled (UNICEF 1991, p. 33). Because more poor women than men live outside the cash nexus, mainly those in rural areas, they are more vulnerable to inflation, social conflict, and uncertainty (Turshen 1999).

In *Globalization, Women and Health in the 21st Century* edited by Kickbusch et al. (2005), the effects of global economic restructuring and adjustment on health is a recurring theme across the chapters. In her chapter, Doyal explicitly lays out a dual framework for examining how gender relations shape the impact of globalization on health and how the globalization of health affects gender relations. Anthropologist Lewando-Hunt considers the health effects of women's social movements and Manish Desai reviews women's international health movements and organized resistances to health restructuring and reform policies from a critical social movement perspective. [See also Elson (1995) and Zuckerman's (2002) discussion of gender and PRSPs, and Haddad et al. (1995) for an economist's review of gender dimensions of economic adjustment.]

Debt and structural adjustment burdens also correlate with political conflict (Leatherman & Thomas 2009). A recent volume reviews the relationship between global health and political conflict and violence (Rylko-Bauer et al. 2009). In this compendium, Quesada carefully describes the relationship of structural adjustment to direct violence in Nicaragua, Heggenhougen describes similar dynamics in Guatemala, and Farmer builds on the argument advanced by Uvin (1998) that structural adjustment and the inequalities it generated contributed to the 1994 Rwandan genocide. Leatherman & Thomas (2009) suggest that structural violence in Peru, worsened by neoliberal reforms, created the conditions for political violence.

HUMAN RIGHTS, RESISTANCE, AND THE HEALTH "COMMONS": TOWARD AN ANTHROPOLOGY OF STRUCTURAL ADJUSTMENT

The 30-year structural adjustment experiment has constituted an assault on the public sector as an essential purveyor and guarantor of population health and welfare. The anthropologists reviewed here bear witness to the human cost. If, as Farmer (2001, 2005, 2008) argues, social and economic rights are human rights, the role of a robust public sector and government emerges as vital; not sufficient, but necessary to guarantee the right to survive. Viewed in this light, structural adjustment's systematic dismantling of public services for health, education, agriculture, water, and safety nets is rightly seen as a war on the poor; its violence measured in increased morbidity, malnutrition, excess mortality, DALYs, and the harder-to-quantify destruction of community that anthropologists have tried to depict. In practical terms, the struggle for public health in the structural adjustment era, then, is the struggle to preserve, renew, and revitalize the idea and role of the public sphere. Anthropologist Smith-Nonini (2006) argues in a recent essay that to operationalize a right to health, a health system should be seen as a commons, not as a market, where priorities are set for the public good, risk is shared, and health providers are accountable to their communities. To argue for a health commons directs anthropologists toward new sites of engagement, application, and resistance.

For example, the large-scale international response to the AIDS crisis underscores the urgency to rebuild a public sector capable of managing millions on treatment; the sheer logistics of the challenge now supersede ideology as practitioners realize that AIDS treatment on a mass scale simply cannot succeed in poor countries through a SAP-created patchwork of NGOs, charities, missions, and private providers (Pfeiffer & Nichter 2008). It requires functioning national health systems with an adequate workforce, expanded training institutions, and major infrastructure rebuilding (McCoy et al. 2005). Hence the new trends in global health toward health system strengthening, operations research, and implementation science (Madon et al. 2007). However, such system and public institution strengthening is blocked by the IMF at virtually every turn, as carefully documented by Rowden (2009) in his recent scathing critique of the IFIs and the AIDS crisis. Most egregiously, IMF-negotiated wage bill caps codified into Medium Term Expenditure Frameworks prevent the hiring of a sufficient health workforce (as well as teachers and social workers for that matter) and cap health sector spending where per capita financing rates are still a fraction of the minimum defined by the WHO. To complicate matters, PEPFAR funding reauthorized at over $50 billion over five years now dwarfs every other source of health sector support in most of its target countries. In Mozambique in 2009, PEPFAR dollars constituted nearly 60% of all funding for health. While an anthropology of PEPFAR is now being forged and the biopolitics of pharmaceuticals, therapeutic citizenship, abstinence policies, and condom distribution explored, we are curiously silent about the single most important dimension of PEPFAR funding; by policy it is channeled to private NGOs rather than to public sector health systems. Ironically, however, PEPFAR is public funding and therefore subject to political contestation and public accountability. Medical anthropologists can be effective advocates both in the countries where they come from and where they do fieldwork to help ensure that this historic opportunity is not squandered on transient NGOs and an imagined or avaricious private sector. This scale of funding can build sustainable public sector health institutions to last for a generation in most PEPFAR countries.

And the political ground is shifting. The recent financial crisis in rich countries has shaken market fundamentalism and rattled the Chicago school (Cassidy 2010). The rise of China as a financial and political player in the developing world, especially in Africa, creates, for better or worse, the first external challenge in centuries to Western hegemony for which SAPs are the latest chapter. The ascendance of the left in Latin America over the past decade constitutes a direct confrontation with the Washington Consensus (Petras 1997, Wallerstein 2002). As Muntaner and colleagues

(2006) report, the new Venezuelan approach to primary health care, *Mision Barrio Adentro*, represents massive public investment in multisectoral health for the poor and flatly rejects structural adjustment. The new approach embraces the most comprehensive versions of primary health care elaborated over 30 years earlier. As Paluzzi & Garcia (2008) optimistically declare, "Alma Ata is alive and well in Venezuela".

New social movements have coalesced in rich countries to challenge structural adjustment, such as the People's Health Movement, myriad organizations that emerged from the antiglobalization movement and so-called Battle in Seattle in 1999, and consortia led by Washington, D.C.–based *ActionAid* that travels the United States giving macroeconomic literacy trainings about structural adjustment (Rowden 2009). A large consortium of international NGOs is calling for an NGO Code of Conduct for Health Systems Strengthening that seeks to reign in the abuses of NGOs that drain resources from public sectors (Pfeiffer et al. 2008).

So, should anthropologists study, or at least grapple with IMF conditionalities, negotiations around wage bill ceilings, Medium Term Expenditure Frameworks, and NGO codes of conduct? We argue here that the apparatus and mechanics of structural adjustment matter— they indicate sites and points of struggle, engagement, and resistance (Rowden 2009). An anthropology of structural adjustment and public health should become unapologetically applied, engaged in the pragmatics of service delivery in the public sector, and committed to uncovering the institutional and political processes through which adjustment unfolds and can be challenged. With these changing political winds, a surprising surge in resources, and a growing recognition that health is a human right, it is perhaps more important than it has ever been for anthropologists to engage with our colleagues in other realms, disciplines, and arenas to resurrect the public sector and celebrate a new health commons.

DISCLOSURE STATEMENT

The authors are not aware of any affiliations, memberships, funding, or financial holdings that might be perceived as affecting the objectivity of this review.

ACKNOWLEDGMENTS

We gratefully acknowledge the outstanding research assistance provided by Anna Zogas, doctoral student in the Department of Anthropology at the University of Washington.

LITERATURE CITED

Abadía-Barrero CE, Castro A. 2006. Experiences of stigma and access to HAART in children and adolescents living with HIV/AIDS in Brazil. *Soc. Sci. Med.* 62:1219–28

Adulana JA, Olomajeye JA. 1999. The impact of government's alleviation of poverty program on the urban poor in Nigeria. *J. Black Stud.* 29(5):695–705

Arrighi G. 2002. The African crisis: world systemic and regional aspects. *New Left Rev.* 15:5–36

Allotey P, Reidpath D, Kouame A, Cummins R. 2003. The DALY, context and the determinants of the severity of disease: an exploratory comparison of paraplegia in Australia and Cameroon. *Soc. Sci. Med.* 57(5):949–58

Anand S, Hanson K. 1998. DALYs: efficiency versus equity. *World Dev.* 26(2):307–10

Baer H, Singer M, Susser I, eds. 2003. *Medical Anthropology and the World System*. Westport, CT: Praeger. 2nd ed.

Bakker I, Gill S. 2003. *Power, Production and Social Reproduction: Human In/security in the Global Political Economy*. Basingstoke, UK: Palgrave/Macmillan

Bassett MT, Bijlmakers L, Sanders DM. 1997. Professionalism, patient satisfaction and quality of health care: experience during Zimbabwe's structural adjustment program. *Soc. Sci. Med.* 45(12):1845–52

Biehl J. 2005. *Vita: Life in a Zone of Social Abandonment*. Berkeley: Univ. Calif. Press

Biehl J. 2007. *Will to Live: AIDS Therapies and the Politics of Survival*. Princeton, NJ: Princeton Univ. Press

Birn A, Zimmerman S, Garfield R. 2000. To decentralize or not to decentralize, is that the question? Nicaraguan health policy under structural adjustment in the 1990s. *Int. J. Health Serv.* 30(1):111–28

Birungi H. 1998. Injections and self-help: risk and trust in Ugandan health care. *Soc. Sci. Med.* 47(10):1455–62

Breman A, Shelton C. 2007. Structural adjustment programs and health. See Kawachi & Wamala 2007, pp. 219–33

Briggs CL, Mantini-Briggs C. 2003. *Stories in the Time of Cholera: Racial Profiling During a Medical Nightmare*. Berkeley: Univ. Calif. Press

Buse K, Walt G. 1997. An unruly mélange? Coordinating external resources to the health sector: a review. *Soc. Sci. Med.* 45(3):449–63

Cassidy J. 2010. After the blowup. *New Yorker*, Jan. 11:28

Castro A. 2006. Adherence to antiretroviral therapy: merging the clinical and social course of AIDS. *PLoS Med.* 2(12):e338

Castro A, Farmer P. 2005. Understanding and addressing AIDS-related atigma: from anthropological theory to clinical practice in Haiti. *Am. J. Public Health* 95:53–59

Castro A, Singer M, eds. 2004. *Unhealthy Health Policy: A Critical Anthropological Examination*. Walnut Creek, CA: AltaMira Press

Chabot J, Harnmeijer JW, Streefland PH, eds. 1996. *African Primary Health Care in Times of Turbulence*. Amsterdam: R. Trop. Inst.

Chapman R. 2003. Endangering safe motherhood in Mozambique: prenatal care as pregnancy risk. *Soc. Sci. Med.* 57(2):355–74

Chapman R. 2004. A nova vida: the commoditization of reproduction in central Mozambique. *Med. Anthropol.* 23(3):229–61

Cliff J. 1991. The war on women in Mozambique: health consequences of South African destabilization, economic crisis, and structural adjustment. In *Women and Health in Africa*, ed. M Turshen, 2:15–34. Trenton, NJ: Afr. World Press

Cliff J. 1993. Donor dependence or donor control?: The case of Mozambique. *Community Dev. J.* 28:237–44

Coburn D. 2000. Income, inequality, social cohesion and the health status of populations: the role of neoliberalism. *Soc. Sci. Med.* 51:139–50

Comaroff J. 2007. Beyond bare life: AIDS, (bio)politics, and the neoliberal order. *Public Cult.* 19(1):197–219

Comaroff J, Comaroff J. 2001. *Millennial Capitalism and the Culture of Neoliberalism*. Durham: Duke Univ. Press

Connelly MP. 1996. Gender matters: global restructuring and adjustment. Social politics: international studies in gender. *State Soc.* 3(1):12–31

Cornia GA, Rosignoli S, Tiberti L. 2009. An empirical investigation of the relation between globalization and health. See Labonté et al. 2009, pp. 34–62

Craig D, Porter D. 2003. Poverty Reduction Strategy Papers: a new convergence. *World Dev.* 31(1):53–69

De Beyer JA, Preker AS, Feachem RG. 2000. The role of the World Bank in international health: renewed commitment and partnership. *Soc. Sci. Med.* 50(2):169–76

Desclaux A. 2004. Equity in access to AIDS treatment in Africa: pitfalls among achievements. See Castro & Singer 2004, pp. 115–32

Elson D. 1995. Gender awareness in modeling structural adjustment. *World Dev.* 23(11)

Escobar A. 1995. *Encountering Development: The Making and Unmaking of the Third World*. Princeton: Princeton Univ. Press

Farmer P. 2001. *Infections and Inequalities: The Modern Plagues*. Berkeley: Univ. Calif. Press

Farmer P. 2004. Political violence and public health in Haiti. *New Engl. J. Med.* 350:1483–86

Farmer P. 2005. *Pathologies of Power: Health Human Rights and the New War on the Poor*. Berkeley: Univ. Calif. Press

Farmer P. 2008. Challenging orthodoxies: the road ahead for health and human rights. *Health Hum. Rights* 10(1):5–19

Farmer P, Connors M, Simmons J, eds. 1996. *Women, Poverty and AIDS: Sex, Drugs and Structural Violence*. Monroe, ME: Common Courage Press

Fassin D. 2007. *When Bodies Remember: Experiences and Politics of AIDS in South Africa*. Berkeley: Univ. Calif. Press

Ferguson J. 2006. *Global Shadows: Africa in the Neoliberal World Order*. Durham, NC: Duke Univ. Press

Foley E. 2009. *Your Pocket Is What Cures You: The Politics of Health in Senegal*. New Brunswick, NJ: Rutgers Univ. Press

Fort M, Mercer MA, Gish O. 2004. *Sickness and Wealth: The Corporate Assault on Global Health*. Cambridge, MA: South End Press

Foster K. 2005. Clinics, communities, and cost recovery: primary health care and neoliberalism in postapartheid South Africa. *Cult. Dyn.* 17(3):239–66

Freedman LP. 2005. Achieving the MDGs: health systems as core social institutions. *Development* 48(1):19–24

Gershman J, Irwin A. 2000. Getting and grip on the global economy. See Kim et al. 2000a, pp. 11–43

Gill L. 2000. *Teetering on the Rim: Global Restructuring, Daily Life, and the Armed Retreat of the Bolivian State*. New York: Columbia Univ. Press

Gladwin CH, ed. 1991. *Structural Adjustment and African Women Farmers*. Gainesville: Univ. Fla. Press

Gloyd S. 1996. NGOs and the "SAP"ing of health care in rural Mozambique. *Hesperian Foundation News*, Spring. Berkeley: Hesperian Found.

Green A, Mathias A. 1997. *Non-Governmental Organizations and Health in Developing Countries*. London: MacMillan

Gwatkin DR, Guillot M, Heuveline P. 1999. The burden of disease among the global poor. *Lancet* 354(9178):586–89

Haddad L, Brown LR, Richter A, Smith L. 1995. The gender dimensions of economic adjustment policies: potential interactions and evidence to date. *World Dev.* 23(6):881–96

Hammonds R, Ooms G. 2004. World Bank policies and the obligation of its members to respect, protect and fulfill the right to health. *Health Hum. Rights* 8(1):26–60

Handa S, King D. 2003. Adjustment with a human face? Evidence from Jamaica. *World Dev.* 31(7):1125–45

Hanlon J. 1996. *Peace Without Profit: How the IMF Blocks Rebuilding in Mozambique.* Portsmouth, NH: Heinemann

Harris RL, Seid M, eds. 2004. *Globalization and Health.* Leiden/Boston: Brill

Harvey D. 2005. *A Brief History of Neoliberalism.* Oxford: Oxford Univ. Press

Hunter M. 2007. The changing political economy of sex in South Africa: the significance of unemployment and inequalities to the scale of the AIDS pandemic. *Soc. Sci. Med.* 64(3):689–700

IMF/World Bank. 2002. *Review of the poverty reduction strategy paper (PRSP) approach: early experience with interim PRSPs and full PRSPs.* Washington, DC: IMF/World Bank

Janes C. 2004. Going global in century XXI: medical anthropology and the new primary health care. *Hum. Organ. Soc. Appl. Anthropol.* 63(4):457–71

Janes CR, Chuluundorj O. 2004. Free markets and dead mothers: the social ecology of maternal mortality in post-Socialist Mongolia. *Med. Anthropol. Q.* 18(2):230–57

Janes CR, Corbett KK. 2009. Anthropology and global health. *Annu. Rev. Anthropol.* 38:167–83

Jitta J, Whyte SR, Nshakira N. 2003. The availability of drugs: What does it mean in Ugandan primary care? *Health Policy* 65:167–79

Justice J. 2000. The politics of child survival. See Manderson & Whiteford 2000, pp. 23–38

Kalipeni E. 2004. Structural adjustment and the health care crisis in Malawi. *Proteus* 21(1):23–30

Kawachi I, Wamala S, eds. 2007. *Globalization and Health.* Oxford: Oxford Univ. Press

Keshavjee S. 2004. The contradictions of a revolving drug fund in post-Soviet Tajikistan. See Castro & Singer 2004, pp. 97–113

Kickbusch I, Hartwig KA, List JM. 2005. *Globalization, Women, and Health in the 21st Century.* New York: Palgrave MacMillan

Kim JY, Millen JV, Irwin A, Gershman J. 2000a. *Dying for Growth: Global Inequality and the Health of the Poor.* Monroe, ME: Common Courage Press

Kim JY, Shakow A, Bayona J, Rhatigan J, Rubin de Celis EL. 2000b. Sickness amidst recovery: public debt and private suffering in Peru. See Kim et al. 2000a, pp. 127–54

Kyaddonoo D, Whyte SR. 2003. Working in a decentralized system: a threat to health workers' respect and survival in Uganda. *Int. J. Health Plan. M.* 18(4):329–42

Labonté R, Schrecker T, Packer C, Runnels V, eds. 2009. *Globalization and Health: Pathways, Evidence and Policy.* New York: Routledge

Laurell AC. 2000. Structural adjustment and the globalization of social policy in Latin America. *Int. Sociol.* 15(2):306–25

Leatherman T, Thomas RB. 2009. Structural violence, political violence, and the health costs of civil conflict: a case study from Peru. In *Anthropology in Public Health: Bridging Differences in Culture and Society,* ed. R Hahn, MC Inhorn, 7:196–220. Oxford: Oxford Univ. Press. 2nd ed.

Loewenson R. 1993. Structural adjustment and health policy in Africa. *Int. J. Health Serv.* 23(4):717–30

Loevinsohn B, Harding A. 2005. Buying results? Contracting for health service delivery in developing countries. *Lancet* 366(9486):676–81

Loftus A. 2006. *A Political Ecology of Water Struggles in Durban, South Africa.* Oxford, UK: Oxford Univ. Press

Lundy P. 1996. Limitations of quantitative research in the study of structural adjustment. *Soc. Sci. Med.* 42(3):313–24

Lurie P, Hintzen P, Lowe RA. 1995. Socioeconomic obstacles to HIV prevention and treatment in developing countries: the roles of the International Monetary Fund and the World Bank. *AIDS* 9(6):539–46

Madon T, Hofman KJ, Kupfer L, Glass RI. 2007. Implementation science. *Science* 318:1728–29

Manderson L, Whiteford L. 2000. *Global Health Policy, Local Realities: The Fallacy of the Level Playing Field.* Boulder, CO: Lynne Rienner

Maternowska MC. 2006. *Reproducing Inequities: Poverty and the Politics of Population in Haiti.* New Brunswick, NJ: Rutgers Univ. Press

Maupin J. 2008. Remaking the Guatemalan midwife: health care reform and midwifery training programs in highland Guatemala. *Med. Anthropol.* 27(4):353–82

Maupin JN. 2009. "Fruit of the accords": healthcare reform and civil participation in highland Guatemala. *Soc. Sci. Med.* 68(8):1456–63

Mburu FM. 1989. Non-government organizations in the health field: collaboration, integration, and contrasting aims in Africa. *Soc. Sci. Med.* 29(5):591–97

McCoy D, Bennett S, Witter S, et al. 2008. Salaries and incomes of health workers in sub Saharan Africa. *Lancet* 371(9613):675–81

McCoy D, Chopra M, Loewenson R, Aitken JM, Ngulube T, et al. 2005. Expanding access to antiretroviral therapy in sub-Saharan Africa: avoiding the pitfalls and dangers, capitalizing on the opportunities. *Am. J. Public Health* 95(1):18–22

Morgan LM. 1993. *Community Participation in Health: the Politics of Primary Care in Costa Rica.* Cambridge, UK: Cambridge Univ. Press

Murray CJL, Lopez AD, eds. 1996. *The global burden of disease: a comprehensive assessment of mortality and disability from diseases, injuries, and risk factors in 1990 and projected to 2020.* Geneva: WHO

Muntaner C, Guerra Salazar RM, Benach J, Armada F. 2006. Venezuela's Barrio Adentro: an alternative to neoliberalism in health care. *Int. J. Health Serv.* 36(4):803–11

Navarro V. 2004. The world situation and WHO. *Lancet* 363(9417):1321–23

Nguyen VK, Ako CY, Niamba P, Sylla A, Tiendrébéogo I. 2007. Adherence as therapeutic citizenship: impact of the history of access to antiretroviral drugs on adherence to treatment. *AIDS* 21(Suppl. 5):S31–35

Nichter M. 2008. *Global Health: Why Cultural Perceptions, Social Representations, and Biopolitics Matter.* Tuscon: Univ. Ariz. Press

Nwajiuba CU, Nwoke BEB, Nwajiuba CA. 2007. Structural adjustment program and public health issues in relation to migration: Nigeria. *Development* 50(4):101–5

Okuonzi S. 2004. Dying for economic growth? Evidence of a flawed economic policy in Uganda. *Lancet* 364(9445):1632–37

Ooms G, Van Damme W, Baker BK, Zeitz P, Schrecker T. 2008. The "diagonal" approach to global fund financing: a cure for the broader malaise of health systems? *Glob. Health* 4(6)

Ooms G, Schrecker T. 2005. Expenditure ceilings, multilateral financial institutions, and the health of poor populations. *Lancet* 365(9473):1821–23

Parker RG, Easton D, Klein CH. 2000. Structural barriers and facilitators in HIV prevention: a review of international research. *AIDS* 14(Suppl. 1):S22–32

Paluzzi JE. 2004. Primary Health Care since Alma Ata: lost in the Bretton Woods? See Castro & Singer 2004, pp. 63–78

Paluzzi JE, Garcia FA. 2008. Health for all: Alma Ata is alive and well in Venezuela. *Soc. Med.* 3(4):217–20

Petras J. 1997. Latin America: the resurgence of the Left. *New Left Rev.* I/223:17–47

Petryna A, Lakoff A, Kleinman A, eds. 2006. *Global Pharmaceuticals: Ethics, Markets, Practices.* Durham: Duke Univ. Press

Pfeiffer J. 2002a. African independent churches in Mozambique: healing the afflictions of inequality. *Med. Anthropol. Q.* 16(2):176–99

Pfeiffer J. 2002b. Cash income, intrahousehold cooperative conflict, and child health in central Mozambique. *Med. Anthropol.* 22:87–130

Pfeiffer J. 2003. International NGOs and primary health care in Mozambique: the need for a new model of collaboration. *Soc. Sci. Med.* 56(4):725–38

Pfeiffer J. 2004. Condom social marketing, pentecostalism, and structural adjustment in Mozambique: a clash of AIDS prevention messages. *Med. Anthropol. Q.* 18(1):77–103

Pfeiffer J. 2005. Commodity fetichismo, the holy spirit, and the turn to pentecostal and African independent churches in central Mozambique. *Cult. Med. Psychiat.* 29(3):255–83

Pfeiffer J, Gimbel-Sherr K, Augusto O. 2007. The holy spirit in the household: pentecostalism, gender, and neoliberalism in Mozambique. *Am. Anthropol.* 109(4):688–700

Pfeiffer J, Nichter M. 2008. What can critical medical anthropology contribute to global health? A health systems perspective. *Med. Anthropol. Q.* 22(4):410–15

Pfeiffer J, Johnson W, Fort M, Shakow A, Hagopian A, et al. 2008. Strengthening health systems in poor countries: a code of conduct for nongovernmental organizations. *Am. J. Pub. Health* 98(12):2134–40

Piot P. 2001. *Aid and human security.* Address at U. N. Univ., Tokyo, 2 Oct.

Poku N. 2006. *AIDS in Africa: How the Poor Are Dying.* Cambridge, UK: Polity Press

Pottier J. 1999. *Anthropology of Food: the Social Dynamics of Food Security*. Cambridge, UK: Blackwell

Ridde V. 2008. "The problem of the worst-off is dealt with after all other issues": the equity and health policy implementation gap in Burkina Faso. *Soc. Sci. Med.* 66(6):1368–78

Rifkin SB, Walt G. 1986. Why health improves: defining the issues concerning "comprehensive primary health care" and "selective primary health care." *Soc. Sci. Med.* 23(6):559–66

Romero-Daza N, Himmelgreen D. 1998. More than money for your labor: migration and the political economy of AIDS in Lesotho. See Singer 1997, pp. 185–204

Rowden R. 2009. *The Deadly Ideas of Neoliberalism: How the IMF has undermined public health and the fight against AIDS*. London: Zed Books

Rylko-Bauer B, Whiteford LM, Farmer P. 2009. *Global Health in Times of Violence*. Santa Fe, NM: School Adv. Res. Press

Sachs JD. 2005. *The End of Poverty: Economic Possibilities for Our Time*. New York: Penguin Press

Sahn DE, Bernier R. 1995. Have structural adjustments led to health sector reform in Africa? *Health Policy* 32(3):193–214

Sahn DE, Dorosh PA, Younger SE. 1997. *Structural Adjustment Reconsidered: Economic Policy and Poverty in Africa*. Cambridge, UK: Cambridge Univ. Press

Sanders T. 2001. Save our skins: structural adjustment, morality, and the occult in Tanzania. In *Magical Interpretations, Material Realities: Modernity, Witchcraft and the Occult in Postcolonial Africa*, eds. HL Moore, T Sanders, 8:160–83. London: Routledge

Sassen S. 2003. The repositioning of citizenship: emergent subjects and spaces for politics. *New Centennial Rev.* 3(2):41–66

Schoepf BG, Schoepf C, Millen JV. 2000. Theoretical therapies, remote remedies: SAPs and the political ecology of poverty and health in Africa. See Kim et al. 2000a, pp. 91–126

Schoepf BG. 2001. International AIDS research in anthropology: taking a critical perspective on the crisis. *Annu. Rev. Anthropol.* 30:335–61

Schoepf BG, Engundu W, with Russel D, Schoepf C. 1991. Women and structural adjustment in Zaire. See Gladwin 1991, pp. 151–68

Singer M. 1997. *The Political Economy of AIDS*. Amityville, NY: Baywood

Singer M, Baer H. 1995. *Critical Medical Anthropology*. Amityville, NY: Baywood

Smith-Nonini S. 1998. Health "antireform" in El Salvador: community health, NGOs and the state in the neoliberal era. *PoLAR* 21(1):99–113

Smith-Nonini S. 2006. Conceiving the health commons: operationalizing a "right" to health. *Soc. Anal.* 50(3):233–45

Sparr P, ed. 1994. *Mortgaging Women's Lives: Feminist Critiques of Structural Adjustment*. London: Zed Books

Stiglitz J. 2002. *Globalization and its Discontents*. New York: W.W. Norton

Streefland P. 2005. Public health care under pressure in subsaharan Africa. *Health Policy* 71:375–82

Susser I. 2009. *AIDS, Sex, and Culture: Global Politics and Survival in Southern Africa*. Oxford, UK: Blackwell

Towghi F. 2004. Shifting policies toward traditional midwives: implications for reproductive health care in Pakistan. See Castro & Singer 2004, pp. 79–95

Turshen M. 1999. *Privatizing Health Services in Africa*. New Brunswick, NJ: Rutgers

UNICEF. 1987. *Adjustment with a Human Face*. New York: UNICEF

UNICEF. 1988. *The Bamako Initiative recommendations to the Executive Board for program co-ordination 1989–1993*. New York: UNICEF

UNICEF. 1991. *The Situation of Women and Children in Mozambique*. Maputo: United Nations

Uvin P. 1998. *Aiding Violence: The Development Enterprise in Rwanda*. West Hartford, CT: Kumarian Press

Van Der Geest S, Macwan'gi M, Kamwanga J, Mulikelela D, Mazimba A, Mwangelwa M. 2000. User fees and drugs: What did the health reforms in Zambia achieve? *Health Policy Plan.* 15(1):59–65

Vavrus F. 2005. Adjusting inequality: education and structural adjustment policies in Tanzania. *Harvard Educ. Rev.* 75(2):174–201

Wallerstein I. 2002. New revolts against the system. *New Left Rev.* 22:27–35

Wamala S, Kawachi I. 2007. Globalization and women's health. See Kawachi & Wamala 2007, pp. 171–84

Wamala S, Kawachi I, Mpepo BP. 2007. Poverty Reduction Strategy Papers: bold new approach to poverty eradication or old wine in new bottles? See Kawachi & Wamala 2007, pp. 234–49

Whiteford L, Whiteford S, eds. 2005. *Globalization, Water, and Health: Resource Management in Times of Scarcity*. Oxford: James Currey

Whyte SR, White MA, Meinert L, Kyaddondo B. 2004. Treating AIDS: dilemmas of unequal access in Uganda. *SAHARA J–J. Soc. Asp. H.* 1(1):14–26

World Bank. 1981. *Accelerated Development in Sub-Saharan Africa*. Washington, DC: World Bank (*The Berg Report*)

World Bank. 1987. *Financing Health Services in Developing Countries: An Agenda for Reform*. Washington, DC: World Bank

World Bank. 1993. *World Development Report: Investing in Health*. Washington, DC: World Bank

World Bank. 2007. *Healthy Development: the World Bank Strategy for Health, Nutrition, and Population Results*. Washington, DC: World Bank

World Health Organization. 2001. *Report of the Commission on Macroeconomics and Health: Macroeconomics and Health—Investing in Health for Economic Development*. Geneva: WHO

Zuckerman E. 2002. 'Engendering' poverty reduction strategy papers (PRSPs): the issues and the challenges. *Gender Dev.* 10(3):88–94

Preindustrial Markets
and Marketing:
Archaeological Perspectives

Gary M. Feinman[1] and Christopher P. Garraty[2]

[1] Department of Anthropology, The Field Museum, Chicago, Illinois 60605-2496;
email: gfeinman@fieldmuseum.org

[2] Statistical Research, Inc., Tucson, Arizona 85712; email: cpgarraty@yahoo.com

Annu. Rev. Anthropol. 2010. 39:167–91

First published online as a Review in Advance on
June 14, 2010

The *Annual Review of Anthropology* is online at
anthro.annualreviews.org

This article's doi:
10.1146/annurev.anthro.012809.105118

0084-6570/10/1021-0167$20.00

Key Words

economic anthropology, exchange, marketplaces, preindustrial
economies

Abstract

Markets are key contemporary institutions, yet there is little agreement
concerning their history or diversity. To complicate matters, markets
have been considered by different academic disciplines that approach
the nature of such exchange systems from diametrically opposed perspectives that impede cross-disciplinary dialogue. This paper reviews
the theoretical and methodological issues surrounding the detection,
development, and significance of markets in the preindustrial past. We
challenge both the view that marketing is natural and the perspective
that market exchange is unique to modern capitalist contexts. Both of
these frameworks fail to recognize that past and present market activities are embedded in their larger societal contexts, albeit in different
ways that can be understood only if examined through a broadly shared
theoretical lens. We examine the origins, change, and diversity of preindustrial markets, calling for multiscalar, cross-disciplinary approaches
to investigate the long-term history of this economic institution.

[B]road concepts such as "markets" and "states," or "socialism" and "capitalism," do not take us very far in thinking about patterns of order in human society . . . . Markets are diverse and complex entities. Markets for different types of goods and services may take on quite different characteristics. Some may work well under impersonal conditions. Others may depend upon personal considerations involving high levels of trust among trading partners. In other words, the options are much greater than we imagine, and we can see this is true if we don't allow our minds to be trapped within narrowly constrained intellectual horizons. (Ostrom 2003, p. 1)

INTRODUCTION

[W]e turned to look at the great market place and the crowds of people that were in it, some buying and others selling, so that the murmur and hum of their voices and words that they used could be heard from more than a league off. Some of the soldiers among us who had been in many parts of the world, in Constantinople, and all over Italy, and in Rome, said that so large a market place and so full of people, and so regulated and arranged, they had never beheld before (Díaz del Castillo 1956, pp. 218–19).

Upon entering the Basin of Mexico in the sixteenth century, Díaz del Castillo and other Spanish conquerors were awestruck by the bustling central Aztec marketplace at Tlatelolco, which shared an island location with the Aztec imperial capital, Tenochtitlán (now Mexico City). Another account (López de Gómara 1966, p. 160) related that this marketplace was "so large . . . that it will hold seventy thousand or even one hundred thousand people, who go about buying and selling . . . not only from the vicinity, but from farther off." This latter account situates this central market on an island in Lake Texcoco, the hub of a network of smaller markets scattered in towns around the lake in the Basin of Mexico. A third account (Torquemada 1943, p. 580) documents marketplace transactions: "[A]pproaching the

exchange, neither one nor the other says a word; she who arrives presents the item she brought and the other, seated, looks at it. If she is interested, she takes it into her hand. Judging that it is too little, she squeezes it and looks at the rest of what the other has brought to sell, which is a signal that she likes what is offered, but that the quantity is too small, that she demands more. And in this manner they haggle with each other until she feels that what she is offered is sufficient; and if the one who is standing does not want to offer more, she reclaims her item and moves on to the next merchant, still without saying anything."

As documented by these sources (see also Cortés 1977), it has long been recognized that the Aztec marketplace at Tlatelolco was crowded, stocked with a wide array of local and exotic goods (Sahagún 1950–1982, book 10, pp. 65–78), and stood at the apex of a hierarchical network of marketplaces (Berdan 1985; Blanton 1996, pp. 68–80). At the same time, Torquemada (1943, p. 580) provided perspective on how prices were set, while evidencing economic transfers that took place between individuals who seemingly were not close social associates. Various currencies, including copper axes, reams of cloth, and cacao seeds, were used in this system of markets (Berdan 1982, p. 43), and the apparent counterfeiting of cacao pods hints at a motive to profit (Oviedo y Valdés 1851–1855, p. 316; Sahagún 1950–1982, book 10, p. 65). Observations such as these make clear that Aztec markets were not qualitatively different from more modern ones, leading us to question the unbridgeable chasm that some scholars have posited between the operational principles of ancient and modern economies.

Yet, despite the size and complexity of the Aztec market system, the critical role of market activities in the prehispanic Mesoamerican world has received relatively little attention in anthropological archaeology, particularly before the past two decades (Blanton 1983; Braswell 2010; Feinman & Nicholas 2004, 2010; Garraty 2009; Hirth 1998, 2009; Smith 2010; Stark & Ossa 2010). Neither the historical roots of this system (Blanton 1996,

Minc 2006) nor the nature of marketplace exchange in other regions of Mesoamerica before the Spanish Conquest have been thoroughly investigated (but see Braswell 2010, Braswell & Glascock 2002, Dahlin et al. 2010, Feinman et al. 1984, Feinman & Nicholas 2004, Hirth 1998, Nichols et al. 2002, Pluckhahn 2009, Stark & Ossa 2010). Rather, most studies of Mesoamerican economies take the existence of markets largely for granted and devote little attention to their scale, structure, level of integration, or role in domestic economic strategies. In the case of the Aztecs, most analyses have stressed the links between marketplace exchange and other mechanisms of distribution, such as tribute and long-distance merchant activities (Berdan 1977, 1983), as well as political oversight of market activities (Carrasco 1978; 1983, pp. 73–79; Hassig 1982; Hicks 1987; Kurtz 1974). In fact, the importance of ancient Mesoamerican markets generally has been downplayed in synthetic treatments of the region's economies (e.g., Carrasco 1978, 2001; Sanders et al. 1979, pp. 404–5). When pre-Hispanic Mesoamerican economies have been considered, emphasis has been placed on the presumed lack or limited scope of land and labor markets rather than on the sizable volume of marketplace exchange for nonfactor commodities (e.g., food, craft goods), price-setting mechanisms, or the degree of economic commercialization (Carrasco 1978, 1983).

Despite the recognized importance of marketplaces in many regions of the preindustrial world (e.g., Blanton & Fargher 2010; Claessen 1978, table 2), such as Greece (Morris 1994, p. 366; Osbourne 1991, pp. 136–40), Rome (de Ligt 1993; Geraghty 2007; Greene 2000; Storey 2004; Temin 2001, 2004, 2006), Mesopotamia (Gledhill & Larsen 1982, Hudson 2002, Silver 1983), medieval Europe (Grantham 1999), China (Shen 2003; Tao 1999, pp. 119–20), and Africa (Curtin 1984, p. 58; Fleisher 2010; Law 1992; Uzoigwe 1972), archaeological syntheses have devoted insufficient attention to early markets compared with other issues relevant to premodern economies, such as tribute or craft production (Minc 2006, p. 82;

Smith 2004). Prior to a recent contribution (Garraty & Stark 2010), few archaeological volumes have tackled premodern markets and marketplaces in comparative perspective (compare Hodges 1988), an intellectual lacuna that is hard to understand without delving into the disciplinary histories and rigidified cross-field academic boundaries that have tended to segregate much of economics from the study of economic history (Findlay 2005, p. 19; Solow 1985, 2005) and has fostered a basic decommercialization of ancient economies (Adams 1974; Oka & Kusimba 2008, p. 345).

In archaeology, the limited attention given to market exchange and marketplaces owes much to the broad influence of Polanyi (1944, 1947; Polanyi et al. 1957) and those who translated and developed key tenets of his approach in economic anthropology (e.g., Bohannan & Dalton 1962; Dalton 1961, 1968, 1975, 1978; Sahlins 1972) and classics (Finley 1999). Although the longstanding formalist-substantivist debate in economic anthropology has been declared over (Halperin 1984, Isaac 1993), its unfortunate legacies include the tendency among archaeologists to view the issue of preindustrial market development and the relative nature and degree of market exchange through the optic of an oversimplified "market/no-market dichotomy" (Wilk 1996, pp. 3–14; 1998, p. 469). Perhaps, related to these conceptual limitations and despite recent advances (Abbott 2010, Feinman & Nicholas 2010, Hirth 1998, Minc 2006, Stark & Garraty 2010), archaeologists still lack a sophisticated set of procedures or toolkit for unequivocally detecting marketplaces, market exchange, and the diversity of market-related activities, especially when investigating times and places where documentary sources do not exist (Hirth 1998, Stark & Garraty 2010).

Nevertheless, despite these conceptual and methodological hurdles, the historical diversity and importance of preindustrial marketplace exchange and market systems has begun to gain greater attention in a number of disciplines over the past two decades (e.g., Friedland & Robertson 1990, Garraty & Stark 2010, Lie

Market exchange: economic transactions where the economic forces of supply and demand are highly visible and where prices or exchange equivalences exist

Marketplaces:
physical places in
which market
exchanges are
generally conducted at
customary times

**Market concept or
model:** an idealized
conception that an
economic (market)
system is the
cumulative effect of
market transactions
between self-interested
buyers and sellers

1997). With the contemporary global financial
crisis, the core tenets of economic theory are
also undergoing an unprecedented reevaluation
(e.g., Arnsperger & Varoufakis 2006, Buiter
2009, Cassidy 2009, Dequech 2007–2008,
Hodgson 2009, Krugman 2009) that even in
these early stages has opened the door for
greater communication among social scientific
disciplines concerning market operations,
development, and diversity (Ensminger 2002,
p. xviii). In the face of these intellectual shifts,
the time is appropriate to take stock of what
is known about preindustrial marketplaces and
market exchange (Swedberg 2005, p. 249). We
approach this topic by first offering a series of
working definitions. We then briefly discuss
the history of theoretical debates across the
social sciences to take stock of the present
state of knowledge, while also outlining recent
conceptual reconsiderations that broaden the
opportunity for cross-disciplinary dialogue.
We review recent archaeological approaches
toward the identification of marketplaces and
market exchange (see also Stark & Garraty
2010). Final sections look forward to critical issues for future studies of preindustrial
markets, as ideas regarding the origins of and
variation in market exchange systems require
a long-term historical perspective (Braudel
1985).

KEY DEFINITIONS

It is paradoxical that at a time when markets pervade almost all aspects of our lives and economic
theory is applied to research issues across the
academic spectrum (e.g., Becker 1976, Levitt
& Dubner 2005), the market still can be described as "the hollow core at the heart of economics" (Lie 1997, p. 342). Economists as well
as other scholars have devoted relatively little
attention to defining and methodically distinguishing market exchange, marketplaces, market systems, and the market model (Barber
1977, p. 19; Coase 1988, pp. 7–8; North 1977,
p. 710; Pryor 1977, p. 31; Rosenbaum 2000;
Swedberg 1994, p. 257). In addition, the concepts that economists do employ often are not

well aligned with those outlined in other disciplines (Dilley 1992b, pp. 1, 13; 1996; Swedberg
1994, 2005). The challenge here is to develop
a set of working definitions that neither stultify
research nor become the central focus of academic discussion and that encourage analytical
practice as well as dialogue across a range of disciplines. We seek definitions that neither narrowly equate the market with Euro-American
capitalism nor are so broad that they subsume
all human exchange, which extends back more
than 12,000 years (Bar-Yosef 2002, p. 367).

We find that many existing definitions of
market-related concepts tend to be overly broad
or restrictively narrow for the purpose of understanding preindustrial market systems. For
instance, Bitzenis & Marangos (2007, p. 604)
broadly describe the market as "a process in
which individuals interact with one another
in pursuit of their separate economic objectives." In a similar vein, Gravelle & Rees (1992,
p. 3) see that "a market exists whenever two
or more individuals are prepared to enter into
an exchange transaction, regardless of time or
place." Yet, Bitzenis & Marangos (2007, p. 604)
adopt a much narrower definition of the concept of market economy, dichotomously contrasting such economies with state-controlled
or planned economies and thus conflating market exchange systems with the presence of a
"free," self-regulating market. This definition
exemplifies a longstanding and erroneous perspective that presumes an oppositional and antagonistic relationship between "public" state
and "private" market aspirations and objectives
(a topic we explore below).

Ironically, Polanyi (1944, p. 68), whose
ideas often are juxtaposed with those of neoclassical economists, likewise adopted a narrow
definition of market exchange as "an economic
system controlled, regulated, and directed
by markets alone." He further adds, "All
goods and services, including the use of land,
labor and capital, are available for purchase in
markets and have, therefore, a price" (Polanyi
1957a, p. 247). For Polanyi (1944, pp. 43,
54–55; 1957a, pp. 247, 266–69), consequential
market exchange did not exist prior to the

advent of Western capitalism (e.g., Humphreys 1969, pp. 166, 184), a development that he placed in nineteenth-century England. In part, the writings of Polanyi and his associates (e.g., Dalton 1975, pp. 86–91; Sahlins 1972, p. 300; compare Cook 1966) erroneously prompted an analytical dichotomy between recent Euro-American market systems and other non-Western (as well as pre-nineteenth-century European) economies in the disciplines of anthropology, archaeology, and ancient history (Blanton & Fargher 2010; Hejeebu & McCloskey 1999, p. 291).

Our definitions are broader than Polanyi's but narrower than the above conceptualization by Gravelle and Rees, as we recognize that marketplaces and market exchange have a long history and must encompass significant empirically documented variability. We conceptualize market exchange as economic transactions where the forces of supply and demand are visible and where prices or exchange equivalencies exist. In theory, market exchanges may be atomized/impersonal or personal/embedded (Granovetter 1985). However, in practice (as we discuss in the next section), all market transactions presuppose social relationships among the parties to an exchange and so are embedded (Barber 1995, Lie 1991, McCloskey 1997), albeit to greatly varying degrees and in distinct ways. Our definition owes much to Pryor (1977, p. 437, see also pp. 31–33, 104–8), and we follow his usage of "visible" as meaning that important changes in relative prices, salient shifts in quantities or availability of goods offered or sought, or the quality of marketed goods available create palpable modulations in supply and demand forces that are perceptible to market participants.

Pryor's definition isolates the economic realm, but market transactions also presuppose a social context that situates relationships between parties to an exchange (Bestor 2001; Fischer 2009; Plattner 1989a, p. 171). The dissemination of supply-demand information is multifaceted and responsive to a variety of social considerations, including notions of value and fairness, word of mouth, bargaining

practices (haggling), the relationships between exchange participants (Dequech 2003, Uzzi 1997), as well as negotiations over price setting involving sellers, merchants, guilds, and trade groups, or by governing officials (Alexander & Alexander 1991; Alexander 1992; Block & Evans 2005, pp. 506–8). We have amplified Pryor's perspective to recognize the influence of social mechanisms on market price formation (Braudel 1985, p. 227; Minor 1965, pp. 51–53; Swedberg & Granovetter 2001, p. 13).

Our definition of market exchange is broad, in accord with the wide temporal and spatial extent of this practice (Abbott 2010, Hirth 2010, Kohler et al. 2000, Lewis 1989). In this regard, we also recognize that in all economies, ancient or modern, market exchange, when present, coexists with other modes of transfer and exchange (e.g., Davis 1992, p. 25; Pryor 1977), as it did in Aztec times (Berdan 1977). Also important for clarifying our broad definition is how market exchange compares with the concept of barter. Barter has been variously defined as interpersonal transactions without formal media of exchange (Humphrey 1985, Humphrey & Hugh-Jones 1992) and as informal and ad hoc exchanges in which commonly held notions of value equivalencies are initially absent, but ultimately achieved (Blanton 2009). Both definitions have merit. In our view, sporadic exchanges based on supply-demand principles theoretically can transpire in an ad hoc fashion without formal media of exchange, but the increasing scale of market participation and establishment of "rules" of market conduct tend to give rise to more formalized arenas for market transactions based on widely shared perceptions of price and value, possibly facilitated by formal media of exchange (although not necessarily by currencies).

For archaeologists and ancient historians, key research questions focus on increasing participation in market exchange, which prompts the emergence of a market institution, including a system of rules, customs, and a physical and legal infrastructure (North 1990, 1991). Once socially institutionalized, market exchanges become more archaeologically visible, but this process is neither natural nor inevitable. Our definition of market exchange does not presuppose a link between the frequency of market exchange and any scalar demographic threshold or level of social complexity. Market exchange may become institutionalized even in small-scale, middle-range societies as exemplified by Abbott's (2010, Abbott et al. 2007) recent argument for market exchange in prehistoric Arizona. When we speak of the physical infrastructure, the most direct example is the marketplace, which we define as arenas where face-to-face market exchanges are conducted at customary times and places. Economically linked marketplaces across regional landscapes are defined as market systems (Christaller 1966; Forman & Riegelhaupt 1970, p. 189; Skinner 1964; C. Smith 1974, 1976), which can take a wide variety of spatial configurations.

On the basis of this perspective, we define markets as social institutions predicated on the market exchange of alienable commodities (Garraty 2010). The social context pertains to the networks of relationships involved in market exchanges and the establishment of prices (e.g., Dequech 2003, Uzzi 1997). By acknowledging the social embeddedness of markets (Granovetter 1985), we do not negate the fundamental role of self-interested economic behavior in market exchange (see also Hirth 2010, Plattner 1989b), although these basic individual interests often may be "satisficed" with other considerations and the minimization of risk (Bowles 1998, Henrich et al. 2005, Levitt & List 2008, E. Ostrom 2000). In formulating these definitions, we have decoupled market-based economic practices from what may be considered the ideological model or concept of the market employed in mainstream economics (Alexander 1992, Carrier 1997, Dilley 1992a). The latter is the idealized conception that an economic (market) system is just the cumulative effect of atomistic market transactions between individual buyers and sellers who act based solely on personal self-interest and independent of social relationships. This conception, which generally is applied to recent Western economic systems, rarely, if ever, conforms to actual practice (Fox 2009).

ADAM SMITH, KARL POLANYI, AND EMBEDDEDNESS

To understand why marketplace exchange has been insufficiently considered and given little significance in preindustrial economies, it is necessary to review the paradigmatic clashes that stretch across disciplines and frame the topic. In anthropology and archaeology, the writings of Polanyi (1944, 1947, 1957a) have long sat at the epicenter of this discussion, while Polanyi's close associate Moses Finley (1999) largely set the debate for the ancient Mediterranean world. The influential works of Polanyi (Block 2003; Halperin 1984, 1994; Humphreys 1969) were in part a reaction to what he viewed as the dehumanizing and culturally specific tenets of classical and neoclassical economic theories (Polanyi 1944, p. 163). Often traced to Adam Smith (1976), classical economics has adopted a positivist approach underpinned by methodological individualism and the view that humans, governed by self-interest, have a natural capacity for "market rationality." In contrast, Polanyi argued that models grounded in individual self-interest and market mentality are solely the product of modern capitalism and that "market society was born in England" (Polanyi 1944, p. 30).

In these contrasting frameworks lie the roots of the long-standing dichotomy between the study of past and present economies. When it came to non-Western economies, Polanyi (1944, pp. 115–117) not only rejected economists' reliance on self-interested individualism, but also argued "that never before our own time were markets more than accessories of economic life" (Polanyi 1944, p. 68). Polanyi (1947) asserted that recent Western economies were qualitatively distinct from other economic systems and outlined criteria for distinguishing recent Euro-American market systems from other economies, including the commoditization of labor and land, the presence of universal money, and perceived inefficiencies of information flows regarding market conditions in the past (see also Dalton 1968). Polanyi and his associates (Bohannan & Dalton 1962, Carrasco 1982, Dalton 1968) also grounded this binary distinction in what we now know are romanticized views of preindustrial societies, which perceived component households as largely self-sufficient economically and sociopolitical integration as more centralized, less multivocal (contentious) than it often actually was (e.g., Blanton & Fargher 2008; Brumfiel 1992; Goldstone 2002, p. 328; Smith 2004). The generations of scholars guided by his perspectives certainly recognized preindustrial and non-Western marketplace exchange (Bohannan & Dalton 1962; Polanyi 1944, pp. 54–55; 1957a, p. 257), but they also starkly contrasted these economic systems to those of the modern West, which they viewed as dominated by self-regulating, "free" markets, autonomous of sociopolitical institutions (Humphrey & Hugh-Jones 1992, pp. 2–3; McCloskey 1997; compare Block 2003).

The unpacking of the issues behind this intellectual chasm provides avenues for serious cross-disciplinary dialogue. The centrality of the "hidden hand" (entirely free self-regulated market exchange) in Adam Smith's legacy to economics (Kennedy 2009, Lubasz 1992) has come into question. Although such notions of the self-regulating market (that freely and efficiently moves to broad economic betterment) are central to recent streams of economic thought (Friedman 1982; compare Harvey 2005; Krugman 1999, 2009; Stiglitz 1999), other economists have become less comfortable with this view, pointing to the critical and essential role of government in the market societies of the contemporary West, especially during times of economic crisis (Baker 2009, Hodgson 2009, Krugman 2009, Polanyi-Levitt 2006). Furthermore, as Hejeebu & McCloskey (2004, p. 139) explain, most economists have fixated on Smith's "hidden hand" argument in *The Wealth of Nations* but failed to appreciate his broader discussion of ethical and social mores. Clearly, Smith recognized that economic action functions relative to societal customs and values (Evensky 2005).

At the same time, the advent of new institutional economics (North 1977, 1990, 1991, Williamson 1975, 1985) signals a recognition that institutions, such as firms and governments, have a key role (along with individuals) in the establishment of order (definitions of property, affirmation of contracts) necessary for the operation of modern Western economies (Nee 2005; Williamson 1975, 1985) as well as others (e.g., Acheson 2002, Ensminger 2002). More recently, modeling at the scale of the individual has begun to expand beyond simple self-interest to include considerations of cooperation, social transmission, and collective management of resources (Bowles 1998, Mansbridge 1990, Ostrom 2000). These recent theoretical developments point to the prescience of some of Polanyi's key arguments concerning the social embeddedness of economic action, but not solely for ancient and non-Western economies (Block 1991, Hodgson 2007).

With Granovetter's (1985) recognition that all economies—past and present, Western and non-Western—were embedded, the differences between market systems become more a matter of degree (i.e., the quantity and complexity of information) than of kind. Following in this vein, new-economic sociologists (Fligstein & Dauter 2007; Lie 1997; Swedberg 1991, 2005) have probed the various ways and differing extents that economies are embedded in social, cognitive, cultural, structural, and political contexts (Barber 1995, Beckert 2009, Dequech 2003, Krippner 2001, Krippner & Alvarez 2007, Uzzi 1997, Zukin & DiMaggio 1990). These range from interplays between mental processes and economic rationality to the role of ongoing interpersonal relations and trust in economic transactions to the ways in which economic institutions are shaped by the struggle for power. Placing market systems in this broader societal context opens a range of comparative questions, while challenging the stark economic dichotomy drawn between the West and the rest of the world (Blanton & Fargher 2008, p. 9; Carrier 1992).

In sum, by using an idealized notion of contemporary Euro-American economies as self-regulating (and not embedded), Polanyi and his associates established a false metric against which they compared economies of the past, thereby underplaying the importance of markets in history. As Hejeebu & McCloskey (2004, pp. 138–39) assert, the recognition that market exchanges have a long history and broad geographic scope clearly does not subscribe one to the extreme "position that the undoubted existence of ancient, archaic, or precolonial markets means that Gilgamesh, when not at war, had the same consumption bundle in his thoughts as a member of Sam's Club. The logic, which is seen, for example, in the Polanyi-inspired work of the great classicist Moses Finley, is this: Markets exhibit dot.coms and Sam's Clubs. Therefore, if ancient Rome does not exhibit dot.coms and Sam's Clubs, it must have lacked markets."

PREINDUSTRIAL MARKETS: EMPIRICAL DEBATES

To date, debates over the nature and role of the market in the past largely have been framed by Polanyi's (1944, pp. 47, 55; 1957a, pp. 250–56) contrast between reciprocity, redistribution, and market exchange. Whereas reciprocity describes face-to-face exchanges of equal amounts of value between social associates, redistribution constitutes a centralized pattern of transfer in which goods move to a central authority and then later are reapportioned out (Bohannan 1963, pp. 231–32; Polanyi 1957a, pp. 250–56; Sahlins 1972). Polanyi (1960, p. 331) was careful to contrast reciprocity, redistribution, and market exchange as three modes or mechanisms of economic allocation that potentially could co-occur in specific contexts. Yet, he also stressed that economies tended to be organized by one of these integrative patterns at any given time (Polanyi 1957a, pp. 254–55; 1960, p. 330), asserting that "each of the three patterns is capable of integrating the economy, ensuring its stability and unity" (Polanyi 1960, p. 330).

In anthropology and archaeology (Fried 1967, pp. 116–18; Sahlins 1958, p. 5, 1972; Service 1975), Polanyi's ideas were crystallized into a tripartite configuration of economic systems that tended to situate reciprocal exchange with egalitarian societies, redistributive economies with hierarchically organized preindustrial societies, and market exchange with Western capitalism (Dalton 1968, p. xiv; Polanyi 1957a). As a consequence, the economies of preindustrial complex societies were thought to be broadly redistributive (Dalton 1975, pp. 92–95; compare Earle 1977; Feinman & Neitzel 1984, p. 73; Smith 2004), a characterization at the foundation of the overly stark dichotomy between command (or planned) economies and "free" market systems. In this comparative synthesis, Service (1975, p. 302) viewed the economies of ancient states as "an organismic redistributional system that...typically involves complex administration." In large part, his view reflected the characterization by Bohannan & Dalton (1962) of African market systems in which they defined well-integrated markets as solely those in which most households rely on the marketplace for all or most of their needed and desired provisions. From this vantage, well-integrated market systems would not have been present in most of the world until the latter half of the twentieth century (Hirth 2010).

As a result of this rigid taxonomic framing, arguments for pre-Hispanic Mesoamerican market exchange generally have either proposed methods to detect market transactions and marketplaces (e.g., Feinman & Nicholas 2010, Garraty 2009, Hirth 1998) and/or outlined the emergence or existence of economic transfer patterns that could not easily be subsumed under meaningful definitions of reciprocity or redistribution (e.g., Blanton 1983; Blanton et al. 1993, pp. 211–17; Feinman et al. 1984; Stark & Ossa 2010). It is revealing of Polanyi's influence that Mesoamericanists have been struggling to distinguish between archaeological signatures of market exchange and redistribution, despite an absence of historical evidence that redistribution was ever a critical mechanism for large-scale provisioning of everyday domestic goods (Hirth 1998, p. 455; Stark & Garraty 2010), except possibly during times of crisis (Duran 1994, pp. 238–41; Hassig 1985). Several scholars have gone so far as to classify the extensive, Aztec regional market system as a large-scale, state-run redistributive network (Carrasco 1982, 1983, 2001; Sanders et al. 1979). Others (e.g., Wolf 1982, pp. 75–77, 79–88; see also Wittfogel 1957) attribute the pre-Hispanic Mesoamerican economy to the tributary mode that also was engineered almost entirely by a ruling elite, and yet there are growing indications that market exchange had a long and significant history in the region.

In this regard, recently discovered murals depicting common people at the Classic period Maya site of Calakmul (Carrasco Vargas et al. 2009) are intriguing. In these paintings, dated preliminarily to the seventh century, Maya commoners serving tamales and ladling maize gruel to others are described in associated glyphic texts as "maize-bread person" and "maize-gruel person." Other persons are generically tagged with "salt-person," "maize-grain person," clay-vessel person," and "tobacco-person." Although the mode of these transfers is not described, the range of specialists circulating goods and the proximity of these painted panels to Calakmul's North Plaza, an area that was previously noted as a possible marketplace (Folan et al. 2001), is suggestive that the mechanism was market exchange (Dahlin et al. 2010).

For the rise of the later Aztec empire, where more ample textual accounts supplement archaeology, the richer empirical foundations have enabled preliminary analyses of shifting degrees of market participation, changing flows of goods, and discussions of the complex interplays between political institutions and markets (e.g., Blanton 1985, 1996; Garraty 2006; Minc 2009; Nichols et al. 2002; Smith 2010). Robust documentary accounts of marketplace exchange for the late pre-Hispanic era (even beyond the Aztec heartland; Pohl et al. 1997), the identification of currencies (Smith 1980, p. 877), and the rarity of evidence for large centralized storage facilities (compare Hassig 1985, p. 107) leave the economic importance of marketplaces and market exchange in ancient Mesoamerica hard to dismiss, although the pre-Aztec origins, history, diversity, geographic breadth, and interconnection with other modes of transfer all remain under debate. The Inca economy, with greater evidence for state storage and labor tribute, has been presented as a nonmarket contrast to that of the Aztec (Stanish 1997, 2010), yet the possibility and extent of marketplace exchange in the Andean world has been too readily discounted and remains to be deciphered (Earle 1985, Stark & Garraty 2010).

In the Mediterranean basin and neighboring regions, dominant metanarratives concerning ancient economies have long revolved around Finley's writings (Greene 2000; Morris 2003; Morris & Manning 2005, p. 15). Although granting markets a more significant role than Polanyi did (Bang 2007, p. 10), Finley's text-dominated conceptions basically adopt a simplified view of past economic systems—domestic self-sufficiency, domination by centralized political institutions, a largely agrarian economy sustained by slave labor, limited trade or potential for growth or innovation—emphasizing binary contrasts with modern European economies (Greene 2000; Scheidel & von Reden 2002, p. 3). Subsequent debates have been less focused on the broad patterns of economic integration (i.e., redistribution versus market exchange) than in anthropological archaeology, yet many of the thematic debates parallel those in other disciplines (Snell 1997; Storey 2004; Temin 2001, p. 181, 2006). As research moves beyond the false primitivist-modernist dichotomy advanced by Finley, significant developments have recognized the complexity of the ancient Greek banking system (Cohen 1992), a marketplace system of exchange in the Roman world that operated according to principles of supply and demand (Paterson 1998, p. 156–57), wage labor and capital markets at the time of the early Roman Empire (Temin 2006), and a significant level of monetization (DeCecco 1985, Kim 2002).

Regional market system: economically linked system of marketplaces across a regional landscape; may have different spatial arrangements

Kessler & Temin (2007, p. 330) argue that "the Roman market rivaled early modern European and colonial American markets in terms of institutional complexity and, perhaps, efficiency" (compare Bang 2007).

Just as the binary oppositions between formalist and substantivist, primitivist and modernist, command economies and free markets, as well as redistribution and market exchange have proven to be analytically unproductive, also untenable is the once axiomatic notion of a transformational past that sets off the past two centuries of Euro-American capitalism as qualitatively unique or exceptional from everything that came before (Block 2000, p. 97). The complex, embedded meanings and roles of currencies and money across time (Hudson 2004, Keister 2002, Maurer 2006, Melitz 1970) are particularly illustrative of the weaknesses of such dichotomous categorical thinking (e.g., Dalton 1961, pp. 12–13; Polanyi 1957a, pp. 264–66). We advocate approaches that neither deny that each historical context has distinctive features, nor gloss over the analytically important differences between the economies of the recent West from those that came before (Goldstone 2002, p. 327; Hall 2001, p. 494). But those differences must be studied and documented through comparable theoretical lenses rather than simply assumed or ignored (Pomeranz 2000, p. 8). The historical circumstances leading to the construction of modern capitalism were long and sinuous (Abu-Lughod 1989; Biddick 1990; Goldstone 2002, p. 329; Lie 1993; Maurer 2006, p. 29; van Bavel et al. 2009) rather than a punctuated outcome of a transformational event that set off unprecedented change in nineteenth-century England or the simple result of a natural process (Block 2000).

On the basis of detailed historical analyses, there is anything but consensus on a specific "hinge point" (the timing or causes) that marked the advent of European market capitalism (e.g., Abu Lughod 1989; Biddick 1990; Braudel 1985; de Vries 2001; Frank 1998; Goldstone 2002; Goody 2004; Polanyi 1944; Pomeranz 2000, 2002; Wallerstein 1974; Wolf

1982). The absence of such agreement stems from the growing realization that agricultural expansion, factor markets, economic growth, innovations in transport, standard coinage or currencies, handicraft production, and rises in commercialization all began in Europe long before the 1800s (Braudel 1985; Britnell 1993; Bryant 2006; Campbell 2009; van Bavel 2006, 2008; van Bavel et al. 2009), and many of these processes and developments were not entirely unique to Europe (Allen 2009; Frank 1998; Pomeranz 2000, pp. 7–8, 2008; Saito 2009; Wong 1997). Immediately before 1800, the performance of grain markets in Western Europe were comparable to those in China, thus neither market efficacy nor breadth is necessary and sufficient to account for subsequent European industrialization (Shiue & Keller 2007). Nevertheless, we remain "vitally interested in what enabled the West to transform the history of human power for however short a period" (Hall 2001, p. 494), but theoretical visions that privilege a single economically rational modernity, isolated and exceptional, are not apt to yield ready answers to that multifaceted question (Eisenstadt 2000; Goldstone 2002, 2008; Sugihara 2003).

ARCHAEOLOGICAL METHODS OF DETECTING MARKET EXCHANGE

We argue above that Polanyi's widespread influence, particularly his narrow definition of market exchange, has been largely responsible for the dearth of scholarly attention to preindustrial markets among archaeologists. Nowhere is this inattention more apparent than in methodological approaches to detecting market activities in the archaeological record. Especially since Hirth's (1998) influential study of market exchange in the central Mexican center of Xochicalco, however, archaeologists have become increasingly aware of the need to develop reliable methods to address this issue.

Hirth (1998; 2009, pp. 89–90) describes four approaches to detecting market exchange. The contextual approach infers the presence of a market system based on logical inference, such as the assumption that a market system is necessary to provision a large urban center or system of centers (e.g., Stanish 2010), but these arguments are predicated on conjecture rather than empirical evidence. The spatial approach involves inferences about market exchange by comparing observed empirical patterns against idealized spatial configurations. Renfrew (1975, 1977), for instance, developed various "falloff curves"—idealized patterns of decline in artifact frequencies with increased distance from a locus of exchange—for market exchange and other exchange mechanisms, which he intended for comparison with empirical data. Similarly, archaeologists have applied central place theory to detect market systems by comparing observed settlement hierarchies on a landscape to geographer Christaller's (1966) idealized hexagonal lattices of evenly spaced market retail centers (e.g., Blanton 1996, Hodder & Orton 1976, Johnson 1972). Neither of these spatial approaches is readily testable or quantifiable, however, and similar to contextual approaches, they ultimately rest on logical inferences.

The configurational approach seeks to detect physical evidence of marketplaces. Although speculative, many Mesoamerican archaeologists have inferred possible marketplaces on the basis of architectural features, such as rock alignments to demarcate stalls, or on spatial configurations of roads, platforms, and plazas (e.g., Becker 2003; Blanton 1978, p. 63; Chase & Chase 2004; Millon 1973). One recent study attempts to detect a marketplace through multiple lines of evidence, including a comparative examination of soil chemistries from a modern marketplace in Guatemala and from a plaza in the ancient Maya center of Chinchucmil posited to have housed market vendors (Dahlin et al. 2007, 2010). Hirth (2009) also considers multiple lines of evidence to detect a market plaza at Xochicalco and infers possible stone-tool production for market exchange through an analysis of minute lithic debitage embedded in the plaza floor. Unlike the two approaches described above,

the configurational approach is predicated on empirical inference. Nevertheless, it remains difficult to rule out alternate, nonmarket hypotheses of plaza function.

Hirth (1998) espouses a distributional approach to detecting market exchange, on the basis of the spatial effects of marketplace provisioning at the level of households. Unlike other exchange mechanisms, marketplace transactions entail equal commodity access to all households, regardless of social rank (Hirth 1998, p. 455). It also produces a larger-scale and more even distribution of goods among households than is likely achievable through nonmarket provisioning (Garraty 2009). The distributional approach is empirically rigorous and quantifiable, as variability in artifact frequency and diversity can be measured among households of different social ranks and over a large area. Yet, various confounding factors potentially muddle its effectiveness; for example, households of different ranks (or across a region) may procure (or manufacture) similar goods for social reasons (e.g., to express a shared social identity), creating similar household artifact composition, even if a market institution is absent.

In addition to Hirth's four approaches, Stark & Garraty (2010) suggest a fifth: the regional production-distribution approach, which considers the distributional scale of quotidian craft goods (e.g., pottery, stone tools) in relation to their locations and scales of production to evaluate the likelihood of market dissemination relative to other, nonmarket mechanisms. As they (Stark & Garraty 2010) explain, this approach considers "whether articles used regularly in commoner households across a region, but which were produced in particular settlements or specialist households, could be efficiently supplied through redistribution or other centrally administered forms of product provisioning" (p. 43). They conclude that, with rare exceptions, only a market system is likely to have accommodated this scale of dissemination. In this sense, their approach could be characterized as contextual in that interpretation is based on logical inference that negates alternate hypotheses rather than "positive" empirical indicators of market activity.

All five approaches suffer from the problem of equifinality: It is rarely, if ever, possible to rule out alternate exchange mechanisms for observed archaeological patterns. In response to this problem, Feinman & Nicholas (2010) employ a multiscalar approach to infer the presence of a market system in the Valley of Oaxaca, Mexico, during the first millennium. They consider evidence at the household, site, and regional scales, and in so doing, they incorporate elements of each of the approaches described above. Their approach thus combats the problem of equifinality by marshaling evidence in support of market activity at various analytical scales.

The multiscalar approach is vital for future efforts to detect market exchange. Ultimately, however, a more important objective is to move beyond detecting the presence/absence of market exchange (Wilk 1998) and develop sophisticated tools and techniques for assessing variability in market system structure and organization. For this task, one potentially productive tactic is to record carefully the archaeological signatures of organizationally different market systems in well-documented contexts and use these data as a basis for inferring market structure and organization in earlier, undocumented contexts. Another vital objective is to investigate how market exchange articulates with other, nonmarket exchange mechanisms within a broader economy. This task will require studies of distributional variability among various goods or classes of goods to discern which items were or were not integrated into market channels. Ideally, archaeologists will creatively refine and tailor their methods to the ideas and concepts they wish to explore rather than rigidly confine them to accommodate perceived limits of archaeological data. Methods of detecting variability among preindustrial markets will be crucial to implement comparative research and, ultimately, create cross-cultural models that capture the dynamic processes and trajectories of early market development in different times and places.

LOOKING FORWARD: KEY COMPARATIVE QUESTIONS

With new theoretical and methodological perspectives, archaeologists can now begin to formulate more targeted questions concerning the variability of markets across time and space as well as shifts in their dynamism and breadth over a long-term history (e.g., Braudel 1985, Collins 1990). Dimensions of market diversity include their interplay with other institutions, such as governing authorities, and the relative significance/breadth of market exchange—degree of commercialization—in specific economic settings (Smith 2004, pp. 75–76). Degree of commercialization highlights the extent to which different commodities are integrated and removed from market channels over a long span, which underscores the dynamism of market processes. For example, commercial development in Europe is frequently depicted as a linear process of increasing commodification of goods and services (Polanyi 1944; Thrift 2000, p. 96) and of markets "colonising ever more areas of daily life" (Williams 2002, p. 221), but historical evidence illustrates both expansion and contraction of commercial integration (Braswell 2010, Lie 1991, Williams 2002). Consider that in Western economies since the early 1800s slaves, child labor, and purchases of political office have been legally decommodified. The dynamic process of commercial expansion and contraction partly reflects changing social attitudes and moral perceptions concerning alienability and transferability of specific classes of goods or labor (Thompson 1971, 1991).

It is also time for a more nuanced examination of the prevailing notion that political power and the extent of commercialism are inversely related (e.g., Blanton et al. 1993; Smith 2004, p. 93; Trigger 2003, pp. 342–55; compare Blanton & Fargher 2010; Block & Evans 2005; Fligstein 1996; Garraty 2006; Greif 2006; Schoenberger 2008). Rather than seeing these forces as fundamentally oppositional, we may examine the range of ways that such institutions are interlinked and how these relations are manifest at different socioeconomic scales

(Garraty 2010). Were resources collected by political authorities and, if so, through what mechanisms? How did variation in the internal governance of polities correlate with their market relations (Blanton & Fargher 2008, 2010; Eisenstadt 1969, p. 27; 1980)? In many past societies, political elites were purveyors of market exchange and commercial expansion (e.g., Blanton et al. 1993, p. 196; Fleisher 2010). Additional studies of past market systems may reveal that political-market relations were as frequently collaborative as antagonistic (Garraty 2006; Hudson 1996, 2002, 2004).

A problem that has been addressed but deserves more concerted attention concerns the origins and institutionalization of market exchange. In many regions of the globe, this issue requires exploration through archaeological investigation because the advent of market exchange and marketplaces predates the first textual sources. To date, proposed models for the beginnings of this economic practice have taken a bottom-up or top-down perspective (Berry 1967, pp. 108–11; Blanton 1983, p. 55; Hirth 2010; C. Smith 1976, pp. 44–45). In part, these different hypotheses stem from distinct scalar and disciplinary vantages (Reeves 1989, pp. 58–60). The former builds on Adam Smith's economic frames and sees the emergence of market activities stemming from the local practices of individual economic actors or traders who— spurred by population growth (Skinner 1964), the division of labor, and/or agricultural intensification (Blanton 1983, pp. 56–58)—respond to expanded movements of goods through the order of the market. A similar perspective emphasizes increased market participation among households to supply domestic goods more efficiently through a single market location rather than relying on multiple nonmarket channels (Hirth 2010).

Top-down approaches stem from the work of Polanyi (1957b), viewing markets as inherently unstable and requiring governmental intervention to sustain them. Such perspectives envision the developmental role of governing institutions as (a) a basis for setting prices (Hudson 1996), (b) a competitive political strategy to wrest power from land-holding elites (Eisenstadt 1969, 1980), (c) a mechanism to encourage agrarian production to meet urban food needs (Hicks 1987, pp. 99–101), (d) a means to control the long-distance circulation of goods through the marketplace (Hodder 1965), or (e) an instrument for converting tribute booty into other resources through market conversion (Carrasco 1978; Garraty 2010, pp. 20–21; Hirth 1998). Many of these works actually discuss the reproduction or expansion of markets rather than the origins of market exchange, and so political institutions may have been less formidable during the earliest stage of market development (e.g., Abbott 2010, Abbott et al. 2007). In reality, market formation and expansion both may stem from top-down and bottom-up dynamics, and explanations for this socioeconomic process may require approaches that transcend a single scale.

Different scales of analysis are crucial to understand preindustrial market development and change (Feinman and Nicholas 2010). Hirth (2010) identifies the household as the proper unit of analysis for understanding these processes. For Hirth, market participation in the past hinged on household-level decisions to obtain necessary or desired goods, and thus the long-term development and sustainability of preindustrial markets rested on the capacity of the market to provide domestic goods continually and at a reasonable price. In contrast, Greif (2006), drawing on ideas and concepts from the new institutional economics, emphasizes the broader, institutional requirements for market development: "Socially beneficial institutions promote welfare-enhancing cooperation and action. They provide the foundations of markets by efficiently assigning, protecting, and altering property rights; securing contracts; and motivating specialization and exchange" (Greif 2006, p. 4). These positions differently define and situate the proper scale of analysis for studying early market development and growth, but for us, both positions merit consideration. Together they illustrate the importance of understanding market processes from the perspective of both the microeconomic scale of household decision making and the macroeconomic scale of institutions that define the social conditions and "rules of the game" (North 1990, p. 3) in which those decisions were made.

Another, less frequently considered scale of analysis focuses on the extrahousehold forms of organization and cooperation that play a role in the spread of supply and price information and create conditions for efficient market exchange at the level of a marketplace or network of marketplaces (e.g., Cook 1976, Plattner 1989c). This scale draws attention to the social parameters of market-information flows and interpersonal relationships among market patrons that facilitate smooth market operations (e.g., Davis 1992, pp. 65–74). It also highlights the need to understand how market actors establish informal social networks (Granovetter 1985) or formal legal constraints (Williamson 1975, 1985) to circumvent malfeasance or opportunism stemming from unequal access to market information. In peasant markets, for instance, many market goers established personalized relationships with trusted associates, including kin or ethnic affiliates (e.g., Geertz 1978, Landa 1999, Schwimmer 1979), to minimize the risk of impropriety or duplicity (Plattner 1989c).

An even broader vantage examines the regional scale of market development and the formation of a commercialized landscape with multiple nodes and a well-defined hierarchy of higher- and lower-order market centers. The broadest conceivable scale concerns the international (possibly global) context of commercial interaction focused on the dynamics of systemic expansion and articulation among polities or conglomerations of polities on an inter-regional scale (Wallerstein 1974), which for pre-Hispanic Mesoamerica has been pivotal for explaining the development and spread of commercial institutions after the Classic-Postclassic transition (ca. A.D. 900) (Blanton & Feinman 1984, Feinman & Nicholas 2010, Smith & Berdan 2003, Stark & Ossa 2010).

Further research also is needed on how and why markets fail (Cassidy 2009) and how market institutions fare in contexts beset by imperial collapse (Schoenberger 2008, pp. 675–76; Tainter 1988, pp. 18–21), revolution (Skinner 1985), or other transformative governmental changes (e.g., Braswell 2010). Again, we reference the Classic-Postclassic (ca. A.D. 900) transition in ancient Mesoamerica (Berdan et al. 2003, p. 316; Blanton & Feinman 1984; Blanton et al. 1993, pp. 207–17; Feinman 1999; Masson et al. 2006, p. 198), which was set off by the collapse of early cities, such as Teotihuacan, Monte Albán, and the Classic Maya centers, and ultimately culminated in increasing exchange volumes and commercialization during the subsequent Postclassic period (900–1520). Likewise in the post-Roman European world, a relatively brief economic contraction may have been followed by a revival of market activities that was underway by the eighth century across Europe (McCormick 2001; Schoenberger 2008, pp. 676–89).

CONCLUSION

The financial crisis of 2008–2009 has brought a new urgency and lens to economic thinking on markets (e.g., Cassidy 2009, Fox 2009, Krugman 2009). No longer can anyone with a rational perspective view modern markets as always self-correcting or inexorably efficient. Likewise, when the U.S. government owns (or recently owned) major shares of top companies in automobile manufacture, insurance, and banking, it is not necessary to focus on "minor details" such as farm subsidies, the tax code, and contract law to realize that the so-called pinnacle of the free market, i.e., the modern American economy, is anything but disembedded from a larger political and societal context: Modern Western markets are neither free nor qualitatively exceptional from all other markets in space and time. Although markets across time and space unquestionably differ significantly in highly important and multiple ways, there also are clear indications that they share certain structural elements and practices. The sole means through which scholars will be able to define and understand those similarities and differences is through dedicated comparative studies using a broadly shared, multiscalar paradigmatic approach that recognizes that all markets are embedded. To probe the dynamics of market systems, scholars must consider both market participants and the wider societal contexts in which those participants exchange and engage.

With the ongoing reevaluation of key aspects of economic theory and free market ideology, as well as the doubt it casts on some of the metrics applied by Polanyi and associates, social scientists and historians appear ready for new dialogues regarding market exchange and markets, past and present. Notions of the free market as anything more than an ideal construct and the hyperindividualizing model of "Homo economicus" now appear incongruent with empirical reality (Levitt & List 2008). As a consequence, the stark dichotomies in regard to markets and economic behavior drawn between current Western peoples and all others, which have framed debate for centuries, clearly do not rest on solid empirical grounding. At the individual level, members from many diverse cultures potentially act rationally, but they tend to do so with a wider set of considerations than basic self-interest (Bowles & Gintis 2006, Henrich et al. 2005, Stanish 2010).

People—Western or non-Western, ancient or modern—should not be envisioned as slavish pawns to power and incapable of acting in their own best interests (Attwood 1997). At the same time, economic actors across time and space participate in larger sociocultural contexts that limit and shape their actions (Guiso et al. 2006). Market behaviors are thus an intermediation between rational individual actions and the societal customs, constraints, and political realities in which specific economic institutions are embedded (e.g., Blanton & Fargher 2009, p. 135). As a consequence, scholars can no longer ignore that economic networks are embedded in larger societal settings that encompass organizations, associations, and power structures that extend well beyond individual actors.

We conclude our discussion with a plea for a multiscalar approach to preindustrial markets that situates these investigations under a broader comparative frame. By definition, such an approach requires communication, comparison, and a basis of understanding that extends well beyond traditional disciplinary boundaries. We suspect that only through greater dialogue and debate in this direction will the history and diversity of markets finally get their intellectual due.

DISCLOSURE STATEMENT

The authors are not aware of any biases that might be perceived as affecting the objectivity of this review.

ACKNOWLEDGMENTS

We thank the editors for the opportunity to prepare this contribution. Some of our thoughts for this paper were stimulated by conversations and the circulation of papers for the volume edited by Garraty & Stark (2010). Richard E. Blanton, Linda M. Nicholas, James Phillips, and Barbara L. Stark provided helpful suggestions on an earlier draft. We also are grateful to Linda M. Nicholas for her editorial assistance.

LITERATURE CITED

Abbott DR. 2010. The rise and demise of marketplace exchange among the prehistoric Hohokam of Arizona. See Garraty & Stark 2010, pp. 61–83

Abbott DR, Smith AM, Gallaga E. 2007. Ballcourts and ceramics: the case for Hohokam marketplace exchange in the Arizona desert. *Am. Antiq.* 72:461–84

Abu-Lughod JL. 1989. *Before European Hegemony: The World System A.D. 1250–1350*. New York: Oxford Univ. Press

Acheson JM. 2002. Transaction cost economics: accomplishments, problems, and possibilities. In *Theory in Economic Anthropology*, ed. J Ensminger, pp. 27–58. Walnut Creek, CA: AltaMira

Adams R McC. 1974. Anthropological perspectives on ancient trade. *Curr. Anthropol.* 15:239–49

Alexander J, Alexander P. 1991. What's a fair price? Price-setting and trading partnerships in Javanese markets. *Man* 26:493–512

Alexander P. 1992. What's in a price? Trading practices in peasant (and other) markets. See Dilley 1992b, pp. 79–96

Allen RC. 2009. Agricultural productivity and rural incomes in England and the Yangtze Delta, c. 1620–c.1820. *Econ. Hist. Rev.* 62:525–50

Arnsperger C, Varoufakis Y. 2006. What is neoclassical economics? *Post-autistic Econ. Rev.* 38(1):1–9 **http://www.paecon.net/heterodoxeconomics/ArnsbergerVaroufkis38.htm**

Attwood DW. 1997. The invisible peasant. In *Economic Analysis Beyond the Local System*, ed. RE Blanton, PN Peregrine, D Winslow, TD Hall, pp. 147–69. Lanham, MD: Univ. Press Am.

Baker D. 2009. Free market myth. *Boston Rev.* Jan./Feb. **http://bostonreview.net/BR34.1/baker.php**

Bang PF. 2007. Trade and empire—in search of organizing concepts for the Roman economy. *Past Present* 195:3–54

Barber B. 1977. Absolutization of the market. In *Markets and Morals*, ed. G Dworkin, G Bermant, PG Brown, pp. 15–31. Washington, DC: Hemisphere Pub.

Barber B. 1995. All economies are "embedded": the career of a concept and beyond. *Soc. Res.* 62:387–413

Bar-Yosef O. 2002. The Upper Paleolithic revolution. *Annu. Rev. Anthropol.* 31:363–93

Becker GS. 1976. *The Economic Approach to Human Behavior*. Chicago: Univ. Chicago Press

Becker MJ. 2003. Plaza plans at Tikal: a research strategy for inferring social organization and processes of culture change at Lowland Maya sites. In *Tikal: Dynasties, Foreigners, and Affairs of State*, ed. JA Sabloff, pp. 253–80. Santa Fe, NM: SAR Press

Beckert J. 2009. The great transformation of embeddedness: Karl Polanyi and the new economic sociology. In *Market and Society: The Great Transformation Today*, ed. C Hann, K Hart, pp. 38–55. Cambridge: Cambridge Univ. Press

Berdan FF. 1977. Distributive mechanisms in the Aztec economy. In *Peasant Livelihood: Studies in Economic Anthropology and Cultural Ecology*, ed. R Halperin, J Dow, pp. 91–101. New York: St. Martin's

Berdan FF. 1982. *The Aztecs of Central Mexico*. New York: Holt, Rinehart, Winston

Berdan FF. 1983. The reconstruction of ancient economies: perspectives from archaeology and ethnohistory. See Ortiz 1983, pp. 83–95

Berdan FF. 1985. Markets in the economy of ancient Mexico. See Plattner 1985, pp. 339–67

Berdan FF, Kepecs S, Smith ME. 2003. A perspective on Late Postclassic Mesoamerica. In *The Postclassic Mesoamerican World*, ed. ME Smith, FF Berdan, pp. 313–17. Salt Lake City: Univ. Utah Press

Berry BJL. 1967. *Geography of Market Centers and Retail Distribution*. Englewood Cliffs, NJ: Prentice Hall

Bestor TC. 2001. Markets: anthropological aspects. In *International Encyclopedia of the Social and Behavioral Sciences*, ed. NJ Smelser, PB Baltes, pp. 9227–31. Amsterdam: Elsevier

Biddick K. 1990. People and things: power in early English development. *Comp. Stud. Soc. Hist.* 32:3–23

Bitzenis A, Marangos J. 2007. Market economy. In *International Encyclopedia of the Social Sciences*, ed. WA Darity Jr., pp. 604–5. Detroit: Macmillan Ref.

Blanton RE. 1978. *Monte Alban: Settlement Patterns at an Ancient Zapotec Capital*. New York: Academic

Blanton RE. 1983. Factors underlying the origin and evolution of market systems. See Ortiz 1983, pp. 51–66

Blanton RE. 1985. A comparison of market systems. See Plattner 1985, pp. 399–416

Blanton RE. 1996. The Basin of Mexico market system and the growth of empire. In *Aztec Imperial Strategies*, ed. FF Berdan, RE Blanton, E Boone, M Hodge, ME Smith, E Umberger, pp. 47–84. Washington, DC: Dumbarton Oaks

Blanton RE. 2009. Variation in economy. In *MyAnthroLibrary*, ed. CR Ember, M Ember, PN Peregrine. Upper Saddle River, NJ: Pearson-Prentice Hall. **http:www.myanthrolibrary.com**

Blanton RE, Fargher L. 2008. *Collective Action in the Formation of Pre-Modern States*. New York: Springer

Blanton RE, Fargher L. 2009. Collective action in the evolution of premodern states. *Soc. Evol. Hist.* 8:133–66

Blanton RE, Fargher L. 2010. Evaluating causal factors in market development in premodern states: a comparative study with some critical comments on the history of ideas about markets. See Garraty & Stark 2010, pp. 207–26

Blanton RE, Feinman GM. 1984. The Mesoamerican world system. *Am. Anthropol.* 86:673–82

Blanton RE, Kowalewski SA, Feinman GM, Finsten LM. 1993. *Ancient Mesoamerica: A Comparison of Change in Three Regions*. Cambridge: Cambridge Univ. Press

Block F. 1991. Contradictions of self-regulating markets. In *The Legacy of Karl Polanyi: Market, State, and Society at the End of the Twentieth Century*, ed. M Mendell, D Salée, pp. 86–106. New York: St. Martin's

Block F. 2000. Remarx: deconstructing capitalism as a system. *Rethink. Marxism* 12:83–98

Block F. 2003. Karl Polanyi and the writing of *The Great Transformation*. *Theory Sociol.* 32:275–306

Block F, Evans P. 2005. The state and the economy. See Smelser & Swedberg 2005, pp. 505–26

Bohannan PJ. 1963. *Social Anthropology*. New York: Holt, Rinehart, Winston

Bohannan P, Dalton G. 1962. Introduction. In *Markets in Africa*, ed. P Bohannan, G Dalton, pp. 1–26. Evanston, IL: Northwestern Univ. Press

Bowles S. 1998. Endogenous preferences: the cultural consequences of markets and other economic institutions. *J. Econ. Lit.* 36:75–111

Bowles S, Gintis H. 2006. The evolutionary basis of collective action. In *The Oxford Handbook of Political Economy*, ed. BR Weingast, DA Whitman, pp. 951–67. Oxford: Oxford Univ. Press

Braswell GE. 2010. The rise and fall of market exchange: a dynamic approach to ancient Maya economy. See Garraty & Stark 2010, pp. 127–40

Braswell GE, Glascock MD. 2002. The emergence of market economies in the Maya world: obsidian exchange in Terminal Classic Yucatán, Mexico. In *Geochemical Evidence for Long-Distance Exchange*, ed. MD Glascock, pp. 33–52. Westport, CT: Bergin & Garvey

Braudel F. 1985. *Civilization and Capitalism, Fifteenth-Eighteenth Century, Vol. 2: The Wheels of Commerce*. London: Fontana

Britnell RH. 1993. *The Commercialisation of English Society 1000–1500*. Cambridge: Cambridge Univ. Press

Brumfiel EM. 1992. Distinguished lecture in archaeology: breaking and entering the ecosystem—gender, class, and faction steal the show. *Am. Anthropol.* 94:551–67

Bryant JM. 2006. The West and the rest revisited: debating capitalist origins, European colonialism, and the advent of modernity. *Can. J. Sociol.* 31:403–44

Buiter W. 2009. The unfortunate uselessness of most 'state of the art' academic monetary economics. *Vox.* Mar. 6; **http://www.voxeu.org/index.php?q=node/3210**

Campbell BM. 2009. Factor markets in England before the Black Death. *Continuity Change* 24:79–106

Carrasco P. 1978. La economia del México prehispánico. In *Economía, Política e Ideología*, ed. P Carrasco, J Broda, pp. 15–74. Mexico City: Instit. Nac. Antropol. Hist.

Carrasco P. 1982. The political economy of the Aztec and Inca states. In *The Inca and Aztec States: 1400–1800*, ed. G Collier, R Rosaldo, J Wirth, pp. 23–42. New York: Academic

Carrasco P. 1983. Some theoretical considerations about the role of the market in ancient Mexico. See Ortiz 1983, pp. 67–82

Carrasco P. 2001. Economic organization and development. In *The Oxford Encyclopedia of Mesoamerican Cultures: The Civilizations of Mexico and Central America*, ed. D Carrasco, 1:363–66. Oxford: Oxford Univ. Press

Carrasco Vargas R, Vázquez López VA, Martin S. 2009. Daily life of the ancient Maya recorded on murals at Calakmul, Mexico. *Proc. Nat. Acad. Sci. USA* 106:19245–49

Carrier JG. 1992. Occidentalism: the world turned upside-down. *Am. Ethnol.* 19:195–212

Carrier JG. 1997. *Meanings of the Market: The Free Market in Western Culture*. Oxford: Berg

Cassidy J. 2009. *How Markets Fail: The Logic of Economic Calamities*. New York: Farrar, Straus, Giroux

Chase AF, Chase DZ. 2004. Exploring ancient economic relationships at Caracol, Belize. In *Research Reports in Belizean Archaeology*, Vol. 1, ed. J Awe, J Morris, S Jones, pp. 115–27. Belmopan: Inst. Archaeol. Nat. Inst. Cult. Hist.

Claessen HJM. 1978. The early state: a structural approach. In *The Early State*, ed. HJM Claessen, P Skalník, pp. 533–96. The Hague: Mouton

Coase RH. 1988. The firm, the market, and the law. In *The Firm, the Market, and the Law*, ed. RH Coase, pp. 1–31. Chicago: Univ. Chicago Press

Cohen EE. 1992. *Athenian Economy and Society: A Banking Perspective*. Princeton, NJ: Princeton Univ. Press

Collins R. 1990. Market dynamics as the engine of historical change. *Sociol. Theory* 8:111–35

Cook S. 1966. The obsolete "antimarket" mentality: a critique of the substantive approach in economic anthropology. *Am. Anthropol.* 68:323–45

Cook S. 1976. The "market" as location and transaction: dimensions of marketing in a Zapotec stoneworking industry. In *Markets in Oaxaca*, ed. S Cook, M Diskin, pp. 139–68. Austin: Univ. Texas Press

Cortés F. 1977. *His Five Letters of Relation to the Emperor Charles V, 1519–1526*. Glorietta, NM: Rio Grande Press

Christaller W. 1966 [1933]. *Central Places in Southern Germany*, trans. CW Baskin. Englewood Cliffs, NJ: Prentice-Hall

Curtin P. 1984. *Cross-Cultural Trade in World History*. Cambridge: Cambridge Univ. Press

Dahlin BH, Jensen CT, Terry RE, Wright DR, Beach T. 2007. In search of an ancient Maya market. *Lat. Am. Antiq.* 18:363–84

Dahlin BH, Bair D, Beach T, Moriarty M, Terry R. 2010. The dirt on food: ancient feasts and markets among the lowland Maya. In *Pre-Columbian Foodways*, ed. JE Staller, MD Carrasco, pp. 191–232. New York: Springer

Dalton G. 1961. Economic theory and primitive society. *Am. Anthropol.* 63:1–25

Dalton G. 1968. Introduction. In *Primitive, Archaic, and Modern Economies*, ed. G Dalton, pp. ix–lii. Garden City, NY: Anchor Books

Dalton G. 1975. Karl Polanyi's analysis of long-distance trade and his wider paradigm. In *Ancient Civilization and Trade*, ed. JA Sabloff, CC Lamberg-Karlovsky, pp. 63–132. Albuquerque: Univ. New Mexico Press

Dalton G. 1978. Comment: what kinds of trade and markets? *Afr. Econ. Hist.* 6:134–38

Davis J. 1992. *Exchange*. Minneapolis: Univ. Minn. Press

DeCecco M. 1985. Monetary theory and Roman history. *J. Econ. Hist.* 45:809–22

de Ligt L. 1993. *Fairs and Markets in the Roman Empire: Economic and Social Aspects of Periodic Trade in a Pre-Industrial Society*. Amsterdam: JC Gieben

Dequech D. 2003. Cognitive and cultural embeddedness: combining institutional economics and economic sociology. *J. Econ. Issues* 37:461–70

Dequech D. 2007–8. Neoclassical, mainstream, orthodox, and heterodox economics. *J. Post Keynesian Econ.* 30:279–302

de Vries J. 2001. Economic growth before and after the industrial revolution: a modest proposal. In *Early Modern Capitalism: Economic and Social Change in Europe 1400–1800*, ed. M Prak, pp. 177–94. New York: Routledge

Díaz del Castillo B. 1956. *The Discovery and Conquest of Mexico, 1517–1521*. New York: Farrar, Straus, Cudahy

Dilley R. 1992a. Contesting markets: a general introduction to market ideology, imagery, and discourse. See Dilley 1992, pp. 1–34

Dilley R, ed. 1992b. *Contesting Markets: Analysis of Ideology, Discourse, and Practice*. Edinburgh: Edinburgh Univ. Press

Dilley R. 1996. Market. In *Encyclopedia of Cultural Anthropology*, ed. D Levinson, M Ember, pp. 728–32. New York: Henry Holt

Durán D. 1994 [1581]. *The History of the Indies of New Spain*. Norman: Univ. Okla. Press

Earle TK. 1977. A reappraisal of redistribution: complex Hawaiian chiefdoms. In *Exchange Systems in Prehistory*, ed. TK Earle, JE Ericson, pp. 213–32. New York: Academic

Earle TK. 1985. Commodity exchange and markets in the Inca state: recent archaeological evidence. See Plattner 1985, pp. 369–97

Eisenstadt SN. 1969. *The Political Systems of Empires: The Rise and Fall of Historical Bureaucratic Societies*. New York: Free Press

Eisenstadt SN. 1980. Cultural orientations, institutional entrepreneurs, and social change: comparative analysis of traditional civilizations. *Am. J. Sociol.* 85:840–69

Eisenstadt SN. 2000. Multiple modernities. *Daedalus* 129:1–29

Ensminger J. 2002. Introduction: theory in economic anthropology at the turn of the century. In *Theory in Economic Anthropology*, ed. J Ensminger, pp. ix–xix. Walnut Creek, CA: AltaMira

Evensky J. 2005. *Adam Smith's Moral Philosophy: A Historical and Contemporary Perspective on Markets, Law, Ethics, and Culture*. Cambridge: Cambridge Univ. Press

Feinman GM. 1999. The changing structure of macroregional Mesoamerica: the Classic-Postclassic transition in the Valley of Oaxaca. In *World-Systems Theory in Practice: Leadership, Production, and Exchange*, ed. PN Kardulias, pp. 53–62. Lanham, MD: Rowman & Littlefield

Feinman GM, Blanton RE, Kowalewski SA. 1984. Market system development in the prehispanic Valley of Oaxaca, Mexico. In *Trade and Exchange in Early Mesoamerica*, ed. KG Hirth, pp. 157–78. Albuquerque: Univ. New Mexico Press

Feinman G, Neitzel J. 1984. Too many types: an overview of prestate societies in the Americas. *Adv. Archaeol. Meth. Theory* 7:39–102

Feinman GM, Nicholas LM. 2004. Unraveling prehispanic highland Mesoamerican economy: production, exchange, and consumption in the Classic period Valley of Oaxaca. In *Archaeological Perspectives on Political Economy*, ed. GM Feinman, LM Nicholas, pp. 167–88. Salt Lake City: Univ. Utah Press

Feinman GM, Nicholas LM. 2010. A multiscalar perspective on market exchange in the Classic period Valley of Oaxaca. See Garraty & Stark 2010, pp. 85–98

Findlay R. 2005. Kindleberger: economics and history. *Atlan. Econ. J.* 33:19–21

Finley MI. 1999 [1973]. *The Ancient Economy*. Berkeley: Univ. Calif. Press

Fischer EF. 2009. Capitalism in context: seeing beyond the "free" market. *Anthropol. News* 50(7):10, 12

Fleisher JB. 2010. Housing the Swahili merchants and regional marketing on the East African Swahili coast, seventh–sixteenth centuries A.D. See Garraty & Stark 2010, pp. 141–59

Fligstein N. 1996. Markets as politics: a political-cultural approach to market institutions. *Am. Sociol. Rev.* 61:656–73

Fligstein N, Dauter L. 2007. The sociology of markets. *Annu. Rev. Sociol.* 33:105–28

Folan WJ, Gunn JD, del Rosario Domínguez Carrasco M. 2001. Triadic temples, central plazas, and dynastic palaces: diachronic analysis of the Royal Court Complex, Calakmul, Campeche, Mexico. In *Royal Courts of the Maya*, ed. T Inomata, SD Houston, pp. 2:223–65. Boulder, CO: Westview

Forman S, Riegelhaupt JF. 1970. Market place and marketing system: toward a theory of peasant economic integration. *Comp. Stud. Soc. Hist.* 12:188–212

Fox J. 2009. *The Myth of the Rational Market*. New York: HarperCollins

Friedman M. 1982 [1962]. *Capitalism and Freedom*. Chicago: Univ. Chicago Press

Frank AG. 1998. *ReOrient: Global Economy in the Asian Age*. Berkeley: Univ. Calif. Press

Fried MH. 1967. *The Evolution of Political Society: An Essay in Political Anthropology*. New York: Random House

Friedland R, Robertson AF. 1990. Beyond the marketplace. In *Beyond the Marketplace: Rethinking Economy and Society*, ed. R Friedland, AF Robertson, pp. 3–49. New York: Aldine de Gruyter

Garraty CP. 2006. *The politics of commerce: Aztec pottery production and exchange in the basin of Mexico, A.D. 1200–1600*. PhD. thesis, Ariz. State Univ., Tempe

Garraty CP. 2009. Evaluating the distributional approach to inferring market exchange: a test case from the Mexican Gulf lowlands. *Lat. Am. Antiq.* 20:157–74

Garraty CP. 2010. Investigating market exchange in ancient societies: a theoretical review. See Garraty & Stark 2010, pp. 3–32

Garraty CP, Stark BL, eds. 2010. *Archaeological Approaches to Market Exchange in Ancient Societies*. Boulder: Univ. Colo. Press

Geertz C. 1978. The bazaar economy: information and search in peasant marketing. *Supp. Am. Econ. Rev.* 68:28–32

Geraghty RM. 2007. The impact of globalization in the Roman Empire, 200 BC-AD 100. *J. Econ. Hist.* 67:1036–61

Gledhill J, Larsen M. 1982. The Polanyi paradigm and a dynamic analysis of archaic states. In *Theory and Explanation in Archaeology: The Southampton Conference*, ed. C Renfrew, MJ Rowlands, BA Seagraves, pp. 197–229. New York: Academic

Goldstone JA. 2002. Efflorescence and economic growth in world history: rethinking the "rise of the West" and the industrial revolution. *J. World Hist.* 13:323–89

Goldstone JA. 2008. Capitalist origins, the advent of modernity, and coherent explanation: a response to Joseph M. Bryant. *Can. J. Sociol.* 33:119–33

Goody J. 2004. *Capitalism and Modernity: The Great Debate*. Cambridge: Polity Press

Granovetter M. 1985. Economic action and social structure: the problem of embeddedness. *Am. J. Sociol.* 91:481–510

Grantham G. 1999. Contra Ricardo: on the macroeconomics of preindustrial economics. *Eur. Rev. Econ. Hist.* 2:199–232

Gravelle H, Rees R. 1992. *Microeconomics*. London: Longman. 2nd ed.

Greene K. 2000. Technological innovation and economic progress in the ancient world: MI Finley reconsidered. *Econ. Hist. Rev.* 53:29–59

Greif A. 2006. *Institutions and the Path to the Modern Economy: Lessons from Medieval Trade*. Cambridge: Cambridge Univ. Press

Guiso L, Sapienza P, Zingales L. 2006. Does culture affect economic outcomes? *J. Econ. Perspect.* 20:23–48

Hall JA. 2001. Confessions of a eurocentric. *Int. Sociol.* 16:488–97

Halperin RH. 1984. Polanyi, Marx, and the institutional paradigm in economic anthropology. *Res. Econ. Anthropol.* 6:245–72

Halperin RH. 1994. *Cultural Economies: Past and Present*. Austin: Univ. Texas Press

Harvey D. 2005. *A Brief History of Neoliberalism*. Oxford: Oxford Univ. Press

Hassig R. 1982. Periodic markets in Precolumbian Mexico. *Am. Antiq.* 47:346–55

Hassig R. 1985. *Trade, Tribute, and Transportation: The Sixteenth-Century Political Economy of the Valley of Mexico*. Norman: Univ. Okla. Press

Hejeebu S, McCloskey D. 1999. The reproving of Karl Polanyi. *Crit. Rev.* 13:285–314

Hejeebu S, McCloskey D. 2004. Polanyi and the history of capitalism: rejoinder to Blyth. *Crit. Rev.* 16:135–42

Henrich J, Boyd R, Bowles S, Camerer C, Fehr E, et al. 2005. "Economic Man" in cross-cultural perspective: behavioral experiments in 15 small-scale societies. *Behav. Brain Sci.* 28:795–855

Hicks F. 1987. First steps toward a market-integrated economy in Aztec Mexico. In *Early State Dynamics*, ed. H Claessen, P van de Velde, pp. 91–107. London: Brill

Hirth KG. 1998. The distributional approach: a new way to identify marketplace exchange in the archaeological record. *Curr. Anthropol.* 39:451–76

Hirth KG. 2009. Craft production in a central Mexican marketplace. *Ancient Mesoam.* 20:89–102

Hirth KG. 2010. Finding the mark in the marketplace: the organization, development, and archaeological identification of market systems. See Garraty & Stark 2010, pp. 227–47

Hodder BW. 1965. Some comments on the origins of traditional markets in Africa south of the Sahara. *Trans. Inst. Br. Geogr.* 36:97–105

Hodder I, Orton C. 1976. *Spatial Analysis in Archaeology*. London: Cambridge Univ. Press

Hodges R. 1988. *Primitive and Peasant Markets*. New York: Basil Blackwell

Hodgson GM. 2007. Evolutionary and institutional economics as the new mainstream? *Evol. Inst. Econ. Rev.* 4:7–25

Hodgson GM. 2009. The great crash of 2008 and the reform of economics. *Cambridge J. Econ.* 33:1205–21

Hudson M. 1996. Privatization: a survey of the unresolved controversies. In *Privatization in the Ancient Near East and Classical World*, ed. M Hudson, BA Levine, pp. 1–32. Cambridge, MA: Peabody Museum Archaeol. Ethnol.

Hudson M. 2002. Reconstructing the origins of interest-bearing debt and the logic of clean states. In *Debt and Economic Renewal in the Ancient Near East*, ed. M Hudson, M van de Mieroop, pp. 7–58. Bethesda, MD: CDL Press

Hudson M. 2004. The archaeology of money: debt versus barter theories of money's origins. In *Credit and State Theories of Money: The Contributions of A. Mitchell Innes*, ed. LR Wray, pp. 99–127. Cheltenham, UK: Eward Elgar

Humphrey C. 1985. Barter and economic disintegration. *Man* 20:48–72

Humphrey C, Hugh-Jones S. 1992. Introduction: barter, exchange, and value. In *Barter, Exchange, and Value: An Anthropological Approach*, ed. C Humphrey, S Hugh-Jones, pp. 1–20. Cambridge: Cambridge Univ. Press

Humphreys SC. 1969. History, economics, and anthropology: the work of Karl Polanyi. *Hist. Theory* 8:165–212

Isaac BL. 1993. Retrospective on formalist-substantivist debate. *Res. Econ. Anthropol.* 14:213–33

Johnson GA. 1972. A test of the utility of Central Place Theory in archaeology. In *Man, Settlement, and Urbanism*, ed. PJ Ucko, R Tringham, GW Dimbleby, pp. 769–85. London: Duckworth

Keister LA. 2002. Financial markets, money, and banking. *Annu. Rev. Sociol.* 28:39–61

Kennedy G. 2009. Adam Smith and the invisible hand: metaphor to myth. *J. Am. Inst. Econ. Res.* 6:239–63

Kessler D, Temin P. 2007. The organization of the grain trade in the early Roman Empire. *Econ. Hist. Rev.* 60:313–32

Kim HS. 2002. Small change and the moneyed economy. In *Money, Labor, and Land: Approaches to the Economies of Ancient Greece*, ed. P Cartledge, EE Cohen, L Foxhall, pp. 44–51. London: Routledge

Kohler TA, Van Pelt MW, Yap LYL. 2000. Reciprocity and its limits: considerations for a study of the prehispanic Pueblo world. In *Alternative Leadership Strategies in the Prehispanic Southwest*, ed. BJ Mills, pp. 180–206. Tucson: Univ. Ariz. Press

Krippner GR. 2001. The elusive market: embeddedness and the paradigm of economic sociology. *Theory Sociol.* 30:775–810

Krippner GR, Alvarez AS. 2007. Embeddedness and the intellectual projects of economic sociology. *Annu. Rev. Sociol.* 33:219–40

Krugman P. 1999. *The Return of Depression Economics*. New York: WW Norton

Krugman P. 2009. How did economists get it so wrong? *New York Times Mag.*, Sept. 6. **http://www.nytimes.com/2009/09/06/magazine/06Economic-t.html?**

Kurtz DV. 1974. Peripheral and transitional markets: the Aztec case. *Am. Ethnol.* 1:685–705

Landa JT. 1999. The law and bioeconomics of ethnic cooperation and conflict in plural societies of Southeast Asia: a theory of Chinese merchant success. *J. Bioecon.* 1:269–84

Law R. 1992. Posthumous questions for Karl Polanyi: price inflation in precolonial Dahomey. *J. Afr. Hist.* 33:387–420

Levitt SD, Dubner SJ. 2005. *Freakonomics: A Rogue Economist Explores the Hidden Side of Everything*. New York: HarperCollins

Levitt SD, List JA. 2008. *Homo economicus* evolves. *Science* 319:909–10

Lewis MW. 1989. Commercialization and community life: the geography of market exchange in a small-scale Philippine society. *Ann. Assoc. Am. Geog.* 79:390–410

Lie J. 1991. Embedding Polanyi's market society. *Sociol. Perspect.* 34:219–35

Lie J. 1993. Visualizing the invisible hand: the social origins of "market society" in England: 1550–1750. *Polit. Soc.* 21:275–305

Lie J. 1997. Sociology of markets. *Annu. Rev. Sociol.* 23:341–60

López de Gómara F. 1966. *Cortés: The Life of the Conqueror by his Secretary*. Berkeley: Univ. Calif. Press

Lubasz H. 1992. Adam Smith and the invisible hand—of the market? See Dilley 1992b, pp. 37–56

Mansbridge JJ, ed. 1990. *Beyond Self-Interest*. Chicago: Univ. Chicago Press

Masson MA, Hare TS, Peraza Lope C. 2006. Postclassic Maya society regenerated at Mayapán. In *After Collapse: The Regeneration of Complex Societie*s, ed. GM Schwartz, JJ Nichols, pp. 188–207. Tucson: Univ. Ariz. Press

Maurer B. 2006. The anthropology of money. *Annu. Rev. Anthropol.* 35:15–36

McCloskey DN. 1997. Other things equal: Polanyi was right and wrong. *East. Econ. J.* 23:483–87

McCormick M. 2001. *Origins of the European Economy: Communications and Commerce A.D. 300–900*. Cambridge: Cambridge Univ. Press

Melitz J. 1970. The Polanyi school of anthropology on money: an economist's view. *Am. Anthropol.* 72:1020–40

Millon R. 1973. *Urbanization at Teotihuacan, Mexico: The Teotihuacan Map*, Vol. 1, Pt. 1. Austin: Univ. Texas Press

Minc LD. 2006. Monitoring regional market systems in prehistory: models, methods, and metrics. *J. Anthropol. Archaeol.* 25:82–116

Minc LD. 2009. Style and substance: evidence for regionalism within the Aztec market system. *Lat. Am. Antiq.* 20:343–74

Minor H. 1965. *The Primitive City of Timbuctoo*. Garden City, NY: Anchor Books. Rev. ed.

Morris I. 1994. The Athenian economy after *The Ancient Economy*. *Clas. Philol.* 89:351–66

Morris I. 2003. Mediterranization. *Mediterr. Hist. Rev.* 18:30–55

Morris I, Manning JG. 2005. Introduction. In *The Ancient Economy: Evidence and Models*, ed. JG Manning, I Morris, pp. 1–44. Stanford, CA: Stanford Univ. Press

Nee V. 2005. The new institutionalisms in economics and sociology. See Smelser & Swedberg 2005, pp. 49–74

Nichols DL, Brumfiel EM, Neff H, Hodge MG, Charlton TH, Glascock MD. 2002. Neutrons, markets, cities, and empires: a 1000-year perspective on ceramic production and distribution in the Postclassic Basin of Mexico. *J. Anthropol. Archaeol.* 21:25–82

North DC. 1977. Markets and other allocation systems in history: the challenge of Karl Polanyi. *J Eur. Econ. Hist.* 6:703–16

North DC. 1990. *Institutions, Institutional Change, and Economic Perfomance*. Cambridge: Cambridge Univ. Press

North DC. 1991. Institutions. *J. Econ. Persp.* 5:97–112

Oka R, Kusimba CM. 2008. The archaeology of trading systems, part I: towards a new trade synthesis. *J. Archaeol. Res.* 16:339–95

Ortiz S, ed. 1983. *Economic Anthropology: Topics and Theories*. Lanham, MD: Univ. Press Am.

Osbourne RG. 1991. Pride and prejudice, sense and sensibility: exchange and society in the Greek city. In *City and Country in the Ancient World*, ed. J Rich, A Wallace-Hadrill, pp. 128–36. New York: Routledge

Ostrom E. 2000. Collective action and the evolution of social norms. *J. Econ. Perspect.* 14:137–58

Ostrom V. 2003. Rethinking the terms of choice. In *Rethinking Institutional Analysis: Interviews with Vincent and Elinor Ostrom*, by PD Aligica, pp. 1–6. Fairfax, VA: Mercatus Cent. George Mason Univ. **http://www.mercatus.org/PublicationDetails.aspx?id=15952**

Oviedo y Valdés GF. 1851–1855. *Historia General y Natural de las Indias, Islas, y Tierra Firme del Mar Océano*. Madrid: Real Acad. Hist.

Paterson J. 1998. Trade and traders in the Roman world. In *Trade, Traders, and the Ancient City*, ed. H Parkins, C Smith, pp. 149–67. New York: Routledge

Plattner S, ed. 1985. *Markets and Marketing*. Lanham, MD: Univ. Press Am.

Plattner S. 1989a. Markets and marketplaces. See Plattner 1989, pp. 171–208

Plattner S. 1989b. Introduction. See Plattner 1989, pp. 1–20

Plattner S. 1989c. Economic behavior in markets. See Plattner 1989, pp. 209–21

Plattner S, ed. 1989. *Economic Anthropology*. Stanford, CA: Stanford Univ. Press

Pluckhahn TJ. 2009. Plazas y mercados en las Mixteca Alta prehispánica. In *Bases de la Complejidad Social en Oaxaca*, ed. NM Robles García, pp. 277–93. Mexico City: Instit. Nac. Antropol. Hist.

Pohl JMD, Monaghan J, Stuiver LR. 1997. Religion, economy, and factionalism in Mixtec boundary zones. In *Códices y Documentos sobre México, Segundo Simposio*, ed. S Rueda Smithers, C Vega Sosa, R Martínez Baracs, 1:205–32. Mexico City: Instit. Nac. Antropol. Hist.

Polanyi K. 1944. *The Great Transformation: The Political and Economic Origins of Our Time*. Boston: Beacon

Polanyi K. 1947. Our obsolete market mentality. *Commentary* 3:109–17

Polanyi K. 1957a. The economy as instituted process. See Polanyi et al. 1957, pp. 243–70

Polanyi K. 1957b. Aristotle discovers the economy. See Polanyi et al. 1957, pp. 64–94

Polanyi K. 1960. On the comparative treatment of economic institutions in antiquity with illustrations from Athens, Mycenae, and Alakh. In *City Invincible*, ed. CH Kraeling, RM Adams, pp. 329–50. Chicago: Univ. Chicago Press

Polanyi K, Arensberg CM, Pearson HW, eds. 1957. *Trade and Market in the Early Empires*. Chicago: Henry Regnery

Polanyi-Levitt K. 2006. Keynes and Polanyi: the 1920s and the 1990s. *Rev. Int. Polit. Econ.* 13:152–77

Pomeranz K. 2000. *The Great Divergence: China, Europe, and the Making of the Modern World Economy*. Princeton, NJ: Princeton Univ. Press

Pomeranz K. 2002. Beyond the East-West binary: resituating development paths in the eighteenth-century world. *J. Asian Stud.* 61:539–90

Pomeranz K. 2008. Land markets in late imperial and republican China. *Continuity Change* 23:101–50

Pryor FL. 1977. *The Origins of the Economy: A Comparative Study of Distribution in Primitive and Peasant Economies*. New York: Academic

Reeves E. 1989. Market places, market channels, market strategies: levels for analysis of a regional system. In *Human Systems Ecology: Studies of the Integration of Political Economy, Adaptation, and Socionatural Regions*, ed. S Smith, E Reeves, pp. 58–80. Boulder, CO: Westview

Renfrew C. 1975. Trade as action at a distance: questions of integration and communication. In *Ancient Civilization and Trade*, ed. JA Sabloff, CC Lamberg-Karlovsky, pp. 3–59. Albuquerque: Univ. New Mexico Press

Renfrew C. 1977. Alternative models for exchange and spatial distribution. In *Exchange Systems in Prehistory*, ed. TK Earle, JE Ericson, pp. 71–90. New York: Academic

Rosenbaum EF. 2000. What is a market? On the methodology of a contested concept. *Rev. Soc. Econ.* 58:455–82

Sahagún B. 1950–1982 [c. 1577]. *General History of the Things New Spain*. Santa Fe, NM/Salt Lake City: Sch. Am. Res./Univ. Utah Press

Sahlins MD. 1958. *Social Stratification in Polynesia*. Seattle: Univ. Wash. Press

Sahlins M. 1972. *Stone Age Economics*. Chicago: Aldine-Atherton

Saito O. 2009. Land, labor, and market forces in Tokugawa Japan. *Continuity Change* 24:169–96

Sanders WT, Parsons JR, Santley RS. 1979. *The Basin of Mexico: Ecological Processes in the Evolution of a Civilization*. New York: Academic

Scheidel W, von Reden S. 2002. Introduction. In *The Ancient Economy*, ed. W Scheidel, S von Reden, pp. 1–8. Edinburgh: Edinburgh Univ. Press

Schoenberger E. 2008. The origins of the market economy: state power, territorial control, and modes of war fighting. *Comp. Stud. Soc. Hist.* 50:663–91

Schwimmer B. 1979. Market structure and social organization in a Ghanian marketing system. *Am. Ethnol.* 12:682–701

Service ER. 1975. *Origins of the State and Civilization: The Process of Cultural Evolution*. New York: WW Norton

Shen C. 2003. Compromises and conflicts: production and commerce in the royal cities of Eastern Zhou, China. In *The Social Construction of Cities*, ed. M Smith, pp. 290–310. Washington, DC: Smithson. Inst.

Shiue CH, Keller W. 2007. Markets in China and Europe on the eve of the industrial revolution. *Am. Econ. Rev.* 97:1189–216

Silver M. 1983. Karl Polanyi and markets in the ancient Near East: the challenge of the evidence. *J. Econ. Hist.* 43:795–829

Skinner GW. 1964. Marketing and social structure in rural China. Part 1. *J. Asian Stud.* 24:3–43

Skinner GW. 1985. Rural marketing in China: repression and revival. *China Q.* 103:393–413

Smelser NJ, Swedburg R, eds. 2005. *The Handbook of Economic Sociology*. Princeton, NJ: Princeton Univ. Press. 2nd ed.

Smith A. 1976 [1776]. *An Inquiry into the Nature and Causes of the Wealth of Nations*. Chicago: Univ. Chicago Press

Smith CA. 1974. Economics of marketing systems: models from economic geography. *Annu. Rev. Anthropol.* 3:167–201

Smith CA. 1976. Regional exchange systems: linking geographic models and socioeconomic problems. In *Regional Analysis, Vol. 1: Economic Systems*, ed. CA Smith, pp. 3–63. New York: Academic

Smith ME. 1980. The role of the marketing system in Aztec society and economy: reply to Evans. *Am. Antiq.* 45:876–83

Smith ME. 2004. The archaeology of ancient state economies. *Annu. Rev. Anthropol.* 33:73–102

Smith ME. 2010. Regional and local market systems in Aztec period Morelos. See Garraty & Stark 2010, pp. 161–82

Smith ME, Berdan FF, ed. 2003. Postclassic Mesoamerica. In *The Postclassic Mesoamerican World*, ed. ME Smith, FF Berdan, pp. 3–13. Salt Lake City: Univ. Utah Press

Snell DC. 1997. Appendix: theories of ancient economies and societies. In *Life in the Ancient Near East, 3100–332 BCE*, ed. DC Snell, pp. 145–58. New Haven, CT: Yale Univ. Press

Solow RM. 1985. Economic history and economics. *Am Econ. Rev.* 75:328–31

Solow RM. 2005 [1997]. How did economics get that way and what way did it get? *Daedalus* 134:87–100

Stanish C. 1997. Nonmarket imperialism in the pre-Hispanic Americas: the Inca occupation of the Titicaca Basin. *Lat. Am. Antiq.* 8:195–216

Stanish C. 2010. Labor taxes, market systems and urbanization in the prehispanic Andes: a comparative perspective. See Garraty & Stark 2010, pp. 185–205

Stark BL, Garraty CP. 2010. Detecting marketplace exchange in archaeology: a methodological review. See Garraty & Stark 2010, pp. 33–58

Stark BL, Ossa A. 2010. Origins and development of Mesoamerican marketplaces: evidence from south-central Veracruz. See Garraty & Stark 2010, pp. 99–126

Stiglitz J. 1999. Beggar-thyself versus beggar-thy neighbor policies: the dangers of intellectual incoherence in addressing the global financial crisis. *South. Econ. J.* 66:1–38

Storey GR. 2004. Roman economies: a paradigm of their own. In *Archaeological Perspectives on Political Economy*, ed. GM Feinman, LM Nicholas, pp. 105–28. Salt Lake City: Univ. Utah Press

Sugihara K. 2003. The East Asian path of economic development: a long-term perspective. In *The Resurgence of East Asia: 500, 150, and 50 Year Perspectives*, ed. G Arrighi, T Hamashita, M Selden, pp. 78–123. London: Routledge

Swedberg R. 1991. Major traditions of economic sociology. *Annu. Rev. Soc.* 17:251–76

Swedberg R. 1994. Markets as social structures. In *The Handbook of Economic Sociology*, ed. NJ Smelser, R Swedberg, pp. 255–82. Princeton, NJ: Princeton Univ. Press

Swedberg R. 2005. Markets in society. See Smelser & Swedberg 2005, pp. 233–53

Swedberg R, Granovetter M. 2001. Introduction to the second edition. In *The Sociology of Economic Life*, ed. M Granovetter, R Swedberg, pp. 1–28. Boulder, CO: Westview. 2nd ed.

Tainter JA. 1988. *The Collapse of Complex Societies*. Cambridge: Cambridge Univ. Press

Tao W. 1999. A city with many faces: urban development in premodern China. In *Exploring China's Past: New Discoveries and Studies in Archaeology and Art*, ed. R Whitfield, W Tao, pp. 111–21. London: Saffron Books

Temin P. 2001. A market economy in the early Roman Empire. *J. Roman Stud.* 91:169–81

Temin P. 2004. The labor market of the early Roman Empire. *J. Interdiscipl. Hist.* 34:513–38

Temin P. 2006. The economy of the early Roman Empire. *J. Econ. Perspect.* 20:133–51

Thompson EP. 1971. The moral economy of the English crowd in the eighteenth century. *Past Present* 50:76–136

Thompson EP. 1991. *Customs in Common: Studies in Traditional Popular Culture*. London: Merlin

Thrift NJ. 2000. Commodity. In *The Dictionary of Human Geography*, ed. RJ Johnston, D Gregory, D Pratt, M Watts, pp. 95–96. Oxford: Blackwell

Torquemada J. 1943. *Monarquia Indiana*. Mexico City: S Chávez Hayhoe

Trigger BG. 2003. *Understanding Early Civilizations: A Comparative Study*. New York: Cambridge Univ. Press

Uzoigwe GN. 1972. Precolonial markets in Bunyoro-Kitara. *Comp. Stud. Soc. Hist.* 14:422–55

Uzzi B. 1997. Social structure and competition in interfirm networks: the paradox of embeddedness. *Admin. Sci. Q.* 42:35–67

van Bavel BJP. 2006. Rural wage labor in the sixteenth-century low countries: an assessment of the importance and nature of wage labor in the countryside of Holland, Guelders and Flanders. *Continuity Change* 21:37–72

van Bavel BJP. 2008. The organization and rise of land and lease markets in northwestern Europe and Italy, c. 1000–1800. *Continuity Change* 23:13–53

van Bavel BJP, de Moor T, van Zanden JL. 2009. Introduction: factor markets in global economic history. *Continuity Change* 24:9–21

Wallerstein I. 1974. *The Modern World-System: Capitalist Agriculture and the Origins of the European World-Economy in the Sixteenth Century*. New York: Academic

Wilk RR. 1996. *Economies and Cultures: Foundations of Economic Anthropology*. Boulder, CO: Westview

Wilk RR. 1998. Comment on "The distributional approach: a new way to identify marketplace exchange in the archaeological record." *Curr. Anthropol.* 39:469

Williams CC. 2002. Beyond the commodity economy: the persistence of informal economic activity in rural England. *Geogr. Ann. B.* 83:221–33

Williamson OE. 1975. *Markets and Hierarchies: Analyses and Antitrust Implications*. New York: Free Press

Williamson OE. 1985. *The Economic Institutions of Capitalism*. New York: Free Press

Wittfogel K. 1957. *Oriental Despotism: A Comparative Study of Total Power*. New Haven, CT: Yale Univ. Press

Wolf ER. 1982. *Europe and the People without History*. Berkeley: Univ. Calif. Press

Wong RB. 1997. *China Transformed: Historical Change and the Limits of the European Experience*. Ithaca, NY: Cornell Univ. Press

Zukin S, DiMaggio P. 1990. Introduction. In *Structures of Capital*, ed. S Zukin, P DiMaggio, pp. 1–36. Cambridge: Cambridge Univ. Press

Consanguineous Marriage and Human Evolution

A.H. Bittles[1,2] and M.L. Black[1]

[1]Centre for Comparative Genomics, Murdoch University, Perth, Western Australia, 6150, Australia; email: abittles@ccg.murdoch.edu.au

[2]Edith Cowan University, Perth, Western Australia, 6027, Australia

Annu. Rev. Anthropol. 2010. 39:193–207

First published online as a Review in Advance on June 21, 2010

The *Annual Review of Anthropology* is online at anthro.annualreviews.org

This article's doi: 10.1146/annurev.anthro.012809.105051

0084-6570/10/1021-0193$20.00

Key Words

selection, homozygosity, reproductive behavior, fertility, health

Abstract

Mate choice among early human groups and in many historical populations was subject to both demographic and social constraints, ensuring that most unions were between couples who had coinherited substantial proportions of their genomes from common ancestors. Even in populations in which close consanguineous marriage was proscribed, community endogamy would have been sufficient to ensure high levels of homozygosity. Consanguineous marriage remains the choice of an estimated 10.4% of the global population, although there has been an overall decline in its popularity, especially in developed countries. Recent studies have indicated that the shift from consanguineous marriage to panmixia has been accompanied by a reduction in homozygosity. The concomitant predicted decrease in incidence of both recessive single-gene disorders and more common adult-onset diseases will have a significant impact on the health of future generations.

INTRODUCTION

The theory of evolutionary change driven by natural selection proposed by Darwin in *The Origin of Species* is dependent on mutational changes that better equip organisms to survive and reproduce in their environments to avoid extinction. This concept remained largely unchallenged until neutral and nearly neutral theories were proposed to explain the large numbers of apparently selection-independent genetic variants revealed by protein electrophoresis (Kimura 1968, 1969; Ohta 1973). Whether neutral mutations are effectively irrelevant or important in evolution remains controversial, as demonstrated by a recent composite proposal hypothesizing that neutral mutations have a preparatory role in evolutionary adaptation prior to selection (Wagner 2008).

Single nucleotide polymorphism (SNP) studies on DNA have identified major regions of the genome that are undergoing positive selection (Voight et al. 2006, Sabeti et al. 2007) or that have already reached fixation (Williamson et al. 2007), and the impact of negative selection on amino acid mutations in disease genes has also been demonstrated (Barreiro et al. 2008). SNP analysis additionally indicates that the rate of adaptive evolution has been accelerating over the course of the past 40,000 years (Hawks et al. 2007).

A DEMOGRAPHIC PERSPECTIVE ON CONSANGUINITY AND EVOLUTION

Unlike palaeoanthropologists, who have access to partial skeletal remains with which to reconstruct the body forms and lives of long-dead individuals, population geneticists and demographers have little contemporary physical evidence of the size and mating structures of early humans. Using calculated rates of mutation, however, investigators generally believe that the out-of-Africa migration of humans, which occurred 60,000–70,000 ybp (years before present) (Behar et al. 2008), involved effective population sizes ranging downward from ~10,000 to as few as ~700 individuals (Harpending et al. 1998, Zhivotovsky et al. 2003, Liu et al. 2006, Tenesa et al. 2007). Given the hunter-gatherer existence of these early groups, which would have favored population dispersal, it seems reasonable to assume a substantial level of intragroup and probable intrafamily mating. Through time, these mating patterns would have involved multiple loops of kin relationships and resulted in high levels of consanguinity (Bittles 2008, Bittles & Black 2010a).

Urban Development and Social Stratification

Following urbanization and with the establishment of increasingly sophisticated city-states in Mesopotamia, Egypt, and the Indus Valley ~3000 ybp, social stratification became increasingly marked within human populations. The net outcome of this change was to restrict mate choice and encourage endogamy and consanguinity, thus counteracting the opportunity for panmixia in the slowly growing, geographically dispersed global population, which by 1000 A.D. is believed to have numbered ~310 million (U.S. Bur. Stat. 2009).

The tribes of Israel provide a relevant and well-documented historical example of the influence of tribal subdivision ~4000–3000 ybp, with the land and social and religious obligations subdivided among 12 sons of Jacob and their descendants. Aside from intrafamilial consanguineous unions, it is difficult to estimate the degree to which historical clan and/or tribal endogamy resulted in genomic homozygosity in numerically small populations. Some indication of the population structure and dynamics of these earlier human groups can, however, be gained by studying present-day societies in which there is marked population stratification, with individuals and families born into patrilineal clans, tribes, castes, and *biraderi*. Thus the Abbad tribe in Jordan, which is composed of some 120,000 individual members, is divided into 76 male lineages of between 250 and 2000 individuals, with 47% of all marriages intralineal and 90% contracted within the tribe (Nabulsi 1995).

SNP: single nucleotide polymorphism

Consanguineous: from the Latin "with the same blood"; persons who share identical alleles inherited from a common ancestor(s)

Homozygosity mapping: genetic mapping for autosomal recessive disorders in which affected persons are expected to have two disease alleles that are identical by descent

Dynastic and Religious Regulation of Close Kin Marriage

With the creation of strong, centralized human societies, religious and civil codification of permitted and prohibited patterns of marriage closely followed. In Egypt, sibling marriage, in which the partners had at least 50% of their genes in common, was both permitted and expected of the ruling Pharaohs during the eighteenth and nineteenth dynasties (prior to 332 B.C.), and incestuous unions also occurred in the ruling dynasties of other prominent civilizations, including the Persian Zoroastrians and the Incas (Middleton 1962, Shaw 1992, Scheidel 1996). Reports on nondynastic incest are rare, although in Athens and Sparta half-sib ($F = 0.125$) unions were permissible alongside first-cousin ($F = 0.0625$) and uncle-niece ($F = 0.125$) marriages (Ottenheimer 1996, Ager 2005). This tradition may explain the occurrence of half- and even full-sib marriage within the Greek Ptolemaic dynasty in Egypt (323–30 B.C.) and the settler population of the Arsinoe region of Lower Egypt during the Roman period of the first to the third centuries A.D. (Scheidel 1997). Papyrus fragments that have survived from the latter period even indicate instances of monogamous brother-sister marriages in successive generations and formal sibling divorces (Scheidel 2004).

Cousin marriage was disfavored in the Classical Rome period (Adam 1865), and it would seem that this tradition influenced attitudes toward first-cousin marriage in the early Christian Church. By the sixth century negative pre-Christian Roman attitudes toward consanguinity had replaced the original tolerance toward first-cousin marriage displayed in the Eastern Empire centered in Constantinople (Bittles 2003). A major outcome of the Protestant Reformation was reversion to the marriage regulations defined in the Biblical book of Leviticus 18:7–18, with first-cousin marriage generally permissible within Protestant denominations (Bittles 2009a). More recent changes within the Roman Catholic Church have resulted in Diocesan dispensation for consanguinity being restricted to marriages between couples related as first cousins or closer ($F \geq 0.0625$), replacing the earlier dispensation requirements, which until 1917 included second-cousin ($F = 0.0156$) and third-cousin unions ($F = 0.0039$), and from the eleventh to the thirteenth centuries also encompassed fourth- through sixth-cousin marriages ($F = 0.00098$–0.00006) (Bittles 2009a).

The marriage guidelines provided in Leviticus 18:7–18 also permit uncle-niece marriage ($F = 0.125$), which along with first-cousin marriage is still favored and practiced in many Sephardi Jewish communities. Within Islam, first-cousin and double-first-cousin ($F = 0.125$) marriages are permitted, but uncle-niece unions are prohibited by the Quran. There is no specific encouragement of consanguinity within Islam; indeed several *hadith* (sayings of the Prophet) endorse marriage between nonrelatives (Hussain 1999), although the Prophet Muhammad married his daughter Fatima to his ward and first-cousin Ali, i.e., a first-cousin-once-removed relationship ($F = 0.0313$). Thus the preference for first-cousin marriage in most Muslim countries, principally of the parallel paternal subtype between a man and his father's brother's daughter, is probably a reflection of both pre-Islamic Arab tradition and the rules introduced in the Quran to enable female inheritance of wealth (Bittles & Hamamy 2010).

As summarized in **Table 1**, among the other major world faiths first-cousin marriage is generally permitted within Buddhism and in the Zoroastrian/Parsi religion. The marriage regulations governing consanguineous unions within Hinduism are significantly more complex. Under the Indo-European tradition that prevails in North India, prior to parental approval of a marriage, the family pedigrees of both partners are examined over an average of seven generations on the male side and five generations on the female side to preclude a consanguineous union (Kapadia 1958). This practice contrasts strongly with marriage among the Dravidian populations of southern India.

Table 1 Religious regulation of first-cousin marriage

Religion	Branch	Regulation
Judaism	Ashkenazi	Permissive
	Sephardi	Permissive
Christianity	Greek and Russian Orthodox	Proscribed
	Coptic Orthodox	Permissive
	Roman Catholic	Diocesan dispensation required
	Protestant	Permissive
Islam	Sunni	Permissive
	Shia	Permissive
	Ibadi	Permissive
Hinduism	Indo-European	Proscribed
	Dravidian	Permissive
Buddhism		Permissive
Sikhism		Proscribed
Confucianism/Taoism		Partially permissive
Zoroastrian/Parsi		Permissive

In the states of Andhra Pradesh, Karnataka, and Tamil Nadu, and to a lesser extent neighboring Kerala, Goa, and southern Maharashtra, first-cousin marriage, preferentially between a man and his mother's brother's daughter, and uncle-niece marriage are popular across Hindu castes and in most Christian denominations (Bittles 2002).

According to Confucian teaching, the marriage of persons with the same family name is forbidden, which means that while a father's brother's daughter first-cousin union is prohibited, as in South Indian Dravidian societies, marriage between a man and his mother's brother's daughter is permissible (Cooper & Zhang 1993). Some flexibility also exists in the Sikh religion, which generally proscribes consanguinity, but first-cousin marriage is tolerated among some Sikh minority groups, mainly living in or originating from Pakistan.

Civil Regulation of Consanguineous Marriage

In almost all countries, no civil proscription on marriage between first cousins exists. The notable exceptions are the People's Republic of China, in which the 1981 Marriage Law prohibited first-cousin marriage but granted partial exemption to ethnic communities (*minzu*) in which such unions were customary; the People's Republic of North Korea, which in the 1994 Family Law formally banned marriage between blood relatives up to and including third cousins and between relatives by marriage up to and including first cousins; and the United States, where first-cousin marriage is illegal or a criminal offense in 31 of the 50 states (Ottenheimer 1996, Paul & Spencer 2008, Bittles & Black 2010a).

To a large degree, the 1981 legislation governing first-cousin marriage in the People's Republic of China was redundant from its inception because of the prior introduction of the One Child Certificate Program in 1979, which, at least in urban centers, very effectively reduced the potential numbers of marriageable first cousins (Wang et al. 2002). The situation with respect to first-cousin marriage in the United States is both confused and confusing. Up to the mid-nineteenth century, most concerns were expressed in terms of the social undesirability of affinal marriages, e.g., between a man and his deceased wife's sister; however, by the end of the nineteenth century, legislation banning first-cousin marriage had been enacted by 12 states (Ottenheimer 1996). In 1970, the National Conference of Commissioners unanimously recommended that all state laws banning first-cousin marriage should be rescinded because of a lack of justificatory evidence regarding ill effects on health. Yet in 2005, the state of Texas formally prohibited first-cousin marriage, although it appears that the primary objective of the banning legislation was to prevent underage marriage within some fundamentalist religious groups.

THE CURRENT GLOBAL PREVALENCE OF CONSANGUINEOUS MARRIAGE

As illustrated in **Figure 1** (see color insert), on the basis of detailed information accessible at the Global Consanguinity Web site (**http://www.consang.net**), close kin marriage continues to be preferential in many major populations with, as noted above, the influence of religion apparent in the regional differences in consanguinity prevalence. Despite anthropological reports indicating consanguineous marriage throughout sub-Saharan Africa, and in Asian countries with large populations, including Bangladesh and Indonesia, few quantitative data on consanguinity are available from these regions. Current information does, however, indicate that some 10.4% of the 6.8 billion global population are related as second cousins or closer ($F \geq 0.0156$) (Bittles & Black 2010a).

The prevalence of consanguineous marriage worldwide is declining, with marked reductions during the twentieth century in the more industrialized countries of Western Europe and North America and in Japan. Given its population of 1.3 billion, the People's Republic of China's legal proscription of first-cousin marriage will also exert a considerable effect on global consanguinity. However, in some countries, the present-day rates of cousin marriage appear to exceed those of the preceding generation, possibly owing to greater numbers of relatives surviving to marriageable age and to

the near-ubiquity of marriage in these societies (Bittles 2008).

During the past 50 years, large-scale emigration of people from countries where consanguinity is preferential to North America, Western Europe, and Oceania has taken place. In general, no decline in the prevalence of consanguineous marriage has been reported in these migrant communities, e.g., the U.K. Pakistani population (Shaw 2000) or the Turkish or Moroccan communities in Belgium (Reniers 1998), although Grjibovski et al. (2009) observed a reduction in first-cousin marriage in the small Norwegian Pakistani community.

Given the large numbers involved, with at least 10 million resident migrants in Western Europe alone, a comprehensive trans-national, cross-community survey would be needed to assess the overall position and to determine if generational differences have occurred. However, as with the British Government's refusal to include a question on first-cousin marriage in the 1871 Census (Darwin 1871), it is questionable whether governmental agencies in any country would wish to be associated with such a socially sensitive undertaking, especially since no civil legal restrictions apply to first-cousin marriage in Western Europe or in Oceania. In jurisdictions such as the United States, where first-cousin marriage is illegal in most states, it is even less likely that a comparable survey would be possible.

THE INFLUENCE OF CONSANGUINITY ON REPRODUCTIVE BEHAVIOR, FERTILITY, AND HEALTH

A large majority of the scientific literature on consanguineous marriage has concentrated on quite specific aspects of the effects of inbreeding on fertility and health. But as indicated in **Figure 2**, any balanced assessment of the overall impact of consanguinity in these areas necessarily requires acknowledging the associated social, economic, and demographic influences, differential reproductive behavior, and early- and late-onset morbidity and mortality.

Figure 2

Influences and outcomes of consanguineous marriage. Reproduced from Bittles & Black (2010a) with permission.

Although first-cousin marriage has been widely used to maintain family wealth and land-holdings, as summarized in **Table 2**, the highest overall prevalence of consanguineous unions is in poor rural communities that have low levels of maternal education, early age at marriage and first birth, short birth intervals, and longer reproductive spans (Bittles et al. 1991, Bittles 1994, Khlat 1997). Each of these factors is independently associated with larger family sizes and higher rates of infant and early childhood mortality.

Consanguinity and Mate Choice

In a study of Swiss university students, on the basis of the level of female attraction to male body odors, a negative relationship was demonstrated between male attractiveness and the degree of major histocompatibility complex (MHC) haplotype similarity between the male

Table 2 Demographic and social correlates of consanguinity

Rural residence
More traditional lifestyle
Lower socioeconomic status
Family tradition of consanguineous marriage
Low level of maternal education
Younger maternal and paternal ages at marriage
Lower spousal age differences
Younger maternal age at first birth
Shorter birth intervals
Extended maternal reproductive span
Larger completed family sizes

and female subjects (Wedekind et al. 1995). A further study, among the S-Leut Hutterites, a highly endogamous Anabaptist sect resident in the state of South Dakota, in the United States, indicated that couples had a lower-than-expected incidence of human leukocyte antigen (HLA) haplotype matches, which suggested either attraction to HLA-dissimilar partners and/or aversion to individuals of the opposite sex who were HLA-similar (Ober et al. 1997). In both cases, the findings could be interpreted as indicative of an evolved mechanism to avoid close inbreeding and to optimize resistance to a wider range of pathogens, and subsequent laboratory studies on the analogous H-2 immune response in mice suggested the action of an olfactory system with chemosensory imprinting (Penn & Potts 1998).

A review of follow-up studies failed to confirm any consistent preference for HLA-dissimilar partners and in some cases even indicated a greater likelihood of increased HLA-sharing between couples (Bittles et al. 2002). Using genome-wide analysis in conjunction with HLA typing to investigate these apparently contradictory results, studies have shown that African couples do not exhibit a significant pattern of similarity/dissimilarity in the MHC region, whereas across the genome they are more similar than random pairs of individuals drawn from the same population. By comparison, European Americans were significantly more MHC-dissimilar than were random pairs of individuals, and this pattern of dissimilarity was more pronounced than in other regions of the genome (Chaix et al. 2008).

These differences between Africans and European Americans indicate that if humans are capable of discriminating between the MHC types of potential partners via odor cues, either the system is specific to certain ancestries or in some instances it can be overridden by other more potent, possibly sociodemographic, cues. From an evolutionary perspective, it is important to note that freedom of mate choice using odor cues is unlikely to have been a major determining factor in early human groups, where potential mates would have been few in number

and females jealously guarded. Similarly, odor-based mate choice is of very limited significance in the many past and present-day populations in which marriage partner choice is largely, if not exclusively, subject to parental prerogative (Bittles et al. 2002).

Consanguinity and Reproductive Behavior

It has not been convincingly demonstrated that consanguinity is associated with elevated rates of pathological sterility (Yanase et al. 1973, Rao & Inbaraj 1977, Edmond & De Braekeleer 1993). As noted in **Table 2**, in most populations in which consanguineous marriage has been studied, maternal age at marriage and at first birth is lower in consanguineous pregnancies (Bittles et al. 1991, 1993). Some evidence also indicates that women in consanguineous unions continue to bear children at later ages (Tunçbilek & Koç 1994), which may be due, in part, to lower contraceptive usage (Hussain & Bittles 1999).

The net result is optimization of the female reproductive span with a higher mean number of children born to consanguineous couples. This outcome is illustrated in **Figure 3**, comparing the numbers of live births to first-cousin and nonconsanguineous couples in 40 studies conducted in 9 countries. First-cousin couples had a larger mean number of live births in 33 of the 40 studies, and for the sample as a whole, they had 0.08 additional births when compared with coresident nonconsanguineous couples ($r^2 = 0.67$, $p < 10^{-9}$). Some care is needed in interpreting these data because, as noted in **Table 2**, consanguineous and nonconsanguineous couples differ significantly in terms of many important sociodemographic variables. However, in Iceland, with access to detailed genealogical data and socioeconomic homogeneity, reproductive success was shown to be greatest at a level of parental relatedness approximating to third to fourth cousins ($F = 0.0039–0.00098$) (Helgason et al. 2008).

Besides optimization of the female reproductive span, evidence from several populations

Random pairs (mating): selection of a spouse irrespective of their ethnic, religious, economic, or social background and genotype

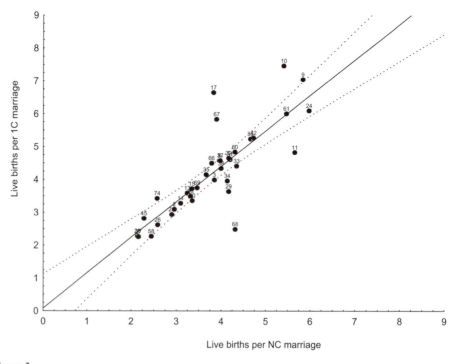

Figure 3

Mean number of live births in first-cousin (1C; $F = 0.0625$: y-axis) versus nonconsanguineous marriages (NC; $F = 0$: x-axis) in 40 study populations.

suggests that the higher mean number of live births in first-cousin marriages may, in part, be a reproductive compensation mechanism for children who die at an early age (Schull et al. 1970, Ober et al. 1999). A mechanism of this type could be dependent on either a conscious decision by parents to achieve their desired family size or cessation of lactational amenorrhea after the death of a breast-fed infant (Bittles et al. 2002).

Consanguinity and Prereproductive Mortality

There has been little evidence of an adverse effect of consanguinity on fetal loss rates (Warburton & Fraser 1964, Al-Awadi et al. 1986, Shami et al. 1991, Khoury & Massad 1992, Al Hussain & Al Bunyan 1997, Jaber et al. 1997, al-Abdulkareem & Ballal 1998, Saad & Jauniaux 2002), although it must be acknowledged that information on early

pre- and even postimplantation losses in pregnancy can be difficult to detect. Most losses are believed to occur during these early stages of pregnancy (O'Connor et al. 1998), whereas the published data are generally based on pregnancies that terminated during the last trimester. Due caution must, therefore, be applied in interpreting the results. Conversely, deaths in the first year of life have consistently been shown to be higher among the progeny of first cousins (Bittles 2001), although it is unclear whether this finding is due primarily to the expression of detrimental recessive genes or whether it can additionally be ascribed to gynecological immaturity, given the younger mean ages at first pregnancy of women in consanguineous relationships.

To estimate the effects of consanguinity on prereproductive mortality, measured from ∼6 months gestation to 12 years of age, Bittles & Black (2010a) conducted a meta-analysis on data compiled from 69 populations

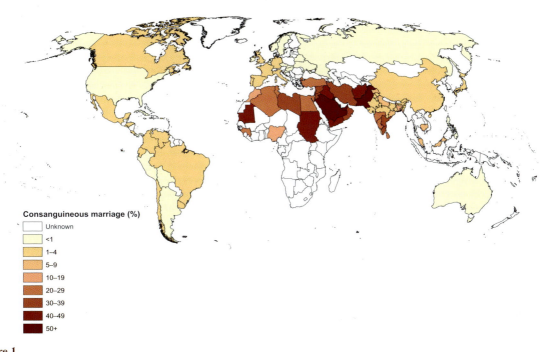

Figure 1

Global distribution of marriages between couples related as second cousins or closer ($F \geq 0.0156$).

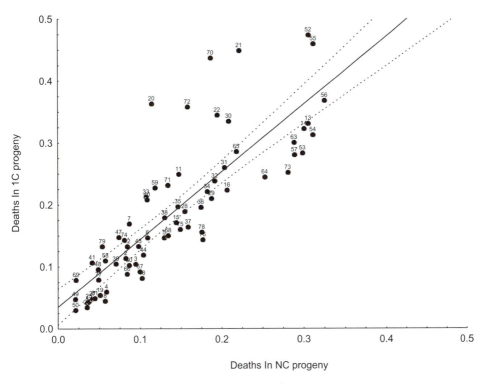

Figure 4

Comparative prereproductive mortality in first-cousin (1C; $F = 0.0625$: y-axis) versus nonconsanguineous progeny (NC; $F = 0$: x-axis) in 69 study populations. Reproduced from Bittles & Black 2010a with permission.

resident in 15 countries located across 4 continents, with a total sample size of 2.14 million. Deaths in first-cousin versus nonconsanguineous progeny were directly compared within specific populations by plotting an unweighted linear regression according to the standard equation $y = a + bx$. The scatter diagram of the results showed a mean excess mortality at first-cousin level of 3.5% ($r^2 = 0.70$, $p < 0.00001$) that is consistent across the range of control mortalities; i.e., the reported levels of excess consanguinity-associated mortality are independent of the basal (nonconsanguineous) death rate in each study population (**Figure 4**). The derived estimate matches the 3.5% excess mortality among first-cousin progeny obtained with Italian data from the early- to mid-twentieth century (Cavalli-Sforza et al. 2004) and compares with an ear-

lier global estimate of 4.4% excess mortality based on a comparable but significantly smaller data set (Bittles & Neel 1994).

As with the data on prenatal losses, the estimated excess mortality in first-cousin progeny must be treated with caution, given the wide range of sociodemographic variables that may influence individual study results, especially because the highest rates of consanguineous marriage are among the more disadvantaged sectors of societies (**Table 2**). With this factor in mind, Bittles (2009b) noted that estimates of consanguinity-associated mortality had declined significantly over the course of the past 30–40 years at a pace that is not readily explicable in terms of generational, and hence genetic, change and primarily reflects improved control for nongenetic variables.

CONSANGUINITY AND SELECTION

In assessing the role of selection across generations, without positive selection it would have been impossible for small, separated human groups to have successfully migrated from their home environments in sub-Saharan Africa some 60,000–70,000 ybp and inhabited the temperate and even the Arctic regions of the globe (Bittles & Black 2010b). This process was particularly important because, in migrating from their ancestral homelands, early human groups (and even present-day migrant communities) would have exposed themselves to previously unencountered pathogenic organisms for which their immune systems were unprimed (Ferwerda et al. 2007). The assumption of positive selection is validated by adaptive evolution observed at the molecular level, principally affecting fertility and reproduction, morphology, skeletal development, brain and nervous system development and function, the immune system, and components of the electron transport chain (Voight et al. 2006, Williamson et al. 2007). In some populations, evidence also indicates that more than one gene in a biological process has undergone positive selection, e.g., *SLC24A5* and *SLC45A2*, both of which influence skin color in Europeans (Sabeti et al. 2007).

Consanguinity and Population Structure

Demographic and social constraints on marriage partner choice strongly suggest that close kin unions continued during the slow population growth of human groups, whether living in scattered rural settlements, villages, small towns, or cities. Even in societies, such as North India, in which first-cousin marriage was prohibited, stringent community endogamy would have resulted in high rates of homozygosity because of multiple loops of remote ancestral relationships (Bittles 2002). Under these circumstances, an excess of recessive diseases can be predicted (Bittles 2008, Reich et al. 2009).

Although estimates of consanguinity obtained by pedigree analysis have usually been restricted to three to four generations, direct assessment of historical and more recent consanguinity is now possible at the genome level using SNPs to measure uninterrupted runs of homozygosity (ROH) (McQuillan et al. 2008). Recent consanguinity is associated with longer ROH; however, even in individuals known to have been outbred for at least 5 and probably more than 10 generations, ROHs measuring up to 4 Mb were common in the genome (McQuillan et al. 2008).

The application of SNP analysis to genomic studies has indicated the effects of bottlenecks, even of small amplitude, owing to periodic epidemics, famines, and warfare (Gherman et al. 2007, Manica et al. 2007, Auton et al. 2009). As previously discussed, by restricting marriage partner choice, bottlenecks would have contributed to increased consanguinity and population stratification. Despite recent urbanization, the effects of population stratification are obvious in countries such as Iran (Ashrafian-Bonab et al. 2007). Perhaps more unexpectedly, population stratification remains a significant factor in modern, industrialized European societies (Novembre et al. 2008, McEvoy et al. 2009).

SNP-based studies have also added a new layer of complexity to our understanding of selection, with the demonstration of sex-specific genetic structure and social organization (Ségurel et al. 2008), sex-biased evolutionary forces (Hammer et al. 2008), and variable parental origins of sequences involved in complex diseases (Kong et al. 2009). The role of *cis*-coding, i.e., noncoding regions, of the genome has additionally become a subject of increased interest in evolutionary processes (Torgerson et al. 2009).

Beneficial Effects of Consanguinity

The social and economic advantages of consanguineous marriage were summarized within **Figure 2**, with ease of marriage arrangements, reduced or zero dowry payments, increased family solidarity and female autonomy, reduced incidence of marital violence, and lower divorce rates all identified as significant (Bittles & Black 2010a, Bittles & Hamamy 2010). From a biological perspective, Sanghvi (1966) proposed that uninterrupted consanguineous unions contracted across multiple generations would have effectively purged deleterious recessive genes from the gene pool. However, there is no evidence that the traditionally preferred high rates of consanguineous unions in populations such as Dravidian South India (Radha Rama Devi et al. 1987) or Arab Israelis (Zlotogora et al. 2000, 2006; Zlotogora 2007) have resulted in significant reductions in the incidence of autosomal recessive disorders. As previously noted, in these communities it is more probable that strict endogamy leading to population stratification and smaller effective population sizes actually results in higher rates of deleterious recessive disorders (Bittles 2008).

Computer simulations of α-thalassemia have been interpreted as suggesting that consanguineous marriage may lead to the accumulation of beneficial mutations that protect against malaria (Denic et al. 2008). However, as in all such simulations, the conclusions reached are critically dependent on the veracity of the underlying demographic assumptions incorporated in the model tested. A case-control study in a region of high malaria endemicity had shown that individuals homozygous for α^+-thalassemia were less likely to experience either malarial or nonmalarial infections (Allen et al. 1997). But the generality of these findings has been questioned by the demonstration of a positive association between homozygosity and fatal invasive bacterial disease in children, involving deaths caused by both gram-positive and gram-negative bacteria (Lyons et al. 2009).

CONCLUSIONS

As predicted by Darwin (1859), the rate at which selection occurs will be positively correlated with population size. Therefore, given the growth in human numbers during the past century, from ~1.7 billion in 1900 to the present 6.8 billion, and the projected total of 9.4 billion in 2050 (Popul. Ref. Bur. 2009), it would seem highly probable that the rate of selection since the beginning of the twentieth century has far exceeded the levels experienced in earlier generations.

Consanguinity would be expected to enhance the expression of rare recessive genes and thus increase selection. Nalls et al. (2009) predicted that the observed reduction in homozygosity/autozygosity in the United States over the course of the twentieth century, ascribed to panmixia and larger effective population sizes, will have caused a reduction in the frequency of recessive single-gene disorders. In terms of the more complex late-onset diseases, such as hypertension, coronary heart disease, and stroke, studies in the Dalmatian Islands, Croatia, have indicated a significant positive association with recent consanguinity (Rudan et al. 2003a,b). By comparison, increased heterozygosity leads to beneficial reductions in blood pressure and total/low-density-lipoprotein (LDL) cholesterol levels (Campbell et al. 2007). Any move toward lower levels of consanguineous marriage should therefore result in increased genome-wide heterozygosity and thus a lower incidence of these increasingly common adult-onset diseases in both developed and developing countries (Campbell et al. 2009), a trend that will be particularly important given rapidly increasing global life expectancies.

Could there be any downside to these changes? Since humans have mainly evolved in small groups, with limited mate choice and high resultant levels of homozygosity, a decline in consanguinity could lead to the disruption of advantageous gene complexes. As originally proposed in the thrifty genotype hypothesis (Neel 1962), the typical health problems of modern westernized humans are far removed from those experienced by our early forebears and largely reflect inappropriate lifestyle and dietary choices, with the consequent development of adult-onset disease phenotypes. Therefore, the degree to which a shift from consanguineous marriage to panmixia actually improves overall human fitness will remain open to speculation until the relevant

Homozygous: an individual who has two identical alleles at a specific gene locus on a pair of homologous chromosomes

Autozygosity: homozygosity due to alleles identical by descent, i.e., inherited from a common ancestor

Genome-wide heterozygosity: the likelihood that an individual will have two different alleles at loci across the genome

predisposing disease genes for present-day ill health have been identified and their possible beneficial role in evolved gene complexes fully assessed.

ACKNOWLEDGMENTS

Financial support to AHB from the National Science Foundation (grant no. 0527751) is gratefully acknowledged.

LITERATURE CITED

Adam W. 1865. Consanguinity in marriage, part 1. *Fortn. Rev.* 3:710–30

Ager SL. 2005. Familiarity breeds: incest and the Ptolemaic dynasty. *J. Hell. Stud.* 125:1–34

al-Abdulkareem AA, Ballal SG. 1998. Consanguineous marriage in an urban area of Saudi Arabia: rates and adverse health effects on the offspring. *J. Community Health* 23:75–83

Al-Awadi SA, Naguib KK, Moussa MA, Farag TI, Teebi AS, El-Khalifa MY. 1986. The effects of consanguineous marriages on reproductive wastage. *Clin. Genet.* 29:384–88

Al Hussain M, Al Bunyan M. 1997. Consanguineous marriages in a Saudi population and the effects of inbreeding on prenatal and postnatal mortality. *Ann. Trop. Paediat.* 17:155–60

Allen SJ, O'Donnell A, Alexander NDE, Alpers MP, Peto TEA, et al. 1997. α^+-Thalassemia protects children against disease caused by other infections as well as malaria. *Proc. Natl. Acad. Sci. USA* 94:14736–41

Ashrafian-Bonab M, Lawson Handley LJ, Balloux F. 2007. Is urbanization scrambling the genetic structure of human populations? A case study. *Heredity* 98:151–56

Auton A, Bryc K, Boyko AR, Lohmueller KE, Reynolds A, et al. 2009. Global distribution of genomic diversity underscores rich complex history of continental human populations. *Genome Res.* 19:795–803

Barreiro LB, Laval G, Quach H, Patin E, Quintana-Murci L. 2008. Natural selection has driven population differentiation in modern humans. *Nat. Genet.* 40:340–45

Behar DM, Villems R, Soodyal HM, Blue-Smith J, Pereira L, et al. 2008. The dawn of human matrilineal diversity. *Am. J. Hum. Genet.* 82:1130–40

Bittles AH. 1994. The role and significance of consanguinity as a demographic variable. *Popul. Dev. Rev.* 20:561–84

Bittles AH. 2001. Consanguinity and its relevance to clinical genetics. *Clin. Genet.* 60:89–98

Bittles AH. 2002. Endogamy, consanguinity and community genetics. *J. Genet.* 81:91–98

Bittles AH. 2003. The bases of Western attitudes to consanguineous marriage. *Dev. Med. Child Neurol.* 45:135–38

Bittles AH. 2008. A community genetics perspective on consanguineous marriage. *Community Genet.* 11:324–30

Bittles AH. 2009a. The background and outcomes of the first cousin marriage controversy in Great Britain. *Int. J. Epidemiol.* 38:1429–39

Bittles AH. 2009b. Consanguinity, genetic drift, and genetic diseases in populations with reduced numbers of founders. In *Human Genetics—Principles and Approaches*, ed. F Vogel, AG Motulsky, SE Antonarakis, M Speicher, pp. 507–28. Heidelberg: Springer. 4th ed.

Bittles AH, Black ML. 2010a. Consanguinity, human evolution and complex diseases. *Proc. Natl. Acad. Sci. USA* 107:1779–86

Bittles AH, Black ML. 2010b. Factors and forces influencing human variation. In *Human Variation—From the Laboratory to the Field*, ed. CGN Mascie-Taylor, A Yasukouchi, S Ulijaszek, pp. 1–16. London: Taylor & Francis

Bittles AH, Grant JC, Shami SA. 1993. An evaluation of consanguinity as a determinant of reproductive behavior and mortality in Pakistan. *Int. J. Epidemiol.* 22:463–67

Bittles AH, Grant JC, Sullivan SG, Hussain R. 2002. Does inbreeding lead to increased human fertility? *Ann. Hum. Biol.* 29:111–31

Bittles AH, Hamamy HA. 2010. Consanguinity and endogamy in Arab countries. In *Genetic Disorders Among Arab Populations*, ed. A Teebi. Heidelberg: Springer. 2nd ed. In press

Bittles AH, Mason WH, Greene J, Appaji Rao N. 1991. Reproductive behavior and health in consanguineous marriages. *Science* 252:789–94

Bittles AH, Neel JV. 1994. The costs of human inbreeding and their implications for variations at the DNA level. *Nat. Genet.* 8:117–21

Campbell H, Carothers AD, Rudan I, Hayward C, Biolglav Z, et al. 2007. Effects of genome-wide heterozygosity on a range of biomedically relevant human quantitative traits. *Hum. Mol. Genet.* 16:233–41

Campbell H, Rudan I, Bittles AH, Wright AF. 2009. Human population structure, outbreeding and human health. *Genome Med.* 1:91–94

Cavalli-Sforza LL, Moroni A, Zei G. 2004. *Consanguinity, Inbreeding, and Genetic Drift in Italy.* Princeton, NJ: Princeton Univ. Press

Chaix R, Cao C, Donnelly P. 2008. Is mate choice in humans MHC-dependent? *PLoS Genet.* 4:e10000184

Cooper E, Zhang M. 1993. Patterns of cousin marriage in rural Zhejing and in Dreams of the Red Chamber. *J. Asian Stud.* 52:90–106

Darwin C. 1859. *The Origin of Species.* London: John Murray

Darwin C. 1871. *The Descent of Man*, Vol. 2. London: John Murray

Denic S, Nagelkerke M, Afarwal MM. 2008. Consanguineous marriages and endemic malaria: Can inbreeding increase population fitness? *Malar. J.* 7:150–58

Edmond M, De Braekeleer M. 1993. Inbreeding effects on fertility and sterility: a case-control study in Saguenay-Lac-Saint-Jean (Québec, Canada) based on a population registry 1838–1971. *Ann. Hum. Biol.* 20:545–55

Ferwerda B, McCall MBB, Alonso S, Gaimarellos-Boruboulis EJ, Mouktaroudi M. 2007. TLR4 polymorphisms, infectious diseases, and evolutionary pressure during migration of modern humans. *Proc. Natl. Acad. Sci. USA* 104:16645–50

Gherman A, Chen PE, Teslovich TM, Stankiewicz P, Withers M, et al. 2007. Population bottlenecks as a potential major shaping force of human genome architecture. *PLoS Genet.* 3:e119

Grjibovski AM, Magnus P, Stoltenberg C. 2009. Decrease in consanguinity among parents of children born in Norway to women of Pakistani origin. *Scand. J. Public Health* 37:232–38

Hammer MF, Mendez FL, Cox MP, Woerner AE, Wall JD. 2008. Sex-biased evolutionary forces shape genomic patterns of human diversity. *PLoS Genet.* 4:e10000202

Harpending HC, Batzer MA, Gurven M, Jorde LB, Rogers AR, Sherry ST. 1998. Genetic traces of ancient demography. *Proc. Natl. Acad. Sci. USA* 95:1961–67

Hawks J, Wang ET, Cochran GM, Harpending HC, Moyzis RK. 2007. Recent acceleration of human adaptive evolution. *Proc. Natl. Acad. Sci. USA* 104:20753–58

Helgason A, Pálsson S, Guðbjartsson DF, Kristjánsson P, Stefánsson K. 2008. An association between the kinship and fertility of human couples. *Science* 319:813–16

Hussain R. 1999. Community perceptions of reasons for preference for consanguineous marriages in Pakistan. *J. Biosoc. Sci.* 31:449–61

Hussain R, Bittles AH. 1999. Consanguinity and differentials in age at marriage, contraceptive use and fertility in Pakistan. *J. Biosoc. Sci.* 31:121–38

Jaber L, Merlob P, Gabriel R, Shohat M. 1997. Effects of consanguineous marriage on reproductive outcome in an Arab community in Israel. *J. Med. Genet.* 34:1000–2

Kapadia KM. 1958. *Marriage and Family in India.* Calcutta: Oxford Univ. Press. 2nd ed.

Khlat M. 1997. Endogamy in Arab countries. In *Genetic Disorders Among Arab Populations*, ed. A Teebi, TI Farag, pp. 63–80. New York: Oxford Univ. Press

Khoury SA, Massad D. 1992. Consanguineous marriage in Jordan. *Am. J. Med. Genet.* 43:769–75

Kimura M. 1968. Evolutionary rate at the molecular level. *Nature* 217:624–26

Kimura M. 1969. Genetic variability maintained in a finite population due to mutational production of neutral and nearly neutral mutations. *Genet. Res.* 11:247–69

Kong A, Steinthorsdottir V, Masson G, Thorleifsson G, Sulem P, et al. 2009. Parental origin of sequence variants associated with complex diseases. *Nature* 462:868–74

Liu H, Prugnolle F, Manica A, Balloux F. 2006. A geographically explicit genetic map of worldwide human-settlement history. *Am. J. Hum. Genet.* 79:230–37

Lyons EJ, Amos W, Berkley JA, Mwangi I, Shafi M, et al. 2009. Homozygosity and risk of childhood death due to invasive bacterial disease. *BMC Med. Genet.* 10:55–59

Manica A, Amos W, Balloux F, Hanihara T. 2007. The effect of ancient population bottlenecks on human phenotypic variation. *Nature* 448:346–49

McEvoy BP, Montgomery GW, McRae AF, Ripatti S, Perola M, et al. 2009. Geographical structure and differential natural selection among North European populations. *Genome Res.* 19:804–14

McQuillan R, Leutenegger AL, Abdel-Rahman R, Franklin CS, Pericic M, et al. 2008. Runs of homozygosity in European populations. *Am. J. Hum. Genet.* 83:359–72

Middleton R. 1962. Brother-sister and father-daughter marriage in ancient Egypt. *Sociol. Rev.* 27:603–11

Nabulsi A. 1995. Mating patterns of the Abbad tribe in Jordan. *Soc. Biol.* 42:162–74

Nalls MA, Simon-Sanchez J, Gibbs JR, Paisan-Ruiz C, Bras JT, et al. 2009. Measures of autozygosity in decline: globalization, urbanization, and its implications for medical genetics. *PLoS Genet.* 5:e1000415

Natl. Conf. Comm. 1970. *Handbook on Uniform State Laws and Proceedings of the Annual Conference Meeting in its Seventy-Ninth Year.* Baltimore: Port City Press

Neel JV. 1962. Diabetes mellitus: a 'thrifty' genotype rendered detrimental by 'progress'? *Am. J. Hum. Genet.* 14:253–62

Novembre J, Johnson T, Bryc K, Kutalik Z, Boyko AR, et al. 2008. Genes mirror geography within Europe. *Nature* 456:98–102

Ober C, Hyslop T, Hauck WW. 1999. Inbreeding effects on fertility in humans: evidence for reproductive compensation. *Am. J. Hum. Genet.* 64:225–31

Ober C, Weitkamp LR, Cox N, Dytch D, Kostyu D, Elias S. 1997. HLA and mate choice in humans. *Am. J. Hum. Genet.* 16:497–504

O'Connor KA, Holman DJ, Wood JW. 1998. Declining fecundity and ovarian aging in natural fertility populations. *Maturitas* 30:127–36

Ohta T. 1973. Slightly deleterious mutant substitutions in evolution. *Nature* 246:96–98

Ottenheimer M. 1996. U.S. laws prohibiting the marriage of relatives. In *Forbidden Relatives: The American Myth of Cousin Marriage*, pp. 19–41. Urbana: Univ. Ill. Press

Paul DB, Spencer HG. 2008. "Its ok, we're not cousin by blood": the cousin marriage controversy in historical perspective. *PLoS Biol.* 6:e320

Penn D, Potts W. 1998. MHC-disassortative mating preferences reversed by cross-fostering. *Proc. R. Soc. Lond. Ser. B* 265:1299–306

Popul. Ref. Bur. 2009. *World Population Data Sheet.* Washington, DC: Popul. Ref. Bur.

Radha Rama Devi A, Appaji Rao N, Bittles AH. 1987. Consanguinity and the incidence of childhood genetic disease in Karnataka, South India. *J. Med. Genet.* 24:362–65

Rao PSS, Inbaraj SG. 1977. Inbreeding effects on human reproduction in Tamil Nadu of South India. *Ann. Hum. Genet.* 41:87–98

Reich D, Thangaraj K, Patterson N, Price AL, Singh L. 2009. Reconstructing Indian population history. *Nature* 461:489–95

Reniers G. 1998. *Postmigration survival of traditional marriage patterns: consanguineous marriage among Turkish and Moroccan immigrants in Belgium.* Interuniv. Pap. Demogr., PPD-1 Work. Pap. 1998–1, Dep. Popul. Stud., Univ. Gent

Rudan I, Campbell H, Carothers A, Wright A, Smolej-Narancic N, et al. 2003a. Inbreeding and the genetic complexity of human hypertension. *Genetics* 163:1011–21

Rudan I, Rudan D, Campbell H, Carothers A, Wright A, et al. 2003b. Inbreeding and risk of late onset complex disease. *J. Med. Genet.* 40:925–32

Saad FA, Jauniaux E. 2002. Recurrent early pregnancy loss and consanguinity. *Reprod. Biomed. Online* 5:167–70

Sabeti PC, Varilly P, Fry B, Lohmueller J, Hostetter E, et al. 2007. Genome-wide detection and characterization of positive selection in human populations. *Nature* 449:913–18

Sanghvi LD. 1966. Inbreeding in India. *Eugen. Q.* 13:291–301

Scheidel W. 1996. Brother-sister and parent-child marriage outside royal families in ancient Egypt and Iran: a challenge to the sociobiological view of incest. *Ethnol. Sociobiol.* 17:319–40

Scheidel W. 1997. Brother-sister marriage in Roman Egypt. *J. Biosoc. Sci.* 29:361–71

Scheidel W. 2004. Ancient Egyptian sibling marriage and the Westermarck effect. In *Inbreeding, Incest, and the Incest Taboo*, ed. AP Wolf, WH Durham, pp. 93–108. Stanford, CA: Stanford Univ. Press

Schull WJ, Furusho T, Yamamoto M, Nagano H, Komatsu I. 1970. The effect of parental consanguinity and inbreeding in Hirado, Japan. IV. Fertility and reproductive compensation. *Humangenetik* 9:294–315

Ségurel L, Martinez-Cruz B, Quintana-Murci L, Balalesque P, Georges M, et al. 2008. Sex-specific genetic structure and social organization in Central Asia: insights from a multi-locus study. *PLoS Genet.* 4:e1000200

Shami SA, Schmitt LH, Bittles AH. 1991. Consanguinity, spousal age at marriage, and fertility in seven Pakistani cities. *Ann. Hum. Biol.* 17:97–105

Shaw A. 2000. Kinship, cultural preference, and immigration: consanguineous marriage among British Pakistanis. *J. R. Anthropol. Inst.* 7:315–34

Shaw BD. 1992. Explaining incest: brother-sister marriage in Graeco-Roman Egypt. *Man* 27:267–99

Tenesa A, Navarro P, Hayes BJ, Duffy DL, Clarke GM. 2007. Recent human effective population size estimated from linkage disequilibrium. *Genome Res.* 17:520–26

Torgerson DG, Boyko AR, Hernandez RD, Indap A, Hu X, et al. 2009. Evolutionary processes acting on candidate *cis*-regulatory regions in humans inferred from patterns of polymorphism and divergence. *PLoS Genet.* 5:e1000592

Tunçbilek E, Koç I. 1994. Consanguineous marriage in Turkey and its impact on fertility and mortality. *Ann. Hum. Genet.* 58:321–29

U.S. Bur. Stat. 2009. *Historical estimates of world population.* **http://www.census.gov/ipc/www.worldhis.html**

Voight BF, Kudaravalli S, Wen X, Pritchard JK. 2006. A map of recent positive selection in the human genome. *PLoS Biol.* 4:e72

Wagner A. 2008. Neutralism and selectionism: a network-based reconciliation. *Nat. Genet.* 9:965–74

Wang W, Qian C, Bittles AH. 2002. Consanguineous marriage in PR China: a study in rural Man (Manchu) communities. *Ann. Hum. Biol.* 29:685–90

Warburton D, Fraser FC. 1964. Spontaneous abortion risks in man: data from reproductive histories collected in a medical genetics unit. *Hum. Genet.* 16:1–15

Wedekind C, Seebeck T, Bettens F, Paepke AJ. 1995. MHC-dependent mate preference in humans. *Proc. R. Soc. Lond. Ser. B* 260:245–49

Williamson SH, Hubisz MJ, Clark AG, Payseur BA, Bustamente CD, Nielsen R. 2007. Localizing recent adaptive evolution in the human genome. *PLoS Genet.* 3:e90

Yanase Y, Fujiki N, Handa Y, Yamaguchi M, Kishimato K, et al. 1973. Genetic studies on inbreeding in some Japanese populations. XII. Studies of isolated populations. *Jap. J. Hum. Genet.* 17:332–36

Zhivotovsky LA, Rosenberg NA, Feldman MW. 2003. Features of evolution and expansion of modern humans, inferred from genomewide microsatellite markers. *Am. J. Hum. Genet.* 72:1171–86

Zlotogora J. 2007. Multiple mutations responsible for frequent genetic diseases in isolated populations. *Eur. J. Hum. Genet.* 15:272–78

Zlotogora J, Hujerat Y, Barges S, Shalev SA, Chakravarti A. 2006. The fate of 12 recessive mutations in a single village. *Ann. Hum. Genet.* 71:202–8

Zlotogora J, Shalev S, Habiballah H, Barjes S. 2000. Genetic disorders among Palestinian Arabs: 3. Autosomal recessive disorders in a single village. *Am. J. Med. Genet.* 92:343–45

Food and the Senses

David E. Sutton

Department of Anthropology, Southern Illinois University, Carbondale IL 62901;
email: dsutton@siu.edu

Annu. Rev. Anthropol. 2010. 39:209–23

First published online as a Review in Advance on
June 21, 2010

The *Annual Review of Anthropology* is online at
anthro.annualreviews.org

This article's doi:
10.1146/annurev.anthro.012809.104957

Key Words

gustemology, synesthesia, taste, distinction, categories

Abstract

This review makes the case for anthropological reflection on the intersection of food and the senses. Given that a focus on food and the
senses allows us to explore some of the most basic boundaries of inside
and outside, private and public, individual and collective, this topic offers an excellent window onto that elusive notion of everyday life that
anthropologists wish to understand theoretically and examine ethnographically. At the same time, food is a key component of ritual, which
has typically been understood as heightening or stimulating sensory
experience to instill social or cosmological values. Food and the senses
overlap in notions of taste as distinction and in an increasing recognition
of the culturally cultivated phenomenon of synesthesia. Furthermore, in
making food and the senses central to understanding wider social issues,
this review argues for the productivity of a concept of "gustemology"
in opening up new realms of ethnographic and theoretical inquiry.

INTRODUCTION

As anthropological topics, both food and the senses were long confined to a sort of limbo whereby many anthropologists may have had the intuition that they were important but, for various reasons, did not have the language to address them either as topics of ethnographic analysis or of theoretical development. As a graduate student in the mid-1980s, I had neither "food" nor "the senses" on the radar screen in my coursework or other training; they were, with notable exceptions, consigned to the realm of ethnographic anecdote. When I began teaching a course on the anthropology of food in the late 1990s, I still had to answer the question, posed by students and colleagues, of what such a course could possibly be about. Roughly 10 years later, explanations seem no longer necessary, and I am faced with a surfeit of excellent choices for readings in a semester-long course. Over the past 20+ years, both the "anthropology of food" and "the senses" have exploded in terms of scholarly production (on the senses, see Howes 2003; and on the anthropology of food, see Mintz & Du Bois 2002, Holtzman 2006). Yet they have run largely on separate, parallel tracks, drawing from similar inspirations, but only occasionally intersecting in terms of extended ethnographic analysis or theoretical synthesis. Thus, this review takes up some of those intersections within a developing, rather than fully mature, field of inquiry—a field with many future possibilities.

EARLY EXPLORATIONS

Although sensory aspects of food may have been mentioned in passing in anthropological accounts going back to Boas's famed salmon recipes, discussion of food and the senses in anthropology is essentially inaugurated by Levi-Strauss and, later, Douglas. This is sensory anthropology in a structuralist key: Basic flavors and other sensory properties (e.g., temperature) are seen in binary oppositions that code for other important structural oppositions.

As Levi-Strauss put it, "They [the senses] are operators, which make it possible to convey the isomorphic character of all binary systems of contrasts connected with the senses, and therefore to express, as a totality, a set of equivalences connecting life and death, vegetable foods and cannibalism, putrefaction and imputrescibility, softness and hardness, silence and noise" (Levi-Strauss 1983 [1964], p. 153). Thus, each of the senses (Levi-Strauss assumes five here) are seen as codes that transmit messages. Interestingly, and in keeping with his interest in cooking as a basic prerequisite of the transition from nature to culture, Levi-Strauss (1983) argues that the "gustatory code" is privileged over the other sensory codes: Its message "is more often transmitted by the others than it is used to translate theirs" (p. 164). Douglas, similarly, draws our attention to the properties of food through a number of basic sensory contrasts that she sees related less to structures of the mind than to structuring meals and, through them, social identities. Contrasts such as sweet versus savoury structure the ordering of a meal, and the taste of sweetness works, by analogy, across meals to relate the everyday pudding (i.e., dessert) to the Sunday pudding or the holiday pudding (Douglas & Gross 1981, p. 11). Douglas gives attention not only to flavor, but also to texture, temperature, color, and other visual patterning elements, once again grouping them into sets of oppositions that structure particular meals and the relationship among different meals, noting, for example, that "the same recurring theme is visible in the sequence from thick gravy to thicker custard to solid icing sugar. One of the structural rules of this food system is progressive desiccation and geometrification of forms through the day" (Douglas 1982, p. 97).

Douglas thus presents an early possibility of taking into account multiple sensory dimensions of food. However, her work, like Levi-Strauss's, is oriented toward abstracting binary patterns in sensory features that reflect other structured aspects of "the food system" and its relationship to "the social system"

(Douglas 1982), i.e., identifying degrees of intimacy and distance and identifying group boundaries (Douglas 1971; see Lalonde 1992 for a detailed critique). Furthermore, her sensory categories, like those of Levi-Strauss, are based on observation, not on informant descriptions or categories. She does suggest some potential cultural variability in the "degree of autonomy" of the rules of combining colors and textures in the food system (Douglas 1982, p. 110) in a particular society, but this angle remains largely speculative in her work.

Bourdieu's highly influential *Distinction: A Social Critique of the Judgment of Taste* (1984) seems like it would be a fruitful avenue for getting away from some of the problems of structuralist abstraction and exploring the sensory aspects of eating, especially given his other work addressing questions of habitus and embodiment (Bourdieu 1990). Although Bourdieu does provide some examples of class-based taste, his analysis takes a wrong turn for our purposes in subsuming gustatory taste under the wider category of aesthetic taste as part of his theory of cultural capital. For Bourdieu, tastes "are the practical affirmation of an inevitable difference" (1984, p. 56), "a system of classificatory schemes" (p. 174), or "the source of the system of distinctive features which cannot fail to be perceived as a systematic expression of a particular class of conditions of existence" (p. 175). It is only very occasionally and briefly in Bourdieu's work that taste becomes "the faculty of perceiving flavours" (p. 474).[1] This subsumption of taste to distinction is an issue discussed by a number of writers as part of a western tradition that specifically devalues taste (and smell) as a lower sense that promotes animal appetites rather than reasoned judgment and that blurs the basic western philosophic distinction between "subjective" and "objective" (Stoller 1989, p. 23; Howes & Lalonde 1991; Borthwick 2000).[2] Taste, then, becomes the capacity to distinguish and name, or categorize, flavors (and to make other aesthetic judgments), rather than an actual multisensory experience, which involves the dissolving of the object into the subject (Borthwick 2000, p. 135).

This latter process of tasting begins to be explored in two much-cited pieces, Stoller & Olkes's "The Taste of Ethnographic Things" (1989) and Seremetakis's essays in *The Senses Still* (1994), both meant as a critique or, better, a throwing down of the gauntlet in the face of mainstream anthropology's lack of sensory awareness. Stoller & Olkes (1989) claim that the "tasteful fieldworker" will eschew the search for "deep-seated hidden truths" and instead "describe with literary vividness the smells, tastes and textures of the land, the people, and the food" (p. 29). They provide one such vivid description of Djebo, a Songhay woman—wife of a younger, unsuccessful brother—and the social frustrations, which she expresses in a sauce called *fukko hoy*, that filled the anthropologists, as well as the other members of her compound, with disgust. The taste of the sauce, then, becomes a form of social action, a way of "express[ing] sensually her anger" (p. 22). It is, however, somewhat troubling that Stoller & Olkes oppose "analytical, theoretical" prose to "tasteful ethnographies [that] are descriptive, nontheoretical and memorable" (p. 32), thus confining the consideration of the senses to

---

[1] His discussion of food and eating, in which he argues that "the body is the most indisputable materialization of class tastes" (p. 190), is suggestive. He pays some attention to the material properties of food, noting that fish is a problematic food for working-class French men because it is "fiddly" and "totally contradicts the masculine way of eating" (p. 190). But in terms of sensory properties or perceptions, it is only the "lightness" of fish that is noted, or the greater interest for the middle classes in the "shape and color" rather than the "consumable substance" of food (p. 196). Thus everything is placed in the abstract oppositions of classification rather than the sensory fullness of experience.

[2] As Borthwick (2000), following Derrida, argues, "In Western thought the division of the senses into categories of objectivity and subjectivity allowed a dialectical process to lift and preserve the objective aspects of the senses to found conceptual knowledge and to devalue what it cancelled, since an immersion in subjectivity cannot found categories of conceptual knowledge. This is especially relevant to taste and smell" (p. 128).

the memorable evocative. In a subsequent article, Stoller & Olkes (2005 [1990]) substantially elaborate their description of the preparation of thin and thick sauces, looking into some of the flavor combinations and the ways that spice and other key ingredients are influenced by seasonality, regional differences, and economic considerations. They also contextualize Djebo's actions within a taste scheme that resonates with Douglas's, in which thin sauces typically express social intimacy and thick sauces formality and the social significance of meal events.

In some ways, Seremetakis's work parallels Stoller & Olkes's because the taste of food, in particular a peach, is used as a kind of revelatory moment (Fernandez 1986) to raise other questions about the senses in anthropology. However, Seremetakis moves considerably further in using this—and other ethnographic and self-reflexive vignettes of drinking a cup of coffee, gathering greens, memories of the tastes and smell of her grandmother's house in the country—to develop an analysis of the relationship of the senses to memory, materiality, modernity, and local epistemologies. She does not elaborate her approach with extended ethnography, but rather, it seems, means her work to be suggestive and provocative. For example, she argues that both material objects such as food and the sense organs (eyes, mouth, etc.) are seen in rural Greece as actively containing and revealing meaning beyond human intention and consciousness: "[T]he sensory is not only encapsulated within the body as an internal capacity or power, but is also dispersed out there on the surface of things as the latter's autonomous characteristics, which then can invade the body as perceptual experience" (Seremetakis 1994, p. 6). Although it is difficult to do justice to Seremetakis's approach in the space of a review article, it should be noted that Seremetakis is one of the first to raise a number of issues developed further below, including the relationship of food and the senses to memory, to synesthesia, and to place-making in the context of state regulatory regimes.

Another suggestive approach is provided by Mintz's extensive writings on sweetness (Mintz 1985, 1996). Although the body of Mintz's work focuses on the political economy of sugar, and he remains attentive to issues of chemical composition and nutritive value, he does not reduce sweetness to the biological, noting that a predisposition toward sweetness "cannot possibly explain differing food systems, degrees of preference, and taxonomies of taste—any more than the anatomy of the so-called organs of speech can 'explain' any particular language" (Mintz 2005 [1985], p. 113). Thus, in tracing the history of sugar in the west, specifically England, the United States, and the Caribbean, he includes extensive discussions of how the taste of sweetness, associated with sugar production, had a distinctive history that altered not only diets and meal practices, but also notions of time, gender and class, senses of self in relation to family, community and labor, and the "locus of desire" (1996, p. 79); indeed, Mintz sees it as at the heart of the European transformations that led to modern consumerist individualism. As he writes, "The first sweetened cup of hot tea to be drunk by an English worker was a significant historical event, because it prefigured the transformation of an entire society, a total remaking of its economic and social basis" (1985, p. 214). Mintz develops these ideas in tracing the relationship of sugar and sweetness to moral ideas. The addictive taste of sugar made it difficult to give up, and, thus, a contentious item of anti-slavery boycott, whereas its taste once again led commentators to suggest it would lead the working classes into idleness and women into other desires and illicit pleasures (1996, pp. 72–76).[3] The use of a particular flavor as a jumping off point for understanding society and its transformations dovetails in interesting ways with Seremetakis's work and also with the concept of "gustemology," which I develop below.

---

[3] Compare Masquelier's (1995) discussion of the illicit pleasures associated with sugar and excessive sweetness as a commentary on contemporary consumption in Niger.

A final precursor to recent work, but one much less cited, is Kuipers's article, "Matters of Taste in Weyewa" (1993 [1984] reprinted in Howes 1991). A linguistic anthropologist, Kuipers explores some of the specific words for taste experience among the Weyewa of highland Sumba, noting a considerably greater diversity than those typical four or five, including words that he translates as "sticky," "soggy," "pungent," "beady," and "fresh." He also notes that many taste experiences do not have particular words except for source identifiers, e.g., "the taste of the mint plant" (1993, p. 545). Kuipers argues that taste terms are always embedded in social and multisensory contexts, making it difficult or pointless to study them in the abstract, as in the equivalent of a Munsell color chart.[4] Like Stoller & Olkes, Kuipers shows the ways that tastes are manipulated in host-guest situations so that bad tastes are used as a marker or as an act of refusal of social intimacy. He raises an important question of what social contexts allow for the use of taste terms, or the discussion of taste, because in Weyewa host-guest interactions it is not considered polite to talk about the taste of food (or other items such as betel and areca nut chew, which are given to guests) while one is consuming it, and any descriptive use of taste terms typically takes place only later, retrospectively. Kuipers also explores the metaphorical use of taste words in ritual contexts to talk about the propitiousness of certain objects and activities: a marriageable girl, or a plantable rice field, or a sacrificial animal are all described as bland to indicate their permissibleness or bitter if they are impermissible. Here these taste terms seem partly to retain and partly to lose their connection to taste experiences because blandness is typically not seen as a good flavor for food, but it takes its meaning in this instance from its opposition to bitterness. The notion of taste terms as descriptive of nonfood experience is further developed below.

These early works on taste, taken together, provide suggestive beginnings for some of the more recent work on food and the senses.[5] They suggest three potential directions for further ethnographic exploration and analysis: (a) the notion of food's sensory qualities as embodied forms of social distinction; (b) the possibility of analyzing a society's key flavor principles and oppositions in ways that suggest combinations different from the familiar salty, sweet, sour, and bitter; and (c) an approach in which taste is central to exploring other aspects of culture. How have these ideas been developed in more recent work?

THE TASTE OF DISTINCTION

Beginning with Bourdieu (see also Goody 1982), a huge literature now explores food as a source and marker of social distinction, but relatively few authors analyze the ways that the senses play into these processes. Some notable exceptions do exist, however. Cowan's work on sweetness in Greece exemplifies the possibilities opened up by such a focus. At once a reflection on the obligatory nature of hospitality in Greece and on changing gendered spaces, Cowan's work is framed by an analysis of the ways that the sweetness of food takes on moral and gendered dimensions in everyday life and neighborly exchanges. Typical afternoon food offered by women to women visitors where Cowan worked in northern Greece includes a several-course delectation of chocolate, spoon sweets (fruits preserved in sugar water), heavily sweetened Turkish/Greek coffee, and a locally produced fruit-flavored liqueur called "the womanly drink" and served in "a richly adorned thin-stemmed glass [of] silver or crystal" (1991, p. 183). As Cowan argues, by ingesting sweet substances, "Sohoian girls and women

---

[4]Indeed, he notes the frustration of some of the few early Torres Straits' researchers (Myers 1904), who complained that Melanesian "natives" could not "perform with accuracy the introspective task of labeling gustatory sensations" based on abstracted flavors such as sucrose, salt, and HCl (Kuipers 1993, p. 539). See also my discussion of synesthesia below.

[5]Even archaeologists, with much less data at hand, have begun to explore the sensory aspects of food (see, e.g., Hamilakis 1999, Joyce & Henderson 2008, Outram 2007).

literally produce themselves as properly feminine persons. Consuming sweets, they do what they 'should' (observe the etiquette of guest-host relations) as well as what they 'want' (since they are thought 'naturally' to desire sweets), a conflation of moral propriety and desire that obscures the coercive aspects of such consumption" (p. 184). Cowan links sweet tastes with sweet feminine dispositions and salty ones with male dispositions, and power with pleasure, suggesting the difficulty of contesting such formulations both because of their "naturalness" and their seeming "triviality" (p. 181).[6]

Another example of hegemonic sensory regimes is Manalansan's (2006) examination of racial and ethnic differences in the context of post-Fordist New York City. Manalansan does not look at tastes of pleasure, but rather at the ways that the smells of food are used to classify, denigrate, and self-exoticize Asian immigrants. While at some level paralleling other work on food and immigrant experiences, Manalansan extends our understanding by focusing on the ways that food smells are stigmatized by a presumed odorless[7] majority population. Odors become such powerful markers because of their sensory properties, in this case their lack of confinement: They do not stay put in kitchens, but mark houses and apartments, clothing and bodies, and thus potentially cross lines of private and public, even potentially marking immigrant neighborhoods as criminalizable as part of New York Mayor Rudolph Giuliani's "quality-of-life" campaign. Thus, Manalansan (2006) notes the embarrassment of a Filipina immigrant at the unexpected visit to her home of her office supervisor after she had cooked *binagoongan*, a pork dish made with fermented shrimp paste: "She reasoned that, at work, she had maintained the respect of her colleagues

through a skillful accumulation of cultural capital, such as having fashionable taste in clothes, speaking seemingly unaccented English and the like. The unexpected visit virtually marked her as an FOB—an ignorant new immigrant 'fresh off the boat'" (p. 46; compare Cantarero & Medina 2000, Jones 2000, Law 2001, Walmsley 2005). Here, notions of distinction and cultural capital, which may be treated as metaphors for taste, are linked to the actual smells of food in the negotiations of everyday life.

Whereas these approaches focus more on the hegemonic use of the senses, others have been interested in tracking the ways that sensory aspects of food do not have to conform to the hegemonic but rather can be releases or escapes from dominant sensory regimes, creating and re-creating identities through sensorily distinct experience and also often drawing on immigrant contexts for their studies. As part of what she calls an alternate "sensory geography," Law (2001) describes the "smellscapes" (compare Low 2005) of Filipina domestics in Hong Kong and how they turn certain public spaces into "sensory landscapes" through sharing home cooking at Sunday picnics in a public square (though watched over by security guards). In my own work on immigrant taste, I consider how alienated Greek migrants "return to the whole" (see Fernandez 1986) through the powerful experiences of taste and smell, encapsulated in such objects as a small vial of olive oil bought at a pharmacy in England (Sutton 2001).[8] In an interesting approach, Lee (2000) collects the stories of elderly first-generation

---

[6]On gendered tastes see e.g., Ritchie (1991, pp. 196–97), Reitz (2007), and a recent theorization of the topic by Hayes-Conroy & Hayes-Conroy (2008).

[7]Or "odor-superior." Manalansan (2006) recounts how a Korean American realtor told his informant to "cook something American such as pot-roast, or even better, apple pie" prior to receiving prospective buyers (p. 47).

[8]A number of scholars have linked food to sensory memory in the context of migration and forced migration both as a balm against alienation and as an active promoter of protest/social change. See Ben-Ze'ev (2004), Choo (2004), Petridou (2001), and further discussion of synesthesia and memory below. One emergent theme is postsocialist nostalgia, showing that food can stand in for other time periods, not just distant places. See e.g., Dunn (2008) on how memories of Soviet tastes drive Georgians to risk botulism in producing their own version of Soviet canned goods, Caldwell (2006) on Soviet restaurant nostalgia, and Lankauskas (2006) on the food nostalgia evoked at a Soviet history museum in Lithuania.

Korean immigrants in Japan who want to eat spicy Kimchee, a strong marker of ethnic difference, but struggle with the gastric troubles it causes them. Lee recounts how one elderly Korean man was "almost apologetic" about his inability to withstand the spicy Korean dishes and his preference for the less spicy, "weaker" Japanese versions. The man explained that after so many years of living in Japan, perhaps his "tongue has changed" (p. 202; see also Ferzacca 2004). This is a rare article in exploring changes in sensory experiences of food, an issue I address further below.

FOOD WORLDS: GUSTEMOLOGIES AND THE SENSES

Anthropologists and other scholars of food have often pointed out the ways in which food is central to cosmologies, worldviews, and ways of life. One interesting extension of such work is to focus on how taste and other sensory experiences of food can become central to such cosmologies, suggesting, in Howes's (2003) formulation, culturally different balances of the senses. As Ritchie (1991), studying Hausa gustatory metaphors, puts it, "different cultures manifest different degrees of 'analytic ability' in different sensory modalities" (p. 192). Taking the lead from Feld's notion of "acoustemology" (Feld 2000) I coin the term gustemology for such approaches[9] that organize their understanding of a wide spectrum of cultural issues around taste and other sensory aspects of food. One intriguing example of such an approach is Farquhar's *Appetites: Food and Sex in Post-Socialist China* (2002). Farquhar's approach is to get at changing subjectivities in China from the Maoist to post-Maoist period. To do so, she develops the notion of a "flavorful temporal formation" as a way of exploring changes in seemingly natural dispositions, emotions, and sensory experiences. In particular, she focuses on the experience of flavors in contemporary Chinese food and herb-based medicine. She says that the different flavors are seen as more than simply peripheral aspects of the medicine, the efficacy of which is found elsewhere; instead, "for a medicine to do anything very complicated it must assault the sufferer with a strong and complex flavor" (2002, p. 63). Thus, flavor has a causal force: "[S]weet herbals build up our overworked spleens" (p. 75).[10] And, "There is no quick, flavorless pill or injection but a whole technology of cooking, tasting and timing as patients wait to feel the results" (p. 70). She then applies these insights about taste to sociopolitical change. In focusing on the connection between bitterness and history, Farquhar describes the ways the concept of suffering in contemporary Chinese literature is termed "eating bitterness" (p. 63). As people experience their changing relations to others and to the Communist Party in relation to their experiences of bitterness, this taste, grounded in their everyday experience of flavor, easily moves between the personal and the political, the contemporary and their memories of "how much bitterness they or their family members have swallowed in the past" (p. 63). Farquhar, thus, does an impressive job of grounding people's changing sense of themselves in relation to larger social forces through their everyday sensory experiences of flavor.[11]

I see Farquhar's approach, despite obvious methodological differences, as similar to Mintz's in focusing on the causal force of a particular flavor and the way this can be found at the very heart of our understanding of society and its transformations. It is interesting to note that Farquhar, like Mintz, focuses on a flavor that borders on the universal. Although she gives historical specificity to bitterness, the

---

[9]Apologies for the mixing of Latin and Greek here, but the strictly Greek "γευmology" would not resonate in English.

[10]Compare Meigs (1984) and Seneviratne (1992) on the ways that food properties are seen to transfer to bodies in different cultural food systems. See also Anderson's (1988) rich description of Chinese food categories.

[11]A number of shorter writings on India are suggestive of this kind of gustemological approach in which not just food but experiences of taste become central to wider experiences of subjectivity, politics, and or/cosmology (see e.g., Appadurai 1981, Pinard 1991, Khare 1992a, Seneviratne 1992).

metaphorical uses of this flavor are instantly recognizable: Ingesting bitter food as a representative of bitter experience can be found in many societies and rituals, not the least of which being the Passover ceremony. The Haggadah makes clear, "These bitter herbs we eat, what is their meaning? Because the Egyptians made the lives of our forebears bitter in Egypt" (cited in Korsmeyer 2005). No doubt similar points could be made about some of the writings on sweetness discussed above. An example of a gustemological approach that challenges the basic tastes in a way similar to Kuipers's is a suggestive piece by Weismantel (2005 [1994]) on the tastes *jayaj* and *mishqui* among the people of Zumbagua, Ecuador. While at first glance corresponding to bitter versus sweet, further examination reveals that *mishqui* can include foods that Weismantel characterized as salty or bland and are considered "tasty." Weismantel shows how these tastes include sensory aspects, but also index male versus female foods, extradomestic versus domestic foods, and foods produced locally through subsistence agriculture versus foods produced through male travel. Like Farquhar, Weismantel (2005) is interested in social change and ties the visceral, sensory aspects of tastes to "the social and economic structures that make consumption possible" (p. 97).

Another approach to gustemology might be found in a number of writings that focus on the sensory aspects of food as part of constructions of senses of place or place-making projects. At a certain level, the attachment of taste to place can be seen as one of the tautologies of food and identity: As one Muscovite young woman explains to the anthropologist, "'People from Russia like Russian tastes'" (Caldwell 2002, p. 307). A number of recent works have begun to unpack these kinds of culinary/sensory sentiments. Trubek's study *The Taste of Place* (2008), which explores the construction of the notion of *terroir* in France, provides the lead here. Trubek defines *terroir* as a "foodview," i.e., a food-centered worldview. She shows how the concept of *terroir*—a taste that is typically naturalized and associated with a specific local place and associated practices

of production and consumption—was, in fact, produced by a particular history of social practices in France over the past two centuries, involving actors such as journalists, writers, chefs, artisans of various stripes, and changing infrastructure and practices such as tourism and rail travel (thus Trubek's approach to taste recalls Mintz, as discussed above). Trubek also usefully contrasts the development of *terroir* in France with specific contexts in the United States (e.g., winemaking in California, niche farming in Vermont) and with an always-encroaching notion of modernity or globalization lurking in the background (compare Seremetakis 1994). Trubek's is the most detailed ethnography of the institutions and practices that shape the ways that taste comes to define place and vice versa (but see also Demossier 2000, Leitch 2000, Leynse 2006, Paxson 2008, Walmsley 2005, and below).

Two innovative methodological approaches to the topic of sensory place-making are provided by Pink (2008) and Marte (2007). Pink takes her cue from phenomenology and from the Slow City movement, which she is studying in a Welsh town, to argue for a "slow ethnography" that involves forms of attention and thick description of the tastes and smells of local coffee shops, farmers' markets, and other places that people walk through and share with others that she sees as "constitutive of place" (2008, p. 181; see also Lemasson 2006). Marte (2007) uses the seemingly more cognitively oriented concept of food maps in discussing the place experience—domestic, public, national, and transnational—of Dominicans and Mexicans in New York City. But she suggests ways to use mapping to explore not only the visual, but also multisensory dimensions of food experience, "mapping" different versions of favorite dishes, mapping side-by-side past and present kitchen spaces, as well as routes taken in search of particular ingredients: "For me, the beauty and productiveness of foodmaps resides in this capacity to encompass so many experiential, representational and geopolitical layers, and still allow one to focus on specific aspects of food relations" (p. 283). Marte's foodmaps would nicely complement Pink's reflexive phenomenology in providing a grounded ethnographic approach to the centrality of the senses in food-based place-making.

If work on *terroir* considers the production of taste through the agricultural production of food, a final suggestive gustemological approach comes from a focus on the production of taste in transforming the raw into the cooked, or the process of cooking in ethnographic works by Adapon in Mexico (2008) and Weiss in Tanzania (1996). Whereas Weiss largely takes his cue from Munn's (1986) concept of value transformations, Adapon adapts Alfred Gell's theory of art and agency (1998) to thinking about cooking, but both works are rare ethnographic treatments of the production of the sensory aspects of cooking as total social facts, or as Adapon (2008) puts it, "an all encompassing social activity" (p. 115; compare Weiss 1996, p. 118).

Weiss's approach is interesting because, while not ignoring other sensory aspects of food, he makes temperature, perceptions, and categorizations of hot and cold, and the different cooking processes involved in producing temperature, central to his understanding of the social life and value transformations of what he calls the "making...of the Haya lived world" (Weiss 1996, title page).[12] Weiss explores, for example, the different ways of cooking bananas (ripening by the hearth, roasting, boiling), both in terms of different notions of temperature and intensity, and how these differences are overlaid with spatial and temporal contrasts, as well as those of gender (men's bananas are cooked slowly by roasting, typically take a long time, and are part of extradomestic circulation). Hot and moist foods are highly valued and typically produced by women through the use of water, a substance associated with women's ability to

"enclose" and transform a "dynamic potential that is then deployed in cooking" (Weiss 1996, p. 89). These distinctions fan out into many domains of Haya sociality, including sexuality [hot spicy foods are said to excite sexual desire, and sexual heat, like cooking heat, can be intense or diffuse (1996, p. 97)], degrees of intimacy, and processes of commoditization [many "hot" foods are seen as commodities rather than domestic staples (133)]. By considering the sensory dimensions of cooking, then, Weiss shows how Haya objectify social values and "construct critical dimensions of themselves and the objective world they inhabit" (p. 126).

Adapon's study explores the agency of Mexican women (and some men) in producing socially valued *sazón* (flavor). Noting that a recipe simply provides a guideline, adjusted by mood and other social factors, she describes the sensory process of cooking as follows: "Ingredients are chosen, touched, and manipulated, assessed by sight, texture and smell, tasted and savored" (2008, p. 16). It is this complex process that makes for the claim that no two cooks ever produce the same flavor, even though they may follow the same recipe and were taught by the same person (p. 21). Adapon's approach becomes more than simply a sensory appreciation of cooking skill, but gustemological in her discussion of cooking as an artwork through which Mexican women's agency is expressed. Without unpacking the details of how Adapon applies Gell's theory and terminology of art to cooking, the author proposes that both the cook and the eater of a meal recognize through a Maussian transfer between people and objects the "social relational matrix surrounding the achievement of flavor and the development of cuisine" (p. 48). Flavor becomes a social agent in itself and food a "trap" (p. 48) through which women can exert power within families and in wider social networks.

SYNESTHETIC CONTRIBUTIONS

Work on food and on the senses has usefully converged through the concept of synesthesia (also spelled synaesthesia), or the union of the

---

[12]Although categories of hot and cold were central staples of structuralist anthropology, often they were not connected in particular to food and not explored experientially but rather as cognitive categories characteristic of certain parts of the world [see Foster (1993) for a review in the context of his theory of the diffusion of humoral medicine].

senses. Synesthesia was implicit in a number of earlier approaches, and it draws into question the western five-sense model (sight, hearing, taste, smell, and touch), making it a useful jumping off point for thinking about other sensory categorizations. Synesthesia also blurs the objectivity and passivity of western sensory models by showing the ways that sensory experience is not simply passively registered but actively created between people.[13] Synesthesia is a reminder of why food and the senses should be considered together: As noted in my discussion of Kuipers, tastes are not separable from the objects being tasted. Bousfield's (1979) writing on the categorization of wine tastes is also a good reminder of this interrelatedness. He argues that when multiple senses and experiences (emotion, sexuality) are used as wine taste descriptors, it is not a matter of assigning names to discrete categories of taste perception: "What is actually happening is that new fields of relationships are being clarified within which a particular taste-experience can be located. The more such relationships can be established for some taste the more it can actually be characterized in its particularity" (1979, p. 201). Finally, synesthesia has been explored as a key to food memories through the notion that memory has multiple interacting sensory registers. These points are summed up by Kirshenblatt-Gimblett (1999): "From color, steam rising, gloss and texture, we infer taste smell and feel.... Taste is something we anticipate and infer from how things look, feel to the hand, smell (outside the mouth), and sound.... Our eyes let us 'taste' food at a distance by activating the sense memories of taste and smell" (p. 3).

Synesthesia is explored in a number of recent ethnographic works. In my own study of food memories in Greece (Sutton 2001), I looked at some of the ways that Kalymnian islanders employed explicit synesthetic metaphors ("listen to that smell") and valued implicit multisensory experiences (Orthodox ritual) in constructing narratives about foods past and making particular ordinary food consumption memorable. As Bousfield's discussion suggests, synesthesia is not a faculty, but rather a socially cultivated skill, developed in particular practices and linguistic devices. And food is often a vehicle for such synesthetic practices. Young (2005), for example, describes the social cultivation of taste-smell-color synesthesia among Pitjantjatjara of the Western Desert of Australia: "Women ask one another, as relatives, holding out an open palm, for a piece of the *kaputu*, the quid or ball of chewed *mingkulpa*, and the quid or part of it passes from mouth to mouth in a mutuality of greenness-taste-odour" (p. 61; compare Seremetakis 1994, p. 26).

A different approach to synesthesia is taken by Meneley. She explores one particular substance—olive oil—from the point of view of some recent approaches to materiality (particularly Keane 2003) to show how "the sensuous qualities of the olive oil itself...lend themselves to participate in larger schemes of value" (Meneley 2008, p. 308). She suggests that the nature of olive oil leads to "synaesthetic bundling," which has led to its use for rubbing on bodies (babies, Olympic athletes), preserving other foods, and taking on the flavors of various herbs and spices, as well as for anointing in Mediterranean religious practices: "Olive oil is a hybrid, sharing qualisigns of preservation that resonate in both the gustatory and spiritual realm" (2008, p. 316). Some of the characteristics of olive oil that she explores and elaborates include its luminosity, immiscibility, liquidity, permeability, cleansing, and warming properties. While recognizing the changing meanings of olive oil as well, especially in the current

---

[13] As Chau (2008, p. 490) rousingly writes, "The process of socializing cannot be done without human sensorial productions of noise, heat, taste, smell, spectacle, etc. (through speaking, shouting, singing, drumming, making music, blasting the speakers, honking, chanting, clapping, dancing, sweating, getting hot, embracing, caressing, cooking, feasting, toasting, bathing, smoking, perfuming, dressing, setting off firecrackers, lighting incense or candles, processing, engaging in games or battles, torturing, etc.). In other words, we sensorialize our world, especially through engaging in intense social activities."

connoisseurship of niche marketing (see Meneley 2007), she argues that starting from these sensory qualities of the oil we can understand why in many different times and places olive oil is not only good to eat, but good to think, and to practice spirituality.

Much of the work cited in this article is at least implicitly synesthetic, recognizing that food is not just taste and smell, but color, texture and temperature. But these explicit considerations of synesthesia remind us that it is both socially cultivated and produced and that some of the distinct material properties of food go beyond the categorization of any five-sense model.

CHANGING TASTES

Whereas changing food habits and cuisines is a staple topic in food studies, once again the sensory aspects of changing tastes are ethnographically underexplored. Rozin & Rozin (2005 [1981]) have written suggestively about the forces of conservation versus boredom in tastes and the influence of socially shaped flavor principles in making innovations acceptable or unacceptable. However, their work is based on social psychology and lacks ethnographic elaboration. Studies of changing taste—while provocative—have, by and large, been speculative about large-scale trends (Haden 2005, Classen et al. 2005 [1994]) or focused on top-down mechanisms, such as official Soviet policies on luxury consumption (Gruknow 2005 [2003]) or Japanese corporate marketing efforts (Cwiertka 2000). Even some of the work discussed above, which takes a historical perspective on taste, tends to be far better at noting change or comparing different periods and to become most fuzzy when it comes to on-the-ground ethnographic observations of mechanisms of change. Wilk's (2006) work on Belizean food is suggestive of ethnographic possibilities, looking at the way Belizean migrant nostalgia and the opening of Belizean restaurants in U.S. cities create a concept of Belizean food in the United States, the taste for which was then imported back to Belize itself: "Just like the brown sugar that had to travel to England for refining, Belizean cuisine was transformed into something much more respectable when the taste came back from abroad" (p. 179).[14]

Two interesting studies examine the role of restaurants in reshaping tastes. Klein (2007) shows how talk about Cantonese cuisine and basic flavor principles allows for the adaption of different ingredients, flavor elements, and regional styles and cooking techniques. Displaying some of the tensions of work on nationalism and the "invention of tradition," Klein argues that nonculinary factors such as regional status hierarchies in China and Hong Kong play a major role in reshaping restaurant food and covering over basic changes in tastes with claims of flavor continuities. Karaosmanoglu (2009), by contrast, shows how the taste of the past is incorporated in restaurants in Istanbul. The past in question is the Ottoman past, and Karaosmanoglu provides a fascinating contrast between high-end restaurants and taverns. In the high-end restaurants, historical research leads to the re-creation of Ottoman dishes, with tastes that customers greet with "astonishment" and "admiration" (p. 347), although these tastes have been somewhat tweaked (less cinnamon, less mixing of salty and sweet) to be acceptable to contemporary palates. In the taverns, by contrast, tastes from the past that have been handed down, apprentice-like from father to son, are preserved in "a modern, middle class setting" so that they will not be "forgotten" (pp. 353–54). Here changes in recipes are more about concerns with global discourses such as health, but in contrast to the high-end restaurants, Ottoman dishes "are defined through a historical continuation and through their

---

[14]Wilk (2006, pp. 105–127) also lays out one of the most extensive schemes for interpreting the ways that foods are localized, describing processes such as "blending," "submersion," "compression," "alternation and promotion." Norton's (2006) work on cultural contact and change in indigenous and European chocolate consumption is suggestive for her focus on taste as sensory and not simply a mode of distinction.

sameness rather than difference. The past is *preserved* rather than *discovered*" (p. 354, emphasis in original). In some ways, this attitude toward the tastes of the past could be captured in Hobsbawm's (1983) distinction between "custom" and "tradition," although Karaosmanoglu sees active invention in both cases.

Finally, a promising approach can be detected in ethnographic studies of the process of taste enculturation, both for children and in niche-marketing/slow-food initiatives. Terrio (2000, p. 40) shows how various French government and food-marketing sources work to reeducate French palates in the proper tasting of chocolate.[15] In particular, Terrio shows how seminars on palate education rely on a wine-tasting model that rewards a vocabulary of distinctions and objectify the five-sense view of perception before suggesting that all the senses come into play in the appreciation of chocolate. What is missing from Terrio's ethnography is how the participants in such a seminar actually take up or refuse such palate retraining. This is where Leynse's work (2006, 2009) with French school children is potentially helpful. Leynse shows the different key settings—classroom, kitchen, dinner table, as well as class trips to vineyards and produce farms—where French children learn cooking skills, skills for talking about food, and the particular categories and modes of sensory appreciation of food. However, she does not see this teaching as a passive enculturation; instead, relying on phenomenological and anthropological approaches to apprenticeship, she indicates some of the ways that these children act back, both through "mistakes and missteps" (2009, p. 15), and potentially incorporate other, contradictory influences in developing practices of taste.

CONCLUSION

Given the worldwide profusion of TV cooking shows, globalized products and ongoing debates about relocalizing food, commoditization of taste distinctions at Starbucks, and even widely reported "new" tastes such as *umami*, it is not surprising that the sensory aspects of food are receiving increased attention in academic scholarship. And although this celebration of food is to be lauded, it should also keep us aware of the politics and economics of food and the potential for our research to fall prey to "Epicureanism" (Holtzman 2006, p. 364). In pursuing our interest in the sensual aspects of food, we should keep our multisensory apparatuses trained on what anthropology has in one way or another always been concerned with: everyday life and the multiple contexts in which the culturally shaped sensory properties and sensory experiences of food are invested with meaning, emotion, memory, and value. In reviewing the literature for this article, it was striking to me that we have moved a long way, theoretically speaking, from the problems of structuralism and other Cartesian approaches to mind and body and outworn dichotomies between the material and the symbolic. The deployment of recent, intertwining approaches from the anthropology of the senses, phenomenology, materiality studies, and theories of value, among others, provides exciting opportunities for rich ethnographic elaboration. And the focus on sensory aspects—experienced like few other things both inside and outside of bodies (and transformed in the crossing of bodily boundaries)—means that these approaches have much to gain from an engagement with food. But our theoretical progress has yet to be matched by any corpus of rich ethnographies that make the sensory aspects of food central to an understanding of lives and experiences; many of the writings on this topic remain in the form of short, suggestive articles or snippets of ethnography in larger works on other topics. In this review I suggest some of the ways that food and the senses could become central ethnographic foci in their own right. Much, indeed, remains to be done.

---

[15]See also Demossier's (2005) ethnography of wine tasting and the creation of wine expertise in France.

DISCLOSURE STATEMENT

The author is not aware of any affiliations, memberships, funding, or financial holdings that might be perceived as affecting the objectivity of this review.

ACKNOWLEDGMENTS

I am grateful for the support of the Department of Anthropology at Southern Illinois University, which provided three excellent research assistants—Kaitlin Fertaly, Katie South, and Qiaoyun Zhang—during the course of writing this article. I could not have done it without you! Thanks also go to a number of people who read outlines, rough drafts, and/or final drafts and offered many helpful suggestions: David Howes, Constance Sutton, Amy Trubek, and Peter Wogan.

LITERATURE CITED

Adapon J. 2008. *Culinary Art and Anthropology*. New York: Berg

Anderson EN. 1988. *The Food of China*. New Haven, CT: Yale Univ. Press

Appadurai A. 1981. Gastro-politics in Hindu South Asia. *Am. Ethnol.* 8:494–511

Ben-Ze'ev E. 2004. The politics of taste and smell: Palestinian rites of return. In *The Politics of Food*, ed. M Lien, B Nerlich, pp. 141–60. Oxford, UK: Berg

Borthwick F. 2000. Olfaction and taste: invasive odours and disappearing objects. *Aust. J. Anthropol.* 11:127–40

Bourdieu P. 1984. *Distinction: A Social Critique of the Judgment of Taste*, transl. R Nice. Cambridge, MA: Harvard Univ. Press. From French

Bourdieu P. 1990. *The Logic of Practice*, transl. R Nice. Stanford, CA: Stanford Univ. Press. From French

Bousfield J. 1979. The world seen as a color chart. In *Classifications in Their Social Context*, ed. RF Ellen, D Reason, pp. 195–220. London: Academic

Caldwell ML. 2002. The taste of nationalism: food politics in postsocialist Moscow. *Ethnos* 67:295–319

Caldwell ML. 2006. Tasting the worlds of yesterday and today: culinary tourism and nostalgia foods in post-Soviet Russia. In *Fast Food/Slow Food: The Cultural Economy of the Global Food System*, ed. R. Wilk, pp. 97–112. Lanham, MD: Altimira

Cantarero L, Medina FX. 2000. Human taste as the expression of sociocultural values. *Bull. Mem. Soc. Anthropol. Paris* 12:351–60

Chau AY. 2008. The sensorial production of the social. *Ethnos* 73:485–504

Choo S. 2004. Eating *satay babi*: sensory perception of transnational movement. *J. Intercult. Stud.* 25:203–13

Classen C, Howes D, Synnott A. 2005 [1994]. Artificial flavours. In Korsmeyer 2005, pp. 337–42

Cowan J. 1991. Going out for coffee? Contesting the grounds of gendered pleasures in everyday sociability. In *Contested Identities: Gender and Kinship in Modern Greece*, ed. P Loizos, E Papataksiarchis, pp. 180–202. Princeton, NJ: Princeton Univ. Press

Cwiertka KJ. 2000. From Yokohama to Amsterdam: Meidi-ya and dietary change in modern Japan. *Japanstudien* 12:45–63

Demossier M. 2000. Culinary heritage and *produits de terroir* in France: food for thought. In *Recollections of France: Memories, Identities and Heritage in Contemporary France*, ed. S Blowen, M Demossier, J Picard, pp. 141–53. Oxford, UK: Berghan

Demossier M. 2005. Consuming wine in France: the wandering drinker and the *vin-anomie*. In *Drinking Cultures: Alcohol and Identity*, ed. T Wilson, pp. 129–54. Oxford, UK: Berg

Douglas M. 1971. Deciphering a meal. In *Myth, Symbol and Culture*, ed. C Geertz, pp. 61–82. New York: Norton

Douglas M. 1982. *In the Active Voice*. London: Routledge

Douglas M, Gross J. 1981. Food and culture: measuring the intricacy of rule systems. *Soc. Sci. Inf.* 20:1–35

Dunn E. 2008. Post-socialist spores: disease, bodies and the state in the Republic of Georgia. *Am Ethnol.* 35:243–58

Farquhar J. 2002. *Appetites: Food and Sex in Postsocialist China*. Durham, NC: Duke Univ. Press

Feld S. 2000. Sound worlds. In *Sound*, ed. P Kruth, H Krobart, pp. 173–200. Cambridge, UK: Cambridge Univ. Press

Fernandez J. 1986. *Persuasions and Performances: The Play of Tropes in Culture*. Bloomington, IN: Indiana Univ. Press

Ferzacca S. 2004. Lived food and judgments of taste at a time of disease. *Med. Anthropol.* 23:41–67

Foster GM. 1993. *Hippocrates' Latin American Legacy: Humoral Medicine in the New World*. Amsterdam: Gordon & Breach

Gell A. 1998. *Art and Agency: An Anthropological Theory*. Oxford: Oxford Univ. Press

Goody J. 1982. *Cooking, Cuisine and Class*. Cambridge, UK: Cambridge Univ. Press

Gruknow J. 2005 [2003]. Champagne and caviar: Soviet kitsch. In Korsmeyer 2005, pp. 249–59

Haden R. 2005. Taste in an age of convenience: from frozen food to meals in the "Matrix." In Korsmeyer 2005, pp. 344–58

Hamilakis Y. 1999. Food technologies/technologies of the body: the social context of wine and oil production and consumption in Bronze Age Crete. *World Archaeol.* 31:38–54

Hayes-Conroy A, Hayes-Conroy J. 2008. Taking back taste: feminism, food and visceral politics. *Gender Place Cult.* 15:461–73

Hobsbawm E. 1983. Introduction: inventing traditions. In *The Invention of Tradition*, ed. E Hobsbawm, T Ranger, pp. 1–14. Cambridge, UK: Cambridge Univ. Press

Holtzman JD. 2006. Food and memory. *Annu. Rev. Anthropol.* 35:361–78

Howes D, ed. 1991. *The Varieties of Sensory Experience*. Toronto: Univ. Tor. Press

Howes D. 2003. *Sensual Relations: Engaging the Senses in Culture and Social Theory*. Ann Arbor, MI: Univ. Michigan Press

Howes D, Lalonde M. 1991. The history of sensibilities. *Dial. Anthropol.* 16:125–35

Jones MO. 2000. What's disgusting, why, and what does it matter? *J. Folk. Res.* 37:53–71

Joyce RA, Henderson JS. 2008. From feasting to cuisine: implications of archaeological research in an early Honduran village. *Am. Anthropol.* 109:642–53

Karaosmanoglu D. 2009. Eating the past: multiple spaces, multiple times—performing "Ottomanness" in Istanbul. *Int. J. Cult. Stud.* 12:339–58

Keane W. 2003. Semiotics and the social analysis of material things. *Lang. Comm.* 23:409–25

Khare RS. 1992a. *Annambrahman*: cultural models, meanings, and aesthetics of Hindu food. In Khare 1992b, pp. 201–20

Khare RS, ed. 1992b. *The Eternal Food: Gastronomic Ideas and Experiences of Hindus and Buddhists*. Albany, NY: State Univ. N. Y. Press

Kirshenblatt-Gimblett B. 1999. Playing to the senses: food as a performance medium. *Perform. Res.* 4:1–30

Klein JA. 2007. Redefining Cantonese cuisine in post-Mao Guangzhou. *Bull. SOAS* 70:511–37

Korsmeyer C, ed. 2005. *The Taste Culture Reader: Experiencing Food and Drink*. Oxford, UK: Berg

Kuipers JC. 1993 [1984]. Matters of taste in Weyewa. *Anthropol. Ling.* 35:538–55

Lalonde M. 1992. Deciphering a meal again, or the anthropology of taste. *Soc. Sci. Inf.* 31:69–86

Lankauskas G. 2006. Souvenirs sensoriels du socialism. *Anthropol. Soc.* 30:45–69

Law L. 2001. Home cooking: Filipino women and geographies of the senses in Hong Kong. *Ecumene* 8:264–83

Lee SS-J. 2000. Dys-appearing tongues and bodily memories: the aging of first-generation resident Koreans in Japan. *Ethos* 28:198–223

Leitch A. 2000. The social life of *lardo*: slow food in fast times. *Asia Pac. J. Anthropol.* 1:103–18

Lemasson J-P. 2006. Le goût et la ville: une difficile rencontre (note de recherché). *Anthropol. Societ.* 30:153–66

Levi-Strauss C. 1983 [1964]. *The Raw and the Cooked: Mythologiques*, Vol. 1, transl. J Weightman, D Weightman. Chicago: Univ. Chicago Press. From French

Leynse WLH. 2006. Journeys through "ingestible topography": socializing the "situated eater" in France. *Eur. Stud.* 22:129–58

Leynse WLH. 2009. *Learning cooking: notes on the cultural parameters of child socialization and cooking in France*. Presented at Annu. Meet. Am. Anthropol. Assoc, 108th, Philadelphia

Low KEY. 2005. Ruminations on smell as a sociocultural phenomenon. *Curr. Soc.* 53:397–417

Manalansan MF. 2006. Immigrant lives and the politics of olfaction in the global city. In *The Smell Culture Reader*, ed. J Drobnick, pp. 41–52. Oxford, UK: Berg

Marte L. 2007. Foodmaps: tracing the boundaries of "home" through food relations. *Food Foodways* 15:261–89

Masquelier A. 1995. Consumption, prostitution and reproduction: the poetics of sweetness in *bori*. *Am. Ethnol.* 22:883–906

Meigs AS. 1984. *Food, Sex, and Pollution: A New Guinea Religion*. New Brunswick, NJ: Rutgers Univ. Press

Meneley A. 2007. Like an extra virgin. *Am. Anthropol.* 109:678–87

Meneley A. 2008. Oleo-signs and quali-signs: the qualities of olive oil. *Ethnos* 73:303–26

Mintz S. 1985. *Sweetness and Power*. New York: Viking Penguin

Mintz S. 1996. *Tasting food, Tasting freedom: Excursions into Eating, Culture, and the Past*. Boston: Beacon

Mintz S. 2005 [1985]. Sweetness and meaning. In Korsmeyer 2005, pp. 110–22

Mintz S, Du Bois C. 2002. The anthropology of food and eating. *Annu. Rev. Anthropol.* 31:99–119

Munn N. 1986. *The Fame of Gawa: A Symbolic Study of Value Transformation in a Massim Papua New Guinea Society*. Cambridge, UK: Cambridge Univ. Press

Myers C. 1904. The taste names of primitivie peoples. *Brit. J. Psychol.* 1:117–26

Norton M. 2006. Tasting empire: chocolate and the European internalization of Mesoamerican aesthetics. *Am. Hist. Rev.* 111:660–91

Outram AK. 2007. Hunter-gatherers and the first farmers: the evolution of taste in prehistory. In *Food: The History of Taste*, ed. P Freedman, pp. 35–61. Berkeley: Univ. Calif. Press

Paxson H. 2008. Post-Pasteurian cultures: the microbiopolitics of raw-milk cheese in the United States. *Cult. Anthropol.* 23:15–47

Petridou E. 2001. The taste of home. In *Home Possessions: Material Culture Behind Closed Doors*, ed. D Miller, pp. 87–104. Oxford, UK: Berg

Pinard S. 1991. A taste of India: on the role of gustation in the Hindu sensorium. In Howes 1991, pp. 221–30

Pink S. 2008. An urban tour: the sensory sociality of ethnographic place-making. *Ethnography* 9:175–96

Reitz JK. 2007. Espresso: a shot of masculinity. *Food Cult. Soc.* 10:7–21

Ritchie I. 1991. Fusion of the faculties: a study of the language of the senses in Hausaland. In Howes 1991, pp. 192–203

Rozin E, Rozin P. 2005. Culinary themes and variations. In Korsmeyer 2005, pp. 34–41

Seneviratne HL. 1992. Food essence and the essence of experience. In Khare 1992b, pp. 179–200

Seremetakis CN, ed. 1994. *The Senses Still: Perception and Memory as Material Culture in Modernity*. Boulder, CO: Westview

Stoller P. 1989. *The Taste of Ethnographic Things: The Senses in Anthropology*. Philadelphia: Univ. Penn. Press

Stoller P, Olkes C. 1989. The taste of ethnographic things. See Stoller 1989, pp. 15–34

Stoller P, Olkes C. 2005 [1990]. Thick sauce: remarks on the social relations of the Songhay, transl. K Hunter. In Korsmeyer 2005, pp. 131–42. From French

Sutton DE. 2001. *Remembrance of Repasts: An Anthropology of Food and Memory*. Oxford, UK: Berg

Terrio SJ. 2000. *Crafting the Culture and History of French Chocolate*. Berkeley: Univ. Calif. Press

Trubek A. 2008. *The Taste of Place: A Cultural Journey into Terroir*. Berkeley: Univ. Calif. Press

Walmsley E. 2005. Race, place and taste: making identities through sensory experience in Ecuador. *Etnofoor* 18:43–60

Weismantel MJ. 2005 [1994]. Tasty meals and bitter gifts. In Korsmeyer 2005, pp. 87–99

Weiss B. 1996. *The Making and Unmaking of the Haya Lived World: Consumption, Commoditization, and Everyday Practice*. Durham, NC: Duke Univ. Press

Wilk R. 2006. *Home Cooking in the Global Village: Caribbean Food from Buccaneers to Ecotourists*. Oxford, UK: Berg

Young D. 2005. The smell of greenness: cultural synaesthesia in the Western Desert. *Etnofoor* 18:61–77

The Anthropology of Credit and Debt

Gustav Peebles

The New School, New York, NY 10011; email: peeblesg@newschool.edu

Annu. Rev. Anthropol. 2010. 39:225–40

First published online as a Review in Advance on June 16, 2010

The *Annual Review of Anthropology* is online at anthro.annualreviews.org

This article's doi:
10.1146/annurev-anthro-090109-133856

Key Words

gift, regulation, time, space, bodies

Abstract

Whether concerned with kinship or with kula, anthropology's interest in credit and debt goes back to the very beginnings of the discipline. Nevertheless, this review dedicates itself primarily to more recent research trends into credit and debt's powerful nature and effects. Following Mauss, credit and debt are treated as an indissoluble dyad that contributes to diverse regulatory mechanisms of sociality, time, space, and the body. Anthropology's overarching contribution to this field of inquiry rotates around its refusal to segregate the moral from the material, seeing the ubiquitous moral debates surrounding credit and debt in various ethnographic settings as coconstitutive of their material effects.

INTRODUCTION

*God forbid that I should be debt-free . . . . all my life
[I have] looked upon debts as the connecting link
between Earth and Heaven, the unique mainstay
of the human race; one, I believe, without which
all mankind would speedily perish . . . . (Rabelais
1955, pp. 295–301)*

When one surveys decades of anthropological literature on credit and debt, an astonishing consistency shines through much of the ethnographic data. Seemingly everywhere that credit and debt are discussed, we find many informants who enunciate a moral stance that credit is considered beneficial and liberating for the creditor (e.g., Nugent 1996, Truitt 2007, Zelizer 1994), whereas indebtedness is more likely to be seen as burdensome and imprisoning for the debtor (e.g., Howe 1998, Lowrey 2006, Taussig 1987). According to this frequently voiced opinion, the former is productive and the latter destructive, which sits in striking contrast with Rabelais's almost Maussian celebration of indebtedness in the epigraph above.[1] This hierarchy between credit and debt is so pervasive that Maine (1866) noticed long ago a deep and sustained favoritism directed toward creditors in many legal systems. In short, a near universal crystallizes out from ethnographic reports, in which local populations describe credit as power and debt as weakness.

Long ago, Mauss (1954) examined the ubiquity of this common belief, and his research led him to develop his now axiomatic paradox regarding credit and debt relations. In *The Gift* (anthropology's foundational text on credit and debt), Mauss asserts that credit and debt greatly contribute to the building of hierarchy and dominance, but they are also the keys to building group solidarity. Malinowski's (1922) evidence that the "handing over of wealth is the expression of the superiority of the giver over the recipient" goes hand-in-hand with

building a cohesive and peaceful trade network still stands as the most famous ethnographic example of this paradox (p. 177). Simmel (1907) made the same point, a contrario, by speaking with such enthusiasm of a future society constituted more by a supposedly freer direct exchange, which would thereby be less colored by the inherently binding domination that he saw in credit and debt relations.

In the years since Mauss's opening salvo in favor of the benefits of debt, careful ethnographic work has lent credence to his notion that credit and debt stand as an inseparable, dyadic unit. As he writes, "[t]he nature and intentions of the contracting parties, the nature of the thing given, are all indivisible (1954, p. 60, see also p. 36). Thus, because debt is always already a dyadic relation that requires its opposite, I henceforth refer to credit/debt rather than trying to distinguish the two, except when working to disentangle the dyad for specific reasons. Although popular understandings of the relationship between credit and debt, as documented by the ethnographers cited here, rely on a hierarchy between the two, anthropology's contribution to this field of inquiry has been not so much in avowing or disavowing the potential legitimacy of this folk theory, but instead in engaging its effects. In some instances, perhaps creditors are socially powerful usurers and debtors are their weak targets, but on other occasions, debtors can be enormously powerful too, as the American Insurance Group revealed to the global public in late 2008. Ethnographic inquiry can hope to clarify such matters, which may be viewed differently by different social parties at different times; indeed, scholars such as Dunn (2004) have even shown us that the same economic resource can be seen as a credit by one owner, but as a debt by a new owner to whom it is transferred.

To explore these matters further, we must first define credit/debt. Bourdieu (1972, pp. 3–9), Guyer (2004), Gell (1992), and Hart (2001), as well as all economists, have insisted that the crucial defining feature of credit/debt is its ability to link the present to the past and the future. As Weber (1922) writes, "The term 'credit' in

---

[1] It is worth noting, however, that this epigraph was voiced by the scoundrel in his text, Panurge, and he was subsequently refuted by the hero, Pantagruel.

the most general sense will be used to designate any exchange of goods presently possessed against the promise of a future transfer of disposal over utilities, no matter what they may be" (p. 81). Seen in this straightforward light, credit is a method of lending concrete resources to an institution or an individual in the present and demanding (or hoping for) a return in the future.

But there is something additionally evocative afoot here for anthropologists. Marx goes so far as to deem credit "fictitious capital" because of its relationship to the speculative future (Marx 1894, p. 595). In this sense, credit/debt can be seen as a method devised for a debtor to borrow speculative resources from his/her own future and transform them into concrete resources to be used in the present (Anderlini & Sabourian 1992, pp. 75–106). For the individual granting the credit, it is the inverse: The creditor is denying him-/herself the use of concrete resources today in exchange for speculative gains in the future. Additionally, for agreements already in motion, credit/debt refers backward to specific actions in the past when an obligation was established. In so doing, contracting parties conjoin their respective futures and pasts, materializing their temporal bond, as it were. This definition of credit/debt as a material link between the past, the present, and the future then has consequences, as shown below, for the regulation and constitution of space and bodies as well. The review is therefore divided into sections addressing social regulation, temporal regulation, spatial regulation, and finally, bodily regulation.

In studying such boundary production and destruction, anthropologists and others have found that Munn's work (1986) has proven particularly inspirational (e.g., Appadurai 1986, Coleman 2004, Foster 1995, Graeber 2001, Harvey 1996, Smith 2008). By relating credit/debt to movement through "spacetime," Munn granted anthropologists a powerful tool for grasping its boundary-building capacity. According to her, credit allowed Gawans to move expansively through spacetime, whereas debt constricted movement in both time and space. Despite this apparent surface dichotomy, Munn clearly treats credit/debt as a Hegelian dialectical relation that creates a regulatory dynamic of "intersubjective spacetime" (e.g., 1986, pp. 63–67). In this model, debt only appears to be constrictive, whereas it is, in fact, equally as generative as credit for the entire movement of the kula ring.

Increasingly, scholars have also been questioning the common hierarchy of credit/debt by taking inspiration from such figures as Bataille (1991), insisting that debt might just as easily be represented as beneficial, and credit a hazard. Thomas (1991), Keane (1997), and Coronil (1997) stand as some of those who are following a general trend encapsulated by Roitman's (2005) helpful formulation of "the productivity of debt." In deeply pursuing the question of how debt might, on occasion, function as a form of abundance instead of lack, Roitman shows how extensive ethnographic data can complicate the standard narratives handed down to us from Adam Smith and his fellow theorists of parsimony. She carefully notes the distinction between "sanctioned" and "unsanctioned" wealth and how these interrelate with one another to "legitimate a system of exclusion and inclusion" (Roitman 2005, p. 84). As for credit, separate contributions by Akin (1999) and Brison (1999) in Akin & Robbins's (1999) much cited collection provide us with equally fascinating instances of the perils of being a lender.

Strathern has argued convincingly that yet another pillar of the popular understanding within many societies of credit/debt must be challenged. According to her, it is vital to attend to the manner in which debts are pushed on debtors by excited creditors. In this assessment, debtors are not necessarily needy; rather, new needs are created to promote the need for new debts (Strathern 1992, pp. 169–91). Masquelier (1997) and Williams (2004) attest to the validity of this insight, by showing the ways in which a sort of predatory lending might manifest itself in widely diverse situations. Even the evidence from Parry's (1986) influential paper and Raheja's (1988) pathbreaking effort in *The*

Poison of the Gift might usefully be viewed in this light, where Gujars carrying "dan" are hoping to gift it to less-than-thrilled future debtors. Long ago, Murphy & Steward (1956) asserted that the colonial trading post might well have a universal capacity to pull people out of traditional life by allowing "the Indian to buy beyond his means" (p. 347). And, of course, Strathern's commentary seems even more convincing today, after America's infamous subprime-lending crisis, which witnessed countless banks and brokers convincing people who could ill afford loans to take them nevertheless.

Works such as these allow us to see that anthropology has focused on the manner in which credit/debt as a dyadic unit helps to determine who stands inside and outside of community borders or who stands above or below (Gudeman 2001). Credit/debt's role in the actual movement of economic resources helps accomplish this, but so too do the constant negotiation and positioning over the morality/immorality/amorality of the dyad itself. Thus it is not only the economic effects of credit/debt that gives it its immensely powerful capacity to construct and destroy community borders or build social hierarchy. It is also the interminable debate about credit/debt itself, what Roitman (2005, p. 73) crisply refers to as the "strategic stance" that we can watch unfold as people position themselves within the economic and moral spectrum of credit/debt relations.

SOCIAL BOUNDARIES

Motives for accumulating economic value (a prerequisite for credit/debt) can vary, as Weber famously pointed out in *The Protestant Ethic and the Spirit of Capitalism* (1905). Since then, anthropologists have been quite adept at attending to the variant modalities and motives of economic storage (or its lack) and its consequent disbursal via credit/debt. Indeed, we have developed a technical vocabulary that can be easily misused by the nonspecialist. Terms of art such as "sharing" (Woodburn 1982),

"reciprocity" (Mauss 1954), "generalized"[2] and "restricted" exchange (Lévi-Strauss 1949, Sahlins 1972), "transfers" (Hunt 2002), and "enactions" (Sneath 2006) all reflect our methodological insistence that the movement of economic resources through time and space via the mechanism of credit/debt cannot be merely reduced to "economic rationality" or "self-maximization." Anthropologists consistently seek out the flow of credit/debt in modalities outside the standard market for such instruments (Firth & Yamey 1964, Gudeman 2001, Gudeman & Rivera 1990, Spyer 1997).

In any discussion concerning anthropology's search for the noneconomic explanations of economic accumulation, the highly regarded work of Weiner (1992) must be mentioned. Weiner convincingly asserts that an "inalienable possession" motivates the circulation of lesser valuables in a credit/debt relationship among exchange partners. One party to the relationship tries to seize the immobile valuable, while the other attempts to hold onto it. In so doing, she focused on how a relative spectrum of alienability allowed for the materialization of social hierarchy to precipitate out of the evident flow of credit/debt. Weiner's focus on the special material objects that creditors withhold as signs of power inspired many ethnographers to look carefully for similar items held outside of the typical credit/debt nexus (e.g., Godelier 1999, and the articles assembled in Myers 2001 represent excellent examples of this notion).

Following a slightly different strain in Mauss's text, much recent work has started to look at the market itself as a place that creates credit/debt bonds between people, even though it is supposedly organized to liquidate trades immediately. For example, Zaloom shows how men on the trading floor (the allegedly callous market incarnated in living form) manage to reinsert the morality of social obligations into Simmel's tit-for-tat trades. She

---

[2]Complicating matters, Lévi-Strauss 1949 and Sahlins 1972 knowingly offer different definitions of generalized exchange.

quotes one trader who sounds almost to be reciting Bourdieu's analysis of the misrecognition inherent in all gift exchange (see also Derrida 1992): "There isn't any quid pro quo. But of course a local will be more willing to do things that would seem on the surface to be irrational...on the understanding or on the belief that later this human being he's trading with will remember" (Zaloom 2006, p. 100). He goes on to explain how one trading partner knowingly carried a loss for him. Zaloom asserts that, "by doing so, he strengthened his relationship of reciprocity with the broker" (Zaloom 2006, p. 100; see also Garsten & Lindh de Montoya 2004, Yanagisako 2002).

Considering important research findings such as these, we need no longer hew so closely to an ideal-typical dichotomy between "gifts and commodities," wherein the former "establishes personal qualitative relationships between subjects transacting," whereas the latter "establishes objective quantitative relationships between objects transacted" (Gregory 1982, p. 41). A full update of the extensive gift-commodity debate is not possible here, but Gell (1992), Miller (1995), Myers (2001), and Robbins (2009) all cover its history more than amply. In a similar vein, Sykes (2005) provides a critique of anthropology itself by way of a careful examination of our theories of the gift.

Rather, regardless of whether the resources transferred are commodities or gifts, an attachment among the creditor, the debtor, and the resources remains, and this is surely one of the defining features of credit/debt. Instead, the main ideal-typical distinction between gifts and standard market forms of credit/debt may be a Graeberian (Graeber 2001) one: As Mauss knew well, they are both transferring resources across the spectrum of time, but the gift "contract" is silent and invisible (or "misrecognized"), whereas the commodity contract is enunciated and visible (for an illuminating study of written contracts, see Alexander 2001). But we should not assume, ipso facto, that this translates into gifts being a better or somehow more moral form of social glue than commodities.

In fact, recent nationwide and global market crises starkly remind us of the lack of alienation between people and things in commoditized credit/debt relations. Certainly, the original creditor or debtor may have become alienated from the products on the basis of their initial exchange (Carrier 1995, Marx 1894), but that does not mean that the product is itself alienated from all humanity, a mere floating and free signifier unattached to all social life (see Shipton 2009, p. 15, for a discussion of how this is not merely a trait of "fast capitalism"). In the global credit crunch, we learned by hard experience that even depersonalized debt (LiPuma & Lee 2004) eventually comes due; the citizenry of the nation-state suddenly discovers, to its chagrin, its nonalienated attachment to debt instruments that it may not even have contractually initiated. Ethnographic examples of related processes are depicted in Coronil (1997), Peebles (2004), Song (2009), and Verdery (1996).[3]

Such instances are actually part of a wider field of inquiry that could be called the socialization of debt, which has been covered in the anthropological record but has not had a great impact on analyses of capitalist credit/debt, even though the phenomenon (known as bankruptcy in capitalist economies) is central to its functioning. For example, Battaglia (1992) provides an evocative description of intergenerational debt forgiveness, whereas Verdery (2003) details the tragic ways in which collective debt is foisted onto individuals while corporations accrue previously collective credit unto themselves. When is credit/debt bequeathable, and when is this practice looked on with horror? Is the debtor a thief or a victim? Is the

---

[3]The large literature on the credit theory of money (which sees money itself as a form of debt) problematizes any claims to a strict separation between direct exchange and credit/debt. Nevertheless, this review article follows the distinction laid out by Mauss and Simmel, restricting the definition of credit and debt relations to economic relations extending over time, whereas money can also be exchanged immediately, precisely so as to avoid the enduring bonds of credit/debt. For a review of the anthropological literature on money, see Maurer's (2006a) thought-provoking and exhaustive recent review in this same journal series.

creditor a miser or a benefactor? Who is protected by the "moral hazard" (as economists call it) of debt forgiveness, and who is permitted to accrue largesse? Nugent (1996), for example, powerfully reminds us of the potentially dangerous outgrowth of such boundaries, wherein entire ethnic groups associated with credit can be labeled villainous by a given population. Such moments wherein credit/debt becomes affixed to individuals or collectivities, and moves between them, allows us to witness the inscription of social boundaries of inclusion, exclusion, hierarchy, and equality (Elyachar 2005, Foster 1995, Greenberg 1995, Verdery & Humphrey 2004).

TEMPORAL BOUNDARIES

In an ideal world, both creditor and debtor are pleased with an agreement that allows for the expansion of economic value for every party involved. But people can also become trapped in a vicious cycle of debt, from which they cannot escape, as Dudley (2000) and Williams (2004) document all too vividly. Weber (1905) might have considered this a variant of his notion of the "iron cage," wherein people are shoehorned into a new future-orientation from their previously present-oriented "economic traditionalism" (pp. 36, 191). Marx (e.g., 1990, p. 342) would likewise proclaim it as an example of living labor's enslavement to dead labor. However, ethnographers can equally point to instances in which debt is seen as a sort of blessing rather than a trap. After providing an illuminating description of the circulation of coins in a village in Mexico, Eiss (2002) explains that laboring to pay back a "sacred debt to the Virgin. . .[brings] value, honor, and grace to their pueblo" (p. 322). Whether good or bad, all these instances show that credit/debt can weld people to particular temporal regimes as people labor to build the increment demanded by the future in exchange for actions in the past.

With credit/debt relations, then, the projection toward the future is critical. Indeed, this notion has long been the transparent dividing line between barter and credit/debt. As

Humphrey & Hugh-Jones (1992) document, for centuries many theorists have alleged that barter cannot create any lasting social ties precisely because of its lack of a temporal horizon. In this narrative, barter is seen as a refusal to enter into credit/debt relations; in a seminal article, Hart (1986) argued that barter thereby serves as a sort of index of the instability or nonexistence of political regimes. Although Humphrey & Hugh-Jones (1992) have critiqued this claim in their benchmark text on barter, they still maintain that barter carries a "relative freedom and [egalitarian] balance" over credit/debt (p. 18; see also Caldwell 2004, Mayer 2001).

Building on Woodburn's (1982) important discussion of "immediate-return" versus "delayed-return" societies, Day et al. (1999) have provided us with a very helpful model for addressing this relationship among time, freedom, and hierarchy. The authors in their volume find that marginalized groups will often flee the compulsion of credit/debt; they do so by constructing a world constituted by abundance. When the world is constituted by plenitude, there is no reason to sacrifice consumption today to better secure tomorrow. There is little reason to engage in credit/debt relations, and their denial of these constitutes a declaration of sovereignty. Brown's (1959) almost pathological search for a liberated, "debtless man" can also be seen as an extreme incarnation of this drive for sovereignty (see also Simmel 1907). Similarly, evidence that some communities mistrust standard banking institutions might also be read as a desire to refuse the binding ties of credit/debt with faceless outsiders and thereby retain sovereignty over their own futures (Elyachar 2003).

Taking these texts together, one could readily imagine a broader interest on the part of anthropologists in connecting the issue of credit/debt with the current interest in sovereignty. And indeed, several people are working in that direction (e.g., Cattelino 2008, Roitman 2007). In fact, Kelly & Kaplan (2001) and Miyazaki (2005) have carried on a highly germane debate about the acceptance and refusal of gifts and how this relates to vital questions of sovereignty. From this literature we learn, among other things, that noticing the emphatic rejection of credit/debt relations is as ethnographically significant as noticing their embrace.

Contrariwise, Comaroff & Comaroff (1990), Ferguson (1990), and Parry & Bloch (1989) have all explored the productive interface between direct exchange and long-term credit/debt. Rather than seeing them as mutually exclusive, these authors show how the negotiation between the two relates to intragroup solidarity and fission. Parry & Bloch (1989) provide a succinct programmatic statement on this matter, whereas the Comaroffs and Ferguson provide clear and convincing examples (so too do the contributors to Parry & Bloch's book). In studying cattle in southern Africa, both the Comaroffs and Ferguson discovered that people did not exclusively position themselves in some scalar competition to acquire the most cattle, but instead embroiled themselves in a discussion over the very question of whether cattle (credit/debt) or cash (direct exchange) should be the basis of society's wealth creation, storage, and disbursal.

If much scholarship has revolved around the way credit/debt binds the present to the future, we must also attend to the way in which it binds the present to the past (see Hart 2001). Most recently, Shipton has shone a very serious light on this matter in the form of a planned trilogy of ethnographic books, two of which have been published to date (Shipton 2007, 2009). Whereas Shipton shows how the ancestors (via graves) are quite literally related to the ownership of land, authors such as Chu and Kwon have investigated the "ghost money" traditions that we often find in Asia (Chu 2010, Kwon 2007). Chu speaks of "cosmic debt," whereas Kwon (2007) informs us that ancient Vietnamese tradition viewed life itself as a type of bank loan: "In old Chinese belief, every birth to this world was based on the allowance of a loan from 'the Treasury of the Other world,' or 'the Bank of Hell'" (p. 77). He tells us that "the postmortem immolation of wealth, real

or symbolic, was almost a legally binding act of debt payment...in ancient China" (Kwon 2007, p. 77). The practices described by Chu, Kwon, and Shipton also readily remind one of the frequent appearance of credit/debt relationships with ancestors that has been so well documented in Melanesia and elsewhere (e.g., Klima 2002, Lambek 2001, Strathern 1988).

Finally, any discussion of credit/debt's ability to contribute to the social mediation and understanding of time would be incomplete if we were to neglect the issue of interest and usury. Gregory's (1997) highly counterintuitive assessment of usury in India (and simultaneous indictment of the World Bank) represents an exciting incursion into the literature. Maurer perhaps stands as the anthropologist who has covered this most extensively and most assiduously. In his work, ranging from offshore finance (2007) to Islamic banking to local currencies (2005), he has covered the nature of interest/usury in great detail. His recent book, *Pious Property* (2006b), presciently provides an insightful and much needed journey through the history of the mortgage (many people's most intimate daily relationship with interest) as a social institution.

Some recent work also attempts to make sense of typically macrolevel objects of analysis related to the study of interest—such as the credit market, the national debt, or the yield curve—via microlevel theories from anthropology. Holmes (2009), Holmes & Marcus (2005), Knorr Cetina & Bruegger (2002), Peebles (2008), Poon (2009), Riles (2006), and Zaloom (2009) all study the production of certain financial techniques and how they represent attempts to govern a given public's shared future. Many of these efforts have been at least partly inspired by Callon's work on the performativity of economics (e.g., Callon 2007).

As anthropological research into the question of interest/usury continues, studies of both microcredit/microfinance, Islamic finance, and local currencies (many, but not all, local currencies proscribe lending at interest) will become increasingly more common. For example, despite celebrations of microcredit/microfinance in the popular media, some ethnographers have noted that its perceived benefits are not always delivered (Elyachar 2005, Lont & Hospes 2004, Moodie 2008, Rahman 1999). Meanwhile, envisioning credit/debt as a socially binding force even when interest is absent (or at 0%, as in Japan between 2001–2006) makes both Islamic finance and the local currency movements fascinating case studies for much of the anthropological theory discussed here (Hart 2001, Maurer 2005).

SPATIAL REGULATION

For interest payments to be collected, there must be either a regulatory authority or a common bond of trust that enforces it. This precondition represents one way in which credit/debt brings together temporal and spatial regulation. Explorations of spatial boundary building and maintenance lead us into the immense literature spawned out of Sahlins's (1972) masterful *Stone Age Economics*. In this text, he famously connects morality, modes of exchange, and spatiality. Inspired by Malinowski's (1922, pp. 177–94) spectrum of possible economic transfers, as well as work by Polanyi (1944), Sahlins considered free gifts, seizure, and everything in between. He writes, "the span of social distance between those who exchange conditions the mode of exchange," wherein enemies suffer theft, strangers tolerate higgling commercialism, and kin and neighbors expect fair and binding credit/debt relations (1972, p. 196). In this model, theft represents an attempt by one party to break the credit/debt dyad by seizing the credit while disavowing the debt. We have here an elegant model for addressing much that remains exciting to scholars today, and one could safely say that many of the authors cited in this review have been at least partly inspired by Sahlins's work.

That said, Zelizer's (1994) groundbreaking evidence of brazen seizure within the nuclear American family makes Sahlins's stimulating effort seem overly schematic. Truitt's sad recounting of the exchange of friendship for loaned money in Vietnam equally calls it into question (Truitt 2007). By ethnographically documenting zones where theft becomes standardized, Roitman (2006) similarly problematizes Sahlins's model for us. She demonstrates that anthropologists cannot take for granted normative claims about the morality of illegal versus legal behavior because illegality has its own rationality that is "both economically strategic and socially productive" (Roitman 2006, p. 264).

Thankfully, Guyer (2004) solves some of these potential shortcomings by providing us with a thoughtful and inspiring rereading of Bohannan's (1955) Polanyian "spheres of exchange" argument.[4] In so doing, she manages to hone our ability to connect credit/debt with the production and regulation of space. Allowing that Bohannan himself thought of "conversions" across spheres as a form of "investment" (i.e., a credit/debt relation), Guyer then points out that "[w]ithout questioning Bohannan's ethnography at all, one can simply lift off the boundedness of the model and connect each sphere to its regional trading networks, to see not barriers but institutions that facilitated asymmetrical exchanges across value registers" (Guyer 2004, p. 28).

In this reading, Bohannon's spheres of exchange take on relevance well outside their normal bailiwick in traditional societies. For example, the sumptuary laws of any governing regime—state or nonstate—can now be seen as attempts to constrain and channel the flow of credit/debt spatially. Many other regulatory mechanisms of credit/debt, such as "rationing" (Guyer 2004, Ledeneva 1998), could be added to this list. Guyer's book can be seen as part of an already growing literature that questions a strict dichotomy between the informal and the formal sectors; instead of formal and informal, we see "tournaments of value" (Appadurai 1986) as well as cooperation among state and nonstate regulatory regimes. Seen in this light,

---

[4]Guyer's book is the result of decades of research and has been so influential that it merited a special edited volume with many timely articles addressing its central themes in *The African Studies Review* (Guyer 2007).

Roitman's (2005) description of a "pluralization of regulatory authority" for all economic transactions may be apt well outside of the Chad Basin.

This work, and others like it, brings to light credit/debt's role in place-making, by connecting it with issues of routinization and the building of consistent transactional pathways and networks (Lowrey 2006, Myers 2000, Nugent 1996, Shipton 2009). We can witness, for example, how places are drawn together via remittances (Buggenhagen 2004, Hernandez & Coutin 2006). But it is also fascinating to pay careful attention to modes of savings and modes of disbursal of these savings, as many ethnographers have done (e.g., Caldwell 2004, Gudeman & Rivera 1990, Maurer 2007, Mayer 2001, Ong 1999, Shipton 1995, Verdery 1996).

Of course, matters of credit/debt relations need not be confined to small communities, and much work within anthropology has considered the role of credit/debt in international or regional systems ever since the vast, interethnic system of the kula was investigated. For example, some anthropologists have provided important discussions of the role of credit/debt for the creation of the colonial system (van Binsbergen & Geschiere 2005, Thomas 1991; see also Stiansen & Guyer 1999 for a discussion of the impact of credit/debt on shifts in temporal reckoning in colonial spaces). Even outside a classic colonial power structure, others have highlighted the colonizing capacity that results from clashing regimes of credit/debt or the international movement of gifts (Gregory 1997, Mandel & Humphrey 2002, Mitchell 2002, Pedersen 2002, Rausing 1997).

Scholars such as Elyachar (2003, 2005, 2006) and Ferguson (1990) have provided influential studies of international movements of credit/debt in the form of states and international organizations that attempt to provide development aid and to solve third-world debt crises with "structural adjustment programs" (see also Smith 2008). As opposed to its movement via such international aid operations, Arrighi (1994), Cronon (1991), Harvey (1990), and Leyshon and Thrift (1997) are all well known for offering macrolevel descriptions of the transformative power of capitalist credit/debt when it moves via profit-oriented banking mechanisms into previously noncapitalist spaces. A history of today's international debt system, so critical to understanding the macrolevel issues afoot in these varied ethnographic settings, can be found in Locke & Ahmadi-Esfahani (1998).

OF BODIES INDIVIDUAL AND NATIONAL

Anthropology may be uniquely situated to insist continually on the relationship between credit/debt and the body. This relationship was developed by Nietzsche (1887), but it was greatly elaborated on by people such as Simmel (1907), Deleuze & Guattari (1972), Brown (1959), and Pietz (1997), all of whom insist on the correlation between debt and bodily punishment. But in some ways, we have little need for a rich philosophical tradition on which to build our claims because we have such an extensive ethnographic one. For example, Chu (2010) inspires us to look very carefully at the intertwinings of credit/debt and bodies by investigating the transnational flow of Chinese migrants, and the debt-slavery into which they enter in their continual efforts to emigrate, not altogether unlike America's old system of indentured servitude (other texts that discuss debt peonage include Dore 2006, Sykes 2005, and Taussig 1987).

While building on Munn's idea that bodies with credit can move through spacetime and bodies in debt are constricted in this same realm, Graeber (2001) has added to this literature on bodies by illuminating the role of visible versus invisible bodily powers and adornment. Leyshon & Thrift (1999) have recently focused on the rise of credit scoring, and thus, the manner in which individual bodies become expressly labeled as either good or bad risks for the banking industry. Finally, Lévi-Strauss (1949) asserted that the bodies of women were traded by men in vast systems of credit/debt that built entire societies. Needless to say, many contested both his empirical and theoretical claims, but considering the flow of living bodies as part of a system that builds enduring relations of credit/debt remains important in the study of kinship (e.g., Hirsch & Strathern 2004; Strathern 1988, 2005).

Finally, the burgeoning globalized trade in human organs or blood, as well as compensation claims based on bodily injury, has become an important object of ethnographic study (Cohen 1999, Copeman 2005, Kirsch 2001, Leach 2005, Ralph 2009, Scheper-Hughes 2000). When body parts are given as gifts, the exchange is seen as moral, but such trades are broadly lambasted when seen as part of a direct exchange.[5] Any future challenges to Mauss's claim that credit/debt builds lasting social ties whereas direct exchange threatens to dissolve them will need to contend with the compelling evidence from these studies.

Relating to the study of bodies, one might say that anthropologists have been contributing to the gradual unraveling of the Lockean tradition that has always projected a straightforward bifurcation between person and object, just as we have worked against separating the credit/debt dyad. Greatly influenced by the pioneering efforts of Strathern, and more recently Latour, anthropologists have shown that the boundary between bodies and objects is much more fluid than the western rationalist tradition of property rights has assumed. Recent research that continues this critique of the universalist pretensions of western theories of property necessarily complicates our standard notion of credit/debt and the spectrum of alienability facilitated by it (Hann 1998, Hirsch & Strathern 2004, Keane 1997, Kirsch 2004, Myers 2001, Pottage & Mundy 2004, Strathern 1988, Thomas 1991, Verdery 2003).

This focus on bodies has gradually expanded, impelling researchers to investigate the capacity of credit/debt to integrate individuals with the corporate body that is the nation-state. Whereas Brantlinger calls "public credit...an ideological, economic corollary of nationalism" (Brantlinger 1996, p. 29), Song (2009) illuminates the manner in which national prestige is tied up with successful national debt payments. In his study of gambling in Greek coffee houses, Papataxiarchis (1999) reveals the fascinating way in which Greeks transfigure their state so as to imagine it as a spendthrift, dappling free gifts on its citizens that need no return. In all cases, we learn not only that citizens and subjects rely on an idiom of credit/debt to become deeply attached to their nation-state, but also that states and citizens are socially constructed, in part, out of the reciprocal flow of material resources between national and individual bodies. Via credit/debt, then, an almost visceral connection between the well-being of the individual body and the national body is reified and reinforced in daily practice.

CONCLUSION

Taking all this research together, we see that the ethnographic task over many years has been to study how the credit/debt nexus is productive of social ties, allegiances, enmities, and hostilities, rather than to make normative pronouncements concerning whether credit is liberating and debt is debilitating. The endless positioning of different social parties within the field of credit/debt is itself ethnographic data, rather than true evidence of one party's upstanding moral rectitude and another's moral lapse. Considering this viewpoint, the history of anthropological study of credit/debt reveals the benefits of not separating the economic effects of credit/debt from the moral debates over it. By contributing to the construction of boundaries of exclusion, inclusion, and hierarchy, the moral tensions and asymmetries that reside within the indissoluble dyad of credit/debt are themselves elemental in helping to generate the specific material effects of credit/debt that unfold in any given ethnographic setting—the material effects that are so privileged in studies by economists.

---

[5] Sharp (2000) offers us a comprehensive review of the literature revolving around the commoditization of the body, although this literature has grown significantly in the past decade.

By providing ethnographies of the dense interlinkages among individual, family, state, and international systems, anthropologists have continually shown an ability to illuminate critical aspects of credit/debt relations that are lost if one turns only to this economics literature studying material effects. Thus, we should be on guard against schematized disciplinary boundaries that attempt to segregate the material (economics) and the moral (anthropology) into two distinct modes of inquiry, rather than seeing them as coconstitutive. As the work reviewed here attests, the anthropological corpus does not, in truth, fit into any such a schematized narrative. Instead, led by Guyer, Hart, Munn, Strathern, and many others, anthropological research on credit/debt can and should spread beyond the discipline, helping to improve not only all social scientists' understanding of the indissoluble dyad, but also our relations with other disciplines with whom we should be engaged in cohesive, long-term exchanges.

DISCLOSURE STATEMENT

The author is not aware of any affiliations, memberships, funding, or financial holdings that might be perceived as affecting the objectivity of this review.

ACKNOWLEDGMENTS

I am grateful to Gabriella Coleman, Michael Ralph, Janet Roitman, Caitlin Zaloom, and most especially, Julienne Obadia for their substantive and editorial advice and critiques as this article gradually came to fruition. All remaining errors are my own.

LITERATURE CITED

Akin D. 1999. Cash and shell money in Kwaio, Solomon Islands. See Akin & Robbins 1999, pp. 103–30

Akin D, Robbins J, eds. 1999. *Money and Modernity: State and Local Currencies in Melanesia.* Pittsburgh, PA: Univ. Pittsburgh Press

Alexander C. 2001. Legal and binding: time, change and long-term transactions. *J. R. Anthropol. Inst.* 7(3):467–85

Anderlini L, Sabourian H. 1992. Some notes on the economics of barter, money and credit. See Humphrey & Hugh-Jones 1992, pp. 75–106

Appadurai A, ed. 1986. *The Social Life of Things: Commodities in Cultural Perspective.* Cambridge, UK: Cambridge Univ. Press

Arrighi G. 1994. *The Long Twentieth Century: Money, Power, and the Origins of Our Times.* New York: Verso

Bataille G. 1991. *The Accursed Share: An Essay on General Economy*, Vol. I, transl. R Hurley. New York: Zone Books. From French

Battaglia D. 1992. The body in the gift: memory and forgetting in Sabarl mortuary exchange. *Am. Ethnol.* 19(1):3–18

Bohannan P. 1955. Some principles of exchange and investment among the Tiv. *Am. Anthropol.* 57:60–70

Bourdieu P. 1977 [1972]. *Outline of a Theory of Practice*, transl. R Nice. Cambridge, UK: Cambridge Univ. Press. From French

Brantlinger P. 1996. *Fictions of State: Culture and Credit in Britain.* Ithaca, NY: Cornell Univ. Press

Brison K. 1999. Money and the morality of exchange among the Kwanga, East Sepik Province, Papua New Guinea. See Akin & Robbins 1999, pp. 151–63

Brown NO. 1959. *Life Against Death: The Psychoanalytical Meaning of History.* Middletown, CT: Wesleyan Univ. Press

Buggenhagen BA. 2004. Domestic object(ion)s: the Senegalese murid trade diaspora and the politics of marriage payments, love, and state privatization. In *Producing African Futures: Ritual and Reproduction in a Neoliberal Age*, ed. B Weiss, pp. 21–53. Leiden: Brill

Caldwell ML. 2004. *Not By Bread Alone: Social Support in the New Russia*. Berkeley: Univ. Calif. Press

Callon M. 2007. What does it mean to say that economics is performative? In *Do Economists Make Markets? On the Performativity of Economics*, ed. D Mackenzie, F Muniesa, L Siu, pp. 311–57. Princeton, NJ: Princeton Univ. Press

Carrier JG. 1995. *Gifts and Commodities: Exchange and Western Capitalism Since 1700*. New York: Routledge

Cattelino JR. 2008. *High Stakes: Florida Seminole Gaming And Sovereignty*. Durham, NC: Duke Univ. Press

Chu JY. 2010. *Cosmologies of Credit: Transnational Mobility and the Politics of Destination in China*. Durham, NC: Duke Univ. Press. In press

Cohen L. 1999. Where it hurts: Indian material for an ethics of organ transplantation. *Daedalus* 128(4):135–65

Coleman S. 2004. The charismatic gift. *J. R. Anthropol. Inst.* 10(2):421–42

Comaroff J, Comaroff JL. 1990. Goodly beasts, beastly goods: cattle and commodities in a South African context. *Am. Ethnol.* 17(2):195–216

Copeman J. 2005. Veinglory: exploring processes of blood transfer between persons. *J. R. Anthropol. Inst.* 11(3):465–85

Coronil F. 1997. *The Magical State: Nature, Money, and Modernity in Venezuela*. Chicago: Univ. Chicago Press

Cronon W. 1991. *Nature's Metropolis: Chicago and the Great West*. New York: W.W. Norton

Day S, Papataxiarchis E, Stewart M, eds. 1999. *Consider the Lilies of the Field: Marginal People Who Live for the Moment*. Boulder, CO: Westview

Deleuze G, Guattari F. 1983 [1972]. *Anti-Oedipus: Capitalism and Schizophrenia*, transl. R Hurley, M Seem, HR Lane. Minneapolis: Univ. Minn. Press. From French

Derrida J. 1992. *Given Time: I. Counterfeit Money*, transl. P Kamuf. Chicago: Univ. Chicago Press. From French

Dore E. 2006. *Myths of Modernity: Peonage and Patriarchy in Nicaragua*. Durham, NC: Duke Univ. Press

Dudley KM. 2000. *Debt and Dispossession: Farm Loss in America's Heartland*. Chicago: Univ. Chicago Press

Dunn EC. 2004. *Privatizing Poland: Baby Food, Big Business, and the Remaking of Labor*. Ithaca, NY: Cornell Univ. Press

Eiss PK. 2002. Hunting for the virgin: meat, money, and memory in Tetiz, Yucatán. *Cult. Anthropol.* 17(3):291–330

Elyachar J. 2003. Mappings of power: the state, NGOs, and international organizations in the informal economy of Cairo. *Comp. Stud. Soc. Hist.* 45(3):571–605

Elyachar J. 2005. *Markets of Dispossession: NGOs, Economic Development and the State in Cairo*. Durham, NC: Duke Univ. Press

Elyachar J. 2006. Best practices: research, finance, and NGOs in Cairo. *Am. Ethnol.* 33(3):413–26

Ferguson J. 1990. *The Anti-Politics Machine: "Development," Depoliticization, and Bureaucratic Power in Lesotho.* Cambridge, UK: Cambridge Univ. Press

Firth R, Yamey BS, eds. 1964. *Capital, Saving and Credit in Peasant Societies: Studies from Asia, Oceania, the Caribbean and Middle America*. Chicago: Aldine

Foster RJ. 1995. *Social Reproduction and History in Melanesia: Mortuary Ritual, Gift Exchange, and Custom in the Tanga Islands*. Cambridge, UK: Cambridge Univ. Press

Garsten C, Lindh de Montoya M, eds. 2004. *Market Matters: Exploring Cultural Processes in the Global Marketplace*. Basingstoke, UK: Palgrave Macmillan

Gell A. 1992. Inter-tribal commodity barter and reproductive gift-exchange in Old Melanesia. See Humphrey & Hugh-Jones 1992, pp. 142–68

Godelier M. 1999. *The Enigma of the Gift*, transl. N Scott. Chicago: Univ. Chicago Press. From French

Graeber D. 2001. *Toward an Anthropological Theory of Value: The False Coin of our Own Dreams*. New York: Palgrave

Greenberg JB. 1995. Capital, ritual, and boundaries of the closed corporate community. In *Articulating Hidden Histories: Exploring the Influence of Eric R. Wolf*, ed. J Schneider, R Rapp, pp. 67–81. Berkeley: Univ. Calif. Press

Gregory CA. 1982. *Gifts and Commodities*. London: Acad. Press

Gregory CA. 1997. *Savage Money: The Anthropology and Politics of Commodity Exchange*. Amsterdam: Harwood Acad. Publ.

Gudeman SF. 2001. *The Anthropology of Economy: Community, Market, and Culture*. Malden, MA: Blackwell

Gudeman SF, Rivera A. 1990. *Conversations in Colombia: The Domestic Economy in Life and Text*. Cambridge, UK: Cambridge Univ. Press

Guyer JI. 2004. *Marginal Gains: Monetary Transactions in Atlantic Africa*. Chicago: Univ. Chicago Press

Guyer JI, ed. 2007. Special Issue: Jane Guyer's marginal gains: monetary transactions in Atlantic Africa. *Afr. Stud. Rev.* 50(2)

Hann CM, ed. 1998. *Property Relations: Renewing the Anthropological Tradition*. Cambridge, UK: Cambridge Univ. Press

Hart K. 1986. Heads or tails? Two sides of the coin. *Man* 21(4):637–56

Hart K. 2001. *Money in an Unequal World: Keith Hart and His Memory Bank*. New York: Texere

Harvey D. 1990. *The Condition of Postmodernity: An Enquiry into the Origins of Cultural Change*. Malden, MA: Blackwell

Harvey D. 1996. *Justice, Nature, and the Geography of Difference*. Malden, MA: Blackwell

Hernandez E, Coutin SB. 2006. Remitting subjects: migrants, money and states. *Econ. Soc.* 35(2):185–208

Hirsch E, Strathern M, eds. 2004. *Transactions and Creations: Property Debates and the Stimulus of Melanesia*. Oxford, UK: Berghahn

Holmes DR. 2009. Economy of words. *Cult. Anthropol.* 24(3):381–419

Holmes DR, Marcus G. 2005. Cultures of expertise and the management of globalization: toward the re-functioning of ethnography. In *Global Assemblages: Technology, Politics, and Ethics as Anthropological Problems*, ed. A Ong, S Collier, pp. 235–52. Malden, MA: Blackwell

Howe L. 1998. Scrounger, worker, beggarman, cheat: the dynamics of unemployment and the politics of resistance in Belfast. *J. R. Anthropol. Inst.* 4(3):531–50

Humphrey C, Hugh-Jones S, eds. 1992. *Barter, Exchange, and Value: An Anthropological Approach*. Cambridge, UK: Cambridge Univ. Press

Hunt RC. 2002. Economic transfers and exchanges: concepts for describing allocations. In *Theory in Economic Anthropology*, ed. J Ensminger, pp. 105–18. Walnut Creek, CA: AltaMira

Keane W. 1997. *Signs of Recognition: Powers and Hazards of Representation in an Indonesian Society*. Berkeley: Univ. Calif. Press

Kelly JD, Kaplan M. 2001. *Represented Communities: Fiji and World Decolonization*. Chicago: Univ. Chicago Press

Kirsch S. 2001. Property effects: social networks and compensation claims in Melanesia. *Soc. Anthropol.* 9(2):147–63

Kirsch S. 2004. Property limits: debates on the body, nature, and culture. See Hirsch & Strathern 2004, pp. 21–39

Klima A. 2002. *The Funeral Casino: Meditation, Massacre, and Exchange with the Dead in Thailand*. Princeton, NJ: Princeton Univ. Press

Knorr Cetina K, Bruegger U. 2002. Traders engagement with markets: a postsocial relationship. *Theory Cult. Soc.* 19(5/6):161–85

Kwon H. 2007. The dollarization of Vietnamese ghost money. *J. R. Anthropol. Inst.* 13(1):73–90

Lambek M. 2001. The value of coins in a Sakalava polity: money, death, and historicity in Mahajanga, Madagascar. *Comp. Stud. Soc. Hist.* 43(4):735–62

Leach J. 2005. Livers and lives: organ extraction narratives on the Rai coast of Papua New Guinea. See van Binsbergen & Geschiere 2005, pp. 123–41

Ledeneva AV. 1998. *Russia's Economy of Favours: Blat, Networking and Informal Exchange*. Cambridge, UK: Cambridge Univ. Press

Lévi-Strauss C. 1969 [1949]. *Elementary Structures of Kinship*, transl. JH Bell, JR von Sturmer, R Needham. Boston: Beacon. From French

Leyshon A, Thrift N. 1997. *Money/Space: Geographies of Monetary Transformation*. New York: Routledge

Leyshon A, Thrift N. 1999. Lists come alive: electronic systems of knowledge and the rise of credit-scoring in retail banking. *Econ. Soc.* 28(3):434–66

LiPuma E, Lee B. 2004. *Financial Derivatives and the Globalization of Risk*. Durham, NC: Duke Univ. Press

Locke CG, Ahmadi-Esfahani FZ. 1998. The origins of the international debt crisis. *Comp. Stud. Soc. Hist.* 40(2):223–46

Lont H, Hospes O, eds. 2004. *Livelihood and Microfinance: Anthropological and Sociological Perspectives on Savings and Debt*. Delft, NL: Eburon Acad. Press

Lowrey K. 2006. Salamanca and the city: culture credits, nature credits, and the modern moral economy of indigenous Bolivia. *J. R. Anthropol. Inst.* 12(2):275–92

Maine H. 2002 [1866]. *Ancient Law*. New Brunswick, NJ: Trans. Publ.

Malinowski B. 1961 [1922]. *Argonauts of the Western Pacific: An Account of Native Enterprise and Adventure in the Archipelagoes of Melanesian New Guinea*. New York: Dutton

Mandel R, Humphrey C, eds. 2002. *Markets and Moralities: Ethnographies of Postsocialism*. Oxford, UK: Berg

Marx K. 1981 [1894]. *Capital*, Vol. III, transl. B Fowkes. Harmondsworth, UK: Penguin. From German

Marx K. 1990 [1867]. *Capital*, Vol. I, transl. B Fowkes. New York: Penguin. From German

Masquelier A. 1997. Vectors of witchcraft: object transactions and the materialization of memory in Niger. *Anthropol. Q.* 70(4):187–98

Maurer B. 2005. *Mutual Life, Limited: Islamic Banking, Alternative Currencies, Lateral Reason*. Princeton, NJ: Princeton Univ. Press

Maurer B. 2006a. The anthropology of money. *Annu. Rev. Anthropol.* 35:15–36

Maurer B. 2006b. *Pious Property: Islamic Mortgages in the United States*. New York: Russell Sage Found.

Maurer B. 2007. Incalculable payments: money, scale, and the South African offshore grey money amnesty. *Afr. Stud. Rev.* 50(2):125–38

Mauss M. 1990 [1954]. *The Gift: The Form and Reason for Exchange in Archaic Societies*. London: Routledge

Mayer E. 2001. *The Articulated Peasant: Household Economies in the Andes*. Boulder, CO: Westview

Miller D. 1995. Consumption and commodities. *Annu. Rev. Anthropol.* 24:141–61

Mitchell T. 2002. *Rule of Experts: Egypt, Techno-Politics, Modernity*. Berkeley: Univ. Calif. Press

Miyazaki H. 2005. From sugar cane to "swords": hope and the extensibility of the gift in Fiji. *J. R. Anthropol. Inst.* 11(2):277–95

Moodie M. 2008. Enter microcredit: a new culture of women's empowerment in Rajasthan? *Am. Ethnol.* 35(3):454–65

Munn ND. 1986. *The Fame of Gawa: A Symbolic Study of Value Transformation in a Massim (Papua New Guinea) Society*. Cambridge, UK: Cambridge Univ. Press

Murphy RF, Steward JH. 1956. Tappers and trappers: parallel process in acculturation. *Econ. Dev. Cult. Change* 4(4):335–55

Myers FR. 2000. Ways of placemaking. In *Culture, Landscape, and the Environment: The Linacre Lectures*, ed. K Flint, H Morphy, pp. 72–110. Oxford: Oxford Univ. Press

Myers FR, ed. 2001. *The Empire of Things: Regimes of Value and Material Culture*. Santa Fe, NM: SAR Press

Nietzsche FW. 1956 [1887]. The genealogy of morals. In *Birth of Tragedy and The Genealogy of Morals*, transl. F Golffing, pp. 147–299. New York: Anchor. From German

Nugent D. 1996. From devil pacts to drug deals: commerce, unnatural accumulation, and moral community in "Modern" Peru. *Am. Ethnol.* 23(2):258–90

Ong A. 1999. *Flexible Citizenship: The Cultural Logics of Transnationality*. Durham, NC: Duke Univ. Press

Papataxiarchis E. 1999. A contest with money: gambling and the politics of disinterested sociality in Aegean Greece. See Day et al. 1999, pp. 158–75

Parry J. 1986. The gift, the Indian gift and the "Indian gift." *Man* 21(3):453–73

Parry J, Bloch MP, eds. 1989. *Money and the Morality of Exchange*. Cambridge, UK: Cambridge Univ. Press

Pedersen D. 2002. The storm we call dollars: determining value and belief in El Salvador and the United States. *Cult. Anthropol.* 17(3):431–59

Peebles G. 2004. The crown capitulates: conflations of national currency and global capital in the Swedish currency crisis. See Garsten & Lindh de Montoya 2004, pp. 180–205

Peebles G. 2008. Inverting the panopticon: money and the nationalization of the future. *Public Cult.* 20(2):233–65

Pietz W. 1997. Death of the deodand: accursed objects and the money value of human life. *Res* 31:97–108

Polanyi K. 1957 [1944]. *The Great Transformation: The Political and Economic Origins of our Time*. Boston, MA: Beacon

Poon M. 2009. From new deal institutions to capital markets: commercial consumer risk scores and the making of subprime mortgage finance. *Account. Org. Soc.* 34(5):654–74

Pottage A, Mundy M, eds. 2004. *Law, Anthropology and the Constitution of the Social: Making Persons and Things*. Cambridge, UK: Cambridge Univ. Press

Rabelais F. 1955. *The Histories of Gargantua and Pantagruel*, transl. JM Cohen. New York: Penguin. From French

Raheja GG. 1988. *The Poison in the Gift: Ritual, Prestation, and the Dominant Caste in a North Indian Village*. Chicago: Univ. Chicago Press

Rahman A. 1999. *Women and Microcredit in Rural Bangladesh: Anthropological Study of the Rhetoric and Realities of Grameen Bank Lending*. Boulder, CO: Westview

Ralph M. 2009. Commodity. *Soc. Text* 27(3):78–84

Rausing S. 1997. Signs of the new nation: gift exchange, consumption and aid on a former collective farm in north-west Estonia. In *Material Cultures: Why Some Things Matter*, ed. D Miller, pp. 189–214. Chicago: Univ. Chicago Press

Riles A. 2006. Real time: unwinding technocratic and anthropological knowledge. In *Frontiers of Capital: Ethnographic Reflections on the New Economy*, ed. MS Fisher, G Downey, pp. 86–107. Durham, NC: Duke Univ. Press

Robbins J. 2009. Rethinking gifts and commodities: reciprocity, recognition, and the morality of exchange. In *Economics and Morality: Anthropological Approaches*, ed. KE Browne, BL Milgram, pp. 43–58. Lanham, MD: AltaMira

Roitman J. 2005. *Fiscal Disobedience: An Anthropology of Economic Regulation in Central Africa*. Princeton, NJ: Princeton Univ. Press

Roitman J. 2006. The ethics of illegality in the Chad Basin. In *Law and Disorder in the Postcolony*, ed. J Comaroff, JL Comaroff, pp. 247–72. Chicago: Univ. Chicago Press

Roitman J. 2007. The right to tax: economic citizenship in the Chad Basin. Spec. Issue. *Cit. Stud.* 11(2):187–209

Sahlins MD. 1972. *Stone Age Economics*. Chicago: Aldine

Scheper-Hughes N. 2000. The global traffic in human organs. *Curr. Anthropol.* 41(2):191–224

Sharp LA. 2000. The commodification of the body and its parts. *Annu. Rev. Anthropol.* 29:287–328

Shipton P. 1995. How Gambians save: culture and economic strategy at an ethnic crossroads. In *Money Matters: Instability, Values, and Social Payments in the Modern History of West African Communities*, ed. J Guyer, pp. 245–76. Portsmouth, NH: Heineman

Shipton P. 2007. *The Nature of Entrustment: Intimacy, Exchange, and the Sacred in Africa*. New Haven: Yale Univ. Press

Shipton P. 2009. *Mortgaging the Ancestors: Ideologies of Attachment in Africa*. New Haven: Yale Univ. Press

Simmel G. 1978 [1907]. *The Philosophy of Money*, transl. T Bottomore, D Frisby. New York: Routledge. From German

Smith JH. 2008. *Bewitching Development: Witchcraft and the Reinvention of Development in Neoliberal Kenya*. Chicago: Univ. Chicago Press

Sneath D. 2006. Transacting and enacting: corruption, obligation and the use of monies in Mongolia. *Ethnos* 71(1):89–112

Song J. 2009. *South Koreans in the Debt Crisis: The Creation of a Neoliberal Welfare Society*. Durham, NC: Duke Univ. Press

Spyer P. 1997. The eroticism of debt: pearl divers, traders, and sea wives in the Aru Islands, eastern Indonesia. *Am. Ethnol.* 24(3):515–38

Stiansen E, Guyer JI, eds. 1999. *Credit, Currencies and Culture: African Financial Institutions in Historical Perspective*. Stockholm: Nordiska Afrikainstitutet

Strathern M. 1988. *The Gender of the Gift: Problems with Women and Problems with Society in Melanesia*. Berkeley: Univ. Calif. Press

Strathern M. 1992. Qualified value: the perspective of gift exchange. See Humphrey & Hugh-Jones 1992, pp. 169–91

Strathern M. 2005. *Kinship, Law and the Unexpected: Relatives Are Always a Surprise*. Cambridge, UK: Cambridge Univ. Press

Sykes KM. 2005. *Arguing with Anthropology: An Introduction to Critical Theories of the Gift*. London: Routledge

Taussig M. 1987. *Shamanism, Colonialism, and the Wild Man: A Study in Terror and Healing*. Chicago: Univ. Chicago Press

Thomas N. 1991. *Entangled Objects: Exchange, Material Culture, and Colonialism in the Pacific*. Cambridge, MA: Harvard Univ. Press

Truitt A. 2007. Hot loans and cold cash in Saigon. In *Money: Ethnographic Encounters*, ed. A Truitt, S Senders, pp. 57–67. Oxford: Berg

van Binsbergen WMJ, Geschiere P, eds. 2005. *Commodification: Things, Agency, and Identities (The Social Life of Things Revisited)*. Münster: Lit Verlag

Verdery K. 1996. *What Was Socialism and What Comes Next?* Princeton, NJ: Princeton Univ. Press

Verdery K. 2003. *The Vanishing Hectare: Property and Value in Postsocialist Transylvania*. Ithaca, NY: Cornell Univ. Press

Verdery K, Humphrey C, eds. 2004. *Property in Question: Value Transformation in the Global Economy*. Oxford: Berg

Weber M. 1978 [1922]. *Economy and Society: An Outline of Interpretive Sociology*, Vol. I, ed. G Roth, C Wittich. Berkeley: Univ. Calif. Press

Weber M. 2003 [1905]. *The Protestant Ethic and the Spirit of Capitalism*, transl. T Parsons. Mineola, NY: Dover. From German

Weiner AB. 1992. *Inalienable Possessions: The Paradox of Keeping-While-Giving*. Berkeley: Univ. Calif. Press

Williams B. 2004. *Debt for Sale: A Social History of the Credit Trap*. Philadelphia: Univ. Penn. Press

Woodburn J. 1982. Egalitarian societies. *Man* 17(3):431–51

Yanagisako SJ. 2002. *Producing Culture and Capital: Family Firms in Italy*. Princeton, NJ: Princeton Univ. Press

Zaloom C. 2006. *Out of the Pits: Traders and Technology from Chicago to London*. Chicago: Univ. Chicago Press

Zaloom C. 2009. How to read the future: the yield curve, affect, and financial prediction. *Public Cult.* 21(2):245–68

Zelizer VA. 1994. *The Social Meaning of Money: Pin Money, Paychecks, Poor Relief, and Other Currencies*. New York: Basic Books

Sense and the Senses: Anthropology and the Study of Autism

Olga Solomon

Division of Occupational Science and Occupational Therapy, University of Southern California, Los Angeles, California 90089; email: olga.solomon@usc.edu

Annu. Rev. Anthropol. 2010. 39:241–59

First published online as a Review in Advance on June 21, 2010

The *Annual Review of Anthropology* is online at anthro.annualreviews.org

This article's doi: 10.1146/annurev.anthro.012809.105012

Key Words

disability, ethnography, intersubjectivity, representation

Abstract

As a clinical category and a sociocultural phenomenon, autism occupies a prominent albeit ambiguous place in ongoing social science and humanities debates about empathy, intersubjectivity, intentionality, epistemological certainty, and moral agency. Autism is used as a counterexample to feeling empathy and understanding other people's beliefs and intentions. Alternatively, it is given as evidence of the limitless potential and neurodiversity of the human mind. This review examines the field of autism research relevant to anthropology of the senses. It considers the production of knowledge about autism as a clinically relevant category at the intersection of sense as culturally organized competence in meaning making and the senses as a culturally normative and institutionally ratified sensory and perceptual endowment. In such a distinction, both sense and the senses are paths toward and objects of the empirical understanding of autism.

AUTISM: THE ANALYTIC LANDSCAPE

Possibly more than any clinical category in Euro-American post–World War II history, autism figures prominently in ongoing social science and humanities debates about intersubjectivity, intentionality, empathy, and the social construction of disability. Autism is discussed in relation to the transmission and maintenance of cultural knowledge (Tomasello 1999, Tomasello et al. 2005, Vinden & Astington 2000) and the constitution of membership in social groups and activities (Ochs 2002). Autism refracts the problems of epistemology in research and clinical practice as well as in the social practices of everyday life (Silverman 2008).

As currently defined in psychiatry and cognitive psychology (APA 2000; Baron-Cohen 2003, 2008; Frith & Hill 2003), autism reaches in contradictory and unexpected ways to the very core of what it means to be human: Autism is used as a counterexample to empathy and intersubjectivity but also as evidence of the limitless potential and neurodiversity of the human mind. Autism as a trope for withdrawal into an isolated and impenetrable world has proliferated at an alarming rate (see Hacking 1999) while making its way into literary criticism (Monroe 1979, Steiner 2002), sociology of meaning (Durig 1996), computer science (Thackara 2001), and climate change research (Hacking 2008).

Autism has become a subject of many disciplines including anthropology, disability studies, education, epidemiology, genetics, neuroscience, occupational science, philosophy, and psychology. Although diverse theories and methods are embraced by those working in these fields, and interdisciplinary collaborations are increasingly common, research on autism tends to cluster around or move between two analytic poles:

1. Basic science and clinical intervention research that focuses on autism as a neurodevelopmental disorder, i.e., on its symptoms, etiology, prevalence, genetics, heterogeneity, and developmental trajectories. This research identifies neuroanatomic structures and neurobiological, cognitive, and sociocommunicative processes characteristic of autism and develops and tests clinical interventions using a range of methods[1] (Amaral et al. 2008, Courchesne et al. 2007, Dapretto et al. 2006, Geschwind & Levitt 2007, Hirstein et al. 2001, Kasari et al. 2008, Levitt & Cambell 2009, Moldin & Rubenstein 2006, Sigman & Capps 1997, Striano & Reed 2009, Volkmar 2005).

2. Ethnographically informed social science research focusing on autism as a personal, family, and community/social group experience as evidenced through the analyses of social interactions, narrative accounts, and participation and engagement in activities in the home and educational, clinical, and other institutional settings (Bagatell 2007, 2010; Grinker 2007, 2010; Prince 2010; Kaufman 2010; Lawlor 2010; Maynard 2005, 2006; Ochs et al. 2001, 2004, 2005; Ochs & Solomon 2004; Park 2008; Solomon 2008, 2010; Sterponi 2004; Sterponi & Fasulo 2010).

These two analytic polarities, one a biomedical view of autism, another a social science view, fall roughly into the emic/etic, experience-near/experience-far dichotomy (Geertz 1974). Although both have been important and the tension between them productive in moving forward, the vast interdisciplinary field of autism research and clinical practice, ethnographic enterprise of autism research has had to "define itself against adjacent and antecedent discourses" (Pratt 1986, p. 27; compare Solomon & Bagatell 2010) to articulate its own native lexicon for describing and understanding this complex condition. This has

---

[1]This is a review of a vast and varied field and of many theories and research directions. To provide a review relevant to anthropological study of autism and anthropology of the senses, the author cites most work in anthropology and either the more recent or the more seminal work outside the field. Absence of a reference does not constitute an intentional omission.

been a formidable task because, as Kleinman (2001) comments, from the height of psychoanalysis to the current era of cognitive neuroscience, anthropology has borrowed its theories and its language of the self from psychology and psychiatry. Thus the lexicon of ethnographically based anthropological research on autism must include terms and concepts that closely describe the everyday experiences of individuals, families, and communities. Such terms as sociality, practice, habitus, and coordination of action have been used to consider individual and collective experience and social engagement, leaving theoretical space for both competence and challenges (Ochs & Solomon 2004, 2010).

Interdisciplinary ethnographic research on autism touches on such quotidian, situated social phenomena as a child's engagement with music (Bakan et al. 2008), school inclusion (Ochs et al. 2001), a child's imaginative practices in an occupational therapy session (Park 2008), children's narrative practices and crafting of selves (Sirota 2004, 2010; Solomon 2004), family interactions about morality and social rules (Sterponi 2004), social interactions with siblings and peers mediated by therapy dogs (Solomon 2010), and mothers' experience of children's engagement in mealtime (Wilkinson 2009). These ethnographic accounts provide a view of how individuals with autism, their families, and others create meaning, engage in activities, construct identities and selves, and pursue possible and imagined futures.

Some of this research integrates both biomedical and social science perspectives into its theoretical framework. The field of occupational science (Clark et al. 1991) addresses both neurobiological function and the engagement in everyday activities. It combines neurobiological and social science approaches to demonstrate that the ability to be aware of and adapt to sensory information, e.g., to have good emotion regulation, balance and motor coordination, is essential for cognitive and social development and that organizing sensory information improves learning and sociality (Ayres 1972, Ayres et al. 2005, Bundy et al. 2002, Fisher et al. 1991, Lawlor 2003, Park 2008, Wilkinson 2009).

Addressing both the biomedical and the social aspects of autism, although in very different ways and from different theoretical perspectives, are philosophical writings that are concerned with the cultural production of kinds of people who are called autistic and their human rights in society (Hacking 1999, 2009a; Nussbaum 2006), as well as cultural-anthropological and sociohistorical analyses that examine shifting definitions of autism across historical periods, physical localities, and experiential narrative planes (Barnbaum 2008, Feinstein 2010, Grinker 2008a, Murray 2008, Nadesan 2005, Osteen 2008, Silverman 2008, Silverman & Brosco 2007).

This review offers an examination of the field of autism research relevant to the anthropology of the senses. It considers the production of knowledge about autism as a clinically relevant category at the intersection of sense as culturally organized competence in meaning making and the senses as a culturally normative and institutionally ratified sensory and perceptual endowment (Foucault 1994). In such a distinction, both sense and the senses are pathways to and objects of empirical understanding of autism. In the case of the latter (the senses), the discussion focuses on the practices of and tensions in seeing autism and the continuously extending empirical reach of the senses through biomedical technology such as functional magnetic resonance imaging (fMRI) to penetrate the autistic brain and further to reveal autism as a neurological disorder. When biomedical vision is thus extended by technology, some scientific narratives of autism become increasingly more authoritarian. Technologically mediated research generates quasi-novel but familiar explanatory frameworks of autistic symptoms (e.g., the deficient mirror neuron system) that objectify and advance existing theories (e.g., lack of empathy, impaired theory of mind).

In the case of the former (sense), this review discusses three existing and three more recent theories of autism from the "experience far" perspective that account for differently understood disruptions in sense making. The three older accounts of autism are theory of mind (Baron-Cohen et al. 1985), weak central coherence (Frith 1989), and executive function (Russell 1997). The three emerging neurobiological accounts are the role of the amygdala in the fear and anxiety associated with autism (Amaral et al. 2003, Amaral & Corbett 2003), the mirror neuron system dysfunction (Dapretto et al. 2006) and early brain overgrowth as a key factor in atypical neural connectivity (Courchesne et al. 2007). The review would have been incomplete without a discussion of the research on cognition and perception in autism that leads to an advantage rather than a deficit. Research by Mottron and colleagues (Mottron et al. 2006, 2009; Mottron & Burack 2001) strongly suggests that individuals with autism demonstrate enhanced perceptual functioning in several areas. This perceptual advantage underlies superior performance in the detection of patterns, visual memory, perfect pitch, and musical talent.

An overview of the experience-near perspective advanced by linguistic anthropological research on autism and social interaction (Ochs 2002; Ochs et al. 2001, 2004; Ochs & Solomon 2010; Solomon 2008, 2010) will illustrate the contributions of anthropology to the study of autism. Suggestions for future directions in anthropological research on autism will be offered in conclusion.

ANTHROPOLOGY AND THE STUDY OF AUTISM

Anthropology has made important contributions to the understanding of human conditions and social processes positioned at the intersections of biomedicine and social science, including agoraphobia (Capps & Ochs 1995), aphasia (Goodwin 2000, 2003, 2004), anorexia (Nasser et al. 2001, Shohet 2008), attention-deficit/hyperactivity disorder (Garro & Yarris 2009), depression (Kleinman 1997, Kleinman & Good 1986), illness and disability experience from family perspectives (Lawlor & Mattingly 2008), mental retardation (Edgerton 1967), pain (Buchbinder 2010,

Throop 2010), posttraumatic stress disorder (Young 1995), schizophrenia (Jenkins & Barrett 2004, Wilce 2004), prenatal diagnosis (Rapp 1998, 1999, 2000; Rapp et al. 2002; Rapp & Ginsburg 2001), and trauma (Lemelson et al. 2007). Autism has been the focus of cultural anthropology (Grinker 2007, 2008a,b), humanistic anthropology (Prince 2010), linguistic anthropology (Ochs 2002; Ochs et al. 2001, 2004, 2005; Ochs & Solomon 2010), medical anthropology (Kaufman 2010), and psychological anthropology (Sirota 2004, 2010).

An anthropological perspective is ontologically oriented to encompass otherness. It is guided by the assumption that "there exist forms of life radically different from ours that are nonetheless fully human, and that, consequently, our own future is potentially more open than we usually imagine" (Sewell 1997, p. 37). Anthropology makes contributions to the study of autism in three ways. First, the anthropological conceptualization of intersubjectivity and empathy is practice-based. It involves little assumption of supernatural intersubjective prowess of the ethnographer and no illusion of a "preternatural capacity to think, feel, and perceive like a native" (p. 56). Rather, there is an assumption of careful attention to and observation of what people "perceive 'with'— or 'by means of', searching out and analyzing the symbolic forms—words, images, institutions, behaviors, in terms of which in each place, people actually represented themselves to themselves and to one another" (p. 58). Second, the anthropological study of autism affords not only an ethnomethodological approach (Garfinkel 1967), but also a hermeneutic, interpretive stance to understand the lived experiences of affected persons.

Finally, the anthropological use of ethnographic methodology allows us to examine in situ the everyday practices of those affected by autism and their families and the production and recirculation of knowledge about autism in family, community, and institutional settings (Davis et al. 2000, Silverman 2008). An ethnographic perspective is meaning centered and is often dedicated to an interpretative explanation of "what institutions, actions, images, utterances, events, customs and the usual objects of social-scientific interest, mean to those whose institutions, actions, customs and so on they are" (Geertz 1983, p. 22), and an ethnographic perspective on autism is no exception. It often employs person-centered, narrative-, and life-history interviewing approaches; thus it follows people into the scenes of their stories and into the midst of their experiences in a world containing, as Sontag (2003) put it, "real suffering" (p. 110). Such research has unavoidable moral implications articulated by Barone (2009): If researchers are witnesses of injustice, are they also agents of social change? As Behar (1996) writes in *The Vulnerable Observer: Ethnography that Breaks Your Heart*, "anthropology is the most fascinating, bizarre, disturbing and necessary form of witnessing [...] where we feel complicitous with structures of power, or helpless to release another from suffering, or at a loss as to whether act or observe" (pp. 5–6).

It was neurologist Oliver Sacks who first linked anthropology and autism. Writing about his first meeting with Temple Grandin, one of the most professionally successful autistic persons to date, Sacks (1995) quotes her description of bewilderment when faced with the complex emotions and intentions of people: "Much of the time, I feel like an anthropologist on Mars" (p. 221). In an earlier piece that implicates, however indirectly, a form of witnessing, Sacks (1970) reports on his experience with autistic twins, John and Michael, at a state hospital. The twins were calendar-calculating savants, and their story demonstrates how difference in cognition and perception, in sense and the senses, becomes highly consequential for the life course of autistic individuals. When Sacks first met them, the twins were in their late twenties and had been institutionalized since childhood. They communicated with each other by a conversational exchange of prime numbers, a communion based on their shared esthetic appreciation of a simultaneously perceived and contemplated, mutually visible, and harmonious numerical landscape.

They were seated in a corner together, with a mysterious secret smile on their faces, [...] enjoying the strange pleasure and peace they now seemed to have.[...] They seemed to be locked in a singular, purely numerical, converse. John would say a number—a six-figure number. Michael would catch the number, nod, smile and seem to savour it. Then he, in turn, would say another six-figure number and now it was John who received and appreciated it richly. They looked, at first, like two connoisseurs wine-tasting, sharing rare tastes, rare appreciations. (Sacks 1970, p. 202)

Such visualizations, Sacks proposes, may be algorithms that are "organized not algebraically but spatially, as trees, spirals, architectures, 'thoughtscapes'" (Sacks 1970, p. 211). When Sacks joined the twins in this conversation offering his own prime number, they looked surprised, then joyful; they moved slightly apart to make space for their new conversational partner; they welcomed him into their social numeral universe. Ten years later they are separated "for their own good" to force them out of this universe and their "unhealthy communication together" (p. 209); they now live apart in halfway houses, do manual jobs under close supervision, and take public transportation if directed and given a bus token. They keep themselves presentable and clean. This semblance of normalcy and independence comes at a high price: Bereft of each other, they lose their numeral world and with it the joy, the "personal and emotional center," the "sense of their lives" (pp. 209–10).

The story ends with Sacks's musing that this loss is never mentioned in the twins' charts and never recognized. The psychiatrists and others who could have done so are syntactically, euphemistically, absent in the story, indexed in passive constructions as powerful but invisible forces: "[I]t was felt that the twins should be separated," "they were separated," "moved to halfway houses," "they are always being hurried and jostled from one job to another," "this is considered a small price to pay." Sacks asked, "What are we supposed to think about such a curious cure?" (p. 210).

What should anthropologists think? In spite of increasing societal concern about autism, it remains "an ultimate, formidable frontier for the field of anthropology" (Ochs & Solomon 2004, p. 141) awaiting to be explored as an area of anthropological inquiry. Anthropology has powerfully hermeneutic theories to bear onto some very important questions, especially in light of the anthropology of the senses. For example, medical anthropology could make a contribution by illuminating the practices of biomedical seeing (DelVeccio Good 2007), the gaze that deemed the twins' numeral universe unhealthy and thus uninhabitable. This is the same gaze that generates and selects clinically relevant types of subjects (Foucault 1973) and categorizes them as autistic and thus in need of being acted upon "for their own good" (Sacks 1970, p. 209), the good that they are not expected to know or understand. Medical anthropologists could think about the "autism epidemic" (e.g. Grinker 2008a, Kaufman 2010) while applying Foucault's (1991) notion of governmentality capturing how individual and populations' health-related conduct is regulated through active self-regulation. This process gains an ethical imperative of health maintenance and self-shaping according to new biomedical knowledge (Briggs 2005, Foucault 1991). Anthropology could shed light on what happens when this ethical imperative is not met, when someone is incapable or unwilling to adopt the dominant medical knowledge and participate in ratified practices of biomedical consumption. Such a situation takes place when parents refuse or are reluctant to vaccinate their children fearing, or blaming after the fact, autism as a consequence of vaccination (Kaufman 2010). Anthropology could illuminate the practices of constituting such persons as failed "biomedical citizens" (Ong 1995, Shah 2001, compare Briggs & Martini-Briggs 2003, p. 272), as "'bad subjects'" (Kulick & Schieffelin 2004, p. 355). It could elucidate how individuals become such subjects, become subjected to social regula-

tions (Butler 1990), related to a biomedical view of autism, how they perform and inhabit these "bad subject" positions, become competent, even expert, in these positions and recruit others into them.

Anthropologists could pursue a biosocial approach to autism (Rabinow 1997) that would examine individual, family, and community experiences and the larger social matrices in which these experiences are embedded, shaped, interpreted, and contested. Anthropologists could ask how and which kinds of sociocultural and sociohistorical processes are shaped into the experiences of autism and how these experiences border/intersect/overlap and/or resonate with other experiences. They could examine the forms of reasoning that underlie logics of structural violence (Farmer 1996, 2004) that produce stories like that of the twins. They also could ask why some narratives become authoritative and why the statements that challenge them (the absent notes in the twins' charts) are preemptively erased from then-public discourse (Briggs 2005). Or anthropologists could ask about the origin story of autism.

AUTISM: THE ORIGIN STORY

Origin stories often address problems of hierarchies and offer interpretations of "how things got to be as they are now" (Wright 2004, p. 6). A careful examination of the origin story of autism could help illuminate how and why the cultural conceptions of autism have been so resistant to change.

Sociohistorical origins of the simultaneous discovery of a cluster of symptoms now called autism by Kanner (1943) and Asperger (1991 [1944]) are repeated in most articles and books on autism and have acquired the feel of a mythic origin story. The story usually focuses on two chronologically parallel but geographically disparate existential planes containing Kanner's child psychiatry clinical practice and Asperger's pediatric practice and educational work. The serene matter-of-fact atmosphere of both accounts usually lacks any contextualization within the historical events of that period.

The story of how autism as a diagnostic category first appeared with miraculous simultaneity in two different geographic locations, Baltimore and Vienna, in the beginning of 1940s usually goes as follows: In 1943, Leo Kanner, an American psychiatrist who immigrated from Austria in 1924 and became the head of the John Hopkins clinic in Baltimore, published an article titled "Autistic Disturbances of Affective Contact" in the journal *Nervous Child*. The article, written in a case-study format, was based on Kanner's clinical work with 11 children he had been treating since 1938. Kanner (1943) writes, "Since 1938, there have come to our attention a number of children whose condition differs so markedly and uniquely from anything reported so far, that each case merits—and, I hope, will eventually receive—a detailed consideration of its fascinating peculiarities" (p. 217).

Through endless recirculation and repetition, descriptions of the children will turn into a trope of autistic isolation and aloneness, strengthening the notion that an autistic child lives in his or her own world: "The most impressive thing is his detachment and his inaccessibility. He walks as if he is in a shadow, lives in a world of his own where he can't be reached"; "[h]e seems almost to draw into his shell and live within himself" (Kanner 1943, pp. 218, 236). At the time of writing this review, Kanner's (1943) article has been cited in research literature more than 3,800 times.

In Vienna, a year later a pediatrician and pedagogue Hans Asperger published his doctoral dissertation, "Autistic Psychopathy in Childhood." Asperger's definition of autism was much more inclusive than Kanner's, encompassing both children with profound challenges and those who seemed only slightly affected. Asperger conceptualized autism as a personality disorder, and his clinical description held a much more optimistic view than did Kanner's about the children's potential for adaptation to the demands of society. He especially emphasized the great value that autistic individuals can have for society and pleaded for giving these children the special education and guidance they need to realize their full potential (Asperger 1991 [1944]).

Asperger and Kanner never met. Asperger remained in Austria as the Chair of Pediatrics at the University of Vienna for 20 years (Frith 1991). His account entered late into sociohistorical processes that shaped autism as a clinical category.

The simultaneous discovery of autism is rarely considered in relation to "Why that now?" question as a product of the political, psychological, philosophic, and aesthetic contexts of the time (McDonough 1999, Nadesan 2005). Although Grinker (2008a) traces the emergence of autism as a diagnostic category against the development of American psychiatry, and Hacking (2006) attributes it to the shared roots of Kanner's and Asperger's training influenced by August Homburger's writing on childhood schizophrenia, the question remains whether larger sociohistorical forces contributed to the sudden appearance of an autism category in the Western clinical taxonomy (Alderson & Goodey 1999). Contemporary accounts of autism may shed some light on this question.

Bruno Bettelheim (1967) compared an autistic child's experience with that of a prisoner in a Nazi concentration camp. In his book *The Empty Fortress: Infantile Autism and the Birth of the Self*, he writes

> Although Anna was not a child of the German concentration camps, her life story was such as to bring them sharply to mind. Through her, the phenomenon of the camps which had long occupied much of my personal and theoretical interest [1943, 1960] became somehow linked with my daily work, the treatment of severely disturbed children. (p. 7)

This story could have been a collective experience shared by European intellectuals who survived Nazi concentration camps and after the war were practicing psychology and psychiatry in the United States. Mira Rothenberg (1960), a Holocaust survivor and a child psychologist who worked with institutionalized

ASD: autism spectrum disorder

autistic children, writes in her book *Children with Emerald Eyes*, "Through all these years I have been fascinated by the variety of fortresses those (autistic) children build for themselves in order to protect themselves against the horrors they sense around them.[...] These children live within such walls [...] often forever" (p. 14).

The enduring quality of this trope of autism as a fortress imprisoning a child within its impenetrable walls foregrounds the heteroglossic nature of language. In the Bakhtinian perspective, words are not monologic and singularly voiced at the moment of speaking but "prior to the moment of appropriation, the word does not exist in a neutral and impersonal language [...], but rather, it exists in other people's mouths, in other people's contexts, serving other people's intentions; it is from there that one must take the word and make it one's own" (Bakhtin 1981, pp. 293–94). Foucault sounds eerily Bakhtinian when he writes, "A meaning has taken shape that hangs over us, leading us forward in our blindness, but awaiting in the darkness for us to attain awareness before emerging into the light of day and speaking. We are doomed historically to history, to the patient construction of discourses about discourses, and to the task of hearing what has already been said" (Foucault 1973, p. xvi).

SEEING AUTISM

Practices of professional vision and their roles in building theory and interpreting data have long been of interest to linguistic anthropology. Goodwin (1994) articulates how members of a profession engage in competing discursive practices that shape the subjects of their scrutiny in a way that creates "objects of knowledge" (p. 606): theories, artifacts, and domains of expertise that distinguish them from other professions. With its Janus-like quality of being relevant to both the clinical and the social, autism creates an analytic bridge between clinical practice and social practice, between clinical knowledge and practical knowledge, and it makes visible the shifts in clinical ontologies and

the politics of scientific evidence (Jensen 2007). Autism illuminates the role of social theory for understanding clinical practices of diagnosis and intervention because, as Taylor (1985) notes, "social theory arises when we try to formulate explicitly what we are doing, describe the activity which is central to the practice, and articulate the norms that are essential to it" (p. 93).

Although empirical understanding of autism has seen significant advances in neuroimaging and biosensing technologies (e.g., Dapretto et al. 2006, Goodwin et al. 2008), to date there are no objective biological biomarker tests that unequivocally establish the presence of autism, and diagnosis is based on the subjective judgment of individual clinicians or interdisciplinary evaluation teams who negotiate a collective consensus of a diagnosis (Goldknopf 2002).

The challenges of seeing autism become especially prominent when the heterogeneity of autism, its hallmark characteristic, is considered together with the notions of ethnicity, race, gender, socioeconomic status, family culture, and communication during clinical encounters. Notions of ethnicity, race, and socioeconomic status are shaped as discrete theoretical objects in some disciplines and not in others (Goodwin 1994) and cannot capture the variation in individual and group cultural practices (Gutierrez & Rogoff 2003). Moreover, heterogeneity, a defining characteristic of autism spectrum disorders, has never been examined as a sociocultural rather than clinical phenomenon where an interpretation of atypical behavior is examined against sociocultural expectations of normative development under default socioeconomic circumstances.

In an Orwellian sense, although everyone appears to be created equal in vulnerability to autism spectrum disorders (ASDs), some categories of people are more equal than others. ASDs affect, on average, 4 times more males than females, but the females tend to be more severely affected, and the ratio changes across the autism spectrum from 2 males to 1 female at the most severely affected end of the spectrum to 15 males to 1 female at the highest functioning end (Wing 1981). Baron-Cohen, the author of the theory of mind hypothesis, suggests that autism is an extreme version of the male brain that tends to systematize information at the expense of empathizing with others (Baron-Cohen 2002, 2003).

Some social groups appear to be more and some less equal when it comes to receiving a diagnosis of ASD; thus being at risk for autism is not only a genetic issue because of family history but also deeply embedded in structures of health care access and delivery as well as in practices of caregiver-physician interaction in clinical encounters. There are children who are at risk not for being diagnosed with autism but rather for being misdiagnosed with other psychiatric conditions or not diagnosed at all. Population-level demographic studies, for example, indicate an unprecedented scale of health and service disparities in autism diagnosis for African American children. A national study that correlates the age of diagnosis in Medicaid-enrolled children with ASDs found that sociodemographic characteristics as well as local health care resources and state policies contribute to disparities in the age of diagnosis, a situation that requires rethinking what being "at risk for autism" means. African American children receiving Medicaid are diagnosed on average at 7.9 years of age, 18 months later than are Caucasian children on Medicaid, who are diagnosed at 6.3 years of age (Mandell et al. 2002, 2009; Stahmer & Mandell 2007). It is significant that these disparities persist for African American children independently of IQ levels, whereas for other racial/ethnic groups it applies only for children with IQs lower than 70, a cutoff for mental retardation (Mandell et al. 2009). The picture that emerges from these studies is of systematic delays in diagnosis and challenges to secure appropriate services once the diagnosis is received.

In spite of such persistent challenges to clinical certainty, autism has become an urgent public health concern. The Centers for Disease Control and Prevention have published a new estimate of the prevalence of ASDs, increasing it from 1 in 150 (CDC 2007) to one in 110 (CDC 2009), meaning that autism should be currently seen in 1 in 110 children and 1 in 70 boys. Investigators have engaged in ongoing and contentious debates about whether these numbers reflect an autism epidemic (Blaxill 2004, Kirby 2005) or if these estimates are finally approximating the actual prevalence of ASDs in the general population (Grinker 2008a,b, 2010; Wing 2003). The fact that it is not seen and thus not accurately diagnosed in some groups of children shows a strong influence of structural, sociocultural, and communicative processes that underlie seeing autism and generate disparities in autism diagnosis.

Anthropology can make an important contribution to illuminating these processes. Epidemiological surveillance methods used by the Centers for Disease Control and Prevention to establish the prevalence of ASDs involve examinations by trained clinician reviewers of children' health and education records to identify documented behaviors that meet the fourth edition, text revision, of the *Diagnostic Statistical Manual (DSM-IV-TR)* criteria for autistic disorder, Asperger disorder, or pervasive developmental disorder not-otherwise specified (CDC 2009). These records are metadiscursive texts that are interactionally achieved and institutionally ratified as descriptions of a child's social behavior or his or her performance on standardized tests. These records are a product of institutional practices that authoritatively entextualize and represent a child's behavior in a clinically relevant way. Outside the realm of the text, this interpretation of the child's behavior may be subjected to multiple and competing interpretations by family members, teachers, clinicians, and children themselves (McDermott 2001; McDermott et al. 2006; Mehan 1993, 1996; Varenne & McDermott 1999), but these different voices may never become entextualized to become part of the child's record.

The process of creating the new *Diagnostic Statistical Manual* Fifth Edition (*DSM-V*) could also benefit from an anthropological perspective. There are heated debates about the *DSM-V*, an authoritative diagnostic meta-text published by the American Psychiatric Association that instructs clinicians on the criteria for diagnosing psychiatric disorders. The new *DSM* is intended to be a paradigm shift in diagnostic practices, a turn toward a more objectively derived diagnosis through the use of a dimensional approach: biomarker testing and neuroimaging (Kupfer 2005). For autism, it reflects a change in the procedural knowledge and practical logic in diagnosis, a movement away from subjective characterizations and toward objective biological measures so far undefined. At the time of this writing, attending to the debates about the psychiatric conditions that will not be included in the new *DSM*, such as two autism spectrum disorders, Asperger's disorder and pervasive developmental disorder not-otherwise-specified, brings into focus the remarkable fluidity of psychiatric diagnoses and the complex interaction of sociocultural and sociohistorical forces that bring them into and out of being, a topic of interest for anthropology.

The American Academy of Pediatrics (AAP) has published guidelines for evaluating all children receiving preventive health care services for developmental delays and ASDs beginning at nine months of age (Zwaigenbaum et al. 2009). The impact of these recommendations in the production of persons diagnosed as autistic is difficult to underestimate (Hacking 2006), bringing to mind Foucault's (1979) notion of Panopticon, the symbolic surveillance tower that serves as a mechanism by which power observes, evaluates, categorizes, and orders individual behavior. The Panopticon is a technology of discipline that brings together knowledge, the control of the body, and the control of space (Foucault 1979). The AAP recommendations, however reasonable and timely, will likely face the challenge of overdiagnosis. In the current era of "autism anxiety" (McDonough 1999), however, it is unlikely that the AAP guidelines will be resisted, although the recent American Medical Association's recommendations regarding breast and prostate cancer screening (Esserman et al. 2009) indicate that more is not always better and that false positives and overdiagnoses present a serious concern.

THEORIES OF AUTISM ACROSS INTERDISCIPLINARY BORDERS

Cognitive psychological research on autism in the 1990s pursued a core deficit question to identify which characteristics of autism were central and which were peripheral to explain the specific profile of autistic individuals' limitations and abilities (Sigman & Capps 1997). Three theories of autism competed for a place of core deficit to account for disruptions in sense making, specifically, a deficit in theory of mind (Baron-Cohen et al. 1985), a theory of weak central coherence (Frith 1989), and an impairment in executing function (Russell 1997).

A theory of mind account of autism explains impairments in pragmatics of language use and in nonverbal social behavior. A deficit in theory of mind hinders a person's ability to perceive a cause-and-effect relationship between mental states and actions, resulting in "abnormalities in understanding other minds" (Baron-Cohen 2000, p. 3).

Linguistic anthropologist Elinor Ochs and colleagues (2004) conducted an ethnographic study of the everyday social interactions of children with autism and extended the scope of inquiry of intersubjectivity in autism from the interpersonal domain to the sociocultural one. Arguing for a distinction between social as interpersonal and social as sociocultural, Ochs et al. (2004) proposed that persons with autism should not be viewed only as individuals in relation to other individuals as has been the case in psychological research. Rather, they should be considered as participating members of social groups and communities, as sociocultural beings who display both social abilities and difficulties that are relative to the socioculturally organized expectations of competence and conduct (see Solomon 2008 for review).

A theory of weak central coherence (WCC) in autism is based on theories of gestalt perception (Frith 1989). It argues that human beings have a built-in propensity to see meaning and structure, to form coherence, and to generalize over as wide a range of stimuli and contexts as possible, and that the drive for central coherence is impaired in autism, which accounts for highly detail-oriented, decontextualized information processing.

The linguistic anthropological analysis of everyday talk involving high-functioning children with autism expanded the study of information processing in autism into an analysis of social interaction. Considering Garfinkel's and Bourdieu's perspectives on practice (e.g., Bourdieu 1990, Garfinkel 1967) to examine children's engagement in social encounters that require fluid, contingent, and practical strategies and behavior, Ochs & Solomon (2004) showed that certain social interactions were easier to participate in than others. The children's social fluency resided primarily in their ability to act relevantly and generatively in response to locally prior and upcoming actions. Linking their predications to the propositional content of locally prior and anticipated utterances was somewhat more challenging. Linking actions to their own and others' actions over a more extensive span of social interaction was significantly more difficult, although the greatest difficulty lay in grasping more global themes constructed across an extended series of utterances.

The third cognitive theory of executive function impairment in autism (Russell 1997) implies, broadly, a deficit in the ability to plan and carry out actions to attain future goals. The impairment in executive function, however, is not specific to autism and is characteristic of other disorders such as attention deficit disorder, obsessive compulsive disorder, and Tourette syndrome. Russell's executive function impairment theory sought to account for challenges concerning agency, specifically with the perception of self and others as social agents and the ability to distinguish between mental and physical states (1997).

In a linguistic anthropological study of sociality in autism, Ochs & Solomon (2010) identified varied degrees of sociality across different social situations. The researchers defined sociality as a range of possible coordination with others that is configured by individual experience, development, and neuropsychological and other conditions. Although challenges of autism hinder sociality, certain configurations of social encounters appear to support social coordination. This research suggests that sociality, and by extension executive function, in autism is less a property of the individual and more a property of social interaction.

Three recent neurobiological accounts suggest various brain structures and processes responsible for the challenges of autism. Atypical brain development has long been a suspect in the search for the etiology of autism, and increasing evidence indicates that this may be the case. Early brain overgrowth, local overconnectivity, and atypical lateralization, followed by an arrest in brain development later in childhood, are being investigated as causes underlying autistic impairments (Courchesne et al. 2007). The role of the amygdala, a part of the brain that processes social information and detects potential threats, has been proposed as an explanation for intense fears and heightened anxiety in autism (Amaral et al. 2003, 2008; Amaral & Corbett 2003). If this theory is correct, individuals with autism inhabit a social world filled with fear and anxiety. This theory would account for pragmatic challenges of autism such as atypical gaze behavior and for a preference for routines and sameness in the environment.

The theory of mirror neuron system dysfunction in autism (Dapretto et al. 2006) suggests that whereas in normal development the human mirror neuron system is involved in the execution and observation of movement as well as in language, imitation, empathy, and social learning, in autistic individuals, the mirror neuron system is impaired, which may explain challenges specific to autism. The mirror neuron system is a powerful and seductive notion that, like theory of mind in the 1990s, is touted as a prerequisite for being human. The function of the human mirror neuron system, however, is far from understood, and is not limited to humans (e.g. Gallese 1996, Rizzolatti et al. 1996). However, like other similarly powerful notions from the past, it becomes dangerously entangled in practices of othering, in social constructions implying that people with autism are less human.

Othering can also go in the opposite direction where individuals with autism out-perform their neurologically unaffected counterparts in tasks in which autistic tendencies are an advantage rather than a deficiency. Nevertheless, such superior abilities are often seen not as a sign of giftedness but as a sign of underlying impairment resulting in savant abilities (see Solomon 2009). Studies of perception in autism by Mottron and colleagues (Mottron et al. 2006, Mottron & Burack 2001) suggest that in several areas individuals with autism possess enhanced perceptual functioning owing to, for example, strong low-level information processing and greater than typical activation of perceptual areas during a range of visuospatial, language, working-memory, and reasoning tasks (Mottron et al. 2009). These areas include one-dimensional visual and auditory discrimination that may result in hyperlexia, superior detection of patterns such a calendaric and prime number calculations (as the twins John and Michael exhibited in Sacks's story); artistic talent and enhanced visual memory remeniscent of Jesse Park and Stephen Wiltshire's paintings; and perfect pitch and musical talent, which characterize the remarkable jazz career of musician Matt Savage. It was perhaps Sacks's clinical genius that allowed him to see this process. He wrote (Sacks 1970): "The twins seem to employ the direct cognition . . . . They see directly a universe and heaven of numbers" (p. 209). This account of autistic cognition empathizes locally oriented, enhanced perceptual functioning owing to low-level hierarchical information processing. In this sense, an individual affected by autism may be perceiving reality more directly than typical development affords. This is an area where anthropology is uniquely positioned to make an important contribution to understanding the perceptual challenges and cognitive potentialities of those affected by autism and to consider carefully the impact of autism on the lives of individuals, families, and communities.

CONCLUSION

This article considers the connections between sense and the senses in the understanding of autism and reviews research that speaks to these connections in anthropology and other disciplines. Of special interest are the ways in which the senses are extended by bio- and other kinds of technology designed to see autism as a certain, albeit sociohistorically and biosocially configured, kind of a neurological and psychological disorder. The review seeks to interrogate the tension between the epistemology of scientific evidence, its sociohistorical contexts, and the personal experiences of autism, and to extricate theoretically the discussion away from cognitive accounts and into a more dangerous world of "bad" subjects (Kulick & Scheiffelin 2004), vulnerable observers (Behar 1996), politics of representation (McDermott 2001; Mehan 1993, 1996; Osteen 2008), and structural violence (Farmer 1996, 2004). Yet it feels that the review barely scratches the theoretical surface and that much remains unconsidered.

Further examination of how institutionalized structures of power and processes of representation intersect and shape the lives of individuals with autism and their families across settings is needed. Careful consideration of practices of resistance to these structural forces should be a necessary part of this work. According to recent estimates, for example, ~5% of inmates in U.S. prisons may have an ASD (Hall et al. 2007), and their interactions with police forces and other disciplinary and law-enforcement entities often turn dangerous and even deadly for those with ASDs (Debbaudt & Rothman 2001).

A careful consideration grounded in a phenomenological approach (Duranti 2006) should be given to the subjective, sensory, and perceptual experiences of autism that go beyond savant abilities or disabling impairments and that are based on personal narratives and practices of being and self-awareness (McGeer 2004, Page 2009, Prince 2010).

Awaiting anthropological inquiry are the tensions between notions of fiction or fantasy regarded in the research community as quite opposite to the science of autism (Grinker 2010, Schopler 2001, Schreibman 2005, Singh et al. 2007) and parental practices of imagination and hope for children's futures. There seems to be a remarkable silence, an absence of discourse about hope in biomedicine's views on autism in spite of advances in biotechnology. The work of narrative imagination and emplotment (Mattingly 1998) and crafting of possible selves is carried out primarily by individuals with autism and their families (Sirota 2010). A biotechnical embrace that engages families and clinicans together in practices of medical imagination (e.g., DelVecchio Good 2001, 2007) has been slow in coming for individuals with autism and their families because biomedicine has been reluctant to imagine their possible lives and futures.

Humanistic anthropologist Michael Jackson (1998) writes, "In most cultures, people assume a cut off point between a world they count as theirs and a world they consider other. (...The) lines of distinction inevitably entail questions as to how one negotiates, controls, and crosses them" (p. 167). Dawn Edding Prince, an anthropologist who was diagnosed with Asperger syndrome in adulthood, reflects on these questions: "I feel a profound duty to admit the illusion of my distinctiveness and I object to the freezing properties of objectivity. Knowing that there is much illusion in the world I feel sure that my way of being is only a disability of context, that what have been labeled symptoms of autism in the context of my culture are inherited gifts of insight and action." (Prince 2010, p. 62).

DISCLOSURE STATEMENT

The author is not aware of any affiliations, memberships, funding, or financial holdings that might be perceived as affecting the objectivity of this review.

LITERATURE CITED

Alderson P, Goodey C. 1999. Autism in special and inclusive schools: "There has to be a point to their being there." *Disabil. Soc.* 14(2):249–61

Amaral DG, Schumann CM, Nordahl CW. 2008. Neuroanatomy of autism. *Trends Neurosci.* 31(3):137–45

Amaral D, Bauman M, Mills Schumann C. 2003. The amygdala and autism: implications from non-human primate studies. *Genes Brain Behav.* 2(5):295–302

Amaral D, Corbett B. 2003. The amygdala, autism and anxiety. *Novartis Found Symp.* 251:177–87; discussion 187–97, 281–97

Am. Psychiatr. Assoc. (APA). 2000. *Diagnostic and Statistical Manual of Mental Disorder.* Washington, DC: Am. Psychiatr. Assoc. IVth ed., text rev.

Asperger H. 1991 [1944]. Die Autistischen Psychopathen im Kindesalter. Autistic Psychopathy. *Eur. Arch. Psychiatry Clin. Neurosci.* 117(1):76–136

Ayres AJ. 1972. Types of sensory integrative dysfunction among disabled learners. *Am. J. Occup. Ther.* 26(1):13–18

Ayres AJ, Robbins J, McAfee S, Bodison S, Brunn LB 2005. *Sensory Integration and the Child: Understanding Hidden Sensory Challenges.* Los Angeles: West. Psychol. Serv.

Bagatell N. 2007. Orchestrating voices: autism, identity and the power of discourse. *Disabil. Soc.* 22(4):413–26

Bagatell N. 2010. From cure to community: transforming notions of autism. *Ethos* 38(1):34–58

Bakan M, Koen B, Kobylarz F, Morgan F, Goff L. 2008. Following Frank: response-ability and the co-creation of culture in a medical ethnomusicology program for children on the autism spectrum. *Ethnomusicology* 52(2):163–202

Bakhtin M. 1981. *The Dialogical Imagination.* Austin: Univ. Tex. Press

Baron-Cohen S. 2000. Theory of mind and autism: a fifteen year review. In *Understanding Other Minds: Perspectives from Developmental Cognitive Neuroscience*, ed. S Baron-Cohen, H Tager-Flusberg, D Cohen, pp. 3–20. Oxford: Oxford Univ. Press. 2nd ed.

Baron-Cohen S. 2002. The extreme male brain theory of autism. *Trends Cogn. Sci.* 6(6):248–54

Baron-Cohen S. 2003. *The Essential Difference: The Truth About the Male and Female Brain.* New York: Basic Books

Baron-Cohen S. 2008. *Autism and Asperger Syndrome: The Facts.* New York: Oxford Univ. Press

Barone T. 2009. Comments on Coulter and Smith: narrative researchers as witnesses of injustice and agents of social change? *Educ. Res.* 38(8):591–97

Barnbaum D. 2008. *The Ethics of Autism: Among Them, But Not of Them.* Bloomington/Indianapolis: Indiana Univ. Press

Behar R. 1996. *The Vulnerable Observer: Ethnography that Breaks Your Heart.* Boston: Beacon

Bettelheim B. 1967. *The Empty Fortress: Infantile Autism and the Birth of the Self.* New York: Simon & Schuster

Blaxill M. 2004. What's going on? The question of time trends in autism. *Public Health Rep.* 119(6):536–51

Bourdieu P. 1990. *The Logic of Practice.* New York: Stanford Univ. Press

Briggs CL. 2005. Communicability, racial discourse, and disease. *Annu. Rev. Anthropol.* 34(1):269–91

Briggs CL, Martini-Briggs C. 2003. *Stories in the Time of Cholera: Racial Profiling During a Medical Nightmare.* Berkeley: Univ. Calif. Press

Buchbinder M. 2010. Giving an account of one's pain in the anthropological interview. *Cult. Med. Psychiatry* 34:108–31

Bundy A, Lane S, Murray E, Fisher A. 2002. *Sensory Integration: Theory and Practice.* Philadelphia: FA Davis

Butler J. 1990. *Gender Trouble: Feminism and the Subversion of Identity.* New York: Routledge.

Capps L, Ochs E. 1995. *Constructing Panic: The Discourse of Agoraphobia.* Harvard, MA: Harvard Univ. Press

Cent. Dis. Control Prev. 2007. Prevalence of autism spectrum disorders—autism developmental disabilities monitoring network, United States, 2002. *Surveill. Summ.* 56(1):12–28

Cent. Dis. Control Prev. 2009. Prevalence of autism spectrum disorders—autism developmental disabilities monitoring network, United States, 2006. *Surveill. Summ.* 58(1):1–20

Clark F, Parham D, Carlson M, Frank G, Jackson J. 1991. Occupational science: academic innovation in the service of occupational therapy's future. *Am. J. Occup. Ther.* 45(4):300–10

Courchesne E, Pierce K, Schumann C, Redcay E, Buckwalter JA. 2007. Mapping early brain development in autism. *Neuron* 56(2):399–413

Dapretto M, Davies M, Pfeifer J, Scott AA, Sigman M. 2006. Understanding emotions in others: mirror neuron dysfunction in children with autism spectrum disorders. *Nat. Neurosci.* 9(1):28–30

Davis J, Watson N, Cunningham-Burley S. 2000. Disabled children, ethnography and unspoken understandings: the collaborative construction of diverse identities. In *Research with Children: Perspectives and Practices*, ed. P Christiansen, A James, pp. 220–59. New York: Routledge

Debbaudt D, Rothman D. 2001. Contact with individuals with autism: effective resolutions. *FBI Law Enforc. Bull.* 7(4):20–24

DelVecchio Good M. 2001. The biotechnical embrace. *Cult. Med. Psychiatry* 25(4):395–410

DelVecchio Good M-J. 2007. The medical imagery and the biotechnical embrace: subjective experiences of clinical scientists and patients. In *Subjectivity: Ethnographic Investigations*, ed. J Biehl, B Good, A Kleinman, pp. 362–80. Berkeley: Univ. Calif. Press

Duranti A. 2006. The social ontology of intentions. *Discourse Stud.* 8(1):31–40

Durig A. 1996. *Autism and the Crisis of Meaning.* New York: State Univ. N. Y. Press

Edgerton RB. 1967. *The Cloak of Competence: Stigma in the Lives of the Mentally Retarded.* Berkeley: Univ. Calif. Press

Esserman L, Shieh Y, Thompson I. 2009. Rethinking screening for breast cancer and prostate cancer. *JAMA* 302(15):1685–92

Farmer P. 1996. On suffering and structural violence: a view from below. *Daedalus* 125(1):261–83

Farmer P. 2004. *Pathologies of Power: Health, Human Rights, and the New War on the Poor.* Berkeley: Univ. Calif. Press

Feinstein A. 2010. *A History of Autism: Conversations with the Pioneers.* Chichester, UK: Wiley-Blackwell

Fisher A, Murray E, Bundy A. 1991. *Sensory Integration: Theory and Practice*. Philadelphia: FA Davis

Foucault M. 1973. *The Birth of the Clinic: An Archaeology of Medical Perception*. London: Tavistock

Foucault M. 1979. *Discipline and Punish*. New York: Random House

Foucault M. 1991. *The Foucault Effect: Studies in Governmentality: With Two Lectures by and an Interview with Michel Foucault*. Chicago: Univ. Chicago Press

Foucault M. 2000. The political technology of individuals. In *Power: Essential Works of Foucault 1954–1984*, Vol. III, ed. J Faubio, pp. 403–17. New York: New Press

Frith U. 1989. A new look at language and communication in autism. *Int. J. Lang. Commun. Disord.* 24(2):123–50

Frith U. 1989. *Autism: Explaining the Enigma*. New York: Blackwell

Frith U. 1991. Asperger and his syndrome. In *Autism and Asperger Syndrome*, ed. U Frith, pp. 1–36. Cambridge, UK: Cambridge Univ. Press

Frith U, Hill E. 2003. Autism: mind and brain. *Philos. Trans. R. Soc. Ser. B* 358(1430):277–80

Gallese V, Fadiga L, Fogassi L, Rizzolatti G. 1996. Action recognition in the premotor cortex. *Brain* 119:593–609

Garfinkel H. 1967. *Studies in Ethnomethodology*. New York: Prentice Hall

Garro L, Yarris K. 2009. "A massive long way": interconnecting histories, a "special child," ADHD, and everyday family life. *Cult. Med. Psychiatry* 33(4):559–607

Geertz C. 1974. "From the native's point of view": on the nature of anthropological understanding. *Bull. Am. Acad. Arts Sci.* 28(1):26–45

Geertz C. 1983. *Local Knowledge*. New York: Basic Books

Geschwind DH, Levitt P. 2007. Autism spectrum disorders: developmental disconnection syndromes. *Curr. Opin. Neurobiol.* 17(1):103–11

Goldknopf E. 2002. Referring indirectly to diagnoses in a psychiatric clinic. *Crossroads Lang. Interact. Cult.* 4(4):59–91

Goodwin C. 1994. Professional vision. *Am. Anthropol.* 96:606–33

Goodwin C. 2000. Gesture, aphasia and interaction. In *Language and Gesture: Window into Thought and Action*, ed. D McNeill, pp. 84–98. Cambridge, UK: Cambridge Univ. Press

Goodwin C. 2003. Conversational frameworks for the accomplishment of meaning in aphasia. In *Conversation and Brain Damage*, ed. C Goodwin, pp. 90–116. Oxford: Oxford Univ. Press

Goodwin C. 2004. A competent speaker who can't speak: the social life of aphasia. *J. Linguist. Anthropol.* 14(2):151–70

Goodwin M, Velicer W, Intille S. 2008. Telemetric monitoring in the behavior sciences. *Behav. Res. Methods* 40(1):328–41

Grinker R. 2007. A secret garden. *N. Sci.* 194(2598):49–55

Grinker R. 2008a. *Unstrange Minds: Remapping the World of Autism*. New York: Basic Books

Grinker R. 2008b. What in the world is autism? A cross-cultural perspective. *Zero Three* 28(4):5–10

Grinker R. 2010. Commentary: On being autistic, and social. *Ethos* 38(1):176–83

Gutierrez K, Rogoff B. 2003. Cultural ways of learning: individual traits or repertoires of practice. *Educ. Res.* 32(5):19–25

Hacking I. 1999. *The Social Construction of What?* Cambridge, MA: Harvard Univ. Press

Hacking I. 2006. Genetics, biosocial groups and the future of identity. *Daedalus* 135(4):81–95

Hacking I. 2006. What is Tom saying to Maureen? *Lond. Rev. Books* 28(9):3–7

Hacking I. 2008. Why physics is easy and autism is hard. In *A Vision of Transdisciplinarity: Laying Foundations for a World Knowledge Dialogue*, ed. F Darbellay, M Cockell, J Billotte, pp. 6–39. Boca Raton, FL: Taylor & Francis

Hacking I. 2009a. Autistic autobiography. *Philos. Trans. R. Soc. Biol. Sci.* 364(1522):1467–73

Hacking I. 2009b. How we have been learning to talk about autism: the role of stories. *Metaphilosophy* 40(3–4):499–516

Hall AV, Schwartz-Watts D, Abramson R. 2007. *The incidence rate of ASD in the correction population*. Presented at Int. Meet. Autism Res., Seattle, WA

Hirstein W, Iversen P, Ramachandran V. 2001. Autonomic responses of autistic children to people and objects. *Proc. Biol. Sci.* 268(1479):1883–88

Jackson M. 1998. *Minima Ethnographica: Intersubjectivity and the Anthropological Project*. Chicago: Univ. Chicago Press

Jenkins J, Barrett R. 2004. *Schizophrenia, Culture, and Subjectivity: The Edge of Experience*. Cambridge, UK: Cambridge Univ. Press

Jensen U. 2007. The struggle for clinical authority: shifting ontologies and the politics of evidence. *BioSocieties* 2(01):101–14

Kanner L. 1943. Autistic disturbances of affective contact. *Nerv. Child* 2:217–50

Kasari C, Paparella T, Freeman S, Jahromi LB. 2008. Language outcomes in autism: randomized comparison of joint attention and play interventions. *J. Consult. Clin. Psychol.* 76(1):125–37

Kaufman SR. 2010. Regarding the rise in autism: vaccine safety doubt, conditions of inquiry, and the shape of freedom. *Ethos* 38(1):8–33

Kirby DF. 2005. *Evidence of Harm. Mercury in Vaccines and the Autism Epidemic: Medical Controversy*. New York: St. Martin's Press

Kirmayer L, Lemelson R, Barad M. 2007. *Understanding Trauma: Integrating Biological, Clinical, and Cultural Perspectives*. Cambridge, UK: Cambridge Univ. Press

Kleinman A. 1997. *Writing at the Margin: Discourse between Anthropology and Medicine*. Berkeley: Univ. Calif. Press

Kleinman A. 2001. Why psychiatry and cultural anthropology still need each other. *Psychiatry: Interpers. Biol. Process.* 64(1):14–16

Kleinman A, Good B. 1986. *Culture and Depression: Studies in the Anthropology and Cross-Cultural Psychiatry of Affect and Disorder*. Berkeley: Univ. Calif. Press

Kulick D, Schieffelin B. 2004. Language socialization. In *A Companion to Linguistic Anthropology*, ed. A Duranti, pp. 349–68. New York: Wiley

Kupfer DJ. 2005. Dimensional models for research and diagnosis: a current dilemma. *J. Abnorm. Psychol.* 114(1):557–59

Lawlor M. 2003. The significance of being occupied: the social construction of childhood occupations. *J. Occup. Ther.* 57(2):424–34

Lawlor M. 2010. Commentary: Autism and anthropology? *Ethos* 38(1):171–75

Lawlor M, Mattingly C. 2008. Understanding family perspectives on illness and disability experience. In *Willard and Spackman's Occupational Therapy*, ed. C Elizabeth, E Cohn, B Schell, pp. 2–12. Philadelphia: JB Lippincott. 11th ed.

Lawlor MC. 2010. Narrative, development, and engagement: intersections in therapeutic practice. In *Narrative, Self and Social Practice*, ed. U Jensen, C Mattingly. Aarhus, Denmark: Aarhus Univ. Press. In press

Lemelson R, Kirmayer LJ, Barad M. 2007. Trauma in context: integrating cultural, clinical, and biological perspectives. In *Understanding Trauma: Integrating Biological, Clinical and Cultural Perspectives*, ed. L Kirkmayer, R Lemelson, M Barad, pp. 451–74. Cambridge, UK: Cambridge Univ. Press

Levitt P, Cambell D. 2009. The genetic and neurobiologic compass points toward common signaling dysfunctions in autism spectrum disorders. *J. Clin. Investig.* 119(4):747–54

Mandell D, Listerud J, Levy S, Pinto-Martin JA. 2002. Race differences in the age at diagnosis among Medicaid-eligible children with autism. *J. Am. Acad. Child Adolesc. Psychiatry* 41(12):1447–53

Mandell D, Wiggins L, Carpenter L, Daniels J, DiGuiseppi C. 2009. Racial/ethnic disparities in the identification of children with autism spectrum disorders. *Am. J. Public Health* 99(3):493–98

Mattingly C. 1998. *Healing Dramas and Clinical Plots: The Narrative Structure of Experience*. Cambridge, UK: Cambridge Univ. Press

Maynard D. 2005. Social actions, gestalt coherence, and designations of disability: lessons from and about autism. *Soc. Probl.* 52(4):499–524

Maynard D. 2006. Cognition on the ground. *Discourse Stud.* 8(1):105–15

McDermott R. 2001. The acquisition of a child by a learning disability. In *Understanding Learning: Influences and Outcomes*, ed. S Chaiklin, J Lave, pp. 269–305. New York: Cambridge Univ. Press

McDermott R, Goldman S, Varenne H. 2006. The cultural work of learning disabilities. *Educ. Res.* 35(6):12–17

McDonough P. 1999. Autism and the modern identity: autism anxiety in popular film. *Disabil. Stud. Q.* 19(3):184–91

McGeer V. 2004. Autistic self-awareness. *Philos. Psychiatry Psychol.* 11(1):235–52

Mehan H. 1993. Beneath the skin and between the ears: a case study in the politics of representation. In *Understanding Practice: Perspectives on Activity and Contexts*, ed. S Chaiklin, J Lave, pp. 241–68. Cambridge, UK: Cambridge Univ. Press

Mehan H. 1996. The construction of an LD student: a case study in the politics of representation. In *Natural History of Discourse*, ed. M Silverstein, G Urban, pp. 253–76. Chicago: Univ. Chicago Press

Moldin SO, Rubenstein JLR. 2006. *Understanding Autism: From Basic Neuroscience to Treatment*. Boca Raton: Taylor & Francis

Monroe W. 1979. Diagnosing literary autism. *Chic. Rev.* 31(1):43–49

Mottron L, Burack JA. 2001. Enhanced perceptual functioning in the development of autism. In *The Development of Autism: Perspectives from Theory and Research*, ed. JA Burack, T Charman, N Yirmiya, PR Zelazo, pp. 131–48. Mahwah, NJ: Lawrence Erlbaum

Mottron L, Dawson M, Hubert B, Soulieres I, Burack JA. 2006. The enhanced perceptual functioning model of autism. *J. Autism Dev. Disorders* 36:27–43

Mottron L, Dawson M, Soulières I. 2009. Enhanced perception in savant syndrome: patterns, structure and creativity. *Phil. Trans. R. Soc. Biol. Sci.* 364:1385–91

Murray S. 2008. *Representing Autism: Culture, Narrative, Fascination*. Liverpool: Liverpool Univ. Press

Nadesan M. 2005. *Constructing Autism: Unravelling the "Truth" and Understanding the Social*. London: Routledge

Nasser M, Katzman M, Gordon R. 2001. *Eating Disorders and Cultures in Transition*. New York: Routledge

Nussbaum M. 2006. *Frontiers of Justice*. New York: Belknap

Ochs E. 2002. Becoming a speaker of culture. In *Language Acquisition and Language Socialization: Ecological Perspectives*, ed. C Kramsch, pp. 99–120. London: Continuum

Ochs E, Solomon O. 2004. Practical logic and autism. In *A Companion to Psychological Anthropology*, ed. R Edgerton, C Casey, pp. 140–67. Oxford: Blackwell

Ochs E, Solomon O. 2010. Autistic sociality. *Ethos* 38(1):72–96

Ochs E, Kremer-Sadlik T, Sirota K, et al. 2004. Autism and the social world: an anthropological perspective. *Discourse Stud.* 6(2):147–83

Ochs E, Kremer-Sadlik T, Solomon O, Sirota KG. 2001. Inclusion as social practice: views of children with autism. *Soc. Dev.* 10(3):399–419

Ochs E, Solomon O, Sterponi L. 2005. Limitations and transformations of habitus in child-directed communication. *Discourse Stud.* 7(4–5):547–83

Ong A. 1995. Making the biopolitical subject: Cambodian immigrants, refugee medicine and cultural citizenship in California. *Soc. Sci. Med.* 40(9):1243–57

Osteen M. 2008. *Autism and Representation*. London: Routledge

Page T. 2009. *Parallel Play: Growing Up with Undiagnosed Asperger's*. New York: Doubleday.

Park M. 2008. Making scenes: imaginative practices of a child with autism in a sensory integration-based therapy session. *Med. Anthropol. Q.* 22(3):234–56

Pratt M. 1986. Fieldwork in common places. In *Writing Culture: The Poetics and Politics of Ethnography*, ed. J Clifford, GE Marcus, pp. 27–50. Berkeley: Univ. Calif. Press

Prince DE. 2010. An exceptional path: an ethnographic narrative reflecting on autistic parenthood from evolutionary, cultural, and spiritual perspectives. *Ethos* 38(1):59–71

Rabinow P. 1997. Artificiality and enlightenment: from sociobiology to biosociality. In *The Science Studies Reader*, ed. M Biagioli, pp. 407–16. New York: Routledge

Rapp R. 1998. Refusing prenatal diagnosis: the meanings of bioscience in a multicultural world. *Sci. Technol. Hum. Values* 23(1):45–70

Rapp R. 1999. *Testing Women, Testing the Fetus: The Social Impact of Amniocentesis in America*. New York: Routledge

Rapp R. 2000. Extra chromosomes and blue tulips: medico-familial interpretations. In *Living and Working with the New Medical Technologies: Intersections of Inquiry*, ed. M Lock, A Young, A Cambrosio, pp. 184–208. Cambridge, UK: Cambridge Univ. Press

Rapp R, Ginsburg F. 2001. Enabling disability: rewriting kinship, reimagining citizenship. *Public Cult.* 13(3):533–56

Rapp R, Heath D, Taussig KS. 2002. Genealogical dis-ease: where hereditary abnormality, biomedical explanation, and family responsibility meet. In *Relative Matters: Reconfiguring Kinship Studies*, ed. S Franklin, S McKinnon, pp. 384–412. Durham, NC: Duke Univ. Press

Rizzolatti G, Fadiga L, Fogassi L, Gallese V. 1996. Premotor cortex and the recognition of motor actions. *Cogn. Brain Res.* 3:131–41

Rothenberg M. 1960. *Children with Emerald Eyes: Histories of Extraordinary Boys and Girls*. Berkeley, CA: N. Atl. Books

Russell J. 1997. *Autism as an Executive Disorder*. Oxford: Oxford Univ. Press

Sacks O. 1970. *The Man Who Mistook His Wife for a Hat and Other Clinical Tales*. New York: Touchstone

Sacks O. 1995. *An Anthropologist on Mars: Seven Paradoxical Tales*. New York: Knopf

Schopler E. 2001. Treatment for autism. From science to pseudo-science or anti-science. In *The Research Basis for Autism Intervention*, ed. E Schopler, N Yirmiya, C Shulman, LM Markus, pp. 9–24. New York: Kluwer Acad./Plenum

Schreibman L. 2005. *The Science and Fiction of Autism*. Cambridge, MA: Harvard Univ. Press

Shah N. 2001. *Contagious Divides: Epidemics and Race in San Francisco's Chinatown*. Berkeley: Univ. Calif. Press

Sewell W Jr. 1997. Geertz, cultural systems, and history: from synchrony to transformation. Spec. Issue: The Fate of "Culture": Geertz and Beyond. *Representations* 59:35–55

Shohet M. 2008. Narrating Anorexia: "full" and "struggling" genres of recovery. *Ethos* 35(3):344–82

Sigman M, Capps L. 1997. *Children with Autism: A Developmental Perspective*. Cambridge, MA: Harvard Univ. Press

Silverman C. 2008. Fieldwork on another planet: social science perspectives on the autism spectrum. *BioSocieties* 3(3):325–41

Silverman C, Brosco J. 2007. Understanding autism: parents and pediatricians in historical perspective. *Arch. Pediatr. Adolesc. Med.* 161(4):392–98

Singh J, Hallmayer J, Illes J. 2007. Interacting and paradoxical forces in neuroscience and society. *Nat. Rev. Neurosci.* 8(2):153–60

Sirota KG. 2004. Positive politeness as discourse process: politeness practices of high-functioning children with autism and Asperger Syndrome. *Discourse Stud.* 6(2):229–51

Sirota KG. 2010. Narratives of distinction: personal life narrative as a technology of the self in the everyday lives and relational worlds of children with autism. *Ethos* 38(1):97–119

Solomon O. 2004. Narrative introductions: discourse competence of children with autistic spectrum disorders. *Discourse Stud.* 6(2):253–76

Solomon O. 2008. Language, autism, and childhood: an ethnographic perspective. *Annu. Rev. Appl. Linguist.* 28(1):150–69

Solomon O. 2009. Giftedness and creativity in autism. In *Encyclopedia of Giftedness, Creativity, and Talent*, ed. BA Kerr, pp. 82–83. Thousand Oaks: Sage

Solomon O. 2010. What a dog can do: children with autism and therapy dogs in social interaction. *Ethos* 38(1):145–70

Solomon O, Bagatell N. 2010. Autism: rethinking the possibilities. *Ethos* 38(1):1–7

Sontag S. 2003. *Regarding the Pain of Others*. New York: Picador

Stahmer A, Mandell D. 2007. State infant/toddler program policies for eligibility and services provision for young children with autism. *Adm. Policy Ment. Health Ment. Health Serv. Res.* 34(1):29–37

Steiner G. 2002. *Grammars of Creation*. Oxford: Yale Univ. Press

Sterponi L. 2004. Construction of rules, accountability and moral identity by high-functioning children with autism. *Discourse Stud.* 6(2):207–28

Sterponi L, Fasulo A. 2010. "How to go on": intersubjectivity and progressivity in the communication of a child with autism. *Ethos* 38(1):120–44

Striano T, Reid V. 2009. *Social Cognition: Development, Neuroscience and Autism*. Malden: Wiley-Blackwell

Taylor C. 1985. *Philosophy and the Human Sciences*. Cambridge, UK: Cambridge Univ. Press

Thackara J. 2001. The design challenge of pervasive computing. *Interactions* 8(3):46–52

Throop CJ. 2010. *Suffering and Sentiment: Exploring the Vicissitudes of Pain and Experience in Yap (Waqab), Federated States of Micronesia*. Berkeley: Univ. Calif. Press

Tomasello M. 1999. *The Cultural Origins of Human Cognition*. Cambridge, MA: Harvard Univ. Press

Tomasello M, Carpenter M, Call J, Behne T, Moll H. 2005. Understanding and sharing intentions: the origins of cultural cognition. *Behav. Brain Sci.* 28(05):675–91

Varenne H, McDermott R. 1999. *Successful Failure: The School America Builds*. Boulder, CO: Westview

Vinden PG, Astington JW. 2000. Culture and understanding other minds. In *Understanding Other Minds: Perspectives from Developmental Cognitive Neuroscience*, ed. S Baron-Cohen, H Tager-Flusberg, D Cohen, pp. 503–19. Oxford: Oxford Univ. Press. 2nd ed.

Volkmar F. 2005. *Handbook of Autism and Pervasive Developmental Disorders: Assessment, Interventions, and Policy*. Hoboken, NJ: Wiley

Wilce J. 2004. Language and madness. In *A Companion to Linguistic Anthropology*, ed. A Duranti, pp. 414–30. Malden: Blackwell

Wilkinson K. 2009. *Mother's perspectives on everyday life with children with autism: mealtimes explored*. PhD diss., Univ. South. Calif. 277 pp.

Wing L. 1981. Autistic spectrum disorders. *Br. Med. J.* 312(7027):327–28

Wing L. 2003. *The Autistic Spectrum: A Guide for Parents and Professionals*. London: Robinson

Wright J. 2004. *Origin Stories in Political Thought: Discourses on Gender, Power, and Citizenship*. Toronto: Univ. Tor. Press

Young A. 1995. *The Harmony of Illusions: Inventing Posttraumatic Stress Disorder*. Princeton, NJ: Princeton Univ. Press

Zwaigenbaum L, Bryson S, Lord C, Rogers S, Carter A. 2009. Clinical assessment and management of toddlers with suspected autism spectrum disorder: insights from studies of high-risk infants. *Pediatrics* 123(5):1383–91

Gender, Militarism, and Peace-Building: Projects of the Postconflict Moment

Mary H. Moran

Department of Sociology and Anthropology, Colgate University, Hamilton, New York
13346; email: mmoran@colgate.edu

Annu. Rev. Anthropol. 2010. 39:261–74

First published online as a Review in Advance on
June 21, 2010

The *Annual Review of Anthropology* is online at
anthro.annualreviews.org

This article's doi:
10.1146/annurev-anthro-091908-164406

0084-6570/10/1021-0261$20.00

Key Words

war, violence, humanitarian intervention, postconflict societies

Abstract

Scholars have argued for decades about the relationship between biological sex and organized violence, but feminist analysts across numerous
disciplines have documented the range and variety of gendered roles in
times of war. In recent years, research has brought new understanding
of the rapidity with which ideas about masculinity and femininity can
change in times of war and the role of militarization in constructing and
enforcing the meaning of manhood and womanhood. In the post–Cold
War period, "new wars" (Kaldor 1999) have mobilized gender in multiple ways, and peace-building is often managed by external humanitarian
organizations. A strange disconnect exists between the massive body of
scholarly research on gender, militarism, and peace-building and on-
the-ground practices in postconflict societies, where essentialized ideas
of men as perpetrators of violence and women as victims continue to
guide much program design.

INTRODUCTION

For anthropologists and other scholars grappling with the relationship between gender, militarism, and peace-building, the dispersal of materials across disciplines and genres can present a formidable challenge. Although massive, interdisciplinary academic and policy literatures exist in the separate areas of militarism and peace-building (and their cognates, including violence, terror, peace-keeping, and postconflict rebuilding), a significant portion ignores the question of gender and simply assumes that these processes are experienced in similar ways by all humans. Paris's influential book *At War's End: Building Peace After Conflict* (2004), for example, contains no index entries for "women," "men," or "gender" and presents detailed case studies in a classical international relations continuum to explore the impact of different types of peace treaties on the desired outcome of a conflict-free society. A recent argument for rethinking the conventional wisdom with regard to standard practices for implementing democratic reform and reconciliation among formerly contesting parties likewise avoids gendered language, referring only to disembodied "belligerents" and "key leaders" (Wolpe & McDonald 2008). Feminist writers, on the other hand, have often addressed the role of violence in maintaining gender inequality. The threat or use of physical force that is glorified and institutionalized in formal, state-based militaries can also be deployed in neighborhoods, households, and bedrooms, resulting in the systematic subordination of women (Elshtain 1987; Reardon 1985). Attempts to read these different literatures side by side suggest that it is apparently still common for political theorists and policy makers to exclude a gender perspective from their analyses; however, since the 1990s a series of United Nations conventions and changes in international law have made it more difficult to ignore. United Nations (UN) Security Council Resolution 1325, passed in October of 2000, calls for the "increased representation of women at all decision-making levels in national, regional, and international institutions and mechanisms for the prevention, management, and resolution of conflict" (United Nations 2000). The resolution was itself a product of both the 1995 Fourth World Conference on Women in Beijing and the "Windhoek Declaration" (also known as the "Namibia Plan of Action"), a document emanating from a seminar organized by the Lessons Learned Unit of the UN Department of Peace Keeping Operations, which called for a "gender mainstreaming" approach at all levels of conflict intervention and peace support (United Nations Secur. Counc. 2001). International criminal tribunals established by the security council to investigate and prosecute war crimes in the former Yugoslavia, Rwanda, and Sierra Leone have pushed the legal definitions of gender-based violence and rape into the categories of crimes against humanity, leading to the emergence of new bodies of international law. An emerging body of critical legal scholarship is beginning to question the universalist assumptions built into transitional justice mechanisms and other strategies that seek to empower women, but too many postconflict reform projects continue to be grounded in static, overly simplified, or locally inappropriate notions of gender. In this review, I trace the points of articulation and disconnect between disparate literatures while pointing out the consequences of naturalizing either femininity or masculinity.

The UN, the World Bank, and other multinational organizations regularly employ gender specialists, who are sometimes anthropologists, in their fact-finding and program-development process, and the ever-growing humanitarian and nongovernmental organization (NGO) communities are particularly sensitive to questions of gender inclusiveness. Two points become clear in any initial survey of the literature, however: (*a*) With some notable exceptions, the term gender is still commonly used as synonym for "women" and, (*b*) although most analysts of gender explicitly position themselves as feminists, a wide variety of theoretical positions and disciplinary perspectives are represented in the body of work on this topic. The literature is further divided into scholarly studies and policy recommendations, rapid assessment reports, and guidebooks for gender mainstreaming practices in such post-conflict projects as the demobilization of armed combatants, male and female, trauma counseling, and the retraining of both former fighters and civilians for economic development in the postwar period. Other peace-building projects with explicit gender components include transitional justice measures such as legal code reform, constitutional and governance restructuring, truth and reconciliation commissions, land tenure reform, and performances of "traditional" modes of conflict resolution. Given the space limitations of this article, I address the scholarly literature only, although the reader will find many references to broader sources of information in the references of these works.

MILITARY MEN, PACIFIST WOMEN?

The overall literature on gender, militarism, and peace has been shaped for close to 50 years by debates about the relationship between these terms; initially, innate biological differences were offered as an explanation for the near universal participation of men as warriors and women as victims and/or peace activists. Within anthropology and other disciplines, debates centered on the question of whether warfare was an inevitable outcome of male biology and was therefore impossible to eradicate from human life. Goldstein (2001) has exhaustively reviewed the cross-cultural evidence from anthropology, psychology, primate studies, and human biology and concluded that "minor biological differences" in combination with "cultural molding of tough, brave men who feminize their enemies to encode domination" (p. 406) best explain men's near monopoly on organized violence, although neither factor is sufficient alone (see also Gusterson 2007). The impact of feminist theories in a number of academic fields, defining gender as fluid, variable, and multiple systems of femininities and masculinities, made possible a new formulation

of the relationship. We know now that times of extreme violence, upheaval, and disruption are also times of profound change for gender ideologies and for relations between men and women. Rather than institutionalizing static, biologically determined patterns of behavior, militarization can promote rapid shifts in the way men and women behave toward each other, the work they do, and what they expect of each other and of themselves. Intimately connected with the process of organizing human and material resources into permanent, legitimate institutions concerned with armed force, militarism requires men and women to consider how their supposedly natural talents and abilities may be put to the service of a larger cause. In contemporary nation-states, militarization often encourages a new and explicit conceptualization of citizenship that may involve highly gendered notions of membership, contribution, and sacrifice. Feminist political scientist Cynthia Enloe, among others, has noted that neither brave soldiers nor patriotic mothers and widows are born; they are produced through gendered processes that require the deployment and mobilization of material and symbolic resources (1983, 1989, 1993). In some times and places, these processes reinforce and naturalize gender inequality, but they can also have the opposite effect. Anthropologists, with their long-standing constructionist view that genders are historically and geographically variable, have been slow to apply these theoretical insights to questions of militarization as a process, perhaps because, as Gusterson (2007) suggests, they have only recently begun to consider the discipline's own positioning in the context of nineteenth- and twentieth-century militarization (p. 156; see also di Leonardo 1985).

Feminist scholars in fields such as philosophy, religion, political science, and international relations as well as anthropology began questioning the stark characterization of men as warriors and women as peacemakers in the early 1980s and have continued to do so in the face of enduring representations of these stereotypes in journalism and popular media (Cancian &

Gibson 1990; Cockburn 1998, 2002, 2007; Cooke & Woollacott 1993; Elshtain 1987; Elshtain & Tobias 1990; Enloe 1983, 1989, 1993; Fraser & Jeffery 1993; Harris & King 1989; Hatty 2000; Jacobs et al. 2000; Lorentzen & Turpin 1998; Macdonald et al. 1998; Meintjes et al. 2001; Melman 1998; Reardon 1985, 1993; Ruddick 1983, 1989; Tickner 1992; Turshen & Twagiramariya 1998; Vickers 1993; Zalewski & Parpart 1998). A series of related topics have been addressed in this literature, including the differing experiences of men and women during wartime; differential rates of representation by sex among casualties and in refugee communities; the targeting of women for particular kinds of violence, usually rape or sexual mutilation; the consequences of men's military mobilization for domestic violence, including marital rape and spousal abuse; women's economic well-being, access to land, jobs, and other resources; and the impact of national military spending on the provision of state services. The growing literature on masculinity, particularly its militarized varients (Bowker 1998; Braudy 2003; Connell 1987, 1995, 2000; Gill 1997; Gillis 1989; Gutman 1997; Helman 1999; Highgate 2003; Kwon 2001; Moon 2005; Moran 1995; Peterson 1992; Wicks 1996), has contributed to the analysis of war and peace as gendered processes. Inspired by Anderson's work on nationalism (1991), studies of contemporary forms of citizenship closely linked to military service showed that these were foundational to hegemonic masculinities subordinating most women and some men. The highly influential body of work by Enloe (1983, 1989, 1993, 2000, 2004, 2007) connected the incorporation of women into national armies, the global distribution of American military bases, world economic restructuring, and prostitution and sex trafficking, among other topics, to shifts in gender ideologies on a global scale. Responses to Enloe's ideas formed the basis of an early collection on militarism, gender, and nationalism in anthropology (Sutton 1995) and paved the way for other anthropological studies of militarism and gender (Lutz 2001, 2009; Nordstom 1997, 2004; Sunindyo 1998). From this body of research, militarism came to be seen as a process affecting all societies worldwide, regardless of whether they were actively engaged in war at any given time.

NEW WARS, NEW QUESTIONS

As local conflicts spread across the globe in the post–Cold War period of the 1990s, American anthropologists who had been able to ignore the militarization of their own nation-state were confronted by what Kaldor has termed "new wars" breaking out in their traditional field locations in Africa, Latin America, Eastern Europe, and elsewhere (Gusterson 2007, Kaldor 1999). The gender regimes of an increasing number of places were suddenly and demonstrably being transformed by processes of militarization; but rather than the state-sponsored, industrially driven pattern that had characterized the west in the first half of the twentieth century, these new wars were more likely to involve nonstate actors and directed much of their violence at civilian populations. Women were no longer confined to the home-front or even to the rear positions but instead were incorporated much more directly into the violence as both victims and perpetrators. As far back as the 1960s and 1970s, some Marxist feminists had speculated about revolutionary mobilization as a liberating process for women, one that would grant them full citizenship for their service in militarized state-making and would force their male counterparts to accept them as full equals. As outcomes of anticolonial and identity-inspired wars of liberation became clear, however, these hopes were largely disappointed (Afshar & Eade 2004, Altinay 2004, Bernal 2000, Conover & Sapiro 1993, El-Bushra 2004, Feinman 2000, Gautam et al. 2001, Goldman 1982, Hauge 2007, Jalusic 1999, Kumar 2001, Lomsky-Feer & Ben-Ari 1999, Luciak 2001, Lyons 2002, Makley 2007, Mama 1998, Manchandra 2001, Milles 2000, Molyneux 1985, Montoya et al. 2002, Moser & Clark 2001, Narikkar 2005, Pankhurst 2008b,

Shayne 2004, Tetreault 1994, Turshen 2002, Unger 2000, Utas 2005). Similar discussion swirled around the question of opening combat roles to women in the highly technologized militaries of the United States and other developed countries. Innovations in weapons design, resulting in smaller and lighter yet more lethal small arms, largely obviated the older discourses about whether women were biologically unsuited for combat. As these weapons flooded into the "new war" sites of Asia, Africa, and Latin American, the phenomenon of the "child soldier" became a focus of much research (Kaldor 1999, Rosen 2007).

At the same time, a different literature focused on women's antiwar efforts, no longer assuming these were natural expressions of essential female nature but rather responses to the differentially devastating impact of the new wars on civilians. There had already been a vigorous debate about the relationship between motherhood and peace-building, some of which reprised the older naturalizing arguments but more importantly raised the issue of "moral maternity" (Ruddick 1989) as a basis for women's solidarity and organizing. Feminists recognized the strategic value of such moral claims but worried that they played into the essentialized femininities that had long been excluded from the male realm of politics. Women's grassroots movements for peace, sometimes crossing class and sectional lines, were credited in some instances with almost phenomenal success, not always accurately. Some of these movements undeniably led to new forms of agency and empowerment as women invoked moral positions as peacemakers in the face of seemingly intractable conflict (African Women Peace Support Group 2004; Amiri 2005; Anderlini 2007; Bouta et al. 2005; Castillo 1997; Clifton & Gell 2001; Cockburn 1998, 2007; Dolgopol 2006; Durham & Gurd 2005; Fitzgerald 2002; Gardner & El Bushra 2004; Giles & Hyndman 2004; Haq 2007; Harris & King 1989; Hunt 2004, 2005; Jacoby 2005; Jok 1999; Korac 2006; Manchandra 2001; Mason 2005; Marshall 2000; Mendez 2005; Moghadam 2001, 2005; Moola 2006; Moran & Pitcher 2004; Nakaya 2004; Pankhurst 2004; Povey 2004; Powers 2006; Rabrenovic & Roskas 2001; Ramet 1999; Rehn & Sirleaf 2002; Sharoni 1995; Zalewski & Parpart 1998). Careful attention to the different strategies used by women activists in diverse times and places has cast doubt on any single-cause theory of how conflicts are resolved and lasting peace is achieved.

Amid the tragedy and terror came a growing realization that the gains in organizational capacity and personal empowerment achieved by some women peace activists were difficult to sustain in the postconflict period. Furthermore, not all women had access to the limited number of leadership positions, even when these were transformed into electoral victories during peace time. It remains unclear just how empowering the experience of participating in peace demonstrations can be for ordinary women, although some individuals might translate these activities into personal decisions that improve their lives and relationships. For the most part, women's visible roles in advocating for peace were often confined to street protests and other unofficial sites, whereas the conference rooms where treaties were negotiated remained male-only enclaves and postwar governmental positions went largely to the well-connected (Abdela 2004; African Women Peace Support Group 2004; Coles 2007; Corrin 2004; Frazier 2002; Mertus 1999, 2000; Porter et al. 1999; Rajasingham-Senanayake 2001). It was in this context, as well as in the aftermath of embarrassing reports about the sexual exploitation of displaced and refugee women by UN peace-keeping troops and civilian employees, that UN Resolution 1325 was passed. In effect, the resolution posits that the postwar moment represents a brief window of time in which wartime gains can be consolidated.

THE AFTERMATH

In the context of postwar peacekeeping by multinational organizations, new questions arose: Could militarized male troops adapt their behavior and expectations to peace-keeping missions? Would the presence of female soldiers among the foreign troops create new models for empowering local women, often presumed to have been historically oppressed? What possibilities for reconfiguring gender relations did the aftermath of violent conflict offer (Breines et al. 2000, Carey 2001, Cock 1994, Cockburn 2002, DeGroot 2001, Highgate & Henry 2004, Karame 2001, Koyama & Myrtiren 2007, Mackay 2004, Mazurana et al. 2005, Meintjes et al. 2001, Merry 2006, Olsson & Tryggestad 2001, Pankhurst 2008b, Skjelbaek 2001, Stiehm 2001, Terry 2002, Whitworth 2004, Williams 2001).

With increasing intervention from both multinational and nonstate entities in these local conflicts, external actors worked to ensure that the more positive gender transformations of wartime, like women's new access to a public voice, could be continued in the peace-time context. Although terrible for those who had to experience it, extreme violence was believed to have the paradoxical effect of opening opportunities for more progressive, egalitarian gender relations in places that had previously been highly patriarchal. The moral claims of women who had acted as peace-makers as well as a general sense that men had failed to sustain reasonable governments created the context for legislative reforms, including gender quotas for elected representation at the national level (Bauer & Britton 2006, Tripp et al. 2009). But even as some postconflict societies, such as Uganda and Rwanda, registered enormous electoral gains for women parliamentary candidates and Liberians elected the first female president on the African continent, other analysts noted the significant backlash occurring for ordinary women. Rape and other forms of gendered violence have actually been seen to increase in the postconflict moment, over wartime levels, and attempts at legal reform often founder on limited institutional and human capacity to staff courts and retrain police, as well as on a lack of political will from successor governments (Pankhurst 2008b, Rehn & Sirleaf 2002, Turshen 2001, Vayrynen 2004). Where militarization had been seen as the source of women's problems, the "return to peace" sometimes included a "retraditionalization" or reassertion of prewar patriarchy (Turshen 2001).

Although the academics cited above have frequently been critical of the postwar reconstruction efforts of multinational institutions and NGOs, many practitioners in the humanitarian community remain fiercely committed to the idea of the postwar moment as a time when gender can be radically reconstructed. The gender mainstreaming called for in UN Resolution 1325 has generated a series of gender projects that are now included in the standard package of postconflict programming. These projects include attention to the disarming and demobilization of both male and female combatants, the training of foreign peacekeepers in their responsibilities regarding the sexual exploitation of local populations, the provision of extensive medical and psychosocial services to victims of sexual violence, and attempts to provide training in marketable skills and small-business development to displaced civilians and excombatants. Some of these programs founder on unexamined gender assumptions, as when men are offered training in auto mechanics and women are presented with classes in dress making or cloth dying, often in places where few people can afford either cars or new clothing (Utas 2003). Other peace-building projects, such as transitional justice and governance reform programs, as well as a host of democracy promotion and classical economic development programs, may not be explicitly about gender, yet their underlying assumptions about both the beneficiaries of the proposed changes and the sources of resistance reflect naturalized ideas of men and women. Implementation of these gender initiatives, even when funded by donations from the United States, European Union, or UN, is commonly contracted to private NGOs and humanitarian groups. Their activities have become a vibrant new area of ethnographic investigation by anthropologists (Abramowitz 2009; Abusharaf 2006; Anderson 1999; Boesten 2008; Burnet 2008; Coulter 2006; Crew & Harrison 1998; Fuest 2007, 2008; Hemmet 2007; Macrae 2001;

Rose 2000; Rosen 2007; Shaw 2007; Snajdr 2007; Summerfield 1999; Tate 2007; Terry 2002; Weissman & Terry 2004; Unvin 1998).

The idea that militarization and war create new opportunities for women has not always been supported by the evidence, as mentioned above. Why, then, should agents on the ground, both local activists and representatives of international organizations, persist in seeing at least some postwar situations as containing limitless possibilities and blank slate opportunities, assuming that gender as well as other relations of power have been erased and progressive outsiders can guide the survivors to a new, neoliberal paradise? Extreme violence might well lead people who have experienced it to be open to new ideas, but many who advocate this position tend to naturalize and essentialize violence as an outgrowth of male aggression, held in check by "good" social institutions (see Pankhurst 2008b, pp. 293–313). Having seen the horrors unleashed by undemocratic, or overly militarized, or nonliberal regimes, citizens are expected to demand social and cultural controls over men as a group, in the form of women's civil and legal rights, enhanced rape laws, and new codes of domestic relations, not only for their own sake but as a check on future wars. This position, however, not only assumes that all men are to blame for the violence, but also discounts women's prewar sources of legitimate political authority. Reduced to its essence, this is the message of such popular documentary films as Abigail Disney's *Pray the Devil Back to Hell*, which represents the women's peace movement in Liberia as arising entirely from the war itself. No mention is made in the film of the rich history of collective action by Liberian women, nor of the powerful ritual, social, and political positions they have held in the past. The horrors of war, paradoxically, are credited with freeing women to discover their own untapped potential and achieve liberation from their oppressive, patriarchal menfolk.

Another common assumption is that it is the dissolution of previous social relations, along with mass casualties that disproportionately impact men, that opens political space for women in postconflict societies. In the absence of the usual personnel to fill positions of authority, new candidates, often with the help of external change agents, step in to fill the gap. Although not as dismissive of men as the first model, this construct likewise assumes that prewar society had no space for women in authority-bearing roles and that women's emergence as peace activists, organizers, and pressure groups is a radical break with the past. Finally, many of the external change agents subscribe to what can only be described as a civilizing mission oriented toward universalizing neoliberal discourses of individual human rights, gender equality, and other progressive goals. The postwar moment is explicitly framed as a valuable but limited window of opportunity, which will close quickly if not exploited to the maximum (Abramowitz 2009, Merry 2006).

In my own experience, returning to my previous research site in Liberia after more than 14 years of civil war, I found a widely circulated discourse that "women are traditionally considered property" was being invoked as an explanation for continuing high levels of rape and domestic violence in the postwar period. This was striking because I had never heard such an expression in the years before the war and because it was repeated by both foreign aid workers and by Liberians working with them. Both indigenous Liberian societies and the national political culture had been unabashedly patriarchal long before the war, but women had also held visible, highly authoritative positions in both rural and urban contexts. Although adult women were said to be "married to" their husbands' families and unions were celebrated with the exchange of bridewealth, women retained membership in their own families of origin and exercised considerable rights over the labor of junior household members and collective resources in their roles as sisters and aunts. Moreover, they often acted collectively to assert their authority over areas considered within their sphere of expertise (including food production and marketing), to check the abuses of male leaders, and to demand protection for individual women (Moran 2006). Yet, in the postwar period, everyone seemed to be asserting that sexual violence was somehow intrinsic to Liberian culture, although Abramowitz (2009) has turned to the ethnographic record to document carefully the history of sanctions applied to rapists and violent domestic abusers in the past, including banishment from the community and capital punishment. She argues that humanitarian organizations, many of them with explicitly feminist identities, have imposed "a specific framing of Liberian and African cultural history and heritage as being intrinsically, totally, and irreversibly patriarchal, dominant, violent, and oppressive" (p. 195; see also Hodgson 2005, Fassin & Pandolfi 2010). Very similar framings have been offered of the traditional culture of Iraq and Afghanistan to support U.S. military interventions ideologically in those countries and elsewhere (Abu-Lughod 2002; Kandiyoti 2008; Moghadam 2001, 2005; Razach 2004).

Feminist or women's NGOs sometimes fail to recognize the power they wield in postconflict societies with high unemployment, limited infrastructure, and few sources of access to the resources and prestige controlled by foreigners. Members of one Liberian NGO described to me the agonizing decision to turn down an offer of funding from a foreign aid group that wanted to set up women's health clinics specifically for "rape victims." As the Liberian nurse heading the organization explained, not only would such clinics have stigmatized any woman seen entering the door, but also clinic workers would have been forced to deny health care to other women equally in need of their services, a requirement the staff found simply unethical. In their desire to address the special needs of women in postconflict societies, external actors can impose new, apparently life-long identities (such as rape survivor) and narrative frameworks that may be difficult for local activist women to resist. Likewise, postconflict survivors who fall into categories that are not recognized by powerful actors may have difficulty gaining access to services offered by the humanitarian community. Since 2006, I have been conducting interviews in Liberia

with male noncombatants. Such men are nearly invisible in the scholarly and policy literature, which devotes enormous attention to the problem of reintegrating violent male excombatants but ignores the experience of men whose victimization often echoes that of women and children. Standard practices for disarming, demobilizing, and reintegrating former combatants typically include cash payments and vouchers for school tuition or vocational training and other relocation expenses in return for turning in a weapon or ammunition. Men and boys who had spent the entire war trying to avoid recruitment into armed factions and who had resisted the lure of looting and violence, however, qualified for no assistance because most programs for "noncombatants" consisted of rape counseling and were directed at women. When I expained my project to a highly placed United Nations political affairs officer in Liberia, she expressed amazment that I could find any "men who did not fight" to interview. As one of my informants stated, "We are truly the forgotten men." The masculine identities embraced by these men as alternatives to the militarized version of manhood so visible during the war could be models for the violent excombatants in need of rehabilitation who so concern the international agencies, if only these men were recognized. One of the most important themes to emerge, in more than 80 interviews I have conducted so far, is the role of senior women in either sending younger male kin to war or refusing them permission to join the armed factions. The authority of mothers, grandmothers, and aunts to deploy young mens' labor power to defense or other tasks is obscured by the discourse of prewar patriarchy just as the hiding and protection of men from involuntary recruitment are overlooked when women's recognized peacemaking activities are limited to public demonstrations.

The massive body of scholarly work on gender, militarism, and peace-building seems not to have been incorporated into the essentialized, simplified images of violent men and suffering women that are neatly packaged for marketing and consumption by western aid donors. Interventions by anthropologists, with a more critical and longer time perspective on particular places, are sorely needed. According to Pankhurst (2008b), further specifying of the varieties of masculinity to emerge in times of both war and peace is particularly crucial; "we need to understand more about men who do not resort to violence, even when they have all the life experiences that would lead us to expect them to do so" (p. 312). She notes that the term femininity is not deployed in the same generalizing and deterministic manner as has been the case for masculinity; feminist scholars of militarism and peace-building have been careful to differentiate the "various and contrasting social roles, identities, sources of and constraints on power and control, access to and use of their own labor" for women, but they have neglected this task for men (p. 313). Attending to gender in all its aspects, she suggests, may be the best course for understanding how societies move from war to sustainable peace, and perhaps even for understanding how militarism as a process can be reversed or re-structured. My current research with Liberian men who did not fight in the civil war attempts to take up this challenge, as no doubt will many others.

DISCLOSURE STATEMENT

The author is not aware of any affiliations, memberships, funding, or financial holdings that might be perceived as affecting the objectivity of this review.

ACKNOWLEDGMENTS

The preparation of this review was assisted by several undergraduate students at Colgate University. Lauren Robinson helped to compile many of the sources in the initial phases of the project. Laura Simoko and Amy Pennenga read and summarized materials and formatted the bibliography. Discussions with Laura Simoko, Anne Pitcher, Sharon Abramowitz, and participants at the May 2009 Liberian Studies Association meetings in Monrovia, Liberia, helped me to frame the organization of this material. Thanks go to Jordan Kerber for proofreading and editorial assistance.

LITERATURE CITED

Abdela L. 2004. Kosovo: missed opportunities, future lessons. See Afshar & Eade 2004, pp. 87–99

Abramowitz SA. 2009. *Psychosocial Liberia: managing suffering in post-conflict life*. PhD thesis. Harvard Univ. 380 pp.

Abu-Lughod L. 2002. Do Muslim women really need saving? Anthropological reflections on cultural relativism and its others. *Am. Anthropol.* 104:1–8

Abusharaf RM. 2006. *Female Circumcision: Multicultural Perspectives*. Philadelphia: Univ. Penn. Press

African Women and Peace Support Group. 2004. *Liberian Women Peacemakers: Fighting for the Right to be Seen, Heard, and Counted*. Trenton, NJ: Afr. World

Afshar H, Eade D, eds. 2004. *Development, Women, and War: Feminist Perspectives*. Oxford, UK: Oxfam

Altinay AG. 2004. *The Myth of the Military-Nation: Militarism, Gender and Education in Turkey*. New York: Palgrave Macmillan

Amiri R. 2005. Fine lines of transformation: Afghan women working for peace. See Durham & Gurd 2005, pp. 243–50

Anderlini SN. 2007. *Women Building Peace: What They Do, Why It Matters*. Boulder, CO: Lynne Rienner

Anderson B. 1991. *Imagined Communities: Reflections on the Origin and Spread of Nationalism*. London/New York: Verso

Anderson MB. 1999. *Do No Harm: How Aid Can Support Peace—Or War*. Boulder, CO: Lynne Rienner

Bauer G, Britton HE, eds. 2006. *Women in African Parliaments*. Boulder, CO: Lynne Rienner

Bernal V. 2000. Equality to die for? Women guerilla fighters and Eritrea's cultural revolution. *PoLAR* 23(2):61–76

Boesten J. 2008. Marrying your rapist: domesticated war crimes in Peru. In *Gendered Peace: Women's Struggles for Post-War Justice and Reconstruction*, ed. D Pankhurst, pp. 205–28. New York: Routledge

Bouta T, Frerks G, Bannon I. 2005. *Gender, Conflict, and Development*. Washington, DC: World Bank

Bowker LH, ed. 1998. *Masculinities and Violence*. Thousand Oaks: Sage

Braudy L. 2003. *From Chivalry to Terrorism: War and the Changing Nature of Masculinity*. New York: Knopf

Breines I, Connell R, Eide I, eds. 2000. *Male Roles, Masculinities and Violence: A Culture of Peace Perspective*. Paris: UNESCO

Burnet J. 2008. Gender balance and the meanings of women in governance in post-genocide Rwanda. *Afr. Aff.* 107/428:361–86

Cancian FM, Gibson JW. 1990. *Making War, Making Peace: The Social Foundations of Violent Conflict*. Belmont, CA: Wadsworth

Carey HF. 2001. "Women and peace and security": the politics of implementing gender sensitivity norms in peacekeeping. See Olsson & Tryggestad 2001, pp. 49–68

Castillo RAH. 1997. Between Hope and Adversity: the Struggle of Organized Women in Chiapas since the Zapatista Uprising. *J. Latin Am. Anthropol.* 3(1):102–20

Clifton D, Gell F. 2001. Saving and Protecting Lives by Empowering Women. *Gender Dev.* 9(3):8–18

Cock J. 1994. Women and the Military: Implications for Demilitarization in the 1990s in South Africa. *Gender Society.* 8(2):152–69

Cockburn C. 2007. *From Where We Stand: War, Women's Activism, and Feminist Analysis*. New York: Zed

Cockburn C. 2002. *The Postwar Moment: Militaries, Masculinities and International Peacekeeping, Bosnia and the Netherlands*. London: Lawrence & Wishart

Cockburn C. 1998. *The Space Between Us: Negotiating Gender and National Identities in Conflict*. New York: Zed

Coles K. 2007. *Democratic Designs: International Intervention and Electoral Practices in Postwar Bosnia-Herzegovia*. Ann Arbor, MI: Univ. Mich. Press

Connell RW. 1987. *Gender and Power*. Cambridge UK: Polity Press

Connell RW. 1995. *Masculinities*. Cambridge, UK: Polity Press

Connell RW. 2000. *The Men and the Boys*. Cambridge, UK: Polity Press

Conover PJ, Sapiro V. 1993. Gender, Feminist Consciousness, and War. *Am. J. Pol. Sci.* 37(4):1079–99

Cooke M, Woollacott A, eds. 1993. *Gendering War Talk*. Princeton: Princeton Univ. Press

Corrin C. 2004. Developing Policy on Integration and Re/Construction in Kosova. See Afshar & Eade 2004, pp. 60–86

Coulter C. 2006. *Being a bush wife: women's lives through war and peace in Northern Sierra Leone*. PhD thesis. Uppsala Univ. 432 pp.

Crewe E, Harrison E. 1998. *Whose Development? An Ethnography of Aid*. New York: Zed

DeGroot GJ. 2001. A Few Good Women: Gender Stereotypes, the Military, and Peacekeeping. See Olsson & Tryggestad 2001, pp. 23–38

di Leonardo M. 1985. Morals, mothers, and militarism: antimilitarism and feminist theory. *Fem. Stud.* 11:600–17

Dolgopol U. 2006. Women and peace building: what we can learn from the Arusha peace agreement. *Aust. Fem. Stud.* 21(50):257–73

Durham H, Gurd T, eds. 2005. *Listening to the Silences: Women and War*. Boston: Martinus Nijhoff

Edwards L, Roces M, eds. 2000. *Women in Asia: Tradition, Modernity and Globalisation*. Ann Arbor: Univ. Mich. Press

El-Bushra J. 2004. Fused in combat: gender relations and armed conflict. See Afshar & Eade 2004, pp. 152–71

Elshtain JB. 1987. *Women and War*. New York: Basic Books

Elshtain JB, Tobias S, eds. 1990. *Women, Militarism, and War: Essays in History, Politics, and Social Theory*. Savage, MD: Rowman & Littlefield

Enloe C. 1983. *Does Khaki Become You? The Militarisation of Women's Lives*. Boston: South End

Enloe C. 1989. *Bananas, Beaches and Bases: Making Feminist Sense of International Politics*. Berkeley: Univ. Calif. Press

Enloe C. 1993. *The Morning After: Sexual Politics at the End of the Cold War*. Berkeley: Univ. Calif. Press

Enloe C. 2000. *Maneuvers: The International Politics of Militarizing Women's Lives*. Berkeley: Univ. Calif. Press

Enloe C. 2004. *The Curious Feminist: Searching for Women in a New Age of Empire*. Berkeley: Univ. Calif. Press

Enloe C. 2007. *Globalization and Militarism: Feminists Make the Link*. Lanham, MD: Rowman & Littlefield

Fassin D, Pandolfi M, eds. 2010. *Contemporary States of Emergency: The Politics of Military and Humanitarian Interventions*. Cambridge, MA: MIT Press

Feinman IR. 2000. *Citizenship Rites: Feminist Soldiers and Feminist Antimilitarists*. New York: New York Univ. Press

Fitzgerald MA. 2002. *Throwing the Stick Forward: The Impact of War on Southern Sudanese Women*. Nairobi: UNIFEM and UNICEF

Fraser TG, Jeffery K, eds. 1993. *Men, Women and War*. Dublin, Irel.: Lilliput

Frazier LJ. 2002. Forging democracy and locality: democratization, mental health, and reparations in Chile. See Montoya et al. 2002, pp. 91–114

Fuest V. 2007. Paradoxical implications of the aid business in Liberia and elsewhere. *Anthropol. News* 48(8):10–11

Fuest V. 2008. This is the time to get in front: changing roles and opportunities for women in Liberia. *Afr. Aff.* 107/427:201–24

Gardner J, El Bushra J, eds. 2004. *Somalia—The Untold Story: The War Through the Eyes of Somali Women*. Sterling, VA: Pluto

Gautam S, Banskota A, Manchanda R. 2001. Where there are no men: women in the Maoist insurgency in Nepal. See Manchanda 2001, pp. 214–51

Giles W, Hyndman J, eds. 2004. *Sites of Violence: Gender and Conflict Zones*. Berkeley: Univ. Calif. Press

Gill L. 1997. Creating citizens, making men: the military and masculinity in Bolivia. *Cult. Anthropol.* 12(4):527–50

Gillis JR, ed. 1989. *The Militarization of the Western World*. New Brunswick, NJ: Rutgers Univ.

Goldman NL, ed. 1982. *Female Soldiers—Combatants or Noncombatants? Historical and Contemporary Perspectives*. Westport, CT: Greenwood

Goldstein JS. 2001. *War and Gender: How Gender Shapes the War System and Vice Versa*. Cambridge, UK: Cambridge Univ. Press

Gusterson H. 2007. Anthropology and militarism. *Annu. Rev. Anthropol.* 36:155–75

Gutmann MC. 1997. Trafficking in men: the anthropology of masculinity. *Annu. Rev. Anthropol.* 26:385–409

Haq F. 2007. Militarism and motherhood: the women of the Lashkar-i-Tayyabia in Pakistan. *Signs* 32:1023–46

Harris A, King Y. 1989. *Rocking the Ship of State: Toward a Feminist Peace Politics*. Boulder, CO: Westview

Hatty SE. 2000. *Masculinities, Violence and Culture*. Thousand Oaks, CA: Sage

Hauge W. 2007. *The Demobilization and Political Participation of Female Fighters in Guatemala*. Oslo: Int. Peace Res. Inst.

Helman S. 1999. Militarism and the construction of the life-world of Israeli males: the case of the reserves system. See Lomsky-Feder & Ben-Ari 1999, pp. 191–224

Hemmet J. 2007. *Empowering Women in Russia: Activism, Aid, and NGOs*. Bloomington, IN: Indiana Univ. Press

Highgate P. 2003. *Military Masculinities: Identity and the State*. New York: Greenwood

Highgate P, Henry M. 2004. Engendering (in)security in peace support operations. *Secur. Dialogue* 35:481–98

Hodgson D. 2005. *The Church of Women: Gendered Encounters Between Maasai and Missionaries*. Bloomington: Indiana Univ. Press

Hunt S. 2004. *This Was Not Our War: Bosnian Women Reclaiming the Peace*. Durham, NC: Duke Univ. Press

Hunt S. 2005. Moving beyond silences: women waging peace. See Durham & Gurd 2005, pp. 251–72

Jacobs S, Jacobson R, Marchbank J. 2000. *State of Conflict: Gender, Violence, and Resistance*. New York: Zed

Jacoby TA. 2005. *Women in Zones of Conflict: Power and Resistance in Israel*. Ithaca, NY: McGill-Queen's Univ. Press

Jalusic V. 1999. Women in post-socialist Slovenia: socially adapted, politically marginalized. See Ramet 1999, pp. 109–30

Jok JM. 1999. Militarism, gender and reproductive suffering: the case of abortion in Western Dinka. *J. Int. Afr. Inst.* 69(2):194–212

Kaldor M. 1999. *New and Old Wars: Organized Violence in the Global Era*. Cambridge, UK: Polity

Kandiyoti D. 2008. The politics of gender and reconstruction in Afghanistan: old dilemmas or new challenges? In *Gendered Peace Women's Struggles for Post-War Justice and Reconciliation*, ed. D Pankhurst, pp. 155–86. New York: Routledge

Karamé KH. 2001. Military women in peace operations: experiences of the Norwegian battalion in UNIFIL 1978–1998. See Olsson & Tryggestad 2001, pp. 85–96

Korac M. 2006. Gender, conflict and peace-building: lessons from the conflict in the former Yugoslavia. *Women's Stud. Int. Forum* 29:510–20

Koyama S, Myrttinen H. 2007. Unintended consequences of peace operations on Timor Leste from a gender perspective. In *Unintended Consequences of Peacekeeping Operations*, ed. C Aoi, C de Coning, R Thakur, pp. 23–43. New York: United Nations Univ. Press

Kumar K. 2001. *Women and Civil War: Impact, Organizations and Action*. Boulder, CO: Lynne Rienner

Kwon I. 2001. A feminist exploration of military conscription: the gendering of the connections between nationalism, militarism and citizenship in South Korea. *Int. Fem. J. Polit.* 3(1):26–54

Lomsky-Feder E, Ben-Ari E, eds. 1999. *The Military and Militarism in Israeli Society*. Albany: State Univ. N. Y. Press

Lorentzen LA, Turpin J. 1998. *The Women and War Reader*. New York: N. Y. Univ. Press

Luciak IA. 2001. *After the Revolution: Gender and Democracy in El Salvador, Nicaragua, and Guatemala*. Baltimore, MD: Johns Hopkins Univ. Press

Lutz C. 2001. *Homefront: A Military City and the American Twentieth Century*. Boston: Beacon Press

Lutz C, ed. 2009. *The Bases of Empire: The Global Struggle Against US Military Posts*. New York: N. Y. Univ. Press

Lyons BJ. 2002. "To act like a man": masculinity, resistance, and authority in the Ecuadorian Andes. See Montoya et al. 2002, pp. 45–64

Macdonald S, Holden P, Ardener S, eds. 1988. *Images of Women in Peace and War: Cross Cultural and Historical Perspectives*. Madison, WI: Univ. Wis. Press

Mackay A. 2004. Training the uniforms: gender and peacekeeping operations. See Afshar & Eade 2004, pp. 100–8

Macrae J. 2001. *Aiding Recovery? The Crisis of Aid in Chronic Political Emergencies*. New York: Zed

Makley CE. 2007. *The Violence of Liberation: Gender and Tibetan Buddhist Revival in Post-Mao China*. Berkeley: Univ. Calif. Press

Mama A. 1998. Khaki in the family: gender discourses and militarism in Nigeria. *Afr. Stud. Rev.* 41(2):1–18

Manchanda R, ed. 2001. *Women, War and Peace in South Asia: Beyond Victimhood to Agency*. Thousand Oaks: Sage

Marshall DR. 2000. *Women in War and Peace: Grassroots Peacebuilding*. Washington, DC: United States Inst. Peace

Mason C. 2005. Women, violence and nonviolent resistance in East Timor. *J. Peace Res.* 42(6):737–49

Mazurana D, Raven-Roberts A, Parpart J, eds. 2005. *Gender, Conflict and Peacekeeping*. Lanham, MD: Rowman & Littlefield

Meintjes S, Pillay A, Turshen M, eds. 2001. *The Aftermath: Women in Post-Conflict Transformation*. New York: Zed

Melman B, ed. 1998. *Borderlines: Genders and Identities in War and Peace, 1870–1930*. New York: Routledge

Méndez L. 2005. Women's role in peacemaking: personal experiences. See Durham & Gurd 2005, pp. 43–50

Merry SE. 2006. *Human Rights and Gender Violence: Translating International Law into Local Justice*. Chicago: Univ. Chicago Press

Mertus J. 1999. Women in Kosovo: contested terrains, the role of national identity in shaping and challenging gender identity. See Ramet 1999, pp. 171–86

Mertus J. 2000. *War's Offensive Against Women: The Humanitarian Challenge of Bosnia, Kosovo, and Afghanistan*. Bloomfield, CT: Kumarian

Milles J. 2000. Militarism, civil war and women's status: a Burma case study. See Edwards & Roces 2000, pp. 265–87

Moghadam V. 2001. Globalization, militarism and women's collective action. *NWASA J.* 13:60–67

Moghadam V. 2005. Peacebuilding and reconstruction with women: reflections on Afghanistan, Iraq and Palestine. *Development* 48:63–72

Molyneux M. 1985. Mobilization without Emancipation? Women's interests, the state, and revolution in Nicaragua. *Fem. Stud.* 11(2):227–54

Montoya R, Frazier LJ, Hurtig J, eds. 2002. *Gender's Place: Feminist Anthropologies of Latin America*. New York: Palgrave Macmillan

Moola S. 2006. Women and peace-building: the case of Mabedlane women. *Agenda: A J. About Women Gender* 69:124–33

Moon S. 2005. *Militarized Modernity and Gendered Citizenship in South Korea*. Durham, NC: Duke Univ. Press

Moran MH. 1995. Warriors or soldiers? Masculinity and ritual transvestism in the Liberian civil war. See Sutton 1995, pp. 73–88

Moran MH. 2006. *Liberia: the Violence of Democracy*. Philadelphia: Univ. Penn. Press

Moran MH, Pitcher MA. 2004. The "basket case" and the "poster child": explaining the end of civil conflicts in Liberia and Mozambique. *Third World Q.* 25(3):501–19

Moser C, Clark F. 2001. *Victims, Perpetrators, and Actors: Gender, Armed Conflict, and Political Violence*. London: Zed

Nakaya S. 2004. Women and gender equity in peacebuilding: Somalia and Mozambique. In *Building Sustainable Peace*, ed. T Keating, WA Knight, pp. 143–66. Edmonton: Univ. Alberta Press

Narikkar N. 2005. Sri Lanka first: the business of peace. See Durham & Gurd 2005, pp. 37–42

Nordstom C. 1997. *A Different Kind of War Story*. Philadelphia: Univ. Penn. Press

Nordstom C. 2004. *Shadows of War: Violence, Power, and International Profiteering in the Twenty-First Century*. Berkeley: Univ. Calif. Press

Olsson L, Tryggestad TL, eds. 2001. *Women and International Peacekeeping*. Portland, OR: Frank Cass

Pankhurst D. 2004. The 'sex war' and other wars: towards a feminist approach to peace building. See Afshar & Eade 2004, pp. 8–42

Pankhurst D, ed. 2008a. *Gendered Peace: Women's Struggles for Post-War Justice and Reconciliation*. New York: Routledge

Pankhurst D. 2008b. Post-war backlash violence against women: What can "masculinity" explain? See Pankhurst 2008a, pp. 293–320

Parris R. 2004. *At War's End: Building Peace After Civil Conflict*. Cambridge, UK: Cambridge Univ. Press

Peterson VS, ed. 1992. *Gendered States: Feminist (Re)Visions of International Relations Theory*. Boulder, CO: Lynne Rienner

Porter F, Smyth I, Sweetman C. 1999. *Gender Works: Oxfam Experience in Policy and Practice*. Oxford, UK: Oxfam

Povey ER. 2004. Women in Afghanistan: passive victims of the *Borga* or active social participants? See Afshar & Eade 2004, pp. 172–87

Powers JM. 2006. *Blossoms on the Olive Tree: Israeli and Palestinian Women Working for Peace*. Westport, CT: Praeger

Rabrenovic G, Roskos L. 2001. Civil society, feminism and the gendered politics of war and peace. *NWASA J.* 13:40–54

Rajasingham-Senanayake D. 2001. Ambivalent empowerment: the tragedy of Tamil women in conflict. See Manchanda 2001, pp. 102–30

Ramet SP, ed. 1999. *Gender Politics in the Western Balkans: Women and Society in Yugoslavia and the Yugoslav Successor States*. University Park: Penn. State Univ. Press

Razach S. 2004. *Dark Threats and White Knights: The Somalia Affair, Peacekeeping, and the New Imperialism*. Toronto: Univ. Tor. Press

Reardon BA. 1985. *Sexism and the War System*. New York: Teach. Coll. Press

Reardon BA. 1993. *Women and Peace: Feminist Visions of Global Security*. Albany: State Univ. N. Y. Press

Rehn E, Sirleaf EJ. 2002. *Women, War, Peace: An Independent Expert's Assessment on the Impact of Armed Conflict on Women and Women's Role in Peace-Building*. New York: UNIFEM

Rose L. 2000. African women in post-conflict societies: rethinking legal research and program implementation methodologies. *PoLAR* 23:107–26

Rosen DM. 2007. Child soldiers, international humanitarian law, and the globalization of childhood. *Am. Anthropol.* 109:296–306

Ruddick S. 1983. Pacifying the forces: drafting women in the interests of peace. *Signs* 8(3):471–89

Ruddick S. 1989. *Maternal Thinking: Toward a Politics of Peace*. Boston: Beacon

Sharoni S. 1995. *Gender and the Israeli-Palestinian Conflict: The Politics of Women's Resistance*. Syracuse, NY: Syracuse Univ. Press

Shaw R. 2007. Memory frictions: localizing the truth and reconciliation commission in Sierra Leone. *Int. J. Transit. Justice* 1:183–207

Shayne JD. 2004. *The Revolution Question: Feminisms in El Salvador, Chile, and Cuba*. New Brunswick, NJ: Rutgers Univ. Press

Skjelbæk I. 2001. Sexual violence in times of war: a new challenge for peace operations? See Olsson & Tryggestad 2001, pp. 69–84

Snajdr E. 2007. Ethnicizing the subject: domestic violence and the politics of primordialsim in Kazakhstan. *J. R. Anthropol. Inst.* 13:603–20

Stiehm JH. 2001. Women, peacekeeping and peacemaking: gender balance and mainstreaming. See Olsson & Tryggestad 2001, pp. 39–48

Summerfield D. 1999. A critique of seven assumptions behind psychological trauma programs in war-affected areas. *Soc. Sci. Med.* 48:1449–62

Sunindyo S. 1998. When the earth is female and the nation is mother: gender, the armed forces and nationalism in Indonesia. *Fem. Rev.* 58:1–21

Sutton CR, ed. 1995. *Feminism, Nationalism and Militarism*. Arlington, VA: Am. Anthropol. Assoc.

Tate W. 2007. *Counting the Dead: The Culture and Politics of Human Rights Activism in Columbia*. Berkeley: Univ. Calif. Press

Terry F. 2002. *Condemned to Repeat? The Paradox of Humanitarian Action*. Ithaca, NY: Cornell Univ. Press

Tétreault MA, ed. 1994. *Women and Revolution in Africa, Asia, and the New World*. Columbia, SC: Univ. S. C. Press

Tickner JA. 1992. *Gender in International Relations: Feminist Perspectives on Achieving Global Security*. New York: Columbia Univ. Press

Tripp AM, Casimiro I, Kwesiga J, Mungwa A. 2009. *African Women's Movements: Changing Political Landscapes*. Cambridge, UK: Cambridge Univ. Press

Turshen M. 2001. Engendering relations of state to society in the aftermath. See Meintjes et al. 2001, pp. 78–96

Turshen M. 2002. Algerian women in the liberation struggle and the civil war: from active participants to passive victims. *Soc. Res.* 69:889–911

Turshen M, Twagiramariya C. 1998. *What Women Do in Wartime: Gender and Conflict in Africa*. London: Zed

Unger E. 2000. Re-gendering Vietnam: from militant to market socialism. See Edwards & Roces 2000, pp. 291–314

United Nations. 2000. Resolution 1325 on women, peace, and security. *S/RES/1325*. U. N. Secur. Counc.

United Nations Secur. Counc. 2001. Windhoek declaration. *Int. Peacekeeping* 8(2):115–20

Unvin P. 1998. *Aiding Violence: The Development Enterprise in Rwanda*. West Hartford, CT: Kumarian

Utas M. 2003. *Sweet battlefields: youth and the Liberian civil war*. PhD thesis. Uppsala Univ. 288 pp.

Utas M. 2005. Victimcy, girlfriending, soldiering: tactic agency in a young woman's navigation of the Liberian war zone. *Anthropol. Q.* 78:403–30

Vayrynen T. 2004. Gender and UN peacekeeping operations: the confines of modernity. *Int. Peacekeeping* 11:125–42

Vickers J. 1993. *Women and War*. Atlantic Highlands, NJ: Zed

Weissman F, Terry F. 2004. *In the Shadow of "Just Wars": Violence, Politics and Humanitarian Action*. Ithaca, NY: Cornell Univ. Press

Whitworth S. 2004. *Men, Militarism and UN Peacekeeping*. Boulder, CO: Lynne Rienner

Wicks S. 1996. *Warriors and Wildmen: Men, Masculinity, and Gender*. Westport, CT: Bergin & Garvey

Williams S. 2001. Oxfam, gender and the aftermath of war. *Gender Dev.* 9(3):19–28

Wolpe H, McDonald S. 2008. Democracy and peace-building: rethinking the conventional wisdom. *Round Table* 97/394:137–45

Zalewski M, Parpart J, eds. 1998. *The "Man" Question in International Relations*. Boulder, CO: Westview

Anthropologies of the United States

Jessica R. Cattelino

Department of Anthropology, University of California, Los Angeles, California 90095;
email: jesscatt@anthro.ucla.edu

Annu. Rev. Anthropol. 2010. 39:275–92

First published online as a Review in Advance on
June 21, 2010

The *Annual Review of Anthropology* is online at
anthro.annualreviews.org

This article's doi:
10.1146/annurev.anthro.012809.104927

Key Words

American cultures, location work, cultural critique, settler colonialism

Abstract

This article reviews recent research in sociocultural anthropology that
has been conducted in and about the United States. I show that anthropologists of the United States have been concerned to locate the
anthropological field in three ways: spatial investigations of region, community, and territory; epistemological and methodological projects of
cultural critique and defamiliarization; and reconsideration of the place
of Native North America in the anthropology of the United States.
Emergent inquiry into settler colonialism and the politics of indigeneity
has the potential to strengthen the anthropology of the United States
by accounting for the ways that being a settler society structures all
American lives.

INTRODUCTION

This article reviews research in sociocultural anthropology that has been conducted in and about the United States since Moffatt's (1992) review. Focusing on the United States risks reinforcing nation-state boundaries, but I take the nation-state and its borders less as givens than as objects of analysis. I show that anthropologists of the United States have been concerned to locate the anthropological field (as discipline, ethnographic site, and theoretical domain) in three ways. First, they have undertaken spatial projects that include regional ethnographies, community studies, and explorations of American power at and beyond U.S. borders. Second, epistemological and methodological projects have located Americanist anthropology in cultural critique and defamiliarization. A third area is emergent: ethnographic research that locates Native North America not as distinct from the anthropology of the United States but rather as critical to it.

Americanist anthropology[1]—the anthropology of the United States—uniquely affords the opportunity to examine the discipline's location work. By "location-work," Gupta & Ferguson (1997) refer to the "idea that anthropology's distinctive trademark might be found not in its commitment to 'the local' but in its attentiveness to epistemological and political issues of location" (p. 39). I undertake location work by outlining the contributions of U.S.-based research to the discipline of anthropology and to critical thinking about American cultures.

The cultural anthropology in and of the United States is long-standing and vast, and omissions are unavoidable. Indeed, exceptionalist discourse about Americanist anthropology's novelty or marginality should be put to rest. In this review, ethnographies are the major sources, supplemented by theoretical

and methodological writings about Americanist anthropology.

AMERICAN GEOGRAPHIES

Anthropologists often organize studies by space, but this practice does not necessarily lead to the naturalization of cultural boundedness. Instead, scholars in and of the United States have investigated the spatialization of the nation-state and citizenship through migration, the production and ideology of localized community, the racialization of place, the cultural politics of environment and the public/private distinction, and the operation of American power and cultural forms beyond U.S. borders.

Movement and Migration

Migration studies can challenge or reinforce static conceptions of national space. Many recent studies of migration to the United States criticize early work for either reifying the "there" and the "here" or for presuming that individuals migrate across spaces but retain unexamined identities in the course of doing so (Rouse 1995). Recent anthropology has turned away from studying assimilation to show how migrant subjects are produced by law and politics and, conversely, how migration constitutes nation-state borders and citizenship.

Law and citizenship figure centrally. Coutin's (2000) study of Salvadoran "legalizing moves" in the United States points to the importance of law as regulating movement and borders and as carving out the substance of being American. De Genova ties migration to spatialized nationalism and the production of illegality; his study of "Mexican Chicago" (2005) aims to resignify the boundaries of nation in an iconic American city.

None of these authors reduces migration to legal processes. Ong shows that, although flexibility has been a privileged dimension of citizenship and subjectivity for transnational elites (1999), Asian immigrants are institutionally and differentially rendered more black or white within American racial hierarchies

---

[1]For reasons of interest below, the "Americanist tradition" has referred to the anthropological study of Native North America, with emphasis on its four-field approach (Fogelson 1999).

(2003; see also Park 1996). Fader's (2009) study of child socialization and language among Hasidic women and girls analyzes a form of illiberal (and yet sometimes multiculturalist) religiosity that challenges standard American immigration narratives. Pérez's ethnography of Puerto Rican migration to the mainland (2004), like Manalansan's (2003) of Filipino gay men in New York City, shows gender and sexuality to organize migration. Pérez documents women's "kin work" (di Leonardo 1992) that maintains transnational networks.

Peoples and Places

Within U.S. borders, anthropological topics and subjects can become pinned to locations. When associations of people with place become patterned, they distort demographic distributions. More importantly, they (inadvertently) reinforce policy decisions that distribute economic and cultural resources unequally across American spaces. For example, as Morgen & Maskovsky (2003) note, poverty studies are conducted more often in urban than in rural contexts (with the exception of Appalachia; see also Goode & Maskovsky 2001 on poverty). Generally, post–World War II anthropologists have deemphasized rural America (Adams 2007) and have associated it with whiteness [but see Stack (1996) on African Americans returning "home" to the rural South and Kosek (2006) on Hispanos and the politics of nature in northern New Mexico]. By contrast, studies of African American, Asian American, Latino, and ethnicized white communities are most often based in urban neighborhoods.

American Indians are strongly associated with the reservation, even though the majority live in urban areas. Ramirez (2007) counters the dominant scholarly view that urban indigenous people are displaced by celebrating urban "hubs" that connect indigenous peoples and places. Biolsi (2005) and Wagoner (2002) analyze indigenous places in spaces of overlap with non-Indians. Simpson (2003) examines Mohawk nationalism in border crossing between the United States and Canada. Even

reservation-based ethnographies need not take for granted the space of the reservation. Basso's (1996) "ethnography of lived topographies" (p. 111) among Western Apaches shows how speaking about places and with place-names creates moral imperatives, histories, and place itself.

Community studies are an old tradition in the anthropology of the United States, and they cement a disciplinary affinity with qualitative sociology (especially urban studies; see, e.g., Sanjek 1998) that dates at least to Lynd & Lynd's *Middletown* (1929) and Warner's *Yankee City* (1941–1959). Early studies generally overstated the representativeness of their samples for an analysis of American society and culture (for a critique, see Lassiter et al. 2004). Nonetheless, they identified themes in American life that have proven enduring, such as the relationships among religion, individualism, and community (for studies of New Age spirituality, faith-based activism, and ex-gay conversion, respectively, see Brown 1997, Elisha 2008, and Erzen 2006). Over time, clusters form of geographically based studies (a recent example is Silicon Valley: see English-Lueck 2002 on technology and the dilemmas of cultural complexity; Ramirez 2007, Shankar 2008, and Zlolniski 2006).

Some anthropologists undertake community studies in which they examine the relationship between identity and place for racially marked Americans. Working against associations of people of color with bounded place, they analyze the commitments that create and maintain places such as Desi Land in Silicon Valley (Shankar 2008) or Black Corona in Queens, New York (Gregory 1998). Jackson (2001) explores the idea and observational terrain of "Harlemworld": He analyzes how, when, and under which conditions Harlem residents understand race to be performative (see also Kondo 1997), and he (2005) argues for the analytical and descriptive value of racial sincerity relative to racial authenticity. Stoller (2002) globalizes Harlem in an ethnography of West African traders who market to African Americans. Goldschmidt (2006) argues that African Americans understand difference on the basis of race, and Hasidic Jews on the basis of religion, in their shared neighborhood of Crown Heights, Brooklyn. A tradition follows Stack (1974) in humanizing the agentive residents of poor and racially marked neighborhoods (e.g., Bourgois 1995 on drug dealing; Bourgois & Schonberg 2009 on addiction; Wojcicka Sharff 1998). Newman (1999, 2008) explores strategies of the working poor in Harlem and connects these to shifting federal and local policy. Newton (1993) charts the work of creating a gay and lesbian town.

Some community studies, more than others, go beyond a case-study approach to raise analytical questions of broader interest. Gregory (1998) and Stewart (1996), for example, interrogate space as process and possibility while engaging the legacy of neighborhood and region, respectively, in American scholarship and cultural politics. For Gregory (1998), "community describes not a static, place-based social collective but the power-laden field of social relations whose meanings, structures, and frontiers are continually produced, contested, and reworked in relation to a complex range of sociopolitical attachments and antagonisms" (p. 11). He analyzes how, for example, a neighborhood clean-up "reworked the racialized economy of space" (p. 127). Hartigan (1999) shows how the racial identities of—and racial ascriptions by—whites in Detroit are situated by class and spatial positions (on whiteness see Brodkin Sacks 1998, Frankenberg 1993). Dávila's (2004) study of the "cultural politics of urban space" (p. 2) in gentrifying East Harlem points to a contradiction whereby Puerto Rican culture is commodified as the basis for neighborhood revitalization even while race and ethnicity are delegitimized as bases for political claims to representation and equality. Doukas (2003) locates community in and against the history of U.S. corporate expansion.

Community is a cultural category in the United States. Ortner (1997) moves away from community studies to investigate the "post-community," arguing that "the fate of 'communities' is precisely one of the issues at stake in contemporary American society" (p. 62). Greenhouse et al. (1994) examine the myth of community and the role of law as an available discourse for Americans to talk about community. Ortner's (2003) ethnography of class and culture among her New Jersey high-school classmates investigates the production and dispersion of community in modern America. As these and other scholars show, anthropological research can retain the benefits of community studies while querying the shifting historical and spatial contours of community in the United States.

The Cultural Politics of American Places

Anthropology has the power to name spatial and cultural units where they might otherwise remain invisible or disconnected. Doing so is political. For example, in a social history of debt, Williams (2004) insists on seeing the connections within a single economy between creditors and debtors and between credit card holders who carry no balance and those whose steep interest rate payments make easy credit possible for the former. Others orient readers to social movements as units: Morgen (2002), for example, argues that the national story of the women's health movement must be told via local groups (see also Durrenberger & Erem 2005 on the labor movement). Valentine (2007) tracks the emergence of transgender as a social category.

Americanist anthropologists increasingly take environment as an object of social analysis. Checker (2005) tracks the relationship between civil rights and environmentalism in environmental justice claims by African American residents of a polluted neighborhood in Georgia (see also Brodkin 2009). Sayre (2002) combines political ecology with ethnography to show how environmentalists in southern Arizona misplaced blame for the decline of masked bobwhite populations on cattle ranching rather than on cattle and real estate speculation (see also Sheridan 2007). Kosek's (2006) study of race, class, nation, and the political life of forests in New Mexico suggests that, at least in some regions, "nature has been the primary target through which bodies and populations—both human and nonhuman—have been governed, and it has been the primary site through which institutions of governance have been formed and operated" (p. 25). These ethnographies reveal the politics of nature's production in America.

Anthropologists often couple analysis of the domestic sphere with a critique of the public/private distinction, including with regard to labor (Lamphere et al. 1993) and homelessness (Dehavenon 1996). Others analyze the race, class, and gender dimensions of home and its defense, from neighborhood governance (Ruben & Maskovsky 2008) to domestic violence control (Merry 2001) to the growth of gated communities (Low 2003; see also Chesluk 2007 on the redevelopment of New York's Times Square). Rapp & Ginsburg (2001) chart forms of citizenship and kinship produced around the public circulation of representations of disability (on disability see Frank 2000, Landsman 2008; on kinship formations, see Franklin & McKinnon 2001, Gailey 2010, Lewin 1993). Stewart (2007) captures aspects of ordinary life in America that often go overlooked, including attachments and ways of affecting and being "affected" (p. 2) that create "little worlds" (p. 109) of shifting coherence and composition.

The United States beyond Nation-State Borders

An exciting possibility for location work extends Americanist research beyond U.S. borders. I do not refer to globalization generally but rather to analyses that stretch the ethnographic investigation of the United States to American formations elsewhere. Maskovsky (2009) argued that "we must first and foremost take seriously the postcolonial critique of area studies' complicity with imperialism and place U.S. empire at the center of analysis" (p. 6). This charge is important. In addition to empire, however, there is room to analyze other modes by which American cultural forms move beyond nation-state boundaries with, for example, military action, rule of law, U.S.-based nongovernmental organizations, American expatriots, and U.S. corporations abroad.

An obvious starting point is the military. Including Gill's (2004) study of the School of the Americas as an instrument of U.S. imperialism in the spread of an "American way of life" (p. 8) and Lutz's (2001) ethnography of the "homefront" at Fort Bragg, this work reconsiders the relationship between home and abroad, state and community, culture and power. Gusterson's (1996) study of the Lawrence Livermore Laboratory articulates national with international culture and politics, as nuclear science exerts "downward pressures" on American culture and as family relations, religion, class, and gender exert "upward pressures" on nuclear practice and policy (p. 223). Masco (2006) argues that Manhattan Project nuclear scientists created not only new technology and changing global-local configurations but also new forms of national consciousness. Price's histories of anthropology in World War II (2008) and the Cold War (2004) show how military engagement produced the area studies institutions that shape the discipline. Americanist scholars are beginning to investigate overseas military bases (Lutz 2009). Vine (2009) tells the story of residents displaced by the legally murky establishment of a U.S. and British military installation on Diego Garcia. Silliman (2008) connects U.S. frontier ideology to overseas warfare through metaphors of American Indians that are deployed by the U.S. military in the Middle East.

Similar work on U.S.-based multinational corporations and business practice focuses less on generalized processes of globalization than on the circulation of particular American cultural forms (see, e.g., Zaloom 2006 on commodities traders in Chicago and London). In line with Susser (1996) and Collins (2003), industrial workers for American-owned companies domiciled outside U.S. borders can be understood as an expansion of the domestic labor force and as potentially altering the cultural logics of work and poverty in America.

Chapters in Maskovsky & Susser (2009) examine the "internal costs of empire." Similarly, Morgen & Maskovsky (2003) urge anthropologists to position U.S. welfare reform policy in relation to global economic processes. Such projects facilitate new analyses of American space, power, and cultural production.

EPISTEMOLOGICAL LOCATIONS

Americanist anthropology can destabilize or reinforce the discipline's epistemological foundations: There is no intrinsic effect of Americanist research on knowledge production. Nonetheless, there are identifiable tendencies. These include cultural critique, concern with the circulation and positioning of anthropological knowledge, and a rethinking of the relationship between theory and data. Before turning to these themes, it is helpful to identify relevant disciplinary traditions.

Disciplinary Traditions

Anthropological research in the United States is widespread and longstanding. Moffatt (1992) explained the growth of Americanist research beginning in the 1980s as the effect of postcolonial critiques of anthropology, interdisciplinarity, and declining funding for international research (p. 205). Additionally, my review of the literature suggests that increasing numbers of women in the discipline contributed to the growth of U.S.-based research, especially second book projects. Yet U.S.-based research is hardly new. Oft-forgotten anthropological research in the United States—by Boasians or urban anthropologists working with the Chicago School of Sociology, at field schools in Indian Country, and in other traditions—was especially prominent prior to World War II. I do not intend to review this history except to cite two imperatives put forth by di Leonardo (1998). She insists on contextualizing anthropology's intellectual history with reference to American political and economic history, and she calls for Americanist anthropologists to undertake interdisciplinary training akin to that of colleagues who work elsewhere.

Anthropological research may or may not theorize America as such. De Genova (2007) follows Marcus (1999) in arguing that anthropology in the United States has not added up to an anthropology of the United States. De Genova pins this absence on American exceptionalism, anthropologists' failure to think of the United States as just another nation-state, and the ongoing existence of blinders to American empire. One might add another view: that scholars have been reluctant to generalize about the United States, perhaps because they are attuned to the dual pitfalls of transferring the anthropological gaze from foreign to "domestic exotics" (di Leonardo 1998) and of allowing white "heartland" communities to stand for America (on identity in America, see Baker 2004). De Genova's solution is to emphasize political economy, but anthropologists of the United States can also take another turn: from reified culture to the study of cultural activism (Ginsburg 2002; see also Checker & Fishman 2004 and Harding 1999) and cultural production. By refusing to oppose structural analysis to cultural critique, an analysis of cultural production can approach questions about capitalism and inequality in domains such as high fashion (Kondo 1997), film making (Ginsburg 2002), rock and roll (Mahon 2004) and country music (Fox 2004), museums (Clifford 1997, Erikson & Wachendorf 2002, Handler & Gable 1997), and magazines (Lutz & Collins 1993). Stewart (1996) presents an arresting account of cultural production and poetics that unsettles realist narratives of Appalachia and America.

Cultural Critique

Along with exploring the production of culture, anthropologists have engaged in cultural critique that defamiliarizes the taken-for-granted in contemporary American life. Marcus & Fischer (1986) contended that anthropologists generally venture afar with "marginal or hidden agendas of critique of their own culture, namely, the bourgeois, middle-class life of mass liberal societies, which industrial capitalism has produced" (p. 111). Written into their analysis was a (descriptive, but also normalizing) vision of which—and whose—America stood in relation to other places and peoples. Despite that limit, they rightly called for more rigorous cultural analysis of American culture, noting that cross-cultural juxtaposition relies on careful study in both places, and they identified a long tradition of epistemological critique. Marcus & Fischer identified the most promising agents of cultural critique as anthropologists whose previous research was located elsewhere, not in the United States (p. 113). Ginsburg (2006), however, argues that there is a recent trend in American-educated anthropologists who train to work in the United States.

What can anthropologists first trained to conduct research in the United States contribute to epistemological critique and cross-cultural juxtaposition? First, such a project—what one might call first-instance Americanist anthropology—has the potential to produce rigorous analysis of American cultures, political economy, and history that often is presumed rather than developed in cultural critique. If interdisciplinary and ethnographically grounded, first-instance Americanist anthropology should challenge the class and race presumptions prevalent in cultural critique. To put it another way, we must question what constitutes the familiar that is supposedly defamiliarized through cultural critique. Second, first-instance Americanists should bring to interdisciplinary American Studies a comparative engagement with the ethnographic record, not forgoing but rather relying on—and contributing to—the discipline's distinctive modes of empirical research and theorization.

An important example of cultural critique has been the study of gender. Inspired by the women's movement, feminist anthropologists in the 1970s and 1980s spread across the globe to establish an ethnographic record of global gender variation and differently gendered power relations. The resulting record was of great importance to feminist theory and practice. Meanwhile, anthropologists of the United States examined a range of topics that included gender negotiation (Ginsburg & Tsing 1990)

and the transformative potential of theorizing reproduction (Ginsburg & Rapp 1994; see also Ragoné 1994, Rapp 1999). The politics of gender and reproduction in the United States influenced research elsewhere, which in turn shaped their investigation in the United States.

In one mode of cultural critique, anthropologists have located America in the identification of forms of knowledge or naturalized domains of social life—e.g., market economy and neoliberal economic theory—that are associated with the United States. For example, in ethnographies of investment bankers and commodities traders, respectively, Ho (2009) and Zaloom (2006) show that the association of the market with (raced, classed, and gendered) America reinforces U.S. global power and restructures American corporations, ideologies of success, and inequalities (see also Martin 1994 on flexible bodies). In the United States, markets are models for social relations and exchange practices, from garage sales (Herrmann 1997) to alternative forms of currency (Maurer 2005). "American consumer culture," as Chin (2001) argues in her examination of African American youth consumption, is not only an arena for working out social inequality but also a measure of social value (see also Jain 2006 on injury and product safety law). Dávila (2001) shows how marketing to Latinos is implicated in hierarchies of race, culture, and nation. In her analysis of the cultural politics of manic depression, Martin (2007) demonstrates mania's historical affinity with a U.S. neoliberal economic order that privileges flexibility, creativity, and productivity.

Circulation and Position

Americanist research raises questions of broader significance about the force and movement of anthropological ideas (Brettell 1993). di Leonardo 1998 (see also Baker 1998) offers a trenchant critique of how anthropological knowledge circulates in ways that create power inequalities. She cautions against the "anthropological gambit" (1998, p. 57), by which scholars deploy irony, humor, or sentimentality to imply that "we" really are like "them" (where who counts as "we" reinscribes privilege).

Debates over conducting anthropological research at home went on for decades and seem to have run out of steam with recognition of the field's epistemic and demographic multiplicity. Rather than arguing about subject positions and objectivity, anthropologists are now more likely to discuss specific at-home fieldwork dilemmas. These include pressure to convert or adhere to Christianity (Harding 1999) or Hasidic Judaism (Fader 2009), the politics of desire and subjective instability in interracial fieldwork (Chin 2006), the space of cultural biography alongside autobiography (Frank 2000), or the imperative for public action to accompany theorization of concepts such as racism and antiracism (Mullings 2005). Maurer (2005) takes the epistemological correspondence between anthropological description and everyday theories of money as an opportunity to explore the ethics and politics of anthropological method. Going beyond commonplace reflexivity, Jackson (2005) adopts a superhero avatar ("Anthroman") to engage creatively the positional and performative dimensions of fieldwork while theorizing class and racial performativity.

Theory as Cultural Resource and Practice

Americanist research encounters recursive risks and evidentiary potential when deploying social theory that is produced in American and European academies. Moffatt (1992) noted that "folk forms" of scholarly concepts circulate in American culture and that those concepts are themselves drawn from "the common culture" (p. 222). I raise a different but related question: What if anthropologists attend to theory as part of the cultural repertoire available for social scientific analysis? Is social theory also data for anthropologists of the United States?

Anthropologists have grappled with the status of non-Western theory and with the challenge of deploying culturally inflected Euro-American social theory to analyze other peoples' lives. Americanist anthropology, by contrast, risks deploying theory that is produced within American cultural arenas without attending to the potential for autoreinforcement when concepts are used to explain proximate social lives and imaginaries. What if Americanists considered social theory to be a form of cultural production? Harrison (2008), among others, reminds us that the terrain of theory in the United States is already structured by race and class. Many have examined the cultures of science, technology, and medicine in the United States (e.g., Dumit 2004; Kelty 2008; Martin 1994, 2007; Rapp 1999; Saunders 2009), and a number of researchers (e.g., Helmreich 1998, Masco 2006) have demonstrated the cultural embeddedness and impact of scientific investigation. In addition to undertaking a located cultural analysis of social theory, Americanist anthropologists can build theory at its creative ethnographic edge.

Anthropologies of the United States do not categorically shake the epistemological foundations of a discipline whose dominant modalities have been familiarization and defamiliarization. The contingency of Americanist anthropologies' effects suggests that it is time to set aside the question of what changes with an anthropology of the United States (as if change were inevitable) and instead to ask what anthropologies of the United States can change, and how.

CONDITIONS OF INDIGENEITY AND SETTLER COLONIALISM

Of all location work undertaken by Americanist anthropologists, perhaps none has been so vexed as the relationship to Indian country. Emergent inquiry into settler colonialism and the politics of indigeneity has the potential to strengthen the anthropology of the United States by accounting for the ways that being a settler society structures all American lives. Such an approach can enhance the anthropology of Native North America by identifying the ongoing conditions and limits of settler colonialism while also attending to forms of indigenous political and cultural distinctiveness.

By "conditions of indigeneity," I mean both the everyday conditions of indigenous peoples' lives and also the structures that condition indigeneity in the contemporary world. Anthropologists, in general, wisely resist debates about who is really indigenous in favor of analyzing claims and practices of indigeneity under changing historical conditions. In recent years, scholarly attention in the Anglophone settler states (especially Australia, New Zealand, and Canada) has turned to settler colonialism as a distinct configuration of citizenship, territory, economy, and cultural politics.

Near, and Yet So Far

The anthropology of the United States and the anthropology of Native North America have been maintained largely as separate anthropological traditions. For example, Moffat defined the scope of his review as follows: "American in this article means 'of the continental United States [excluding native American peoples]'" (Moffatt 1992, p. 205n1, brackets in original). Native America's marginal status in the anthropology of the United States (combined with its ongoing legitimacy as a distinct site of anthropological study) reflected and reinforced the positioning of indigenous peoples as outside the time and space of modern American life. Perhaps for related reasons, Deloria's trenchant critique of "anthros" (1988 [1969]), in combination with efforts by Native communities to gain control over their representation and knowledge production, led to some research restrictions and generated scholarly reflections on the ethics, politics, and subjective positioning of anthropological research in Indian country (e.g., Biolsi & Zimmerman 1997, Field 2008, Medicine 2001, Simpson 2007, Starn 2004, Whiteley 1998).

My goal is neither to revisit these questions of history and method nor to review generally the recent research on indigenous peoples in the United States (for the latter, see Strong 2005; see also Kan & Strong 2006). Nor am I simply criticizing anthropologists of the United States for failing to include Indian country.

Instead, I consider the location work that is accomplished by analyzing the United States and Native North America in terms of settler colonialism and the politics of indigeneity. To analyze the United States as a settler society is not to displace other conceptualizations (e.g., as a former slave state or an ongoing site of migration) but rather to capture the complexity of American political, economic, and cultural formations.

Before turning to this conceptual terrain, it is vital to recognize that a number of anthropologists have treated indigenous communities neither as outside of the time and space of the United States nor as laboratories for the study of acculturation. For example, Blu's (2001 [1980]) study of Lumbee identity and racial formation during the Civil Rights era took Lumbee political activity to be the outcome of combined internal and outsider ideas of who Lumbees are. Sider (2003, updating an earlier study published in 1993) showed Lumbee identity to be inextricably bound up with inequalities produced by the state and capital. A number of anthropologists have examined how American Indian blood reckoning both participates in American racial logics and also is contoured by the specificity of Indian claims to tribal sovereignty and nationhood (Strong & Van Winkle 1996, Sturm 2002; see also Kauanui 2008 for a historical account of Hawaiian blood and sovereignty).

Others have centered Native America in the racial and geopolitical organization of U.S. society and anthropological inquiry. Baker (2010) argues that concepts of culture first developed by anthropologists of Native North America formed the template for anthropological theories of race deployed in subsequent debates over "the Negro problem." De Genova (2006) contends that Native American racialization is the "ideological template" (p. 10) for Latino and Asian racialization. Although powerful, his model relies on an overly restrictive account of indigenous peoples as foreign. Borneman (1995), likewise, centers Native Americans in his history of anthropology as "foreign policy" arguing that the discipline has always been concerned with the foreign and paradigmatically with the Indian (who subsequently became domesticated, after which anthropology moved overseas). Nonetheless, as Native American Studies scholars have shown (e.g., Deloria 1998), American Indians have long been part of settler American domestic imaginaries (and especially of American exceptionalism): Indigenous peoples can form or threaten the boundaries of citizenship and sovereignty in settler states (see also Biolsi 2005, Simpson 2003). If, as Borneman (1995) argues, "anthropology's unique location from which it makes continued contributions to knowledge" is "[f]ieldwork among the foreign" (p. 669), where does this leave Americanist anthropology? Shifting the anthropological focus to settler colonialism brings into view new ethnographic and analytical questions about politics, sovereignty, economy, and representation in the United States.

Politics

Relatively little research focused on the politics of indigeneity until after the Red Power movement and the indigenous critique of anthropology forced a reorganization of the anthropology of Indian country (but see Blu 2001 [1980]). Some anthropologists have addressed federal Indian law and policy on Indian reservations (e.g., Biolsi 1992, 2001; Miller 2001; Richland 2008). Nesper's (2002) ethnography of the "walleye wars" over Ojibwe treaty rights provides an account not only of political conflict with whites but also of political organizing and internal diversity within Ojibwe communities. Fowler (2002) explores Cheyenne-Arapaho political consciousness and practice in the context of federal self-determination policy (whereby federally recognized tribal governments administered tribal social services). Blu (2001), Cramer (2005), and Miller (2003) have explored the racial, legal, and regional politics of recognition whereby some but not other indigenous groups can gain federal acknowledgment as (semi)sovereigns. Merry's (2000) historical ethnography of law, culture, and colonization in Hawai'i explores the "civilizing process" (p. 8)

whereby Euro-American law became a marker of sovereignty to which Hawaiians appealed as evidence of nationhood. Some of these works point the way toward an analysis of the everyday practices and structures of feeling (see O'Nell 1996 on depression) entailed by the politics of indigeneity. Research on politics among indigenous peoples can contribute to ethnographic and theoretical understandings of citizenship, recognition, and law in settler states.

Sovereignty

American Indian nations retain (limited) sovereignty within the U.S. federalist system and also stake claims to inherent sovereignty outside their relationships to the United States. Increasing attention among anthropologists to indigenous sovereignty dovetails with recent trends in Native American Studies, indigenous political movements, and anthropology outside of Indian country. Relative to others, anthropologists are likely to study sovereignty's local manifestations and limits (Fowler 2002) and attend to the lived dimensions of sovereignty beyond formal political claims. Anthropological investigations of indigenous sovereignty also have the (unrealized) potential to inform theories of sovereignty beyond the indigenous context. Meanwhile, anthropologists working in nonindigenous contexts have increasingly taken sovereignty to be an object of inquiry (see Hansen & Stepputat 2006). Their work aids in theorizing settler-state sovereignties. Indigenous sovereignty, however, is differently configured and, therefore, is essential to any larger project of theorizing sovereignty.

Sovereignty takes a particularly territorialized (and temporalized; see Bruyneel 2007) form for indigenous people in settler states. Nonetheless, Biolsi (2005) observes that American Indian sovereignty is rarely territorially exclusive but rather is shared, to varying degrees, with other sovereigns. Cattelino (2008; see also Spilde 1998) examines Florida Seminole sovereignty in the casino era as constituted through practices of autonomy but also in relations of interdependency with other sovereigns (including other indigenous peoples; see Jackson 2003 on interindigenous relations). Indigenous forms of sovereignty, when not taken solely to be failed sovereignties, point to the limits of dominant theories of sovereignty as autonomy. Attention to these limits, in turn, has implications for anthropological investigation of U.S. sovereignty.

As Strong & Van Winkle (1993) write, Native American nations "challenge and constrain the boundaries and sovereignty of the United States" (p. 9). Simpson (2003) examines Mohawk narratives of, and embodied practices at, the U.S.-Canadian border to show how indigenous nationalism unsettles settler-state sovereignty. At a historical moment when indigenous claims and practices are increasingly articulated in the terms of sovereignty, anthropologists working in Indian country can investigate aspects of sovereignty that are of critical concern to indigenous lives and social theory alike.

Economy

Anthropological study of indigenous economic action has the potential to upend the settler colonial conflation of indigenous peoples with poverty. Anthropologists have examined American Indian marginalization in wage labor (Littlefield & Knack 1996), capital accumulation (Faiman-Silva 1997, Pickering 2000), economic development (Dombrowski 2001), job training in boarding schools (Lomawaima 1994), and welfare state redistribution (Berman 2003). Tribal government operation of casinos has forced reconsideration in public culture and policy alike of American Indians' place within American economic and political landscapes (Cattelino 2008; Darian-Smith 2002, 2003; Spilde 1998). The task is not simply to offer an empirical corrective (showing that Indians can be rich or capitalists) or a celebration of counter-stereotypes that overlooks exploitative economic relations within Indian country. Instead, rethinking indigenous economy poses a political and theoretical challenge to the cultural logics whereby indigenous people are perceived to occupy a space of economic difference, pastness, and lack of regulation or lawlessness (Darian-Smith 2002, Erikson 1999, Simpson 2008). Anthropological inquiry may unsettle the "double bind of American Indian need-based sovereignty" (Cattelino 2010), whereby indigenous wealth is taken to be a sign of cultural loss and assimilation to an "American" way of life and thereby to undermine the difference on which tribal sovereignty is based.

Representation

One condition of settler colonialism is that indigenous lives and differences are contested on the terrain of representation (Bodinger de Uriarte 2007, Castile 1996, Ginsburg 2002, Krech 1999, Mithlo 2009, Mullin 2001, Prins 2002, Strong 2004). Struggles over "who owns Native culture," as Brown (2003) puts it, often involve legal disputes over cultural and intellectual property (see also Coombe 1998). Brown rightly identifies cultural activism as key to indigenous claims. That said, his appeal to an open domain of ideas and images downplays the harm of transparency and translation to some indigenous forms of knowledge production (see, e.g., Whiteley 1998 on Hopi cultural representation as instrumental value) and the selective deployment of openness within settler societies. The production and contestation of tradition is explored by Jackson (2003) in Yuchi ceremonial performance and Richland (2008) in language use in Hopi courts (see also Samuels 2004 and Fienup-Riordan 2000). While noting that cultural claims sometimes deploy essentialisms (Mithlo 2009) and that indigenous difference is often figured narrowly as cultural (Mullin 2001), anthropologists can complement the well-established literature on white images of Indians with attention to indigenous cultural activism.

Toward an Anthropology of Settler Colonialism

Scholars in indigenous studies are increasingly writing and thinking in terms of settler colonialism. Wolfe (1999, p. 2) describes settler colonialism as "a structure not an event," and he differentiates settler colonialism's target of land dispossession from the expropriation of labor in dependent colonies. He, like Fogelson (1999), connects past-oriented anthropological research in Native America to American nationalism. Settler colonialism creates a set of structures, practices, ideological formations, and dilemmas that are open to social scientific analysis. These, I suggest, include but by no means are limited to the dilemmas that indigenous peoples' everyday practices of citizenship pose to settler states, distinctive epistemologies and disciplinary formations, settler quandaries of how to claim national histories and territories when these are laced with traces of invasion, and pressure on the crafting of shared futures.

The anthropology of Native North America cannot be subsumed by the study of the United States. On the other hand, it cannot stand entirely outside of the time and space of the United States. Critical ethnographic engagement with the conditions of indigeneity may illuminate aspects of life in this settler society that too often go unexplored not only in scholarship but also in public culture. If anthropology was built partly on the study of American Indians, then it is time to critically reclaim the discipline's foundations as built in, on, and with Indian country. Along with ongoing investigation of the space of America and the epistemological position of Americanist anthropology, it is this type of location work that will maintain the vitality of the anthropology of the United States.

DISCLOSURE STATEMENT

The author is not aware of any affiliations, memberships, funding, or financial holdings that might be perceived as affecting the objectivity of this review.

ACKNOWLEDGMENTS

I am grateful to two exemplary research assistants: Alexander Blanchette at the University of Chicago and Katja Antoine at UCLA. This article benefited from comments by Faye Ginsburg, Jason Jackson, Sherry Ortner, and Audra Simpson. Research was supported by the Institute for Advanced Study in Princeton, the Lichtstern Fund in the Department of Anthropology at the University of Chicago, and the Division of Social Sciences and Department of Anthropology at UCLA.

LITERATURE CITED

Adams J. 2007. Ethnography of rural North America. *N. Am. Dialogue* 10(2):1–6

Baker LD. 1998. *From Savage to Negro: Anthropology and the Construction of Race, 1896–1954*. Berkeley: Univ. Calif. Press

Baker LD. 2004. *Life in America: Identity and Everyday Experience*. Malden, MA: Blackwell

Baker LD. 2010. *Anthropology and the Racial Politics of Culture*. Durham, NC: Duke Univ. Press

Basso KH. 1996. *Wisdom Sits in Places: Landscape and Language Among the Western Apache*. Albuquerque: Univ. N. M. Press

Berman T. 2003. *Circle of Goods: Women, Work, and Welfare in a Reservation Community*. Albany: State Univ. N. Y. Press

Biolsi T. 1992. *Organizing the Lakota: The Political Economy of the New Deal on the Pine Ridge and Rosebud Reservations*. Tucson: Univ. Ariz. Press

Biolsi T. 2001. *"Deadliest Enemies": Law and the Making of Race Relations On and Off Rosebud Reservation*. Berkeley: Univ. Calif. Press

Biolsi T. 2005. Imagined geographies: sovereignty, indigenous space, and American Indian struggle. *Am. Ethnol.* 32(2):239–59

Biolsi T, Zimmerman LJ, eds. 1997. *Indians and Anthropologists: Vine Deloria, Jr. and the Critique of Anthropology.* Tucson: Univ. Ariz. Press

Blu KI. 2001 [1980]. *The Lumbee Problem: The Making of an American Indian People.* Lincoln/London: Univ. Nebr. Press

Blu KI, with introduction by RD Fogelson. 2001. Region and recognition: Southern Indians, anthropologists, and presumed biology. In *Anthropologists and Indians in the New South*, ed. RA Bonney, JA Paredes, pp. 27–51. Tuscaloosa: Univ. Ala. Press

Bodinger de Uriarte JJ. 2007. *Casino and Museum: Representing Mashantucket Pequot Identity.* Tucson: Univ. Ariz. Press

Borneman J. 1995. American anthropology as foreign policy. *Am. Anthropol.* 97(4):663–72

Bourgois PI. 1995. *In Search of Respect: Selling Crack in El Barrio.* Cambridge/New York: Cambridge Univ. Press

Bourgois PI, Schonberg J. 2009. *Righteous Dopefiend.* Berkeley: Univ. Calif. Press

Brettell CB. 1993. Introduction: Fieldwork, text, audience. In *When They Read What We Write: The Politics of Ethnography*, ed. CB Brettell, pp. 163–76. Westport, CT: Bergin and Garvey

Brodkin K. 1998. *How Jews Became White Folks and What That Says About Race in America.* New Brunswick, NJ: Rutgers Univ. Press

Brodkin K. 2009. *Power Politics: Environmental Activism in South Los Angeles.* New Brunswick, NJ: Rutgers Univ. Press

Brown MF. 1997. *The Channeling Zone: American Spirituality in an Anxious Age.* Cambridge, MA: Harvard Univ. Press

Brown MF. 2003. *Who Owns Native Culture?* Cambridge, MA: Harvard Univ. Press

Bruyneel K. 2007. *The Third Space of Sovereignty: The Postcolonial Politics of U.S.-Indigenous Relations.* Minneapolis: Univ. Minn. Press

Castile GP. 1996. The Commodification of Indian Identity. *Am. Anthropol.* 98(4):743–49

Cattelino JR. 2008. *High Stakes: Florida Seminole Gaming and Sovereignty.* Durham, NC: Duke Univ. Press

Cattelino JR. 2010. The double bind of American Indian need-based sovereignty. *Cult. Anthropol.* 25(2):235–62

Checker M. 2005. *Polluted Promises: Environmental Racism and the Search for Justice in a Southern Town.* New York: N. Y. Univ. Press

Checker M, Fishman M, eds. 2004. *Local Actions: Cultural Activism, Power, and Public Life in America.* New York: Columbia Univ. Press

Chesluk B. 2007. *Money Jungle: Imagining the New Times Square.* New Bruswick, NJ: Rutgers Univ. Press

Chin EM. 2001. *Purchasing Power: Black Kids and American Consumer Culture.* Minneapolis: Univ. Minn. Press

Chin EM. 2006. Confessions of a Negrophile. *Transform. Anthropol.* 14(1):44–52

Clifford J. 1997. *Routes: Travel and Translation in the Late Twentieth Century.* Cambridge, MA: Harvard Univ. Press

Collins JL. 2003. *Threads: Gender, Labor, and Power in the Global Apparel Industry.* Chicago: Univ. Chicago Press

Coombe RJ. 1998. *The Cultural Life of Intellectual Properties: Authorship, Appropriation, and the Law.* Durham, NC: Duke Univ. Press

Coutin SB. 2000. *Legalizing Moves: Salvadoran Immigrants' Struggle for U.S. Residency.* Ann Arbor: Univ. Mich. Press

Cramer RA. 2005. *Cash, Color, and Colonialism: The Politics of Tribal Acknowledgment.* Norman: Univ. Okla. Press

Darian-Smith E. 2002. Savage capitalists: law and politics surrounding Indian casino operations in California. In *Studies in Law, Politics, and Society*, ed. A Sarat, P Ewick, 26:109–40. Amsterdam: JAI

Darian-Smith E. 2003. *New Capitalists: Law, Politics, and Identity Surrounding Casino Gaming on Native American Land.* Belmont, CA: Wadsworth/Thomson Learn.

Dávila AM. 2001. *Latinos, Inc.: The Marketing and Making of a People.* Berkeley: Univ. Calif. Press

Dávila AM. 2004. *Barrio Dreams: Puerto Ricans, Latinos, and the Neoliberal City.* Berkeley: Univ. Calif. Press

De Genova N. 2005. *Working the Boundaries: Race, Space, and "Illegality" in Mexican Chicago*. Durham, NC: Duke Univ. Press

De Genova N. 2006. Introduction: Latino and Asian racial formations at the frontiers of U.S. nationalism. In *Racial Transformations: Latinos and Asians Remaking the United States*, ed. N De Genova, pp. 1–20. Durham, NC: Duke Univ. Press

De Genova N. 2007. The stakes of an anthropology of the United States. *CR: The New Centennial Rev.* 7(2):231–77

Dehavenon A. 1996. *There's No Place Like Home: Anthropological Perspectives on Housing and Homelessness in the United States*. Westport, CT: Bergin & Garvey

Deloria PJ. 1998. *Playing Indian*. New Haven: Yale Univ. Press

Deloria VJ. 1988 [1969]. Anthropologists and other friends. In *Custer Died for Your Sins: An Indian Manifesto*, pp. 78–100. Norman: Univ. Okla. Press

Di Leonardo M. 1992. The female world of cards and holidays: women, families, and the work of kinship. In *Rethinking the Family: Some Feminist Questions*, ed. B Thorne, M Yalom, pp. 246–61. Boston: Northeast. Univ. Press

Di Leonardo M. 1998. *Exotics at Home: Anthropologies, Others, American Modernity*. Chicago: Univ. Chicago Press

Dombrowski K. 2001. *Against Culture: Development, Politics, and Religion in Indian Alaska*. Lincoln: Univ. Nebr. Press

Doukas D. 2003. *Worked Over: The Corporate Sabotage of an American Community*. Ithaca, NY: Cornell Univ. Press

Dumit J. 2004. *Picturing Personhood: Brain Scans and Biomedical Identity*. Princeton, NJ: Princeton Univ. Press

Durrenberger EP, Erem S. 2005. *Class Acts: An Anthropology of Service Workers and Their Union*. Boulder, CO: Paradigm

Elisha O. 2008. Moral ambitions of grace: the paradox of compassion and accountability in evangelical faith-based activism. *Cult. Anthropol.* 23(1):154–89

English-Lueck J. 2002. *Cultures@Silicon Valley*. Palo Alto, CA: Stanford Univ. Press

Erikson PP. 1999. A-whaling we will go: encounters of knowledge and memory at the Makah Cultural and Research Center. *Cult. Anthropol.* 14(4):556–83

Erikson PP, with Ward H, Wachendorf K. 2002. *Voices of a Thousand People: The Makah Cultural and Research Center*. Lincoln/London: Univ. Nebr. Press

Erzen T. 2006. *Straight to Jesus: Sexual and Christian Conversions in the Ex-Gay Movement*. Berkeley: Univ. Calif. Press

Fader A. 2009. *Mitzvah Girls: Bringing Up the Next Generation of Hasidic Jews in Brooklyn*. Princeton, NJ: Princeton Univ. Press

Faiman-Silva SL. 1997. *Choctaws at the Crossroads: The Political Economy of Class and Culture in the Oklahoma Timber Region*. Lincoln: Univ. Nebr. Press

Field LW. 2008. *Abalone Tales: Collaborative Explorations of Sovereignty and Identity in Native California*. Durham, NC: Duke Univ. Press

Fienup-Riordan A. 2000. *Hunting Tradition in a Changing World*. New Brunswick, NJ: Rutgers Univ. Press

Fogelson RD. 1999. Nationalism and the Americanist tradition. In *Theorizing the Americanist Tradition*, ed. LP Valentine, R Darnell, pp. 75–83. Toronto: Univ. Tor. Press

Fowler L. 2002. *Tribal Sovereignty and the Historical Imagination: Cheyenne-Arapaho Politics*. Lincoln/London: Univ. Nebr. Press

Fox AA. 2004. *Real Country: Music and Language in Working-Class Culture*. Durham, NC: Duke Univ. Press

Frank G. 2000. *Venus on Wheels: Two Decades of Dialogue on Disability, Biography, and Being Female in America*. Berkeley: Univ. Calif. Press

Frankenberg R. 1993. *White Women, Race Matters: The Social Construction of Whiteness*. Minneapolis: Univ. Minn. Press

Franklin S, McKinnon S. 2001. *Relative Values: Reconfiguring Kinship Studies*. Durham, NC: Duke Univ. Press

Gailey C. 2010. *Blue-Ribbon Babies and Labors of Love: Race, Class, and Gender in U.S. Adoption Practice*. Austin: Univ. Tex. Press

Gill L. 2004. *The School of the Americas*. Durham, NC: Duke Univ. Press

Ginsburg FD. 2002. Screen memories: resignifying the traditional in Indigenous media. In *Media Worlds: Anthropology on New Terrain*, ed. FD Ginsburg, L Abu-Lughod, B Larkin, pp. 39–57. Berkeley: Univ. Calif. Press

Ginsburg FD. 2006. Ethnography and American studies. *Cult. Anthropol.* 21(3):487–95

Ginsburg FD, Rapp R, eds. 1994. *Conceiving the New World Order: The Global Politics of Reproduction*. Berkeley: Univ. Calif. Press

Ginsburg FD, Tsing AL, eds. 1990. *Uncertain Terms: Negotiating Gender in American Culture*. Boston: Beacon

Goldschmidt H. 2006. *Race and Religion Among the Chosen People of Crown Heights*. New Brunswick, NJ: Rutgers Univ. Press

Goode J, Maskovsky J, eds. 2001. *New Poverty Studies: The Ethnography of Power, Politics, and Impoverished People in the United States*. New York: N. Y. Univ. Press

Greenhouse CJ, Yngvesson B, Engel DM. 1994. *Law and Community in Three American Towns*. Ithaca/London: Cornell Univ. Press

Gregory S. 1998. *Black Corona: Race and the Politics of Place in an Urban Community*. Princeton, NJ: Princeton Univ. Press

Gupta A, Ferguson J. 1997. Discipline and practice: "the field" as site, method, and location in Anthropology. In *Anthropological Locations: Boundaries and Grounds of a Field Science*, ed. A Gupta, J Ferguson, pp. 1–46. Berkeley: Univ. Calif. Press

Gusterson H. 1996. *Nuclear Rites: A Weapons Laboratory at the End of the Cold War*. Berkeley: Univ. Calif. Press

Handler R, Gable E. 1997. *The New History in an Old Museum: Creating the Past at Colonial Williamsburg*. Durham, NC: Duke Univ. Press

Hansen TB, Stepputat F. 2006. Sovereignty revisited. *Annu. Rev. Anthropol.* 35(1):295–315

Harding S. 1999. *The Book of Jerry Falwell: Fundamentalist Language and Politics*. Princeton, NJ: Princeton Univ. Press

Harrison FV. 2008. *Outsider Within: Reworking Anthropology in the Global Age*. Urbana: Univ. Ill. Press

Hartigan J. 1999. *Racial Situations: Class Predicaments of Whiteness in Detroit*. Princeton, NJ: Princeton Univ. Press

Helmreich S. 1998. *Silicon Second Nature: Culturing Artificial Life in a Digital World*. Berkeley: Univ. Calif. Press

Herrmann GM. 1997. Gift or commodity: What changes hands in the U.S. garage sale? *Am. Ethnol.* 24(4):910–30

Ho K. 2009. *Liquidated: An Ethnography of Wall Street*. Durham, NC: Duke Univ. Press

Jackson JB. 2003. *Yuchi Ceremonial Life: Performance, Meaning, and Tradition in a Contemporary American Indian Community*. Lincoln: Univ. Nebr. Press

Jackson JL. 2001. *Harlemworld: Doing Race and Class in Contemporary Black America*. Chicago: Univ. Chicago Press

Jackson JL. 2005. *Real Black: Adventures in Racial Sincerity*. Chicago: Univ. Chicago Press

Jain SL. 2006. *Injury: The Politics of Product Design and Safety Law in the United States*. Princeton, NJ: Princeton Univ. Press

Kan S, Strong PT, eds. 2006. *New Perspectives on Native North America: Cultures, Histories, and Representations*. Lincoln: Univ. Nebr. Press

Kauanui JK. 2008. *Hawaiian Blood: Colonialism and the Politics of Indigeneity and Sovereignty*. Durham, NC: Duke Univ. Press

Kelty CM. 2008. *Two Bits: The Cultural Significance of Free Software*. Durham, NC: Duke Univ. Press

Kondo DK. 1997. *About Face: Performing Race in Fashion and Theater*. New York: Routledge

Kosek J. 2006. *Understories: The Political Life of Forests in Northern New Mexico*. Durham, NC: Duke Univ. Press

Krech S. 1999. *The Ecological Indian: Myth and History*. New York: Norton

Lamphere L, Zavella P, Gonzales F, with Evans PB. 1993. *Sunbelt Working Mothers: Reconciling Family and Factory*. Ithaca, NY: Cornell Univ. Press

Landsman G. 2008. *Reconstructing Motherhood and Disability in the Age of "Perfect" Babies*. New York: Routledge

Lassiter LE, Goodall H, Campbell L, Johnson MN, eds. 2004. *The Other Side of Middletown: Exploring Muncie's African American Community*. Walnut Creek, CA: AltaMira

Lewin E. 1993. *Lesbian Mothers: Accounts of Gender in American Culture*. Ithaca, NY: Cornell Univ. Press

Littlefield A, Knack MC, eds. 1996. *Native Americans and Wage Labor: Ethnohistorical Perspectives*. Norman/London: Univ. Okla. Press

Lomawaima KT. 1994. *They Called It Prairie Light: The Story of Chilocco Indian School*. Lincoln: Univ. Nebr. Press

Low SM. 2003. *Behind the Gates: Life, Security, and the Pursuit of Happiness in Fortress America*. New York: Routledge

Lutz CA. 2001. *Homefront: A Military City and the American Twentieth Century*. Boston: Beacon

Lutz CA, ed. 2009. *The Bases of Empire*. New York: N. Y. Univ. Press

Lutz CA, Collins JL. 1993. *Reading National Geographic*. Chicago: Univ. Chicago Press

Lynd RS, Lynd HM. 1929. *Middletown: A Study in Modern American Culture*. New York: Harvest Books, Harcourt Brace

Mahon M. 2004. *Right to Rock: The Black Rock Coalition and the Cultural Politics of Race*. Durham, NC: Duke Univ. Press

Manalansan MFI. 2003. *Global Divas: Filipino Gay Men in the Diaspora*. Durham, NC: Duke Univ. Press

Marcus GE. 1999. How anthropological curiosity consumes its own places of origin. *Cult. Anthropol.* 14(3):416–22

Marcus GE, Fischer MMJ. 1986. *Anthropology as Cultural Critique: An Experimental Moment in the Human Sciences*. Chicago: Univ. Chicago Press

Martin E. 1994. *Flexible Bodies: Tracking Immunity in American Culture from the Days of Polio to the Age of AIDS*. Boston: Beacon

Martin E. 2007. *Bipolar Expeditions: Mania and Depression in American Culture*. Princeton, NJ: Princeton Univ. Press

Masco J. 2006. *The Nuclear Borderlands: The Manhattan Project in Post-Cold War New Mexico*. Princeton, NJ: Princeton Univ. Press

Maskovsky J. 2009. Some new directions in anthropology "at home." *N. Am. Dialogue: Newsl. Soc. Anthropol. N. Am.* 12(1):6–9

Maskovsky J, Susser I. 2009. *Rethinking America: The Imperial Homeland in the 21st Century*. Boulder, CO: Paradigm

Maurer B. 2005. *Mutual Life, Limited: Islamic Banking, Alternative Currencies, Lateral Reason*. Princeton, NJ: Princeton Univ. Press

Medicine B. 2001. *Learning to Be an Anthropologist and Remaining "Native": Selected Writings*. Urbana: Univ. Ill. Press

Merry SE. 2000. *Colonizing Hawai'i: The Cultural Power of Law*. Princeton, NJ: Princeton Univ. Press

Merry SE. 2001. Spatial governmentality and the new urban social order: controlling gender violence through law. *Am. Anthropol.* 103(1):16–29

Miller BG. 2001. *The Problem of Justice: Tradition and Law in the Coast Salish World*. Lincoln: Univ. Nebr. Press

Miller BG. 2003. *Invisible Indigenes: The Politics of Nonrecognition*. Lincoln: Univ. Nebr. Press

Mithlo NM. 2009. *Our Indian Princess: Subverting the Stereotype*. Santa Fe, NM: Sch. Adv. Res.

Moffatt M. 1992. Ethnographic writing about American culture. *Annu. Rev. Anthropol.* 21:205–29

Morgen S. 2002. *Into Our Own Hands: The Women's Health Movement in the United States, 1969–1990*. New Brunswick, NJ: Rutgers Univ. Press

Morgen S, Maskovsky J. 2003. The anthropology of welfare "reform": new perspectives on U.S. urban poverty in the post-welfare era. *Annu. Rev. Anthropol.* 32(1):315–38

Mullin MH. 2001. *Culture in the Marketplace: Gender, Art, and Value in the American Southwest*. Durham, NC: Duke Univ. Press

Mullings L. 2005. Interrogating racism: toward an antiracist anthropology. *Annu. Rev. Anthropol.* 34(1):667–93

Nesper L. 2002. *The Walleye War: The Struggle for Ojibwe Spearfishing and Treaty Rights*. Lincoln: Univ. Nebr. Press

Newman KS. 1999. *No Shame in My Game: The Working Poor in the Inner City*. New York: Knopf/Russell Sage Found.

Newman KS. 2008. *Chutes and Ladders: Navigating the Low-Wage Labor Market*. Cambridge, MA: Harvard Univ. Press

Newton E. 1993. *Cherry Grove, Fire Island: Sixty Years in America's First Gay and Lesbian Town*. Boston: Beacon

O'Nell TD. 1996. *Disciplined Hearts: History, Identity, and Depression in an American Indian Community*. Berkeley: Univ. Calif. Press

Ong A. 1999. *Flexible Citizenship: The Cultural Logic of Transnationality*. Durham, NC: Duke Univ. Press

Ong A. 2003. *Buddha Is Hiding: Refugees, Citizenship, the New America*. Berkeley: Univ. Calif. Press

Ortner SB. 1997. Fieldwork in the postcommunity. *Anthropol. Humanism* 22(1):61–80

Ortner SB. 2003. *New Jersey Dreaming: Capital, Culture, and the Class of '58*. Durham, NC: Duke Univ. Press

Park K. 1996. Use and abuse of race and culture: Black-Korean tension in America. *Am. Anthropol.* 98(3):492–99

Pérez GM. 2004. *The Near Northwest Side Story: Migration, Displacement, and Puerto Rican Families*. Berkeley: Univ. Calif. Press

Pickering KA. 2000. *Lakota Culture, World Economy*. Lincoln: Univ. Nebr. Press

Price DH. 2004. *Threatening Anthropology: McCarthyism and the FBI's Surveillance of Activist Anthropologists*. Durham, NC: Duke Univ. Press

Price DH. 2008. *Anthropological Intelligence: The Deployment and Neglect of American Anthropology in the Second World War*. Durham, NC: Duke Univ. Press

Prins HEL. 2002. Visual media and the primitivist perplex: colonial fantasies and indigenous imagination in the decolonization of the fourth world. See Ginsburg 2002, pp. 58–74

Ragoné H. 1994. *Surrogate Motherhood: Conception in the Heart*. Boulder, CO: Westview

Ramirez RK. 2007. *Native Hubs: Culture, Community, and Belonging in Silicon Valley and Beyond*. Durham, NC: Duke Univ. Press

Rapp R. 1999. *Testing Women, Testing the Fetus: The Social Impact of Amniocentesis in America*. New York: Routledge

Rapp R, Ginsburg F. 2001. Enabling disability: rewriting kinship, reimagining citizenship. *Public Cult.* 13(3):533–56

Richland J. 2008. *Arguing with Tradition: The Language of Law in Hopi Tribal Court*. Chicago: Univ. Chicago Press

Rouse R. 1995. Questions of identity: personhood and collectivity in transnational migration to the United States. *Crit. Anthropol.* 15(4):351–80

Ruben M, Maskovsky J. 2008. The homeland archipelago: neoliberal urban governance after September 11. *Crit. Anthropol.* 28(2):199–217

Samuels DW. 2004. *Putting a Song on Top of It: Expression and Identity on the San Carlos Apache Reservation*. Tucson, AZ: Univ. Ariz. Press

Sanjek R. 1998. *The Future of Us All: Race and Neighborhood Politics in New York City*. Ithaca, NY: Cornell Univ. Press

Saunders B. 2009. *CT Suite: The Work of Diagnosis in the Age of Noninvasive Cutting*. Durham, NC: Duke Univ. Press

Sayre NF. 2002. *Ranching, Endangered Species, and Urbanization in the Southwest: Species of Capital*. Tucson: Univ. Ariz. Press

Shankar S. 2008. *Desi Land: Teen Culture, Class, and Success in Silicon Valley*. Durham, NC: Duke Univ. Press

Sheridan TE. 2007. Embattled ranchers, endangered species, and urban sprawl: the political ecology of the New American West. *Annu. Rev. Anthropol.* 26(1):121–38

Sider GM. 2003. *Living Indian Histories: Lumbee and Tuscarora People in North Carolina*. Chapel Hill: Univ. N. C. Press

Silliman SW. 2008. The "old west" in the Middle East: U.S. military metaphors in real and imagined Indian country. *Am. Anthropol.* 110(2):237–47

Simpson A. 2003. *To the reserve and back again: Kahnawake Mohawk narratives of self, home and nation*. PhD diss., McGill Univ.

Simpson A. 2007. On ethnographic refusal: indigeneity, 'voice' and colonial citizenship. *Junctures* 9:67–80

Simpson A. 2008. Subjects of sovereignty: indigeneity, the revenue rule, and juridics of failed consent. *Law Contemp. Probl.* 71:191–215

Spilde KA. 1998. *Acts of sovereignty, acts of identity: negotiating interdependence through tribal government gaming on the White Earth Indian Reservation.* PhD diss., Univ. Calif., Santa Cruz

Stack C. 1974. *All Our Kin: Strategies for Survival in a Black Community.* New York: Harper & Row

Stack CB. 1996. *Call to Home: African Americans Reclaim the Rural South.* New York: BasicBooks

Starn O. 2004. *Ishi's Brain: In Search of America's Last "Wild" Indian.* New York: Norton

Stewart K. 1996. *A Space on the Side of the Road: Cultural Poetics in an "Other" America.* Princeton, NJ: Princeton Univ. Press

Stewart K. 2007. *Ordinary Affects.* Durham, NC: Duke Univ. Press

Stoller P. 2002. *Money Has No Smell: The Africanization of New York City.* Chicago: Univ. Chicago Press

Strong PT. 2004. Representational practices. In *A Companion to the Anthropology of North American Indians*, ed. T Biolsi, pp. 341–59. Malden, MA: Blackwell

Strong PT. 2005. Recent ethnographic research on North American Indigenous peoples. *Annu. Rev. Anthropol.* 34:253–68

Strong PT, Van Winkle B. 1993. Tribe and nation: American Indians and American nationalism. *Soc. Anal.: J. Soc. Cult. Pract.* 33:9–26

Strong PT, Van Winkle B. 1996. "Indian blood": reflections on the reckoning and refiguring of Native North American identity. *Cult. Anthropol.* 11(4):547–76

Sturm C. 2002. *Blood Politics: Race, Culture, and Identity in the Cherokee Nation of Oklahoma.* Berkeley: Univ. Calif. Press

Susser I. 1996. The construction of poverty and homelessness in US cities. *Annu. Rev. Anthropol.* 25(1):411–35

Valentine D. 2007. *Imagining Transgender: An Ethnography of a Category.* Durham, NC: Duke Univ. Press

Vine D. 2009. *Island of Shame: The Secret History of the U.S. Military Base on Diego Garcia.* Princeton, NJ: Princeton Univ. Press

Wagoner PL. 2002. *They Treated Us Just Like Indians: The Worlds of Bennett County, South Dakota.* Lincoln: Univ. Nebr. Press

Warner WL. 1941–1959. *Yankee City.* New Haven, CT: Yale Univ. Press

Whiteley PM. 1998. *Rethinking Hopi Ethnography.* Washington, DC: Smithson. Inst. Press

Williams B. 2004. *Debt for Sale: A Social History of the Credit Trap.* Philadelphia: Univ. Penn. Press

Wojcicka Sharff J. 1998. *King Kong on Fourth Street: Families and the Violence of Poverty on the Lower East Side.* Boulder, CO: Westview

Wolfe P. 1999. *Settler Colonialism and the Transformation of Anthropology: The Politics and Poetics of an Ethnographic Event.* London/New York: Cassell

Zaloom C. 2006. *Out of the Pits: Traders and Technology from Chicago to London.* Chicago: Univ. Chicago Press

Zlolniski C. 2006. *Janitors, Street Vendors, and Activists: The Lives of Mexican Immigrants in Silicon Valley.* Berkeley: Univ. Calif. Press

Exhibiting Archaeology: Archaeology and Museums

Alex W. Barker

Museum of Art and Archaeology, University of Missouri, Columbia, Missouri 65211-1421;
email: barkeraw@missouri.edu

Annu. Rev. Anthropol. 2010. 39:293–308

First published online as a Review in Advance on
June 21, 2010

The *Annual Review of Anthropology* is online at
anthro.annualreviews.org

This article's doi:
10.1146/annurev.anthro.012809.105115

Key Words

representation, curation, authority, interpretation

Abstract

From their beginnings, archaeology museums have reflected a complex
and dynamic balance between the demands of developing, documenting,
and preserving objects on the one hand and sharing knowledge, access,
and control on the other. This balance has informed and inflected the
ways that museums present the past, including both practical aspects
of pedagogy and exhibition design as well as more critical and contested issues of authority, authenticity, and reflexivity in interpretation.
Meeting the complex requirements of curation, deliberate collections
growth, management, and conservation, as well as the need to respond
to continuing challenges to the museum's right and title to hold various
forms of cultural property, archaeological museums play an active role
in both preserving and shaping the public's view of the past and reflect
the prospects and perils of being at once a temple to the muses and a
forum for sometimes contentious public discourse.

INTRODUCTION

Museums were once the primary venue for archaeological research, and although the academy supplanted the museum in this role over the course of the twentieth century (Willey & Sabloff 1980), museums are still recognized as "the main institutional connection between archaeology as a profession and discipline, and wider society" (Shanks & Tilley 1992, p. 68). By any measure, they remain powerful forces for the communication of archaeological information. A 2001 survey in Great Britain found that visiting museums and galleries was a more popular activity than watching soccer games or any other live sporting event (MORI, p. 7), and a 2000 statistically representative survey of 1016 American adults found that 88% had visited museums interpreting archaeological materials (Ramos & Duganne 2000, p. 21).

Scholars differ over what constitutes a museum (Ginsburgh & Mairesse 1997, Hudson 1998), however, and in many respects an appropriate definition depends on the context of the discussion and why a definition is sought (Alexander & Alexander 2008, Weil 1990). For our purposes, I focus on informal educational institutions [equivalent to Paris & Hapgood's (2002, p. 39) informal learning environments], which hold archaeological collections and interpret them through regular exhibitions for one or more audiences; I set aside entities which interpret the past without the benefit of actual objects (such as science centers), and repositories which hold objects without an explicit charge to interpret them for the public. Many issues identified here cross these admittedly arbitrary boundaries, but the need of museums to balance constantly the conflicting demands of access and interpretation on the one hand and preservation and stewardship on the other creates a dynamic tension less evident in these other kinds of entities, where priority is given to one or the other side of the equation. This balance also organizes the discussion that follows, considering in turn the changing role of museums, complexities of interpreting the past for multiple audiences, the epistemological dimensions of museum interpretation, curation and conservation of the past's tangible remains, and challenges to the rights of museums to claim good title to various categories of cultural objects.

THE CHANGING ROLE OF MUSEUMS

Most of the earliest archaeological museums were founded either as a byproduct of antiquarian research or to promote social betterment through access to works of art and science [see Pearce (1995) for a general history of collecting in the European tradition and see Swain (2007) for an abbreviated history of archaeological museum collecting]. Museums themselves have evolved from private entities through public charities into nonstock corporations or units of government (Hall 1992). This shift had the effect of moving many museums from a narrow focus on the interests and passions of the individuals who built the collection (e.g., Larson 2009, McMullen 2009) to a broadly defined emphasis on public betterment, and more recently a better-defined emphasis on meeting the needs of specific audiences, largely owing to shifts in governance that placed key stakeholders in governance positions. Hudson (1998) argues that it can be asserted

> ...with confidence that the most fundamental change that has affected museums...is the now universal conviction that they exist in order to serve the public. The old-style museum felt itself to be under no such obligation. It existed, it had a building, it had collections and a staff to look after them. It was reasonably adequately financed, and its visitors, usually not numerous, came in to look, to wonder and to admire what was set before them. They were in no sense partners in the enterprise. The museum's prime responsibility was to its collections, not its visitors. (p. 43)

The public service and educational roles of museums were articulated by late-nineteenth and early-twentieth-century museum leaders including John Cotton Dana (1920), William

Henry Flower (1898), Franz Boas (1974 [1905]), G. Brown Goode (1891), Alexander Ruthven (1931), and Harlan Smith (1912), among others. Earlier generations had implicitly assumed this educational role; indeed Thomsen is remembered not only for the three-age system but for his tireless educational efforts. In an age when access to the British Museum was limited to 60 persons a day, each screened by the porter to make sure they were the right sort (Hudson 1987), Thomsen met and led tours of the Danish National Museum by groups of every kind to promote both general knowledge of the past and through that knowledge social betterment of the masses. Lord Elgin took a similar view in exporting the contested marbles from the East pediment of the Parthenon to London, suggesting the marbles might have "some benefit on the progress of taste" (St. Clair 1998). Although more recent generations of scholars have carefully deconstructed these views to examine the ideological stances and stereotypes informing them (e.g., Hamilakis 1999, Hitchens et al. 1998), it is worth recalling that the conscious motivations of these early antiquarians were largely educational. More recently, this educational role of museums has been affirmed by major professional organizations; in *Excellence and Equity*, the American Association of Museums (AAM) (1992) stated that museums must place education—in the broadest sense of the word—at the center of their public service role and make their educational role central to their activities.

This educational role is crucial to both the development of modern archaeological museums and the wide range of critical approaches to them because it requires that museums move from passive repositories to active arbiters and interpreters of the past. Throughout the nineteenth century (and I suggest well into the twentieth) most museum archaeologists believed "in the explanatory power and epistemological transparency of objects, specimens, things" (Conn 2004, p. 117). The more subtle role of museums in creating or altering perceptions about the past is now well established, although

one could argue that recognition of this role is part of a logical historical progression in how the tangible objects of the past have been understood and used in constructing epistemological frameworks (e.g., Anderson 2004).

For much of the eighteenth and nineteenth centuries, museums were concerned with organizing and arranging objects to document the time periods and cultures that produced them (e.g., Holmes 1902). Objects were treated as index fossils, whose form and character allowed archaeologists or antiquarians to draw valid inferences regarding the dating of sites and the identification of cultural complexes associated with the site or site component. The advent of chronometric techniques in the twentieth century allowed and promoted a focus on cultural process rather than culture history and altered the ways in which material culture implicated, inscribed, and informed processual studies. More recently, postprocessual studies have recruited both museum objects and the institutions that house them in critical reexaminations of how material objects were appreciated and appropriated by agents in societies past and present—critiques that react against processual excesses while to some degree premised on the epistemological emphases they established.

EXPLANATION AND PRESENTATION

Although the educational mandate of archaeological museums is clear, whether they have been particularly effective achieving that mandate through exhibitions remains debatable (e.g., see articles in McManus 1996). One sobering statistic emerged from surveys of public attitudes toward archaeology; although 88% of respondents said they had visited a museum exhibiting archaeological materials, only 9% reported learning anything about archaeology from museums (Ramos & Duganne 2000, p. 12). Television remains the most popular vehicle for learning about the past (Ramos & Duganne 2000), and relatively few media— even formal instructional textbooks—teach about the past consistently. A 1990 study, for example, found "textbooks from all parts of the world that ignore contemporary understandings of the prehistoric past" (MacKenzie & Stone 1990, p. 3).

Available data suggest that people interpret the past in light of their own experiences and cultural constructs; we see the past not as it was but as we are. This mindset is more than a naïve extension of one's own views, but an active strategy pursued even when presented with seemingly authoritative information that contradicts these constructs (Wineburg 2001). Although it has long been recognized by museum professionals that people want to play an active role in interpreting the past and making it meaningful, in all the complex meanings of the term (Davis 2000, Falk & Dierking 2000, Jameson 1997, Rosenzweig & Thelen 1998, Rowan & Baram 2004, Stone & Molyneaux 1994), recent studies suggest this desire may be crucial to learning success (e.g., Roschelle 1995). Dierking (2002) argues that three overlapping leaning contexts contribute to the way children (at least) interact with and apprehend objects. The personal context includes motivation and expectation, interest, prior knowledge and experience, and dimensions of choice and control. The sociocultural context includes within-group sociocultural mediation, specifically social aspects of learning within the immediate group, and mediation facilitated by others, including parents, teachers, docents, or others. Finally, the physical context includes advance preparation, setting and immediate environment, design elements of the experience, and subsequent reinforcing events and experience (see also Falk & Dierking 2000). Despite best efforts, however, none of these three primary contexts are entirely within a museum's control.

Davis (2005) offers a constructivist approach to student learning in archaeology, identifying six distinct types of learning strategies. The types are distinguished by whether the learner sees knowledge as constructed or acquired, the degree of proficiency achieved in this knowledge, and whether they tend to articulate and process this knowledge as narratives or analytical processes (pp. 99–103). Individual learners may shift fluidly between strategies depending on context, structure of information, and proficiency. Different kinds of experiences and pedagogical practices are needed to effectively engage students employing different learning strategies. Museum-based programs tend to have shorter encounter times with visitors or students than do other kinds of venues, they tend to be more dependent on self-guided activities, and they require greater knowledge of visitor preconceptions well in advance of exhibition creation or programmatic activities. Thus, successful programs often depend on detailed visitor studies to understand the needs and background of diverse audiences (p. 142). She notes that many of the techniques she has found successful "require significant investments of both time and money," which she recognizes "may seem extravagant or even impossible, given the kinds of constraints that many schools and nonprofit organizations have to contend with" (p. 160).

Pedagogical approaches in museums generally focus on either objects or ideas, what Weil (1990, 1995) called emphasis on the "isness" of objects or their "aboutness" (see also Witcomb 1997). Greenblatt (1991) united these apparently disparate paradigms as focusing on different dimensions of objects, which he called "wonder" and "resonance" [wonder being the ability of an object to stop the viewer in his or her tracks (read masterwork) and resonance being the ability of objects to evoke a larger world or set of cultural forces], arguing that successful exhibitions required elements of both and that "the poetics and politics of representation are most completely fulfilled in the experience of wonderful resonance and resonant wonder" (p. 54). Exhibitions, then, can succeed by offering elements that provide wonder and other elements (or moments) that contextualize and embed the object through resonance.

A broad range of museum literature examines the morphology or logistics of exhibitions, including such elements as traffic flow, sight lines, dwell time (or the amount of time a visitor spends in front of a particular element), and diligence (whether visitors fully examine exhibit elements and signage or select a subset of available options); treatments of both individual installations and more general best practices can be found in journals including *Visitor Studies Today* or *Visitor Behavior, Art Education, Journal of Museum Education, Curator, Museum Management and Curatorship*, and *Exhibitionist: A Journal of Reflexive Practice*; see also general works on exhibit development and design such as Dean (1994) and Lord & Lord (2002). Pearce (1990) suggests three additional dimensions in archaeological exhibits. "Depth" is the relative number of distinct spaces that must be crossed to move from one exhibit element to another. "Rings" measure the number of alternative paths a visitor may use to traverse an exhibition without backtracking, and "entropy" measures the relative linearity or simplicity of the layout. More than measures of visitor behavior, however, Pearce (1990) argues that these dimensions directly structure how information is perceived by the visitor. Shallow depth and low ring factors "present knowledge as if it were a map of a well-known terrain where the relationship of each part to the other, and all to the whole, is thoroughly understood" (p. 150). By contrast, she argues, exhibits with a high entropy value, considerable depth, and high ring factor "show knowledge as a proposition which may stimulate further, or different, answering propositions" (p. 150).

Cotton & Wood (1996) provide a detailed discussion of the thinking that went into the design of a specific archaeological exhibition, *People Before London*, a prehistory installation at the Museum of London. In an intriguing twist, curators and designers went beyond take-home messages regarding specific cultural units or time periods and posed direct, reflexive questions to the visitor, including "Can you believe what we say?", to problematize the issue of authority in archaeological exhibitions.

AUTHORITY AND INTERPRETATION

Museums and their use of objects have faced critiques from feminists (Porter 1996), structuralists (Bal 1992), poststructuralists (Bennett 1995), postmodernists (Crimp 1995), and postcolonial theorists (Clifford 1997, Rigg 1994; see also Sherman 1994 for a more general treatment of critiques of museum-as-institution) and a range of postprocessualist critiques from within archaeology itself (Shanks & Tilley 1992). Many of the broader anthropological critiques regarding formalism, primitivism, authenticity, and historicism in museum settings (Jones 1993) can also be generalized to apply to archaeological museum exhibitions (see also Crew & Sims 1991). Bourdieu (1984) has argued that museums serve primarily to maintain existing class distinctions; although his arguments were originally specific to art museums, they have been expanded by other scholars and applied to archaeological, heritage, and cultural museums more generally (Bennett et al. 1991, Merriman 1989). Museum exhibitions can reify and perpetuate stereotypical understandings; Wood (1997) shows that stereotypical presentations of gender roles persist in many archaeological museums. By contrast, Wood & Cotton (1999) carefully consider how gender was presented in *People Before London*. The appearance of past peoples as conjectural is also emphasized at the Keiller Museum in Wiltshire, England, where a single figure is depicted with two very different sets of clothing, hairstyles, and tattoos on either side of his body. Although aptly illustrating the ambiguity of presentations of the past, Swain (2007) notes that the figure "comes across as a rather badly dressed 1980s shop dummy" (p. 214). Interpreting people of the past also raises complex issues regarding representation and the role of living communities in controlling, framing, and interpreting their own pasts (e.g., Ames 1991, 1992; Colwell-Chanthaphonh & Ferguson 2006; Hendry 2005; Isaac 2005; Karp et al. 1992; Kuklick 1991; Lawlor 2006; Levy 2006; Simpson 2007; Sleeper-Smith 2009; see also Peers 2007).

For Bourdieu (Bourdieu & Johnson 1993) museums play a key role in consecrating objects, embodying and perpetuating theories of how objects should be appropriately apprehended, understood, and contextualized. Whitehead

(2009), following Vergo's (1994) notion that museums create their own contexts, argues further that museums create an environment that encourages certain kinds of theorizing (an argument analogous in many respects to the reception aesthetics views of Wolfgang Iser (1980) and Hans Robert Jauss (1982) in literary theory).

This view of objects, whether individually or as exhibitions, as signs that can be read reflects a textual view of representation which had permeated history by the late-eighteenth and nineteenth centuries (Conn 2004), and is commonplace in studies of museum interpretation (e.g., van Kraayenoord & Paris 2002). Pearce (1990, 1992) employs a Saussurean construct to understand how visitors understand and "read" archaeological exhibitions. Perhaps the most familiar examples of this approach are the postprocessual critiques of archaeology by Hodder (1986) and of museums by Shanks & Tilley (1992). Vogel (1991) has suggested that "the fact that museums recontextualize and interpret objects is a given, and requires no apologies." Instead, museums should "allow the public to know that [museums are] not a broad frame through which the art and culture of the world can be inspected, but a tightly focused lens that shows the visitor a particular point of view." She concludes "it could hardly be otherwise" (p. 201).

One of the most intriguing theoretical works affecting interpretation of archaeological artifacts is that of the late Alfred Gell (1998). Gell's approach is equally radical but is based on an utter rejection of meaning as an appropriate way of understanding things and on the bankruptcy of precisely the textual approaches on which Shanks and Tilley depend as useful avenues for anthropological understanding of objects. "I entirely reject," Gell writes "the idea that anything, except language itself, has 'meaning' in the intended sense" (Gell 1998, p. 6). Instead Gell sees objects as ways of doing something, as social entities imbued with the ability to act as 'secondary agents,' and examines "the practical mediatory role of art objects in the social process."

Although Gell's approach presents a series of interpretive problems for both scholars and those who view displays of objects understood from this perspective, it represents a bold departure from existing treatments of objects and their practical contextualization. However, this approach also entails the proposition that an exhibition is likewise a work of art designed to have an effect, is itself an artifact of the kind and with the properties of the works it presents, and should be understood in terms of the social relationships it mediates—an approach that fits comfortably within visitor-centric constructs commonly encountered in museum studies as a discipline (Black 2005).

The centrality of issues of authority and authenticity have been apparent since the very beginning of museums. The Library and Musaeum of Alexandria (better remembered today for its destruction than for its encyclopedic stature) received important works to be copied, then quietly returned the copy rather than the original to the lender to ensure the authority and authenticity of its holdings (Bagnall 2002, p. 356; Heller-Roazen 2002, p. 133). Institutions such as the Musaeum (then and now) play an important role in nation building and definition of a group's social identity (Crinson 2001, Kaplan 1994, Kohl 1998, Launius 2007, Linenthal & Engelhardt 1996), but only recently have these practices become the subject of direct ethnographic inquiry (Handler & Gable 1997, Davis 2005). One such study examines the Musaeum itself: Butler (2007) uses ethnographic approaches to study the new Bibliotheca Alexandrina, a joint Egyptian/UNESCO project completed in 2002.

CURATION AND CONSERVATION

Collections lie at the heart of the museum, the *sine qua non* of the museum as an institution. As Swain has argued (2007, p. 91), of all the elements that constitute a museum (staff, buildings, donors, galleries, collections, etc.), any one could be removed without changing the fundamental character of the institution, except the collections. They define the profile and prospects of the institution in ways more profound and lasting than do mission statements or current circumstances. The importance of appreciating why humans collect and use tangible things to make sense of the past is recognized both through a range of individual scholarly studies (e.g., Pearce 1992, 1995, Wertsch 2002; see also articles in Knell 1999, Krech & Hall 1999, Pearce 1994) and entire journals (e.g., *Journal of the History of Collections* or *Collections: A Journal for Museums and Archives Professionals*, among others).

Pearce (1997) has identified six distinct kinds of objects comprising archaeological collections in museums: (*a*) chance finds, usually received as single pieces or small groups and generally lacking meaningful documentation; (*b*) private collections amassed by individuals, with or without accompanying documentation; (*c*) material from museum-based excavation projects, usually accompanied by complete documentation; (*d*) material from excavations by other bodies or institutions, with the level of accompanying documentation varying by age and quality of excavation; (*e*) materials accepted from fieldwork or cultural resources management (CRM) projects, often through curation agreements, which should in general be accompanied by levels of documentation specified in the curation agreement; and (*f*) material from metal detectorists, a category more commonly separable in British museums than elsewhere.

It remains unclear, however, whether all collections objects are equal. Thomas (cited in Swain 2007) has argued for the concept of the "total collection," in which every object in the collection is equally valued; Swain (2007, p. 95) by contrast argues for an implicit hierarchy in practice in which some exhibitable or complete objects often have greater perceived value than do others. The truth likely lies somewhere in between, with the relative value or utility of an object depending on the specific purposes or needs on which it is called to address.

Whitehead (2009) has argued that museums are constitutive rather than reflective of their fields; museums do not simply show art but by doing so define its nature. Archaeological museums do the same, establishing the ground on which (and from which) different conceptions of the past are contested. Archaeologists do not actually study the past, but instead study those remains of the past that persist into the present to make inferences about that past; time is perhaps the most salient analytical dimension in archaeology but one which must always be inferred. Archaeological museums played a crucial role both in the development of culture history as an approach and in the construction of alternative temporocultural frameworks for classifying archaeological remains in time and space prior to the advent of chronometric dating techniques (Lyman et al. 1997). Although the importance of museums and museum-affiliated archaeologists (including, among others, Thomsen, Worsaae, Holmes, Wissler, Flinders Petrie, Uhle, Lothrop, Kidder, Woolley, Phillips, McKern, Ford, and Willey) is generally understood in this regard, the profound importance and immediacy of collections are not fully appreciated. Thomsen is widely credited with the three-age system, but it had been previously proposed for Scandinavian archaeology by Vedel-Simonsen and seconded by both Magnus Bruzelius (prior to Thomsen's reorganization of the National Museum collections) and Sven Nilsson. Heizer (1962) traces a long continental ancestry, including mention in the works of Mercati, Eccard, Borlase, Rothe, Pennant, Hodgson, Büsching, and Goguet, among others. It was less the proposal of the three-age system (which after all could be pressed earlier to the times of Hesiod and Lucretius) than its application to physical museum collections by Thomsen in 1836 and G.C. Friedrich Lisch in 1837, with its utility confirmed through excavations by J.J.A. Worsaae in Denmark published in the 1840s, that makes Thomsen's contribution a watershed. Later in the nineteenth century the same logic—but a different set of organizing principles—were used by Otis Mason to organize the archaeological material in the Smithsonian. Instead of a threefold system based on the stuff of which bladed weapons were made, Mason used Lewis

Henry Morgan's evolutionary sequence from savagery through barbarism to civilization to provide both a context for understanding material variability and a rationale for the directionality of change (Sullivan & Childs 2003, pp. 5–6; later Mason was instrumental in defining New World culture areas in a continuing attempt to better map changes in material form onto both time and later space). McKern's development of the midwestern taxonomic method was similarly a museum-based iterative process of organizing data—largely physical collections—into units that could be meaningfully discussed and compared by archaeologists; it differed from the systems of Thomsen and Otis (among others) in being explicitly nonevolutionary in character. Precisely because McKern was interested in understanding temporal and historical relationships, he explicitly excluded them from the classificatory framework.

Whereas archaeological curators wrestle with the problem of how best to document and depict time, archaeological conservation attempts to forestall its effects. Cheating time is only partially effective at best, but enormous strides have been made in both the theory and the practice of conservation, both in field (Sease 1994) and in laboratory (Cronyn & Robinson 1990, May & Jones 2006). As part of a larger tendency to foreground museological processes, numerous exhibitions and publications have discussed and described how archaeological materials are conserved. For the most part, these works have addressed technical issues of preserving objects from deleterious chemical changes and inhibiting inherent vice (Podany & Maish 1993), but a growing number of works have discussed the balance between the preservation of objects on the one hand and natural processes of decay or weathering on the other, which may have been integral to their function within the communities which produced them (Bernstein 1992, Hull-Walski & Flynn 2001). This growing conservation literature details both consultation and compromise between traditional academic forms of conservation and community-based standards of care and treatment, which emphasize the social dimension

of archaeological objects (Clavir 2002, Kreps 2003). Literature written by and for indigenous groups and tribal museums has also begun to address museological conservation, object handling protocols, and collections management issues (see articles in Ogden 2004).

A broad and growing literature examines appropriate collections management and curatorial procedures (Buck et al. 2007, Cassar 1995, Fahy 1995, Knell 1994, Simmons 2006), and specific treatments aimed at archaeologists or that examine specific kinds of archaeological remains have appeared (Cassman et al. 2007, Pearce 1990, Sullivan & Childs 2003, Swain 2007). Although these contributions provide guidance regarding conceptual issues and best practices, for the most part they presume that adequate resources in time, space, staff, and funding are available—an enviable position rarely found in practice. Curation of archaeological collections has been described as in a state of crisis since 1982 (Bawaya 2007, Marquardt et al. 1982, Thompson 1999, Trimble & Marino 2003; see also Owen 1999 for a critique of the role of museums in fieldwork), with few immediate prospects for relief in sight. This crisis, coupled with high rates of site destruction, has led some to ask whether it is ethical to excavate new sites if extant museum collections are sufficient to address a given research question (Barker 2003).

TITLE AND CULTURAL PROPERTY ISSUES

Another central challenge facing archaeological museums in the twenty-first century involves the question of title to cultural objects (Messenger 1989). Traditionally, the process of accessioning objects intrinsically involved an assertion of title, an approach deeply rooted in Lockean notions of private property and ownership (Malaro 1998). Changing legal and ethical frameworks have problematized these assumptions, however. The Native American Graves Protection and Repatriation Act (NAGPRA) (McKeown et al. 1998, McLaughlin 2004, Trope & Echo-Hawk

2000) challenged both the right of museums to hold certain categories of objects and whether goodness of title could be asserted for objects acquired from groups where individual ownership—and hence the ability of an individual to convey good title—could not be assumed. The development of the so-called McClain doctrine, which allows foreign countries from whom objects have been looted to seek damages in U.S. courts under the National Stolen Property Act under certain circumstances, has also problematized the degree to which museums can assert good title to objects for which full provenance cannot be established. The McClain doctrine holds that antiquities whose ownership is clearly vested in foreign governments may be stolen property if they were excavated illegally and removed without appropriate permissions; for the doctrine to apply, the antiquities must have been recovered within the borders of the nation-state bringing action, the antiquities laws vesting ownership in the state must be sufficiently clear to give notice to U.S. citizens that removal of antiquities is illegal, and finally the antiquities must have been excavated or removed after the effective date of the statutes vesting ownership in the state (Gerstenblith 2004, Yasaitis 2005).

Although the McClain doctrine, NAGPRA, and related legal precepts provide legal foundations for various kinds of claims, many instances of restitution to foreign governments are based less on litigation than on leverage. The well-publicized case of the Euphronios krater is one example. The Metropolitan Museum purchased the vessel in 1972 for what was then a record sum, giving it pride of place in its galleries as expressing a crucial moment in the development of representational art. The Italian government had long sought its return, claiming the vase had been looted from the Greppe Sant'Angelo near Cerveteri, Italy, within a year or so of its purchase. In 2006, the Metropolitan agreed to return the Euphronios krater and several other contested objects to Italy in return for a series of long-term loans of comparable objects (Watson & Todeschini 2006).

The threat of litigation and continued negative publicity led the Metropolitan's leadership to decide a negotiated settlement was preferable to establishing an unpalatable precedent (Waxman 2008). Other museums have resisted calls for the return of putatively stolen objects. Egypt claims that a funerary mask of Ka Nefer Nefer was stolen from one of its store rooms and purchased by the St. Louis Art Museum, but despite the apparent presence of the item in a 1953 Egyptian inventory the Museum has, to date, declined calls for the mask's return.

Applicable ethical guidelines under which museums acquire antiquities have undergone significant changes in recent years. Through the 1990s, the primary requirements were that objects not be illegally acquired or have been imported illegally into the country in which the museum is located. Particularly for U.S.-based museums, this ethical standard set a relatively low bar because export restrictions and foreign patrimony laws were generally not observed in determining the legality of import of objects. In 2004, the Association of Art Museum Directors (an organization representing the 200 largest art museums in the United States, Canada, and Mexico) introduced guidelines that recommended museums not acquire objects that could not be shown to have left their source countries at least 10 years before acquisition by the museum (AAMD 2004). These guidelines were widely criticized by a number of archaeological groups, including the Archaeological Institute of America, the Council for Museum Anthropology, the Society for American Archaeology, and the Archaeology Division of the American Anthropological Association as providing a blueprint for the allowable sale of looted antiquities rather than restricting their trade. These organizations instead called on museums to require that antiquities be shown to have left their country of probable origin prior to the 1970 UNESCO Convention on the Illegal Sale and Trafficking in Cultural Objects or be accompanied by documentation showing that they had been legally imported into the United States and legally exported from their country of origin. In 2008, the American

Association of Museums recommended new guidelines for American museums in general, which required transparency in acquisitions guidelines, research on provenance of newly acquired objects, and determination that objects had left their country of probable origin prior to the 1970 UNESCO Convention date (AAM 2008). The Association of Art Museum Directors (AAMD) revised its standards as well, allowing more room for interpretation than the American Association of Museums (AAM) but similarly adopting the fixed 1970 date for provenance of antiquities and establishing a Web-based registry for listing of artifacts with potentially problematic provenance (AAMD 2008).

The use of Web-based information registries for objects of this kind is not new. In 2000, AAM and AAMD had developed and launched the Nazi Era Provenance Internet Portal in consultation with the Presidential Advisory Commission on Holocaust Assets in the United States (PCHA) to provide information to potential claimants of objects in U.S. museums that changed hands in continental Europe between 1933–1945, along with detailed procedures for conducting provenance research on such objects (Yeide et al. 2001).

These represent only some of the challenges to the right of museums to hold good title to particular objects or kinds of cultural property. Hutt (2004) has identified six perspectives on objects from the past, which inform and inflect both legal cases and public debate regarding cultural property claims. Moralist perspectives generally use normative rather than legal language to argue for a particular position perceived as the right or honorable resolution to a contested claim. Nationalist perspectives hold that cultural property is inalienable, hence an entity accepting a nation's patrimony can never hold good title. Internationalist perspectives, which she alternatively names "paternalist theory," argue just the opposite, that significant objects of cultural property transcend nationalist laws and are the common property of humankind, and those who can control them should. Property law perspectives focus on identifying who among competing claimants has the right of ownership, regardless of other moral or scientific claims. Scientific perspectives appeal to the public benefit of inquiry and the loss of knowledge by all if inquiries are prevented. The market theory perspective focuses on private property interests and the promotion of free trade in objects and emphasizes mechanisms that permit goodness of title to be restored to objects to facilitate their exchange.

While Hutt's (2004) identification of different perspectives is a useful heuristic vehicle, the perspectives reflect a particular viewpoint or bias with which many theorists and legal scholars might take issue, notably the premise that native claimants are *prima facie* rightful owners of cultural property under common law, that patrimonial rights and property law perspectives are the same (common law would generally view property rights as a more complex and separable bundle of rights allowing no such sweeping generalizations), and that nationalist perspectives hold that cultural property is inalienable, rather than the more limited claim that national laws vesting ownership of antiquities in the nation-state should be internationally respected. She presents an intriguing diagram (2004, p. 31) showing possible relationships between the various perspectives and notes that the scientific perspective might be able to establish the validity of nationalist claims, but she does not suggest that scientific analysis could similarly warrant the validity of patrimonial claims by putative descendants.

Increasing rates of site destruction and a series of high-profile restitution cases have intensified debates over the role of the antiquities trade, licit and illicit, in looting, site destruction, and loss of cultural heritage (Atwood 2004, Bogdanos & Patrick 2005, Carman 2005, Renfrew 2006, Watson & Todeschini 2006, Waxman 2008). For some, the role of looting and the illicit (and sometimes legal) trade in antiquities is plain (Brodie et al. 2001), whereas others see such criticisms as a direct or indirect attack on private collecting (Fitz Gibbon 2005).

Just as individual scholars find themselves caught between ethical prohibitions against publication of unprovenanced material on the one hand and the loss of information from such materials on the other (e.g., Owen 2005), some museum staff feel caught between the ethical prohibition against accepting unprovenanced antiquities and the loss of these objects to the private market. These concerns have been most widely voiced by advocates of so-called encyclopedic art museums, such as the Metropolitan Museum in New York, the British Museum in London, and the Art Institute in Chicago (Cuno 2008, 2009). Apologists for encyclopedic museums cast the antiquities debate as pitting archaeologists against museums (e.g., Watt 2009), although much of the debate really centers on whether archaeological contexts have significant value in art museum contexts, a debate less between archaeologists and museums than between disciplinary emphases on different kinds of contexts within different kinds of museums. Art historians emphasize assigned or assumed contexts based on extrinsic classification of the object (e.g., Boardman 2009), whereas archaeologists focus on observed contexts that allow the validity of extrinsic classifications to be assessed (Barker 2004). The former view privileges the authority of the museum or museum curator, whereas the latter decenters that privileged position by allowing significance to be determined through multiple kinds of contexts (archaeological, aesthetic, pedagogical patrimonial, etc.), which may be assigned by different entities or individuals.

PROSPECTS

McLean (1999) has succinctly depicted the terrain in which archaeological museums now operate: "Our times seem to be framed by an increasingly complex and layered dialectic of privilege, expert knowledge, and prescriptive meaning-making on the one hand, and access, popular culture, and the negotiation of meaning on the other" (p. 103). To this might be added a decentering of the privileged place museums have held as keepers of cultural property and myriad economic and governance challenges. To some, this perspective suggests a bleak future.

But although the terrain may be difficult, it should seem familiar. The tension between the dual aspects of the museum—responsible for both holding collections and making them available for its publics—has always lain at the heart of the museum enterprise. Museums are at once sacred groves and public attractions (Jeffers 2003), consecrated as temples to the Muses on the one hand and committed to service as a public forum on the other. Like our understandings of the past and our needs as a diverse and disparate society, museums will continue to change. That is and will continue to be their nature, suggesting a bright rather than bleak future for the keepers of the past.

DISCLOSURE STATEMENT

The author is not aware of any affiliations, memberships, funding, or financial holdings that might be perceived as affecting the objectivity of this review.

ACKNOWLEDGMENTS

Archaeology and museums each represent dynamic disciplines with wide-ranging and growing fields of associated scholarship. Their intersection is broad and deep, and only its outlines are sketched here. I humbly apologize to my colleagues whose many significant and stimulating contributions have not been included here owing to limitations of space; it is remarkable how rapidly the assigned space goes from impossible to fill to woefully inadequate. I am grateful to Lee Lyman and Lana Coggeshall for their thoughtful comments on some of the issues presented here and to my colleagues in the Council for Museum Anthropology for much fruitful and enjoyable discussion.

LITERATURE CITED

Alexander EP, Alexander M. 2008. *Museums in Motion: An Introduction to the History and Functions of Museums*. Lanham, MD: AltaMira

Am. Assoc. Mus. 1992. *Excellence and Equity: Education and the Public Dimension of Museums: A Report*. Washington, DC: American Association of Museums

Am. Assoc. Mus. 2008. Standards regarding archaeological material and ancient art, American Association of Museums. *Int. J. Cult. Prop.* 15:401–3

Ames M. 1991. Biculturalism in museums. *Mus. Anthropol.* 15:7–15

Ames M. 1992. *Cannibal Tours and Glass Boxes: The Anthropology of Museums*. Vancouver: Univ. B.C. Press

Anderson G. 2004. *Reinventing the Museum: Historical and Contemporary Perspectives on the Paradigm Shift*. Walnut Creek, CA: AltaMira

Assoc. Art Mus. Dir. 2004. *Report of the AAMD Task Force on the Acquisition of Archaeological Material and Ancient Art*. New York: Association of Art Museum Directors

Assoc. Art Mus. Dir. 2008. *Report of the AAMD Subcommittee on the Acquisition of Archaeological Materials and Ancient Art*. New York: Association of Art Museum Directors

Atwood R. 2004. *Stealing History: Tomb Raiders, Smugglers, and the Looting of the Ancient World*. New York: St. Martin's

Bagnall R. 2002. Alexandria: library of dreams. *Proc. Am. Philos. Soc.* 146:348–62

Bal M. 1992. Telling, showing, showing off. *Crit. Inq.* 18:556–94

Barker A. 2003. Archaeological ethics: museums and collections. See Zimmerman 2003, pp. 71–84

Barker A. 2004. Stewardship, collections integrity and long-term research value. In *Our Collective Responsibility: The Ethics and Practice of Archaeological Collections Stewardship*, ed. ST Childs, pp. 25–42. Washington, DC: Soc. Am. Archaeol.

Bawaya M. 2007. Archaeology: curation in crisis. *Science* 317:1025–26

Bennett T. 1995. *The Birth of the Museum*. New York: Routledge

Bennett T, Bulbeck C, Finnane M. 1991. *Accessing the Past*. Brisbane: Inst. Cult. Policy Stud.

Bernstein B. 1992. Collaborative strategies for the preservation of North American Indian culture. *J. Am. Inst. Conserv.* 31:23–29

Black G. 2005. *The Engaging Museum: Developing Museums for Visitor Involvement*. London: Routledge

Boardman J. 2009. Archaeologists, collectors, and museums. See Cuno 2009, pp. 107–24

Boas F. 1974 [1905]. The educational functions of anthropology museums. In *The Shaping of American Anthropology, 1883–1911; A Franz Boas Reader*, ed. GW Stocking, pp. 297–301. New York: Basic Books

Bogdanos M, Patrick W. 2005. *Thieves of Baghdad: One Marine's Passion for Ancient Civilizations and the Journey to Recover the World's Greatest Stolen Treasures*. New York: Bloomsbury

Bourdieu P. 1984. *Distinction: A Social Critique of the Judgment of Taste*. London: Routledge & Kegan Paul

Bourdieu P, Johnson R. 1993. *The Field of Cultural Production: Essays on Art and Literature*. New York: Columbia Univ. Press

Brodie N, Renfrew C, Doole J, McDonald Inst. Archaeol. Res., eds. 2001. *Trade in Illicit Antiquities: The Destruction of the World's Archaeological Heritage*. Cambridge, UK: McDonald Institute for Archaeological Research

Buck RA, Gilmore JA, Am. Assoc. Mus. 2007. *Collection Conundrums: Solving Collections Management Mysteries*. Washington, DC: American Association of Museums

Butler B. 2007. *Return to Alexandria: An Ethnography of Cultural Heritage, Revivalism, and Museum Memory*. Walnut Creek, CA: Left Coast

Carman J. 2005. *Against Cultural Property: Archaeology, Heritage and Ownership*. London: Duckworth

Cassar M. 1995. *Environmental Management: Guidelines for Museums and Galleries*. London/New York: Routledge

Cassman V, Odegaard N, Powell JF. 2007. *Human Remains: Guide for Museums and Academic Institutions*. Lanham, MD: AltaMira

Clavir M. 2002. *Preserving What Is Valued: Museums, Conservation, and First Nations*. Vancouver: Univ. B.C. Press

Clifford J. 1997. *Routes: Travel and Translation in the Late Twentieth Century*. Cambridge, MA: Harvard Univ. Press

Colwell-Chanthaphonh C, Ferguson TJ. 2006. Memory pieces and footprints: multivocality and the meanings of ancient times and ancestral places among the Zuni and Hopi. *Am. Anthropol.* 108:148–62

Conn S. 2004. *History's Shadow: Native Americans and Historical Consciousness in the Nineteenth Century*. Chicago: Univ. Chicago Press

Cotton J, Wood B. 1996. Retrieving prehistories at the Museum of London: a gallery case-study. See McManus 1996, pp. 53–71

Crew SR, Sims JE. 1991. Locating authenticity: fragments of a dialogue. See Karp & Lavine 1991, pp. 159–75

Crimp D. 1995. *On the Museum's Ruins*. Cambridge, MA: MIT Press

Crinson M. 2001. Nation-building, collecting and the politics of display. *J. Hist. Collect.* 13:231–50

Cronyn JM, Robinson WS. 1990. *The Elements of Archaeological Conservation*. London/New York: Routledge

Cuno JB. 2008. *Who Owns Antiquity? Museums and the Battle over our Ancient Heritage*. Princeton, NJ/Woodstock, UK: Princeton Univ. Press

Cuno JB. 2009. *Whose Culture? The Promise of Museums and the Debate over Antiquities*. Princeton, NJ: Princeton Univ. Press

Dana JC. 1920. *The New Museum*. Woodstock, VT: Elm Tree

Davis ME. 2005. *How Students Understand the Past: From Theory to Practice*. Walnut Creek, CA: AltaMira

Davis P. 2000. Museums and the promotion of environmental understanding and heritage conservation. In *Cultural Resource Management in Contemporary Society: Perspectives on Managing and Presenting the Past*, ed. FP McManamon, A Hatton, pp. 310–18. London: Routledge

Dean D. 1994. *Museum Exhibition: Theory and Practice*. London/New York: Routledge

Dierking LD. 2002. The role of context in children's learning from objects and experiences. See Paris 2002, pp. 3–18

Fahy A. 1995. *Collections Management*. London/New York: Routledge

Falk JH, Dierking LD. 2000. *Learning from Museums: Visitor Experiences and the Making of Meaning*. Walnut Creek, CA: AltaMira

Fitz Gibbon K. 2005. *Who Owns the Past? Cultural Policy, Cultural Property, and the Law*. New Brunswick, NJ: Rutgers Univ. Press

Flower WH. 1898. *Essays on Museums, and Other Subjects Connected with Natural History*. London: MacMillan

Gell A. 1998. *Art and Agency: An Anthropological Theory*. Oxford/New York: Clarendon

Gerstenblith P. 2004. From Steinhardt to Schultz: the McClain doctrine and the protection of archaeological sites. See Richman & Forsyth 2004, pp. 100–18

Ginsburgh V, Mairesse F. 1997. Defining a museum: suggestions for an alternative approach. *Mus. Manag. Curatorship* 16:15–33

Goode GB. 1891. *The Museums of the Future*. Washington, DC: Gov. Print. Off.

Greenblatt S. 1991. Resonance and wonder. See Karp & Lavine 1991, pp. 42–56

Hall PD. 1992. *Inventing the Nonprofit Sector and Other Essays on Philanthropy, Voluntarism, and Nonprofit Organizations*. Baltimore, MD: Johns Hopkins Univ. Press

Hamilakis Y. 1999. Stories from exile: fragments from the cultural biography of the Parthenon (or "Elgin") marbles. *World Archaeol.* 31:303–32

Handler R, Gable E. 1997. *The New History in an Old Museum: Creating the Past at Colonial Williamsburg*. Durham, NC: Duke Univ. Press

Heizer RF. 1962. The background of Thomsen's three age system. *Technol. Cult.* 3:259–66

Heller-Roazen D. 2002. Tradition's destruction: on the Library of Alexandria. *October* 100:133–53

Hendry J. 2005. *Reclaiming Culture: Indigenous People and Self-Representation*. Houndsmills, UK/New York: Palgrave Macmillan

Hitchens C, Browning R, Binns G. 1998. *The Elgin Marbles: Should They Be Returned to Greece?* London/New York: Verso

Hodder I. 1986. *Reading the Past: Current Approaches to Interpretation in Archaeology*. Cambridge, UK/New York: Cambridge Univ. Press

Holmes WH. 1902. Classification and arrangement of the exhibits of an anthropology museum. *Science* 16:487–504

Hudson K. 1987. *Museums of Influence*. Cambridge, UK/New York: Cambridge Univ. Press

Hudson K. 1998. The museum refuses to stand still. *Mus. Int.* 50:43–50

Hull-Walski D, Flynn GA. 2001. Merging traditional indigenous curation methods with modern museum standards of care. *Mus. Anthropol.* 25:31–40

Hutt S. 2004. Cultural property law theory: a comparative assessment of contemporary thought. See Richman & Forsyth 2004, pp. 17–36

Isaac G. 2005. Mediating knowledges: Zuni negotiations for a culturally relevant museum. *Mus. Anthropol.* 28:3–18

Iser W. 1980. *The Act of Reading: A Theory of Aesthetic Response*. Baltimore, MD: Johns Hopkins Univ. Press

Jameson JH, ed. 1997. *Presenting Archaeology to the Public: Digging for Truths*. Walnut Creek, CA: Altamira

Jauss HR. 1982. *Toward an Aesthetic of Reception*. Minneapolis: Univ. Minn. Press

Jeffers CS. 2003. Museum as process. *J. Aesthet. Educ.* 37:107–19

Jones AL. 1993. Exploding canons: the anthropology of museums. *Annu. Rev. Anthropol.* 22:201–20

Kaplan FS, ed. 1994. *Museums and the Making of "Ourselves": The Role of Objects in National Identity*. London: Leicester Univ. Press

Karp I, Kreamer CM, Lavine S. 1992. *Museums and Communities: The Politics of Public Culture*. Washington, DC: Smithson. Inst. Press

Karp I, Lavine S, eds. 1991. *Exhibiting Cultures: The Poetics and Politics of Museum Display*. Washington, DC: Smithson. Inst. Press

Knell SJ. 1994. *Care of Collections*. London/New York: Routledge

Knell SJ. 1999. *Museums and the Future of Collecting*. Aldershot, UK/Brookfield, VT: Ashgate

Kohl PL. 1998. Nationalism and archaeology: on the constructions of nations and the reconstruction of the remote past. *Annu. Rev. Anthropol.* 27:223–46

Kraayenoord CEv, Paris SG. 2002. Reading objects. See Paris 2002, pp. 215–34

Krech S, Hail BA, eds. 1999. *Collecting Native America, 1870–1960*. Washington, DC: Smithson. Inst. Press

Kreps CF. 2003. *Liberating Culture: Cross-Cultural Perspectives on Museums, Curation, and Heritage Preservation*. London/New York: Routledge

Kuklick H. 1991. Contested monuments: the politics of archaeology in Southern Africa. In *Colonial Situations: Essays in the Contextualization of Ethnographic Knowledge*, ed. G Stocking, pp. 135–69. Madison: Univ. Wis. Press

Larson F. 2009. *An Infinity of Things: How Sir Henry Wellcome Collected the World*. New York: Oxford Univ. Press

Launius RD. 2007. American memory, culture wars, and the challenge of presenting science and technology in a national museum. *Public Hist.* 29:13–30

Lawlor M. 2006. *Public Native America: Tribal Self-Representations in Casinos, Museums, and Powwows*. New Brunswick, NJ: Rutgers Univ. Press

Levy J. 2006. Prehistory, identity, and archaeological representation in Nordic Museums. *Am. Anthropol.* 108:135–47

Linenthal ET, Engelhardt T. 1996. *History Wars: The Enola Gay and Other Battles for the American Past*. New York: Metrop. Books/Henry Holt

Lord B, Lord GD. 2002. *The Manual of Museum Exhibitions*. Walnut Creek, CA: AltaMira

Lyman RL, O'Brien MJ, Dunnell RC. 1997. *The Rise and Fall of Culture History*. New York: Plenum

MacKenzie R, Stone P. 1990. Introduction: the concept of the excluded past. In *The Excluded Past: Archaeology in Education*, ed. PG Stone, R MacKenzie, pp. 1–11. London: Unwin Hyman

Malaro MC. 1998. *A Legal Primer on Managing Museum Collections*. Washington, DC/London: Smithson. Inst. Press

Marquardt WH, Montet-White A, Scholz SC. 1982. Resolving the crisis in archaeological records curation. *Am. Antiq.* 47:409–18

May E, Jones M. 2006. *Conservation Science: Heritage Materials*. Cambridge, UK: R. Soc. Chem.

McKeown TC, Murphy A, Schansberg J. 1998. Ethical and legal issues: complying with NAGPRA. In *The New Museum Registration Methods*, ed. RA Buck, JA Gilmore, pp. 311–20. Washington, DC: American Association of Museums

McLaughlin RH. 2004. NAGPRA, dialogue, and the politics of historical authority. See Richman & Forsyth 2004, pp. 185–201

McLean K. 1999. Museum exhibitions and the dynamics of dialogue. *Daedalus* 128:83–107

McManus PM. 1996. *Archaeological Displays and the Public: Museology and Interpretation*. London: Inst. Archaeol., Univ. Coll. London

McMullen A. 2009. Reinventing George Heye: nationalizing the Museum of the American Indian and its collections. See Sleeper-Smith 2009, pp. 65–105

Merriman N. 1989. Museum visiting as a cultural phenomenon. In *The New Museology*, ed. P Vergo, pp. 149–71. London: Reaktion

Messenger PM, ed. 1989. *The Ethics of Collecting Cultural Property*. Albuquerque: Univ. N. M. Press

MORI. 2001. *Attitudes Towards the Heritage: Research Study Conducted for English Heritage*. London: English Heritage

Ogden S. 2004. *Caring for American Indian Objects: A Practical and Cultural Guide*. St. Paul: Minn. Hist. Soc. Press

Owen D. 2005. An archaeological dilemma. *Science* 309:1816

Owen J. 1999. Who is steering the ship? Museums and archaeological fieldwork. See Knell 1999, pp. 132–40

Paris SG, ed. 2002. *Perspectives on Object-Centered Learning in Museums*. Mahwah, NJ: Lawrence Erlbaum

Paris SG, Hapgood SE. 2002. Children learning with objects in informal learning environments. See Paris 2002, pp. 37–54

Pearce SM. 1990. *Archaeological Curatorship*. Leicester, UK/New York: Leicester Univ. Press

Pearce SM. 1992. *Museums, Objects and Collections: A Cultural Study*. Washington, DC: Smithson. Inst. Press

Pearce SM. 1994. *Interpreting Objects and Collections*. London/New York: Routledge

Pearce SM. 1995. *On Collecting: An Investigation into Collecting in the European Tradition*. London/New York: Routledge

Pearce SM. 1997. Archaeology as collection. In *Representing Archaeology in Museums*, ed. GT Denford. *Soc. Mus. Archaeol.* 22:6–12

Peers LL. 2007. *Playing Ourselves: Interpreting Native Histories at Historic Reconstructions*. Lanham, MD: AltaMira

Podany TC, Maish SL. 1993. Can the complex be made simple? Informing the public about conservation through museum displays. *J. Am. Inst. Conserv.* 32:101–8

Porter G. 1996. Seeing through solidity: a feminist perspective on museums. In *Theorizing Museums: Representing Identity and Diversity in a Changing World*, ed. S Macdonald, G Fyfe, pp. 105–126. Oxford, UK: Blackwell

Ramos M, Duganne D. 2000. *Exploring Public Perceptions and Attitudes About Archaeology*. Washington, DC: Soc. Am. Archaeol.

Renfrew C. 2006. *Loot, Legitimacy and Ownership: The Ethical Crisis in Archaeology*. London: Duckworth

Richman JR, Forsyth M, eds. 2004. *Legal Perspectives on Cultural Resources*. Walnut Creek, CA: Altamira

Rigg V. 1994. Curators of the colonial idea: the museum and the exhibition as agents of bourgeois ideology in nineteenth-century New South Wales. *Public Hist. Rev.* 3:188–203

Roschelle J. 1995. Learning in interactive environments: prior knowledge and new experience. In *Public Institutions for Personal Learning*, ed. JH Falk, LD Dierking, pp. 37–51. Washington, DC: American Association of Museums

Rosenzweig R, Thelen DP. 1998. *The Presence of the Past: Popular Uses of History in American Life*. New York: Columbia Univ. Press

Rowan Y, Baram U, eds. 2004. *Marketing Heritage: Archaeology and the Consumption of the Past*. Walnut Creek, CA: Altamira

Ruthven AG. 1931. *A Naturalist in a University Museum*. Ann Arbor, MI: Privately printed

Sease C. 1994. *A Conservation Manual for the Field Archaeologist*. Los Angeles: Inst. Archaeol., Univ. Calif.

Shanks M, Tilley CY. 1992. *Re-Constructing Archaeology: Theory and Practice*. London/New York: Routledge

Sherman DJ. 1994. Quatremere/Benjamin/Marx: art museums, aura and commodity fetishism. In *Museum Culture: Histories, Discourses, Spectacles*, ed. DJ Sherman, I Rogoff, pp. 123–43. Minneapolis: Univ. Minn. Press

Simmons JE. 2006. *Things Great and Small: Collections Management Policies*. Washington, DC: American Association of Museums

Simpson MG. 2007. Charting the boundaries: indigenous models and parallel practices in the development of the post-museum. In *Museum Revolutions: How Museums Change and are Changed*, ed. S Knell, S MacLeod, S Watson, pp. 235–49. London: Routledge

Sleeper-Smith S. 2009. *Contesting Knowledge: Museums and Indigenous Perspectives*. Lincoln: Univ. Neb. Press

Smith HI. 1912. The educational work of a great museum. *Science* 36:659–64

St. Clair W. 1998. *Lord Elgin and the Marbles*. Oxford/New York: Oxford Univ. Press

Stone P, Molyneaux BL, eds. 1994. *The Presented Past: Heritage Museums and Education*. London: Routledge

Sullivan LP, Childs ST. 2003. *Curating Archaeological Collections: From the Field to the Repository*. Walnut Creek: Altamira

Swain H. 2007. *An Introduction to Museum Archaeology*. Cambridge/New York: Cambridge Univ. Press

Thompson RH. 1999. The crisis in archaeological collections management. *CRM* 23:4–6

Trimble MK, Marino EA. 2003. Archaeological curation: an ethical imperative for the twenty-first century. See Zimmerman 2003, pp. 99–114

Trope JF, Echo-Hawk WR. 2000. The Native American Graves Protection and Repatriation Act: background and legislative history. In *Repatriation Reader: Who Owns American Indian Remains?*, ed. DA Mihesuah, pp. 123–68. Lincoln: Univ. Neb. Press

Vergo P. 1994. The rhetoric of display. In *Towards the Future of the Museum: New European Perspectives*, ed. R Mills, L Zavala, pp. 149–59. London: Routledge

Vogel S. 1991. Always true to the object, in our fashion. See Karp & Lavine 1991, pp. 191–204

Watson P, Todeschini C. 2006. *The Medici Conspiracy: The Illicit Journey of Looted Antiquities, from Italy's Tomb Raiders to the World's Greatest Museums*. New York: Public Aff.

Watt JCY. 2009. Antiquities and the importance—and limitations—of archaeological contexts. See Cuno 2009, pp. 89–106

Waxman S. 2008. *Loot: The Battle over the Stolen Treasures of the Ancient World*. New York: Times Books

Weil SE. 1990. *Rethinking the Museum and other Meditations*. Washington, DC: Smithson. Inst. Press

Weil SE. 1995. *A Cabinet of Curiosities: Inquiries into Museums and their Prospects*. Washington, DC: Smithson. Inst. Press

Wertsch JV. 2002. Epistemological issues about objects. See Paris 2002, pp. 0.113–18

Whitehead C. 2009. *Museums and the Construction of Disciplines: Art and Archaeology in Nineteenth-Century Britain*. London: Duckworth

Willey GR, Sabloff JA. 1980. *A History of American Archaeology*. San Francisco: Freeman

Wineburg SS. 2001. *Historical Thinking and Other Unnatural Acts: Charting the Future of Teaching the Past*. Philadelphia: Temple Univ. Press

Witcomb A. 1997. One the side of the object: an alternative approach to debates about ideas, objects and museums. *Mus. Manag. Curatorship* 16:383–99

Wood B. 1997. Does size matter? Effective presentation of archaeology in small museums. In *Representing Archaeology in Museums*, ed. GT Denford. *Soc. Mus. Archaeol.* 22:6–12

Wood B, Cotton J. 1999. The representation of prehistory in museums. In *Making Early Histories in Museums*, ed. N Merriman, pp. 28–43. Leicester, UK/New York: Leicester Univ. Press

Yasaitis KE. 2005. National ownership laws as cultural property protection policy: the emerging trend in *United States v. Schultz*. *Int. J. Cult. Prop.* 12:95–113

Yeide NH, Walsh A, Akinsha K, Am. Assoc. Mus. 2001. *The AAM Guide to Provenance Research*. Washington, DC: American Association of Museums

Zimmerman LJ, Vitelli KD, Hollowell JJ, eds. 2003. *Ethical Issues in Archaeology*. Walnut Creek, CA: AltaMira

The Audacity of Affect: Gender, Race, and History in Linguistic Accounts of Legitimacy and Belonging

Bonnie McElhinny

Anthropology and Women and Gender Studies Institute, University of Toronto, Toronto, Ontario, M5S 1C6, Canada; email: bonnie.mcelhinny@utoronto.ca

Annu. Rev. Anthropol. 2010. 39:309–28

First published online as a Review in Advance on June 21, 2010

The *Annual Review of Anthropology* is online at anthro.annualreviews.org

This article's doi:
10.1146/annurev-anthro-091908-164358

Key Words

language, labor, imperialism, public discourse

Abstract

This review considers research on language and affect, with particular attention to gender, that has appeared in the past two decades in ways informed by the recent effloresence of work on affect in feminist, queer, (post)colonial, and critical race studies. The review is selective: It focuses on a few key ways that recent research is responding to gaps identified in earlier research and opening up promising areas for future research. This review thus attempts to connect linguistic anthropological and discourse analytic studies more fully with contemporary debates in feminist, queer, antiracist, and postcolonial studies. In general, I look at the rise of more fully historical approaches; in particular, I look at (*a*) affect in imperial and other global encounters; (*b*) language, neoliberalism, and affective labor; and (*c*) terror and hate, compassion, and conviviality in public speech. It also considers why we are, at this particular moment, witnessing such interest in affect.

INTRODUCTION

Two decades ago, Besnier (1990) offered an authoritative, comprehensive account of work on language and affect. Since then, there has been a remarkable effloresence of work on affect in feminist, queer, (post)colonial, and critical race studies (Ahmed 2004; Berlant 2000, 2004; Brown 1995; Butler 1997, 2004; Cheng 2001; Cvetkovich 2003; Gilroy 2005; Povinelli 2006; Sedgwick 2003). This review attempts to connect linguistic anthropological and discourse analytic studies more fully with contemporary debates in feminist and critical studies while offering a selective account of some ways in which recent research is responding to some gaps identified in earlier research (see Wilce 2009b for a complementary approach). In general, I look at the rise of more fully historical approaches; in particular, I look at language and affect as manifest in (*a*) imperial and other global interactions; (*b*) neoliberalism and affective labor; and (*c*) hate and terror, compassion, and conviviality in public speech. Such an approach also requires us to consider why so many scholars are currently preoccupied with affect.

Studies of affect intersect with a range of different topics and recent surveys, including studies of language and religion (Keane 1997), music (Feld & Fox 1994, Fox 2004), queer linguistics (Kulick 2000), socialization (Garrett & Baquedano-López 2002), and conversation analysis (Sidnell 2007); I attempt to address a complementary literature. A number of conversational analytic studies focus explicitly on affect in ways that provide a nuanced challenge to the simplistic dichotomizations of nonverbal and verbal communication evident in some recent theoretical discussions of affect (Evaldsoon 2004; C. Goodwin 2006, 2007; M.H. Goodwin 2006; M.H. Goodwin & C. Goodwin 2000); Svasek (2005) rightly notes that a focus on embodiment is re-emerging in opposition to a discursive approach to emotion, in ways that I believe ignore recent work on multimodality in linguistic anthropology (C. Goodwin 2006).

Most articles on affect spend considerable time parsing out distinctions among emotion,

affect, feeling, and sentiment. For instance, Sedgwick (2003) defines affect as building blocks for complex emotions, whereas Lutz & White (1986) reverse this terminology, reviewing a series of neurocultural and psychiatric accounts that locate universal emotions in an overlay of affect. For other recent and influential definitions of emotion, feeling, affect, impression, and sentiment, see Clough (2007), Ducey (2007), Massumi (2002), Pavlenko (2005), Richard & Rudnyckyj (2009), and Stoler (2005). Some scholars attempt to distinguish the biological from the social, the universal from the cultural, the private from the public, the explicit from the ineffable, whereas others choose a single term (typically "affect," "desire," or "sentiment") to try to transcend such distinctions. Besnier (1990, p. 42) notes that anthropologists are often suspicious of binary distinctions because of the ways they encode a western ideology of self and society. Rather than attempting to fix the definitions of these words, a linguistic anthropological approach instead considers what this proliferation of semantic parsing and taxonomic specification might reflect about differences in intellectual geneaologies (whether Darwin, Deleuze and Guattari, Fanon, Foucault, Freud, Lacan, Spinoza, socialist feminism), their various epistemological and political claims, and the dilemmas of the current political moment. In Ahmed's (2004, p. 4) formulation, we should ask not what emotions are, but what work emotions do. Following Williams (1976), we might treat affect as a keyword. Williams's (1977) notion of "structures of feeling" also remains useful for the ways it tries, in some ways, to transcend these distinctions. Although the concept is often now extracted from and used without attention to the debates about hegemony and ideology within which it is embedded, for Williams a focus on structure allows a focus on social rather than personal experience to acknowledge institutions, formations, and positions not as fixed products, but rather as forming and formative processes (p. 132), whereas a focus on feeling emphasizes a distinction from the formal, explicit, and systematic beliefs that he calls ideology (although Eagleton 1991 would argue that feeling is not opposed to ideology, but rather what makes ideology stick). Williams (1973) uses structures of feeling to analyze literary texts; inspired by Williams, Stewart (2007) adopts an ethnographic approach to "ordinary affects" in the United States. Note, however, that Said (1994) critiques Williams as inattentive to his own imperial location; he adapts Williams's notions into "structures of attitude and reference" for analyzing colonial discourse. Stoler (1991), meanwhile, critiques Said for the way gender figures only symbolically in his work. One of the most compelling recent applications of the notions of structures of feeling, which takes into account all these dimensions, is Tadiar's (2009b) analysis of how the circulation of popular songs of lament in the Philippines in the 1970s and 1980s, which were linked to earlier colonial and national struggles, maintained a cultural literacy and social feeling, which contributed to the popular revolt against the Marcos dictatorship. Attending to structures of feeling requires just such attention to history, politics, and economy (see also Richard & Rudnyckyj 2009).

HISTORICIZING STUDIES OF LANGUAGE AND AFFECT

Influential works on emotion in linguistic and sociocultural anthropology that appeared in the late 1980s and early 1990s challenged universalizing approaches to emotion grounded in biological, psychological, or psychotherapeutic accounts, developing instead a social constructivist, culturally sensitive approach (Besnier 1990; Harré 1986; Irvine 1982; Lutz & Abu Lughod 1990; Lutz & White 1986, 1990; Ochs & Schieffelin 1989; White 1993). These studies also challenged binary approaches to thinking about emotion and reason, which tended to associate emotion with negative characteristics such as irrationality, instinct, or irresponsibility, all not incidentally associated with negatively stereotyped groups, such as women, racialized groups, children, and/or the poor, while they also examined the significant roman-

tic strand of thought associating emotion with authenticity, lack of estrangement or alienation, purity, and honesty. Accounts of why studies of affect flourished at this particular moment often focus on intellectual history, but also could be written with attention to the increasing impact of (and continuing backlashes against) scholars previously underrepresented in the academy, as well as broader social and political struggles.

Many of these earlier review articles drew on a comparative or cross-cultural methodology. Some aspects of comparative approaches used to decenter western assumptions about human behavior have been extensively debated in recent years in anthropology and transnational feminist studies (Clough 2007, Gingrich & Fox 2002, Grewal & Kaplan 1994, Kingfisher 2002); commentators note that the language of social construction on which such comparisons draw is rather weak (Lyon 1995, Massumi 2002, Rose 1999). Stearns (1993) even argues that history permits a "deeper exploration of the causation operating in the social context of emotions…than that possible in crosscultural comparisons" (p. 26). An approach to affect attentive to history and political economy considers when certain kinds of emotional display emerge as novel or problematic and who gets to decide they are such (Reddy 2001; Stearns 1993; Stoler 2001, 2005). Rose (1999), drawing on Foucault, suggests that we need to trace "in very concrete and material forms, the actual history of those forms of rationality that comprise our present, the ways of thinking and acting with which they have been caught up, the practices and assemblages which they have animated, and the consequences for our understanding of our present, and of ourselves in that present" (p. x). From his perspective, the interesting questions are thus where and when objects emerge, which authorities can pronounce on them, the concepts and explanatory regimes through which they are specified, and how certain constructions acquire the status of truth. Richard & Rudnyckyj (2009) note that current work on "the economy of affect" differs from earlier feminist studies of "emotion work" by focusing on "the way in which subjects circulate within and are formed through affect, rather than the circulation of emotions between subjects" (p. 69). Considering these questions begins to address two intertwined and continuing gaps in the literature on language and emotion noted by earlier scholars: (*a*) the need for further studies on hegemony, emotion, and social structure (Besnier 1990, Lutz & White 1986), and (*b*) the need for more historical approaches (Abu Lughod & Lutz 1990; see also Wilce 2004).

A historicized approach requires us to ask ourselves why we are, at this particular moment, witnessing such interest in affect. Some commentators offer explanations couched in terms of histories of theory, arguing, for instance, that a focus on affect redresses the inadequacies of a focus on performativity and performance in gender and queer theory (Sedgwick 2003) or that it challenges academic divisions of labor between studies of the individual, or the biological, and the social, between biology/psychology and anthropology (Abu Lughod & Lutz 1990, White 1993). Others see it as a form of political exhaustion, which ends up as a tacit affirmation of the status quo (Wiegele 2005). One of the most comprehensive accounts of the rise of interest in affect in western settings is Rose (1999). His work responds to earlier (Abu Lughod & Lutz 1990, p. 6) calls for a genealogy of emotion comparable with Foucault's genealogy of sexuality, asking how emotions came to be constituted in their current form as physiological forces, located within individuals, and granting access to an inner truth about the self and why preoccupations with sexuality and emotion are among the defining features of late capitalism in the west. He notes that in many western nations, "citizenship is primarily realized through acts of free but responsibilized choice in a variety of private, corporate, and quasi-public practices from working to shopping" (Rose 1999, p. xxiii). Such a view of citizenship leads, simultaneously, to a celebration of choice and self-realization through consumption, as well as to a focus on diseases of the will, or failures of self-control. As affect becomes commodified, a focus also emerges on parsing authenticity and sincerity. Essays in Gal & Woolard's (2001) volume on languages and publics consider the politics of anonymity and authenticity and the role they play in constructing authority. It is worth emphasizing, however, that Rose's analysis stays close to the west, especially the United Kingdom (see Rofel's 2007 call for a more global perspective). Adams et al. (2009) suggest that the contemporary fascination with affect can be understood as an intensification of regimes of anticipation (perhaps in contrast with regimes of truth). They argue hope and fear are becoming increasingly prominent political vectors because of their importance in generating an urgent sense of the future, in ways that authorize action in the present (p. 249). Anticipatory regimes are like finance capitalism in the way they generate new fields of expansion and focus on managing risk, which itself becomes a commodity generating credit and insurance industries. A postcolonial perspective complicates and extends Rose's picture by analyzing how attention to affect is inspired by colonial rules and violence, anxieties and desires about imperial decline and mimicry, and the aftermath and ongoing effects of empire evident in global migration flows and increasingly multicultural metropoles, settler colonial states, and postcolonial states (Ahmed 2004, Césaire 1972, Fanon 1967, Gilroy 2005, Memmi 1965, Stoler 2005). The scholarly preoccupation with affect, emotion, desire, and feeling thus arises out of and extends a passional economy, but it can also serve to critique it.

AFFECT IN IMPERIAL AND OTHER GLOBAL ENCOUNTERS

A call for historical approaches to language and affect resonates with an emergent and rich body of research in sociolinguistics and linguistic anthropology that considers attempts to change ideas of personhood and other practices in the name of "modernization" (Bauman & Briggs 2003), under (neo)imperial, (post)colonial, national, supranational, and nongovernmental organization regimes. In both history and linguistic anthropology, an emerging area of concern is alterations of emotional expression in the light of imperial contacts. Such work challenges the Weberian ideologies about the rationality and reasonableness of colonial states which were one of colonialism's most insidious and effective technologies of rule (Stoler 2005) and extends the long-standing radical feminist notion of how the personal is political to a new realm, as it considerably revises definitions of both personal and political in ways attentive to racial and imperial hierarchies. Studies of language and colonialism so far have tended to focus more on the development of philology and comparative linguistics (Errington 2008, Said 1978). More work remains to be done to consider the ways affect figures in such sources. Reyes's (2008, pp. 217–25) analysis of how Spanish missionaries and Filipino nationalists addressed the image of a putatively sexually permissive Filipina in dictionaries, confessional manuals, and codes of etiquette suggests one way researchers can track ideologies of morality, desire, and sentiment in lexicographical sources. Kuipers (1998) exemplifies a historical approach to the ethnography of communication in his discussion of the transformations of Weyewa ritual speech traditions after the arrival of Dutch administrators and missionaries in Sumba in the late nineteenth century. He documents how linguistic features that express anger, which were once important symbols of masculinity and spiritual authority, came to be sanctioned as primitive and defiant.

Weidman (2006, 2007) notes that in postcolonial South India, Karnatic or South Indian classical music is now valued as a sign of uncolonized Indian distinctiveness. Her geneaological work considers how the revaluing of music as a sign of bourgeois respectability for upper-caste family women in the colonial period was linked with the interiorization of music and expression within the body, an interiority inflected by gender and race in that Indian womanhood was thus constructed as pure and untouched by western influence.

McElhinny (2005, 2007b, 2009) offers another example of colonial and national elite attempts to intervene in local interactional practices in the name of public health and modernity. In the midst of concern about high infant mortality in the early twentieth century, Filipino child-rearing strategies were stigmatized in educational, public health, and public welfare discourses in the American-occupied Philippines as overly indulgent in ways that can be linked to metropolitan concerns about production of the "new industrial man" and to racialized critiques of the cultural practices of Filipinos whom U.S. President McKinley called "little brown brothers" (McElhinny 2005). Education in English was about education in hygienic and appropriate forms of comportment and interaction and vice versa.

Conversion is, Rafael (1988) argues, an attempt to restructure desire and forge novel affective bonds (p. ix). His analysis of Tagalog understandings of indebtedness and shame encoded in the terms *utang na loob* and *hiya*, and the ways these were applied to Christian practices, highlights some of the ways that translation was not, at least at first, about internalizing Christianity under Spanish colonial rule in the Philippines, but about evading it. Keane (1999) considers debates about the ideologies of "sincerity" and speaking agency in light of the encounter between Dutch Calvinist missionaries and their converts and unconverted ancestral ritualists on the island of Sumba in Indonesia.

Language is not only shaped within spheres of direct imperial influence but also indirectly, as part of emergent social formations of modernity, capitalism, and nationalism. Inoue (2006) provides one of the most compelling examples of the geneology of affect called for by Abu Lughod & Lutz (1990) by documenting the ways the emergence of a notion of "women's language" in nineteenth- and twentieth-century Japan was part of a development of a specific gendered form of Japanese modernity, as an ambivalent reaction in part to Western modernity and in part to growing inequalities among Japanese women. Inoue shows the ways discussions of schoolgirl speech as "unpleasant to the ear" were mobilized to construct bourgeois subjects disclosing inner truths, asserting individualistic consumer tastes and styles, and talking about romantic love, friendship, and linkages to family and nation.

Mitchell (2009) considers the conditions under which people become willing to die for a language in a newly independent India by examining evidence of emotional commitments (protests, suicides) to mother tongues (especially Telugu) in the mid-twentieth century alongside evidence of how languages came to be viewed as primary and natural foundations for such attachment. In particular, she addresses the personification and gendering of languages in southern Indian as mothers, goddesses, and victims, arguing that emotional attachments to language should not simply be seen in the same way as they are in European histories, but within the distinctive light of a newly independent state and earlier Indian ideologies about multilingualism (see also Ramaswamy 1997).

Ahearn's (2001) compelling linguistic ethnography examines a transformation in structures of feeling in a shift from arranged marriages and capture marriage toward love marriage in Nepal. Arguing that development discourses are not only a set of economic programs, but also a set of ideas about how to think and act, she examines transformations in ideologies about love, marriage and gender, and love letters and literacy. Romantic love is changing from being a source of shame and embarrassment to being a source of empowerment and pride because it is associated with development, westernization, success, and autonomy.

Transformations in the light of encounters with modern practices may seem to suggest a negative evaluation of earlier practices [see Sahlins's (1992) claim that encounters with modernity that lead to change are associated with feelings of humiliation]. However, a series of recent papers challenge such an argument. Robbins (2005) argues that Christianity also offers ways to overcome humiliation and provides the grounds for critique of development discourses by challenging emphases on worldly success. Schieffelin (1990, 2000) provides a compelling picture of some of the ways

that mission activities, including literacy activities, among the Kaluli in Papua New Guinea led to differences in social organization, as well as in the ways individuals imagined themselves. The ways that the impact of schools, churches, and significant outmigration have transformed literacy and emotion practices in Nukulaelae are the subject of Besnier's (1995) monograph. Besnier's (2007) analysis of "cosmopolitan" sites in Tonga also questions any simple association of modernity with humiliation. His analysis of a beauty pageant for transgendered men in Tonga shows how embracing a cosmopolitan identity can be one strategy for challenging the silencing of sexual and emotional desires within the gender and sexual structures of Tongan society; for mainstream Tongans, however, having those who are locally abject embody an external world that is regarded with ambivalence allows them to treat both the external world and transgendered men as laughable and harmless. Philips (2007) addresses the irony of the continuing high value placed on traditional women's weaving in the context of significant outmigration in Tonga, even though the practice is not materially rewarding. Her analysis of love songs and sexual teasing, which occur as women weave *ngatu*, shows how some of the women who have benefited least from the introduction of new female occupations, forms of church affiliation, or migrant labor police each other's sexuality, especially in the light of overseas husbands, as they offer humorous challenges to the tender portraits of love offered by popular songs.

Kulick's (1992) analysis of why children in Papua New Guinea are no longer speaking Taiap, their village's language, but instead are speaking Tok Pisin, argues that invoking macrosociological forces alone, such as migration, industrialization, urbanization, and proletarianization, does not allow one to explain or predict language shift. Kulick argues, instead, that changing notions of self are significant. Individualistic displays of selfishness, haughtiness, and anger are seen as sometimes necessary but are devalued over and against displays of cooperativeness. The first display has become linked with Taiap, women, and the past, whereas the second has come to be associated with men, whiteness, Tok Pisin, Catholicism, and modernity.

Mendoza-Denton (2008) considers the ways that distinctions between the Global North and South play out in the linguistic and semiotic practices of young Latinas in California. Her study analyzes clowning, and the possibilities for its misrecognition by cultural outsiders, as well as "smile now, cry later," an ideology of comportment and a form of distributed memory linked to the difficulties of immigration that is elaborated and circulated in drawings, photographs, and poems among youth.

In an encyclopedic survey, Wilce (2009a) documents the encoding of ideas about emotion and propriety in laments as he considers how attempts to eliminate lament in Bangladesh, Greece, Ireland, Papua New Guinea, and northern Pakistan and Afghanistan in imperial and national modernizing movements were often attempts to eliminate the subversive voices, often female, associated with the practice. Lament is subject to the contradictions of nostalgia (Hill 1992): That which is eliminated is, often enough, yearned for, re-created, or co-opted to represent national or other identities.

INTERROGATING RATIONAL CHOICE: NEOLIBERALISM AND AFFECTIVE LABOR

A number of recent works in sociolinguistic and linguistic anthropology (Blommaert 2003, Coupland 2003, Heller 2003, McElhinny 2007a, Valentine 2006, Wilce 2005) consider the ways neoliberalization and globalization are leading to the creation of new identities for workers, parents, students, citizens, and consumers, an integral piece of which is emotion management (Hochschild 1983). Neoliberalism is "a theory of political economic practices that proposes that human well-being can best be advanced by liberating individual entrepreneurial freedoms and skills within an institutional framework characterized by strong private property rights, free markets, and free trade" (Harvey 2005, p. 2); however,

Harvey cautions us to understand neoliberalist theory not as a description of social reality but as a claim to the future (see also Fairclough 2000). Proponents of neoliberalism attempt to transform divisions of labor, welfare provisions, reproductive activities, and "habits of the heart" (Harvey 2005, p. 3). (This last phrase was originally used in Bellah et al. 1996.) Rose (1996) elaborates some of the new regimes of self associated with neoliberalism, in which the ideal adult person is responsible, autonomous, self-sufficient, and entrepreneurial. This self is not incidentally or accidentally also the idealized western masculine self (Kingfisher 2002). Linguistic anthropological and sociolinguistic studies in a variety of different sites have attempted to consider how and where neoliberal changes of heart are actively engineered while they inflect the notion of neoliberalism with further regional, historical, and cultural specificity and consider how resistances to an emphasis on rational choice and utility maximization are formulated. Welfare states in, for example, Canada, New Zealand, and the United States, which previously offered extended support for single poor women with children created "workfare" programs in the 1980s and 1990s, in ways that emphasized identities as workers at the expense of identities as mothers and with explicit or implicit pressures toward heterosexual marriage. Kingfisher (2007) analyzes conversations among welfare providers and poor single mothers in New Zealand with an eye to understanding convergences and divergencies between the common sense and institutional understandings of responsibility and romantic attachment that such policies engendered. Neoliberal retrenchments have led to changing notions of care in, for example, the health care sector in many countries. Cutbacks reduce time for patient care, speed up work, increase surveillance, and lead to staff conflicts. Ducey's (2007) analysis of the ways U.S. health care workers talk about the meaning of work highlights the significance of semiotic practices in changing workers' attitudes toward current work in ways that do not necessarily lead to better pay or improved working conditions. As state cutbacks occur, volunteer labor may be celebrated. Sociocultural studies such as Muehlebach (2007) of how affective services that states cannot or will not provide any longer are devolved onto civil society organizations such as churches and neighborhoods are as yet largely unelaborated by linguistic anthropologists (although see Pujolar 2007).

Institutional indifference in the context of globalization needs to be theorized and described as carefully as other forms of affect (Herzfeld 1992). Briggs with Briggs (2003) intertwine linguistic anthropological theories and methods with medical anthropology to analyze the political economy of representations of indigenous groups in Venezuela in political, media, medical, and anthropological discourses as outside the reach of modernity. Indigenous people are thus cast as natural victims of cholera rather than victims of the negative effects of neoliberal forms of globalization and of structural adjustment such as constrictions on access to health care, increasing poverty, and diminished access to running water and effective sewage facilities (see also Briggs 2005).

The restructuring of the socialist state in China from a Maoist planned economy to a Dengist market economy has led to a new emphasis on gender binaries and essentialism, as well as concern about a new crisis of masculinity (compare Gal & Kligman 2000 on economic transitions in east central Europe). Yang's (2006, 2007a) work uses sociolinguistic analysis to understand the effects of restructuring in China, a country that still pays homage to socialist discursive forms. She finds that factory directors encourage unemployed working-class men to "speak bitterness," just as workers were earlier encouraged to vent concerns about other kinds of work issues in ways that divert men's social anger from class conflicts to gender, sexual conflicts, or family issues, with implications for, e.g., talk about domestic violence (2007b). Yang also examines new individualizing technologies of regulating self and emotion offered under the guise of a socialist ethics devoted to antipoverty measures (*song wennuan*) in media

representations as well as in trade union representatives' visits to poor households.

Gee et al. (1996) note that from the end of World War II until the early 1970s, the old industrial mass-market capitalism in western countries had large national markets for consumer goods. As markets become more heavily saturated with consumer goods, and industrial work moved to countries in the Global South (these sites still require further linguistic analysis), companies began to focus on creating new kinds of customers and new kinds of desires; they retooled workforces accordingly. If work under the old capitalism was alienating, and workers were forced to sell their labor, they are now asked to invest "their hearts, minds and bodies fully in their work" (p. 7). Gee et al. analyze the key words of the new work order evident in new capitalist texts. They also consider whether ESL (English as a second language) classes and team meetings at a Silicon Valley company with a multilingual workforce, offered in the name of empowering workers to collaborate as a team, may work as a new form of surveillance and regulation. In the United Kingdom, Cameron (2000) considers the rise of communication factories (call centers), where the Fordist logic of the assembly line governs interactional routines, and certain personality traits (being outgoing, friendly, enthusiastic, sincere) are set as industry standards. [For more on call centers, see Heller (2007).] Cameron argues that present-day service regimes make greater demands on workers because they do not require only courtesy but also the simulation of positive feelings and because most westerners see speech style as evidence of personality rather than something which is readily changed. Communication and affect are increasingly central in service jobs in health care, education, finance, entertainment, and advertising, where for the workers and their clients the production of feelings of well-being and even passion are key (Hardt 1999).

In a study of neoliberal discourses in Japan, Inoue (2007) tracks the emergence of a new word, *jiko sekinin* ("self-responsibility"), in government documents that discuss Japanese civilians taken hostage by an armed group in Iraq as well as in documents focused on interpersonal interaction in work sites. Inoue considers the ways interpersonal communication has been diagnosed as a key site for problematic gender relations in the aftermath of neoliberal reforms occurring alongside new equal-employment opportunity legislation and the ways that women workers have been encouraged to redress miscommunications through more logical, rational, and assertive speech. For other studies of changing norms of interaction and personhood within neoliberalizing economies, see Richard & Rudnyckyj (2009) on how grassroots networks in Mexico forge solidary transnational networks with foreign donors and on how a Jakarta steel company attempted to train workers in a manner that was more disciplined and emotionally open with a spiritual practice that instructed workers in the ways that their actions were observed by Allah. See also Lempert (2006) on changes in the notions of moral discipline among Tibetan Buddhist monks in India as neoliberal ideologies about civility take hold, and Matza (2009) on the deployment of neoliberal technologies in host-caller exchanges on a Moscow talk show.

Affective labor is not always paid labor. Lutz & White (1986, p. 421) note that the relationship between emotions and family is one of the most studied aspects of emotions in history, just as it has been in linguistic anthropology in which studies of language socialization, especially but not exclusively in households, were and are a crucial site for the development of linguistic studies of affect (see Capps & Ochs 1995, Garrett & Baquedano-López 2002, Ochs 1988, Ochs & Schieffelin 1989, Schieffelin 1990). Socialist feminists also pioneered studies of affect in ways often neglected in recent studies, in their analyses of reproductive labor (child care, housework, elder care, kin connections) in households and its relationship to gendered segregation in paid labor (for reviews, see Hennessy & Ingraham 1997, Jaggar 1983). (Negri 1999 draws on this work, without citing it.) Socialist feminists have also tracked changes in such interactions as modes of production

change. Collier (1997) is particularly useful for highlighting changes in affective and interactional norms for parents, especially mothers, in the transformation from an agricultural to an industrial economy in Spain; see also Pitt (2002) for neoliberal transformations of motherhood.

The provision of reproductive labor has become significantly more commodified since the earlier feminist work on affect in families, with marked accelerations since the 1990s (Constable 2009, Clough 2007, Ehrenreich & Hochschild 2002). See, for instance, di Leonardo (1992) on paid greeting cards and the work of kinship, Hall (1995) on paying for sex talk, and Leidner (1993) on paying for the preparation and serving of food. Studies of paid caregiving have received particular attention because of the ways they highlight the interaction of the negative impact of structural adjustment policies in the Global South with the privatization of health, elder care, and child care in the Global North and the tragic irony of Third World women supporting their own families by leaving them to care for First World families. Colen's (1995) notion of "stratified reproduction" captures how "physical and social reproductive tasks are accomplished differentially according to inequalities that are based on hierarchies of class, race, ethnicity, gender, place in a global economy, and migration status and that are structured by social, economic, and political forces" (p. 78). An important element of stratified reproduction is emotional labor. The most extended linguistic analysis is Lorente's (2007) wonderful study of how English is understood by the Philippine state and maid agencies in Singapore, which sell Filipino domestic labor, and by the Filipino domestic workers themselves. Lorente's study documents how emotional and character traits are mapped onto those who command linguistic varieties: Filipino workers are seen as modern, in key part because of their fluency in English, whereas Indonesian and Sri Lankan domestic workers are portrayed as traditional, and thus passive, shy, and compliant. In Canada, where one's particular English accent, and not simply fluent command of English, matters, it is the

Filipino workers who are portrayed as "traditional" (England & Stiell 1997, Pratt 1999).

Studies of paid caregiving consider how gender divisions of labor within heterosexual families are shored up by racialized hierarchies while they signal the advent of new kinds of household formations. Lancaster (2003), inspired by Gramsci's analyses of the role of sex in the formation of a Fordist economy, has undertaken ground-breaking historical work on heteronormativity and desire within post-Fordist formations. He argues that, in the west, mid-twentieth-century relations of mass production and mass consumption relied on heteronormative families as sites of production and consumption, but it is less clear that contemporary capitalism, with its focus on flexibility, mobility, individuation, and desire, requires heternormativity. (On language, identity, and consumption, see e.g., Besnier 2007, Bucholtz 2007, Fairclough 2001, Gaudio 2003, Lefkowitz 2003, Piller & Takahashi 2006.) Instead, Lancaster (2003) argues that late capitalism is "foremost about harnessing desires and marketing them to disparate populations, thereby soliciting new needs, new wants, new identities, and new experiments in lifestyle" (p. 315). Social movements are agents and beneficiaries of this transition from Fordism to post-Fordism in ways that have created new forms of life, families, and desire, including "flexible relationships, temporary unions, negotiable role expectations, recombinant families, gay families, open relationships" (p. 319). The relatively recent rise of queer linguistics can be understood as shaped by, as it studies, this context (see Kulick 2000, for one review; see also Cameron & Kulick 2003, Leap 1995, Leap & Boellstorff 2004, Livia & Hall 2007, McIlvenny 2002). Linguistic analyses of desire and romantic love (Harvey & Shalom 1997, Shibamoto Smith 2004, Walton et al. 2002) can benefit from considering how desire is intimate, national, and cosmopolitan, all at once, as it is situated within these economic transformations, in the ways that Besnier (2007), Lancaster (2003), and Rofel (2007) analyze. Eckert (2002) offers just such a perspective in a helpful contribution to a recent debate on the nature of desire and identity among Bucholtz & Hall (2004), Cameron & Kulick (2003), and Kulick (2000). Dave's research (2010, n.d.) exemplifies such an approach in her consideration of the politics of becoming "Indian and lesbian" within India's structural adjustments in the 1990s, the resultant transnationalization of social service provision and increase in foreign funds for NGOs, and postcolonial debates about what is considered "authentic" tradition and nation. She analyzes the film *Fire*, letters that lesbian women wrote to one another, activists' debates about how to name themselves, and political and media discourse to consider the conditions under which queer politics became intelligible and the ways queer affect became contained within a potential conservative discourse of national belonging.

The linguistic and other behaviors one is required to display at work may shape, in complex ways, how one expresses emotion in the putatively unrestrained context of leisure-time interactions. Dunk (1991) considers how jokes, banter, and scatological humor produced by white working-class men involved in resource extraction industries in northern Ontario focus on release in ways that contrast with the importance of self-control in middle-class culture. This behavior thus expresses a form of class resistance, which is nonetheless easily diverted into racial prejudice (particularly against indigenous people) and sexism. The significance of self-reliance in rural working-class settings helps explain why retraining discourses that focus on instilling individual initiative and an entrepreneurial spirit for finding jobs are not more actively challenged by working-class men when they lose their jobs in these resource-extraction industries (Dunk 1996). How, whether, and why language and affect in leisure-time practices are linked to changing forms of work remain a rich area for research. We might consider, for instance, the forms of expressiveness evident in the remarkable rise in Pentecostal churches in the United States, with their predominantly lower-middle-class female constituency, documented by Shoaps

(2002). Is there any link, however complicated, between the policing of affect in service work and the embrace of forms of release from it?

TERROR AND HATE, COMPASSION AND CONVIVIALITY IN THE PUBLIC SPHERE

Projects of racialization developed in the context of long histories of colonization, neoliberal rule, and labor exploitation develop taxonomies of human types, which are arranged into a hierarchy and linked with the allocation of resources in ways that exalt Whiteness and Whites and denigrate Color and people of Color (see Hill 2008, pp. 20–21). Ahmed (2004) argues that the production of such hierarchies is about the "production of the effect of likeness and unlikeness...this separation of others into bodies that *can be* loved and hated" (p. 54, emphasis in original). This performative and discursive approach to understanding emotion is concealed, she argues, in hate crime legislation, where it is assumed that a group identity is in place and works as the cause, rather than the effect, of the crime. Ahmed (2004) is interested instead in "how language works as a form of power in which emotions align some bodies with others" (p. 195), that is, how the idea that people make invidious distinctions and "prefer their own" is naturalized (see also Leudar et al. 2004). Such work builds on Anderson's (2006) claims about the ways that nationalism commands emotional legitimacy by creating bonds of fraternal solidarity. Nonetheless recent works query whether Anderson's work conflates the trope of imagined community with the reality (see Silverstein 2000) in their considerations of previously colonized nations defined by outmigration (Rafael 2000) or in settler colonial nations fractured by racism (Thobani 2007), while the authors agree that nationalism is "a kind of affect productive of a community of longing" (Rafael 2000, p. 204).

The formulation of emotion as an investment in social norms for differentiation and inclusion is useful in thinking through a series of recent thoughtful works on fear, hate, and terror, whether expressed as xenophobia, homophobia, racism, sexism, or anti-Semitism and studied as conflict or violence (Armstrong 1997, Evaldsoon 2005, Morrish 1997, O'Connor 1995, among others), as well as in considering debates about what counts as hate speech (Butler 1997, Matsuda et al. 1993). See Adams et al. (2009) on how fear and anxiety are used to govern subjects (p. 249) and McElhinny (2003) on how fear is used to justify state violence. After September 11, 2001, linguists drew on critical discourse analysis and systemic functional analysis to consider the discursive elaboration of "terrorism" evident in representations of 9/11 and the occupations of Afghanistan and Iraq (Chatterjee 2009, Collins & Glover 2002, Edwards 2004, Erjavec & Volcic 2007, Hodges & Nilep 2007, Lazar & Lazar 2004, Martin 2004). Many of these studies build on the earlier findings of Said (1978) to consider how stereotypes of the violent Muslim are constructed and reconstructed in a variety of settings.

One of the critiques of Said's work has been that it focuses on perduring, unchanging stereotypes. Others consider how, as certain forms of invidious discourse have become unacceptable in the light of social movements, distinctions take different forms. Hill (2008) notes that one challenge for linguists in the United States is to consider how a current folk theory, which understands racism as beliefs held by ignorant people, leads to the denial of racism. She tracks the ways that public discussions about racial gaffes, slurs, and "joking" linguistic appropriations serve to recirculate racist discourse (see also Labrador 2009) because they may allow certain commentators to adopt stances distancing themselves from racism. We have no space here for a detailed list of all recent works on racist discourse, but a few key sources are Billig (2001), Downing (1999), Hill (2008), Henry & Tator (2002), Meek (2006), Rathzel (1997), Reisigl & Wodak (2001), Reyes (2009), Rickford & Rickford (2000), Santa Ana (1999), Van Dijk & Smitherman (1988), Wellman

(1997), Van Dijk (1991), and Wetherell & Potter (1992).

The focus on hate is necessarily linked with ideologies of love and compassion; however, ideologies of compassion or pity can also be forms of othering, particularly when empathy, sympathy, or compassion become ways of re-inforcing one's own superiority and justifying interventions into others' lives, as is frequently the case in colonial, imperial, welfare, non-governmental, and international interventions, as well as in many of the caring professions such as social work, nursing, and teaching (Berlant 2004; Chouliaraki 2004; Thobani 2007, p. 126). Indeed, in the aftermath of the January 2010 earthquake in Haiti, Caribbean diasporic activists critiqued the circulation of images of Haitians as international supplicants and called for "solidarity, not pity" (Trotz 2010). More work needs to be done on the full range of interactions here as well, but some initiatives include Graham (2003), Hall et al. (2006), Kingfisher (1996, 2007), McElhinny (1994), and Sarangi & Slembrouck (1996), and select papers in Drew & Heritage (1992) and Sarangi & Roberts (1999).

What might it mean for nations, or other collectivities, to acknowledge past and current wrong-doing linked to and perpetuating invidious racial and other distinctions? Ahmed (2004) identifies an area for further linguistic analysis by asking how national and international apologies work (p. 101). Does an apology show emotion? Attach responsibility? Provide an interpretation of the injustice? She analyzes the discourse of reconciliation in Australia, as well as requests for apologies from African countries directed toward European and North American countries involved in the slave trade, whereas Nobles (2008) considers the political, legal, and affective effects of apologies to indigenous groups in Australia, Canada, New Zealand and the United States and to African Americans for historical injustices in the United States. The range of apologies illustrated in both of these works, plus those in Gibney et al. (2007), deserves further linguistic analysis along the lines of Hill's (2000) work on promising.

HOPE?

How do progressive scholars use the analytic lens of affect to think toward a better future? The account by Adams et al. (2009) of how anticipation works asks us to challenge the temporal logics that lead to an intense focus on hope and fear, and thus to rethink what the notion of the future authorizes at various political moments. [See, e.g. Miskimmin (2007) for the ways that Aboriginal families recalibrate notions of what "at risk" means in ways more favorable to their own political and personal projects.] However, others argue that one of the critical barriers to progressive politics is the lack of some form of optimism, hope, or joy (Ehrenreich 2007, Harvey 2000, Miyazaki 2004, Zournazi 2002). Gee et al. (1996) argue that many studies of critical literacy in recent years have developed in ways that preclude participating in positive political transformation because they have confined themselves to negative critique (131). Gilroy (2005) advocates for the notion of conviviality, or for considering processes of cohabitation and interaction that make multi-culture an ordinary feature of social life in metropolitan centers. If Gilroy's analysis can, perhaps because of a focus on popular culture sites that are putatively postracial, be charged with moving too quickly toward a moment when we can say we are beyond racism (compare, e.g., Rampton 1995), his account nonetheless challenges linguistic anthropologists to consider how, when, and where sites of everyday sociability, workplace interactions, political solidarity, and consumption foster critical discussions and transformations, as they continue to analyze shortfalls, myopias, and problems. To this end, we might consider, to name just a few, the kinds of hope and concern evident in the account by Gee et al. (1996) of literacy practices in a Nicaraguan cooperative; Chun's (2009) analysis of how an Asian American comic's mockery of stereotypes of Asian American accents is also a critique of racist discourse; Pratt's (2009) collaborative work with the Philippine Women's Center in Vancouver on the role and forms of witnessing and testimony that effect political transformation; Gaudio's (2009) account of the ways different Nigerian publics make sense of a comic movie about 'yan daudu, men who are said to talk and act like women; Morgan's (2009) analysis of a hip-hop workshop in Los Angeles as a struggle to control language and life; Tadiar's (2009a) analysis of how poems, songs, novels, and stories create imagined revolutionary communities; Goldstein's (2003) production of research-informed theater to provoke critical discussions of multilingualism, multiculturalism, social violence, and oppression in Canadian schools and communities; and Tannock's (1999) analysis of the negotiation of different ways of dealing with diversity in a U.S. neighborhood–based youth organization. An audacious hope for linguistic anthropology is to play an even larger role in constructing a longer list.

DISCLOSURE STATEMENT

The author is not aware of any affiliations, memberships, funding, or financial holdings that might be perceived as affecting the objectivity of this review.

ACKNOWLEDGMENTS

I thank the following for inspiring scholarship, comments, questions, and conversations on the topics discussed in this article: Niko Besnier, Nais Dave, Lisa Davidson, Miyako Inoue, Martin Manalansan, Andrea Muehlebach, Michelle Murphy, Lisa Rofel, Jesook Song, and Jie Yang. All my recent work has been informed by heartfelt exchanges within the Kritical Kolectibo at University of Toronto. Thanks go to Kori Allan for her research assistance and to Jie for giving me the opportunity to present an early draft at a conference on market and affect at Simon Fraser University. I extend a particular thank you to Sue Gal for warm and supportive advice as I stared down a deadline for this article.

LITERATURE CITED

Abu-Lughod L, Lutz C. 1990. Introduction: Emotion, discourse and the politics of everyday life. See Lutz & Abu-Lughod 1990, pp. 1–23

Adams V, Murphy M, Clarke A. 2009. Anticipation: technoscience, life, affect, temporality. *Subjectivity* 28:246–65

Ahearn LM. 2001. *Invitations to Love: Literacy, Love Letters and Social Change in Nepal*. Ann Arbor: Univ. Mich. Press

Ahmed S. 2004. *The Cultural Politics of Emotion*. Edinburgh: Edinburgh Univ. Press

Anderson B. 2006. *Imagined Communities: Reflections on the Origin and Spread of Nationalism*. New York: Verso. Revised ed.

Armstrong J. 1997. Homophobic slang as coercive discourse among college students. See Livia & Hall 1997, pp. 326–34

Bauman R, Briggs CL. 2003. *Voices of Modernity: Language Ideologies and the Politics of Inequality*. Cambridge/New York: Cambridge Univ. Press

Bellah RN, Madsen R, Sullivan W, Swidler A, Tipton S. 1996. *Habits of the Heart: Individualism and Commitment in American Life*. Berkeley: Univ. Calif. Press

Berlant L, ed. 2000. *Intimacy*. Chicago: Univ. Chicago Press

Berlant L. 2004. *Compassion: The Culture and Politics of an Emotion*. New York: Routledge

Besnier N. 1990. Language and affect. *Annu. Rev. Anthropol.* 19:419–51

Besnier N. 1995. *Emotion and Authority: Reading and Writing on a Polynesian Atoll*. Cambridge, UK: Cambridge Univ. Press

Besnier N. 2007. Language and gender research at the intersection of the global and local. *Gend. Lang.* 1(1):67–78

Billig M. 2001. Humour and hatred: the racist jokes of the Ku Klux Klan. *Discourse Soc.* 12:267–89

Blommaert J. 2003. Commentary: A sociolinguistics of globalization. *J. Socioling.* 7(4):607–23

Briggs CL. 2005. Communicability, racial discourse and disease. *Annu. Rev. Anthropol.* 34:269–91

Briggs CL, with Mantini-Briggs C. 2003. *Stories in the Time of Cholera: Racial Profiling During a Medical Nightmare.* Berkeley: Univ. Calif. Press

Brown W. 1995. *States of Injury.* Princeton, NJ: Princeton Univ. Press

Bucholtz M. 2007. Shop talk: branding, consumption and gender in American middle-class youth interaction. See McElhinny 2007c, pp. 371–403

Bucholtz M, Hall K. 2004. Theorizing identity in language and sexuality research. *Lang. Soc.* 33(4):501–47

Butler J. 1997. *Excitable Speech: A Politics of the Performative.* New York: Routledge

Butler J. 2004. *Precarious Life: The Powers of Mourning and Violence.* London: Verso

Cameron D. 2000. *Good to Talk? Living and Working in a Communication Culture.* London: Sage

Cameron D, Kulick D. 2003. *Language and Sexuality.* Cambridge, UK: Cambridge Univ. Press

Campbell K, Podesva R, Roberts S, Wong A. 2002. *Language and Sexuality: Contesting Meaning in Theory and Practice.* Palo Alto: Cent. Study Lang. Inform.

Capps L, Ochs E. 1995. *Constructing Panic: The Discourse of Agoraphobia.* Cambridge, MA: Harvard Univ. Press

Césaire A. 1972. *Discourse on Colonialism,* transl. J Pinkham. New York: Mon. Rev. Press

Chatterjee P. 2009. Terrorism: state sovereignty and militant politics in India. In *Words in Motion: Toward a Global Lexicon,* ed. C Gluck, A Lowenhaupt Tsing, pp. 240–65. Durham, NC: Duke Univ. Press

Cheng A. 2001. *The Melancholy of Race.* Oxford: Oxford Univ. Press

Chouliaraki L. 2004. Watching 11 September: the politics of pity. *Discourse Soc.* 15:185–98

Chun E. 2009. Ideologies of legitimate mockery: Margaret Cho's revoicings of mock Asian. See Reyes & Lo 2009, pp. 261–87

Clough P. 2007. Introduction. See Clough & Halley 2007, pp. 1–33

Clough PT, Halley J, eds. 2007. *The Affective Turn: Theorizing the Social.* Durham, NC: Duke Univ. Press

Colen S. 1995. 'Like a mother to them': stratified reproduction and West Indian childcare workers and employers in New York. In *Conceiving the New World Order: The Global Politics of Reproduction,* ed. F Ginsburg, R Rapp, pp. 78–102. Berkeley: Univ. Calif. Press

Collier J. 1997. *From Duty to Desire: Remaking Families in a Spanish Village.* Princeton, NJ: Princeton Univ. Press

Collins J, Glover R, eds. 2002. *Collateral Language: A User's Guide to America's New War.* New York: N. Y. Univ. Press

Constable N. 2009. The commodification of intimacy: marriage, sex, and reproductive labor. *Annu. Rev. Anthropol.* 28:49–64

Coupland N. 2003. Introduction. Sociolinguistics and globalization. *J. Socioling.* 7(4):465–72

Cvetkovich A. 2003. *An Archive of Feelings: Trauma, Sexuality and Lesbian Public Cultures.* Durham, NC: Duke Univ. Press

Dave N. n.d. Indian and Lesbian: affect and commensuration in India's "lesbian emergence." Manuscript under review

Dave N. 2010. To render real the imagined: making lesbian locality out of unruly geographies in India. *Signs* 35(3):595–619

Downing J. 1999. Hate speech and First Amendment absolutism discourses in the US. *Discourse Soc.* 10:175–89

Drew P, Heritage J. 1992. *Talk at Work: Interaction in Institutional Settings.* Cambridge, UK: Cambridge Univ. Press

Ducey A. 2007. More than a job: meaning, affect, and training health care workers. See Clough & Halley 2007, pp. 187–209

Dunk T. 1991. *It's a Working Man's Town: Male Working Class Culture in Northwestern Ontario.* Montreal: McGill-Queen's Univ. Press. 2nd ed.

Dunk T. 1996. Culture, skill, masculinity and whiteness. In *The Training Trap: Ideology, Training and the Labour Market,* ed. T Dunk, S McBride, RW Nelson, pp. 1–12. Winnipeg: Fernwood

Eagleton T. 1991. *Ideology*. London: Longman

Eckert P. 2002. Demystifying sexuality and desire. In *Language and Sexuality: Contesting Meaning in Theory and Practice*, ed. K Campbell-Kibler, R Podesva, S Roberts, A Wong, pp. 99–110. Stanford, CA: Cent. Study Lang. Inf., Stanford Univ.

Edwards J. 2004. After the fall. *Discourse Soc.* 15:155–84

Ehrenreich B. 2007. *Dancing In the Streets: A Collective History of Joy*. New York: Metropolitan

Ehrenreich B, Hochchild A, eds. 2002. *Global Woman: Nannies, Maids and Sex Workers in the New Economy*. New York: Metropolitan

England K, Stiell B. 1997. "'They think you're as stupid as your English is': constructing foreign domestic workers in Toronto. *Environ. Plan. A* 29(2):195–215

Erjavec K, Volcic Z. 2007. "War on terrorism" as a discursive battleground: Serbian recontextualization of G.W. Bush's discourse. *Discourse Soc.* 18:123–37

Errington J. 2008. *Linguistics in a Colonial World*. Oxford, UK: Blackwell

Evaldsson A. 2004. Shifting moral stances: morality and gender in same-sex and cross-sex game interaction. *Res. Lang. Soc. Interact.* 37:331–63

Evaldsson A. 2005. Staging insults and mobilizing categorizations in a multiethnic peer group. *Discourse Soc.* 16:763–86

Fairclough N. 2000. *New Labour, New Language?* New York: Routledge

Fairclough N. 2001. *Language and Power*. London: Longman

Fanon F. 1967. *Black Skin, White Masks*. New York: Grove

Feld S, Fox A. 1994. Music and language. *Annu. Rev. Anthropol.* 23:25–53

Fox A. 2004. *Real Country: Music and Language in Working-Class Culture*. Durham, NC: Duke Univ. Press

Gal S, Kligman G. 2000. *The Politics of Gender After Socialism: A Comparative Historical Essay*. Princeton, NJ: Princeton Univ. Press

Gal S, Woolard K, eds. 2001. *Languages and Publics: The Making of Authority*. Manchester, UK: St. Jerome

Garrett P, Baquedano-López P. 2002. Language socialization: reproduction and continuity, transformation and change. *Annu. Rev. Anthropol.* 31:339–61

Gaudio RP. 2003. Coffeetalk: Starbucks and the commercialization of casual conversation. *Lang. Soc.* 32:659–91

Gaudio RP. 2009. *Allah Made Us: Sexual Outlaws in an Islamic African City*. Oxford, UK: Wiley-Blackwell

Gee JP, Hull G, Lanshear C. 1996. *The New Work Order: Behind the Language of the New Capitalism*. Sydney: Allen & Unwin

Gibney M, Howard-Hassmann RE, Coicaud JM, Steiner N. 2007. *The Age of Apology: Facing Up to the Past*. Philadelphia: Univ. Penn. Press

Gilroy P. 2005. *Postcolonial Melancholia*. New York: Columbia Univ. Press

Gingrich A, Fox R, eds. 2002. *Anthropology, By Comparison*. London: Routledge

Goldstein T. 2003. Hong Kong, Canada. In *Teaching and Learning in a Multilingual School: Choices, Risks, and Dilemmas*, ed. T Goldstein, pp. 133–81. Philadelphia: Lawrence Erlbaum

Goodwin C. 2006. Human sociality as mutual orientation in a rich interactive environment: multimodal utterances and pointing in aphasia. In *Roots of Human Sociality*, ed. N Enfield, S Levinson, pp. 96–125. London: Berg

Goodwin C. 2007. Participation, stance and affect in the organization of activities. *Discourse Soc.* 18:53–73

Goodwin C, Goodwin MH. 2000. Emotion within situated activity. In *Linguistic Anthropology: A Reader*, ed. A Duranti, pp. 239–57. Oxford, UK: Blackwell

Goodwin MH. 2006. *The Hidden Life of Girls: Games of Stance, Status and Exclusion*. Oxford, UK: Blackwell

Graham M. 2003. Emotional bureaucracies: emotions, civil servants and immigrants in the Swedish welfare state. *Ethos* 30(3):199–226

Grewal I, Kaplan A. 1994. *Scattered Hegemonies: Postmodernity and Transnational Feminist Practices*. Minneapolis: Univ. Minn. Press

Hall C, Slembrouck S, Sarangi S. 2006. *Language Practices in Social Work: Categorisation and Accountability in Child Welfare*. London: Routledge

Hall K. 1995. Lip service on the fantasy lines. In *Gender Articulated: Language and the Socially Constructed Self*, ed. K Hall, M Bucholtz, pp. 183–216. New York/London: Routledge

Hardt M. 1999. Affective labor. *Boundary* 26(1):89–100

Harré R. 1986. *The Social Construction of Emotions*. Oxford, UK: Blackwell

Harvey D. 2000. *Spaces of Hope*. Berkeley: Univ. Calif. Press

Harvey D. 2005. *A Brief History of Neoliberalism*. Oxford: Oxford Univ. Press

Harvey K, Shalom C, eds. 1997. *Language and Desire: Encoding Sex, Romance and Intimacy*. London: Routledge

Heller M. 2003. Globalization, the new economy, and the commodification of language and identity. *J. Socioling.* 7(4):473–92

Heller M. 2007. Gender and bilingualism in the new economy. See McElhinny 2007c, pp. 287–304

Hennessey R, Ingraham C, eds. 1997. *Materialist Feminism: A Reader in Class, Difference and Women's Lives*. New York: Routledge

Henry F, Tator C. 2002. *Discourses of Domination: Racial Bias in the Canadian English-Language Press*. Toronto: Univ. Tor. Press

Herzfeld M. 1992. *The Social Production of Indifference: Symbolic Roots of Western Bureaucracy*. Oxford, UK: Berg

Hill JH. 1992. "Today there is no respect": nostalgia, "respect" and oppositional discourse in Mexicano (Nahuatl) language ideology. *Pragmatics* 2(3):263–80

Hill JH. 2000. "Read my article": ideological complexity and the overdetermining of promising in American presidential politics. See Kroskrity 2000, pp. 259–92

Hill JH. 2008. *The Everyday Language of White Racism*. Oxford, UK: Wiley-Blackwell

Hochschild A. 1983. *The Managed Heart: Commercialization of Human Feeling*. Berkeley: Univ. Calif. Press

Hodges A, Nilep C, eds. 2007. *Discourse, War and Terrorism*. Amsterdam: John Benjamins

Inoue M. 2006. *Vicarious Language: Gender and Linguistic Modernity in Japan*. Berkeley: Univ. Calif. Press

Inoue M. 2007. Language and gender in an age of neoliberalism. *Gend. Lang.* 1(1):79–92

Irvine J. 1982. Language and affect: some cross-cultural issues. In *Contemporary Perceptions of Language: Interdisciplinary Dimensions*, ed. H Byrnes, pp. 133–43. Washington, DC: Georgetown Univ. Press

Jaggar A. 1983. *Feminist Politics and Human Nature*. Totowa, NJ: Rowman & Littlefield

Keane W. 1997. Religious language. *Annu. Rev. Anthropol.* 26:47–71

Keane W. 1999. From fetishism to sincerity: on agency, the speaking subject, and their historicity in the context of religious conversion. *Comp. Stud. Soc. Hist.* 39(4):674–93

Kingfisher C. 1996. Women on welfare: conversational sites of acquiescence and dissent. *Discourse Soc.* 7:531–57

Kingfisher C. 2002. *Western Welfare in Decline: Globalization and Women's Poverty*. Philadelphia: Univ. Penn. Press

Kingfisher C. 2007. What D/discourse analysis can tell us about neoliberal constructions of (gendered) personhood: some notes on commonsense and temporality. *Gend. Lang.* 1(1):93–106

Kroskrity P, ed. 2000. *Regimes of Language: Ideologies, Polities and Identities*. Santa Fe, NM: Sch. Am. Res. Press

Kuipers J. 1998. *Language, Identity and Marginality in Indonesia: The Changing Nature of Ritual Speech on the Island of Sumba*. Cambridge, UK: Cambridge Univ. Press

Kulick D. 1992. *Language Shift and Cultural Reproduction: Socialization, Self and Syncretism in a Papua New Guinean Village*. Cambridge/New York: Cambridge Univ. Press

Kulick D. 2000. Gay and lesbian language. *Annu. Rev. Anthropol.* 29:243–85

Labrador RN. 2009. "We can laugh at ourselves": Hawai'i ethnic humor, local identity and the myth of multiculturalism. See Reyes & Lo 2009, pp. 261–87

Lancaster RN. 2003. *The Trouble With Nature: Sex in Science and Popular Culture*. Berkeley: Univ. Calif. Press

Lazar A, Lazar MM. 2004. The discourse of the new world order: "out-casting" the double face of threat. *Discourse Soc.* 15:223–42

Leap W, ed. 1995. *Beyond the Lavender Lexicon: Authenticity, Imagination and Appropriation in Lesbian and Gay Languages*. Amsterdam: Gordan and Breach

Leap W, Boellstorff T, eds. 2004. *Speaking in Queer Tongues: Gay Language and Globalization*. Urbana: Univ. Ill. Press

Lefkowitz D. 2003. Investing in emotion: love and anger in financial advertising. *J. Linguist. Anthropol.* 13(1):71–97

Leidner R. 1993. *Fast Food, Fast Talk: Service Work and the Routinization of Everyday Life*. Berkeley: Univ. Calif. Press

Lempert M. 2006. Disciplinary theatrics: public reprimand and the textual performance of affect at Sera Monastery, India. *Lang. Commun.* 26:15–33

Leonardo M. 1987. The female world of cards and holidays: women, families and the work of kinship. *Signs* 12(4):440–53

Leudar I, Marsland V, Nekvapil J. 2004. On membership categorization: 'us', 'them' and 'doing violence' in political discourse. *Discourse Soc.* 15:243–66

Lewis M, Haviland J, eds. 1993. *Handbook of Emotions*. New York: Guilford

Livia A, Hall K, eds. 1997. *Queerly Phrased: Language, Gender and Sexuality*. Oxford: Oxford Univ. Press

Lorente BP. 2007. *Mapping English linguistic capital: the case of Filipino domestic workers in Singapore*. PhD thesis. Natl. Univ. Singapore. 260 pp.

Lutz C, Abu-Lughod L, eds. 1990. *Language and the Politics of Emotion*. Cambridge, UK: Cambridge Univ. Press

Lutz C, White G. 1986. The anthropology of emotions. *Annu. Rev. Anthropol.* 15:405–36

Lutz C, White G. 1990. Engendered emotion: gender, power, and the rhetoric of emotional control in American discourse. See Lutz & Abu-Lughod 1990, pp. 69–91

Lyon M. 1995. Missing emotion: the limitations of cultural constructionism in the study of emotion. *Cult. Anthropol.* 10(2):244–63

Martin JR. 2004. Mourning: how we get aligned. *Discourse Soc.* 15:321–44

Massumi B. 2002. *Parables for the Virtual: Movement, Affect, Sensation*. Durham, NC: Duke Univ. Press

Matsuda M, Lawrence C III, Delgado R, Crenshaw K, eds. 1993. *Words that Wound: Critical Race Theory, Assaultive Speech, and the First Amendment*. Boulder, CO: Westview

Matza T. 2009. Moscow's echo: technologies of the self, publics, and politics on the Russian talk show. *Cult. Anthropol.* 24(3):489–522

McElhinny B. 1994. An economy of affect: objectivity, masculinity and the gendering of police work. In *Dislocating Masculinity: Comparative Ethnographies*, ed. A Cornwall, N Lindisfarne, pp. 159–71. New York: Routledge

McElhinny B. 2003. Fearful, forceful agents of the law: ideologies about language and gender in police officers' narratives about the use of physical force. *Pragmatics* 13(2):253–84

McElhinny B. 2005. "Kissing a baby is not at all good for him": infant mortality, medicine and colonial modernity in the U.S.-occupied Philippines. *Am. Anthropol.* 107(2):183–94

McElhinny B. 2007a. Language, gender and economies in global transitions: provocative and provoking questions about how gender is articulated. See McElhinny 2007c, pp. 1–38

McElhinny B. 2007b. Recontextualizing the American occupation of the Philippines: erasure and ventriloquism in colonial discourse around men, medicine and infant mortality. See McElhinny 2007c, pp. 205–36

McElhinny B, ed. 2007c. *Words, Worlds, Material Girls: Language and Gender in a Global Economy*. Berlin: Mouton de Gruyter

McElhinny B. 2009. Producing the A-1 baby: puericulture centres and the birth of the clinic in the U.S. occupied Philippines 1906–1946. *Philipp. Stud.* 57(2):219–60

McIlvenny P, ed. 2002. *Talking Gender and Sexuality*. Amsterdam: John Benjamins.

Meek B. 2006. And the Injun goes "how": representations of American Indian English in white public space. *Lang. Soc.* 35:93–128

Memmi A. 1965. *The Colonizer and the Colonized*. Boston: Beacon

Mendoza-Denton N. 2008. *Homegirls: Language and Cultural Practice among Latina Youth Gangs*. Oxford, UK: Blackwell

Miskimmin S. 2007. When Aboriginal equals "at risk": the impact of institutional discourse on Aboriginal Head Start families. See McElhinny 2007c, pp. 107–30

Mitchell L. 2009. *Language, Emotion and Politics in South India: The Making of a Mother Tongue*. Bloomington: Indiana Univ. Press

Miyazaki H. 2004. *Method of Hope: Anthropology, Philosophy and Fijian Knowledge*. Stanford, CA: Stanford Univ. Press

Morgan MH. 2009. *The Real Hiphop: Battling for Knowledge, Power and Respect in the LA Underground*. Durham, N.C.: Duke Univ. Press

Morrish L. 1997. "Falling short of God's ideal": public discourse about lesbians and gays. See Livia & Hall 1997, pp. 334–68

Muehlebach A. 2007. *The moral neoliberal: welfare state and ethical citizenship in contemporary Italy*. PhD thesis. Univ. Chicago. 392 pp.

Negri A. 1999. Value and affect. *Boundary* 2(26):77–88

Nobles M. 2008. *The Politics of Official Apologies*. Cambridge, UK: Cambridge Univ. Press

Ochs E. 1988. *Culture and Language Development: Language Acquisition and Socialization in a Samoan Village*. Cambridge/New York: Cambridge Univ. Press

Ochs E, Schieffelin B. 1989. Language has a heart. *Text* 9(1):7–25

O' Connor P. 1995. Discourse of violence. *Discourse Soc.* 6:309–18

Pavlenko A. 2005. *Emotions and Multilingualism*. Cambridge/New York: Cambridge Univ. Press

Philips S. 2007. Symbolically central and materially marginal: Women's talk in a Tongan work group. See McElhinny 2007c, pp. 41–76

Piller I, Takahashi K. 2006. A passion for English: desire and the language market. In *Bilingual Minds: Emotional Experience, Expression, and Representation*, ed. A Pavlenko, pp. 59–83. Clevedon, UK: Multiling. Matt.

Pitt K. 2002. Being a new capitalist mother. *Discourse Soc.* 13:251–67

Povinelli EA. 2006. *The Empire of Love: Toward a Theory of Intimacy, Genealogy, and Carnality*. Durham, NC: Duke Univ. Press

Pratt G. 1999. From registered nurse to registered nanny: discursive geographies of Filipina domestic workers in Vancouver. *Econ. Geogr.* 75(3):215–36

Pratt G, in collaboration with the Philippine Women Centre of BC. 2009. Circulating sadness: witnessing Filipino mothers' stories of family separation. *Gend. Place Cult.* 16(1):3–22

Pujolar J. 2007. African women in Catalan language courses: struggles for class, gender and ethnicity in advanced liberalism. See McElhinny 2007c, pp. 305–48

Rafael V. 1988. *Contracting Colonialism: Translation and Christian Conversion in Tagalog Society under Early Spanish Rule*. Ithaca, NY: Cornell Univ. Press

Rafael V. 2000. *White Love and Other Events in Filipino History*. Durham, NC: Duke Univ. Press

Ramaswamy S. 1997. *Passions of the Tongue: Language Devotion in Tamil India 1891–1970*. Berkeley: Univ. Calif. Press

Rampton B. 1995. *Crossing: Language and Ethnicity among Adolescents*. London: Longman

Rathzel N. 1997. Gender and racism in discourse. In *Gender and Discourse*, ed. R Wodak, pp. 57–80. London: Sage

Reddy W. 2001. Emotional expression as a type of speech act. In *The Navigation of Feeling: A Framework for the History of Emotions*, pp. 63–111. Cambridge/New York: Cambridge Univ. Press

Reisigl M, Wodak R. 2001. *Discourse and Discrimination: Rhetorics of Racism and Anti-Semitism*. London: Routledge

Reyes A. 2009. Asian American stereotypes as circulating resource. See Reyes & Lo 2009, pp. 43–62

Reyes A, Lo A, eds. 2009. *Beyond Yellow English: Toward a Linguistic Anthropology of Asian Pacific America*. Oxford: Oxford Univ. Press

Reyes RAG. 2008. *Love, Passion and Patriotism: Sexuality and the Philippine Propaganda Movement 1882–1892*. Seattle: Univ. Wash. Press

Richard A, Rudnyckyj D. 2009. Economies of affect. *J. R. Anthropol. Inst.* 15:57–77

Rickford JR, Rickford RJ. 2000. *Spoken Soul: The Story of Black English*. Oxford, UK: Wiley

Robbins J. 2005. Humiliation and transformation: Marshall Sahlins and the study of cultural change in Melanesia. In *The Making of Global and Local Modernities in Melanesia: Humiliation, Transformation and the Nature of Cultural Change*, ed. J Robbin, H Wardlow, pp. 3–21. Surrey: Ashgate

Rofel L. 2007. *Desiring China: Experiments in Neoliberalism, Sexuality and Public Culture*. Durham, NC: Duke Univ. Press

Rose N. 1996. *Inventing Our Selves: Psychology, Power and Personhood*. Cambridge, UK: Cambridge Univ. Press

Rose N. 1999. *Governing the Soul: The Shaping of the Private Self*. London: Free Assoc. 2nd. ed.

Sahlins M. 1992. The economics of develop-man in the Pacific. *Res* 21:1–25

Said E. 1978. *Orientalism*. New York: Vintage

Said E. 1994. *Culture and Imperialism*. New York: Vintage

Santa Ana O. 1999. "Like an animal I was treated": Anti-immigrant metaphor in US public discourse. *Discourse Soc.* 10:191–224

Sarangi S, Roberts C. 1999. *Talk, Work, and Institutional Order: Discourse in Medical, Mediation, and Management Settings*. Berlin: Mouton de Gruyter

Sarangi S, Slembrouck S. 1996. *Language, Bureaucracy and Social Control*. London: Longman

Schieffelin B. 1990. *The Give and Take of Everyday Life: Language Socialization of Kaluli Children*. Cambridge/New York: Cambridge Univ. Press

Schieffelin B. 2000. Introducing Kaluli literacy: a chronology of influences. See Kroskrity 2000, pp. 293–328

Sedgwick E. 2003. *Touching Feeling: Affect, Pedagogy, Performativity*. Durham, NC: Duke Univ. Press

Shibamoto Smith JS. 2004. Language and gender in the (Hetero)romance: "reading" the ideal hero/ine through lover's dialogue in Japanese romance fiction. In *Japanese Language, Gender, and Ideology: Cultural Models and Real People*, ed. S Okamoto, JS Smith, pp. 113–30. Oxford: Oxford Univ. Press

Shoaps R. 2002. "Pray earnestly": the textual construction of personal involvement in Pentecostal prayer and song. *J. Linguist. Anthropol.* 12(1):34–71

Sidnell J. 2007. Comparative studies in conversation analysis. *Annu. Rev. Anthropol.* 36:229–44

Silverstein M. 2000. Whorfianism and the linguistic imagination of nationality. See Kroskrity 2000, pp. 85–138

Stearns P. 1993. History of emotions: the issue of change. See Lewis & Haviland 1993, pp. 17–28

Stewart K. 2007. *Ordinary Affects*. Durham, NC: Duke Univ. Press

Stoler AL. 1991. Carnal knowledge and imperial power: gender, race, and morality in colonial Asia. In *Gender at the Crossroads of Knowledge: Feminist Anthropology in the Postmodern Era*, ed. M di Leonardo, pp. 51–101. Berkeley: Univ. Calif. Press

Stoler AL. 2001. Tense and tender ties: the politics of comparison in North American history and (post) colonial studies. *J. Am. Hist.* 88(2):829–65

Stoler AL. 2005. Affective states. In *A Companion to the Anthropology of Politics*, ed. D Nugent, J Vincent, pp. 4–20. Oxford, UK: Blackwell

Svašek M. 2005. Emotions in anthropology. In *Mixed Emotions: Anthropological Studies of Feeling*, ed. K Milton, M Svašek, pp. 1–24. Oxford, UK: Berg

Tadiar N. 2009a. Guerilla passion and the unfinished cultural revolution. In *Things Fall Away: Philippine Historical Experience and the Makings of Globalization*, pp. 299–333. Durham, NC: Duke Univ. Press

Tadiar N. 2009b. Popular laments. *Cult. Stud.* 23(1):1–26

Tannock S. 1999. Working with insults: discourse and difference in an inner-city youth organization. *Discourse Soc.* 10:317–50

Thobani S. 2007. *Exalted Subjects: Studies in the Making of Race and Nation in Canada*. Toronto: Univ. Tor. Press

Trotz A. 2010. *We must stand with Haiti: solidarity, not help*. **http://www.stabroeknews.com/2010/features/01/18/we-must-stand-with-haiti-solidarity-not-help./**

Valentine G. 2006. Globalizing intimacy: the role of information and communication technologies in maintaining and creating relationships. *Women's Stud. Q.* 34:365–93

Van Dijk T. 1991. *Racism and the Press*. London: Routledge

Van Dijk T, Smitherman G. 1988. *Discourse and Discrimination*. Detroit, MI: Wayne State Univ. Press

Walton M, Weatherall A, Jackson S. 2002. Romance and friendship in pre-teen stories about conflicts: "We decided that boys are not worth it." *Discourse Soc.* 13:673–89

Weidman A. 2006. *Singing the Classical, Voicing the Modern: The Postcolonial Politics of Music in South India*. Durham, NC: Duke Univ. Press

Weidman A. 2007. Stage goddesses and studio divas in South India: on agency and the politics of voice. See McElhinny 2007c, pp. 131–56

Wellman D. 1997. Minstrel shows, affirmative action talk, and angry white men: marking racial otherness in the 1990s. In *Displacing Whiteness: Essays in Social and Cultural Criticism*, ed. R Frankenberg, pp. 311–32. Durham, NC: Duke Univ. Press

Wetherell M, Potter J. 1992. *Mapping the Language of Racism: Discourse and the Legitimation of Exploitation*. New York: Columbia Univ. Press

White G. 1993. Emotions inside out: the anthropology of affect. See Lewis & Haviland 1993, pp. 29–40

Wiegele K. 2005. *Investing in Miracles: El Shaddai and the Transformation of Popular Catholicism in the Philippines*. Honolulu: Univ. Hawaii Press

Wilce J. 2004. Passionate scholarship: recent anthropologies of emotion. *Rev. Anthropol.* 33:1–17

Wilce J. 2005. Narrative transformations: emotion, language and globalization. In *Companion to Psychological Anthropology*, ed. C Casey, R Edgerton, pp. 123–39. Oxford, UK: Blackwell

Wilce J. 2009a. *Crying Shame: Metaculture, Modernity and the Exaggerated Death of Lament*. Oxford, UK: Wiley-Blackwell

Wilce J. 2009b. *Language and Emotion*. Cambridge/New York: Cambridge Univ. Press

Williams R. 1973. *The Country and the City*. Oxford: Oxford Univ. Press

Williams R. 1976. *Keywords*. Oxford: Oxford Univ. Press

Williams R. 1977. *Marxism and Literature*. Oxford: Oxford Univ. Press

Yang J. 2006. *Ritualized transition: language, gender and neoliberal restructuring in China*. PhD thesis. Univ. Tor.

Yang J. 2007a. "Re-employment stars": language, gender and neoliberal restructuring in China. See McElhinny 2007c, pp. 77–105

Yang J. 2007b. *Zuiqian* 'deficient mouth': language, gender and domestic violence in urban China. *Gend. Lang.* 1(1):105–16

Zournazi M. 2002. *Hope: New Philosophies for Change*. New York: Routledge

Soundscapes: Toward a Sounded Anthropology

David W. Samuels,[1] Louise Meintjes,[2]
Ana Maria Ochoa,[3] and Thomas Porcello[4]

[1] Department of Music, New York University, New York, NY 10003;
email: dws2004@nyu.edu

[2] Departments of Music and Cultural Anthropology, Duke University, Durham,
North Carolina 27708-0665; email: meintjes@duke.edu

[3] Department of Music, Columbia University, New York, NY 10027;
email: ao2110@columbia.edu

[4] Department of Anthropology, Vassar College, Poughkeepsie, New York 12604;
email: thporcello@vassar.edu

Annu. Rev. Anthropol. 2010. 39:329–45

First published online as a Review in Advance on
June 21, 2010

The *Annual Review of Anthropology* is online at
anthro.annualreviews.org

This article's doi:
10.1146/annurev-anthro-022510-132230

0084-6570/10/1021-0329$20.00

Key Words

aurality, film sound, listening, music, recording technology, sound art

Abstract

A generation of scholars in multiple disciplines has investigated sound in
ways that are productive for anthropologists. We introduce the concept
of soundscape as a modality for integrating this work into an anthropological approach. We trace its history as a response to the technological
mediations and listening practices emergent in modernity and note its
absence in the anthropological literature. We then trace the history of
technology that gave rise to anthropological recording practices, film
sound techniques, and experimental sound art, noting productive inter-
weavings of these threads. After considering ethnographies that explore
relationships between sound, personhood, aesthetics, history, and ideology, we question sound's supposed ephemerality as a reason for the
discipline's inattention. We conclude with a call for an anthropology
that more seriously engages with its own history as a sounded discipline and moves forward in ways that incorporate the social and cultural
sounded world more fully.

INTRODUCTION

In 2004 Feld commented in *American Ethnologist*, "Until the sound recorder is presented and taught as a technology of creative and analytic mediation, which requires craft and editing and articulation just like writing, little will happen of an interesting sort in the anthropology of sound" (Feld & Brenneis 2004, p. 471). What would a sounded anthropology be? How might the discipline of anthropology develop if its practitioners stopped thinking of the field recording only as a source of data for the written work that then ensues and rather thought of the recording itself as a meaningful form? What if discussions of recording moved beyond inquiries about the state of the art in recording technology to how best to present and represent the sonorous enculturated worlds inhabited by people?

A generation of scholars in various disciplines has been asking questions about sound, listening, the voice, and the ear (Erlmann 2004, Feld et al. 2004, Finnegan 2002, Kruth & Stobart 2000, Nancy 2007) in ways that make such reflection in anthropology both possible and possibly productive. Prominent among these questions is Clifford's provocative jibe, echoed by Erlmann (2004), "but what of the ethnographic ear?" (Clifford 1986, p. 12). We propose that an alertness toward sound and sound recording and production is useful to anthropology at large. First we outline and contextualize genealogies of the theoretically generative concept of soundscape. Then we review emerging ethnographic work on sound and sound recording through which the relevance of the soundscape concept to anthropology is made explicit. At the same time, this ethnography refines theory about soundscape, even if it does not all make use of the term. In combination, soundscape theory and ethnographies of sound prompt us to call for an aural reflexive turn in the discipline and offer tools with which to do it. We build on the model of Canadian composer R. Murray Schafer (1994 [1977]), which we contend has advantages for anthropologists. He frames the soundscape as a publicly circulating entity that is a produced effect of social practices, politics, and ideologies while also being implicated in the shaping of those practices, politics, and ideologies. Soundscape opens possibilities for anthropologists to think about the enculturated nature of sound, the techniques available for collecting and thinking about sound, and the material spaces of performance and ceremony that are used or constructed for the purpose of propagating sound.

FROM SOUND TO SOUNDSCAPE

The history of the soundscape concept is intimately linked to histories of mediation and to changing technologies that make particular kinds of listening possible. It is inseparable from the critical encounter with sound that these changes themselves enable. Indeed, after World War II a number of concepts for thinking about sound emerged simultaneously. Each responded to recording technology by addressing sound's intimate connections to contexts of time and place. Following Latour (1993), we infer from these overlapping concerns that the invention of sound machines was part of a collection of epistemological practices of purification of sound, which sought to abstract sound from its immediate surroundings while noting its connectivity to place.

We trace the term soundscape to Schafer (1994 [1977]), who brought it into wide circulation when he called for "a total appreciation of the acoustic environment" (p. 4). Soundscape was somewhat analogous to landscape insofar as it attempted to contain everything to which the ear was exposed in a given sonic setting. Like "landscape," as well, the term contains the contradictory forces of the natural and the cultural, the fortuitous and the composed, the improvised and the deliberately produced. Similarly, as landscape is constituted by cultural histories, ideologies, and practices of seeing, soundscape implicates listening as a cultural practice.

Schafer's concern with the noise pollution of modern technology dictated the form of his presentation: The soundscape moves historically from natural to rural to town to city and thence through the industrial and electric revolutions, becoming ever louder and less tuned to a human(ist) scale. In its historical movement from "hi-fi" to "lo-fi" soundscapes, this presentation masks the ways in which the concept of soundscape is itself anchored in a form of listening that became possible only through the development of technological forms of mediation and recording.

Schafer's initial engagement with the concept thus emerged out of a somewhat romantic materialist environmentalism, and his presentation performs a recurrent worry about technology's dismantling of the natural soundscape. This concern manifested in two ways: First, Schafer often returned to a discussion of technology's ability to drown out the human scale of the natural soundscape—"noise" is represented as the enemy of "sound"; second, his desire for the holism of the soundscape led him to critique the ways in which sound recordings could time- and place-shift the sources of a sound's natural context—from a specific "here" and "now" of natural occurrence to a multiplicity of "heres" and "nows" through the aegis of mediation. For this sundering of sound and scape, Schafer coined a second term, schizophonia. As a result of Schafer's concern with noise pollution and the composition of the emerging city soundscape, one place that the concept has found a fertile home is in urban studies (Arkette 2004, Atkinson 2007, Gidlof-Gunnarsson & Öhrström 2007).

The concept overlaps and layers with a more widely circulating academic discourse about sound, under such rubrics as "sound studies" and "anthropology of sound" and in scholarly attention to listening. Some of this work uses the term soundscape and other attendant concepts developed by Schafer in detailed form or dedicates one chapter to the concept (Picker 2003, Smith 1999). Other work appropriates the term but not the wide-ranging approach to the public sphere and to cultural histories that characterize Schafer's understanding of sound and culture. Still other important work approaches the sonic from within studies of science, technology, and communication (Bijsterveld 2008, Sterne 2003, Thompson 2002).

Soundscape studies has had particular traction in Scandinavia, where radio documentary, sound art, and interdisciplinary scholarship have intersected in formative ways (Järviluoma 2004). With some exceptions, however (Feld 1990 [1982], Helmreich 2007, Rice 2008, Ridington 1988), the soundscape concept has circulated more widely outside of anthropology than within it and more widely outside of North America than within it. This failure to take root could be in part because Schafer's neologism was broadly contemporaneous with the publication of Spivak's translation of Derrida's *Of Grammatology* (1976), which heralded a disciplinary turn away from voice and sound as presence toward a focus on textuality and inscription. Another reason may be the loose way in which the term has sometimes circulated. Some music scholars have employed "soundscape," either explicitly (Shelemay 2006) or implicitly (Dudley 2002, Jones 2003, Manuel 1994), as a new cover term for "the context in which music occurs" but without exploring the sonic aspects of that context that the soundscape concept can activate. Others, especially in the realm of popular music studies (Albiez 2003, Kronengold 2005), use the term to refer to the internal sonic or tonal texture of a musical performance or ensemble, a usage that overlaps with the way electroacoustic composers have used the term (Truax 2008, Westerkamp 2002). These uses invite an unfortunate reductive approach to both ethnography and the theory of the soundscape and limit the possibilities for a cross-fertilization of music studies and anthropology of sound. Yet the notion of soundscape may find more traction in the anthropological mainstream now than in past decades. The return to the body, the senses, and embodiment as areas of anthropological research and sources of local knowledge, along with Appadurai's (1990) framing of modernity and the global cultural economy as an intertwined collection of "-scapes," raises the profile of sound and soundscape as productive arenas for research.

In language and music studies, work that picks up on Bakhtinian notions of dialogism, polyphony, and the chronotope presents the voice as an utterance shaped and sounded in relation to other voices and to situated events (Inoue 2006, Silverstein 2005). Recent work on the acoustic dimensions of voice and the politics of time (Cavarero 2005, Grosz 2004), as well as studies on orality and remediation, further mobilizes questions about context and vocal sound. Together, these approaches bring attention to the linguistic transformation of speech acts when recontextualized to new media (Bauman 2010). This, along with work that decenters a Eurocentric approach to the relation between media and mediation (García Canclini 2005, Martín-Barbero 2001, Shohat & Stam 2003), identifies the aural as imbricated in theory and politics and, thereby, as critical to the ethnographic endeavor.

TECHNOLOGIES OF SONIC INSCRIPTION AND EXPERIENCE

New forms of technological mediation in the late nineteenth century helped constitute a particular modern(ist) engagement with sound, intensified cultural practices of listening (Connor 2004, Kahn 1992), and prompted shifts in practices of signification. Some of the earliest audio recordings included oratory, storytelling, and other verbal arts that until then had been performed face to face. The introduction of the new medium, in part, changed the modes of performing these genres. On the one hand, recording demanded that performance practices adapt to the art and technologies of recording, which led to distinctions between studio and live performances. On the other hand, live performance was itself transformed by the new access to playback (Katz 2004). These shifts can be seen linguistically and socially in a newly emergent focus on prosody, new practices of indexicality, new modes of eliciting audience response, and new contextualization cues for hypothetical audiences. This remediation of oral genres reconstituted those genres and their relationships to time and space (Bauman 2010, Bauman & Feaster 2004). At once futurist and nostalgic, sound recording also shifted the felt nature of memory, time, and place, disrupting the naturalized chronotope of live performance and producing an epistemological divide between face-to-face and mediated communication in a way that the invention of the telephone had not. Sound recording as well promised to bring the fullness of performed vocal and sonic presence of the past to future generations, and as a technology of memory, sound recording was quickly incorporated into the idea of the archive. The archival impetus still strongly undergirds anthropological field methodology with sound, configured anew by issues around new forms of electronic access, the emerging dominance of digital technology, and questions of ethics, informed consent, and cultural property rights to control archival collections (Christen 2006, Fabian 2008, Kelty et al. 2008). But recording as archival documentation is not the only effect of the development of inscriptive technologies for sound. Considerations of the adjacent and overlapping histories of motion picture sound, studio recording, and experimental sound art also contribute to the emergence of the concept of soundscape and to anthropology's productive engagement with it.

Sterne (2003) challenges the technological determinism of many histories of sound and listening, arguing that such inventions were themselves made possible because of an antecedent early-nineteenth-century interest in the ear, listening, deafness, and acoustics in fields such as medicine, psychoacoustics, and physiology. Gitelman (1999) demonstrates further that the idea of "new technologies" of sound reproduction is far from new. Before the invention of sound machines, the inscription of sound resulting from listening practices took place through "legible representations of aural experience" (p. 15): inscriptive practices that involved musical notation and words about sound and aural perception. Gitelman challenges readers to recognize the ways in which technologies of the legible made and continue to make sound circulation possible. Thus the problem that Schafer frames as schizophonia is not in fact determined by the emergence of sound recording technology. One could argue that the gramophone changed the stakes, but still the existence of recordings forced researchers in the areas of music, language, and other sounded cultural practices to rethink already existing scriptural procedures of notation and transcription (Rehding 2005). Likewise, the thin line between the Edison cylinders and the piano arrangements of nonwestern musical forms created by early ethnomusicologists (Troutman 2009) attested to the dialogic relationship between sound and sight.

Recent scholarly trends demonstrate recognition of these historical practices of legible aural inscription. These include the search for traces of the aural and practices of listening in literatures of different historical periods (Connor 2004, Picker 2003), for the sound of the voice in its written modes (Smith 1999), and for the trace left by different genres of inscription on the critical work of music making (Szendy 2008). Together with critical work on the philosophical grammar of vocality and writing (Cavarero 2005, Derrida 1976), the study of discourses and practices surrounding the invention of sound machines (Brady 1999, Sterne 2003), and the search for how specific historical periods predating the emergence of mechanical sound reproduction sounded (Johnson 1995, Rath 2003, Smith 2004b), this work on auditory history enables scholars to confront the presumption of western ocularcentrism. The dilemma that emerges is whether alternative sensorial histories have always been there as "subterranean histories" (Hirschkind 2006) at the margins of a mainstream history dominated by visuality or if the resounding of such histories gives rise in effect to a radically different temporal cartography: that "an auditory rather than a predominantly visual approach to the past produces a different cultural history" (Johnson 2005, p. 259).

Historians working in the realm of sound (Connor 2000, Corbin 1998, B. Johnson 2005, J. Johnson 1995, Schmidt 2000, Smith 1999), often "strongly drawn to epochs and subjects that *precede* sound recording" (Thomas 2007, p. 107; emphasis in original), have made us aware that an ocularcentric history is based on an erasure of the place of the ear in constituting knowledges and different practices crucial to modernity. Anthropologists working with sound, however (Feld 1996a,b; Hirschkind 2006; Meintjes 2004), question the epistemic foundation of histories that claim an ocularcentricity of modernity through fieldwork that explores the acoustic construction of knowledge.

SOUND IN FILM

Soundscape and its companion concepts appeared in conjunction with a number of alternative approaches to thinking about questions of sound, culture, place, history, acoustic space, and technology. One of the key terms from these alternative traditions is the idea of "acousmatic" sound associated with experimental composer Pierre Schaeffer and the *musique concrète* movement in France (Schaeffer 1966). Thinking of sound on tape as itself a "sound object" (*l'objet sonore*), that is, an entity independent of its acoustic origin, Schaeffer framed this relationship between the sound object and its missing source as acousmatic, borrowed from Pythagorean philosophy but which in its modern coinage referred to sounds "of which the cause is invisible" (Chion 1983, p. 18). The term shares ground with schizophonia, but without the sense of anxiety about the separation of sounds from their naturally occurring contexts that marks Murray Schafer's work.

Discussions of film sound that focus on the acousmatic enter the purview of anthropology because they strongly implicate relationships of sound, place, and space. Even prior to the commercial success of the Vitaphone process (Lastra 2000, pp. 92–122), musical accompaniment was usually heard in the theaters that exhibited so-called "silent" films, and the traces of the presence of musicians on the film set can be seen in the rhythmic coordination of movements of the actors on the screen in the finished film (C. Abbate, manuscript in preparation). Film editing was often analogized as musical, however problematic the analogy may be. Conversely, A. Monchick (manuscript in preparation) argues that musical composition in Germany between the World Wars was broadly influenced by montage and other tropes of cinematic technique.

Given the ways in which filmmaking influenced ideologies of sound and hearing, sound film studies promise a rich area of engagement for anthropologists considering sound, space, context, listening, technology, and aesthetic production. The historical development of synchronized sound in motion pictures (Crafton 1997) was partially constituted by the technological apparatus that enabled filmmakers to separate production of the visual narrative from that of the aural narrative. This process made possible the production of soundtracks that took full advantage of the recording studio's ability to enhance the listener's experience of attending to and focusing on particular sounds and even particular features of sounds. Recent film scholarship has witnessed an explosion of literature on the soundtrack (Altman 2007, Buhler et al. 2009, Chion 1994, Donnelly 2001, Goldmark et al. 2007, Kassabian 2000). Much of this work continues to concentrate on the role of music in the experience of film viewership, exploring, for example, the nature of diegetic and nondiegetic music in film, that is, the question of whether the source of a musical sound is in the story and meant for the characters or in the score and meant for the audience. Chion (1994) has challenged scholars to think of film as an audio-visual experience and to understand sound in film as synergistic with vision. Chion's emphasis on acousmatic sound acknowledges the mediated means by which filmmakers use the soundtrack to (re)create the material reality in which the film takes place.

Growing attention to the produced nature of the aural experience of film is echoed by a terminological move from film sound to sound design in articulating how soundtracks are constructed, and construed, as more than the musical score that accompanies the narrative arc of a film (Beck & Grajeda 2008,

Sider 2003). A number of film scholars have therefore avoided using "soundtrack" in favor of "soundscape," a term in film studies traced more often to Stilwell (2001) than to Schafer. Stilwell's framing of soundscape is intended to prod scholars to think holistically about film soundtracks, not only as the music that accompanies the sequence of scenes in a film, but as a complex layering of dialogue, music, and sound effects that together helps to anchor the viewer's experience of the film.

SOUND ARTS, SOUND RECORDING, SOUNDSCAPE

Strongly influenced by *musique concrète* and Schaeffer's twinned notions of the sound object and acousmatics, as well as other postwar experimental music traditions in Europe and the United States (LaBelle 2006), sound art is another refraction of relationships between sound, space, technology, expression, and culture that emerged in tandem with the idea of the soundscape. A number of electroacoustic composers associate their work directly with Schafer's concepts (Truax 2008, Westerkamp 2002). Architects, visual and performance artists, music composers, documentary recordists, and scholars have all written about sound art, sound installations, and recorded soundscapes, often in the same collected volumes (Carlyle 2007, Drobnick 2004, Gray & Yan 2007, Licht 2007, Rudi 2009; also see Soundscape: The Journal of Acoustic Ecology). The in situ ethnographic field recording has also served as a precedent for some sound art in ways that intersect directly with anthropological interests and with framings of the soundscape (see Kahn 1999, pp. 101–22).

As a social science, however, anthropology's engagement with sound has, for the most part, been different from that within the arts and humanities. Despite exceptions such as "deep listening," (Becker 2004, Oliveros 2005), anthropology has largely treated the work of sound artists as tangential to its enterprise. Anthropologists' disregard is returned in kind by sound artists who often dismiss ethnographic field recordings for their rudimentary production techniques and their largely archival impetus. Zhang (2007), for example, criticizes field recordings as low-fi and academic rather than commercial and as preservationist rather than creative in impulse, arguing for the creative license to manipulate what he records. Such rhetorical stances, however, limit the ways in which sound art can be considered as a form of ethnographic argument as well as creative material for social analysts to think with. It limits, as well, the ways that sound artists might treat ethnography as making a contribution to artistic work, especially with regard to representing alternative positions of audition.

Soundscape composition reveals and sometimes replicates a limitation of Schafer's soundscape concept—its assumption that sound is only a matter of the vibrations of the source, leaving undertheorized the social, ideological, or political positionalities of listeners. Documentary sound art and soundscape composition take on the challenge of representing sound in a social or environmental context. Some projects add environmental sounds. Others blend music into environmental recordings (Cradick 1993, Cusack 2003, Sarno 1995). Still other sound artists are concerned primarily with expressing their own aesthetic or politics. Lockwood's *A Sound Map of the Danube* (2008) and DeLaurentis's activist *Our Streets!* (2006) are affective and carefully observed and heard, but the listening position of these multivocal soundscapes is solely that of the composer/recordist. Documentary sound art centered on musical expression sometimes blends environmental sounds into the representation of musical performances. In his *Voices of the Rainforest* (1991a), by contrast, Feld was less interested in providing listeners with a sense of "Kaluli music in context" than in shaping a representation of a Kaluli way of listening, dialogically mixed with Kaluli artists and listeners. Thus, it differs from many recordings framed as musical soundscapes, whether by sound artists or by scholars.

Although anthropological or ethnomusicological field recording has continued to have an archival focus on documenting expressive forms in performance, recent work has expanded the goals of documenting music, oratory, storytelling, language elicitation, or the like by situating the expressive arts within an acoustic environment in which listeners are active social participants. Earlier literature gestures in this direction. Turnbull's classic *Mbuti Pygmies of the Ituri Rainforest* (Turnbull & Chapman 1992 [1957]) is an early foray in this direction. Influenced by Turnbull, Guillaume & Surgue (1982) produced a recording that attempted to offer listeners "an impression of what life among the Aka 'sounds like.'" But Feld's Kaluli recordings and his discussion of them (1991b) especially challenged ethnographers to rethink the aural representation of culture. Influenced in part by Rouch's film playback and feedback experiments in the 1950s, 1960s, and 1970s, Feld has produced experimental collaborative projects (Annan & Feld 2008, Ryan & Feld 2007) that blur the boundaries between documentary, ethnographic, and compositional work, raising questions about the premise of these distinctions in the first place and theorizing the aesthetics of recordings (see Feld 2000, Feld & Brenneis 2004, Zemp 1996).

Except for linguistic anthropology and ethnomusicology, anthropological training has tended to invest little in learning to work with sound recording and editing technologies, in developing techniques of interpretation for acoustic "texts," and in refining ethnographic language to articulate the poetics of sonic forms. In producing recordings, however, field recordists make decisions behind which lie histories of ideas about what needs to be made audible. For example, they must consider how to bridge the seeming divide between representing local soundscapes in their own terms (however the ethnographer might understand this) and translating local performances into terms that are legible in foreign markets and other listening contexts (the classroom, the archive, or the lecture, for example). The best field recordings are those in which the recordist has paid close attention to these questions, their quality due in part to the way the researchers have been guided through their research by deep and nuanced listening. Such recordings are derived as well from extensive ethnographic knowledge and consultation about the sounds recorded, combined with concerns on the part of the recordist with the politics and poetics of representation. These recordings are themselves statements: creative, interpretive, empirical, hermeneutic, analytical texts rendered in acoustic form. The recordings of Turnbull (Turnbull & Chapman 1992[1957]), Arom & Renaud (1990 [1975]), and Berliner (1995 [1973]), for example, have enjoyed as sustained a life as have their monographs. (See also Zemp 1990 [1974].)

ETHNOGRAPHIES OF SOUND AND THE SOUNDSCAPE

Recording the Rainforest

In the late 1970s through the 1980s, with Turnbull (1961) as a precursor, music ethnographers working in rainforest societies made a vital contribution to globalizing soundscape studies (Basso 1985, Feld 1990 [1982], Roseman 1991, Seeger 1987). The dense rainforest canopy was a sensorially exceptional ecological environment in which one could hear further than one could see. With this emphasis on acoustic experience, their ethnographies showed social worlds to be at once imbricated in spiritually, ecologically, and sonically dense environments. Working in the shadows of structuralism, using Turnerian approaches to ritual as performance, and taking art to be a component of symbolic action, these studies sought an understanding of social coherence. For them, the interrelationship between the arts played a role in producing a sense of communality. Studies of music in these places demonstrated how sound structure as social structure blurred the distinctions between nature and culture and between musical and acoustic analysis. Their focus on the idea of coherence—as social, sounded, and symbolic— combined with detailed ethnographic research to reveal that the soundscape was dense with significance, led them to a particularly cohesive sense of how such significance operated—a co-hesion that was modified in these authors' own later work (Feld 1996a, 2000; Seeger 2003), as well as work in other aural environments.

Recording Cosmopolitanism and Struggle

The holistic approaches to sound, history, environment, and place of these rainforest ethnographies provided the inspiration for successive work on aurality in metropolitan, ambient, and cosmopolitan environments and in places in which forms of social struggle made coherence itself difficult to find. Scholars taking an ethnographic approach to sonic practices in urban environments (Wallach 2008), zones of conflict (White 2008), or virtual communities (Bennett & Peterson 2004), for example, focus on the contemporary encounter between sound in performance and the means of production, reproduction, and consumption. Studies that examine the ways that sound technologies are embroiled in the shaping of sonic aesthetics, whether through manipulation of musical instruments (Berger & Fales 2005), technologies of distribution (Sutton 1996), mediated devotional practices (Hirschkind 2006, Lee 1999), or patterns of circulation and reception (Novak 2008, Solomon 2009) also call attention to the ways in which listening is space- and place-specific, as well as to the multiple ways of listening to the acoustic components of sound. Work that highlights megacities as products of voyages and circulation and the daily movements of people within them has led to ethnographies of emplaced auditory landscapes and media usage, leading to an understanding of media and the construction of the urban landscape as mutually constitutive of each other (García Canclini et al. 1996, Gray 2007, Hansen 2006, Hirschkind 2006, Sakakeeny 2010).

Studio Production and Listening Practices

Key to much of the work that puts sound into a more contested framework is a willingness to grapple with multiple dimensions of sound that are manipulable in the recording process and that have become part of the palette of expressive resources used by recording artists, sound engineers, and producers: timbre (or sound color), spatialization (via use of echo or reverberation as well as stereo-field or surround-sound manipulation), ambience, and distortion. Space in particular has received a great deal of attention because it is a highly constructed artifact of the mediations inherent in production and listening practices. Thus running parallel to the concept of the soundscape is that of the sound stage, a three-dimensional recorded representation of a space from which performance emerges (Moylan 2002). Recordings have always included some representation of the space of performance, ranging from close-miked recordings, which seek to create the artifice that the performance is occurring outside of any physical space whatsoever (Brady 1999), to the classical concert-hall recording approaches, which seek to position the listener as an "ideal ear" (or ears) in an audience (Chanan 1995), to spaces that are invented, imaginary, or in which the spatial features are themselves part of the composer's (or producer's) compositional palette (Blesser & Salter 2007, Doyle 2005, Porcello 2005, Zak 2001).

Other work has emphasized the role of mediating technologies in the politics of aesthetics in music. Ethnographers working directly in recording studios have attended to negotiations involving musicians, engineers, producers, and other interests in the production of recordings (Bates 2008, Meintjes 2003). Music scholars increasingly listen to music with an ear to the sound engineering practices that underpin the recording (Katz 2004, Porcello 2005), and an increasing number of sound engineers and producers have sought to theorize the recording process (Moylan 2002). Others have looked at the intersection of sound production and communities of listeners or consumers (Fikentscher 2003, Wong 2003).

New Forms of Place in the Global Economy

A fourth engagement with soundscape, mediation, and culture ethnographically traces the cultural productivity of formally dislocated sounds, positing a creative and cultural productivity to various schizophonic moments in the production of new forms of identity, performance, and memory. The globalizing music industry (Burnett 1996, Taylor 1997) and the circulation of new technologies of production have bequeathed a preponderance of new forms of emplacement for music and sound, including hip hop in Japan (Condry 2006), new forms of reggae in Jamaica (Veal 2007), country music in Native American communities (Samuels 2004) as well as other new forms of Native American musical identities (Browner 2009, Lassiter et al. 2002), the global circulation of hip hop (Alim et al. 2008), and new forms of musical expression in exile (Diehl 2002). This topic has become central to ethnomusicology, but covering the complete scope of its emerging literature is beyond the range of this article. We note, however, the legacy of the chronotope implicit in ethnographies that probe the relationship between time, place, and personhood through the voice (Fox 2004, Samuels 2004, Webster 2009, Weidman 2006). Grappling with the means of understanding an auditory intimacy while maintaining a sense of socially, geographically, and historically emplaced relationships, this work explores shifting constitutions of personhood as registered in the voice in the modern global ecumene.

Most of this work continues to be in dialogue with the politics of schizophonic emplacement as crucial to the political understanding of sonic production, finding new social meanings in the tensions heard in sounds that are or are not "naturally" associated with the new places in which they are found. In recent extensions of this scholarship, work attentive to the politics of place and time further displaces the relation between sound and place as the central node of political concern by an attention to sound and the politics of circulation (Lemos & Castro 2008, Novak 2008, Ochoa & Botero 2009).

This reworking of place is partly a product of decentering the politics of production and circulation to different critical domains: the coming of age of a generation for whom global consumption of media products is not necessarily seen as oppositional to their local appropriation in certain parts of the world, which decenters place as the arbiter of authenticity or signification (Novak 2008); the appropriation of technology for uses that question the historical divide between the religious and the secular, thus displacing technology as the exclusive scientific-secular domain of emplacement (Hirschkind 2006, Larkin 2008); the politics of sound production and circulation increasing as a contested legal terrain that blurs the line between copyright laws, illegal forms of appropriation (generally glossed as "piracy"), and the emergence of new juridical regimes of circulation that recognize alternative modes of production (creative commons, social commons, free software, etc.) (Lemos & Castro 2008, Ochoa & Botero 2009); and the questioning of the politics of circulation by indigenous groups who increasingly contest ideas of copyright and free circulation in efforts to develop their own politics of circulation of cultural objects (Christen 2009).

THE SONIC, THE SPATIAL, THE MATERIAL, THE EPHEMERAL

Scholars and composers have long suggested that one of the difficulties posed by sounds, as compared with images, is the inability to extract sounds from their temporal constraints. Sound recording allows for the temporal dislocation of a sound from its time and place of origin, but does not facilitate the ability to do the auditory equivalent of sustaining the gaze on an image for as long or as short as one desires. Thus even though sounds can be reproduced and replayed, sound is often considered to have, by its nature, a kind of temporality that the visual may not share.

This way of thinking about the temporality of sound has often led to an essentialization of sound as ephemeral, or at least elusive. One can see the material remains of Pompeii or Mesa Verde, for instance, and describe with some accuracy their architecture, spatial and material

properties, etc.; but one can only imagine, infer, or at best indirectly reconstruct what they sounded like. Witmore's (2006) discussion of developing techniques in archaeological mapping implies that methods of visual inscription enhanced the idea of the permanence of visual objects, whereas methods of sound inscription, ironically, underscored the impermanence of sonic objects. The salvage ethnography work of early anthropologists was similarly predicated on a premise that loss of sound producers (the last speakers of native languages or performers of expressive genres) without recording them was to lose those sounds forever (Brady 1999, Ames 2003).

Compelling and provocative research by sound scholars in a number of disciplines has demonstrated the ways that the most permanent productions of material culture are associated with and shaped by the so-called intangibility of sound. Exploring the ways in which spaces of sonic performance both shape and are shaped by ideologies of proper aural practices and listening, this work covers a range of built, modified, and natural spaces used for sonorous practices, including painted Paleolithic caves (Reznikoff 2006), churches and cathedrals (Wright 1989), concert halls (Thompson 2002), and theater spaces (Arms & Crawford 1995, B. Smith 1999). As Sterne's essay on the Mall of America (1997) shows, even in a material structure distinctly nonsonorous in purpose, we ought not ignore its role as an ambient sounding environment.

The soundscape concept provides some response to the ephemerality dilemma by offering a means to materialize sounds, their interrelations, and their circulation, much as Urban (1991) argues for the materiality of discourse. Yet the soundscape tends to be theorized as strongly geographic, leaving the complexities of sound's temporality largely unexplored. Time in much soundscape work tends to mean diurnal time or historical time rather than duration. This definition, along with the neglect of the socially and culturally positioned listener, weakens the engagement of soundscape with politics and power. A similar limitation results from the absence of the human voice in most soundscape work. In Schafer's chronicle of the soundscape, the human voice is progressively drowned out by modernity, the pleasant cries of street vendors replaced by the cold amplitude of machinery. This inattentiveness to the voice prevents Schafer's own history from including such well-known events in the histories of European languages as The Great Vowel Shift in English, the ascendancy of *langue d'oil* over *langue d'oc* in France, or any number of standardizations revealing power and ideology at the level of sound—including a great deal of contemporary work in linguistics and lingustic anthropology on the politics of language revitalization. Recent work on the voice from a number of disciplines (Cavarero 2005, Feld et al. 2004, Fox 2004, Levin 2006, Urciuoli 1996) offers ways to integrate the human voice into the soundscape in ways that help anthropologists interrogate the historicized and ideological relations of bodies to their physical and cultural surroundings.

CONCLUSION: SOUNDED ANTHROPOLOGY

In speaking of a sounded anthropology, we are not proposing a break from the discipline as it has been framed. We are attempting to incorporate into the current work and profile of the discipline an acknowledgment that anthropology's history of entwinement with histories of technology, aesthetics, and mediation has led it to a critique of representation in the visual field while largely neglecting issues of sound, recording, and listening.

Histories of inscription and studies of orality and the voice and of recording provide anthropologists theoretical tools with which to reexamine their own disciplinary history as also a sounded one, with the sounded component of the discipline as more than simply a methodological means toward the end of accurate written analysis. These same rapidly growing bodies of literature also offer guidance on how to listen to compositional form, sound design, and acoustic properties as artful and social, making distinctly possible the development of a sounded anthropology.

The rich literature on inscription combined with the idea of the soundscape and with patterns of globalization—the distribution of particular sounds, their audibility, and their value—reminds us that configurations of sound have political implications for a public, which is always a cosmopolitan listening public. Disciplinarity, coloniality, and the cultural politics of globalization are epistemologically linked (Ochoa 2006). The postcolonial move that draws sounded ways of knowing and thinking closer into the center of anthropology recognizes the politics of aurality. Such a move can partner anthropology about sound with anthropology in sound. Critical discussion of field recordings, soundscape recordings, and sound art projects as ethnographic endeavors along with the rapidly expanding literature on studio production practices, circulation processes, ethnographies of listening, the poetics of the voice, and the politics of globalization in relation to expressive culture offers anthropology a possible path toward a reflexive aural turn. Treating recordings as integral components of a sounded anthropology and equal partners in a theoretical conversation stands to refine and advance that conversation.

Were anthropology to consider its critical deafness to its own use of sound technology, to processes of acoustic mediation, and to the potential of sounded aesthetics as ethnography, anthropology might more productively engage with the artifacts of its own early history, and ethnographers could bring aural sensibilities to the worlds inhabited by the people with whom they work and consider those sounded worlds as more than performance genres to be extracted from their contexts. Finally, anthropologists would be reminded that recordings of those extracted performances themselves are interpretive statements. As constructions of the events recorded, they are not simply abstractions.

What, then, of the ethnographic ear? Clifford's call will continue to resonate until anthropologists attend to the soundscape and the politics of aurality. It is our hope that by tracing the genealogies and histories of the concept of the soundscape we will promote such attention and enable anthropologists and other scholars of culture to engage the full potential of sound—and in sound—for the theoretical project of anthropology.

DISCLOSURE STATEMENT

The authors are not aware of any affiliations, memberships, funding, or financial holdings that might be perceived as affecting the objectivity of this review.

ACKNOWLEDGMENTS

The authors thank Steven Feld, Tim Taylor, Dave Novak, Priscilla Wald, Aaron Fox, and Martin Daughtry, who read earlier versions of this manuscript. Simon Calle, Nicole Devoe, Karl Hoffstad, Mark Pechak, and Spencer Peterson ably assisted in the collection and discussion of bibliographic materials. Paul Berliner and the graduate students in the Anthropology of Sound seminar at Duke University helped us think through many of our ideas. Thomas Solomon made important contributions to our conversation, especially from the Scandinavian perspective.

LITERATURE CITED

Albiez S. 2003. Know history!: John Lydon, cultural capital and the prog/punk dialectic. *Pop. Music* 22:357–74

Alim S, Ibrahim A, Pennycook A. 2008. *Global Linguistic Flows: Hip Hop Cultures, Youth Identities, and the Politics of Language*. London: Routledge

Altman R. 2007. *Silent Film Sound*. New York: Columbia Univ. Press

Ames E. 2003. The sound of evolution. *Modernism/Modernity* 10(2):297–325

Annan NO, Feld S. 2008. *Bufo Variations*. Santa Fe: Voxlox. CD

Appadurai A. 1990. Disjuncture and difference in the global cultural economy. *Theory Cult. Soc.* 7:295–310

Arkette S. 2004. Sounds like city. *Theory Cult. Soc.* 21(1):159–68

Arms RG, Crawford BE. 1995. Resonant cavities in the history of architectural acoustics. *Technol. Cult.* 36(1):104–35

Arom S, Renaud P. 1990 [1975]. *Cameroon: Baka Pygmy Music/Cameroun: La Musique des Pygmées Baka*. Ivry-sur-Seine: Auvidis CD 8029

Atkinson R. 2007. Ecology of sound: the sonic order of urban space. *Urban Stud.* 44(10):1905–17

Basso EB. 1985. *A Musical View of the Universe: Kalapalo Myth and Ritual Performances*. Philadelphia: Univ. Penn. Press

Bates E. 2008. *Social interactions, musical arrangement, and the production of digital audio in Istanbul recording studios*. PhD diss. Univ. Calif., Berkeley

Bauman R. 2010. The remediation of storytelling: narrative performance on early commercial sound recordings. In *Telling Stories: Building Bridges Among Language, Narrative, Identity, Interaction, Society and Culture*. Rep. Georgetown Univ. Round Table Discuss. Lang. Ling., 2008, ed. A De Fina, D Schiffrin, pp. 23–43. Washington, DC: Georgetown Univ. Press

Bauman R, Feaster P. 2004. Oratorical footing in a new medium: recordings of presidential campaign speeches, 1896–1912. *Proc. Annu. Symp. Lang. Soc., 11th, Austin, April 11–13, 2003. Tex. Ling. Forum* 47:1–19

Beck J, Grajeda T. 2008. *Lowering the Boom: Critical Studies in Film Sound*. Urbana: Univ. Ill. Press

Becker J. 2004. *Deep Listening: Music, Emotion, and Trancing*. Bloomington: Indiana Univ. Press

Bennett A, Peterson RA, eds. 2004. *Music Scenes: Local, Translocal, and Virtual*. Nashville, TN: Vanderbilt Univ. Press

Berger HM, Fales C. 2005. "Heaviness" in the perception of heavy metal guitar timbres: the match of perceptual and acoustic features over time. See Greene & Porcello 2005, pp. 181–97

Berliner P. 1995 [1973]. *Zimbabwe: The Soul of Mbira*. Nonesuch Explorer Ser. CD 72054–2. New York: Nonesuch Records

Bijsterveld K. 2008. *Mechanical Sound: Technology, Culture and Public Problems of Noise in the Twentieth Century*. Cambridge, MA: MIT Press

Blesser B, Salter R. 2007. *Spaces Speak, Are you Listening? Experiencing Aural Architecture*. Cambridge, MA: MIT Press

Brady E. 1999. *A Spiral Way: How the Phonograph Changed Ethnography*. Jackson: Univ. Press Miss.

Browner T, ed. 2009. *Music of the First Nations: Tradition and Innovation in Native North Amercan Music*. Urbana: Univ. Ill. Press

Buhler J, Neumeyer D, Deemer R. 2009. *Hearing the Movies: Music and Sound in Film History*. New York: Oxford Univ. Press

Burnett R. 1996. *The Global Jukebox: The International Music Industry*. London: Routledge

Carlyle A, ed. 2007. *Autumn Leaves: Sound and the Environment in Artistic Practice*. Paris: Double Entendre

Cavarero A. 2005. *For More than One Voice: Toward a Philosophy of Vocal Expression*. Stanford, CA: Stanford Univ. Press

Chanan M. 1995. *Repeated Takes: A Short History of Recording and its Effects on Music*. New York: Verso

Chion M. 1983. *Guide des Objets Sonores: Pierre Schaeffer et al. Recherché Musicale*. Paris: Buchet/Chastel, Inst. Natl. Commu. Audiovisuelle

Chion M. 1994. *Audio-Vision: Sound on Screen*. New York: Columbia Univ. Press

Christen K. 2006. Ara Irititja: protecting the past, accessing the future—indigenous memories in a digital age. *Mus. Anthropol.* 29(1):56–60

Christen KA. 2009. *Aboriginal Business: Alliances in a Remote Australian Town*. Santa Fe: Sch. Adv. Res. Press

Clifford J. 1986. Introduction: partial truths. In *Writing Culture: The Poetics and Politics of Ethnography*, ed. J Clifford, GE Marcus, pp. 1–26. Berkeley: Univ. Calif. Press

Condry I. 2006. *Hip-Hop Japan: Rap and the Paths of Cultural Globalization*. Durham, NC: Duke Univ. Press

Connor S. 2000. *Dumbstruck: A Cultural History of Ventriloquism*. New York: Oxford Univ. Press

Connor S. 2004. Sound and the self. See Smith 2004a, pp. 54–68

Corbin A. 1998. *Village Bells: Sound and Meaning in the 19th-Century French Countryside*. New York: Columbia Univ. Press

Cradick M. 1993. *Heart of the Forest: The Music of the Baka Forest People of Southeast Cameroon*. Salem, MA: Hannibal Rec., CD HNCD 1378

Crafton D. 1997. *The Talkies: American Cinema's Transition to Sound, 1926–1931*. New York: Scribner

Cusack P. 2003. *Baikal Ice: Spring*. Thornton Heath, UK: ReR. CD PC2

Delaurentis C. 2006. Our streets. In *On Interpreting the Soundscape*, curated by P Cusack. *Leonardo Music J.* Cambridge, MA: MIT Press. Vol. 16, LMJ16 CD

Derrida J. 1997 [1976]. *Of Grammatology*, transl. GC Spivak. Baltimore, MD: Johns Hopkins Univ. Press. Correct. ed. From French

Diehl K. 2002. *Echoes from Dharamsala: Music in the Life of a Tibetan Refugee Community*. Berkeley: Univ. Calif. Press

Donnelly K, ed. 2001. *Film Music: Critical Approaches*. London: Continuum

Doyle P. 2005. *Echo and Reverb: Fabricating Space in Popular Music Recording, 1900–1960, Music /Culture*. Middletown, CT: Wesleyan Univ. Press

Drobnick J. 2004. Listening awry. In *Aural Cultures*, ed. J Drobnick, pp. 9–18. Banff: XYZ Books

Dudley S. 2002. Dropping the bomb: steelband performance and meaning in 1960s Trinidad. *Ethnomusicology* 46(1):135–64

Erlmann V. 2004. But what of the ethnographic ear? Anthropology, sound, and the senses. In *Hearing Cultures: Essays on Sound, Listening and Modernity*, ed. V Erlmann, pp. 1–20. Oxford: Berg

Fabian J. 2008. *Ethnography as Commentary: Writing from the Virtual Archive*. Durham, NC: Duke Univ. Press

Feld S. 1990 [1982]. *Sound and Sentiment: Birds, Weeping, Poetics, and Song in Kaluli Expression*. Philadelphia: Univ. Penn. Press

Feld S. 1991a. *Voices of the Rainforest: A Day In The Life Of The Kaluli People*. Salem, MA: Rykodisc. CD 10173

Feld S. 1991b. Voices of the rainforest: politics of music. *Public Cult.* 4(1):131–40

Feld S. 1996a. Pygmy pop, a genealogy of schizophonic mimesis. *Yearb. Trad. Music* 28:1–35

Feld S. 1996b. Waterfalls of song: an acoustemology of place resounding in Bosavi, Papua New Guinea. In *Senses of Place*, ed. S Feld, KH Basso, pp. 91–136. Santa Fe, NM: Sch. Am. Res. Press

Feld S. 2000. A sweet lullaby for world music. *Public Cult.* 12(1):145–71

Feld S, Brenneis D. 2004. Doing anthropology in sound. *Am. Ethnol.* 41(4):461–74

Feld S, Fox AA, Porcello T, Samuels D. 2004. Vocal anthropology: from the music of language to the language of song. In *A Companion to Linguistic Anthropology*, ed. A Duranti, pp. 321–45. Malden, MA: Blackwell

Fikentscher K. 2003. There's not a problem I can't fix 'cause I can do it in the mix: on the performative technology of the 12-inch vinyl. In *Music and Technoculture*, ed. RTA Lysloff, LC Gay Jr. pp. 290–315. Middletown, CT: Wesleyan Univ. Press

Finnegan R. 2002. The sounding world and its creation. In *Communicating: The Multiple Modes of Human Interconnection*, pp. 59–91. London: Routledge

Fox AA. 2004. *Real Country: Music and Language in Working-Class Culture*. Durham, NC: Duke Univ. Press

García Canclini N. 2005. *Antropología urbana en México*. México City: Consejo Nac. Cult. Artes, Univ. Autónoma Metrop., Fondo Cult. Econ.

García Canclini N, Castellanos A, Mantecón AR. 1996. *La Ciudad de Los Viajeros: Travesías e Imaginarios Urbanos, México 1940–2000*. México City: Univ. Autónoma Metrop., Unidad Iztapalapa, Grijalbo

Gidlof-Gunnarsson A, Öhrström E. 2007. Noise and well-being in urban residential environments: the potential role of perceived availability to nearby green areas. *Landsc. Urban Plan.* 83(2–3):115–26

Gitelman L. 1999. *Scripts, Grooves and Writing Machines: Representing Technology in the Edison Era*. Stanford, CA: Stanford Univ. Press

Goldmark D, Kramer L, Leppert R, eds. 2007. *Beyond the Soundtrack: Representing Music in Cinema*. Berkeley: Univ. Calif. Press

Gray L, Yan J, eds. 2007. *Sound and the City*. London: Br. Counc.

Gray LE. 2007. Memories of empire, mythologies of the soul: fado performance and the shaping of saudade. *Ethnomusicology* 53(1):106–30

Greene PD, Porcello T, eds. 2005. *Wired for Sound: Engineering and Technologies in Sonic Cultures*. Middletown, CT: Wesleyan Univ. Press

Grosz E. 2004. *The Nick of Time, Politics, Evolution and the Untimely*. Durham, NC: Duke Univ. Press

Guillaume H, Surgue B. 1982. *Chasseurs Pygmées*. Paris: Off. Rech. Sci. Tech. Outre-Mer (ORSTOM), Soc. Etud. Ling. Anthropol. France (SELAF), CETO 795

Hansen TB. 2006. Sounds of freedom: music, taxis, and racial imagination in urban South Africa. *Public Cult.* 18(1):185–208

Helmreich S. 2007. An anthropologist underwater: immersive soundscapes, submarine cyborgs, and transductive ethnography. *Am. Ethnol.* 34(4):621–41

Hirschkind C. 2006. *The Ethical Soundscape: Cassette Sermons and Islamic Counterpublics*. New York: Columbia Univ. Press

Inoue M. 2006. *Vicarious Language: Gender and Linsguistic Modernity in Japan*. Berkeley: Univ. Calif. Press

Järviluoma H. 2004. On the fringes of musical inquiry: soundscape research. *Finn. Music Q.* 1:30–35

Johnson B. 2005. Hamlet: voice, music, sound. *Pop. Music* 24(2):257–67

Johnson J. 1995. *Listening in Paris: A Cultural History*. Berkeley: Univ. Calif. Press

Jones S. 2003. Reading between the lines: reflections on the massive "Anthology of Folk Music of the Chinese Peoples." *Ethnomusicology* 47(3):287–337

Kahn D. 1992. Histories of sound once removed. In *Wireless Imagination: Sound, Radio and the Avant Garde*, ed. D Kahn, G Whitehead, pp. 1–30. Cambridge, MA: MIT Press

Kahn D. 1999. *Noise, Water, Meat: A History of Sound in the Arts*. Cambridge, MA: MIT Press

Kassabian A. 2000. *Hearing Film: Tracking Identifications in Contemporary Hollywood Film Music*. London: Routledge

Katz M. 2004. *Capturing Sound: How Technology Has Changed Music*. Berkeley: Univ. Calif. Press

Kelty CM, Fischer MMJ, Golub A, Jackson JB, Christen K, et al. 2008. Anthropology of/in circulation: the future of open access and scholarly societies. *Cult. Anthropol.* 23(3):559–88

Kronengold C. 2005. Accidents, hooks and theory. *Pop. Music* 24:382–97

Kruth P, Stobart H, eds. 2000. *Sound. Darwin College Lectures*. Cambridge, UK: Cambridge Univ. Press

LaBelle B, ed. 2006. *Background Noise: Perspectives on Sound Art*. New York: Continuum

Larkin B. 2008. *Signal and Noise: Media, Infrastructure, and Urban Culture in Nigeria*. Durham, NC: Duke Univ. Press

Lassiter LE, Ellis C, Kotay R. 2002. *The Jesus Road: Kiowas, Christianity, and Indian Hymns*. Lincoln: Univ. Neb. Press

Lastra J. 2000. *Sound Technology and the American Cinema*. New York: Columbia Univ. Press

Latour B. 1993. *We Have Never Been Modern*. New York/London: Harvester Wheatsheaf

Lee TS. 1999. Technology and the production of Islamic space: the call to prayer in Singapore. *Ethnomusicology* 43(1):86–100

Lemos R, Castro O. 2008. *Tecnobrega: Pará Reinventing the Music Business*. Rio de Janeiro: Aeroplano Ed.

Levin T. 2006. *Where Rivers and Mountains Sing: Sound, Music, and Nomadism in Tuva and Beyond*. Bloomington: Indiana Univ. Press

Licht A. 2007. *Sound Art: Beyond Music, Between Categories*. New York: Rizzoli

Lockwood A. 2008. *A Sound Map of the Danube*. New York: Lovely Music. 3 CD set. LCD2083

Manuel P. 1994. Puerto Rican music and cultural identity: creative appropration of cuban sources from Danza to Salsa. *Ethnomusicology* 38(2):249–80

Martín-Barbero J. 2001. *Al Sur de la Modernidad: Comunicación, Globalización y Multiculturalidad*. Pittsburgh: Inst. Int. Lit. Iberoamericana, Univ. Pittsburgh

Meintjes L. 2003. *Sound of Africa!: Making Music Zulu in a South African Studio*. Durham, NC: Duke Univ. Press

Meintjes L. 2004. Shoot the sergeant, shatter the mountain: the production of masculinity in Zulu ngoma song and dance in postapartheid South Africa. *Ethnomusicol. Forum* 13(3):173–201

Moylan W. 2002. *The Art of Recording: The Creative Resources of Music Production and Audio*. New York: Van Nostrand Reinhold

Nancy J-L. 2007. *Listening*, transl. C Mandell. New York: Fordham Univ. Press. From French

Novak D. 2008. 2.5 by 6 meters of space: Japanese music coffeehouses and experimental practices of listening. *Pop. Music* 27:15–34

Ochoa AM, Botero C. 2009. Notes on practices of musical exchange in Colombia. *Pop. Comm. on Lat. Am.* 7(3):158–68

Ochoa Gautier AM. 2006. Sonic transculturation, epistemologies of purification and the aural public sphere in Latin America. *Soc. Ident.* 12(6):803–25

Oliveros P. 2005. *Deep Listening: A Composer's Sound Practice*. Lincoln, NE/Kingston, NY: iUniverse/Deep Listening

Picker JM. 2003. *Victorian Soundscapes*. New York: Oxford Univ. Press

Porcello T. 2005. Music mediated as live in Austin; sound, technology, and recording practice. See Greene & Porcello 2005, pp. 103–17

Rath RC. 2003. *How Early America Sounded*. Ithaca/London: Cornell Univ. Press

Rehding A. 2005. Wax cylinder revolutions. *Music Q.* 88(1):123–50

Reznikoff I. 2006. The evidence of the use of sound resonance from Palaeolithic to Medieval times. In *Archaeoacoustics*, ed. C Scarre, G Lawson, pp. 77–84. Cambridge, UK: Cambridge Univ. Press

Rice T. 2008. "Beautiful murmurs": stethoscopic listening and acoustic objectification. *Senses Soc.* 3(3):293–306

Ridington R. 1988. Why baby why: Howard Broomfield's documentation of the Dunne-Za soundscape. *Can. J. Nat. Stud.* 8(2):251–74

Roseman M. 1991. *Healing Sounds from the Malaysian Rainforest: Temiar Music and Medicine*. Berkeley: Univ. Calif. Press

Rudi J, ed. 2009. *Sound Art*. Spec. issue of *Org. Sound*, Vol. 14, No. 1

Ryan V, Feld S. 2007. *The Castaways Project*. Santa Fe: VoxLox. CD, DVD 207

Sakakeeny M. 2010. "Under the bridge": an orientation to soundscapes in New Orleans. *Ethnomusicology* 54(1):1–27

Samuels D. 2004. *Putting a Song on Top of It: Expression and Identity on the San Carlos Apache Reservation*. Tucson: Univ. Ariz. Press

Sarno L. 1995. *Bayaka: The Extraordinary Music of the Babenzele Pygmies and Sounds of Their Forest Home*. Roslyn, NY: Ellipsis Arts. CD 3490

Schaeffer P. 1966. *Traité des Objets Musicaux, Essai Interdisciplines*. Paris: Ed. Seuil

Schafer RM. 1994 [1977]. *The Soundscape: Our Sonic Environment and the Tuning of the World*. Rochester, VT: Destiny

Schmidt LE. 2000. *Hearing Things: Religion, Illusion and the American Enlightenment*. Cambridge, MA: Harvard Univ. Press

Seeger A. 1987. *Why Suya Sing: A Musical Anthropology of an Amazonian People*. Cambridge/New York: Cambridge Univ. Press

Seeger A. 2003. Globalization from a local perspective in Brazil: the Suyá Indians and *música sertaneja*. In *Musical Cultures of Latin America, Global Effects, Past and Present. Selected Reports in Ethnomusicology*, ed. S Loza, 11:121–28. Los Angeles: Ethnomusicology

Shelemay KK. 2006. *Soundscapes: Exploring Music in a Changing World*. New York: Norton. 2nd ed.

Shohat E, Stam R. 2003. *Multiculturalism, Postcoloniality and Transnational Media*. New Brunswick, NJ: Rutgers Univ. Press

Sider L, ed. 2003. *Soundscape: The School of Sound Lectures, 1998–2001*. London: Wallflower

Silverstein M. 2005. Axes of evals: token versus type interdiscursivity. *J. Ling. Anthropol.* 15(1):6–22

Smith B. 1999. *The Acoustic World of Early Modern England: Attending to the O-Factor*. Chicago: Univ. Chicago Press

Smith MM, ed. 2004a. *Hearing History: A Reader*. Athens/London: Univ. Ga. Press

Smith MM. 2004b. Introduction. Onward to audible pasts. See Smith 2004a, pp. ix–xxii

Solomon T. 2009. Berlin-Frankfurt-Istanbul: Turkish hip-hop in motion. *Eur. J. Cult. Stud.* 12(3):305–27

Sterne J. 1997. Sounds like the Mall of America: programmed music and the architectonics of commercial space. *Ethnomusicology* 41(1):22–50

Sterne J. 2003. *The Audible Past. Cultural Origins of Sound Reproduction*. Durham/London: Duke Univ. Press

Stilwell R. 2001. Sound and empathy: subjectivity, gender and the cinematic soundscape. See Donnelly 2001, pp. 167–87

Sutton RA. 1996. Interpreting electronic sound technology in the contemporary Javanese soundscape. *Ethnomusicology* 40(2):249–68

Szendy P. 2008. *Listening, A History of our Ears*. New York: Fordham Univ. Press

Taylor T. 1997. *Global Pop: Global Music, Global Markets*. London: Routledge

Thomas M. 2007. The rush to record: transmitting the sound of Aboriginal culture. *J. Aust. Stud.* 90:107–21

Thompson E. 2002. *The Soundscape of Modernity: Architectural Acoustics and the Culture of Listening in America, 1900–1933*. Cambridge, MA: MIT Press

Troutman JW. 2009. *Indian Blues: American Indians and the Politics of Music, 1879–1934*. Norman: Univ. Okla. Press

Truax B. 2008. Soundscape composition as global music: electroacoustic music as soundscape. *Org. Sound* 13(2):103–9

Turnbull C, Chapman FS. 1992 [1957]. *Mbuti pygmies of the Ituri rainforest*. Washington, DC: Smithson. Folkways CD 40401

Turnbull CM. 1961. *The Forest People*. New York: Simon and Schuster

Urban G. 1991. *A Discourse-Centered Approach to Culture: Native South American Myths and Rituals*. Austin: Univ. Tex. Press

Urciuoli B. 1996. *Exposing Prejudice: Puerto Rican Experiences of Language, Race, and Class*. Boulder, CO: Westview

Veal M. 2007. *Dub: Soundscapes and Shattered Songs in Jamaican Reggae*. Middletown, CT: Wesleyan Univ. Press

Wallach J. 2008. *Modern Noise, Fluid Genres: Popular Music in Indonesia, 1997–2001*. Madison: Univ. Wis. Press

Webster A. 2009. *Explorations in Navajo Poetry and Poetics*. Albuquerque: Univ. N. M. Press

Weidman A. 2006. *Singing the Classical, Voicing the Modern: The Postcolonial Politics of Music in South India*. Durham: Duke Univ. Press

Westerkamp H. 2002. Linking soundscape composition and acoustic ecology. *Org. Sound* 7(1):51–56

White BW. 2008. *Rhumba Rules: The Politics of Dance Music in Mobutu's Zaire*. Durham, NC: Duke Univ. Press

Witmore C. 2006. Vision, media, noise and the percolation of time: symmetrical approaches to the mediation of the material world. *J. Mat. Cult.* 11(3):267–92

Wong DA. 2003. *Speak it Louder: Asian Americans Making Music*. New York: Routledge

Wright C. 1989. *Music and Ceremony at Notre Dame of Paris, 500–1550*. New York: Cambridge Univ. Press

Zak A. 2001. *The Poetics of Rock: Cutting Tracks, Making Records*. Berkeley: Univ. Calif. Press

Zemp H. 1990 [1974]. *Polyphonies des Îles Salomon/Polyphonies of the Solomon Islands*. France: Chant du monde, Distribution Harmonia Mundi. CD LDX 274 663

Zemp H. 1996. The/an ethnomusicologist and the record business. *Yearb. Trad. Music* 28:36–56

Zhang X. 2007. Let your ears grow like weed. See Gray & Yan 2007, pp. 35–38

RELATED RESOURCES

Following the invention of sound-recording technologies, sound archives were foundational to the history of anthropology, ethnomusicology, folkloristics, and linguistics. They remain important for work in and through sound and culture, along with a recent generation of Web sites offering access to natural, musical, linguistic, historical, and other archival collections of the sonorous world. Following is a list of some of the collections available online.

ARCHIVES OF INDIGENOUS LANGUAGE AND CULTURE

Archive of Indigenous Languages of Latin America. **http://www.ailla.utexas.org/site/welcome. html**

Australian National Film and Sound Archives. **http://www.nfsa.gov.au/**

British Library Sound Archive. **http://www.bl.uk/nsa**

International Library of African Music. **http://www.ru.ac.za/ilam**

Mukurtu Wumpurrarni-Kari Archive. **http://www.mukurtuarchive.org/**

Plateau People's Web Portal. **http://plateauportal.wsulibs.wsu.edu/html/ppp/index.php**

ONLINE SOUNDSCAPES

Archive Sonoro. **http://www.archivosonoro.org/paisajes_sonoros/**

Helmi Järviluoma's Acoustic Environments in Change project (an updating of Murray Schafer's 1975 Five European Villages project). **http://www.6villages.tpu.fi**

World Soundscape Project at Simon Fraser University. **http://www.sfu.ca/~truax/wsp.html**

ACOUSTIC ECOLOGY WEB SITES

Cornell University's Macaulay Library of Natural Sounds. **http://macaulaylibrary.org/ index.do**

The Owl Project at the MIT media lab. **http://owlproject.media.mit.edu/**

World Forum for Acoustic Ecology (featuring the journal *Soundscape*). **http://interact. uoregon.edu/MediaLit/wfae/home/**

SOUND MAPS OF VARIOUS CITIES

Montreal sound map. **http://cessa.music.concordia.ca/soundmap/en/**

New Orleans sound map. **http://www.opensoundneworleans.com/core/**

New York sound map. **http://fm.hunter.cuny.edu/nysae/nysoundmap/soundseeker.html**

Tony's Schwartz's seminal recordings of the NYC streetscape. **http://www.tonyschwartz.org/ #audio**

Property and Persons: New Forms and Contests in the Era of Neoliberalism

Eric Hirsch

Department of Anthropology, Brunel University, Uxbridge, Middlesex UB8 3PH,
United Kingdom; email: eric.hirsch@brunel.ac.uk

Annu. Rev. Anthropol. 2010. 39:347–60

First published online as a Review in Advance on
June 21, 2010

The *Annual Review of Anthropology* is online at
anthro.annualreviews.org

This article's doi:
10.1146/annurev.anthro.012809.105036

Key Words

culture, heritage, intellectual property, land, ownership, technology

Abstract

The past few decades have witnessed an eruption of property claims
worldwide. The new form of cultural property has emerged. There has
also been a marked growth in claims of intellectual property that are
now applied to an expanded array of things and contexts. Older property
forms, such as landownership, are deployed in new contexts, generating
novel contests about the capacity of land to be exclusively owned. The
ideology of neoliberalism and new technologies of biology, information,
and communication are central to these transformations in property
relations. In their distinctive ways, each has contributed to the expansion
of property claims while continually disrupting the division of persons
and things central to property. The article considers how contests about
new and old property forms are simultaneously generative of new forms
of persons, such as indigenous persons, whose outlook and conduct
potentially undermine the legitimacy of conventional property claims.

INTRODUCTION

In 2004, Kolimangh Clay Products based in the Imbuon village of Chambri Lakes, Papua New Guinea, began litigation against Post PNG. The company took the legal action because it claimed that Post PNG had used images of some of their work on two stamps that were issued in 2004 and that were in circulation for two years. The images were of ornamental sculpture and of spirits called Sengi. Kolimangh Clay Products make traditional clay pots and other traditional items and had, they asserted, protected their work under copyright. The company claimed that Post PNG had infringed their copyright, under a recently passed law in Papua New Guinea. The legal action was taken in order to receive payments for the use of the sacred images found on the two stamps (Kenneth 2009).

What is of interest about this story is both how it is very familiar, as disputes about copyright are commonplace, and also unusual, as it is played out in a place not conventionally associated with such legal contests. What the case signals is a transformed view of property in places like Papua New Guinea, and that village people there are prepared to use legal means to protect their property. Although the company claimed it was their property, from what is known anthropologically about Papua New Guinea societies it is unlikely that there is communal, let alone individual, ownership in this case (Strathern 2005). Post PNG presumably assumed that these were a local, cultural resource and the property of no one in particular. Such conflicts about copyright are of course a well-known story for Euro-American people, stretching back more than 300 years, when authors began to seek legal ownership of their work through the new copyright legislation (Rose 1993). But this change in outlook in places like Papua New Guinea, or similar changes among aboriginal peoples in Australia and Central, North, and South America, is fairly recent. How can this change be accounted for? There is no simple answer but the influences of a new ideology and new technology are significant, and they are important because of the way in which they have enabled persons and things, and their relations to be perceived in new ways. In areas such as Papua New Guinea and similarly globally, these new ways are those of property. At the same time, old forms of property and property dispute, e.g., land ownership, have taken on a new saliency in many places of the world where such forms of ownership are new and where the distinction between persons and things in this context raises interesting analytical problems.

The article reviews anthropological scholarship of the past 20 years, from a period of new ideological and technological innovations and the new forms of property and new forms of persons that have arisen in their wake. The article suggests that the global acceleration and intensification of contests and conflicting claims regarding diverse property forms are mutually connected with contests about both the constitution and boundaries of persons and things; the latter is a long-standing anthropological concern (Leenhardt 1979, Mauss 1985). What is new is the capacity to perceive this in an increasing range of context, and the new kinds of property and persons that emerge as a result of these transformed contexts (see Demian 2004). The article considers examples from novel properties associated with biotechnologies to older property forms, such as landownership in areas of the world where this is a new relation between people. Property claims have expanded but so too have the claims that question the legitimacy of conventional property theory and the division of persons and things it presupposes.

IDEOLOGY AND TECHNOLOGY

Thirty years ago a new ideology began to take hold institutionally and in the popular imagination among Euro-Americans. The ideology was always seen as controversial, but its emergence was an outgrowth of the development project that dominated nations and the international order after the second world war

(Escobar 1994; Ferguson 1994; McMichael 1998, p. 99). Nowadays this ideology goes under various labels: neoliberalism (closely associated with globalization), or neoconservatism; its earlier manifestations were dubbed as Thatcherism and Reaganomics (see Harvey 2005). In this ideology (private) property relations and rights took on a new and more intense significance, a globalized privatization regime (Mirowski & Sent 2002). This was evident in all domains of economic, political, and social life including that of technology and science. It was, for example, in 1980 that the U.S. Supreme Court ruled in the landmark *Diamond v. Chakrabarty* decision that a genetically engineered microorganism that had been designed for clearing up oil spills could be patented in the same way as a nonliving invention. The Court justified its decision with the understanding that patentable subject matter was "anything under the sun that is made by man" (*Diamond v. Chakrabarty, 447 U.S. 303*, quoted in Hayden 2003, p. 26; Rabinow 1996a, pp. 131–32). The ruling was a harbinger of a new kind of property thinking informing science and technology in particular and other domains more generally. Biotechnology and its property claims began to flourish as an outcome of this ruling. How have these property contests been implicated with notions of personhood and social relations? In a landmark decision a decade later, *Moore v. Regents of California* decided that a cell line deriving from John Moore's spleen tissue was not his property but that of the university scientists who created it in the laboratory. In a related manner, the ability to copy artistic and scholarly creations through the use of digital technologies has expanded exponentially, engendering recurrent debates about the boundaries of ownership. Most recently, Google's program to digitize millions of books has raised not only legal issues about copyright but also questions about its power to control access to information about persons and their social relations (this concern is of course applicable to all Web-based activity). The company "may be able to aggregate data about your reading, email, consumption, housing, travel, employment, and many other

activities" (Darnton 2009, p. 3). Whose information and intellectual property is this: the person who created it through the conduct of his or her social relations or a corporation that created it through their powerful technology? Contests about the boundary between what can be owned by particular individuals, large or small, in such a case, has accelerated considerably (see Maurer & Schwab 2006).

With the fall of the Berlin Wall and the collapse of the Soviet Union anthropologists were confronted with a plethora of new, hybrid property regimes (see Benda-Beckmann et al. 2006; Humphrey 2002; Verdery 2004, 2003, 1998). Not only were there new ways of owning former collective property but also new ways of knowing property and new ways to be a person thereby (Anderson 1998; Humphrey 2002, pt. III; see also Nadasdy 2003). The volume edited by Hann (1998) was planned and published several years after these momentous changes highlighting the transformative power of neoliberalism. The volume signaled a renewed interest in property, a category that had preoccupied previous generations of anthropologists from different theoretical persuasions (Bloch 1975, Gluckman 1965, Goody 1962, Gudeman 1986, Hirschon 1986, Leach 1961, Malinowski 1935; see also Riles 2004). There has also been an upsurge of interest in cultural and intellectual property as the societies studied by anthropologists have been the site of contests regarding products of their cultural life and their usable knowledge (for reviews, see Brown 2003, Strathern 2006). Is the name Crazy Horse, for example, the (cultural) property of the Sioux peoples among whom he was a nineteenth century Lakota statesman or the trademark and intellectual property of a U.S.-based malt liquor manufacturer that has sold the product since 1992 (Brown 2003, pp. 77–78; Coombe 1998, pp. 199–204)? With regard to different but related property contests, Strathern (1996, p. 30) makes the important general point that "[o]wnership gathers things momentarily to a point by locating them in the owner [whether a corporation, culture or individual author or inventor], halting endless dissemination, effecting an identity." The gathering and halting are often less than simple matters. They involve not only the attribution of property to an owner, but also the fabrication of distinct persons and things. Is Crazy Horse a thing available for creative innovation or a person with distinct rights in law, or somehow both?

The new ideology in conjunction with the new technologies of information and communication facilitated extensive financial liberalization. The management of global economic relations was now the priority in contrast to the previous priority given to national markets and national development. This change in priority has led, among other matters, to what Maurer (2004) refers to as cyberspatial properties (Internet banking products, electronic commerce transactions, and web-based offshore finance services): These properties challenge the moral claims of property because of the way by which they call into question regulatory frameworks and state jurisdiction. The enormous expansion of resource extraction throughout the global South and the proliferation of land and property contests in its wake are further evidence of the priority given to global economic connections (see Sawyer 2004, Tsing 2005). The regulation of this new economic regime is by a host of multilaterals such as the International Monetary Fund (IMF), the World Bank, and the World Trade Organization (WTO) (see Miller 1998). The WTO, in particular, has rules about freedom in investment and trade as well as on intellectual property protection that are binding on all members.

THE FICTIONS OF PERSONS AND THINGS: BIOTECHNOLOGY, INFORMATION, AND INTELLECTUAL PROPERTY CLAIMS

In their recent volume, Verdery & Humphrey (2004) draw on Pocock (1985) and Tully (1993), historians of political thought, among others, to historically contextualize the conceptual work of property in the Euro-American setting and to understand the powerful influence it has exerted internationally. One of the issues their contributors and they address is what makes a thing property? Anthropologists have become increasingly preoccupied with this question as only things can be property, although "[p]roperty law... is surrounded by assumptions that act out the idea that one can have property in persons, or aspects of persons, even though the law is built on its denial" (Strathern 2005, p. 136). The legal scholar Radin (1993, p. 17) states that personhood, our personal endowments, and capacities associated with the body cannot be described as property. At the same time, though, as things such as blood and organs are construed as severable fungible commodities, it becomes increasingly difficult to object to these being considered marketable property. Nowadays, the legal notion of self-ownership is the arena in which property in persons is suggested, whereas legal thinkers once took this "as the radical divide that separated persons from things . . . Insofar as persons (as subjects) own themselves, no one else can own them (as objects)" (Strathern 2005, p. 136). What makes a thing property, then, of course depends on what a thing is and what property is. Is property a relation, a bundle of rights, a concept that does particular kinds of work? Is it all three? As Humphrey & Verdery (2004, pp. 6–7) suggest, defining property is an illusive enterprise because conceptions of property alter as notions of persons and things change, in relation to both ideological and technological transformations. As has been debated by anthropologists, persons, things, and property are local notions that do not exist everywhere as they do in standard Euro-American property theory or everyday understandings (see Strathern 1988).

The recent eruption of intellectual property claims is particular evidence of the historical shift in what counts as property and what ideological work the concept does (Humphrey & Verdery 2004, p. 6). Ideas can be property, intellectual property, but only if they assume a material form (such as a book, musical score, or technical artifact) and where originality can be demonstrated. In an argument of significance to recent anthropological debates in this area, the legal scholar Barron notes: "[I]n law, originality is... the description of a causal relationship between a person and a thing: to say that a work is original in law is to say nothing more than this it originates from [can be attributed to] its creator" (Barron 1998, p. 56). Specifying DNA in itself is not subject to claims of originality or creativity. However, "combining sequenced DNA to form new databases of information" is construed as creative and these databases are often subject to copyright (Parry 2004, p. 43). As Parry (2004, pp. 44–45) suggests, echoing Strathern (2005) above, as such things are transformed into information it becomes ever easier to sustain the fiction that persons cannot be property by continually subverting this distinction (see Pottage 2004, p. 34).

Information, then, especially digitized information, has become a new kind of thing and thus potentially property (or derivatives, following Parry 2004). In a related manner, things not previously conceptualized as property, such as pollution (e.g., sulfur dioxide emissions traded on a futures market) or parts of the body, including ova and organs, have now been transformed into things that can be owned (see Kirsch 2004, Konrad 2005, Sharp 2006). Information, in particular, is part of numerous domains: it "can be 'about' anything... which is the reason it can connect entities such as humans, transgenic mice, and digital organisms" (Helmreich 2001, p. 136). In this respect, it is not unlike the relation, a central analytical construct in anthropology, which can be applied to any order of connection (Strathern 2005). As such, new kinds of information lead to new kinds of relations. Consider the case of genetic information: "Intensive research over the past decades has revealed what practitioners of the new genetics would take as the elementary structures of the universe within and the geography of the genome. Each organism, in their language, possesses a 'genome' that contains instructions necessary for constructing and maintaining a living example of that organism... 'Genes' are seen as the most important part of

the genome thanks to the biological information they contain" (Palsson 2007, p. 8). So, for example, legal instruments define genetic information as the property of those to whom it pertains. Specific information about the human genome, in turn, creates potential relations with family and kin so that they are or not (as the case may be) in the know. At the same time, "... the very idea that people should claim property in genetic information is vigorously opposed by sections of the biotechnology industry" as they see the imposition of ownership on genetic information as inhibiting research and as interfering with profits (Strathern 2005, pp. 49, 74–75; Rapp et al. 2001). In other ways, though, the biotechnology industry vigorously polices its intellectual property claims (see Crook 2000). Examples from agricultural biotechnology are the Monsanto companies so-called Terminator Seed and the Mexican enola bean (Hayden 2003, pp. 223–24, 254 n.3). The former is an engineered seed that has been designed to produce infertile offspring so that the investment of the company is protected. This property forces farmers to buy their seeds from the company each year. The latter refers to a patent taken out on the mayacoba, a yellow bean that is widely used in northern Mexico. The patent was taken out on the renamed enola bean after several generations had been grown in the United States and it was claimed to have a unique yellow color compared to other beans regularly found in the country of origin. The patent holder then sued distributors of the bean from northern Mexico from where it originated, claiming they had infringed his patent. The second case, in particular, raises the whole issue about the propriety of property where the thing in question is a widespread cultural staple.

The debates around research on the human genome are analogous to the contested claims surrounding the enola bean. In the early days of the Human Genome Project, critics of biotechnology companies suggested that DNA was being patented. The critics failed to give patent its technical interpretation: that is, the rights to prevent others from exploiting the assay kits that derived from DNA analysis, or the programs with which DNA was identified. Instead, the critics promoted the idea that what was happening were claims over the substance, i.e., DNA itself. This was the case in Iceland where critics of deCODE Genetics promoted the idea that the state and commercial company were selling Icelandic DNA (Palsson & Rabinow 1999, p. 15; see Hoyer 2002). The rhetoric of an encroachment on commons— a sense that property was being taken away— raised the question of who created the patented entities. The ordinary view came to assume that persons were being patented like things. As a result of these contests, the human genome is now widely conceived as a common human creation and resource, whereas before the legal claims were made, it would not have entered commonplace perceptions in this way (Hirsch 2004, p. 179). People in the United States, Britain, or elsewhere (see Simpson 2007; see Bamford 2007) may think of their genome as their genetic inheritance (part of the person). Simultaneously, aspects of the genome are subject to property (as a thing)—such a Craig Venter's declaration to map the human genome as a commercial venture, but which did not materialize in the way planned (Palsson 2007, pp. 153–54).

A different way of viewing the idea of a common resource (or culture) transformed into individual property (a patented invention) is disclosed by anthropological research into biotechnological innovations. Consider the case of PCR (polymerase chain reaction), the exemplary biotechnology invention, documented in the ethnography by Rabinow (1996a; see also Hirsch 2004, p. 183). PCR transformed molecular biology as through its use genetic material can be quickly identified and manipulated for experimentation. Rabinow's study interrogates the questions of who invented PCR: when did this new property form emerge? PCR emerged not only through the work (conceptual and manual) of different persons in their distinctive domains, but also through the negotiations between domains (Rabinow 1996a, pp. 111–33). Was the inventor the scientist who perceived the possibility, the technician who

made it operate, or the group that transformed it subsequently into a commercially viable technology? Whereas the boundaries between the conceptual, technical, and experimental are significant in the organizational matrix of a scientific establishment (such as Cetus Corporation where Rabinow conducted his study), they become obscure when one attempts to assign an advent point for a new form such as PCR. In other words, the new form appears to comprise the multiple relations and negotiations that brought it about. When Rabinow (1996a, p. 8) asked a former Cetus scientist, "Who invented PCR?", he was told, "Conception, development, and application are all scientific issues— invention is a question for the patent lawyers."

CULTURE, LAND, AND INTANGIBLE HERITAGE

Because individuals—whether persons, universities, or corporations—are deemed the originators of new property forms in conventional property law, the creations of cultures have, until recently, been perceived as outside property claims (see Sykes 2005, pp. 187–204). The question of who owns native culture has arisen in these neoliberal times. Brown (2003, pp. 44–55) analyzes the high-profile case of Johnny Bulun Bulun and George Milpurrurru, a painter and a senior clan official from Arnhem Land, respectively, who in the late 1990s brought a lawsuit against a firm that had used unauthorized images of the artist's work. Brown notes that the art of Australian Aboriginals among other native peoples was understood as uncopyrightable because their creations were folkloric and did not demonstrate the originality deemed necessary by copyright. In such cases, the creator was deemed by outsiders, such as R&T Textiles Pty Ltd, to be a culture and hence lacked the causal relation between individual creator and individual creation, described by legal scholars such as Barron (1998). The plaintiffs insisted that the case was about land as much as it was about copyright, stressing "the supposedly unbreakable link between land tenure and traditional art" (Brown 2003, p. 47). The art is inseparable from the land that is the source of persons and knowledge that makes the art as a thing possible in the first place. Following on from the Mabo decision earlier in the decade (*Mabo and Others v. Queensland*, see Brown 2003, pp. 46–47), land was no longer assumed to be unoccupied and under the power of the Crown (see Povinelli 2004, pp. 189–92). Rather, native title was established by one criterion: that of demonstrating on-going connection to the land. The legal and political concern about the Bulun Bulun case in Australia more generally was that it could "usher in a new era in which traditional painting was used as evidence in land-claims litigation" (Brown 2003, p. 48; see Morphy 1991; Myers 2005).

As this case and others from Australia and North and Central America documented by Brown (2003) and the case of Papua New Guinea cited at the beginning of the article indicate, longstanding legal instruments for dealing with intellectual property claims such as copyright, patent, and trademarks have taken on a new prominence, especially in everyday discourse and understandings (see Whimp & Busse 2000). This heightened prominence is related to both the expanded number of claims made in the name of intellectual property and the proliferation of contexts that are subject to intellectual property claims (see Coombe 1998). This is evident most recently in the United Nations Educational, Scientific, and Cultural Organization (UNESCO)-inspired conference about intangible heritage, called appropriately *Sharing Culture*, (**http://sharing. cultures2009.greenlines-institute.org/**). But if native cultures are perceived as tightly integrated wholes, then any protection proposed for one aspect of a culture will negatively affect other aspects of the culture. It is this outlook and the proliferating number of contests concerning infringements of native cultures that account for the drafting of the UN document *Protection of the Heritage of Indigenous People* (or the Daes Report after the Greek jurist who issued the document) published in 1997. The notion of Total Heritage Protection is how this is dubbed by Brown (2003,

pp. 209–18) in his critical analysis, where he states: "In the name of defending indigenous traditions, [the UN document] forces the elusive qualities of entire civilizations—everything from attitudes and bodily postures to agricultural techniques—into ready-made legal categories, among which 'heritage' and 'culture' are only the most far-reaching. In the interest of promoting diversity, Total Heritage Protection imposes procedural norms that have the paradoxical effect of flattening cultural differences" (Brown 2003, pp, 217–18). The goal of such heritage protection is to protect people now known as indigenous, a new kind of person and people that has emerged out of proprietary contests over the past two decades (see Posey 1996; see Kuper 2003).

Although concepts of property are essential to Euro-American self-understandings, this is not necessarily the case more generally: It is a contested issue, for instance, whether forms of inclusive and exclusive property are found in places such as Melanesia (see Carrier 1998, Strathern 1998, Bainton 2009). Deciphering the genome enabled the creation of new potential forms of property. It also created new potential ways for people to define themselves (see Hacking 2006). In a similar way, the concept of owning land, something that has never been owned before is a potentially new concept to peoples across the globe. In places such as Papua New Guinea or other areas of the southwest Pacific, becoming a landowner and the ideology of landownership is a novel and contested enterprise. Land as property in these contexts effects potentially new boundaries and relations between persons and things.

In the late 1990s, Ernst (1999) coined the term entification to describe the new relation Melanesian peoples had to develop with their land as their land was transformed into property for resource extraction and they were transformed into (customary) landowners as a result (see Filer 1997). Ernst's term refers to "the process of making 'entities' or things from what have been contingent categories" (Ernst 1999, p. 89). Conventionally, Melanesians did not treat their land as property, as individually owned (see Hogbin & Lawrence 1967, Lamour 1991) in the way common among Euro-Americans, for example. With the advent and great expansion of resource extraction throughout the region, Melanesians began to adopt a new form of property but in a way fraught with conflict and continual dispute. As Filer (1997) notes for the Papua New Guinea context: "[W]e can propose that public identification of the mass of Papua New Guineans as customary landowners is a phenomenon which owes a good deal to the mineral prospecting boom of the early 1980s" (see Filer et al. 2000; Tsing 2005, pp. 66–68). Whereas Western legal techniques assume that land as property can be routinely defined, where the boundary between persons and things can be effectively fabricated, Melanesian conceptions of the relations of persons and things further question this assumption and create new ways of imaging property. This is based less on exclusive claims of ownership than on networks of transactions (see Kalinoe & Leach 2001, Hirsch & Strathern 2004; see also Latour 1993).

A parallel case highlights another dimension of the new, complex, and contested connections between land and property that returns to some of the issues about heritage protection mentioned above. In this instance, it is a conflict between land as a site of heritage and cultural property and land as a site of landownership and potential resource extraction. The Kokoda Track (or Trail) was the place of an important battle during World War II between Australians, Papua New Guineans, and the Japanese, which is said in Australian folk traditions to have "turned the fortunes of the Japanese in the Pacific" (see Nelson 2003, 2007). The track is on land of the Koiari- and Orokaiva-speaking peoples. Over the decades since the war, the track has become a trekking destination for many Australians seeking to retrace the steps of the heroic Australian soldiers or diggers (and local fuzzy wuzzy angels, as they were known). In fact, for many it has become a site of pilgrimage and a journey of self-discovery (Nelson 2007, p. 77): a part of Australian heritage and

cultural property, eclipsing the previous place of Gallipoli and the Anzac legend from World War I (Kapferer 1988, pp. 121–47). Evidence of this importance and prominence can be gauged by the number of books and articles written about Kokoda in the past decade (e.g., FitzSimons 2005, Lindsay 2002) and the fact that it was the subject of major Australian film in 2006 (*Kokoda—39th Batallion*).

However, also in 2006 an Australian mining company found significant deposits of copper and gold in the area of the track and sought to exploit them. The mining company had the support of many of the local people. They see the mining operations as a better road to development than that offered by the ecotourism of the trekkers, although it is clear that mining operations are inevitably fraught with ecological and social problems (see Kirsch 2006). Simultaneously, there was much Australian opposition including that from the then-leader of the opposition, Kevin Rudd. This, in turn, prompted local protests and in early 2008 local people blocked the track and held placards, one reading "Rudd wants fuzzy wuzzy angels to live in perpetual poverty" (*The Australian* 2008). Later in 2008, after much political contest the mining plans were blocked by the Papua New Guinea Mining Minister, while Papua New Guinea and Australia had already sought in 2006 to have the area listed as a World Heritage Site, further ensuring that it could not be mined in the future. The case raises the question of whose land and property this is. It is clearly within the territorial boundaries of Papua New Guinea, and that of the local people. But many Australians argue that the land and region more generally was saved by heroic actions of the diggers and the fuzzy wuzzy angels assisting them. They perceive their personhood and national heritage bound up with this area in a way fundamentally different from that of many of the local landowners. It appears in this particular case that the Australian government could assert its powerful influence in the region to protect this sign of its national identity. As Brown (2003, p. 15) notes: "Settler societies such as the United States and Australia have long used monuments and other material expressions of heritage to unify their ethnically diverse populations" (see Coombe 1998, pp. 139–40; Lowenthal 1998; Rowlands 2004). In this case, the interests of the local community of landowners were subordinated to a national heritage politics and discourse of personal actualization. The views of the powerful were that the area should be part of Papua New Guinea (and by implication Australian) cultural property and not simply the property of a local community of customary landowners (Hirsch 2008; see van Meijl 2009).

WHERE ARE THE LOCAL BENEFACTORS: BIOPROSPECTING OR BIOPIRACY?

The image of a local community associated with their natural resources figures centrally in neoliberal framings of property relations. This is especially evident in bioprospecting, a distinctive offspring of neoliberalism, which is, in turn, closely connected with the UN-sponsored Convention on Biological Diversity (CBD), which became effective in 1993. The objectives of the Convention, spelled out in Article 1, are as follows:

> . . . the conservation of biological diversity, the sustainable use of its components and the fair and equitable sharing of the benefits arising out of the utilization of genetic resources, including by appropriate access to genetic resources and by appropriate transfer of relevant technologies, taking into account all rights over those resources and to technologies, and by appropriate funding.

An anthropological literature since the 1990s has emerged from studies of this new way of organizing property claims (see Brush 1999, Brush & Stabinsky 1996). Bioprospecting seeks to realize the goals of the CBD by conserving nature or wilderness, especially in the nations of the South, while transforming plant material into information and thus into potentially valuable patents and drug therapies: a way to con-

serve biodiversity while simultaneously sharing the benefits of patented discoveries with local stakeholders, the benefit-recipients. The sharing with benefit-recipients takes the form of "intellectual property-modelled claims to compensation" (Hayden 2003, p. 128). The CBD "reinforces the notion that [a neoliberal vision of nature] should be treated effectively, as biomass for biotech" (Hayden 2003, p. 63). The benefits derived from nature are shared, in principle, by the interested parties in this arrangement: The interested parties for the most part are pharmaceutical industries, universities, and scientists from the global North, on the one hand, and indigenous, local people from the global South in places like Mexico or Peru, on the other (see Greene 2004). However, there is a fundamental tension at the heart of these interests not unlike that expressed at Kokoda (discussed above), where it was shown that local landowner interests are in conflict with national ideologies and multilateral agreements (i.e., the World Heritage status of UNESCO). In the case of bioprospecting, to what extent do existing multilateral agreements conflict and run counter to the ideas contained in the CBD? For instance, Trade Related Aspects of Intellectual Property Rights (TRIPS) [which is part of GATT (Global Agreement on Tariffs and Trade) and the WTO] require intellectual property protection that is markedly different from that of the CBD. As Hayden (2003, p. 95) argues:

> TRIPS requires that member states recognize patents on microorganisms and the biological processes used to produce them; at the same time, it holds no requirement for benefit-sharing or even obtaining consent when companies patent compounds based on natural products from nations such as Mexico. And unlike the CBD, if member nations do not sign TRIPS, they are subject to trade sanctions.

In this way, nations of the global South are being forced to comply with the intellectual property regime of TRIPS instead of the redistributive mechanisms of the CBD. Regardless of these potential conflicts, bioprospecting can only operate if the scientists are able to properly identify the benefit-recipients that come with their plants (Hayden 2003, p. 128). This identification is especially a problem when, for example, the plant material collected derives from a place with no discernible locals, such as the sides of roads: "[P]lant ecologists understand roads in general as crucial to the spread of "exotic" species, serving as incredibly effective moving corridors along which plants travel with great efficiency" (Hayden 2003, p. 175). The potential for property to be realized requires that the thing being utilized is the managed resource of a person or community at the local level. When it comes to roadside flora, it is virtually impossible to specify the individual stakeholders of the local plant life. Much of the flora used in the collections made also derives from markets and in this case "(most) obligations end when the money changes hands" (Hayden 2003, p. 144). In short, the plant collections made in the name of bioprospecting have always been multiply authored and generally do not conform to the Western presupposition that individual local benefactors can be routinely specified in order that the proceeds from intellectual property can be shared. As with the problem of landownership throughout the southwest Pacific or the case of medical and scientific discoveries and authorship, the resources transformed into different forms of property are never unentangled; they can never be straightforwardly located in a local community as such communities are more the product of Euro-American idealizations (see Anderson 2008, McSherry 2001; see Thomas 1991).

More generally, though, bioprospecting raises the specter of biopiracy—what critics of bioprospecting perceive as a version of (old) colonialist forms of resource extraction and unequal exchange (see Conklin 2002). The biopiracy discourse is also associated with a new kind of person mentioned above, that of the indigenous person or peoples (see Dove 2006). Shortly after the Human Genome Diversity Project was meant to begin in 1994, the World Council of Indigenous Peoples dubbed

it the "Vampire Project" (Palsson 2007, p. 158). However, as Brown (2003, p. 215) reminds us, who is indigenous and the boundaries of the indigenous are similarly difficult to specify, like that of property ownership itself. He describes a North American example where a law defines Indians and Alaska Natives as only those people registered as members of a tribe or community: "One result is that people who are clearly Indians, but lack the requisite tribal membership, are prevented from identifying their [arts and crafts] work as Native American."

CONCLUSION

Property as Euro-Americans conventionally understand it, whether intellectual, cultural, or of more conventional things such as land, requires a boundary to be formed, a network of relations to be cut, and the claims of other persons to be severed so that a singular identity can be effected (Strathern 1996). To do so requires the assertion of law as much as power. Property entails a thing created; in the case of intellectual property, a person is attributed as creator and potential owner. The relation between created and creator requires that the competing claims of others are bounded off. But in all forms of property the boundary is often contested, especially when the specification of persons and things derive from very different presuppositions about origins, relations, and creativity. As people contest or accommodate these assertions of property, entailing distinct fabrications of persons and things, there emerge new ways to be a person or collective of persons. As I indicated at the beginning of this article, 300 years ago the modern author emerged through struggles with printers and booksellers to institute copyright over the authorial text (Rose 1993). In more recent times, there has emerged directly or indirectly, through contests around property claims, indigenous people, new forms of landowners, kinds of people formed around a genetic risk factor, what Rabinow (1996b; see Hacking 2006) labeled as a form of biosociality, among others. As property claims expand and intensify in these uncertain neoliberal times, the fabrication of persons and things will be increasingly contested. The old Euro-American certainties about the boundaries of persons and things (as much as the boundaries of the social and biological or of nature and culture) will continue to decompose and recompose in combination with the way in which these certainties are embedded in technological innovations, such as the human genome or digitized information (Strathern 2005). Or the way local communities around the world demonstrate the limited applicability of these distinctions while continuing to raise questions about the appropriateness of dividing up diverse resources (e.g., cultural or intellectual) according to ideas of property. As the neoliberal emphasis on the expansion of property continues apace, so too do the contests about the division of persons and things that property theory both presupposes and, necessarily, continually subverts.

DISCLOSURE STATEMENT

The author is not aware of any affiliations, memberships, funding, or financial holdings that might be perceived as affecting the objectivity of this review.

ACKNOWLEDGMENTS

I thank Karen Richards for her very helpful comments on a draft of this article.

LITERATURE CITED

Anderson D. 1998. Property as a way of knowing on Evenki lands in Arctic Siberia. See Hann 1998, pp. 64–84

Anderson W. 2008. *The Collectors of Lost Souls: Turning Kuru Scientists into Whitemen*. Baltimore: Johns Hopkins Univ. Press

Australian. 2008. Locals close Kokoda in mine protests. *The Australian* Feb. 7

Bainton N. 2009. Keeping the network out of view: mining, distinctions and exclusion in Melanesia. *Oceania* 79:1

Bamford S. 2007. *Biology Unmoored: Melanesian Reflections on Life and Biotechnology*. Berkeley: Univ. Calif. Press

Barron A. 1998. No other law? Authority, property and aboriginal art. In *Intellectual Property and Ethics*, ed. L Bently, S Maniatis. London: Sweet & Maxwell

Benda-Beckmann K, Benda-Beckmann F, Wiber M, eds. 2006. *Changing Property of Properties*. Oxford, UK: Berghahn

Bloch M. 1975. Property and the end of affinity. In *Marxist Analysis in Social Anthropology*, ed. M Bloch, pp. 203–28. London: Malaby Press

Brown M. 2003. *Who Owns Native Culture?* Cambridge, MA: Harvard Univ. Press

Brush S. 1999. Bioprospecting in the public domain. *Cult. Anthropol.* 14:535–55

Brush S, Stabinsky D. 1996. *Valuing Local Knowledge: Indigenous Peoples and Intellectual Property Rights*. Washington, DC: Island Press

Carrier J. 1998. Property and social relations in Melanesian anthropology. See Hann 1998, pp. 85–103

Carrier J, Miller D, eds. 1998. *Virtualism: A New Political Economy*. Oxford, UK: Berg

Coombe R. 1998. *The Cultural Life of Intellectual Properties: Authorship, Appropriation, and the Law*. Durham, NC: Duke Univ. Press

Conklin B. 2002. Shamans versus pirates in the Amazonian treasure chest. *Am. Anthropol.* 104:1050–61

Crook T. 2000. Length matters: a note on the GM debate. *Anthropol. Today* 16:8–11

Darnton R. 2009. Google and the new digital future. *NY Rev. Books*, Dec. 19:3–4

Demian M. 2004. Seeing, knowing, owning: property claims as revelatory acts. See Hirsch & Strathern 2004, pp. 60–82

Dove M. 2006. Indigenous people and environmental politics. *Annu. Rev. Anthropol.* 35:191–208

Ernst T. 1999. Land, stories and resources: discourse and entification in Onabasulu modernity. *Am. Anthropol.* 101:88–97

Escobar A. 1994. *Encountering Development: The Making and Unmaking of the Third World.* Princeton, NJ: Princeton Univ. Press

Ferguson J. 1994. *The Anti-politics Machine: Development, Depoliticization and Bureaucratic Power in Lesotho.* Minneapolis: Univ. Minn. Press

Filer C. 1997. Compensation, rent and power in Papua New Guinea. In *Compensation for Resource Development in Papua New Guinea*, ed. S Toft, pp. 156–89. Boroko, PNG: Law Reform Comm. (Monogr. 6); Canberra, Aust.: Aust. Natl. Univ. Natl. Cent. Dev. Stud. (Pac. Policy Pap. 24)

Filer C, Henton D, Jackson R. 2000. *Landowner Compensation in Papua New Guinea's Mining and Petroleum Sectors.* Port Moresby, P.N.G.: PNG Chamber Mines Petrol.

FitzSimons P. 2004. *Kokoda.* Sydney: Hodder Headline

Gluckman M. 1965. *Politics, Law and Ritual in Tribal Society.* Oxford: Basil Blackwell

Goody J. 1962. *Death, Property and the Ancestors: A Study of the Mortuary Customs of the Lodagaa of West Africa.* Stanford, CA: Stanford Univ. Press

Greene S. 2004. Indigenous people incorporated? Culture as politics, culture as property in pharmaceutical bioprospecting. *Curr. Anthropol.* 45:211–37

Gudeman S. 1986. *Economics as Culture.* London: Routledge

Hacking I. 2006. Genetics, biosocial groups and the future of identity. *Daedalus* Sept.:81–95

Hann C, ed. 1998. *Property Relations: Renewing the Anthropological Tradition.* Cambridge, UK: Cambridge Univ. Press

Harvey D. 2005. *A Brief History of Neoliberalism.* Oxford, UK: Oxford Univ. Press

Hayden C. 2003. *When Nature Goes Public: The Making and Unmaking of Bioprospecting in Mexico.* Princeton, NJ: Princeton Univ. Press

Helmreich S. 2001. Transsubstantiating fatherhood and information flow in artificial life. In *Relative Values: Reconfiguring Kinship Studies*, ed. S Franklin, S McKinnon, pp. 116–43. Durham, NJ: Duke Univ. Press

Hirsch E. 2004. Boundaries of creation: the work of credibility in science and ceremony. See Hirsch & Strathern 2004, pp. 176–92

Hirsch E. 2008. *Whose landscape and heritage? Contrasting ways of understanding the past in Papua New Guinea and Australia.* Keynote address at Glob. Heritage Semin., Aarhus Univ., 3–5 Dec.

Hirsch E, Strathern M, eds. 2004. *Transactions and Creations: Property Debates and the Stimulus of Melanesia.* Oxford, UK: Berghahn

Hirschon R. 1986. *Women and Property/Women as Property.* London: Routledge

Hogbin I, Lawrence P. 1967. *Studies in New Guinea Land Tenure.* Sydney: Sydney Univ. Press

Hoyer K. 2002. Conflicting notions of personhood in genetic research. *Anthropol. Today* 18:9–13

Humphrey C. 2002. *The Unmaking of Soviet Life: Everyday Economies After Socialism.* Ithaca, NY: Cornell Univ. Press

Humphrey C, Verdery K. 2004. Introduction: raising questions about property. See Verdery & Humphrey 2004, pp. 1–25

Kalinoe L, Leach J, eds. 2001. *Rationales of Ownership: Ethnographic Studies of Transactions and Claims to Ownership in Contemporary Papua New Guinea.* New Delhi: UBSPD

Kapferer B. 1988. *Legends of People, Myths of State: Violence, Intolerance, and Political Culture in Sri Lanka and Australia.* Washington, DC: Smithson. Inst. Press

Kenneth G. 2009. Govt to pay group K52m. *Papua New Guinea Post-Courier* Feb. 2

Kirsch S. 2004. Property limits: debates on the body, nature and culture. See Hirsch & Strathern 2004, pp. 21–39

Kirsch S. 2006. *Reverse Anthropology: Indigenous Analysis of Social and Environmental Relations in New Guinea.* Stanford, CA: Stanford Univ. Press

Konrad M. 2005. *Nameless Relations: Anonymity, Melanesia and Reproductive Gift Exchange Between British Ova Donors and Recipients.* Oxford, UK: Berghahn

Kuper A. 2003. The return of the native. *Curr. Anthropol.* 44:389–402

Lamour P, ed. 1991. *Customary Land Tenure: Registration and Decentralisation in Papua New Guinea (IASER Monogr. 29).* Boroko, P.N.G.: Natl. Res. Inst.

Latour B. 1993. *We Have Never been Modern*. Trans. C Porter. London: Harvester Wheatsheaf

Leach E. 1961. *Pul Eliya, a Village in Ceylon: A Study of Land Tenure and Kinship*. Cambridge, UK: Cambridge Univ. Press

Leenhardt M. 1979. *Do Kamo: Person and Myth in the Melanesian World*. Trans. V Crapanzano. Chicago: Univ. Chicago Press

Lindsay P. 2002. *The Spirit of Kokoda: Then and Now*. Sydney: Hardie Grant

Lowenthal D. 1998. *The Heritage Crusade and the Spoils of History*. Cambridge, UK: Cambridge Univ. Press

Malinowski B. 1935. Coral Gardens and their magic—a study of the methods of tilling the soil and of agricultural rites. In *The Trobriand Islands–Vol. 1: The Language Of Magic and Gardening*. London: Allen & Unwin

Maurer B. 2004. Cyberspatial properties: taxing questions about proprietary regimes. See Verdery & Humphrey 2004, pp. 297–318

Maurer B, Schwab G, eds. 2006. *Accelerating Possession: Global Futures of Property and Personhood*. New York: Columbia Univ. Press

Mauss M. 1985. A category of the human mind: the notion of person; the notion of self. In *The Category of the Person: Anthropology, Philosophy, History*, ed. M Carrithers, S Collins, S Lukes, pp. 1–25. Cambridge, UK: Cambridge Univ. Press

McMichael P. 1998. Development and structural adjustment. See Carrier & Miller 1998, pp. 95–116

McSherry C. 2001. *Who Owns Academic Work?: Battling for Control of Intellectual Property*. Cambridge, MA: Harvard Univ. Press

Miller D. 1998. Conclusion: a theory of virtualism. See Carrier & Miller 1998, pp. 187–216

Mirowski P, Sent E-M, eds. 2002. *Science Bought and Sold: Essays in the Economics of Science*. Chicago: Univ. Chicago Press

Morphy H. 1991. *Ancestral Connections: Art and an Aboriginal System of Knowledge*. Chicago: Univ. Chicago Press

Myers F. 2005. Some properties of culture and persons. In *Code: Collaborative Ownership and the Digital Economy*, ed. R Ghosh, pp. 45–60. Cambridge, MA: MIT Press

Nadasdy P. 2003. *Hunters and Bureaucrats: Power, Knowledge and Aboriginal-state Relations in the Southwest Yukon*. Vancouver: Univ. Br. Columbia Press

Nelson H. 2003. Kokoda: the track from history to politics. *J. Pac. Hist.* 38:109–27

Nelson H. 2007. Kokoda: and two national histories. *J. Pac. Hist.* 42:73–88

Palsson G. 2007. *Anthropology and the New Genetics*. Cambridge, UK: Cambridge Univ. Press

Palsson G, Rabinow P. 1999. The human genome project in Iceland. *Anthropol. Today* 15:14–18

Parry B. 2004. Bodily transactions: regulating a new space of flows in "bio-information." See Verdery & Humphrey 2004, pp. 29–48

Pocock J. 1985. *Virtue, Commerce, and History: Essays on Political Thought and History, Chiefly in the Eighteenth Century*. Cambridge, UK: Cambridge Univ. Press

Posey D. 1996. *Traditional Resource Rights: International Instruments for Protection and Compensation for Indigenous Peoples and Local Communities*. Cambridge, UK: Int. Union Conserv. Nat.

Pottage A. 2004. Introduction: the fabrication of persons and things. In *Law, Anthropology, and the Constitution of the Social: Making Persons and Things*, ed. A Pottage, M Mundy, pp. 1–39. Cambridge, UK: Cambridge Univ. Press

Povinelli E. 2004. At home in the violence of recognition. See Verdery & Humphrey 2004, pp. 185–206

Rabinow P. 1996a. *Making PCR: A Story of Biotechnology*. Chicago: Univ. Chicago Press

Rabinow P. 1996b. *Essays on the Anthropology of Reason*. Princeton, NJ: Princeton Univ. Press

Radin M. 1993. *Re-interpreting Property*. Chicago: Univ. Chicago Press

Rapp R, Heath D, Taussig K-S. 2001. Genealogical disease: Where hereditary abnormality, biomedical explanation, and family responsibility meet. In *Relative Values: Reconfiguring Kinship Studies*, ed. S Franklin, S McKinnon, pp. 384–409. Durham, NC: Duke Univ. Press

Riles A. 2004. Property as legal knowledge: means and ends. *J. R. Anthropol. Inst.* 10:775–95

Rose M. 1993. *Authors and Owners: The Invention of Copyright*. Cambridge, MA: Harvard Univ. Press

Rowlands M. 2004. Cultural rights and wrongs: uses of the concept of property. See Verdery & Humphrey 2004, pp. 207–28

Sawyer S. 2004. Crude properties: the sublime and slime of oil operations in the Ecudorian Amazon. See Verdery & Humphrey 2004, pp. 85–111

Sharp L. 2006. *Strange Harvest: Organ Transplants, Denatured Bodies, and the Transformed Self*. Berkeley: Univ. Calif. Press

Simpson B. 2007. On parrots and thorns: Sri Lankan perspectives on genetics, science and personhood. *Health Care Anal.* 15:41–49

Strathern M. 1988. *The Gender of the Gift: Problems with Women and Problems with Society in Melanesia*. Berkeley: Univ. Calif. Press

Strathern M. 1996. Potential property: intellectual rights and property in persons. *Soc. Anthropol.* 4:17–32

Strathern M. 1998. Divisions of interest and languages of ownership. See Hann 1998, pp. 214–32

Strathern M. 2005. *Kinship, Law and the Unexpected: Relatives Are Always a Surprise*. Cambridge, UK: Cambridge Univ. Press

Strathern M. 2006. Intellectual property and rights: an anthropological perspective. In *Handbook of Material Culture*, ed. C Tilley, W Keane, S Kücheler, M Rowlands, P Spyer, pp. 447–62. London: Sage

Sykes K. 2005. *Arguing With Anthropology: An Introduction to Critical Theories of the Gift*. London: Routledge

Thomas N. 1991. *Entangled Objects: Exchange, Material Culture, and Colonialism in the Pacific*. Cambridge, MA: Harvard Univ. Press

Tsing A. 2005. *Friction: An Ethnography of Global Connection*. Princeton, NJ: Princeton Univ. Press

Tully J. 1993. *An Approach to Political Philosophy: Locke in Contexts*. Cambridge, UK: Cambridge Univ. Press

Van Meijl T, eds. 2009. Pacific discourses about cultural heritage and its protection. *Int. J. Cult. Prop.* 16:221–370 (Spec. Iss.)

Verdery K. 1998. Property and power in Transylvania's decollectivization. See Hahn 1998, pp. 160–80

Verdery K. 2003. *The Vanishing Hectare: Property and Value in Postsocialist Transylvania*. Ithaca, NY: Cornell Univ. Press

Verdery K. 2004. The obligations of ownership: restoring rights to land in postsocialist Transylvania. See Verdery & Humpnrey 2004, pp. 139–60

Verdery K, Humphrey C, eds. 2004. *Property in Question: Value Transformations in the Global Economy*. Oxford, UK: Berg

Whimp K, Busse M, eds. 2000. *Protection of Intellectual, Biological and Cultural Property in Papua New Guinea*. Canberra, Aust.: Asia Pac. Press

Education, Religion, and Anthropology in Africa

Amy Stambach

Educational Policy Studies and Anthropology, University of Wisconsin, Madison, Wisconsin 53706; email: aestambach@wisc.edu

Annu. Rev. Anthropol. 2010. 39:361–79

First published online as a Review in Advance on June 21, 2010

The *Annual Review of Anthropology* is online at anthro.annualreviews.org

This article's doi:
10.1146/annurev.anthro.012809.105002

Key Words

Christianity, Islam, mission education, development, secular-modernity

Abstract

Taking as its starting point classic accounts of native education and culture contact, this article reviews key trends and orientations that have shaped the anthropological study of education and religion in Africa. It identifies three frames that capture the development of research chronologically from the 1930s onward: (*a*) a functionalist focus on Christian-inflected adaptive education; (*b*) applied and sociohistorical emphases on education as, respectively, an engine for driving secular change and a medium through which to shape new ritualized practices and religious beliefs; and (*c*) a more recent concentration on youth education as a key site for analyzing politicized religious identity and youths' radicalization. I argue that this trajectory of research foregrounds two phenomena that anthropology also underanalyzes: first, the close association of religious missions with the development of today's highly secularized yet religiously inflected regional and global institutions that support educational programming in Africa; and second, a marginalization of the study of Islam in Africa, which reflects a Christianized cultural legacy in anthropological studies of religion and education.

INTRODUCTION

The subject of religion and education in Africa has provoked considerable discussion among anthropologists, political scientists, sociologists, and historians alike, some of whom in recent years have examined connections between education and youths' political socialization (Bangstad 2004, Coe 2005, Fumanti 2006, Sharp 2003, Williams 2004). Others have focused on the palliative capacity of schooling to integrate religious communities into a harmonious order (Brenner 2007, Cheney 2007, Chidester 2006, Eickelman 2007, Keller 2006). Still others have examined education in the context of the rise of new and geographically dispersed religious communities (Ahmed 2008, Brouwer et al. 1996, Chande 2000, Cooper 2006, Sharkey 2008, Stambach 2010, Umar 2001).

For reasons that some of yesterday's functionalist principles remain evident in twenty-first-century development policies (including in Education for All and the Millennium Development Goals), this review focuses on the legacy of British social anthropology in the study of African missions and schools. It compares today's discussions about religion and education with those of the 1930s when anthropologists including Bronislaw Malinowski (1936), Monica Hunter (1936), Otto F. Raum (1938), and Isaac Schapera (1934) wrote about anthropology's relation to colonial education policy. The first section links arguments about the organization and function of African "indigenous education" (Fortes 1938, Hoernlé 1931, Krige 1937, Rattray 1932) to commentaries about the selective use of mission schooling to reshape social life (Dougall 1930, Eiselen 1934, Mumford 1930). The second section examines research on social conflict and African-missionary encounters, including works of anthropologists who studied education, migration, and urbanization in Africa in the mid-twentieth century (LaFontaine 1970, Mayer 1961, Musgrove 1952, Wilson 1951) and who focused, in the 1980s and 1990s, on the moral logics of Christian missions (Beidelman 1982, Comaroff & Comaroff 1997, Fabian 1983a, Pels 1999). The third section describes research on contemporary youth culture (Coe 2005, Cole & Durham 2007, Durham 2000, Ignatowski 2008, Ngwane 2001a), including anthropological demographers' accounts of health education programs (Bratton 2010, Bledsoe 1990, Johnson-Hanks 2006, Renne 2003) that prefigure some of today's analyses of faith-based social-services (Hearn 2002, Stambach 2010).

In view that the anthropological study of African missions is itself closely tied to Christianized schooling, but that this historical connection has been underemphasized in anthropologists' reflections (Bowie 2000), part of the final section addresses research on Muslim education, including the recent growth of analyses of some organizations' use of education for economic development. The article argues that one explanation for ongoing connections among religion, education, and economic development lies in recognizing that yesterday's "native education" question has become today's "Muslim concern"—not in any straightforward way, but through incremental associations. Put simply, non-Christians' economic impoverishment about which Malinowski and others wrote nearly a century ago maps partly onto today's concerns about Muslims' civic and educational underrepresentation. Popular media and academic outlets alike imply connections among religion, opportunity, and education (e.g., Africa News 2008, Lord 2008). Some see Muslims' civic underrepresentation as evidence of schools' religified norms (Hemed 1996). Others seek to resolve this problem by using education to bring excluded persons back into the main of society. However because schools in Africa are associated historically with European Christian missions, the mechanism of social inclusion and reform—education—is itself regarded by those who are excluded as sometimes a part of the problem in the first place.

Drawing on the argument that education is both an antidote to and a cause of religious-based social stratification, this review concludes with a call for more conversation between studies of Islam and studies of Christianity. It also advocates for greater awareness within anthropology of the religious forms that are culturally embedded in ostensibly secular as well as Christian and Islamic forms of schooling.

FUNCTIONALIST FOCUS ON ADAPTIVE EDUCATION

To get into the matter of how religion, education, and anthropology entwine, consider first a page from CMS (Church Mission Society) missionary J. Lewis Krapf's (1860) account, *Travels, Researches, and Missionary Labors During an Eighteen Years' Residence in Eastern Africa*. Walking from coastal Mombasa toward Mount Kilimanjaro in 1844, Krapf encountered Muslim missionaries living and working along the mountain foothills. He condemned these Arab-Muslims for enslaving Africans and hauling out elephant tusks. He criticized sheikhs for teaching "fables" (p. 107) and luring converts to Islam with food and patronage. "From [the work of these missionaries] it may be seen," Krapf declared, "how religion, politics, and trade are combined in the case of the followers of Mahomet" (p. 114). Several paragraphs later, Krapf himself combined religion, politics, and trade in his own picture of CMS work when he argued that befriending Muslim caravan leaders was important for transporting Christianity to the interior.

Fast-forward Krapf's account about 65 years to the 1925 Phelps-Stokes Commission Report on Education in Africa (Jones 1925). In the introduction, the president of the funding agency, Anson Phelps Stokes, writes that "the modern Christian missionary has been in Africa, as elsewhere, the advance agent of civilization" (p. xv), but henceforth, following the commission's advice, science not religion will guide education planning. Phelps Stokes did not mention Muslim missions; they appear to have moved off this East African landscape. Instead, he focuses exclusively on Christian missionaries as integral to European colonization. Christian agents are fundamental, Phelps Stokes suggests, less for introducing new beliefs concerning the existence of God than for their use of discipline, logic, and reason to address Africans' practical needs. Indeed, adaptive, scientific, or practical education was to become a policy centerpiece in interwar British colonial Africa.

To help develop this focus, the Phelps-Stokes Commission called on social scientists, including anthropologists, to provide information about the "Native population" (Jones 1925, pp. 140–41). Ethnological information was intended to assist in adapting European methods to local conditions and to produce a new class of vocationally skilled Africans. Yet the displacement of religion by scientific method did not happen wholly or easily: Christianity proved to be a key part of both the colonial mission and the tenets of interwar anthropology—a key point for understanding the salvational overtones of functionalism in relation to development policy.

The chief representative of functionalist anthropology to colonial administrators was Malinowski. Malinowski (1936) supported the Phelps-Stokes Commision's endorsement of adaptive education and reasoned that if only anthropologists could figure out how native education operated, anthropologists might be in a position to help Africans adjust to colonialism. Malinowski's unabashed Eurocentrism affronts today's sensibilities. But his view of adaptive education as a means to raise up Africans in preparation for independence was typical among his students and contemporaries (e.g., Hoernlé 1931, Mair 1934, Schapera 1934). Anticipating the transfer of power to Britain's created class of native authorities, Malinowksi equated Christian schooling with social development. He noted that "to give the Native unstintingly our knowledge and our Christianity" is crucial to enabling Africans to claim "full citizenship and...personal dignity" (p. 484). Like his funders, the Rockefeller and Carnegie Foundations, whose work Kuklick (1991, pp. 209–16) and Salamone (2000) document differently (see also Kuper 1983,

Phelps-Stokes Commission Report on Education in Africa: Two-volume description of schooling in Africa, written by Thomas Jesse Jones, Commission Chair, based on a fourteen-month trip across the continent

Mafeje 1976, Schumaker 2001), Malinowski seemed to recognize that imperial projects such as colonialism are forged in the instructional mode: through a combination of working on and through existing pedagogical methods and in introducing new ideas directly, including didactically through schooling.

Malinowski (1936) identified two areas in which anthropologists might inform policy. First, "the Native" might be schooled in a form of "inverted anthropology" by which Africans would learn the habits and norms of Europeans (including Europeans' propensity to preach one thing but then do otherwise, as Malinowski observed Africans observed, pp. 503–4). Second, anthropologists might help colonial educators school Africans in a manner that did not undermine aspects of traditional "family life, age-grades or chieftanships" (p. 513).

The first idea did not pan out. The anthropological study of European culture did not become a part of the colonial curriculum for Africans. But the second gained the attention of funding agencies, and many of the now-classic accounts of African education were undertaken in part with a promise to inform the decisions of colonial educators. Hunter's (1936) dissertation on culture contact between Europeans and Pondo was introduced by Jans Christian Smuts, South African Education Secretary; Raum's (1940) study of indigenous Chagga childhood included practical conclusions for policy and school organization; and Little's (1951) exploration of Mende socialization compared boys' initiation to "Western education" (see also Hoernlé 1931, Krige 1937, Mair 1934, Richards 1956). Roughly all but one of these early ethnographies—by Nadel (1942) on Nupe Muslim teachers in Bida—associated African schooling with Christian missions.

In documenting culture, most functionalists and some German ethnologists (e.g., Gutmann 1926, Richter 1912) pieced together a normative picture of indigenous life. They defined education as "the relation between consecutive generations" that possessed "characteristics of mutuality and reciprocity" (Raum 1938, p. 209). Colonial administrators used anthropology to

train African teachers and students. Dougall, for instance, an administrator with a Jeanes School in Kenya, argued that teachers should draw on "whatever of native custom or idea is capable of use and improvement" (Dougall 1930, p. 54), and Tanganyika Superintendent of Education W. Bryant Mumford, who pursued a PhD at the University of Toronto while serving in the colonial office, conducted his own ethnological studies (1930) on grounds that his research could inform his practice.

As suggested by this emphasis on indigenous culture and change, functionalists wrote about precontact Africa and about changes wrought by missionaries but said little about a history of Muslim presence. Raum (1938), for instance, reminded readers of the presence of a "third-generation of Christian families" (p. 218) but said nothing of Muslims who predated Christians and remained present. And Malinowski (1936), writing about his extended research trip to Raum's field site on Mount Kilimanjaro, reported that

> one of the symptoms which shocked me was the fact that everywhere there existed this profound rift between the Christian and non-Christian section of every tribe. At a dance there would be a group of people standing aside, looking on with keen interest and yet contemptuous, with envy and yet with a show of superiority—these were the Christians....On the social side [this rift] means that a modernized African child develops a contempt for his African peers. (pp. 497–98)

Yet Malinowski was quiet on the subject of the Wanyika and Wakamba descendents whose previous generation Krapf had described as "fanatic" and "heathen" Mohamedans (p. 103). Nor did Malinowski's contemporaries widely document the patterns of Islamization and religious experiences among Muslims. Only relatively recently have these experiences been analyzed by historians (e.g., Chande 2000, Levtzion 2000, Robinson 2000). Instead, British functionalist anthropologists and their colonial administrator colleagues—including Dougall, Musgrove, Mumford, and Jackson—stressed the importance of blending African beliefs and practices with Christian education.

Another way of putting this is to say that functionalist anthropologists associated a liberal-secular kind of Christianity with both the education and the anthropological study of "native" Africans. They wove analysis of social activity with analysis of Africans' sense of changing identity. In so doing, functionalists' work fluctuated between studying indigenous institutions (their primary focus) and describing social change. Focusing on the drivers of education rendered problematic a straightforward idea of separation between religion and schooling. Analyzing the beliefs and practices developed by a modernized African child made it difficult to secure a clear distinction between religious identity and mode of schooling, including at times those of anthropologists. Malinowski (1936), for instance, described "the work of such bodies as the Universities' Mission" as "profess[ing] and even practis[ing] the enlightened anthropological outlook" of social science liberalism (p. 495). In an amazing maneuver of professional reflexivity, the likes of which would not be widely discussed until two or three generations later, Malinowski and contemporaries acknowledged that anthropologists' own education and mission in Africa shared enlightenment tenets with both missionaries and administrators and, in an adapted form with Africans. They presented anthropological understanding of the Other as a means for knowing how best to modify western schooling so that this form of education could be grafted onto, and used selectively to change, African indigenous forms.

Malinowski clearly made this point about the adaptation and fusion of European forms to African schooling in 1934 when he said to his New Education Fellowship audience in South Africa, at which John Dewey was present, "African education lives in family life, in the structure of kinship and community .... European schooling and African education have to be harmonized and carried on simultaneously, with conscious direction and

adjustment" (Malinowski 1936, p. 514; see also Johnson 1943, pp. 630–31). It was precisely this form of adapted schooling that the next generation of anthropologists questioned and sought to change; yet they were less critical of policy makers' instrumental use of anthropology than was their subsequent generation, which by the early twenty-first century sought to unpack the connected categories of religion and secularity and of missionization and development policy.

APPLIED AND SOCIOHISTORICAL EMPHASES ON CHANGE AND ENCOUNTER

To forward this discussion about African missions and education to the second half of the twentieth century, consider that two largely unintersecting lines of analysis emerged, both from functionalist anthropology: applied and historical-dialectical strands. Both emphasized social change and cultural encounter, and both focused on secular modernity.

Applied anthropological studies of education figured Africa as a cold war province for staving off the expansion of communism (Camilleri 1986, p. iii; Malassis 1976). This ideological and instrumental approach developed in the later days of what the British Colonial Office referred to as the process of "devolution" of the administration of African governments to Africans. Applied studies of education coincided with a new carving up of Africa by Western-European and North American governments seeking the cooperation of Africans in the control of capital markets. Speaking at a British Colonial Office conference on African education in 1952, Margaret Read, a graduate of the London School of Economics, reported that "An American of shrewd political insight said to me after his recent visits to Africa that he thought the ultimate pivotal stability of the free world lies in Africa" (Read 1955, p. 116). Read headed the Department of Education in Tropical Areas (formerly the Colonial Department) at the London University Institute of Education. A student of Malinowski, she had written her dissertation

UNESCO: a UN specialized agency composed of 193 member states dedicated to using education, science, and cultural exchange to promote development and reduce poverty

on Ngoni education in Malawi (Read 1956). She remarked that the American's comment "sounds perhaps like a bit of grandiose journalism" but that it was a "sober and considered opinion, based...partly on the nature of the democratic institutions introduced particularly in British Africa" (p. 116).

Among these institutions Read included the then-recently established (in 1945) United Nations specialized agency UNESCO (United Nations Education, Scientific, and Cultural Organization), which, along with philanthropic and governmental agencies located primarily in the United States, Britain, and France, was keen to educate a mass cadre of vocationally oriented, technically skilled Africans. UNESCO's International Bureau of Education (IBE) portrayed this citizenry as western, democratic, and pluralistic. It did so all in a way that sought to preclude the fall of soon-to-be-self-governing states to Soviet hands. "The education systems of those countries where cultural confrontations or social adaptation of colonial origin are still familiar," wrote an unnamed author with the Bureau, "could have a very unpredictable effect" on citizenries' directions for the future.

To counterbalance this effect, the IBE supported studies that applied anthropological knowledge to the development of educational outcomes. Camilleri's little known but perceptive study is a case in point. It "identifies the educational situations in which the failure to take the cultural dimension into account can have negative effects" (publisher's description), and it evinces liberal institutions' elision of religion with western culture and secular humanism. Writing about Moroccan schooling and other "educational problems," Camilleri (1986) contrasted "theocentrically oriented" Arabic texts with the "humanistic ideology" of "Westernized" education (pp. 117–18). He religified Arabic curricula yet secularized western forms, and in so doing (to paraphrase Madan 1987, p. 754) prescribed a transfer of modern secularism without regard to the idea that anthropology itself emerged from a dialectic of modern science and (at least in

part) Protestantism. The assumption that the individual is responsible for his or her own salvation, including enlightenment through education, is very much a modernist idea, one that, like the idea that school characteristics affect implementation, is well represented in comparative studies of education and in many international education statements and policies (e.g., USAID 2004, World Bank 2008).

One implication of the imbrication of Christianity, education, and anthropology in post–World War II and postcolonial Africa is that religion could appear to fade away. Education was seen as standing on its own, with little indication of those "advanced agents of civilization" (missionaries) about whom Phelps Stokes had written previously. The greater concern of the era was "Godless communism," ironic because liberal agencies of the mid-century had also put "God" away. Indeed in the discourse of UNESCO's IBE, the moral economy of the Christian missionary had transformed into the secular humanism of development missions— much as the Protestant ethic of Weber's (1905) observations had converted to the spirit of capitalism. Read saw this transformation-in-the-making from her vantage working in an institute of education, but how did other anthropologists of Read's day think about African missions, religion, and schools?

A short answer is that many anthropologists saw their task as a matter of accounting for a tension between African communities and schooling. Most intellectual descendents of the functionalist school focused more on conflict and change than did their predecessors. Hunter, who had written about "school people" as European-dressed people (1936), later wrote (as Wilson 1951) that "the profession of Christianity and school education tend to coincide" (p. 128), schooled people tended to be "skeptical of witchcraft" (p. 128), and differences between generations had become a measure of "the effects of Christian missions on the community" (from the preface, p. iii). Also stressing conflict and change, Gluckman's student Elizabeth Colson and her colleague

Thayer Scudder (Scudder & Colson 1980) studied the life course and outcomes of students in Gwembe, Zambia. Theirs was a longitudinal study that documented social stratification and emerging class cleavages connected to the presence of the Methodist mission. It prefigured other studies on social stratification and education (Bond 1982, Brook 1996, Masemann 1974, Roberts 1982).

A longer explanation of mid-century analyses would attend to anthropologists' focus on the changing significance of African schools in relation to a broader international economy. Interested in understanding how people coped with population changes and urbanization, LaFontaine (1970), for instance, described youth groups, including those in Kinshasa who recruited themselves from within schools and churches. She focused on economic reform. Leacock (1976) compared the myths of education in New York City and Zambian schools (see also Herskovits 1943 for a different kind of Africa and New World comparison). And Mayer (1961), varying Hunter's point, described unschooled Africans as wearing bright red garments and seeing school as destroying the "home economy" (p. 136).

A problem with some of this latter research on schooled and unschooled Africans was that it projected its own cultural categories of African tradition and European modernity onto a social field that was heterotopic, not defined (as functionalists saw it) by dualistic categories of old and new or past and present. Mayer (1961), for instance, wrote that "to see a dance for Red youth and a concert for School youth, a sacrifice in one homestead and a prayer meeting in the next, or even a Red and a School family meal, is to realize that they belong to two different worlds, in spite of the language and the peasant background being one" (p. 20). He also observed the merging of these categories as rural communities urbanized, raising the question, how can Red and School be both different and combinable?

A contemporary of Mayer, Fallers avoided the pitfall of seeing Europe's vision of a traditional past in present-day African life. Fallers (1961) described a new, younger age set of schooled, nonhereditary "chiefs, committed to Christianity and progress" who promoted the inseparabilty of western education and African social structure. "How can Africans be 'modern' without being 'western'?" he asked, noting that the Baganda *kibaki* (leader) "enthusiastically embraced Western education [and] Christianity" but also retained "a deep sense of cultural identity" even as (like some other African leaders, see Benbow 2005) he had been educated abroad. School-educated Africans, Fallers remarked, were simultaneously traditional and modern—an observation foreshadowed in the work of Schapera, who argued there was one new and "specifically South African culture" emerging (see Thomas 2009, p. 35).

Fallers's focus on Africans' differential appropriation of colonization introduced a theme of colonial encounter that was better handled by scholars influenced by French structuralists such as Bourdieu (1977), Foucault (1979), Lévi-Strauss (1963), Saussure (1966), and (though to a lesser extent) Derrida (1976). Each of these four Durkheimian-inspired writers animated (at least indirectly) British anthropology by theorizing how people themselves operationalize their own collective representations in ways that signify new social possibilities. Instead of cataloging and labeling as traditional or modern various social practices, French structuralists discerned how habits and ideas are shaped in the course of everyday life and ritual action. Their approach to analyzing social meaning also laid the foundations for analyzing education and pedagogy. They showed that understanding the way, manner, or form in which something exists is also a matter of understanding how it is taught and habituated. However, few scholars, until a cadre of anthropologists working in the 1980s and 1990s, wrote of cultural practice in terms of education or pedagogy. Instead, the focus of analysis was on ritual and belief. Turner (1967), for instance, stressed aspects of Ndembu ritual, not ritual teaching; and Lienhart (1961), writing before Turner, wrote of Dinka experience and divinity in terms of religion and not in terms of lessons or knowledge that results from habituation or direct experience.

One exception to this observation of the underemphasis of education in favor of ritual is the work of Colonna (1975). Colonna examined French education in the metropole and African colony. Her general argument that schooling sustains distance between colonizer and colonized even as it effects profound change in the morals and lifestyles of Algerians presaged a theme developed by Fabian (1983a) and varied by others more recently (Macola 2003, Milbourne 2000, Reimer 2008), namely, that a driving force in the colonial field of education (including, for Fabian, language policies) was a "will to control spontaneous processes and to bend them to the purposes of the colonizing society" (Fabian 1983a, p. 182). Where Fabian focused most famously on colonial authorities' will to power and anthropologists' use of time to constitute Europe's colonial Other (Fabian 1983b), he and others applied this insight about the disciplining use of social technologies to the study of African Christianity (De Craemer 1977, Engelke 2007, Fabian 1971, MacGaffey 1982).

Arguably the most influential of these historically inspired studies of African Christianity are the works of Jean and John Comaroff. The former's *Body of Power, Spirit of Resistance* (1985) embeds an argument about the pedagogic dimensions of African ritual. It builds on Turner's (1967) analysis of Ndembu rites of passage, Richards's (1956) exploration of Bemba initiation, and Evans-Pritchard's (1937) ethnographic picture of the pedagogic qualities of Azande apprenticeship—although again the main emphases of Comaroff's early work are ritual and belief, not education. In *Of Revelation and Revolution: Christianity, Colonialism, and Consciousness in South Africa* (Volume 1), the Comaroffs together lay the foundation of what was to have become a later volume on the power of schooling to change people and places. They describe evangelism as "inseparable from education" because both "aimed at the system-atic, moral reconstruction of the person in a world in which individuals were increasingly viewed as capable of being formed and reformed by social institutions" (1997, p. 233). Like the works of Gluckman and Schapera, which influence them, the Comaroffs emphasize "conflict between colonizer and colonized, ruler and ruled" as a source and engine of innovation; and in a broad leap from, although consistent with, the line of thinking introduced by Fabian, they discern connections between the colonial pedagogy of the missions and modern black consciousness (Comaroff 1996, p. 19; see also Jackson 1997, Fumanti 2006).

Continuing the practice of theorizing the past and present as unfolding in ongoing conversation (a practice well analyzed by Ngwane 2001b), Pels (1999) employs a historical-dialectical framework to study contacts between missionaries and Waluguru in late colonial Tanganyika. Implicitly a corrective to Beidelman's work (1982)—which had been path-breaking in its time for showing how the "missionary urge moves into secular work" (Karp 1984) but was also criticized as were others for overlooking Africans' understandings of religion (Spear & Kimambo 1999)—Pels employed a Foucauldian frame to show how "missionaries had to adapt to local relations of power, and how this balance of power had to adapt to the educational discipline which the colonial state imposed through the missionaries, not always with the latters' whole-hearted support" (1999, pp. 40–41). In the vein of Feierman's *Peasant Intellectuals* (1990), which analyzes Pare control of (and disregard for) British policies, Pels determines that African communities did not so much resist as redeploy the signs and practices of policy in ways that required colonizers to respond to African communities, not solely vice versa (see also Hodgson 2005, Mathabatha 2005, Simmons 2000, Summers 2003).

Another way of describing both applied and historical-dialectical bodies of research is to say that as a whole, anthropologists of the latter twentieth-century were interested in the rise of secular modernity—either as a way of life to be fostered through schooling (applied research) or as a problem to be understood in African contexts (sociohistorical work). Applied researchers viewed schools as engines for driving social change; sociohistorical researchers viewed schools as institutional locii for studying, not forcing, secular-modernizing processes. Regardless of which strand—applied or sociohistorical—writers tended to stay close to the topic of European colonialism in Africa, with one consequence that scholarship on Christianity and on Islam developed separately, seldom jointly or as a broader subject to be discussed under the broad umbrella of African schools and missions.

In developing separately, applied and sociohistorical works did not address as fully as the discipline might have questions about culture outside anthropology's own historical-cultural backyard of social science liberalism. Such liberalism was itself borne in the sentiment of ecumenical Christianity (Asad 1993, Bowie 2000, Madan 1987) and derived primarily from British-influenced studies of missions and indigenous education located in southern Africa, where Islam was arguably less prominent than in northern, western, central, or eastern Africa. Two exceptions to this "either indigenous or Christian" model can be found in the works of Nadel (1942) and Fallers (1961) who wrote about Christianity, Islam, and "traditional cults" (p. 684). However, these works were treated as exceptions and, in Fallers's case, the analysis was not very extensive. As a result, when anthropologists—and with them historians—began to think more broadly about schools and African missions, these works (particularly those on Islam) appeared to identify a new phenomenon that was, in fact, more embedded than absent throughout Africa (Levtzion 2000, Robinson 2000). Simply put, anthropological analysis of Christian ritual and pedagogy led the field down a narrow path and disposed anthropologists to overlook a complex interplay between the religious and pedagogic practices of both Islam and Christianity.

ON YOUTH AND ACTION-AID ORGANIZATIONS

To take a few steps back from the early twenty-first century before moving closer to the present: The late 1990s saw the growth of market-driven neoliberal public policies, including changes that allowed religious groups greater opportunity to join forces with, or in some cases to supplant, state-sponsored public schools. It also saw a low-grade crisis, as it were, in the very tenets of modernity, including a loss of faith in the abilities of state-sponsored schools to jump-start national economies and provide citizens with new opportunities (Weiss 2004).

Along with this further giving-way of the myth of modern education about which Leacock had already hinted in the 1970s, new questions about the meaning of national identity and of religion and education began to emerge. By the early twenty-first century, questions of education were couched first with regard to youths' social location and vulnerability, and second in terms of nonstate agencies' abilities to temper—or as the case might be, to fuel—youths' political and religious conscientization.

Building productively on LaFontaine's view that youth is a social not age category (adulthood in much of Africa, for example, is discerned through the passing of events such as child bearing and marriage, not always or entirely in terms of years), Durham (2000) and Cole (Cole & Durham 2007) describe youth as an indexical term that socially locates people in relation to one another. When youth are so located, Durham suggests, they are sometimes regarded by persons of an older generation as having strong, and to a degree inordinate, agency—especially when they are students. Bastian (2000) illustrates this point in an analysis of Christian missions' use of schools to reconfigure gender relations among students and graduates, especially of school-educated Igbo women around their evangelist husbands.

Observations about school-empowered women and youth also arise in works about political engagement and popular culture (Sharp 2003, Simpson 1999, Stambach 2000a, Weiss 2009, Williams 2004). With reference to West Africa, Cruise O'Brien (1996) writes about youths' implications in the development of multiparty democracy. Far from being the docile generation ready to inherit the lessons of their elders, the second generation of independence-era Senegal was school-educated but lacked jobs. A socially unmoored group, unemployed graduates were subject to political persuasion, including by a Sufi brotherhood who tried to lead Senegalese youth to vote a particular way. Students and graduates did not follow. Instead they allied with labor groups—a student-worker alliance that provoked military intervention. Pointing out an obvious but strangely overlooked point in much of this literature (although see Abernethy 1969, Mbabuike 2001), Cruise O'Brien (1996) calls education a potentially dangerous force that if not met with jobs and opportunity can become part of a "recipe for future disaster" (p. 59).

Reynolds's (1995) analysis of schoolchildren's involvement in the 1976 South African uprisings underscores this point (Soweto Township students protested against the use of Afrikaans as the language of instruction on grounds that unlike English it prevented their social mobility), as does the work of Ngwane (2001b), who illustrates how schooling and initiation rites are sites around which debates and struggles for control between adults and schooled youth take shape. Ngwane's (2003) analysis of Christmastime in South Africa shows connections among religion, education, and migrant labor. Household economies, Ngwane explains, are closely tied to the calendars of younger generations of labor-seeking youth.

The question of overschooled, underemployed graduates is also suggested in studies of public life and nationalism. Focusing on a generation born well after independence, Coe (2005) examines how state schools foster the development of nation-state culture by objectifying and transforming local beliefs and practices. She looks at how Basel missionary-derived projects in Akuapem (Ghana) that represent music and dance as African tradition paradoxically alienate students and local communities from their past in the course of seeking to attract and incorporate students into the project of nation building. Cheney's (2007) analysis of Ugandan nationalism brings to the fore international religious organizations' involvement in African education, and Ignatowski's (2008) contributions illustrate how people strategically and poetically deploy songs in ways that seek to advance particular visions of social and political justice. Each of these works draws on a line of analysis traceable to Hobsbawm & Ranger (1983), who view tradition as produced, not given. Each describes how people make sense of schooling and deploy it for their own ends (see also Bishop 2007, Bloch 1993, Bonini 2006, Phillips 2009, Stambach 2000b).

Reversing the usual policy formulation that years in school positively correlate with reduced rates of mortality and fertility, Bledsoe (1990) argues in an influential essay on school fees and the marriage process that "those girls who manage to avoid pregnancy and childbirth can stay in school longer" (p. 304). She illustrates that schooling itself does not necessarily foster reduced fertility, but reduced fertility enables ongoing schooling. Johnson-Hanks (2006) builds on this insight. She examines school graduates' reasons for having fewer children than un- or less-schooled counterparts. Citing Mann's (1985) study of marriage and education in colonial Lagos, Johnson-Hanks notes that Christianity, western education, and British manners and customs create a distinctive lifestyle for schooled Cameroonians. Likewise, other anthropologists examine the social contexts of fertility decisions among school students and graduates (e.g., Hollos 1998, Renne 2003).

Moving analysis even further in the direction of understanding the flows as well as breaks in the movement of education around the world, a recent body of research details the moral economies of education and students' lives. Wendland's (2010) analysis of

Malawian medical school students' experiences shows that the application of knowledge to action is not everywhere the same. Malawian students and interns develop a "contradictory consciousness" in the course of practicing their profession. Like students about whom Meinert (2009) and Bratton (2010) write, Malawian doctors know the norms of science but recognize that—despite its universalizing claims—science is enacted differently in different places, often as a function of wealth and poverty. In revealing the social limits and contingencies of science, Malawian doctors' work illuminates how contradictory consciousness becomes a starting place for protest and rebellion (compare Gramsci 1971). Their understanding underscores that if, as Cruise O'Brien indicates (1996, pp. 58–59), "mass education creates problems for the future," then solutions to this problem must include but also come from beyond the institution of mass education.

Enter at this point in the story "action-aid organizations," all of which provide services beyond the single realm of education. Among these organizations are Médecins Sans Frontières, Heifer International, and Rafiki Foundation. Some are faith-based, others not, but many identify as their mission the deliverance of youth and children from poverty. Public policies and leaders are mixed in their reviews of the significance of such organizations. Some see these entities as undercutting the political and moral authority of states to educate their own citizens. Others see them as necessary supplements to "weak states" and as correctives to years of massive underfunding of social and public services. A novel development at the turn of this century within international organizations such as UNESCO and the World Bank has been to use religious groups as action-aid providers to expand religious understanding and—at least ideally—to reduce religious-political tensions (see Marshall & Keogh 2005, UNESCO 2008, Varghese 2009). The reasoning behind this sometimes flawed approach is that religious groups can educate children and promote development without

eclipsing states' overarching function. Not unlike the argument of Malinowski, who commented, as quoted above, on the similarities between University Missions and the science of anthropology, today's reasoning behind faith groups' involvment in mass schooling and public outreach campaigns is that religious education and public governance are connected. Both employ ethical-moral principles that can be traced to the conjoined histories of states and religion. But where Christianity in much of the twentieth-century was "secularized and generalized as bourgeois ideology" (Comaroff & Comaroff 1997, p. 63), religion has more recently taken on populist, literalist, and sometimes illiberal forms that drive wedges among popular practices, Islam, and Christianity.

Writing about power relations in southwestern Tanzania, for instance, Green (2003) notes that the Catholic Church seeks to mediate between the state and the family and to address contradictions "between institutional opulence and poverty" (p. viii). Not unlike the disparities indicated in the categories of schooled versus red-dressed or scholar's associations (or, for that matter, by Malinowski's observations of Christians and non-Christians), differences between the haves and have-nots are cast along lines of (among other markers) religion and education. Green (2003) observes "the gap between Christianity and popular practice grows ever wider" (p. 142), and Cheney's (2007) work makes it clear that development missions play a key role in bridging divisions, including the highly secularized yet religiously inflected agencies of UNICEF (United Nations Children's Fund), USAID (United States Agency for International Development), and the Global Movement for Children. The Global Movement for Children draws on resources from (among others) Save the Children, Plan International, UNICEF, and World Vision International. The latter is a Christian aid organization that emphasizes the importance of building economic infrastructure from a multidenominational religious base. For additional research on the ways in which religious organizations operate as action-aid organizations in the early twenty-first century, see, for instance, Bornstein (2002), Hearn (2002), Stambach (2010), and A.C. Kwayu (forthcoming dissertation).

DISCUSSION

In all, the past decade of research on youth and religion has focused on generational transformations associated with education and on the appearance of new social service providers, including new (and new roles for old) religious groups. These past 10 years reflect a longer legacy of functionalist thinking in anthropology and development policy, including an understanding of education as salvational and as leading people toward a better, as-yet unattainable end—although, to be sure, not all analyses treat schools this way.

The challenge now is to broaden this trajectory and look at what scholarship has missed. In part, anthropological analysis of religion and education in Africa underanalyzes what it also foregrounds: the political-economic and socioreligious dimensions of African missions and schools. Existing work has studied Christian missions and analyzed the morality of development aid. It has defined missions in terms of Christian evangelism coming from Europe and North America, and it has built reliably on anthropology's historical record of interest in localized education and the objectification of tradition (indeed, functionalist ethnographies contributed to this objectification). The strength of this work is its deep, detailed focus. Its weaknesses are also the same. With tempered comparison, anthropological research on religion broadly defined—taken together with a consideration of anthropology's history—could advance a space within the discipline that accounts for the study of religiosity and secularity, missions and schools, civilizing missions and development projects, Christianity and Islam—and the integration of all these phenomena simultaneously.

Specialists of Islam in Africa already know the deep interconnections of world and so-called traditional religions (Ahmed 2008, Babou 2003, Brenner 2001). Many also know that European and international policy in Africa oscillate historically between supporting but largely excluding Muslim schools and groups (Chande 2000, Guillermou 2005, Reichmuth 2000). Some radical groups exploit and protest religious-based class inequities and are driven underground (Hemed 1996); others mobilize publicly around a human rights agenda that promotes religious freedom and equal educational opportunity (Clarke 2009, Loimeier 2005). Literate Muslim women in various places take charge in ways that challenged liberal feminism, using their knowledge to reinscribe custom (Mahmood 2005, p. 8) or in other cases to redefine it (Masquelier 2009, Renne 2003). In addition, higher education and the development of private Arabic schools in all corners of the continent are increasingly merging "religious knowledge" with "marketable" instruction (Loimeier 2005, p. 405) and moving new forms of understanding into a public, sometimes politicized arena (Bangstad 2004, Eickelman 1992, Janson 2005, Renders 2002).

Once the student of Evans-Pritchard, Talal Asad set the stage for this consideration. Quoting Peter Brown (1967, pp. 236–38) on St. Augustine, Asad (1993) wrote that it is "not the mind that move[s] spontaneously to religious truth, but power that create[s] the conditions for experiencing that truth" (p. 35). Later referring to the works of Mauss, Asad, following others (Bourdieu 1977, Durkheim 1915), suggested that learning is embodied, that it does not only, or primarily, involve the cognitive grasping of information (as today's policy makers and government leaders might have it, focusing on standards). Instead, learning involves the habituation of bodily practices and a certain disciplinarity of souls. Asad's point is in reference to Christianity, but his larger interest is in unpacking the particular logic (mainly Protestant, he argued) of anthropology by analyzing Islam through a practice-theoretical lens. Where Bourdieu before him illuminated the ritualistic dimensions of pedagogy, Asad brought forward the pedagogic qualities of religious life.

FINAL THOUGHTS

Perhaps anthropology's own mission in the academy across the past 80-odd years has been to educate students in an either/or school of thought. Either study Christianity, or spirit possession and witchcraft, or Islam. Either specialize in education or write about ritual and belief. Either study the United States or Africa or another location and think about how schools create national, more so than global or translocal, citizens. If an analyst follows the content and flow of human-social interaction, however, religion and education (and places) connect.

This article has traced such connections (following the path and legacy of British anthropology) through the 1930s to the present. It has argued that functionalist anthropology embeds religified ideas about salvational schools and that anthropologists' focus on civilizing missions, and on today's counterpart, secular-modernity, might be broadened to adopt a more flexible understanding of the content and scope of missions and schools, and of Christianity and Islam, in Africa as elsewhere.

SUMMARY POINTS

1. The anthropological study of religion and education in Africa is closely tied to Christianized schooling.

2. There is a need within anthropology for more conversation between studies of Islam and studies of Christianity.

3. If education is broadly studied and conceptualized, and secular-modernity is seen as (perhaps paradoxically) not irreligious, clear distinctions between education and religion, and between schools and development, fall away.

4. This blurring of the fields of education and religion creates a space for grasping more broadly than is typically understood (or at least than is currently analyzed and articulated) world religions' differential place in secular-modern international and action-aid organizations.

DISCLOSURE STATEMENT

The author is not aware of any affiliations, memberships, funding, or financial holdings that might be perceived as affecting the objectivity of this review.

LITERATURE CITED

Abernethy DB. 1969. *The Political Dilemma of Popular Education: An African Case*. Stanford, CA: Stanford Univ. Press

Afr. News. 2008. Nigeria: Civil Society Groups Task Governments on Education. *Afr. News* April 21

Ahmed C. 2008. The Wahubiri wa Kislamu (preachers of Islam) in East Africa. *Afr. Today* 54(4):3–18

Asad T. 1993. The construction of religion as an anthropological category. In *Genealogies of Religion: Discipline and Reasons of Power in Christianity and Islam*, ed. T Asad, pp. 27–54. Baltimore, MD: Johns Hopkins Univ. Press

Babou CA. 2003. Educating the Murid: theory and practices of education in Amadu Bamba's thought. *J. Relig. Afr.* 33(3):310–27

Bangstad S. 2004. The changed circumstances for the performance of religious authority in a Cape Muslim community. *J. Relig. Afr.* 34(1–2):39–61

Bastian M. 2000. Young converts: Christian missions, gender and youth in Onitsha, Nigeria 1880–1929. *Anthropol. Q.* 73(3):145–58

Beidelman TO. 1982. *Colonial Evangelism: A Socio-Historical Study of an East African Mission at the Grassroots.* Bloomington: Indiana Univ. Press

Benbow RJ. 2005. *Education, nationalism, and resistance: a comparative analysis of Banda, Azikiwe, and Nkrumah in Africa and the United States, 1898–1945.* MA thesis. Univ. Wis. Madison. 122 pp.

Bishop E. 2007. Schooling and the encouragement of farming amongst pastoralists in Tanzania. *Nomadic Peoples* 11(2):9–29

Bledsoe C. 1990. School fees and the marriage process for Mende girls in Sierra Leone. In *Beyond the Second Sex: New Directions in the Anthropology of Gender*, ed. PR Sanday, RG Goodenough, pp. 281–310. Philadelphia: Univ. Penn. Press

Bloch M. 1993. The uses of schooling and literacy in a Zafimaniry village. In *Cross-Cultural Approaches to Literacy*, ed. B Street, pp. 87–109. Cambridge, UK: Cambridge Univ. Press

Bond GC. 1982. Education and social stratification in northern Zambia: the case of the Uyombe. *Anthropol. Educ. Q.* 13(3):251–67

Bonini N. 2006. The pencil and the shepherd's crook: ethnography of Maasai education. *Ethnogr. Educ.* 1(3):379–92

Bornstein E. 2002. Developing faith: theologies of economic development in Zimbabwe. *J. Relig. Afr.* 32(1):4–31

Bourdieu P. 1977. *Outline of a Theory of Practice.* Cambridge, UK: Cambridge Univ. Press

Bowie F. 2000. *The Anthropology of Religion: An Introduction.* Oxford, UK: Blackwell

Bratton AR. 2010. *An Anthropological Study of Factors Affecting the Construction of Sexuality in Ghana: Teenage Pregnancy, School Education and Virgins' Clubs.* Lewiston, NY: Edwin Mellen Press

Brenner L. 2001. *Controlling Knowledge: Religion, Power, and Schooling in a West African Muslim Society.* Bloomington: Indiana Univ. Press

Brenner L. 2007. The transformation of Muslim schooling in Mali: the madrasa as an institution of social and religious mediation. See Hefner & Zaman 2007, pp. 199–223

Brook DL. 1996. From exclusion to inclusion: racial politics and South African educational reform. *Anthropol. Educ. Q.* 27(2):204–31

Brown P. 1967. *Augustine of Hippo.* London: Faber and Faber

Brouwer S, Gifford P, Rose SD. 1996. *Exporting the American Gospel: Global Christian Fundamentalism.* New York: Routledge

Camilleri C. 1986. *Cultural Anthropology and Education.* Paris: Kogan Page

Chande A. 2000. Radicalism and reform in East Africa. See Levtzion & Pouwells 2000, pp. 349–69

Cheney KE. 2007. *Pillars of the Nation: Child Citizens and Ugandan National Development.* Chicago: Univ. Chicago Press

Chidester D. 2006. Religion and the transformational state in South Africa. *Soc. Anal.* 50(3):61–83

Clarke KM. 2009. *Fictions of Justice: The International Criminal court and the Challenge of Legal Pluralism in Sub-Saharan Africa.* New York: Cambridge Univ. Press

Coe C. 2005. *Dilemmas of Culture in African Schools: Youth, Nationalism, and the Transformation of Knowledge.* Chicago: Univ. Chicago Press

Cole J, Durham D, ed. 2007. *Generations and Globalization: Youth, Age, and Family in the New World Economy.* Bloomington: Indiana Univ. Press

Colonna F. 1975. *Instituteurs Algérians 1883–1939.* Paris: Press. Found. Natl. Sci. Polit. Excerpt reprinted in Cooper F, Stoler AL. 1997. Chapter 10: Educating conformity in French colonial Algeria. In *Tensions of Empire: Colonial Cultures in a Bourgeois World*, ed. F Cooper, AL Stoler, pp. 346–70. Berkeley: Univ. Calif. Press

Comaroff J. 1985. *Body of Power, Spirit of Resistance: The Culture and History of a South African People.* Chicago: Univ. Chicago Press

Comaroff J. 1996. Reading, rioting and arithmetic: the impact of mission education on black consciousness in South Africa. *Bull. Inst. Ethnol. Acad. Sin. (Taipei)* 82:19–63

Comaroff JL, Comaroff J. 1997. *Of Revelation and Revolution: Christianity, Colonialism, and Consciousness in South Africa*, Vol. 1. Chicago: Univ. Chicago Press

Cooper BM. 2006. *Evangelical Christians in the Muslim Sahel*. Bloomington: Indiana Univ. Press

Cruise O'Brien DB. 1996. A lost generation? Youth identity and state decay in West Africa. In *Postcolonial Identities in Africa*, ed. R Werbner, T Ranger, pp. 55–74. London: Zed

De Craemer W. 1977. *The Jamaa and the Church: A Bantu Catholic Movement in Zaire*. Oxford, UK: Clarendon

Derrida J. 1976. *Of Grammatology*, trans. GC Spivak. Baltimore: Johns Hopkins Univ. Press. From French

de Saussure F. 1966. *Course in General Linguistics*, ed. C Bally, A Sechehaye, A Riedlinger, trans W Baskin. New York: McGraw-Hill

Dougall JW. 1930. School education and native life. *Afr. J. Int. Afr. Inst.* 3(1):49–58

Durham D. 2000. Youth and the social imagination in Africa: introduction to parts 1 and 2. *Anthropol. Q.* 73(3):113–20

Durkheim E. 1915 [1965]. *The Elementary Forms of the Religious Life*, transl. JW Swain. New York: Free Press. From French

Eickelman DF. 1992. Mass higher education and the religious imagination in contemporary Arab societies. *Am. Ethnol.* 19(4):643–55

Eickelman DF. 2007. Madrasas in Morocco: their vanishing public role. See Hefner & Zaman 2007, pp. 131–48

Eiselen WM. 1934 [1967]. Christianity and the religious life of the Bantu. See Schapera 1934b [1967], pp. 65–82

Engelke M. 2007. *A Problem of Presence: Beyond Scripture in an African Church*. Berkeley: Univ. Calif. Press

Evans-Pritchard EE. 1937. *Witchcraft, Oracles and Magic Among the Azande*. Oxford, UK: Clarendon

Fabian J. 1971. *Jamaa: A Charismatic Movement in Katanga*. Evanston, IL: Northwestern Univ. Press

Fabian J. 1983a. Missions and the colonization of African languages: developments in the former Belgian Congo. *Can. J. Afr. Stud.* 17(2):165–87

Fabian J. 1983b. *Time and the Other: How Anthropology Makes Its Object*. New York: Columbia Univ. Press

Fallers LA. 1961. Ideology and culture in Uganda nationalism. *Am. Anthropol.* 63(4):677–86

Feierman S. 1990. *Peasant Intellectuals: Anthropology and History in Tanzania*. Madison: Univ. Wis. Press

Fortes M. 1938. Social and psychological aspects of education in Taleland. See Middleton 1970, pp. 14–74

Foucault M. 1979. *Discipline and Punish: The Birth of the Prison*, transl. A Sheridan. New York: Vintage

Fumanti M. 2006. Nation-building and the battle for consciousness: state ceremonialism and contested discourses on education in past-Apartheid Namibia. *Soc. Anal.* 50(3):84–108

Gramsci A. 1971. *Selections from the Prison Notebooks*, ed./transl. Q Hoare, GN Smith. New York: International

Green M. 2003. *Priests, Witches, and Power: Popular Christianity after Mission in Southern Tanzania*. Cambridge, UK: Cambridge Univ. Press

Guillermou Y. 2005. La mosquée dans l'école ou contre l'école? Appareil éducatif, inégalités sociales et luttes idéologiques en Algérie. *J. Des Anthropol.* 100–101:117–38

Gutmann B. 1926. *Das Recht der Dschagga*, transl. AM Nagler. Hum. Relat. Area Files. New Haven, CT: Yale Univ. Press

Hearn J. 2002. The 'invisible' NGO: US evangelical missions in Kenya. *J. Relig. Afr.* 32(1):32–60

Hefner RW, Zaman MQ, eds. 2007. *Schooling Islam*. Princeton, NJ: Princeton Univ. Press

Hemed HS. 1996. *The academic performance of Muslim and Christian seminaries as a factor reproducing religious based educational inequalities in Tanzania*. MA thesis. Univ. Dar es Salaam

Herskovits MJ. 1943. Education in Africa: its pattern and role in social change. See Middleton 1970, pp. 250–71

Hobsbawm E, Ranger T, ed. 1983. *The Invention of Tradition*. Cambridge, UK: Cambridge Univ. Press

Hodgson D. 2005. *The Church of Women: Gendered Encounters between Maasai and Missionaries*. Bloomington: Indiana Univ. Press

Hoernlé AW. 1931. An outline of the native conception of education in Africa. *Africa* 4:145–63

Hollos M. 1998. The status of women in Southern Nigeria: Is education a help or a hindrance? In *Women and Education in Sub-Saharan Africa: Power, Opportunities, and Constraints*, ed. M Bloch, JA Beoku-Betts, R Tabachnick, pp. 247–76. Boulder, CO: L. Rienner

Hunter M. 1936. *Reaction to Conquest: Effects of Contact with Europeans on the Pondo of South Africa*. London: Oxford Univ. Press

Ignatowski C. 2008. *Journey of Song: Public Life and Morality in Cameroon*. Bloomington: Indiana Univ. Press

Jackson S. 1997. Critical pedagogy and the public sphere: comparative perspectives in education in South Africa and the United States. *Soc. Dyn.* 23(2):19–56

Janson M. 2005. Roaming about for God's sake: the upsurge of the *Tabligh Jamaat* in the Gambia. *J. Relig. Afr.* 35(4):450–81

Johnson CS. 1943. Education and the cultural process: introduction to symposium. *Am. J. Soc.* 48(6):629–32

Johnson-Hanks J. 2006. *Uncertain Honor: Modern Motherhood in an African Crisis*. Chicago: Univ. Chicago Press

Jones TJ. 1925. *Education in East Africa: A Study of East, Central, and South Africa by the Second African Education Commission under the Auspices of the Phelps-Stokes Fund*. Rep. Afr. Educ. Comm. London: Edinburgh House

Karp I. 1984. Review of *Colonial Evangelism: A Socio-Historical Study of an East African Mission at the Grassroots* by TO Beidelman, Indiana Univ. Press, 1982. *Am. Ethnol.* 11(1):215–16

Keller E. 2006. Scripture study as normal science: Seventh-Day Adventist practice on the east coast of Madagascar. In *The Anthropology of Christianity*, ed. F Cannell, pp. 273–94. Durham, NC: Duke Univ. Press

Krapf JL. 1860. *Travels, Researches, and Missionary Labours, During an Eighteen Years' Residence in Eastern Africa*. Boston: Ticknor & Fields

Krige EJ. 1937. Individual development. In *The Bantu-Speaking Tribes of South Africa*, ed. I Schapera, pp. 95–118. London: Routledge & Kegan Paul

Kuklick H. 1991. *The Savage Within: The Social History of British Anthropology: 1885–1945*. Cambridge, UK: Cambridge Univ. Press

Kuper A. 1983. *Anthropology and Anthropologists: The Modern British School*. New York: Routledge

LaFontaine JS. 1970. Two types of youth groups in Kinshasa (Léopoldville). In *Socialization: The Approach from Social Anthropology*, ed. P Mayer, pp. 191–213. London: Tavistock

Leacock EB. 1976. Education in Africa: myths of "modernization." In *The Anthropological Study of Education*, ed. CJ Calhoun, FAJ Ianni, pp. 240–50. Paris: Mouton

Levine RA. 2007. Ethnographic studies of childhood: a historical overview. *Am. Anthropol.* 109(2):247–60

Lévi-Strauss C. 1963. *Structural Anthropology*, transl. C Jacobson, BG Schoepf. New York: Basic Books

Levtzion N. 2000. Islam in the Bilad al-Sudan to 1800. See Levtzion & Pouwels 2000, pp. 63–91

Levtzion N, Pouwels RL, eds. 2000. *The History of Islam in Africa*. Athens: Ohio Univ. Press

Lienhart RG. 1961. *Divinity and Experience: The Religion of the Dinka*. Oxford, UK: Clarendon

Little K. 1951. The social cycle and initiation among the Mende. See Middleton 1970, pp. 207–25

Loimeier R. 2005. Translating the Qur'an in sub-Saharan Africa: dynamics and disputes. *J. Relig. Afr.* 35(4):403–23

Lord K. 2008. Implicit religion: a contemporary theory for the relationships between religion, state, and society. *J. Contemp. Relig.* 23(1):33–46

MacGaffey W. 1982. Education, religion, and social structure in Zaire. *Anthropol. Educ. Q.* 13(3):238–50

Macola G. 2003. Historical and ethnographical publications in the vernaculars of colonial Zambia: missionary contributions to the "creation of tribalism." *J. Afr. Relig.* 33(4):343–64

Madan TN. 1987. Secularism in its place. *J. Asian Stud.* 46(4):747–59

Mahmood S. 2005. *Politics of Piety: The Islamic Revival and the Feminist Subject*. Princeton, NJ: Princeton Univ. Press

Mafeje A. 1976. The problem of anthropology in historical perspective: an inquiry into the growth of the social sciences. *Can. J. Afr. Stud.* 10(2):307–33

Mair LP. 1934. The study of culture contact as a practical problem. *Afr. J. Int. Afr. Inst.* 7(4):415–22

Malassis L. 1976. *The Rural World: Education and Development*. Paris: UNESCO

Malinowski B. 1936. Native education and culture contact. *Int. Rev. Missions* 25:480–515

Mann K. 1985. *Marrying Well: Marriage, Status, and Social Change among the Educated Elite in Colonial Lagos*. New York: Cambridge Univ. Press

Marshall K, Keough L. 2005. *Finding Global Balance: Common Ground between the Worlds of Development and Faith*. Washington, DC: World Bank

Masemann V. 1974. "Hidden curriculum" of a West African girls' boarding school. *Can. J. Afr. Stud.* 8(3):479–94

Mathabatha S. 2005. Missionary schools, student uprisings in Lebowa, and the Sekhukhuneland students' revolts, 1983–1986. *Afr. Stud.* 64(2):263–84

Mayer P. 1961 [1971]. *Townsmen or Tribesmen: Conservatism and the Process of Urbanization in a South African City*. Cape Town: Oxford Univ. Press

Mbabuike MC. 2001. Beyond politics and praxis: educational challenges in contemporary Africa. *Dialect. Anthropol.* 26:325–42

Meinert L. 2009. *Hopes in Friction: Schooling, Health, and Everyday Life in Uganda*. Charlotte, NC: Information Age

Middleton J, ed. 1970. *From Child to Adult: Studies in the Anthropology of Education*. New York: Am. Mus. Nat. Hist.

Milbourne KE. 2000. Craft and creativity: artists and missionary outreach in Barotseland. *Mus. Anthropol.* 24(1):42–56

Mumford WB. 1930. Malangali School. *Afr. J. Int. Afr. Inst.* 3(3):265–92

Musgrove F. 1952. A Uganda secondary school as a field of culture change. *Afr. J. Int. Afr. Inst.* 22(3):234–49

Nadel SF. 1942. Education for citizenship among the Nupe. See Middleton 1970, pp. 173–206

Ngwane Z. 2001a. Real men reawaken their fathers' homesteads, the educated leave them in ruins': the politics of domestic reproduction in post-apartheid rural South Africa. *J. Relig. Afr.* 31(4):402–26

Ngwane Z. 2001b. "The long conversation": the enduring salience of nineteenth-century missionary colonial encounters in post-apartheid South Africa. *Interv. Int. J. Postcolon. Stud.* 3(1):65–75

Ngwane Z. 2003. "Christmas Time" and the struggles for the household in the countryside: rethinking the cultural geography of migrant labour in South Africa. *J. S. Afr. Stud.* 29(3):681–99

Pels P. 1999. *A Politics of Presence: Contacts between Missionaries and Waluguru in Late Colonial Tanganyika*. Amsterdam: Harwood

Phillips K. 2009. Hunger, healing, and citizenship in central Tanzania. *Afr. Stud. Rev.* 52(1):23–45

Rattray RS. 1932. *The Tribes of the Ashanti Hinterland*. Oxford, UK: Clarendon

Raum OF. 1938. Some aspects of indigenous education among the Chaga. *J. R. Anthropol. Inst. Great Br. Irel.* 68:209–21

Raum OF. 1940 [1967]. *Chaga Childhood: A Description of Indigenous Education in an East African Tribe*. New York: Oxford Univ. Press

Read M. 1955. *Education and Social Change in Tropical Areas*. London: Nelson

Read M. 1956. *The Ngoni of Nyasaland*. London: Oxford Univ. Press

Reichmuth S. 2000. Islamic education and scholarship in sub-Saharan Africa. See Levtzion & Pouwells 2000, pp. 419–40

Reimer FJ. 2008. Becoming literate, becoming human: adult literacy and moral reconstruction in Botswana. *Anthropol. Educ. Q.* 39(4):444–64

Renders M. 2002. An ambiguous adventure: Muslim organisations and the discourse of "development" in Senegal. *J. Relig. Afr.* 32(1):61–82

Renne EP. 2003. Changing assessments of abortion in a northern Nigerian town. In *The Sociocultural and Political Aspects of Abortion: Global Perspectives*, ed. AM Basu, pp. 119–38. London: Praeger

Reynolds P. 1995. Youth and the politics of culture in South Africa. In *Children and the Politics of Culture*, ed. S Stephens, pp. 218–40. Princeton, NJ: Princeton Univ. Press

Richards A. 1956. *Chisungu: A Girls' Initiation Ceremony among the Bemba of Northern Rhodesia*. London: Faber & Faber

Richter M. 1912. *Die Wirtschaftsleben der südafrikanischen Bantuneger*. PhD diss. Dresden Univ.

Roberts PA. 1982. Whose school? Conflicts over school management in Sefwi Wiawso, Ghana. *Anthropol. Educ. Q.* 13(3):268–78

Robinson D. 2000. Revolutions in the western Sudan. In *The History of Islam*, ed. N Levtzion, RL Pouwels, pp. 131–52. Oxford, UK: James Currey

Rogoff B. 2003. *The Cultural Nature of Human Development*. Oxford: Oxford Univ. Press

Salamone FA. 2000. The International African Institute: the Rockefeller Foundation and the development of British social anthropology in Africa. *Transform. Anthropol.* 9(1):19–29

Schapera I. 1934a [1967]. The old Bantu culture. See Schapera 1934b [1967], pp. 3–36

Schapera I, ed. 1934b [1967]. *Western Civilization and the Natives of South Africa: Studies in Culture Contact.* London: Routledge & Kegan Paul

Schumaker L. 2001. *Africanizing Anthropology: Fieldwork, Networks, and the Making of Cultural Knowledge in Central Africa*. Durham, NC: Duke Univ. Press

Scudder T, Colson E. 1980. *Secondary Education and the Formation of an Elite: The Impact of Education on Gwembe District, Zambia*. New York: Academic

Sharkey HJ. 2008. *American Evangelicals in Egypt: Missionary Encounters in an Age of Empire*. Princeton, NJ: Princeton Univ. Press

Sharp LA. 2003. Laboring for the colony and nation: the historicized political consciousness of youth in Madagascar. *Crit. Anthropol.* 23(1):75–91

Simmons D. 2000. Signs of the times: missionaries and tribal genesis in southern Rhodesia. *Transform. Anthropol.* 9(2–3):3–18

Simpson A. 1999. The labours of learning: education in the postcolony. *Soc. Anal.* 43(1):4–13

Spear T, Kimambo IN, ed. 1999. *East African Expressions of Christianity*. Athens: Ohio Univ. Press

Stambach A. 2000a. Evangelism and consumer culture in northern Tanzania. *Anthropol. Q.* 73(3):171–79

Stambach A. 2000b. *Lessons from Mount Kilimanjaro: Schooling, Community, and Gender in East Africa*. New York: Routledge

Stambach A. 2006. Revising a four-square model of a complicated whole: on the cultural politics of religion and education. *Soc. Anal.* 50(3):1–18

Stambach A. 2010. *Faith in Schools: Religion, Education, and American Evangelicals in East Africa*. Stanford, CA: Stanford Univ. Press

Summers C. 2003. *Colonial Lessons: Africans' Education in Southern Rhodesia, 1918–1940*. Oxford, UK: James Currey

Thomas LM. 2009. Love, sex, and the modern girl in 1930s southern Africa. In *Love in Africa*, ed. J Cole, LM Thomas, pp. 31–57. Chicago: Univ. Chicago Press

Turner V. 1967. Betwixt and between. In *The Forest of Symbols: Aspects of Ndembu Ritual*, ed. V Turner, pp. 93–111. Ithaca, NY: Cornell Univ. Press

Umar MS. 2001. Education and Islamic trends in nortnern Nigeria: 1970s–1990s. *Afr. Today* 48(2):127–50

UNESCO. 2008. *Interreligious dialogue programme.* **http://portal.unesco.org/culture/en/ev.php-URL_ID=35270&URL_DO=DO_TOPIC&URL_SECTION=201.html**

Varghese NV. 2009. Private sector as a partner in higher education development in Africa. *ADEA-WGHE-AAU-IIEP Policy Brief*. Paris: UNESCO

Weber M. 1905 [1958]. *The Protestant Ethic and the Spirit of Capitalism*. New York: Scribner's

Weiss B. 2004. Introduction. In *Producing African Futures: Ritual and Reproduction in a Neoliberal Age*, ed. B Weiss, pp. 1–20. Leiden: Brill

Weiss B. 2009. *Street Dreams and Hip Hop Barbershops: Global Fantasy in Urban Tanzania*. Bloomington: Indiana Univ. Press

Wendland C. 2010. *A Heart for the Work: Journeys through an African Medical School*. Chicago: Chicago Univ. Press

Williams CA. 2004. Student political consciousness: lessons from a Namibian mission school. *J. S. Afr. Stud.* 30(3):539–57

Wilson M. 1951. *Good Company: A Study of Nyakyusa Age-Villages*. Oxford: Oxford Univ. Press

World Bank. 2008. *Accelerating catch-up: tertiary education for growth in sub-Saharan Africa.* **http://siteresources.worldbank.org/INTAFRREGTOPEDUCATION/Resources/e-book_ACU.pdf**

RELATED REVIEWS

Bucholtz M. 2002. Youth and cultural practice. *Annu. Rev. Anthropol.* 31:525–52

Fischer WF. 1997. Doing good? the politics and antipolitics of NGO practices. *Annu. Rev. Anthropol.* 26:439–64

Hefner RW. 1998. Multiple modernities: Christianity, Islam, and Hinduism in a globalizing age. *Annu. Rev. Anthropol.* 27:83–104

The Anthropology of Genetically Modified Crops

Glenn Davis Stone

Department of Anthropology, Washington University, St. Louis, Missouri 63130;
email: stone@wustl.edu

Annu. Rev. Anthropol. 2010. 39:381–400

First published online as a Review in Advance on
June 21, 2010

The *Annual Review of Anthropology* is online at
anthro.annualreviews.org

This article's doi:
10.1146/annurev.anthro.012809.105058

0084-6570/10/1021-0381$20.00

Key Words

biotechnology, agriculture, developing countries, political economy,
commodification

Abstract

By late in the twentieth century, scientists had succeeded in manipulating organisms at the genetic level, mainly by gene transfer. The major impact of this technology has been seen in the spread of genetically modified (GM) crops, which has occurred with little controversy in some areas and with fierce controversy elsewhere. GM crops raise a very wide range of questions, and I address three areas of particular interest for anthropology and its allied fields. First are the political-economic aspects of GM, which include patenting of life forms and new relationships among agriculture, industry, and the academy. Second is the wide diversity in response and resistance to the technology. Third is the much-debated question of GM crops for the developing world. This analysis is approached first by determining what controls research agendas and then by evaluating actual impacts of crops to date.

INTRODUCTION

The last half of the twentieth century saw a momentous series of developments in microbiology. By the time the structure of DNA was published in 1953, biologists knew that bacteria could exchange genes via small extrachromosomal rings called plasmids. By the early 1970s, biologists at Stanford University had learned to isolate some individual genes, cut them out with restriction enzymes, and recombine them on plasmids to move genes between bacteria (Halford 2003, Lurquin 2001). By 1983, biologists at both Monsanto Corp. and Washington University had succeeded in moving genes into plants, marking the beginning of transgenic or genetically modified (GM) crops.[1] Because the genetic code is uniform across life forms, genes could now be transferred across phyla and kingdoms; the first GM plants contained a bacterial gene. Although this technology has seen limited application in bacteria and animals, its major impact has been in crop plants.[2]

In 1988, China became the first country to grow a commercial GM crop: tobacco, modified to resist tobacco mosaic virus (Pray 1999). In the United States, the first GM crop was released in 1994: Calgene's ill-fated "Flavr Savr" tomato, with a gene altered to delay rotting (Harvey 2004, Martineau 2001). The next two years saw arrivals of the two plant transformations that have overwhelmingly dominated GM plantings ever since: herbicide tolerance and insect resistance. Herbicide tolerance is usually from a gene for immunity to glyphosate weedkiller, allowing the farmer to spray weeds without harming the crop. Insect resistance is via a gene from the *Bacillus thuringiensis* (Bt) bacterium, which produces an insecticide, and these crops are often called Bt crops. Major industrial crops—soybean, maize, cotton, and canola—with one or both traits were adopted by many farmers in the United States and Canada with little initial controversy.

But by the late 1990s, the situation had become much more turbulent. The spread of GM crops had stumbled badly in western Europe, and opposition to GM crops and foods had emerged in many parts of the world. High-profile, highly evocative campaigns were launched both for and against GM crops. By 1999, debates turned increasingly to the developing world; new crops were cast as either an agricultural and public health savior or as an ominous threat. Even though GM crops were being developed almost entirely for large-scale industrial agriculture, and were being planted in miniscule amounts in developing countries, there was a surge of publicity on GM crops for the third-world poor: vitamin-enhanced rice to "save a million kids a year," high-protein sweet potato, virus-resistant cassava, and fungus-resistant banana (Moffat 1999, TIME Mag. 2000). The industry-supported ISAAA (International Service for the Acquisition of Agri-Biotech Applications) began to issue reports emphasizing GM crop adoptions in developing countries. Opponents of genetically modified organisms (GMOs) also favored the discursive terrain of the developing world, where they depicted GM crops as a danger to farmer sovereignty and the environment. The trajectory of controversy has been covered by journalists (Charles 2001, Lambrecht 2001, Pringle 2003) and social scientists (Jasanoff 2005); the refocusing of the debate on the developing world has been examined in anthropology (Glover 2010; Stone 2002b, 2005b).

The latest figures show that by 2009 GM crops had spread to 134 million ha (**Table 1**),

---

[1] Like so many aspects of this technology, the terminology is contested. *Genetic modification* (GM) is used here because it is a neutral and accurate term for altering organisms at the genetic level; it is also widely used by advocates and opponents alike. The meaning is the same as *genetic engineering*, but that term implies a greater degree of control than exists at some key points in the process. The term *transgenic* is common but inaccurate for the cases in which genes have been altered in place rather than transferred. *Recombinant DNA*, the original descriptor for this technology, is still the most exact term, but it is unwieldy and out of common usage. Corporate media prefers the nickname *biotech crops*, but biotechnology encompasses a wide range of technologies of which GM is only one particularly controversial subcategory. *Biotechnology* here refers specifically to agricultural biotechnology.

[2] Many introductions to plant genetic modification have been published, ranging from brief (Stone 2002c) to moderately thorough (Halford 2003, Lurquin 2001) to more technical (Liang & Skinner 2004).

Table 1   GM crop plantings in 2009. Compiled from James 2010[a,b]

Country	Area (million hectares)	Soybean (all HT)	Maize (mostly stacked)	Cotton (mostly Bt)	Other (mostly HT canola)
United States	64.0	45%	47%	5%	3%
Brazil	21.4	76%	23%	1%	
Argentina	21.3	88%	10%	2%	
India	8.4			100%	
Canada	8.2	17%	15%		78%
China	3.7			100%	
Paraguay	2.2	100%			
South Africa	2.1	11%	89%	<1%	
Uruguay	0.8	88%	11%		
Bolivia	0.8	100%			
Philippines	0.5		100%		
Australia	0.2			82%	18%
Burkina Faso	0.1			100%	
Spain	0.1		100%		
Mexico	0.1	23%		77%	
(minor plantings in 10 other countries)					

[a]Abbreviations: Bt, *Bacillus thuringiensis*; GM, genetically modified; HT, herbicide tolerant.

[b]Crop-specific figures are row percentages, i.e., breakdowns of each country's total GM hectares, not the percentage of the country's entire planting of the crop is GM.

yet they remain largely a technology for large-scale industrial commodity crops; the most common GM crop (by far) is herbicide tolerant (HT) soybean, followed by HT and Bt maize. However, land planted to GM crops has risen in developing countries, led by Bt cotton (Herdt 2006, Showalter et al. 2009). Other GM crops include HT canola, sugarbeets, and alfalfa; virus-resistant papaya and squash; and blue carnations. Bt eggplant and rice may be nearing release in India and China.

What is the real significance of this development in agricultural technology? Notwithstanding claims that this technology was only a logical continuation of scientific progress, the moment that the first gene was inserted into a bacterium was in many senses a watershed. Humans obviously have a long history of shaping the organisms (and ecosystems) around them, but this was the first instance of humans designing a life form at the genetic level. Although the technology is still primitive (compared with

what it will be), the power to alter and transfer genes is revolutionary. It is also a power long anticipated by speculative fiction, which had pointedly asked whose interests would dictate how life forms would be designed. Huxley (1932) provided perhaps the best known answer in *Brave New World*, in which life forms were developed according to the interests of corporate sales and state control.

Perspectives on what the impacts of this technology have been (and will be) vary wildly, and a vigorous struggle has taken place over the framings through which it is understood. The framing favored by industry and allied academic proponents is that ever-growing food needs require continuation of the long history of improving plants and animals. But a technology as multifaceted as crop genetic modification lends itself to other framings (Heller 2007, Jasanoff 2005), and anthropologists may gain greater insight from other historic trajectories in which this technology fits.

SSTW: small-scale
third world

One such trajectory is the progressive commodification of agriculture; this has been a long-term spasmodic process, with the previous spasm—the adoption of synthetic insecticides with the resulting problem of insect resistance—creating the need now being filled by Bt crops. Another trajectory is the ongoing enclosure of the genome; genetic modification facilitated and was facilitated by patenting of life forms. Closely related is the rise of biopower, theorized by Foucault (1978) as the state's increasing preoccupation with life itself. Another trajectory is the march of neoliberal economics; the Flavr Savr tomato appeared the same year that the World Trade Organization (WTO) was created, with its mandate to globalize trade and harmonize intellectual property (IP) regimes. Another is the continuing reconfiguration of the academy's relationships to both industry and the state; the parallels in the timelines of genetic modification and what is often called academic capitalism are striking.

Many of these perspectives on GM crops intersect core anthropological concerns, just as the "move south" of the GM debate did in the late 1990s. Anthropology has played an increasing, but certainly not leading, role in addressing these issues; allied and overlapping fields such as cultural geography, STS (science and technology studies), and especially sociology also have growing literatures, which will be selectively considered here along with anthropology. Some of the issues listed above have yet to receive significant attention, but others have. I focus here on three areas of anthropological interest on which literatures are available: (*a*) the role of genetic modification in the changing political economy of agriculture, (*b*) the cultural and national variation in response and resistance, and most importantly (*c*) impacts in the global south—i.e., smaller-scale, less industrialized, often relatively resource-poor producers, often in developing countries. These characteristics of farmers are hardly isomorphic, but owing to space limitations, I follow Soleri et al. (2008) in lumping them as small-scale third-world (SSTW) farmers.

POLITICAL ECONOMY OF GM CROPS

The industry-favored framings noted above obscure political-economic aspects of the technology by naturalizing GM crops as part of the long history of plant manipulation. This framing responds to claims (by Charles 2006, among others) that science was transgressing realms that belong to God, and to depictions (by Greenpeace, for instance) of GM crops as "frankenfood." The "plant manipulation as progress" narrative is standard in histories of biotechnology from corporate media departments, showing a natural progression from grain domestication to genetic modification (Monsanto Corp. 2001); these are published by grateful newspaper editors as unproblematic backgrounders. In this view, domestication is genetic modification (e.g., Fedoroff 2003, Pinstrup-Andersen & Schioler 2000) and the term genetic modification itself is only a political construction (Herring 2008a). The narrative is often coupled with the Malthusian specter of famine (Scoones 2002; Stone 2002b, 2005b; Stone & Glover 2011), casting hunger as a condition of nature (Ross 1998).

Countering this framing is work viewing the technology in the context of expanding corporate control over agriculture (Lewontin 2000). Central to this literature is concern for commodification in agricultural production. Orthodox Marxist theories of commodification were always an awkward fit on the farm, in large part because farmers produce their own seed (Goodman et al. 1987, Kloppenburg 2004, Mann & Dickinson 1978). Instead, capital has penetrated and commodified agriculture through a history of spasms led by developments in science and technology that "pull away the natural ground from the foundation" of agriculture (Kloppenburg 2004, Marx 1858), obligating the farmer to purchase inputs (Goodman 2003, Goodman et al. 1987, Lewontin 2000). Thus hybrid breeding created seeds that performed well for only one generation, inducing farmers to repurchase seeds (Berlan & Lewontin 1986, Fitzgerald 1990, Lewontin &

Berlan 1986). Hybrids also allowed private seed companies to capture the value from public research at land-grant colleges and agricultural experiment stations (Kloppenburg 2004).

With hybrids, farm mechanization, pesticides, and other agro-technological spasms, the United States has been a leader; this is not only because conditions in the United States favored labor-saving technologies, as induced-innovation theorists argue (Binswanger & Ruttan 1978, Koppel 1995), but because integrating industry into agriculture was an alternative to extracting cheap farm commodities from colonies or neo-colonies (Foster 2002, McMichael 2000).

This process of state-supported transformation of agriculture to integrate industrial inputs is described as "appropriationism" (Goodman et al. 1987), and it fits the rise of GM crops. Just as the state had invested in earlier agro-industrial technologies, the United States has invested heavily to ensure global leadership in integrating biotechnology into agriculture (Busch et al. 1991). GM crops, like hybrids before, bring new mechanisms to prevent seed replanting and for agricultural capital to benefit from public investment—particularly government-supported academic research, largely because of judicial and legislative developments just prior to the advent of GM plants. In the United States, life forms were statutorily ineligible for patents until the 1980 Chakrabarty Supreme Court decision allowed patenting of a bacterium because it had been genetically modified (Hamilton 1993). Patenting was soon extended to plants. These important changes in IP rights are covered well by legal scholars (Golden 2001, Stein 2005; also see comparative analysis in Jasanoff 2005). Economic impacts of these developments have been covered extensively (e.g., Evenson & Raney 2007, Santaniello et al. 2000), as have social perspectives on these changes in IP laws (Bowring 2003, Fleising & Smart 1993, Marsden et al. 2003, Rabinow 1996).

At the international scale, Kloppenburg (2004) puts these IP rights into a broader pattern of plunder of biological resources of the global south. Brush (1993) examines the spread of new IP rights and the impact of biotechnology on indigenous knowledge before the WTO, whereas Otero and coworkers (Otero 2008, Pechlaner & Otero 2008) and Buttel (2003) examine GM crops in the context of the march of neoliberal economic regimes. Cleveland & Murray (1997) argue that industrial-world IP rights mechanisms are problematic for indigenous farmers, and McAfee (2003) considers IP regimes against the backdrop of the Convention of Biological Diversity. Back in the United States, the Chakrabarty ruling coincided with the 1980 Bayh-Dole legislation allowing results of publicly funded research to be sold into private hands, further weakening boundaries between industry and the academy (Etzkowitz & Leydesdorff 1997b) in the era of "informational capital" (Heller 2001). Genetic modification has therefore been both a catalyst for and a beneficiary of the rise of "academic capitalism" (Slaughter & Leslie 1997, Slaughter & Rhoades 2004), also called the "capitalization of knowledge" (Etzkowitz 1997) or the new university-industrial complex (Kenney 1986). These new relationships have had profound consequences for research priorities in biotechnology (specific impacts relevant to developing countries are discussed below). Further analysis of these evolving relationships among "plants, power and profit" is found in a rich vein of work by Busch and coworkers (Busch 2000, Busch & Lacy 1983, Busch et al. 1991, Middendorf et al. 2000).

The political-economic entailments of GM crops will not be understood for some time, but it is clear that the technology facilitates and is facilitated by key changes in the relationships among industry, the academy, the state, and the farm. Attempts to naturalize GM with assertions like "people have been selecting plant genes for 5000 years [sic]" (Langreth & Herper 2010) seem tantamount to claiming the textile mills of the early industrial revolution to be a simple continuation of the age-old act of making cloth.

REACTIONS AND RESISTANCE

Unlike other categories of biotechnology (such as tissue culture, marker-assisted breeding, and medicine production by GM bacteria), GM crops have often been the subject of heated controversy. Although some have attributed opposition to ignorance (e.g., Braun 2002; see Gusterson 2005), this view fares poorly under scrutiny (Bonny 2003, Bryan 2001, Jasanoff 2005, Priest 2004). Others trace opposition to problems of symbolism, quaint attitudes,[3] or "pagan beliefs" (Bond 1999), and Herring (2009a) attributes European hostility and Asian enthusiasm for GMOs to continent-wide God concepts—all rather unconvincing, although religious perspectives on GMOs are a valid topic (Mirza 2004, Reichman 2004). Citing Haraway's (1997) view of GMOs as a revolutionary form of hybridity, Kwiecinski ascribes anti-GM views to taboos as described by Douglas: GMOs "break the boundaries of fixed, neat categories and thus pollute the entire system of ordering the universe" (Kwiecinski 2009) (although Haraway is more inclined to celebrate the new hybridity).

Discourses and images of "unnaturalness" and disturbing symbols do appear in debates on GM crops (Gusterson 2005), but conflicts over GM crops have also been fierce because there is so much at stake—ecologically, economically, and politically. There has been virtually no opposition to the use of GM bacteria to produce medicines, but GM crops are released into the environment, where their genes will flow and from where they cannot be recalled (Ellstrand 2001, Snow 2005). This technology will produce economic winners and losers (Clapp 2006, Isaac 2002, Wu 2004), and the new niche for the corporate sector in farming stirs deep and long-standing political divisions (Stone 2005b).

These tensions have played out in a variety of ways. If we consider broad patterns of attitudes toward GM crops (and foods), there is no doubt that western Europe has been distinct in its general skepticism (and often hostility). But the European response has been neither simple nor uniform. Development and regulation of GM plants are closely entangled with national law and politics, and an interesting literature has arisen that charts country-specific reactions. Jasanoff (2005) compares framings of the new technology in the United States, the United Kingdom, and Germany, highlighting the uniqueness of the United States's resolutely product-centered approach and exclusion of broader social questions. The U.S.-U.K. divergence on GM crops has attracted particular interest (Gaskell et al. 1999, 2007; Munro & Schurman 2009; Schurman & Munro 2003). Peters et al. (2007) compare U.S. and German attitudes toward institutions. In France, Heller (2006, 2007) traces a history in which disenfranchised smallholders successfully steered the national framing about "quality" and the importance of place. In Hungary, Harper (2004) describes national sentiment driven in part by umbrage over the smearing of the Hungarian scientist who questioned the safety of GM crops. In Norway, Wandel (2005) sees the primary bone of contention being power over labeling. Finucane & Holup (2005) look generally at cultural variation in risk perception and other cultural factors (Finucane 2002) to explain views of GM foods, whereas Gaskell et al. (2000) survey and attempt to explain the widely differing levels of support across European nations.

Reactions and responses in developing countries have also been examined, albeit less closely. Pelaez & Da Silva (2008) examine attempts to create a GM-free territory in Brazil. Comparing resistance movements in India, South Africa, and Brazil, Scoones (2008) finds new hybrid networks confronting global issues that are given shape in local political contexts. Herring (2008b) looks critically at GM opposition in India, which he sees as gaining legitimacy from a "reciprocal authenticity

---

[3] When controversy erupted over the "terminator" technology that uses genetic modification to produce nonviable seeds, a Monsanto spokesman waxed anthropological in attributing opposition to there being "something psychologically offensive about sterile seed in every culture" (Feder 1999).

dynamic" between ex-colonial powers and local global narratives (Herring 2009b). Attitudes in Africa and Europe are also linked in important ways, including use of African food shortages to challenge European opponents (Clapp 2005).

A growing body of work examines differences in the media coverage of these debates. Priest (2001, 2004) considers the ways in which varying attitudes play out in the media, including in Africa, and economists have studied effects of media on consumer choice (e.g., Kalaitzandonakes et al. 2004). Given the range of potent cultural symbols touched by GM crops, the discourse and language in the global debates have been rich subjects. Cook (2004) shows how phraseology used by politicians, journalists, and scientists reflects struggles over the technology; Nelson (2005) traces impacts of academic discourse on public perceptions; Gusterson (2005) decodes the discourse of "frankenfood."

IMPACTS

The available summaries of GM crops' economic and environmental impacts in developing countries (e.g., Brookes & Barfoot 2006, Herdt 2006, Raney 2006) leave unanswered questions of broader sociocultural impacts (Stone 2011). But it is impossible to put actual impacts into context without considering which technologies are being provided to these populations, and what is driving crop modification projects. We therefore divide the discussion of impacts into upstream issues of why GM crops are (or, more commonly, are not) developed for the needs of SSTW farmers and downstream issues of how the crops have actually affected these groups.

Upstream

Thomson (2002, p. 1) opens her book on GM crops for Africa by charging the press with bias for reporting on fears of GM foods but not on how GM technologies are saving Asian children from blindness or African sweet potatoes from viruses. This is a curious charge because

no such crops are, or have ever been, in use. In fact, virtually all the world's GM acres are planted to crops developed for industrial farming. The ISAAA's annual reports emphasize the spread of GM crops into developing countries, but even in developing countries the GM acres are planted overwhelmingly to Bt cotton (Smale et al. 2006) and HT soy (Du Bois & de Sousa 2008). A decade after appearing on the cover of *Time*, Golden Rice is still not available (although GM blue carnations and glowing zebrafish are), and the heralded virus-resistant sweet potatoes (Cook 2002) were never released. But could, and will, this powerful technology be used to benefit SSTW agriculture?

There have long been ardent debates on whether the very structure of GM research militated against SSTW technologies (Beachy 1991, Crouch 1991). Biotechnologists have for years insisted that GM crops can and must be part of the feeding of the third world[4] and have been joined by some social scientists (Collier 2008; Herring 2008a,b; Paarlberg 2000, 2008). Paarlberg blames misguided western sentiments for starving Africa by obstructing development of pro-SSTW biotechnologies, based on his belief that African poverty results directly from low labor productivity in the absence of modern science such as GM crops (2008). This view contrasts extensive research on productivity in low-technology smallholder agriculture in Africa and elsewhere (Netting 1993; Pretty & Hine 2000; Pretty et al. 2006; Richards 1985, 1997). Anthropologists with expertise in agriculture in the developing world have generally taken more nuanced positions: Scoones (2002) does not dismiss GM crops but explores hidden assumptions in SSTW biotechnology advocacy; Tripp (2001a,b), although skeptical of some claims by anti-GM campaigners, points to key informational problems with GM crops, along with institutional

---

[4]For example, "unless we will accept starvation or placing parks and the Amazon Basin under the plow, there really is no alternative to applying biotechnology to agriculture" (McGloughlin 1999).

challenges (Tripp 2009c); Stone (2002b, 2005b) dismisses Malthusian justifications for GM crops but also identifies potentially valuable uses for the technology. Others have found the green revolution to be a useful lens through which to contemplate what a "gene revolution" might be able to accomplish (Brooks 2005, Conway 1998, Parayil 2003, Spielman 2007, Tripp 2009a, Vroom 2009).

The paucity of GM crops for SSTW farming is partly explained by the incentives and institutional relations shaping research and development. Genetic modification requires a vastly more advanced infrastructure, expertise, and expense than do earlier methods of seed improvement, and most of the basic research and innovation needed to create functional GM crops has been (and will be) done in academic institutions (Etzkowitz & Leydesdorff 1997a). But university research on GM crops increasingly mirrors the research profile of industry (Welsh & Glenna 2006), with public good being defined in a way that promotes university-industry relationships (Glenna et al. 2007). IP laws combine with incentive structures among academic researchers, universities, and corporations with devastating effects for SSTW biotechnology (DeVries & Toenniessen 2001, p. 273). Offerings to SSTW farmers also suffer when the technological regime of genetic modification becomes established enough to lock out competing considerations such as agroecological engineering (Vanloqueren & Baret 2009).

These general institutional relationships have been illuminated by studies of specific institutions conducting plant (and other) biotechnology; a pioneering example in anthropology was Rabinow's (1996) account of the commercialization of PCR (a technology playing a key role in plant genetic modification). Hodges (manuscript under review) follows the struggles over a potentially pro-SSTW technology in an institute collaborating with private firms; Kleinman (2003) observed incentives driving research while embedded in a plant biotechnology lab; Charles (2001) describes interactions between academic and corporate pioneers of plant biotechnology; and Scoones'

(2006) fieldwork on the biotechnology frontier in Bangalore examines how public policies interact with public and private research to shape development of GM products.

How GM crop development for SSTW agriculture should proceed is an open question. Virtually all stakeholders claim to be allied with the small farmer (Freidberg & Horowitz 2004), but discussions on research priorities usually occur with little knowledge of the complexities of agro-food systems and how technologies are embedded in social situations (Richards 2005). Collaborations between biotechnologists and social scientists are rare (but see Hall 2005, Richards et al. 2009), although social science provides valuable concepts for envisioning impacts of technological change, such as the technographic approach to how socially embedded technologies are actually used (Richards 2005, Thompson & Scoones 2009). Indigenous biologists may have a special contribution to make in choosing GM crop projects (Holmes & Graham 2009).

Anthropological perspectives have been used to advocate some specific GM technologies for SSTW farms. Cassava, an ecologically advantageous pro–poor crop that is difficult to breed conventionally, would benefit from GM for bio-fortification (Stone 2002b) and virus resistance (Stone 2005b). Bt brassicas (e.g., cabbage) could benefit small-scale vegetable producers (Vroom 2009). Apomixis (plant asexual reproduction) could be a step towards "uncommodification" of seeds (Bicknell and Bicknell 1999, Richards 2004, Stone 2002b), although after years of struggle between competing interests, GM apomictic maize is at least a decade from farmer fields (M. Hodges, manuscript under review).

It is ironic that the two most publicized GM technologies for SSTW farming are not in use at all, common perceptions notwithstanding. Golden Rice is a multigene technology for producing beta carotene (a vitamin A precursor) in the rice endosperm. As its announcement in 2000 coincided with the discursive shift to the developing world, it was lavishly publicized by the biotechnology industry and criticized vociferously by skeptics (Massieu & Chauvet 2005, RAFI 2000). A decade later it remains far from release, despite claims even by biotechnology leaders that it has already helped save many lives (Krock 2009). GM opponents found their own poster child when genetic modification was used to create a gene use restriction technology to produce crops with nonviable seeds.[5] Activists nicknamed this the "Terminator" and used it to depict GM crops as a threat to farmer independence and to impugn industry motives (Steinbrecher & Mooney 1998). This technology too is widely believed to be in common use, and/or to be in all GM seeds, but in reality it never advanced beyond testing.[6]

Downstream

Whatever the potential for pro-SSTW technologies, GM crops have been moving into developing countries, and economists and agricultural researchers have generated a substantial literature on farm-level impacts. Even-handed and thorough overviews of economic impacts are provided by Smale and colleagues at the International Food Policy Research Institute (IFPRI) (Smale et al. 2009). This body of research, in particular on Bt cotton (Smale et al. 2006; Tripp 2009b,d), shows predominantly positive economic impacts although the empirical record is varied and still short-term.[7] But a simple and essentialized summary of the crops' impacts is demanded by many, and this demand is met by two entrenched and contradictory narratives: one of general agronomic failure, especially of the pivotal crop of Bt cotton (critiqued by Herring 2009b), and one of resounding success (critiqued by Glover 2009).

An anthropological purview extends beyond yields to broader impacts on farmers and their practices (Stone 2011). As debates on GM crops turned to the developing world, biotechnologists pressed the case that genetic modification was especially suited to SSTW farmers because it was a self-contained technology that could aid cultivation without altering agricultural practice or even being understood by the farmer. In *Nature*, Kenyan biotechnologist Florence Wambugu (1999, p. 16) wrote that "[t]he great potential of biotechnology to increase agriculture in Africa lies in its 'packaged technology in the seed,' which ensures technology benefits without changing local cultural practices."[8]

However, many researchers who actually study agriculture are less inclined to see GM seeds as a "no-brainer" self-contained technology. Soleri et al. (2008) show that less market-oriented farmers use a more nuanced set of criteria for seed selection. Chataway (2005) and Tripp (2001a, 2009c) show that, far from being independent of agricultural practices and institutions, impacts of GM seeds are closely tied to a range of institutions involved in farming. Byerlee & Fischer (2002) show how prospects for GM technology in SSTW farming vary with indigenous research capacities, and Hall (2005) contrasts examples of progress in pro-SSTW biotechnologies in Asia and Africa. Indeed a key reason that GM seeds have had such varied impacts, and have raised such a wide range of questions, is the great variation in agriculture-related institutions and practices around the world. We have noted how many aspects of GM seeds are country specific, and

---

[5] This particular technology was developed by the U.S. Department of Agriculture and licensed to Delta Pine & Land, a cotton seed company. It was not the technology per se that initially caused uproar, but the 1998 announcement that Delta was being bought by Monsanto Corp., the *bête noire* of environmental movements (Charles 2001).

[6] It is interesting that many people who are disturbed by so-called terminator technology, which is not in use, are unaware that nonreplantability is the hallmark of hybrid seeds, which are widely used in industrial and SSTW farming.

[7] The research is also not free of biases. For instance, most Bt cotton studies comparing adopters and nonadopters suffer from selection bias because early adopters are not a random group but rather a sample biased toward successful farmers (Crost et al. 2007, Stone 2011).

[8] This narrative reached an apogee when biotechnologist Bruce Chassy explained that GM seeds were not too complex for farmers because "[g]enetic farming is the easiest way to cultivate crops. All that farmers have to do is to plant the seeds and water them regularly" (Thaindian News 2008). This statement, probably stunning to anyone who has actually studied farmers, was reprinted by biotechnologist C.S. Prakash (2008) as being from "a fellow biotech expert."

a survey of literature on downstream impacts can be organized along country lines.

Argentina and Brazil account for the great majority of the GM acres in developing countries (**Table 1**). Argentina has been featured in industry publicity that often elides "small farmers" with "developing countries"; in reality, most GM acres in Argentina are planted to commodity soybeans on highly industrialized farms averaging almost 500 ha (Qaim & Traxler 2005, Teubal 2008). Widespread adoption of GM soy has been eased by Argentina's weak IP protection (Raney 2006, Trigo & Cap 2003). Argentina also offers an intriguing contrast to other areas of the world (including in Latin America) where civil society ferment has impeded biotechnology; here the technology has been "secured in material, institutional and discursive arenas of power, producing a particular expression of 'bio-hegemony'" (Newell 2009). Brazil, by contrast, has seen social struggles over regulation (Pelaez & Schmidt 2004), which have important variations among regions (Jepson et al. 2008).

An extensive literature has been published on GM crops in Mexico. Social issues in small-scale Bt cotton farming are an interesting topic here: Traxler & Godoy-Avila (2004) consider how IP enforcement affects cotton farmers' seed saving, their relationship to gins, and the gins' relationship to Monsanto Corp. But the major issue in Mexico has been flow of transgenes into farmer varieties of maize. In 1998, Mexico banned planting of GM maize out of concern for gene flow into the many landraces in this center of diversity. In 2001, ecologists Quist & Chapela (2001) reported transgene contamination in landrace seeds and also asserted that the transgene had unstably integrated into the corn genome. Furor followed (more over the second claim than over the more important first one), including unusual attacks on the ecologists (Monbiot 2002, Worthy et al. 2005). Subsequent studies first failed to confirm the transgene contamination (Ortiz-García et al. 2005) and then succeeded (Piñeyro-Nelson et al. 2009). Effects of transgene introgression on local ecology and farming

practices are uncertain but troubling for Mexico (Fitting 2011, Gepts 2005, Soleri et al. 2006, Soleri & Cleveland 2006) as they are elsewhere in Latin America (Soleri et al. 2008). GM maize in Mexico has also been seen against the backdrop of trade liberalization (Fitting 2006).

South Africa, the only African country to approve GM crops, has been the scene of important collisions of interests (Freidberg & Horowitz 2004). GM maize and cotton have been grown there since 1996 on large farms, but there has been enormous interest in plantings of Bt cotton by Zulu smallholders in Makhathini Flats, KwaZulu-Natal. This case became a staple in the literature on GM crops after early reports of yield increases and rapid adoption seemed to exemplify benefits of GM crops for SSTW farmers (ISAAA 2002). However, it is not clear whether adoption of the technology indicates its benefit or lack of choice (Witt et al. 2006). Investigators later determined that the benefits were tied to the vertical integration in the local cotton industry and to extra services provided to Bt planters (Gouse et al. 2003, Smale et al. 2006), and economists judged this case a "technological triumph but institutional failure" (Gouse et al. 2005).

India, with its strong biology infrastructure, enormous population of farmers, and energetic civil society, has had a particularly heated debate on GM crops in which Indian writer Vandana Shiva has emerged as a leading opponent (Shiva 2000, 2005; Shiva et al. 1999; Shiva & Jafri 1998). India has seen a bitter dispute on the role of Bt cotton in farmer suicide. Biotechnology opponents linked GM seeds with farmer suicide even before the seeds had been adopted (Christian Aid 2000, Shiva & Jafri 1998), but biotechnology supporters also use farmer suicide to bolster their position (Stone 2002a). A growing body of research (Kantor 2008, Mohanty & Shroff 2004, Sridhar 2006, Vakulabharanam 2005) has not settled the matter; an IFPRI study (Gruère et al. 2008) shows that both the adoption timeline and the cost/benefit patterns exonerate Bt cotton, but activists (Shiva 2008) and British princes (Lean 2008) still blame GM seeds.

Anthropological research in a high-suicide area in Andhra Pradesh, India, found a more complex relationship between Bt cotton and farmer desperation. Just as Tripp (2001a,b) had warned of informational issues with the spread of GM seeds, studies in Andhra Pradesh found unrecognizability and frenetic change in the cotton seed market to have wrecked the "agricultural skilling" process (Stone 2005a, 2007a). GM seeds were hardly the cause of the suicides, but they did exacerbate the root causes. In Gujarat, Shah (2008) saw the spread of Bt cotton as conforming to a technological culture shaped by the green revolution; Bt cotton reinforced the hegemony of global and local elites (2005). But Gujarat also saw the unauthorized release of "stealth seeds" (Herring 2007), with stolen Bt technology bred into locally adapted cotton. This triggered a burst of farmer breeding and prosperity in Gujarat's cotton sector, contrasting the skilling problems that bedeviled farmers in Andhra Pradesh (Stone 2007b).

China is a unique case because of its early release of GM seeds and because GM crops are developed there largely by the state (Pray 1999). Bt cotton, available since 1997, is now planted widely (**Table 1**). As in Argentina, the cost of seeds in China is low owing to weak IP protection (Smale et al. 2006). Studies by economists of field-level impacts showed years of increased yields and reduced pesticide applications (Huang et al. 2009, Smale et al. 2006), followed by surging populations of pests not targeted by Bt, eroding the earlier benefits (Ho et al. 2009). Broader impacts of Bt cotton in China have been little studied, although some recent work focuses on livelihoods (Wang et al. 2009) and farmers' knowledge about the new seeds and trust in institutions (Ho et al. 2009). It is interesting that the successes of Bt cotton in China were facilitated by the breaking of the rules: The Bt trait has been bred in many locally adapted varieties of cotton, without authorization and without complying with biosafety regulations (Huang et al. 2009). Taken with the findings in Gujarat and Argentina, this case raises questions not only about whether GM crop technologies can be regulated, but also of whether they tend to work best in developing-world agriculture when they circumvent regulation.

Although the focus here is on sociocultural impacts in SSTW farming, there may have been significant impacts on industrial farmers in North America. For instance, biotechnology firms send detectives into farmers' fields and promote farmers turning each other in for noncompliance, which is punished by attempts at public shaming and lawsuits (Weiss 1999). The possibility of a "culture of surveillance" (Mehta 2005b) remains to be studied by rural sociology or anthropology.

ANTHROPOLOGY AND GM CROPS

The advent of GM crops obviously raises a range of questions of major interest in anthropology, and I have surveyed key issues and findings under the rubrics of political economy, responses and resistance, and impacts in developing countries. Although anthropology has shed important light in each of these areas, the overall contribution has not maintained the level of engagement that was signaled by pioneering work on biotechnology (Rabinow 1996). In particular there is need for research on more synthetic, indirect, and social aspects of the technology (Stone 2011). Many key questions about GM crops have been recognized but remain largely unresearched, including gendered effects (Bryant & Pini 2006, Morse & Bennett 2008), impacts on social cohesion (Mehta 2005b), and how biotechnology research changes in institutional cultures in developing countries (Richards 1994, Richards & Ruivenkamp 1996). Meanwhile, the demand for anthropologically informed analysis is frequently being filled by others. Thus when domestication of maize was compared with GM maize, the analysis was performed by a microbiologist (Fedoroff 2003), and it was a rheumatologist (Kwiecinski 2009) who questioned whether anthropological approaches help to explain people's irrational reactions to GM crops and food. Social aspects of biotechnology are often handled in major academic forums with coarse generalizations (e.g., Da Silva 1992).

GM crops are not going away, and they will continue to have highly consequential impacts on research agendas and institutional relationships, on IP rights, on civil society, on rural environments, and on farmers. An expanded role for anthropology, especially involving primary fieldwork, is definitely needed, whether it is to "take sides" or to concentrate on "how the sides came to be the way they are" (Murcott 2001).

DISCLOSURE STATEMENT

The author is not aware of any affiliations, memberships, funding, or financial holdings that might be perceived as affecting the objectivity of this review.

ACKNOWLEDGMENTS

Some of the material in this review is based on work supported by the National Science Foundation under Grants 0314404 and 0078396. I am also grateful to J.R. Bowen, A.G. Glore, and A.E. Stone.

LITERATURE CITED

Beachy RN. 1991. The very structure of scientific research does not mitigate against developing products to help the environment, the poor, and the hungry. *J. Agric. Environ. Ethics* 4:159–65

Berlan J-P, Lewontin RC. 1986. The political economy of hybrid corn. *Mon. Rev.* 38:35–47

Bicknell RA, Bicknell KB. 1999. Who will benefit from apomixis? *Biotechnol. Dev. Monit.* 37:17–20

Binswanger HP, Ruttan VW, eds. 1978. *Induced Innovation: Technology, Institutions, and Development.* Baltimore: Johns Hopkins Univ. Press

Bond M. 1999. Dr Truth. *New Sci.* 2218:74–77. **http://www.newscientist.com/article/mg16422185.000-dr-truth.html**

Bonny S. 2003. Why are most Europeans opposed to GMOs? Factors explaining rejection in France and Europe. *Electron. J. Biotechnol.* 6:50–71

Bowring F. 2003. *Science, Seeds and Cyborgs: Biotechnology and the Appropriation of Life.* London: Verso

Brannigan MC, ed. 2004. *Cross-Cultural Biotechnology.* Lanham, MD: Rowman & Littlefield

Braun R. 2002. People's concerns about biotechnology: some problems and some solutions. *J. Biotechnol.* 93:3–8

Brookes G, Barfoot P. 2006. Global impact of biotech crops: socio-economic and environmental effects in the first ten years of commercial use. *AgBioForum* 9:39–151. **http://www.agbioforum.org/v9n3/v9n3a02-brookes.htm**

Brooks S. 2005. Biotechnology and the politics of truth: from the Green Revolution to an Evergreen Revolution. *Sociol. Ruralis* 45:360–79

Brush SB. 1993. Indigenous knowledge of biological resources and intellectual property rights: the role of anthropology. *Am. Anthropol.* 95:653–86

Bryan W. 2001. Creating public alienation: expert cultures of risk and ethics on GMOs. *Sci. Cult.* 10:445–81

Bryant L, Pini B. 2006. Towards an understanding of gender and capital in constituting biotechnologies in agriculture. *Sociol. Ruralis* 46:261–79

Busch L. 2000. *The Eclipse of Morality: Science, State and Market.* New York: Aldine de Gruyter

Busch L, Lacy WB. 1983. *Science, Agriculture, and the Politics of Research.* Boulder, CO: Westview

Busch L, Lacy WB, Burkhardt J, Lacy LR. 1991. *Plants, Power, and Profit: Social, Economic, and Ethical Consequences of the New Biotechnologies.* Cambridge, UK: Blackwell

Buttel FH. 2003. The global politics of GEOs: the Achilles' heel of the globalization regime? See Schurman & Kelso 2003, pp. 152–73

Byerlee D, Fischer K. 2002. Accessing modern science: policy and institutional options for agricultural biotechnology in developing countries. *World Dev.* 30:931–48

Charles D. 2001. *Lords of the Harvest: Biotech, Big Money, and the Future of Food*. Cambridge, MA: Perseus

Charles HRH. 2006. Lady Eve Balfour memorial lecture, 1996. In *Speaking of Earth: Environmental Speeches that Moved the World*, ed. A Tal, pp. 195–200. Rutgers, NJ: Rutgers Univ. Press

Chataway J. 2005. Introduction: Is it possible to create pro-poor agriculture-related biotechnology? *J. Int. Dev.* 17:597–610

Christian Aid. 2000. *Selling Suicide, Farming, False Powers and Genetic Engineering in Developing Countries*. London: Christian Aid

Clapp J. 2005. The political economy of food aid in an era of agricultural biotechnology. *Glob. Gov.* 11:467–85

Clapp J. 2006. Unplanned exposure to genetically modified organisms: divergent responses in the global south. *J. Environ. Dev.* 15:3–21. **http://jed.sagepub.com/cgi/content/abstract/15/1/3**

Cleveland DA, Murray SC. 1997. The world's crop genetic resources and the rights of indigenous farmers. *Curr. Anthropol.* 38:477–515

Collier P. 2008. The politics of hunger: how illusion and greed fan the food crisis. *Foreign Aff.* 87(6):67–68

Conway G. 1998. *The Doubly Green Revolution: Food for all in the Twenty-First Century*. Ithaca, NY: Comstock

Cook G. 2004. *Genetically Modified Language: The Discourse of Arguments for GM Crops and Food*. London/New York: Routledge

Cook LJ. 2002. Millions served. *Forbes Mag.* Dec. 23 **http://www.forbes.com/forbes/2002/1223/302.html**

Crost B, Shankar B, Bennett R, Morse S. 2007. Bias from farmer self-selection in genetically modified crop productivity estimates: evidence from Indian data. *J. Agric. Econ.* 58:24–36. **http://www3. interscience.wiley.com/journal/120700319/abstract**

Crouch M. 1991. The very structure of scientific research mitigates against developing products to help the environment, the poor, and the hungry. *J. Agric. Environ. Ethics* 4:151–58

Da Silva EJ. 1992. Biotechnology: socio-economic considerations, intercultural perspectives and international viewpoints. In *Biotechnology: Economic and Social Aspects, Issues for Developing Countries*, ed. EJ Da Silva, C Ratledge, A Sasson, pp. 189–217. Cambridge, UK: Cambridge Univ. Press

DeVries J, Toenniessen G. 2001. *Securing the Harvest: Biotechnology, Breeding and Seed Systems for African Crops*. New York: CABI Int.

Du Bois CM, de Sousa ISF. 2008. Genetically engineered soy. In *The World of Soy*, ed. CM Du Bois, C-B Tan, S Mintz, pp. 74–96. Urbana: Univ. Ill. Press

Ellstrand NC. 2001. When transgenes wander, should we worry? *Plant Physiol.* 125:1543–45. **http://www.plantphysiol.org/cgi/reprint/125/4/1543**

Etzkowitz H. 1997. The entrepreneurial university and the emergence of democratic corporatism. See Etzkowitz & Leydesdorff 1997b, pp. 141–52

Etzkowitz H, Leydesdorff L. 1997a. Introduction: Universities in the global knowledge economy. See Etzkowitz & Leydesdorff 1997b, pp. 1–8

Etzkowitz H, Leydesdorff L, eds. 1997b. *Universities and the Global Knowledge Economy: A Triple Helix of University-Industry-Government Relations*. London: Pinter

Evenson RE, Raney T, eds. 2007. *The Political Economy of Genetically Modified Foods*. Cheltenham, UK: Edward Elgar

Feder BJ. 1999. Plant sterility research inflames debate on biotechnology's role in farming. *New York Times* April 19: A18

Fedoroff NV. 2003. Prehistoric GM corn. *Science* 302:1158–59

Finucane ML. 2002. Mad cows, mad corn and mad communities: the role of socio-cultural factors in the perceived risk of genetically-modified food. *Proc. Nutr. Soc.* 61:31–37

Finucane ML, Holup JL. 2005. Psychosocial and cultural factors affecting the perceived risk of genetically modified food: an overview of the literature. *Soc. Sci. Med.* 60:1603–12

Fitting E. 2006. Importing corn, exporting labor: the neoliberal corn regime, GMOs, and the erosion of biodiversity in Mexico. *Agric. Hum. Values* 23:15–26

Fitting E. 2011. *The Struggle for Maize: Campesinos, Workers, and Transgenic Corn in the Mexican Countryside*. Durham, NC: Duke Univ. Press

Fitzgerald D. 1990. *The Business of Breeding: Hybrid Corn in Illinois 1890–1940*. Ithaca, NY: Cornell Univ. Press

Fleising U, Smart A. 1993. The development of property rights in biotechnology. *Cult. Med. Psychiatry* 17:43–57

Foster JB. 2002. Marx's ecology in historical perspective. *Int. Soc.* 97:71–86

Foucault M. 1978. *The History of Sexuality*. Vol. 1: *The Will to Knowledge*. London: Penguin

Freidberg S, Horowitz L. 2004. Converging networks and clashing stories: South Africa's agricultural biotechnology debate. *Afr. Today* 51:2–25

Gaskell G, Allum N, Bauer M, Durant J, Allansdottir A, et al. 2000. Biotechnology and the European public. *Nat. Biotechnol.* 18:935–38

Gaskell G, Bauer MW, Durant J, Allum NC. 1999. Worlds apart? The reception of genetically modified foods in Europe and the U.S. *Science* 285:384–87

Gaskell G, Jackson J, Ten Eyck T, Einsiedel E, Priest SH. 2007. Transatlantic tensions over GM crops and foods: diverging perspectives. In *Genomics and Society: Legal, Ethical and Social Dimensions*, ed. G Gaskell, MW Bauer, pp. 346–66. London: Earthscan

Gepts P. 2005. Introduction of transgenic crops in centers of origin and domestication. See Kleinman et al. 2005, pp. 119–34

Glenna L, Lacy W, Welsh R, Biscotti D. 2007. University administrators, agricultural biotechnology, and academic capitalism: defining the public good to promote university-industry relationships. *Sociol. Q.* 48:141–63

Glover D. 2009. *Undying promise: agricultural biotechnology's pro-poor narrative, ten years on*. Work. Pap. 15, STEPS Centre, Brighton. **http://www.steps-center.org/PDFs/Bt%20Cotton%20web.pdf**

Glover D. 2010. The corporate shaping of GM crops as a technology for the poor. *J. Peasant Stud.* 37:67–90

Golden JM. 2001. Biotechnology, technology policy, and patentability: natural products and invention in the American system. *Emory Law J.* 50:101–91

Goodman D. 2003. The brave new worlds of agricultural technoscience: changing perspectives, recurrent themes, and new research. See Schurman & Kelso 2003, pp. 218–38

Goodman D, Sorj B, Wilkinson J. 1987. *From Farming to Biotechnology: A Theory of Agro-Industrial Development*. Oxford, UK: Basil Blackwell

Gouse M, Kirsten J, Jenkins L. 2003. Bt cotton in South Africa: adoption and the impact on farm incomes among small-scale and large scale farmers. *Agrekon* 42:15–29

Gouse M, Kirsten J, Shankar B, Thirtle C. 2005. KwaZulu Natal: technological triumph but institutional failure. *AgBiotechNet* 7:1–7

Gruère GP, Mehta-Bhatt P, Sengupta D. 2008. Bt cotton and farmer suicides in India: reviewing the evidence. *IFPRI Discuss. Pap. 808* **http://www.ifpri.org/pubs/dp/ifpridp00808.asp**

Gusterson H. 2005. Decoding the debate on "Frankenfood". In *Making Threats: Biofears and Environmental Anxieties*, ed. B Hartmann, B Subramanian, C Zerner, pp. 109–33. Lanham, MD: Rowman & Littlefield

Halford NG. 2003. *Genetically Modified Crops*. London: Imp. Coll. Press

Hall A. 2005. Capacity development for agricultural biotechnology in developing countries: an innovation systems view of what it is and how to develop it. *J. Int. Dev.* 17:611–30

Hamilton ND. 1993. Who owns dinner? Evolving legal mechanisms for ownership of plant genetic resources. *Tulsa Law J.* 28:587–657

Haraway DJ. 1997. *Modest_Witness@Second_Millennium.FemaleMan©_Meets_OncoMouse*™. New York: Routledge

Harper K. 2004. The genius of a nation versus the gene-tech of a nation: science, identity, and genetically modified food in Hungary. *Sci. Cult.* 13:471–92

Harvey M. 2004. The appearance and disappearance of GM tomato: innovation strategy, market formation and the shaping of demand. See Jansen & Vellema 2004, pp. 68–90

Heller C. 2001. McDonald's, MTV and Monsanto: resisting biotechnology in the age of informational capital. In *Redesigning Life? The Worldwide Challenge to Genetic Engineering*, ed. B Tokar, pp. 405–19. Montreal/Kingston: McGill-Queen's Univ. Press

Heller C. 2006. Post-industrial "quality agricultural discourse": techniques of governance and resistance in the French debate over GM crops. *Soc. Anthropol.* 14:319–34

Heller C. 2007. Techne versus technoscience: divergent (and ambiguous) notions of food "quality" in the French debate over GM crops. *Am. Anthropol.* 109:603–15

Herdt RW. 2006. Biotechnology in agriculture. *Annu. Rev. Environ. Resour.* 31:265–95

Herring RJ. 2007. Stealth seeds: bioproperty, biosafety, biopolitics. *J. Dev. Stud.* 43:130–57

Herring RJ. 2008a. Opposition to transgenic technologies: ideology, interests and collective action frames. *Nat. Biotechnol.* 9:458–63

Herring RJ. 2008b. Whose numbers count? Probing discrepant evidence on transgenic cotton in the Warangal district of India. *Int. J. Mult. Res. Approaches* 2:145–59

Herring RJ. 2009a. China, rice, and GMOs: navigating the global rift on genetic engineering. *Asia-Pac. J.* 3-2-09 **http://japanfocus.org/articles/print_article/3012**

Herring RJ. 2009b. Persistent narratives: Why is the "failure of Bt cotton in India" story still with us? *AgBio-Forum* 12:14–22. **http://www.agbioforum.missouri.edu/v12n1/v12n1a02-herring.htm**

Ho P, Zhao JH, Xue D. 2009. Access and control of agro-biotechnology: Bt cotton, ecological change and risk in China. *J. Peasant Stud.* 36:345–64

Holmes C, Graham JE. 2009. Genetically modified organisms as public goods: plant biotechnology transfer in Colombia. *Cult. Agric.* 31:26–38

Huang J, Chen R, Mi J, Hu R, Osir E. 2009. Farmers' seed and pest control management for Bt cotton in China. See Tripp 2009b, pp. 105–34

Huxley A. 1932. *Brave New World*. London: HarperCollins

ISAAA. 2002. *The Makhatini Story: Bt Cotton and Sustainable Development*. Ithaca, NY: Int. Serv. Acquis. Agri-Biotech Appl.

Isaac G. 2002. *Agricultural Biotechnology and Transatlantic Trade: Regulatory Barriers to GM Crops*. Wallingford, CT/New York: CABI Int.

James C. 2010. Global status of commercialized biotech/GM crops: 2009. *ISAAA Brief No. 41*. Ithaca, NY: Int. Serv. Acquis. Agri-Biotech Appl.

Jansen K, Vellema S, eds. 2004. *Agribusiness and Society: Corporate Responses to Environmentalism, Market Opportunities and Public Regulation*. London: Zed

Jasanoff S. 2005. *Designs on Nature: Science and Democracy in Europe and the United States*. Princeton, NJ/Oxford: Princeton Univ. Press

Jepson WE, Brannstrom C, De Souza RS. 2008. Brazilian biotechnology governance: consensus and conflict over genetically modified crops. In *Food for the Few: Neoliberal Globalism and Biotechnology in Latin America*, ed. G Otero, pp. 217–42. Austin: Univ. Tex. Press

Kalaitzandonakes N, Marks LA, Vickner SS. 2004. Media coverage of biotech foods and influence on consumer choice. *Am. J. Agric. Econ.* 86:1238–46

Kantor HS. 2008. *Poisoned futures: pesticide usage and agrarian suicide in Vidarbha, India*. MA thesis, Univ. Chicago

Kenney M. 1986. *Biotechnology: The University Industrial Complex*. New Haven, CT: Yale Univ. Press

Kleinman DL. 2003. *Impure Cultures: University Biology and the World of Commerce*. Madison: Univ. Wis. Press

Kleinman DL, Kinchy AJ, Handelsman J, eds. 2005. *Controversies in Science and Technology: From Maize to Menopause*. Madison: Univ. Wis. Press

Kloppenburg JR Jr. 2004. *First the Seed: The Political Economy of Plant Biotechnology, 1492–2000*. Madison: Univ. Wis. Press. 2nd ed.

Koppel BM. 1995. *Induced Innovation Theory and International Agricultural Development*. Baltimore, MD/London: Johns Hopkins Univ. Press

Krock B. 2009. Researchers look to enriched crops to solve childhood malnutrition. *Student Life* (Wash. Univ.) Sept. 28. **http://www.studlife.com/news/2009/09/28/researchers-look-to-enriched-crops-to-solve-childhood-malnutrition/**

Kwiecinski J. 2009. Genetically modified abominations? *EMBO Rep.* 10:1187–90. **http://dx.doi.org/10.1038/embor.2009.230**

Lambrecht B. 2001. *Dinner at the New Gene Cafe: How Genetic Engineering Is Changing What We Eat, How We Live, and the Global Politics of Food*. New York: St. Martins Press

Langreth R, Herper M. 2010. The planet versus Monsanto. *Forbes Mag.* Jan. 18. **http://www.forbes.com/forbes/2010/0118/americas-best-company-10-gmos-dupont-planet-versus-monsanto.html**

Lean G. 2008. Charles: "I blame GM crops for farmers' suicides." *Independent (London)*, Oct. 5

Lewontin RC. 2000. The maturing of capitalist agriculture: farmer as proletarian. See Magdoff et al. 2000, pp. 93–106

Lewontin RC, Berlan J-P. 1986. Technology, research, and the penetration of capital: the case of U.S. agriculture. *Mon. Rev.* 38:21–34

Liang GH, Skinner DZ, eds. 2004. *Genetically Modified Crops: Their Development, Uses, and Risks.* Binghamton, NY: Haworth

Lurquin PF. 2001. *The Green Phoenix: A History of Genetically Modified Plants.* New York: Columbia Univ. Press

Magdoff F, Foster J, Buttel F, eds. 2000. *Hungry for Profit: The Agribusiness Threat to Farmers, Food, and the Environment.* New York: Mon. Rev. Press

Mann S, Dickinson J. 1978. Obstacles to the development of capitalist agriculture. *J. Peasant Stud.* 5:466–81

Marsden TK, Bridge G, McManis P. 2003. The next new thing? Biotechnology and its discontents. *Geoforum* 34:165–75

Martineau B. 2001. *First Fruit: The Creation of the Flavr SavrTM Tomato and the Birth of Genetically Engineered Food.* New York: McGraw-Hill

Marx K. 1858. *The Grundrisse.* **http://www.marxists.org/archive/marx/works/1857/grundrisse/ch10.htm**

Massieu Y, Chauvet M. 2005. Contesting biotechnology: cross-continental concerns about genetically modified crops. In *Cross-Continental Agro-Food Chains: Structures, Actors and Dynamics in the Global Food System,* ed. B Pritchard, N Fold, pp. 66–77. London: Routledge

McAfee K. 2003. Biotech battles: plants, power and intellectual property in the new global governance regimes. See Schurman & Kelso 2003, pp. 174–94

McGloughlin M. 1999. Ten reasons why biotechnology will be important to the developing world. *AgBioForum* 2:163–74. **http://www.agbioforum.org/v2n34/v2n34a04-mcgloughlin.htm**

McMichael P. 2000. Global food politics. See Magdoff et al. 2000, pp. 125–43

Mehta MD, ed. 2005a. *Biotechnology Unglued: Science, Society, and Social Cohesion.* Vancouver: Univ. B. C. Press

Mehta MD. 2005b. The impact of agricultural biotechnology on social cohesion. See Mehta 2005a, pp. 13–26

Middendorf G, Skladny M, Ransom E, Busch L. 2000. New agricultural biotechnologies: the struggle for democratic choice. See Magdoff et al. 2000, pp. 107–23

Mirza B. 2004. Islamic perspectives on biotechnology. See Brannigan 2004, pp. 105–14

Moffat AS. 1999. Crop engineering goes south. *Science* 285:370–71

Mohanty BB, Shroff S. 2004. Farmers' suicides in Maharashtra. *Econ. Pol. Wkly.* 39:5599–606

Monbiot G. 2002. The fake persuaders. *Guardian* May 14. **http://www.monbiot.com/archives/2002/05/14/the-fake-persuaders/**

Monsanto Corp. 2001. A brief biotech timeline. **http://www.biotechknowledge.com/biotech/bbasics.nsf/timeline.html**

Morse S, Bennett R. 2008. Impact of Bt cotton on farmer livelihoods in South Africa. *Int. J. Biotechnol.* 10:224–39

Munro W, Schurman R. 2009. Chain (re)actions: comparing activist mobilization against biotechnology in Britain and the U.S. In *Frontiers in Commodity Chains Research,* ed. J Bair, pp. 207–30. Stanford, CA: Stanford Univ. Press

Murcott A. 2001. Public beliefs about GM foods: more on the makings of a considered sociology. *Med. Anthropol. Q.* 15:9–19

Nelson S. 2005. Deconstructing genetically modified organisms? Academic discourse on GMOs and its effect on popular understandings of food and agriculture. *Int. J. Technol. Manage. Sustain. Dev.* 4:21–33

Netting RM. 1993. *Smallholders, Householders: Farm Families and the Ecology of Intensive, Sustainable Agriculture.* Stanford, CA: Stanford Univ. Press

Newell P. 2009. Bio-hegemony: the political economy of agricultural biotechnology in Argentina. *J. Latin Am. Stud.* 41:27–57

Ortiz-García S, Ezcurra E, Schoel B, Acevedo F, Soberón J, Snow A. 2005. Absence of detectable transgenes in local landraces of maize in Oaxaca, Mexico (2003–2004). *Proc. Natl. Acad. Sci. USA* 102:12338–43

Otero G, ed. 2008. *Food for the Few: Neoliberal Globalism and Biotechnology in Latin America.* Austin: Univ. Tex. Press

Paarlberg R. 2000. Genetically modified crops in developing countries: promise or peril? *Environment* 42:19–27

Paarlberg R. 2008. *Starved for Science: How Biotechnology Is Being Kept out of Africa*. Cambridge, MA/London: Harvard Univ. Press

Parayil G. 2003. Mapping technological trajectories of the Green Revolution and the Gene Revolution from modernization to globalization. *Res. Policy* 32:971–90

Pechlaner G, Otero G. 2008. The third food regime: neoliberal globalism and agricultural biotechnology in North America. *Sociol. Ruralis* 48:351–71

Pelaez V, Da Silva LR. 2008. Social resistance to biotechnology: attempts to create a genetically modified-free territory in Brazil. *Int. J. Tech. Glob.* 4:207–22

Pelaez V, Schmidt W. 2004. Social struggles and the regulation of transgenic crops in Brazil. See Jansen & Vellema 2004, pp. 232–61

Peters HP, Lang JT, Sawicka M, Hallman WK. 2007. Culture and technological innovation: impact of institutional trust and appreciation of nature on attitudes towards food biotechnology in the USA and Germany. *Int. J. Public Opin. Res.* 19:191–220

Piñeyro-Nelson A, Heerwaarden JV, Perales HR, Serratos-Hernández JA, Rangel A, et al. 2009. Transgenes in Mexican maize: molecular evidence and methodological considerations for GMO detection in landrace populations. *Mol. Ecol.* 18:750–61

Pinstrup-Andersen P, Schioler E. 2000. *Seeds of Contention: World Hunger and the Global Controversy Over GM Crops*. Baltimore, MD: Johns Hopkins Univ. Press

Prakash CS. 2008. Genetic engineering can help solve food crisis: US expert. *AgBioWorld*. **http://www.gmofoodforthought.com/2008/07/genetic_engineering_can_help_s.html**

Pray CE. 1999. Public and private collaboration on plant biotechnology in China. *AgBioForum* 2:48–53

Pretty J, Hine R. 2000. The promising spread of sustainable agriculture in Asia. *Nat. Resour. Forum* 24:107–21

Pretty J, Noble AD, Bossio D, Dixon J, Hine RE, et al. 2006. Resource-conserving agriculture increases yields in developing countries. *Environ. Sci. Technol.* 40:1114–19

Priest SH. 2001. *A Grain of Truth: The Media, The Public, and Biotechnology*. Lanham, MD: Rowman & Littlefield

Priest SH. 2004. Biotechnology, media and public opinion across national boundaries. *Ecquid Novi: Afr. J. Stud.* 25:80–93

Pringle P. 2003. *Food, Inc: Mendel to Monsanto—The Promises and Perils of the Biotech Harvest*. New York: Simon & Schuster

Qaim M, Traxler G. 2005. Roundup ready soybeans in Argentina: farm level and aggregate welfare effects. *Agric. Econ.* 32:73–86

Quist D, Chapela I. 2001. Transgenic DNA introgressed into traditional maize landraces in Oaxaca, Mexico. *Nature* 414:541–43

Rabinow P. 1996. *Making PCR: A Story of Biotechnology*. Chicago: Univ. Chicago Press

RAFI. 2000. Golden rice and trojan trade reps: a case study in the public sector's mismanagement of intellectual property. *RAFI Communique* 66. **http://www.etcgroup.org/upload/publication/305/01/com_goldenrice.pdf**

Raney T. 2006. Economic impact of transgenic crops in developing countries. *Curr. Opin. Biotechnol.* 17:174–78

Reichman E. 2004. Why is this gene different from all other genes? The Jewish approach to biotechnology. See Brannigan 2004, pp. 93–104

Richards P. 1985. *Indigenous Agricultural Revolution*. London: Hutchinson

Richards P. 1994. The shaping of biotechnology: institutional culture and ideotypes. *Biotechnol. Dev. Monit.* 18:24. **http://www.biotech-monitor.nl/1813.htm**

Richards P. 1997. Toward an African green revolution? An anthropology of rice research in Sierra Leone. In *The Ecology of Practice: Studies of Food Crop Production in Sub-Saharan West Africa*, ed. AE Nyerges, pp. 201–52. Amsterdam: Gordon and Breach

Richards P. 2004. Private versus public? Agenda-setting in international agro-technologies. See Jansen & Vellema 2004, pp. 261–84

Richards P. 2005. Plant biotechnology and the rights of the poor: a technographic approach. In *Science and Citizens: Globalization and the Challenge of Engagement*, ed. M Leach, I Scoones, B Wynne, pp. 199–212. London: Zed

Richards P, Bruin-Hoekzema MD, Hughes SG, Kudadjie-Freeman C, Offei S, et al. 2009. Seed systems for African food security: linking molecular genetic analysis and cultivator knowledge in West Africa. *Int. J. Technol. Manage.* 45:196–214

Richards P, Ruivenkamp G. 1996. New tools for conviviality: society and biotechnology. In *Nature and Society: Anthropological Perspectives*, ed. P Descola, G Palsson, pp. 275–95. London: Routledge

Ross EB. 1998. *The Malthus Factor: Population, Poverty, and Politics in Capitalist Development.* London: Zed

Santaniello V, Evenson RE, Zilberman D, Carlson GA, eds. 2000. *Agriculture and Intellectual Property Rights: Economic, Institutional and Implementation Issues in Biotechnology.* Wallingford, UK: CABI

Schurman RA, Kelso DDT, eds. 2003. *Engineering Trouble: Biotechnology and Its Discontents.* Berkeley: Univ. Calif. Press

Schurman RA, Munro WA. 2003. Making biotech history: social resistance to agricultural biotechnology and the future of the biotechnology industry. See Schurman & Kelso 2003, pp. 111–29

Scoones I. 2002. Can agricultural biotechnology be pro-poor? A skeptical look at the emerging 'consensus'. *IDS Bull.* 33(4):114–19. **http://www.steps-center.org/PDFs/IS_bull33_4.pdf**

Scoones I. 2006. *Science, Agriculture and the Politics of Policy: The Case of Biotechnology in India.* New Delhi: Orient Longman

Scoones I. 2008. Mobilizing against GM crops in India, South Africa and Brazil. *J. Agrar. Change* 8:315–44

Shah E. 2005. Local and global elites join hands: development and diffusion of Bt cotton technology in Gujarat. *Econ. Pol. Wkly.* 40:4629–39

Shah E. 2008. What makes crop biotechnology find its roots? The technological culture of Bt cotton in Gujarat, India. *Eur. J. Dev. Res.* 20:432–47

Shiva V. 2000. *Stolen Harvest: The Hijacking of the Global Food Supply.* Cambridge, MA: South End

Shiva V. 2005. *India Divided: Diversity and Democracy under Attack.* New York: Seven Stories

Shiva V. 2008. *Toxic Genes and Toxic Papers: IFPRI Covering Up the Link Between Bt Cotton and Farmers Suicides.* New Delhi: Res. Found. Sci. Technol. Ecol. **http://www.zcommunications.org/zspace/commentaries/3748**

Shiva V, Emani A, Jafri AH. 1999. Globalisation and threat to seed security: case of transgenic cotton trials in India. *Econ. Pol. Wkly.* 34:601–13

Shiva V, Jafri AH. 1998. *Seeds of Suicide: The Ecological and Human Costs of Globalization of Agriculture.* New Delhi: Res. Found. Sci. Technol. Ecol.

Showalter AM, Heuberger S, Tabashnik BE, Carrièred Y. 2009. A primer for using transgenic insecticidal cotton in developing countries. *J. Insect Sci.* 9:22. **http://www.insectscience.org/9.22/#b89-9-22**

Slaughter S, Leslie LL. 1997. *Academic Capitalism: Politics, Policies, and the Entrepreneurial University.* Baltimore, MD/London: Johns Hopkins Univ. Press

Slaughter S, Rhoades G. 2004. *Academic Capitalism and the New Economy: Markets, State and Higher Education.* Baltimore, MD: Johns Hopkins Univ. Press

Smale M, Zambrano P, Cartel M. 2006. Bales and balance: a review of the methods used to assess the economic impact of Bt cotton on farmers in developing economies. *AgBioForum* 9:195–212. **http://www.agbioforum.org/v9n3/v9n3a06-zambrano.htm**

Smale M, Zambrano P, Gruère G, Falck-Zepeda J, Matuschke I, et al. 2009. Measuring the economic impacts of transgenic crops in developing agriculture during the first decade: approaches, findings, and future directions. *No. 10, Food Policy Rev.* Washington, DC: Int. Food Policy Res. Inst. (IFPRI). **http://econpapers.repec.org/RePEc:fpr:fprevi:10**

Snow AA. 2005. Genetic modification and gene flow: an overview. See Kleinman et al. 2005, pp. 107–18

Soleri D, Cleveland DA. 2006. Transgenic maize and Mexican maize diversity: risky synergy? *Agric. Hum. Values* 23:27–31

Soleri D, Cleveland DA, Cuevas FA. 2006. Transgenic crops and crop varietal diversity: the case of maize in Mexico. *BioScience* 56:503–13

Soleri D, Cleveland DA, Glasgow G, Sweeney SH, Cuevas FA, et al. 2008. Testing assumptions underlying economic research on transgenic food crops for Third World farmers: evidence from Cuba, Guatemala and Mexico. *Ecol. Econ.* 67:667–82. doi:10.1016/j.ecolecon.2008.01.031

Spielman DJ. 2007. Pro-poor agricultural biotechnology: Can the international research system deliver the goods? *Food Policy* 32:189–204

Sridhar V. 2006. Why do farmers commit suicide? The case of Andhra Pradesh. *Econ. Pol. Wkly.* 41:1559–65

Stein H. 2005. Intellectual property and genetically modified seeds: the United States, trade, and the developing world. *Northwest. J. Technol. Intellect. Property* 3:160–78. **http://www.law.northwestern.edu/journals/njtip/v3/n2/4/Stein.pdf**

Steinbrecher RA, Mooney PR. 1998. Terminator technology: the threat to world food security. *Ecologist* 28:276–79

Stone GD. 2002a. Biotechnology and suicide in India. *Anthropol. News* 43(5). **http://artsci.wustl.edu/~anthro/research/biotech_suicide.html**

Stone GD. 2002b. Both sides now: fallacies in the genetic-modification wars, implications for developing countries, and anthropological perspectives. *Curr. Anthropol.* 43:611–30

Stone GD. 2002c. Crop biotechnology backgrounder (online enhancement to "Both Sides Now: Fallacies in the Genetic-Modification Wars, Implications for Developing Countries, and Anthropological Perspectives"). *Curr. Anthropol. (online)* Vol. 43

Stone GD. 2005a. Biotechnology and the political ecology of information in India. *Hum. Organ.* 63:127–40

Stone GD. 2005b. A science of the gray: Malthus, Marx, and the ethics of studying crop biotechnology. In *Embedding Ethics: Shifting Boundaries of the Anthropological Profession*, ed. L Meskell, P Pels, pp. 197–217. Oxford: Berg

Stone GD. 2007a. Agricultural deskilling and the spread of genetically modified cotton in Warangal. *Curr. Anthropol.* 48:67–103

Stone GD. 2007b. The birth and death of traditional knowledge: paradoxical effects of biotechnology in India. In *Biodiversity and the Law: Intellectual Property, Biotechnology and Traditional Knowledge*, ed. C McManis, pp. 207–38. London: Earthscan

Stone GD. 2011. Field vs. farm in Warangal: Bt cotton, higher yields, and larger questions. *World Devel.* In press

Stone GD, Glover D. 2011. Genetically modified crops and the food crisis: discourse and material impacts. *Dev. Pract.* In press

Teubal M. 2008. Genetically modified soybeans and the crisis of Argentina's agriculture model. See Otero 2008, pp. 189–216

Thaindian News. 2008. Genetic engineering can help solve food crisis: US expert. **http://www.gmofoodforthought.com/2008/07/genetic_engineering_can_help_s.html**

Thompson J, Scoones I. 2009. Addressing the dynamics of agri-food systems: an emerging agenda for social science research. *Environ. Sci. Policy* 12:386–97

Thomson JA. 2002. *Genes for Africa: Genetically Modified Crops in the Developing World*. Landsdowne, South Afr.: Univ. Cape Town Press

TIME Mag. 2000. Cover. *TIME Mag.* Aug. 7

Traxler G, Godoy-Avila S. 2004. Transgenic cotton in Mexico. *AgBioForum* 7:57–62

Trigo EJ, Cap EJ. 2003. The impact of the introduction of transgenic crops in Argentinean agriculture. *AgBioForum* 6:87–94. **http://www.agbioforum.org/v6n3/v6n3a01-trigo.htm**

Tripp R. 2001a. Can biotechnology reach the poor? The adequacy of information and seed delivery. *Food Policy* 26:249–64

Tripp R. 2001b. "Twixt cup and lip"—biotechnology and resource-poor farmers. *Nat. Biotechnol.* 19:93

Tripp R. 2009a. Biotechnology and agricultural development. See Tripp 2009b, pp. 1–22

Tripp R, ed. 2009b. *Biotechnology and Agricultural Development: Transgenic Cotton, Rural Institutions and Resource-Poor Farmers*. London/New York: Routledge

Tripp R. 2009c. Transgenic cotton and institutional performance. See Tripp 2009b, pp. 88–104

Tripp R. 2009d. Transgenic cotton: assessing economic performance in the field. See Tripp 2009b, pp. 72–87

Vakulabharanam V. 2005. Growth and distress in a South Indian peasant economy during the era of economic liberalisation. *J. Dev. Stud.* 41:971–97

Vanloqueren G, Baret PV. 2009. How agricultural research systems shape a technological regime that develops genetic engineering but locks out agroecological innovations. *Res. Policy* 39:971–83

Vroom W. 2009. *Reflexive Biotechnology Development: Studying Plant Breeding Technologies and Genomics for Agriculture in the Developing World*. Wageningen, The Neth.: Wageningen Acad.

Wambugu F. 1999. Why Africa needs agricultural biotech. *Nature* 400:15–16

Wandel M. 2005. Genetically modified food in Norway: a consumer perspective. See Mehta 2005a, pp. 70–94

Wang G, Wu Y, Gao W, Fok M, Liang W. 2009. Impact of Bt cotton on the farmer's livelihood system in China. *Life Sci. Int. J.* Spec. Ed. on Cotton Policies, 1:132–39. **http://halshs.archives-ouvertes.fr/halshs-00324390/**

Weiss R. 1999. Seeds of discord; Monsanto's gene police raise alarm on farmers' rights, rural tradition. *Washington Post* Feb. 3:A1

Welsh R, Glenna L. 2006. Considering the role of the university in conducting research on agri-biotechnologies. *Soc. Stud. Sci.* 36:929–42

Witt H, Patel R, Schnurr M. 2006. Can the poor help GM crops? Technology, representation and cotton in the Makhathini Flats, South Africa. *Rev. Afr. Pol. Econ.* 109:497–513

Worthy K, Strohman R, Billings P, Delborne J, Duarte-Trattner E, et al. 2005. Agricultural biotechnology science compromised: the case of Quist and Chapela. See Kleinman et al. 2005, pp. 135–49

Wu F. 2004. Explaining public resistance to genetically modified corn: an analysis of the distribution of benefits and risks. *Risk Anal.* 24:715–26

Water Sustainability: Anthropological Approaches and Prospects

Ben Orlove[1] and Steven C. Caton[2]

[1] School of International and Public Affairs, Columbia University, New York, NY 10027;
email: bso5@columbia.edu

[2] Department of Anthropology, Harvard University, Cambridge, Massachusetts 02138;
email: caton@wjh.harvard.edu

Annu. Rev. Anthropol. 2010. 39:401–15

First published online as a Review in Advance on
June 21, 2010

The *Annual Review of Anthropology* is online at
anthro.annualreviews.org

This article's doi:
10.1146/annurev.anthro.012809.105045

Key Words

value, equity, governance, politics, regimes, integrated water resource
management

Abstract

Water has become an urgent theme in anthropology as the worldwide
need to provide adequate supplies of clean water to all people becomes
more challenging. Anthropologists contribute by seeing water not only
as a resource, but also as a substance that connects many realms of social
life. They trace the different forms of valuing water, examine the often
unequal distribution of water, explore the rules and institutions that
govern water use and shape water politics, and study the multiple, often
conflicting knowledge systems through which actors understand water.
They offer ethnographic insights into key water sites—watersheds, water regimes, and waterscapes—found in all settings, though with widely
varying characteristics. Anthropologists provide a critical examination
of a concept called integrated water resource management (IWRM),
which has become hegemonic in the global discourse of sustainable
development.

INTRODUCTION

We propose to study water as a "total social fact" (Mauss 1990). Although Mauss had prestations or "service exchanges" principally in mind when he spoke of the total social fact, he did not limit this kind of fact to them. It suffices that

> in these 'total' social phenomena, as we propose calling them, all kinds of institutions are given expression at one and the same time—religious, juridical, and moral, which relate to both politics and the family; likewise economic ones, which suppose special forms of production and consumption, or rather, of performing total services and distribution. This is not to take into account the aesthetic phenomena to which these facts lead, and the contours of the phenomena that these institutions manifest. (p. 3)

In the conclusion of the essay, Mauss explains that in his approach "[one] has the advantage of...seeing the social 'things' themselves, in concrete form and as they are" (p. 80).

Although we have the tendency to reduce water to a biological fact when thinking about its nature, it is integral, even essential, to many if not most domains or institutions of society—economic, political, religious, leisure, etc., as Strang (2004, p. 5) recognizes in her discussion of the "essentiality" of water. In this way, water is social and total in precisely the encompassing sense that Mauss had in mind. At the same time, water as a social fact takes concrete forms, even though physically and in the abstract we conceive of it as a continuous and homogeneous substance. When washing our bodies, we think of personal hygiene, and yet it matters to us whether water is delivered by a spigot into a bath or by a shower head into a stall whether the spray is strong or weak, sharp or gentle; and let us not even approach the cultural nuances of water temperature and softness. In these concrete forms, water is totalistically connected to the domain of public health and to popular notions of water as an invigorating as well as a sensually pleasurable substance, as a morning social ritual, and as a political-economic aesthetic (as seen in accessories of showerheads, metal fixtures, shower stalls, bathroom tiles, mirrors, etc.). The choices and meanings are no less complex for a Ugandan farmer, who squats or sits on a low bench, first transferring water (usually, but not always, heated over an open wood fire) from a jerrycan or pot into a plastic basin, and then dipping out the tepid or warm or hot water (using either a plastic cup with a handle or the two hands pressed together to form a kind of scoop) and splashing it over the back and the rest of the body. The farmer may or may not use soap or washing powder; the spilled water may be absorbed by an earthen floor or mopped off a concrete floor.

Mauss was interested in the form or structure that prestations take (the acts of giving, receiving, and countergiving), which the concreteness of water does not usually have, but it might be said to have a system, although again perhaps not quite as Levi-Strauss had envisioned in his logico-mathematical model of kinship (Lévi-Strauss 1949). Water connects domains of life such that the water used in one will affect the water used in others, and if the notion of system suggests more integration of these domains than is warranted, perhaps "connectivity" might be a better term for what we seek to define. That is, water connects different domains of social life to each other in ways that are not haphazard or accidental because they depend on each other. Water's connectivity is mediated by levels of social organizational complexity (Hannerz 1992). Getting water from something as apparently simple as a spigot is, in fact, no simple matter because it depends on a physical infrastructure that is both extensive and complex, not to mention a bureaucracy ranging from the most local unit (a water-user association or a village water works utility, for example) to national authorities and international governance structures such as the World Bank. Water's management and control also entail legal systems, oversight agencies, and courts of law to regulate water use and adjudicate violations or conflicts.

Less apparent in Mauss's definition, but which we insist is critical to understanding water as a "a total social fact," is what we call the materiality of water. Its molecular properties give it many distinctive characteristics (transparency; incompressibility; chemical neutrality; odorlessness and tastelessness; an ability to exist as a gas, a liquid, and a solid at the temperatures and pressures found on the surface of our planet; an ability to dissolve many substances and to be absorbed by many substances). These properties combine into two key material attributes. Because a given volume of water is fixed by incompressibility but threatened with losses through evaporation, leakage, and absorption by soil, the quantity of water is a crucial matter. And because water can receive so many chemical and biological contaminants, only some of which are readily evident to the human senses of sight, smell, and taste, the quality of water is also a crucial matter. This article, concerned as it is with sustainability, addresses these two aspects, which might seem to be simple universal attributes but which, as we suggest, reflect the highly specific materiality of water in its interactions with human bodies and human-made structures (Hamlin 1990, Orlove 1998, Orlove & Caton 2009). To be sure, quantity and quality are always experienced as social constructions—a recent study (Wilk 2006) traces historical shifts in meanings of potable water in several countries, and another shows the changing concerns over pollution (Beamish 2000)—but they are not only that. Thus, Americans feel the need for a minimum amount of water to sustain their general sense of well-being. These needs are couched in a naturalizing discourse of bodily or societal needs; however, as water becomes scarce in California's Central Valley or in the aquifers under the High Plains, material pressures are put on these constructions, forcing people to begin questioning them and in time perhaps to adopt new water-use practices. The point, however, is not to determine where social constructions end and materialities begin, but to see how complexly they are intertwined. The point may be even more subtle in the case of water

quality, as illustrated in an ethnographic case study by Alley (2002); the water of the Ganges is known to be polluted, but Hindus perform their ablutions in it because of their belief in the restorative powers of Mother Ganga. Sometimes cultural beliefs trump material realities in stunning ways. And as Alley also shows, the point is not to dispel supposedly misguided cultural beliefs in favor of scientific truth (which is contested in any case) but to see that these are always complexly interconnected, thereby affecting how water policy can be implemented.

A widespread tendency exists among anthropologists to locate water's primary locus in the domain of agriculture and to extrapolate widely from this foundation. After all, one of the most influential works in Marxist social science is Wittfogel's (1957) hydrological theory of the rise of the state. Indeed, a focus on the provisioning of water in the agricultural sphere marks some of the most interesting work done in archaeology (Scarborough 2003) as well as in social anthropology (Fleuret 1985; Geertz 1972; Gelles 2000; Glick 1970; Guillet 1998; Ilahiane 1996, 2001; Lansing 1991; Rodríguez 2006; Varisco 1983; Wilkonson 1977). Surely one of the most brilliant ethnographic studies of water provisioning in the agricultural sphere is the analysis of the complex intertwining of Balinese religious ritual and irrigation practices by J. Stephen Lansing (1991). Yet, it is a fact of water's totality that it is extracted from and used in many other spheres besides agriculture, and for many more purposes than irrigation. It circulates through practically all domains of social life, rural as well as urban (Swyngedow 2004, Swyngedow et al. 2002), is handled differently by men and women (Bennet 1995, Bennet et al. 2005, Cleaver & Elson 1995, Elmendorf 1981, Harris 2005, Tortajada 2003), and is important in economic sectors other than agriculture, such as industry, fishing, tourism, and sports.

To name the totality of connections that water may have in any given society, we adopt Hastrup's term "waterworld" (2009a). (We also share Hastrup's sense that many waterworlds, pressed by climate change, growing demand, and social inequality, are in crisis.) This

Materiality (also elementality and essentiality): the physical attributes of water that affect its relation to the human body and environment and that shape its use

Social construction: the meanings and values people give to things so that they can be discussed and incorporated into action

Waterworld: the totality of connections (see connectivity) that water may have in a given society

connectivity means that water can mark the boundaries of groups and communities, defined by shared involvement with water (Orlove 1993). Raffles (2002) offers a particularly rich ethnography of a waterworld, showing how a major waterway has changed over time and has also been imagined as a politically fraught space. A counterexample is Mitchell's widely read book (2002) on colonialism, modernity, and power in Egypt; despite its attention to forms of control of persons, property, and knowledge, this book pays scant attention to the Nile and to the role of water management and regulation in the shifts in political order.

FIVE CENTRAL THEMES IN WATERWORLDS

To sum up the discussion so far, we have remarked on two of the central features of water, its connectivity and its materiality, that ought to be of paramount concern to anthropologists. The totality of connections in any specific case comprises what we call a waterworld. We now suggest that any anthropological analysis of a waterworld ought to be concerned with five principal themes: value, equity, governance, politics, and knowledge.

Value: Natural Resources and Human Rights

How do nature (or environment) and culture (or society) intersect in waterworlds? One way to answer that question is to say that water is valued on the one hand as a resource for human well-being and productive activity, and hence is part of economic systems, and on the other hand as a right that has meaning from its connections to our place as conscious social beings who live in a natural and cultural world, and hence is part of political systems. Moreover, the value of water can be negative as well as positive because of hazards such as flood and erosion, the risks of waterborne diseases, and lesser threats such as rot. And the rights to water are associated with obligations to use water prudently and to support water systems.

Anthropologists are particularly well-suited to consider the ways that water, a substance with specific properties, is understood and used differently in a variety of social settings (Bachelard 1942, Hamlin 1990). The connectivity of water associates it with survival, sanitation, production, pleasure, and other aspects of social life. In Levi-Strauss's term, it is "good to think" (Renne 1991, Shapiro 1995, Sheridan 2002). And water can be also termed "good to experience" (Anderson & Tabb 2002, Orlove 1997). Water is a substance that richly engages the senses (touch, sight, hearing, and taste) as mediated through social products and practices that have specific cultural value, as Limbert (2001) has shown in her beautifully rendered ethnography of the "senses of water" in an Omani town.

Equity: Access and Distribution

How is this valued substance to be shared among the members of a society or the inhabitants of the world? This matter is tied to two other linked issues: of justice, on the one hand, and of political economy, on the other. A crucial concern is the equity of access to safe drinking water for people of all classes, of all ethnic and racial groups, of all ages, and of both genders. The competition among uses and economic sectors is also crucial (Donahue & Johnston 1997). Political scientists have studied the complex factors and strategic interests that shape water distribution within and between nations (Fischer 2006), as well as the consequences of treating water as a commodity and allowing the market to allocate it in the name of efficiency (Whiteley et al. 2008). Peters (1994) offers a telling account of the factors that have led to a grossly unequal distribution of water in colonial and postcolonial Botswana.

Governance: Organization and Rules

How far do institutional economics and economic sociology lead us in understanding the organizations that manage and distribute water? This question is particularly complex for the case of water, with its multiple scales that link storage facilities with dispersed users. The uneven availability of water worldwide promotes the development of large-scale water-distribution systems. Considerable capital and labor must be invested to build and maintain water facilities. Indeed, recent discussions of common-property resources draw heavily from examples of irrigation works, which have been a locus both of participatory governance (Ostrom 1990) and of state parasitism (Wittfogel 1957). This study of water organization is a particularly promising site for the integration of economic, sociological, and anthropological perspectives on water, as Geertz (1972) noted in his contrast of irrigation in Indonesia and Morocco and as Mosse (1997) describes in his account of the patterning of irrigation institutions in semiarid zones in India. These questions of governance can be particularly important at times of crisis and scarcity, and the uncertainty surrounding the resilience of water supply may be as much a question of governance as it is a question of the physical availability of water (Johnston 2003, Roth et al. 2005, Wagner 2009).

Politics: Discourse and Conflict

How do the three previous questions lead us to understand the struggles to control water in civil society and the public sphere? As Ernst (2003) shows in his study of political conflicts over regulation of Chesapeake Bay, three categories or concepts seem to dominate the analytical talk about water sustainability: conservation, justice, and governance. The term governance is useful, but its association with the notion of management may presume the agreement of all parties on the goals that they share and on the values that they place on water: The debates and conflicts over these goals and values lead us to the sphere of politics. With its propensity to flow, and with its ready partibility, water is almost without exception shared among people and among localities and is therefore linked to collectivities. The organizations that manage water operate within a broader political and regulatory context. These public contexts draw on a variety of forms of discourse, including property laws and human rights (Boelens & Doornbos 2001, Derman & Ferguson 2003). As Guillet (1998) indicates, water law is often a crucial site of contestation between earlier regional customary law and nationalist reform. The political contestations over the construction of dams and distribution of water show these interacting forces with particular clarity because they lead water to shift between different individuals and groups (McCully 2001, Scudder 2006, McCormick 2007). In a discussion of dam-building in colonial and neo-colonial Rhodesia and post-colonial Zimbabwe, Hughes (2006) shows that the striking visual transformation of the landscape by water projects can become a subject of contestation as important as the actual distribution of water for drinking and agriculture. Many anthropologists look to see how different groups insert themselves in the larger debates over water sustainability. This question leads researchers to examine the strategies of water sustainability discourse and to compare the framings that consider practical challenges with solutions and the framings that address broader relations among states, societies, and environments. The power of such representations can lead to massive mobilizations, whether in Bolivia, where municipalities privatized water supplies (McNeish 2006), or in Peru, where mines altered traditional systems for irrigation and potable water in rural areas (Li 2009b). To be sure, the question of discourse as it relates to the problem of water sustainability is not only one of politics. When faced with such scarcities in the past, Muslim societies have responded with rain prayers, an ethnographic example of which can be found in the analysis by Caton (2006) of a recent drought in Yemen that occasioned elaborate and quite intense mosque supplications for rain.

Knowledges: Local/Indigenous and Scientific Systems

Water management, whether ancient or modern, depends on various kinds of knowledge.

Watershed: an area of land through which water drains downhill to a lowest point; a possible management unit

Anthropology and other researchers have long studied the great diversity of irrigation practices and the knowledge they entail. Needham (1971) documented the debates between Confucian and Taoist approaches to irrigation in Imperial China, and Carney (2001) showed how the rice plantations in coastal areas of the antebellum South depended not only on the labor of African slaves and their descendants but also on Africans' specific knowledge of water management in humid lowland environments. Researchers in the Andes trace the complex conceptual systems that underlie water management in terraced agriculture in steep canyons (Gelles 2000, Trawick 2003). Water use in the household requires a kind of knowledge (often undervalued) that is different from what is required in the agricultural field, a matter of gender difference.

In contrast, anthropologists have conducted fewer studies of water scientists and their knowledge, although we can glimpse what such studies might look like when we read the ethnographies of Walley (2004) on conservation experts in the development of a Tanzanian marine park, of Mehta (2001, 2005) on the construction of scarcity in India by water experts who have little grasp of local understandings and management, and especially of Helmreich (2009) on scientific narratives about ocean life and its beginnings (see also, Alatout 2007a,b; Li 2009a; Molle 2008, 2009; Nichter 1985; Orlove et al. 2010; Paolisso & Maloney 2000). These works can be classified within the history of science as well as within science and technology studies (Haraway 1989; Jasanoff 1995; Latour 1987, 2004; Latour & Woolgar 1986; Rabinow 1999; Shapin & Schaffer 1985). An example of anthropological research that links the study of science, the state, transnational institutions, and capital in Yemen appears in a later section of this review.

THREE SITES IN WATERWORLDS

Having reviewed general attributes of water and central themes in the study of water sustainability, we now suggest that anthropological analyses of waterworlds could productively explore three specific sites: watersheds, water regimes, and waterscapes.

Watersheds

The term watershed (or water catchment) is widely used in scientific and policy contexts. The notion is simple and powerful: Because water flows downhill, each spot in the world can be assigned to a specific topographical basin. The water in each connected basin forms a watershed, and each watershed can be managed and governed as a unit. The boundaries of a watershed define a set of participants in this management, which includes natural scientists, government officials, members of local organizations, and ordinary citizens. In the past few decades, many watershed councils have been formed that are generally nonprofit participatory organizations that seek environmental quality and sustainable development. Other groups also promote more effective, equitable, and sustainable water management in a participatory way; the semiarid region of northeastern Brazil contains a number of examples (Broad et al. 2007, Lemos & Farios de Oliveira 2004, 2005). At a much larger scale, some watersheds, such as the Rhine River basin (Cioc 2002), extend across national boundaries and are managed by organizations whose members span nations.

Although we recognize that these councils and other groups have done much work that addresses basic human needs and rights and that is broadly sustainable, we include a few words of caution about the term watershed. The conceptual boundaries that humans use reflect cultural systems as well as the natural world, so it gives us as anthropologists pause to hear that an administrative unit has an a priori material or natural existence. Other environmental and ecological categories, such as "forest" and "wetland," include both natural and social elements, given the complex nature of their characteristics and boundaries.

Watersheds may be simpler, more straightforward units than forests and wetlands, but they are not entirely and unproblematically present in nature, as Strang shows in her account (2004) of the River Stour in England. First, watersheds vary enormously in scale, with a single watershed sometimes containing smaller subwatersheds, thus making the selection of a particular scale in part a social choice. [The Colorado River Compact of 1922, which divided the Colorado River watershed into upper and lower basins, is a particularly clear example of such a choice (Reisner 1986).] Second, water moves in many ways. Groundwater, a crucial resource in many regions, is located in basins whose boundaries do not always correspond with watersheds so that residents of a given watershed may dig wells that directly affect the residents of another watershed. Deforestation in one watershed may reduce the amount of water vapor that is carried to another watershed downwind of it, creating water scarcity in this second watershed. And the long human history of digging canals, leveling hills, and constructing dikes has also led water to move from one watershed to another. In this way, watersheds are not always the well-bounded management units that water managers and others often assume them to be.

Moreover, the notion of watershed tends to go hand-in-hand with the notion of stakeholder, understood as the residents, property holders, and public bodies within the boundaries of the watershed, all of whom, presumably, seek to assure sustainable water use because of their commitments to the watershed. The participatory democratic practices of watershed councils and other groups rest on this notion of the responsible stakeholder. But such a focus on watersheds can rest on a naïve and simplistic view of ecological citizenship. Stakeholders may engage in exclusionary practices while caring deeply about areas far from the ones in which they live [the idea of stakeholder can be linked to the archaic and widely rejected principle of allowing only property owners to vote (Holston 2008)], and even among the stakeholders who gain seats at the discussion table, there are some who are more powerful than others (Broad et al. 2007, Roncoli et al. 2009).

Water Regimes

A second term, water regime, had a specific meaning within the field of hydrology referring to the pattern of water flow in a freshwater ecosystem, but it is increasingly used in political science and other fields. The term regime comes from the field of international relations, in which it is defined as "sets of implicit or explicit principles, norms, rules, and decision-making procedures around which actors' expectations converge in a given area" (Krasner 1983, p. 2); it has helped explain how nations might cooperate. It can be similarly employed to examine cooperation and coordination among water users, who, like nations, could seem to be autonomous and to have conflicting interests. For example, the political scientist Stefan Lindemann (2008) traces the multiple factors that have led to successful management of water quality in the Rhine and Elbe watersheds. But the term can also apply to specific national systems for regulating and managing water. Buller (1996) compares the French and British rules and institutions in the period of increasing integration into European frameworks. Galaz (2004) contrasts the water regimes in periods of public and corporate provision of water in Chile. He offers useful insights into the ways that the more recent water regime, consistent with other politics of privatization and market regulation of resources, weakens the rights of several groups of water users and reduces their ability to voice their concerns.

Anthropologists and other researchers have made important contributions to the study of water regime changes. Researchers have shown regime changes to be slow because physical infrastructure, reflecting earlier rules and institutions, remains in place, because water regulations overlap with other often entrenched legal institutions, and because social understandings do not shift overnight. Bakker (2001) discusses opposition of the shift from a state- to a market-centered regime in Britain, where people, accustomed to being treated as citizens with rights to water, do not readily accept becoming consumers purchasing water

Water regime: the aggregate of institutional rules and practices for managing water resources in a specific setting or watershed

as a commodity. Similarly, research on the indigenous fishing villages of Lake Titicaca in Peru examines conflicts between local and state regimes that govern water, manage economically important aquatic plants, and grant rights to fish and to travel on the lake (Orlove 2002). Moreover, the notion of water regime can be associated with resilience because the rules and institutions that form part of specific water regimes shape response to external pressures such as climate change (Hastrup 2009b).

Waterscapes

A third term, waterscape, has been used since the mid-nineteenth century, by analogy with the word landscape, to describe works of art that depict scenery with bodies of water. In recent years, natural scientists have spoken of waterscape ecology as an aquatic specialization within landscape ecology, the discipline that studies the interactions of contiguous ecosystems. This term gained attention after its appearance in an influential 1999 article by the geographer Erik Swyngedouw, in which he considers Spain in the period from 1890 to 1930. He draws on political economy approaches within geography to examine the production of waterscapes, emphasizing the ideological dimensions of place in the construction of dams and canals and the creation of new administrative units based on watersheds. Other works examine the visual, experiential, and cultural aspects of waterscapes more extensively (Baviska 2007). Historian David Blackbourn's (2006) account of the reshaping of rivers, marshes, lakes, and coasts in nineteenth- and twentieth-century Germany is a good example, paralleling similar efforts, although on a smaller scale, in Iceland (Pálsson & Huijbens 2009). These and other studies show that water is not merely an economically valuable resource that flows through spaces, but is also a culturally and experientially meaningful substance present in places. Although humans are never fully aquatic, they are often, perhaps always, hydrophilic, and the human sense of place often engages with water

as well as with land, as Strang shows in her analysis of two very different Australian waterscapes (2009, p. 30) and Orlove documents in his accounts of the cultural importance of glaciers (2009a,b). A number of examples can be found in the anthropological literature; of particular importance are the accounts of irrigated rice landscapes in East Asia and Southeast Asia by Conklin (1980), Bray (1986), Lansing (1991), and others.

A number of studies consider all three sites: watersheds, water regimes, and waterscapes. Rodríguez's (2006) ethnography of community-managed irrigation in northern New Mexico examines watersheds, showing that the social boundaries of parishes and the hydrological boundaries of basins are close but not always overlapping because local residents redirect water between drainages. The study considers water regimes by tracing conflicts between customary practices and new state regulations. It also depicts the sensory and ritual aspects of waterscapes and shows how the annual cleaning of canals and other ritual practices by local residents inscribe them in the landscape and in the multilayered ethnic history of their region.

INTEGRATED WATER RESOURCE MANAGEMENT

Integrated water resource management (IWRM) has become the new and, many would claim, the hegemonic paradigm for discussing, legitimizing, and implementing policies regarding the management of the world's water resources, subsuming within it the notion of sustainability of 1970s and 1980s development discourses. This notion was enshrined in the World Water Council's *World Water Vision* (of the 2000 World Water Forum), which states that "to ensure the sustainability of water, we must view it holistically, balancing competing demands on it—domestic, agricultural, industrial (including energy), and environmental. Sustainable management of water resources requires systemic, integrated decision-making"

(Cosgrove & Rijsberman 2000, p. 1). However, there is no fixed or universally agreed-upon definition of IWRM, nor does it lead to uniform policies in the international organizations that advocate it or the states that are, voluntarily or not, attempting to implement it in their water resources management, although certain basic themes or principles are evident even if their formulation remains necessarily abstract.

First, IWRM argues that solutions to water problems cannot be found in only one sector of society, such as agriculture, because water is used across society as a whole (a view that we share in our notion of water as a total social fact); therefore a broad, multisectoral approach must be taken, one that attempts to integrate what is happening with water in each sector into a holistic view of the overall situation, delimited in IWRM usually by country or national boundary, if the water resource, as is often the case for rivers, is shared. Second, although it has a healthy respect for normal and universal scientific knowledge in being able to help solve problems, as one might expect of a paradigm that has emerged primarily from expert scientific networks, IWRM at the same time evinces skepticism toward narrow technological solutions for overcoming the world's water problems (a reaction, in part, to large-dam construction that came under heavy fire in the past two decades) by suggesting that these methods must be integrated with other approaches—bureaucratic, legislative, economic, political, cultural, etc.—depending on the water problems in question.

A third theme is the stress on the management of water resources, implying that it is unlikely that significant new sources will be found (through desalination, the discovery of underground aquifers, massive transfers from watersheds with low human populations, and other such methods) to alleviate water scarcity or contamination and that instead a finite and rapidly diminishing resource must be managed. The idea of management that is invoked is bureaucratic, though at varying levels of complexity and integration. The basic or fundamental level

is usually seen to be the watershed (for reasons given above in our discussion of watersheds), but it is understood by water managers that this notion is not enough because the regulation of watersheds must be integrated to meet the total demands on water by the various sectors and groups in society. To accomplish this integration, one should enlist the help of regional and national levels of bureaucracy such as governorates or provinces as well as the nation-state.

In some versions of IWRM, a fourth theme is evident: educating water users in a society about its water problems and the steps to alleviate them, starting with the ordinary citizen whose water-conservation practices are constructed as a civic duty to the nation as well as a gift of water (to invoke Mauss once again) to future generations. In other versions of IWRM, a fifth theme, akin to what we have referred to as value, also becomes important. For example, in the World Bank's (2003) "Water Resources Sector Strategy," water is explicitly valued as an economic good or commodity, leading to market solutions to managing the allocation of the world's water; the resulting patterns of distribution are not necessarily optimal for the world's poor. But there is another valuation of water: as a basic human right to be equitably distributed among all peoples of the world according to need, which is not consonant with water's market value (although in theory the two values are not necessarily incommensurable). This is the view taken, for example, in the 1997 *Comprehensive Assessment of the Freshwater Resources of the World* by the United Nations Commission on Sustainable Development. Still other views argue that three values—economic efficiency, social equity, and environmental sustainability—must be coordinated (Glob. Water Partnersh. 2000). The fact that all these valuations of water can be put forward in versions of IWRM demonstrates how contradictory the concept can be.

IWRM emerged as a discursive construct over the previous two decades, mainly in the work of international cadres of water experts (a broad array that includes, for example, scientists such as engineers or experts on water pollution, members of nongovernmental organizations concerned with equitable water distribution, international aid and development experts involved in water conservation and water-delivery projects, economists who study water as a commodity, and members of international agencies such as the Food and Agriculture Organization or the World Water Council concerned with water distribution) and as such is not the brainchild of any one organization. [For a history of the concept, see White (1998), and for a critical analysis, see Conca (2006).] IWRM is discussed in academic conferences and scientific journals and ratified in world treaty agreements. It is, in short, an example of the impact of expert knowledge on water policies in the world today, which we refer to above as a crucial component to an anthropological understanding of water.

IWRM has a vision of the waterworld with many parallels to our own, namely of water as a total social fact. It also includes all the themes (value, equity, governance, politics, and knowledge) that we hold to be essential to address the problems of water scarcity and degradation. For example, with its emphasis on management, IWRM is a regime—a global regime—for governing the world's water resources (just as with forests or the atmosphere, water is seen as a global and not just a national resource). Thus it falls under what we have termed the politics of water, although we hasten to add that IWRM's explicit or stated political engagements do not go beyond two concerns: the supposed democratic participation in decision making regarding local-level water management, and equitable and affordable access to safe drinking water, especially for the world's poor.

What IWRM does not venture into is the complex political question of how its principles will be struggled over and fought out in concrete settings, a prime subject for anthropological inquiry. It is the politics that lies between conceptualization and practice that is crucial for understanding results, a politics of local actors supposedly nearest to the source of water in the ground, a politics of national bureaucra-

cies established to manage water resources, and a politics of international donor agencies that are supposed to assist them (Mehta 2005, Oré 2005, Strang 2009). Moreover, IWRM's narrative of normal science overlooks the disagreements among scientists over precise measurements and ignores the pressures to arrive at a broad consensus to conceal these rifts or disagreements. In contrast, Budds (2009) provides an ethnographic analysis of hydrological assessment in Chile that documents the intense political struggles about the construction of measures and interpretation of statistics, showing that such struggles frustrate planning and lead to skepticism over the authority of science.

As for the valuation of water, what is meant by a basic right or a commodity is hardly questioned, as if these matters were settled long ago in philosophical and scientific discourses and need not be revisited in settings where these concepts are highly contested or do not hold sway. Anthropology has an important role to play in keeping these questions open rather than to consign the discipline to the study of how the "natives" value and use water locally. That said, the meanings and values placed on water by its users and the contestations over these among those same users (along class, gender, and ethnic lines, as well as urban versus rural divides) will fundamentally affect how water can be managed at the watershed in the first place, and here anthropology has an obvious and perhaps singular contribution to make to the understanding of water's valuation. This incomplete treatment of the valuation of water reflects the tendency of IWRM to overlook waterscapes because it assumes that water is a resource that is used for specific ends, rather than a meaningful substance that is present in specific settings.

Let us illustrate an anthropological study of IWRM and these themes by examining the way it has been put into practice in a concrete situation: the Republic of Yemen. For a partial example of how anthropology might do an ethnography of IWRM, the reader should consider the article by Caton (2007), which is concerned with water sustainability in Yemen.

Four sites were studied, all of which are closely connected to IWRM as a concept and as a practice: a 2005 scientific conference in Yemen on integrated watershed management, in which experts affirmed the primacy of IWRM practices; the Yemen Center for Water and the Environment, which teaches IWRM to Yemeni water engineers with the assistance of Dutch IWRM experts, an example of the transnational circulation of expert knowledge; an assessment of Yemen's water-management policies and practices conducted by international donors (Dutch, German, and British) invested in Yemen's five-year water plan, an example of the global governance of water resources; and finally, but not least, an examination of how expert knowledge gets transmuted into local knowledge at the watershed level by international development experts working in a water basin north of Yemen's capital, San'a. Political contestations among experts were clearly visible in every site as were conflicts between national and international management agencies with their own legitimacies at stake. IWRM experts welcomed anthropological knowledge as helpful for understanding local stakeholders at the watershed level but were unsurprisingly ambivalent about the prospect of them becoming subjects of anthropological research as well.

HOW ANTHROPOLOGY CAN ENGAGE WITH WATER ISSUES

What have we learned about the world's water problems? There is no one solution, whether technological, economic, bureaucratic, or political, that works globally. A combination of approaches must be applied in each case, depending on the particular materialities and connectivities in specific contexts.

However, waterworlds must be studied ethnographically, in all their components, including the often-neglected waterscapes as well as the more commonly examined watersheds and water regimes. The wide range of people, agencies, and processes involved in addressing concrete water problems all require sustained scrutiny. Too often in the past, water consumers have been the sole concern, along with their national governments; this mindset is no longer sufficient when one realizes the profound presence and involvement of the transnational community of water experts. It is likely, therefore, that an anthropology of water can fruitfully link up with science and technology studies, even while continuing to connect with other specific, longer-established approaches, such as political ecology and material culture studies, and with the broad integrative styles of analysis that characterize the discipline.

DISCLOSURE STATEMENT

The authors are not aware of any affiliations, memberships, funding, or financial holdings that might be perceived as affecting the objectivity of this review.

ACKNOWLEDGMENTS

We offer our thanks to the many people whose research, insight, and comments have helped us to develop our thinking on the subject of water sustainability. Sadly, space constraints do not allow us to name the numerous colleagues and associates who contributed to this review, so we will mention only the groups in which they participated: the Water Sustainability Field of the Dissertation Proposal Development Fellowship Program, supported by the Social Science Research Council; the two-year workshop, sponsored by the Department of Energy at the Center for Middle East Studies at Harvard, on the politics of water sustainability; the cultural ecology seminar on water sustainability at the University of California, Davis; and Waterworlds, a Center for Anthropological Climate Research, funded by the European Research Council, at the Department of Anthropology, University of Copenhagen.

LITERATURE CITED

Alatout S. 2007a. From water abundance to water scarcity (1936–1959): a 'fluid' history of Jewish subjectivity in historic Palestine and Israel. In *Reapproaching Borders: New Perspectives on the Study of Israel-Palestine*, ed. S Sufian, M Levine, pp. 199–219. Lanham, MD: Rowman and Littlefield

Alatout S. 2007b. State-ing natural resources through law: the codification and articulation of water scarcity and citizenship in Israel. *Arab World Geogr.* 10(1):16–37

Alley KD. 2002. *On the Banks of the Ganga: When Wastewater Meets a Sacred River*. Ann Arbor: Univ. Mich. Press

Anderson SC, Tabb BH. 2002. *Water, Leisure and Culture: European Historical Perspectives*. Oxford: Berg

Bachelard G. 1942. *L'eau et les rêves, essai sur l'imagination de la matière*. Paris: J. Corti

Bakker K. 2001. Paying for water: water pricing and equity in England and Wales. *Trans. Inst. Br. Geogr.* 26(2):143–64

Baviska A, ed. 2007. *Waterscapes: The Cultural Politics of a Natural Resource*. Delhi: Perm. Black

Beamish T. 2000. Accumulating trouble: complex organization, a culture of silence, and a secret spill. *Soc. Probl.* 47(4):473–98

Bennet V, ed. 1995. *The Politics of Water: Urban Protest, Gender and Power in Monterrey, Mexico*. Pittsburgh: Univ. Pittsburgh Press

Bennet V, Dávila-Poblerte S, Rico MN, eds. 2005. *Opposing Currents: The Politics of Water and Gender in Latin America*. Pittsburgh: Univ. Pittsburgh Press

Blackbourn D. 2006. *The Conquest of Nature: Water, Landscape, and the Making of Modern Germany*. New York: Norton

Boelens R, Doornbos B. 2001. The battlefield of water rights: rule making amidst conflicting normative frameworks in the Ecuadorian highlands. *Hum. Organ.* 60(4):343–55

Bray F. 1986. *The Rice Economies: Technology and Development in Asian Societies*. Oxford/New York: Blackwell

Broad K, Pfaff A, Taddei R, Sankarasubramanian A, Lall U, de Souza FD. 2007. Climate, stream flow prediction and water management in northeast Brazil: societal trends and forecast value. *Clim. Change* 84(2):217–39

Budds J. 2009. Contested H_2O: science, policy and politics in water resources management in Chile. *Geoforum* 40(3):418–30

Buller H. 1996. Privatization and Europeanization: the changing context of water supply in Britain and France. *J. Environ. Plann. Manag.* 39(4):461–82

Carney J. 2001. *Black Rice: The African Origins of Rice Cultivation in the Americas*. Cambridge, MA: Harvard Univ. Press

Caton SC. 2006. What is an authorizing discourse? In *Powers of the Secular Modern: Talal Asad and His Interlocutors*, ed. D Scott, C Hirschkind, pp. 31–56. Stanford, CA: Stanford Univ. Press

Caton SC. 2007. Yemen, water, and the politics of knowledge. **http://globetrotter.berkeley.edu/ GreenGovernance/papers/Yemen%20Water%20Politics%20of%20Knowledge.pdf**

Cioc M. 2002. *The Rhine: An Eco-Biography, 1815–2000*. Seattle: Univ. Wash. Press

Cleaver F, Elson D. 1995. *Women and Water Resources: Continued Marginalisation and New Policies*. London: Int. Inst. Environ. Dev.

Conca K. 2006. *Governing Water: Contentious Transnational Politics and Global Institution Building*. Cambridge, MA: MIT Press

Conklin HC. 1980. *Ethnographic Atlas of Ifugao: A Study of Environment, Culture, and Society in Northern Luzon*. New Haven, CT: Yale Univ. Press

Cosgrove W, Rijsberman FR, eds. 2000. *World Water Vision: Making Water Everybody's Business*. London: Earthscan

Derman B, Ferguson A. 2003. Value of water: political ecology and water reform in southern Africa. *Hum. Organ.* 62(3):277–88

Donahue JM, Johnston BR, eds. 1997. *Water, Culture, and Power: Local Struggles in a Global Context*. Washington, DC: Island Press

Elmendorf M. 1981. *Women, Water and the Decade*. Water and Sanitation for Health Project, Techn. Rep. 6 (Order Tech. Dir. 35). Washington, DC: Agency Int. Dev.

Ernst H. 2003. *Chesapeake Bay Blues: Science, Politics, and the Struggle to Save the Bay.* Lanham, MD: Rowman & Littlefield

Fischer MM. 2006. Changing Palestine-Israel ecologies: narratives of water, land, and conflict, and political economy then and now, and life to come. *Cult. Polit.* 2(2):159–92

Fleuret P. 1985. The social-organization of water control in the Taita-Hills, Kenya. *Am. Ethnol.* 12(1):103–18

Galaz V. 2004. Stealing from the poor? Game theory and the politics of water markets in Chile. *Environ. Polit.* 13(2):414–37

Geertz C. 1972. The wet and the dry: traditional irrigation in Bali and Morocco. *Hum. Ecol.* 1:23–39

Gelles P. 2000. *Water and Power in Highland Peru: The Cultural Politics of Irrigation and Development.* New Brunswick, NJ: Rutgers Univ. Press

Glick TF. 1970. *Irrigation and Society in Medieval Valencia.* Cambridge, MA: Harvard Univ. Press

Glob. Water Partnersh. 2000. *Integrated water resources management.* Tech. Advis. Committee Backgr. Pap. No 4, Glob. Water Partnersh., Stockholm

Guillet D. 1998. Rethinking legal pluralism: local law and state law in the evolution of water property rights in northwestern Spain. *Comp. Stud. Soc. Hist.* 40(1):42–70

Hamlin C. 1990. *A Science of Impurity: Water Analysis in Nineteenth Century Britain.* Berkeley: Univ. Calif. Press

Hannerz U. 1992. *Cultural Complexity: Studies in the Social Organization of Meaning.* New York: Columbia Univ. Press

Haraway D. 1989. *Primate Visions: Gender, Race, and Nature in the World of Modern Science.* New York: Routledge

Harris L. 2005. Negotiating inequalities: democracy, gender, and the politics of difference in water user groups of southeastern Turkey. In *Turkish Environmentalism: Between Democracy and Development*, ed. AF Arsel, M Aldershot, pp. 185–200. Hampshire, UK: Ashgate

Hastrup K, ed. 2009a. *The Question of Resilience: Social Responses to Climate Change.* Copenhagen: R. Dan. Academy Sci. Lett.

Hastrup K. 2009b. Waterworlds: framing the question of social resilience. See Hastrup 2009a, pp. 11–30

Helmreich S. 2009. *Alien Ocean: Anthropological Voyages in Microbial Seas.* Berkeley: Univ. Calif. Press

Holston J. 2008. *Insurgent Citizenship: Disjunctions of Democracy and Modernity in Brazil.* Princeton, NJ: Princeton Univ. Press

Hughes D. 2006. Hydrology of hope: farm dams, conservation, and whiteness in Zimbabwe. *Am. Ethnol.* 33(2):269–87

Ilahiane H. 1996. Small-scale irrigation in a multiethnic oasis environment: the case of Zaouit Amelkis village, southeast Morocco. *J. Polit. Ecol.* 3:89–106

Ilahiane H. 2001. The ethnopolitics of irrigation management in the Zis Oasis, Morocco. In *Communities and the Environment: Ethnicity, Gender, and the State in Community-Based Conservation*, ed. A Agrawal, CC Gibson, pp. 89–110. New Brunswick, NJ: Rutgers Univ. Press

Jasanoff S. 1995. *Science at the Bar: Law, Science and Technology in America.* Cambridge, MA: Harvard Univ. Press

Johnston BR. 2003. The political ecology of water: an introduction. *Capital. Nat. Soc.* 14(3):73–90

Krasner SD. 1983. *International Regimes.* Ithaca, NY: Cornell Univ. Press

Lansing JS. 1991. *Priests and Programmers: Technologies of Power in the Engineered Landscape of Bali.* Princeton, NJ: Princeton Univ. Press

Latour B. 1987. *Science in Action: How to Follow Scientists and Engineers Through Society.* Cambridge, MA: Harvard Univ. Press

Latour B. 2004. *Politics of Nature: How to Bring the Sciences into Democracy.* Cambridge, MA: Harvard Univ. Press

Latour B, Woolgar S. 1986. *Laboratory Life: The Construction of Scientific Facts.* Princeton, NJ: Princeton Univ. Press

Lemos MC, Oliveira JLF. 2004. Can water reform survive politics? Institutional change and river basin management in Ceará, Northeast Brazil. *World Dev.* 32(1):2121–37

Lemos MC, Oliveira JLF. 2005. Water reform across the state/society divide: the case of Ceará, Brazil. *Int. J. Water Resour. Dev.* 21(1):133–47

Levi-Strauss C. 1949. *Elementary Forms of Kinship*. Boston: Beacon

Li F. 2009a. Documenting accountability: environmental impact assessment in a Peruvian mining project. *PoLAR* 32(2):218–36

Li F. 2009b. *How pollution comes to matter: the science and politics of 21st century mining in Peru*. PhD thesis. Univ. Calif., Davis. 273 pp.

Limbert ME. 2001. The senses of water in an Omani town. *Soc. Text* 69(19):35–55

Lindemann S. 2008. Understanding water regime formation—a research framework with lessons from Europe. *Glob. Environ. Polit.* 8(4):117–40

Mauss M. 1990. *The Gift: The Form and Reason for Exchange in Archaic Societies*. London: Routledge

McCormick S. 2007. The governance of hydro-electric dams in Brazil. *J. Lat. Am. Stud.* 39:227–61

McCully P. 2001. *Silenced Rivers: The Ecology and Politics of Large Dams*. London: Zed

McNeish JA. 2006. Stones on the road: the politics of participation and the generation of crisis in Bolivia. *Bull. Lat. Am. Res.* 25(2):220–32

Mehta L. 2001. The manufacture of popular perceptions of scarcity: dams and water-related narratives in Gujarat, India. *World Dev.* 29(12):2025–41

Mehta L. 2005. The politics and poetics of water: the naturalization of scarcity in western India. New Delhi: Orient Longman

Mitchell T. 2002. *Rule of Experts: Egypt, Techno-Politics, Modernity*. Berkeley: Univ. Calif. Press

Molle F. 2008. Nirvana concepts, narratives and policy models: insights from the water sector. *Water Altern.* 1(1):23–40

Molle F. 2009. River-basin planning and management: the social life of a concept. *Geoforum* 40(3):484–94

Mosse D. 1997. The symbolic making of a common property resource: history, ecology and locality in a tank-irrigated landscape in south India. *Dev. Change* 28(3):467–504

Needham J, with the collaboration of Wang L, Lu GD. 1971. *Science and Civilisation in China*, Vol. IV, Part 3: I. Cambridge, UK: Cambridge Univ. Press

Nichter M. 1985. Drink boiled water: a cultural analysis of a health education message. *Soc. Sci. Med.* 21(6):667–69

Oré MT. 2005. *Agua: bien común y usos privados: riego, estado y conflictos en La Achirana del Inca*. Lima: Fondo Ed. Pontificia Univ. Católica del Perú

Orlove B. 1993. Putting race in its place: order in colonial and postcolonial Peruvian geography. *Soc. Res.* 60(2):301–36

Orlove B. 1997. Meat and strength: the moral economy of a Chilean food riot. *Cult. Anthropol.* 12(2):234–68

Orlove B. 1998. Down to earth: race and substance in the Andes. *Bull. Lat. Am. Res.* 17(2):207–22

Orlove B. 2002. *Lines in the Water: Nature and Culture at Lake Titicaca*. Berkeley: Univ. Calif. Press

Orlove B. 2009a. Glacier retreat: reviewing the limits of adaptation to climate change. *Environment* 51(3):22–34

Orlove B. 2009b. The past, the present, and some possible futures of adaptation. In *Adaptation to Climate Change: Thresholds, Values, Governance*, ed. WN Adger, I Lorenzoni, K O'Brien, pp. 131–63. Cambridge, UK: Cambridge Univ. Press

Orlove B, Caton SC. 2009. Water as an object of anthropological inquiry. See Hastrup 2009a, pp. 31–47

Orlove B, Roncoli C, Kabugo M, Majugu A. 2010. Indigenous climate knowledge in southern Uganda: the multiple components of a dynamic regional system. *Climatic Change* 100(2):243–65

Ostrom E. 1990. *Governing the Commons: The Evolution of Institutions for Collective Action*. Cambridge, UK: Cambridge Univ. Press

Pálsson G, Huijbens EH. 2009. The marsh of modernity: iceland and beyond. See Hastrup 2009a, pp. 48–69

Paolisso M, Maloney RS. 2000. Recognizing farmer environmentalism: nutrient runoff and toxic dinoflagellate blooms in the Chesapeake Bay region. *Hum. Organ.* 59(2):209–21

Peters PE. 1994. *Dividing the Commons. Politics, Policy, and Culture in Botswana*. Charlottesville: Univ. Press Va.

Rabinow P. 1999. *French DNA: Trouble in Purgatory*. Chicago: Univ. Chicago Press

Raffles H. 2002. *In Amazonia: A Natural History*. Princeton, NJ: Princeton Univ. Press

Reisner M. 1986. *Cadillac Desert: The American West and its Disappearing Water*. New York: Viking

Renne E. 1991. Water, spirits, and plain white cloth: the ambiguity of things in Bunu social-life. *Man* 26(4):709–22

Rodriguez S. 2006. *Acequia: Water Sharing, Sanctity, and Place*. Santa Fe, NM: Sch. Adv. Res.

Roncoli C, Kirshen P, Etkin D, Sanon M, Somé L, et al. 2009. From management to negotiation: technical and institutional innovations for integrated water resource management in the Upper Comoe River Basin, Burkina Faso. *Environ. Manag.* 44(4):695–711

Roth D, Boelens R, Zwarteveen M, eds. 2005. *Liquid Relations: Contested Water Rights and Legal Complexity*. New Brunswick, NJ: Rutgers Univ. Press

Scarborough V. 2003. *The Flow of Power: Ancient Water Systems and Landscapes*. Santa Fe, NM: Sch. Adv. Res.

Scudder T. 2006. *The Future of Large Dams: Dealing with Social, Environmental, Institutional and Political Costs*. London: Earthscan

Shapin S, Schaffer S. 1985. *Leviathan and the Air Pump: Hobbes, Boyle, and the Experimental Life*. Princeton, NJ: Princeton Univ. Press

Shapiro D. 1995. Blood, oil, honey, and water: symbolism in spirit possession sects in northeastern Brazil. *Am. Ethnol.* 22(4):828–47

Sheridan MJ. 2002. An irrigation intake is like a uterus: culture and agriculture in precolonial North Pare, Tanzania. *Am. Anthropol.* 104(1):79–92

Strang V. 2004. *The Meaning of Water*. Oxford, UK: Berg

Strang V. 2009. *Gardening the World: Agency, Identity and the Ownership of Water*. Oxford, UK: Berghahn

Swyngedouw E. 1999. Modernity and hybridity: nature, regeneracionismo, and the production of the Spanish waterscape, 1890–1930. *Ann. Assoc. Am. Geogr.* 89(3):443–65

Swyngedouw E. 2004. *Social Power and the Urbanization of Water*. Oxford: Oxford Univ. Press

Swyngedouw E, Kaika M, Castro E. 2002. Urban water: a political-ecology perspective. *Built Environ.* 28(2):124–37

Tortajada C. 2003. Professional women and water management: case study from Morocco—a water forum contribution. *Water Int.* 28(4):532–39

Trawick P. 2003. *The Struggle for Water in Peru: Comedy and Tragedy in the Andean Commons*. Palo Alto, CA: Stanford Univ. Press

United Nations Comm. Sustain. Dev. 1997. *Comprehensive Assessment of the Freshwater Resources of the World*. New York: United Nations Dept. Econ. Soc. Aff.

Varisco DM. 1983. *Sayl* and *ghayl*: the ecology of water allocation in Yemen. *Hum. Ecol.* 11(4):365–83

Wagner J. 2009. Water governance today. *Anthropol. News* 51(1):5, 9

Walley CJ. 2004. *Rough Waters: Nature and Development in an East African Marine Park*. Princeton, NJ: Princeton Univ. Press

White G. 1998. Reflections on the 50-year international search for integrated water management. *Water Policy* 1(1):21–27

Whiteley J, Ingram H, Perry RW, eds. 2008. *Water, Place, and Equity*. Cambridge, MA: MIT Press

Wilk R. 2006. Bottled water: the pure commodity in the age of branding. *J. Consum. Cult.* 6(3):303–25

Wilkonson JC. 1977. *Water and Tribal Settlement in South-East Arabia*. Oxford, UK: Clarendon

Wittfogel KA. 1957. *Oriental Despotism: A Comparative Study of Total Power*. New Haven, CT: Yale Univ. Press

World Bank. 2003. *Water Resources Sector Strategy: Strategic Directions for World Bank Engagement*. Washington, DC: World Bank

World Water Counc. 2000. *World Water Vision*. London: Earthscan

Cooperative Breeding and its Significance to the Demographic Success of Humans

Karen L. Kramer

Department of Human Evolutionary Biology, Harvard University, Cambridge, Massachusetts 02138; email: kkramer@fas.harvard.edu

Annu. Rev. Anthropol. 2010. 39:417–36

First published online as a Review in Advance on June 21, 2010

The *Annual Review of Anthropology* is online at anthro.annualreviews.org

This article's doi: 10.1146/annurev.anthro.012809.105054

Key Words

life history, intergenerational transfers, allocare, demography

Abstract

The demographic success of humans compared with other closely related species can be attributed to the relatively rapid pace of reproduction and improved chances of survival. The assistance that mothers receive from others to help raise children is a common theme in explaining this gain in surviving fertility. Cooperative breeding in its broad definition describes such a social system in which nonmaternal helpers support offspring who are not their own. In traditional societies, kin and nonkin of different ages and sex contribute both to child care and to provisioning older children. This review discusses empirical evidence for human cooperative breeding and its demographic significance and highlights the ways in which humans are similar to and different from other cooperative breeders. An emphasis is placed on cross-cultural comparison and variability in allocare strategies. Because helping in humans occurs within a subsistence pattern of food sharing and labor cooperation, both kin selection and mutualism may explain why children are often raised with nonmaternal help. Cooperative breeding is relevant to debates in anthropology concerning the evolution of human life history, sociality, and psychology and has implications for demographic patterns in today's world as well as in the past.

INTRODUCTION

The human capacity for population growth is one of the remarkable stories of our evolutionary history. Demographically it can be attributed to short birth intervals and high survivorship. But it is also fundamentally shaped by features of human parenting, sociality, and economic organization. Cooperative breeding combines these features and is a useful framework to consider child-rearing patterns characteristic of humans.

Cooperative breeding refers to a parenting and social system in which nonparental members of the social group help support offspring. Cooperative breeding models were originally developed to describe the parenting behavior of certain insects, birds, and mammals (Brown 1974, Emlen 1991[1978], Skutch 1987, Solomon & French 1997). Turke's (1988) seminal study among Micronesian islanders first introduced humans as cooperative breeders into anthropology. Turke showed that mothers who bore girls, who are valuable helpers to their mothers, early in their reproductive careers had greater completed fertility than if their first-born children were boys. Since then, anthropologists have paid increasing attention to humans as cooperative breeders.

Cooperative breeding has been documented for ~3% of bird species and for a similar percentage of mammals. Although uncommon, cooperative breeding occurs across diverse mammalian taxa: predominantly wild canids, foxes, meerkats, rodents, and several species of primates, including humans (Brown 1987, Clutton-Brock et al. 2001, Emlen 1991[1978], Nicolson 1987). Among nonhuman cooperative breeders, helpers may guard, nurse, or transport young, help forage for food, defend territory boundaries, or build and clean nests. The occurrence of these helping behaviors across species ranges from rare to habitual. Reflecting this pattern, the classification of species as cooperative breeders varies among researchers depending on definitional criteria. Cooperative breeding occurs in other primates but is not a parenting strategy shared by our closest relatives.

Are Humans Cooperative Breeders?

Definition of the term cooperative breeding has undergone recent debate and reconsideration (Clutton-Brock 2006, Cockburn 1998, Russell 2004, Strassman & Kurapati 2010). Because its usage lacks consensus, especially in its application to humans, cooperative breeding is used here in its broadest historic sense as a social system in which nonmaternal individuals help support offspring who are not their own. Another term, such as social parenting, may also be suitable. In lieu of developing a new vocabulary, the cooperative breeding literature provides a rich theoretic and empirical background with which to comparatively situate human parenting.

Because human mothers routinely rely on the help of others to raise young, humans share many features in common with other cooperative breeders. But human parenting and reproduction are also distinct in several key ways. First, the formation of cooperative breeding in many species of birds and mammals is broadly associated with delayed dispersal. Sexually mature offspring may delay leaving their natal territory and initiating reproduction when constraints exist either in mating opportunities or in the availability of resources or territory to reproduce successfully (Emlen 1995, Woolfenden & Fitzpatrick 1984). In several studies of historic Europe, late age at marriage has been related to ecological constraints (Strassman & Clarke 1998, Voland et al. 1991). Delayed dispersal, however, is not a necessary condition for human cooperation in raising children. Second, cooperative breeding in many species of birds and mammals tends to be associated with female reproductive suppression and reproduction by one or a small group of dominant females. In contrast, human mothers acquire help without suppressing the reproductive effort of other females in the group. This may be partly because two classes of helpers common in traditional societies but not among nonhuman cooperative breeders—juveniles and grandmothers—are not competing for mating opportunities or direct reproductive help. Nor do they compromise their own reproductive effort during life stages when they help. Third, among humans, childrearing help occurs within the broader context of food sharing in which individuals of all ages and sex participate. One reason cooperative breeding may be uncommon among mammalian species is because dependency of young terminates with weaning, limiting opportunities for help (Russell 2004). Since human juveniles are also dependent, it introduces the potential for helping behaviors aside from child care. Because juvenile provisioning occurs within a general subsistence pattern of food sharing and labor cooperation, the costs, benefits, and pathways to cooperative breeding in humans may be very different than those for other animals.

The goal of this overview is to discuss the importance of and empirical evidence for human cooperative breeding and to consider its demographic significance. The first section outlines key human life-history characteristics associated with cooperative breeding. The second section identifies helpers and addresses the roles that fathers, older adults, and siblings play in helping raise human young. The third and fourth sections discuss two important cooperative breeding questions: Does help benefit mothers and young, and why should others help? The fifth section addresses the demographic implications of cooperative breeding in relationship to the quality/quantity trade-off. The cross-cultural examples in these sections focus on modern natural-fertility, subsistence populations. In these small-scale populations, typically wealth is labor-based and children grow up in close proximity to kin and have little access to health care and education. Given the variation in labor patterns among modern foragers and the overlap in demographic parameters and child-rearing practices with subsistence agriculturalists and pastoralists (Bentley et al. 1993, Kramer & Boone 2002), natural fertility, rather than subsistence classification, is considered the more meaningful criteria for discussing cooperative breeding. A distinction is made between natural-fertility and postdemographic transition populations because family planning, paying for child care,

schooling, and institutional subsidies alter the need and economic options for providing help. The final section explores implications of cooperative breeding for postdemographic transition populations.

HUMAN LIFE HISTORY AND COOPERATIVE BREEDING

Human mothers and children are unusual with respect to a number of life-history features compared with our closest primate relatives (**Figure 1**). Children are weaned at a young age, reach sexual maturity late, and are more than twice as likely to survive to reproductive age (Kaplan et al. 2000). The common explanation for this remarkable improvement in child survivorship is that, unlike other primates who are independent of their mothers once they are weaned, human children continue to be fed, clothed, sheltered, and otherwise assisted. Nonhuman primate mothers may let juveniles forage in close proximity, offer agonistic support, and help negotiate social position. But before the birth of the next offspring, juveniles are independent food providers. In contrast, human juveniles are subsidized throughout much of their growth and development.

Short birth intervals, a relatively high probability of survival, and postweaning dependency commit mothers to raising children of various ages concurrently. Many mammals have litters, and mothers support multiple young of the same age. But raising dependents of different ages presents a unique challenge to human mothers because infants, young children, and older children require different time and energy investments. Infant survival is dependent on mother's milk. Young children, whose dental and digestive maturation is incomplete, yet whose brain growth is calorically demanding, need calorie-rich, but easily digestible food (Bogin 1999). Older children eat adult foods and often require investments in training, education, and status to become competitive adults. Because of these disparate time and energy expenditures, mothers are faced with a time allocation problem throughout their

Life history: age-related time and energy allocations to growth, reproduction, and survival across the life course

Natural fertility population: a population in which fertility is not limited, regulated, or controlled through conscious means

Subsistence population: a hunter-gatherer, agricultural, or pastoral society with little involvement in wage labor or market economy, and in which households generally consume what they produce, and produce what they consume

Demographic transition: the trend in recent centuries toward declining mortality and fertility

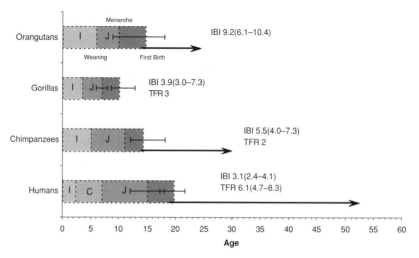

Figure 1

Comparative primate life-history parameters showing mean age at weaning, age at menarche, age at first birth. Error bars show ranges for age at menarche and first birth. Arrows show life expectancy given survival to reproductive age. Birth intervals (IBI) and total fertility rate (TFR) given where available. Sources: Orangutans age at weaning (Galdikas & Wood 1990); age at first birth, birth intervals, life span (Wich et al. 2004, p. 393); age at menarche (Knott 2001). Gorillas age at weaning (Fossey 1979); age at menarche, age at first birth, birth intervals (Watts 1991); TFR (Kaplan et al. 2000). Chimpanzees age at weaning (Pusey 1983); age at menarche (Pusey 1990); age at first birth, birth intervals (Knott 2001); TFR, life span (Kaplan et al. 2000). Humans age at weaning (Kaplan et al. 2000); age at menarche (Eveleth & Tanner 1990, pp. 162–65); age at first birth (Kaplan et al. 2000, mean for Ache, !Kung, Hiwi, and Hadza); life span (Kaplan et al. 2000); TFR (Bentley et al. 1993, mean for 57 groups of foragers, horticulturalists, and agriculturalists); birth intervals (Alvarez 2000, mean for Ache, !Kung, Amele, and Turkana), lower range (Kramer 2002), upper range (Howell 1979, 2000).

reproductive careers: how to provide high-quality child care without sacrificing activities that support older children (Hewlett 1991a, Hill & Hurtado 1996, Hill & Kaplan 1988, Hrdy 1999).

In managing these competing demands, mothers tend not to compromise the time they allocate to child care, but instead adjust time spent in other activities. The care that infants receive from their mothers is similar cross-culturally. **Table 1** includes all known published sources of the proportion of child care that young children receive from various caretakers. Mothers on average provide only ~50% of the care a young child receives. This regularity partly reflects that breastfeeding constitutes a predictable and large proportion of child care. Although rare instances of allonursing occur in humans, under most circumstances the time mothers spend nursing

is not adjustable, regardless of the availability of helpers. Cross-cultural research suggests that mothers with a nursing infant and older children balance the competing demands of providing for children of different ages by reducing time spent in domestic activities, foraging activities, or field work, activities that more directly benefit older children (Hames 1988; Hurtado et al. 1985, 1992; Kramer 2004; Marlowe 2003). How mothers resolve this reduction in time spent in other activities has led to provocative debate in anthropology about who helps mothers raise their young.

WHO HELPS MOTHERS RAISE THEIR YOUNG?

Numerous cross-cultural studies document the social support mothers receive to help raise young. Although a variety of kin and nonkin

Table 1 Mean proportion of direct child care received by a child[a]

	Mothers	Fathers	Siblings	Grandmothers	Other related/unrelated
Ye'kwana[b] (Hames 1988, p. 245)	49%	2.7%	♀ 16.7% ♂ 1.9%	11.2%	20.6%
Aka[c] (Hewlett 1988, p. 269)	42.7%	15.8%	–	–	13.2%
Efe (P. Ivey, unpublished data)	50%	6%	♀ 13% ♂ 14%	9%	9%
Agta (Goodman et al. 1985, p. 1206)	51.7%	4.4%	♀ 10.2% ♂ 1.1%	7.6%	–
Maya (Kramer 2005a, p. 227)	46.1%	1.6%	♀ 31.6% ♂ 4.6%	1.2%	11.2%[d] 2.8%
Alyawara[e] (Denham 1974, p. 264)	53%	<1%	31%	–	16%
Trinidad[f] (Flinn 1992, p. 66)	44.2%	10.3%	16.3%	–	29.3%
Mardu[g] (Scelza 2009, p. 451)	32.2%	1.7%	5.0%	14.3%	29.8% (12.6)[h]
Toba (Valeggia 2009)	50%	–	♀ 33% ♂ 4%	13%	–

[a]Unless otherwise indicated, direct child care includes nursing, feeding, carrying, holding, and grooming (dressing, bathing, delousing, minor medical). Values are for infants, in most cases defined as children under the age of one year. A dash indicates data not reported for category. Values may not add up to 100%.

[b]Includes children 0–40 months.

[c]Values for mothers and fathers includes children 1–18 month(s) old. Other may include siblings and grandmothers.

[d]Help by related individuals shown on top (of this, aunts comprise 8.4%), unrelated on bottom.

[e]Values reported for carrying children only. Values for male and female siblings reported as an aggregate.

[f]Includes children 0–4 years old. Other includes grandparents. Values for male and female siblings reported as an aggregate.

[g]Includes children 0–3 years old. Values for male and female siblings reported as an aggregate.

[h]Percent of child care observations in which more than one caretaker was present, and most often includes the mother. In an additional 4.4% of observations, no caretaker was present.

help mothers, attention has centered on males, older adults, and children. A selection of these studies is discussed below.

Male Investment

The help of males in avian studies, where ideas about cooperative breeding were developed, was traditionally considered to be parental investment. When genetic testing opened up the possibility of ascertaining paternity, it became clear that in many cases male helpers were not biological fathers. To avoid making assumptions about paternity, current literature often refers to male assistance as allocare or allomothering (Hrdy 2001).

Male investment is unusual among animals but occurs in a number of cooperative breeding species (Woolfenden & Fitzpatrick 1984), including nonhuman primates (Bales et al. 2000, Goldizen 1987, McKenna 1987). In human societies, males assist relatively little in child care (**Table 1**). A notable exception is Aka (central African foragers) fathers, who provide a high proportion of infant care (Hewlett 1988). While males generally help little with children, they are important economic contributors in many traditional societies (Draper & Hames 2000, Hewlett 1991a, Hurtado & Hill 1991, Irons 1983, Kaplan et al. 2000, Marlowe 1999). In a comprehensive review of male contribution to forager diets, Lancaster et al. (2000) find that males in most societies provide the majority of calories and most of the protein. Male provisioning may be particularly important during lactation (Hurtado et al. 1992, Quinlan &

Paternity certainty: the extent to which a male is certain he is the biological father

Quinlan 2008). Hadza women, for example, forage less, and their husbands more, when they have young nurslings (Marlowe 2003).

Although males make valuable food contributions, these inputs are quite variable. A number of studies emphasize that this variation is best understood as a response to how much others help (Fouts 2008, Griffin & Griffin 1992, Quinlan & Quinlan 2008). For example, Fouts (2008) finds that among Indian Bofi foragers and Kashi agriculturalists the presence of a grandmother is associated with decreased male parenting effort. Among the Agta, foragers native to the Philippines, fathers spend more time in child care early in a marriage when a mother does not have a daughter old enough to assist (Griffin & Griffin 1992).

Other studies emphasize that variation in male assistance reflects the value of their help. Aka fathers, for example, vary their investment depending on the opportunity costs of other ways to spend their time. Aka fathers who have fewer resources to offer spend more time with their children and provide more child care than do wealthier, higher-status fathers (Hewlett 1988). Among the Ache, food provisioning has higher fitness payoffs than does time spent in other activities, such as child care (Hill & Kaplan 1988). Although children may benefit from male investment, especially where male resources are important to the diet, motivation for male provisioning has alternatively been explained as mating effort (Bliege Bird 1999, Hawkes 1991, Hawkes et al. 2001).

Older Adults

Grandparents in traditional populations often live in close proximity to or reside with younger generations. Many empirical studies have focused specifically on grandmothers, who may care for young children while daughters spend time away from home foraging or in other economic pursuits. In other circumstances, mothers with newborns reduce time spent in economic activities while grandmothers take on these support tasks (Hawkes et al. 1989, 1997; Hurtado et al. 1992; Leonetti et al. 2005).

The few studies for which time allocation data are reported specifically for older adults indicate that they remain hard workers until late in life (Hawkes et al. 1989, 1997; Kaplan 1994; Kramer 2005b; Turke 1988). A comparative time allocation study for which age-specific consumption data are also available shows that a high proportion of Piro and Machiquenga, two groups of Peruvian horticulturalists, and Maya older adults produce more than they consume. As net producers, these older adults not only continue to support themselves, but also produce surpluses that can be transferred to underproducers (Lee et al. 2002).

In traditional societies in which residence patterns are primarily kin based, male and female kin may have differential effects on survival and growth. The willingness to help has been associated with paternity certainty, with respect to both fathers and male relatives. A number of studies have found, for example, that maternal grandparents are more inclined to invest in grandchildren than are paternal grandparents (Fox et al. 2010, Leonetti et al. 2004, Sear et al. 2000, Voland & Beise 2002).

Juveniles

Juveniles are an important but often overlooked source of help (Kramer 2002, 2005b). Children who are still young enough to receive child care also often care for their younger siblings (Flinn 1988, Hames 1988, Kramer 2005b, Nag et al. 1978, Weisner & Gallimore 1977, Whiting & Edwards 1988). Although children receive food and resources from mothers and others, juveniles in many traditional societies contribute to their own and their siblings' needs from a young age. In addition to food production, juveniles participate in a range of other subsistence and domestic tasks. The time children allocate to these activities varies widely across cultures (**Figure 2**). This figure includes all known published sources on the time children spend working in preindustrial societies. Variation in the time spent in productive activities crosscuts modes of subsistence. Notably, forager children have both high and

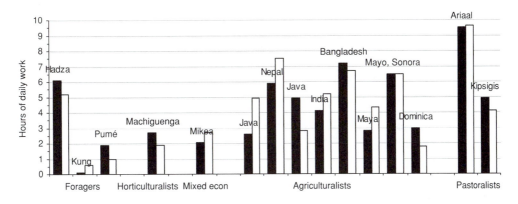

Figure 2

Time that children in natural-fertility populations allocate to food production and domestic tasks. Values include the time children spend foraging, hunting, fishing, working in the fields, caring for animals, hauling water, collecting fire wood, processing and preparing food, and performing other domestic tasks. These values do not include time spent in child care. Age categories reported in published sources vary from group to group but roughly include children ages 3–12. Sources (left to right): Hadza (Hawkes et al. 1997, p. 556), !Kung (Draper & Cashdan 1988, p. 349), Pumé (K. Kramer & R. Greaves, n.d.), Machiguenga (Johnson 1975, p. 305), Mikea (Tucker & Young 2005, p. 155), Java (Nag et al. 1978, p. 295), Nepal (Nag et al. 1978, p. 296), Java (White 1975, p. 141), India (Skoufias 1994, p. 340), Bangladesh (Cain 1977, p. 216), Maya (Kramer & Boone 2002, p. 308), Mayo (Erasmus 1955, p. 330), Dominica (Quinlan et al. 2005, p. 475), Ariaal (Fratkin 1989, p. 434), and Kipsigis (Borgerhoff Mulder et al. 1997, p. 43).

the lowest participation in economic activities. This suggests that children's help varies with specific subsistence ecologies, the kinds of subsistence tasks available to children, costs to participate, dangerousness of the environment, and how children learn to become competent adults, rather than whether a child is a forager, agriculturalist, or pastoralist per se (Kramer 2005b).

The age patterning of child care differs from economic activities in that it is younger, not older, children who allocate the most time to child care. Children in many traditional societies allocate considerably more time to economic activities than to child care (Kramer 2005a, 2009). This is an important point because much of the research on the helping behavior of children has focused on child care, which while valuable underrepresents their economic role.

In sum, researchers emphasize the contributions of different age and sex classes of potential helpers. Given that the importance of male and female resources to the diet and mortality schedules vary widely across environments, there is strategic value to mothers having access to a range of helpers. Under preindustrial

mortality schedules, women are more likely to have a surviving mother when they are young. Later in her reproductive career, when a mother is most pressed by competing demands to care for older and younger children, a mother is more likely to have productive-aged children and adult sisters. Depending on society and individual circumstances, husbands and male relatives may provide resources and child care throughout a mother's reproductive career. Small-scale populations are subject to pronounced stochastic variation in age and sex distribution. Although grandmothers, fathers, and siblings are often posed as alternative sources of help, different classes of helpers may be important at different points in a woman's reproductive career and under variable ecological and demographic conditions.

DO HELPERS HELP?

Benefits of Help to Mothers and Young

An important question in the cooperative breeding literature is whether help actually benefits maternal fitness. Even though

Table 2 Studies documenting the effect that helpers have on maternal and child outcomes, stratified by type of helper

Males/fathers	Grandparents	Juveniles
Hill et al. 1985	Hawkes et al. 1989, 1997	Bereczkei 1998
Hill & Hurtado 2009	Jamison et al. 2002	Bereczkei & Dunbar 2002
Hurtado et al. 1992	Leonetti et al. 2005	Bove et al. 2002
Lancaster et al. 2000	Sear et al. 2000, 2002	Bulatao & Lee 1983
Lancaster & Lancaster 1983, 1987	Sear & Mace 2008	Cain 1977
Leonetti et al. 2004, 2007	Voland & Beise 2002	Crognier et al. 2001, 2002
Lee 1979		Hagen & Barrett 2009
Kaplan et al. 2000		Kramer 2002, 2005a,b, 2009
Marlowe 1999, 2001, 2003		Lee & Kramer 2002
Quinlan & Quinlan 2008		Reynolds 1991
		Turke 1988, 1989
		Zeller 1987

mothers may receive assistance, evidence for positive effects on fitness across cooperative breeding species is inconclusive (overview in Clutton-Brock 2006, Russell 2004). In humans, help provisioning juveniles and assisting in child care is associated with mothers giving birth at younger ages and at shorter birth intervals, and offspring having improved survival probabilities and better growth outcomes (**Table 2**). However, the complexities of human subsistence make it difficult to distinguish between the benefits of help per se and the general effects of group living, food sharing, and labor transfers.

The benefits of help on maternal and child outcomes have been assessed with both demographic parameters and individual time allocation and return rate data. Several studies using demographic variables as an assay for help have shown that the presence of a grandmother in a household, particularly maternal grandmothers, produces positive effects on grandchild survival and growth (Fox et al. 2010, Jamison et al. 2002, Sear et al. 2000, Voland & Beise 2002). Among the Hadza, foragers in sub-Saharan Africa, mothers' foraging efforts are correlated with children's weight, but only for nonnursing mothers. After the birth of a new child, children's weight is correlated with the foraging efforts of older adults (O'Connell et al. 1999). Using time allocation data, others have found that sibling contributions are associated with higher maternal fertility (Kramer 2005b, 2009; Lee & Kramer 2002; Turke 1988). Other research documents that mothers and children benefit from male provisioning returns (Kaplan et al. 2000; Lancaster et al. 2000; Marlowe 2001, 2003).

Intergenerational Resource Flows

These studies draw attention to several points that distinguish human and nonhuman cooperative breeders. Because juveniles in other species of cooperative breeding mammals are independent foragers, help is directed primarily to unweaned young. Helping behaviors such as allonursing, babysitting, and transporting young are clear examples of the unidirectional nature of interactions between helpers and infants. Older individuals help younger individuals with no expectation of an infant reciprocating. However, because weaned human children also receive care, much of what helpers provide is support to juveniles. Helping an infant is distinct from helping a juvenile because infants do not give back, but juveniles in most traditional societies make food and labor transfers not only to their siblings, but also to older generations, including those who help them. Likewise, helpers who provide food and other goods also receive subsidies from others, often times including those they help. These complex social interactions and bidirectional resource flows among individuals of different ages and sex add a layer of complexity to modeling the benefits, motivations, and costs of human cooperative breeding.

Subsistence economies are characterized by widespread labor cooperation and food sharing (Alvard & Nolin 2002; Gurven et al. 2000; Hames 1990, 2000; Smith & Boyd 1990). These resource and labor transfers may occur among individuals within biological families and with more distantly related kin. Cooperating units vary in composition and size, but rarely does an individual of any age do all the tasks necessary to grow, survive, and reproduce. Among Pumé foragers living on the *llanos* of Venezuela, a father may bring home hunted game that is shared with other members of his extended family, but he also consumes roots that his wife, daughters, and others collect and process, as well as fish that his juvenile son catches. A Maya boy harvests enough maize to meet his own consumption as well as that of his siblings. However, he does not consume the maize he harvests until after it has been shelled, leached, soaked, ground, and cooked, tasks that his older sisters and mother perform (Kramer 2005a). This pattern of pooled labor and bidirectional resource flows raises a question about why helpers help and the cost to help in human cooperative breeding.

WHY HELP? PATHWAYS TO COOPERATIVE BREEDING

Although help raising young may benefit mothers, it poses an evolutionary puzzle. Why should others help raise offspring that are not their own? Why divert valuable time, energy, and resources to another when they could be directed to one's own survival and fitness? This is an important question because it addresses the collective action problem that arises from helping. Traditional explanations for cooperative behaviors center on indirect and direct benefits (Emlen 1995) and forms of reciprocity (Trivers 1971, 2006). Recently, greater attention has been given to mutualism, by-product mutualism, and coercion (Clutton-Brock 2006).

HAMILTON'S RULE

Hamilton's rule predicts that altruistic behavior among relatives will be favored by natural selection if rb > c, where r is the coefficient of relatedness, b is the benefit to the recipient, and c is the cost to the helper.

These explanations are reviewed with respect to their applicability to cooperative breeding in humans.

Kin Selection

Prior to Hamilton's (1964) articulation of inclusive fitness theory, there was no satisfying way to explain helping behavior, which was seen as an enigmatic expression of altruism. Hamilton's rule (see sidebar, Hamilton's Rule) provided a framework to view helping as an adaptive behavior by formulating a means to weigh whether benefits accrued by helpers compensate for the cost of their help (Brown 1987, Emlen & Wrege 1991, Vehrencamp 1978). Hamilton's rule predicts that helping is favored and more likely to evolve among closely related kin.

Kin selection has broad appeal as the evolutionary basis for cooperative breeding. As an explanation for why helpers help, kin selection is supported by the close genetic relatedness often noted between helpers and those they support and the amount of allocare they provide (Anderson 2005, Emlen & Wrege 1991, Hames 1988, Ivey 2000, Koenig & Mumme 1991, Skutch 1987). Child rearing in traditional societies is typically kin based. If a caretaker benefits directly, the benefit is the same regardless of whether he or she helps kin or nonkin. But if the caretaker helps a closely related child, he or she also benefits indirectly. Grandparents are closely related to their grandchildren. Full siblings are even more closely related, as are biological fathers. Although helpers are often related to the young they help, this relationship does not necessarily explain why they provide support.

Bidirectional resource flows: resource exchanges and labor flows that occur generationally both downward from older to younger generations and upward from children to adults

Collective action problem: arises when an individual or group of individuals partakes in benefits without providing benefits in return

Indirect and direct benefits (of helping): direct benefits enhance a helper's own survival, mating opportunities, or fecundity. An indirect benefit increases the fitness of closely related kin

Mutualism: the benefits of a cooperative act shared by both the helper and the recipient (e.g., forms of food sharing)

Kin selection as the explanation for cooperative breeding has been reexamined from two perspectives (Chapais 2001, 2006). First, the emphasis placed on indirect benefits may eclipse direct benefits to the helper and overstate the cost to help (Clutton-Brock 2002, Clutton-Brock et al. 2001, Griffin & West 2002). Although help may benefit offspring, there may be little fitness cost to helpers. Second, kin-biased behaviors may be motivated by factors other than kin selection (Coall & Hertwig 2010, de Waal 2008, Silk 2006). These reevaluations are particularly relevant to humans among whom helping young occurs within the general context of food sharing and labor cooperation.

Mutualism and Bidirectional Transfers

The importance of provisioning young is a predominant focus in human parenting, reproduction, and life-history research. The emphasis on children as the recipients of care, however, overlooks an important aspect of resource sharing and labor cooperation in subsistence economies. Transfers flow downward from older to younger generations, but also upward from children to adults. It is not surprising that these intergenerational transfers tend to occur among related kin and in the context of sibling help. But they may have important effects on the cost to raise children, on the cost to help, and perhaps on the motivation to help.

Cost to raise children. Because dependency of human young extends into juvenility, the energetic burden on others to support children is often assumed to increase. While children growing up in industrialized nations are expensive to raise, children in many traditional and evolutionary contexts may be less costly than often characterized.

Although juveniles depend on others for some of what they need to survive, they have complex relationships with their caretakers. In most traditional societies, children provide some portion of what they need. For instance,

during some seasons Hadza children provide 50% of their own caloric requirements by age five (Blurton Jones et al. 1989). When subsistence work is defined to include processing and household tasks, Maya girls produce 50% of what they consume by age six (Robinson Sullivan et al. 2008). Detailed time allocation data reveal that juveniles can produce some of what they need at the level of their own consumption and some in excess of their consumption: Fetching water, harvesting, fishing, foraging for fruit, and collecting shellfish are good examples. Children may satisfy their own consumption needs through these tasks, but their surplus at these tasks may be redistributed among other members of the sharing group. Human subsistence includes many necessary activities in addition to food provisioning. However, few studies measure the time and energy children spend in these food-processing and domestic tasks. The emphasis on food production underestimates juveniles' economic contributions.

Although children receive help, in societies where they make economic contributions (see **Figure 1**), children underwrite a proportion of their own costs, as well as those of others. Where bidirectional transfers between mothers and young have been quantified, children's subsistence efforts allow their mothers to support more children than they otherwise could without help (Kramer 2005b, Lee & Kramer 2002).

Cost to help and proximate mechanisms. Recent research has questioned whether kin-biased behaviors may be motivated by factors in addition to kin selection (Coall & Hertwig 2010, de Waal 2008, Silk 2006). Some researchers have raised the point that kin selection is an ultimate cause focused on fitness payoffs. Because these payoffs are often time delayed, kin selection per se may be insufficient to explain helping behaviors. Several emotional mechanisms have been forwarded as motivation: empathy, fairness, sympathy (de Waal 2008, Hrdy 2009, Preston & de Waal 2002).

Helpers, especially children, may be coerced or strongly urged to help (Becker 1981) or punished for not cooperating. Alternatively, what appears to be altruistic help may more appropriately be characterized as an aspect of the long-term mutualism (or short-term reciprocal altruism) of food sharing and labor transfers that are the basis of human subsistence. It is important to emphasize that kin selection, coercion, and mutualism are not mutually exclusive explanations for cooperative breeding but may explain different aspects of very complex human economic and social interactions.

In subsistence economies, self- and allo-provisioning are often part of the same general suite of subsistence activities, e.g., some portion of the returns from the time a grandmother spends digging for roots she consumes and some portion her grandchild consumes. Other than child care, the time and energy spent provisioning juveniles, who consume adult resources, are integrated into the same suite of tasks helpers otherwise do to support themselves. This point is obvious, but it is not well incorporated into ideas about the costs of food sharing, cooperation, and helping.

Relative to other primates, humans are impressively efficient food producers. Chimpanzees spend 50%–75% of their daily time budget foraging (Newton-Fisher 1999). Human foragers spend about half that time (Altmann 1987, Gragson 1989, Lee 1979). This efficiency reduces costs associated with helping. For example, postreproductive Pumé women have significantly higher return rates than do reproductive-aged women for wild roots, which comprise about 35% of the diet. These older women do not spend more time foraging, indicating that the difference in return rates is because they are more efficient at the task. Their greater efficiency may have some energetic cost, but the increase in total cost to provide some of their food returns to others is not expected to be great.

In sum, cooperative breeding in humans and other animals is often kin based. Indirect benefits may explain why helpers assist in child care and other unidirectional helping behaviors where the individual who is being helped is not likely to reciprocate. However, mutualism in addition to kin selection may pertain to juvenile food provisioning where both the helper and the individual being helped are often engaged in a long-term economic relationship. While juveniles depend on subsidies from others, the challenge is to distinguish help per se from general economic interdependence that extends across ages/sex. Although adults may produce surpluses that exceed the levels of their own consumption (Hawkes et al. 1989, Kaplan 1994, Kramer 2005b), they also rely on exchanges from others, including from younger generations.

DEMOGRAPHIC SIGNIFICANCE OF COOPERATIVE BREEDING

The quality/quantity trade-off, developed both in evolutionary biology and in economics to model optimal reproductive solutions, is a useful heuristic to compare parental investment strategies across species. The quantity/quality trade-off predicts that offspring survival will either plateau or decline at higher levels of fertility (Trivers 1972). This expectation follows from the principle of allocation and its implication for reproduction. Because time and resources are limited, mothers cannot both have more children and produce higher-quality offspring, often measured by survivorship. Or can they?

Compared with other closely related species of similar size, human mothers have both higher fertility rates and offspring who are twice as likely to survive to reproductive age (Kaplan et al. 2000). An alteration of the quality/quantity trade-off is not uncommon in cooperative breeders (Hrdy 2005). Because resources available to invest in offspring often vary among parents, problems with phenotypic correlation can obscure trade-offs within populations (Hill & Hurtado 1996, Smith & Fretwell 1974). However, one explanation why the quality/quantity trade-off is resituated in cooperative breeders is that resources available for reproduction and parental care are not solely a function of maternal production.

For most mammals, the energy available for reproduction is limited by a mother's ability to produce energy. Mothers must increase their foraging efforts to fund the metabolic costs of reproduction and lactation. For cooperative breeders, these costs may be mitigated to some extent by helpers. For example, among nonhuman primates, help carrying infants allows mothers to forage more efficiently and reallocate energy from carrying, an energetically demanding activity, to lactation and the production of young (French 1997, Goldizen 1987, Koenig 1995, Mitani & Watts 1997, Tardif 1997). The association of helpers with a reduction in maternal time spent in energetically costly activities, such as food provisioning, has also been observed in humans (Hurtado et al. 1985, 1992; Kramer 2004; Marlowe 2003).

If the energy available for reproduction and childrearing is not limited by a mother's production, it attenuates constraints on the pace of reproduction. This has particular significance to humans because investment in offspring is decoupled from lactation. Young weaned children (under age 7) are similar to infants in their almost complete dependency on others for growth and survival. However, from a mother's perspective, there is a significant distinction. The shift in dependency from milk to food allows mothers to bear children at shorter birth intervals because they are not energetically constrained by lactation. In addition to early weaning compared with closely related primates, help allows mothers to produce higher-quality juveniles without compromising the rate of reproduction.

The modern human diet poses challenges to juveniles, and also to adults, to be self-sufficient. Compared with other primates, day ranges are enormous, annual ranges are vast, food is often transported long distances back to camp, and many foods require sophisticated technology and skills to access and process. When these changes occurred and their sequential

development are debated topics beyond the scope of this review. Humans solving complicated problems of access to a great variety of high-quality foods using technology, food processing, and large foraging ranges establishes a time allocation constraint for any individual to be self-reliant. Economic interdependence co-occurs with behaviors that reduce both a mother's sole responsibilities to fund child rearing and the risks of juvenile self-reliance. Socially supported resource provisioning and offspring care have become elaborated beyond a sexual division of labor to include both bidirectional transfers and complex reciprocity. These strategies have made humans successful reproducers through both an increase in the pace of reproduction and improved chances of offspring survival.

IMPLICATIONS FOR THE PRESENT

Two distinct demographic processes are ongoing in the world today. Developed nations have passed through the demographic transition and population growth rates are low, in some cases below replacement. Yet, in many developing nations and traditional societies, fertility and population growth rates remain high. The implications of cooperative breeding to pre- and postdemographic transition populations are discussed separately because family planning and economic options available to raise children, which affect the need for and cost of help, are very different in contracepting, market-economy contexts and natural fertility populations.

Predemographic Transition Populations

In most natural fertility societies today, and for much of human history, reproduction and parenting occur in the context of extended families and under circumstances in which maternal work and child care are easily combined and shared among family and kin. The persistence of high fertility following the reduction in child mortality in many nonindustrialized and traditional communities can be seen as a further expansion of cooperative breeding. Assistance in raising young, which traditionally came from kin and others, is today augmented by governments and institutions. In many natural fertility populations, child survival has increased through nonkin sources of nutritional and medical assistance. Concomitant with the increase in child survival, birth rates have also increased, leading to rapid population growth (Dyson & Murphy 1985, Kramer & Greaves 2007, Kramer & McMillan 2006, Romaniuk 1980).

Postdemographic Transition Populations

Mothers in postdemographic transition populations face new challenges to the same time allocation dilemma of how to provide competent child care while maintaining their economic production. In postdemographic transition populations, childbearing occurs much less often in a kin-based context. As generational time lengthens and families are more prone to geographic dispersion, child-rearing support networks often diminish or evaporate. The reduction of completed family size to approximately two children means that in both the current and the immediately previous generation, siblings, aunts, and uncles are in short supply (Cohen 2003). Unlike the trend in traditional societies, mothers who work outside the home often spend more time in economic pursuits and less time in child care.

In these populations, mothers can solve the competing demands of providing for children of different ages by delaying first birth, extending birth intervals, and limiting family size through contraception. Even though families are small, help from others is often still essential, but support shifts to nonkin-based assistance, paying for child care or institutional assistance. An interesting outcome is that,

although mothers make allocation decisions and rely on help, the central evolutionary question about why helpers help no longer pertains if caretakers are paid. The child care industry rests on a relationship between parents and caretakers that is based in money and trust.

The benefits of help in postdemographic-transition contexts are difficult to identify when evaluated against traditional measures of fitness because of the confounding effects of the demographic transition. Currencies other than reproductive success, such as risk adversity, may be more appropriate in evaluating helper effects in posttransitional industrialized societies. Although many traditional kin roles may be supplanted, grandparenting, for example, continues to have an important effect on the fertility decisions of working mothers (Coall & Hertwig 2010).

CONCLUDING REMARKS

Similarities and differences between human and nonhuman cooperative breeders are rooted in the diverse social and economic interactions that characterize human behavior. For example, that children offset some portion of their own costs, by helping their siblings while also receiving help, underscores the complexity of demonstrating the dynamics of human cooperative breeding in as comparably clear costs and benefits as described for other animals. Resolving how humans fit into the framework of cooperative breeding will benefit from further theoretical debate and empirical research. Because humans target high-quality resources with complex access problems, both juveniles and adults are constrained from being self reliant. High fertility and survival rates are accomplished through our particular subsistence and social behaviors and by utilizing many forms of offspring support. Human cooperative breeding is embedded in a complex sociality, food sharing, and long-term reciprocal relationships that occur across all ages and sex. These conditions provide rich fodder for future research directions.

SUMMARY POINTS

1. The combined effects of short birth intervals, juvenile dependency, relatively high fertility, and survivorship commit human mothers to raise young of different ages. Because mothers routinely depend on the help of others, human parenting has been characterized as cooperative breeding. Males, older adults, a mother's children, other kin, and nonkin help support mothers, their infants, and older children. Although different classes of helpers (father, grandmothers, siblings) often are posed as alternative sources of help, the range of evidence for nonmaternal support of young suggests that who helps is facultative and varies across a mother's reproductive career.

2. Unlike other cooperative breeders among whom help is directed primarily to unweaned young and their mothers, human juveniles also are subsidized, not only with food, but with shelter, material goods, etc. Although they are subsidized in part, juveniles in most subsistence populations also help support their siblings and make food and labor transfers to older generations. The analytic challenge is to distinguish help per se from general economic interdependence.

3. Because cooperative breeding occurs within a subsistence pattern of food sharing and labor cooperation, it affects helping behavior in two significant ways. First, the economic relationship between older and younger generations is bidirectional. If these transfers are considered, children growing up in traditional societies may not be as costly as often characterized. Second, the opportunity and energetic cost for adults to help juveniles may be relatively low because the time and energy spent provisioning others are embedded in the same set tasks they do to support themselves.

4. Although helpers often are closely related to those they help, kin selection may not be the only explanation for human cooperative breeding. Help directed to infants may be motivated by inclusive fitness benefits. But provisioning juveniles may be based in long-term mutualistic food-sharing and labor cooperation in which juveniles also participate.

FUTURE ISSUES

1. Within-population comparisons (e.g., Hill & Hurtado 2009) across a greater range of populations will further illuminate the relative importance of various age and sex classes of helpers and the extent to which help is facultative or a determined life-history trait. A wider range of data on children's age-specific production and consumption will improve our understanding of the need and opportunities for help and their cross-cultural variation.

2. Many studies infer helper effects from demographic stipulation (the number of grandparents, siblings, or other relatives living or resident in household). The extent to which the presence of a potential helper is an adequate proxy for allocare, resource provisioning, or other forms of help is unclear. Supporting time allocation, economic, and resource flow data are critical to distinguish statistical association from causation and further develop causal links and comprehensive explanations of the effects of help on child and maternal outcomes.

3. Modern human cooperative breeding occurs within a subsistence strategy that itself involves cooperation and sharing across all ages and sex. Combining what is known more generally about cooperation and food sharing will improve the understanding of human cooperative breeding.

4. Alloparenting in other cooperative breeders is often associated with delayed dispersal. In many traditional societies, parents encourage girls to marry and initiate childbearing at a young age. In other societies, the lapse between sexual maturity and age at first birth may last up to a dozen years (Whiting et al. 1986). Examining cross-cultural differences in the activity profiles and ecological constraints of girls who remain in their natal families well past sexual maturity may clarify the role of delayed dispersal in human compared with nonhuman cooperative breeders.

DISCLOSURE STATEMENT

The author is not aware of any affiliations, memberships, funding, or financial holdings that might be perceived as affecting the objectivity of this review.

ACKNOWLEDGMENTS

Researchers working with cooperative breeding birds and mammals have laid much of the foundation for our understanding of cooperative breeding. This rich background provides many interesting parallels to human cooperative breeding. Much appreciation goes to the Maya and Pumé for the many years spent observing the interactions of mothers, children, and extended families at work and play. This overview benefited from discussions with Sarah Hrdy, Peter Ellison, Russell Greaves, Hilly Kaplan, Jane Lancaster, and Benjamin Chabot-Hanowell.

LITERATURE CITED

Altmann JC. 1987. *Hunter-Gatherers Today. An Aboriginal Economy in North Australia*. Canberra: Aust. Inst. Aborig. Stud.

Alvard M, ed. 2004. *Socioeconomic Aspects of Human Behavioral Ecology, Volume 23: Research in Economic Anthropology*. Amsterdam: Elsevier

Alvard M, Nolin D. 2002. Rousseau's whale hunt? Coordination among big game hunters. *Curr. Anthropol.* 43:533–59

Alvarez HP. 2000. Grandmother hypothesis and primate life histories. *Am. J. Phys. Anthropol.* 113:435–50

Anderson KG. 2005. Relatedness and investment in children in South Africa. *Hum. Nat.* 16:1–31

Bales K, Dietz J, Baker A, Miller K, Tardif S. 2000. Effects of allocare-givers on fitness in infants and parents of Callitrichid primates. *Folia Primatol.* 71:27–38

Becker GS. 1981. *A Treatise on the Family*. Cambridge, MA: Harvard Univ. Press

Bentley G, Goldberg T, Jasienska G. 1993. The fertility of agricultural and nonagricultural traditional societies. *Popul. Stud.* 47:269–81

Bentley G, Mace R, eds. 2009. *Substitute Parents. Biological and Social Perspectives on Alloparenting in Human Societies*. New York: Berghahn

Bereczkei T. 1998. Kinship network, direct childcare, and fertility among Hungarians and Gypsies. *Evol. Hum. Behav.* 19:283–98

Bereczkei T, Dunbar RIM. 2002. Helping-at-the-nest and sex-biased parental investment in Hungarian Gypsy population. *Curr. Anthropol.* 43:804–12

Betzig L, Borgerhoff Mulder M, Turke P, eds. 1988. *Human Reproductive Behavior: A Darwinian Perspective.* Cambridge, UK: Cambridge Univ. Press

Bliege Bird R. 1999. Cooperation and conflict: the behavioral ecology of the sexual division of labor. *Evol. Anthropol.* 8:65–75

Blurton Jones N, Hawkes K, O'Connell J. 1989. Measuring and modeling costs of children in two foraging societies: implications for schedule of reproduction. In *Comparative Socioecology. The Behavioral Ecology of Humans and Other Mammals*, ed. V Standen, R Foley, pp. 367–90. Oxford: Blackwell

Bogin B. 1999. *Patterns of Human Growth.* Cambridge, UK: Cambridge Univ. Press

Borgerhoff Mulder M, Moore MD, Kerr A. 1997. Time allocation among the Kipsigis of Kenya. In *Cross-Cultural Studies in Time Allocation*, Vol. XIV. New Haven, CT: Hum. Relat. Area Files

Bove RB, Valeggia CR, Ellison PT. 2002. Girl helpers and time allocation of nursing women among the Toba of Argentina. *Hum. Nat.* 13:457–72

Brown JL. 1974. Alternate routes to sociality in jays—with a theory for the evolution of altruism and communal breeding. *Am. Zool.* 14:63–80

Brown JL. 1987. *Helping and Communal Breeding in Birds.* Princeton, NJ: Princeton Univ. Press

Bulatao RA, Lee RD, eds. 1983. *Determinants of Fertility in Developing Countries.* New York: Academic

Cain M. 1977. The economic activities of children in a village in Bangladesh. *Popul. Dev. Rev.* 3:201–27

Chapais B. 2001. Primate nepotism: What is the explanatory value of kin selection? *Int. J. Primatol.* 22:203–29

Chapais B. 2006. Kinship, competence and cooperation in primates. See Kappeler & van Schaik 2006, pp. 47–64

Clutton-Brock TH. 2002. Breeding together: kin selection and mutualism in cooperative vertebrates. *Science* 296:69–72

Clutton-Brock TH. 2006. Cooperative breeding in mammals. See Kappeler & van Schaik 2006, pp. 173–90

Clutton-Brock TH, Brotherton PNM, O'Riain MJ, Griffin AS, Gaynor D, et al. 2001. Contributions to cooperative rearing in meerkats. *Anim. Behav.* 61:705–10

Coall DA, Hertwig R. 2010. Grandparental investment: past, present, and future. *Behav. Brain Sci.* 33:1–59

Cohen JE. 2003. Human population: the next half century. *Science* 302:1172–75

Cockburn A. 1998. Evolution of helping behavior in cooperatively breeding birds. *Annu. Rev. Ecol. Syst.* 29:141–77

Crognier E, Baali A, Hilali M-K. 2001. Do "helpers at the nest" increase their parents' reproductive success? *Am. J. Hum. Biol.* 13:365–73

Crognier E, Villena M, Vargas E. 2002. Helping patterns and reproductive success in Aymara communities. *Am. J. Hum. Biol.* 14:372–79

Denham WW. 1974. Infant transport among the Alyawara tribe, Central Australia. *Oceania* 64:253–77

de Waal F. 2008. Putting the altruism back into altruism: the evolution of empathy. *Annu. Rev. Psychol.* 59:279–300

Draper P, Cashdan E. 1988. Technological change and child behavior among the !Kung. *Ethnology* 27:339–65

Draper P, Hames R. 2000. Birth order, sibling investment and fertility among Ju/Hoansi (!Kung). *Hum. Nat.* 11:117–56

Dyson T, Murphy M. 1985. The onset of fertility transition. *Popul. Dev. Rev.* 11:399–440

Emlen ST. 1991[1978]. Evolution of cooperative breeding in birds and mammals. In *Behavioral Ecology: An Evolutionary Approach*, ed. JR Krebs, NB Davies, pp. 301–37. London: Blackwell. 3rd ed.

Emlen ST. 1995. An evolutionary theory of the family. *Proc. Natl. Acad. Sci. USA* 92:8092–99

Emlen ST, Wrege PH. 1991. Breeding biology of white-fronted ee-eaters at Nakuru. The influence of helpers on breeder fitness. *J. Anim. Ecol.* 60:309–26

Erasmus C. 1955. Work patterns in a Mayo village. *Am. Anthropol.* 57:322–33

Eveleth PB, Tanner JM. 1990. *Worldwide Variation in Human Growth.* Cambridge, UK: Cambridge Univ. Press

Flinn MV. 1988. Parent-offspring interactions in a Caribbean village: daughter guarding. See Betzig et al. 1988, pp. 189–200

Flinn MV. 1992. Paternal care in a Caribbean village. See Hewlett 1991b, pp. 57–84

Fossey D. 1979. Development of the mountain gorilla (*Gorilla gorilla beringei*): the first thirty-six months. In *The Great Apes*, ed. DA Hamburg, ER McCown, pp. 139–86. Menlo Park, CA: Benjamin-Cummings

Fouts HN. 2008. Father involvement with young children among the Aka and Bofi foragers. *Cross-Cult. Res.* 42:290–312

Fox M, Sear R, Beise J, Ragsdale G, Voland E, Knapp LA. 2010. Grandma plays favorites: X-chromosome relatedness and sex-specific childhood mortality. *Proc. R. Soc. B* 277:567–73

Fratkin E. 1989. Household variation and gender inequality in Ariaal pastoral production: results of a stratified time-allocation survey. *Am. Anthropol.* 91:430–40

French JA. 1997. Proximate regulation of singular breeding in Callitrichid primates. See Solomon & French 1997, pp. 34–75

Galdikas BM, Wood JW. 1990. Birth spacing patterns in humans and apes. *Am. J. Phys. Anthropol.* 83:185–91

Goldizen AW. 1987. Tamarins and marmosets: communal care of offspring. See Smuts et al. 1987, pp. 34–43

Goodman M, Griffin P, Estioko-Griffin A, Grove J. 1985. The comparability of hunting and mothering among the Agta hunter-gatherers of the Philippines. *Sex Roles* 12:1199–209

Gragson TL. 1989. *Allocation of time to subsistence and settlement in a Ciri Khonome Pumé village of the Llanos of Apure, Venezuela.* PhD thesis. Penn. State Univ., Pittsburgh

Griffin AS, West SA. 2002. Kin selection: fact and fiction. *Trends Ecol. Evol.* 17:15–21

Griffin PB, Griffin MB. 1992. Fathers and childcare among the Cagayan Agta. See Hewlett 1991b, pp. 297–320

Gurven M, Allen-Ararve W, Hill K, Hurtado M. 2000. "It's a wonderful life": signaling generosity among the Ache of Paraguay. *Evol. Hum. Behav.* 21:263–82

Hagen EH, Barrett HC. 2009. Cooperative breeding and adolescent siblings. *Curr. Anthropol.* 50:727–37

Hames R. 1988. The allocation of parental care among the Ye'Kawana. See Betzig et al. 1988, pp. 237–51

Hames R. 1990. Sharing among the Yanomano: Part I, The effects of risk. In *Risk and Uncertainty in Tribal and Peasant Economics*, ed. E Cashden, pp. 89–105. Boulder, CO: Westview

Hames R. 2000. Reciprocal altruism in Yanomano food exchange. In *Adaptation and Human Behavior: An Anthropological Perspective*, ed. L Cronk, N Chagnon, W Irons, pp. 397–416. New York: Aldine de Gruyter

Hamilton WD. 1964. The genetical evolution of social behavior, I and II. *J. Theor. Biol.* 9:12–45

Hawkes K. 1991. Showing off: test of an hypothesis about men's foraging goals. *Ethol. Sociobiol.* 12:29–54

Hawkes K, O'Connell J, Blurton Jones N. 1989. Hardworking Hadza grandmothers. In *Comparative Socioecology: The Behavioral Ecology of Humans and Other Mammals*, ed. V Standen, RA Foley, pp. 341–66. London: Basil Blackwell

Hawkes K, O'Connell J, Blurton Jones N. 1997. Hadza women's time allocation, offspring provisioning and the evolution of long postmenopausal life spans. *Curr. Anthropol.* 38:551–77

Hawkes K, O'Connell J, Blurton Jones N. 2001. Hunting and nuclear families. *Curr. Anthropol.* 42:681–709

Hewlett B. 1988. Sexual selection and paternal investment among Aka pygmies. See Betzig et al. 1988, pp. 263–76

Hewlett B. 1991a. Demography and childcare in preindustrial societies. *J. Anthropol. Res.* 47:1–37

Hewlett B, ed. 1991b. *Father-Child Relations: Cultural and Biological Contexts*. New York: Aldine

Hewlett BS, Lamb ME, eds. 2005. *Hunter Gatherer Childhoods. Evolutionary, Developmental and Cultural Perspectives*. New Brunswick, NJ: Transaction

Hill K, Hurtado AM. 1996. *Ache Life History*. New York: Aldine de Gruyter

Hill K, Hurtado AM. 2009. Cooperative breeding in South American hunter-gatherers. *Proc. R. Soc. B* 276:3863–70

Hill K, Kaplan H. 1988. Tradeoffs in male and female reproductive strategies among the Ache: part 1. See Betzig et al. 1988, pp. 277–89

Hill K, Kaplan H, Hawkes K, Hurtado AM. 1985. Men's time allocation to subsistence work among the Ache of Eastern Paraguay. *Hum. Ecol.* 13:29–47

Howell N. 1979, 2000. *Demography of the Dobe !Kung*. New York: Academic

Hrdy SB. 1999. *Mother Nature*. New York: Pantheon

Hrdy SB. 2001. Mothers and others. *Nat. Hist.* 110:50–62

Hrdy SB. 2005. Comes the child before the man: how cooperative breeding and prolonged postweaning dependence shaped human potential. See Hewlett & Lamb 2005, pp. 65–91

Hrdy SB. 2009. *Mothers and Others: The Evolutionary Origins of Mutual Understanding*. Cambridge, MA: Belknap

Hurtado M, Hawkes K, Hill K, Kaplan H. 1985. Female subsistence strategies among Ache hunter-gatherers of eastern Paraguay. *Hum. Ecol.* 13:1–28

Hurtado M, Hawkes K, Hill K, Kaplan H. 1992. Trade-offs between female food acquisition and child care among Hiwi and Ache foragers. *Hum. Nat.* 3:1–28

Hurtado MA, Hill K. 1991. Paternal effect on offspring survivorship among Ache and Hiwi hunter-gatherers: implications for modeling pair-bond stability. See Hewlett 1991b, pp. 31–55

Irons W. 1983. Human female reproductive strategies. In *Social Behavior of Female Vertebrates*, ed. S Wasser, pp. 169–213. New York: Academic

Ivey PK. 2000. Cooperative reproduction in Ituri Forest hunter-gatherers: Who cares for Efe infants? *Curr. Anthropol.* 41:856–66

Jamison CS, Cornell LL, Jamison PL, Nakazato H. 2002. Are all grandmothers equal? A review and a preliminary test of the "Grandmother Hypothesis" in Tokugawa Japan. *Am. J. Phys. Anthropol.* 119:67–76

Johnson A. 1975. Time allocation in a Machiguenga community. *Ethnology* 14:301–10

Kaplan H. 1994. Evolutionary and wealth flows theories of fertility: empirical tests and new models. *Popul. Dev. Rev.* 20:753–91

Kaplan H, Hill K, Lancaster JB, Hurtado AM. 2000. A theory of human life history evolution: diet, intelligence, and longevity. *Evol. Anthropol.* 9:156–85

Kappeler PM, van Schaik CP, eds. 2006. *Cooperation in Primates and Humans*. Berlin: Springer-Verlag

Knott C. 2001. Female reproductive ecology of the apes. In *Reproductive Ecology and Human Evolution*, ed. PT Ellison, pp. 429–63. Hawthorne, NY: Aldine de Gruyter

Koenig A. 1995. Group size, composition, and reproductive success in wild common marmosets (*Callithrix jacchus*). *Am. J. Primatol.* 35:311–17

Koenig W, Mumme R. 1991. Levels of analysis, functional explanations, and the significance of helper behavior. In *Interpretation and Explanation in the Study of Animal Behavior, Vol. 1*, ed. M Bekoff, D Jamieson, pp. 268–303. Boulder, CO: Westview

Kramer K. 2009. Does it take a family to raise a child? See Bentley & Mace 2009, pp. 77–99

Kramer KL. 2002. Variation in juvenile dependence: helping behavior among Maya children. *Hum. Nat.* 13:299–325

Kramer KL. 2004. Reconsidering the cost of childbearing: the timing of children's helping behavior across the life cycle of Maya families. See Alvard 2004, pp. 335–53

Kramer KL. 2005a. Children's help and the pace of reproduction: cooperative breeding in humans. *Evol. Anthropol.* 14:224–37

Kramer KL. 2005b. *Maya Children: Helpers at the Farm*. Cambridge, MA: Harvard Univ. Press

Kramer KL, Boone JL. 2002. Why intensive agriculturalists have higher fertility: a household labor budget approach to subsistence intensification and fertility rates. *Curr. Anthropol.* 43:511–17

Kramer KL, Greaves RD. 2007. Changing patterns of infant mortality and fertility among Pumé foragers and horticulturalists. *Am. Anthropol.* 109:713–26

Kramer KL, McMillan GP. 2006. The effect of labor saving technology on longitudinal fertility changes. *Curr. Anthropol.* 47:165–72

Lancaster J, Altmann J, Rossi A, Sherrod L, eds. 1987. *Parenting Across the Life Span*. New York: Aldine de Gruyter

Lancaster J, Lancaster C. 1983. Parental investment: the hominid adaptation. In *How Humans Adapt: A Biocultural Odyssey*, ed. D Ortner, pp. 33–58. Washington, DC: Smithson. Inst. Press

Lancaster JB, Kaplan H, Hill K, Hurtado AM. 2000. The evolution of life history, intelligence and diet among chimpanzees and human foragers. In *Perspectives in Ethology. Evolution, Culture and Behavior*, ed. F Tonneau, NS Thompson, pp. 47–72. New York: Kluwer Acad.

Lancaster JB, Lancaster C. 1987. The watershed: change in parental-investment and family-formation strategies in the course of human evolution. See Lancaster et al. 1987, pp. 187–205

Lee RB. 1979. *The !Kung San: Men, Women and Work in a Foraging Society*. Cambridge, UK: Cambridge Univ. Press

Lee RD, Kaplan H, Kramer KL. 2002. *Children and the elderly in the economic life cycle of the household: a comparative study of three groups of horticulturalists and hunter-gatherers*. Presented at Annu. Meet. Popul. Assoc. Am., Atlanta, Georgia

Lee RD, Kramer KL. 2002. Children's economic roles in the Maya family life cycle: Cain, Caldwell and Chayanov revisited. *Popul. Dev. Rev.* 28:475–99

Leonetti DL, Nath DC, Hemam NS. 2007. In-law conflict: women's reproductive lives and the roles of their mothers and husbands among the matrilineal Khasi. *Curr. Anthropol.* 48:861–90.

Leonetti DL, Nath DC, Hemam NS, Neill DB. 2004. Do women really need marital partners for support of their reproductive success? The case of the matrilineal Khasi of N.E. India. See Alvard 2004, pp. 151–74

Leonetti DL, Nath DC, Heman NS, Neill DB. 2005. Kinship organization and the impact of grandmothers on reproductive success among the matrilineal Khasi and patrilineal Bengali of Northeast India. In *Grandmotherhood: The Evolutionary Significance of the Second Half of Life*, ed. E Voland, A Chasiotis, W Schiefenhövel, pp. 194–214. New Brunswick, NJ: Rutgers Univ. Press

Marlowe F. 1999. Show-offs or providers? The parenting effort of Hadza men. *Evol. Hum. Behav.* 20:391–404

Marlowe F. 2001. Male contributions to diet and female reproductive success among foragers. *Curr. Anthropol.* 42:755–60

Marlowe F. 2003. A critical period for provisioning by Hadza men: implications for pair bonding. *Evol. Hum. Behav.* 24:217–29

McKenna JJ. 1987. Parental supplements and surrogates among primates: cross-species and cross-cultural comparisons. See Lancaster et al. 1987, pp. 143–84

Mitani JC, Watts DP. 1997. The evolution of non-maternal caretaking among anthropoid primates: Do helpers help? *Behav. Ecol. Sociobiol.* 40:213–20

Nag M, White B, Peet R. 1978. An anthropological approach to the study of the economic value of children in Java and Nepal. *Curr. Anthropol.* 19:293–306

Newton-Fisher NE. 1999. The diet of chimpanzees in the Budongo Forest Reserve, Uganda. *Afr. J. Ecol.* 37:344–54

Nicolson NA. 1987. Infants, mothers, and other females. See Smuts et al. 1987, pp. 330–42

O'Connell JF, Hawkes K, Blurton Jones NG. 1999. Grandmothering and the evolution of *Homo erectus*. *J. Hum. Evol.* 36:461–85

Preston SO, de Waal FBM. 2002. Empathy: its ultimate and proximate bases. *Behav. Brain Sci.* 25:1–72

Pusey AE. 1983. Mother-offspring relationship in chimpanzees after weaning. *Anim. Behav.* 31:363–77

Pusey AE. 1990. Behavioural changes in adolescence in chimpanzees. *Behavior* 115:203–46

Quinlan RJ, Quinlan MB. 2008. Human lactation, pair-bonds, and alloparents. *Hum. Nat.* 19:87–102

Quinlan RJ, Quinlan MB, Flinn MV. 2005. Local resource enhancement and sex-biased breastfeeding in a Caribbean community. *Curr. Anthropol.* 46:471–80

Reynolds P. 1991. *Dance Civet Cat: Child Labor in the Zambezi Valley*. Athens: Ohio Univ. Press

Robinson Sullivan R, Lee R, Kramer K. 2008. Counting women's labor: a reanalysis of children's net productivity in Mead Cain's Bangladeshi village. *Popul. Stud.* 62:25–38

Romaniuk A. 1980. Increase in natural fertility during the early stages of modernization: evidence from an African case study, Zaire. *Popul. Stud.* 34:293–310

Russell AF. 2004. Mammals: comparisons and contrasts. In *Ecology and Evolution of Cooperative Breeding Birds*, ed. WD Koenig, JI Dickinson, pp. 210–27. Cambridge, UK: Cambridge Univ. Press

Scelza BA. 2009. The grandmaternal niche: critical caretaking among Martu Aborigines. *Am. J. Hum. Biol.* 21:448–54

Sear R, Mace R. 2008. Who keeps children alive? A review of the effects of kin on child survival. *Evol. Hum. Behav.* 29:1–18

Sear R, Mace R, McGregor I. 2000. Maternal grandmothers improve nutritional status and survival of children in rural Gambia. *Proc. R. Soc. B* 267:461–67

Sear R, Steele F, McGregor IA, Mace R. 2002. The effects of kin on child mortality in Gambia. *Demography* 39:43–63

Silk J. 2006. Practicing Hamilton's rule: kin selection in primate groups. See Kappeler & van Schaik 2006, pp. 25–46

Skoufias E. 1994. Market wages, family composition and the time allocation of children in agricultural households. *J. Dev. Stud.* 30:335–60

Skutch AF. 1987. *Helpers at Birds' Nests. A Worldwide Survey of Cooperative Breeding and Related Behavior*. Iowa City: Univ. Iowa Press

Smith CC, Fretwell SD. 1974. The optimal balance between size and number of offspring. *Am. Nat.* 108:499–506

Smith EA, Boyd R. 1990. Risk and reciprocity: hunter-gatherer socioecology and the problem of collective action. In *Risk and Uncertainty in Tribal and Peasant Economies*, ed. E Cashdan, pp. 167–91. Boulder, CO: Westview

Smuts B, Cheney D, Seyfarth R, Wrangham R, Struhsaker T, eds. 1987. *Primate Societies*. Chicago: Univ. Chicago Press

Solomon NG, French JA, eds. 1997. *Cooperative Breeding in Mammals*. Cambridge, UK: Cambridge Univ. Press

Stecklov G. 1999. Evaluating the economic returns to childbearing in Côte d'Ivoire. *Popul. Stud.* 53:1–17

Strassman BI, Clarke AL. 1998. Ecological constraints on marriage in rural Ireland. *Evol. Hum. Behav.* 19:33–55

Strassman BI, Kurapati NT. 2010. Are humans cooperative breeders? Most studies of natural fertility populations do not support the grandmother hypothesis. *Behav. Brain Sci.* 33:35–38

Tardif SD. 1997. The bioenergetics of parental care in marmosets and tamarins. See Solomon & French 1997, pp. 11–33

Trivers RL. 1971. The evolution of reciprocal altruism. *Q. Rev. Biol.* 46:25–57

Trivers R. 1972. Parental investment and sexual selection. In *Sexual Selection and the Descent of Man*, ed. B Campbell, pp. 136–79. Chicago: Aldine

Trivers RL. 2006. Reciprocal altruism: 30 years later. See Kappeler & van Schaik 2006, pp. 67–83

Tucker B, Young A. 2005. Growing up Mikea. Children's time allocation and tuber foraging in southwest Madagascar. See Hewlett & Lamb 2005, pp. 147–71

Turke P. 1988. Helpers at the nest: childcare networks on Ifaluk. See Betzig et al. 1988, pp. 173–88

Turke P. 1989. Evolution and demand for children. *Popul. Dev. Rev.* 15:61–90

Valeggia CR. 2009. Flexible caretakers: responses of Toba families in transition. In *Substitute Parents: Biological and Social Perspective on Alloparenting across Human Societies*, eds. Bentley G, Mace R, pp. 100–14. New York: Berghahn

Vehrencamp SL. 1978. The adaptive significance of communal nesting in groove-billed anis (*Crotophaga sulcirostris*). *Behav. Ecol. Sociobiol.* 4:1–33

Voland E, Beise J. 2002. Opposite effects of maternal and paternal grandmothers on infant survival in historical Krummhörn. *Behav. Ecol. Sociobiol.* 52:435–43

Voland E, Siegelkow E, Engel C. 1991. Cost/benefit oriented parental investment by high status families: the Krummhörn case. *Ethol. Sociobiol.* 12:105–18

Watts DP. 1991. Mountain gorilla reproduction and sexual behavior. *Am. J. Primatol.* 24:211–26

Weisner T, Gallimore R. 1977. My brother's keeper: child and sibling caretaking. *Curr. Anthropol.* 18:169–90

White B. 1975. The economic importance of children in a Javanese village. In *Population and Social Organization*, ed. M Nag, pp. 127–46. The Hague: Mouton

Whiting BB, Edwards CP. 1988. *Children of Different Worlds. The Formation of Social Behavior*. Cambridge, MA: Harvard Univ. Press

Whiting JWM, Burbank VK, Ratner MS. 1986. The duration of maidenhood across cultures. In *School-Age Pregnancy and Parenthood*, ed. JB Lancaster, BA Hamburg, pp. 273–302. New York: Aldine de Gruyter

Wich SA, Utami-Atmoko SS, Mitra Setia T, Rijksen HR, Schürmann C, et al. 2004. Life history of wild Sumatran orangutans (*Pongo abelii*). *J. Hum. Evol.* 47:385–98

Woolfenden GE, Fitzpatrick JW. 1984. *The Florida Scrub Jay. Demography of a Cooperative-Breeding Bird*. Princeton, NJ: Princeton Univ. Press

Zeller AC. 1987. A role for women in hominid evolution. *Man* 22:528–57

Defining Behavioral Modernity in the Context of Neandertal and Anatomically Modern Human Populations

April Nowell

Department of Anthropology, University of Victoria, British Columbia V8W 3P5, Canada;
email: anowell@uvic.ca

Annu. Rev. Anthropol. 2010. 39:437–52

The *Annual Review of Anthropology* is online at
anthro.annualreviews.org

This article's doi:
10.1146/annurev.anthro.012809.105113

0084-6570/10/1021-0437$20.00

Key Words

Aurignacian, Châtelperronian, cognition, demography

Abstract

This review summarizes current thinking about the concept of modern behavior in the context of Neandertals and anatomically modern humans. The decoupling of modern anatomy and modern behavior has prompted researchers to reframe studies of the emergence of modern humans as a debate that explicitly focuses on the origins of behavioral modernity making its intersection with modern anatomy a point of discussion rather than a given. Four questions arise from this debate: (*a*) What is modern behavior? (*b*) Is the emergence of modern behavior sudden or more gradual? (*c*) Is modern behavior unique to modern humans or more widely shared with other species, most notably the Neandertals? (*d*) Is the emergence of modern behavior primarily the result of new cognitive abilities or social, cultural, demographic, and historic factors? This review briefly addresses each of these questions and in the process offers some thoughts on the current state of the debate.

INTRODUCTION

AMH: anatomically modern humans

UP: Upper Paleolithic; ca. 40,000 BP–10,000 BP

BP: years before present

MP: Middle Paleolithic; ca. 250,000–40,000 BP

MSA: Middle Stone Age

Mousterian: MP stone tool industry normally associated with Neandertals but also made by AMH populations in the Levant

Levant: Geographic region that includes Jordan, Israel, Syria and Lebanon

EUP: early Upper Paleolithic; i.e., ca. 40,000 BP–28,000 BP

The purpose of this review is to summarize current thinking about the concept of modern behavior in the context of Neandertals and anatomically modern humans (AMHs). Two decades ago it was widely accepted that "modern" behavior and modern anatomy evolved in tandem in Europe approximately 40,000 years ago at the start of the Upper Paleolithic (UP). It was argued that the emergence of AMHs (*Homo sapiens sapiens*) coincided with an explosion of modern behaviors (e.g., language, cave art, specialized tools, complex social organization, extensive trade networks, etc.). However, the intensification of paleoanthropological research outside of Europe began to paint a different picture of our origins. As mounting evidence (an important point of contact between genetics and fossils) pointed to an African origin for modern humans at 130,000 years before present (BP) there appeared to be a "lag" between the emergence of modern anatomy and the emergence of modern behavior (see discussion in Noble & Davidson 1996). Recent studies suggest modern anatomy evolved even earlier by at least 160,000–195,000 BP (White et al. 2003) in the Middle Paleolithic/Middle Stone Age (MP/MSA), thereby increasing this gap, although the work by Marean and colleagues (2007) at Pinnacle Point in South Africa may have brought them closer together. At this site, evidence for the exploitation of aquatic resources, ochre use, and bladelet technology was uncovered dating to 164,000 BP. Early evidence of symboling behavior in the form of personal adornment, however, dates to only 77,000 BP in South Africa and possibly to 90,000–100,000 BP in Israel and Algeria (d'Errico & Vanhaeren 2007 and references therein; Bar-Yosef Mayer et al. 2009).

What has led to the decoupling of modern anatomy and modern behavior more than anything, however, is the increasingly complex picture of the relationship between stone tool industries and the species that made and used them. For example, it is no longer possible to equate Neandertals with Mousterian industries wherever and whenever they occur and AMHs with UP industries only. In the Levant, both Neandertal and AMH populations are found in association with Mousterian tools during the MP, whereas in Western Europe during the early Upper Paleolithic (EUP), AMH and some Neandertal populations made UP industries while other Neandertal groups continued to make Mousterian tools (Weniger 2006, Straus 2009) and follow what Soffer (2009) has called MP lifeways.

This decoupling of modern anatomy and modern behavior has prompted researchers to reframe studies of the emergence of modern humans as a debate that explicitly focuses on the origins of behavioral modernity with its intersection with modern anatomy being a point of discussion rather than a given (e.g., McBrearty & Brooks 2000, Wadley 2001, Bar-Yosef 2002, d'Errico 2003, d'Errico et al. 2003, Henshilwood & Marean 2003, Shea 2003, Bower 2005, Brumm & Moore 2005, Conard 2006a, Hovers & Belfer-Cohen 2006, Zilhão et al. 2006, Harrold 2007, O'Connell & Allen 2007, Zilhão 2007, d'Errico 2007, Habgood & Franklin 2008, Norton & Jin 2009; see also Shennan 2001). Specific issues that have arisen as a result of this debate include (*a*) what specifically constitutes modern behavior and what the archaeological signatures of modern behavior are; (*b*) whether the appearance of modern behavior is sudden (revolutionary and continuously built upon) (e.g., Bar-Yosef 2002, Mellars 2005) or gradual (appearing and disappearing at different times and places—more mosaic in character and only gradually becoming more generalized) (e.g., Chase 2006, Straus 2009); (*c*) whether modern behavior is, by definition, unique to modern humans (e.g., Mellars 2005) or is more widely shared with other species, most notably the Neandertals (e.g., Hayden 1993, Deacon & Wurz 2001, d'Errico 2003, Zilhão 2006); and (*d*) whether the appearance of modern behavior is primarily the result of new cognitive abilities (e.g., Davidson & Noble 1989, Noble & Davidson 1991, Parkington 2001,

Lewis-Williams 2002, Klein 2003, Wynn & Coolidge 2007) or cultural, historical, social, and demographic factors (e.g., Shennan 2001; Chase 2006; Hovers & Belfer-Cohen 2006; d'Errico & Vanhaeren 2007; Kuhn & Stiner 2007a,b; Powell et al. 2009; Hopkinson 2010). This review briefly considers each of these questions in turn and in the process offers some thoughts on the current state of the debate.

WHAT IS MODERN BEHAVIOR?

The greatest hindrance to resolving the debate surrounding the origins of modern behavior is the lack of consensus regarding what exactly is meant by this term. This is due to the lack of a well-developed body of theory defining modern human behavior (Henshilwood & Marean 2003). As Chase (2003) points out, if we take the term modern behavior literally we would have to include all modern behaviors such as practicing agriculture and sending email but it is clear that this is not what Paleolithic archaeologists mean when they use the term. As such, Chase (2003) outlines four ways of thinking about the way we define modern behavior and each has implications for how we use fossil and archaeological data. First, by definition, modern behavior can be thought of as behavior associated with AMHs—the key would be to identify behaviors that were somehow tied with the emergence of AMHs. Behaviors that postdate the evolution of AMHs or that are shared with earlier hominins would be irrelevant. Researchers who take this approach include Mellars (2005) and Bickerton (2007) (see also Hill et al. 2009 for a variant of this approach). Second, if AMHs initially shared the behavioral repertoire of earlier hominins but then a "constellation of traits…appear more or less simultaneously and these indicate a neurological change that is morphologically invisible in the fossil record, then it is this constellation of traits that constitutes 'modern behavior'" (Chase 2003, p. 637). Klein's (1995, 2000, 2001, 2008) research, which is discussed below, is a good example of this way of thinking about modern behavior.

Chase's (2003) third approach to the definition of modern behavior is based not on the archaeological or fossil records per se but instead more theoretically on what researchers perceive to be behaviors that get to the heart of the matter of what makes AMHs unique—what McBrearty & Brooks (2000, p. 533, citing the work of Greene 1999) have described as "a search for the soul, for the inventive spark that distinguishes humans from the rest of the animal kingdom." In other words, there is some sense that what researchers are trying to define is when our species became human in all senses of that word—something that takes us beyond the biological landmarks of bipedality and the like and gets to the essence of what it means to be human. For many researchers this "essence" has to do with symbolic capacity (Davidson & Noble 1989; Noble & Davidson 1991, 1996; Stringer & Gamble 1993; Wadley 2001; Henshilwood & Marean 2003; Marean et al. 2007; Soffer 2009). Essentially this approach requires researchers to justify their choice of a particular behavior as a means of separating AMHs from all other hominins. As Chase (2003, p. 637) observes, in this case, "the fossil and archaeological records are used not to define modernity but to trace its evolution or to test the model." Finally, behavioral modernity may be defined on the basis of the list of traits that separate the MP from the UP (e.g., Mellars 1973, 1989). For Chase (2003), this approach has the least utility but it also has the longest history and it is here where we begin.

Historically, lists of traits used to define modern behavior were largely based on the UP record of Western Europe and the nature of the transition from the MP (i.e., Neandertals) to the UP (i.e., modern humans) in this region. This is partly an accident of history because so much research, especially early research, into the Paleolithic was conducted here but it is also a result of the richness of the Western European record (McBrearty & Brooks 2000, Henshilwood & Marean 2003, White 2003, McBrearty 2007, Harrold 2009). In a very real sense, it dictated what researchers expected to see in other parts of the world. Twenty years ago, Paul Mellars and Chris Stringer (Mellars & Stringer 1989, Mellars 1990; see also Mellars 1973, White 1982; papers in Mellars et al. 2007a; and see Mellars 2007 for a retrospective on this conference) organized a conference at Cambridge on the *Origins and Dispersal of Modern Humans*, "which helped to make the origins of modern humans and modern behavior central concerns in paleoanthropology" (Harrold 2009, p. 283). Mellars (1989, pp. 340–45) compiled a list of traits that included a transition from flake to blade technologies, the appearance of specialized tool types such as burins and endscrapers, the rapid proliferation of novel tool types, the extensive use of artifacts shaped from nonlithic materials (e.g., bone, antler, ivory), and an increase in the degree of the standardization of tool types. Traits such as these in combination with the sudden appearance of personal ornaments, a broadening of the subsistence base, increase in settlement and population size, and long-distance trade (Mellars 1973) became a checklist against which the archaeological records of other regions were compared. Thus the definition, timing, and revolutionary nature of the onset of modern behavior were dictated by what archaeologists were seeing in the MP and UP records of Western Europe (see, for example, Binford 1985, 1989; Klein 1989; Noble & Davidson 1991; Bar-Yosef 1998). Although Mellars (2005, p. 24; 2007) insists that these trait lists were "never intended or presented as any kind of global characterization of 'modern' behavioral patterns across Europe as a whole, let alone on a more continental scale," they were certainly taken that way.

Indeed, the publication of the seminal paper by McBrearty & Brooks (2000), *The Revolution That Wasn't*, was a reaction to these Eurocentric models. Although these authors continued the tradition of compiling a trait list of modern behavior, it is a significant contribution to the field because they emphasized the importance of the archaeological record outside of Europe. They argued that the archaeological record of Western Europe was erroneously being used as a template for understanding the emergence of modern behavior globally. Rather than being a "finishing school," Western Europe was, in fact, a "cul-de sac." McBrearty & Brooks (2000, p. 454) argued that "models derived from the unique record of European prehistory do not explain events in Africa where the origin of modern people actually occurred." Furthermore, they emphasized the gradual nature of the emergence of modern behaviors—associated with the emergence of modern humans but building on the behavioral repertoire of previous hominins and being expressed in certain contexts under certain circumstances (see also McBrearty 2007).

Drawing on the African archaeological record, McBrearty & Brooks define modern behavior as being comprised of four sets of behaviors (2000; following d'Errico 2003, figure 3): (*a*) abstract thinking; (*b*) planning depth; (*c*) behavioral, economic, and technological innovativeness; and (*d*) symbolic behavior. The archaeological signatures or the "on the ground" correlates of these behaviors can also be divided into four groups (McBrearty & Brooks 2000; following d'Errico 2003, p. 191, figure 4): (*a*) ecology (e.g., "range extension of previously unoccupied regions [and] increased diet breadth"); (*b*) technology (e.g., new technologies and the use of new materials such as bone, standardization of tool forms, evidence of hafting, and composite tools; the development of specialized tools, geographic and temporal variation in tool forms, and increased pyrotechnical skills); (*c*) economic and social organization [e.g., long-distance exchange networks; use of exotic materials; "specialized hunting of large, dangerous animals[,] scheduling and seasonality in resource exploitation[,] site reoccupation[,] intensification of resource extraction (aquatic and vegetable), long distance exchange networks[,]... [and] structured use of domestic space"]; and (*d*) symbolic behavior (e.g., "regional artifact styles[,] personal adornment[,] use of pigments[,] image and representation[,] notched and incised objects[,] and burials with grave goods" and/or a ritual dimension).

Harrold (2007, pp. 23–24) describes the paper by McBrearty & Brooks (2000) as "the most systematic treatment" of the definition of modern behavior and argues that "in the absence of an accepted theory and definition of 'modern-ess' in behavior...[it is] preferable to look at discreet characteristics of the archaeological record." For others (Soffer 2009, p. 45), any "'modernity' kitchen list" is problematic because these "criteria are more than slippery because they are neither universal nor eternal." Accordingly, Marean (2007, p. 367) observes that in the field today "there is a growing consensus around a definition [of modern behavior] that has symbolic capacity at its core." In fact, Henshilwood (2007, p. 123; see also Henshilwood & Marean 2003) argues researchers should use the term "fully symbolic *sapiens* behavior" rather than modern behavior, whereas Chase (2003, p. 637; see also Chase 2006) prefers the term "symbolically organized behavior." Similarly, Texier et al. (2010) write, "symbolically mediated behavior has emerged as one of the few universally accepted markers of behavioral modernity" (p. 6180). For Wadley (2001, p. 201), "the storage of symbolic information outside the human brain is...the first undisputed evidence for cultural modernity...modern human behavior in this context is distinguished by a symbolic use of space and material culture to define social relationships." Soffer (2009, p. 46) writes that for her the "essence of modernity is institutionalized interdependence...invented social categories that distinguish us from all our hominioid relatives and hominid ancestor," whereas Stringer & Gamble (1993, p. 207; see also Gamble 1999) maintain that "symbolically organized behavior is the main structural difference that distinguishes moderns from the ancients." This way of thinking about modern behavior falls under Chase's (2003) third approach, which is theoretically based. For the majority of researchers then, it is symbolic behavior including language and codified social relationships that defines modern behavior.

REVOLUTION OR EVOLUTION?

It is clear that the traditional notion of a "Human Revolution" in modern behavior

beginning at 40,000 BP at the transition from the MP to the UP in Western Europe is now effectively dead owing to the number of personal ornaments, engraved ochre, and other material correlates of modern behavior that have been recovered from the MP/MSA of the Near East, North Africa, and Sub-Saharan Africa (e.g., d'Errico et al. 2005, 2009; Vanhaeren et al. 2006; Bouzouggar et al. 2007; Bar-Yosef Mayer et al. 2009; Henshilwood et al. 2009) and on the basis of behaviors associated with the colonization of Australia around 42,000–45,000 BP (Davidson & Noble 1992, Holdaway & Cosgrove 1997, Brumm & Moore 2005, O'Connell & Allen 2007, Balme et al. 2009, Davidson 2010; see also Habgood & Franklin 2008).

The question of whether modern behavior is the result of a revolution (a sudden break with earlier behavior) or evolution (more gradual, mosaic development), however, remains pertinent—simply, the location and date of the possible revolution has changed to Africa at either 50,000 BP (corresponding to a final "fine-tuning" of the AMH brain) or closer to 200,000 BP (roughly the first appearance of AMHs in the fossil record) or even earlier (in, for example, the last common ancestor of AMH and Neandertal populations). In a sense, the arena has changed but the players and their positions have remained largely the same. Mellars (2007), for instance, has revised the timing but not the nature of his human revolution in light of the African evidence. He (2007, p. 4) suggests that between 80,000–60,000 BP there appeared a "whole succession of significant technological and other cultural developments in southern Africa, for which comparable evidence from the earlier stages of the MSA sequence is largely, if not entirely lacking." This succession of developments (new techniques of blade production, classic forms of UP-like tools, complex bone tools, engraved pieces of ochre, pierced shells, etc.) represents (contra McBrearty & Brooks 2000, McBrearty 2007) an abrupt break with what came before it and is associated with AMH only. We return to this issue below.

By contrast, Straus (2009) argues that many of the traits used to define modern behavior

(Mellars 1989, 2005) such as prismatic blade technology, worked bone, control and complex use of fire, specialized hunting, creation of art objects, and deliberate burial actually developed during the MP or even the Lower Paleolithic (LP)—in fact, some researchers see a greater break between the EUP and the later UP (i.e., between the Aurignacian and the Gravettian) than they do between the MP and the UP (e.g., Riel-Salvatore & Clark 2001). As a result, Straus maintains that is it no longer tenable to characterize modern behavior as "not here" (i.e., MP) one moment and then "here" (i.e., UP) the next. Instead, he describes the emergence of modern behaviors as more of a change in the frequency distribution of these traits.

Straus (2009) further argues that researchers need to recognize that the UP is highly variable. As he points out, the UP "explosion of art" is far more circumscribed geographically than is commonly acknowledged. This observation underscores the behavioral variability in the UP. Straus (2009, p. 10) writes, "variation should not be seen as something to be reduced but rather as a phenomenon to be studied in order to get at the complexity of hominid behavior and adaptations. Just as the MP increasingly shows signs of 'modernity' so too would a 'noisier' UP come closer to reflecting the diversity of human strategies during a far shorter but climatically eventful period of time." Thus, for many researchers (e.g., d'Errico 2003, Hovers & Belfer-Cohen 2006, Zilhão 2006, d'Errico & Vanhaeren 2007, Soffer 2009, Straus 2009), "innovations indicative of modern cognition are not restricted to our species and appear and disappear in Africa, Europe, and the Near East between 200 and 40 ka before becoming fully consolidated (d'Errico et al. 2009, p. 16051)."

As this discussion shows, whether the emergence and development of modern behavior is seen as gradual or revolutionary depends on one's definition of modern behavior and one's evaluation of the evidence for modern behavior. Accordingly, McBrearty (2007, p. 139) identifies a number of issues in identifying modern behavior: "(1) The behavior must involve material objects; (2) the material objects must be

preserved; (3) the objects must be accurately dated; (4) the species of the maker of the objects must be correctly identified; and (5) archaeologists must agree that the objects are the product of behavior that reveals advanced cognition or symbolic thought." Not all modern behaviors, regardless of the definition used, will leave lasting traces. Similarly, in the case of early evidence for symboling, it can be difficult to distinguish anthropogenic from naturally produced grooves and perforations. Thus, the science of taphonomy is particularly crucial to an understanding of the emergence of modern behavior (e.g., Davidson 1990, d'Errico & Villa 1997; Chase & Nowell 1998; Nowell & d'Errico 2007; d'Errico et al. 2005, 2009; Vanhaeren et al. 2006; see also discussions in Chase & Dibble 1992, Henshilwood & Marean 2003, Soffer 2009). A related issue is the value or significance placed on an idiosyncratic object. Take, for instance, the Berekhat Ram artifact (d'Errico & Nowell 2000). This is a 233,000-year-old artifact described by some as a figurine but it is separated by thousands of years and thousands of kilometers from the next widely accepted examples of figurines. Is the incipient beginnings of symboling what is most important for our understanding of the emergence of modern behavior or is evidence of the existence of a symbol-based social system necessary? One's answer to this question will affect how the nature of the emergence of modern behavior is perceived. It has little to do with the archaeological record and is more theoretically based. The issues of dating and species identification are touched on below.

MODERN BEHAVIOR: THE PURVIEW OF MODERN HUMANS ONLY?

Is modern behavior by definition unique to modern humans or is it more widely shared with other hominin species such as the Neandertals? With regards to Neandertals specifically, the majority of this debate has focused on the relationship between the roughly contemporaneous Châtelperronian and Aurignacian industries at sites in Western Europe and the story they tell about Neandertal behavioral/cognitive capabilities. The Châtelperronian industry is an in-situ development from local Mousterian industries associated with Neandertals at sites such as St. Césaire and Arcy-Sur-Cure in France (Hublin et al. 1996; Bailey & Hublin 2006a,b), whereas the Aurignacian industry is intrusive to Western Europe, probably originating somewhere in the Zagros Mountains (Olszewski & Dibble 1994), and is associated with the migration of AMHs into Europe. What is most salient about the Châtelperronian industry is that in addition to MP tool types it includes UP tool types, worked bone, and items of personal adornment. As Harrold (2009) notes, before Neandertals were discovered in association with what are now often called transitional industries, this was (and still is by many researchers) considered a true UP industry (see also Clark & Riel-Salvatore 2009 and references therein).

The question at the crux of the matter is whether Neandertals developed a UP culture independently or whether the personal ornaments in the Châtelperronian layers are the result of acculturation, trade with AMHs, imitation of AMHs, or simply contamination (the mixing of layers) (e.g., White 1992; d'Errico et al. 1998; Mellars et al. 1999, 2007b; Mellars 2005; Hublin & Bailey 2006; Zilhão 2006; Chase 2007; Zilhão et al. 2010). With the recent discovery at two Spanish sites of perforated marine shells, some containing a mixture of pigments, and a shell that is painted orange on its white exterior (all taken as evidence of body painting and personal adornment) associated with Neandertals and a late Mousterian industry at 50,000 BP (only slightly earlier than the traditional dates for the Châtelperronian) (Zilhão et al. 2010), a resolution to this debate becomes even more pertinent.

Proponents of an independent origin of UP cultures among Neandertals (d'Errico et al. 1998, Bordes 2003, Zilhão 2006, Zilhão et al. 2010) argue that "the Châtelperronian (like other 'transition industries') represents the independent flowering of a Neandertal Upper Paleolithic, and demonstrates that Neandertals were the cognitive and cultural equals of AMH" (Harrold 2009, p. 290). Most importantly, they argue that all Châtelperronian layers predate the Aurignacian and therefore could not be the result of contact with AMHs. Resolution of the Châtelperronian-Aurignacian chronology has been hindered by the accuracy and precision of our dating methods (Pettitt & Pike 2001, Klein 2003, Mellars 2005, Hublin & Bailey 2006, Stringer 2006, Weniger 2006, Harrold 2009). The key sites all date to between 50,000 and 30,000–35,000 BP—just at the limits of radiocarbon dating with few alternatives that have received wide acceptance. Issues raised include what calibration curves to use, how much of a role contamination has played, and the relationship between samples and what they are believed to date (Harrold 2009). Many researchers feel that the dates for this crucial period are too imprecise to say anything (Weniger 2006), whereas others feel they show overlap between the two industries (Mellars 2005).

In a new development, although calibration curves have been available for radiocarbon dates going back approximately 26,000 years, only now is a reliable curve available for dates up to 50,000 years ago (Reimer et al. 2010). Although this may help sort out the dating conundrum, will it resolve the debate? Mellars (2005), for instance, has argued that even if all Châtelperronian sites predate the Aurignacian, this industry could still be the result of acculturation because of what he has termed the bow wave effect—the spread of "modern ideas" ahead of modern humans. Some have argued that if there was extensive cultural contact the fact that Neandertals could make and use personal adornment says a great deal about their capacity for modern behavior, whereas others (White 1992; see also White 2007) contend such an act was imitation without understanding the meaning or power of personal ornaments and the adorned body (for an excellent discussion of this issue, see Chase 2007).

Another issue that will not be resolved by a more precise chronology is the fact that we have no fossils associated with the

Transitional industries: stone tool industries that technologically and typologically bridge MP and UP industries, normally associated with non-AMH populations

earliest Aurignacian industries, although AMHs are found with later ones (Trinkaus 2005, Straus 2009). Similarly, Bar-Yosef (2006) argues that the Châtelperronian is, in fact, made by AMHs. In his view, the fragmentary Neandertal remains at Arcy-Sur-Cure made their way into the Châtelperronian layers as humans dug postholes that breached underlying Mousterian layers. This brings us back to the point raised by McBrearty (2007) about the necessity and difficulty of ascertaining the species of the makers of the objects we believe speak to modern behavior. Better dates will not address the issue of how to interpret stratigraphic data from decades-old excavations.

Mellars (2005, p. 12; see also Mellars 2006a,b; Hublin & Bailey 2006), for his part, has responded to this debate by writing that "if the Neanderthals did independently develop the whole range of behavior that traditionally has been regarded as the hallmark of fully 'modern' humans, this would arguably be the most important thing we have learned about the Neanderthals since their original discovery more than 150 years ago." He argues that it is an "impossible coincidence" that after 200,000 years of what he describes as behavioral and technological stasis that Neandertals should suddenly and independently "invent" UP/modern behaviors when such behaviors have been linked with AMH populations since their emergence as a species. Some (e.g., d'Errico et al. 1998) have argued that the contact between populations produced the need to differentiate oneself from the "other," resulting in more overt symbol use among late Neandertals, but that the capability for symbolic behavior was always there and was expressed to greater or lesser degrees as the situation warranted (see also Chase 2006). If as Straus (2009) and others have argued we need to think about shifting frequencies of modern behavior throughout the Paleolithic and you include Neandertal behaviors such as purposeful burial, adhesive manufacture (Koller et al. 2001), site modification (Henry et al. 2004), use of aquatic resources (Karkanas et al. 2002), etc. then there is no sudden invention. It very clearly comes back to what you accept as evidence of modern behavior.

COGNITION OR CULTURE?

Is modern behavior the result of cognitive changes or social, cultural, historical, and demographic factors? The major difficulty in answering this question is that, as with modern behavior, the term cognition is often poorly defined in archaeology—a cognitive change is fundamentally a sort of "black box." The most common cognitive explanations include a fully phonemic, syntactical, and symbol-based language; symbol-use and self-reflexivity; enhanced working memory; multiple intelligences; or the incorporation of "different minds," each allowing for some degree of greater communication, forethought, planning, and creativity (e.g., Donald 1991, 2001; Davidson & Noble 1989, 1993; Byers 1994; Noble & Davidson 1991, 1996; Deacon & Wurz 2001; Lewis-Williams 2002; Klein 2003; Mithen 1996, 2005; Wynn & Coolidge 2004, 2007; Bickerton 2007; Lieberman 2007; Rossano 2009; Spikins 2009). Others have argued that modern behavior is simply the result of a change in the diet that had profound effects on the formation of brain tissue (Parkington 2001; see also Unger et al. 2006).

Wynn & Coolidge (2004, 2007; Coolidge & Wynn 2004, 2005) provide one of the most clearly articulated models for a cognitive change underpinning modern behavior. They argue that essentially modern cognition was in place long before the emergence of AMHs and that "the neural change leading to modernity was modest and added to the abilities already possessed by premodern populations" (Wynn & Coolidge 2004, p. 468). Specifically, they suggest that the primary difference between Neandertals and modern humans relates to working memory. They argue that a "relatively simple" mutation led to enhanced working memory in modern humans (Wynn & Coolidge 2007), whereas Neandertals experienced a more restricted working memory that would have placed limits on their ability to solve new tasks and to deviate from well-established patterns of behavior. For these researchers, essentially modern cognition (*a*) evolved prior to the emergence of AMHs, (*b*) was characteristic of the common ancestor of Neandertals and AMHs (i.e., *Homo antecessor*), (*c*) was the result of mosaic evolution, and (*d*) represents a final "fine tuning" of the AMH mind but one that had profound implications.

Klein (2000, 2003), in his "spontaneous mutation" model argues that at 50,000 BP a genetic mutation occurred in African "near-modern" populations that is directly responsible for modern behavior. It likely involved the "neural capacity" for language and symbol use. For Klein's model to hold true, AMH populations in Africa from 160,000 BP to essentially 50,000 BP are only slightly more modern than contemporary populations of Neandertals living in Europe and the Levant. In this model, AMH populations reach the Levant by only 45,000 BP, meaning that hominins at the Levantine sites of Qafseh and Skhul are not considered AMHs. Thus there is no need to explain their association with Mousterian tools or the possible local extinction of AMH populations in the Levant at approximately 75,000 BP (Shea 2008). Strictly speaking, following Klein's model, the engraved pieces of ochre and perforated tick shells from Blombos (d'Errico et al. 2005, Henshilwood et al. 2009) and the engraved ostrich eggshell containers from Diepkloof Rock Shelter would not be considered evidence of modern behavior (see also Shea 2003; Barham & Mitchell 2008, p. 270). Both are MSA sites with relevant artifacts dating to 70,000–77,000 BP and 65,000–55,000 BP, respectively.

McBrearty & Brooks (2000) also see modern human behavior originating in Africa but they attribute it to a speciation event. The same biological processes that selected for modern anatomy 160,000 years ago (see White et al. 2003) also resulted in language, the capacity for symbolic behavior, and the whole suite of behaviors outlined above, but they see the development of modern behaviors after this point as being somewhat gradual and context specific

(Barham & Mitchell 2008). As d'Errico (2007, p. 123) notes, the African models by Klein as well as McBrearty and Brooks assume that biological differences between Neandertals and AMHs precluded Neandertals from developing "culturally and cognitively modern behavior." The difference between the two models lies primarily in the timing and whether the initial African populations are fully behaviorally modern.

A final example of this approach is Lewis-Williams (2002) who takes a slightly different tack. He argues that it is not so much that Neandertals were less intelligent but that they had a different type of "consciousness." On the basis of the archaeological record of the EUP in Western Europe, he argues that Aurignacian people brought with them "the ability to form, entertain and manipulate mental imagery in social contexts, to conceive of a spiritual realm, and to prepare the dead for that realm...[and they] must have realized that Neandertals did not have these abilities" (Lewis-Williams 2002, p. 94).

In contrast to the cognitive models, there is a growing movement in the field to understand the material culture and lifeways of Late Pleistocene hominins as historically situated phenomena (see discussion in Conkey 1997). In other words, many researchers explain differences between Neandertal and AMH populations, the emergence of modern behavior, and the transition from the MP/MSA to the EUP/LSA with reference to social, cultural, historical, and demographic factors instead of (or in addition to) cognitive ones arguing this is most parsimonious with archaeological, paleoneurological, and life history data (e.g., Chase 1999, 2001, 2006; Bar-Yosef & Kuhn 1999, Shennan 2001, Hockett & Haws 2005, Henry et al. 2004, Holloway et al. 2004, Wolpoff et al. 2004, Brumm & Moore 2005; Hovers & Belfer-Cohen 2006, Conard 2006a, O'Connell 2006, d'Errico 2007, Barham 2007, Kuhn & Stiner 2007b, Habgood & Franklin 2008, Powell et al. 2009, Soffer 2009, Straus 2009, Zilhão et al. 2010; see also Nowell & White 2010).

For example, Chase (1999, 2001, 2006) argues that symbolic behavior could have existed long before it became archaeologically visible, and it is only when symbolism came to organize social behavior beyond communication that this fundamental shift is detectable in the archaeological record. His (2006) review of the evidence for symbolic behavior suggests to him that this change appeared sporadically in different places and at different times and included both AMH and Neandertal populations. For Chase, "modern behavior," much like agriculture, which is a change in adaption, originated not in response to a genetic change but to fluctuating local conditions.

Similarly, Shennan (2001, Powell et al. 2009) proposes an elegant model to explain the processes of cultural innovation and transmission in relation to population size. His model accounts for the seemingly inexplicable flashes of modern behavior that we see throughout the Paleolithic—what Mellars (1996) in another context referred to as the "incipient beginnings" of symbol use. These pulses of modern behavior seem to appear and disappear with no directional trend (e.g., see Soriano et al. 2007). Using a computer simulation, Shennan (2001, p. 6) demonstrates that as population size increases so does the likelihood that innovations will occur, be retained, and spread (see also Powell et al. 2009; Nowell & White 2010; Hopkinson 2010, for a discussion of metapopulation ecology).

On the basis of genetic data, we know that during Oxygen Isotope Stage (OIS) 4 modern human populations fragmented and that some local populations of AMH went extinct (Lahr 1996, Lahr & Foley 1998, Shennan 2001, Kuhn & Stiner 2007b). This may be because of the global impact of the eruption of Mt. Toba at approximately 74,000 BP (Ambrose 1998) followed by the onset of harsh glacial conditions (Lahr 1996, Lahr & Foley 1998) or for some as yet unknown reason. In this view, it was not until 60,000 years ago that climatic conditions ameliorated enough to allow for population growth and renewal (Lahr 1996, Lahr & Foley 1998) and not until the EUP that

long-distance exchange networks may have increased the amount of contact populations had with each other (Shennan 2001). This recovery and expansion in population size is thought to be supported not only by genetic data but also by evidence of the broadening of the human diet and the increase in the number of archaeological sites (Kuhn & Stiner 2007b).

Once the climatic conditions eased at the end of OIS 4 then local populations would have begun to increase. Shennan (2001) suggests that "cultural innovations would have become increasingly effective" in increasing overall population fitness and the likelihood that innovations would be maintained and spread, leading to dramatic changes in the archaeological record. Because the rate of innovation retention and spread increases so dramatically as small populations grow, this could look like an explosion in the archaeological record and thus explain the explosion of art and personal adornment in the later Aurignacian. In fact, Kuhn & Stiner (2007b, p. 48) argue as follows:

> [R]ather than the appearance of novel cognitive abilities, the integration of beads and other ornaments into the material cultures of both sub-Saharan Africa and Eurasia reflects changing social and demographic conditions. Increasing populations associated with the origins and dispersal of anatomically modern *Homo sapiens* changed the social landscape, putting nearly everyone in more frequent contact with strangers. This heightened level of interaction fostered heightened sensitivity to group boundaries as a means of delimiting and defining bodies.

It is clear that there is a genetic component to all behavior at some level and that the capacity for modern behavior however broadly or narrowly defined is the result of a change in cognitive abilities be it at 50,000 or 500,000 BP or earlier. More importantly, the relationship between the capacity for modern behavior and the expression of modern behavior is key (see Clark 2002, Chase 2006), and in my view, the latter is likely governed by these historically situated variables.

CONCLUSION

This review summarizes current thinking about the concept of modern behavior in the context of Neandertals and AMHs. In particular, it presents different perspectives on four questions related to this debate: What do we mean by modern behavior? Is modern behavior unique to modern humans? Does modern behavior emerge suddenly or gradually? Is modern behavior best explained by cognitive or historically situated factors? Although approaches to these questions vary widely, there are some points of consensus. The majority of researchers would agree that (*a*) the relationship between modern anatomy and modern behavior is more complex than once envisioned and these components are best decoupled; (*b*) however broadly defined, modern behavior has symboling at its core; (*c*) the archaeological record of the African MSA has rendered invalid the idea of a "human revolution" occurring for the first time in the UP of Western Europe; (*d*) late Neandertals demonstrate modern behavior in some form or to some degree; and (*e*) social, demographic, and cultural factors are key to understanding patterning and variability in the archaeological record. The questions we seek to answer will undoubtedly benefit from additional archaeological and fossil finds such as the new research by Zilhão and colleagues (2010) as well as new or more refined methods of excavation, analysis, and dating, but these sorts of innovations are unlikely in and of themselves to resolve the debate. As discussed, these individual questions are highly interrelated and perspectives on them often have little to do with the actual "on the ground" data. It is not a case of finding more things. That the bones and stones associated with modern behavior do not speak for themselves has never been more clear, and the only way to move the field forward on this debate is by developing a more robust and integrated theoretical framework within which to study modern behavior, the notion of transitions, cognition, and historically situated phenomena.

DISCLOSURE STATEMENT

The author is not aware of any affiliations, memberships, funding, or financial holdings that might be perceived as affecting the objectivity of this review.

ACKNOWLEDGMENTS

I thank Philip Chase, Iain Davidson, Mark Moore, Nicolas Rolland, and Genevieve Von Petzinger for comments on this paper.

LITERATURE CITED

Ambrose S. 1998. Late Pleistocene human population bottlenecks, volcanic winter, and differentiation of modern humans. *J. Hum. Evol.* 34:623–51

Bailey S, Hublin J-J. 2006a. Dental remains from the Grotte du Renne at Arcy-Sur-Cure (Yonne). *J. Hum. Evol.* 50:485–508

Bailey SE, Hublin J-J. 2006b. Did Neanderthals make the Châtelperronian assemblage from La Grotte du Renne (Arcy-sur-Cure, France)? In *Neanderthals Revisited: New Approaches and Perspectives* (Vertebrate Paleobiology and Paleoanthropology Ser.), ed. K Havarti, T Harrison, pp. 191–209. New York: Springer

Balme J, Davidson I, MacDonald J, Stern N, Veth P. 2009. Symbolic behavior and peopling of the southern arc route to Australia. *Quaternary Int.* 202:59–68

Barham L. 2007. Modern is as modern does? Technological trends and thresholds in the south-central African record. See Mellars et al. 2007a, pp. 165–76

Barham L, Mitchell P. 2008. *The First Africans: African Archaeology From the Earliest Tool-Makers to Most Recent Foragers*. Cambridge: Cambridge Univ. Press

Bar-Yosef O. 1998. On the nature of transitions: the Middle to Upper Paleolithic and the Neolithic revolution. *Cambr. Archaeol. J.* 8:141–63

Bar-Yosef O. 2002. The Upper Paleolithic revolution. *Annu. Rev. Anthropol.* 31:395–417

Bar-Yosef O. 2006. Neandertals and modern humans: a different interpretation. See Conard 2006b, pp. 467–82

Bar-Yosef O, Kuhn S. 1999. The big deal about blades: laminar technologies and human evolution. *Am. Anthropol.* 101:322–38

Bar-Yosef Mayer D, Vandermeersch B, Bar-Yosef O. 2009. Shells and ochre in Middle Paleolithic Qafzeh Cave, Israel: indications for modern behavior. *J. Hum. Evol.* 56:307–14

Bickerton D. 2007. Did syntax trigger the human revolution? See Mellars et al. 2007a, pp. 99–105

Binford LR. 1985. Human ancestors: changing views of their behavior. *J. Anthropol. Archaeol.* 4:292–327

Binford LR. 1989. Isolating the transition to cultural adaptations: an organizational approach. In *Emergence of Modern Humans: Biocultural Adaptations in the Late Pleistocene*, ed. E Trinkaus, pp. 18–41. Cambridge: Cambridge Univ. Press

Bordes J-G. 2003. Lithic taphonomy of the Châtelperronian/Aurignacian interstratifications in Roc de Combe and Le Piage (Lot, France). In *The Chronology of the Aurignacian and of the Transitional Technocomplexes: Dating, Stratigraphies, Cultural Implications*, ed J Zilhão, F d'Errico, pp. 223–44. Lisbon: Instit. Portuguese Arqueol.

Bouzouggar A, Barton N, Vanhaeren M, d'Errico F, Collcutt S, et al. 2007. 82,000-year-old shell beads from North Africa and implications for the origins of modern human behavior. *Proc. Natl. Acad. Sci. USA* 104:9964–69

Bower J. 2005. On 'Modern Behavior' and the evolution of human intelligence. *Curr. Anthropol.* 46(1):121–22

Brumm A, Moore M. 2005. Symbolic revolutions and the Australian archaeological record. *Cambr. Archaeol. J.* 15:157–75

Byers M. 1994. Symboling and the Middle to Upper Paleolithic transition: a theoretical and methodological critique. *Curr. Anthropol.* 35:369–99

Camps M, Chauhan P, eds. 2009. *Sourcebook of Paleolithic Transitions*. New York: Springer

Chase PG. 1999. Symbolism as reference and symbolism as culture. In *The Evolution of Culture: An Interdisciplinary View*, ed. RIM Dunbar, C Knight, C Power, pp. 34–99. Edinburgh: Edinburgh Univ. Press

Chase PG. 2001. "Symbolism" is two different phenomena: implications for archaeology and paleontology. In *Humanity From African Naissance to Coming Millennia, Colloquia in Human Biology and Paleoanthropology*, ed. PV Tobias, MA Raath, J Moggi-Cecchi, GA Doyle, pp. 199–212. Florence: Firenze Univ. Press

Chase PG. 2003. Comment on "The origin of modern behavior: a review and critique of models and test implications" by Henshilwood and Marean. *Curr. Anthropol.* 44(5):637

Chase PG. 2006. *The Emergence of Culture: The Evolution of a Uniquely Human Way of Life*. New York: Springer

Chase PG. 2007. The significance of acculturation depends on the meaning of culture. See Mellars et al. 2007a, pp. 55–66

Chase PG, Dibble HL. 1992. Scientific archaeology and the origins of symbolism: a reply to Bednarik. *Cambridge Archaeol. J.* 2:43–51

Chase P, Nowell A. 1998. Taphonomy of a suggested Middle Paleolithic bone flute from Slovenia. *Curr. Anthropol.* 39(4):549–53

Clark GA. 2002. Neandertal archaeology—implications for our origins. *Am. Anthropol.* 104:50–67

Clark GA, Riel-Salvatore J. 2009. What's in a name? Observations on the compositional integrity of the Aurignacian. In *The Mediterranean From 50,000–25,000 BP. Turning Points and New Directions*, ed M Camps, C Szmidt, pp. 323–38. Oxford: Oxbow Books

Conard N. 2006a. Changing views of the relationship between Neandertals and modern humans. See Conard 2006b, pp. 5–20

Conard N, ed. 2006b. *When Neandertals and Modern Humans Met*. Tübingen: Kerns Verlag

Conkey M. 1997. Beyond art and between the caves: thinking about context in the interpretive process. In *Beyond Art: Pleistocene Image and Symbol*, ed. M Conkey, O Soffer, D Stratmann, NG Jablonski, pp. 343–68. San Francisco: Mem. Calif. Acad. Sci.

Coolidge F, Wynn T. 2004. A cognitive and neuropsychological perspective on the Châtelperronian. *J. Anthropol. Res.* 60:55–73

Coolidge F, Wynn T. 2005. Working memory, its executive functions, and the emergence of modern thinking. *Cambr. Archaeol. J.* 15(1):5–26

Davidson I. 1990. Bilzingsleben and early marking. *Rock Art Res.* 7:52–56

Davidson I. 2010. The colonization of Australia and its adjacent islands and the evolution of modern cognition. *Curr. Anthropol.* 51(Suppl. 1):S177–89

Davidson I, Noble W. 1989. The archaeology of perception: traces of depiction and language. *Curr. Anthropol.* 30(2):125–56

Davidson I, Noble W. 1992. Why the first colonization of the Australian region is the earliest evidence of modern human behavior. *Perspect. Hum. Biol. Archaeol. Oceania* 27:113–19

Davidson I, Noble W. 1993. Tools and language in human evolution. In *Tools, Language and Cognition in Human Evolution*, ed. KR Gibson, T Ingold, pp. 363–88. Cambridge: Cambridge Univ. Press

Deacon HJ, Wurz S. 2001. Middle Pleistocene populations of southern Africa and the emergence of modern behavior. In *Human Roots: Africa and Asia in the Middle Pleistocene*, ed. L Barham, K Robson-Brown, pp. 55–63. Bristol: West. Acad. Spec. Press

d'Errico F. 2003. The invisible frontier. A multiple species model for the origin of behavioral modernity. *Evol. Anthropol.* 12:188–202

d'Errico F. 2007. The origin of humanity and modern cultures: archaeology's view. *Diogenes* 54:122–33

d'Errico F, Henshilwood C, Lawson G, Vanhaeren M, Tillier A-M, et al. 2003. Archaeological evidence for the emergence of language, symbolism, and music—an alternative multidisciplinary perspective. *J. World Prehist.* 17(1):1–70

d'Errico F, Henshilwood C, Vanhaeren M, van Niekerk K. 2005. *Nassarius kraussianus* shell beads from Blombos Cave: evidence for symbolic behavior in the Middle Stone Age. *J. Hum. Evol.* 48:3–24

d'Errico F, Nowell A. 2000. Origins of symboling in the Near East: a new look at the Berekhat Ram figurine. *Cambr. Archaeol. J.* 10(1):123–67

d'Errico F, Vanhaeren M. 2007. Evolution or revolution? New evidence for the origins of symbolic behavior in and out of Africa. See Mellars et al. 2007a, pp. 275–86

d' Errico F, Vanhaeren M, Barton N, Bouzouggar A, Mienis H, et al. 2009. Additional evidence on the use of personal ornaments in the Middle Paleolithic of North Africa. *Proc. Natl. Acad. Sci. USA* 106:16051–56

d'Errico F, Villa P. 1997. Holes and grooves. The contribution of microscopy and taphonomy to the problem of art origins. *J. Hum. Evol.* 33:1–31

d'Errico F, Zilhão J, Julien M, Baffier D, Pelegrin J. 1998. Neandertal acculturation in Western Europe? A critical review of the evidence and its interpretation. *Curr. Anthropol.* 39:S1–44

Donald M. 1991. *Origin of the Modern Mind: Three Stages in the Evolution of Culture and Cognition.* Cambridge, MA: Harvard Univ. Press

Donald M. 2001. *A Mind So Rare: The Evolution of Human Consciousness.* New York: Norton

Gamble C. 1999. *Paleolithic Societies of Europe.* Cambridge: Cambridge Univ. Press

Greene K. 1999. V. Gordon Childe and the vocabulary of revolutionary change. *Antiquity* 73:97–109

Habgood PJ, Franklin NR. 2008. The revolution that didn't arrive: a review of Pleistocene Sahul. *J. Hum. Evol.* 55(2):187–222

Harrold F. 2007. On the fate of the Neandertals and the Middle-Upper Paleolithic transition in Western Europe. In *New Approaches to the Study of Early Upper Paleolithic 'Transitional' Industries in Western Eurasia: Transitions Great and Small*, ed. J Riel-Salvatore, GA Clark, pp. 19–32. Oxford: Archaeopress

Harrold F. 2009. Historical perspectives on the European transition from Middle to Upper Paleolithic. See Camps & Chauhan 2009, pp. 283–99

Hayden B. 1993. Cultural capacities of Neandertals: a review and re-evaluation. *J. Hum. Evol.* 24:113–46

Henry DO, Hietala HJ, Rosen AM, Demidenko YE, Usik V, Armagan TL. 2004. Human behavioral organization in the Middle Paleolithic: Were Neanderthals different? *Am. Anthropol.* 106:17–31

Henshilwood CS. 2007. Fully symbolic *sapiens* behavior: innovation in the Middle Stone Age at Blombos Cave, South Africa. See Mellars et al. 2007a, pp. 123–32

Henshilwood CS, Marean C. 2003. The origin of modern human behavior. *Curr. Anthropol.* 44:627–51

Henshilwood CS, d'Errico F, Watts I. 2009. Engraved ochres from the Middle Stone Age levels at Blombos Cave, South Africa. *J. Hum. Evol.* 57:27–47

Hill K, Barton M, Hurtado AM. 2009. The emergence of human uniqueness: characters underlying behavioral modernity. *Evol. Anthropol.* 18:187–200

Hockett B, Haws JA. 2005. Nutritional ecology and the human demography of Neandertal extinction. *Quaternary Int.* 137:21–34

Holdaway S, Cosgrove R. 1997. The archaeological attributes of behaviour: difference or variability? *Endeavour* 21(2):66–71

Holloway R, Broadfield DC, Yuan M. 2004. *The Human Fossil Record, Volume Three: Brain Endocasts. The Paleoneurological Evidence.* New Jersey: Wiley-Liss

Hopkinson T. 2010. The transmission of technological skills in the Paleolithic: insights from metapopulation ecology. In *Investigating Archaeological Cultures: Cultural Transmission and Material Culture Variability*, ed. B Roberts, M Vander Linden. New York: Springer. In press

Hovers E, Belfer-Cohen A. 2006. Now you see it, now you don't—modern human behavior in the Middle Paleolithic. In *Transitions Before The Transition: Evolution and Stability in the Middle Paleolithic and Middle Stone Age*, ed E Hovers, SL Kuhn, pp 205–304. New York: Springer

Hublin J-J, Bailey SE. 2006. Revisiting the last Neandertals. See Conard 2006b, pp. 105–28

Hublin J-J, Spoor F, Braun M, Zonneveld F, Condemi S. 1996. A late Neanderthal associated with Upper Paleolithic artifacts. *Nature* 381:224–26

Karkanas P, Rigaud J-P, Simek JF, Albert RM, Weiner S. 2002. Ash, bones and guano: study of the minerals and phytolithis in the sediments of Grotte XVI, Dordogne, France. *J. Archaeol. Sci.* 29:721–32

Klein R. 1989. Biological and behavioral perspectives on modern human origins in southern Africa. In *The Human Revolution: Behavioral and Biological Perspectives on the Origins of Modern Humans*, ed. P Mellars, CB Stringer, pp. 529–46. Edinburgh: Edinburgh Univ. Press

Klein RG. 1995. Anatomy, behavior, and modern human origins. *J. World Prehist.* 9:167–98

Klein RG. 2000. Archaeology and the evolution of human behavior. *Evol. Anthropol.* 9:17–36

Klein RG. 2001. Southern Africa and modern human origins. *J. Anthropol. Res.* 57:1–16

Klein RG. 2003. Whither the Neandertals? *Science* 299:1525–27

Klein RG. 2008. Out of Africa and the evolution of human behavior. *Evol. Anthropol.* 17:267–81

Koller J, Baumer U, Mania D. 2001. High-tech in the Middle Paleolithic: Neandertal manufactured pitch identified. *Eur. J. Archaeol.* 4:385–97

Kuhn S, Stiner M. 2007a. Body ornamentation as information technology: towards an understanding of the significance of early beads. See Mellars et al. 2007a, pp. 45–54

Kuhn S, Stiner M. 2007b. Paleolithic ornaments: implications for cognition, demography and identity. *Diogenes* 54:40–48

Lahr MM. 1996. *The Evolution of Modern Human Diversity.* Cambridge: Cambridge Univ. Press

Lahr MM, Foley R. 1998. Towards a theory of modern human origins: geography, demography and diversity in recent human evolution. *Yearbk. Phys. Anthropol.* 41:137–76

Lewis-Williams D. 2002. *The Mind in the Cave.* London: Thames & Hudson

Lieberman P. 2007. The evolution of human speech: its anatomical and neural bases. *Curr. Anthropol.* 48:39–66

Marean CW. 2007. Heading north: an Africanist perspective on the replacement of Neanderthals by modern humans. See Mellars et al. 2007a, pp. 367–79

Marean CW, Bar-Matthews M, Bernatchez J, Fisher E, Goldberg P, et al. 2007. Early human use of marine resources and pigment in South Africa during the Middle Pleistocene. *Nature* 449:905–8

McBrearty S. 2007. Down with the revolution. See Mellars et al. 2007a, pp. 133–51

McBrearty S, Brooks A. 2000. The revolution that wasn't: a new interpretation of the origin of modern behavior. *J. Hum. Evol.* 39:453–563

Mellars P. 1973. The character of the Middle-upper Paleolithic transition in south-west France. In *The Explanation of Culture-Change*, ed. C Renfrew, pp. 255–76. London: Duckworth

Mellars P. 1989. Technological changes at the Middle-Upper Paleolithic transition: economics, social and cognitive perspectives. See Mellars & Stringer 1989, pp. 338–65

Mellars P. 1990. *The Emergence of Modern Humans: An Archaeological Perspective.* Ithica: Cornell Univ. Press

Mellars P. 1996. *The Neanderthal Legacy: An archaeological Perspective from Western Europe*. Princeton: Princeton Univ. Press

Mellars P. 2005. The impossible coincidence: a single species model for the origins of modern human behavior in Europe. *Evol. Anthropol.* 14:12–27

Mellars P. 2006a. A new radiocarbon revolution and the dispersal of modern humans in Eurasia. *Nature* 439:931–35

Mellars P. 2006b. Archaeology and the dispersal of modern humans in Europe: deconstructing the Aurignacian. *Evol. Anthropol.* 15:167–82

Mellars P. 2007. Rethinking the human revolution: Eurasian and African perspectives. See Mellars et al. 2007a, pp. 1–14

Mellars P, Boyle K, Bar-Yosef O, Stringer C, eds. 2007a. *Rethinking the Human Revolution*. Cambridge: MacDonald Institute

Mellars P, Gravina B, Bronk Ramsey C. 2007b. Confirmation of the Neandertal/modern human interstratifcation at the Châtelperronian type-site. *Proc. Natil. Acad. Sci. USA* 104:3657–62

Mellars P, Otte M, Straus L, Zilhão J, d'Errico F. 1999. California forum on theory in anthropology: the Neandertal problem, continued. *Curr. Anthropol.* 40:341–64

Mellars P, Stringer C, eds. 1989. *The Human Revolution*. Edinburgh: Univ. Edinburgh Press

Mithen S. 1996. *The Prehistory of the Mind*. London: Thames & Hudson

Mithen S. 2005. *The Singing Neanderthals*. London: Weidenfield and Nicolson

Noble W, Davidson I. 1991. The evolutionary emergence of modern human behavior: language and its archaeology. *Man* 26:223–53

Noble W, Davidson I. 1996. *Human Evolution, Language and Mind: A Psychological and Archaeological Inquiry*. Cambridge: Cambridge Univ. Press

Norton CJ, Jin JJH. 2009. The evolution of modern human behavior in East Asia: current perspectives. *Evol. Anthropol.* 18:247–60

Nowell A, d'Errico F. 2007. The art of taphonomy and the taphonomy of art. *J. Archaeol. Method Theory* 14(1):1–26

Nowell A, White M. 2010. Growing up in the Middle Pleistocene: life history strategies and their relationship to Acheulian industries. In *Stone Tools and the Evolution of Human Cognition*, ed. A Nowell, I Davidson, pp. 67–82. Boulder: Univ. Press Col.

O'Connell JF. 2006. How did modern humans displace Neandertals? Insights from hunter-gatherer ethnography and archaeology. See Conard 2006b, pp. 43–64

O'Connell JF, Allen J. 2007. Pre-LGM Sahul (Pleistocene Australia-New Guinea) and the archaeology of early modern humans. See Mellars et al. 2007a, pp. 395–410

Olszewski D, Dibble HL. 1994. The Zagros Aurignacian. *Curr. Anthropol.* 35(1):68–75

Parkington J. 2001. Milestones: the impact of systematic exploitation of marine foods on human evolution. In *Humanity From African Naissance to Coming Millennia, Colloquia in Human Biology and Paleoanthropology*, ed. PV Tobias, MA Raath, J Moggi-Cecchi, GA Doyle, pp. 327–36. Florence: Firenze Univ. Press

Pettitt P, Pike AWG. 2001. Blind in a cloud of data: problems with the chronology of Neanderthal extinction and modern human expansion. *Antiquity* 75:415–20

Powell A, Shennan S, Thomas MG. 2009. Late Pleistocene demography and the appearance of modern human behavior. *Science* 324(5932):1298–301

Riel-Salvatore J, Clark GA. 2001. Grave markers: Middle and Early Upper Paleolithic burials and the use of chronotypology in contemporary Paleolithic research. *Curr. Anthropol.* 42:449–79

Reimer PJ, Baillie MGL, Bard E, Bayliss A, Beck JW, et al. 2010. IntCal09 and Marine09 radiocarbon age calibration curves, 0–50,000 years cal BP. *Radiocarbon* 51:1111–50

Rossano M. 2009. Ritual behavior and the origins of modern cognition. *Cambr. Archaeol. J.* 19(2):243–56

Shea J. 2003. Neandertals, competition and the origin of modern human behavior in the Levant. *Evol. Anthropol.* 12:173–87

Shea J. 2008. Transitions or turnovers? Climatically forced extinctions of *Homo sapiens* and Neandertals in the east Mediterranean Levant. *Quaternary Sci. Rev.* 27(23–24):2253–70

Shennan S. 2001. Demography and cultural innovation: a model and its implications for the emergence of modern human culture. *Cambr. Archaeol. J.* 11:5–16

Soffer O. 2009. Defining modernity, establishing rubicons, imagining the other—and the Neanderthal enigma. See Camps & Chauhan 2009, pp. 43–64

Soriano S, Villa P, Wadley L. 2007. Blade technology and tool forms in the Middle Stone Age of South Africa: the Howiesons Poort and post-Howiesons Poort at Rose Cottage Cave. *J. Archaeol. Sci.* 34:681–703

Spikins P. 2009. Autism, the integrations of 'difference' and the origins of modern human behavior. *Cambr. Archaeol. J.* 19(2):179–201

Straus LG. 2009. Has the notion of 'transitions' in Paleolithic prehistory outlived its usefulness? The European record in wider context. See Camps & Chauhan 2009, pp. 3–18

Stringer CB. 2006. The Neanderthal–*H. sapiens* interface in Eurasia. In *Neanderthals Revisited: New Approaches and Perspectives*, ed. E Delson, RDE McPhee, pp. 315–23. New York: Springer

Stringer CB, Gamble C. 1993. *In Search of the Neandertals*. New York: Thames & Hudson

Texier P-J, Porraz G, Parkington J, Rigaud J-P, Poggenpoel C, et al. 2010. A Howiesons Poort tradition of engraving ostrich eggshell containers dated to 60,000 years ago at Diepkloof Rock Shelter, South Africa. *Proc. Natl. Acad. Sci. USA* 107(14):6180–85

Trinkaus E. 2005. Early modern humans. *Annu. Rev. Anthropol.* 34:207–30

Unger PS, Grine FE, Teaford MF. 2006. Diet in early *Homo*: a review of the evidence and a new model of adaptive versatility. *Annu. Rev. Anthropol.* 35:209–28

Vanhaeren M, d'Errico F, Stringer C, James SL, Todd JA, Mienis HK. 2006. Middle Paleolithic shell beads in Israel and Algeria. *Science* 12:1785–88

Wadley L. 2001. What is cultural modernity? A general view and a South African perspective from Rose Cottage Cave. *Cambr. Archaeol. J.* 11(2):201–21

Weniger G-C. 2006. Neandertals and early modern humans—human contacts on the borderline of archaeological visibility. See Conard 2006b, pp. 21–32

White R. 1982. Rethinking the Middle/Upper Paleolithic transition. *Curr. Anthropol.* 23(2):169–92

White R. 1992. Beyond art: toward an understanding of the origins of material representation in Europe. *Annu. Rev. Anthropol.* 21:537–64

White R. 2003. *Prehistoric Art: The Symbolic Journey of Humankind*. New York: Abrams

White R. 2007. Systems of personal ornamentation in the early Upper Paleolithic. See Mellars et al. 2007a, pp. 287–303

White TD, Asfaw B, DeGusta D, Tilbert H, Richards GD, et al. 2003. Pleistocene *Homo sapiens* from Middle Awash, Ethiopia. *Nature* 423:742–47

Wolpoff M, Mannnheim B, Mann A, Hawkes J, Caspari R, et al. 2004. Why not the Neandertals? *World Archaeol.* 36:527–46

Wynn T, Coolidge F. 2004. The expert Neandertal mind. *J. Hum. Evol.* 46:467–87

Wynn T, Coolidge F. 2007. Did a small but significant enhancement in working memory capacity power the evolution of modern thinking? See Mellars et al. 2007a, pp. 79–90

Zilhão J. 2006. Neandertals and moderns mixed, and it matters. *Evol. Anthropol.* 15:183–95

Zilhão J. 2007. The emergence of ornaments and art: an archaeological perspective on the origins of behavioral modernity. *J. Archaeol. Res.* 15:1–54

Zilhão J, Angelucci D, Badal-García E, d'Errico F, Daniel F, et al. 2010. Symbolic use of marine shells and mineral pigments by Iberian Neandertals. *Proc. Natl. Acad. Sci. USA* 107(3):1023–28

Zilhão J, d'Errico F, Bordes J-G, Lenoble A, Texier J-P, Rigaud J-P. 2006. Analysis of Aurignacian interstratifications at the Châtelperronian type-site and implications for the behavioral modernity of Neandertals. *Proc. Natl. Acad. Sci. USA* 103:12643–48

The Southwest School of Landscape Archaeology

Severin Fowles

Department of Anthropology, Barnard College, Columbia University, New York, New York 10027; email: sf2220@columbia.edu

Annu. Rev. Anthropol. 2010. 39:453–68

First published online as a Review in Advance on June 21, 2010

The *Annual Review of Anthropology* is online at anthro.annualreviews.org

This article's doi: 10.1146/annurev.anthro.012809.105107

Key Words

American Southwest, Pueblo cultural landscapes, ethnoepistemology

Abstract

A distinctive school of landscape archaeology is emerging in the American Southwest. The Southwest School, as here defined, has its roots in a unique set of historical relationships among archaeologists, ethnographers, indigenous people, and an intoxicating physical setting that has long provided scholarly inspiration. The most significant contribution of this school, however, is the manner in which it has begun to engage Native American intellectuals, not as data to be studied, but as interlocutors with distinct epistemological stances who have their own contributions to make toward the theorization of cultural landscapes generally. As such, the Southwest School stands poised to offer an important alternative to the more widely read landscape approaches currently popular in British archaeology.

INTRODUCTION

Does a peculiarly North American tradition of landscape archaeology exist? Might we even identify a distinctive school of landscape archaeology within the arid confines of the American Southwest? If so, what are its defining characteristics, and what historical influences—intellectual, social, political—have given shape to these characteristics? Moreover, how might we distinguish the Southwest School from the more visible and widely read landscape studies within British archaeology (e.g., Bender 1998, Bender et al. 2007, Bradley 1998, Tilley 1994)?

Archaeologists in the American Southwest, generally speaking, have grown suspicious of newly defined schools, as they have of prophetic calls for paradigm change. Whereas a former generation of Southwesternists may have authored and promoted a "behavioral archaeology" or been devotees of an explicitly "processual archaeology," those of the contemporary scene are typically happy to let Europeans keep their postprocessual, interpretive, symbolic, symmetrical, etc., archaeologies and the inevitable polemics that accompany them. In the Southwest, the bulk of archaeologists tend to regard themselves as salt-of-the-earth empiricists and stubborn realists who remain hard at work within what Kuhn would describe as a period of normal science: New data are amassed and new methods developed to address core intellectual questions of longstanding concern (see Hegmon 2003). Which is to say that Southwestern archaeologists, unlike their colleagues overseas, still read and cite texts from the 1970s with impunity. This is as true in the study of ancient Southwest landscapes as it is in the analysis of village organization or pottery manufacture.

That said, the landscape studies coming out of Southwest archaeology over the past 15 years look a great deal different from those of the prior generation, and this difference must be accounted for. Indeed, when all such studies are laid out on the table, it is difficult not to conclude that we are looking at a quiet revolution of sorts. Superficially, this revolution might be regarded as part and parcel of the interpretative turn within archaeology generally, which itself is simply part of the broader textual turn within late-twentieth-century social theory. Thus have ancient Southwestern landscapes come to be viewed as texts with embedded meanings—particularly cosmological or religious meanings—to be read (e.g., Marshall 1997, Ortman 2009, Sofaer 2008, Snead 2009). One might also note the growing influence, in some circles, of British-style phenomenological approaches, signaling Southwest archaeology's engagement with both the critique of earlier interpretive approaches and the widespread effort to attend more closely to the material entanglements between humans and their physical surroundings (e.g., Darling 2009; Potter 2004; Snead 2002a; Van Dyke 2007, 2009).

But to describe the contemporary scene in this way—to track its development solely through its engagement with theory developed elsewhere—is to miss entirely what is most interesting about landscape archaeology in the Southwest. Yes, it is characterized by more frequent references to continental philosophy and its various reworkings within British archaeological theory; however, many of these external influences and intellectual borrowings strike me as comparatively minor and fleeting fashions. The more sustained and meaningful influence, I suggest, has arisen out of a newly intensified engagement with the native philosophical tradition of the Pueblos and other local groups—that is, with a body of indigenous knowledge that was once viewed simply as "ethnographic data" to be analyzed through some other theoretical lens but that is now beginning to be regarded as an intellectual epistemology in its own right. Within the emerging Southwest School of landscape studies, in other words, "theory" is not the unique contribution of Western intellectuals but is also to be found in the teachings of Alfonso Ortiz (1969, 1972), Emory Sekaquaptewa (Sekaquaptewa 1972, Sekaquaptewa & Washburn 2004), Ed Ladd (1994), Rina Swentzell (1985, 1988,

1990, 1993), Tessie Naranjo (1995, Naranjo & Swentzell 1989), Gregory Cajete (1994, 2000), and other native interlocuters, many of whose insights, needless to say, are only accessible to archaeologists in anonymous form through the medium of early-twentieth-century ethnographers. Other recent comparisons of British and American traditions of landscape archaeology (e.g., David & Thomas 2008, Johnson 2007) have missed this central point.

Below, I review the development of landscape studies within Southwest archaeology, after which I highlight three regional foci that provide a sense of the range of work currently in vogue. My goal in this review, simply put, is to argue that a distinctive Southwest School does indeed exist or, at least, very nearly exists. Whenever possible, I also attempt to outline the shape of this school through a comparison with British landscape studies, highlighting points of convergence and divergence.

THE GROWTH OF SOUTHWEST LANDSCAPE ARCHAEOLOGY

Cultural landscapes—as networks of natural and constructed places perceived and made meaningful by particular human communities (for programmatic statements within Southwest archaeology, see Anschuetz et al. 2001, Snead 2008, Van Dyke 2007)—have been a special intellectual concern for Southwest archaeologists and anthropologists since the late-nineteenth century for three primary reasons. First, the natural features of the region are striking; mesas, canyons, deserts, and mountains present the visitor with an alternately enchanted and bleak spectacle that has long prompted reflection on the sway of place within both native and non-native discourse (**Figure 1**, see color insert). Second, Pueblo and other indigenous groups in the region continue to occupy traditional territories that, while much reduced in scale, are nevertheless on substantially the same ground as during precolonial times. Unlike the many forcibly displaced tribes of the Eastern Woodlands and West Coast, Southwestern communities know their

surroundings by virtue of many hundreds—if not thousands—of years of intimate residency, a fact that has greatly empowered the direct historical approach. Third, the aridity of the Southwest has left many Ancestral Pueblo sites impressively visible at the surface, prompting repeated inquiry into how local native peoples relate to a meaningful landscape filled with ruins—or as many Pueblo people put it, with the "footprints of the ancestors" (Kuwansisiwma & Ferguson 2004).

The first harbingers of a landscape approach date back to the late-nineteenth and early-twentieth centuries when anthropologists regularly relied on Pueblo oral histories of ancestral sites and clan movements through the landscape as a basis for archaeological interpretation (e.g., Fewkes 1900, Mindeleff 1989). Unencumbered by any real means of establishing the chronological position of sites or indeed by much comparative data at all, archaeologists were typically forced to attend closely to indigenous memories and perceptions of the sites that densely surrounded their villages. Consultation with native groups at this time may have been more a matter of blunt necessity than of scholarly respect; nevertheless, some of the resultant work was striking in its detail and humanistic insights.

Perhaps the most impressive study of the period was, in fact, a work of fiction. Adolf Bandelier's (1971) *The Delight Makers* was a wildly innovative dramatization of the pre-Columbian Keres occupation of Frijoles Canyon, New Mexico, based on ethnography, archaeology, and, most significantly, Bandelier's visits to the well-preserved ruins of Frijoles in the company of friends from Cochiti Pueblo. The text is rarely cited today, which is a pity, for *The Delight Makers* was both an early experiment in collapsing Western temporalities—the text flickers back and forth between myth and history, past and present, often intentionally conflating the two—and a pioneering study of cultural landscapes, in the sense that Bandelier presents us with a humanistic reading of, for example, the embodied experience of visiting mountaintop shrines and the emotions of an ostracized woman traveling along paths through a foreign and primarily male terrain. Contemporary archaeologists in the Southwest are only now returning to these sorts of issues (e.g., Ortman 2009, Potter 2004, Snead 2009) as they are to more experimental forms of writing (e.g., Collwell-Chanthaphonh 2005).

Be that as it may, two other key texts in Pueblo landscape studies emerged soon thereafter in the same portion of the Rio Grande Valley. The first was Harrington's (1916) *Ethnogeography of the Tewa*, one of the earliest anthropological compendia of native place names and geographical meanings. Harrington's goal was exhaustive documentation rather than interpretation, but his research was instrumental in demonstrating the potential richness of inquiry into native perceptions of place. The second text was Ortiz's (1969) landmark study, *The Tewa World*, which has come to be the major reference point for the archaeology of Southwestern landscapes [with Basso (1996) a close second]. A native of Ohkay Owingeh (San Juan) Pueblo and a structuralist by training, Ortiz gathered all the material documented by Harrington, drew extensively from the teachings of tribal elders, and presented a heady vision of an elaborate Tewa ontology and cosmology rendered materially in the hills, caves, and shrines of the Rio Grande Valley.

With the publication of *The Tewa World*, Southwest archaeology was poised to embark on a new research agenda focused on pre-Columbian landscapes, questions of cosmology, and scholarly collaboration with native intellectuals. But it would be 30 years before this promise would be truly met, a fact that is all the more surprising given that the 1970s and 1980s saw a great many influential land-claims cases in the Southwest that should have directed widespread attention to native sacred geographies (Ellis 1974a,b; Ferguson & Hart 1985; Glowacka et al. 2009; Goodman 1987; Gordon-McCutchan 1995; Gulliford 2000; Zedeño 1997). Indeed, this same period saw the publication of important texts on the meaning, spirituality, and aesthetics of Pueblo landscapes in art history (Scully

1972), architecture (Saile 1977, 1989, 1990), and geography (Jackson 1984) that might have provided additional inspiration. Instead, the discipline moved in precisely the opposite direction, devoting the lion's share of its energies to the growth of a processual archaeology with new commitments to science over humanism, to the study of economics and politics over religion and ideology, and to modeling behavior rather than deciphering meaning. Within the processualist paradigm, the natural environment was typically studied as a more-or-less patchy array of economic resources to be exploited, and the spatial distribution of sites was investigated to shed light on questions of sociopolitical organization and exchange. By and large, Southwest archaeologists of the 1970s and 1980s were interested in space rather than place, as these terms have come to be conventionally used (see Casey 1997).

The notable exception to this trend was in research on Chaco, the great center of the northern Southwest during the Pueblo II period (AD 900–1150) and long a focus of archaeological work. There, questions of meaning, ideology, and cosmology simply could not be ignored, particularly following the discovery of the elaborate Chacoan roads (Kincaid 1983, Nials et al. 1987, Roney 1992), whose excessive construction, strict linearity, and accompanying shrines defied straightforward functional analyses. Study of Chaco's sacred geography was properly born with Fritz's (1978, 1987) highly original analysis of symmetries and alignments in the distribution of monumental constructions that dot the core canyon area. Fritz argued that the Chacoan landscape was structured by certain basic ideological principles that organized everything from the internal layout of kivas and Great Houses, to their arrangement throughout the canyon, and ultimately to the cosmic order writ large: "Chacoan architecture was an essential component of the memory of Chacoan culture, referents encoded in stone and space, the organizing principles of secular and sacred existence" (Fritz 1978, p. 55). This reads as quite a contemporary statement, though it must be said that Fritz's overall project remained anchored in the question of systemic adaptation: In the end, he still reduced the symbolism of the built landscape to an ideological buttress for political control, very much in keeping with orthodox processualist arguments. Nevertheless, Fritz's essay was soon followed by a series of studies of Chacoan archaeoastronomy by Anna Sofaer and the Solstice Project (Sofaer 2008; Sofaer et al. 1979, 1989), which did indeed foreground questions of Puebloan worldview and further demonstrated the degree to which Chacoans used their landscape as a monumental medium for materializing core beliefs. Research along these lines intensified in the 1990s and continues apace today (see below).

To a certain extent, these early Chacoan studies laid the groundwork for the subsequent explosion of interest in cultural landscapes that has come to characterize much of the Southwest during the past 15 years. And by the end of the 1990s, the more humanistic approach of British postprocessual archaeologies was also having its effect. Nevertheless, the single greatest impact on the field during this period clearly came from the passage of Native American Graves Protection and Repatriation Act (NAGPRA) legislation in 1990 and the sudden imperative to explore carefully the links of contemporary native communities to their ancestral and sacred sites. "The most effective implementation of humanistic approaches," writes Lekson (1996, p. 891), "comes not through academic debate and scholarly exchange but through law and regulation"—a true statement if ever there was one. Indeed, only when archaeologists were legally compelled to engage the perspectives of native individuals in the present did they seriously begin to theorize the situated perspectives of native individuals in the past.

The immediate intellectual fallout of NAGPRA was a return to long-neglected research into migration, indigenous accounts of past clan movements, and the like (Cameron 1995, Clark 2001, Reid 1997, Spielmann 1998, Stark et al. 1995, Varien 1999), which has, more recently, developed into a growing theoretical interest in what it means to be on the move in a landscape generally (sensu Bender 2001). Bernardini (2005, 2008), for instance, has looked to the itinerant past of the Hopi to explore the way serial migrations become sedimented into detailed "topogenies" that link genealogies of ancestral places to contemporary identities. Others have attended more closely to the actual material remnants of trails and roads as a means of thinking about the aesthetics of movement, its links to social memory, and the manner in which movement produces particular sorts of subjectivities (Anschuetz & Wilshusen 2010; Fowles 2010, Snead 2002a, 2008; Van Dyke 2004, 2007). In a fascinating recent study, Darling (2009) also links the spiritual journeys recounted in O'odham (Pima) songs to the physical traces of movement along pre-Columbian trails in southern Arizona. The result is an understanding of what Darling refers to as a "cognitive geography" that is necessarily situated both in the mind and in the physical terrain as lines of song and lines of trails (compare Ingold 2007).

Of course, the major impact of NAGPRA—and of late-twentieth century native activism generally—has been the manner in which it has prompted a profound methodological shift toward collaborative approaches, most of which have naturally come to focus on the interpretation of past and living landscapes (Anschuetz et al. 2002, Colwell-Chanthaphonh & Ferguson 2006, Ferguson et al. 2009, Ferguson & Anyon 2001). Post-NAGPRA collaboration between archaeologists and indigenous Southwest communities could fill a review article of its own, so let me simply highlight two key theoretical implications of this work, vis-à-vis landscape studies generally.

First, collaboration with native peoples has left many Southwest archaeologists critical of British-style phenomenological approaches. Lekson expresses this succinctly:

> Phenomenological archeology seems peremptory in its methodology de novo and more than a little naive in its claim for human universals... spatial perceptions are learned; they are nurtured, not natural. Visiting sites with

Pueblo colleagues, I can attest that their spatial keys are not mine. Pueblo people look for and see different things than I do, and the things they see are essential to their understanding of place. (Lekson 2009a, p. 580)

British archaeologists studying ancestral Britons may feel justified in speculating on the embodied experience of their prehistoric subjects, but for Southwest archaeologists to do so borders on being disrespectful to native communities who contest the ability of Western scientists to represent the thoughts, perceptions, and emotions of non-Westerners. More than simply a matter of Southwestern politics, this should be read as a basic critique of archaeology's engagement with phenomenology (see Snead 2008, pp. 11–14)— or at least of the garden-variety engagement with phenomenology that typically amounts to little more than a straightforward claim to see through another's eyes and feel through another's body.

Second, and somewhat paradoxically, the increased attention to native voices has also challenged orthodox understandings of the supposed chasm between Western and non-Western spatialities; the former is typically characterized as cartographic, Euclidean, disembodied, and top-down, whereas the latter is assumed to be embodied, subjective, and forever sensuous. The simple fact, as Lekson (1999, pp. 166–170) more than anyone has demonstrated, is that Pueblo people clearly chart out abstract space and impose their own linear grids on the landscape even though they, like all other humans, also experience places at a bodily scale (see also Fowles 2009). Much Ancestral Pueblo architecture and spatial planning, in fact, was not "vernacular" at all. It was measured, sighted, and formally specified by priestly architects, often with spiritual help:

> The water spider spread his legs to the north
> and to the south, to the west and to the east,
> and then he said to the priests and the chiefs,
> "Now indeed I have measured it. Here is the
> center of the earth and here you must build
> your city!" (Carr 1979, p. 17)

More than simply a matter of Pueblo history, these points should be read as a corrective to dominant trends in archaeological theory that implicitly set up a divide between an embodied "premodernity" and a disembodied "modernity," as if only post-Renaissance Westerners ever authored a detached and abstract spatial discourse.

Beyond critique, however, native landscape philosophies may also be read as the source of a number of theoretical positions that Southwest archaeologists increasingly share with their British colleagues. "The land. The people. They are in relation to each other . . . The land has worked with us. And the people have worked with it," wrote Simon Ortiz (1980, p. 35) of Acoma well before a relational ontology was adopted in certain postprocessual circles. Similarly, one can find elegant indigenous statements arguing—sometimes implicitly, sometimes explicitly—for the collapse of the nature-culture divide, for an object biography approach to the analysis of material things in the landscape, and for revisions to modernist understandings of temporality (e.g., Cajete 1994, 2000; Ortiz 1972, p. 137; Silko 1986, 1995, 1996; Swentzell 1985; see also Saile 1977, 1989). Basso's (1996) widely read discussion of Western Apache place-making has had special impact in this regard and has even prompted some Southwestern archaeologists to begin to investigate the relationship between landscape, narrative, and morality in the past. Snead (2008, pp. 142–44), for example, looks to the case of Burnt Corn Pueblo, a violently destroyed village in the Galisteo Basin, and considers what sorts of teachings would have resided in a landscape that included both the pueblo's charred ruins and the grim stories that undoubtedly surrounded them.

This is not to say that Southwest landscape studies have entirely flipped from a scientific to a humanistic mode of inquiry, far from it. Analyses of settlement patterns, agricultural systems and the like continue to be regarded as critical. But there is now a widespread sense that questions of meaning are at least as important as questions of behavior and that a rigorous investigation of past landscapes must also seek to understand the way in which they were perceived and experienced on the ground by culturally situated individuals. In this latter project, indigenous Southwestern philosophies of time, space, and morality have come to provide vital guidance—not by determining archaeological interpretations but—by helping to disrupt and denaturalize the taken-for-granted Western orientations of earlier processual studies. It is instructive, in this sense, to look back not so very long ago to the influential 1992 publications on Chaco's ritual landscapes (Fowler & Stein 1992, Stein & Lekson 1992, Roney 1992), which were written in the last pre-NAGPRA days of Southwest archaeology. What does one find? Not a single reference to Pueblo ethnography, nor any acknowledgment that Chaco Canyon continues to be a major ritual landscape for descendant Pueblo and Navajo communities in the present. This is not really a criticism. As with all texts, these were products of their times, and the times remained preoccupied with escaping the perceived confines of Pueblo ethnography and the direct historic approach. My point is simply that such omissions would be almost inconceivable today, two decades later.

THE CONTEMPORARY SCENE

Currently, landscape archaeology in the Southwest is dominated by three regional foci (**Figure 2**, see color insert), each of which is further distinguished by a special attention to a particular time period and, to a certain extent, varying theoretical emphases. (*a*) In the Western Pueblo region, for instance, the past 25 years have seen a growing number of collaborative projects exploring the relationship of the modern Hopi and Zuni Pueblos to their ancestral landscapes. As ethnographic as they are archaeological, these projects are largely oriented toward questions of heritage, memory, and cultural affiliation. (*b*) The Eastern Pueblo or Rio Grande region, in contrast, has produced a great many studies of ancestral landscapes dating from the Pueblo III through the Pueblo

Revolt periods (AD 1275–1700). Although frequently in dialogue with native scholars, Eastern Pueblo research gravitates more strongly toward the direct historical approach, drawing upon twentieth-century ethnography to explore issues of pre-Columbian cosmology and community identity, among other issues. (*c*) The third region is the Chacoan heartland, where long-standing interests in Pueblo II period (AD 900–1150) cosmology, pilgrimage, and ritual practice are being expanded to address new questions of monumentality, memory, aesthetics, and the politics of space. Needless to say, valuable Southwest landscape studies are also being produced in other regions, even if I lack the space to discuss them here.

Living Landscapes of the Western Pueblos

Recent collaborative research into Hopi and Zuni cultural landscapes bears the clear mark of having emerged out of the 1970s and 1980s land-claims struggles, during which time archaeologists were invited to help document traditional land-use patterns, the extent of ancestral Pueblo geographic movements, and the current cultural significance of surrounding natural and constructed features (Dodge 2007, Ferguson & Hart 1985, Goodman 1987). To a degree not seen for many decades, archaeologists came to reassume the role of the ethnographer or, more accurately, the ethnogeographer. This is a curious fact of Southwest archaeology that has received little commentary to date. In the wake of Deloria's (1969) damning critiques of the ethnography of Native America and its modes of objectification, ethnographers largely packed their things and left the Pueblo region (formerly the heartland of American anthropology), leaving archaeologists to pick up the pieces and to continue representing the discipline as a whole (but see Whiteley 1998, 2008). Consequently, a greater blurring of the subdisciplines exists here than perhaps anywhere else in the world.

The blurring has gone both ways. Those few ethnographers who did find a spot for themselves in the new era of 1980s postcolonialism increasingly wore the hat of the archaeologist. Young (1985, 1987, 1988), for instance, undertook fascinating research into Zuni perceptions of rock art and the context in which it was set, a subject of obvious importance to landscape archaeologists. Young learned that the Zuni clearly responded to a different and more diverse set of cues than did most Western archaeologists, the latter of whom tend to regard isolated icons as texts to be interpreted. "For the Zunis," she suggested, "the power of certain visual images, their affecting presence, lies in their ability to evoke stories of the myth time and consequently to make the past coexistent with the present" (1987, p. 11). Rock art and other iconic features of the landscape became meaningful when they indexed the agency of the ancestors who, in this way, continued to act in the present and to convey messages to the living (compare Gell 1998).

More recently, archaeologists such as T.J. Ferguson and Chip Colwell-Chanthaphonh have continued to work with the Hopi and Zuni tribes in a similar vein, producing a number of remarkable collaborative studies of the manner in which Pueblo individuals perceive and make meaningful a landscape filled with indexes of ancestral and spirit beings (Colwell-Chanthaphonh 2003, 2005; Colwell-Chanthaphonh & Ferguson 2006; Colwell-Chanthaphonh et al. 2008; Ferguson et al. 2009; Ferguson & Anyon 2001; Ferguson 1995; Kuwansisiwma & Ferguson 2004; see also Adler 2005; Bernardini 2005, 2009). Much of the focus in this research has been on the affective and semiotic experience of visitation to sacred places. In their work in the San Pedro Valley of Arizona, for instance, Colwell-Chanthaphonh & Ferguson (2006, p. 150) observe that "for many of the tribal consultants, actually visiting places creates a unique experience in which place becomes inseparable from traditional narratives: Stories recall places and places recall stories." Native commentators in the Southwest, in this sense, regularly confirm Ingold's (1993, p. 155) parallel observation that "whereas with space, meanings are *attached to*

the world, with the landscape they are *gathered from* it." Or as Hieb (2006, p. 118) has observed of the Hopi, "the landscape . . . serves as an archive, a repository of 'mementos' . . . both cultural (for example, shrines, petroglyphs, ancestral dwellings) and natural (for example, springs, significant places) that give meaning and, more importantly, create and maintain 'a place to make life'" (see also Malotki 1993, 2002).

There is much of interest in this work to landscape archaeology generally. Of particular importance are the recent efforts of Ferguson & Colwell-Chanthaphonh (2006, pp. 32–39) to address the multiple temporalities and spatialities at work in Pueblo engagements with ancestral sites. Adopting what they refer to as a "cultural landscape matrix," they begin with the premise that both space and time can vary along gradients from absolute to relative to representational, which more or less chart a movement from a history embodied in external or physical properties to a history that is located within a cultural or mythic imaginary. Archaeologists interested in so-called landscapes of memory would do well to bear this sort of complexity in mind.

Just as important, though more implicit, is the manner in which collaborative studies of Hopi and Zuni landscapes further complicate phenomenological methodologies. British archaeology has tended to follow in the philosophical tradition of Husserl, Heidegger, and Merleau-Ponty, indulging in general claims about the nature of the human body, experience, and the like. If one's intellectual project is more philosophical than anthropological—as Tilley's (1994), Thomas's (1996), and others' often seem to be—then one body comes to be regarded as good as any other for illuminating the general manner in which the world is given to humans. This sort of approach has been widely criticized by those more attuned to the diversity of physical and cultural bodies in the world as well as the historical specificity of human subjectivity (see Barrett & Ko 2009, Brück 2005). Despite its recognition of this critique, however, British archaeology still seemed taken aback when Ramilisonina, a Malagasy archaeologist, visited Stonehenge and quickly developed an interpretation markedly different from the thousands of Western scholars who had previously visited and mulled over the site (Parker Pearson & Ramilisonina 1998). Ramilisonina perceived the monument through a Malagasy body with Malagasy eyes, and discussion of his insights might have afforded an opportunity to rethink and refine phenomenology as a methodology. Instead, it was debated as a matter of ethnographic analogy (Parker Pearson et al. 2006). (Stonehenge, it was concluded, may have deployed wood and stone to reference the living and dead, similar to the way such materials have been used in Madagascar during recent centuries.) In contrast, collaborative studies of Hopi and Zuni landscapes during the past 20 years have always regarded the confrontation and dissonance between Western and non-Western modes of perception as the very foundation of fieldwork. Unlike British phenomenologists who record their personal experiences on site, Southwestern collaborative archaeologists walk about a site in the company of cultural others, recording their perceptions and the way the site is given to them. The result may be thought of as a comparative or cross-cultural phenomenological methodology, although as I have indicated there are good reasons why it has not been presented in these terms.

Ancestral Landscapes of the Eastern Pueblos

In the Rio Grande Valley, a distinct variant of landscape archaeology has developed. Here, engagement with native communities has been on somewhat different terms, in part because Eastern Pueblo cultural preservation offices tend to be less active than those at Hopi and Zuni, but also because a long history of close coresidence with Hispanic and Anglo-American populations has heightened efforts to keep indigenous knowledge private. That said, the region has been home to a number of Pueblo intellectuals whose independent contributions to landscape studies have been substantial (Cajete 1994, 2000; Naranjo 1995; Ortiz 1969; Swentzell 1990), and archaeologists interested in Eastern Pueblo landscapes tend to draw deeply from their insights (Snead 2002b).

One of the most striking characteristics of contemporary landscape studies in the Rio Grande Valley is the degree to which they sit comfortably beside earlier processualist studies in which human-environment interactions were viewed as an objective matter of ecological adaptation. Snead (2006, 2008) and Anschuetz (2002, 2005, Anschuetz et al. 2001) have drawn our attention to this apparent paradox explicitly, using their research in the region as a way to advocate for an integrative or multivalent approach to landscape archaeology that does not rely on a single set of overarching premises. They accept, in other words, that landscapes are both real and imagined, objective and subjective, past and present, space and place, nature and culture. And rather than seeking to overcome these oppositions (be it through phenomenology, actor-network theory, or some other overarching paradigm), both Snead and Anschuetz suggest we take them seriously and learn from the tensions therein. Thus are we encouraged to focus, for instance, on "the ongoing interplay between the cultural ecology of archaeologists and the spiritual ecology of the Tewa" (Anschuetz 2005, p. 63; see also Anschuetz 2001).

Some archaeologists—particularly those committed to a view of archaeological theory as a thing of revolutions in which scholarly ancestors are continuously overthrown—may find this integrative approach unsatisfying insofar as it does not reject the call of the 1970s to view societies as systems adapted to their surrounding natural environments. However, it is the "fashionable" archaeologist who dislikes older texts simply because they are older (or who advises her students to engage solely with new or emerging theoretical paradigms) who ironically stands most firmly entrenched within the modernist cult of progress. In contrast, Anschuetz, Snead, and others could be said to have taken Native American epistemologies to heart, permitting truth claims to be situational and adopting a view of the past as a living guide for the present. (Here, the landscape is archaeology itself and "the past" is the range of enlightening theoretical frameworks that precedes the latest intellectual revolution.) In the Rio Grande Valley, the results of this sort of approach can be seen in Snead's (2008) recent book, which interweaves culture history, rational economics, phenomenology, interpretive approaches, and much else to flesh out the varied relationships between the Ancestral Pueblos and their landscapes. Or one might look to Anschuetz's (2002, 2005, 2006) studies of pre-Columbian Tewa agriculture not only as a matter of rainfall, ground absorption, and soil chemistry, but also as a materialized philosophy—"an extension of Pueblo thought and being" (Anschuetz 2005, p. 59, quoting Gregory Cajete)—that must be understood using indigenous principles of breath, center, emergence, movement, and connectedness.

Recent studies in the Rio Grande Valley have also come to focus strongly on the relationship between landscape and cosmology. Building from Ortiz's (1969) analysis of the Tewa cosmos, a number of projects have attempted to trace village-centered sacred geographies back in time using a direct historical approach. Snead & Preucel (1999), for instance, have demonstrated that the seventeenth-century site of Kotyiti and the fifteenth-century site of Pueblo Los Aguajes—both ancestral Keresan—carefully modified their surrounding landscapes through the construction of cardinally oriented shrines that placed the village in the center of the cosmos and that, in the case of Kotyiti, grounded efforts at religious revitalization in the physical engagement with place (see also Liebmann et al. 2005). In the ancestral Northern Tiwa area to the north, Fowles (2009) further demonstrates that such efforts in cosmic centering through shrine construction went hand in hand with the initial appearance of large aggregated villages in the Rio Grande Valley at the start of the fourteenth century. Ortman (2009) carries this genealogy one step further by tracing the pattern back to the

thirteenth-century village of Castle Rock in the Mesa Verde region, long regarded as the ancestral homeland of many Eastern Pueblo groups.

Southwest specialists will find these studies particularly interesting because they collectively define a wide-ranging Pueblo cosmology that emerged in the aftermath of—and, it seems, in pointed response to—the Chacoan ritual landscapes of the eleventh and twelfth centuries. For archaeologists more generally, their significance lies in their potential theoretical contributions to existing interpretive approaches, insofar as, here, the goal is not just to unearth past meanings through material remains, but also to address issues of historical contingency and the evolution of quite specific systems of signification in the landscape through time.

Chacoan Landscapes of the Eleventh and Twelfth Centuries

Chaco has long been at the vanguard of landscape archaeology in the American Southwest, and its prominence has only intensified in the past decade. Indeed, important debates over the nature of Chacoan complexity, ideology, cosmology, political influence, and ritual practice have increasingly been addressed through a landscape approach, broadly conceived. In part, this is due to the fact that the National Park Service has more or less prohibited new excavations at Chacoan sites, thereby encouraging the use of survey data and the analysis of spatial relationships. However, the greater reason is that ancient Chacoan leaders were deeply engaged in the manipulation of the landscape through the construction of monuments, shrines, roads, and the like. As Stonehenge provides a focal point for British landscape archaeology, so Chaco does for the Southwest.

During the past decade, two major works have defined a new agenda for Chacoan landscape studies: Lekson's (1999; also 2009b) wonderfully iconoclastic study of what he refers to as "the Chaco meridian" and Van Dyke's (2007; also 2004, 2009) thoughtful phenomenological analysis of the relationships between human perception, Chacoan architecture, and the varied landforms of the Colorado Plateau. Although the methodologies of these two works could hardly be more different, both share a view of the Chacoan polity as strongly hierarchical, headed by elites whose power stemmed largely from their control over an elaborate ritual landscape. (This is notable insofar as it marks the quiet retreat of more egalitarian readings of Chaco in contemporary scholarship.) Just as significantly, both Lekson's and Van Dyke's books are also legibly post-NAGPRA texts; each in its own way depends heavily on Pueblo philosophies of space, time, and historical contingency.

Lekson's argument, by now, will be familiar to most. In brief, he offers an interpretation of the pre-Columbian history of the Southwest in terms of a long-distance movement between three primary centers (Chaco, Aztec, and Paquime), each of which was oriented on a common north-south line that was consciously employed, argues Lekson, as a spatial means of both defining the Pueblo cosmos and legitimizing an evolving system of hierarchical leadership. His argument owes much to earlier analyses of Chacoan spatial geometries as ideology imprinted upon the landscape (Doxtater 1990, Fowler & Stein 1992, Fritz 1978, Marshall 1997, Sofaer 1997, Stein et al. 2007, Stein & Lekson 1992), but he encourages the reader to think at such an expanded geographic scale that entirely novel political implications arise.

With respect to landscape theory, Lekson makes two especially important contributions. First, as noted above, he challenges the widespread assumption that abstract conceptions of space are distinctly modern phenomena. Innumerable studies have looked at how past societies made place out of space. But Lekson is the only archaeologist I know of who has turned this on its head and looked at how abstract space was culturally fashioned out of place—a special accomplishment given that his subject is not only non-Western but also, broadly speaking, "Neolithic." Second, Lekson has deeply taken on board the teachings of Pueblo oral history, which regularly reference particular ancestral sites where leaders went astray and sought unacceptable forms of social power. Chaco, he suggests, was just such a landscape of transgression, and it was the simultaneously geographic and moral movement away from the Chacoan landscape in the thirteenth century that Lekson regards as having come to define the modern form of Pueblo egalitarianism. Just as Basso (1996, pp. 58–60) writes of the Western Apache as stalked by places that figure in tales of morality, so too are we led to view Chaco Canyon—or "White House," in the idiom of myth (Lekson & Cameron 1995)—as an ancestral place that continues to stalk the contemporary Pueblos.

Van Dyke (2007), in contrast, draws our attention to the sensuous experience of the Chacoan landscape, very much in the spirit of Tilley's (1994) phenomenological method. In so doing, she intervenes into past debates regarding the legitimization of Chacoan leadership by thinking in tangible terms about the aesthetics of the built landscape and its ability to inculcate particular sorts of subjectivities. What is seen, what remains hidden, how one is led to move through different spaces—these are the spatial constraints and affordances upon which Van Dyke focuses, and her argument is that this is where political legitimization takes on a bodily reality. Importantly, Van Dyke places special emphasis on the relationship between landscape and memory, arguing that—however much the subconscious experience of a spatial order may have affected individuals—it was the explicit discursive reference to the past that was the bread and butter of political legitimization (Van Dyke 2009). This leads her to consider the manner in which monuments in the landscape would have consciously indexed prior world orders, transforming taken-for-granted worldviews into overt political ideologies. Van Dyke's approach owes much to British scholarship (compare Barrett 1999), but her core argument regarding the relationship between landscape, cosmology, and political power is equally indebted to Ortiz (1969) and other native commentators.

CONCLUSIONS

Does a distinctive Southwest School of landscape archaeology exist, then? Nearly, I think. Certainly, the work produced in the region during the past 15 years has its own unique intellectual history, having emerged out of an extended dialogue among archaeologists, ethnographers, a remarkable physical setting, and an indigenous population with deep historical ties to place as well as increasing political influence over the future of Southwestern landscapes. Certainly, there are also distinguishing theoretical and methodological characteristics: the widespread recognition of the importance of collaboration with native groups; the effective use of the direct historical approach not just to find meaning in the past, but also to explore how and why meanings change; a concerted effort to marry ecological or systemic analyses with more humanistic lines of inquiry, rather than privileging one over the other; a reasoned hesitancy to engage with phenomenology—the list could go on.

In reviewing the literature, however, I have found one striking theme rise above all others. From a point 30 years ago when serious engagement with native perspectives was rare, landscape archaeology in the Southwest has now moved through an extended period in which native knowledge has come to be accepted as viable historical data, and it is fast approaching a new era in which native epistemologies [what Cajete (2000) refers to as "native science"] are understood as precisely that—epistemologies or bodies of theory about the world that may be profitably drawn upon in a rigorous manner alongside the classic writings of the Western intellectual tradition. This, I suggest, is the great promise of the Southwest School as it may soon come to be.

DISCLOSURE STATEMENT

The author is not aware of any affiliations, memberships, funding, or financial holdings that might be perceived as affecting the objectivity of this review.

LITERATURE CITED

Adler M. 2005. Collaborative knowledge: carrying forward Richard Ford's legacy of integrative ethnoscience in the U.S. Southwest. See Hegmon & Eiselt 2005, pp. 6–26

Anschuetz KF. 2001. Soaking it all in: northern New Mexican Pueblo lessons of water management and landscape ecology. In *Native Peoples of the Southwest: Negotiating Land, Water, and Ethnicities*, ed. L Winston, pp. 49–78. Westport, CT: Greenwood Publ. Grp.

Anschuetz KF. 2002. A healing place: Rio Grande Pueblo cultural landscapes and the Petroglpyh National Monument. See Anschuetz et al. 2002, pp. 6.1–6.18

Anschuetz KF. 2005. Landscapes as memory: archaeological history to learn from and to live by. See Hegmon & Eiselt 2005, pp. 52–72

Anschuetz KF. 2006. Tewa fields, Tewa traditions. See Price & Morrow 2006, pp. 57–73

Anschuetz KF, Ferguson TJ, Francis H, Kelley KB, Scheick CL, eds. 2002. *"That Place People Talk About": The Petroglyph National Monument Ethnographic Landscape Report*. Santa Fe: Rio Grande Found. Comm. Cult. Landsc.

Anschuetz KF, Wilshusen RH, Scheick CL. 2001. An archaeology of landscapes: perspectives and directions. *J. Archaeol. Res.* 9(2):157–211

Anschuetz KF, Wilshusen RH. 2010. Ensouled places: ethnogenesis and the making of the Dinétah and Tewa Basin landscapes. In *Changing Histories, Landscapes, and Perspectives: The Twentieth Anniversary Southwest Symposium*, ed. P Nelson, C Strawhacker. Denver: Univ. Colorado Press. In press

Bandelier AF. 1971 [orig 1916]. *The Delight Makers: A Novel of Prehistoric Pueblo Indians*. New York: Harcourt Brace

Barrett JC. 1999. The mythical landscapes of the British Iron Age. In *Archaeologies of Landscape: Contemporary Perspectives*, ed. W Ashmore, AB Knapp, pp. 253–65. Oxford: Blackwell

Barrett JC, Ko I. 2009. A phenomenology of landscape: a crisis in British landscape archaeology? *J. Soc. Archaeol.* 9(3):275–94

Basso K. 1996. *Wisdom Sits in Places: Landscape and Language among the Western Apache*. Albuquerque: Univ. New Mex. Press

Bender B. 1998. *Stonehenge: Making Space*. Oxford: Berg

Bender B. 2001. Landscapes on-the-move. *J. Soc. Archaeol.* 1(1):75–89

Bender B, Hamilton S, Tilley C. 2007. *Stone Worlds: Narrative and Reflexivity in Landscape Archaeology*. Walnut Creek, CA: Left Coast Press

Bernardini W. 2005. *Hopi Oral Tradition and the Archaeology of Identity*. Tucson: Univ. Ariz. Press

Bernardini W. 2008. Identity as history: Hopi clans and the curation of oral tradition. *J. Anthropol. Res.* 64(4):483–509

Bernardini W. 2009. *Hopi History in Stone: The Tutuveni Petroglyph Site*. Tucson: Ariz. State Mus.

Bradley R. 1998. *The Significance of Monuments: On the Shaping of Human Experience in Neolithic and Bronze Age Europe*. New York: Routledge

Brück J. 2005. Experiencing the past? The development of a phenomenological archaeology in British pre-history. *Archaeol. Dialog.* 12(1):45–72

Cajete G. 1994. *Look to the Mountain: An Ecology of Indigenous Education*. Durango: Kivakí

Cajete G. 2000. *Native Science: Natural Laws of Interdependence*. Santa Fe: Clear Light

Cameron CM. 1995. Migration and the movement of Southwestern peoples. *J. Anthropol. Archaeol.* 14:104–24

Carr P. 1979. *Mimbres Mythology*. Southwest. Stud. Monogr. No. 56. El Paso: Western Press

Casey ES. 1997. How to get from space to place in a fairly short stretch of time: phenomenological prole-gomena. In *Senses of Place*, ed. S Feld, KH Basso, pp. 13–52. Santa Fe: SAR

Clark JJ. 2001. *Tracking Prehistoric Migrations: Pueblo Settlers among the Tonto Basin Hohokam*. Anthropol. Pap. 65. Tucson: Univ. Ariz. Press

Colwell-Chanthaphonh C. 2003. Signs in place: Native American perspectives of the past in the San Pedro Valley of southeastern Arizona. *Kiva* 69(1):5–29

Collwell-Chanthaphonh C. 2005. Portraits of a storied land: an experiment in writing the landscapes of history. *Anthropol. Q.* 78(1):151–77

Collwell-Chanthaphonh C, Ferguson TJ. 2006. Memory pieces and footprints: multivocality and the meanings of ancient times and ancestral places among the Zuni and Hopi. *Am. Anthropol.* 108(1):148–62

Collwell-Chanthaphonh C, Ferguson TJ, Anyon R. 2008. Always multivocal and multivalent: conceptualizing archaeological landscapes in the San Pedro Valley. In *Archaeologies of Placemaking: Monuments, Memories, and Engagement in Native North America*, ed. PE Rubertone, pp. 59–80. Walnut Creek, CA: Left Coast Press

Darling JA. 2009. O'odham trails and the archaeology of space. See Snead et al. 2009, pp. 61–83

David B, Thomas J. 2008. Landscape archaeology: introduction. In *Handbook of Landscape Archaeology*, ed. B David, J Thomas, pp. 27–43. Walnut Creek, CA: Left Coast Press

Deloria V Jr. 1969. *Custer Died For Your Sins: An Indian Manifesto*. New York: MacMillan

Dodge WA. 2007. *Black Rock: A Zuni Cultural Landscape and the Meaning of Place*. Jackson: Univ. Press Miss.

Doxtater D. 1990. Reflections of the Anasazi cosmos. In *Social Space: Human Spatial Behavior in Dwellings and Settlements*, ed. O Gron, E Englestad, I Lindblom, pp. 155–84. Odense: Odense Univ. Press

Doyel DE, ed. 1992. *Anasazi Regional Organization and the Chaco System*. Anthropol. Pap. 5. Albuquerque: Maxwell Mus. Anthropol.

Ellis FH. 1974a [1962]. Anthropological data pertaining to the Taos land claim. In *Pueblo Indians I*, pp. 29–150. New York: Garland

Ellis FH. 1974b. Anthropology of Laguna land claims. In *Pueblo Indians II*. New York: Garland

Ferguson TJ. 1995. An anthropological perspective on Zuni land use. In *Zuni and the Courts*, ed. ER Hart, pp. 103–20. Lawrence: Univ. Press Kansas

Ferguson TJ, Anyon R. 2001. Hopi and Zuni cultural landscapes: implications of history and scale for cultural resources management. In *Native Peoples of the Southwest: Negotiating Land, Water, and Ethnicities*, ed. L Weinstein, pp. 99–122. Westport: Bergin & Garvey

Ferguson TJ, Berlin GL, Kuwanwisiwma LJ. 2009. Kukhepya: searching for Hopi trails. See Snead et al. 2009, pp. 20–41

Ferguson TJ, Colwell-Chanthaphonh C. 2006. *History is in the Land: Multivocal Tribal Traditions in Arizona's San Pedro Valley*. Tucson: Univ. Ariz. Press

Ferguson TJ, Hart ER. 1985. *A Zuni Atlas*. Norman: Univ. Okla. Press

Fewkes JW. 1900. Tusayan migration traditions. *Annu. Rep. Bur. Am. Ethnol.* 19(2):575–633. Washington, DC: Gov. Print. Off.

Fowler AP, Stein JR. 1992. The Anasazi Great House in space, time and paradigm. See Doyel 1992, pp. 101–22

Fowles SM. 2009. The enshrined Pueblo: villagescape and cosmos in the northern Rio Grande. *Am. Antiquity* 74(3):448–66

Fowles SM. 2010. Movement and the unsettling of the Pueblos. In *The Anthropology of Migration*, ed. G Cabana, J Clark. Gainesville: Univ. Fla. Press. In press

Fritz JM. 1978. Paleopsychology today: ideational systems and human adaptation in prehistory. In *Social Archaeology: Beyond Subsistence and Dating*, ed. C Redman, pp. 37–59. New York: Academic

Fritz JM. 1987. Chaco Canyon and Vijayanagara: proposing spatial meaning in two societies. In *Mirror and Metaphor*, ed. D Ingersoll, G Bronitsky, pp. 314–49. Lanham: Univ. Press Am.

Gell A. 1998. *Art and Agency: An Anthropological Theory*. Gloucester: Clarendon

Glowacka M, Washburn D, Richland J. 2009. *Nuvatukya'ovi*, San Francisco Peaks: balancing Western economies with Native American spiritualities. *Curr. Anthropol.* 50(4):547–61

Goodman JM. 1987. *A Navajo Atlas*. Norman: Univ. Okla. Press

Gordon-McCutchan RC. 1995. *The Taos Indians and the Battle for Blue Lake*. Santa Fe, NM: Red Crane Books

Gulliford A. 2000. *Sacred Objects and Sacred Places: Preserving Tribal Traditions*. Boulder: Univ. Press Colo.

Harrington JP. 1916. The Ethnogeography of the Tewa Indians. *Annu. Rep. Bur. Am. Ethnol. Years 1907–1908, 29th*, pp. 29–636. Washington, DC: Gov. Print. Off.

Hegmon M. 2003. Setting theoretical egos aside: issues and theory in North American archaeology. *Am. Antiquity* 68:213–43

Hegmon M, Eiselt BS, eds. 2005. *Engaged Anthropology: Research Essays on North American Archaeology, Ethnobotany, and Museology*. Ann Arbor: Univ. Mich. Mus. Anthropol.

Hieb LA. 2006. The narrative construction of landscape. See Price & Morrow 2006, pp. 113–23

Ingold T. 1993. The temporality of the landscape. *World Archaeol.* 25(2):152–74

Ingold T. 2007. *Lines: A Brief History*. New York: Routledge

Jackson JB. 1984. *Discovering the Vernacular Landscape*. New Haven: Yale Univ. Press

Johnson M. 2007. *Ideas of Landscape*. Oxford: Blackwell

Kincaid C, ed. 1983. *Chaco Roads Project Phase I: A Reappraisal of Prehistoric Roads in the San Juan Basin*. Albuquerque: US Dep. Interior Bur. Land Manage.

Kuwansisiwma L, Ferguson TJ. 2004. Ang Kuktota: Hopi ancestral sites and cultural landscapes. *Expedition* 46(2):25–29

Ladd EJ. 1994. The Zuni ceremonial system: the kiva. In *Kachinas in the Pueblo World*, ed. P Shaafsma, pp. 17–21. Albuquerque: Univ. New Mex.

Lekson SH. 1996. Landscape with ruins: archaeological approaches to built and unbuilt environments. *Curr. Anthropol.* 37(5):886–92

Lekson SH. 1999. *The Chaco Meridian: Centers of Political Power in the Ancient Southwest*. Walnut Creek, CA: AltaMira

Lekson SH. 2009a. A new deal for Chaco Canyon? Review of Ruth Van Dyke, "The Chaco experience: landscape and ideology at the center place." *Curr. Anthropol.* 50(4):579–80

Lekson SH. 2009b. *A History of the Ancient Southwest*. Santa Fe: SAR

Lekson SH, Cameron CM. 1995. The abandonment of Chaco Canyon, the Mesa Verde migrations, and the reorganization of the pueblo world. *J. Anthropol. Archaeol.* 14:184–202

Liebmann M, Ferguson TJ, Preucel RW. 2005. Pueblo settlement, architecture, and social change in the Pueblo Revolt era, AD 1680–1696. *J. Field Archaeol.* 30(1):45–60

Malotki E, ed. 1993. *Hopi Ruin Legends*. Lincoln: Univ. Nebr. Press

Malotki E, ed. 2002. *Hopi Tales of Destruction*. Bison Books

Marshall MP. 1997. The Chacoan roads: a cosmological interpretation. See Morrow & Price 1997, pp. 62–74

Mindeleff V. 1989 [1891]. *A Study of Pueblo Architecture in Tusayan and Cibola*. Washington, DC: Smithsonian Inst.

Morrow BH, Price VB, eds. 1997. *Anasazi Architecture and American Design*. Albuquerque: Univ. New Mex. Press

Naranjo T. 1995. Thoughts on migration by Santa Clara Pueblo. *J. Anthropol. Archaeol.* 14:247–50

Naranjo T, Swentzell R. 1989. Healing spaces in the Pueblo world. *Am. Indian Cult. Res. J.* 13(3–4):257–65

Nials F, Stein JR, Roney JR. 1987. *Chacoan Roads in the Southern Periphery: Results of Phase II of the BLM Chaco Roads Project*. Santa Fe: New Mex. Bur. Land Manage.

Ortiz A. 1969. *The Tewa World*. Chicago: Univ. Chicago Press

Ortiz A. 1972. Ritual drama and the Pueblo world view. In *New Perspectives on the Pueblos*, ed. A Ortiz, pp. 135–62. Santa Fe: SAR

Ortiz S. 1980. We have been told many things but we know this to be true. *INAD Literary J.* 1(1):35

Ortman SG. 2009. Action, place, and space in the Castle Rock community. In *The Social Construction of Communities: Agency, Structure, and Identity in the Prehispanic Southwest*, ed. MD Varien, JM Potter, pp. 125–54. New York: AltaMira

Parker Pearson M, Ramilisonina. 1998. Stonehenge for the ancestors: the stones pass on the message. *Antiquity* 72:308–26

Parker Pearson M, Pollard J, Richards C, Thomas J, Tilley C, et al. 2006. The Stonehenge Riverside Project. *J. Mater. Cult.* 11(1/2):227–61

Potter J. 2004. The creation of person, the creation of place: hunting landscapes in the American Southwest. *Am. Antiquity* 69(2):322–38

Price VB, Morrow BH, eds. 2006. *Canyon Gardens: The Ancient Pueblo Landscapes of the American Southwest*. Albuquerque: Univ. New Mex. Press

Reid JJ. 1997. Return to migration, population movement, and ethnic identity in the American Southwest: a peer reviewer's thoughts on archaeological inference. In *Vanishing River: Landscapes and Lives of the Lower Verde Valley*, ed. SM Whittlesey, R Ciolek-Torrello, J Altschul, pp. 629–38. Tucson: SRI

Roney JR. 1992. Prehistoric roads and regional integration in the Chacoan system. See Doyel 1992, pp. 123–31

Saile DG. 1977. Making a house: building rituals and spatial concepts in the Pueblo Indian world. *Architect. Assoc. Q.* 9(2–3):72–81

Saile DG. 1989. Many dwellings: views of a Pueblo world. In *Dwelling, Place and Environment: Towards a Phenomenology of Person and World*, ed. D Seamon, R Mugerauer, pp. 159–81. New York: Columbia Univ. Press

Saile DG. 1990. Understanding the development of Pueblo architecture. See Markovich et al. 1990, pp. 49–63

Scully V. 1972. *Pueblo: Mountain, Village, Dance*. New York: Viking

Sekaquaptewa E. 1972. Preserving the good things of Hopi life. In *Plural Society in the Southwest*, ed. EM Spicer, RH Thompson, pp. 239–60. Albuquerque: Univ. New Mex. Press

Sekaquaptewa E, Washburn D. 2004. *They go along singing*: reconstructing the Hopi past from ritual metaphors in song and image. *Am. Antiquity* 69(3):457–86

Silko LM. 1986. Landscape, history, and the Pueblo imagination. *Antaeus* 57(Autumn):882–94

Silko LM. 1995. Interior and exterior landscapes: the Pueblo migration stories. In *Landscape in America*, ed. GF Thompson, pp. 155–69. Austin: Univ. Texas Press

Silko LM. 1996. *Yellow Woman and a Beauty of Spirit: Essays on Native American Life Today*. New York: Touchstone Books

Snead JE. 2002a. Ancestral Pueblo trails and the cultural landscape of the Pajarito Plateau, New Mexico. *Antiquity* 76:756–65

Snead JE. 2002b. 'An imperishable record': history, theory, and the cultural landscape of the Northern Rio Grande. In *Traditions, Transitions, and Technologies: Themes in Southwestern Archaeology in the Year 2000*, ed. SH Schlanger, pp. 16–32. Niwot: Univ. Press Colo.

Snead JE. 2006. Mirror of the Earth: water, landscape, and meaning in the Precolumbian Southwest. In *Precolumbian Water Management: Ideology, Ritual, and Power*, ed. L Lucero, B Fash, pp. 205–20. Tucson: Univ. Ariz. Press

Snead JE. 2008. *Ancestral Landscapes of the Pueblo World*. Tucson: Univ. Ariz. Press

Snead JE. 2009. Trails of tradition: movement, meaning, and place. See Snead et al. 2009, pp. 42–60.

Snead JE, Erickson CL, Darling JA, eds. 2009. *Landscapes of Movement: Trails, Paths, and Roads in Anthropological Perspective*. Philadelphia: Univ. Penn. Mus. Archaeol. Anthropol.

Snead JE, Preucel RW. 1999. The ideology of settlement: ancestral Keres landscapes in the northern Rio Grande. In *Archaeologies of Landscape*, ed. W Ashmore, AB Knapp, pp. 169–97. Oxford: Blackwell

Sofaer A. 1997. The primary architecture of the Chacoan culture: a cosmological expression. See Morrow & Price 1997, pp. 88–131

Sofaer A, Solstice Project Contributors. 2008. *Chaco Astronomy: An Ancient American Cosmology*. Santa Fe: Ocean Tree Books

Sofaer A, Marshall M, Sinclair R. 1989. The Great North Road: a cosmographic expression of the Chaco culture of New Mexico. In *World Archaeoastronomy*, ed. A Aveni, pp. 365–76. Cambridge: Cambridge Univ. Press

Sofaer A, Zinser V, Sinclair R. 1979. A unique solar marking construct: an archaeoastronomical site in New Mexico marks the solstices and equinoxes. *Science* 206(4416):283–91

Spielmann KA, ed. 1998. *Migration and Reorganization: The Pueblo IV Period in the American Southwest*. Anthropol. Res. Pap. 51. Tempe: Ariz. State Univ.

Stark MT, Clark JJ, Elson MD. 1995. Causes and consequences of migration in the thirteenth century Tonto Basin. *J. Anthropol. Archaeol.* 14:212–46

Stein J, Friedman R, Blackhorse T, Loose R. 2007. Revisiting downtown Chaco. In *The Architecture of Chaco Canyon, New Mexico*, ed. S Lekson, pp. 199–224. Salt Lake City: Univ. Utah Press

Stein JR, Lekson SH. 1992. Anasazi ritual landscapes. See Doyel 1992, pp. 87–100

Swentzell R. 1988. Bupingeh: the pueblo plaza. *El Palacio* Winter:14–19

Swentzell R. 1990. Pueblo space, form, and mythology. In *Pueblo Style and Regional Architecture*, edited by NC Markovich, WFE Preiser, FG Sturm, pp. 23–30. New York: Van Nostrand Reinhold

Swentzell R. 1993. Mountain form, village form: unity in the Pueblo world. In *Ancient Land, Ancestral Places: Paul Logsdon in the Pueblo Southwest*, pp. 139–47. Santa Fe: Mus. New Mex. Press

Swentzell R. 1997 [1985]. An understated sacredness. See Morrow & Price 1997, pp. 186–89

Thomas J. 1996. *Time, Culture, and Identity*. London: Routledge

Tilley C. 1994. *A Phenomenology of Landscape: Places, Paths and Monuments*. Oxford: Berg

Van Dyke RM. 2004. Memory, meaning, and masonry: the Late Bonito Chacoan landscape. *Am. Antiquity* 69(3):413–31

Van Dyke RM. 2007. *The Chaco Experience: Landscape and Ideology at the Center Place*. Santa Fe, NM: SAR

Van Dyke RM. 2009. Chaco reloaded: discursive social memory on the post-Chacoan landscape. *J. Soc. Archaeol.* 9(2):220–48

Varien M. 1999. *Sedentism and Mobility in a Social Landscape*. Tucson: Univ. Ariz. Press

Whiteley P. 1998. *Rethinking Hopi Ethnography*. Washington, DC: Smithson. Inst. Press

Whiteley P. 2008. *Hopi concepts of landscape and person as indices of biocultural loss*. Presented at CBC Symp., April 3. New York: Am. Mus. Nat. Hist. **http://anthro.amnh.org**

Young MJ. 1985. Images of power and the power of images: the significance of rock art for contemporary Zunis. *J. Am. Folklore* 98(387):3–48

Young MJ. 1987. Towards an understanding of "place" for Southwestern Indians. *New Mex. Folklore Rec.* 16:1–13

Young MJ. 1988. *Signs from the Ancestors*. Albuquerque: Univ. New Mex. Press

Zedeño MN. 1997. Landscapes, land use, and the history of territory formation: an example from the Puebloan Southwest. *J. Archaeol. Method Theory* 4(1):67–103

Archaeology of the Eurasian Steppes and Mongolia

Bryan Hanks

Department of Anthropology, University of Pittsburgh, Pittsburgh, Pennsylvania 15260;
email: bkh5@pitt.edu

Annu. Rev. Anthropol. 2010. 39:469–86

First published online as a Review in Advance on
June 21, 2010

The *Annual Review of Anthropology* is online at
anthro.annualreviews.org

This article's doi:
10.1146/annurev.anthro.012809.105110

0084-6570/10/1021-0469$20.00

Key Words

pastoralism, horse domestication, warfare, steppe empires, complex
societies

Abstract

International interest in the prehistory and archaeology of the Eurasian
steppes and Mongolia has increased dramatically since the collapse of
the Soviet Union in 1991. This article surveys important new evidence and interpretations that have emerged from several collaborative
projects in the past two decades. A particular emphasis is placed on issues that are crucial to regional studies in the steppe ecological zone;
however, it also is suggested that steppe prehistory must come to play
a more significant role in developing more comprehensive understandings of world prehistory. Key developments connected with the steppe
include the diffusion of anatomically modern humans, horse domestication, spoke-wheeled chariot and cavalry warfare, early metal production
and trade, Indo-European languages, and the rise of nomadic states and
empires. In addition to these important issues, thoughts are offered on
some of the current challenges that face archaeological scholarship in
this region of the world.

INTRODUCTION

It is an unfortunate fact that, of the numerous introductory textbooks published on world prehistory and archaeology in the Anglo-American market, few if any provide any detail on the Eurasian steppe region. In fact, if one glances at the world maps in any of these books it would seem that nothing significant to prehistory had ever occurred in the northern Eurasian region, including the vast steppe zone. Notable exceptions to this include well-known Upper Paleolithic sites in Eastern Europe such as Mezhirich and Kostenki and sites in northeastern Eurasia such as Mal'ta and Dyuktai Cave (**Figure 1**, see color insert). Although this limited view of the archaeology and prehistory of the steppe region may have been acceptable at the height of the Cold War era, we have, since 1991, been living in a very different geopolitical atmosphere. Archaeological field work in the regions of the former Soviet Union has been a distinct reality for many international scholars, and their collaborative programs of research have produced significant new discoveries. Nevertheless, the data, theories, and models stemming from such work have circulated primarily among specialists of these regions and have infrequently entered the mainstream consciousness of archaeologists working in other parts of the world. One need only turn to the textbooks used in survey courses on world prehistory for clear evidence of this notion.

Regrettably, this problem extends beyond the classroom and is of more serious concern in terms of comparative understandings of the various trajectories of development that have shaped the human past and more recent present. For example, anthropological archaeology in North America, which has favored global comparative study, has rarely enlisted case studies from the vast steppe region in the study of the evolution of village and urban life, the emergence of complex societies, innovation and diffusion of new technologies, conflict and warfare, and the rise of early states. This exclusion has occurred for various reasons; one of the most significant reasons is the earlier lack of publications in languages other than Russian and other regional languages. This situation has changed substantially in the past two decades as important new publications in other languages have been produced. Many of these have stemmed from productive international conferences held in the territories of the former Soviet Union, Europe, Asia, and the United States (e.g., Boyle et al. 2002, Bemmann et al. 2009, Hanks & Linduff 2009, Jones-Bley & Zdanovich 2002, Levine et al. 1999, Mei & Rehren 2009, Peterson et al. 2006b, Popova et al. 2007). What has emerged from this new scholarship is a clear sign that the archaeology of the Eurasian steppe zone contributes in significant ways to both regional scholarship and broader anthropological interpretations of human change and development in the past. As we enter the twenty-first century, the steppe region and adjacent territories must figure more prominently in the pursuit of refined models and theories for the human past and contribute more visibly to the development of global heritage. One important, recent contribution to this literature has been the publication of Eurasian steppe developments within comparative discussions on early social complexity and the emergence of early states (Grinin et al. 2004, 2008). These publications, part of a series titled, "Social Evolution and History Monographs," have been published in Russia in English and have included chapter contributions by several international scholars. Other publications, notably those by Nikolai Kradin, have emphasized the importance of steppe pastoralist sociopolitical developments and offered important new models that contribute productively to comparative discussions on anthropological archaeology (Kradin 2002, Kradin et al. 2003). Such publications are forcing the door open to broader theoretical discussions of Eurasian steppe archaeology and history.

As a specific aim, this article offers a concise chronological survey of several recent projects and publications in Eurasian steppe prehistory, starting with anatomically modern human settlement in the Upper Paleolithic (~40,000 B.P.) and extending through to the Xiongnu confederation (~155 A.D.) (**Table 1**). The

Table 1 General chronology of periods and archaeological sites discussed in text

Archaeological period	Approximate date range	Key developments discussed
Upper Paleolithic	46,000 to 10,000 B.P.	Peopling of northern Eurasia, accelerator mass spectrometry (AMS) dating
Mesolithic-Early Neolithic	10,000 to 6000 B.C.	Complex hunter-gatherer adaptations
Neolithic-Eneolithic	10,000 to 3500 B.C.	Horse domestication, Indo-European Languages
Bronze Age	3500 to 1200 B.C.	Metallurgy, spoke-wheeled chariots, inter-regional trade, stone monuments
Final Bronze–Early Iron Age	1200 to 300 B.C.	Mobile pastoralism, large-scale kurgans, cavalry warfare
Xiongnu Polities	500 B.C. to A.D. 155	Regional surveys, China-steppe interaction, elite tombs

selected topics and sites covered are restricted to the grassland steppe and adjacent arid steppe and forest-steppe ecological zones. Owing to space limitations, it is not possible to discuss more than two or three case studies for each defined chronological phase. Therefore, all the case studies chosen represent important recent research undertaken in the steppe region by international teams and an overview of new data and interpretations emerging from such work. More specifically, projects that are relatively well published in English have been selected to be useful to nonregional specialists. Unfortunately, presenting such a broad chronological overview severely limits the space available for more detailed discussion of one or more of the periods; however, the aim here is to provide a point of departure for nonspecialists and an up-to-date outline of the current state of archaeological research in the steppe region that is international in scope. Scholars seeking more in-depth theoretical treatments and culture history overviews should consult the numerous conference volumes and other more recent publications that focus on specific regions and time periods cited throughout the article.

The first part of the following discussion chronicles recent discoveries in the greater Eurasian steppe zone, stretching from Ukraine in the west to the far eastern region of Russia. The second part focuses more specifically on recent archaeological projects in the region of present-day Mongolia. Mongolia emerged recently as an extremely vibrant area of archaeological study, and several successful international projects are based there. Thus, a variety of new evidence is emerging that is having a clear impact on how prehistoric and early historic developments in the Mongolian region relate to adjacent territories and developments in China, Central Asia, and Russia. The article concludes with a more personal reflection on the changing nature of scholarship in the steppe region and outlines some of the critical issues that continue to challenge research in the region.

THE EURASIAN STEPPES

Upper Paleolithic (~46,000 to 10,000 B.P.)

Archaeological evidence from the vast steppe territory has played an important role in our understanding of late glacial environmental change and the spread of anatomically modern humans throughout northern Eurasia. Upper Paleolithic habitation sites in the Eastern European plain associated with the Eastern Gravettian complex (e.g., Mezhirich, Kostenki, Dolní Věstonice) have become well known to foreign scholarship (Hoffecker 2002). Archaeological evidence from these sites has indicated an amazing adaptation to the inhospitable Pleistocene environments of the open plains of northern Eurasia and has produced some of the earliest evidence for fired clay animal and female figurines (Soffer & Vandiver 1997). Recent analysis of burnt clay objects from sites such as Pavlov I (Czech Republic), originally recovered during excavations of the early Soviet

Period, have revealed evidence of corded fiber impressions (Adovasio et al. 1996). Additional research has produced more evidence of early perishables, such as textile and basketry production by 28,000 B.P., connected with additional finds from Central Europe, France, and Russia (Soffer et al. 2000). These studies have indicated that such technologies were much more widespread across Europe and the western steppe region during the late Pleistocene than previously thought.

Another significant development in the scholarship of the Upper Paleolithic has been the achievement of several large-scale radiocarbon dating programs. This new data has provided the opportunity to reassess not only previous dates for many known sites but also to understand better the sequences of occupation and to develop new demographic models relating to early colonization processes across the vast northern Eurasian plains. Whereas recent excavation programs focusing on habitation sites in far northeastern Siberia have connected importantly with the peopling of the Americas (Goebel 2004), other studies have sought to develop better understandings of Paleolithic occupation of the East European Plain (Dolukhanov et al. 2001, 2002), Southern Siberia, and the Russian Far East (Kuzmin & Orlova 2000, Kuzmin & Keates 2005).

These areas played a key role in what have been conceptualized as pulses of occupation and reoccupation by late Upper Paleolithic groups in response to changing environmental conditions, particularly for the extreme conditions of the Late Glacial Maximum (LGM) (~20,000–18,000 B.P.). For example, Goebel has argued that this period saw a sharp decline in human population in Siberia, and it was not until 18,000 B.P. with the retreat of glacial fields, less extreme environmental conditions, and the emergence of a microblade technology that the northern regions were once again occupied by humans (Goebel 2002). The analysis and dating of Upper Paleolithic sites such as Studenoe-2 in the Transbaikal region of Siberia have indicated that the microblade industry appeared as early as 17,800 B.P. (Goebel et al. 2000).

A counterargument to the depopulation of Siberia in the LGM emerged in 2005 as a result of an intensive study of 437 radiocarbon dates (Kuzmin & Keates 2005). The authors of this article have suggested that investigators can model occupation sequences by applying radiocarbon dating of occupation episodes (dates from individual sites that fall within 1000 ^{14}C). Their data analysis suggests that the number of occupations in Siberia did not decline during the LGM period; rather, there was a gradual increase of occupation episodes from 36,000 to 16,000 B.P. and then a sharp increase after 16,000 B.P.

It is hoped that continued research and dating of this region in the near future will provide further assessment of these new models. The eastern and northeastern zones of Siberia will certainly continue to be critically investigated as the occupation sequences and lithic industries are of particular importance for questions surrounding the early peopling of Eastern Asia and the Americas. Nevertheless, future research focused on the Upper Paleolithic must continue to expand beyond the eastern and western limits of the northern Eurasian region (e.g., Derev'anko et al. 1998). For example, 15 Upper Paleolithic sites are known from the southern Ural Mountains region of Russia. Several of these are cave sites, such as Kapova (Shulgan-Tash) in the Republic of Bashkortosan, that have significant evidence of cave paintings and occupation sequences (Danukalova & Yakovlev 2006). Future research at sites such as these is greatly needed to develop improved models of Upper Paleolithic colonization and adaptation processes across the vast Eurasian steppe plain.

Mesolithic to Early Neolithic Hunter-Forager Societies (~10,000 to 6,000 B.C.)

The relationship of early Holocene hunter-forager groups in Europe to the appearance and diffusion of early Neolithic technologies such as pottery production and domesticated plants and animals has been a strong focus of

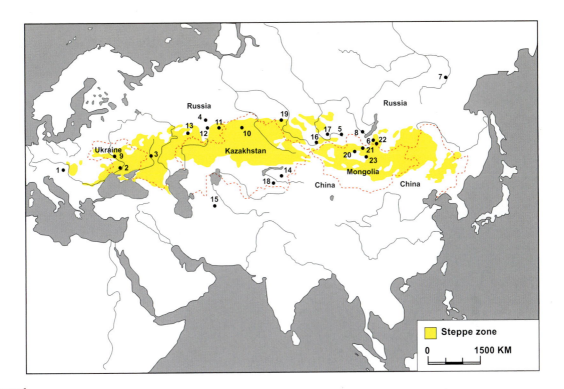

Figure 1

Upper Paleolithic Sites: 1, Dolní Věstonice and Pavlov I; 2, Mezhirich; 3, Kostienki; 4, Kapova (Shulgan-Tash); 5, Mal'ta; 6, Studenoe-2; 7, Dyuktai Cave. **Mesolithic Sites:** 8, Lokomotiv. **Eneolithic-Neolithic Sites:** 9, Dereivka; 10, Botai. **Bronze Age Sites:** 11, Sintashta; 12, Karagaly (Gorny); 13, Krasnosamarskoe; 14, Sermirech'ye Valley; 15, Bactria-Margiana Archaeological Complex. **Iron Age Sites:** 16, Pazyryk; 17, Arzhan I and II; 18, Talgar Fan; 19, Čiča; 20, Urt Bulagyn; 21, Egiin Gol River Valley; 22, Tsaraam Valley; 23, Kharkhorum.

research within European prehistory (Cavalli-Sforza 1996, Harris 1996, Price 2000). However, such developments within the larger northern Eurasian and Eurasian steppe zones were little known to foreign scholarship during the Soviet Period. A large international project in Lake Baikal, the Baikal Archaeology Project (BAP), has recently added significantly to understandings of regional change in the southern Siberian region of Russia.

The BAP project, which is a multi-institution, multidisciplinary research program, has generated substantial data and numerous publications on the development of early Holocene communities and the nature of economic and social change that occurred during this period (see Weber et al. 2010, 2007; links to the project's Web site may be found on the University of Alberta Department of Anthropology's Web site). Research has focused intently on the excellent preserved habitation sites and large cemeteries, including the well-known Lokomotiv cemetery, which was first discovered in 1897 and subsequently excavated during the Soviet Period. This cemetery is considered to be the largest Neolithic cemetery in northern Asia and has produced well-preserved human remains with a variety of grave goods including fishing and hunting tools, other domestic artifacts, and personal adornments (Mooder et al. 2005). A major component of BAP research has focused on the detailed physical and chemical analysis of human remains from Lokomotiv and other cemeteries, including genetics, associated grave goods, and chronological phasing of burials. The picture that has emerged from this research suggests that two main groups of hunter-gatherers occupied this region of Lake Baikal: first, the Early and Late Kitoi phases from the Late Mesolithic and Early Neolithic (6,800–4,900 cal. B.C.), and second, the Serovo and Glazkovo phases from the Middle-Late Neolithic and later Bronze Age (~4,200 to 1,000 cal B.C.). A period from which no graves have been recovered occurred between ~4,900 to 4,200 cal. B.C. (Weber et al. 2002, 2005) and represents an important temporal lacuna of cemetery use that is likely connected with a transition in social organization and ritual activity. Results from the BAP project continue to uncover important trajectories of hunter-gatherer adaptations in the region including the role that social identity, status, and kinship played in the emergence of social complexity.

In addition to the highly successful fieldwork and publications stemming from the project, numerous undergraduate and graduate students from North America and Russia have taken part in the project, and they have subsequently produced several theses and dissertations. The BAP stands as one of the most successful initiatives of its kind operating in the northern Eurasian region and illustrates the effective role that multidisciplinary research can play in the study of hunter-gatherer social complexity and the complex array of adaptive strategies that were connected to changing social and environmental landscapes during the Holocene.

Neolithic-Eneolithic Horse Domestication and Indo-European Languages (~6,000 to 3,500 B.C.E.)

Animal and plant domestication is one of the major transformations connected with the Neolithic of the Old World. Certainly some of the most persistent and contentious questions of this period pertain to when and where the horse was first domesticated and how the use of this animal for subsistence, traction, and riding evolved in conjunction with human social, cultural, and technological change. Much of the debate over these unknowns has focused on the Eurasian steppe region. Three recent publications connected with this area of research provide excellent overviews of the debates and useful introductions into the complexity of the archaeological data linked to early horse domestication (Drews 2004, Kelekna 2009, Olsen et al. 2006).

For much of the twentieth century, the dominant view of horse domestication and early riding was attached to theories for the emergence of the Proto-Indo-European language, its geographical "homeland," and the subsequent spread of Indo-European languages. Marija Gimbutas (1970) was one of the most outspoken scholars in this regard. Gimbutas argued for several incoming waves of horse-riding, patriarchal warriors (kurgan culture) from the steppe region into "Old Europe," which, she argued, brought about the destruction of the more peaceful, sedentary (and matriarchal) European societies. Important excavations during the Soviet Period at sites such as Dereivka on the Lower Dnieper River produced archaeological remains dating to the Neolithic and Eneolithic (copper age) that appeared to be linked to early horse domestication and riding. This evidence became the focus of intense scrutiny and debate in the 1980s and 1990s.

The recovery of horse bones from settlements such as Dereivka was believed to offer strong proof for the early domestication and riding of horses and their significance within cultic and ritual activities. By the 1990s, however, Gimbutas's kurgan culture model of invading horsemen waned as a result of limited archaeological evidence for such migrations into Europe. Several scholars continued to support the theory of horse domestication and riding by the Eneolithic (Anthony & Brown 1991, Mallory 1989). Other scholars have argued that the presence of horse remains from settlement contexts might reflect forms of exploitation, such as hunting, taming, or domestication, but does not prove that horses were actually ridden at this time (Häusler 1996, Levine et al. 1999). Subsequent studies by Anthony & Brown (2000) of bit wear on the lower premolar teeth of prehistoric horse remains, coupled with experimental harnessing and bit-wear studies on modern horses, added important new data to the argument. Many scholars currently still remain unconvinced that horse riding became a significant factor in the steppe region, particularly in terms of mounted warfare, until the late second to early first millennium B.C. (Bokovenko 2000, Levine 2004, Levine et al. 2003, Renfrew 2002, and most recently, Drews 2004). Out of these debates has emerged a much greater appreciation for the fact that the trajectory of human-horse relationships developed over a much longer period than was previously thought and that horse domestication as a complex process unfolded over several millennia (Olsen et al. 2006).

New lines of evidence have emerged very recently on the DNA of modern horses (Lindgren et al. 2004, Jansen et al. 2002, McGaherrn et al. 2006) that point toward a multiorigin, rather than diffusion from a single point, for horse domestication within the Eurasian region. Additional data are needed, and such studies will ultimately need to be connected more effectively to ancient DNA analyses of horse remains from key archaeological sites. Nevertheless, such studies, particularly when combined with additional archaeological and zoological analyses, will begin to unravel the contentious debates surrounding early horse domestication. For example, important new studies coming from Eneolithic period sites in Kazakhstan (Botai culture, 3,500 B.C.) have integrated bit wear, metric studies of horse lower limb bones (metapodials), and the detailed analysis of organic residue collected from recovered pottery vessels (Outram et al. 2009, Travis 2008). Previous studies of the horse remains from Botai culture settlements in Kazakhstan, which represent nearly 99% of all large faunal remains recovered from these sites, suggest that the Botai groups hunted horses as one of their primary sources of food (Olsen 2000, 2003). A recent study (2009) by Outram and colleagues, which uses three lines of evidence, suggests that horses at Botai were also possibly ridden and mares were exploited for their milk. The analysis of pottery residues focused on the classification of the values of fatty acids and distinguished between non-ruminant and ruminant carcass and ruminant dairy fats. Although additional supporting data are certain to be forthcoming in the near future, these lines of evidence are perhaps the strongest support yet for the model that Botai groups were utilizing horses in several different ways, including their use as a meat source and a secondary products adaptation that included milking, and on the basis of the bit-wear evidence, some horses were even being ridden.

These results are currently some of the earliest evidence available for horse taming and the initial stages of domestication for the Eurasian steppe region.

THE EURASIAN STEPPE BRONZE AGE: ECONOMY, TRADE, AND INTERACTION (~3,500–1,200 B.C.E.)

The Bronze Age of the Eurasian steppe region has been synonymous with the emergence of much larger-scale patterns of movement, interaction, and trade between regional communities and polities. International field projects and numerous recent publications in English have offered a variety of new perspectives on this period and the substantial role that it played in the broader Eurasian region (Anthony 2007, Chernykh 2009, Frachetti 2008, Kohl 2007, Koryakova & Epimakhov 2007, Linduff 2004).

One of the key developments that appeared at this time was the emergence of spoke-wheeled chariot technology. Excavations by Soviet scholars in the southeastern Ural Mountains region of Russia in the 1970s and 1980s yielded the remains of Middle Bronze Age fortified settlements, spectacular burials with lavish animal sacrifice (including domesticated horses, cattle, and sheep/goats), and in some cases the remains of chariots placed with the dead (Gening et al. 1992). As Anthony (2007) has pointed out, the excavation and publication of the eponymous settlement site of Sintashta and its associated cemetery (both situated in the Sintashta River valley) stimulated a new era in the archaeology of the steppe region (p. 371). Subsequent radiocarbon dating of other Sintashta settlements and cemeteries (~2,100–1,750 cal. B.C.) has established that the chariot technology found at these sites is among the earliest in the world (Anthony & Vinogradov 1995, Epimakhov 2005, Hanks et al. 2007, Kuznetsov 2006, Vinogradov 2003).

Another important characteristic of the settlements is evidence for smelting furnaces and copper metallurgy recovered from houses within the fortified walls (Zdanovich & Zdanovich 2002). These data have led to strong debate over the scale of production of bronze metals, possibly for trade with polities of the Bactria Margiana Archaeological Complex (BMAC) situated well south of the Urals in the arid Central Asian region (see Hiebert 2002, Kohl 2007 for overview of BMAC). Not all scholars agree with this model, and a variety of opinions on the emergence, spread, and decline of the Sintashta archaeology pattern have been published recently (Anthony 2007; chapters by Hanks and Anthony & Frachetti in Hanks & Linduff 2009; chapters in Jones-Bley & Zdanovich 2002).

Although the exact nature and scale of Sintashta metallurgy may be debated, the Late Bronze Age Kargaly mining complex and settlement of Gorny (see Chernykh 2004 and Kohl 2007 for overviews in English), which is located in the southwestern Ural Mountains of Russia, have yielded extraordinary evidence for intensive mining of copper ores. The Kargaly mining complex was situated within a vast deposit of copper ores distributed within an estimated 500-km^2 zone. The recovery of more than 2.3 million animal bones (99.8% were domestic animals, of which 80% were cattle) from a 1000-m^2 excavation at the Gorny site has prompted Chernykh to suggest that this was a specialist community of miners that may have traded copper ores or smelted copper metals for subsistence goods in the form of domestic animals (see Kohl 2007, pp. 170–78 for overview in English). Recent archaeological and palynological work at the site has indicated that a peak in exploitation during the Late Bronze Age Srubnaya period (1700–1400 B.C.) gave way to a substantial decline after ~1,400 B.C. (Diaz del Rio et al. 2006). Interestingly, this evidence has been modeled as a potential decline in smelting as a result of the degradation of available resources such as timber for metal production, which ultimately led to the exploitation and trade of copper ores rather than processed metals by local groups (Vicent et al. 2006).

The trajectory that chariot technology, metals production, and more expansive trade may have taken in the Bronze Age finds great expression in what regional scholars have called the Late Bronze Age "Andronovo Horizon." This development is actually made up of several different archaeological cultures (e.g., Alakul', Fydorovka) spread over a vast territory of north central Eurasia and Central Asia, and in some cases the penetration of steppe groups and/or technology and trade items into what is today northwestern China (Kuz'mina 2008, Mei 2000, Mei & Shell 2002). The excavation of well-preserved mummies in the Xinjiang region of China that have European physical features and were clothed with nonlocal forms of textiles has also initiated great discussion over migration processes at this time (Mallory & Mair 2000, Mair 1998; see Barber 1999 for textiles). Interregional trade and migration in Bronze Age Eurasia have been modeled from a variety of different perspectives, including the use of world systems theory and core-periphery dynamics (Kohl 1996, 2007; Koryakova 2002). Unfortunately, such large-scale models are often lacking more detailed regional data that connect better with local adaptations, socioeconomic change, and the mosaic of environmental landscapes that comprise the Eurasian steppe region.

In response to this lack of data, several recent projects have focused on detailed investigations of specific ecological zones and the complexity associated with both pastoralist and agro-pastoralist economies and mobility patterns within these areas during the Late Bronze Age. Recent projects in the Samara Valley region of Russia (Anthony et al. 2005; Popova 2006; Peterson et al. 2006a,b) and in South Eastern Kazakhstan (Frachetti 2002, 2004, 2008, 2009; Frachetti & Benecke 2009) have produced detailed archaeological and paleoenvironmental data. These results are providing an important window into the complexity and variability of Bronze Age steppe communities and their subsistence and productive economies. Such projects are setting a new standard for archaeological research on early pastoralist communities in the Eurasian steppe region and are beginning to overturn the traditional model of the distinctly different worlds of the pastoralist northern steppe versus the agricultural southern sown.

Early Iron Age Societies, Mobile Pastoralism, and Mounted Warfare (1,200–300 B.C.)

Scholars of the former Soviet Union have long known that the transition from the Bronze to the Iron Age was one of sweeping social and technological change. In fact, many scholars have been quite divided over whether classic mobile pastoralism (nomadism) developed first during the Bronze Age or not until the first millennium B.C. and the emergence of the Iron Age (see Frachetti 2008, Koryakova & Epimakhov 2007, and Kohl 2007 for recent overviews of this). As outlined above, scholarship has also been quite divided over the earliest appearance of horse domestication and the rise of mounted warfare, yet evidence in the steppe zone for mounted warfare sharply increased by ~900 B.C. The excavation of numerous kurgan (burial mound) mortuary complexes throughout the steppe region, which include in many cases sacrificed horses with riding accoutrements, indicates that horse riding at this time was part of much broader changes taking place in mobile subsistence economies, sociopolitical organization, and new forms and scales of regional and interregional warfare (Hanks 2002, Parzinger 2006).

The excavation of lavishly furnished Scythian tombs in the Crimea and Ukrainian western steppe zone in the eighteenth through twentieth centuries provided a dynamic image of the Eurasian steppe Iron Age and reflected the emergence of new dimensions of social and political power connected with territorial conflict and control. Additional discoveries in the Altai Mountains by Soviet scholars Sergei Rudenko and Mikhail Gryaznov in the 1950s through 1980s brought to light well-preserved frozen burials (Pazyryk tombs) and one of the earliest and largest Iron Age burial complexes in the steppe region, which has been dated to the ninth century B.C. (Arzhan I) (Bokovenko

2006; Gryaznov 1950, 1980, 1984; Rudenko 1970). More recent discoveries by Russian and German scholars in the Altai Mountains (Arzhan II) and Minusinsk Basin of Siberia have added further evidence about the widespread development of mounted warfare, new forms of funerary and other ritual monuments, and the development of the so-called animal-style art pattern (Bokovenko 2000, 2006; Chugunov et al. 2001, 2003, 2004; Parzinger 2006).

Whereas the scholarship of the Eurasian steppe Iron Age has persistently emphasized funerary monuments, in large part because easily observable settlement evidence declines during this period (believed to be connected with nomadism), several recent field research programs have focused specifically on settlement patterning in the steppe and forest-steppe environmental zones. In particular, the work of Chang and colleagues has added importantly to our understanding of socioeconomic change in Kazakhstan connected with the emergence of the Saka-Wusun period and what appears to be an intensification of domesticated cereal production and an agro-pastoral economic regime (Chang et al. 2003, Chang & Tourtellotte 1998, Miller-Rosen et al. 2000). This is the exact period during which conventional scholarship would have us believe that groups in this region were primarily nomadic. Another project in Western Siberia has also clearly documented the diachronic development of economy and diet of Late Bronze to Early Iron Age populations at the multiphase fortified settlement site of Čiča (Privat et al. 2005). These projects have shown that the study of settlement evidence when available in the steppe region, in conjunction with funerary monuments, is absolutely crucial to the process of building more comprehensive understandings of the dynamic nature of Early Iron Age steppe societies and their social and economic foundations.

MONGOLIA

Perhaps it is due, in part, to the intense scholarly interest in China's early historic relationships with the northern periphery and Xiongnu confederation (and later Chinggis Khan Empire) that the prehistoric past of Mongolia has only recently emerged as a topic of great interest to international scholarship (Christian 1998). In fact, a long history of archaeological field research has taken place in Mongolia, stemming from the Soviet Period, which has played a significant role in identifying early developments in the eastern steppe zone and the Altai-Sayan Mountains to the west and northwest of Mongolia (Bemmann et al. 2009, Novgorodova 1989; Volkov 1967, 1981). Although the territory of present-day Mongolia was important from the Paleolithic to Neolithic in terms of human settlement and the emergence of pastoral and agro-pastoral adaptations, most field projects in recent years have focused on the Bronze and Iron Age periods. What has emerged from this work are the further identification and documentation of numerous early mortuary complexes and other ritual monuments and some of the first systematic, large-scale regional surveys (systematic pedestrian surface collection) conducted in the Eurasian steppe zone.

Bronze and Iron Age Ritual Monuments and Regional Surveys (1,500–500 B.C.E.)

Early research by Soviet scholars led to the documentation of a wide variety of Bronze and Iron Age stone burial and ritual monuments within the Mongolia region, and these have greatly attracted international attention in recent years. Field research over the past two decades by Mongolian and international teams has led to the excavation, mapping, and radiocarbon dating of large stone monument complexes, called khirigsuurs, dated to the Late Bronze Age and Early Iron Age (Allard et al. 2002, Allard & Erdenebaatar 2005, Frohlich 2006). Although some of these sites have yielded poorly preserved human remains, it is unclear whether they were all constructed as funerary monuments. Recent field expeditions sponsored by the Smithsonian Institution have also led to the excavation, recording, and dating of standing

Animal-style art: a traditional form of art in the steppes often depicting cervids, felines, and fanciful hybrid animals

Khirigsuurs: Mongolian word for funerary monument or ritual construction variously made of earth and/or stones

stone monuments called deer stones in an effort to preserve these important monuments, which have unfortunately been prone to looting and destruction (Fitzhugh & Bayarsaikhan 2008, Frohlich et al. 2008). The deer stones, often adorned with stylized cervids and/or anthropomorphic images of warriors with accompanying bows, daggers, axes, and other symbols of warfare, are widely distributed within the steppe zone and have been dated from the Late Bronze Age through to the Medieval Period within the Mongolian region.

Research at larger khirigsuur sites in central Mongolia has revealed complex ritual activity that appears to have existed at a surprising scale in terms of human labor. For example, Urt Bulagyn, one of the two largest khirigsuur complexes in the Khanuy River Valley, is composed of a large central mound of stone 5 m tall and 26 m in diameter. This mound is surrounded by a rectangular fence of surface stones measuring 60 m by 90 m. Placed around the outer perimeter of the fence are 1,752 smaller stone cists. Several of these cists have been excavated and dated (1,040 to 750 cal. B.C.), and each of them contained the remains of an east-facing horse skull and/or vertebrae or leg bones of a horse (Allard et al. 2006, Fitzhugh 2009). An additional 1,100 small stone piles are situated at the periphery of the satellite stone cists, and these typically contain burnt animal bone remains. Such ritual evidence, and what appears to reflect a significant mobilization of human labor in the construction of these sites, has generated a great deal of discussion among scholars about regional social integration and the emergence of new forms of hereditary ranking and political authority (Houle 2009; Wright 2006, 2007).

In addition to research focused specifically on the mapping and excavation of stone monuments, several large regional survey projects have produced results that better substantiate diachronic settlement and human demographic patterning. An excellent example of this analysis is the multiyear Egiin Gol River Valley survey carried out in north central Mongolia from 1996 to 2000. This project employed systematic pedestrian survey to cover a 310-km² area.

As a result, 550 archaeological sites were identified that dated from the Upper Paleolithic to the mid-twentieth century (Soviet Period) (Honeychurch 2004; Honeychurch & Amartuvshin 2006, 2007). The collection of data through this project has provided, for the first time, a much better understanding of the trajectories of pastoral and agro-pastoral regimes that developed in Mongolia. Such developments can now be modeled in conjunction with local socioeconomic adaptations as well as interregional contact with sedentary states such as China. This progress is particularly significant because much discussion has been waged on the role that these sedentary states and polities had in stimulating a greater degree of sociopolitical complexity among pastoralist groups through a dependency on agricultural products (Barfield 1989; Di Cosmo 1994, 2002). Archaeological research in Mongolia is now defining a much more complex set of sequences connected with the emergence of early steppe polities in the Bronze Age, many of which set the stage for the later emergence of the Xiongnu confederation and Mongolian Empire.

Iron Age Developments and the Xiongnu Polities (500 B.C.E.–A.D. 155)

In addition to new research on the Mongolian Bronze Age, several recent field projects by Mongolian and international teams have added substantially to our understanding of the Early Iron Age (Erdenebaatar 2004) and later Xiongnu developments (Brosseder 2007, Crubézy et al. 1996, Crubézy et al. 2006, Torbat 2006). Much of this research has focused on the excavation of funerary tombs in the region and in particular on the large and richly furnished tombs of the Xiongnu elite (Miller et al. 2006). Evidence gathered from sites in both Mongolia and just across the border in Russia (Tsaraam Valley; Minyaev & Sakharovskaya 2007a,b) indicates a complex array of social and political relationships that were played out through gift exchange with the Chinese states and the appropriation of various aspects of Chinese customs that became rearticulated through local traditions and social practices (Miller 2009). Such archaeological evidence provides an important comparative perspective when trying to interpret the historical biases connected with early Chinese texts on the Xiongnu. Archaeology is therefore in an important position to provide greater detail on local contexts relating to the cultural practices of the Xiongnu elites and also to chart the ways in which the Xiongnu confederation developed and responded to the ebb and flow of its political and economic relationship with China. Interestingly, recent survey projects and excavations have provided important evidence on the rise of urban centers by the Xiongnu period, which later came to be important components in the social, economic, and political structure of the Uighur and later Mongolian Empire (Rogers et al. 2005). Recent work at such sites as Kharkhorum is effectively extending our understanding of the long-term traditions of development that emerged out of the large-scale political networks of Mongolian expansionist states.

The scale and intensity of archaeological research and publication for Mongolia have risen considerably in the past decade. As such, Mongolia has become the setting for some of the most important and productive new research in Eurasian steppe prehistory. Whereas much of this research has traditionally been focused on the relationship between China and nomadic polities to the north, more recent research is highlighting not only the nature of external contact and social change but also internal developments within Mongolia stretching back to the Early Bronze Age. Archaeological fieldwork from this region will no doubt continue to challenge currently held views on pastoralist societal development and the emergence of large-scale steppe polities and states in the eastern zone of the Eurasian steppe.

CONCLUDING THOUGHTS

As noted at the beginning of this article, the study of the social, economic, and political developments in the steppe region has rarely factored into anthropological comparative models for understanding social evolution and change within world prehistory. Numerous archaeological projects in the past few years, some of which have been touched on here, have addressed these issues and signal an important shift in the role that the archaeology of Mongolia and the Eurasian steppes will play in the coming years. A substantial rise in the number of international publications and conferences over the past two decades also suggests that Eurasian steppe prehistory is moving more firmly into the spotlight of global prehistory and, we hope, will become more effectively recognized by scholars working in other regions of the world.

The international projects that have been outlined here do indicate, however, that there has been a more intentional focus on the archaeology of the Eneolithic through Iron Age and that these periods of study have overshadowed new research on earlier periods such as the Upper Paleolithic, Mesolithic, and Neolithic. Thus, numerous important issues and questions still remain to be addressed more effectively for the steppe zone. Such issues include the earliest sequences of northern Eurasian colonization by anatomically modern humans within the central Eurasian steppe plain in addition to the excellent research that has been achieved thus far for the western and eastern regions. Issues connected with the Mesolithic to Neolithic transition, such as changing environmental conditions and social and technological adaptations, remain to be more fully understood for many parts of the steppe zone. As noted above, the BAP has been highly successful in this endeavor, yet multidisciplinary research of this quality and intensity is desperately needed in other regions as well. In addition, numerous questions still surround the nature of plant and animal domestication and their diffusion throughout the steppe zone and adjacent territories. To date, archaeological research has indicated that numerous trajectories of adaptation are connected with pastoralist and agro-pastoralist economies, and such developments remain to be more fully recognized for many areas. The issues outlined here are, for the most part, practical concerns in terms of developing and expanding the nature and scale of future archaeological research. Nevertheless, a number of other critical challenges remain to be overcome in the archaeology of the Eurasian steppe zone in the twenty-first century.

Future Goals and Challenges

As an archaeologist involved in collaborative field research in the steppe region since 1998, I have had the unique opportunity both to contribute to and to witness a dynamic transition in the nature of scholarship connected with this region of the world. Academic institutions and scholarly programs within the countries of the former Soviet Union have undergone profound change over the past 20 years, and the discipline of archaeology and the way in which field research is conducted have been radically impacted. As Trigger (1989) has noted, archaeology during the height of the Soviet Period was state sponsored, and more than 500 field expeditions were supported annually and more than 5,000 scholarly reports published (p. 207). Organized through the vast infrastructure of the Academy of Sciences, field reports and publications produced in Russian were centralized and made available through state archives. In the late 1980s, with the emergence of Perestroika and the collapse of the Soviet Union in 1991, funding for the Academy of Sciences was decimated. As Chernykh (1995) has stated, several institutes were left without even sufficient funds to cover basic utility costs for their facilities (p. 140). This situation has improved in recent years but varies substantially on the basis of the role that independent state governments play in their support of archaeology.

Nevertheless, over the past decade a number of important developments have transpired. For example, regional archaeological publications are being produced in a variety of national languages (Kazakh, Mongolian, Ukrainian, etc.), however; the emphasis on centralized information and data storage is no longer a certainty for many regions. The scale of international collaboration in field research and publication has risen sharply and readers are encouraged to compare the projects discussed in this article with the publication by Masson & Taylor (1989) on the state of Soviet Archaeology in 1989. It is indeed remarkable how much has changed in just over two decades. One of the most prominent leaders in stimulating and supporting new forms of international collaboration is the Deutsches Archäologisches Institut (DAI) in Germany and its Eurasian Department (Eurasien-Abteilung, formed in 1995). A new branch has also recently been formed in Ulaanbaatar, Mongolia, and is further supporting German-Mongolian collaborative projects. DAI efforts in recent years have successfully funded several new programs of field research across the Eurasian steppe region, produced numerous bilingual publications, formed new journals such as *Eurasia Antiqua*, and developed several new monograph series (Parzinger 2002). DAI-sponsored collaborations have also provided an important foundation for the international exchange of students and other scholars, which is certain to play a vital role in educating the next generation of Eurasian steppe scholars both regionally and internationally.

Unfortunately, although there is much about which to be optimistic concerning recent developments, several important challenges remain. One of the most important is truly a quiet crisis and is connected with the decline of students pursuing advanced degrees and professional careers in academic archaeology in countries of the former Soviet Union. The lack of positions in universities and comparatively low salaries reflect the difficult transition that has confronted higher education in these regions. Although international collaboration may help to stimulate some growth, the reality is that the archaeological curriculum, which has traditionally been based within history departments, will need to undergo change just as other academic disciplines (e.g., economics, business, natural sciences) have done. In addition, the role that archaeology will come to play within dynamically changing socioeconomic conditions in the independent states is yet to be realized.

Unfortunately, exactly where the next generation of regional scholars in archaeology will come from is uncertain and is an increasingly pressing concern (L. Koryakova, E. Chernykh, and S. Hansen, personal communication).

The intellectual nature of archaeological scholarship has also shifted substantially since 1991 with the decline of state-sponsored and obligatory use of the Marxist ideology. And, with the fragmentation of any nation-state, what follows is often the emergence of new national, ethnocultural agendas that appropriate the past in the construction of new sociopolitical agendas for the present (Lamberg-Karlovsky 2002; Shnirleman 1998, 1999). Regrettably, traditional understandings of prehistory and history are often in the position of being (re)written during such tumultuous processes, and steppe archaeology has not been immune to this tendency. As Eurasian prehistory is drawn more effectively into global archaeology, we hope the danger of heritage appropriation and misuse will become more visible on the international stage and held more accountable. This issue again connects very importantly with the education of the next generation of regional scholars and can only be challenged through the epistemological foundation and integrity of academic scholarship.

These challenges and many more will remain a reality for Eurasian steppe archaeology in the near future. Nevertheless, substantial progress has been made, and I look forward to the contribution that the archaeology of this region can make to global prehistory and the discipline of archaeology more generally. As a personal aside, I am impatiently waiting for the day when that large blank space in Anglo-American introductory textbooks fills in both to acknowledge and to address effectively the important role this region has played in the human past—something that Soviet and post-Soviet regional specialists have understood for a very long time.

DISCLOSURE STATEMENT

The author is not aware of any affiliations, memberships, funding, or financial holdings that might be perceived as affecting the objectivity of this review.

ACKNOWLEDGMENTS

I gratefully acknowledge the numerous colleagues and students in Eurasia who have so positively contributed to my knowledge and understanding of Eurasian steppe archaeology. All mistakes and omissions within this article remain the sole responsibility of the author.

LITERATURE CITED

Adovasio J, Soffer O, Klíma B. 1996. Upper Palaeolithic Fibre Technology: interlaced woven finds from Pavlov I, Czech Republic, c. 26,000 years ago. *Antiquity* 70:526–34

Allard F, Erdenebaatar D. 2005. Khirisgsuurs, ritual, and nomadic pastoralism in the Bronze Age of Mongolia. *Antiquity* 17:1–18

Allard F, Erdenebaatar D, Batbold N, Miller B. 2002. A Xiongnu cemetery found in Mongolia. *Antiquity* 76:637–38

Allard F, Erdenebaatar D, Houle J-L. 2006. Recent archaeological research in the Khanuy River Valley. See Peterson et al. 2006b, pp. 202–24

Anthony D. 2007. *The Horse, the Wheel, and Language: How Bronze-Age Riders from the Eurasian Steppes Shaped the Modern World.* Princeton, NJ: Princeton Univ. Press

Anthony D, Brown D. 1991. The origins of horseback riding. *Antiquity* 65:22–38

Anthony D, Brown D. 2000. Eneolithic horse exploitation in the Eurasian steppes: diet, ritual and riding. *Antiquity* 74:75–86

Anthony D, Brown D, Brown E, Goodman A, Kokhlov A, et al. 2005. The Samara Valley Project. Late Bronze Age economy and ritual in the Russian steppes. *Eurasia Antiq.* 11:395–417

Anthony D, Vinogradov N. 1995. The birth of the chariot. *Archaeology* 48(2):36–41

Barber E. 1999. *The Mummies of Ürümchi*. New York: Norton

Barfield T. 1989. *The Perilous Frontier: Nomadic Empires and China 221 BC to AD 1757*. Oxford, UK: Blackwell

Bemmann J, Parzinger H, Pohl E, Tseveendorzh D, eds. 2009. *Current archaeological research in Mongolia*. Pap. Int. Conf., 1st, "Archaeological Research in Mongolia," Ulaanbaatar, 19–23 Aug. 2007. *Bonn Contrib. Asian Archaeol.*, Vol. 4. Bonn, Germ.: Vor- und Frühgeschichtliche Archäologie Rheinische Friedrich-Wilhelms-Universität Bonn

Bokovenko N. 2000. The origins of horse riding and the development of ancient central Asian nomadic riding harnesses. In *Kurgans, Ritual Sites, and Settlements: Eurasian Bronze and Iron Age*, ed. J Davis-Kimball, pp. 304–10. Oxford, UK: Archaeopress

Bokovenko N. 2006. The emergence of the Tagar culture. *Antiquity* 80(310):860–79

Boyle K, Renfrew C, Levine M. 2002. *Ancient Interactions: East and West in Eurasia*. Cambridge, UK: McDonald Inst. Monogr.

Brosseder U. 2007. Les Xiongnu et leurs relations internationales. In *Mongolie, les Xiongnu de l'Arkhangaï*, ed. J-P Desroches, G André, pp. 82–84. Ulaanbaatar, Mong.: ADMON

Cavalli-Sforza LL. 1996. The spread of agriculture and nomadic pastoralism: insights from genetics, linguistics and archaeology. See Harris 1996, pp. 51–69

Chang C, Norbert B, Grigoriev F, Rosen A, Tourtellotte P. 2003. Iron Age society and chronology in South-East Kazakhstan. *Antiquity* 77:298–312

Chang C, Tourtellotte P. 1998. The role of agro-pastoralism in the evolution of steppe culture in the semirech-eye area of Southern Kazakhstan during the Saka/Wusun Period (600 BCE–400 CE). See Mair 1998, pp. 264–79

Chernykh EN. 1995. Postscript: Russian archaeology after the collapse of the USSR—infrastructural crisis and the resurgence of old and new nationalisms. In *Nationalism, Politics, and the Practice of Archaeology*, ed. PL Kohl, C Fawcett, pp. 139–48. Cambridge, UK: Cambridge Univ. Press

Chernykh EN. 2004. Kargaly: the largest and most ancient metallurgical complex on the border of Europe and Asia. See Linduff 2004, pp. 223–37

Chernykh EN. 2009. Formation of the Eurasian steppe belt cultures viewed through the lens of archaeomet-allurgy and radiocarbon dating. See Hanks & Linduff 2009, pp. 115–45

Christian D. 1998. *A History of Russia, Central Asia and Mongolia*. Vol. 1: *Inner Eurasia from Prehistory to the Mongol Empire*. Oxford, UK: Blackwell

Chugunov K, Parzinger H, Nagler A. 2001. Der Fürst von Arzhan. Ausgrabungen im skythischen Fürstengrabhügel Arzhan 2 in der südsibirischen Republik Tuva. *Antike Welt* 32(6):607–14

Chugunov K, Parzinger H, Nagler A. 2003. Der skythische Fürstengrabhügel von Arzhan 2 in Tuva. Vorbericht der russischdeutschen Ausgrabungen 2000–2002. *Eurasia Antiq.* 9:113–62

Chugunov K, Parzinger H, Nagler A. 2004. Arzhan 2: la tombe d'un prince scythe en Sibérie du Sud. Rapport préliminaire des fouilles Russo-Allemandes de 2000–2002. *Arts Asiat.* 59:5–29

Crubézy E, Martin H, Batsaikhan Z, Erdenbaatar D, Giscard P, et al. 1996. Pratiques funéraires et sacrifices d'animaux en Mongolie á la période proto-historique. *Paléorient* 22(1):89–107

Crubézy E, Ricaut F, Martin H, Erdenebaatar D, Coqueugnot H, et al. 2006. Inhumation and cremation in medieval Mongolia: analysis and analogy. *Antiquity* 80:894–905

Danukalova G, Yakovlev A. 2006. A review of biostratigraphical investigations of Paleolithic localities in the Southern Urals region. *Quat. Int.* 149(1):37–43

Derev'anko A, Shimkin D, Powers W. 1998. *The Paleolithic of Siberia: New Discoveries and Interpretations*, transl. I Laricheva. Novosibirsk: Inst. Archaeol. Ethnogr., Sib. Div., Russ. Acad. Sci.; Chicago: Univ. Ill. Press

Diaz del Rio P, Lopez Garcia P, Antonio Lopez Saez J, Isabel Martinez Navarrete M, Rodriquez Alcalde AL, et al. 2006. Understanding the productive economy during the Bronze Age through archaeo-metallurgical and palaeo-environmental research at Kargaly (Southern Urals, Orenburg, Russia). See Peterson et al. 2006, pp. 343–57

Di Cosmo N. 1994. Ancient Inner Asian nomads: their economic basis and its significance in Chinese history. *J. Asian Stud.* 53(4):1092–126

Di Cosmo N. 2002. *Ancient China and Its Enemies: The Rise of Nomadic Power in East Asia*. Cambridge, UK: Cambridge Univ. Press

Dolukhanov P, Shukurov A, Sokoloff D. 2001. Radiocarbon chronology of Upper Palaeolithic sites in eastern Europe at improved resolution. *J. Archaeol. Sci.* 28:699–712

Dolukhanov P, Shukurov A, Tarasov P, Zaitseva G. 2002. Colonization of Northern Eurasia by modern humans: radiocarbon chronology and environment. *J. Archaeol. Sci.* 29:593–606

Drews R. 2004. *Early Riders: The Beginnings of Mounted Warfare in Asia and Europe*. London: Routledge

Epimakhov A. 2005. *Ranniye Kompleksniye Obshyestva Severa Tzentral'noi Evrazii (po materialam mogil'nika Kamennyi Ambar 5), Kniga 1*. Chelyabinsk, Russia: Nauk

Erdenebaatar D. 2004. Burial materials related to the history of the Bronze Age on the territory of Mongolia. See Linduff 2004, pp. 189–221

Fitzhugh W. 2009. Pre-Scythian ceremonialism, deer stone art, and cultural intensification in Northern Mongolia. See Hanks & Linduff 2009, pp. 378–411

Fitzhugh W, Bayarsaikhan J. 2008. *American-Mongolian Deer Stone Project: Field Report 2007*. Ulaanbaatar, Mong.: Natl. Mus. Mong. History

Frachetti M. 2002. Bronze Age exploitation and political dynamics of the Eastern Eurasian steppe zone. See Boyle et al. 2002, pp. 161–70

Frachetti M. 2004. *Bronze Age pastoral landscapes of Eurasia and the nature of social interaction in the mountain steppe zone of Eastern Kazakhstan*. PhD diss. Univ. Penn. 593 pp.

Frachetti M. 2008. *Pastoralist Landscapes and Social Interaction in Bronze Age Eurasia*. Berkeley: Univ. Calif. Press

Frachetti M. 2009. Differentiated landscapes and non-uniform complexity among Bronze Age societies of the Eurasian steppe. See Hanks & Linduff 2009, pp. 19–46

Frachetti M, Benecke N. 2009. From Sheep to (some) horses: 4500 years of herd structure at the pastoralist settlement of Begash (south-eastern Kazakhstan). *Antiquity* 83:1023–37

Frohlich B. 2006. Burial mound survey in Hovsgol Aimag, Mongolia. In *Mongolian Deer Stone Project Field Report 2005*, ed. W Fitzhugh, pp. 67–82. Washington, DC: Arct. Stud. Cent. Smithson. Inst.

Frohlich B, Amgalantugs T, Hunt D. 2008. Bronze Age burial mound excavation in the Hovsgol Aimag, Northern Mongolia. In *The American-Mongolian Deer Stone Project: Field Report for 2007*, ed. W Fitzhugh, J Bayarsaikhan, pp. 101–3. Washington, DC: Arct. Stud. Cent. Smithson. Inst.

Gening VF, Zdanovich GB, Gening VV. 1992. *Sintashta. Arkheologicheskii Pamyatnik Ariiskikh Plemen Uralo-Kazakhstanskikh Stepei*. T. 1. Chelyabinsk, Russia: Uzhno-Ural'skoe knizhnoe Izd-vo

Gimbutas M. 1970. Proto-Indo-European culture: the Kurgan culture during the fifth, fourth, and third millennia B.C. In *Indo-European and Indo-Europeans*, ed. G Cardona, H Hoenigswald, A Senn, pp. 155–97. Philadelphia: Univ. Penn. Press

Goebel T. 2002. The "Microblade Adaptation" and re-colonization of Siberia during the late Upper Pleistocene. *Archaeol. Pap. Am. Anthropol. Assoc.* 12:117–32

Goebel T. 2004. The early Upper Paleolithic of Siberia. In *The Early Upper Paleolithic East of the Danube*, ed. J Brantingham, K Kerry, pp. 162–95. Berkeley: Univ. Calif. Press

Goebel T, Waters M, Buvit I, Konstantinov M, Konstantinov A. 2000. Studenoe-2 and the origins of microblade technologies in the Transbaikal, Siberia. *Antiquity* 74:567–75

Grinin L, Beliaev D, Korotayev A. 2008. *Hierarchy and Power in the History of Civilizations: Ancient and Medieval Cultures*. Moscow: Uchitel

Grinin L, Carneiro R, Bondarenko D, Kradin N, Korotayev A. 2004. *The Early State, its Alternatives and Analogues*. Volgograd, Russia: Uchitel

Gryaznov M. 1950. *Pervii Pazyrykskii Kurgan*. Leningrad: Hermitage-Art.

Gryaznov M. 1980. *Drevnie Kochevniki v Tsentre Azii*. Moscow: Nauka

Gryaznov M. 1984. *Der Großkurgan von Arzan in Tuva, Südsibirien*. München: Verlag C.H. Beck

Hanks B. 2002. The Eurasian steppe "Nomadic World" of the first millennium BC: inherent problems within the study of Iron Age nomadic groups. See Boyle et al. 2002, pp. 183–97

Hanks B, Epimakhov A, Renfrew C. 2007. Towards a refined chronology for the Bronze Age of the Southern Urals, Russia. *Antiquity* 81:333–67

Hanks B, Linduff K. 2009. *Social Complexity in Prehistoric Eurasia: Monuments, Metals and Mobility*. Cambridge, UK: Cambridge Univ. Press

Harris D. 1996. *The Origins and Spread of Agriculture and Pastoralism in Eurasia*. London: Univ. Coll. Lond. Press

Häusler A. 1996. Invasionen aus den nordpontischen steppen nach Mitteleuropa im Neolithikum und in der Bronzezeit: realität oder phantasieprodukt? *Archäologische Inf.* 19:75–88

Hiebert F. 2002. Bronze Age interaction between the Eurasian steppe and Central Asia. See Boyle et al. 2002, pp. 237–48

Hoffecker J. 2002. *Desolate Landscapes*. New Brunswick, NJ: Rutgers Univ. Press

Honeychurch W. 2004. *Inner Asian warriors and Khans: a regional spatial analysis of Nomadic political organization and interaction*. PhD diss. Univ. Mich., Ann Arbor, 314 pp.

Honeychurch W, Amartuvshin C. 2006. States on horseback: the rise of Inner Asian confederations and empires. In *Asian Archaeology*, ed. M Stark, pp. 255–78. Cambridge, UK: Blackwell

Honeychurch W, Amartuvshin Ch. 2007. Hinterlands, urban centers and mobile settings: the "new" Old World archaeology from the Eurasian steppe. *Asian Perspect.* 46(1):36–64

Houle J-L. 2009. Socially integrative facilities and the emergence of societal complexity on the Mongolian steppe. See Hanks & Linduff 2009, pp. 358–77

Jansen T, Forster P, Levine M, Oelke H, Hurles M, et al. 2002. Mitochondrial DNA and the origins of the domestic horse. *Proc. Natl. Acad. Sci. USA* 99:10905–10

Jones-Bley K, Zdanovich D. 2002. *Complex Societies of Central Eurasia from the 3rd to the 1st Millennium BC—Regional Specifics in Light of Global Models*. Vol. I and II. J. Indo-Eur. Stud. Monogr. Ser. 45. Washington, DC: Inst. Study Man

Kelekna P. 2009. *The Horse in Human History*. Cambridge, UK: Cambridge Univ. Press

Kohl P. 1996. The ancient economy, transferable technologies and the Bronze Age world-system: a view from the Northeastern frontier of the Ancient Near East. In *Contemporary Theory in Archaeology*, ed. R Pruecel, I Hodder, pp. 143–65. Oxford, UK: Blackwell

Kohl P. 2007. *The Making of Bronze Age Eurasia*. Cambridge, UK: Cambridge Univ. Press

Koryakova L. 2002. The social landscape of central Eurasia in the Bronze and Iron Ages: tendencies, factors, and limits of transformation. In *Complex Societies of Central Eurasia from the Third to the First Millennia BC: Regional Specifics in the Light of Global Models*, ed. K Jones-Bley, G Zdanovich, pp. 97–117. Washington, DC: Inst. Study Man

Koryakova L, Epimakhov A. 2007. *The Urals and Western Siberia in the Bronze and Iron Ages*. Cambridge, UK: Cambridge Univ. Press

Kradin N. 2002. Nomadism, evolution and world-systems: pastoral societies in theories of historical development. *J. World-Syst. Res.* 8(3):368–88

Kradin N, Bondarenko D, Barfield T. 2003. *Nomadic Pathways in Social Evolution*. Moscow: Russ. Acad. Sci.

Kuzmin Y, Keates S. 2005. Dates are not just data: paleolithic settlement patterns in Siberia derived from radiocarbon records. *Am. Antiquity* 70(4):773–89

Kuzmin Y, Orlova L. 2000. The neolithization of Siberia and Russian Far East: radiocarbon evidence. *Antiquity* 74:356–64

Kuz'mina E. 2008. *The Prehistory of the Silk Road*. Philadelphia: Univ. Penn. Press

Kuznetsov P. 2006. The emergence of Bronze Age chariots in Eastern Europe. *Antiquity* 80:638–45

Lamberg-Karlovsky CC. 2002. Archaeology and language: the Indo-Iranians. *Curr. Anthropol.* 43(1):63–88

Levine M. 2004. Exploring the criteria for early horse domestication. In *Traces of Ancestry: Studies in Honour of Colin Renfrew*, ed. M Jones, pp. 115–26. Cambridge, UK: McDonald Inst. Monogr.

Levine M, Rassamakin Y, Kislenko A, Tatarintseva N. 1999. *Late Prehistoric Exploitation of the Eurasian Steppe*. Cambridge, UK: McDonald Inst. Monogr.

Levine M, Renfrew C, Boyle K. 2003. *Prehistoric Steppe Adaptation and the Horse*. Cambridge, UK: Cambridge Univ. Press

Lindgren G, Backström N, Swinburne J, Hellborg L, Einarsson A, et al. 2004. Limited number of patrilines in horse domestication. *Nat. Genet.* 36(4):335–36

Linduff K. 2004. *Metallurgy in Ancient Eastern Eurasia from the Urals to the Yellow River*. New York: Mellon

Mair V. 1998. *The Bronze Age and Early Iron Age Peoples of Eastern Central Asia*. Washington, DC: Inst. Study Man. 2 vols.

Mallory J. 1989. *In Search of the Indo-Europeans: Language, Archaeology and Myth*. London: Thames and Hudson

Mallory J, Mair V. 2000. *The Tarim Mummies: Ancient China and the Mystery of the Earliest Peoples from the West*. London: Thames and Hudson

Masson VM, Taylor T. 1989. Special Section: Soviet Archaeology in the Steppe Zone. *Antiquity* 63:779–83

McGahern A, Bower M, Edwards C, Brophy P, Sulimova G, et al. 2006. Evidence for biogeographic patterning of mitochondrial DNA sequences in Eastern horse populations. *Anim. Genet.* 37(5):494–97

Mei J. 2000. *Copper and Bronze Metallurgy in Late Prehistoric Xinjiang: Its Cultural Context and Relationship with Neighboring Regions*. BAR Int. Ser. 865. Oxford: Archaeopress

Mei J, Rehren T. 2009. *Metallurgy and civilization: Eurasia and beyond*. Proc. Int. Conf. Beginnings Use Metals Alloys (BUMA VI), 6th, Beijing, PRC. London: Archetype

Mei J, Shell C. 2002. The Iron Age cultures in Xinjiang and their steppe connections. See Boyle et al. 2002, pp. 213–34

Miller B. 2009. *Power politics in the Xiongnu Empire*. PhD diss. Univ. Penn., Phila. 435 pp.

Miller B, Allard F, Erdenebaatar D, Lee C. 2006. A Xiongnu Tomb complex: excavations at Gol Mod 2 cemetery (2002–05). *Mongol. J. Anthropol. Archaeol. Ethnol.* 2(2):1–21

Miller-Rosen A, Chang C, Grigoriev F. 2000. Paleoenvironments and economy of Iron Age Saka-Wusun agro-pastoralists in southeastern Kazakhstan. *Antiquity* 74(285):611–23

Minyaev S, Sakharovskaya L. 2007a. Elitnii Kompleks zahoronenii Siunnu v padi Tsaram. *Rossiiskaya Arkheol.* 1:194–201

Minyaev S, Sakharovskaya L. 2007b. Investigation of a Xiongnu royal complex in the Tsaraam Valley—part 2: the inventory of Barrow no. 7 and the chronology of the site. *Silk Road* 5(1):44–56

Mooder K, Weber A, Bamforth F, Lieverse A, Schurr T, et al. 2005. Matrilineal affinities and prehistoric Siberian mortuary practices: a case study from Neolithic Lake Baikal. *J. Archaeol. Sci.* 32(4):619–34

Novgorodova E. 1989. *Drevnyaya Mongoliya*. Moscow: Nauka

Olsen S. 2000. Reflections of ritual behavior at Botai, Kazakhstan. *Proc. Annu. UCLA Indo-Eur. Conf.*, 11th, ed. K Jones-Bley, M Huld, A Della Volpe, pp. 183–207. *J. Indo-Eur. Stud. Monogr.* Ser. No. 35

Olsen S. 2003. The exploitation of horses at Botai, Kazakhstan. See Levine et al. 2003, pp. 83–104. Cambridge, UK: McDonald Inst. Monogr.

Olsen S, Grant S, Choyke A, Bartosiewicz L. 2006. *Horses and Humans: The Evolution of Human-Equine Relationships*. Oxford, UK: Archaeopress

Outram A, Stear N, Bendrey R, Olsen S, Kasparov A, et al. 2009. The earliest horse harnessing and milking. *Science* 323:1332–35

Parzinger H. 2002. The German Archaeological Institute: tasks and prospectives in archaeological investigations of Eurasia. *Rossiiskaya Arkheol.* 3:59–78

Parzinger H. 2006. *Die Frühen Völker Eurasiens: Vom Neolithikum Bis Zum Mittelalter*. München: Verlag C.H. Beck

Peterson D, Kuznetsov P, Mochalov O. 2006a. The Samara Bronze Age Metals Project: investigating changing technologies and transformations of value in the Western Eurasian steppes. See Peterson et al. 2006b, pp. 322–42

Peterson D, Popova L, Smith A. 2006b. *Beyond the Steppe and the Sown: Proceedings of the 2002 University of Chicago Conference on Eurasian Archaeology*. Colloquia Pontica 13. Leiden: Brill

Popova L. 2006. *Political pastures: navigating the steppe in the Middle Volga Region (Russia) during the Bronze Age*. PhD diss. Univ. Chicago

Popova L, Hartley C, Smith A. 2007. *Social Orders and Social Landscapes*. Newcastle upon Tyne, UK: Cambridge Scholars

Price TD. 2000. *Europe's First Farmers*. Cambridge, UK: Cambridge Univ. Press

Privat K, Schneeweis J, Benecke N, Vasil'ev S, O'Connell T, et al. 2005. Economy and diet at the Late Bronze Age/Iron Age site of Cica. Artefactual, archaeozoological and biochemical analyses. *Eurasia Antiq.* 11:419–48

Renfrew C. 2002. Pastoralism and interaction: some introductory questions. See Boyle et al. 2002, pp. 1–12

Rogers D, Ulambayar E, Gallon M. 2005. Urban centres and the emergence of empires in Eastern Inner Asia. *Antiquity* 79:801–18

Rudenko S. 1970. *Frozen Tombs of Siberia*. London: Dent and Son

Shnirelman V. 1998. Archaeology and ethnic politics: the discovery of Arkaim. *Mus. Int.* 50(2):33–39

Shnirelman V. 1999. Passions about Arkaim: Russian nationalism, the Aryans, and the politics of archaeology. *Inner Asia* I:267–82

Soffer O, Adovasio J, Illingworth J, Amirkhanov H, Praslov N, Street M. 2000. Palaeolithic perishables made permanent. *Antiquity* 74:812–21

Soffer O, Vandiver P. 1997. The ceramics from Pavlov I—1957 excavation. In *Pavlov I: 1957 Excavations*, ed. J Svoboda, pp. 383–402. Brno, Czech Rep.: Archeol. Ustav AV CR

Torbat TS. 2006. The origin of Xiongnu archaeological culture based on funeral rites. *Mong. J. Archaeol. Anthropol. Ethnol.* 2.2(271):22–36

Travis J. 2008. Trail of mare's milk leads to first tamed horses. *Science* 322:368

Trigger B. 1989. *A History of Archaeological Thought*. Cambridge, UK: Cambridge Univ. Press

Vicent J, Ormeno S, Martinez-Navarrete M, Delgado J. 2006. The Kargaly Project: modeling Bronze Age landscapes in the steppe. In *From Space to Place: 2nd International Conference on Remote Sensing in Archaeology*, ed. S Campana, M Forte, pp. 279–84. BAR Int. Ser. 1568. Oxford: Archaeopress

Vinogradov N. 2003. *Mogil'nik bronzovogo veka Krivoe Ozero v Yuzhnom Zaural'ye*. Chelyabinsk, Russia: Yuzhno-Ural'skoe knizhnoe izd-vo

Volkov V. 1967. *Bronzovyi i rannii Zheleznyi vek Severnoi Mongolii*. Ulaanbaatar, Mong.: Nauk

Volkov V. 1981. *Olennie Kamni Mongolii*. Ulaanbaatar, Mong.: Nauk

Weber A, Katzenberg M, Goriunova O. 2007. *Khuzhir-Nuge XIV, a Middle Holocene Hunter-Gatherer Cemetery on Lake Baikal, Siberia: Osteological Materials*. North. Hunter-Gatherers Res. Ser. 3. Edmonton: CCI Press

Weber A, Katzenberg MA, Schurr T. 2010. *Prehistoric Hunter-Gatherers of the Baikal Region, Siberia: Bioarchaeolgical Studies of Past Life Ways*. Philadelphia: Univ. Penn. Press

Weber A, Link D, Katzenber MA. 2002. Hunter-gatherer culture change and continuity in the Middle Holocene of the Cis-Baikal, Siberia. *J. Anthropol. Archaeol.* 21:230–99

Weber A, McKenzie H, Beukens R, Goriunova O. 2005. Evaluation of radiocarbon dates from the Middle Holocene hunter-gatherer cemetery Khuzhir-Nuge XIV, Lake Baikal, Siberia. *J. Archaeol. Sci.* 32:1480–500

Wright J. 2006. *The adoption of pastoralism in Northeast Asia, monumental transformations in the Egiin Gol Valley, Mongolia*. PhD diss. Harvard Univ., Cambridge, Mass., 382 pp.

Wright J. 2007. Organizational principles of Khirigsuur monuments in the lower Egiin Gol Valley, Mongolia. *J. Anthropol. Archaeol.* 26:350–65

Zdanovich G, Zdanovich D. 2002. The "country of towns" of Southern Trans-Urals and some aspects of steppe assimilation in the Bronze Age. See Boyle et al. 2002, pp. 249–63

Ethnographic Approaches to Digital Media

E. Gabriella Coleman

Department of Media, Culture, and Communication, New York University, New York,
NY 10003; email: biella@nyu.edu

Annu. Rev. Anthropol. 2010. 39:487–505

First published online as a Review in Advance on
June 21, 2010

The *Annual Review of Anthropology* is online at
anthro.annualreviews.org

This article's doi:
10.1146/annurev.anthro.012809.104945

0084-6570/10/1021-0487$20.00

Key Words

ethnography, communication, computers, cell phones

Abstract

This review surveys and divides the ethnographic corpus on digital media into three broad but overlapping categories: the cultural politics of digital media, the vernacular cultures of digital media, and the prosaics of digital media. Engaging these three categories of scholarship on digital media, I consider how ethnographers are exploring the complex relationships between the local practices and global implications of digital media, their materiality and politics, and their banal, as well as profound, presence in cultural life and modes of communication. I consider the way these media have become central to the articulation of cherished beliefs, ritual practices, and modes of being in the world; the fact that digital media culturally matters is undeniable but showing how, where, and why it matters is necessary to push against peculiarly narrow presumptions about the universality of digital experience.

No mode of production and therefore no dominant social order and therefore no dominant culture in reality includes or exhausts all of human practice, human energy or human intention.

Raymond Williams

INTRODUCTION

Whenever and wherever individuals and groups deploy and communicate with digital media, there will be circulations, reimaginings, magnifications, deletions, translations, revisionings, and remakings of a range of cultural representations, experiences, and identities, but the precise ways that these dynamics unfold can never be fully anticipated in advance. In some instances, digital media have extended their reach into the mundane heart of everyday life, most visibly with cell phones—gadgets now vital to conduct business affairs in remote areas of the world, as well as in bustling global cities. In other instances, digital artifacts have helped engender new collectivities: Web-cam girls, gamers, hackers, and others, whose senses of self, vocation, and group sociabilities are shaped significantly, although not exclusively nor deterministically, by digital technologies.[1]

The diversity and pervasiveness of digital media can make them difficult to study, but also can make them compelling objects of ethnographic inquiry. Still, anthropologists have been slow to enter this terrain—at least until recently, when the trickle of 1990s publications became a steady stream. Here I survey and divide this growing ethnographic corpus on digital media into three broad but overlapping categories. The first category explores the relationship between digital media and what

might be called the cultural politics of media. This work examines how cultural identities, representations, and imaginaries, such as those hinged to youth, diaspora, nation, and indigeneity, are remade, subverted, communicated, and circulated through individual and collective engagement with digital technologies. The second category explores the vernacular cultures of digital media, evinced by discrepant phenomena, digital genres, and groups—hackers, blogging, Internet memes, and migrant programmers—whose logic is organized significantly around, although not necessarily determined by, selected properties of digital media. The final category, what I call prosaics of digital media, examines how digital media feed into, reflect, and shape other kinds of social practices, like economic exchange, financial markets, and religious worship. Attention to these rituals, broad contexts, and the material infrastructures and social protocols that enable them illuminates how the use and production of digital media have become integrated into everyday cultural, linguistic, and economic life.[2]

The distinctions I draw among these three fields should not imply that they are neat and tidy categories; indeed anthropological work in the past two decades has often contested these boundaries. Even though groupings such as the prosaics of digital media and the vernacular culture of digital media overlap, I use the terms provisionally and tactically to emphasize different frames of analysis that have been brought to bear on the ethnographic study of digital media. To grasp more fully the broader significance of digital media, its study must involve various frames of analysis, attention to history, and the

---

[1] Although the term digital media may be familiar to most readers, it is worth highlighting that digital media encompasses a wide range of nonanalog technologies, including cell phones, the Internet, and software applications that power and run on the Internet, among others. Despite this diversity—and with the exception of cell phones—many digital technologies are still not within reach of most of the world's population. For the latest trends on Internet use around the world, see: **http://www.internetworldstats.com/stats.htm**

[2] This review does not consider in much depth virtual worlds, the role of digital tools in reshaping ethnographic inquiry, or many publications covered in earlier *ARA* reviews on similar topics (Cook 2004, Eisenlohr 2004, Wilson & Peterson 2002). For reflections on methods see Burrell (2009) and Hine (2005), and for reviews on virtual worlds see Boellstorff (2008) and Malaby & Burke (2009). Fischer (2007) provides four genealogies in science and technology studies, including many examples that engage with digital media. For a media studies review of critical information studies see Vaidhyanathan (2006).

local contexts and lived experiences of digital media—a task well suited to the ethnographic enterprise.

To elaborate my tripartite structure further, I open by historicizing ethnographic work on digital media in light of broader shifts in the popular and scholarly literature. Then, engaging my three categories of scholarship on digital media, I consider how ethnographers are exploring the complex relationships between local practices and global implications of digital media, their materiality and politics, and their banal, as well as profound, presence in everyday life and modes of communication. The presumption that digital technologies are the basis of planetary transformations is widespread, but unfounded. I take my task to be one of "provincializing" digital media [to borrow a phrase coined by postcolonial theorist Dipesh Chakrabarty (2000)]. To provincialize digital media is not to deny their scale and global reach, particularly in the circulation of finance capital and in the aspirations of transnational corporations (Boyer 2007, Sassen 2002, Zaloom 2006); rather, it allows us to consider the way these media have become central to the articulation of cherished beliefs, ritual practices, and modes of being in the world; the fact that digital media culturally matters is undeniable but showing how, where, and why it matters is necessary to push against peculiarly narrow presumptions about the universality of digital experience.

MAPPING THE TERRAIN

Just a little more than a decade ago, the study of digital media was marked by a notable division of labor. Although anthropologists published influential methodological and theoretical reflections on the cultural implications of digital media—many of which remain relevant even today (Appadurai 1996, Escobar 1994, Fischer 1999, Kirshenblatt-Gimblett 1996)—few scholars attempted to conduct ethnographic research primarily in terms of emergent digital technologies (for a few exceptions, see Baym 2000, Danet 2001, Kendall 2002, Miller & Slater 2000, Pfaffenberger 1996). This is despite the explosion of scholarly and popular work that heralded the coming of a new posthuman subject residing in a "digital age" or "network society" (Castells 1996, Hayles 1999, Negroponte 1996, Turkle 1995). These technologies supposedly ushered in, according to Manuel Castells (1996), an "historically new reality" (p. 92)—one that is "fundamentally altering the way we are born, we live, we sleep, we produce, we consume, we dream, we fight, or we die" (p. 31). By now it is well known that much of this initial literature was concerned with two problematic motifs: rupture and transformation. A few anthropologists were quick to challenge these kinds of broad claims, for instance, casting doubt on the autonomous power of technology to engender change (Hakken 1999, 2003). Others noted that, far from stimulating novelty, digital technologies in many instances facilitated social reproduction, catalyzing "expansive realizations" of self and culture, as Miller and Slater aptly phrased it (2000).

By the turn of the century, owing in part to the Silicon Valley "dot-com" bust, the breathless, utopian enthusiasm engulfing digital media had subsided, as had the epochal scholarly pronouncements concerning the digital age. But by 2004, scholarly and especially popular hype about digital technologies resurfaced, following the proliferation of what has been branded as Web 2.0 technologies—a term used to distinguish contemporary social media (Wikis, blogs, embedded videos) from their immediate predecessors, the static Web pages and message forums that had characterized what was retroactively dubbed Web 1.0. A new wave of publications by scholars, journalists, and pundit-entrepreneurs would once again insist, with varying degrees of specificity, that social media allowed for more communicative interactivity, flexibility, social connectivity, user-generated content, and creativity, facilitating more democratic participation than did previous digital platforms and greater interaction among larger swaths of the global populace (Shirky 2008, Weinberger 2007).

Despite a surge of scholarship contesting the liberatory image of Web 2.0's participatory architectures (Hindman 2009, Lovink 2008, Mosco 2004, Scholz 2008) and the continued reality of the digital divide (Warschauer 2004), the digital age remains a powerful structuring emblem with material and cultural consequences. Ginsburg (2008), for instance, critiques this governing metaphor by examining how it resurrects outdated modernization theories, working to influence the agenda of development projects and marginalize groups, such as indigenous communities, who are rarely included in academic or popular accounts on digital media:

> This techno-imaginary universe of digital eras and divides…has the effect of reinscribing onto the world a kind of "allochronic chronopolitics"… in which "the other" exists in a time not contemporary with our own. This has the effect of restratifying the world along lines of a late modernity, despite the utopian promises by the digerati of the possibilities of a 21st-century McLuhanesque global village. (pp. 130–31).

If, as Ginsburg notes, sweeping visions of the digital age betray a constitutive myopia built on very particular exclusions, there is another irony as well: The term native is now commonly used by scholars and policy makers—most often in the titles of their books and reports—to denote the momentous and deep cultural changes that follow from the use of digital media (Adams & Smith 2008, Zeitlyn 2009). The use of digital media is, no doubt, culturally and politically meaningful. But even if we momentarily set aside important questions of access and capacity, the evidence remains unconvincing that digital media are the sole or even the most important grounds for producing a shared subjectivity or a wholly new sensorium, still less a life world that might characterize a vast population, such as an entire generation of young people in North America—the very thing that "native" connotes.[3]

Despite these limits, it would be a mistake to overlook how digital media have cultivated new modes of communication and selfhood; reorganized social perceptions and forms of self-awareness; and established collective interests, institutions, and life projects. Indeed, anthropologists, as well as sociologists and media theorists, have increasingly attended to more particular kinds of groups, practices, and communicative genres that are underwritten and sustained via engagement with digital technology. Whether it is a dense ethical practice rooted in legal and technical tinkering online (Coleman 2009, Kelty 2008); the genre-specific attributes of blogs (Doostdar 2004; Herring & Paolillo 2006; Reed 2005, 2008), the status and microcelebrity gained by Webcasting (Senft 2008), or the blurring of work and pleasure among Silicon Valley hightech workers (English-Leuck 2002, Malaby 2009), it is clear that groups substantially can and do culturally dwell in digital technology (Ingold 2000). These examples, however, are more circumscribed in time and place (and often require substantial skills and media literacy) than what is all too often portrayed in the popular, and even some of the scholarly, literature.

Of course, these are not the only digital genres or groups whose engagement with digital technologies merits ethnographic investigation. Indeed, the cultural significance of digital media extends far beyond those groups most immediately organized around these technologies. To privilege these "cultural locations" (Gupta & Ferguson 1997) over others—to emphasize well-defined groups over alternate forms of collectivity—would limit our understanding of the important role digital media play in a wide range of social, linguistic, and political processes and projects: postcolonial economies and aesthetics (Larkin 2008, Silvio 2007, Smith 2007); perception and visual representations of self, memory,

---

[3] Tribal motifs have long been part of the scholarly study of digital media owing in part to Marshall McLuhan's popularization of this connection (see Boyer 2007). The term digital generation functions in a similarly problematic fashion to connote the fundamental changes that follow from the use of digital media.

space, and the built environment (Cohen 2005, DeNicola 2006); and the cultural logic of capitalism, globalization, and corruption (Boyer 2007; Mazzarella 2004, 2006; Schull 2008), among others explored in this review.

Furthermore, to assess more richly the cultural and political life of digital media, we must attend to the role of social and technical protocols, infrastructure, and platforms (servers, cell phone towers, underwater cables, video sharing sites, conventions for chatting) that enable and constrain the circulation and use of digital media (Bowker 2007, DeNardis 2009, Gillespie 2007, Gitelman 2006, Larkin 2008, O'Donnell 2009, Ratto 2005) and do so, as Larkin (2008) insists, in light of their actual and material day-to-day operations. Whether it is willful avoidance of the Internet (Wyatt et al. 2002), the "unimagined user" (Burrell 2010), or a crumbling, slow infrastructure (Larkin 2008), these are the small but necessary details that render the materiality of media (and hence its particular affordances and constraints) not only heterogeneous but fully cultural, social, and above all, political.

DIGITAL MEDIA AND THE POLITICS OF CULTURAL REPRESENTATION

People the world over use Internet applications (email, social networking sites, video chat) and cell phones to stay in touch with family and friends living overseas. Digital technologies are thus central to diasporic groups in part because, as Bernal (2005) argues in her work on Eritrea, diaspora and information technologies stand in a "homologous" relationship to each other because "in both cyberspace and the spaces of diaspora . . . location is ambiguous, and to be made socially meaningful, it must be actively constructed" (p. 661). Bernal also insists that conflict is part of the social architecture of many diasporic communities, a motif emerging in other studies on diaspora and information technologies (Axel 2004, Whitaker 2004).

For many diasporic groups, unfiltered and affordable access has been central to support interactions that stretch from familial relations to pressing political projects (Burrell & Anderson 2008, Forte 2003, Landzelius 2006, Miller & Slater 2000, Panagakos & Horst 2006). In contrast, some indigenous groups seek to restrict the circulation of specific (i.e., sacred) forms of cultural knowledge, meaning imperatives other than unhampered circulation are also at stake. Cultural protocols might dictate restrictions on viewing material, such as images, owing to the ritual state of the viewer (initiated versus uninitiated, for example). In other instances, restrictions might follow after the death of an individual. A number of studies examine how indigenous groups, with the aid of ethnographers and nongovernmental organizations, have thus crafted (in painstaking detail) digital databases, interactive multimedia projects, and cultural mappings to represent, circulate, and at times, exclude various cultural motifs, norms, values, and folklore (Christen 2006, 2009; Christie 2008; Cohen & Salazar 2005; Salazar 2005; Srinivasan 2006). These digital projects represent what scholars have identified as "digital ontologies," which map "the community's overall structure of priorities and issues" (Srinivasan 2006, p. 510). These mappings, which often bypass the need for traditional forms of digital literacy, provide new visual representations of anthropological knowledge as well as resources for the community that respect cultural protocols.

These digital projects and their scholarly accounts also sustain a new chapter in the project of "dewesternizing media studies" (Curran & Park 2000; see also Ginsburg et al. 2002) all too rarely reflected in the scholarly or advocacy literature on the commons and digital access (Benkler 2006, Lessig 2004). To be sure, these advocates have built a politically vital project because it provides a legal and ethical counterweight to the ever-growing tangle of intellectual property restrictions. The particular debate over "free culture," however, perhaps too heavily relies on binaries like "'open and closed' or 'proprietary and free'" that overlook other modes of circulation and access than those of capitalist proprietorship and liberal access

(Christen 2009, p. 4; Leach 2005; Myers 2005; Strathern 2005). One way to revamp scholarly thinking on the relation between culture and access is by considering national patrimony and cultural repatriation, whose politics must account for the material properties of media, colonial histories, and the multiplicity of protocols for organizing knowledge (Geismar 2008, Geismar & Mohns 2010).

The interplay between open and restricted access is also pertinent to questions of identity and digital media. One of the richest studies on the topic of identity, ethnicity, and race, is offered by Nakamura (2007) who examines how default virtual representations—white and masculine—"are intensified, modulated, reiterated, and challenged" by users online (p. 34). A recent monograph on white supremacy digs deep into the social life of racism online, appraising the role of "cloaked" Web sites whose design obscures the source, intention, and authorship of the content—a mode of presentation increasingly common on many political and corporate Web sites (Daniels 2009). It is surprising that only a handful of ethnographers have pursued in-depth studies on ethnicity, race, and digital media (Eglash & Bennett 2009). Youth and digital media, however, have been the subject of substantial ethnographic inquiry, although studies are generally limited to industrialized nations such as the United States, Brazil, and Japan (boyd 2009, boyd & Marwick 2009, Herring 2008, Horst 2010, Ito 2009, Ito et al. 2009, Palfrey & Gasser 2008). One recent collaborative project points an ethnographic lens at the intersection between digital media and American youth, including the changing dynamics of friendship, the reconfigurations between publicity and privacy, and the role of gaming and playing (Ito et al. 2009).

Many places in the world, even in North America, are untouched by the Internet grid— a condition commonly dubbed the digital divide—although this notion is more complex than a simple binary of haves and have-nots. Cell phones, often adopted where no telephone land line infrastructure has been built, and being small, "portable" (Ito et al. 2005), and more affordable than computers, have populated the world over. There are no signs that this trend will abate. Used to transmit voice, send texts, and take pictures, cell phones have become important multimodal tools not only for economic activity, but for extending sociality and kin networks (Horst & Miller 2006, Ito et al. 2005, Wallis 2008); reinforcing friendships and transforming patterns of social coordination, status, and visibility (Ito et al. 2005, Caron & Caronia 2007, Katz 2008, Ling & Donner 2009, McIntosh 2010); and providing new avenues for intimacy and sexuality (Humphreys & Barker 2007, Pertierra 2006, Wallis 2010). Cell phones, generally a domesticated object, can assume extraordinary symbolic power, for example, when deployed during spectacular street protests, as in the People's Revolution in the Philippines in 2001 (Pertierra 2006, Rafael 2003). Other scholars zero in on the more mundane features of cell phones, such as the ring tone, making the banal appear strange and extraordinary to arrive imaginatively at the logic of late capitalism (Gopinath 2005).

DIGITAL MEDIA VERNACULARS

Scholars are increasingly applying an ethnographic lens to practices, subjects, modes of communication, and groups entirely dependent on digital technologies for their existence (Baron 2008, Biao 2007, Boellstorff 2008, English-Leuck 2002, Juris 2008, Malaby 2009, Senft 2008, Taylor 2006). The bulk of this work, however, continues to confound sharp boundaries between off-line and online contexts and between the past and the present (Kelty 2008, Sreberny & Khiabany 2010), for instance by turning to remediation, usefully defined by Silvio (2007) in terms of desire and attention: "To be compelling, a new media product must capture the psychic and social experiences of a particular time and place, and these include the experiences of older media, as well as the hopes and anxieties around the introduction of new media technologies themselves" (p. 286).

Other scholars examine the way digital media have become centrally implicated in centuries-old debates, such as those surrounding liberal rights, personhood, and institutional governance. For instance, ethnographers have given ample attention to free software and open source software hackers and developers—programmers and systems administrators who freely make, truck, and barter in the underlying recipes of software, source code, via novel licensing arrangements that invert, and thus politically challenge, the *raison d'etre* of copyright law (Coleman 2009, Coleman & Golub 2008, Coombe & Herman 2004, Leach et al. 2009, Lin 2007). Much of this scholarship is concerned with transformations as well as continuities within liberal and Enlightenment ideals. For instance, Kelty treats free software as a "recursive public" whereby continuous and collaborative modification of software is what marks this "geek" public as distinctive from those publics mediated primarily by print culture (2008). In other parts of the world, the liberalism of open source is often submerged, although not entirely eclipsed, as it melds with national projects (Chan 2008a) as well as pan-regional imaginaries of the European Union (Karanovic 2008).

Furthermore, whereas some digital networks allow for decentralized networks or loosely associated groups, some of which would have been "unimaginable" (Lysloff 2003, p. 236) before the Internet (Shirky 2008), other online projects not only are part of vibrant public cultures but have become "routinized" (Weber 1947). Many open source projects—and close cousins, most famously Wikipedia—have become partially centralized organizations, with complex governance procedures and policy instructions edging close to guilds of times past, and even bureaucracies (Coleman & Hill 2004, O'Neil 2009, Reagle 2010).

If some geeks extend and transform liberalism, others renew and transform leftist, radical traditions. Juris's (2008) monograph, a detailed ethnographic account of the social justice, counter-globalization movement, identifies the affinities between technical decentralization and the organizational and political decentralization of many activist collectives who collaborate virtually to expose the abuses of corporate globalization (compare Milberry 2008). Digital activism uses other formats as well, including "banal activism" in suburban Malaysia (Postill 2008), the technological activism of nongovernmental organizations (McInerney 2009), immigrant mobilization and Web 2.0 (Costanza-Chock 2008), and the vibrant sphere of political blogging in Iran (Doostdar 2004, Sreberny & Khiabany 2010).

Indeed, the 2009 postpresidential election protests in Iran provide a powerful reminder of the double-edged sword of digital activism: Social media tools can simultaneously support grass-roots political mobilizations as well as government surveillance and human rights violations. For instance, during the course of these dramatic protests, citizens could purchase low-cost CDs loaded with anticensorship software, ensuring that a steady stream of images and videos were catapulted onto social media networks and the mainstream news (Sreberny & Khiabany 2010). The government, however, also used digital media to fortify its surveillance apparatus (Morozov 2009). "So long as 'free' is paid for by surveillance" as one activist technology scholar has put it, "the Internet will represent a Faustian bargain for radical social movements" (Saxon 2009).

If some technologists make and use digital media to fight the injustices of capitalism, others are enmeshed in flexible post-Fordist capitalism. The latter have been the subjects of studies—many regionally focused on South Asia—whereby the most abstract features of informational capitalism are brought to the foreground through nuanced ethnographic excavation (Amrute 2008, Aneesh 2006, Biao 2007). For example, Biao (2007) examines body shops—small outfits that place itinerant South Asian programmers into software companies in Australia, the United States, and Malaysia for short-term contact work. He reveals not only the lived experience of these migrant programmers, but also the economic and cultural conditions sustaining this practice. These laborers, who at the turn of the century filled a massive global labor shortage (owing to the Y2K bug), now respond to fluctuations in a volatile market, rationalized, in part, by ideologies of meritocracy (Biao 2007, p. 111). Companion studies critical of informational capitalism attend to some of the most intractable and long-lasting by-products of digital media: the toxic waste of screens, computers, cell phones, and other electronics, which, despite its undeniable materiality and ubiquity, has received meager scholarly or journalistic attention (Maxwell & Miller 2008).

Some of the richest ethnographic studies explore digital media in light of language ideologies change, informality, virtuosity, revitalization, play, and morality (Axel 2006; Baron 2008; Cook 2004; Crystal 2008; Danet & Herring 2007; Eisenlohr 2004; Gershon 2010; Jones & Schieffelin 2009a,b; Keating & Mirus 2003; Lange 2009; McIntosh 2010). Many challenge the mainstream media's moral panic over the seeming demise of literacy; others make the panic itself the object of analysis (Tagliamonte & Denis 2008, Thurlow 2006). Jones & Schieffelin (2009a,b) provide a rich microanalysis of verbal informality, play, panic, and morality in digital contexts from the perspective of users. They treat thousands of comments left on YouTube videos—addressing an AT&T advertisement about text messaging that went viral—as "user-generated metalinguistic data" (2009b, p. 1063) whereby "young proponents of texting . . . publicize their own opinions about texting as linguistic phenomenon" (p. 1058) and publicize them with a remarkable level of moral acuity.

This ethnographic analysis is methodologically significant because the authors make sense of data—Internet memes, chatting, viral videos, and an astonishing cascade of comments that accompany this material—that may initially seem unsuitable for ethnographic analysis. It illustrates how the study of digital media transforms the possibilities and contours of fieldwork (Burrell 2009, Wesch 2007). Ethnographers will increasingly have to address how to collect and represent forms of digital data whose social and material life are often infused with elements of anonymity, modalities of hybermobility, ephemerality, and mutability and thus pose new challenges to empirical, let alone ethnographic, analysis.

In contrast to the microanalysis of YouTube comments, Baron's (2008) monograph covers multiple modes of online communication—from social networking to chatting—to argue that the informality of many types of digital communication is part of a broader informalization in American public, familial, and work life. Examining the Iranian blogosphere, Doostdar (2004) takes on what Iranian critics call blogging's "vulgar spirit"— referring to informalities of language such as grammar mistakes. McIntosh (2010) addresses the informality and playfulness of texting to demonstrate how Giriamian youth construct a "fantasized persona" (p. 338) that is not bound to local customs. Among many elders, however, "mobile-phone technology and language are saturated with a kind of witchcraft that threatens Giriama identity" (p. 347).

Even if texting and IMing are predicated on a disregard for grammar and spelling, scholars have treated these genres in terms of their virtuosity and moral depth (Crystal 2008, Jones & Schieffelin 2009a). To understand the culture and linguistics of digital media, it will be crucial to pay ethnographic attention to what Gershon (2010) defines as media ideologies: "beliefs about how a medium communicates and structures communication" (p. 3), measuring these beliefs against what people actually do with this media, a method she deftly applies in her work on the use of digital media for mediating romance, and especially its end: the break-up (2010).

THE PROSAICS OF DIGITAL MEDIA

The word prosaic invokes much of Bakhtin's work, which attests to the lived experience of language, the contexts in which it is uttered and reuttered (church versus market), the multiplicity of speech genres, and the ideological and material conditions that sustain not only dominant languages, but also the heteroglossic and polyphonic formations, such as dialects, that can disturb the coherence of monologic languages (Morson & Emerson 1990). Looking at digital media in similarly prosaic terms means uncovering the lived experiences of digital media; discussing the conditions in which they are made, altered, and deployed (finance, religion, news); attending to particular genres of communication (blogs, spam, video-sharing sites); and finally placing attention on the material and ideological functions produced and sustained by digital technologies.

Several ethnographic accounts expand our understanding of the cultures of finance and capitalism (Knorr-Cetina & Bruegger 2002a,b; Schull 2008, 2010; Zaloom 2006), complementing existing sociological scholarship on how digital technologies magnify the speed, exploitation, and reach of contemporary global, neoliberal capitalism (Castells 2009, Harvey 1990, Sassen 2002). One the one hand, Zaloom (2006) demonstrates how financial trading firms created a new neoliberal dynamic of competitive hyperindividualism via the introduction of computers alongside new architectural spaces—a model pioneered in Chicago in the 1990s and subsequently adopted by other firms in financial centers around the world. Other studies are oriented phenomenologically, examining in detail how computer screens bring into being an entire world for finance traders (Knorr-Cetina & Bruegger 2002b).

On the other hand, digital media sustains underground, shadow, or unofficial/informal economies: digital piracy (Larkin 2008, Philip 2005, Sundaram 2007); fan fiction (Jenkins 2008, Silvio 2007); "mail-order" brides (Constable 2003, Johnson 2007); and email scams and spam (Brunton 2009; Burrell 2008, 2010; Smith 2007). Internet piracy, in particular, follows from uncoordinated and distributed activity whereby hundreds of thousands of people around the world download music, movies, and increasingly, books. Other types of digital piracy emerge on the streets or markets in global cities where copies of movies and music

are sold at low cost (Larkin 2008, Philip 2005, Sundaram 2007). Digital piracy in its totality partly interferes with the smooth functioning of capitalist and liberal-legal imperatives, tearing into what Derrida (1992) calls the "mystical foundation of authority" and inducing a moral panic in the copyright industries. Along with the hefty financial and ideological support of governments, the copyright industries have retaliated with aggressive educational campaigns in the form of comics, videos, radio ads, and posters (Gillespie 2007) along with doomsday declarations, which have also functioned to represent developing nations "as adolescents growing toward nation- and statehood, awakening to the joys of shop-lifting but still unprepared for full-time shop-keeping" (Philip 2005, p. 207).

The Internet has also become a central conduit and node for one of the most public and politically significant genres of communication: news. As journalism in industrialized nations migrates online, and as regional papers in the United States struggle to survive as advertising revenue dwindles, the scholarly discussion has been fiercely focused on what these transformations mean not only for the future of journalism but, by extension, the future of democracy (Downie & Schudson 2009). Ethnographic accounts complement these existing studies by examining the lives, ideologies, hopes, desires, and perceptions of digital journalists and grassroots bloggers (Boczkowski 2004, Boyer 2010, Klinenberg 2005, Paterson & Domingo 2008, Russell 2010, Srinivasan & Fish 2009). Boyer's (2010) ethnographic work among digital journalists in Germany, for instance, unveils their cybernetic orientation that, although fully rooted in their actual, material, and very particular experiences, becomes conveyed in far more general "definitions and discourse—and ultimately, into the truth—of digital expertise and power" (p. 143).

Many other domains and groups are being refigured and refiguring themselves through their everyday reliance on digital media including religious worshippers (Eisenlohr 2006, Ess et al. 2007, Radde-Antweiler 2008), people with disabilities (Boellstorff 2008, Davidson 2008,

Ginsburg 2007, Keating & Mirus 2003), and patients and their families who are turning to each other via online forums to supplement or supplant doctor's advice, devise treatment strategies, discuss side-effects of medications, seek emotional support, and organize advocacy campaigns (Dumit 2006, Epstein 2008, Gillet 2003, Orgad 2005, Radin 2006).

A number of researchers turn away from groups and frame their analyses of digital media along the axes of perception and self-awareness (Cohen 2005, Reed 2005, Wesch 2009); personality, personal connection, and friendships (Baym 2010, boyd 2009, Humphrey 2009); the shifting lines between publicity and privacy (Lange 2007, Marwick & boyd 2010); affect and addiction (Chan 2008b, Golub & Lingley 2008, Schull 2011); and archive and memory (Bowker 2007). Schull (2008, 2011) provides a wide-ranging ethnographic analysis of slot machine addicts in Las Vegas, for whom gambling becomes a means of self-suspension in which "time, space, the value of money, social relations, and even a sense of the body dissolves" (2008, p. 155; for scholarship on human-machine interaction, see Suchman 2007 and Nardi & Kaptelinin 2006). The technologically mediated repetition of mini-decisions involved in machine gambling affords a sense of safety and control that eludes her informants in an "uncertain human world" of "ever-proliferating choices" and risks (p. 168).

Given the seemingly disembodied interaction that occurs online, digital media, especially the Internet, may seem to be a quintessential nonspace as defined by M. Augé (1995): the bland and uniform spaces of modernity, such as highway rest stops and motels. Ethnographic work, however, tells a very different story. Studies examine how various places and spaces sustain the production and reach of virtual spaces and technologies: regions and cities such as Chennai (Fuller & Narasimhan 2007, 2008); spatially situated ritual events such as gamer and hacker conferences (Coleman 2010, Taylor 2006); and places such as body shops, cyber cafes, and Internet centers (Burrell 2010, Constable 2003, Johnson 2007, Smith 2007,

Tawil-Souri 2009). Others examine the virtual configuration of place (Boellstorff 2008), for instance, whereby the city of London is apprehended via blogging (Reed 2008) or a particular slice of Los Angeles street/musical culture is virtualized and memorialized in stunning detail in Grand Theft Auto San Andreas (Miller 2008).

One of the most detailed studies concerning the importance of place is English-Lueck's (2002) ethnography of Silicon Valley: the unofficial capital of software, hardware, geeks, engineers, and immigrant technology workers. It is a region defined, on the one hand, by "technological saturation" (p. 2), which blurs the line between work, play, and leisure for privileged workers, and, on the other hand, by the reality of immigrant workers with a vastly different relation to technology (Saxenian 2002). Differences appear among digital producers: The Bay Area is home to high-tech giants and smaller start-up firms, institutions whose norms and practices simultaneously sustain countercultural worldviews (Turner 2006), techno-liberal commitments (Malaby 2009), and "New Edge" spiritual celebrations of technology (Zandbergen 2010). Malaby's ethnographic study of the Bay Area Linden Lab, corporate makers of the popular virtual world Second Life, joins an older literature on the intersection between labor, information technologies, and corporate life (Freeman 2000, Ross 2003). This study demonstrates how one of the most distinctive attributes of games, their "contrived contingency" [defined as a "mixture of constraint and open-endedness" (Malaby 2009, p. 68)], is integrated into corporate governance structures by Linden Lab employees in an attempt to minimize the bureaucracies they so overtly shun.

FINAL MEDIATIONS AND MEDITATIONS

Many ethnographic studies of digital media provincialize and thus particularize the role that digital media play in the construction of sociocultural worlds, group identities and representations, protocols of economic exchange, communicative genres, and phenomenological experience. This anthropological imperative posits that the devil is in the details; these details are often aesthetically valued for revealing the splendor of sociocultural life and at times are also ethically deployed to push against faulty and narrow presumptions about the universality and uniformity of human experience. Although there might seem to be an analytical price to be paid by considering the minutiae of social life, resolutely following the details, whether "the social life of things" (Appadurai 1986) or the constitution, extension, and especially translation of people and objects along various networks (Latour 1988), does not imply a delinking from totalities or global processes. Details can be tethered to action, global formations, other material artifacts, and social processes of translation, providing a dynamic view into what Fischer (1999), following Heidegger, aptly describes as "worlding."

To flesh out this point ethnographically, we might consider a digital genre infamous for its ubiquity: the advanced fee fraud, more commonly known as the "419" scam (also known as the "Nigerian" scam), a subgenre of spam, itself a subgenre of email. A 419 email is meant to circulate promiscuously via the Internet so as to arrive at hundreds of thousands of email in-boxes with the intent of duping a handful of users into transferring large sums of money to the originating scammers. If there are scammers and spammers, however, there are also systems administrators—the plumbers of the Internet—tasked with halting the circulatory voyage of spam. Thus, the entrapment of spam is a powerful reminder of the extensive, costly, and often-invisible forms of human labor needed to keep the Internet running "smoothly" (Brunton 2009, Downey 2001). Despite elaborate spam filters, some (but by no means all) 419 emails arrive at their final destination. As individuals sift through the daily deluge of email—an increasingly onerous chore and nuisance (Fisher et al. 2006)—some might come across one or two 419 emails, and a few, apparently, are compelled to wire over their savings to the scammers (Zuckoff 2006). Most people, however,

delete the emails with no further thought. Others may take a moment to reflect on the email, bemused by its "strange" qualities, amazed that anyone would fall for such a scam, but not really able to decipher its full meaning, despite the fact that most are written in English. A few do not just delete the email; they seek to bait the scammers. They have grown so irked that they have banded together as 419 baiters to trap the trappers, a form of Internet vigilantism representative of the cat-and-mouse politics common to the Internet.[4] Systems administrators use the messages that beat their systems to train their filters and tweak their rules, or they report them to collaborative filters; by thus maintaining servers, systems administrators are in almost continuous crafting mode (Sennett 2008), learning skills and tips from others, gaining capacities that are economically lucrative and also constitute vocational mores and sensibilities.

Smith (2007), in his ethnography of the culture of corruption in Nigeria, shows that 419 scams are ethnographically significant because "their themes...[are] directly related to the structure of real fraud and corruption in Nigeria" (p. 36) and are an entryway into "popular perceptions" of corruption among the many low-level scammers, who have been themselves scammed—ensnared in this informal and precarious vocation by the economic marginalization of Nigeria in the global, capitalist economy.

This brief example demonstrates how ethnographically rich the examination of a single digital genre can be and how the study of digital media can touch on many of the analytic frames explored in the previous sections. Thus to entertain a single 419 email, a small communicative artifact, is to entertain a pervasive communicative subgenre (spam); a vocational group (systems administrators); ideologies of cultural difference; the workings of shadow economies,

---

[4]Given the plasticity of software and thus to some degree the Internet, software can be written to route around the restrictions; hence we might identify this tug of war politics as what marks the Internet as politically distinct from older media, such as television. See **http://www.419baiter.com/**

structured in part by the massively unequal distribution of world economic resources; the far-reaching and hidden human labor required to keep the Internet functioning; new types of political responses such as Internet vigilantism; and most richly, the culture and politics of corruption in particular places such as Nigeria.

Although this one digital genre connects various worlds, types of people, and activities, one cannot always entertain all these dimensions at once. What enters our analysis depends on a particular type of mediation, as Weber (1949) famously insisted when he argued that we cannot nakedly apprehend the full force and complexity of any social phenomena. Scholars, he argued, can reach significant cultural and social conclusions via mediation only in the form of the questions and analytic frames brought to bear on the objects and subjects of analysis. Or, in Nietzsche's (1980) more philosophical take on this predicament, "[o]ne blinds some birds to make others sing more beautifully" (p. 41). Despite the massive amount of data and new forms of visibility shored up by computational media, many of these worlds remain veiled, cloaked, and difficult to decipher. Long-term ethnographic research is well suited to tease out some of these veiled dimensions, however tentatively, to unearth the remarkable depth, richness, and variability of digital media in everyday and institutional life.

DISCLOSURE STATEMENT

The author is not aware of any affiliations, memberships, funding, or financial holdings that might be perceived as affecting the objectivity of this review.

ACKNOWLEDGMENTS

Trying to make sense of a large body of scholarship is a humbling experience and would not have been possible without the generosity of others providing critical feedback, suggestions, and resources: Sareeta Amrute, Finn Brunton, Jacob R Gaboury, Faye Ginsburg, Heather Horst, Graham Jones, Jelena Karanovich, Chris Kelty, Genevieve Lakier, Thomas Malaby, Ted Magder, Michael Ralph, Bambi Schieffelin, Martin Scherzinger, and especially my research assistant Jamie Berthe.

LITERATURE CITED

Adams TL, Smith SA, eds. 2008. *Electronic Tribes: The Virtual Worlds of Geeks, Gamers, Shamans, and Scammers.* Austin: Univ. Tex. Press

Amrute SB. 2008. *Producing mobility: Indian ITers in an interconnected world.* PhD thesis. Univ. Chicago. 345 pp.

Aneesh A. 2006. *Virtual Migration: The Programming of Globalization.* Durham, NC: Duke Univ. Press

Appadurai A. 1986. *The Social Life of Things: Commodities in Cultural Perspective.* Cambridge, UK/New York: Cambridge Univ. Press

Appadurai A. 1996. *Modernity at Large: Cultural Dimensions of Globalization.* Minneapolis: Univ. Minn. Press

Augé M. 1995. *Non-Places: Introduction to an Anthropology of Supermodernity*, transl. J Howe. London/New York: Verso. From French

Axel BK. 2004. The context of diaspora. *Cult. Anthropol.* 19(1):26–60

Axel BK. 2006. Anthropology and the new technologies of communication. *Cult. Anthropol.* 21(3):354–84

Baron NS. 2008. *Always On: Language in an Online and Mobile World.* Oxford/New York: Oxford Univ. Press

Baym NK. 2000. *Tune-In, Log Out: Soaps, Fandom, and Online-Community.* Thousand Oaks, CA: Sage

Baym NK. 2010. *Personal Connections in the Digital Age.* Cambridge, UK: Polity

Benkler Y. 2006. *The Wealth of Networks: How Social Production Transforms Markets and Freedom.* New Haven: Yale Univ. Press

Bernal V. 2005. Eritrea on-line: diaspora, cyberspace, and the public sphere. *Am. Ethnol.* 32(4):660–75

Biao X. 2007. *Global "Body Shopping": An Indian Labor System in the Information Technology Industry.* Princeton, NJ: Princeton Univ. Press

Boczkowski P. 2004. *Digitizing the News: Innovation in Online Newspapers.* Cambridge, MA: MIT Press

Boellstorff T. 2008. *Coming of Age in Second Life: An Anthropologist Explores the Virtually Human.* Princeton, NJ: Princeton Univ. Press

Bowker GC. 2007. The past and the Internet. See Karaganis 2007, pp. 20–37

boyd D. 2009. Why youth (heart) social network sites: the role of networked publics in teenage social life. See Ito et al. 2009, pp. 119–42

boyd D, Marwick A. 2009. The conundrum of visibility. *J. Child. Media* 3(4):410–14

Boyer D. 2007. *Understanding Media: A Popular Philosophy.* Chicago: Prickly Paradigm

Boyer D. 2010. Digital expertise in online journalism (and anthropology). *Anthropol. Q.* 83(1):125–47

Brunton F. 2009. *Spam in action: social technology and unintended consequences.* PhD thesis. Univ. Aberdeen. 231 pp.

Burrell J. 2008. Problematic empowerment: West African Internet scams as strategic misrepresentation. *Inf. Technol. Int. Dev.* 4(4):15–30

Burrell J. 2009. The field site as a network: a strategy for locating ethnographic research. *Field Methods* 21(2):181–99

Burrell J. 2010. User agency in the middle range: rumors and the reinvention of the Internet in Accra, Ghana. *Sci. Technol. Hum. Values.* In press

Burrell J, Anderson K. 2008. "I have great desires to look beyond my world": trajectories of information and communication technology use among Ghanaians living abroad. *New Media Soc.* 10(2):203–24

Caron A, Caronia L. 2007. *Moving Cultures: Mobile Communication in Everyday Life.* Montreal: McGills-Queens Univ. Press

Castells M. 1996. *The Rise of the Network Society.* Cambridge, MA: Blackwell

Castells M. 2009. *Communication Power.* Oxford/New York: Oxford Univ. Press

Chakrabarty D. 2000. *Provincializing Europe: Postcolonial Thought and Historical Difference.* Princeton, NJ: Princeton Univ. Press

Chan AS. 2008a. Retiring the network spokesman: the poly-vocality of free software networks in Peru. *Sci. Stud.* 20(2):78–99

Chan AS. 2008b. Through fieldwork: slashdot.org. See Turkle 2008, pp. 125–37

Christen K. 2006. Tracking properness: repackaging culture in a remote Australian town. *Cult. Anthropol.* 21(3):416–46

Christen K. 2009. Access and accountability: the ecology of information sharing in the digital age. *Anthropol. News* April:4–5

Christie M. 2008. Digital tools and the management of Australian Aboriginal desert knowledge. In *Global Indigenous Media: Cultures, Poetics, and Politics,* ed. P Wilson, M Stewart, pp. 270–86. Durham, NC: Duke Univ. Press

Cohen H, Salazar JF, eds. 2005. Digital anthropology. *Media Int. Aust.* 116:5–75

Cohen K. 2005. What does the photo blog want? *Media Cult. Soc.* 27(6):883–901

Coleman EG. 2009. Code is speech: legal tinkering, expertise, and protest among free and open source software developers. *Cult. Anthropol.* 24(3):420–54

Coleman EG. 2010. The hacker conference: a ritual condensation and celebration of a lifeworld. *Anthropol. Q.* 83(1):99–124

Coleman EG, Golub A. 2008. Hacker practice: moral genres and the cultural articulation of liberalism. *Anthropol. Theory* 8(3):255–77

Coleman EG, Hill B. 2004. The social production of ethics in Debian and free software communities. In *Free and Open Source Software Development,* ed. S Koch, pp. 273–95. Hershey, PA: Idea Group

Constable N. 2003. *Romance on a Global Stage: Pen Pals, Virtual Ethnography, and "Mail-Order" Marriages.* Berkeley: Univ. Calif. Press

Cook SE. 2004. New technologies and language change: toward an anthropology of linguistic frontiers. *Annu. Rev. Anthropol.* 33:103–15

Coombe RJ, Herman A. 2004. Rhetorical virtues: property, speech, and the commons on the World-Wide Web. *Anthropol. Q.* 77(3):559–74

Costanza-Chock S. 2008. The immigrant rights movement on the Net: between "Web 2.0" and comunicación popular. *Am. Q.* 60(3):851–64

Crystal D. 2008. *Txtng: The Gr8 Db8*. Oxford/New York: Oxford Univ. Press

Curran J, Park MJ, eds. 2000. *De-Westernizing Media Studies*. London/New York: Routledge

Danet B. 2001. *Cyberpl@y: Communicating Online*. Oxford/New York: Berg

Danet B, Herring S, eds. 2007. *Multilingual Internet: Language, Culture, and Communication Online*. Oxford/New York: Oxford Univ. Press

Daniels J. 2009. *Cyber Racism: White Supremacy Online and the New Attack on Civil Rights*. Lanham, MD: Rowman & Littlefield

Davidson J. 2008. Autistic culture online: virtual communication and cultural expression on the spectrum. *Soc. Cult. Geogr.* 9(7):791–806

DeNardis L. 2009. *Protocol Politics*. Cambridge, MA: MIT Press

DeNicola L. 2006. The bundling of geospatial information with everyday experience. In *Surveillance and Security: Technological Politics and Power in Everyday Life*, ed. T Monahan, pp. 243–64. New York: Routledge

Derrida J. 1992. Force of law: the mystical foundation of authority. In *Deconstruction and the Possibility of Justice*, ed. DG Carlson, D Cornell, M Rosenfeld, pp. 3–67. New York: Routledge

Doostdar A. 2004. The vulgar spirit of blogging: on language, culture, and power in Persian Weblogestan. *Am. Anthropol.* 106(4):651–62

Downey G. 2001. Virtual webs, physical technologies, hidden workers: the spaces of labor in information internetworks. *Tech. Cult.* 42(2):209–35

Downie L, Schudson M. 2009. The reconstruction of American journalism. *Columbia J. Rev.* **http://www.cjr.org/reconstruction/**

Dumit J. 2006. Illnesses you have to fight to get: facts as forces in uncertain, emergent illnesses. *Soc. Sci. Med.* 62(3):577–90

Eglash R, Bennett A. 2009. Teaching with hidden capital: agency in children's computational explorations of cornrow hairstyles. *Child. Youth Environ.* 19(1):58–74

Eisenlohr P. 2004. Language revitalization and new technologies: cultures of electronic mediation and the refiguring of communities. *Annu. Rev. Anthropol.* 33:21–45

Eisenlohr P. 2006. As Makkah is sweet and beloved, so is Madina: Islam, devotional genres and electronic mediation in Mauritius. *Am. Ethnol.* 33(2):230–45

English-Leuck J. 2002. *Cultures@SiliconValley*. Palo Alto, CA: Stanford Univ. Press

Epstein SG. 2008. Patient groups and health movements. In *Handbook of Science and Technology Studie*s, ed. EJ Hackett, O Amsterdama, M Lynch, J Wajcman, pp. 499–540. Cambridge, MA: MIT Press

Escobar A. 1994. Welcome to Cyberia: notes on the anthropology of cyberculture. *Curr. Anthropol.* 35(3):211–31

Ess C, Kawabata A, Kurosaki H. 2007. Cross-cultural perspectives on religion and computer-mediated communication. *J. Comput. Mediated Commun.* 12(3):article 9, **http://jcmc.indiana.edu/vol12/issue3/**

Fischer M. 1999. Worlding cyberspace: towards a crucial ethnography in time, space, theory. In *Critical Anthropology Now: Unexpected Context, Shifting Constituencies, Changing Agendas*, ed. G Marcus, pp. 245–305. Santa Fe, NM: SAR Press

Fischer M. 2007. Four genealogies for a recombinant anthropology of science and technology. *Cult. Anthropol.* 22(4):539–615

Fisher D, Brush AJ, Gleave E, Smith MA. 2006. Revisiting Whittaker & Sidner's "email overload" ten years later. In *Proc. CSCW 2006*, pp. 309–12. New York: ACM Press

Forte MC. 2003. Caribbean aboriginals online: digitized culture, networked representation. *Indig. Aff.* 2:32–37

Freeman C. 2000. *High Tech and High Heels in the Global Economy: Women, Work and Pink-Collar Identities*. Durham, NC: Duke Univ. Press

Fuller C, Narasimhan H. 2007. Information technology professionals and the new-rich middle class in Chennai (Madras). *Mod. Asian Stud.* 41(1):121–50

Fuller C, Narasimhan H. 2008. From landlords to software engineers: migration and urbanization among Tamil brahmans. *Comp. Stud. Soc. Hist.* 50(1):170–96

Geismar H. 2008. Cultural property, museums and the Pacific—reframing the debates. *Int. J. Cult. Prop.* 15(2):109–22

Geismar H, Mohns W. 2010. Database relations: rethinking the database in the Vanuatu Cultural Center and National Museum. *J. R. Anthropol. Inst.* In press

Gershon I. 2010. *The Break-Up 2.0: Disconnecting Over New Media*. Ithaca, NY: Cornell Univ. Press. In press

Ghosh R, ed. 2005. *Code: Collaborative Ownership and the Digital Economy*. Cambridge, MA: MIT Press

Gillespie T. 2007. *Wired Shut: Copyright and the Shape of Digital Culture*. Cambridge, MA: MIT Press

Gillet J. 2003. Media activism and Internet use by people with HIV/AIDS. *Soc. Health Illn.* 25(6):608–24

Ginsburg F. 2007. Found in translation. *Media Res: A MediaCommons Project*. **http://mediacommons.futureofthebook.org/imr/2007/03/28/found-in-translation**

Ginsburg F. 2008. Rethinking the digital age. In *The Media and Social Theory*, ed. D Hesmondhalgh, J Toynbee, pp. 127–44. London/New York: Routledge

Ginsburg F, Abu-Lughod L, Larkin B, eds. 2002. *Media Worlds: Anthropology on New Terrain*. Berkeley: Univ. Calif. Press

Gitelman L. 2006. *Always Already New: Media, History, and the Data of Culture*. Cambridge, MA: MIT Press

Golub A, Lingley K. 2008. "Just like the Qing Empire": Internet addiction, MMOGs, and moral crisis in contemporary China. *Games Cult.* 3(1):59–75

Gopinath S. 2005. Ringtones, or the auditory logic of globalization. *First Monday* 10(12):**http://firstmonday.org/issues/issue10_12/gopinath/index.html**

Gupta A, Ferguson J. 1997. Discipline and practice: "the field" as site, method, and location in anthropology. In *Anthropological Locations: Boundaries and Grounds of a Field Science*, ed. A Gupta, J Ferguson, pp. 1–46. Berkeley: Univ. Calif. Press

Hakken D. 1999. *Cyborgs@Cyberspace? An Ethnographer Looks at the Future*. New York: Routledge

Hakken D. 2003. *The Knowledge Landscapes of Cyberspace*. New York: Routledge

Harvey D. 1990. *Condition of Postmodernity: An Enquiry into the Origins of Cultural Change*. Cambridge, MA: Blackwell

Hayles NK. 1999. *How We Became Posthuman: Virtual Bodies in Cybernetics, Literature, and Informatics*. Chicago: Univ. Chicago Press

Herring SC. 2008. Questioning the generational divide: technological exoticism and adult construction of online youth identity. In *Youth, Identity, and Digital Media*, ed. D Buckingham, pp. 71–94. Cambridge, MA: MIT Press

Herring SC, Paolillo JC. 2006. Gender and genre variation in weblogs. *J. Sociolinguistics* 10(4):439–59

Hindman MS. 2009. *The Myth of Digital Democracy*. Princeton, NJ: Princeton Univ. Press

Hine C. 2005. *Virtual Methods: Issues in Social Research on the Internet*. Oxford/New York: Berg

Horst AH. 2010. Aesthetics of the self: digital mediations. In *Anthropology and the Individual: A Material Culture Approach*, ed D Miller, pp. 99–114. Oxford: Berg

Horst AH, Miller D. 2006. *The Cell Phone: An Anthropology of Communication*. New York: Berg

Humphrey C. 2009. The mask and the face: imagination and social life in Russian chat rooms and beyond. *Ethnos* 74(1):31–50

Humphreys L, Barker T. 2007. Modernity and the mobile phone: exploring tensions about dating and sex in Indonesia. *J. Media Cult.* 10(1):**http://journal.media-culture.org.au/0703/06-humphreys-barker.php**

Ingold T. 2000. *Perception of the Environment: Essays on Livelihood, Dwelling and Skill*. London/New York: Routledge

Ito M. 2009. *Engineering Play: A Cultural History of Children's Software*. Cambridge, MA: MIT Press

Ito M, Baumer S, Bittani M, Boyd D, Cody R, et al. 2009. *Hanging Out, Messing Around and Geeking Out: Living and Learning with New Media*. Cambridge, MA: MIT Press

Ito M, Okabe D, Matsuba M, eds. 2005. *Personal, Portable, Pedestrian: Mobile Phones in Japanese Life*. Cambridge, MA: MIT Press

Jenkins H. 2008. *Convergence Culture: Where Old and New Media Collide*. New York: New York Univ. Press. Rev. ed.

Johnson E. 2007. *Dreaming of a Mail-Order Husband: Russian-American Internet Romance*. Durham, NC: Duke Univ. Press

Jones G, Schieffelin B. 2009a. Enquoting voices, accomplishing talk: uses of be + like in instant messaging. *Lang. Commun.* 29(1):77–113

Jones G, Schieffelin B. 2009b. Talking text and talking back: "my BFF Jill" from boob tube to YouTube. *J. Comp. Mediat. Commun.* 14(4):1050–79

Juris J. 2008. *Networking Futures: The Movements Against Corporate Globalization*. Durham, NC: Duke Univ. Press

Karaganis J, ed. 2007. *Structures of Participation in Digital Culture*. New York: SSRC

Karanovic J. 2008. *Sharing publics: democracy, cooperation, and free software advocacy in France*. PhD Thesis. New York Univ. 287 pp.

Katz JE. 2008. *Handbook of Mobile Communication Studies*. Cambridge, MA: MIT Press

Keating E, Mirus G. 2003. American Sign Language in virtual space: interactions between Deaf users of computer-mediated video communication and the impact of technology on language practices. *Lang. Soc.* 32:693–714

Kelty C. 2008. *Two Bits: The Cultural Significance of Free Software*. Durham, NC: Duke Univ. Press

Kendall L. 2002. *Hanging Out in the Virtual Pub: Masculinities and Relationships Online*. Berkeley: Univ. Calif. Press

Kirshenblatt-Gimblett B. 1996. The electronic vernacular. In *Connected: Engagements with Media*, ed. G Marcus, pp. 21–66. Chicago: Univ. Chicago Press

Klinenberg E, ed. 2005. *Cultural Production in a Digital Age*. Ann. Am. Acad. Pol. Soc. Sci. 597(1). Thousand Oaks, CA: Sage

Knorr-Cetina K, Bruegger U. 2002a. Global microstructures: the virtual societies of financial markets. *Am. J. Soc.* 107(4):905–50

Knorr-Cetina K, Bruegger U. 2002b. Inhabiting technology: the global lifeform of financial markets. *Curr. Soc.* 50(3):389–405

Landzelius K, ed. 2006. *Native on the Net: Indigenous and Diasporic Peoples in the Virtual Age*. London/New York: Routledge

Lange PG. 2007. Publicly private and privately public: social networking on YouTube. *J. Comp. Mediat. Commun.* 13(1):361–80

Lange PG. 2009. Conversational morality and information circulation: how tacit notions about good and evil influence knowledge exchange. *Hum. Organ.* 68(2):218–29

Larkin B. 2008. *Signal and Noise: Media, Infrastructure, and Urban Culture in Nigeria*. Durham, NC: Duke Univ. Place

Latour B. 1988. *Science in Action: How to Follow Scientists and Engineers through Society*. Cambridge, MA: Harvard Univ. Press

Leach J. 2005. Modes of creativity and the register of ownership. See Ghosh 2005, pp. 29–44

Leach J, Nafus D, Krieger B. 2009. Freedom imagined: morality and aesthetics in open source software design. *Ethnos* 74(1):51–71

Lessig L. 2004. *Free Culture: How Big Media Uses Technology and the Law to Lock Down Culture and Control Creativity*. New York: Penguin

Lin Y. 2007. Hacker culture and the FLOSS innovation. In *Handbook on the Research in Open Source Software: Technological, Economic and Social Perspectives*, ed. K St. Amant, B Still, pp. 34–46. Hershey, PA: Inf. Sci. Ref.

Ling R, Donner J. 2009. *Mobile Phones and Mobile Communication*. Cambridge, UK: Polity

Lovink G. 2008. *Zero Comments: Blogging and Critical Internet Culture*. New York: Routledge

Lysloff RTA. 2003. Musical community on the Internet: an online ethnography. *Cult. Anthropol.* 18(2):233–63

Malaby T. 2009. *Making Virtual Worlds: Linden Lab and Second Life*. Ithaca: Cornell Univ. Press

Malaby T, Burke T. 2009. The short and happy life of interdisciplinarity in game studies. *Games Cult.* 4(4):323–30

Marwick A, boyd D. 2010. I tweet honestly, I tweet passionately: Twitter users, context collapse, and the imagined audience. *New Media Soc.* In press

Maxwell R, Miller T. 2008. Ecological ethics and media technology. *Int. J. Commun.* 2:**http://ijoc.org/ojs/index.php/ijoc/article/view/320/151**

Mazzarella W. 2004. Culture, globalization, mediation. *Annu. Rev. Anthropol.* 33:345–67

Mazzarella W. 2006. Internet X-ray: e-governance, transparency, and the politics of immediation in India. *Public Cult.* 18(3):473–505

McInerney PB. 2009. Technology movements and the politics of free/open source software. *Sci. Tech. Hum. Values* 34(2):206–33

McIntosh J. 2010. Mobile phones and Mipoho's prophecy: the powers and dangers of flying language. *Am. Ethnol.* 37(2):337–53

Milberry K. 2008. The Wiki way: prefiguring change, practicing democracy. In *Reconstructing Biotechnologies: Critical Social Analyses*, ed. G Ruivenkamp, S Hisano, J Jongerden, pp. 327–43. Wageningen, The Neth.: Wageningen Acad.

Miller D, Slater D. 2000. *The Internet: An Ethnographic Approach.* Oxford/New York: Berg

Miller K. 2008. Grove Street Grimm: Grand Theft Auto and digital folklore. *J. Am. Folklore* 121(481):255–85

Morozov E. 2009. How dictators watch us on the Web. *Prospect.* Vol. 165:**http://www. prospectmagazine.co.uk/2009/11/how-dictators-watch-us-on-the-web/**

Morson GS, Emerson C. 1990. *Mikhail Bakhtin: Creation of a Prosaics.* Stanford, CA: Stanford Univ. Press

Mosco V. 2004. *The Digital Sublime: Myth, Power, and Cyberspace.* Cambridge, MA: MIT Press

Myers F. 2005. Some properties of culture and persons. See Ghosh 2005, pp. 45–60

Nakamura L. 2007. *Digitizing Race: Visual Cultures of the Internet.* Minneapolis: Univ. Minn. Press

Nardi B, Kaptelinin V. 2006. *Acting with Technology: Activity Theory and Interaction Design.* Cambridge, MA: MIT Press

Negroponte N. 1996. *Being Digital.* New York: Vintage Books

Nietzsche F. 1980. *On the Advantage and Disadvantage of History for Life*, transl. P Preuss. Indianapolis/ Cambridge: Hackett

O'Donnell C. 2009. The everyday lives of video game developers: experimentally understanding underlying systems/structures. *Transform. Works Cult.* Vol. 2:**http://journal.transformativeworks.org/ index.php/twc/article/view/73/76**

O'Neil M. 2009. *Cyberchiefs: Autonomy and Authority in Online Tribes.* London/New York: Pluto

Orgad S. 2005. *Storytelling Online: Talking Breast Cancer on the Internet.* New York: Peter Lang

Palfrey J, Gasser U. 2008. *Born Digital: Understanding the First Generation of Digital Natives.* New York: Basic Books

Panagakos AN, Horst HA. 2006. Return to Cyberia: technology and the social worlds of transnational migrants. *Glob. Netw.* 6(2):109–24

Paterson C, Domingo D, eds. 2008. *Making Online News: The Ethnography of New Media Production.* New York: Peter Lang

Pertierra R. 2006. *Transforming Technologies: Altered Selves—Mobile Phones and Internet Use in the Philippines.* Manila: De Salle Univ. Press

Pfaffenberger B. 1996. "If I want it, it's OK": Usenet and the (outer) limits of free speech. *Inf. Soc.* 12(4):365–86

Philip K. 2005. What is a technological author? The pirate function and intellectual property. *Postcolon. Stud.* 8(2):199–218

Postill J. 2008. Localising the Internet beyond communities and networks. *New Media Soc.* 10(3):413–31

Radde-Antweiler K. 2008. Religion is becoming virtualized: introduction to the special issue on religion in virtual worlds. *Heidelberg J. Rel. Internet*, ed. K Radde-Antweiler, 3.1:**http://online.uni-hd.de/**

Radin P. 2006. "To me, it's my life": medical communication, trust, and activism in cyberspace. *Soc. Sci. Med.* 62(3):591–601

Rafael VL. 2003. The cell phone and the crowd: messianic politics in the contemporary Philippines. *Public Cult.* 15(3):399–425

Ratto M. 2005. Embedded technical expression: code and the leveraging of functionality. *Inf. Soc.* 21(3):205–13

Reagle J. 2010. *Good Faith Collaboration: The Culture of Wikipedia.* Cambridge, MA: MIT Press. In press

Reed A. 2005. My blog is me: texts and persons in UK online journal culture (and anthropology). *Ethnos* 70(2):220–42

Reed A. 2008. Blog this: surfing the metropolis and the method of London. *J. R. Anthropol. Inst.* 14(2):391–406

Ross A. 2003. *No-Collar: The Humane Workplace and Its Hidden Costs.* New York: Basic Books

Russell A. 2010. Salon.com and the shifting culture of journalism. In *The Anthropology of News and Journalism: Global Perspectives*, ed. E Bird, pp. 270–82. Bloomington: Indiana Univ. Press

Salazar JF. 2005. Digitising knowledge: anthropology and new practices of digitextuality. *Media Int. Aust.* 116:64–74

Sassen S. 2002. Towards a sociology of information technology. *Curr. Soc.* 50(3):365–88

Saxenian AL. 2002. *Local and Global Networks of Immigrant Professionals in Silicon Valley*. San Francisco: Public Policy Inst. Calif.

Saxon E. 2009. The price of free. *Social Text Periscope*. **http://www.socialtextjournal.org/periscope/2009/11/the-price-of-free-1.php**

Scholz T. 2008. Market ideology and the myth of Web 2.0. *First Monday*. 13(3):**http://firstmonday.org/htbin/cgiwrap/bin/ojs/index.php/fm/article/view/2138/1945**

Schull N. 2008. Video poker. See Turkle 2008, pp. 153–71

Schull N. 2011. *Addiction by Design: Machine Gambling in Las Vegas*. Princeton, NJ: Princeton Univ. Press. In press

Senft T. 2008. *Camgirls: Celebrity and Community in the Age of Social Networks*. New York: Peter Lang

Sennet R. 2008. *The Craftsman*. New Haven: Yale Univ. Press

Shirky C. 2008. *Here Comes Everybody: The Power of Organizing Without Organizations*. New York: Penguin

Silvio T. 2007. Remediation and local globalizations: how Taiwan's "digital video knights-errant puppetry" writes the history of the new media in Chinese. *Cult. Anthropol.* 22(2):285–313

Smith DJ. 2007. *A Culture of Corruption: Everyday Deception and Popular Discontent in Nigeria*. Princeton, NJ: Princeton Univ. Press

Sreberny A, Khiabany G. 2010. *Blogistan: The Internet and Politics in Iran*. London: Tauris

Srinivasan R. 2006. Indigenous, ethnic and cultural articulations of the new media. *Int. J. Cult. Stud.* 9(4):497–518

Srinivasan R, Fish A. 2009. Internet authorship in Kyrgyzstan: social and political implications. *Comput. Mediat. Commun.* 14(3):559–80

Strathern M. 2005. Imagined collectivities and multiple authorship. See Ghosh 2005, pp. 13–28

Suchman L. 2007. *Human-Machine Reconfigurations: Plans and Situated Actions*. Cambridge, UK/New York: Cambridge Univ. Press

Sundaram R. 2007. Other networks: media urbanism and the culture of the copy in South Asia. See Karaganis 2007, pp. 48–73

Tagliamonte S, Denis D. 2008. Linguistic ruin? LOL! Instant messaging and teen language. *Am. Speech* 83(1):3–34

Tawil-Souri H. 2009. Americanizing Palestine through Internet development. In *Internationalizing Internet Studies: Beyond Anglophone Paradigms*, ed. G Goggin, M McLelland, pp. 32–47. New York: Routledge

Taylor TL. 2006. *Play Between Worlds: Exploring Online Game Culture*. Cambridge, MA: MIT Press

Thurlow C. 2006. From statistical panic to moral panic: The metadiscursive construction and popular exaggeration of new media language in the print media. *J. Comput. Mediated Commun.* 11(3):667–70

Turkle S. 1995. *Life on the Screen: Identity in the Age of the Internet*. New York: Simon and Schuster

Turkle S, ed. 2008. *The Inner History of Devices*. Cambridge, MA: MIT Press

Turner F. 2006. *From Counterculture to Cyberculture: Stewart Brand, The Whole Earth Network, and the Rise of Digital Utopianism*. Chicago: Univ. Chicago Press

Vaidhyanathan S. 2006. Critical information studies: a bibliographic manifesto. *Cult. Stud.* 20(2–3):292–315

Wallis C. 2008. Techno-mobility and translocal migration: mobile phone use among female migrant workers in Beijing. In *Gender Digital Divide*, ed. MI Srinivasan, VV Ramani, pp. 196–216. Hyderabad, India: Icfai Univ. Press

Wallis C. 2010. The traditional meets the technological: mobile navigations of desire and intimacy. In *Youth, Society, and Mobile Media in Asia*, ed. S Hemelryk Donald, T Dirndorfer Anderson, D Spry, pp. 57–69. London: Routledge. In press

Warschauer M. 2004. *Technology and Social Inclusion: Rethinking the Digital Divide*. Cambridge, MA: MIT Press

Weber M. 1947. *Theory of Social and Economic Organization*, transl AR Anderson, T Parsons. Glencoe, IL: Free Press. From German

Weber M. 1949. *On the Methodology of the Social Sciences*, transl. EA Schils, HA Finch. New York: Free Press. From German

Weinberger D. 2007. *Everything Is Miscellaneous: The Power of the New Digital Disorder*. New York: Henry Holt

Wesch M. 2007. *Web 2.0 . . . the machine is us/ing us*. **http://www.youtube.com/watch?v = 6gmP4nk0EOE**

Wesch M. 2009. Youtube and you: experiences of self-awareness in the context collapse of the recording Webcam. *Explor. Media Ecol.* 8(2):19–34

Whitaker MP. 2004. Tamilnet.com: some reflections on popular anthropology, nationalism, and the Internet. *Anthropol. Q.* 77(3):469–98

Wilson S, Peterson LC. 2002. The anthropology of online communities. *Annu. Rev. Anthropol.* 31:449–67

Wyatt S, Thomas G, Terranova T. 2002. They came, they surfed, they went back to the beach: conceptualizing use and nonuse of the Internet. In *Virtual Society? Get Real!: Technology, Cyberbole, Reality*, ed. S Woolgar, pp. 23–40. Oxford/New York: Oxford Univ. Press

Zaloom C. 2006. Markets and machines: work in the technological sensoryscapes of finance. *Am. Q.* 58(3):815–37

Zandbergen D. 2010. Silicon Valley New Age: the coconstitution of the digital and the sacred. In *Religions of Modernity*, ed. S Aupers, D Houtman, pp. 161–85. Leiden: Brill. In press

Zeitlyn D. 2009. *Digital anthropology report 2009: the six tribes of Homo digitalis*. **http://www.talktalk.co.uk/we-love-the-web/digital-anthropology/tribes**

Zuckoff M. 2006. The perfect mark: how a Massachusetts psychotherapist fell for a Nigerian email scam. *New Yorker*, May 15: **http://www.newyorker.com/archive/2006/05/15/060515fa_fact**

Cumulative Indexes

Contributing Authors, Volumes 30–39

Chapter Titles, Volumes 30–39

Linguistics and Communicative Practices

Sociocultural Anthropology

History, Theory, and Methods

Economics, Ecology, Technology, and Development

Social and Political Relationships